A LEIGHTON GENEALOGY

VOLUME ONE

A LEIGHTON GENEALOGY

Descendants of Thomas Leighton
of Dover, New Hampshire

VOLUME ONE

Compiled by
Perley M. Leighton

Based in part on data collected by

Julia Leighton Cornman

New England Historic Genealogical Society

Boston, 1989

Library of Congress Cataloging-in-Publication Data

Leighton, Perley M.
  A Leighton genealogy : descendants of Thomas Leighton of Dover, New
Hampshire / compiled by Perley M. Leighton based in part on data collected b
Julia Leighton Cornman.

  Includes bibliographical references.
  ISBN 0-88082-023-3
  1. Layton family. 2. Leighton, Thomas, 1604-1672 -- Family. 3. New England -- Genealogy. I. Cornman, Julia Leighton, 1852-1921. II. Title.
CS71.L429 1989
929'.2'0973--dc20   89-1335
                                                                    CI

TABLE OF CONTENTS

VOLUME ONE

VOLUME TWO

PREFACE

As a child, I heard from my grandparents the family legend of the three Leighton brothers, English barons who had been forced by evil King John (!) to flee to America, where they settled in Maine and married Indian squaws. Somehow we were the rightful owners of all of Portland, land taken from our ancestors by fraud. Although I came to realize how false these stories were, they did make me curious to discover the truth.

While pursuing graduate studies at Columbia University I discovered at the New York Public Library a manuscript Leighton genealogy compiled by Julia Cornman. Outlined there were my three Leighton lines. (My grandfather's mother was born a Leighton, and so was her mother.) For thirty-odd years since then my hobby has been family research, tracing my wife's Massachusetts and Connecticut ancestry and my own more difficult Maine and New Hampshire lines.

When I learned that Ruth Leighton Froeberg, compiler of a published Belden genealogy, was interested in preparing a Leighton genealogy, I turned over to her my typescript of the Cornman manuscript and my collection of data on downeast Leightons. For some years she corresponded with descendants and checked microfilm rolls, annotating and adding to parts of Julia Cornman's work. When I retired in 1980 she persuaded me to take up the burden of compiling a genealogy--then foreseen as merely an edited version of the Cornman manuscript. That concept has changed indeed.

Years ago Leonard F. Tibbetts, an eminent genealogist of downeast Maine families, had warned me that a genealogy of this Leighton family was impossible--just too many lines to follow. Now I realize how right he was. I realize also that at some point one must quit the search and publish, however incomplete the work.

This family history reflects that of our nation itself. Leightons fought for their homes against hostile Indians, alongside British troops against the French and their Indian allies, and then against the British to win independence. Some took part in "Madison's War" of 1812-1814, and nearly every Leighton of military age served with dogged zeal and an awesome mortality rate in the war to preserve the Union.

Many descendants still live in Maine and New Hampshire, some on land held in the family for over 200 years. Many others joined in the move west: farmers in upstate New York or the fertile central and western plains; lumberjacks in the forests of Michigan, Wisconsin and Oregon; miners in Montana; ranchers and citrus growers in California.

These Leightons have been mostly ordinary people. We can
find in this book sea captains, doctors, lawyers, a bishop,
an author, a brace of poets--but mostly they were farmers,
artisans, merchants, builders, mariners, lumbermen and stone-
cutters.

They were prolific, and their progeny are connected by marriage with many pioneer Maine and New Hampshire families.
The limited gene pool in small communities resulted in a
tight interweaving of families; marriages of cousins was not
only common but perhaps unavoidable.

One motive for undertaking this genealogy was the nagging
itch to set right several widespread errors. In turn, I
anticipate and welcome the inevitable addenda and corrigenda
of other researchers.

Another motive has been the enthusiastic encouragement of
hundreds of descendants, who have made clear their desire to
have the history of the family put into permanent form.

The contributions of others are too many to acknowledge
adequately here. First, of course, the formidable work of
Julia Cornman laid a solid foundation to build upon. Ruth
Froeberg added to that base, and has always retained faith
that publication was a realistic goal. Leonard F. Tibbetts
has generously shared his extensive records on Washington
County families. George F. Sanborn Jr. solved a knotty problem in his own Leighton ancestry, and reviewed the first six
generations of my draft. Gary Boyd Roberts reviewed the rest
of the draft, and has offered helpful editorial suggestions.
The late Margaret Kelley Ashe Colton generously checked Washington County data, often adding firsthand knowledge.

Many descendants have provided family records; their contributions have been noted in the appropriate sections of the
genealogy. The staff at the Maine Historical Society and the
Maine State Archives has been especially helpful, and those
at other libraries and societies have given valuable assis-
tance. Countless state, county and town officials have borne
with my requests, often able from their experience to give
answers to questions I didn't know enough to ask.

I dedicate this work to all those Leighton descendants who
have collaborated in making it possible.

Perley Leighton
177 Myrtle Street
Westbrook, Maine 04092
September 1989

INTRODUCTION

Editorial Patterns and Procedures

Since no genealogy can be truly complete, a compiler who plans to publish one must set both goals and limits. In this Leighton genealogy one goal has been to clarify and prove the relationships within the first six generations, mainly by using town records, deeds and wills.

Another goal was to trace as many lines as possible into the twentieth century; research concerning those born after about 1900 has had to be very limited. By using family scrapbooks and modern state records Leighton descendants now living should be able to place their parents or grandparents within the families described in this book.

Female lines are followed only to a limited degree; the immediate families of Leighton daughters, including their children with their spouses, have been included when the information was available. The grandchildren of Leighton daughters have not been listed.

Adopted children are shown, but their issue is not given. Illegitimate children are treated as if they were legitimate if they bore the Leighton surname.

Sources for information are indicated. So far as practical these are town or state vital records, censuses, gravestone inscriptions, military and pension files and other firsthand records. Data from US Census schedules are often identified in the text by notations such as "in 1850."

Information has sometimes been provided by others (usually descendants); often their family records have been accepted without verification. In fact, some of their sources--such as family Bibles and letters--are unique.

Genealogies, town and county histories and other secondary sources are frequently cited--not necessarily because they are the only or major sources, but often because they offer the reader clues to develop another ancestral line. The data in these could not always be verified; their inclusion does not imply any judgment as to their reliability. Frequently notations point out errors or variant data.

A full description is given when a book or other source is first cited in the text; an abbreviated title is given for subsequent citations, and the full title is listed in the Bibliography.

A number of lines are carried to the present, usually because a descendant has conscientiously gathered family records. Pursuing lines into the twentieth century a genealogist is today hindered by several barriers--accelerated geographical dispersion; just too many people to deal with in some prolific families; the substantial fees charged for most official records; the disappearance of written letters as a means of communication; and often a reluctance or even a refusal to provide information that is "too personal."

It has been impossible to include (or even search out) additional biographical details to give flesh to the barebones skeletons of names, dates and places. Readers should keep in mind that many sources have yet to be investigated, and that they have before them the joys and challenges of learning and preserving more information about their ancestors than this book can offer.

The arrangement of this genealogy follows the Register style. The first line of each family group section has the identification number of the Leighton described and his or her given name or names, and then the number assigned to the person's parents and their names. Lines can be traced back or forward by these numbers. In the Index numbers refer to pages, not to these individual numbers.

Over the centuries the name Leighton has been spelled many different ways: Layton, Laton, Laighton, Laiten etc. No single spelling can be designated the original or correct one because usage was inconsistent. This book does not attempt to indicate the spelling any particular person may have used. The first generations used Layton most of the time. Laighton then became more common, and was retained by the Portsmouth branch of the family. By 1800 Leighton had become standard, although variants continued to appear in census and other records.

Middle names did not come into common use until shortly after 1800. As the century went on, people switched their first and middle names back and forth (with no consideration for the problems they were creating for family historians). Charles F. was perhaps always called Fred; Jane M. may have been known as Jennie, Mary J., or even Polly or Molly. If a person was regularly known by her or his middle name, the first name is placed in parentheses. In the index some attempt is made to clarify such confusions, but readers may still need imagination to correlate some names.

Leightons known to be unrelated to Thomas of Dover are not included. Unfortunately, scores of other Leightons who may well be descended from him have had to be omitted also since no link can yet be proved or even reasonably advanced as an hypothesis.

The Cornman Manuscripts and Papers

Fortunately several collections of information concerning Leighton descendants have been made and preserved. Probably the most useful of these was the work of Julia Leighton Cornman, our genealogical trailblazer.

Julia Leighton [ID# 1106] was born at Lowell MA in 1852, graduated from Salem Normal School in 1872, and became a schoolteacher at Lowell. In 1877 she married Daniel Cornman, a West Point graduate and career army officer. They and their two sons lived for years at or near various army posts. Col. Cornman also served duty tours in Cuba, the Philippines and Mexico. After he retired in 1915 they lived at Washington DC. She died there in 1921 and he in 1924; both are buried in Arlington National Cemetery.

In 1901, while her husband was stationed in the Philippines, Mrs. Cornman seriously set about compiling a Leighton genealogy. She sent printed questionnaires to every Leighton she could find, gathering the names and addresses from other correspondents, postmasters, and directories. She collected official records and interviewed countless descendants, especially in northern New England. About the time her husband retired she apparently put aside her work on the genealogy.

After her death her husband and children realized the value of her research and arranged to have her papers preserved. Her manuscript Leighton genealogy is in the genealogical and local history collection at the New York Public Library: two boxes filled with unpaged sheets, stapled in sections which each describe a branch of the family. A collection of her papers in the manuscript collections of the New England Historic Genealogical Society includes a shorter Leighton genealogy and many other papers--letters, notebooks, family data forms, correspondence logs and material copied from books. (George F. Sanborn Jr., the Society's director of library operations, has made it possible for the compiler to collate the two collections.) In this book references to the Cornman manuscripts are usually to the New York version.

The two compilations of family groupings follow the same pattern--the bare listings of names and dates with almost no further detail. Both contain pencilled additions, erasures and cryptic notes about potential sources or possible relationships. The ink is faded, the paper deteriorating, the penmanship hurried and here and there barely decipherable. Neither compilation appears to be a later, corrected version of the other.

Julia Cornman listed no sources. To unravel the Leighton relationships, she must have checked probate and land records at county courthouses; her papers do not reveal any such searches. Vital records are collected in notebooks, but often with no place indicated. Her address lists bear a checkmark to indicate she had written and another that she had received a reply; they confirm that much of her nineteenth-century data came to her firsthand from descendants. The correspondence which survives, however, relates to people she could not fit into any line or to Leightons who emigrated to the United States long after the colonial period. Information derived from letters or questionnaires she received is cited in this book as coming from the "Cornman Papers."

Eight decades ago Julia Cornman talked and corresponded with people whose parents had been born in the eighteenth century. We may regret that she did not tell us where she obtained her data, but her work has provided a foundation on

which to build. It has been possible to document most of the
events she listed, to add biographical detail to her ungarn-
ished notations, and of course to follow Leighton lines far
beyond what she had been able to do.

Despite a few erroneous deductions and the occasional
perpetuation of others' mistakes, the general integrity of
Mrs. Cornman's work has been borne out by later research.
This compilation might never have been attempted without her
groundwork for inspiration.

English Origins

Leighton was first a placename given to a hamlet or town in
a lea or meadow (or perhaps a place where leeks were grown);
several English localities still bear the name. As a surname
it was not uncommon, especially in Cheshire, Shropshire and
Bedfordshire. Leightons, with many different spellings,
appeared in records as early as the twelfth century.

So far, the ancestry of Thomas Leighton of Dover has not
been determined. Genealogists, who abhor such dead ends as
nature abhors a vacuum, sometimes yield to temptation and
make imaginative linkages to historical personages. In a
letter dated 2 Sept. 1899 found among the Cornman Papers,
John Scales, the historian of New Hampshire and of Dover,
stated:

> Thomas Leighton Sr. was the son of Dr. Alexander
> Leighton, the distinguished theologian and Professor in
> the University of Edinborough, Scotland; he was one of
> the leaders in the fight against the English Church
> during the reign of Charles I and was a staunch sup-
> porter of the Protector Oliver Cromwell. He sent his
> son Thomas to New England with the party that came over
> with Captain Wiggin, having servants, in the English
> style of gentlemen who owned large landed estates,
> cattle and much property. Thomas's older brother Rob-
> ert remained in England and when times changed became
> distinguished as the Archbishop of Glasgow.

Scales even described a Leighton coat of arms which had
been first granted in 1260:

> There was a family Bible that belonged to Thomas Sr,
> and passed on to his son Thomas Jr, in whose possession
> it remained as long as he lived. In this Bible was
> engraved the Leighton Coat of Arms; the description of
> this engraving in the old Bible corresponds exactly
> with that furnished by the Heraldry Office. What
> became of the Bible I do not know

Despite the improbability of this ancestry many genealogies
have confidently shown Thomas of Dover as son of Dr. Alexander Leighton (1568-1649). The Scottish divine and physician had four sons and two daughters but no Thomas among them
(Dictionary of National Biography, 11:880-883). We should
note, moreover, that Thomas of Dover signed all documents
with his mark; it is not likely that Alexander Leighton would
have had an illiterate son.

John Winthrop, governor of the Massachusetts Bay colony, noted in his journal on 10 Oct. 1633 (John Winthrop, The History of New England 1630 to 1649, edited by James Savage [Boston, 1853], 137):

> The same day, Mr. Grant, in the ship James, arrived at Salem, having been but eight weeks between Gravesend and Salem. He brought Capt. Wiggin and about thirty, with one Mr. Leveridge, a godly minister, to Piscataquack, (which the Lord Say and the Lord Brook had purchased of the Bristol men) and about thirty for Virginia, and about twenty for this place, and some sixty cattle.

No list of those passengers survives; the number thirty could have meant either heads of households or individuals. In his History of Durham, N. H., Everett Stackpole listed [p. 3] twenty men as probably in Capt. Wiggin's party; most of these, however, are mentioned in earlier Bay Colony or New Hampshire records. In his History of New Hampshire [1:33] Stackpole "safely mentions" Thomas Leighton among passengers on the James. It is very likely but not at all proven that he had been recruited as a planter during Capt. Wiggin's trip to England in 1632 to seek increased financial backing from Shrewsbury merchants.

Thomas was evidently from the yeoman class of landowners rather than from the gentry. He was a Puritan who displayed no unusual interest in church matters. Nothing is known of his wife Joanna's origin--not even whether the two married in England before the voyage or in Massachusetts or at Dover after his arrival in New England.

Even more persistent than John Scales's Edinburgh legend is that of the "three brothers"--usually listed as Thomas of Dover, William of Kittery and John of Saco. No evidence has been found that any of the early Leighton immigrants were related to one another.

Other New England Leighton Families

Not all New England Leightons are descended from Thomas of Dover, N. H.--far from it. In his Genealogical Dictionary of the First Settlers of New England (3:44), James Savage listed several others who had immigrated before 1650: in Maine, William of Kittery and John of Saco; in Massachusetts, Richard of Rowley with his sons Ezekiel and John, John of Ipswich, and Thomas of Lynn with his sons Samuel and Thomas; and in Rhode Island, the brothers George and Thomas of Portsmouth, and Daniel of Newport.

William[1] had settled at Kittery, Maine, by 1656, and through his son John left many descendants. Almost all the Leightons of York County are of this family; some cropped up living near Thomas's descendants in Somerset and Penobscot Counties, and later in Illinois and Iowa. A good genealogy of this family is Tristram Frost Jordan's An Account of the Descendants of Capt. William Leighton of Kittery, Maine [Albany, 1855]. An unidentified William Layton living at Dover in 1655 and on tax lists there in 1663 and 1666 may have been the William who joined others from this area in

settling Piscataway, N. J.   The Genealogical Dictionary of
Maine and New Hampshire (p. 428) attributed these references
to William of Kittery.

John Layton, freeman of Winter Harbor (Saco) in 1653, had a
son John who left descendants at Portsmouth, N. H.   John of
Winnegance, a Maine pioneer on the Kennebec River, apparently
had no children.

Richard[1] was living at Rowley by 1643 (George B. Blodgette
and Amos E. Jewett, Early Settlers of Rowley, Mass. [Rowley,
1930], 228-30), and left many descendants.   One of them,
Capt. John[4], settled at Littleton and at Westford (Frederick
W. Weis, Ancestors of Frank Chester Harrington and Leora
(Leighton) Harrington [Worcester MA, 1958], 152ff; Edwin R.
Hodgman, History of Westford, Mass. [Lowell, 1883], 460).
Another, Jonathan[4], took his family from Rowley to Maine and
died at Newcastle in 1772.   His four sons and six daughters
left many descendants in Maine (David Q. Cushman, History of
Ancient Sheepscot and Newcastle [Bath, ME, 1882], 398-9).

John of Ipswich named no children in his will, but did name
his brother Richard and his cousin (really nephew) John of
Rowley.   Hodgman's version of the "three brothers" tradition
linked John of Ipswich with William of Kittery and Samuel of
Virginia.   Thomas[1], freeman at Lynn in 1639, had sons Thomas
and Samuel and three daughters.   Many Massachusetts Leightons
descend from this "other" Thomas.

Unrelated Leighton families have not been traced except for
such checking as has been required to set them apart.   Many
Leightons came to the United States directly from the British
Isles or from New Brunswick and Nova Scotia.   Some (often
named Layton) appeared before 1800 on Long Island, N. Y., in
Virginia, and on the opening frontier.

Some are Leightons in name only.   In 1832 Isaac and Abigail
Leathers (or Letheres) of Strafford, N. H., had their family
name changed to Leighton by the legislature; the action also
named their twelve children.   Some immigrants adopted the
name--examples include a Portuguese at Boston, a Finn at
Rockport, Maine, and a Polish Jew at New York.   Scores of
"dangling" Leightons cannot be tied into the family of Thomas
of Dover, nor yet definitely excluded.

Settlement of New Hampshire

The early history of Dover and of the New Hampshire colony
is complicated.   In 1620, a royal charter covering the Province of Maine, then a territory stretching from the Merrimac
to the Sagadahoc River, was granted to the Council of New
England.   The Council in turn awarded a patent for these
lands in 1622 to Sir Ferdinando Gorges and Capt. John Mason.
Neither ever came to New England.   Their agent David Thomson
founded a trading company at Odiorne's Point (Newcastle), and
Edward Hilton was granted rights to establish the first permanent colony at Hilton's Point (Wecohannet or Dover Neck) in
1628.   Walter Neale, agent for a group of London adventurers,
established Strawbery Banke (Portsmouth), and opposed Hilton
by claiming "Bloody Point" (now Newington).

The planters were expected to exploit the new world's
resources--fish and furs, and timber for masts, shipbuilding,
potash and barrel staves--and thereby yield a profit for the
English investors. The original grants were small neighboring plots; the later grants were larger, reflecting the
reality of permanent towns and farms.

In 1629, Gorges and Mason divided their patent along the
Piscataqua River; Mason named his portion "New-Hampshire."
Hilton sold his rights there to a group of merchants at Bristol, England, who sold them to the Puritan Lords Say and
Brooke, who in turn sold shares to a group of Shrewsbury
investors. Capt. Thomas Wiggin, a friend of Gov. John Winthrop, was appointed head of the Dover enterprise; in 1632 he
was in England's west country, seeking increased financial
backing and recruiting settlers for the Piscataqua.

Most of the early New Hampshire settlers were from Massachusetts. By 1640 they numbered nearly 1000, divided among
the towns of Dover, Portsmouth, Hampton and Exeter. Because
they feared Indian attacks and lacked an effective government
these settlers sought the protection of the stronger Bay colony; they decided in 1642 to form a union with Massachusetts.
For the next thirty years New Hampshire was governed from
Puritan Boston.

Settlement spread despite Indian attacks on outlying homes
in 1675-1676 during and after King Philip's War. In 1680 New
Hampshire received its own royal charter as a separate province, but in 1690 during King William's War it again united
with Massachusetts. Until 1740 the two colonies were under
the same royal governor, even after New Hampshire had again
achieved separate status.

A series of British wars against the French and their
Indian allies, sideshows to the dynastic struggles between
England and France in Europe, kept New England in turmoil
from 1689 to 1760. In New Hampshire only a few outlying
towns suffered direct attack, but town militia companies
joined British troops in expeditions against strongholds in
Nova Scotia and Quebec, and against French forces penetrating
south along Lake George.

Despite the wars settlement spread out from the original
towns, and then up the Merrimac and Connecticut Rivers, the
result of Massachusetts and Connecticut populations spilling
north. By 1760 the best arable land was gone. In 1763 the
Treaty of Paris ended French rule in Canada and Indian terror
in the colonies, but in the same year a royal proclamation
prohibited settlement west and north of existing frontiers.
For many New Hampshire families, the future lay east in the
struggling settlements or trackless wilderness of Maine.

Patterns of Migration

The attention usually focused on migrations to the west has
obscured the extent of the Eastern Migration, from New Hampshire and Massachusetts into Maine. Early in the eighteenth
century the colonial government of Massachusetts laid out new
townships in southern Maine and sold them to proprietors who

encouraged settlers by offering generous purchase terms.
Well before 1750 many New Hampshire families had obtained
settlers' rights or had purchased land in what soon became
Cumberland and Lincoln counties, joining other immigrants
from Essex County and Cape Cod.

During the French Wars, New Hampshire soldiers had gone up
the Connecticut and Hudson Rivers toward Canada and down the
Maine coast into Nova Scotia (which then included New Brunswick). From 1760 to 1840 or so the route to new opportunities from southeastern New Hampshire was into Maine --to the
virgin forests downeast, the growing towns in the south, and
the potential farmland inland. By coastal ships and by
inland trails along the Ossipee and the Androscoggin people
flooded into Maine. Several inland towns were originally
settled exclusively by New Hampshire migrants.

The Leighton experience reflects the extent of this east-
ward migration. Of the seven heads of family in the fourth
generation, four settled in Maine; of the 33 heads of family
in the fifth generation 18 were in Maine: two at Falmouth,
ten inland at Mount Vernon and Harmony, and six in what is
now Washington County. A few years later the 1790 federal
census listed 25 descendants of Thomas Leighton in New Hampshire, and 25 in the district of Maine. Other Leightons
joined this eastern movement over the next half-century or
so, establishing branches of the family in Somerset and
Penobscot counties.

This genealogy also reflects the opening of the western
frontiers to settlement after the Revolutionary War. The
Western Reserve Act opened Ohio and Indiana; soon after New
York settlements were encouraged by soldiers' bounty awards
and, after 1825, by the new Erie Canal. Severe weather drove
many to leave Maine, especially after "Eighteen-hundred-and-
Froze-to-Death"--the year without a summer in 1816. Settlers
were welcomed in Illinois, Michigan and Wisconsin in the
1830s and after, and in Iowa in the 1850s. Minnesota drew
New Englanders by the 1860s, especially lumbermen (nicknamed
"Bangor Tigers"). A spurt of migration to northern California in the early 1850s followed the gold rush, and another of
ranchers and farmers to southern California after the Civil
War. When the boundary was drawn by treaty with Great Britain Oregon and Washington were opened to settlers in the
1860s, attracting Yankee loggers and fishermen as well as
farmers.

Leightons are found in each of the western surges. These
down-east natives took west with them their faith in self-
government, in local schooling, in religious freedom and in
economic initiative.

THOMAS LEIGHTON THE IMMIGRANT

1. **THOMAS**[1] (1604-1672) was born in England about 1604 (deposed aged 60 in Dec. 1665), and died at Dover NH 22 Jan. 1671-2 (Vital Records of Dover, N. H. [Heritage Books, 1977], reprinted from Collections of the Dover, N. H., Historical Society [Dover, 1894], 117). He married, perhaps after arriving in New England, JOANNA ---- , born say 1617, who as widow of Job Clements "departed this life being full of daies" at Dover 15 Jan. 1703-4 (VRs Dover, 3).

Although no record of his arrival exists, Thomas Layton (as the name was spelled in early records) was undoubtedly among the planters of Dover (then called Northam) who settled at Cocheco or Dover Point in 1633 under the leadership of Capt. Thomas Wiggin (see Introduction). His home lot of ten acres was on the present border of Dover and Madbury, later bisected by the Post Road which bridged the Piscataquis River; for generations this area was called "Leighton's Hill" (Mary P. Thompson, Landmarks in Ancient Dover, N. H. [Durham, 1892], 118-9.) About two and a half centuries after, in 1885, Mary Ann (Leighton) Rollins had a monument erected "In Memory of the Leighton Household" in the field on the west side of the Back River Road.

Thomas soon acquired extensive land holdings (John Scales, History of Dover, N. H.: Colonial Era [Manchester, 1923, reprinted in 1977], 202, 235-248); in 1639 he was taxed on property valued at 155 pounds--the highest assessment in the town. In 1640 he was granted ten acres of marshland on Great Bay; in 1642 he received # 18 of the 20-acre lots laid out on the west side of the Back River; on 15 Apr. 1646 he was allotted ten acres on Great Bay near Laighton's Cove (on Bloody Point, which later became the town of Newington).

On the tax list of 19 10mo [Dec.] 1646 he had the second-highest assessment (Scales, Dover, 234; for tax lists of 1649 through 1666 see Alonzo Quint, Historical Memoranda concerning Persons and Places in Old Dover, N. H. [Dover, 1900, reprinted in 1983], 140, 349-364). He, William Pomfret and John Dam were granted mill privileges at Bellamy's Bank in 1649 (Quint, Old Dover, 35); he sold his quarter-share in the sawmill there 8 Apr. 1653 (New England Historical and Genealogical Register [NEHGReg], 47[1893]:469). On 10 Jan. 1655 he was granted 100 acres on the west shore of Great Bay, and in 1656 another 30 acres of upland adjoining Laighton's Cove (Thompson, Landmarks, 118-9) and 100 acres on the south side of Frenchman's Creek. In 1656 he bought 20 more acres adjoining his Back Bay property from Ambrose Gibbons. On 11 Jan. 1658-9 he deeded 20 acres to his apprentice John Wingate (New Hampshire Province Deeds [NHPD], 3:43), and on 16 Feb. 1670 he deeded to Thomas, Jr., the house and 160-acre farm north of Royall's Cove which his son was already occupying (NHPD 3:58).

Land was usually laid out to settlers according to their
ability to develop it. Thomas Layton's land acquisitions
suggest that he immigrated bringing the money and tools he
would need to establish himself in the new world. Settlers
had to cut down trees to clear ground for crops, although the
salt marshes might provide hay for their stock. Besides
farming, they engaged in fur-trading, fishing, making pipes-
taves and clapboards, and rendering potash from wood ashes.
Dover settlers developed a lively trade with the West Indies,
especially the Barbados, in dried salt fish and barrel
staves; it is probable that Thomas Leighton invested cargo in
such ventures.

He was influential in shaping the pioneer community. His
name and mark ("T") are on all the early political documents:
the petition against control by Massachusetts Bay 4 Mar. 1640
(N. H. Provincial and State Papers [NHSP], 1:128); the Dover
Combination of 22 Oct. 1640 (10:701); the petition on 9 Oct.
1641 for union with the Bay Colony; a petition against
the Patentees in 1654 (1:212); and on 10 Oct. 1665 a declaration of continued allegiance to Massachusetts (1:284-5). He
was repeatedly chosen as selectman, grand juror and constable
("Extracts from Dover Town Records," New Hampshire Genealogical Record [NHGR], 4[1907]: 247; Quint, Old Dover, 1-10). He
was made a freeman (having full voting rights) in 1653 and
was released from the obligation for military training 26
June 1661 (NHSP, 40:157).

Thomas Layton's will, made 21 Sept. 1671, was admitted to
probate 25 June 1672 (NHSP, 31:126-7, 212). It was unusual
in that his widow was left a life interest in the whole
estate rather than the usual one-third dower right, and that
his children were not to receive their shares until her
re-marriage or death. An inventory of his estate was made 15
Feb. 1671-2 (New Hampshire Province Probate Records [NHPP],
1:145-6; 2:186).

Joanna Layton did marry again, to Job Clements, Sr., at
Dover 16 July 1673 (VRs Dover 109). Son of Robert and Lydia
Clements, he was born at Anstey, Warwickshire, England, about
1615, and died at Dover about 1683; his will was made 4 7mo
[Sept.] 1682 and proved 9 Nov. 1683. He had married first at
Haverhill MA 25 Dec. 1645 Margaret Dummer and second a Lydia.
A prosperous tanner, he became a Dover inhabitant by 1653,
and served on the Provincial Council (Sybil Noyes, Charles T.
Libby and Walter G. Davis, Genealogical Dictionary of Maine
and New Hampshire [Portland 1928-39, reprinted Baltimore
1976], 150).

The historian John Scales has sown confusion about the
early Leightons. In his Piscataqua Pioneers 1623-1775
[Dover, 1919, 122-3], he insisted that Joanna could not have
been the mother of Thomas's children because she was called
his "present wife," and because she must have been too young,
outliving him by more than 30 years. Since she was about 87
when she died, she would have been 25 or so when her first
child was born. The wording "my present wife" appeared in
many wills of the period, part of the contemporary legal jar-
gon and meant to eliminate confusion with any possible past
or future spouse.

In the documents below, spelling and punctuation have been
modernized, and clarification of some terms has been given in
brackets.

Thomas Layton's Will

In the name and fear of God Amen, I Thomas Layton senior of Dover in New England, aged sixty-seven years or thereabouts, being exercised with great infirmity of body, but through the goodness of God of sound mind and memory, not knowing how soon my dissolution may be, do therefore make and conclude this my last Will and Testament in manner and form as followeth.

First, I recommend my soul into the hands of my blessed God and Father and in our Lord Jesus Christ, and my body to the Dust to be buried in a Christian manner at the discretion of my executor and executrix hereafter mentioned.

As for my outward estate, my will is that my present wife Joanna do enjoy (during her natural life if she continue in the estate of widowhood, or during her widowhood if she marry) my whole estate both personal and real, to be improved for her comfortable maintenance; and at her marriage one-third part of the whole, after that--her marriage--to be improved by or for her until her decease.

That my only son and heir Thomas Layton shall have (besides what he hath or shall receive before my decease) all my housing, lands, orchard, marshes, flats, with their privileges or appurtances, either within or out of this town, to be had and held by him, his heirs or assigns forever, after they fall from his mother by marriage or her decease as abovesaid. To him also I give one-quarter part of the movables [furniture and other personal property] which shall be left undisposed of by my wife for her comfortable supply as abovesaid.

He, the said Thomas Layton my son, paying to my daughter Mary, the wife of Thomas Roberts junior, to the value of ten pounds, to my daughter Elizabeth, wife of Philip Cromwell, to the value of forty pounds, to my daughter Sarah (unmarried at present) to the value of forty pounds, which he is to pay to them or to their heirs or assigns within the space or term of two years after the decease of his mother Joanna if they shall demand it, which I by these presents assign to them out of the said estate, together with a quarter part of the movables /to each of them/ which shall be left by my wife Joanna. He, the said Thomas my son, also setting John my Indian servant free, and paying to him the value of five pounds at the decease of the said Joanna. Moreover I do hereby constitute and appoint my son and heir Thomas abovesaid Executor and my wife Joanna Executrix jointly whilst they are both living, and severally after the decease of either of them.

In witness of the premises [statements] I do hereby set my hand and seal this one and twentieth day of September Anno Domini 1671.

John Reynor   Thomas [T] Layton senior
                                       his mark
Thomas X Roberts junior
    his mark

Inventory of Property

An inventory of the Estate of Thomas Layton senior deceased, taken this 15th day of February anno domini 1671 by the persons hereinafter mentioned, at the request of widow Layton and her son Thomas Layton.

		L	S
Impr[imis] the stock			
It[em] Two yoke [pair] of oxen		26	-
It One bull and three steers		15	-
It Two Heifers and a steer		7	-
It Three yearlings and a calf		3	-
It Four cows		18	-
It One and twenty sheep		12	-
It Six grown swine and 3 pigs		6	-
It Poultry		-	7

Tools and instruments of husbandry

It One cart and wheels, one sled, one plow
with plow irons [reinforced edges], one
harrow, three yokes, three chains and a
clevis [shackle], two [ox]bows, three axes,
one beetle [maul] and six wedges, one thwart
[crosscut] saw, one iron shovel, a spade
and a shovel shod [edged with iron], two
hammers, a pair of pincers, a pickax and
a mattock, two pitchforks, two scythes,
one hatchet, one grinding stone   6   6

It Three augers, a square and a pair of comp-
asses, one square adze and one hollowing
adze, one chisel. one gouge, one spokeshave,
one hand-saw, one plow iron, one drawing
knife, one pair of wheel rings [rims], one
crow[bar]   13

It Five canoes   4   -
It Cider press   8

In the Kitchen

It Iron--three pots, one kettle, one gridiron,
one mortar and pestle, two pair of trammels
[fireplace chains and hooks], one pressing
iron, one pair of tongs, one fire pan   2   10
It 2 brass kettles and one copper kettle 3   -
It provisions with their vessels   10   -

In the Hall

It pewter--4 dishes, 2 basins, 3 porringers,
3 saucers, 1 quart pot, 1 saltcellar,
1 beer bowl, 1 chamber pot   1   5
It Wooden ware--1 cupboard and one table, 5
chairs, 4 pails, 3 tubs, platters   2   -

In the parlor

It His own wearing clothes   5   10
It One bed and furniture [bedding] to it 7   -
It One tablecloth and one dozen of napkins 1 -
It 3 chests and one trunk   1   -
It Yarn and cotton, wool   1   9
It woolen and cotton cloth   11   -
It a warming pan   6
It Stock cards and small cards [brushes with
teeth for untangling fibers   9
It two pair of sheep irons [shears]   2

```
        In the Chamber
It Bedding                                          2   10
It Peas [dried]                                     4   12
It Barley                                               6
It 3 spinning wheels                                    6
        In the Garret
It Indian corn                                     12    -
It malt                                                16
        Immovables
It Dwelling house, barn, orchard and pasture
    adjoining                                      100   -
It Lot adjoining to G[oodman] Davis and G.         15    -
    Beard
It Another lot adjoining to G. Davis               25    -
It Lot joining to G. Tibbetts                      50    -
It A twenty-acre lot with marsh and flats on
    the west of Back River                         48    -
It Land and meadow on the West Bay                 50    -
It Oats to thrash, 20 bushels                       2   10
It Blanketing at mill to full [shrink and           5    -
    thicken]
It One Indian slave                                15    -
It Credit [proceeds due from loan]                  2    -
        The whole sum cast up                     475    5
```

The inventory within written was taken at the date there-in specified, finished and cast up on the 21st day of the 4th mo 72. Prised [appraised] by us, Job Clements, John Damme, John Hall.

Joanna Layton executrix, the relict of Thos. Layton, and Thomas Layton executor, son of the above, appeared in court this 25th day of the 4mo [June] 1672, and made oath that this is a true and just inventory of the estate of the late Thomas Layton abovesaid to the best of their knowledge, and that when they know more they will discover it. This they done, as attests

            Elias Stileman, Clerk

Children, born at Dover:

2. i.   THOMAS[2], b. say 1642.
3. ii.   MARY, b. say 1644; m. THOMAS ROBERTS, JR.
4. iii. ELIZABETH, b. say 1646; m. PHILIP CROMWELL.
    iv.   SARAH, b. in 1648; unm. in 1671. Julia Cornman
          (in her manuscript "Leighton Genealogy," New
          York Public Library) placed her as the wife of
          Philip Chesley. In the Noyes-Libby-Davis Gen-
          ealogical Dictionary (p. 139), Charles Thornton
          Libby named Sarah Rollins as Chesley's wife,
          basing his deduction on the choice of Chesley by
          Sarah's father James Rollins as an overseer of
          his will (see his letter of 28 Mar. 1932 to
          Samuel B. Shackford, NEHGS Ms Collections).

SECOND GENERATION

2. **THOMAS**[2] 1642-1677 [1 Thomas[1] and Joanna] was born at Dover say 1642, died there intestate in 1677; married first at Dover about 1670 ELIZABETH NUTTER, born at Dover say 1646, died there between 1671 and 1674, daughter of Hatevil and Anne (----) Nutter (Noyes-Libby-Davis, 516); married second ELIZABETH ---- , who survived him.

The town voted 28 July 1665 to pay a bounty to Thomas, Jr., and others for "Kielling a wolfe" (Quint, Old Dover, 71). On 13 Feb. 1670, the same day that his father deeded him a house and land, Hatevil Nutter deeded him a 40-acre lot between Oyster River and Back River (NHPD, 3:58); these deeds were probably marriage gifts. His drafting of a will six years before he died suggests his health had been poor.

He took the freeman's oath 25 June 1672 (NHSP, 40:277), served as constable in 1673 (40:290) and as juryman in 1676. His estate was inventoried 29 Oct. 1677 at more than 515 pounds (NHPD, 5:20-26; NHSP, 31:186). Administration was granted to Elizabeth Layton, Philip Cromwell and John Tuttle 31 Oct. 1677 (NHSP, 31:200). On 25 June 1678, at the widow's request, Lt. Peter Coffin and Mr. Fryer were appointed additional administrators.

When Hatevil Nutter made his will 24 Dec. 1674, he did not mention his daughter Elizabeth, indicating she was then dead (NHSP 31:157-9). (From him, the name Hatevil persisted generation after generation among his descendants, notably in the Leighton, Roberts and Hall families.) Julia Cornman made a conjecture that Thomas's second wife may have been born a Tuttle, perhaps because John Tuttle was a co-administrator of the estate.

Children by first wife Elizabeth, born at Dover:

5. i. THOMAS[3], b. c1671.
6. ii. JOHN, b. say 1673.

Child by second wife Elizabeth, born at Dover:

7. iii. ELIZABETH, b. say 1676; m. RICHARD PINKHAM.

3. **MARY**[2] 1644- [1 Thomas[1] and Joanna] was born at Dover say 1644; married by 1671 THOMAS ROBERTS, JR., born at Dover about 1636 (deposed as aged 25 in 1661), living about age 70 in 1705, son of Thomas and Rebecca Roberts (Noyes-Libby-Davis, 589; Scales, Dover, 302ff).

He served Dover as selectman in 1670, 1671 and 1694, and was sergeant of the Dover militia company.

Children (**Roberts**), born at Dover, order uncertain:

i.   THOMAS, JR., will 1746-1755; m. SARAH CANNEY, b. 3
      Aug. 1667, dau. of Thomas and Sarah (Taylor) Canney.
ii.   NATHANIEL, will 1746-1753; m. Somersworth 11 Apr.
      1706 ELIZABETH MASON.
iii. JOHN, b. c1680, will 1749-1756; m. 1st 26 Oct. 1704
      DEBORAH CHURCH, b. 15 Aug. 1683, dau. of John and
      Sarah Church; m. 2nd 17 May 1720 FRANCES EMERY,
      b. 17 Dec. 1694, dau. of James and Margeret (Hitch-
      cock) Emery.
iv.   JOANNA, living in 1729; m. 24 Mar. 1690 THOMAS
      POTTS of Oyster River, son of Richard and Margaret
      Potts.
v.   MARY, d. "ancient" in 1745; m. THOMAS YOUNG.
vi.   LYDIA; m. her cousin HATEVIL ROBERTS, son of John and
      Abigail (Nutter) Roberts.
vii. SARAH; m. 8 June 1704 HOWARD HENDERSON, son of
      William and Sarah (Howard) Henderson.

4. ELIZABETH^2 1646-   [1 Thomas^1 and Joanna] was born at
Dover say 1646, survived her husband; married Capt. PHILIP
CROMWELL, born about 1634 (deposed as aged 32 in 1666), died
at Dover 26 May 1708, aged about 74, son of Giles and Alice
(Weeks) Cromwell (Noyes-Libby-Davis, 173). He had married
first by 1663 Elizabeth Tuttle, daughter of John and Dorothy
Tuttle of Dover. He was taxed at Cocheco (Dover) in 1657,
and lived at Oyster River (later Durham), a ships' carpenter
by trade. In 1683 he was commissioned captain of the town
militia (Everett S. Stackpole, Lucien Thompson, Meserve S.
Winthrop, History of the Town of Durham, N. H. [Concord,
1913, reprinted in 1973], 2:83-4).

Note: Elizabeth Layton is mistakenly claimed as an ancestor
by many Hall and Small descendants. Lora Underhill stated in
her Descendants of Edward Small of New England [rev. ed.,
1934, 1:44] that "about 1652 or 1653, Francis Small married
Elizabeth ---- : mentioned by Mr. Charles W. Tuttle as Elizabeth Leighton, who was born ... about 1634." Alonzo Quint
(Old Dover, 257) reported that John^2 Hall "married (1?)
Elizabeth, daughter of Thomas Laighton"; while Joseph B. Hall
stated that Deacon John^1 Hall "married, it is said, Elizabeth
Layton, daughter of Thomas Layton, but of this we are not
sure" (Genealogy of Hatevil Hall and Descendants [undated,
unpaged scrapbook] MHS).

Children (**Cromwell**), all named in Philip's will, the first
      five probably by Elizabeth Tuttle:

i.   JOSHUA, b. say 1665; m. LYDIA ---- .
ii.   SAMUEL, b. say 1668; m. ELIZABETH ---- and RACHEL
      ---- .
iii. JOANNA, living in 1753; m. in 1706 MORRIS HOBBS, b.
      1 Jan. 1677, d. c1753, son of James and Sarah
      (Fifield) Hobbs.
iv.   ALICE.
v.   ELIZABETH; m. 1st in 1695 SAMUEL EDGERLY; m. 2nd
      (per Cornman Ms, but not Noyes-Libby-Davis) JOHN
      AMBLAR.

vi.   SARAH, b. 1668; probably m. JOHN[3] LEIGHTON [# 6]. In
      letters to Samuel B. Shackford 28 Mar. and 8 Apr.
      1932 (Ms Collections, NEHGS), Charles T. Libby based
      this probability on the placement in the Dover town
      records of Ann Cromwell's birth (30 yrs. late) just
      below the birth of John's dau. Lydia.
        Sarah has also been called the wife of TIMOTHY[2]
      WENTWORTH, son of William and Elizabeth (Knight)
      Wentworth, who d. in 1719 leaving 5 children (John
      Wentworth, The Wentworth Genealogy [Boston, 1878],
      1:157).
vii. MERCY, b. say 1672; m. 14 Mar. 1706-7 HATEVIL HALL,
      son of John and Abigail (Roberts) Hall.
viii. ANN, b. 19 Aug. 1674.

THIRD GENERATION

5. THOMAS[3] 1671-1744 [2 Thomas[2] and Elizabeth Nutter] was born at Dover about 1671 (deposed as aged 32 in 1702), died at Newington in 1744; married DEBORAH ---- , born about 1683 (deposed as aged 61 in 1744), survived her husband. Julia Cornman conjectured that she was surnamed Bunker, but without giving any rationale for her guess.

Only six when his father died, he was placed under the guardianship of his uncle Lt. Anthony Nutter, who on 31 Oct. 1677 and 25 June 1678 filed complaints of not receiving sufficient funds for the boy's maintenance (NHSP, 31:200; 40: 338). Nutter died of smallpox 19 Feb. 1685-6; no other guardian was shown in the records.

About 1692, on attaining his majority, Thomas would have been given control of his inherited estate, subject to his grandmother's rights. He signed a petition on 10 Aug. that year which asked the Bay Colony for aid against the Indians (Noyes-Libby-Davis, 13), and another in 1695 asking that Oyster River be a separate parish (NHSP, 9:234). On 18 Apr. 1699 he conveyed part of his Dover land to Richard Pinkham and "my only sister Elizabeth" (NHPD, 5:108). He was sergeant of the Dover militia, and was employed in 1700 to carry messages to the Earl of Bellomont concerning Indian depredations at Cocheco (NHSP, 3:96-7).

He lived on Bloody Point, which in 1714 became the town of Newington. He signed the petition 15 July 1713 which asked the Provincial Council to establish the new parish (NHSP, 9:234), and pledged payment for a pew in the new meetinghouse 25 Oct. 1714 (Noyes-Libby-Davis, 49). The eastern portion of his Dover land, on Frenchman's Creek, he sold to Samuel Emerson 17 May 1714 (NHPD, 9:428-9). As administrator "unto my father Tho Layton dec'd" he turned over to his brother John, in a deed dated 4 Jan. 1717-8, "land granted by Dover to my grandfather Thomas Layton, also land said grandfather bought of Henry Beck" (9:734). He bought more Newington land from Clement Meserve in 1721 and from John Fabyan in 1729, and was a proprietor of Barnstead in 1727 (NHSP, 24:419-20).

He and his son John in 1722 joined with John McDuffee in purchasing a proprietor's share in the newly-laid-out settlement of Rochester (Franklin McDuffee, History of the Town of Rochester N. H. from 1722 to 1890 [Manchester, 1892], 1:40). On 2 Dec. 1729 Thomas and John bought from John Carter of Newington the other third of this Rochester land, lot 93 of the first division (NHPD, 17:122).

In his sixties Thomas began disposing of his holdings. On 17 July 1735 he deeded to his son John 70 acres in Dover, and the same day an adjoining 60-acre lot to his son Hatevil (21:415, 269). His proprietor's share in Barnstead he deeded 22 June 1739 to his grandson William [# 20], minor son of John. On 26 Jan. 1741 he deeded to his son Thomas, Jr., his homestead in Newington and his meetinghouse pew in return for

1000 pounds and a bond to support his parents for life
(25:466-7, 472). He also sold to his son Thomas 6 Mar.
1743-4 his share of their Rochestor rights (28:508).
Thomas died intestate in 1744; his widow was made administratrix 29 Aug., and his estate was inventoried at more than
102 pounds on 15 Nov. (NHPP, 15:357; NHSP, 33:209-10).

Note: Relationships among these early Leightons were
confused by respected historians, and their errors have been
perpetuated in later books and manuscript genealogies. For
example, Walter L. Leighton (A Genealogical Sketch of a
Dover, N. H., Branch of the Leighton Family [Newton MA,
1940], 7) paused in his narrative to observe: "Everett Stackpole confirms to this point the Leighton line as I have it:
Thomas(1), Thomas(2), John(3), Thomas(4), Hatevil(5)." That
line should be Thomas(3), Hatevil(4).
    Rev. Alonzo Quint probably initiated the confusion. In his
notes on early Dover families (NEHGReg, 7[1853]:255-6), he
treated as one this Thomas and his nephew Thomas [# 16] who
married Susannah Chesley, saying casually "(apparently the
same person)." Stackpole gave the error the weight of his
reputation in his History of Durham, N. H. (2:259-50), and
John Scales repeated it in his books and correspondence. Of
course the confusion became worse when the children of the
two Thomases had to be accounted for. Julia Cornman's manuscripts and the Noyes-Libby-Davis Genealogical Dictionary
(p. 427) described the relationships correctly.

Children:

8.   i.   ELIZABETH[4], b. Dover c1703; m. RICHARD DAM.
9.   ii.   JOHN, b. Dover in 1706.
10. iii. ABIGAIL, b. Dover 14 Jan. 1710; m. NEHEMIAH
           FURBER.
11. iv.   HATEVIL, b. Dover in 1712.
12. v.   DEBORAH, b. Newington c1714; m. WILLIAM COLLINS
           and ARTHUR WATERHOUSE.
13. vi.   OLIVE, b. Newington c1720; m. JAMES COLBATH.
14. vii. THOMAS, bp. Newington 13 May 1720.
15. viii. KEZIAH, b. Newington c1722; m. ELEAZER COLEMAN.

6.   **JOHN[3]** 1673-1718 [2 Thomas[2] and Elizabeth Nutter]
was born at Dover say 1673, died there about 1718; married
first SARAH (probably SARAH CROMWELL [# 4]); married second
ELEANOR (MERROW) Meader, born at Reading MA, died at Dover
about 1738, daughter of Henry and Jane (Linders) (Wallis)
Merrow (Noyes-Libby-Davis, 474, 476). Eleanor married first
about 1695 Nathaniel Meader; they had five children before he
was killed by Indians 25 Apr. 1704 at Oyster River (Stackpole, Durham, 2:276).
    John served under Capt. John Woodman for 34 days at the
Oyster River garrison, Dec. 1695 to Jan. 1696 (NHSP, 17:655).
He was chosen guardian of James Nute 16 Dec. 1699 (NHPP,
3:173; NHSP, 31:361). On 22 Nov. 1698 he sold 20 acres on the
Back River to Shadrach Hodsdon (Thompson, Landmarks, 65). He
was deeded land at Dover by Job Clements 15 Mar. 1704 (a
consequence perhaps of the recent death of John's grandmother
Joanna), and bought land at Madbury 29 Mar. 1708 from Samuel
Perkins (NHPD, 5:111, 7:211). He was chosen surveyor of
highways in 1706, 1708 and 1709 (Quint, Old Dover, 160-161).

He sold land in Dover 7 May 1714 to Timothy Conner, and on
the 25th of that month sold 30 acres to John Drew (NHPD,
11:136, 9:315). He received his share of his father's estate
in 1718 (NHPD, 9:734).
John made his will 24 Sept. 1712, leaving his Dover homestead to Thomas and his Madbury property to James (NHPP,
8:200; NHSP, 31:693-4). He bound his son Thomas "to let my
wife Eleanor to have hous rume and fier wood, covenant he
shall hall the wood to the dor and cut itt to put into the
fier as long as shee seese fit to live with him on the place,
with hous rume for her creturs." His son John was given "my
land and marsh up to the back reiver, binding him to pay ten
shillings every year to his mother-in-law [that is, step-
mother] Ellenor as long as she liveth."
The will could not be accepted due to improper wording, and
son Thomas was appointed administrator 4 June 1718, after an
inventory made 8 Apr. showed an estate valued at more than
524 pounds (NHPP, 10:32-4). Widow Eleanor probably died
about 1738; between then and 1742 the other children sold
their rights in their father's estate to their brother Thomas
for 50 pounds each.

Children, all by first wife Sarah, born at Dover:

16.   i.   THOMAS[4], b. in 1696.
17.   ii.   JOHN, b. in 1698.
18.   iii. JAMES, b. in 1699.
19.   iv.   SARAH, b. c1701; m. JAMES CLARK.
      v.   LYDIA, b. 19 Feb. 1703-4 (VRs Dover, 4), res.
            Salem MA; m. 1st Salem 17 Feb. 1725 (VRs) ISAAC
            MEACHAM, d. before 1738, son of John and Mary
            (Cash) Meacham; m. 2nd Salem 14 Sept. 1749
            (VRs) SAMUEL FOWLER of Salisbury.
            In 1738 Lydia Meacham, widow of Isaac, late of
            Salem, blacksmith, quitclaimed her rights in
            her father's estate to her brother Thomas
            (Essex County Probate, 28:14).

7. ELIZABETH[3] 1676-1756 [2 Thomas[2] and Elizabeth] was born
at Dover say 1676, died about 1756; married at Dover RICHARD
PINKHAM, born about 1672 (but deposed aged 77 in 1756), son
of John and Martha (Otis) Pinkham. He married second 27 Nov.
1757 Mary (Hill) Welch of Kittery, widow of Benjamin Welch
(Noyes-Libby-Davis, 556-7; Charles N. Sinnett, Richard Pinkham of Old Dover, N. H., and His Descendants [Concord, 1908],
15-17). He was a carpenter.
They were given land by her brother Thomas 18 Apr. 1699
(NHPD, 5:107). Everett S. Stackpole (History of New Hampshire [N. Y., 1916], 1:33) noted that the wife of Richard
Pinkham was put in the stocks because her husband would not
or could not pay her fine for "entertaining" Quakers and for
attending Quaker worship at Oyster River.

Children (**Pinkham**), born at Dover:

i.   JOHN, b. 19 Aug. 1696; m. ROSE OTIS.
ii.   RICHARD, b. say 1698.
iii. TRISTRAM, b. say 1700; m. 12 Aug. 1728 MARTHA
      HAYES.

FOURTH GENERATION

8. ELIZABETH[4] 1703-1776 [5 Thomas[3] and Deborah] was born
at Dover about 1703, died at Newington 10 Mar. 1776 in her
73rd year; married there 24 Jan. 1724 (NHGR, 2[1904]:169)
RICHARD DAM, born at Dover 26 Aug. 1699, died at Newington 13
May 1776, son of Dea. John and Jane (Rowe) Dam (John Scales,
"Some Descendants of Deacon John Dam of Dover," NEHGReg,
65[1911]:214; Noyes-Libby-Davis, 181; Scales, Dover, 271).
Their children were baptized in the Newington Church (NHGR,
3[1905]:62-3, 108, 110-11, 155; 4[1906]:64).

Children (Dam), born at Newington:

i.   MARY, b. 17 Oct. 1725 (bp. 28 Feb. 1725/6), d.
        in 1732.
ii.   JONATHAN, b. 23 Feb. 1726 (bp. 14 Apr.), d. Roches-
        ter NH 3 Jan. 1802; m. 29 Nov. 1758 MERCY VARNEY,
        b. Dover 15 May 1730, d. in 1818, dau. of Stephen
        and Mercy (Hanson) Varney.
iii.   MARTHA, b. 15 Mar. 1728 (bp. 18 Aug.), d. in 1740.
iv.   BENJAMIN, b. 25 Feb. 1730 (bp. 9 Aug.), d. Newington
        in 1810; m. JANE SIMPSON.
v.   JABEZ, b. 14 Aug. 1732 (bp. 23 Sept. 1733), d. Roch-
        ester 14 Nov. 1813; m. MERIBAH EMERY, b. 20 Mar.
        1740, d. Rochester 24 Feb. 1838.
vi.   SAMUEL. b. 14 Dec. 1734, d. in 1735.
vii.   TIMOTHY, b. 30 Nov. 1736, d. Newington in 1803; m.
        Newington 12 Mar. 1767 ELIZABETH PICKERING.
viii.   JOHN, b. 18 Nov. 1738, d. Durham NH 13 May 1814; m.
        Newington 10 Nov. 1767 ELIZABETH FURBER.
ix.   ABIGAIL, b. 27 June 1740 (bp. 5 July 1752); m. Durham
        16 Dec. 1752 JACOB CROMWELL.
x.   ELIZABETH, b. 5 July 1742 (bp. 27 Aug.); m. ----
        MATHER.

9. JOHN[4] 1706-1756 [5 Thomas[3] and Deborah] was born at
Dover in 1706, died there in Nov. 1756; married at Portsmouth
7 Nov. 1728 (NEHGReg, 24[1870]:360) ABIGAIL HAM, born there
15 Nov. 1710, survived her husband, daughter of Samuel and
Elizabeth Ham (Noyes-Libby-Davis, 303; Stackpole, Durham,
2:260-1, 238-9). In his will made 11 Sept. 1731, Samuel Ham
bequeathed 20 pounds to his daughter Abigail, wife of John
Leighton (NHSP, 32:420).
    In 1722 John joined with his father in buying part of a
proprietor's share in Rochester (McDuffee, Rochester, 1:40);
on 19 Sept. 1745 he was deeded his late father's share by his
brother Thomas (NHPD, 105:11). He sold 20 acres of land at
Dover to Stephen Pinkham 8 July 1734 (46:194), but bought
other Dover land from his father 17 July 1735 (21:415). He
and his brother Hatevil on 27 Mar. 1751 sold to James Tuttle

25 of the 150 acres in lot 163, Barrington, which had been
purchased by his father and Joseph Hicks (86:95).
His will, made 8 Oct. 1756 and proved 24 Nov., named his
son John as executor; an inventory valued at 1294 pounds was
taken 23 Feb. 1757 (NHPP, 20:16, 41:439; NHSP, 35:505-6).
His wife and his sons William and Hatevil each received a
third of the property, after gifts of 40 pounds to each of
the other eight children.
Although he was a Dover yeoman, some of his children were
baptized at Newington (NHGR, 3[1906]:156; VRs Dover, 53;
NEHGReg, 7[1853]:256). The name of the fourth child is not
clear in the original record.

Children, born at Dover:

20.   i.   WILLIAM⁵, b. Dover 20 Aug. 1729.
21.   ii.   HATEVIL, b. Dover 13 May 1731.
22.   iii. TOBIAS, b. Dover 9 May 1736.
      iv.   ?MOSES, bp. Newington 30 Sept. 1736; nfr.
      v.   PAUL, bp. Newington 30 Sept. 1736, d.y.
23.   vi.   PAUL, b. Dover 3 Apr. 1738.
24.   vii. ABIGAIL, b. 2 May 1740; m. JOHN KELLEY.
25.   viii. JONATHAN, bp. 20 Oct. 1742.
26.   ix.   OLIVE, b. 29 Oct. 1743; m. SAMUEL KELLEY.
27.   x.   MARY, b. 19 Feb. 1746; m. CHRISTOPHER NUTTER.
28.   xi.   DEBORAH, b. 23 Oct. 1747; m. EBENEZER TUTTLE.
29.   xii. JAMES, b. 12 Oct. 1749.

   10. ABIGAIL⁴ 1710-1779 [5 Thomas³ and Deborah] was born at
Dover 14 Jan. 1710, died at Newington 28 Apr. 1779; married
there 5 Dec. 1732 (NHGR, 2[1905]:171) NEHEMIAH FURBER, born
there 21 Jan. 1710, died there 10 June 1789, son of William,
Jr., and Sarah (Nute) Furber (Stackpole, Durham, 2:260).
They were admitted to the Newington Church 21 July 1765
(NHGR, 4[1907]:156), and their children were baptized there
(3[1906]:155-9; 4:18, 60, 63).

Children (Furber), born at Newington:

i.   ELIZABETH, b. 26 Apr. 1733 (bp. 30 May 1736); m. 16
       July 1753 THOMAS VINCENT.
ii.   MARY, b. 5 May 1735, d. 18 Apr. 1736, 11m.
iii.   JERUSHA, b. 6 Jan. 1738 (bp. 29 Jan.); m. 10 July
       1759 THOMAS PICKERING.
iv.   ABIGAIL, b. 12 June 1740 (bp. 22 June).
v.   DEBORAH, b. 19 Apr. 1742; m. 1st 11 Oct. 1764 Capt.
       LUKE WELLS; m. 2nd JOHN PICKERING.
vi.   SARAH, b. 1 Mar. 1745 (bp. 10 Mar.); m. Rochester 16
       July 1761 TIMOTHY ROBERTS.
vii.   NEHEMIAH, b. 24 Apr. 1748, d. 23 Feb. 1754.
viii. LEVI, b. 16 May 1751 (bp. 26 May), d. 19 Jan. 1829;
       m. 4 Oct. 1770 ROSAMUND FABYAN, b. 14 June 1752,
       d. 18 Feb. 1802, dau. of Samuel and Elizabeth
       (Huntress) Fabyan.

   11. HATEVIL⁴ 1712-1770 [5 Thomas³ and Deborah] was born at
Dover about 1712, died probably at Gouldsboro ME say 1770;
married at Newington 7 Dec. 1732 (NHGR, 2[1905]: 171) SARAH

TRICKEY, born at Dover about 1714 (baptized as an adult 4
Apr. 1725), died at the home of her son Thomas at Gouldsboro
(Cornman Ms), daughter of Thomas and Mary (Gambol) Trickey
(Noyes-Libby-Davis, 693).
Hatevil signed the petitions of 6 Feb. 1733 and 3 Jan. 1734
seeking establishment of Newington as a township (NHSP,
9:168, 174), and purchased land there from his father 17 July
1735 (NHPD, 21:264). He joined with his wife in deeding to
her mother Mary their share of the life rights in the Trickey
family farmstead 3 Nov. 1738 (NHPD, 23:465).
He and his cousins Thomas, John and James appeared on the
roll of Capt. Thomas Millett's company 21 July 1740 (NHSP,
9:173-4). He was listed 24 May 1744 as an ensign in Capt.
Ichabod Tibbett's company of scouts (Chandler E. Potter,
"Military History of N. H. ... 1623-1861," Adjutant General
Report, part 1, vol. 2 [Concord, 1868], 2:54). He served in
Capt. Paul Gerrish's company with his brothers Mark, Gideon
and John 19 Sept. to 11 Oct. 1755 (2:141-153).
Hatevil and Sarah were admitted to the Newington Church 18
July 1742 (NHGR, 4(1906):15). With his brother John, he sold
land in Barrington to James Tuttle 17 Mar. 1752 (NHPD,
13:533).
The increase in population and the end of hostilities with
the French and Indians in 1759 stimulated New Hampshire families to seek land beyond the province's borders. In 1763 the
British crown prohibited further expansion westward, closing
off that opportunity. Many New Hampshire men had seen the
forests, harbors and potential farmlands of eastern Maine
while serving in expeditions against the French in Nova Scotia. A wave of emigration into Maine was set in motion which
continued for decades.
Prior to 1760 there was not an English family settled east
of the Penobscot River, but pioneers were soon to seek new
homes there. On 3 Oct. 1763, one group of men at Majabagaduce (now Castine and Penobscot) made a petition to Gov.
Francis Bernard of Massachusetts Bay, stating that

    ...most of your Petitioners were Soldiers in his
    Majesties Service in the Pay of this Province & were
    Dismissed from the Service after the Peace was settled
    & being Humbly of opinion that some of the Lands they
    had Conquered would be as likely to fall to their Share
    as to others, they settled upon the aforesd tract of
    Land, a Place where no English inhabitants had ever
    before settled & at Great Peril Labour & Expence they
    Cleared & cultivated Some Small Spots of Land and have
    got themselves Comfortable houses, Suffering beyond
    Expression the Last Winter & having grappled through
    those Difficulties they have been able this Summer to
    Raise sauce & a few necessaries to Support their fami-
    lies & have been in hopes to have had their Settlements
    confirmed to them, & accordingly Petetioned to the Gen-
    eral Court for this purpose Long before the sd Land was
    granted to 60 others, but your Petetioners being Poor &
    not able to attend and further their Petetion they are
    informd it never reached the General Court & that now
    the fruit of their heavy toil & Labour is like to be
    reapt by others unless your Petetioners will Submit to
    very hard terms offered them by the new proprietors...

Among those signing this petition were Hatevil Laighton and
his son Thomas, and Thomas Laighton of Dover [# 16] and three
of his sons (James Phinney Baxter, ed., Documentary History
of the State of Maine [Portland, 1909], 13:315-6). No
Leightons signed a similar petition drawn 3 June 1785, which
sought establishment of Penobscot township (Bangor Historical
Magazine, 3[1887]:77-8); Penobscot was made a town in 1787.
The General Court did lay out, and conditionally grant to
proprietors, six townships between the Penobscot and Union
Rivers, and another six east of the Union River. The king's
ministers, however, withheld the royal assent for establishing these towns; they favored plans to set up a New Ireland
in eastern Maine, peopled by emigrants more submissive to
British authority. In 1764, Robert Gould and Francis Shaw
obtained extensive grants, which were later swallowed up in
William Bingham's purchase. Beginning soon after 1763, when
the Treaty of Paris was signed, settlers moved in, taking up
lots no proprietor could then sell.
Hatevil and his son Thomas were among them, settling at
Gouldsboro, then designated as township #3. By 1772 the population east of the Penobscot had reached 13,000, but the
inhabitants were unable to levy local taxes or hire teachers
and ministers, and were improving land they might never be
able to purchase.
Hatevil and Lemuel Trickey deeded land in Dover 17 Dec.
1763 to Hatevil Leighton, Jr. [# 21], son of John and Abigail
(NHPD, 75:400). On 27 Mar. 1765 Hatevil of Gouldsboro and
his wife Sarah deeded other Dover holdings to Amos Peaslee
(NHPD, 99:150), proving that they had by then cast their lot
on the down-east coast.

Children, born at Newington and baptized in the Newington
    Church (NHGR, 3[1906]:156-9, 4[1907]:64, 109; VRs Dover,
    152-3, 186):

        i.   DEBORAH[5], b. say 1733 (bp. 30 Sept. 1736), d.
              Newington 23 Mar. 1819.
        ii.   ISAAC, bp. 30 Sept. 1736, said to have settled
              at Machias ME (Cornman Ms). He served in NH
              under Capt. John Titcomb 6 Mar. to 5 Nov. 1757
              during an expedition to Crown Point (Potter,
              Mil. Hist., 186).
30.   iii. JEMIMA, bp. 7 Oct. 1739; m. SAMUEL LIBBY.
        iv.   MARK, bp. 7 Oct. 1739, d. West Point NY in 1803
              (Cornman Ms); unm. He served in the 5th Co.,
              Col. Blanchard's Rgt., during an expedition to
              Canada in 1755, and under Capt. Paul Gerrish,
              Col. Peter Gilman's Rgt., 19 Sept. to 14 Dec.
              1755 (Potter, 2:144, 150-3). He served from
              Rochester under Capt. Moore, Col. Goffe's Rgt.,
              at Ft. William Henry in 1757 (NHSP, 18;531-2),
              and the same year under Capt. Hercules Mooney,
              Col. Nathaniel Meserve's Rgt., at Crown Point
              (Potter, 2:188). In 1759, he was hired by the
              town of Rochester to serve in place of a Quaker
              (NHSP 11:718), and was part of the 600-man
              force sent to Canada in 1760 (Potter, 2:236).
31.   v.   THOMAS, b. 1 Sept. 1740.
        vi.   GEORGE, bp. Dover 2 June 1745; nfr.
32.   vii. SARAH, bp. Dover 28 Sept. 1746; m. JEREMIAH
              TRACY.

33. viii. HATEVIL, b. 28 Feb. 1750.
     ix.   KEZIAH, bp. Dover 13 Dec. 1752; m. Rochester 26
           Feb. 1777 JAMES WILLEY (Stackpole, Durham,
           2:389). Julia Cornman noted that it was "said
           that she went into the British Provinces with
           her husband at the close of the War" (Cornman
           Papers, Ms Collection, NEHGS).
34. x.   SAMUEL, bp. Newington 18 Oct. 1756.
     xi.   DAVID, bp. Newington 18 Oct. 1756; nfr.
     xii. MARY, bp. 24 July 1759, d. 25 July 1800; unm.
     xiii. VALENTINE, b. say 1760, res. Kittery after war,
           lived to file for bounty land (Act of 1788,
           ext. 1803, 1806); m. Durham 15 Apr. 1784 SARAH
           WILLEY, d. 3 Feb. 1785. A child d. 14 Nov.
           1785, aged 9m (Stackpole, Durham, 1:148).
           In July 1779 he enlisted at Durham for the
           war's duration, and served in several units of
           the Continental Line (NHSP, 15:684-5; 16:103,
           207, 227, 269-75, 639). He had settled in ME
           before his military service; his brother Thomas
           took up land at Steuben through Valentine's
           settler's right there.
               James Willey of Durham petitioned 18 Oct.
           concerning settlement of Valentine's bounty
           land claim; warrant #2364-100 was issued 19
           Aug. 1845 to the heirs: nephew James Willey,
           and nieces Lucretia Vincent, Sally Huntress,
           and Deborah Watson (National Archives-Military
           Service Records).

12. DEBORAH[4] 1714-   [5 Thomas[3] and Deborah] was born at
Dover about 1714, lived at Portsmouth; married first at New-
ington 9 Oct. 1735 (NHGR, 2[1905]:172) Capt. WILLIAM COLLINS,
born at Portsmouth in 1711, whose estate was administered 30
Jan. 1738-9 (NHSP, 32:744), probably son of John and Sarah
Collins; married second ARTHUR WATERHOUSE, baptized at Ports-
mouth 16 Aug. 1711, died in 1746, son of Richard and Sarah
(Fernald) Waterhouse.
   Deborah was appointed administrator of Arthur's estate 30
July 1746; her son Samuel was placed under the guardianship
of Thomas Bickford 25 Mar. 1747, and the widow's share was
set forth, in minute detail, 26 Aug. (NHSP, 33:390; George H.
Waterhouse, Descendants of Richard Waterhouse of Portsmouth
[TMs, 1934, MHS], 1:119).

Child (Collins), born at Portsmouth:

i.   SARAH.

Children (Waterhouse), born at Portsmouth:

ii.   SAMUEL, bp. 18 Feb. 1738, d. c1820; m. 16 Oct.
      1769 HANNAH BICKFORD.
iii. RICHARD, bp. 19 Dec. 1741, d. infant.
iv.   DEBORAH, bp. 24 March 1744-5;, d. infant.

13. OLIVE[4] 1720-1800 [5 Thomas[3] and Deborah] was born at
Newington about 1720, died at Middleton NH before 1800; married JAMES COLBATH (sometimes Coolbreath), born at Newington

about 1714, died at Middleton before 1800, son of George and Mary (Pitman) Colbath (Ezra S. Stearns, Genealogical and Family History of the State of New Hampshire [NY, 1908], 4:1751-2; Cornman Ms). James joined the Newington church 1 Dec. 1739, and Olive 26 Sept. 1742 (NHGR, 3[1906]:158; 4:15). On 7 May 1746, James applied for court permission to keep a public tavern. He had extensive land holdings in Newington and Barnstead, and operated a gristmill at Newington. In 1754 he was deeded land at Portsmouth by Joseph Colbath; in 1784, he and Olive deeded this land to their son Benning. About 1785 they moved to the part of Rochester which later became Farmington, and then settled at Middleton, where they are buried.

Children (**Colbath**), born at Newington (baptisms listed in NHGR, 3[1905]:58; 4[1906]:17, 19, 64, 110):

i. LEIGHTON, b. 3 Nov. 1739 (bp. 1 Dec.); m. Newington 3 Dec. 1761 DEBORAH[5] LEIGHTON, bp. there 12 Nov. 1743, d. in 1819, dau. of Thomas and Mary (Smithson) Leighton [# 35].
ii. KEZIAH.
iii. HUNKING, b. 17 Feb. 1743/4, d. Farmington 28 Jan. 1825; m. 4 Mar. 1776 SUSAN KNIGHT, b. in 1744, d. 14 Mar. 1816.
iv. DEBORAH, bp. 9 Oct. 1746.
v. WINTHROP, bp. 16 June 1751; m. 25 Nov. 1773 ELEANOR WALKER.
vi. AMY, bp. 9 July 1758.
vii. DEPENDENCE, b. in 1761, d. 26 July 1840; m. HANNAH ROLLINS. He res. Boothbay ME.
viii. BENNING, b. 28 May 1762, d. Farmington 21 Sept. 1824; m. MARY ROLLINS, b. 26 May 1761, d. 9 Aug. 1825, dau. of Samuel and Mary (Huntress) Rollins.

14. THOMAS[4] 1720-   [5 Thomas[3] and Deborah] was baptized at Newington 13 May 1720 (NEHGReg, 22[1868]:299), living there in 1771; married at Newington 28 Oct. 1742 (NHGR, 2[1905]:173) MARY SMITHSON, daughter of John and Deborah (Pickering) Smithson, baptized at Portsmouth 18 Mar. 1721/2 (NEHGReg, 81[1927]:419; Noyes-Libby-Davis, 552).

Thomas, Jr., was deeded his father's homestead in Newington 27 Jan. 1741-2, after giving bond to support his parents for life (NHPD, 25:466-7, 472), and on 6 Mar. 1743/4 was deeded his father's Rochester land (28:508). Thomas and Mary joined the Newington church 26 Sept. 1741 (NHGR, 4[1907]:15); their children were baptized there (4:16, 18, 59, 61, 108).

He deeded to his brother John 19 Sept. 1745 half of a 60-acre lot in Rochester, which was "originally granted to my father Thomas who made a verbal agreement to give 30 acres (for some time enclosed and possessed by him) to my brother John" (NHPD, 105:11). On 11 Mar. 1755 he sold half of lot 43, 2nd division, at Rochester to James Place (64:251). He served under Capt. Samuel Gerrish, Col. Nathaniel Meserve's Rgt., 12 May to 21 Nov. 1756 (Potter, Mil. Hist., 2:173), marching to Crown Point. He sold to John Downing 4 July 1759 30 acres at Newington, part of the land Thomas, Sr., bought from John Fabyan (NHPD, 58:251).

On 18 June 1771, he mortgaged his home lot to Nicholas Pickering, and then deeded it, along with his meetinghouse

pew, to his son George on condition that he redeem the mortgage and support his parents for life (Rockingham County
Deeds [RockCD], 101:375).

Children, born at Newington:

35.   i.   DEBORAH^5, b. 28 Oct. 1743; m. LEIGHTON COL-
            BATH.
36.   ii.   MARY, bp. 3 Mar. 1744/5; m. SIMEON PEARL.
37.   iii. GEORGE, b. 2 June 1745.
      iv.   THOMAS, bp. 25 May 1746 (NHGR, 4[1907]:19); nfr.
      v.   JOHN SMITHSON, bp. 10 Apr. 1748 (4:59), d.y.
38.   vi.   JOHN SMITHSON, bp. 26 Nov. 1749.
      vii. JOSEPH, bp. 3 Nov. 1751 (4:64), d. while a
            soldier 13 Nov. 1777; unm. He was on the roll
            of Capt. Winborn Adams's Co. 2 June 1775, and
            in Capt. Nicholas Rawlings's co., Col. Abraham
            Drake, in Sept. 1777 (NHSP, 14:187; 15:325).
39.   viii. JOEL, b. 24 Sept. 1751.
      ix.   LUKE, bp. 14 Dec. 1753 (NHGR 4[1907]105); nfr.
40.   x.   ELIZABETH, bp. 15 Feb. 1756; m. THOMAS PINDER.

15. KEZIAH^4 1722-   [5 Thomas^3 and Deborah] was born at
Newington about 1722; married there 20 Sept. 1739 (NHGR,
2[1905]:172) ELEAZER COLEMAN, born there 26 June 1719, son of
Eleazer and Anne (Nutter) Coleman. He served under Capt. Job
Clements in 1748 (NHSP, 14:18).

Children (**Coleman**), born at Newington (baptisms listed in
   NHGR, 4[1907]:14, 59, 61):

i.   WILLIAM, bp. 20 Dec. 1741.
ii.   TEMPERANCE, bp. 12 June 1747.
iii. ELEAZER, JR., bp. 15 Jan. 1749.

16. THOMAS^4 1696-1763 [6 John^3 and Sarah] was born at
Dover in 1696, died 16 Jan. 1763 (Cornman Ms); married say
1718 SUSANNAH CHESLEY, born at Dover about 1696, died at
Gouldsboro ME 19 Jan. 1786 (Cornman Ms), daughter of Thomas
and Ann (Huntress) Chesley (Noyes-Libby-Davis, 140; Stackpole, Durham, 2:53). He was a farmer and cordwainer.
   About 1719 he received his Dover home from his father's
estate. On 21 Jan. 1722/3 he sold to John Ham, Jr., with his
wife Susannah signing also, 14 acres he had purchased from
John Drew on the Dover plains (NHPD, 16:414). In settlement
of a legacy from their father, he deeded to his brother John
20 acres in Dover 28 Mar. 1729 (16:399); he repurchased this
land from John 7 Oct. 1735 (28:16). Thomas and Susannah quit
their rights in her father's estate to her brother Thomas
Chesley 9 July 1737 (23:76).
   With Joseph Hicks he bought 150 acres in Barrington from
John Cutts of Portsmouth 29 Dec. 1735 (26:408). Probably
for speculation he and Samuel Chesley purchased by mortgage
from George Jaffrey 960 acres in Barrington's Two-Mile Streak
1 Oct. 1737 (23:10, 344). Thomas sold to Samuel Chesley the
rights to 200 acres in Barrington 10 May 1739 (24:642), and
over the next few years they sold off parcels of their land,
including 50 acres in lot 6 to his brother James 7 Apr. 1743
(36:200). Thomas was deeded Dover land by his brother John

26 June 1741 (26:409); on 7 May 1753 Thomas, gent., and John, yeoman, completed the division of their Dover property (40:535). He bought of Timothy Emerson of Durham 40 acres in the sixth range at Barrington, 14 Nov. 1751 (64:422-3).

Thomas served as sergeant in Capt. Thomas Millett's company in 1740 (NHSP, 40:535), and was listed as lieutenant in Capt. Ichabod Tibbetts's company of scouts on 24 May 1744 (Potter, Mil. Hist., 2:54).

Thomas and his family prepared to move east for new opportunities. On 1 Apr. 1762 he with Susannah sold 100 acres on Dover's Back River to Thomas Wallingford of Somersworth, reserving a burying place (NHPD, 68:180). This land at the foot of Mahomet's or Leighton's Hill had been owned by the first Thomas (Thompson, Landmarks, 141). In 1763, he and his sons Thomas, Samuel and Theodore were among those at Majabagaduce on the Penobscot, petitioning for land grants there. (See Hatevil [#11] for this petition.) Unsuccessful, they moved further east to Gouldsboro, taking up land not yet legally open to settlement.

The source for his date of death in 1763, and his wife's in 1786, contributed by Julia Cornman, is not known. However, on 30 March 1765 Josiah Tucker was named administrator of the estate of "Thomas Leiton of a place called Goldsbury, coaster" [a shipper of goods and materials between coastal ports], with Robert Gould and Francis Shaw, both of Boston, as sureties (Lincoln County Probate 1760-1800 [Portland, 1895], 17). The probate papers can no longer be found.

Children, born at Dover (VRs, 18, 47):

41. i.   JOHN[5], b. 27 June 1719.

     ii.   SARAH, b. 10 Aug. 1721, nfr. Sarah was shown in in the Cornman genealogy as wife of Richard Swain, but that Sarah was dau. of James and Sarah (Leighton) Clark [# 19].

    iii. DOROTHY, b. 18 Oct. 1723. Her husband is not certain. She has been called the wife of Jacob Buzzell of Madbury, who was an early settler at Bangor ME in 1769.

          Circumstantial evidence supports a marriage to Isaac Allen of Dover and Falmouth. Deeds involving Isaac and Dorothy (one naming him Isaac of "Majistagaduse") with George and Joseph Leighton suggest a close relationship (e.g., Cumberland County Deeds 3:244 in 1762, and 11:463 in 1782). Isaac's sister Martha m. Dorothy's brother John. Isaac served in Capt. Millett's Co. in 1748, along with Thomas[4] and 5 other Leightons. Charles Thornton Libby (Libby Family in America [Portland, 1882], 222) called Mary Allen, wife of Arthur Libby, the dau. of Isaac Allen and Dolly Leighton.

          Thus Isaac, son of Jacob and Mary (Spencer) (Jones) Allen of Dover, probably m. Dorothy Leighton and settled at Falmouth with her two brothers.

          To further complicate the matter, a different Isaac Allen m. Abigail Hall, sister of the wives of George and Joseph Leighton, making both Isaac Allens brothers-in-law to George and Joseph Leighton.

42. iv.   THOMAS, b. 13 Nov. 1725.
43. v.   GEORGE, b. 18 Nov. 1727.
44. vi.   SAMUEL, b. 20 Dec. 1729.
45. vii. GIDEON, b. 14 Feb. 1731.
46. viii. JOSEPH, b. 23 Apr. 1733.
47. ix.   ELIZABETH, b. 11 Mar. 1737; ?m. ISAAC DREW.
48. x.   THEODORE, b. 22 Mar. 1739.
49. xi.   SUSANNAH, b. 6 Dec. 1742; ?m. EPHRAIM RICKER.

   17. JOHN[4] 1698-   [6 John[3] and Sarah] was born at Dover
in 1698, lived at Edgecomb ME in 1778; married first SARAH
----, and second RUTH ---- . His wives are known only from
their names on deeds, releasing dower rights. Sarah so
signed in 1742; Ruth's name appeared in 1750, but was absent
in 1762.
   In 1722, John bought a third of lot 117 in Rochester with
Benjamin Mason and William Dam (McDuffee, Rochester, 1:40);
on the list of proprietors in 1737 he was called "Capt. John
Laighton" (TRs 1:2). On 6 Feb. 1733 he signed a petition for
Rochester to become a town (NHSP, 9:168-171). He frequently
held town offices: commissioner, selectman, assessor and surveyor (McDuffee, 2:531, 535). On 10 Jan. 1741-2, Sarah and
Lydia Layton, probably his wife and daughter, entered into
the covenant of the Rochester church and were baptized
(McDuffee, 2:588). He signed petitions seeking military protection in 1744, 1746 and 1747 (NHSP, 9:725-7; 13:334-5). On
29 Nov. 1749, the selectmen asked that the court "do account
Mr. John Leighton a Sutabel Person to Keep a tavren in
Rochester, he living in a Part of the town whare it is much
wanting" (N. H. Province Court Record #24759).
   Why he was called captain is not clear, but he had extensive service as a soldier. He was a corporal in Capt. Thomas
Millett's company 21 July 1740 (NHSP, 9:173-4, 725-7), and
later the same year enlisted under Capt. Thomas Wallingford
for a proposed expedition to the West Indies (18:113). He
was one of nine scouts with Capt. Benjamin Mathes during the
winter of 1744-45 (Stackpole, Durham, 1:113). He served from
24 Apr. to 9 Aug. 1755 under Capt. John Tasker, and under
Capt. Roberts Rogers at Ft. William Henry 25 Nov. 1755 to 6
June 1756 (Potter, Mil. Hist., 2:137, 156). He took part in
Capt. Ephraim Berry's march against Crown Point 14 Mar. to 27
Nov. 1760, but had to be left behind sick at the blockhouse
on the Connecticut River (2:248-9). Often his sons served in
the same company with him.
   In 1729 John's brother Thomas transferred to him the Dover
land due from their father's estate. John and Sarah sold 20
acres of it to William Dam 1 Oct. 1735, and another 20 acres,
the former Back River homestead, to Shadrach Hodgdon 28 Nov.
1737 (NHPD, 21:353, 25:138); on the same date he bought from
Hodgdon 250 acres in Rochester. On 1 June 1742 he sold
Jonathan Young 36 of those Hodgdon acres, and on 22 July that
year bought of Jonathan Wentworth 60 acres adjacent to his
Rochester homestead (58:339; 27:210). He sold to his brother
Thomas 26 Aug. 1743 the marsh and flats near Royal Cove at
Dover, formerly their father's property, and 26 Aug. 1743
sold him the rest of his Dover property (28:16). With his
wife Ruth he sold 120 acres, half of lot 43, second division,
to James Place 20 Oct. 1750 (64:252). He and Walter Bryant
were hired to survey the town's third division (McDuffee,
1:48); their map, completed 28 Aug. 1753, is in the Rochester

Town Hall vault. John Leighton and "his son Jonathan Leighton, both of Rochester," joined in purchasing 60 acres, adjoining land of John and of James Place, from Joseph Colbath and John Kent 2 July 1754 (78:368-370).

About 1760, with others from NH, John settled in Lincoln County in the District of Maine, taking up land along the Damariscotta River at Townsend, a plantation which now includes Boothbay and part of Edgecomb.

John's sons we know by their deeds; in 1762 "John Laighton of a place called Townsend" acknowledged at Dover deeds to four of his sons--naming each as "my son." To his son Jonathan on 30 Mar. he sold his share of the 60 acres they had bought jointly, land on which Jonathan was living, and all his rights as a proprietor to undivided land. To his son David he sold on Mar. 18 sixty acres in lot 69, 1st division, which David then lived on and had improved, and on the same date he sold Rochester land and buildings to Samuel. To his son Benjamin he sold on 30 Mar. other land in Rochester, and on the same day sold to David Place 32 acres of the Colbath-Kent property (NHPD, 78:372-4; 68:89; 105:12, 14; 70:332-4). Without naming him his son, John on 18 June 1771 sold to Solomon Laighton of Freetown (now Edgecomb) 122 acres on the Damariscotta River (Lincoln County Deeds, 8:169-70).

On 9 March 1766, John Laighton, Solomon Laighton, "bengamen laighton" and Simon Pearl were signers of a petition to Gov. Francis Bernard protesting the selection of Frankfort (now Dresden) as shire town, and asking that the court sit instead at the more-populous Wiscasset (Documentary History of the State of Maine, Collections of the Maine Historical Society, Second Series, 13:441-3). John witnessed in 1778 a deed between Solomon and John Smithson Leighton (LincCD, 13:44).

An unverifed reference stated that his will was proved at Wiscasset 16 Dec. 1772. No such record exists, although a Jonathan Leighton did die at Newcastle 15 Aug. 1772. That Jonathan Laiten (as that family usually spelled the name) had immigrated to ME from Rowley MA with his sons John, Jonathan, Moses, Ezekiel and Richard, settling at nearby Sheepscot (now Newcastle). The descendants of Richard[1] Leighton of Ipswich and Rowley settled mainly in Lincoln County.

Children by first wife Sarah, born at Dover and Rochester:

50. i.   LYDIA[5], b. c1726; m. JAMES ROGERS, JR.
51. ii.   JONATHAN, b. c1728.
52. iii. SAMUEL, b. 20 June 1729.
53. iv.   DAVID, b. 14 Oct. 1730.
54. v.   BENJAMIN, b. c1735.
55. vi.   SOLOMON, b. c1739.

Probable child by second wife Ruth:

     vii. JAMES, listed in the 1790 census at Washington
           Plantation (Mount Vernon) with one male under
           16 and one female, but not in the 1800 census.
           On 18 Apr. 1804, at the Mount Vernon town meet-
           ing, Solomon Leighton was asked to maintain his
           "half-brother James Leighton," and was voted a
           dollar a month for the expenses. On 6 Apr.
           1807, Samuel Leighton was voted $12 for the
           keep of James the year past (TRs 2:115, 154).
           James disappeared from town records thereafter.

18. JAMES[4] 1699-1759 [6 John[3] and Sarah] was born at Dover
in 1699, died there 8 July 1759, about 60y (VRs Dover, 160);
married HANNAH BUZZELL, born at Dover (baptized as an adult
23 June 1723), daughter of John and Sarah Buzzell (Noyes-
Libby-Davis, 123-4; Helen Gertrude Buzzell, Buzzell-Orr and
Related Families [TMs, 1964, MHS], 2:10; Stackpole, Durham,
2:49-50). Her father's will made 24 Nov. 1737 named his-
daughter Hannah Leighton (NHPP, 32:671).
     A blacksmith, James moved from Dover about 1732 to settle
on the Madbury property inherited from his father in 1718. He
signed the petition to make Rochester a town 6 Feb. 1733
(NHSP, 9:168-70), and bought of Thomas Bennett of New Durham
48 acres in Rochester, lots 111 and 128, fourth division, 23
Apr. 1738 (NHPD, 52:2). He sold 20 acres of Dover land to
Nathaniel Davis 9 Apr. 1739, and on 26 Apr. that year transferred to his brother Thomas rights to the estate of their
father John (24:402; 28:17). He purchased 50 acres in Barrington's Two-Mile Streak from his brother Thomas and from
Samuel Chesley 7 Apr. 1743 (36:100). He evidently did not
occupy his Rochester or Barrington property.

     Children, born at Madbury (NEHGReg, 29[1875]:268-9) and
     baptized there (VRs Dover, 144, 146):

     56. i.   JAMES[5], bp. 18 Mar. 1739.
     57. ii.   ISAAC, bp. 18 Mar. 1739.
     58. iii. AARON, b. 22 June 1741.

     19. SARAH[4] 1701-1770 [6 John[3] and Sarah] was born at Dover
about 1701, died at Wells ME in 1770, 69y; married at Dover
16 11mo [Jan.] 1717-8 (VRs Dover, 8; NHGR, 2[1905]:126) JAMES
CLARK, who died at Wells in 1767 (will made in 1754, proved
in 1768), son of Abraham and Elizabeth (Drew) Clark of Oyster
River (Stackpole, Durham, 2:76-7, Noyes-Libby-Davis, 143).
     They were Quakers. On 26 Aug. 1742, they quitclaimed to
her brother Thomas their interest in the estate of her father
John (NHPD, 28:15).

     Children (Clark), order uncertain:

     i.   JONATHAN, b. 1728; m. 1st in 1752 (and for it dis-
           owned) IZETTE DOWNING, dau. of Joshua and Susanna
           Downing of Newington; m. 2nd Barrington 5 Sept. 1770
           MARY (FRIEND) Tibbetts, dau. of Abraham and Abigail
           Friend of Somersworth.
     ii.   SARAH, m. "out" Dover c1752 RICHARD SWAIN, JR.
     iii   JAMES.
     iv.   REMEMBRANCE. b. 25 Dec. 1732, d. 5 Nov. 1819; m. 31
           Aug. 1763 SARAH BRIDGES.
     v.   MARTHA, b. 23 Aug. 1735, d. 17 July 1819; m. Dover
           24 Nov. 1762 DAVID VARNEY, b. Dover 28 Nov. 1726, d.
           there 3 Oct. 1802, son of Stephen and Mercy (Hanson)
           Varney.

FIFTH GENERATION

20. **WILLIAM**[5] 1729-   [9 John[4] and Abigail Ham] was born at Dover 30 Aug. 1729 (VRs Dover, 53), baptized at Newington 30 Sept. 1736 (NHGR, 3[1905]:156), lived at Farmington in 1806; married ELIZABETH ---- .
On 22 June 1736, his grandfather Thomas Laighton, Sr., of Newington deeded his rights to land at Barnstead "for and in consideration of the natural love and affection that I bare unto my well-beloved grandson William Laighton, the son of my eldest son John of Dover, who is yet a minor" (NHPD, 30:531). William Leighton "Jr." was on the Dover parish rate list in 1753 (NHSP, 11:518-9). He inherited land at Dover from his father in 1736 (NHPP, 35:505-6). With his wife Elizabeth, he sold his Barnstead land to Francis Drew of Dover 16 Apr. 1754 (NHPD, 63:50). William served under Capt. John Hazzen, Col. John Goffe's Rgt., 10 June to 27 Nov. 1760, marching against Crown Point (Potter, Mil. Hist., 2:244).
He and his brother Hatevil were made grantees of a new town, Peeling [now Woodstock], 23 Sept. 1763, but the province did not complete action on the grant (NHSP, 25:647). On 6 and 7 Nov. 1778 he and Hatevil exchanged Dover properties (Strafford County Deeds, 3:218, 226). William bought land from an Isaac Drew [see # 47] of Wolfeboro NH 2 Apr. 1791 (13:489). A William Leighton signed the petition 6 June 1798 for incorporation of Farmington as a town (NHSP, 13:346-7). On 16 Oct. 1800, William of Dover sold to John of Dover his share of their father's estate, the homestead where he was then living; no wife was named in that deed (StrCD, 36:84-5).
William appeared in the 1790 Dover census with one male under 16 and three females. In 1800, his household contained a male and a female over 45, and a female 26-44. His wife and probable children have not been identified.

21. **HATEVIL**[5] 1731-1800 [9 John[4] and Abigail Ham] was born at Dover 13 May 1731 (VRs, 53), baptized at Newington 30 Sept. 1736, died at Farmington 17 Apr. 1800 (TRs); married at Dover 3 Nov. 1778 (NEHGReg, 25[1871]:57) ABIGAIL NOCK, daughter of James and Anne (Twombley) Nock (later usually spelled Knox). Abigail married second at Dover 27 Mar. 1805 (NHGR, 1[1903]:164) John Gove, born at Hampton Falls NH 5 Apr. 1746, died at Weare NH 25 Aug. 1826, son of Edward and Judith (Hoag) Gove. Gove had seven children by Martha Dow, but none by Abigail (William Henry Gove, The Gove Book [Salem MA, 1922], 105; William Little, History of Weare, N. H. [Lowell MA, 1888], 867).
Hatevil, a joiner by trade, was called "Hatevil, Jr." as the younger man of that name at Dover. He served under Capt. Paul Gerrish, Col. Peter Gilman's Rgt., in 1755 (Potter, Mil. Hist., 2:151). On 17 Dec. 1763, his uncle Hatevil [# 11] and Lemuel Trickey sold to Hatevil, Jr., of Dover

a certain tract of land on the westerly side of the
said Hatevil Leighton's other lands and on the easterly
side of William Leighton's and the said Hatevil
Leighton Jr land, being on the south side of the said
Hatevil Leighton's orchard and so to run on a straight
line down to Royal Cove keeping a breadth to complete
two acres and one half acre (NHPD, 75:400-1).

Hatevil served with his brothers Tobias and James under
Capt. Winborn Adams in 1775, and was listed as an ensign in
Col. David Gilman's Rgt. 14 Mar. 1776 (NHSP, 14:123, 187;
Stackpole, Durham, 1:123). In the DAR Index this service has
been credited to Hatevil Leighton of Pembroke ME [# 33], but
it seems unlikely that the latter would have left his family
to enlist in NH. Unfortunately, no pension record exists to
verify which of the two served in the war.

Hatevil probably joined the Society of Friends when he married into a Quaker family, after his military service. With
his wife Abigail he sold to his brother Jonathan land on the
Back River in Dover 2 Feb. 1783, and bought from him part of
lot 38, in Rochester's second division (StrCD, 33:405-6); in
that year he settled in the section of Rochester that became
Farmington in 1798. He appeared on the Dover tax lists from
1751 to 1782, and on the Rochester lists from 1783 on.

In 1790, his Rochester household included his wife, a male
16 or older, three sons under 16, and three daughters. He
and his wife again sold land at Dover to his brother Jonathan
27 Jan. 1791 (StrCD, 12:418). Hatevil and Richard Furber
bought jointly part of lot 38 in the second division of
Rochester, and divided it 12 Nov. 1799; on 22 Feb. 1800
Jonathan sold him land there (StrCD, 31:414; 33:405-6).

Hatevil's will, made 6 Feb. 1800 and proved 20 May, named
his son John as executor (StrCP, 6:146-9, 378). It provided
that John would receive a two-thirds share upon coming of
age, but widow Abigail was to control all the property until
daughter Abigail was 18. John was to receive his father's
joiner's tools; each of the eight children was named.
Hatevil's name appeared on tax lists until 1805, when his
estate was taxed to his son John.

Children, births in Farmington TRs:

59. i.   ANNA[6] [Nancy], b. Dover 15 Feb. 1780; m. SAMUEL
           FURBER.
60. ii.   JAMES, b. Dover 1 Nov. 1781.
61. iii. JOHN, b. Rochester 2 Nov. 1783.
     iv.   MARK, b. Rochester 5 Oct. 1786, living in 1800.
62. v.   ELIZABETH, b. Rochester 24 Nov. 1788; m. JOSEPH
           MEADER, JR.
     vi.   HANNAH, b. Rochester 23 Jan. 1791, d. in 1819;
           unm.
63. vii. EPHRAIM, b. Rochester 22 Sept. 1794.
     viii. ABIGAIL, b. Farmington 1 Dec. 1798, d. in 1840;
           unm. (Cornman Ms note: perhaps m. 27 Jan. 1833
           Henry Knox [both of Dover, in VRs Dover, 99]).

22. TOBIAS[5] 1736-1812 [9 John[4] and Abigail Ham] was born at
Dover 9 May 1736 (baptized 30 Sept.) (VRs Dover, 53), died at
Madbury in 1812; married there before 1774 ANN TUTTLE, died
in 1812, daughter of John and Elizabeth (Nute) Tuttle (George
Frederick Tuttle, Descendants of William and Elizabeth Tuttle

[Rutland VT, 1883], xxix; Stackpole, Durham, 2:261). He was
a joiner by trade.
Tobias had an extensive military record. He served under
Capt. Trueworthy Ladd, Maj. Thomas Tash's Battalion, 19 Aug.
to 30 Oct. 1757, in the garrison at No. 4 (Charlestown NH)
(Potter, Mil. Hist., 193). When the Revolutionary War began,
he was listed as aged 37, formerly of Durham, in Capt. Winborn Adams's Co., Col. Enoch Poor's Rgt., on 2 June 1775, and
was company sergeant 25 May to 1 Aug. (NHSP, 14:107, 122-4).
He was made ensign at New Castle 17 June 1776 (NHSP, 8:94-5),
and then commissioned 19 Sept. 1776 as lieutenant in Capt.
Caleb Hodgdon's Co., Col. Pierce's Rgt. (Potter, Mil. Hist.,
2:291, 374); he served in that regiment under Capt. Abraham
Perkins 7 Dec. 1776 to 7 Jan. 1777.
    In the 1790 Durham census, his household included one son
under 16 and seven daughters. He bought land from Abigail
Pinkham of Durham 25 Oct. 1793, and a lot from Dorothy Jones
in Madbury 12 Dec. 1798--which he sold that day to Daniel
Symes (StrCD, 17:107; 29:148, 150). In 1800, he and his wife
were living at Madbury alone.
    His will, made 27 Apr. and proved 1 Aug. 1812, named his
son William as executor, and mentioned his wife and each of
his nine children (StrCP, 13:132; 20:150).

    Children, born at Durham or Madbury, order uncertain:

64. i.   ABIGAIL⁶, b. say 1764; m. Dover 2 June 1782
            BENJAMIN ODIORNE.
65. ii.   ELIZABETH; m. JOHN GOWDEY (or GOUDEY).
     iii. ANN; called Ann Thompson in her father's will.
     iv.   DEBORAH, res. Barrington; m. 22 Sept. 1788
            TIMOTHY LANGLEY.
66. v.   WILLIAM, b. say 1772.
     vi.   DOROTHY, b. say 1775; m. 10 Dec. 1793 JACOB
            SPENCER of Nottingham.
     vii. SARAH; unm. in 1812.
67. viii. OLIVE, b. 8 Oct. 1780; m. BENJAMIN BACHELDER.
     ix.   HANNAH, b. say 1782; m. Belfast ME 12 Dec. 1802
            SAMUEL NICKERSON.

    23. PAUL⁵ 1739-1814 [9 John⁴ and Abigail Ham] was born at
Dover 3 Apr. 1739 (VRs Dover, 53), died at Portsmouth NH 9
March 1814, 76y (TRs); married at Portsmouth 8 Aug. 1765
(NEHGReg, 82[1928]:292) MARY MILLS, born at Portsmouth 28
Mar. 1747, died there 28 May 1823, 77y, daughter of Luke and
Hannah (Lang) Mills (Portsmouth VRs; Howard P. Moore, The
Lang Family [Rutland VT, 1935], 60; Cornman Ms).
    Note: Paul and his descendants spelled their name Laighton.
    He lived at Portsmouth, where he operated a ships' block-
making shop. In 1773 he was named a grantee of the proposed
town of Success, which was never organized (NHSP, 25:553-7).
He signed a petition in 1777 to expel Tories from the town
(17:139), but no record of any military service exists for
him. He did however join with his brothers in outfitting the
privateer Grand Turk, which was captured by the British on
its second voyage, causing a ruinous financial loss. His
brother-in-law Eligood Mills had been an officer on the ship
(NEHGReg, 79 [1925]:218-220).
    With Newmarket residents, he petitioned 1 June 1785 for a
bridge (NHSP, 13:34). In both the 1790 and 1800 censuses, he

and his wife were shown with seven sons and two daughters. Mary's will was made 5 Sept. 1816, and her property inventoried 3 Aug. 1823 (RockCP #10676). She left her personal property (including the family Bible and church pew) to her daughter Hannah, and made other bequests to the widow and daughters of her son James; her son Samuel was executor.

Julia Cornman stated that Mary Mills's mother was Dutch, and that her father was lost at sea in 1754; her source was probably a query in the Maine Historical and Genealogical Recorder, ed. S. M. Watson [Portland, 1884-1898], 9(1898):63.

Children, born at Portsmouth (TRs; baptisms in NEHGReg, 82[1928]:45):

68. i.   LUKE MILLS⁶, b. 10 Feb. 1766.
     ii.   JOHN, b. 5 Sept. 1767, d. 14 Sept. 1768.
     iii. JOHN, b. 20 Mar. 1769. d. 4 Sept. 1784.
     iv.   DEBORAH, b. 6 Feb. 1771, d. 24 Nov. 1789; unm.
69. v.   ABIGAIL, b. 4 Feb. 1773; m. CHARLES BLUNT.
     vi.   HANNAH, b. 14 Nov. 1774; m. Boston in Feb. 1792
           GEORGE HOMANS.
     vii. MARY, b. 28 Nov. 1776, d. 25 Oct. 1777.
     viii. WILLIAM, b. 20 July 1778, d. Martinique, French
           West Indies, estate admin. 20 June 1810; m. 1st
           ---- BOWEN; m. 2nd 2 May 1809 REBECCA MUSHSEA,
           dau. of John Mushsea of Portsmouth. She m. 2nd
           Portsmouth 25 May 1828 Samuel Hutchins. In the
           1800 Portsmouth census, William had two daus.
           under 5 in his household.
70. ix.   MARK, b. 22 Mar. 1780 (bp. 26 Mar., as Arthur).
71. x.   JAMES, b. 26 June 1782.
72. xi.   JOHN, b. 17 Oct. 1784.
73. xii. SAMUEL, b. 3 Nov. 1787.
74. xiii. PAUL, b. 20 Apr. 1789.

24. ABIGAIL⁵ 1740-1797 [9 John⁴ and Abigail Ham] was born at Dover 2 May 1740 (bapt. 4 Sept.) (VRs, 53; NHGR, 3[1905]: 159), died 30 Dec. 1797; married 9 Dec. 1761 JOHN KELLEY (recorded as Keille), born at Dover 23 Apr. 1731, died 18 Dec. 1819, son of James and Deborah (Stiles) Kelley. John married second 2 Sept. 1798 widow Phebe Trefethen, who died 8 Apr. 1821 (Stackpole, Durham, 2:238-9).

Children (Kelley), born at Dover (VRs, 54):

i.   BENJAMIN, b. 23 Aug. 1763, d. 5 May 1857; m. 1st 18
     Feb. 1790 SARAH FLAGG, b. 1 Nov. 1772, d. 21 Sept.
     1797; m. 2nd 30 Apr. 1800 KEZIAH SAWYER, b. 12 Jan.
     1762.
ii. HANNAH, b. 22 Mar. 1765; m. Dover 24 Mar. 1785
     EPHRAIM HAM, b. Dover in 1760, d. there in 1817,
     son of Ephraim and Lydia (Ham) Ham (NEHGReg,
     26[1872]:393).

25. JONATHAN⁵ 1742-1832 [9 John⁴ and Abigail Ham] was born at Dover 20 Jan. 1742, baptized 20 Oct. (NEHGReg, 7[1917]: 256), died there 29 Dec. 1832; married there 3 Dec. 1777 MARY BAMPTON, born there 2 Aug. 1755, died there 13 May 1831, daughter of Ambrose and Rebecca (Hill) Bampton (NHGR,

4[1907]:40). Jonathan was accepted into membership at the
Dover meeting 23 Sept. 1775, before his marriage into the
Quaker family (NHGR, 1[1903]:63, 114). He appeared on the
Madbury census in 1790, and at Dover in 1800.
On 22 Feb. 1783 he sold to his brother Hatevil land in
Rochester, lot 38, second divison (StrCD, 33:405-6). After
the death of Nathaniel Bampton, Jonathan and Mary Leighton,
Ambrose Bampton, and Benjamin and Anna Paul divided the
estate 6 Apr. 1806 (StrCD, 51: 212, 65:216, 71:42).

Children, born at Dover (NHGR, 5[1908]:32):

75. i.   JOHN⁶, b. 3 Oct. 1778.
    ii.   AMBROSE, b. 3 Mar. 1780, d. 8 Sept. 1786.
    iii. ANNE, b. 21 Sept. 1781, d. 11 Sept. 1786.
    iv: ELIZABETH, b. 30 June 1785, d. 30 Aug. 1786.

26. OLIVE⁵ 1743-   [9 John⁴ and Abigail Ham] was born at
Dover 29 Oct. 1743 (VRs, 53); married in 1759 SAMUEL KELLEY
(recorded as Kielle), born at Dover 8 Nov. 1738 (baptized 8
Jan. 1744, VRs, 49, 151), son of James and Deborah (Stiles)
Kelley (Stackpole, Durham, 2:238).

Children (Kelley), probably born at Dover, order uncertain:

i.   MARY, b. 1760; m. 30 Sept. 1784 SAMUEL ESTES.
ii.   JOHN, d. at sea; unm. He was a sea captain.
iii. DEBORAH, b. 1765; m. ISAAC YOUNG.
iv.   ANNA; m. 1st SAMUEL DEMERITT; m. 2nd JOSEPH CLARK.
v.   HANNAH; unm.
vi.   SAMUEL, d. at sea of yellow fever; unm. He was a
      sea captain.
vii. SARAH; unm.
viii. BENJAMIN, b. 18 Feb. 1787; m. NANCY⁶ LEIGHTON [# 80].

27. MARY⁵ 1746-   [9 John⁴ and Abigail Ham] was born at
Dover 19 Feb. 1746 (baptized 12 Oct.) (VRs, 53); married at
Newington 21 Mar. 1777 CHRISTOPHER NUTTER, baptized at New-
ington 18 Mar. 1755 (NHGR, 4[1907]:107), son of Samuel and
Sarah (Hoyt) Nutter. In 1790, they were living at Durham
with two sons and a daughter.

Child (Nutter), others not found:

i.   ALICE; m. JOHN HIGHT, b. Newington 27 Nov. 1768,
      d. Barnet VT 4 Jan. 1826, son of Dennis and Eliza-
      beth (Fabyan) Hight (Georgia Hight Truslow, Hight
      Families [np, 1979], 16).

28. DEBORAH⁵ 1747-1831 [9 John⁴ and Abigail Ham] was born
at Dover 23 Oct. 1747 (VRs, 53). died there 2 Mar. 1831;
married at Dover 30 Nov. 1768 EBENEZER TUTTLE, born at Dover
5 Feb. 1737, died there 13 Dec. 1796, 57y, son of Thomas and
Mary (Brackett) Tuttle, and a Quaker (NHGR, 4[1907]:163; VRs
Dover, 200; Tuttle Desc., xxviii; Mary Tuttle Gaylord, The
Tuttles - Branch of Simon [Verona VA, 1981], 41). Eben's
will, made 29 Apr. 1796, was proved 13 Jan. 1797 (Scales,
Dover, 360).

Children (**Tuttle**), born at Dover (VRs, 194, 200):

i.   TOBIAS, b. 25 Aug. 1769, d. 30 Sept. 1822; m. 24
        Aug. 1796 PHOEBE AUSTIN, b. 28 Feb. 1770, dau. of
        Elijah and Hannah (Roberts) Austin; perhaps m. 2nd
        in Sept. 1812 CATHERINE COLEMAN.
ii.   THOMAS, b. 17 May 1772, d. 22 Aug. 1817; unm.
iii.   ABIGAIL, b. 13 May 1775; m. Portsmouth 8 July 1828
        SAMUEL NASON.
iv.   MARY, b. 14 May 1778, d. 5 Apr. 1787.
v.   JOHN, b. 17 July 1782, also d. 5 Apr. 1787.
vi.   HOPE, b. 5 Oct. 1786.
vii.   EBENEZER, d. 12 July 1811.

29. **JAMES**[5] 1749-1824 [9 John[4] and Abigail Ham] was born at
Dover 12 Oct. 1749 (VRs, 53), died at Durham 22 Feb. 1824,
75y (GS); married first at Dover in 1777 SARAH THOMPSON, born
at Durham 16 Feb. 1759, died there 16 Jan. 1807, 48y (GS),
daughter of Judge Ebenezer and Mary (Torr) Thompson (Stackpole, Durham, 2:363); married second at Durham in Jan. 1810
ABIGAIL (MATHES) Mooney, born about 1772, died at Durham 11
May 1827, 56y, daughter of Valentine and Dolly (Rogers)
Mathes (Rosamund J. Allen, Valentine Hill--His Descendants
and Related Families [TMs, nd, MHS], 3; Stackpole, Durham,
2:292). Burials are at Durham Falls.
     Abigail had married first 12 Jan. 1792 Capt. Jeremiah Burn-
ham Mooney, son of Lt. Benjamin and Hannah (Burnham) Mooney,
who died at Durham 17 Mar. 1807 leaving three children: John,
Dorothy and Hannah. His will, proved 16 Apr. 1807, left to
Abigail for life a third of his property (StrCP, 10:350-2;
15:261-2).
     James Laighton, tailor of Durham, aged 25, enlisted in
Capt. Winborn Adams's Co., Col. Enoch Poor's Rgt., 26 May
1775, and served "before Boston" until he was discharged 1
Aug. (NHSP, 14:107, 122-4, 187-8). His naval service has
been exaggerated (Stackpole, Durham, 2:261). His pension
application (NA-MSR, #S44506) stated that he served under
Capt. John Paul Jones "over a year," but he then amended it
to "about one Year." Actually, he signed on as mariner in
Sept. 1777 for service on the Ranger, the newly-completed
Continental war-ship, perhaps motivated by the $40 enlistment
bonus. The ship sailed from Portsmouth 1 Nov., cruised the
English Channel, raided the coast of Scotland, and seized the
British war-sloop Drake. When the Ranger put into a French
port for repairs, Jones was replaced as commander by Capt.
Thomas Simpson; the Ranger then sailed back to Portsmouth,
where James was discharged in the autumn of 1778.
     He was chosen as a Durham selectman in 1790, and purchased
a pew in the new meetinghouse in 1792 (Stackpole, Durham,
1:366, 203). James deeded land to his sons-in-law: to Edward
Moulton 1 May 1811, and to Ephraim Hanson 10 Mar. 1817
(StrCD, 67:264; 94:344). The county records contain over 30
deeds by which he bought or sold property.
     In his application for a pension 3 Apr. 1818, he pleaded
financial hardship; he was placed on the pension roll as of 6
Apr., but was removed for insufficient need (NHSP, 30:68).
He re-applied in 1820, listing assets totaling $1462, offset
by debts of $1564, and naming his dependents: a wife, 40; the
Mooney step-children Dorothy, 25, and Hannah, 16 ; Ebenezer,
23, and Susanna, 8--all "doing poorly" and unable to work.

His will, made 14 Jan. 1824, was proved 31 Mar.; Valentine
Smith was named executor. The inventory taken 27 Apr. showed
real estate of $4500; all the personal property was listed as
belonging to his wife (StrCP, 30:36; 32:70-3; 33:68). The
will named his wife Abigail, Ebenezer as residual heir and
executor, and the daughters Susan Laighton, Nancy Kelley and
Martha Lancaster. Benjamin Kelley was made the guardian of
Ebenezer (35:498).

Children by Sarah, born at Durham (TRs; NHGR, 1[1903]:98):

76   i.   ELIZABETH[6], b. 19 Apr. 1778; m. DANIEL REYNOLDS.
77. ii.   MARY. b. 1 Oct. 1780; m. EDWARD MOULTON.
78. iii. SARAH, b. 1 Dec. 1782; m. JAMES WOODHOUSE.
79. iv.   ABIGAIL, b. 11 Feb. 1787; m. EPHRAIM HANSON.
     v.   JOHN, b. 16 Oct. 1789, res. Manchester NH; unm.
           He was said to have d. in Russia.
80. vi.   ANN [Nancy], b. 6 July 1792; m. BENJAMIN KELLEY.
81. vii. MARTHA, b. 2 Oct. 1794; m. JOSIAH LANCASTER.
     viii. EBENEZER, b. 1 Jan. 1797, d. Durham 10 Aug.
           1875, 78y; unm. He was placed under guardian-
           ship in 1867, insane.

Child by Abigail, born at Durham (ibid.):

82. ix.   SUSANNAH, b. 23 Nov. 1810; m. CHARLES MATHES.

30. JEMIMA[5] 1739-   [11 Hatevil[4] and Sarah Trickey] was
baptized at Newington 7 Oct. 1739 (NHGR, 3[1905]:158), died
at Gouldsboro ME; married at Falmouth ME in 1762 Capt. SAMUEL
LIBBY, born at Falmouth 1 Feb. 1737, died at Gouldsboro in
Mar. 1825, son of William and Elizabeth (Goodwin) Libby. He
had married first Mary Frost, who died childless in 1762
(Libby Family, 60, 105; Noyes-Libby-Davis, 427-8).
In 1776 Samuel was commissioned captain of the 5th Co.,
Col. Benjamin Foster's 6th Lincoln Co. Rgt., and assigned to
guard the Maine coast from Castine to Machias (Massachusetts
Soldiers and Sailors of the Revolutionary War [MSS] [Boston,
1896-1908], 9:772).

Children (Libby), born at Gouldsboro:

i.   MARY, b. in 1763, d. in 1848; unm. She was the first
      white female ch. b. at Gouldsboro.
ii.   JOSEPH, b. 25 Apr. 1765, d. Gouldsboro 12 Sept. 1822;
      m. Gouldsboro 27 Oct. 1799 BATHSHEBA GIBBS, b. Roch-
      ester MA 31 May 1765, d. 22 Apr. 1858, dau. of
      Sylvanus and Thankful (Pope) Gibbs.
iii. ELIZABETH [Betsey], b. in 1770, d. in 1842; unm.
iv.   ABIGAIL; m. in 1791 JOB GIBBS.
v.   LYDIA, b. in 1780, d. Deblois ME; m. Gouldsboro int.
      7 May 1798 GOWEN WILSON, JR., b. in 1775, d. Cherry-
      field 9 Aug. 1847, 72y, son of Gowen and Abigail
      (Ingersoll) Wilson.

31. THOMAS[5] 1740-1803 [11 Hatevil[4] and Sarah Trickey] was
born at Newington 1 Sept. 1740 and baptized 26 Oct. (NHGR
3[1905]:159), died at Steuben ME 12 Feb. 1803 (VRs); married
at Falmouth ME 12 Nov. 1766 (VRs) LYDIA TRACY, born there
10 Feb. 1748, died at Steuben 16 Jan. 1789, daughter of

Jonathan and Abigail (Riggs) Tracy (Tracy, Hist. Address,
10-17).
Like his father, he petitioned for land at Majabagaduce on
the Penobscot in 1763, and with him went east to Gouldsboro
(James A. Milliken, The Narraguagus Valley: Some Account of
the Early Settlement and Settlers [Machias, 1886; reprint
Portland, 1910], 7-9). He then settled, in say 1765, on lot
#1 at Township #4, organized as Steuben 27 Feb. 1795. His
holding was on Leighton Point, now Dyer's Point (BHM,
8[1893]:236; 9[1894]:226).
He was called Thomas Second or Junior, since his older second cousin Thomas [# 42] had settled at Steuben at the same
time. People have confused the two, often combining them
into one person. Although the military service cannot be
assigned with certainty, it seems reasonable that the younger
Thomas is the one who enlisted as private from No. 4 under
Capt. Henry Dyer 7 Sept. 1777, serving 11 days at Machias
harbor, and who served again as a private under Capt. John
Hall in Aug. and Sept. 1779 at Castine (MSS, 9:414, 544).
Thirty years after taking up land at Steuben, he and other
settlers finally gained land titles. To prevent evictions
and exploitation by proprietors, the Massachusetts General
Court on 21 June 1793 resolved that settlers be given rights
to purchase land for an amount adjusted to allow for their
improvements; that they be paid for the improvements if they
did not exercise their right; and that the Commonwealth
receive a third of the receipts (BHM, 1[1885]:31).
Samuel Freeman of Portland, agent for the Proprietors, sold
to settlers 100-acre lots as laid out on a plan drawn by
Lothrop Lewis. On 2 June 1794, he deeded to Thomas Leighton,
Jr., for 15 pounds lot #75 (Washington Co. Deeds, 1:503).
The same day, Thomas was deeded 200 acres, lots 1 and 27, as
assignee of his brother Valentine, "settler" (1:541). At a
tax auction he purchased for 21 silver dollars 100 acres "on
head of a creek making for Dyer's Bay, and also on said his
sawmill stream," adjoining land of his son Jonathan (3:34).

Children, born at Steuben (TRs):

83. i.   JONATHAN[6], b. 23 Nov. 1767.
84. ii.   MARK, b. 8 Jan. 1770.
85. iii. CHARITY, b. 15 May 1772; m. DANIEL GODFREY.
86. iv.   ALEXANDER, b. 4 Aug. 1775.
87. v.   HATEVIL, b. 24 Aug. 1779.
88. vi.   PAMELIA, b. 4 Apr. 1780; m. JOHN PATTEN.
89. vii. ISRAEL, b. 10 Dec. 1782.
90. viii DANIEL, b. 14 Apr. 1785.
91. ix.   ISAIAH, b. 4 Nov. 1788.
92. x.   ASA, b. 14 Apr. 1791.

32. SARAH[5] 1746-1834 [11 Hatevil[4] and Sarah Trickey] was
baptized at Dover 28 Sept. 1746 (VRs, 153; born in 1744 per
GS), died at Sunbury Co. NB in 1834 (GS); married in 1771
JEREMIAH TRACY, born at Falmouth ME 9 Aug. 1744, died at
Gladstone Parish NB in 1812 (GS), son of Jonathan and Abigail
(Riggs) Tracy (Tracy, Hist. Address, 16). Burials are in
Pioneer Cemetery, Gladstone Parish.
They first lived at Gouldsboro, from which he served as a
soldier at Machias and on an expedition against Majabagaduce
in 1779 (MSS, 16:6). About 1784 they settled in Sunbury Co.

NB, on the St. John River near Oromocto. In 1810 he was
granted land up the north branch of the Oromocto River, near
present Tracy Settlement (Miriam L. Phillips, Facts and Folk-
lore / Tracy and Little Lake Area [Fredericton NB, 1985]. He
was said to have had six sons and four daughters, six of the
children born in NB (1851 census, Parish of Blissville, Sunbury Co.; research of descendant June Tracy MacNair). Julia
Cornman did not mention Sarah.

Children (**Tracy**), order uncertain:

i.   ABIGAIL, b. in ME say 1771, d. in NB 13 May 1813; m.
      ANDREW SMITH, b. 20 Aug. 1756, d. 15 Dec. 1842.
ii.   SOLOMON, b. in ME say 1773, d. in NB 11 Apr. 1856; m.
      MARY PHILLIPS, b. in Jan. 1778, d. 10 May 1844.
iii. MARY, b. in ME 1 Oct. 1774, d. in Aug. 1844 (or 15
      July 1838); m. LEMUEL NASON, son of John and Sarah
      (Jenkins) Nason.
iv.   ISRAEL, b. in ME, d. in 1870; m. FANNIE BRIGGS (or m.
      ANNIE HOYT and removed to Ontario, per Phillips).
v.   ?ASA, returned to Gouldsboro.
vi.   LYDIA, b. in NB; m. SOLOMON TUCKER.
vii. SARAH, b. in NB; m. JOHN MILLS.
viii. SAMUEL, b. in NB 1785, d. Lakeville NB 23 July 1861;
      m. LUCY JONES.
ix.   JEREMIAH, b. Oromocto NB 27 Nov. 1786 (66 in 1851),
      res. Blissville, Sunbury Co.; m. 7 Apr. 1807 MARY
      WEBB, b. 14 Nov. 1787, d. 13 Apr. 1843, dau. of
      Richardson and Bessie (Thomas) Webb.
x.   JONATHAN, b. 27 Nov. 1786 (twin?-65 in 1851), d. in
      Sept. 1869; m. RACHEL WEBB, b. in 1787, d. 2 Oct.
      1849, 59y (GS), sister of Mary above.

33. **HATEVIL**[5] 1750-1819 [11 Hatevil[4] and Sarah Trickey] was
born at Newington NH 28 Feb. 1750, baptized there 18 Aug.
1751 (NHGR, 4[1907]:64), died at Pembroke ME in 1819; married
at Dover NH in 1772 MARTHA [Patty] DENBOW, born at Dover 27
July 1751, daughter of John and ---- (Tibbetts) Denbow.
    A boy of 15, Hatevil settled about 1765 with his brother
Thomas at Narraguagus (the Steuben-Cherryfield area). In 1768
he set off for Machias, and explored as far as Campobello
Island. He, Capt. Robert Wilson and William Clark took up
500 acres at Pennamaquam by "squatter sovereignty" in 1770,
intending to harvest trees rather than to settle. They cut
and shipped timber, and had a sawmill near completion when
both his partners were drowned at Cobscook Falls. Pennamaquam, or Tp No. 2, east district, was incorporated as Dennysville in 1818, and the portion earliest settled was set off
as the town of Pembroke in 1832.
    In the spring of 1773, he became the first settler at what
is now Pembroke, building a home for his family on Leighton's
Point. In 1932 a marker was placed on a boulder marking the
site ("Pembroke 1832-1932," Eastport Sentinel, 2 Mar., 10
Aug. 1932; Peter E. Vose, Centennial History of Dennysville,
Me. [Portland, 1886], 108; Leighton, Gen. Sketch, 6-9; Gerald
G. Wilder, Pembroke, Maine, Families [manuscript, Peavey
Library, Eastport]). His name is in the DAR Index [409], but
the service credited was more likely that of his cousin
Hatevil [# 21]. He was listed at No. 2 in 1790 as "Hatewell
Laton," and was in the 1800 and 1810 censuses also.

On 18 Aug. 1790, Clement Denbow sold him 30 acres with buildings adjoining Hatevil's land on Cobscook Bay; on 20 May 1792 a 72-acre lot on Denbow Neck, Cobscook Bay (now in Lubec, then the 3rd division of Eastport); and 21 Nov. 1801 more land on Denbow's Neck (WashCD, 2:435, 1:240, 3:132). With his wife Patty, Hatevil sold to Hatevil, Jr., of Eastport 27 July 1809 lot #1 on Denbow's Neck (11:347-8).

His son John was appointed administrator of his estate 12 May 1819, after widow "Paty" declined the duty. The inventory made 22 June 1819 included his homestead of 130 acres near Cobscook Falls. In 1824 John was given a warrant to divide the land among the heirs, all listed; on Apr. 17 he was authorized to divide the homestead into two lots and to arrange that eleven heirs accept payment for their shares (WashCP, 4:473, 480, 501; 5:220-2, 453).

Children, the first born at Newington NH or Narraguagus, and the others at No. 2 (Dennysville TRs):

93.   i.   JOHN PATTEN^6, b. 25 Dec. 1772.
94.   ii.   SARAH, b. 2 May 1774; m. ADNA HERSEY.
95.   iii. HATEVIL, b. 8 Aug. 1775.
96.   iv.   SAMUEL, b. 25 Dec. 1776.
97.   v.   MARGARET, b. 20 Sept. 1778; m. ROBERT ASH, JR.
98.   vi.   MARY, b. 28 May 1780; m. WILLIAM BELL.
99.   vii. PHOEBE, b. in 1782; m. JOHN CAREW and JOHN
            KELLEY.
100. viii. HANNAH, b. in 1784; m. JOHN NUTTER.
101. ix.   REBECCA, b. 8 May 1786; m. JAMES DENSMORE.
102. x.   CLEMENT, b. in 1790.
103. xi.   ABIGAIL, b. 29 July 1792; m. GEORGE NUTTER.
104. xii. MARTHA [Patty], b. in June 1795; m. CLEMENT
            DENSMORE.
105. xiii. ELIJAH, b. in 1796.

34. SAMUEL^5 1756-1831 [11 Hatevil^4 and Sarah Trickey] was baptized at Newington NH 18 Oct. 1756 (NHGR, 4[1907]:109), died at Perry ME 3 Dec. 1831 (VRs); married ELIZABETH FROST, born 9 Oct. 1757, died at Perry 4 Oct. 1843 (VRs), daughter of William Frost.

He lived first at Gouldsboro with his father, and was likely the Samuel who enlisted in Capt. Nathan Shaw's Co. at Gouldsboro 7 Sept. 1775, serving 4 months, 3 days, defending the coast (MSS, 9:413).

He lived at Pembroke, and then about 1780 became the first settler at Pleasant Point, or Township No. 9 east of Machias, incorporated as Perry in 1818 (BHM, 3[1887]:96; 9[1889]:226). On 6 June 1788 Samuel of Cobscook Bay sold to John Crane his rights (4 days and a half, or 1/6 and 1/48) in a sawmill "known as Old Cobscook tide mills" on the Cobscook River, and lot #9 of 100 acres bounded by the tidemill and pond (WashCD, 1:137). (The name Cobscook was then applied to all the land bordering the Bay.) He sold 100 acres at No. 9 to John Crane 5 Dec. 1792 (1:331).

Note: Julia Cornman's major error was to confuse various Samuel Leightons. She placed here Samuel of Columbia [# 44], and instead identified Samuel of Perry as a son of David of Rochester [# 53].

Children, born at Perry (Eastport VRs):

106.   i.   SAMUEL[6], b. 26 Mar. 1779.
       ii.   JOHN, b. 10 Jan. 1781, d. c1849; m. SARAH
             JONES, b. Milton MA 28 Nov. 1786 (Perry VRs),
             dau. of Samuel and Mary Jones. No ch. In
             1804 John bought land on Moose Island (East-
             port) adjoining land he and his brother Samuel
             owned, and another Moose Island lot in 1805
             (WashCD, 4:234-6). Sarah of Perry, widow of
             John, intestate, was named administratrix 18
             Jan. 1850 (WashCP, 15:489).
107.   iii. SALLY, b. 10 Apr. 1783; m. SAMUEL WHEELER.
108.   iv.   MARK, b. 1 Aug. 1785.
       v.   GEORGE, b. 4 July 1787; d. Perry 25 Apr. 1818,
             30y; m. MARY CUTTER. He served from Eastport
             in Lt. Bela Wilder's detachment in 1812 (Mass-
             achusetts Volunteer Militia ... War of 1812-
             1814 [Adjutant General's Records, Boston,
             1913], 161.
       vi.   ALICE. b. 30 Aug. 1789, d. 24 May 1793.
       vii. NANCY, b. 29 June 1791, d. 15 Feb. 1806; m.
             Eastport 24 Mar. 1805 (int. 13 Dec. 1804)
             STEPHEN STIMPSON.
       viii. LYDIA, b. in 1793; m. in 1817 JOHN SMALL, prob-
             ably son of Ebenezer and Abigail[6] (Leighton)
             Small [# 131]. Lydia was listed in Wilder's
             Pembroke Families, but not in the Cornman Ms.

35. **DEBORAH**[5] 1743-1831 [14 Thomas[4] and Mary Smithson] was
born at Newington NH 28 Oct. 1743 (baptized 12 Nov.) (NHGR,
4[1907]:16), died 2 Mar. 1831; married at Newington 3 Dec.
1761 (3[1905]:4) LEIGHTON COLBATH, born 3 Nov. 1739 (baptized
1 Dec.), died at Exeter ME in 1830, son of James and Olive[4]
(Leighton) Colbath [# 13] (Cornman Ms; records of descendants
Lois Pospisal and W. Robert Mill). He served under Capt.
Timothy Langdon in 1775 defending the coast at Boothbay.

Children (**Colbath**), order uncertain:

i.   LEMUEL, b. 10 Oct. 1762.
ii.   MARY.
iii.   ?JOHN.
iv.   ?JAMES; m. ABIGAIL ---- in 1794.
v.   OLIVE, b. in 1776, d. in 1854; m. JOSEPH FOYE, b. in
       1774, d. in 1839 (GS, Barnstead NH).
vi.   LEIGHTON.

36. **MARY**[5] 1745-1806 [14 Thomas[4] and Mary Smithson] was
baptized at Newington 3 Mar. 1744/5 (NHGR, 4[1907]:18), died
probably at Edgecomb ME in 1806; married SIMEON PEARL, born
in NH about 1740, died about 1806. He married second at
Edgecomb 7 Aug. 1806 (TRs) Abigail Gove, who was still living
there in 1828.
    Simeon settled at Freetown (Edgecomb) about the time John
Leighton [# 17] did, and with him signed the petition in 1761
concerning Wiscasset as shiretown. His land on Salt Marsh
Cove adjoined that of Benjamin Leighton [# 54]. He owned a
sawmill; John Smithson Leighton [# 38] became his partner in

a lumber business. He was 2nd Lieutenant of Capt. Timothy
Langdon's Co. in 1775 (MSS, 12:24).
  In 1785, he, a bricklayer at Falmouth, sold a lot at Edgecomb to Henry Williams, with John Smithson Leighton a witness
(LincCD, 18:171-2); he (styled gent.) and his wife and son
Silas were at Falmouth in 1787 (CumbCD, 14:315). They did
not remain there; in 1790 "Simeon Paul" was listed at Washington Town (Mount Vernon), and in 1800 he and his wife were
at Mount Vernon with a second female, probably Hannah.

  Children (**Pearl**), born probably at Edgecomb:

i.   RUTH, b. 31 Dec. 1760, d. Georgetown ME 13 Jan. 1857,
       96y 13d; m. 17 Sept. 1782 BENJAMIN RIGGS, b. Glou-
       cester MA 27 Mar. 1759, d. Georgetown 2 Jan. 1846,
       86y 8m 5d, son of Moses and Mary (Ellery) Riggs
       (NEHGReg, 80[1926]:24-5). He was a JP, and a Maine
       delegate to the Mass. General Court. Burials are in
       the Riggs Cemetery, Georgetown.
ii.   CATHERINE, d.y.
iii.   SARAH, d.y.
iv.   ABRAM, d.y.
v.   SAMUEL, d.y.
vi.   MARY; m. 1st NEAL BEAN; m. 2nd THOMAS^6 LEIGHTON
       [# 113].
vii.   LYDIA; m. EZEKIEL^6 LEIGHTON [# 189].
viii. SILAS, d. Mt. Vernon c1860. In 1790, he had 2
       females in his household, and had 6 ch. in 1800.
ix   BETSEY; m. EMERSON STAIN.
x.   HANNAH, b. 3 June 1783; m. JOSEPH^6 LEIGHTON
       [# 114].

  37. GEORGE^5 1745-1817 [14 Thomas^4 and Mary Smithson] was
born at Newington NH 2 June 1745, died at Gardiner ME 21 Mar.
1817 (VRs); married at Stratham NH in 1779 (int. Greenland 17
May, per pension record) DEBORAH PERKINS, born about 1761 (78
in 1839), died at Gardiner 29 Sept. 1844, 85y (VRs).
  George signed the Association Test at Newington in 1776.
He served as private in Col. John Langdon's Light Horse Vol-
unteers in Aug. 1778 on a sortie to RI (NHSP, 15:577), and as
ensign and then lieutenant of cavalry under Col. Hercules
Mooney in June 1779, again to RI (NHSP, 8:829, 15:654).
  He and Deborah joined the Newington church 26 Nov. 1780,
baptizing their daughter Molly Smithson on the same date
(NHGR, 5[1908]:78). On 12 Oct. 1782, he sold to Nicholas
Pickering 31 acres with buildings on Great Bay, Newington,
where he was then living (StrCD, 114:417), and on 27 May 1783
bought 39 acres at Meredith of John Dockham (113:446). On 16
Mar. 1784 George, gentleman of Meredith, sold 30 acres "where
I now live" to Joel Leighton of Newington (RockCD, 116:339).
  From 1784 to 1792, he bought several holdings at Meredith--
from David Bachelder, John Gilman, John Dockham and the town
(5:465; 13:291. 446; 14:302), and was licensed to operate a
tavern there (NHSP, 18:751-2). In the 1790 Meredith census
his household included another male 16 or older, two younger
males, and four females besides his wife.
  In 1791-2, he sold off his Meredith properties, mainly to
Benjamin Page, Gordon Lawrence and Isaac and Jonathan Farrar,
and settled at Pittston ME, in that portion west of the Kennebec River that became Gardiner in 1803. On 7 Sept. 1798

George Leighton of Pittston, gent., sold to Rufus Gray land
purchased from Robert McCausland in 1797 (LincCD, 43:188).
In 1800 his household at Pittston included his wife, three
males and four other females; in 1810 he was listed at Gardiner with his wife, two males and two other females.
On 14 Aug. 1837 his widow applied for a pension, but failed
to prove she had been married to George while he was still in
service. (John Smithson Leighton filed a supporting affidavit.) On 29 Apr. 1853 Molly Sanborn, Elizabeth Plaisted and
Sarah McCausland made a successful pension application in
their mother's right, stating they were the only surviving
children (NA-MSR # R 6274).

Children, probably others unidentified:

109.   i.   MARY SMITHSON^6, bp. Newington 26 Nov. 1780;
             m. PEARSON SANBORN and JAMES WAKEFIELD.
110.   ii.   ELIZABETH, b. c1786; m. ICHABOD PLAISTED.
111.   iii. NATHANIEL, b. Pittston 18 Dec. 1791.
112.   iv.   SARAH, b. c1800; m. HENRY McCAUSLAND.

38.   **JOHN SMITHSON**^{5} 1749-1849 [14 Thomas^4 and Mary Smith-
son] was baptized at Newington NH 26 Nov. 1749 (NHGR
4[1907]:61), died at Rome ME 22 Mar. 1849, 100y (VRs); married first at Freetown (now Edgecomb) ME 11 July 1771 (TRs)
SARAH BAREY, died at Mount Vernon ME 22 March 1799; married
second at Mt. Vernon int. 13 Feb. 1802 LOIS (WOODMAN) Scott.
(Although middle names were uncommon until after 1800, he
was always known by his full name.)
His wife Lois had a son Nathaniel W. Scott, born at Machias
ME 22 Mar. 1792. On 23 Sept. 1808 Lois Leighton of Rome sold
her dower right to a tract on the Machias River, owned by the
late George Scott (WashCD, 5:240).
About 1770 he settled at Freetown (now Edgecomb) in Lincoln
County ME, where Capt. John [# 17] and his sons Benjamin and
Solomon had settled earlier, and joined Simeon Pearl in his
lumbering business. After Edgecomb became a town in 1774, he
served as tithingman in 1775, hay constable in 1777, constable in 1781, selectman in 1783, and surveyor of highways in
1786 (TRs).
He bought about 100 acres along the Damariscotta River from
his second cousin Solomon 8 July 1778; on 21 June 1779 he
bought from Solomon and Sarah an adjoining tract (LincCD,
13:44, 21:184). From Simeon Pearl, gent., he bought on 7
Apr. 1784 a further 250 acres on the west side of the Damariscotta, including Salt Marsh Cove, Mill Creek and the mill
privilege 1784 (18:32).
In 1785, he began selling off land, perhaps being over-
extended. In fact, on 20 June 1785, he was ordered by the
court to pay Roger Standley of Boothbay over 44 pounds, with
the "sheriff to see judgment satified and to put said John in
Pownalborough gaol until amount is paid." To pay this debt
he delivered 28 acres on 15 Sept. 1785, "part of the 100 acre
lot whereon John Smithson Laighton dwells" (18:213-5).
By 1787 he had removed to Washington Plantation (organized
in 1792 as Mount Vernon), settling at Whittier's Mills, now
within Mount Vernon village. On 3 Dec. 1787 he sold to
Edward Emerson of Edgecomb 200 acres at Washington, including
half a crop of winter rye and a dwelling house (21:184).

John Smithson Laighton was not listed in the 1790 census, but was living at Mount Vernon in 1800, with three males under 5, perhaps grandchildren; in 1810 he and his wife were listed at Rome, with a young girl.

Children by Sarah, born at or near Edgecomb:

113. i.   THOMAS[6], b. c1771.
114. ii.   JOSEPH, b. 26 May 1779.
     iii. LYDIA, d.y.
     iv.   MARY; probably m. ANDREW[6] LEIGHTON [# 195].

39.   JOEL[5] 1751-1810 [14 Thomas[4] and Mary Smithson] was born at Newington NH 24 Sept. 1751 (baptized 3 Nov.), died at Exeter NH 29 Oct. 1810, 56y; married first at Newington 21 Oct. 1778 (NHGR, 3[1905]:9) ELIZABETH HUNTRESS, baptized at Newington 21 Aug. 1757, died at Exeter 4 Sept. 1802, daughter of William and Susanna (Downing) Huntress; married second BETSEY (HAIGHT) Smith, born 10 Aug. 1768, died at Bloomfield (Skowhegan) ME. Betsey had married first Hezekiah Smith, and married third Peter Labree (Cornman Ms; Louise H. Coburn, Skowhegan on the Kennebec [1941], 659).
    Joel served in Capt. David Copp's company in 1775, and as sergeant under Capt. Joseph Parsons, Col. Senter's Battalion, 4 July 1777 to 6 Jan 1778 on duty in RI (NHSP, 15:249, 256, 259, 262; 16:29).
    He and Elizabeth joined the Newington church 8 Oct. 1780 (NHGR, 5[1908]:78), and their children were baptized there. In 1781 he was chosen selectman. In 1790 he was listed at Newington with his wife and ten others, and in 1800 with eight others. He was a joiner by trade.
    He had bought land in 1784 from his brother George (RockCD, 116:339), was deeded land at Barnstead by his father-in-law William Huntress 3 May 1785 (StrCD, 9:122), and had purchased a 95-acre lot at Meredith in 1793 (16:530). In a series of transactions from 1783 on, he sold off land tract by tract. Joel, joiner of Newington, sold to Ephraim Pickering, Esq., in 1784 the 30 acres on Great Bay, Newington, "which I live on" (RockCD, 115:343). In 1788 he sold his Barnstead lots to Ebenezer Place, Jr. (StrCD, 9:127). In 1783, Joel of Durham sold 80 acres at Candia to Abraham Fitts (RockCD, 115:53), and in 1796 he sold his Meredith property to Joseph Neal (122:213).
    Soon after 1800, he and his family moved to Exeter, where he kept a tavern. In 1805 he was administrator of the estate of Hezekiah Smith, late of Brentwood and first husband of his second wife. Joel, innkeeper, sold his homestead to his stepson John Smith of Portsmouth in 1807 (RockCD, 179:295), and in 1808 he and his wife sold John her rights as widow "for $3 hard money" (184:58). He sold 60 acres of land to his son Samuel also in 1808 (183:115).

Children by Elizabeth, all but Lydia listed in Newington TRs.

115. i.   SAMUEL[6], b. 28 Mar. 1779.
116. ii.   TEMPERANCE PICKERING, b. 20 Apr. 1780; m.
           MOSES RANDLETT.
117. iii. THOMAS, b. 23 Dec. 1781.
118. iv.   WILLIAM, b. 20 Sept. 1784.

119. v.   MARY SMITHSON, b. 5 Sept. 1786; m. JOHN SMITH.
120. vi.   ELIZABETH, b. 20 Sept. 1788; m. INCREASE
            RANDLETT.
121. vii. JOEL, b. 15 Apr. 1790.
122. viii. MEHITABLE FABYAN, b. 3 Dec. 1793; m. BENJAMIN
            SMITH.
      ix.   LYDIA S., b. Exeter 3 July 1796; m. Sharon VT
            JOHN B. WHEELER. Only ch. Charles William
            b. 12 Apr. 1818 (Cornman Ms).

40. **ELIZABETH**⁵ 1756-   [14 Thomas and Mary Smithson] was
baptized at Newington 15 Feb. 1756 (NHGR, 4[1907]:108); married there 4 Jan. 1779 (3[1906]:7) THOMAS PINDER, baptized at
Durham NH 23 Dec. 1755, son of Joseph and Hepzibah (Davis)
Pinder (Stackpole, Durham, 2:305).

Children (**Pinder**), born at Newington:

i.   BENJAMIN, d. 19 Nov. 1814; m. Newmarket NH 24 Nov.
      1791 SUSANNA PERKINS.
ii.   JAMES BICKFORD, bp. 5 Aug. 1781.
ii.   JOSEPH LEIGHTON, bp. 5 Aug. 1781; prob. m. 21 June
      1801 MARY DOE.

41. **JOHN**⁵ 1719-1778 [16 Thomas⁴ and Susanna Chesley] was
born at Dover 27 June 1719, died at Barrington NH in 1778;
married by 1749 MARTHA ALLEN, daughter of Jacob and Mary
(Spencer) (Jones) Allen. Jacob Allen's will made 8 July 1752
gave five pounds to his daughter Martha Leighton (NHPP,
34:246-9).
     John's father deeded him 125 acres in the Two-Mile Streak
of Barrington in 1739, land which his father and his uncle
Samuel Chesley had purchased (Morton H. Wiggin, History of
Barrington N. H. [np, 1966], 27-9). As Sgt. John Laighton he
appeared on the 1742 Barrington tax list; in 1758 he was on
the minister's roll of Durham residents (NHGR, 5[1908]:41).
He bought additional land at Barrington 30 Nov. 1745 from his
parents (NHPD, 32: 561-2). Portions of his holdings he sold
off in 1749, 1754, 1756, 1762 and 1766. On 7 May 1753 he and
his brother Thomas divided their jointly-owned property
(40:535).
     He was among the four Leightons who served under Capt. Paul
Gerrish, Col. Peter Gilman's Rgt., from 19 Sept. to 14 Dec.
1755, marching to Albany when the French threatened Lake
George (Potter, Mil. Hist., 144, 150-3).
     John's will, made 4 Nov. 1777, was proved 10 June 1778, his
son James being named executor. The inventory, allowed 11
Aug. 1778, was valued at 73 pounds (StrCP, 1:312-4, 322-3,
378-9; 2:455; 3:344-5; NHSP, 33:248). The family homestead
was left to James (sold out of family hands by him in 1795
when he moved to Farmington); the other children received six
shillings each. His widow was given a third of the income
from his property, and a third of the movables.

Children, born at Barrington:

123. i.   THOMAS⁶, b. c1753.
      ii.   DOROTHY, b. c1755; m. Barrington 19 Aug. 1773
            EBENEZER JACKSON, bp. Durham 5 Oct. 1741,

son of William and Abigail (Follett) Jackson
(Stackpole, Durham, 2:227).
124. iii. JEDEDIAH, b. 31 July 1756.
125. iv.   LUCY, b. 4 Mar. 1758; m. WILLIAM HILL.
126. v.   JAMES, b. 8 May 1759.
      vi.   HANNAH, b. in 1761, d. Strafford 18 Dec. 1826,
            65y 5m 2d (GS); unm.

42. THOMAS⁵ 1725-1813 [16 Thomas⁴ and Susannah Chesley]
was born at Dover 13 Nov. 1725 (VRs, 18), died at Steuben ME
9 Mar. 1813 (TRs); married at Dover 30 Nov. 1745 MARGARET
MURRAY, born at Barrington 17 June 1727, died at Steuben of
childbed 4 Feb. 1773, aged 45 (TRs), daughter of Thomas Murray. In Maine records he was called Thomas, Sr., and Elder
Thomas.
     He served in the colonial war: in 1755 in the 5th Co. of
Col. Blanchard's Rgt. against Canada; in 1756 under Capt.
Samuel Gerrish on a march to Crown Point; in 1757 in Col.
Meserve's 5th Co.; and in the 5th Co. again in 1760, marching
to Crown Point as part of the attack on Canada (Potter, Mil.
Hist., 173, 236).
     He and his brother divided their Barrington property 7 May
1753 (NHPD, 40:535); he and Margaret then sold their Barring-
ton land to John Bickford 19 Apr. 1759 (64:59).
     In 1763, Thomas was in Maine at Majabagaduce, petitioning
for a grant of land (see #11), but settled instead about 1764
at No. 4 (now Steuben), on a lot at the head of Pigeon Hill
Bay still owned by a descendant. His household included his
parents. His second cousin Thomas, Jr., [# 31] settled at
Steuben at the same time; the two have often been confused
(Milliken, 6-7, 8-11; BHM, 8[1893]:222, 236; 9[1894]:226).
     Because of his age and previous experience, he was likely
the Thomas who served as sergeant under Capt. Reuben Dyer
from May to July 1777 on an expedition against Saint John NB
(MSS, 9:414). His sons Joseph and Robert were also in the
same company.
     In 1790 he was listed in the census for Plantation #4,
which was incorporated as Steuben in 1795. On 12 July 1786
Thomas, "now living in the 4th township called Titmanan"
(Petit Manan Point), conveyed to Stephen Waite of Falmouth
100 acres "possessed by him [Thomas] 3 years before this
date" (WashCD, 1:54).
     Six townships east of Union River had been conditionally
set up in 1760, but never approved by the Crown. The grants
were confirmed to the original proprietors in 1785, on the
condition that they quiet the claims of inhabitants who had
settled on and improved lots of 50 acres or more before the
peace with Britain (BHM, 1[1885]:31). "Settlers' rights"
thus allowed purchase of land at low prices.
     Elder Thomas preferred to settle at No. 5, incorporated in
1791 as Harrington; he bought from the commissioners 100
acres of land and marsh, lot 25 at Harrington, on 4 June 1794
(WashCD, 4:219-20).
     On 26 Sept. 1805 he sold Ebenezer Small of Cherryfield a
portion of lot 25 in Steuben east of the mill stream, with
house, barn and mill privileges; and to his son Benjamin land
granted as his settler's right (4:220-3). On 8 Feb. 1806,
Small sold back most of lot 25; on 17 Feb. Thomas sold to his
son James "one quarter of the land [at Steuben] dyked by me,
James and Benjamin," northwest of Benjamin's land (5:37-8).

On 21 Aug. 1807, Thomas bought 66 acres at Harrington, again exercising his settler's right, and on the same day sold this to Gad Townsley of Steuben (5:37-8).

Children, the older born at Madbury, recorded in the Barrington VRs:

	i.	BENJAMIN^6. b. 4 Aug. 1746, d. 20 Sept. 1756.
127.	ii.	ANN, b. 29 Jan. 1747; m. TRISTRAM PINKHAM.
128.	iii.	ELIZABETH, b. 25 Aug. 1750; m. ELEAZER DAVIS and RICHARD PINKHAM.
129.	iv.	SARAH, b. 5 June 1752; m. ---- LEIGHTON and THOMAS STEVENS.
130.	v.	JOSEPH, b. 1 Apr. 1755.
131.	vi.	ROBERT, b. 28 Jan. 1758.
132.	vii.	ABIGAIL, b. 2 May 1760; m. JAMES TRACY and EBENEZER SMALL.
133.	viii.	MARY, b. 16 Jan. 1762; m. THOMAS WEST.
134.	ix.	THOMAS, b. Steuben 18 June 1765.
135.	x.	ROSS, b. Steuben 14 Nov. 1766.
136.	xi.	JAMES, b. Steuben 20 Mar. 1769.
137.	xii.	BENJAMIN F., b. Steuben 4 Feb. 1773.

43. GEORGE^5 1727-   [16 Thomas^4 and Susannah Chesley] was born at Dover NH 18 Nov. 1727 (VRs, 47), living at Falmouth ME in 1817 when his son Pelatiah died; married at Dover 20 1mo 1753 (NHGR, 4[1907]:44) DOROTHY HALL, born at Dover 22 Aug. 1733, died at Falmouth say 1777, daughter of Hatevil and Sarah (Furbush) Hall (David B. Hall, The Halls of New England [Albany, 1883], 165; Hall Desc., #1). Cumberland County probate records were completely destroyed by fire in 1907. Burials are in an old granite tomb at Hardy Road, near Blackstrap Road. Like the Halls, George was a Quaker.

They settled at Falmouth before 1760, where he became a prosperous landowner. He bought of John Frink 104 acres 12 Aug. 1762 (CumbCD, 3:260). County land records show dozens of George's transactions; he often purchased rights to common and undivided land from proprieters or their heirs. His wife Dorothy signed with him waiving her dower rights up to 1775, but not in 1778. Most holdings were described as north of the Presumpscot River, but some were at Cape Elizabeth.

He sold to "my son Hatevil" 4 Dec. 1787 64 acres with buildings, the land Hatevil was living on (26:7). On 4 Dec. also he sold 36 acres to James Hicks, and 30 more to "my daughter Abigail, wife of James Hicks" (16:101-2). He sold on 3 Jan. 1797 70 acres to his son Paul (25:529), 119 acres to son David (50:137), and 132 acres west of George's homestead to son Silas (50:138); and on 23 Feb. 37 more acres to James Hicks (36:401). He sold to "my son Jedediah" 145 acres adjoining Pelatiah's land, and a separate 21-acre lot, on 4 Dec. 1787 (37:455-6). On 10 May 1804 he sold two small lots to son Hatevil (48:464-5). To Pelatiah, he sold 149 acres adjoining the North Yarmouth line 17 Nov. 1806 (75:353).

George was listed by Carleton E. and Sue G. Fisher in their Soldiers, Sailors and Patriots of the Revolutionary War / Maine [1982, p. 457], giving as their source the 1776-7 orderly book of Maj. Daniel Ilsley (MHS Ms. Collection). George "Laten" was named there, not as a soldier but in a Memorandum of Sundry Men's Bills, indicating payment made for providing and hauling timber.

Children, births of the last five in Falmouth TRs:

138. i.   PELATIAH[6], b. c1753.
139. ii.   JEDEDIAH, b. in 1757.
140. iii. SARAH, b. in 1758; m. JOHN WEBB, JR.
141. iv.   HATEVIL, b. 24 July 1760.
142. v.   ABIGAIL, b. 4 June 1762; m. JAMES HICKS.
143. vi.   DAVID, b. 18 Dec. 1767.
144. vii. PAUL, b. 3 May 1770.
145. viii. SILAS, b. Sept. 1771.

44. SAMUEL[5] 1729-1812 [16 Thomas and Susannah Chesley] was
born at Dover NH 20 Dec. 1729 (VRs, 47), died at Columbia ME
21 Mar. 1812 (VRs); married first at Falmouth ME int. 13 Oct.
1755 (TRs) DORCAS BUNKER, baptized at Dover 13 Oct. 1744,
died at Columbia about 1799, daughter of Zachariah and Deborah (Varney) Bunker; married second about 1800 SARAH (INGER-
SOLL) Rolfe, baptized at North Yarmouth ME 13 Oct. 1745 (but
born about 1738), daughter of William and Sarah (Parker)
Ingersoll and widow of Moses Rolfe (NEHGReg, 122[1968]:292).
    With his father, he was at Majabagaduce in 1763 (see #11),
and with him settled first at Gouldsboro. Shortly after, he
was the pioneer settler at Columbia, then No. 12 and 13.
    During the Revolutionary War he was in Capt. Francis Shaw's
Co. for 4 months in 1775 defending the coast; under Capt.
Thomas Parritt in June 1777; in Capt. Henry Dyer's detachment
in Aug. and Sept. 1777, serving at Machias; in Capt. John
Hall's Co. at Majabagaduce in Aug. 1779; and again under
Capt. Henry Dyer in 1780 (MSS, 9:413, 544, 664).
    In 1790, Samuel and his sons Parritt and Isaac were the
only heads of household at Columbia, which was incorporated
in 1796. On 6 June 1795 he sold to Eli Forbes 100 acres at
Columbia south of the Great Heath (WashCD, 1:493-4).
    Again, Julia Cornman's manuscript confused the Samuels.
She showed here the Samuel Leighton of Farmington [# 52] who
married Abigail Goodwin, and the Samuel above she placed as
Samuel [# 34], a son of Hatevil.

Children, all by Dorcas:

        i.   THEODORE[6], b. say 1757, d.y. Narraguagus.
        ii.   DEBORAH, b. say 1759. Perhaps the DORCAS
              LEIGHTON named as 1st wife of Asa Tracy, b.
              Falmouth 4 Aug. 1760, d. Gouldsboro 23 Dec.
              1831, son of Jonathan and Abigail (Riggs)
              Tracy (N. B. Tracy, Historical Address before
              the Fourth Annual Reunion of the Tracy Family
              at Gouldsboro, Maine [Auburn 1900], 23). Asa
              m. 2nd say 1800 Dorcas Bunker; he had 10 ch, 5
              by each wife (Edward C. Moran, Jr., Bunker
              Genealogy [np, 1965], 1:11). No other refer-
              ences to this Dorcas Leighton have been found.
        iii. SARAH, b. say 1761; m. JOHN PARRITT, son of
              Thomas Parritt.
146.   iv.   ISAAC, b. 25 Feb. 1763.
147.   v.   ESTHER, b. c1765; m. SAMUEL TUCKER.
148.   vi.   (THOMAS) PARRITT, b. say 1766.
149.   vii. PHINEAS, b. Columbia say 1768.
150.   viii. HANNAH, b. Columbia 31 July 1770; m. MOSES
              WORCESTER, JR.

151. ix. SUSAN, b. Columbia in 1773; m. RICHARD GOWELL
           MERRITT.
      x.   JOHN C., b. Columbia c1780, lived at Cherry-
           field in 1850, aged 60, with Dolly, 70; m.
           (prob. 2nd) Addison 4 Feb. 1833 DOLLY PINKHAM,
           presumably that dau. of Theodore Leighton who
           m. 1st TRISTRAM PINKHAM [# 167]. Phineas
           Leighton of Eastport sold to John of Cherry-
           field 26 June 1813 a lot at Cherryfield near
           Epping Plains, 100 acres with house and barn
           (WashCD, 8:8). In 1820, John Leighton was
           listed at Addison with one female and 2 males
           under 10.

45. GIDEON⁵ 1731-1776 [16 Thomas⁴ and Susannah Chesley]
was born at Dover 14 Feb. 1731 (VRs, 47), died at Barrington
10 June 1776, 45y; married at Dover in 1761 ABIGAIL TITCOMB,
born in 1743, died in 1837, 94y, daughter of William and Jane
(Emmons) Titcomb. Gideon was killed by a falling timber
while dismantling a sawmill (Wiggin, Barrington, 32), and is
buried in the Otis family cemetery at Strafford. Thomas Foss
was appointed guardian of Gideon's children in July 1779
(StrCP, 2:18).
     Abigail married second at Barrington 23 Jan. 1777 (VRs)
William Gray, Jr., and had five Gray children; she married
third at Barrington 12 Oct. 1789 (VRs) John Pearl (Stearns,
N. H. Genealogies, 3:1320-1). Her will, made 8 Mar. 1821,
was proved 1 Oct. 1838; Gideon Gray was executor (StrCP,
50:130; 52: 493; 54:6; 55:27).
     Gideon and his brother Theodore served "to the amount of 7
years in the holl" in the French war (NHSP, 11:711). He was
a scout from Durham under Capt. Joseph Bickford during the
defense of Epsom in 1754, and was a private in Capt. Paul
Gerrish's Co., Col. Peter Gilman's Rgt., in 1755 on the march
to Albany (Potter, Mil. Hist., 126-7, 144, 150-3). In 1758
he served under Capt. Thomas Tash, and was promoted to ensign
(NHSP, 11:154, 711; 14: 228). He served in the Revolutionary
War also, and was listed as corporal under Capt. Samuel Hayes
in 1775 (NHSP, 30:11).

     Children, born at Barrington (TRs):

     152. i.   STEPHEN, b. 4 Sept. 1763.
     153. ii.   JOSEPH, b. 17 May 1766.
     154. iii. ANDREW, b. 22 May 1767.
     155. iv.   LEVI, b. c1773.

46. JOSEPH⁵ 1733-1803 [16 Thomas⁴ and Susannah Chesley]
was born at Dover 23 Apr. 1733 (VRs, 47), died at Falmouth ME
14 June 1803, "fell dead while working on the highway"; married first at Falmouth 6 Oct. 1757 MERCY HALL, born at Dover
6 Oct. 1738, died at Falmouth 2 Mar. 1792, daughter of
Hatevil and Sarah (Furbish) Hall (Falmouth TRs; Halls of NE,
166; Hall Desc., #4); married second at Kittery ME 13 Dec.
1792 HANNAH WILSON, born there 4 Feb. 1760, died at Falmouth
22 Aug. 1813, daughter of Joseph and Mary (Mansfield) Wilson
(Everett S. Stackpole, Old Kittery and Her Families [1903,
reprinted 1970], 800; Cornman Ms).

Like his brother George he settled at Falmouth, married a
daughter of Hatevil Hall, and was a Quaker. He too bought
much land at Falmouth and North Yarmouth. In 1757 he and
Isaac Allen purchased together from Josiah Noyes 50 acres
east of the Presumpscot (CumbCD, 4:321), and he bought rights
to undivided land from various owners. In 1790 he, his son
Andrew and Richmond Loring divided jointly-owned land in the
North Yarmouth Gore east of Goose Pond Brook (17:423), and on
16 Apr. 1798 he, Andrew and Richard Mountford divided other
North Yarmouth property (30:139). On 8 Sept. 1792 he deeded
92 acres east of the Gray Road to his son Ezekiel (19:331-2).

Children by first wife Mercy, born at Falmouth:

156. i.   SUSANNAH⁶, b. 1 May 1758; m. GEORGE HUSTON.
      ii.   HANNAH, b. 10 Jan. 1761; m. ROBERT⁶ LEIGHTON
            [# 131].
157. iii. ANDREW, b. 7 June 1762.
158. iv.   STEPHEN, b. 7 May 1764.
159. v.   MARY W., b. 9 Dec. 1765; m. JAMES WEYMOUTH.
160. vi.   EZEKIEL, b. 19 July 1767.
      vii. LYDIA, b. 22 Sept. 1770, d. 28 Feb. 1848; m.
            JAMES HICKS. No ch. He m. 1st her cousin
            ABIGAIL LEIGHTON [# 142].
      viii. DANIEL, b. 7 Mar. 1772, d. in 1784.
      ix.   OLIVE, b. and d. 13 Mar. 1774.
      x.   PHEBE, b. and d. 11 May 1775.
161. xi.   ELIZABETH, b. 20 June 1776; m. JAMES WINSLOW.
      xii. ROBERT, b. 15 Aug. 1778, d. 15 June 1780.
162. xiii. SARAH, b. 15 Aug. 1780; m. WILLIAM HADLOCK.

Children by second wife Hannah, born at Falmouth:

163. xiv. JEREMIAH, b. 21 May 1793.
164. xv.   JANE, b. 28 July 1794; m. NATHANIEL ABBOTT.
      xvi. DORCAS, b. 2 Mar. 1796, d. 2 Dec. 1798.
165. xvii. ANN, b. 9 Aug. 1797; m. HENRY HUSTON.
166. xviii DORCAS, b. 2 Oct. 1801; m. EBENEZER LIBBY.

47. ELIZABETH⁵ 1737-   [16 Thomas⁴ and Susannah Chesley]
was born at Dover 11 Mar. 1737 (VRs, 47); perhaps married
ISAAC DREW and lived at Wolfeboro NH (Cornman Ms). Verification of this marriage has been elusive. Isaac was a common
name in Drew families.

Children (**Drew**), from Cornman Ms:

i.   BETSEY, b. 25 July 1764.
ii.   JOHN LEIGHTON, b. 7 Mar. 1769.
iii. ISAAC.

48. THEODORE⁵ 1739-   [16 Thomas⁴ and Susannah Chesley]
was born at Dover 22 March 1739 (VRs, 47), lived at Cherryfield ME in 1821; married HANNAH ---- , born 29 Nov. 1746,
died at Cherryfield 9 May 1817 (TRs). By tradition, she was
named Plummer, and was from Newburyport MA; she did have a
granddaughter named Hannah Plummer Pinkham.
      Theodore served in the French War in 1759 (NHSP, 11:711),
and by 1760 was at Falmouth ME. In 1763 he was with his

father at Majabagaduce (see #11), and probably lived with him
at Gouldsboro and Steuben. On 3 Jan. 1772 he purchased 60
acres from William McNeil at Cherryfield (then No. 11, or
Narraguagus) on the west side of Mill River (LincCD, 10:110;
Milliken, 2-11, 20-25; BHM, 9[1894]:223-6).
He served in the Revolutionary War in Capt. John Hall's
Co., Col. Benjamin Foster's Rgt., on an expedition to Castine
in 1779 (MSS, 9:544). His household in 1790 at Cherryfield
included his wife and his six daughters; in 1800 one daughter
still lived at home.
He bought of Nathaniel Denbo on 6 Aug. 1782 120 acres at
Cherryfield, land and meadow "with a dwelling house and 2
hovels" (WashCD, 1:128-9). On 22 Apr. 1816 he mortgaged to
William Willey the 80-acre lot where he lived, provided that
his heirs maintain and support Theodore and Hannah (8:376);
but on 15 Sept. 1821 he sold this property to Robert Tucker
of Cherryfield, with Tucker obliged to sue William Willey for
possession (14:336).
Julia Cornman did not list Theodore's family, nor did James
Milliken. Dr. Thomas Roderick, a geneticist and genealogist,
has traced the inheritance of hemophilia among descendants.

Children, born at Cherryfield (VRs):

167.   i.   RACHEL[6], b. 20 Aug. 1780; m. BENJAMIN PINKHAM.
168.   ii.   DOROTHY, b. 18 June 1782; m. TRISTRAM PINKHAM.
169.   iii. ELIZABETH, b. 7 May 1784; m. WILLIAM TUCKER.
170.   iv.   SUSANNAH, b. 15 Jan. 1786; m. DANIEL TRACY.
       v.   HANNAH, b. 9 Apr. 1788; nfr.
       vi.   SARAH, b. 17 Dec. 1790; nfr.

49. SUSANNAH[5] 1742-   [16 Thomas and Susannah Chesley]
was born at Dover 6 Dec. 1742 (VRs, 47); perhaps married in
1769 EPHRAIM RICKER, born at Berwick in 1736, died in 1820,
son of George, Jr., and Jemima (Busby) Ricker (William B.
Lapham, Records of Some of the Descendants of George and Mat-
urin Ricker [Augusta, 1899], 10; also in MG&B, 3[1878]:10).
They lived at Somersworth NH and Berwick ME.

Children (**Ricker**), place and order of birth uncertain:

i.   TOBIAS, res. Buckfield ME; m. ABIGAIL WARREN, b. 12
       May 1764, dau. of Tristram and Mary (Neal) Warren of
       Buckfield.
ii.   GEORGE, b. 14 Dec. 1771, d. Auburn ME in 1854; m.
       DORCAS PHILBRICK of Buckfield. He was a Baptist
       minister.
iii.   DANIEL, res. Warren and Freedom; m. ---- . He was a
       Baptist minister.
iv.   JAMES, b. 24 June 1777, res. Hartford ME; m. 1st 26
       Apr. 1801 NANCY WESCOTT; m. 2nd 26 June 1806 ELIZA-
       BETH BERRY.
v.   DOLLY; m. THOMAS ALLEN of Hartford.
vi.   SALLY; m. STEPHEN PEARCE.

Note: Julia Cornman included this family in her Leighton
genealogy, probably relying upon Lapham as her source. No
proof has been found that Ephraim's wife Susannah Leighton
was descended from either Thomas[1] Leighton of Dover or from
William[1] Leighton of Kittery.

An hypothesis could be justified that Thomas's daughter
Susannah was the wife of Josiah Tucker, Sr., as yet known
only by her first name. Josiah was with the Leightons at
Majabagaduce in 1763, and was administrator of Thomas's
estate in 1765. Born in NH, he lived at Gouldsboro and Cherryfield. Josiah and Susanna had a son Theodore, a very
uncommon name at the time. Josiah Tucker's children were
listed in Milliken's Narraguagus (p. 6).

   50. LYDIA^5 1726-   [?17 John^4 and Sarah] was born
probably at Dover about 1726; married at Rochester 26 Nov.
1747 (NHGR, 4:145) JAMES ROGERS, JR. He was selectman at
Rochester from 1756 to 1758.
   Her identity is not proven; Julia Cornman listed her as a
daughter of John.

   Child (**Rogers**), perhaps others:

   i.   JAMES, bp. Rochester 8 Apr. 1753; m. there 28 Sept.
         1779 SUSANNAH PINKHAM.

   51. JONATHAN^5 1728-1797 [17 John^4 and Sarah] was born at
Dover say 1728, died at Alton NH about 1797; married probably
at Rochester about 1752 SARAH ---- , who died at Alton about
1820. Sarah was listed with a daughter in the 1810 Alton
census; the two were town-supported paupers in 1817 (TRs
3:324-709). On 3 Mar. 1821 the town voted payment to David
Langley for having made Sarah's coffin (TRs 3:436).
   Jonathan and his father on 2 July 1754 joined in purchasing
60 acres at Rochester adjoining other property of his father
(NHPD, 78:372-4). On 30 Mar. 1762, his father (by then residing in ME) deeded to Jonathan his share of this land, and
his proprietor's rights to undivided land (78:372-4). By
that time, Jonathan had already made his home on this lot.
   He served in the French War under Capt. Samuel Gerrish,
Col. John Goffe's Rgt., 8 Mar. to 27 Nov. 1760, on an expedition to Crown Point (Potter, Mil. Hist., 236). He and his
brothers signed a petition 8 Feb. 1762 seeking representation
for Rochester in the General Assembly (NHSP, 13:336). He was
named frequently in town records from 1765 to 1788 as holding
various town offices. "Mr. Jonathan Layton" sold land on the
Salmon Falls River at Rochester to Remembrance Clark 13 Feb.
1765--six acres in lot 56, fourth division, land originally
granted to Thomas Leighton (NHPD, 79:357). In support of the
new Rochester meeting-house, he purchased a pew 18 Sept.
1780. He was among Rochester petitioners to the General
Assembly 30 Aug. 1785 (NHSP, 13:341), but by 1790 he had
settled his family at New Durham Gore.
   In 1762 the General Assembly had granted to proprietors a
charter for New Durham, a township bordering Rochester and
Barnstead. New Durham Gore, a section which bordered on Lake
Winnipesaukee, was set up as a separate parish in 1777; it
was incorporated as Alton in 1796.
   In the 1790 New Durham census, Jonathan had a household of
one male over 16, two under 16, and two females. His nephew
Jonathan, Jr. [# 182], was also listed at New Durham.
   Jonathan and Sarah on 4 Nov. 1790 sold to his second cousin
Jabez Dame 90 acres in Rochester, part of the land he and his
father had bought in 1754 (StrCD, 13:384-6). On 17 Nov. 1790

he and others divided jointly-owned lots in the Gore, located
in the present Alton village (3:149-53), and he bought more
land from James Rogers 4 June 1794 (17:367). He was probably
the Jonathan chosen town moderator in 1796; the first town
meeting was held at his home 10 Apr. 1797 (TRs 1:47-8).

On 8 Mar. 1794 and again on 6 June 1796, inhabitants of the
Gore petitioned for incorporation as the town of "Roxbry"
(NHSP, 11:52-7). Among those signing were Jonathan Laighton,
Jr., Jonathan Leighton and Jonathan Leighton 3d. The
research of George F. Sanborn, Jr., has identified these
three, and has constructed the family of Jonathan, Sr.

Former usage was to call the younger of two men with the
same name in the same locality "Junior," no matter how or
whether they were related. On petitions and deeds, we find
Jonathan[5] and his son Jonathan 3d living at Alton Village and
Alton Bay, and Jonathan, Jr., son of David and nephew of Jonathan, at East Alton. From this usage, a date for Jonathan's
death may be estimated. On 10 June 1797, his nephew signed a
deed as Jonathan, Jr., but on 5 Dec. 1797 he did not use
"Jr." in another deed (25:161-2; 25:232-3). It is thus probable that Jonathan[5] died between the two dates.

Julia Cornman listed Dolly, wife of John Rogers, as a
daughter of Jonathan. The marriage of John and Molly Rogers
was recorded in the Rome ME VRs as 5 Sept. 1784, along with
the births of ten children between 1787 and 1811. However,
the marriage intentions filed 10 May 1784 at Edgecomb ME
named them as John Rogers and Mary Poole (TRs 1:251).

Known children, born at Rochester:

171. i.   ELIZABETH[6], b. 18 July 1753; m. JOHN ROLLINS.
     ii.   SUSANNAH, b. c1760, living at Alton in 1850,
           aged 90, with nephew Frederick B. Rollins;
           unm. She lived with her mother in 1810, and
           in 1816-7 when both were paupers supported by
           the town (TRs 3:321, 359, 361-2, 395).
172. iii. JONATHAN, b. c1762.
173. iv.   LYDIA, b. 24 Apr. 1767; m. JONATHAN PLACE and
           STEPHEN WENTWORTH.
174. v.   MARY, b. 30 Mar. 1769; m. JAMES ROBERTS.
175. vi.   SARAH, b. 1 July 1772; m. ICHABOD ROLLINS.
176. vii. HANNAH, b. 1 Feb. 1774; m. JOSHUA HANSON.

52. SAMUEL[5] 1729-1812 [17 John and Sarah] was born at
Dover 20 June 1729, died at Farmington NH 21 Mar. 1812, 82y
9m (GS); married ABIGAIL GOODWIN, born 29 [sic] Feb. 1733,
died at Farmington 2 Aug. 1814, 81y 5m (GS). They are buried
in the Silver Street Cemetery.

He was deeded land and buildings at Rochester by his father
18 Mar. 1762 (NHPD, 105:12). He signed the petition for town
representation in the General Assembly 8 Feb. 1762 (NHSP,
13:336). On 12 Apr. 1777 he and Abigail deeded lot 93 in
Rochester's first division to John McDuffee (StrCD, 1:521).

Samuel held many town offices at Rochester: surveyor of
highways eight times between 1759 and 1784, constable in 1761
and 1770, assessor from 1766 to 1772, and selectman in 1773-4
and 1784-1786 (McDuffee, Rochester, 2:532-3; Stearns, N. H.
Genealogies, 3:1206).

He was evidently not himself a member of the Rochester
church; Sarah and Hannah were baptized "upon their mother's

account at a lecture at Jno Layton's" 23 June 1756 (NHGR,
6[1909]:113). In 1790 he, his wife and daughter Jane were
living at Rochester. His home was at Farmington after a section of Rochester was set off as a new town in 1797.
      Julia Cornman confused him with Samuel [# 44], a son of
Thomas and Susannah (Chesley). An unresolved problem con-
cerns her listing of children Samuel and Jacob. On 31 July
1757, the Rochester church records showed baptisms of Samuel
and Jacob Layton (McDuffee, Rochester 2:593). Mrs. Cornman
listed them as twin sons of David [# 53], born 12 July 1757,
but also listed Samuel, son of Samuel, as born the same day.
The church record did not name a parent. Other evidence
makes clear that Samuel did have a son Samuel; David had a
son Jacob, but apparently not a son named Samuel.

      Children, born at Rochester (TRs):

        i.   HANNAH⁶, b. 29 July 1752, d. 11 Aug. 1795; m.
              Middleton NH 17 Oct. 1771 (VRs) DANIEL DREW.
       ii.   SARAH, b. 5 Apr. 1755, d. 3 Oct. 1776; unm.
177. iii.   SAMUEL, b. 12 July 1757 (per Cornman Ms).
178.   iv.   GEORGE, b. 4 Nov. 1764.
        v.   JANE, b. 24 Aug. 1768, d. 25 Dec. 1794; m. 26
              Dec. 1793 ENOCH WENTWORTH, b. 11 May 1764, d.
              in 1806, son of Benjamin and Rebecca (Hodsdon)
              Wentworth. No ch. Enoch m. 2nd Rochester
              10 Nov. 1796 Anna Young: 2 ch. (Wentworth
              Gen., 2:255).
       vi.   BENJAMIN, b. 12 June 1770, d. 4 Oct. 1771.

    53. DAVID⁵ 1730-1811 [17 John⁴ and Sarah] was born at
Dover 14 Oct. 1730, died at Harmony ME 14 Dec. 1811, 81y 2m;
married at Rochester 19 Dec. 1751 (NHGR, 4[1907]:146) ANNA
CHAMBERLAIN, born there 18 July 1733, died at Harmony 29
Sept. 1816, 83y, daughter of William and Mary (Tibbetts)
Chamberlain (Harmony VRs). In his will made 23 Apr. 1753,
her father gave 40 pounds to his daughter Anna Leighton
(NHSP, 34:365).
      David and Anna joined the Rochester church 22 Sept. 1754
and had their daughter Dolly baptized there (NHGR, 4[1907]:
74), as were their other children (6[1909]:74-5, 114-8).
      With his brothers Jonathan, Samuel and Solomon he signed
a petition 30 Aug. 1785 for Rochester's representation in the
General Assembly (NHSP, 13:336).
      His father deeded him 18 Mar. 1762 lot 69 in Rochester's
first division, the property he was already living on and
farming (NHPD, 68:29). On 6 Oct. that year he sold this lot
to James Place (78:370), and the same day bought Lt. Ebenezer
Chamberlain's home lot (69:34; 70:136-8), part of which he
sold to Abner Dam 9 Feb. 1785 (StrCD, 6:203). David Latain
of the Gore bought 100 acres, part of lot 2, first range, in
the Gore from proprietor Theodore Atkinson 30 Nov. 1768
(NHPD, 102:387). He sold part of this latter 25 June 1772 to
Nathaniel Buzzell, on condition that within a year Buzzell
build and occupy a dwelling on it, and within three years
have three acres cleared for mowing or planting (103:283-4).
On 20 Sept. 1777, he sold to "my loving son Jacob" a 60-acre
tract, lot 48 in the second division (StrCD, 5:446).
      David served as ensign under Capt. Daniel McDuffee, Col.
Stephen Evans's Rgt., 8 Sept. to 15 Dec. 1777, marching

against the British at Saratoga (NHSP, 15:297), and was
the recruiting officer for Capt. David Place's Co. (TRs 293).
In 1780, 1784 and 1788 he was town surveyor (McDuffee,
Rochester, 594-7, 606-11).
David bought land from Abner Dam 9 Feb. 1785, sold part of
his home lot in the second division to Ephraim Perkins 8 July
1785, and bought a 240-acre lot from Samuel and John Clements
the same day (StrCD, 6:203; 5:40; 6:265). This Clements property he sold to his son William 18 March 1789 (19:68), and
part of his lot 48 to his son Ephraim 18 Feb. 1796 (22:98).
David and Anna were listed in the 1790 Rochester census
with a male under 16, another 16 or older, and a daughter; he
was on the tax list of the second parish there in 1795.
In 1800, when David was 70, he and Anna joined his son
Willliam in settling at Harmony ME, making the two-week journey by ox-cart, driving their livestock with them (George T.
Little, Genealogical and Family History of the State of Maine
[NY, 1909] 4:2056-8). Harmony, first settled in 1796 as
Vaughntown, was incorporated in 1803. David bought lot 6,
9th range, from Abel Gould 27 Sept. 1806 (KenCD, 11:449).

Note: Tobias Leighton, descendant of William[1] of Kittery,
settled at Harmony about the same time; his progeny lived in
the same general area, and are easily confused with David's.

Children, born at Rochester (TRs):

179. i.   DOROTHY[6] [Dolly], b. 5 Aug. 1752; m. ROBERT
            WALKER.
      ii.   JOHN, b. 12 Feb. 1755 (bp. 13 Apr.); nfr.
180. iii. JACOB, b. 12 July 1757 (bapt. 31 July).
181. iv.   EPHRAIM, b. 13 Feb. 1760.
182. v.   JONATHAN, b. 12 Feb. 1762.
183. vi.   WILLIAM, b. 17 July 1764.
184. vii. ELIZABETH, b. 2 Dec. 1766; m. ELEAZER
            HODGDON.
185. viii. ANNA, b. 16 Nov. 1770; m. JONATHAN WATSON.
186. ix.   DAVID, b. 9 Nov. 1773.
187. x.   MOSES, b. 25 Mar. 1776.

54. BENJAMIN[5] 1735-1824 [17 John[4] and Sarah] was born at
Dover NH about 1735, died at Mount Vernon ME 8 Jan. 1824;
married at Wiscasset ME 16 May 1763 (int. 30 Mar., "Lincoln
County Marriages," BHM, 9[1894]:138) JANE WEBBER, born say
1742, died at Mt. Vernon 5 Mar. 1823, perhaps daughter of
Gershom and Marcy (Young) Webber of York ME.
Benjamin Laighton, tanner of Rochester, served with his
father and his brother Solomon under Capt. Ephraim Berry,
Col. John Goffe's Rgt., 13 Mar. to 27 Nov. 1760, during the
campaign to Albany and Crown Point (Potter, Mil. Hist.,
248-9).
His father deeded him land in Rochester 18 Mar. 1762 (NHPD,
105:14), but soon afterward Benjamin joined his father in
Lincoln County ME. On 3 Nov. 1766 "bengamand laighton"
signed a petition for Wiscasset to be shire town (see # 17),
and on 26 Jan. 1774 he among those petitioning for a new town
(incorporated as Edgecomb in Mar. 1774). He was a member of
the militia (TRs 11), hay constable in 1775, and surveyor of
highways in 1776-1777.

Benjamin Laighton of Freetown (Edgecomb) on 13 Oct. 1772 deeded to his brother Samuel undivided land in Rochester's third division, the proprietors' rights originally owned by Thomas Leighton, John Leighton and John Carter (NHPD, 105:15). On 5 May 1778 he sold to Simeon Pearl the Rochester land his father had given him (StrCD, 3:125).

In 1789 he and his family moved to Mount Vernon (called Washington Plantation until 1792), and appeared there in the 1790 census with eight children.

He petitioned the proprieters 15 Jan. 1798, claiming that their surveyor had defrauded him (Kennebec Purchase Papers, Box 10, MHS Collections). On 17 Mar. 1802 the proprietors deeded him lot 155 containing 100 acres as his settler's right (Kennebec County Deeds 3:66). He sold the northerly half of this lot to Nathaniel Brainerd 27 Apr. 1804 (12:6). On 8 Apr. 1811 he sold 100 acres with a dwelling to his son Timothy, and 55 acres to his nephew Andrew (47:222; 24:221).

Julia Cornman included among his children a Jane, born at Edgecomb 30 Aug. 1774, died at Palermo ME 28 July 1834, who married Francis Richie Carr. Lincoln County records showed intentions filed at Wiscasset 12 Nov. 1796 by Richey Carr and Jane Laiten, both of New Milford (Alna). She appeared elsewhere as of Whitefield. It is almost certain she was a descendant of Jonathan[4] Laiten of Rowley and Newcastle.

Children, born at or near Edgecomb:

188. i.   EPHRAIM[6], b. in Jan. 1765.
189. ii. EZEKIEL, b. 21 May 1768.
190. iii. ISAAC, b. in Sept. 1770.
191. iv. TIMOTHY, b. c1773.
      v.   ?SUSANNAH. Enoch Carll, b. 25 Dec. 1770, d. Zurich, Wayne Co. NY 8 Jan. 1852; m. 1st about 1790 a Susannah Leighton, d. Zurich 18 Jan. 1829; m. 2nd Mrs Polly M. Dennis. Enoch and Susannah had 10 ch. at Mt. Vernon 1791-1814. A farmer and cattle-drover, he settled in NY in 1815; several grandchildren lived in MI.
           A page preserved from a letter to Julia Cornman from a son of Nathan and Abigail (Carll) Leighton [# 613] identified Enoch as Abigail's uncle, and Susannah as somehow related to Nathan. Enoch and Susannah had a grandson David Leighton Carll. It seems probable that Enoch Carll, Benjamin Carll the father of Abigail, and Margaret Carll the wife of Moses Leighton [# 194] were siblings.
192. vi. LYDIA; m. DAVID DOLLOFF.
193. vii. DAVID, b. 22 Sept. 1785.
      viii. POLLY, b. c1789; m. DANIEL G. ALLEN, b. c1791, res. Rome in 1850. Ch. Benjamin; Daniel, Jr., b. c1831 (19 in 1850).

55. SOLOMON[5] 1739-1807 [17 John[4] and Sarah] was born probably at Rochester about 1739 (36 in 1775), died at Mount Vernon ME 9 Nov. 1807 (TRs); married at Dover NH 26 Jan. 1759 (NHGR, 2[1905]:126) SARAH VARNEY, born at Dover, not indicated on the 1800 census, daughter of Moses and Phoebe (Tuttle) Varney. The Friends' records showed that she "married out" to Solomon (2:146).

Solomon served against the French under Capt. John Titcomb, Col. Nathaniel Meserve's Rgt., 1 May to 13 Oct. 1756 (Potter, Mil. Hist., 166), and enlisted for two years' service in 1759 from Rochester; he served in Capt. Ephraim Berry's Co., Col. John Goffe's Rgt., during an expedition against Crown Point 13 Mar. to 27 Nov. 1760, along with John and Benjamin Leighton (Potter, 248-9; NHSP 11:712). He was among the signers of a petition 8 Feb. 1762 asking that Rochester be represented in the General Assembly (NHSP, 13:336).

Moses Varney's will, proved at Dover 25 Apr. 1765, named his daughter Sarah, wife of Solomon Leighton. When Moses's estate was distributed 26 July 1765, James Varney stated that he had previously purchased his sister Sarah's share (NHSP, 36:404-6). By that time, Solomon and Sarah had settled at Edgecomb, Lincoln County ME.

On 18 June 1771 John Laton of Freetown (Edgecomb) sold to Solomon Laighton of Freetown 122 acres along the Damariscotta River, adjoining land Solomon already owned (LincCD, 8:169). Solomon returned to Rochester to serve in the Revolutionary War, sworn in as husbandman, aged 36, of Damariscotta (NHSP, 17:12). He enlisted under Capt. Jonathan Wentworth, Col. Enoch Poor's Rgt., 28 May 1775, and was still there 12 Oct. (14:127, 188). On 8 May 1776 he was listed at Edgecomb as first lieutenant, Capt. Ebenezer Gove's Co., Col. William Jones's Third Lincoln County Rgt. (MSS, 9:414; TRs). He was surveyor of highways at Edgecomb in 1775 and 1778.

Solomon quitclaimed a 100-acre tract on the west side of the Damariscotta River to John Smithson Leighton 3 July 1778, and on 21 June 1779 another tract adjoining the above (LincCD, 13:44; 21:184-5). John Laighton witnessed these deeds.

Solomon and his family settled at Mount Vernon (then Washington Plantation); he was listed there with wife and six others in 1790. When the town was organized in 1792, he (styled gent.) was on the first board of selectmen (Henry D. Kingsbury and Simeon L. Deyo, ed., Illustrated History of Kennebec County, Maine [New York, 1892], 2:931). In 1800, he headed a household of six, but with no female of Sarah's age.

Like his brother Benjamin, he had difficulty obtaining title to his Mt. Vernon land, and addressed his grievance to the Proprietors of the Kennebec Purchase, whose patent rights derived from the Colony of New Plymouth (MHS Collections Box 10, 500-536):

The Petition of Solomon Laighton
Humbly Showeth
that he settled on Land in the Late Town of Washington Now Mount Vernon within your said Purchase on the Lot of Land now numbered one hundred and fifty six in the fifth Range of Lotts in the year A D. 1789 and was at the expence with his brother Benjamin Laighton in surveying said Lotts in the South part of said Town Rigonlly [originally] Surveyed by Dummer Esqr and your petitioner not Doughting but he should hold the Same on as Settler's Lott altho by the conduct of Dr. Williams your Surveyor said Lotts were Returned and marked as a proprietors Lott but your Petitioner went further than that he moved on Said Lot in the fall of the year 1789 --with a Famerly of nine children and hath ever Since Resided there on and there is now no Less than five famerlys settled on said Lott Including your Petetioner

who with your Comp'y Refusing your petitioner a grant
of said Lott must be Ruined your petitioner therefore
humbly prays you to give him a grant of said Lott
Agreeable to your Letter of Direction to said Williams
as in Duty Bann will ever pray
    Jany-11-1798   Solomon Laighton

    Settlers' rights had to be given by the proprieters to
those who had settled upon and improved lots which had been
laid out but not yet deeded; proprietor's lots were sold at
higher prices to families moving into an already established
community.
    Solomon did receive the grant of Mt. Vernon land from the
Plymouth proprietors (KenCD, 3:650) and gave to his son
Andrew the south part of lot 157 26 Aug. 1801 (24:222). He
deeded 75 acres of lot 156 to his son Samuel 20 Nov. 1805
(15:295), another part of the lot to his son Benjamin, Jr.,
20 Nov. 1805, and on the same date still more of lot 156,
between land of Jedediah and Andrew, to his son Samuel
(15:295-6).
    Julia Cornman placed Solomon as a son of Thomas[3] [# 5] and
Deborah; he was so listed in Noyes-Libby-Davis (p. 427) as
"possibly." The petition above, as well as other circumstan-
tial evidence, proves he was a son of John and Sarah.
    The date of his marriage and of the births of children were
entered in the Mt. Vernon town records (2:305).

Children, the first two or three probably born at Rochester
    and the rest at Edgecomb:

194. i.   MOSES[6], b. 6 Feb. 1760.
195. ii.   ANDREW, b. 16 Aug. 1761.
     iii. HANNAH, b. 31 Aug. 1763; nfr.
196. iv.   JOHN, b. 22 May 1766.
     v.   ESTHER, b. 31 Oct. 1767; nfr.
197. vi.   DANIEL, b. 16 Sept. 1770.
198. vii. PELATIAH, b. 13 Feb. 1772.
199. viii. SAMUEL, b. 10 Feb. 1774.
200. ix.   BENJAMIN, b. 12 Nov. 1776.

   56.   JAMES[5] 1739-1795 [18 James[4] and Hannah Buzzell] was
baptized at Dover 18 Mar. 1739 (VRs, 144), died at Barrington
NH in 1795; married PATIENCE TWOMBLEY, who survived him,
daughter of Isaac and Lydia Twombley (Cornman Ms).
    With James Evans he purchased 50 acres in lot 23, Barring-
ton, on 10 Feb. 1762 (NHPD, 68:178), and later bought out
Evans's share. This land was passed on to eldest sons for
five generations, remaining the family homestead until 1891
(Wiggin, Barrington, 30-31). He also purchased 156 acres in
lot 143, fourth range (Martha Leighton Tracy, The Lineage of
Reuben Leighton [TMs, Ithaca NY, nd], 5.). He was elected
surveyor of highways in 1778 and 1791, and was named constable in 1779--and fined for refusing to serve. In the 1790
census, his household included a wife and eight others.
    His will, made 5 July 1795, gave his widow Patience a half-
right in his property during her widowhood, the homestead to
James, and one-third of lot 143 to Reuben, Isaac and Aaron.
All nine children were named, those under-aged receiving
small bequests. At his request, no inventory was tallied or
recorded (StrCP, 5:12-5, 22-24).

Children, born at Barrington:

201. i.   MARY[6], b. in 1757; m. NATHANIEL CHURCH.
202. ii.   SARAH, b. 5 Feb. 1762; m. WILLIAM BABB.
203. iii. JAMES, b. 23 Apr. 1768.
204. iv.   REUBEN, b. 4 June 1770.
205. v.   PATIENCE, b. c1772; m. BENJAMIN WATSON.
206. vi.   ISAAC, b. in 1774.
207. vii. AARON, b. 11 Apr. 1776.
208. viii. JONATHAN, b. 26 Apr. 1778.
209. ix.   EZEKIEL, b. 21 Nov. 1780.
      x.   LYDIA, res. Freedom NH in 1840; m. STEPHEN
            DROWN of Barrington.
      xi.   HANNAH, d. Barrington in 1825; unm.

57. ISAAC[5] 1739-   [18 James[4] and Hannah Buzzell]
was baptized at Dover 18 Mar. 1739 (VRs 144), lived at Barrington in 1800; married in 1764 ANNA EVANS, born at Madbury
in 1744, died in 1817, daughter of Robert and Elizabeth Evans
(Tracy, Reuben Leighton, 4; Cornman Ms).
     Isaac served under in Capt. John Titcomb's company 6 Mar.
to 5 Nov. 1757, including duty at Fort William Henry, which
was brutally seized by Indians on 3 Aug. (Potter, Mil. Hist.,
186). He was called Capt. Isaac in town records.
     On 7 Apr. 1762, jointly with John and Sarah Roberts of Mad-
bury and Jacob and Hannah Buzzell of Barrington, Isaac purchased part of lot 26 at Barrington from Samuel Hale; the
same day he also bought out the Roberts and Buzzell shares
(NHPD, 68:144-5). Isaac and Anna quitclaimed to her brother
Thomas Evans their rights in the estate of her father Robert
Evans (92:254).
     Isaac served in the Revolutionary War, enrolling under
Capt. David Copp 25 Nov. 1775 (NHSP, 17:28-9). The 1790 census for Barrington showed Isaac heading a household of wife,
three sons and two daughters. He sold to his son Andrew 24
Mar. 1794 the 70 acres in lot 26 (StrCD, 33:187).

Children, born at Barrington:

210. i.   HANNAH[6], b. in 1765; m. SAMUEL HALL.
211. ii.   ANDREW, b. in 1766.
      iii. ELIZABETH, b. in 1769, d. Brookfield NH in
            1840; m. LEVI KENISON.
212. iv.   REMEMBRANCE, b. in 1771.
213. v.   ISAAC, b. 8 Mar. 1775.
      vi.   ANNA, b. in 1777, d. prob. Nottingham in 1816;
            m. in 1808 EDMUND EVANS. Ch. Levi Leighton
            Evans m. Strafford 9 July 1837 Mariah Leighton
            of Barrington (Cornman Ms).

58. AARON[5] 1741-1816 [18 James[4] and Hannah Buzzell]
was born at Dover 22 June 1741 (baptized 9 Aug., VRs, 144),
died at Barnstead NH 7 Sept. 1816 (GS); married at Madbury 21
Oct. 1779 (pension record) MARY [Molly] MURRAY, born at
Northwood NH 15 Feb. 1757, died at Strafford 8 Oct. 1840, 84y
(TRs; Tracy, Reuben Leighton, 4; Wiggin, Barrington 58-9).
Burials are in the Clark lot, Ridge Cemetery, Center Straf-
ford. He was a cordwainer.
     On 28 Mar. 1769 he sold land in the Two-Mile Streak to Ben-

jamin Hall (NHPD, 98:42).   He bought 10 acres in Barrington
from Joseph Young 20 Apr. 1778, but sold them 13 Sept. that
same year to Jeremiah Johnson (StrCD, 2:177-9).
    As a yeoman, age 30, he enlisted in May 1775 under Capt.
Benjamin Titcomb, Col. Enoch Poor's Rgt., for service at Cambridge, and was discharged 6 Dec. (NHSP, 14:114, 142, 193).
Family tradition held that he served throughout the War, from
Bunker Hill to Cornwallis's surrender.   He was on the sick
list of Capt. Bell's Co., aged 28, of Madbury, in July 1776
(14:310), and was on the roster of men raised by Capt. Joseph
Badger in 1776 for a Canada expedition (14:363).   His widow
claimed he had eight months' service in 1776, including three
months sick with smallpox at Ft. Independence, but this was
not credited.   He served 15 Sept. 1777 to 7 Jan. 1778 under
Capt. Enoch Page, Col. Joseph Senter's Rgt., in Rhode Island
(15:249-53). His pension was based on 23 months and two days
of military duty.
    The 1790 Barrington census showed him with his wife and
five children, and in 1800 with six besides his wife.   In
1810 they lived at Barnstead.
    He sold land in the Two-Mile Streak adjoining his homelot
to Andrew Young 2 Sept. 1793 (StrCD, 21:446).   On 26 Jan.
1801, he was issued a taverner's license (TRs 1:711).
    He bought 40 acres of lot 16 in the half-mile range from
Ebenezer Whitehouse 12 Feb. 1808 (StrCD, 61:161), and sold 30
acres of it to Moses Furber 3 Sept. 1811 (98:126).   On 5 Nov.
1814 he sold land at Effingham to Lydia Buzzell (80:569).
    His widow Mary, aged 81 of Strafford, applied for a pension
3 Sept. 1838, which was approved 13 July 1839.   The record
showed that she was issued a new certificate, and that Daniel
Murray of Newmarket was collecting the pension, on 17 Mar.
1843--over two years after her death (NA-MSR #W16630).

    Children, born at Barrington:

214.   i.   MARK[6], b. 8 June 1780.
215.   ii.   SARAH, b. 12 Oct. 1781; m. DANIEL CLARK.
       iii. MOLLY, b. 25 Mar. 1783, d. 15 Nov. 1785.
216.   iv.   WILLIAM HALE, b. 3 Jan. 1785.
217.   v.   JOHN, b. 29 Dec. 1786.
218.   vi.   TIMOTHY MURRAY, b. 28 Apr. 1789.
       vii. POLLY, b. 31 Aug. 1792, d. 7 Aug. 1815; m. 3
             Aug. 1814 DANIEL FOSS, b. 2 Dec. 1792, d. 17
             Apr. 1870. No ch.
219.   viii. PATIENCE TWOMBLEY, b. 22 Aug. 1795; m. SAMUEL
             MELLOWS.
       ix.   DANIEL MURRAY, b. 10 Aug., d. 11 Aug., 1797.
       x.   ANDREW, b. 6 June 1799, d. 6 Mar. 1820.

SIXTH GENERATION

59. ANNA[6] [Nancy] 1780-1848 [21 Hatevil[5] and Abigail Knox] was born at Dover NH 15 Feb. 1780, died at Farmington 31 Dec. 1848; married at Rochester 21 May 1804 (int. 9 May) (NHGR, 5[1908]:55) SAMUEL EMERSON FURBER, born 24 Sept. 1779, died at Farmington 17 Mar. 1842, son of Capt. Samuel and Mary (Emerson) Furber (Cornman Ms; Farmington TRs). She appeared also as Nancy Ann in town records.

Children (**Furber**), born at Farmington:

i.	JOHN F., b. 20 Dec. 1801, d. 4 Dec. 1829.	
ii.	RICHARD, b. 1 Oct. 1803.	
iii.	ABIGAIL, b. 7 Dec. 1805.	
iv.	MARK L., b. 21 Feb. 1808; m. Dover 5 July 1832 ELIZA RICKER.	
v.	EMERSON, b. 21 Nov. 1816, d. Farmington 2 June 1895; m. MARY [Polly] YOUNG, d. 14 Mar. 1901, 61y 20d.	
vi.	HANNAH, b. 17 Oct. 1819, d. 7 Oct. 1823.	

60. JAMES[6] 1781-1854 [21 Hatevil[5] and Abigail Knox] was born at Dover 1 Nov. 1781, died at Farmington 1 Sept. 1854, 72y 10m; married there 3 Nov. 1811 SARAH SEAVEY, born at Rochester 17 Nov. 1790 (baptized 13 May 1792), daughter of Ebenezer and Prudence Berry (Marden) Seavey (Sylvia F. Getchell, Marden Family Genealogy [np, 1974], 161; NHGR, 6[1909]:127; Farmington, Rochester and Weare TRs).
They removed to Weare NH in 1817, but returned to Farmington in 1830 (Little, Weare, 932). They belonged to the Society of Friends.

Children:

220.	i.	DANIEL[7], b. Farmington 16 Nov. 1812.
	ii.	HANNAH, b. Weare 24 Jan., d. 29 Nov., 1819.
	iii.	ANNA A, b. Weare 27 Apr. 1822, d. 18 Apr. 1823.

61. JOHN B.[6] 1783-1859 [21 Hatevil[5] and Abigail Knox] was born at Rochester 2 Nov. 1783, died at Weare NH 22 Oct. 1859; married at Rochester 13 Apr. 1809 (as John, Jr., on int. 24 Mar.) MARY EMERSON [Polly] FURBER, born 23 Jan. 1792, died at Weare 28 Oct. 1868, daughter of Capt. Samuel and Mary (Emerson) Furber.
By 1830 they had settled at Weare (town VRs; Little, Weare, 324, 932-3; Cornman Ms).

Children:

        i.   MARK[7], b. prob. Farmington 24 Jan. 1810, d.
              Weare 11 Mar. 1834.
221.   ii.   MARY E., b. Farmington 26 Oct. 1813; m.
              NATHAN C. DOW.
        iii. ELIZA, b. Weare 14 Mar. 1822, d. there 2 Dec.
              1826.

62.   ELIZABETH[6] [Betsey] 1788-   [21 Hatevil[5] and Abigail
Knox] was born at Farmington 24 Nov. 1788; married at Rochester 4 Dec. 1808 (Farmington int. 12 Nov.) JOSEPH MEADER, JR.,
born at Durham NH 24 Apr. 1785, son of Joseph and Abigail
(Frye) Meader. They lived at Lee and Alton NH, and Bangor ME
(Granville Meader, John Meader of Piscataqua [Baltimore,
1975], 1:24; Stackpole, Durham, 2:278). He was a carpenter.

Children (**Meader**), from Alton TRs:

i.   JOHN, b. Alton 3 Sept. 1809.
ii.   MARY, b. Alton 8 May 1812, d. Barnstead 30 Dec.
       1893; m. ---- MURPHY.

63.   EPHRAIM[6] 1794-1872 [21 Hatevil[5] and Abigail Knox]
was born at Farmington 22 Sept. 1794, died at Weare 29 Feb.
1872; married there 24 Aug. 1820 HANNAH BREED, born 4 May
1798, died at Weare 22 Apr. 1889, daughter of Stephen and
Rhoda (Chase) Breed. A carpenter and carriagemaker, he also
manufactured bedsteads at Folly Mill (Little, Weare, 541,
933; Cornman Ms). They were Quakers.

Children, born at Weare (NHGR, 2[1904]:30):

222.   i.   DAVID BREED[7], b. 22 Dec. 1821.
        ii.   CLARISSA, b. 15 Mar. 1838, d. 12 May 1851.

64.   ABIGAIL[6] 1764-   [22 Tobias[5] and Ann Tuttle]
was born at Durham or Madbury say 1764; married at Dover 2
June 1782 BENJAMIN ODIORNE, born at Portsmouth NH in May
1762, son of Benjamin and Patience (Kennard) Odiorne. They
lived at Rochester. About 1792, Benjamin mysteriously disappeared while he was carrying a large sum of money (James C.
Odiorne, Genealogy of the Odiorne Family [Boston, 1875], 70;
records of Joseph Odiorne).

Children (**Odiorne**), birthplace uncertain:

i.   PATIENCE, b. 5 June 1782, d. 22 July 1819; m. in Mar.
       1802 MESCHACH HURD, b. Alton NH 22 Oct. 1779.
ii.   JOHN, b. Dover; m. Rochester 29 Mar. 1810 LYDIA
       WENTWORTH, d. Wheelock VT, dau. of Paul and Deborah
       (Naylor) Wentworth (Wentworth Gen., 2:84).
iii.   ANNA, b. 13 Feb. 1787, d. Dec. 1859; m. THOMAS
       RICHARDSON of Rochester.
iv.   THEOPHILUS DAM, b. c1790, d. Durham in 1835; m.
       SARAH ----.
v.   LYDIA, b. 1791, d. Rochester 19 Apr. 1857; m. Dover
       25 Dec. 1806 THOMAS WENTWORTH, b. Rochester 7 Feb.
       1779, d. there 6 July 1867, son of Isaac and Abigail
       (Nutter) Wentworth (Wentworth Gen., 2:394).

65. ELIZABETH[6]   -   [22 Tobias[5] and Ann Tuttle]
was born probably at Madbury; married JOHN GOUDEY, probably
son of James and Elizabeth (Potter) Goudey of Marblehead MA
and Wakefield NH. They settled at Leighton's Corners, Ossipee (Mahlon M. Gowdy, Gowdy Family History [Lewiston ME,
1919], 2:438, 441). Two of their five children are listed in
the family history.

Children (**Goudey**), others unknown:

i.   WILLIAM, d. Ossipee; unm.
ii. NATHANIEL (twin); m. 18 Oct. 1827 LYDIA TASKER.

66. WILLIAM[6] 1772-1824 [22 Tobias[5] and Ann Tuttle]
was born at Madbury say 1772, died at Dover 16 Dec. 1824;
married MARY LIBBY, born in 1772, died at Concord NH 28 Dec.
1870, daughter of Benjamin and Abigail (Wingate) Libby (Cornman Ms). Two children, names unknown, were lost at sea.

Children, born at Madbury:

223. i.   BENJAMIN[7], b. 1813.
     ii.   ELIZABETH, b. 2 Nov. 1816, d. Concord 29 July
           1887, 71y; m. MOSES CASS, d. there 9 Sept.
           1870, 50y (GS, Old North Cem.). Ch. Ellen d.
           27 Sept. 1845, aged 3.
224. iii. WILLIAM ALEXANDER, b. 13 May 1820.
     iv.   ABIGAIL, d.y.

67. OLIVE[6] 1780-1838 [22 Tobias[5] and Ann Tuttle]
was born at Madbury 8 Oct. 1780, died 3 Sept. 1838; married
at Belfast ME about 1797 BENJAMIN BACHELDER, born 20 Nov.
1773, died 7 Feb. 1859, 85y 2m 20d, son of Capt. Benjamin and
Esther Bachelder (Warren V. Sprague, Sprague Families in
America [np, 1913], 421). He went to OH, and was settled at
Goshen IN in 1827.

Child (**Bachelder**), born at Belfast (perhaps others):

i.   NANCY, b. 4 Sept. 1797, d. 29 Oct. 1870; m. 16 Oct.
     1825 RESOLVED FULLER, b. Pomfret CT 16 Sept. 1780,
     son of Job and Susannah (Russell) Fuller. He had m.
     1st 1806 Elizabeth Nash (William H. Fuller, Some
     Descendants of Thomas Fuller of Woburn [np, 1919],
     4:152).

68. LUKE MILLS[6] 1766-1834 [23 Paul[5] and Mary Mills]
was born at Portsmouth NH 10 Feb. 1766 (baptized 9 Mar.),
died there 26 Dec. 1834; married there 1 Apr. 1789 ELIZABETH
MENDUM, born 3 June 1767, died at Portsmouth 3 Mar. 1854
(Portsmouth TRs; Cornman Ms). He and his brothers spelled
their name "Laighton." A mast and sail maker, he served as
town selectman from 1807 to 1810 (NHGR, 2[1905]:162). He and
Elizabeth belonged to the South Church.
     His will was made 28 Apr. 1832 (RockCP, #12852), and the
inventory taken 7 Mar. 1835. His son Charles was named
executor; his widow was given life use of his real estate,

which included three houses, a shop, a wharf and docks. The listing of tools, materials and expensive home furnishings showed him to have been a prosperous businessman.

Children, born at Portsmouth (TRs; baptisms in NEHGReg, 82 [1928]:412):

    i.   DEBORAH[7], b. 1 Aug. 1789, d. 16 Dec. 1803.
    ii.   JOHN, b. 31 Mar., d. 27 Sept., 1792.
    iii. LUKE MILLS, b. 31 July 1793, d. 12 Jan, 1826, lost on the Zephyr near Boston Light.
    iv.   CHARLES, b. 21 Sept. 1794, d. 24 Oct. 1797.
    v.   EDWARD, b. 17 Oct. 1795, d. 25 Oct. 1797.
    vi.   JOHN, b. 7 Jan. 1797, d. 15 June 1815.
    vii. ELIZABETH, b. 25 Aug. 1798; m. Portsmouth 16 Nov. 1829 THOMAS FOLSOM, b. Exeter NH 12 Jan. 1772, d. there 26 Nov. 1845, son of Capt. Thomas and Elizabeth (Gilman) Folsom. No ch. He m. 1st Nancy Adams, who died in 1820: one son. A hotel-keeper, he had been a brigade quartermaster in the War of 1812 (Elizabeth K. Folsom, Genealogy of the Folsom Family [Rutland VT, 1938], 1:257).

225. viii. CHARLES EDWARD, b. 17 Nov. 1799.
    ix.   MARY E., b. 17 Jan. 1801; m. 1st ---- BACHEL-DER; m. 2nd Exeter 15 May 1834 THOMAS WIGGIN.
    x.   ALEXANDER L., b. 21 Aug. 1802, d. 20 Mar. 1805.
    xi.   JAMES, b. 8 Jan. 1804, d. 4 May 1824.
    xii. DEBORAH, b. 9 Apr. 1805.
    xiii. OLIVE, b. 11 June 1806, d. 4 Feb. 1837; unm.
    xiv. ALEXANDER, b. 21 Oct. 1807, d. 2 Aug. 1829.
226. xv.   WILLIAM, b. 15 May 1810.

69. ABIGAIL[6] 1773-1860 [23 Paul[5] and Mary Mills] was born at Portsmouth 4 Feb. 1773 (NEHGReg, 82 [1928]:45), died there in Feb. 1860; m. in Sept. 1795 Capt. CHARLES BLUNT, born at Portsmouth 3 Aug. 1768, died at Havana, Cuba, 19 Mar. 1823, son of John and Hannah (Sherburne) Blunt.
A sea captain, he was murdered when his ship was seized by pirates (Portsmouth TRs; Roscoe C. Blunt, Jr., The Blunts: A History [np, nd] MHS).

Children (**Blunt**), born at Portsmouth:

    i.   JOHN B., b. 10 Dec. 1796.
    ii.   CHARLES EDWARD, b. 13 Feb. 1799.
    iii. EVELINA, b. 19 Aug. 1801; m. 6 June 1822 JOHN NATH-ANIEL SHERBURNE, b. 20 Sept. 1793, d. in June 1859.
    iv.   ROBERT, b. 9 July 1803.

70. MARK[6] 1780-1832 [23 Paul[5] and Mary Mills] was born at Portsmouth 22 Mar. 1780 (baptized 26 Mar. as "Arthur"), died there 2 Aug. 1832; married at New Castle NH 1 July 1801 DEBORAH SEAVEY, born in 1780, died at Kennebunk ME in 1862, daughter of John Sr. and Deborah Seavey (Cornman Ms; Portsmouth VRs).
A contractor, Mark Laighton built the first bridge to the naval yard at Kittery. In 1850 Deborah was living at Portsmouth, aged 67, with her daughter Almira Dennett.

Children, born at Portsmouth:

       i.   SAMUEL[7], b. in 1802, d. at sea in March 1827
              on the Eliza; m. 21 Nov. 1822 CATHERINE
              VAUGHAN.
227. ii.   JOSEPH WALTON, b. in 1803.
228. iii. THOMAS BELL, b. 2 Feb. 1805.
      iv.   MARK, drowned during childhood.
229. v.   WILLIAM, b. 7 Aug. 1809.
      vi.   DEBORAH, d. infant.
230. vii. ELIZABETH W., b. in 1812; m. RICHARD GIL-
              PATRICK.
      viii. MARK, b. in 1814, not heard from after 1840.
              His nephew Oscar stated that Richard H. Dana
              had mentioned Mark in one of his stories:
              "He wrote, 'No danger on the ship with Mark
              Laighton at the wheel.' That was the last
              word that ever reached us about Uncle Mark"
              (Ninety Years at the Isles of Shoals [Andover
              MA, 1929], 8)
231. ix.   ALMIRA, b. 11 Mar. 1816; m. MARK DENNETT.
232. x.   DEBORAH, b. 6 June 1820; m. JOSEPH CHEEVER.

71. JAMES[6] 1782-1811 [23 Paul[5] and Mary Mills]
was born at Portsmouth 26 June 1782 (baptized 1 July), died
at sea 15 Sept. 1811; married at Kittery ME 1 Sept. 1805
(NEHGReg, 83 [1929]:25) MARY DEERING PAGE, born 5 Apr. 1784,
died at Portsmouth 19 Sept. 1874, daughter of Edward and Mary
(Deering) Page (or Paige) (Portsmouth TRs; Cornman Ms).
While captain of the brig Sally, he and all aboard were lost
in a gale. Mary was admitted to South Church and her children were baptized 5 July 1818 (NEHGReg, 81[1927]:421).
   Widow Polly was executrix of James's will 5 Sept. 1816.
His mother's will included bequests to Polly and her three
daughters. In 1870 Mary, 86, was living with William Simes.

Children, born at Portsmouth:

233. i.   OLIVE BOURNE[7], b. 11 July 1807; m. WILLIAM
              SIMES.
234. ii.   ANN HAM, b. 11 Jan. 1809; m. DANIEL BADGER.
      iii. ABIGAIL BLUNT, b. 28 Feb. 1812 (posthumous);
              m. WILLIAM JAMES[7] LEIGHTON [# 236].

72. JOHN[6] 1784-1866 [23 Paul[5] and Mary Mills] was baptized
at Portsmouth 17 Oct. 1784, died there 3 Feb. 1866; married
first there 9 Oct. 1808 (NEHGReg, 83[1929]:25) ELIZABETH HOWE
(Eliza on marriage record), born 12 Mar. 1789, died at Portsmouth 24 Feb. 1815; married second at Portsmouth 2 Mar. 1816
widow MARY (DAMRELL) Vaughan, born at Lubec ME 23 Nov. 1785,
died at Portsmouth 19 Nov. 1880 (Portsmouth VRs; Cornman Ms).
Mary had married first William Vaughan, born at Portsmouth 14
Aug. 1780, son of William and Katherine (Broughton) Vaughan
(NEHGReg, 82 [1928]:143).
   John was navy agent at the Portsmouth naval yard at Kittery
from 1829 to 1841. He was a selectman at Portsmouth from
1829 to 1831 and in 1840, mayor in 1851, and then a state
legislator (NHGR, 2[1905]:157-165).

Children by Elizabeth, born at Portsmouth:

235. i.   GEORGE HOWE[7], b. 6 Sept. 1809.
236. ii.   WILLIAM JAMES, b, 22 Jan. 1812.
237. iii. EDWARD JOHN, b. 14 July 1814.

Children by Mary, born at Portsmouth:

238. iv.   BENJAMIN DAMRELL, b. 18 Mar. 1817.
239. v.   MARY ELIZABETH, b. 3 Oct. 1818; m. SAMUEL J.
           DODGE.
     vi.   OCTAVE, b. 13 May 1820, d. 6 Mar. 1821.
240. vii. OCTAVE V., b. 25 Jan. 1822.
     viii. LAFAYETTE, b. 9 Nov. 1823, d. Portsmouth 27
           Apr. 1877; m. Westford MA 20 June 1849
           LYDIA R. FREEMAN, b. 21 Nov. 1825, d. Ports-
           mouth 3 Jan. 1883. No ch. He was a grocer.
241. ix.   ELLEN AUGUSTA, b. 8 Oct. 1825; m. FRANCIS
           SABINE and THOMAS LEWIS.
     x.   ALBERT, b. 11 June 1827, d. 11 June 1828.
242. xi.   ALBERT, b. 8 Jan. 1829.

73.   SAMUEL[6] 1787-1834 [23 Paul[5] and Mary Mills]
was born at Portsmouth 3 Nov. 1787 (bapt. 5 Nov.), died there
19 Sept. 1834; married at Kittery 29 Dec. 1807 MARY FERNALD,
born 25 Mar. 1788, died at Portsmouth 1 Mar. 1834, daughter
of Mark and Eunice (Leach) Fernald (Portsmouth VRs; Cornman
Ms). His spar-making shop was next to Luke Laighton's water-
front businesses. He was selectman in 1827-8 and 1833 (NHGR,
2[1905]:157).
His son Littleton was appointed guardian of William F. and
the other younger children on 15 Oct. 1834.

Children, born at Portsmouth:

243. i.   SARAH RICHARD[7], b. 7 May 1808; m. JOHN LAKE.
244. ii.   LITTLETON MILLS, b. 12 Sept. 1809.
     iii. MARTHA RADCLIFF, b. 19 July 1811, d. Bangor
           18 Nov. 1878; m. Portsmouth 16 Nov. 1834
           LEONARD MARCH (NEHGReg, 83[1929]173; Cornman
           Ms). Ch. Mary b. in 1836, d. 21 Apr. 1899;
           m. ---- Barr.
245. iv.   PAUL, b. 26 June 1813.
246. v.   WILLIAM FERNALD, b. 13 Nov. 1815.
     vi.   SAMUEL, b. 29 May 1817, d. 22 Feb. 1882; m.
           Portsmouth 2 Aug. 1845 (int. Sandown NH 22
           July) ELIZA B. RICKER, b. in 1817, d. 4 Apr.
           1902. No ch. A sea captain, he res. New
           Orleans (Cornman Ms). In 1900 widow Eliza
           res. Portsmouth with sisters Martha and Maria.
     vii. MARY OLIVIA, b. 6 July 1819, d. Bangor ME
           1 Apr. 1903;; m. Bangor int. 10 Dec. 1842
           Col. MOSES PATTEN, b. Bangor 13 July 1810,
           d. there 28 May 1846, son of Moses and Sally
           Patten (Thomas W. Baldwin, Patten Genealogy
           [Boston, 1908], 140; BHM, 6[1890]:55). No ch.
247. viii. MARK FERNALD, b. 18 Mar. 1821.
     ix.   NATHAN PARKER, b. 23 Feb. 1823, d. Danvers MA
           30 Apr. 1896; m. GEORGIANA WEBSTER, b. 21 Mar.
           1823, d. Boston 11 May 1891 (VRs).

Ch. GEORGIANNA P.[8] b. Boston in June 1844,
d. there 17 Jan. 1855, 10y 7m (VRs).
x.   SUSAN, b. 20 Mar., d. 21 Mar. 1825.
xi.   ROBERT BLUNT, b. 7 Apr. 1825, d. Key West FL
      9 Apr. 1846; unm.
xii. JOSEPH EDWARD, b. 11 Nov. 1828, d. Seattle WA
      5 July 1884; unm.
248. xiii. CLARA, b. 26 Feb. 1831; m. WILLIAM STRICK-
      LAND.

74. PAUL[6] 1789-   [23 Paul[5] and Mary Mills] was born at
Portsmouth 20 Apr. 1789 (bapt. 26 Apr.), lived at Boston MA;
married there 8 Feb. 1811 SARAH W. RICHARDS (Cornman Ms),
born there about 1795, daughter of George Richards. At 63
she married second at Boston 6 June 1858 (VRs) Jedediah Snow,
73, son of Uriah Snow of Stoughton MA.

Children, perhaps others:

i.   daughter[7], b. 1816, d. Portsmouth 16 Feb.
      1817, aged 5 1/2 mos.
ii.   child, b. Portsmouth 11 Mar. 1820.
iii. ANDREW J., b. 8 Jan. 1830, d. Easton MA 18
      Oct. 1865, 35y 9m 10d (VRs). Alice Clary
      Chase (Mrs. Daniel E., Jr.) of Somerville MA
      wrote that she was descended from Andrew;
      mention was made of Andrew's grandson Paul
      Leighton Butler (Cornman Papers).

75. JOHN[6] 1778-1819 [25 Jonathan[5] and Mary Bampton] was
born at Dover 3 Oct. 1778 (VRs, 181), died there 23 June
1819; married at Dover in Mar. 1799 ABIGAIL SHACKFORD, born
at Newington NH 2 Feb. 1779, died at Dover 10 July 1820,
daughter of John and Ruth Webb (Adams) Shackford (Cornman
Ms). He was disowned by the Friends' meeting for marrying
outside the faith (NHGR, 5[1908]:32).

Children, born at Dover:

249. i.   MARY ANN[7], b. 20 Jan. 1800; m. JOHN ROLLINS.
250. ii.   RUTH, b. say 1802; m. JAMES CURTIS and
           JONATHAN LOCKE.
251. iii. SETH, b. say 1803.
     iv.   JOHN, b. in 1816, d. Salem MA 2 Nov. 1825,
           buried at Dover.

76. ELIZABETH[6] 1778-1851 [29 James[5] and Sarah Thompson] was
born at Durham 19 Apr. 1778, died 12 Sept. 1851, 71y; married
6 Aug. 1797 DANIEL REYNOLDS, born at Londonderry NH 7 Oct.
1771, died at Alton Bay NH 24 Oct. 1809, son of Col. Daniel
Reynolds/Runnels. He was a teacher and deputy sheriff
(Stackpole, Durham, 2:317; Cornman Ms).

Children (**Reynolds**):

i.   HANNAH, b. 9 Dec. 1797, d. 3 Mar. 1872; m. 17 Feb.
      Feb. 1817 DANIEL MASON, d. 3 Mar. 1872. He was a
      superintendent, Boston & Providence RR.

ii.   DANIEL, b. 9 July 1799; m. 14 Nov. 1824 SARAH
      WATSON, b. 21 May 1803, d. 8 Nov. 1888.
iii. MARY, b. 1 May 1801, d. in 1802.
iv.   EBENEZER THOMPSON, b. in May 1803. d. 29 May 1852; m.
      5 Mar. 1824 ABIGAIL WYATT, b. 3 June 1802, d. 30
      Apr. 1876.
v.   STEPHEN, b. 1 Jan. 1805, d. in 1881; m. Shelburne NH
      1 Sept. 1831 SALLY GARLAND, b. 24 Nov. 1809, d. 20
      Mar. 1880.
vi.   ADDISON, b, 15 Jan. 1808, d. 4 Sept. 1884; m. 13 Jan.
      1833 ELIZABETH ROGERS, b. 4 Sept. 1812.
vii. ELIZA, b. 23 July 1809; m. 15 Aug. 1828 Rev. CONVERSE
      L. McCURDY.

77.   MARY[6] 1780-1869 [29 James[5] and Sarah Thompson] was
born at Durham 1 Oct. 1780, died at Saco ME 6 Dec. 1869; married at Rochester NH 15 May 1803 EDWARD S. MOULTON, born in
NH 15 Oct. 1778, died at Saco 16 Aug. 1855 (Cornman Ms).
    Her father deeded land to them in 1811 (StrCD, 67:264). In
1850 their daughter Abigail lived with them at Saco. He was
a goldsmith.

Children (**Moulton**):

i.   MARY THOMPSON, b. 9 Dec. 1803; m. DAVID FERNALD.
ii.   SARAH LEAH, b. 7 Nov. 1807, d. 6 Sept. 1835; m.
      LEWIS WAKEFIELD.
iii. ELIZABETH, b. 24 Feb. 1810, d. So. Berwick ME
      9 Oct. 1893; m. 18 July 1835 WILLIAM HUNTRESS.
iv.   MARTHA A., b. 18 May 1812; m. JOHN CHADWICK.
v.   LYDIA PIERCE, b. 27 Sept. 1815, d. 21 Oct. 1841; m.
      JOHN CHADWICK, who m. 2nd her sister Martha.
vi.   ABIGAIL, b. 14 Nov. 1820, d. 18 Dec. 1886; unm.

78.   SARAH[6] 1782-1868 [29 James[5] and Sarah Thompson] was
born at Durham 1 Dec. 1782, died 23 Apr. 1868; married 8 Oct.
1801 JAMES L. WOODHOUSE, born 10 Aug. 1780, died 3 June 1862
(Cornman Ms; Dover VRs). They lived at Dover.

Children (**Woodhouse**):

i.   EMILY, b. 3 Jan. 1802, d. 16 July 1806.
ii.   JAMES L., b. 29 Oct. 1803; m. PANTHEA WILSON.
iii. SARAH L., b. 29 Oct. 1805, d. 17 Sept. 1842; m. 6 May
      1829 GEORGE W. ROBERTS of Somersworth.
iv.   JOHN L., b. 11 Nov. 1807; m. 1st LYDIA A. RAND; m.
      2nd MELISSA A. PATTERSON.
v.   OLIVE W., b. 25 Aug. 1811, d. 8 Oct. 1892.
vi.   SUSAN P., b. 15 Feb. 1814.
vii. EBENEZER, b. 10 May 1816, d. 10 May 1817.
viii. GEORGE W., b. 10 July 1819, d. 21 Nov. 1850; m.
      ELIZA F. TIBBETTS.
ix.   MARY P., b. 19 Oct. 1824.
x.   ANNETTE I.; m. ---- BAKER.

79.   ABIGAIL[6] 1787-1873 [29 James[5] and Sarah Thompson] was
born at Durham 11 Feb. 1787, died 6 June 1873; married in
1808 EPHRAIM HANSON, born at Dover 16 Sept. 1780, died 20

Sept. 1824, son of John Burnham and Elizabeth (Rogers) Hanson
(Stackpole, Durham, 2:207; Cornman Ms). Her father deeded
land to them in 1817 (StrCD, 94:344).

Children (**Hanson**), born probably at Durham:

i. SARAH, b. 29 Dec. 1809, d. 1 Nov. 1890; m. in 1839
    JONATHAN T. DODGE.
ii. JOHN LEIGHTON, b. 5 Sept. 1811, d. 20 Nov. 1864; m.
    in Sept. 1835 ELIZA WIGGIN.
iii. JOSEPH GAGE, b. 10 Oct. 1814; m. in Sept. 1836
    ROSETTA CORNWALL.
iv. JAMES LEIGHTON, b. 29 Dec. 1816, d. 14 Jan. 1865; m.
    1st in 1840 ANN M. MERRIAM; m. 2nd in 1852 AMANDA M.
    PRATT.
v. MARTHA E., b. 8 Jan. 1819.
vi. LYDIA A., b. 23 Apr. 1821, d. 19 Oct. 1873; m. in
    1865 SILAS A. QUINCY.
vii. CHARLES H., b. 20 Oct. 1823, d. in 1850; unm.

80. **ANN**[6] [Nancy] 1792-1862 [29 James[5] and Sarah Thompson]
was born at Durham 6 July 1792, died there 6 May 1862; mar-
ried BENJAMIN KELLEY, born at Madbury 18 Feb. 1787, lived at
Durham, son of Samuel and Olive (Leighton) Kelley [# 26].
   He was selectman at Madbury in 1816, but they settled at
Durham, where he was served the town as moderator, town
clerk, selectman, state representative and tavern-keeper
(Stackpole, Durham, 2:239-40).

Children (**Kelley**), born at Durham (VRs):

i. SARAH ANN, b. 21 Dec. 1809, d. 12 May 1855; m. JOHN
    ODELL.
ii. JOHN L., b. 23 Oct. 1811, d. Manchester NH 1 May
    1887; m. 8 Sept. 1838 MARY E. HURD. Lt. Col. during
    the Civil War, he was in 1877 mayor of Manchester.
iii. LYDIA, b. 31 Jan. 1814; m. 23 Sept. 1840 ANDREW L.
    SIMPSON, a sea captain.
iv. SAMUEL, b. 22 Apr. 1816, res. Durham; m., had ch.
v. OLIVE, b. 15 Apr. 1818, d. 11 Sept. 1819.
vi. OLIVE, b. 19 Nov. 1820, d. 3 Sept. 1891; m. GEORGE
    ROSS of Boston.
vii. BENJAMIN, b. 22 Jan. 1823, d. 5 Sept. 1842; unm.
viii. MARY ELIZABETH, b. 11 Mar. 1825; unm.
ix. MOSES NOBLE, b. 19 Apr. 1828, res. Durham; m. MARY
    J. BEAN. A son Charles Granville, b. Boston 23
    Aug. 1853, settled in TX under the Leighton name,
    and left descendants there named Leighton.
x. JAMES L., b. 14 Jan. 1830, d. 12 Mar. 1833.
xi. CHARLES TIBBETTS, b. 30 Apr. 1832.

81. **MARTHA**[6] 1794-1879 [29 James[5] and Sarah Thompson] was
born at Durham 2 Oct. 1794, died 12 June 1879; married at Lee
NH 9 Mar. 1820 Dr. JOSIAH LANCASTER, born at Sanbornton NH 3
June 1793, died at Hartford ME 17 Aug. 1836, 43y 2m, son of
Thomas and Sarah (Sargent) Lancaster. He set up a medical
practice at Hartford ME (Josephine S. Ware, The Lancaster
Genealogy [Rutland VT, 1934], 38-9; Moses T. Runnels, History
of Sanbornton, N. H. [Boston, 1882], 2:435; Cornman Ms).

Children (**Lancaster**):

i.   SARAH ANN, b. Lee 16 Feb. 1821, d. 5 Sept. 1822,
      1y 7m.
ii.   JAMES L., b. Lee 4 Dec. 1823, res. Boston; m. 1st 28
      June 1849 CATHERINE ARMSTRONG, d. 5 July 1851; m.
      2nd 8 Nov. 1854 ELIZA SHEPARD.
iii. SARAH S., b. Hartford 29 June 1830, d. in 1879; unm.
      She was a teacher at Hyde Park MA.
iv.   EDWARD M., b. Hartford 29 Mar. 1832, d. 13 June 1919;
      m. 28 July 1864 ANNA WINSLOW STACKPOLE. He was also
      a teacher at Hyde Park.
v.   CHARLES L., b. Hartford 16 June 1835, d. 9 Feb.
      1836.

82.   SUSANNAH[6] 1810-1887 [29 James[5] and Abigail Mathes] was
born at Durham 23 Nov. 1810, died at Santa Barbara CA 17 Mar.
1887; married at Durham 9 Nov. 1835 (VRs) her cousin CHARLES
LANE MATHES, born 30 Apr. 1809, died at Burlington NJ 7 Apr.
1866, son of Benjamin and Martha (Lane) Mathes (Stackpole,
Durham, 2:268; Cornman Ms).
In 1850 they lived at Dover.

Children (**Mathes**):

i.   ABIGAIL, b. 5 Oct. 1836, res. San Diego CA.
ii.   ANN MARTHA, b. 4 July 1839, d. in July 1854.
iii. CAROLINE, b. 30 Aug. 1842, d. San Diego 19 Feb.
      1901; unm.
iv.   SUSAN M., b. 8 Mar. 1845, d. 25 Nov. 1895; m. in Nov.
      1892 EDWIN SMITH.

83.   JONATHAN[6] 1767-1847 [31 Thomas[5] and Lydia Tracy] was
born at Steuben ME (then No. 4) 23 Nov. 1767, died there 25
June 1847, 79y 7m; married 15 Dec. 1791 ANNAH DYER, born at
Steuben 16 Feb. 1771, died there 23 May 1861, 90y 3m 7d,
daughter of Capt. Henry and Betty (Simonton) Dyer (Steuben
VRs; William M. Pierce, Old Hancock County Families [Ells-
worth ME, 1933], 50-1). He was the first male English child
born east of Castine.
    On 2 June 1794 Jonathan received from the proprietors'
agent a deed for his settler's right to lot 49 of 100 acres
at No. 4 (WashCD, 4:363-4), which he and Annah sold 6 July
1806 to his brother Hatevil (4:364-5). He sold his brother
Isaiah [# 91] 100 acres, lot 27, 29 June 1810 (6:208).
    Annah was living with her son Jonathan at her death. Her
obituary in the Machias Union 30 May 1861 noted that she was
survived by 11 children, 57 grandchildren, 89 great-grand-
children, and one great-great-grandchild.

Children, born at Steuben:

252. i.   JONATHAN[7], b. 26 Nov. 1792.
      ii.   LYDIA, b. 15 Apr. 1794, res. Milltown ME
            (Calais); m. 1st Steuben 19 Mar. 1814 NATHAN
            GODFREY, b. 10 Apr. 1788, son of Ichabod and
            Lydia (Wakefield) Godfrey; m. 2nd Calais
            STEPHEN HILL. No ch.

253. iii. ANNA, b. 3 June 1795; m. BENJAMIN GODFREY.
254. iv.   CHARITY, b. 30 Oct. 1796; m. SAMUEL NASH and
            WILLIAM NASH.
255. v.   HENRY DYER, b. 18 Apr. 1799.
256. vi.   HANDY, b. 21 Sept. 1800.
257. vii. TRYPHENA, b. 19 July 1802; m. WILLIAM B. NASH.
258. viii. THOMAS, b. 1 Mar. 1804.
259. ix.   PERSIS TOWNLEY, b. 19 Jan. 1807; m. OLIVER
            CLEAVES.
260. x.   IRENE, b. 14 Jan. 1809; m. ISAAC SMALL.
261. xi.   ELIZABETH DYER, b. 25 Jan. 1811; m. OLIVER
            RANDALL.
      xii. MARY THERESA, b. 11 Dec. 1812; m. JOHN COY
            of Milburn NB.
262. xiii. ALMON, b. 4 Jan. 1818.

84. MARK[6] 1770-1832 [31 Thomas[5] and Lydia Tracy] was born
at Steuben 8 Jan. 1770, died there 1 Apr. 1832, 62y; married
SALLY CATES, born 18 Oct. 1774, died at Steuben 2 June 1829,
55y (GS) (Steuben VRs; Little, Me. Genealogies, 4:2060).
They are buried on the site of the old Mark Leighton Inn on
Milbridge Road. Mark purchased lot 29, 100 acres, as his
settler's right 2 June 1794 (WashCD, 8:307).
James Gordon Bennett, while a young teacher at Steuben,
boarded with Mark and Sally, and by family tradition continued to correspond with them when he was publisher of the New
York Tribune.

Children, born at Steuben:

263. i.   ABIGAIL[7], b. 24 Feb. 1796; m. JAMES SMITH.
264. ii.   ELISHA, b. 4 Apr. 1798.
265. iii. WARREN, b. 22 June 1800.
266. iv.   PAMELIA, b. 11 Aug. 1802; m. JAMES PARKER.
267. v.   SEWELL, b. 28 Oct. 1804.
268. vi.   LYDIA, b. 16 June 1806; m. JOHN STEWART,
            JONAH DYER and PATRICK KELLEY.
      vii. FREEMAN, b. 1 Jan. 1807; prob. unm. In 1850 he
            lived in Elsie Phinney's household, and in
            1860 with his sister Amy Kelley. He was a
            farmer.
269. viii. NAOMI, b. 12 Dec. 1811; m. JAMES CLARK.
270. ix.   AMY, b. 4 Nov. 1814; m. JAMES KELLEY and
            JOEL GAY.
271. x.   BELINDA NASH, b. 8 Dec. 1818; m. ALFRED
            SMITH.

85. CHARITY[6] 1772-1844 [31 Thomas[5] and Lydia Tracy]
was born at Steuben 15 May 1772, died there 6 May 1844; married in 1790 DANIEL GODFREY, born at Falmouth ME 25 Feb.
1761, died at Cherryfield ME 12 Apr. 1837, son of Benjamin
and Olive (Wilson) Godfrey (town VRs; family Bible). Daniel
was a sea captain. In 1790 the census showed him living
at Steuben alone.
The Godfrey family Bible, passed down through James, is now
owned by Edgar Lamson Leighton, Jr., Temple NH (The Maine
Seine, 8:[1986]68-70).

Children (**Godfrey**), all but the first born at Steuben:

i.   LYDIA M., b. Gouldsboro 21 Nov. 1793, d. Cherryfield
       4 Apr. 1876; m. there 19 Mar. 1820 WILLIAM SMALL, b.
       there 19 June 1791, d. 23 June 1879, son of Elisha
       and Priscilla (Strout) Small.
ii.   FREDERICK, b. 24 Aug. 1795, d. Steuben in 1867; m.
       21 June 1825 JOANNA HASKELL, b. 6 Apr. 1806, d. 12
       Jan. 1896, dau. of Zebulon and Susanna (Sherman)
       Haskell. He was a sea captain.
iii.   ELIZA, b. 26 June 1797, d. 2 Nov. 1813; unm.
iv.   LEWIS, b. 24 June 1799, d. Steuben 24 Jan. 1886;
       married 17 Nov. 1822 BETSEY FOSTER, b. in 1803, d.
       27 Mar. 1879, dau. of James and Lydia (Stevens)
       Foster. He was also a sea captain.
v.   FLORA, b. 5 June 1801, d. 5 June 1873; m. 9 Jan. 1825
       LEONARD HASKELL, b. Rochester MA 15 Feb. 1801, d. 19
       Oct. 1873, son of Zebulon and Susanna (Sherman)
       Haskell.
vi.   JAMES, b. 18 Jan. 1805, d. 8 Sept. 1871; m. 28 Jan.
       1832 ALMIRA DYER YEATON, b. 25 Mar. 1809, d. 20 Oct.
       1878. He was a shipbuilder.
vii.   OLIVE, b. 26 Feb. 1808, d. 17 Jan. 1858; m. 3 Apr.
       1830 LEONARD SMITH, son of Justus and Polly (Allen)
       Smith.
viii. PAMELIA, b. 27 Apr. 1810, d. Milbridge 8 Mar. 1855;
       m. 3 Apr. 1830 ALBERT HAYFORD, b. Salem MA 3 Feb.
       1806, d. 12 June 1862.

86. ALEXANDER[6] [Sandy] 1775-1849 [31 Thomas[5] and Lydia
Tracy] was born at Steuben 4 Aug. 1775, died there 11 June
1849; married about 1800 MARY J. [Polly] LAWRENCE, born at
Steuben 17 Aug. 1781, died there 28 Dec. 1856, 76y, daughter
of John, Jr., and Jennie (Rolfe) Lawrence (Steuben VRs). He
was a blacksmith.
He bought at a tax auction 21 July 1797 100 acres above
Pinkham's Falls at Steuben (WashCD, 2:364-5). On 28 Jan.
1800 he and his brother Hatevil bought from William Shaw of
Quincy MA lot 9, of 100 acres (3:38-9).

Children, born at Steuben:

272.   i.   DIREXA[7], b. 13 Feb. 1802; m. WILLIAM SMITH.
273.   ii.   JANE, b. 28 Oct. 1803; m. ROBERT SMITH.
274.   iii.   (HORATIO) NELSON, b. 18 Apr. 1805.
275.   iv.   ABIGAIL, b. 18 Apr. 1808; m. EZRA SMITH.
276.   v.   ANNA, b. 21 July 1810; m. WILLIAM STEVENS.
277.   vi.   DANIEL L., b. 19 Apr. 1813.
278.   vii.   CAROLINE, b. 2 Sept. 1817; m. STILLMAN SMITH.
279.   viii. NANCY, b. 25 Sept. 1819; m. JOHN PIERCE.
280.   ix.   JOHN. b. 9 Jan. 1822.

87. HATEVIL[6] 1779-1858 [31 Thomas[5] and Lydia Tracy] was
born at Steuben 24 Aug. 1779 (VRs; Cornman Ms has 24 Nov.
1777, a more probable year), died there 9 Oct. 1858, about
81; married MARY [Polly/Molly] DUNBAR, born at Steuben 18
June 1780, died there 13 May 1867, at 87, daughter of Obed
and Abigail (Humphrey) Dunbar (Steuben VRs; his extensive
obituary, Machias Union).

Deacon Hatevil Leighton was a farmer. He bought land with
his brother Alexander in 1800, and from his brother Jonathan
in 1806. In 1850, the couple lived at Steuben; in 1860,
Polly was living with Elisha Parker.

Children, born at Steuben:

281. i.   ZERVIAH[7], b. 27 Nov. 1802; m. NATHAN PERRY.
      ii.   JOHN PATTEN, b. 4 Nov., d. 5 Dec., 1804.
      iii. SOPHRONIA, b. 27 Oct. 1805, d. 4 Sept. 1806.
282. iv.   LEONICE BUCKMAN, b. 11 Sept. 1807; m. SAMUEL
            CLEAVES.
283. v.   ELEANOR SMITH, b. 29 July 1809; m. ELISHA
            PARKER.
284. vi.   GEORGE ULMER, b. 27 Aug. 1811.
      vii. WILLIAM PATTEN, b. 11 Aug. 1814, d. Trinidad,
            Cuba, in 1840; unm.
285. viii. WEALTHY DYER, b. 22 Feb. 1817; m. WILLARD F.
            HALL.
      ix.   SOPHRONIA HANDY, b. 24 Jan. 1820, d. 29 Feb.
            1890; m. Gouldsboro 16 Apr. 1842 ELIJAH
            DOANE. No ch. (She and James L. Pinkham
            filed int. 28 Nov. 1839.
      x.   MARY JANE, b. 22 Feb. 1824, d. Milbridge 9
            Feb. 1849, 25y (GS); m. FRANCIS [Frank] MAR-
            TIN of Sullivan, son of Capt. Roland and Mary
            Martin (Johnson, Sullivan and Sorrento, 344).
            Burials are at East Sullivan. Ch. Charles
            L. b. 7 Feb. 1848, d. 25 Aug. 1926 (GS);
            m. Amelia Inman of Franklin.

88. PAMELIA[6] [Permelia] 1780-1819 [31 Thomas[5] and Lydia
Tracy] was born at Steuben 4 Apr. 1780, died there 3 Dec.
1819 during a typhus epidemic which also took five of her
children; married about 1798 JOHN PATTEN, born at Cherryfield
in 1779, died at Machias ME 25 Feb. 1855, son of Isaac and
Amy (Allen) Patten (Steuben and Cherryfield VRs; Baldwin,
Patten Genealogy, 124-9; Milliken, 16).
     John Patten married second at Steuben 1 Aug. 1821 Nancy
(Alline) Patten, born 4 Aug. 1784 (1786 per GS), died in
1872, daughter of Dr. Benjamin and Ann (Lowell) Alline of
Boston and Steuben and widow of Tobias Patten, brother to
John. John had three children by Nancy (BHM, 8[1893]:236).

Children (**Patten**), born at Cherryfield:

i.   ISAAC, b. 5 June 1799; m. (perhaps 2nd) Cherryfield
      11 Apr. 1830 JOAN WATTS, b. 16 Mar. 1810, dau. of
      David and Abigail (Noyes) Watts.
ii.   AMY, b. 5 Jan. 1801, d. 2 Dec. 1819; unm.
iii. SALLY, b. 23 Oct. 1803, d. 31 Oct. 1819; unm.
iv.   LYDIA, b. 23 Dec. 1805, d. 21 Oct. 1819.
v.   JULIA, b. 23 Feb. 1807; m. Cherryfield 31 Jan. 1828
      ALEXANDER F. CAMPBELL, b. there 29 June 1803, d. in
      Nov. 1882, son of James and Susannah (Coffin)
      Campbell.
vi.   JANE, b. 27 Apr. 1809; m. 16 Apr. 1829 GEORGE W.
      NASH, son of Holmes and Mary (Drisko) Nash of
      Addison.
vii. WILLIAM, b. 9 June, d. 29 Aug., 1811.

viii. JOHN, b. 9 June 1811 (twin), d. 3 Nov. 1819.
ix.   CHARITY, b. 30 Jan. 1813; m. Harrington int. 9 Dec.
      1833 BRADBURY COLLINS, b. in Mar. 1814.
x.   LOVE M., b. 24 Nov. 1815, d. 20 July 1893; m. Cherry-
      field 16 Nov. 1841 LEMUEL DYER SAWYER of Calais, b.
      Cape Elizabeth ME 8 May 1801, son of Nathan and
      Abigail (Dyer) Sawyer.
xi.   MARY, b. 23 Apr., d. 23 Oct., 1819.

89. ISRAEL[6] 1782-1830 [31 Thomas[5] and Lydia Tracy] was
born at Steuben 10 Dec. 1782, died there 19 May 1830; married
first AMY [Emma] SMITH, born at Lincolnville ME in 1784, died
at Unionville (Steuben) 14 Apr. 1817; married second at Harrington int. 1 Aug. 1817 PRISCILLA STROUT, died in 1841,
daughter of Thomas and Mary (Knowles) Strout (Steuben VRs;
Cornman Ms).
    Samuel Freeman, agent for the proprietors, deeded to Israel
1 Aug. 1822 the 100-acre "Vendue Lot" he had purchased at
auction (WashCD, 14:333-4).
    His son Alva was appointed administrator of Israel's estate
12 July 1830, and Benjamin Godfrey was appointed 2 Oct. as
guardian of Arthur and James G., over 14, and of Priscilla's
four children, all under 14. An inventory 30 Sept. included
the 100-acre homestead, and 63 acres of unimproved land. The
estate was distributed 2 Jan. 1832, a third to the widow
Priscilla, and two-thirds to Eliza and the minor children
(WashCD, 7:169-70, 337-8, 371; 8:17).

Children by Emma, born at Steuben:

    i.   ALVA[7], b. 25 Feb. 1807; m. Steuben int. 2
          Dec. 1833 ANN EATON of Robbinston.
    ii.   ELIZA, b. 10 Oct. 1809; m. ---- SMITH.
    iii. ARTHUR, b. 14 July 1813, d. Boston in Aug.
          1846, bur. in Mt. Auburn Cemetery, Cambridge.
          His brother James petitioned the court 5
          Aug. 1847 to settle the estate of Arthur of
          Addison, stating that their father Israel had
          died 15 years before, and his widow in 1841;
          that Arthur had died leaving no wife nor chil-
          dren but having 2 brothers and 2 sisters, and
          that his only estate was one-sixth of his
          father's homestead (WashCP, 15:51).
    iv.   JAMES, b. 15 Nov. 1815; unm.

Children by Priscilla, born at Steuben:

    v.   SEAMAN, b. 25 Dec. 1818, d. Steuben 10 Jan.
          1899, 81y 16d; m. there 7 May 1851 ELIZA
          WILLARD SHAW, b. 16 Apr. 1824, d. 23 Feb.
          1890, dau. of Willard Nichols and Nancy D.
          (Stevens) Shaw. He was a house carpenter.
          Ch. JOSEPHINE SHAW[8] b. 12 May 1852, d. 29 Oct.
          1920; unm. She was a teacher and Steuben
          postmistress.
286. vi. NICHOLAS H., b. 14 Aug. 1820.
     vii. PHOEBE GAY, b. 14 Apr. 1825, res. Steuben in
          1850 with William and Sybil Rich.
     viii.KINGSBURY, b. 6 May 1827, d.y.

90.   DANIEL[6] 1785-1849 [31 <u>Thomas</u>[5] and <u>Lydia Tracy</u>] was
born at Steuben 14 Apr. 1785, died there 24 Jan. 1849, 63y 9m
(GS, E. Steuben); married at Darrell, Sunbury Co. NB 8 Aug.
1810 ABIGAIL NASON, born at Lubec ME 18 June 1795 (in Steuben
VRs), died at East Steuben 6 Apr. or 4 June 1888, daughter of
Lemuel and Mary (Tracy) Nason [# 32] (Cornman Ms; Steuben
VRs). Widow Abigail was living in her son John's household
in 1850 and after.

Children:

	i.	DANIEL[7], d. infant.
287.	ii.	MARY, b. Oromocto NB 28 Oct. 1819; m. JUSTUS BICKFORD.
288.	iii.	THOMAS, b. Steuben 17 Dec. 1820.
289.	iv.	ABIGAIL, b. Steuben 7 Dec. 1823; m. HENRY B. CRANE.
290.	v.	JOHN NASON, b. Steuben 5 Aug. 1825.
291.	vi.	ISRAEL, b. Steuben 15 Nov. 1830.
292.	vii.	LEONARD H., b. Steuben 4 July 1835.

91.   ISAIAH[6] 1788-1857 [31 <u>Thomas</u>[5] and <u>Lydia Tracy</u>] was
born at Steuben 4 Nov. 1788, died at Cherryfield 23 Nov.
1857, 69y 19d (GS); married 14 Mar. 1811 MARY [Polly] SMALL,
born 14 Apr. 1789, died at Cherryfield 28 Oct. 1868, 79y 6m
14d, daughter of Elisha and Priscilla (Strout) Small (town
VRs; Underhill, <u>Small Desc.</u>, 1:175). Burials are in Pine
Grove Cemetery. A farmer, he held several Cherryfield town
offices. In 1850, their household included his mother Lydia
and two boarders.
Amos was granted administration of his father's estate 2
Mar. 1858; the inventory made 26 Mar. listed the 70-acre
homestead and an undeveloped lot. Heirs listed besides widow
Mary were Elisha, Amos and the three minor children of Lydia
Hutchins (WashCP, I:188, 192).

Children, born at Cherryfield (town record book):

	i.	ELISHA S.[7], b. 23 Apr. 1812, d. Cherryfield 3 Oct. 1884, 72y 5m 10d (GS); m. Hancock 20 Nov. 1843 CAROLINE LANCASTER, b. there 1 May 1817, d. Cherryfield 7 May 1901, 84y 6d, dau. of Silas Lancaster. One ch. CHARLES ISAIAH[8] b. 19 Dec. 1847, d. Cherryfield 12 Feb. 1917, 69y 1m 21d; unm. Burials are in the Small Cemetery. In 1850, an AMBROSE LEIGHTON, 19, was in his household.
	ii.	(WILLIAM) SHERMAN, b. 30 May 1813, d. Cherryfield 30 Apr. 1842 (GS); m. there int. 13 July 1839 MATILDA JONES, b. in 1812, d. Cherryfield 18 Sept. 1850 (GS). His widow applied for administration 2 Aug. 1842 (WashCP, 11: 30, 127). She m. 2nd Milbridge 2 Apr. 1844 James Parker Lawrence.
293.	iii.	AMOS P., b. 26 Mar. 1817.
	iv.	LYDIA, b. 9 Sept. 1819; m. 20 July 1850 WALTER D. HUTCHINS. In 1860 Walter, 38, lived at Cherryfield with a son Horace O., 7.

92. ASA[6] 1791-1861 [31 Thomas[5] and Lydia Tracy] was born at Steuben 14 Apr. 1791 (VRs), died at Milbridge in Dec. 1861; married LORUHAMAH FICKETT, born at Harrington 10 Oct. 1794, living at Milbridge in 1870, 75y, daughter of James and Mary (Howell) Fickett (town VRs). He was a mason and farmer.

His farm was on the west side of the Narraguagus River, in the part of Harrington set off to Milbridge in 1848. The home was razed in 1960. On 11 Oct. 1827, he gave a mortgage to Christopher Tracy of Durham ME for purchase of 20 acres, "part of the lot I now live on" (WashCD, 18:322-3).

Loruhamah's name (from the Book of Hosea 1:6-8) hardly appeared twice spelled the same. In 1870, she was living with her daughter Isabelle Small.

Children, the first seven listed in Steuben VRs, the rest in Milbridge records:

294. i.   CYNTHIA FICKETT[7], b. 17 Apr. 1814; m. JOHN L. GRIFFIN.
      ii.   ELIZA GODFREY, b. 29 Oct. 1815; m. DAVID B.[7] LEIGHTON [# 409].
295. iii. JOANNA FICKETT, b. 6 May 1817; m. JOHN STROUT.
296. iv.   OLIVER TRAIN, b. 13 May 1819.
297. v.   MARY B., b. 22 Sept. 1821; m. SAMUEL HOOPER, PETER COLE, and LEONARD J. WHITE.
298. vi.   HANNAH STROUT, b. 4 July 1823; m. EPHRAIM STROUT.
299. vii. ISABELLE STROUT, b. 13 Apr. 1825; m. MYRICK SMALL.
      viii. (ROBERT) PALMER, b. 28 Feb. 1827, d. Cherryfield 20 Feb. 1896 (GS); m. Harrington 13 June 1851 (VRs) MARTHA C. [Mattie] SMALL, b. Harrington 30 May 1835, d. Cherryfield 15 Dec. 1908, 73y 6m 15d (VRs; 1834-1909 per GS), dau. of James W. and Jane (Wakefield) Small. No ch. Burials are in Pine Grove Cemetery. He was a blacksmith.
300. ix.   LEWIS R., b. 23 Feb. 1829.
301. x.   ELLEN, b. 9 Jan. 1833; m. SIMPSON S. GORDON.
302. xi.   GEORGE F., b. 14 Oct. 1834.

93. JOHN PATTEN[6] 1772-1838 [33 Hatevil[5] and Martha Denbow] was born probably at Narraguagus (Cherryfield) 25 Dec. 1772, died at Pembroke 17 Oct. 1838 (probate record; in 1839, 68y, GS); married at Pembroke 3 Oct. 1796 SARAH MAHAR, born at Pembroke 28 May 1776, died there 19 July 1877, 99y 2m, daughter of Edmund and Rebecca (Riley) Mahar (BHM, 9[1894]: 221; Dennysville and Pembroke VRs). Family burials are in Clarkside Cemetery.

John and Sarah lived on his father's homestead, he having bought out the shares of his siblings (Vose, Dennysville, 108; Wilder, Pembroke Families).

Township 2 east of Machias (Pennamaquan) became the town of Dennysville in 1818; the part earliest settled was then separated as Pembroke in 1832.

John bought from Isaiah Hersey a 50-acre lot on "Sipp Bay" (Hersey's Neck, on Scipio Bay) 24 Aug. 1811, and an adjoining lot of 60 acres from Theodore Lincoln 22 May 1824 (WashCD, 12:117; 15:340-1).

His estate was admitted to probate 5 Feb. 1839, after his widow Sarah asked that her son John be named co-administrator. The inventory was presented 29 [sic] Feb. 1839 and again on 29 Oct. 1840, listing the heirs (WashCP, 9:501; 11:89-90, 222-3). John's nephew Adna, who became administrator, sold to Hatevil J. Leighton 9 Dec. 1843 Leighton's Point Farm, and to widow Sarah the 100-acre Cutler lot and 50-acre Hersey lot (WashCD, 53:224, 346).

In the 1850 census Sarah, 70, and her daughter Sarah, 50, were listed next door to her sons Hatevil and Thomas.

Children, born at Dennysville:

303. i.   ELEANOR M.[7], b. 17 Feb. 1797; m. JOSIAH
           BRIDGES.
      ii. SARAH [Sally], b. 10 Apr. 1799, d. Pembroke 1
           Oct. 1854 (GS); unm. (WashCP, IV:368).
304. iii. JOHN, b. 31 Aug. 1801.
305. iv. HATEVIL J., b. 28 Sept. 1803.
306. v.   EDMUND, b. 12 Sept. 1805.
307. vi. THOMAS, b. 14 Feb. 1808.
308. vii. LUCY, b. 19 Feb. 1810; m. WILLIAM WILBUR.
      viii. ANNA, b. c1814, d. 11 May 1820, 6y (GS)[7]
      ix. ELIZA ANN, b. 20 Sept. 1816; m. HATEVIL[7]
           LEIGHTON [# 317].
      x.   ANN MARIA PHELPS, b. 25 July 1818; m. JOHN[7]
           LEIGHTON [# 321).
309. xi. MARY JANE, b. 19 Oct. 1819; m. JOSIAH WILBUR.
      xii. AARON, d. 18 May 1820, aged 1m (GS).
310. xiii. AARON NEWELL, b. 18 July 1823.

94. **SARAH**[6] [Sally] 1774-1848 [33 Hatevil[5] and Martha Denbow] was born at Dennysville 2 May 1774, died at Pembroke 5 May 1848 (VRs); married ADNA HERSEY, born at Hingham MA 23 June 1778, died at Pembroke 4 Aug. 1851, son of Isaiah and Rebecca (Sprague) Hersey (History of the Town of Hingham, Mass. [The Town, 1893], 2:308-9; Wilder, Pembroke Families). They lived at Passamaquoddy.

On 17 Apr. 1824, Adna and Sally sold to her brother John her rights in the estate of their father Hatevil (WashCD, 15:341).

Sarah had an illegitimate son by one Denbo or Densmore (per Wilder), whom she and Adna raised.

Child (**Leighton**), born at Pembroke:

311. i.   GEORGE[7], b. 24 Mar. 1794.

Children (**Hersey**), born at Pembroke:

      ii. SAMUEL, b. 26 Mar. 1800, d. 24 Oct. 1881; m. THIRZA
           HERSEY, b. 4 Dec. 1801, d. 18 Aug. 1868, dau. of
           Perez and Catherine (Benner) Hersey.
      iii. ADNA, b. 5 Nov. 1801, d. 9 Jan. 1871; m. 16 Dec.
           1828 MERCY DeFOREST, dau. of Henry and Sarah
           (Wentworth) DeForest.
      iv. MARTHA, b. 9 July 1805, d. in Sept. 1820.
      v.   HANNAH, b. 22 Jan. 1806; m. ABIJAH[7] LEIGHTON
           [# 340].
      vi. ISAAC, b. 30 Mar. 1808, d. 1 Feb. 1831; unm.

vii.   SARAH, b. 26 Nov. 1809; m. JOHN CAMPBELL, b. St.
       George NB 19 July 1809, d. Pembroke 30 Dec. 1882.
viii. JOHN, b. 5 Mar. 1811, d. 5 Oct. 1837; unm.
ix.   MARY BELL, b. 9 July 1812; m. COLIN CAMPBELL.
x.   WILLIAM BELL, b. 12 Jan. 1820; m. EMMA RANDALL.

95. HATEVIL[6] 1775-1844 [33 Hatevil[5] and Martha Denbow] was
born at Dennysville 8 Aug. 1775, died at Lubec ME 26 Jan.
1844, 69y 6m; married in 1799 MARY [Polly] MAHAR, born at
Dennysville 13 Sept. 1783, died at Lubec 30 Sept. 1829,
daughter of Edmund and Rebecca (Riley) Mahar (Dennysville,
Pembroke and Lubec VRs; Wilder, Pembroke Families; Vose,
Dennysville, 108). Burials are in Pembroke Cemetery.
       He bought from the Mass. General Court 14 Feb. 1805 lots 1
and 23 on Lowell's Neck containing 100 acres in the 3rd divison of Tp No. 2, which became Lubec (WashCD, 11:347), and lot
19 of 19 acres 17 Sept. 1823 (15:354-5). (When Maine became
a state in 1820, Massachusetts retained ownership of large
tracts of land.) His purchase was conditional; he or his
heirs had to build a house 16 by 20 feet, and improve six
acres suitable for tillage or pasturage.
       With Sally and six children, he was living at Lubec in 1811
("Inhabitants and Residents of Lubec in 1811," Downeast
Ancestry, 10[1986]:103). He served, as "Hatwell," under
Capt. J. W. Reynolds, Lt. Col. Oliver Shead's Rgt., 15 July
to 28 Aug 1812 at Eastport (MA Mil. 1812-14, 166). However,
the British soon gained control of the area east of the
Penobscot and administered it as part of Canada.
       Clement and Patty Densmore sold Hatevil of Lubec 16 Apr.
1820 the lot on Leighton's Point, Dennysville, which Patty
had received from her father (WashCD, 14:412-3). Hatevil
sold to the Portland, Scarborough and Phippsburg Mining Co.
on 23 June 1834 his mineral rights at Lubec (27:294).
       On 2 Apr. 1844 James Leighton, "next of kin" to Hatevil of
Lubec, was made administrator of Hatevil's estate. James
presented an inventory and plan for distribution (including a
map laying out 13 thirty-acre lots), naming the eleven living
children, and the minor children of both Samuel and Margaret
(WashCP, 11:472; 13:142, 179, 408-11).

       Children, listed in Eastport and Lubec VRs, although most
       were born at Dennysville/Pembroke:

312.   i.   JAMES[7], b. 16 June 1800.
313.   ii.   ISAAC, b. 17 Jan. 1802.
       iii. REBECCA, b. 22 Apr. 1804; m. JOHN[7] LEIGHTON
             [# 305].
314.   iv.   MARGARET, b. 10 Jan. 1806; m. HORATIO GATES
             ALLEN.
315.   v.   SAMUEL. b. 31 Oct. 1807.
316.   vi.   MARK, b. 23 Dec. 1809.
       vii. MARY, b. 27 Oct. 1811; m. HATEVIL J.[7] LEIGHTON
             [# 305].
317.   viii. HATEVIL, b. 10 Aug. 1813.
318.   ix.   KEZIAH, b. 12 June 1816; m. JAMES HUCKINS, JR.
319.   x.   MARTHA, b. 18 Sept. 1818; m. WILLIAM BRYANT.
       xi.   ANNA, b. 25 Apr. 1820; m. AARON WHITFIELD[8]
             LEIGHTON [# 757].
320.   xii. AARON, b. 8 July 1822.
321.   xiii. JOHN M., b. say in 1825.

96. SAMUEL[6] 1776-1863 [33 Hatevil[5] and Martha Denbow] was
born at Dennysville 25 Dec. 1776, died at Pembroke 18 Dec.
1869, 87y (GS); married first at Hingham MA 25 Dec. 1800 LEAH
HERSEY, born at Hingham 2 Apr. 1781, died at Pembroke of
childbed 12 or 25 Sept. 1812, daughter of Isaiah and Rebecca
(Sprague) Hersey (Hist. of Hingham, 2:308-9; Vose, Dennysville, 108; Dennysville and Pembroke VRs).
    He marrried second at Pembroke 21 Dec. 1813 TABITHA (Le-
SURE) Pomeroy, who died 5 Sept. 1848, widow of Benjamin Pomeroy of Dennysville. Traditionally, she was Acadian, from the
Wolfville area of NS, descended from an Isle of Jersey family
(Wilder, Pembroke Families; Leighton, Gen. Sketch, 10-11).
    He bought from Hosea Smith in 1811 a lot running from Hardy
Point to the Union Meetinghouse. Often a hundred shad were
taken during one tide in his weir on the West Branch. He
sold land to Edwin Blake 9 May 1818 (WashCD, 10:70), and sold
to his brother John his share of their father's estate.
    According to Wilder, his second wife ran through all his
money and drove him mad; thereafter he was called "Crazy
Sam." In 1825 his son Adna was appointed guardian of Samuel,
"a lunatic, non compos or distracted person." Samuel, aged
71, was living with his son Hatevil in 1850, and in 1860, at
84, with Samuel, Jr. Burials are in Pembroke Cemetery.

Children by Leah, born at Dennysville:

322. i.   ADNA[7], b. 22 Feb. 1801.
323. ii.   LEAH, b. 7 Feb. 1803; m. WILLIAM LINCOLN and
              ISAAC GARDNER.
324. iii.   SAMUEL, b. 23 Feb. 1805.
325. iv.   ISAIAH, b. 7 Dec. 1807.
326. v.   JUSTIN L., b. 22 Apr. 1809.
      vi.   ELIZA ANN, b. 5 Sept. 1812, d. 1 Sept. 1886; m.
              Pembroke 23 Nov. 1837 PETER GILMAN FARNS-
              WORTH, b. Norridgewock ME 1 July 1809, d.
              Pembroke 3 Dec. 1849, son of Col. Jonas and
              Maria (Gould) Farnsworth (Farnsworth Mem.,
              261). Ch. Isaac Hobart b. 30 Dec. 1840; unm.

Children by Tabitha, born at Dennysville:

327. vii.   HATEVIL, b. 26 Apr. 1814.
      viii.   CHARLES HENRY, b. in 1816, d. infant.
328. ix.   CHARLES HENRY, b. 1 May 1818.
      x.   OLIVE, b. 5 Feb. 1820, d. 15 Jan. 1829 as a
              result of burns.

97. MARGARET[6] 1778-   [33 Hatevil[5] and Martha Denbow]
was born at Dennysville 20 Sep. 1778; married ROBERT ASH,
JR., born perhaps at Gouldsboro ME 27 Nov. 1772, died at St.
George NB in Jan. 1816, killed by the fall of a tree, son of
Robert and Catherine Ash. Robert married first 26 Oct. 1795
Elizabeth [Betsey] Benner, who drowned in the Magaguadavic
River at St. George 20 Jan. 1808; they had five children
(Karin E. and Gerald F. Gower, "Ancestry of James Ash," Gen-
erations, N. B. Genealogical Society, Sept. 1988, 29, 31-2).
    Widow Margaret Ash of St. George deeded her rights in her
father's estate to her brother Hatevil 30 Apr. 1824 (WashCD,
15:353-4).

Children (**Ash**), born in Charlotte Co. NB:

i.   child, d. before father.
ii.   JEMIMA BELL, b. c1812, d. Second Falls, Charlotte
      Co. in Jan. 1878; m. 11 June 1835 SMITH CRAIG.
iii. HATEVILLE LEIGHTON, b. 10 Mar. 1813; m. 5 Dec. 1839
      ELIZABETH GILL BARTON.
iv.   HIRAM, b. c1815.

98. MARY[6] 1780-1857 [33 Hatevil[5] and Martha Denbow] was
born at Dennysville 28 May 1780, died 4 Jan. 1857; married
WILLIAM BELL, born in NH in 1777, died 2 Apr. 1861, son of
Robert and Jemima (Merrill) Bell.
He owned a tidemill with Capt. John Crane and then with
John Crane, Jr. They lived at Trescott and at Whiting (town
VRs; Gladys Hall Forslund, History of Whiting, Maine [np,
1975], 67; Cornman Ms).

Children (**Bell**), born at Trescott (VRs):

i.   MARY, b. 10 Sept. 1799, d. Trescott 14 Nov. 1866; m.
      WILLIAM DENSMORE, b. 10 May 1792, d. Trescott 19
      Oct. 1869, son of John and Hannah Densmore.
ii.   ELIZABETH, b. 2 Oct. 1800; m. ABRAHAM WHEELER.
iii. HATEVIL, b. 19 Feb. 1802; m. REBECCA CRANE, b. 10
      May 1809, d. 13 May 1899, dau. of Abijah and Rebecca
      Crane.
iv.   RHODA C., b. 13 Mar. 1803.
v.   WILLIAM, b. 23 June 1804; m. ZERVIAH G. CRANE, b. 1
      Aug. 1815, d. 11 Apr. 1900, dau. of Abijah and
      Rebecca Crane.
vi.   JEMIMA, b. 27 Mar. 1812, d. 7 Feb. 1848; m. JOHN
      LITTLE, b. in 1814, d. 17 Aug. 1848.
vii. MARTHA. b. 20 Oct. 1814.
viii. ROBERT, b. 15 Oct. 1816, went to CA in 1849; m.
      LUCY COMSTOCK.
ix.   PHILENA ANN, b. 6 Jan. 1817; m. GEORGE LITTLE.
x.   JOSEPH, b. 25 Dec. 1820; m. REBECCA EDES WARD.
xi.   CLARISSA CAROLINE, b. 27 June 1824, living in
      1914; unm.

99. PHOEBE[6] 1782-   [33 Hatevil[5] and Martha Denbow] was
born at Dennysville in 1782; married first in Nov. 1808 JOHN
CAREW of Perry, born at Dublin, Ireland, died at Perry 16
July 1816; married second JOHN KELLEY of Perry (Wilder, Pembroke Families).
Carew was a British naval officer who had deserted at Halifax NS and become a plantation clerk at Perry. He had married first Nancy (Frost) Preble, who died soon after.
On 19 Apr. 1824 John and Phebe "Kaley" of Perry quitclaimed
her rights in her late father's estate to her brother John
(WashCD, 15:353).

Children (**Carew**), born at Pembroke:

i.   JOHN, b. 5 Mar. 1811, d. 5 Nov. 1894.
ii.   JAMES.

100. HANNAH[6] 1784-   [33 Hatevil[5] and Martha Denbow] was
born at Dennysville in 1784; married at Lubec 21 Nov. 1808
JOHN NUTTER (Downeast Ancestry, 10:(1986):104).

Children (**Nutter**), born at Dennysville:

i.   JOHN, b. 6 Dec. 1808.
ii.   HANNAH, b. 15 Aug. 1810.
iii. MARGARET, b. c1818; m. JAMES DENSMORE [# 101].

101. REBECCA[6] 1786-   [33 Hatevil[5] and Martha Denbow]
was born at Pembroke 8 May 1786; married JAMES DENSMORE of
Trescott, born 11 Oct. 1783, died at Lubec, son of John and
Hannah Densmore (Cornman Ms). James and Rebecca of No. 9
quit their rights in the estate of her father to her brother
Hatevil on 7 June 1824 (WashCD, 15:352-3).

Children (**Densmore**), order uncertain:

i.   JAMES, b. 1809 (41 in 1850); m. MARGARET NUTTER,
      32 in 1850, dau. of John and Hannah[7] (Leighton)
      Nutter [# 100]
ii.   ORRIN; m. Lubec JULIA RAY.
iii. WILLIAM, b. c1817 (33 in 1850); m. ELIZA FICKETT,
      b. c1823 (27 in 1850).
iv.   ELIZABETH; unm.
v.   MARY ANN; m. ---- MARSTON.
vi.   REBECCA, d. Lubec 8 June 1897, 64y 1m (VRs); unm.

102. CLEMENT[6] 1790-1853 [33 Hatevil[5] and Martha Denbow]
was born at Dennysville in 1790, died at Trescott in 1853;
married first at Dennysville 4 Oct. 1812 (VRs) MARY WILDER,
died at Trescott in 1841, daughter of Zenas Wilder; married
second PRUDENCE ---- , 56 in 1850; married third MARY J.
FRANCIS of Gouldsboro 19 Jan. 1852 (Trescott and Dennysville
VRs; Wilder, Pembroke Families; Cornman Ms).
He lived at Trescott in 1830 and 1840, and in 1850 his
household there included George Campbell, 10.

Children by first wife Mary (Trescott VRs):

       i.   MARY[7]; m. (SAMUEL) HALL CHASE, son of Eleazer
             Chase (Drisko, Machias, 396).
       ii.   EUNICE; m. CHARLES PALMER.
329.   iii. REBECCA B., b. 18 Sept. 1818; m. GEORGE W.
             CAMPBELL.
       iv.   LYDA, b. 10 Feb. 1823, prob. d.y.
       iv.   KEZIAH [Cusiah], b. 12 Apr. 1827, d. 21 May
             1891; m. 20 Feb. 1848 WILSON HADLEY.
330.   v.   ISAAC C., b. Trescott 26 May 1828.
331.   vi.   JOSEPH HATEVIL, b. Machias 30 Mar. 1831.
332.   vii. JAMES HENRY (twin), b. Machias 30 Mar. 1831.
333.   viii. EPHRAIM FRANKLIN, b. in 1834.
       ix.   LUCINDA, b. 7 Jan. 1839.

103. ABIGAIL[6] 1792-   [33 Hatevil[5] and Martha Denbow]
was born at Dennysville 29 July 1792, lived there on Garnett's Neck; married 29 Aug. 1812 GEORGE NUTTER, born 12 Jan.

1793, son of Mathias and Betsey Nutter (Dennysville and Pembroke VRs).
On 17 Apr. 1824 they quitclaimed to her brother John
her share in their father's estate (WashCD, 15:339-40).

Children (**Nutter**):

i.   MAUDE, b. 11 Apr. 1812.
ii.   ROYAL, b. 19 Apr. 1813.
iii. MARY, b. 18 June 1814.
iv.   ETHEL, b. 7 Jan. 1818.
v.   ABIGAIL, b. 17 June 1823.
vi.   GEORGE FURBER, b. Pembroke 30 Sept. 1824.
vii. SEWARD BUCKNAM, b. Pembroke 14 Jan. 1828.
viii. LORENZO SABIN, b. Pembroke 10 Sept. 1829.

104. MARTHA[6] [Patty] 1795-1869 [33 Hatevil[5] and Martha
Denbow] was born at Dennysville in June 1795 (in Wilder,
1793), died in Feb. 1869; married CLEMENT DENSMORE, born 12
July 1790, died in 1872, son of John and Hannah Densmore
(Wilder, Pembroke Families; Cornman Ms).
They lived at Dennysville, then at Lubec in 1840, and were
listed at Bangor in 1850.
On 16 Apr. 1820, Clement and Patty sold to her brother
Hatevil the lot she inherited at Leighton Point from her
father (WashCD, 14:412-3). In 1850, Joseph and Eliza Case
lived with them at Bangor.

Children (**Densmore**):

i.   CLEMENT, b. c1806 (44 in 1850); m. ELIZA TUCKER.
ii.   ELIZA LIBBY, b. 7 Dec. 1812, d. 10 May 1889; m.
      JOSEPH CASE, b. Feb. 1810, d. 10 Sep 1861.
iii. JAMES TALBOT, b. in 1822, d. Apr. 1902; m. SARAH A.
      STICKSON.

105. ELIJAH[6] 1792-1882 [33 Hatevil[5] and Martha Denbow] was
born at Dennysville 29 July 1796, died at Eastport ME 26 Dec.
1882; married at Whiting 12 Oct. 1817 MARY ANN SAUNDERS, born
in NB about 1796 (53 in 1850) (town VRs; Cornman Ms).
They lived at Trescott (censuses of 1850 through 1880). He
was called Abijah in Vose's Dennysville History. In 1870 and
1880 they were part of their son Stephen's household.

Children, born at Trescott (VRs):

334. i.   WILLIAM HENRY[7], b. 29 Apr. 1818.
335. ii.   ELSAIDE, b. 15 Jan. 1820; m. JACKSON BRIDGES.
336. iii. JAMES EVERETT, b. 4 Feb. 1822.
337. iv.   ELEANOR, b. 17 Mar. 1824; m. JACOB SYLVA.
      v.   SARAH JANE, b. 18 June 1826.
      vi.   ACHSA SAWYER, b. 28 Dec. 1828; m. Pembroke 3
            Dec. 1848 (4 Nov. Trescott VRs) (JAMES) HENRY
            MAHAR, b. 27 Oct. 1822, son of James and Sarah
            (Dunbar) Mahar. They settled at Wiscasset
            ME. Ch. William and Byron.
338. vii. MARY CORDELIA, b. 12 May 1831; m. HENRY
            RICHARDSON.

339.   viii. STEPHEN S., b. 1 Dec. 1833.
        ix.   ANN MARAH, b. 15 May 1837, res. Portland; m.
               NEAL J. JOHNSON. Ch. Frank and Fred.
        x.   (MARGARET) ELIZA, b. 29 July 1840, res. Port-
               land; m. Eastport 4 July 1863 (Machias Union)
               JOHN A. KNIGHTS of Lubec. Ch. Maude.

106.   SAMUEL[6] 1779-1864 [34 Samuel[5] and Elizabeth Frost]
was born at Eastport 26 Mar. 1779, died there 23 Sept. 1864,
85y (Machias Union); married there 8 Dec. 1800 JANE COCHRANE,
born about 1780 (70 in 1850), probably daughter of Eastport's
first settler, James Cochrane (Eastport VRs; Cornman Papers).
    Samuel was a mariner. He and his brother John, then both
minors, bought from Caleb Boynton, Jr., 1 Aug. 1796 land on
Moose Island (Eastport) (WashCD, 2:34), and on 17 Jan. 1803
they bought of Jonathan Poor of Essex Co. an adjacent 3/4
acre (3:302-3). Samuel bought from Perez Burr of Freeport
lot 12 in the 3rd division, 108 acres on Denbo's Neck, 30 May
1805, and bought a small plot from James Cochrane on 11 June
that year (4:157-8).

Children, born at Eastport:

        i.   ALICE[7], b. 13 Nov. 1801.
        ii.   ELIZA, b. 25 Dec. 1803.
340.   iii.   ABIJAH, b. 7 Sept. 1806.
341.   iv.   SARAH, b. 30 Dec. 1808; m. JOHN CAPEN.
342.   v.   SAMUEL, b. 5 June 1811.
        vi.   JANE, b. 24 Nov. 1815, d. 20 Feb. 1818.
343.   vii.   GEORGE, b. 9 Apr. 1820.

107.   SALLY[6] 1783-   [34 Samuel[5] and Elizabeth Frost] was
born at Perry 10 Apr. 1783; married at Eastport 13 Mar. 1803
SAMUEL WHEELER (Cornman Ms; Eastport VRs).

Children (**Wheeler**), born at Eastport:

i.   SALLY, b. 14 Jan. 1804, res. Calais; m. ---- SHAW.
ii.   LORING FIELD, b. 22 Oct. 1807, d. 28 Feb. 1844.
iii.   ASENATH ANN, b. 19 Mar., d. 27 Aug., 1810.
iv.   SAMUEL BIGELOW, b. 27 Aug. 1811.
v.   ANDREW HOWARD, b. 11 Sept. 1815, d. 27 Nov. 1817.
vi.   JAMES PUTNAM (twin), b. 11 Sept. 1815.
vii.   WILLIAM TREW, b. 30 May 1817, d. in June 1843.
viii.   MARY FIELD, b. 25 July 1819, d. 10 Sept. 1821.
ix.   LUCY ANN, b. 19 May 1821.

108.   MARK[6] 1785-1868 [34 Samuel[5] and Elizabeth Frost] was
born at Perry (Eastport VRs) 1 Aug. 1785, died there 25 May
1868 (25 Apr. per Machias Union); married at Eastport 15
Dec. 1809 OLIVIA SOPHIA WENTWORTH, born at Saint John NB 19
Apr. 1795, died at Perry 4 Jan. 1881 (Perry and Eastport VRs;
Cornman Ms; Wilder, Pembroke Families).
    He was a farmer, and a fou
house in 1828 (BHM, 9[1894]:1
Joshua Gove's household.

Children, most births listed in Perry VRs:

	i.	SALINA[7], b. Eastport 15 Feb., d. 8 Mar. 1811.
344.	ii.	ALMIRA D.. b. Eastport 5 Apr. 1812; m. THOMAS HIBBARD.
345.	iii.	SARAH RICHARD, b. 3 Apr. 1814; m. HENRY FROST.
346.	iv.	JOHN D., b. 10 Apr. 1816 (Eastport VRs).
347.	v.	EMILY, b. 15 Dec. 1818; m. JAMES MAHAR and ANDROS ELDRIDGE.
348.	vi.	THOMAS PARKER, b. 7 Feb. 1820.
349.	vii.	NANCY, b. 21 May 1823; m. DANIEL HIBBARD.
350.	viii.	MARK, b. 13 July 1826.
	ix.	WILLIAM WOODWORTH, b. 23 Sept. 1828, d.y.
	x.	ELSIE JANE, b. 1 Feb. 1831, d. in 1850; unm.
351.	xi.	CHARLOTTE OLIVIA, b. 27 Oct. 1833; m. JOSHUA GOVE.
	xii.	REBECCA C., b. 5 Mar. 1837, d. Perry 27 Feb. 1893; m. 29 Aug. 1859 WILLIAM H. POTTER, b. c1838 (32 in 1870). Ch. William D. b. c1860, Isabella M. b. c1862, and May b. c1863.

109.   MARY SMITHSON[6] [Polly] 1780-   [37 George[5] and Deborah Perkins] was baptized at Newington NH 26 Nov. 1780 as Molly Smithson Leighton (NHGR, 5[1908]:78), lived at Washington ME in 1853 when she and her sisters applied for their mother's pension; married first at Gardiner ME int. 4 Jan. 1806 (JOHN) PEARSON SANBORN [Sandburn], born at Bristol ME 15 Sept. 1774, died in NY in 1815 en route home from military service, son of Richard and Abigail (Kelley) Sanborn. He had married first at Gilmanton NH Betsey Gilman: three children (V. C. Sanborn, Genealogy of the Family of Samborne or Sanborn [1899], 260). Polly married second at Gardiner 10 Feb. 1819 JAMES WAKEFIELD, born at Gardiner 8 Sept. 1788, son of Dominicus and Martha (Door) Wakefield (Homer Wakefield, Wakefield Memorial [np, 1897], 127-8).

Children (**Sanborn**), born at Gardiner (VRs):

i.   NANCY L., b. 17 Feb. 1806; m. Gardiner int. 22 Mar. 1824 ASA DOW.
ii.   EZRA L. SMITHSON, b. 16 Mar. 1808, d. Gardiner 20 Feb. 1885; m. Gardiner 26 Feb. 1835 his cousin ELIZABETH PLAISTED [#110]. No ch. They res. Searsmont and Thomaston.
iii.   DEBORAH P., b. 4 June 1810, d. 5 May 1884; m. 28 Apr. 1836 EDWIN C. KIMBALL of Belfast ME, b. 5 May 1813, d. 17 May 1879, son of Luther and Eunice (Tripp) Kimball of Kennebunkport (Morrison, Kimball Family, 1109).
iv.   LYDIA K., b. 10 Oct. 1812; m. Gardiner 16 Apr. 1836 ABRAHAM LORD, who d. 16 Apr. 1836.

110.   ELIZABETH[6] 1786-1857 [37 George[5] and Deborah Perkins] was born in NH about 1786 (67 in 1853), died at Gardiner 16 Oct. 1857, 70y 8m; married at Gardiner int. 28 Feb. 1806 (VRs) ICHABOD PLAISTED, born at Berwick 2 Oct. 1763, died at Gardiner 11 Mar. 1836, 72y, son of William and Jane (Hight) Plaisted.

Ichabod had married first at Pittston in 1793 Charity Church, who died in Oct. 1884, leaving a son Ichabod (BHM, 9[1894]:8:143).

Children (**Plaisted**), born at Gardiner (VRs):

i.   ELIZABETH, b. c1808, d. Gardiner 4 Feb. 1885, 77y; m. her cousin EZRA SANBORN [# 109].

ii.   GEORGE, b. 11 Mar. 1813, d. Boston 27 Dec. 1886, 73y (Gardiner record); m. Gardiner int. 1 Oct. 1836 FANNY JACKINS.

iii.   WILLIAM, b. 17 Apr. 1815, d. Gardiner 12 Oct. 1864.

iv.   FRANCIS A., b. 2 Jan. 1829; m. Gardiner 6 Nov. 1858 THANKFUL P. RIDLEY.

111. NATHANIEL[6] 1791-1849 [37 George[5] and Deborah Perkins] was born at Pittston (Gardiner) ME 18 Dec. 1791, died at Milan, Ripley Co., IN 10 July 1849; married first at Augusta ME 4 Apr. 1813 (VRs) (Gardiner int. 13 Mar.) NANCY MAXWELL, born at Shapleigh ME 11 Nov. 1792, died at Gardiner in 1833 (her obituary, Morning Star of 26 Sept. 1833), daughter of David Maxwell of Industry ME; married second at Gardiner 22 Sept. 1834 (int. 6 Sept.) MARY GETCHELL, born 22 Sept. 1807, died at Milan 3 Nov. 1887.

He served in Capt. Jacob Davis's Co. in Sept. 1814 (MA Mil. 1812-14, 272). He purchased through a mortgage from Robert Hallowell Gardiner 29 Aug. 1816 about 53 acres in the westerly part of lot 63, from the north bank of the Cobbosseecontee River to the Litchfield Road (KenCD, 26:434).

A merchant, he settled in IN about 1835. His children were all under 10 when he died (town VRs; records of his son David --Cornman Papers).

Children. all by second wife Mary, born at Milan:

i.   NANCY[7], b. 17 Sept. 1836, d. 20 July 1838.

ii.   MARY NANCY, b. 8 Sept. 1839, d. in Jan. 1892; m. 1st in 1861 SAMUEL BOLDREY; m. 2nd HAROLD S. ABBOTT.

352. iii. GEORGE NATHANIEL, b. 14 July 1841.
353. iv. JOSEPH, b. 14 Aug. 1843
354. v.   DAVID GARDINER, b. 18 Aug. 1845.
355. vi. NATHANIEL, b. 2 Nov. 1849.

112. SARAH[6] [Sally] 1800-1884 [37 George[5] and Deborah Perkins] was born in NH (per census) about 1800, died at Gardiner 4 Feb. 1884, 80y; married there 11 Feb. 1819 HENRY [Harry] McCAUSLAND III, born about 1794 (46 in 1840), died at Gardiner 23 Mar. 1863, 70y, son of Henry, Jr., and Abiah (Stackpole) McCausland (Gardiner VRs). He was a shoemaker.

In 1840, his household included a female 80-90; in 1860, it also contained George C., 9, and Elizabeth, 40. Sally was living with her son John in the 1870s.

Children (**McCausland**), probably all born at Gardiner:

i.   JULIA, b. c1820 (30 in 1850), d. Gardiner 2 Dec. 1869, 49y; unm.

ii.   MARY H., b. in Dec. 1826, a widow at Gardiner in
        1900; m. Dover NH 19 Oct. 1857 (Gardiner VRs) JOHN
        HOLT.
iii.   CHARITY, b. in Sept. 1829, res. Gardiner in 1900;
        unm.
iv.   CATHERINE A., b. in July 1832, living a widow at
        Gardiner in 1900; m. there 20 Jan. 1861 GEORGE W.
        FLYNT. No ch.
v.   DEBORAH, b. c1835 (15 in 1850); m. Gardiner 9 Jan.
        1858 ROBERT A. SAGER.
vi.   JOHN H., b. c1837 (12 in 1850), d. Farmingdale ME
        4 Aug. 1890, 53y.
vii.   EMMA J., b. c1840 (10 in 1850).
viii.   CHRISTIANA, b c1842 (18 in 1860, not listed in the
        1850 census).

113. THOMAS[6] 1771-1855 [38 John Smithson[5] and Sarah Barey]
was born probably at Edgecomb ME about 1771, died at Mount
Vernon ME 9 June 1855, 83y 8m (GS); married at Mount Vernon
int. 8 Apr. 1798 (VRs) MARY [Polly] (PEARL) Bean, born about
1772, died at Mt. Vernon 20 June 1841 (1844 per GS), 69y,
daughter of Simeon and Mary[5] (Leighton) Pearl [# 36].
    She had married first Neal Bean. On 11 Apr. 1803 Silas
Pearl, Polly's brother, deeded to Thomas the westerly half of
lot 180 (KenCD, 16:77). Burials are in Bean Cemetery.

Children, born at Mount Vernon (TRs 2:316):

        i.   SARAH[7], b. 5 May 1799, d.y.
        ii.   ZERVIAH, b. 29 Aug. 1801.
        iii.   SALLY, b. 27 July 1803, d. Mt. Vernon 27 Mar.
                1872, 68y; unm.
356.   iv.   SUSANNAH, b. 7 Dec. 1805; m. JAMES LAWRENCE.
357.   v.   WARNER R., b. 15 May 1808.
        vi.   JAMES RIGGS, b. 19 Apr. 1810, d. Dover ME 21
                Nov. 1846, 36y (in Gospel Banner of 5 Dec.
                1846; 1848 per GS); m. Mt. Vernon 26 Feb. 1833
                DORINDA WHITTIER, b. there 13 Aug. 1808,
                dau. of John and Climena (Blake) Whittier
                (Charles Collyer Whittier, Descendants of
                Thomas Whittier and Ruth Green [Rutland VT,
                1937], 111). He was a militia captain.
                Burials are in Old Dover village cemetery.
                Ch. Jane V. 1835-1837; and Minnie and Dorinda
                C., who both d. infants.
358.   vii.   ELIZA ANN, b. 12 Sept. 1812; m. NATHANIEL T.
                ROBINSON.
        viii.   ALICE, b. 7 Dec. 1815, d. 27 June 1816.

114. JOSEPH[6] 1779-1851 [38 John Smithson[5] and Sarah Barey]
was born probably at Edgecomb 26 May 1779 (per Mount Vernon
VRs), died at Mount Vernon 26 July 1851, 72y (GS); married at
Rome ME 29 Oct. 1801 (int. Aug. 1799) HANNAH PEARL, born
probably at Edgecomb 3 June 1783 (Mt. Vernon VRs), died at
Mt. Vernon 11 Nov. 1866, 83y 5m (GS), daughter of Simeon and
Mary[5] (Leighton) Pearl [# 36].
    Burials are in Bean Cemetery. In 1850 his household
included his wife and his sons Lemuel and Delano.

Children, born at Mt. Vernon (TRs 2:318):

    i.   LEMUEL[7], b. 1 Mar. 1803, d. 1 Mar. 1871, 68y
           (GS); m. 12 Feb. 1856 widow MELINDA YOUNG,
           b. c1809, d. Belgrade 13 Apr. 1875 (GS). A
           Granville Leighton, son of Lemuel, d. Mt.
           Vernon 18 Sep. 1867, 24y. Burials are in Old
           Yard Cemetery. In 1870 Lemuel res. Belgrade,
           67, with Belinda, 61.
359. ii.   JOHN SMITHSON, b. 8 Feb. 1805.
360. iii. JOSEPH, b. 30 Aug. 1806.
361. iv. SIMEON, b. 23 May 1809.
     v.   WILLIAM, b. 14 Aug. 1811, d. Mt. Vernon 13
           Oct. 1826.
     vi.   RUTH, b. 1 Aug., d. 8 Sept., 1814.
362. vii. BENJAMIN R., b. 18 July 1815.
363. viii. THOMAS, b. 8 Apr. 1818.
     ix.   JAMES HARVEY, b. 16 July 1821, d. 28 May 1823.
364. x.   DELANO, b. 16 July 1824.
     xi.   SARAH JANE, b. 8 May 1828; m. her cousin WARNER
           R. LEIGHTON [# 357] and CHESMAN ROBINSON.

115. SAMUEL[6] 1779-1823 [39 Joel[5] and Elizabeth Huntress]
was born at Newington NH 28 Mar. 1779, died at Exeter NH 21
Oct. 1823; married 17 Feb. 1808 MARY LANE, born at Hampton NH
13 July 1778, died at Exeter 22 Sept. 1860, daughter of
Daniel Ward and Mehitable (Fogg) Lane (Exeter VRs; Jacob
Chapman and James H. Fitts, Lane Genealogies [Exeter NH,
1891], 1:72-73; Phyllis O. Whitten, Samuel Fogg 1628-1692
[Washington DC, 1976], 1:322).

Children, born at Exeter:

    i.   SAMUEL[7], b. 2 Jan. 1809, d. 13 Feb. 1811.
    ii.   GEORGE ALBERT, b. 13 June 1809, d. Charles-
          town MA 8 Feb. 1855; m. there 8 May 1842 (VRs)
          PHOEBE ANN ANDREWS. No ch.
    iii. CHARLES WILLIAM BUTLER, b. 3 July 1812, d.
          2 Feb. 1857; unm.
365. iv. MARY LANE, b. 27 Mar. 1814; m. ORISON MELVIN.
366. v.   HARRIET PEARSON, b. 16 Aug. 1816; m. LEVI
          STEVENS.
     vi.   JOHN LANE, b. 10 Feb. 1818, d. Boston 21 Oct.
          1868 (VRs); m. Boston 2 May 1843 LOUISA
          THURSTON, b. in 1824, dau. of Stephen and Mary
          Thurston.
367. vii. JOEL A., b. 17 Feb. 1820.
    viii. THOMAS LANE, b. 3 June 1822, d. Lowell MA 2
          May 1894; m. Lowell 22 Aug. 1847 PHOEBE JANE
          ROWE, b. Laconia NH in 1821, d. Boston 19 Jan.
          1893, dau. of Jeremiah and Lydia Rowe. No ch.

116. TEMPERANCE PICKERING[6] 1780-   [39 Joel[5] and Eliza-
beth Huntress] was born at Newington 20 Apr. 1780, baptized 8
Oct. (NHGR, 5[1908]:78); married at Epping NH 19 July 1803
(4[1907]:90) MOSES RANDLETT [as Ranlet], born at Epping 27
Nov. 1781, died there 29 Nov. 1824, 43y, son of Daniel and
Mehitable (Langan) Randlett (Joseph M. Odiorne, A Rundlett-
Randlett Genealogy [Farmington ME, 1976], 121).

Children (**Randlett**), born at Epping:

i.   DANIEL, b. 9 Oct. 1804, d. 5 Nov. 1850; m. Exeter
     NH 18 Nov. 1827 SARAH G. SMITH, d. there 1 Nov.
     1877, 70y.
ii. MARY ANN, b. 17 Feb. 1807, d. 14 May 1860, 54y;
     m. Lowell MA 6 Dec. 1836 AMOS PAUL.
iii. THOMAS LEIGHTON, b. 12 Aug. 1809, d. in 1883; m.
     Newburyport MA 21 June 1831 MARGARET BARTLETT.
iv. CHARLES WILLIAM, b. 28 June 1819.

117.   THOMAS[6] 1781-1806 [39 Joel[5] and Elizabeth Huntress]
was born at Newington 23 Dec. 1781, baptized 20 Nov. 1785
(NHGR, 5[1908]:80), died at Palmyra ME 24 July 1806, 24y 7m;
married at Exeter NH 7 Mar. 1804 (VRs) ELIZABETH MITCHELL,
born about 1784, died at Palmyra 25 Dec. 1863, 79y 5m (GS).
He died insolvent, and administrator Ebenezer Nay, appointed
31 Mar. 1807, sold his property at vendue 15 June (KenCP).
   His widow married second Ebenezer Nay, born about 1780,
died at Palmyra 30 Oct. 1869, 88y 11m (GS). Burials are in
Warren Hill Cemetery, Palmyra. Palmyra was incorporated as a
town in 1807.

Children:

     i.   CHARLES W.[7], b. 8 Mar. 1804.
368. ii. ELIZABETH A., b. 24 July 1805; m. JOHN FOLSOM.

118.   WILLIAM[6] 1784-   [39 Joel[5] and Elizabeth Huntress]
was born at Newington 20 Sept. 1784, baptized 20 Nov. 1785
(NHGR, 5[1908]:80); married MARY STAPLES, born about 1786,
died 20 Sept. 1843, 57y (Cornman Ms).

Children:

     i.   MARY E.[7], b. 8 May 1815.
     iii. WILLIAM, b. 20 Sept. 1816.

119.   MARY SMITHSON[6] 1786-1845 [39 Joel[5] and Elizabeth
Huntress] was born at Newington 5 Sept. 1786, died 15 Mar.
1845; married JOHN SMITH, born 22 Sept. 1789 (Cornman Ms).
John was probably her step-brother.

Children (**Smith**):

i.   CATHERINE N., b. 10 Oct. 1810, d. 12 Dec. 1890; m.
     26 July 1830 ABEL WESTON.
ii. SOPHIA L., b. 7 Aug. 1815.

120.   ELIZABETH[6] 1788-1846 [39 Joel[5] and Elizabeth Hunt-
ress] was born at Newington 20 Sept. 1788, died 1 Mar. 1846;
married 4 Mar. 1813 INCREASE RANDLETT [as Rundlet], born at
Epping NH 2 Sept. 1788, died 27 July 1871, son of Joseph and
Priscilla (Wilson) Randlett (Odiorne, Rundlett/ Randlett,
125-6).
   Increase lived in VT, and then settled at Palmyra ME
where he was a farmer.

Children (**Randlett**):

i.   JOEL L., b. in VT 17 Jan. 1815, d. 5 Aug. 1872; m. 22
      Jan. 1847 MARY J. WALKER, b. in ME in 1819.
ii.   ELIZABETH ANN, b. 6 Oct. 1816; m. 17 June 1848
      JOHN E. BAILEY.
iii. MARY JANE, b. 6 Apr. 1818, d. in May 1880; m. 14
      Aug. 1844 B. W. WELLINGTON.
iv.   FANNY M., b. 11 Feb. 1820; m. OLIVER SAMUEL NAY,
      b. 30 Jan. 1812, d. 7 Sept. 1867, son of Ebenezer
      and Elizabeth (Mitchell) Nay [# 117].
v.   JOSEPH W., b. 1 Feb. 1822, d. 10 Mar. 1823.
vi.   CHARLES, b. in VT 9 Jan. 1823, d. 13 Sept. 1854.
vii. CATHERINE, b. 29 June 1825; m. STEPHEN A. ROBINSON.
viii. ABIGAIL, b. 2 May 1829, d. 17 June 1860.
ix.   AARON H., b. in ME 20 Sept. 1831; m. Detroit ME 28
      Sept. 1858 AMELIA A. HOLWAY, b. in 1837, dau. of
      Freeman and Julia Holway.

121. JOEL[6] 1790-1851 [39 Joel[5] and Elizabeth Huntress] was
born probably at Newington 15 Apr. 1790, died at Bloomfield
(Skowhegan) ME 25 Oct. 1857 (VRs); married there 25 Jan. 1824
BETSEY LABREE, born at Brentwood NH 15 Dec. 1799, died at
Skowhegan 12 July 1864, daughter of Peter Labree, third hus-
band of Joel Sr.'s second wife Betsey Haight (Bloomfield and
ME VRs; Coburn, Skowhegan, 2:659; Cornman Ms).
   In 1822 he settled at Bloomfield, buying lot 16; on 3 Mar.
1824 he bought from Bryce McClellan another 30 acres (KenCD,
14:125). He was assessor and surveyor of highways in 1829.
In 1850 he was listed as a farmer at Bloomfield, with his
wife and all his children but Maria.

Children, born at Bloomfield:

      i.   MARIA FRANCES[7], b. 30 Dec. 1824, d. 22 June
            1826.
369. ii.   ALBERT FRANCIS, b. 5 Feb. 1826.
      iii. TERESA ORNE, b. 12 Feb. 1828, d. 25 Sept. 1866;
            unm.
      iv.   ELLEN MARIA, b. 3 Mar. 1830, d. Skowhegan 29
            Dec. 1911, 81y 9m 21d; unm.
      v.   AUGUSTUS VINTON, b. 21 Jan. 1832, d. Skowhegan
            1 Jan. 1898, 65y 11m 13d; unm. He was an
            architect.
370. vi.   MARY ELIZABETH, b. 11 Aug. 1834; m. JAMES B.
            HUSSEY, who d. 30 Nov. 1911.
371. vii. EMILY JOSEPHINE, b. 7 Oct. 1836; m. HENRY M.
            FRANCIS.
      viii. EDWIN HATHAWAY, b 11 Mar. 1839, d. Skowhegan
            2 July 1869; m. 6 Sept. 1868 VIENNA A. BROWN.
            No ch.

122. **MEHITABLE FABYAN**[6] 1793-   [39 Joel[5] and Elizabeth
Huntress] was born at Newington 3 Dec. 1793, lived at Lowell
MA; married at Epping 10 Aug. 1815 (NHGR, 3[1906]:119) as his
first wife BENJAMIN M. SMITH of Wolfeboro NH (Benjamin F.
Parker, History of Wolfeborough N. H. [The Town, 1901], 393;
Cornman Ms).

Children (**Smith**):

i.   AARON, b. 26 Mar. 1816.
ii.   RUFUS.

123.   THOMAS[6] 1753-1782 [41 John[5] and Martha Allen] was
born at Barrington NH about 1753, died at Somersworth NH in
Oct. 1782 (probate records); married at Dover 23 Nov. 1775
(VRs, 174) MERCY HORNE, born perhaps at Berwick ME 14 Oct.
1758, daughter of William and Phoebe (Heard) Horne (Ralph
Peak, Heard Family [TMs, MHS, 1968], 1:122; Cornman Ms;
records of David Dunlap). He bought land of William Willey
of Somersworth 31 May 1779 (StrCD, 2:369).
    Mercy (as Mary Laton) married second at Somersworth NH int.
24 Apr. 1784 Richard Hoyt, born at West Amesbury MA 30 Mar.
1756, son of Timothy and Hannah Hoyt. He had married first
Mary Martin of Salisbury MA 9 Sept. 1779, who died 16 July
1783 (David W. Hoyt, A Genealogical History of the Hoyt,
Haight and Hight Families [Boston 1857, reprinted 1984], 69).
    Administration of Thomas's estate was granted to his widow
Mercy 12 Feb. 1783; it was inventoried at over 855 pounds.
William Horne was appointed guardian of the children, and the
widow was granted funds for support of her sons from the time
Thomas had died until they should reach age 7: William, from
5y 7m, John from 4y, and Edward from 1y 6m. Her dower rights
were defined 13 July 1785 (StrCP, 1:531; 2:52, 197, 511-3).
Richard and Mercy Hoit leased her dower third of Thomas's
land to her son William 16 May 1796.

Children, born probably at Somersworth:

372. i.   WILLIAM[7], b. 13 May 1776.
      ii.   JOHN, b. in 1778, nfr.
373. iii. EDWARD, b. 16 Apr. 1781.

124.   JEDEDIAH[6] 1756-1837 [41 John[5] and Martha Allen] was
born at Barrington NH 31 July 1756, died at Strafford 24 June
1837, 81y (Morning Star of 19 July, as Jerediah); married at
Strafford NH 20 Apr. 1784 REBECCA SWAIN, born 25 Mar. 1760,
died at Strafford 24 Dec. 1837, 77y (records of descendants
Kathleen Crousen, Alice Haubrich and Lena Waldron Leighton;
Cornman Ms). Burials are in the Leighton/Hill lot, Province
Road Cemetery, Bow Lake, Strafford.
    He served during the Revolution under Capt. John Drew, Col.
Enoch Poor's Rgt., from Nov. 1775 to Jan. 1776 at Cambridge,
and under Capt. Peter Drowne, Col. Stephen Peabody's Rgt., in
RI (NHSP, 15: 469, 481, 506).
    He put together large landholdings. On 15 June 1782 he
bought from Caleb Wakeman lot 10 in Rochester's third divi-
sion (StrCD, 4:225); part of lot 236, range 3 in Barrington
from Thomas Evans 2 Feb. 1786 (6:504); part of lot 235 from
Richard and John Swaine 14 Sept. 1789 (11:537); parts of lot
236 from Moses Canney 2 Mar. 1797 and from Isaac Waldron 29
Oct. 1798 (24:320; 28:463); more of lot 235 from Joshua Foss,
Jr., 29 Oct. 1798 (28:458); and land in the half-mile streak
from Isaiah Swaine 1 Jan. 1808 (56:263).
    The Barrington censuses of 1790 and 1800 listed him with
more children than he had--perhaps other relatives. His home
became Strafford after the town was organized in 1820.

He filed for a pension 22 Aug. 1832, aged 76, of Strafford
(#S 8840, NA-MSR). His will, written 24 Oct. 1833 and proved
19 July 1837, named his wife, his six living children, and
two grandchildren, the sons of John Allen. He named his son
James residual heir and executor, and left $10 to each of the
other children.

Children:

	i.	PATIENCE[7], b. Barnstead 9 Oct. 1785, d. 22 Apr. 1868, aged 83; unm., blind.
374.	ii.	RICHARD, b. Strafford 19 Feb. 1787.
375.	iii.	JOHN ALLEN, b. 6 Jan. 1789.
	iv.	MARTHA, b. 23 Mar. 1792, d. 22 Dec. 1797.
376.	v.	SALLY, b. Barnstead 1 Sept. 1794; m. JOHN HILL [# 125].
377.	vi.	JAMES, b. Barrington 5 Oct. 1796.
378.	vii.	HANNAH, b. Barrington 22 Nov. 1798; m. WILLIAM H. HILL [# 125].
	viii.	REBECCA, b. 28 July 1804, d. Strafford 20 Jan. 1885, 80y 5m 22d; unm., blind.
	ix.	FIDELIA, b. 17 Nov. 1808, d. Strafford 25 Jan. 1868, 59y.

125. LUCY[6] 1758-1841 [41 John[5] and Martha Allen] was born
at Barrington 4 Mar. 1758, died at Barnstead 17 June 1841;
married at Barrington 24 Feb. 1780 WILLIAM HILL, born there
24 Jan. 1758, died at Gilmanton NH 20 Sept. 1806, in a fall
from his horse, son of John Hill. He was an officer in the
Revolutionary War, and received a pension for his six years'
service (records of descendants Kathleen Crousen, Alice Haubrich and Lena Waldron Leighton).

Children (**Hill**), born at Barnstead:

i.   SALLY, b. 16 May 1781, d. Barnstead 15 Apr. 1837,
       56y 5m 16d; m. NATHANIEL TASKER, b. 9 Sept. 1764,
       d. 22 Mar. 1817, 53y 6m 14d.

ii.   JOHN, b. 11 May 1785, d. 14 Apr. 1845; m. SALLY[7]
       LEIGHTON [# 376].

iii.   SAMUEL, b. 17 Jan. 1787, d. Strafford 13 Mar. 1867;
       m. Greenland NH in 1812 HANNAH DOW, b. 22 Mar.
       1794, d. Strafford 16 June 1889, 95y 3m, dau. of
       Isaiah and Betsey (Burns) Dow (Robert P. Dow, The
       Book of Dow [Claremont NH, 1929], 183).

iv.   JOSEPH, d. Starksboro VT.

v.   BETSEY, d. Starksboro; m. LIONEL HILL.

vi.   WILLIAM L., b. 29 Mar. 1795; m. HANNAH[7] LEIGHTON
       [# 378].

126. JAMES[6] 1759-1837 [41 John[5] and Martha Allen] was born
at Barrington 8 May 1759, died at Farmington 25 Sept. 1837,
77y; married ABIGAIL HORNE, died at Farmington 27 Apr. 1853,
90y 2m. According to Ralph Peak (Heard Fam., 1:122), she was
born at Berwick ME 18 Feb. 1763, daughter of William and
Phoebe (Heard) Horne. (Family tradition gave her father's
name as Nathaniel.) Burials are in the old family cemetery
on James's farm, off Hornetown Road.

He inherited his father's Barrington homestead in 1778, and was listed there in 1790 with three children. He settled at Rochester, in the part incorporated in 1798 as Farmington, and was on the Rochester second parish tax list in 1795. He was at the first town meeting at Farmington 11 Mar. 1799.

On 30 Aug. 1795, as administrator for his father, he sold about 70 acres at Barrington to John Wingate (StrCD, 18:30). He purchased part of lot 115, Rochester's third division, from Tristram Horne 3 June 1796, and more land there from Thomas Pinkham 23 Jan. 1797 (37:222; 23:358). In 1800 he was listed at Farmington with six children. He took a mortgage on his Milton property from his son Thomas 20 Mar. 1816 (88:371). He bought part of lot 116, third division, from his brother Jedediah 27 July 1829, but sold it back to him 20 Mar. 1834 (140:501; 174:581). He was taxed on 190 acres in 1837; in 1838 his property was assessed to his son Tristram.

He built a substantial home (called his "mansion house" in his will), which has been restored--and its Leighton burial lot rehabilitated). Photos and descriptions are in the Boston Globe, 28 Apr. 1968, pages 72-73, and Yankee, Jan. 1980, pages 50-53.

James's will, made 31 Aug. 1820 and proved 27 Oct. 1837, named his wife and all his living children, and appointed Tristram as executor (StrCP 50:104; 53:123-8); an inventory was taken 5 Feb. 1838 (52:283). He gave his wife one-third; gave Tristram half of the 50 acres of Shannon land acquired in 1807, and Jedediah the other half; gave to William 25 acres bought from John Swain about 1812; gave to James the Farmington homestead; gave to Thomas 15 acres with house and mill at Milton; and gave the cows and movables to Patty Ham. He made three codicils--15 Nov. 1820, 30 Oct. 1834 and 26 Aug. 1836. In these he increased William's share in recognition of his marriage, and while forgiving Thomas a mortgage on the Milton property, gave him only a life interest, so the estate would go to Thomas's heirs.

Widow Abigail's portion was designated as 146 of the homestead's 170 acres (53:299-301). She was living with Tristram in 1850. Her will, made 5 Aug. 1851 and proved 3 May 1853, left her estate to Tristram, with minor gifts to Patty Ham, and to Nancy and Abigail Hussey (65:356; 68:17).

Record searches were assisted by descendant Lewis L. Knox.

Children, first four born at Barrington, others at
   Farmington (VRs):

379.   i.   THOMAS[7], b. 8 June 1784.
380.   ii.   MARTHA, b. 15 Feb. 1787; m. GEORGE HAM, JR.
381.   iii. TRISTRAM, b. 30 Nov. 1789.
382.   iv.   JEDEDIAH, b. 22 Oct. 1791.
       v.   WILLIAM, b. 31 May 1798, d. Farmington 31 Oct.
             1847, 54y 7m (GS); m. there int. 21 Feb.
             1830 ABIGAIL LEIGHTON of Somersworth. No
             ch. His will, made 31 Oct. and proved 7
             Dec. 1847, left $2.50 to his wife, and named
             Tristram as residual heir (StrCP, 50:344;
             62:229; 64:72-3).
       vi.   PHEBE, b. 28 Feb. 1801, d. 28 Feb. 1807.
       vii. JAMES A., b. 20 Jan. 1806, d. Farmington 20
             Jan. 1838, 31y 7m (GS); unm.
       viii. ANDREW, d.y.

127. ANN[6] 1747-1825 [42 Thomas[5] and Margaret Murray] was
born at Barrington NH 29 Jan. 1747, died at Steuben ME 13
Nov. 1825; married TRISTRAM PINKHAM, JR., born at Dover NH
about 1748, died at Steuben 13 Dec. 1825, son of Tristram and
Martha (Hayes) Pinkham (Sinnett, Pinkham Gen., 19; Katherine
F. Richmond, John Hayes of Dover, N. H. [Tyngsboro MA, 1936],
1:99; BHM, 8[1893]:236).
    Tristram was a signer of the Majabagaduce petition in 1763
(see #11). He built a tidemill at Long Cove, Steuben, and
served at Machias in Capt. Daniel Sullivan's Co. in Nov. 1780
(MSS, 12:428). On 28 Jan. 1826, his heirs joined in a quit-
claim deed, giving title to 79 acres on Pinkham's Bay to his
two youngest sons Richard and Thomas. Signing were William,
Benjamin, Margaret Clark, Susanna Royal, Sarah Sargent,
Susanna in right of her father Tristram, Jr., and four
Leightons in right of their mother Martha (WashCD, 16:411-3).

Children (**Pinkham**), born at Steuben:

i.   MARTHA, b. 5 Dec. 1769; m. GIDEON[7] LEIGHTON
        [# 383].
ii.   MARGARET, b. 4 May 1772; m. THOMAS CLARK.
iii.   SARAH, b. 25 May 1774; m. ANDREW SARGENT of Goulds-
        boro.
iv.   WILLIAM, b. 9 Oct. 1776; m. LUCY STROUT, b. Harr-
        ington 12 Oct. 1773, dau. of Solomon Strout.
v.   BENJAMIN, b. 27 May 1779, d. 15 Apr. 1874; m.
        RACHEL[6] LEIGHTON [# 167].
vi.   TRISTRAM, JR., b. 12 Sept. 1781, d. Steuben 26 Nov.
        1825; m. DOROTHY[7] [Dolly] LEIGHTON [# 168].
vii.   SUSANNA, b. 25 May 1783; m. JOHN ROYAL.
viii.   RICHARD, b. 9 Dec. 1788, d. 19 Dec. 1876; m. 23
        Nov. 1815 cousin ELIZABETH WEST, born 24 Sept.
        1792, d. 28 May 1873, 80y, dau. of Thomas and Eliza-
        beth[7] (Leighton) West [# 133].
ix.   THOMAS, b. 31 July 1791, d. 9 Feb. 1860; m. Steuben
        14 Dec. 1814 cousin MARGARET [Peggy] WEST, b. 30
        Oct. 1794, dau. of Thomas and Elizabeth[7] (Leighton)
        West [# 133].

128. ELIZABETH[6] 1750-   [42 Thomas[5] and Margaret Murray]
was born at Barrington 25 Aug. 1750, died at Steuben aged
over 98; married first ELEAZER DAVIS; married second RICHARD
PINKHAM, born at Dover NH, died at Steuben 28 Mar. 1815, son
of Tristram and Martha (Hayes) Pinkham (Sinnett, Pinkham
Gen., 19; Richmond, John Hayes, 1:99; Steuben VRs).
    Although James Milliken wrote that she and Eleazer Davis
had but one child Samuel, it seems probable that Elizabeth
was a Davis child also. Sinnett called her first husband
Ebenezer Ruel Davis.

Children (**Davis**), born at Steuben:

i.   SAMUEL; m. JANE WILLEY, b. Steuben in 1786, d. in
        1882, dau. of Ichabod and Elizabeth (Bumford)
        Willey.
ii.   ELIZABETH, b. c1776, d. 3 May 1865, 91y; m. 11 June
        1795 WILLIAM WILLEY, b. Cherryfield 25 May 1773,
        d. there 25 Apr. 1852, son of Ichabod and Elizabeth
        (Bumford) Willey.

Children (**Pinkham**), born at Steuben:

iii.   MERCY, b. 4 Sept. 1784; m. HENRY P. ALLINE.
iv.   ROBERT L., b. 15 Apr. 1787, d. 2 Nov. 1867; m.
      Cherryfield 31 Dec. 1821 LYDIA WILLEY, b. 10 Jan.
      1800, d. 7 July 1880, dau. of Ichabod and Sarah
      (Fernald) Willey.
v.   RICHARD, b. 5 Sept. 1790; m. Steuben int. 20 Jan.
      1835 PRISCILLA PINKHAM, b. there 1 Dec. 1808,
      dau. of William and Lucy (Strout) Pinkham.
vi.   JAMES, b. 18 Jan. 1793; m. Steuben int. 11 Aug.
      1822 HANNAH WALLACE, b. Cherryfield 26 Aug.
      1802, dau. of Robert and Mary Wallace.

129. SARAH[6] 1752-   [42 Thomas[5] and Margaret Murray] was
born at Barrington NH 5 June 1752, and lived at Steuben. She
presents a genealogical puzzle. According to James Milliken's Narraguagus Valley (p. 7) "Sarah m. ---- Leighton.
Ch. Eleazer and Gideon." Julia Cornman, on what basis is
unknown, wrote that Sarah married first ---- Leighton, and
second Thomas Stevens; she listed the two sons, and then
stated that they "took name Leighton & have descendants in
Milbridge & Steuben" (Cornman Ms).
No male Leighton appears as a potential husband, and no
trace of Thomas Stevens is found in or near Steuben. The
sons may have been illegitimate, and used the mother's name,
or perhaps were born Stevens, and "took" the Leighton name.

Children (**Leighton**):

383. i.   GIDEON[7], b. say 1770.
384. ii.   ELEAZER, b. say 1780.

130. JOSEPH[6] 1755-1832 [42 Thomas[5] and Margaret Murray]
was born at Barrington NH 1 Apr. 1755 (VRs), or at Madbury 3
Apr. 1754 (pension application), died at Cherryfield in 1832
(GS) or in 1833 (pension file); married about 1779 BETSEY
JORDAN, born about 1759, daughter of Ebenezer and Rebecca
(Brown) Jordan. He lived at Steuben as a child with his
father, and later at Cherryfield (records of Joanna Willey;
Steuben and Cherryfield VRs).
Joseph enlisted in May 1775 under Capt. Reuben Dyer, Col.
Allen's Rgt., and then re-enlisted for a two-year term, serv-
ing at Machias. He was in the same company from 26 May to 23
July 1777 on an expedition against Saint John NB (MSS,
9:413). With his brother Robert, he returned to NH to enlist
in July 1779, as from Madbury, under Capt. Samuel Runnels,
Col. Hercules Mooney's Rgt., for 6 months in RI; he was discharged 15 Jan. 1780 (NHSP, 15:655-6, 684-5; 16:730-1).
In 1790, he was at Steuben with two children, and in 1800
at Cherryfield with eight children. He received a deed 2
Apr. 1794 to lot #50 for his settler's right, but on 6 Apr.
(with wife "Rachel" waiving her dower right) sold this lot on
the western side of Pigeon Hill Bay to his brother James
(WashCD, 3:516-7).
He applied 11 Aug. 1832, aged 78, and 8 Jan. 1833, aged 80,
for a military pension, which he received about the time of
his death (NA-MSR #S 18072).

Children, born at Steuben and Cherryfield:

385. i.   REBECCA[7], b. c1780; m. ELISHA STROUT.
386. ii.   LUCY HOPE, b. Cherryfield 18 Nov. 1793; m.
            AARON LAWRENCE.
387. iii. JOSEPH, b. c1794.
      iv.   ROBERT, b. c1796 (51 in 1850, 64 in 1860), d.
            Cherryfield 31 May 1873; m. there 26 Oct. 1821
            ELIZABETH [Betsey] WILLEY, b. 9 May 1799, d. 9
            Jan. 1875, dau. of William and Elizabeth
            (Davis) Willey [# 127]. No ch.
            DANIEL, 13 [# 879], was listed in their
            household in 1870.
388. v.   RACHEL, b. Cherryfield 20 Oct. 1797; m.
            ORRIN WILLEY.
389. vi.   EBENEZER JORDAN, b. Cherryfield 7 Aug. 1801.
      vii. ELIZABETH, b. say 1805; m. JACOB[7] LEIGHTON
            [# 403].

131. ROBERT[6] 1758-1834 [42 Thomas[5] and Margaret Murray]
was born at Barrington NH 28 Jan. 1758 (VRs) or at Madbury 12
Jan. 1757 (pension application), died at Falmouth ME 16 Nov.
1834; married first at Falmouth 27 Nov. 1781 (Cumb. Co. mar.
record) his cousin HANNAH[6] LEIGHTON, born at Falmouth 10 Jan.
1761, died there 9 Dec. 1813, 53y, daughter of Joseph and
Mercy (Hall) Leighton [# 46] (Hall Desc., #45); married second at Falmouth 2 May 1814 ELIZABETH (FIELD) Cole, daughter
of Zachary and Hannah (Knight) Field and widow of Ebenezer
Cole (Falmouth TRs; Charles S. Tibbetts, Descendants of John
and Richard Knight of Newbury [TMs, 1941, MHS], 97).
    During the Revolutionary War Robert served from No. 4
(Steuben), but enrolled as of Falmouth ME, under Capt. Reuben
Dyer, Maj. Gen. Frank Shaw's Rgt., from 26 May to 23 July
1775 on an expedition against Saint John NB (MSS, 9:413). In
Sept. 1778, he signed as a seaman on the Ranger at Portsmouth
under Capt. Simpson; was aboard when it took eleven ships as
prizes off Halifax, in the West Indies and in the English
Channel; and was discharged in May 1779 (pension declara-
tion). With his brother Joseph, he next enrolled as from
Madbury NH under Capt. Samuel Runnels, Col. Hercules Mooney's
Rgt., 12 July 1779 to 15 Jan. 1780 for service on a campaign
to RI (NHSP, 15:655, 684-5).
    Like his uncles George and Joseph he settled at Falmouth.
In 1790 Robert Laten's household there included four children, and six in 1800. He applied for a pension 11 Aug.
1832, aged 75, outlining in detail his 14 months' service
(#S-16917 NA-MSR).

Children, all by Hannah, born at Falmouth:

390. i.   THOMAS[7], b. 30 Oct. 1783.
391. ii.   SUSANNAH, b. 25 May 1785; m. ROBERT HALL and
            JOHN PRINCE.
392. iii. DANIEL, b. 10 June 1787.
      iv.   MARCY, b. 23 Apr. 1789; m. Falmouth 28 Mar.
            1820 DAVID DUTTON. Ch. Hannah.
393. v.   ROBERT, b. 10 Dec. 1791.
394. vi.   SARAH, b. 17 Sept. 1797; m. JOHN WEST.

132. ABIGAIL[6] [Nabby] 1760-   [42 Thomas[5] and Margaret
Murray] was born at Steuben ME 2 May 1760; perhaps married
first JAMES TRACY; married 23 Feb. 1781 EBENEZER SMALL, son
of John and Priscilla (Strout) Small.   Ebenezer and Nabby
lived at Cherryfield (No. 11) in 1790 with three children,
later were at Lubec, but returned to Cherryfield (Underhill,
Small Desc., 1:177; records of Leonard F. Tibbetts; Downeast
Ancestry, 10[1986]:130).

Children (**Small**), born at Cherryfield, order uncertain:

i.   DEBORAH; m. JAMES COLSON, b. Steuben in 1785, d.
       Steuben 22 Dec. 1860, 75y, son of Samuel and Susan
       (Willey) Colson.
ii.   SAMUEL, res. Lubec; m. MOLLY COLSON, sister of
       James.
iii.   ABIGAIL [Nabby]; m. SAMUEL TUTTLE, b. Lynn MA 20
       Sept. 1779, d. Perry ME 27 Aug. 1858, son of Samuel
       Tuttle (Alva M. Tuttle, Tuttle - Tuthill Lines
       [Columbus OH, 1968], 501).
iv.   MARGARET [Peggy], b. c1788 (62 in 1850), d. Cutler in
       1859 (GS); m. Lubec TIMOTHY LIBBY CATES, b. c1785,
       d. Cutler 12 Feb. 1839, 54y (GS), son of Robert and
       Mary (Holmes) Cates.
v.   THOMAS, b. 3 Apr. 1791, res. Columbia; m. DEBORAH
       TUCKER, b. there 27 Feb. 1790, dau. of Samuel and
       Esther[6] (Leighton) Tucker [# 147].
vi.   JOHN, b. 18 Apr. 1793, res. Lubec and Bucksport;
       m. LYDIA[6] LEIGHTON [# 34].
vii.   LYDIA, b. 20 July 1795; m. JAMES GROSS of Perry.
viii. EBENEZER, b. 23 Oct. 1797; m. Bucksport EUNICE
       HARRIMAN.
ix.   SALLY, b. 7 Nov. 1799; m. 1st Machias 20 Oct. 1818
       JAMES CATES, d. prob. Cutler about 1829, son of
       Robert and Mary (Holmes) Cates; m. 2nd FREDERICK
       RANDALL, who d. Cutler 9 Apr. 1856.
x.   ANNA, b. 15 May 1801; m. int. 17 Nov. 1829 JAMES[7]
       LEIGHTON [# 407].
xi.   DOCTOR HANDY, b. 29 May 1803.

133. MARY[6] [Molly] 1762-1855 [42 Thomas[5] and Margaret
Murray] was born at Steuben 16 Jan. 1762, died there in Oct.
1855; married THOMAS WEST, born in 1754, died at Steuben 28
Nov. 1842.
He was a lieutenant in the Continental Army (Cornman Ms);
in 1790 he was listed at Steuben alone.

Children (**West**), born at Steuben (VRs):

i   ELIZABETH, b. 24 Sept. 1792, d. 28 May 1873; m. 25
       Nov. 1815 RICHARD PINKHAM [# 127].
ii   MARGARET, b. 30 Oct. 1794; m. THOMAS PINKHAM
       [# 127].
iii.   JOHN, b. 15 Feb. 1796, d. Falmouth ME 5 May 1877;
       m. SARAH[7] LEIGHTON [# 394].
iv.   DANIEL, b. 22 May 1798, d. 21 Feb. 1888; m. Steuben
       18 Dec. 1833 NANCY ANN WALLACE, b. Cherryfield 12
       Dec. 1805, d. Steuben 12 July 1878, dau. of Robert
       and Mary Wallace.

v.   ELLIS [?Alice], b. 30 Nov. 1801, d. 11 June 1805.
vi.   ISAAC, b. 29 Aug. 1804, d. 28 Jan. 1898; m. Mil-
      bridge 16 Dec. 1837 NANCY PINKHAM, b. 7 Aug. 1821.
vii. GEORGE WASHINGTON, b. 6 Sept. 1807; m. 5 Sept. 1834
      RHODA ANDERSON, b. 7 July 1815.

134. THOMAS[6] 1765-1853 [42 Thomas[5] and Margaret Murray]
was born at Steuben 18 Jun 1765, died at Milbridge 13 Mar.
1853 (GS); married at Harrington PATIENCE WALLACE, born at
Harrington in 1764, died at Milbridge 24 Dec. 1848, daughter
of Benjamin and Hannah (Penniman) Wallace (Harrington and
Steuben VRs, Cornman Ms).
His farm on the east side of the Narraguagus River was in
the part of Harrington set off to Milbridge in 1848. He was
listed at Harrington in 1790 with his wife and a son under
16. In 1850, at 88, he had James and his family in his
household.

Children, born at Harrington:

395. i.   BENJAMIN[7], b. 4 Jan. 1794.
396. ii.   LUCY, b. 11 Apr. 1796; m. LOUIS J. WALLACE.
397. iii. JAMES, b. 11 Sept. 1798.
398. iv.   ROBERT, b. say 1800.
399. v.   JOANNA, b. in 1802; m. HENRY BRAY and DAVID
            STROUT.
400. vi.   OTIS, b. 16 Apr. 1803.
401. vii. PATIENCE, b. 5 July 1805; m. AMOS GAY and
            WILLIAM WALLACE.
      viii. ABIGAIL, b. in 1807, d. Harrington 24 May
            1844, 37y; unm.

135. ROSS[6] [Robert] 1766-1860 [42 Thomas[5] and Margaret
Murray] was born at Steuben 14 Nov. 1766, died at Cherryfield
in 1860; married there 10 Dec. 1791 MARY CHANDLER. He was
called Robert or Bob.
On 5 Feb. 1834 he deeded his 94-acre homestead to Ross,
Jr., in return for his bond to maintain his parents for life
(WashCD, 27:78-9).
His obituary in the Machias Union 10 Apr. 1860 stated that
he was at 94 the oldest inhabitant of Cherryfield.

Children, born at Cherryfield (VRs):

      i.   ELIZABETH[6], b. 19 Sept. 1792, d. 1 Apr. 1797.
402. ii.   JOHN, b. 3 Apr. 1794.
403. iii. JACOB, b. 10 Dec. 1795.
404. iv.   SAMUEL, b. 21 Dec. 1797.
405. v.   DANIEL, b. 7 June 1800.
      vi.   DAVID, b. 9 June 1802.
406. vii. WILLIAM, b. 25 June 1803.
407. viii. JAMES, b. 7 Oct. 1805.
408. ix.   AARON, b. 9 Mar. 1808.
      x.   ROSS, b. 9 Mar. 1810; m. Gouldsboro 26 Mar.
            1843 (VRs) ALMIRA CARPENTER of Penobscot. He
            prob. had no ch.; in 1850 Almira was living at
            Penobscot in the household of Wilson and Lucy
            Carpenter.

136. JAMES⁶ 1769-   [42 Thomas⁵ and Margaret Murray] was
born at Steuben 20 Mar. 1769, lived at Harrington; married
MARY [Kitty] BROWN, daughter of David and Sarah (Jordan)
Brown (BHM, 9[1894]:207).
He was a farmer. James's family was not documented in the
town records. In 1810 he and Kitty had five children at Harrington, in 1820 seven, and in 1830 eight; he was not listed
in 1840.
Dorothy Phelan Parker (Steuben, Maine, Families [TMs, 1964,
MHS]) listed ten possible children, but her data must be
regarded with great caution.

Children:

	i.	BETSEY⁷, b. Steuben 21 May 1800, d. Milbridge 28 Jan. 1883; m. Harrington 28 July 1826 DANIEL LOVETT, b. in England, son of Isaac and Annie (Sawyer) Lovett. No ch. He m. 2nd Steuben int. 10 Dec. 1840 Delia Corson.
	ii.	?MARGARET; perhaps m. Harrington int. 27 Dec. 1824 JOHN L. SMITH.
409.	iii.	DAVID BROWN, b. 11 Aug. 1805.
410.	iv.	JAMES, b. say 1810.
411.	v.	?JOANN; m. JOEL G. CURTIS.
412.	vi.	LOUISE, b. in 1819; m. JAMES BROWN.
	vii.	MARY; m. Harrington int. 21 Dec. 1835 PATRICK FICKETT, son of James and Mary (Howell) Fick- ett. Ch. Frank b. Milbridge in 1836, d. there 29 Nov. 1901; m. Caroline B. Strout: no ch. Patrick m. 2nd 18 Feb. 1848 Frances Woods.
	viii.	?LUCRETIA; m. JESSE BROWN.
413.	ix.	HANNAH S., b. say 1828; m. GIDEON THOMPSON and ISAAC FINNEMORE.
	x.	?JESSE.

137. BENJAMIN F.⁶ 1773-1868 [42 Thomas⁵ and Margaret Mur-
ray] was born at Steuben 4 Feb. 1773, died there 15 Sept.
1868, 95y; married BETSEY STROUT of Cherryfield, born at
Steuben say 1780, daughter of David Strout (Steuben VRs;
Cornman Ms).
He bought his father's land at Steuben 26 Sept. 1805
(WashCD, 4:222-3). In 1850, Benjamin, 78, farmer, and Bet-
sey, 60, were listed at Steuben, next door to his brother
Thomas.

Children, born at Steuben:

414.	i.	ROBERT⁷, b. 23 Oct. 1800.
415.	ii.	MARY STROUT [Polly], b. 7 Sept. 1802; m. WILLIAM PINKHAM.
416.	iii.	PERSIS, b. 14 Nov. 1804; m. NATHAN HINCKLEY.
417.	iv.	ALICE W., b. 29 Oct. 1806; m. LEVI CORTHELL.
418.	v.	JOSHUA M., b. 10 June 1808.
419.	vi.	JAMES P., b. 18 Apr. 1813.
420.	vii.	THOMAS, b. 3 Sept. 1814.
	viii.	EDWARD, b. 2 Apr. 1820, d. Milbridge 22 Feb. 1897, 78y 9m 21d (VRs); m. Steuben 24 Sept. 1885 (Machias Union) EUNICE D. (MITCHELL) Ray, b. Milbridge 25 Nov. 1841, d. there 17 June 1912, 70y 6m 22d (VRs), dau. of Samuel and

Thankful (Pinkham) Mitchell and widow of
William Ray. No ch. He served in Co. K, 2nd
ME Cavalry Rgt., and then in the US Navy from
1863 to 1865; he was a pensioner.

138. **PELATIAH**[6] 1753-1817 [43 George[5] and Dorothy Hall] was
born at Falmouth ME about 1753, died there 18 Feb. 1817 (aged
64 per GS, Universalist Churchyard, West Cumberland); married
at Falmouth 17 Nov. 1774 (Cumberland Co. record) ELIZABETH
[Betsey] ALLEN, who died at Falmouth 2 July 1826, perhaps
daughter of Jacob and Hannah (Tibbetts) Allen (Hall Desc.,
#14; Falmouth TRs). He was "Peltiah Laten" in the 1790 cen-
sus, listed with seven children. A Quaker, he did not serve
in the Revolutionary War.
    Pelatiah sold to his sons John of North Yarmouth and Thomas
12 Nov. 1798 lots at North Yarmouth (CumbCD, 29:10-11). In
July 1806 he sold to his son Chesley 21 acres at Falmouth
(50:363), and 12 acres there to son Robert of North Yarmouth
29 Sept. 1814 (76:414). On 30 Jan. 1817 he sold to his son
Ezekiel land adjoining the road to North Yarmouth, and the
same day sold to his father George "all my homested" of 40
acres adjoining Robert's land (75:354).

Children, born at Falmouth:

421. i.   JOHN[7], b. 4 June 1775.
422. ii.   THOMAS, b. 14 Feb. 1777.
423. iii. ROBERT, b. 20 June 1779.
424. iv.   CHESLEY, b. in 1781.
425. v.   DORCAS, b. in 1783; m. GEORGE JOHNSON.
426. vi.   CHARLOTTE, b. in 1785; m. JAMES M. LINCOLN.
427. vii. GEORGE, b. 11 Oct. 1787.
428. viii. DOROTHY, b. c1790; m. JOB SHAW.
429. ix.   EZEKIEL, b. 9 May 1794.

139. **JEDEDIAH**[6] 1757-1851 [43 George[5] and Dorothy Hall] was
born at Falmouth about 1757, died there 11 Oct. 1851, 94y 9m
3d (GS; obituary, Morning Star of 7 Jan. 1852, as Jeremiah;
Hall Desc., #15); married first at Falmouth 17 Apr. 1777
EUNICE GERRISH, born at Dover NH 3 Oct. 1755 (VRs 49), died
at Falmouth 1 Oct. 1821 (65y, GS), daughter of Jonathan and
Eunice (Tobey) Gerrish (Orville K. Gerrish, Genealogical
Record of the Gerrish Family [Portland, 1880]); married second at Falmouth 27 Feb. 1823 MARY (MARSTON) Noyes, born in
1781, died at Falmouth 17 Apr. 1866 (83y 8m, GS, Methodist
Cemetery, West Falmouth; obituary, Morning Star of 2 May),
daughter of Benjamin and Ruth (Sawyer) Marston (Nathan W.
Marston, Marston Genealogy [So. Lubec Me., 1888], 208) and
widow of Peter Noyes (Falmouth TRs; Cornman Ms).
    In 1790, Jedediah Laten's household at Falmouth included
his wife and ten others. He purchased land from the Falmouth
proprietors 31 Dec. 1810 (CumbCD, 3:105), as well as other
land earlier. He served as captain in the 3rd Rgt. in 1814,
and was usually called Capt. Leighton.
    When his youngest child was born, he was 70. In 1850, at
93, he was living with his son Jonathan. He and Eunice--and
others of his family--are buried in the private lot off Hardy
Road where his parents rest. In 1860, his widow Mary was
living with her stepson George.

Children by Eunice, born at Falmouth:

    i.   JONATHAN^7, d.y.
430. ii.   NATHANIEL C., b. 21 July 1779.
431. iii. MARY, b. say 1781; m. NATHANIEL HALE.
432. v.   LOIS, b. 17 Sept. 1784; m. CYRUS WILSON.
433. vi.   PETER, b. 18 Feb. 1785.
434. vii. GEORGE, b. 20 Sept. 1789.
435. viii. JOSIAH L., b. 14 Apr. 1792.
436. iv.   EUNICE, b. say 1794; m. JOSIAH GERRISH.

Children by Mary, born at Falmouth:

437. ix.   JONATHAN, b. c1823.
438. x.   ADELINE, b. 17 Dec. 1824; m. JOSEPH$_8$KEEN.
     xi.   LUCY G., b. 29 June 1827; m. ROBERT^8 LEIGHTON
           [# 889].

140. SARAH^6 1758-   [43 George^5 and Dorothy Hall] was
born at Falmouth in 1758, died at Westbrook ME 10 Oct. 1823
(1833?); married in 1777 JOHN WEBB, JR., born 19 May 1754,
died at Westbrook 8 July 1846, son of John Webb (Cornman Ms;
Hall Desc., #16; Falmouth and Westbrook VRs).
   In 1790 he was listed at Falmouth with one male under 16
and seven females. Part of Falmouth was incorporated as
Stroudwater, and then as Westbrook in 1814.

Children (**Webb**), born at Falmouth (now Westbrook):

i.   DOROTHY, b. say 1780; m. Westbrook 8 Nov. 1804
       ANDREW HUNNEWELL.
ii.   ELIZABETH, b. 3 Sept. 1782, d. Westbrook 24 Sept.
       1864; m. 10 June 1806 BRACKETT SAWYER, b. 4 Mar.
       1775, d. Westbrook 21 Apr. 1857, son of Zachary and
       Sarah (Knight) Sawyer.
iii.   ABIGAIL, b. 29 Mar. 1785; m. 16 Dec. 1802 JOHN LORD,
       b. in 1774, d. Falmouth 25 Sept. 1856, son of Natha-
       niel and Mehitable (Jones) Lord.
iv.   SETH, prob. res. in MI; m. POLLY BUZZELL.
v.   LUCY, b. 17 Nov. 1787; m. Kittery ME 20 Apr. 1807
       JAMES LORD, b. 14 Dec. 1781, d. Falmouth 8 Apr.
       1862, son of Simon and Sarah (Gowen) Lord.
vi.   EUNICE, b. 13 Aug. 1789, d. Pownal ME 29 Dec. 1867;
       m. Falmouth (Westbrook) 1 Nov. 1809 WILLIAM TOBEY.
vii.   BETHANA, b. 20 Jan. 1792; m. 1st Falmouth 29 Apr.
       1812 BENJAMIN KNIGHT, lost at sea in 1835, son of
       Joseph Knight; m. 2nd Westbrook CHARLES JAMESON, b.
       31 Jan. 1804, d. 23 Apr. 1858, son of Henry and
       Sarah (Cleaves) Jameson.
viii. PHOEBE, b. 16 June 1794, d. 29 Apr. 1881; m. Scar-
       borough ME 24 Nov. 1814 SIMON LIBBY, b. there 2 Feb.
       1795, d. Richmond ME 5 Aug. 1843, son of Joshua and
       Ruth (Libby) Libby (Libby Fam., 192).
ix.   RUTH, b. 20 Jan. 1795; m. CHARLES JAMESON (see vii.
       above).
x.   MARY, b. 1 Apr. 1801, d. 1 Nov. 1837; m. 1st 5 Nov.
       1818 DAVID BEVERLY, d. in 1818; m. 2nd EBENEZER
       HODGKINS, b. Minot ME 27 Mar. 1800, d. 17 May 1865.

141. HATEVIL[6] 1760-1806 [43 George and Dorothy Hall] was born at Falmouth 24 July 1760, died there 9 July 1806; married at Falmouth 22 Mar. (Cumberland Co. record; Topsham int. 13 Jan.) 1781 LUCY STAPLES, born at Falmouth 3 Nov. 1760, died at Westbrook 10 Dec. 1838, 78y 1m (GS; Hall Desc., #17, Falmouth VRs; Cornman Ms). Both are buried in Pride's Corner Cemetery, Westbrook.

He sold 11 Aug. 1791 to Luke Wooster "land which I purchased of my father George Leighton 4 Dec. 1789" (CumbCD, 20:352). On 2 Apr. 1806 he sold to his son Isaac 64 acres north of the Presumpscot together with buildings, noting that property too had belonged to his father (48:466).

Lucy married second at Westbrook 16 Apr. 1815 James Gowen, born at Kittery 18 Feb. 1753-4, died at Westbrook 26 July 1822, son of Willliam and Mary (Davis) (Chick) Gowen.

Children, born at Falmouth:

439.	i.	EBENEZER[7], b. 14 July 1781.
440.	ii.	ISAAC, b. 19 Aug. 1783.
441.	iii.	DANIEL, b. 3 May 1785.
442.	iv.	ICHABOD, b. 25 Oct. 1787.
443.	v.	SILAS, b. 20 June 1791.

142. ABIGAIL[6] 1762-1811 [43 George[5] and Dorothy Hall] was born at Falmouth 4 June 1762, died there 21 July 1811; married there 15 July 1779 (Cumberland Co. record) JAMES HICKS, born at Falmouth 18 Apr. 1759, died at Falmouth 24 Dec. 1834, son of Lemuel and Martha (Cox) Hicks (Hall Desc., #18; Susan E. Hicks, Ancestry of John A. Hicks of Auburn [TMs, 1952, MHS], 7; Falmouth TRs).

James served in Capt. Joseph Pride's militia detachment in Oct. 1779 (MSS, 7:823-4). In 1790 he was listed at Falmouth with two males under 16 and four females. He married second LYDIA[6] LEIGHTON [# 46]; they had no children.

Children (**Hicks**), born at Falmouth:

i. GEORGE, b. 19 Feb. 1780, d. 21 Sept. 1879; m. 13 May
    1803 HANNAH ALLEN, b. 24 Nov. 1785, d. 27 Nov. 1857,
    dau. of Jacob and Hannah (Tripp) Allen.
ii. DOROTHY, b. 18 June 1781, d. Gray ME in 1819; m.
    EVARDUS KING, b. in England, d. 25 Oct. 1878. He m.
    2nd Eleanor Pennell (Florence H. L. Nelson, (Gray,
    Maine, Families [TMs, nd, MHS], 16).
iii. SAMUEL, b. 8 July 1783, d. Danville 30 Nov. 1856; m.
    1st Falmouth 1 Oct. 1807 ABIGAIL WINSLOW, b. 8 Jan.
    1787, d. 22 Feb. 1834, dau. of Hezekiah and Phoebe
    (Doughty) Winslow; m. 2nd 21 Oct. 1834 NANCY R.
    (ANDERSON) Murray, d. 12 Feb. 1854; m. 3rd in 1854
    JANE BARTLETT, who d. in Nov. 1855, 53y.
iv. SARAH, b. 15 Jan. 1785, d. 21 Sept. 1853; m. 5 Mar.
    1806 LEVI WILSON, b. 28 Dec. 1783, d. 11 Aug. 1864,
    son of Ichabod and Ruth (Huston) Wilson.
v. ESTHER, b. 18 Dec. 1786, d. 22 Mar. 1787.
vi. ESTHER, b. 15 Jan. 1789, d. 6 Feb. 1801.
vii. EUNICE, b. 2 May 1791, d. Cumberland ME 13 Dec. 1847;
    m. 6 Feb. 1811 EPHRAIM MORRISON, b. 6 Sept. 1791,
    son of Jonathan and Sarah (Harford) Morrison. He m.
    2nd Cumberland 22 Feb. 1849 ELIZA (LIBBY) LEIGHTON,

      widow of Daniel[7] [# 506]. Ephraim donated land for
      the Universalist Church and cemetery on Morrison's
      Hill, West Cumberland.
viii. HANNAH, b. 9 Apr. 1793, d. 30 Sept. 1824; m. EDWARD
      GILMAN[7] LEIGHTON [# 449].
ix.   MARTHA, b. 29 Dec. 1794, d. 12 Nov. 1797.
x.   ELIZABETH, b. 1 Nov. 1796, d. 19 July 1839; m. 23
      Jan. 1823 ISAAC WINSLOW, b. 28 Mar. 1794, son of
      Thomas and Elizabeth (Swett) Winslow.
xi.   CYRUS, b. 21 Feb. 1798, d. Falmouth 14 Nov. 1876; m.
      1 Mar. 1822 HANNAH HADLOCK, b. Cumberland 5 Mar.
      1802, d. 2 June 1880, dau. of William and Sarah[6]
      (Leighton) Hadlock [# 162].
xii. MARTHA, b. 3 Jan. 1800, d. 22 May 1814.
xiii. MARY, b. 30 Mar. 1802, res. Albany and Greenwood ME;
      m. in Sept. 1842 MOSES HUMPHREY YOUNG, b. 22 Mar.
      1809, son of Joshua and Mary (Tenney) Young.
xiv. SUSAN, b. 2 Mar. 1804, d. in July 1871; m. JOHN WAKE-
      FIELD. No ch.
xv.   ANDREW, b. 10 Jan. 1807; m. 30 Sept. 1830 SARAH
      HICKS. They removed to Pittsfield ME in 1871.

    143. DAVID[6] 1767-1825 [43 George[5] and Dorothy Hall] was
born at Falmouth 18 Dec. 1767, died there 10 Dec. 1825; married there 20 Sept. 1791 LUCY BAKER, born 5 Feb. 1767, died
at Falmouth 15 Apr. 1837, daughter of Josiah and Susanna
(Gibbs) Baker (Hall Desc., #19; Falmouth VRs; Cornman Ms; his
obituary, Christian Mirror of 27 Jan. 1826). Both are buried
in the Brook Street Cemetery.
    David and Lucy quitclaimed 18 July 1809 her rights to land
at Poland belonging to her late grandfather William Gibbs
(CumbCD, 84:213). David sold land in Falmouth east of his
father's homestead to his sons Levi and Thaddeus 25 Aug.
1817, but re-purchased it 23 Nov. 1820 (77:287; 95:326). On
30 Apr. 1825, he sold to his sons Ephraim and Levi land
adjoining that of his brother Silas (104:104-5).

    Children, born at Falmouth:

444. i.   JUDITH[7], b. 28 Mar. 1792; m. WILLIAM ELDER.
445. ii.   LEVI, b. 23 June 1793.
446. iii. THADDEUS, b. 14 Nov. 1794.
      iv.   URSULA, b. 24 Dec. 1796, d. Falmouth 8 Mar.
            1879 (TRs; GS, 82y); unm. She lived with her
            sister Thankful Cobb.
447. v.   EPHRAIM, b. 14 June 1798.
448. vi.   THANKFUL H., b. 31 Aug. 1800; m. JAMES COBB.

    144. PAUL[6] 1770-1847 [43 George[5] and Dorothy Hall] was
born at Falmouth 3 May 1770, died there 4 July 1847; married
first at Standish ME (VRs) 13 Sept. 1792 PHOEBE GILMAN, born
there 1 Feb. 1763, died at Falmouth 7 Nov. 1816 (48y, obituary, Eastern Argus of 13 Nov.), daughter of Edward Gilman and
his first wife; married second at Falmouth 28 July 1821 widow
URSULA (BAKER) Claridge, born say 1780, died at Falmouth 8
Mar. 1879, daughter of Josiah and Susannah (Gibbs) Baker
(Hall Desc., #20; Cornman Ms; Falmouth TRs; records of
descendant Mae Federhen). Ursula had married first 15 Dec.
1791 William Claridge.

Paul, Phebe and others quitclaimed 25 Jan. 1804 their rights to land inherited from "our honored grandfather Edward Gilman" (CumbCD, 45:415-6). Ursula Claridge had like her sister Lucy quitclaimed her rights in the William Gibbs estate on 28 July 1809 (84:213). On 8 Nov. 1817 Paul sold to his son Edward a lot of 70 acres at Falmouth with its buildings (78:499).

Children, all by Phebe, born at Falmouth:

449. i.   EDWARD GILMAN[7], b. 31 July 1793.
      ii.   JAMES, b. 26 July 1795, d. 5 Sept. 1804.
      iii. NATHAN, b. 23 Sept. 1797, d. 29 Aug. 1799.
      iv.   JOEL, b. 10 Aug., d. 27 Oct. 1799.
450. v.   TIMOTHY, b. 28 Nov. 1800.
      vi.   NATHAN, b. 30 Apr. 1804, res. Falmouth in Isaac Winslow's household in 1850, 47, without wife or ch., and in 1870, 66, was in Nathaniel Packard's household.
451. vii. HENRY [Harry], b. 3 Sept. 1806.
452. viii. ADRIAL WARREN, b. 18 Apr. 1809.
453. ix.   ANN GILMAN, b. 1 May 1812; m. SAMUEL BROWN.

145. SILAS[6] 1771-1856 [43 George[5] and Dorothy Hall] was born at Falmouth in Sept. 1771, died there 28 Jan. 1856 (84y, GS, Brook Road Cemetery); married first at Falmouth 10 Sept. 1791 BETHANE WHITE, born at Uxbridge MA 31 May 1769, daughter of Thomas and Eleanor (Brown) White; married second DORCAS BAKER, daughter of Josiah and Susannah (Gibbs) Baker (Hall Desc., #21; Cornman Ms; research of Janet I. Delorey).
Silas was a farmer. On 10 Jan. 1807 he sold his brother David 120 acres near their father's homestead (CumbCD, 77:285-6). In 1850, aged 78, he was living with his son Asa.
On 8 Apr. 1813 Dorcas Leighton, like her sisters, quitclaimed her rights in the William Gibbs estate (72:311). Perhaps they divorced; on 21 Jan. 1819 "Dorcas Baker, singlewoman," quitclaimed other Gibbs rights (81:229).

Children, probably all by Bethane, born at Falmouth:

454. i.   ELEANOR[7], b. in 1792; m. JEREMIAH PENNELL.
455. ii.   SARAH, b. 31 Aug. 1793; m. SAMUEL PENNELL.
456. iii. ELIAS HALL, b. 9 May 1799.
457. iv.   ASA, b. 17 July 1801.
      v.   NICHOLAS, b. in 1803, res. Gray in 1860; m. ABBIE ---- , b. c1808 (52 in 1860). With them in 1860 were CHARLES, 12, and WILLIAM, 10.
458. vi.   STATIRA, b. 2 Nov. 1805; m. JOB FOSTER.

146. ISAAC[6] 1763-1836 [44 Samuel[5] and Dorcas Bunker] was born in ME 25 Feb. 1763, died at Columbia ME 20 Jan. 1836 (GS); married there about 1790 MARY WORCESTER, born there 28 Feb. 1767, died there 8 Oct. 1844 (GS), daughter of Moses Worcester.
In 1790, he and his wife were listed at No. 12 west of Machias (incorporated in 1796 as Columbia). They settled on uncleared land in the northwestern section called Epping Ridge. Burials are in Epping Cemetery.

This family has been well documented by their grandson
Levi, in "Sketches in Columbia, Maine" and "Leighton Family
of Columbia, Me.," MH&GR, 9[1898]:86-9, 221-3; in the Autobiography of Levi Leighton [Portland, 1890], 9-11; and in
Levi's Centennial Historical Sketch of the Town of Columbia,
1796-1896 [Machias, 1896].

Children, born at Columbia:

459. i.   MOSES[7], b. 19 Oct. 1790.
460. ii.   SAMUEL, b. 22 Sept. 1792.
461. iii. LEVI W., b. 11 Feb. 1794.
462. iv.   LOVICEY, b. 26 May 1797; m. STEPHEN OSGOOD and
            SAMUEL SILSBY.
463. v.   DANIEL, b. 18 Aug. 1799.
464. vi.   HARRISON THATCHER, b. 21 Nov. 1801.
465. vii. AARON, b. 14 Jan. 1804.
466. viii. SARAH, b. 28 Apr. 1806; m. JUSTUS TUCKER.
467. ix.   MARY ANN, b. 13 Oct. 1812; m. JUSTUS RAMSDELL
            and FRANK ALLEN.

147. ESTHER[6] 1765-   [44 Samuel[5] and Dorcas Bunker] was
born probably at Columbia about 1765; married SAMUEL TUCKER,
born say 1755, perhaps brother of Josiah Tucker. They
settled at Lubec, but soon returned to Columbia (Lubec and
Columbia VRs; records of Leonard F. Tibbetts). In 1790 they
were listed at Columbia with three children.

Children (**Tucker**), born at Columbia (first seven also
    listed in Lubec VRs):

i.   ISAAC, d. before 1812; m. Columbia c1809 ABIGAIL
        COFFIN, dau. of Matthew Coffin. She m. 2nd James
        Crowley.
ii.   LYDIA, b. in 1785, res. Springfield ME in 1860; m.
        ISAAC WORCESTER, b. Columbia in 1787, son of Moses
        Worcester.
iii.   DEBORAH, b. 20 Feb. 1790; m. THOMAS SMALL, b. Cherry-
        field 3 Apr. 1791, son of Ebenezer and Abigail[6]
        (Leighton) Small [# 132].
iv.   MARK B., b. 2 July 1793; m. Steuben 8 July 1817 ANNA
        DOWNS, dau. of Allen and Anna (Willey) Downs.
v.   (THOMAS) RUGGLES, b. 25 Oct. 1795, d. in May 1860; m.
        1st Addison int. 28 Jan. 1831 NANCY (LOOK) Norton,
        b. c1805, dau. of Daniel and Lois (Hillman) Look and
        widow of Lot Norton--div.; m. 2nd 5 Apr. 1847
        LAURETTA PHILLIPS, b. c1821, dau. of John F. and
        Martha (Dorr) Phillips. Nancy m. 3rd Israel Perley
        of Jonesport.
vi.   SAMUEL, JR., b. 4 Dec. 1796; m. Steuben int. 9 July
        1814 ANNICE SMITH, b. Taunton MA 24 Dec. 1795, dau.
        of Job and Diadama (Booth) Smith.
vii.   ASA, b. in 1799, d. 10 Dec. 1858; m. 1st Columbia
        int. 16 Nov. 1822 MIRIAM WORCESTER, b. Columbia in
        1805, d. Steuben 4 Apr. 1883, 78y 10m, dau. of Moses
        and Hannah[6] (Leighton) Worcester [# 150]. Miriam m.
        2nd EBENEZER JORDAN[7] LEIGHTON [# 389].
viii.   JUSTUS SMITH, b. 25 Mar. 1802, d. Columbia 19 Jan.
        1883; m. there int. 2 June 1827 SARAH[7] LEIGHTON
        [# 466].

ix.   MARY [Polly], b. 25 July 1804, d. Oconto WI 12 May
      1876; m. int. 5 June 1824 DAVID TABBUTT, b. Columbia
      in 1802, d. Addison 18 Aug. 1853, son of Thomas and
      Catherine (Crowley) Tabbutt.
x.   SARAH [Sally], b. 24 May 1806, d. Columbia Falls 28
      Mar. 1885; m. Columbia int. 27 Nov. 1829 SEWELL
      FRENCH, b. in NH in 1805, d. Columbia 2 June 1884,
      79y.

148.   (THOMAS) PARRITT[6] 1766-1847 [44 Samuel[5] and Dorcas
Bunker] was born probably at Narraguagus say 1766, died at
Indian River (Addison) about 1847; married MIRIAM WORCESTER,
born about 1771, died at Addison in July 1859, 88y, daughter
of Moses Worcester. He was also called Parrat or Parrot.
      He was named for Capt. Thomas Parritt, with whom his father
served during the war; since Parritt did not settle in the
area until the mid-1760s, his namesake could not have been
born in 1759, as Julia Cornman estimated.   In 1790, he was
single, living at No. 12 (Columbia); in 1800 he had four
children there; in 1810 his household was at Indian River.
In 1850, his widow Miriam, aged 79, was in the household of
Ackley and Priscilla (Drisko) Norton [# 471].   His home was
on Leighton's Point.   Descendant Darryl Lamson has exten-
sively researched Parritt's family.

      Children, the first four probably born at Columbia, the
      rest at Addison:

468. i.   ENOCH[7], b. in 1794.
469. ii.   ELI FORBES. b. 24 May 1796.
470. iii. ROBERT BARTON, b. in 1798.
471. iv.   LUCY W., b. in 1800; m. JOHN DRISKO and JOHN
            BURNS.
472. v.   NAHUM H., b. in 1803.
473. vi.   JOHN C., b. 27 Jan. 1805.
474. vii. CURTIS M., b. in 1807.
      viii. DANIEL M., b. in 1810, d. Boston 5 Feb. 1889,
            80y (VRs); prob. had ch. by a 1st wife NANCY
            ---- (Cornman Ms); m. Boston 5 May 1866 (VRs)
            MARGARET LYNCH, b. in 1835, dau. of John and
            Mary Lynch.
475. ix.   BARNABAS BEAL, b. in 1814.
476. x.   MOSES WORCESTER, b. in 1817.
      xi.   son, b. in 1819, d. in 1821.

149.   PHINEAS[6] 1768-1857 [44 Samuel[5] and Dorcas Bunker] was
born say 1768, died at Perry ME 16 Oct. 1857; married first
at Columbia about 1790 ANNIE WORCESTER, born about 1773, died
at Perry of childbed in June 1812, daughter of Moses Worcester; married second in NB (Eastport VRs) 5 Apr. 1813 ANNIE
BABCOCK, born in NB in 1788, died at Perry 16 Oct. 1856
(Perry and Columbia VRs; Cornman Ms; records of Leonard F.
Tibbetts).
      In 1800, he was listed at Columbia with three children; in
1810 the family lived at Bailey's Mistake, Eastport.   On 26
June 1813, Phineas of Eastport sold to his brother John C.
Leighton of Cherryfield 100 acres in Cherryfield with house
and barn, "being the same that I took up and occupied in or

near Epping Plains," adjoining Theodore Leighton's land
(WashCD, 8:8). Phineas lived at Pembroke, and then at Perry.
In 1850, aged 80, he and his wife shared a household with
their sons Oliver and Andrew.

Children by first wife, all but one born at Columbia:

477. i.   DORCAS⁷, b. 14 Sept. 1791; m. WILLIAM SWAIN.
     ii.   OTIS, b. 27 July 1793, not in 1800 census.
     iii. LYDIA, b. 30 Nov. 1795, res. Aroostook County;
           m. 1st ---- ANDREWS; m. 2nd ---- ANDERSON.
478. iv.   HOLLAND, b. 2 Apr. 1798.
     v.   WALTER, served in US Navy during War of 1812,
           prisoner of war in Dartmoor Prison, Devon-
           shire, released at Port Mahan NB, and drowned
           at Castine (Cornman Ms). Perhaps the ELIJAH,
           late of Eastport, mariner, who d. intestate
           and unm. After his father Phineas declined,
           Jonathan Weston accepted administration of his
           estate 13 Mar. 1828. The only asset listed
           was back pay as seaman on frigate Constitution
           (WashCP, 6:104, 215, 316-7).
     vi.   DAMEYETTE; m. Saint John NB 17 July 1833 DAVID
           WOODWORTH. Ch. Julia, Lucy, perhaps others,
           b. Saint John.
479. vii. SABRINA, b. 17 Mar. 1804; m. JAMES B. BRAWN.
     viii. JOSIAH, b. Perry 24 June 1812, d. in Sept.
           1832; m. Eastport 6 Feb. 1831 (Cornman Ms) or
           31 Mar. 1832 (Eastport Sentinel) PARTHENIA
           RUBERT. Ch. MARY ANN⁸ b. there in 1831; m. in
           1858 JOHN DAGGETT: ch. Clarence Daggett b. in
           1859, res. Herring Lake MN (Cornman Ms).

Children by second wife, born at Perry:

480. ix.   ALFRED CARPENTER, b. 16 Apr. 1814.
     x.   JOHN BABCOCK, b. 18 Feb. 1816, d. San Francisco
           CA in Feb. 1874; m. Calais int. 2 Sept. 1848
           SARAH JANE PHELPS, b. Robbinston c1825, d. Red
           Beach (Calais) 2 Nov. 1857, 33y (Machias
           Union). He was a millwright, not listed in
           1870 ME census. Ch. KATE M.⁸ b. c1856, d.
           Calais in 1881; m. there 7 Oct. 1879 JAMES
           CARROLL.
481. xi.   JACOB, b. 30 Sept. 1818.
482. xii. ISAAC, b. 25 Nov. 1820.
483. xiii. OLIVER PERRY, b. 13 Mar. 1823.
484. xiv. ANNIE, b. 16 Dec. 1825; m. JOHN J. BENNER.
485. xv.   ANDREW JACKSON, b. 12 Dec. 1829.

150. HANNAH⁶ 1770-1862 [44 Samuel⁵ and Dorcas Bunker] was
born 31 July 1770, died at Columbia 23 Feb. 1862, 91y 6m 25d;
married MOSES WORCESTER, JR., born at Wooster's Point about
1762, the first white child born at Columbia, died there 13
Oct. 1855, 93y, son of Moses Worcester (Columbia VRs; BHM,
8[1893]:3; records of Leonard F. Tibbetts).
    In the Columbia 1850 census, Moses was shown as 85 and Han-
nah as 80. Her death notice (Machias Union of 11 Mar.) stated
that she left 12 children, 102 grandchildren, 195 great-
grandchildren and 9 great-great-grandchildren.

Children (**Worcester**), born at Columbia:

i.   MARY [Polly], b. 23 July 1792, d. Addison 17 Sept.
      1887, 97y 2m 15d; m. 1st 2 May 1812 ABRAHAM B.
      ALLEN; m. 2nd in 1854 (Machias Union of 5 Dec.)
      OBADIAH ALLEN.
ii.   JUDITH N., b. 2 May 1794, d. 9 July 1869; m. JONA-
      THAN DORR, JR., son of Jonathan and Eunice (Downs)
      Dorr, b. 18 May 1791, d. 22 July 1883.
iii. AMOS, b. 13 Feb. 1796, d. c1876; m. 1st 8 Jan. 1819
      SARAH WARD, d. 16 Nov. 1865; m. 2nd Columbia
      Falls 4 Apr. 1866 JUDITH (NASH) Allen.
iv.   LEONARD, b. 28 Feb. 1798, d. Addison 30 July 1883,
      aged 86; m. Jonesboro ME 23 Dec. 1819 LOVE MOORE
      CORTHELL, b. Columbia 8 Feb. 1802, d. there 28 Sept.
      1882, dau. of Kinsman and Lucy (Hall) Corthell
      (Mary M. Corthell, Corthell Genealogy [np, 1984,
      MHS], 51).
v.   ESTHER, b. 25 May 1800, d. Addison 6 Aug. 1885; m.
      Columbia int. 3 Nov. 1819 DAVID MERRITT, b. in 1792,
      d. 29 Dec. 1876.
vi.   HANNAH, b. 7 June 1802, d. Columbia 13 June 1880; m.
      1st at Columbia 10 Oct. 1824 MOSES LOOK, JR., son of
      Moses and Martha (Haycock) (Miller) Look; m. 2nd
      DANIEL⁷ LEIGHTON [# 463].
vii. MIRIAM, b. in May 1804, d. Unionville (Steuben) 4
      Apr. 1883, 78y 10m (GS); m. 1st Columbia int. 16
      Nov. 1822 ASA TUCKER [# 147]; m. 2nd 25 Oct. 1861
      EBENEZER JORDAN⁷ LEIGHTON [# 389].
viii. DEBORAH, b. in Apr. 1806; d. Newton MA 7 Sept. 1892;
      m. Columbia int. 10 Nov. 1822 GEORGE W. STEVENS.
ix.   ABIGAIL C., b. 9 Mar. 1808, d. Addison 18 July 1901,
      93y; m. Addison 1 Oct. 1826 STILLMAN LOOK, b. c1803,
      son of George and Elizabeth (Stevens) Look.
x.   MOSES 3RD, b. 11 Aug. 1810, d. Columbia 10 Feb. 1879;
      m. Columbia 31 Oct. 1838 DIADAMA SMITH, b. 15 Mar.
      1814, d. Columbia 11 Nov. 1889, 75y 6m 26d, dau. of
      Ebenezer and Deborah (Farnsworth) Smith.
xi.   AARON, d.y.
xii. LOUISA S., b. in 1816; m. 1st int. 12 June 1836
      JOSHUA FARNSWORTH, b. Jonesboro 13 July 1813, son of
      Adrial and Grace (Hall) Farnsworth; m. 2nd Jonesboro
      23 July 1846 HAZZARD SMALL, b. in 1815, d. 26 Aug.
      1858, 44y 3m 17 (Epping GS); m. 3rd Columbia int.
      3 Apr. 1859 HIRAM LOWE, d. 22 Mar. 1878, 67y 11m 7d.

151. **SUSAN**⁶ 1773-   [44 Samuel⁵ and Dorcas Bunker] was
born at Columbia in 1773, lived there at Pleasant River; married RICHARD GOWELL MERRITT, born 9 Sept. 1761, died in 1834,
son of Daniel and Mary (Gowell) Merritt (Addison VRs; records
of Leonard F. Tibbetts).
   Merritt was a Revolutionary soldier, serving in 1780 under
Capt. Henry Dyer (MSS, 10:685). They lived at Addison. In
1790 they were listed at Columbia with a daughter.

Children (**Merritt**), born at Addison--perhaps others:

i.   RICHARD G., JR., b. 11 Dec. 1791, d. 16 Aug. 1870; m.
      1st JANE WASS; m. 2nd Addison int. 17 June 1829
      DORCAS NASH.

ii.   DAVID, b. 16 Nov. 1792, d. Addison 29 Dec. 1876 (GS-
       Merritt Cem.); m. Columbia int. 3 Nov. 1819 ESTHER
       WORCESTER.
iii.   JESSE PLUMMER, b. 28 Oct. 1801, d. Addison 25 Jan.
       1892; m. 1st Addison int. 10 May 1825 NANCY WASS;
       m. 2nd Addison 15 Oct. 1873 LUCINDA (DOYLE) Beal,
       widow of Barnabas Beal.

152.   STEPHEN[6] 1763-1824 [45 Gideon[5] and Abigail Titcomb]
was born at Barrington NH 4 Sept. 1763, died at Strafford NH
6 July 1824, 60y 10m 2d (GS); married first 7 Aug. 1794 MARY
[Polly] EMERSON, born at Madbury 11 Nov. 1774, died at Barrington 11 Mar. 1810, 35y 4m (GS), daughter of Solomon and
Sarah (Demeritt) Emerson (Stackpole, Durham, 2:180); married
second 11 Jan. 1811 DEBORAH WILLEY, born at Barrington 30
Jan. 1781, died there 13 Feb. 1860, 79y (GS) (Barrington VRs;
Stearns, N. H. Genealogies, 3:1320-1). Burials are in a
private lot near Willey's Pond, Strafford.
On 14 July 1779, Thomas Foss was appointed as his guardian
(StrCP, 2:18-9). Stephen lived in the section of Barrington
set off as Strafford in 1820. His will, made 17 Mar. and
proved 5 Aug. 1824, named his wife Deborah as executrix, left
land to Andrew and Stephen and cash bequests to the other
children, and gave Stephen responsibility for the support of
his brother Solomon (StrCP, 30:33; 33:73, 82).

Children by Mary, born at Barrington:

486.   i.   JOHN EMERSON[7], b. 15 Jan. 1796.
       ii.   SOLOMON, b. 10 Aug. 1797, d. Strafford 24 Sept.
              1900, 103y 1m 12d (VR); unm., "idiot."
487.   iii.   GIDEON, b. 24 June 1799.
       iv.   ABIGAIL, b. 28 Feb. 1801, d. Rochester 12 Jan.
              1884; m. AARON RICKER of Somersworth, b. 6
              Oct. 1795, d. Rochester 6 Jan. 1862. Ch.
              Daniel G. b. Strafford 10 Nov. 1822, d.
              Rochester 20 Jan. 1894; m. in 1863 Olive E.
              Hanson of Lowell MA (Cornman Ms).
488.   v.   SARAH, b. 13 Nov. 1802; m. HENRY FOLSOM.
489.   vi.   HANNAH, b. 15 Nov. 1804; m. EBENEZER FOSS.
490.   vii.   MARY E., b. 15 Oct. 1806; m. LUTHER SAMPSON.
491.   viii. ANDREW, b. 7 Apr. 1808.

Children by Deborah, born at Barrington:

       ix.   BETSEY K., b. 24 Jan. 1812, d. 28 Oct. 1851;
              m. MOSES C. WILLEY. No ch.
492.   x.   STEPHEN, b. 18 Apr. 1813.

153.   JOSEPH[6] 1766-1837 [45 Gideon[5] and Abigail Titcomb]
was born at Barrington 17 May 1766 (Farmington TRs), died at
Farmington 21 Apr. 1837, 71y (GS); married first at New Durham NH 5 Nov. 1795 (VRs) HANNAH BABB, born at Barrington 8
Aug. 1772 (or 5 Nov. 1770, Farmington TRs), died at Farmington 24 Mar. 1817, 46y (GS), daughter of Richard and Hannah
(Perkins) Babb (Jean A. Sargent and Ina Babb Mansur, Babb
Families of New England--and Beyond [Laurel MD, 1987], 161);
married second at Dover 30 Nov. (int. Farmington 15 Nov.)
1835 MARY (----) HAYES (D. Hamilton Hurd, ed., History of

Rockingham and Strafford Counties, N. H. [Philadelphia, 1882], 637 John Scales, History of Strafford County, N. H., and Representative Citizens [Chicago, 1914], 488). He was also under Thomas Foss's guardianship as a child. Burials are in the family graveyard on his farm off Ten Rod Road.

In 1798 he purchased several parcels of land in Rochester's third division (Farmington) (StrCD, 27:341; 28:41-2), and additional land at Farmington from 1800 to 1813 (36:110; 52: 404). On 19 Jan. 1804, he sold lot 117 to his brother Levi (44:51).

His will, made 14 Apr. and proved 13 May 1837, gave his property to his son Levi [designated Levi, Jr.] and to his Demeritt grandchildren; the estate included property at Alton as well as at Farmington, and Rochester Bank shares (StrCP, 50:94; 52:110).

Children by Hannah, born at Farmington:

493. i.   LEVI WASHINGTON^7, b. 4 Feb. 1796.
494. ii.   ABIGAIL EMMONS, b. 28 Jan. 1799; m. MARK
            DEMERITT.
      iii. JOHN BABB, b. 30 Aug. 1801, d. 14 Nov. 1819.

154. ANDREW^6 1767-1826 [45 Gideon^5 and Abigail Titcomb] was born at Barrington 22 May 1767, died at Strafford 25 Dec. 1826, 59y 7m 3d (GS); married at Barrington 7 June 1792 (VRs) MARGARET T. BABB, born at Barrington 24 Jan. 1772, died at Strafford 24 Aug. 1848, 76y (obituary, Morning Star; 56y 5m per GS), daughter of Richard and Hannah (Perkins) Babb (Sargent, Babbs of New Eng., 162). Burials are in Ridge Cemetery, Strafford. He too had been a ward of Thomas Foss.

Often jointly with his brother Joseph, Squire Andrew purchased land in Rochester's third and fourth divisons during 1798-1800, in what later was Farmington. In 1809 he was made justice of the peace. His section of Barrington became part of Strafford when it was incorporated in 1820; he served as that town's state representative in 1823.

Children, born at Barrington:

495. i.   SALLY^7, b. in 1793; m. ANDREW HILL.
      ii.   MARY H., b. say 1795; m. Barrington 16
            Dec. 1813 JAMES HALE, son of Thomas Wright
            Hale. Both d. Conway NH. Ch. Martha Susan
            Leighton Hale b. in 1818; m. Samuel D.
            Shackford.
496. iii. HANNAH E., b. 16 Oct. 1800; m. 22 Sept. 1825
            Dr. AARON BUZZELL.
      iv.   ABIGAIL TITCOMB, b. 22 Nov. 1805; m. WILLIAM
            PEAVEY^7 LEIGHTON [# 498].
497. v.   ANDREW DYER, b. 18 Sept. 1812.

155. LEVI^6 1773-1821 [45 Gideon^5 and Abigail Titcomb] was born at Barrington about 1773, died at Farmington 14 Dec. 1821 (VRs; 16 Dec. 1823, 48y, per GS); married at New Durham 17 Apr. 1800 (int. Farmington 26 Feb.) SARAH [Sally] PEAVEY, born at Farmington in 1782, died there 1 Nov. 1854. She married second at Farmington 17 Mar. (int. 7 Feb.) 1830 Benjamin Reed, who died 22 Sept. 1864 (Farmington VRs; Cornman Ms).

He was also under the guardianship of Thomas Foss as a child. Levi, Esq., served ten terms as selectman of Farmington between 1805 and 1819, and was state representative in 1807, 1812 and 1814. A carpenter, he set up the first sawmill in the area with a powered return. His will, made 21 Jan. 1820 and proved 7 Jan. 1822, named his wife, son and four daughters. A codicil made 19 Nov. 1821 provided for his unborn child, and asked his heirs to care for his nephew Solomon. On 29 June 1833 Levi H. Pinkham was named Martha's guardian (StrCP, 28:45-50; 30:3, 192).

Children, born at Farmington:

498.   i.   WILLIAM PEAVEY[7], b. c1801.
499.   ii.   MARY RICHARDSON, b. c1802; m. JOHN HOYT.
500.   iii. MARIA TITCOMB, b. 4 Sept. 1808; m. LEVI H.
              PINKHAM.
       iv.   JANE EMMONS, b. 24 Oct. 1814, d. 24 Nov. 1878;
              m. 13 Oct. 1835 BENJAMIN RANDALL, b. in 1809,
              d. 28 June 1878. No ch. Grandson of Elder
              Benjamin Randall, founder of the Free Will
              Baptist denomination.
       v.   HANNAH MARGARET, b. 8 May 1817, d. 8 Nov. 1890;
              m. GEORGE W. REED, b. 21 May 1823, d. 28 Mar.
              1900, son of Benjamin Reed. Ch. Charles H. b.
              2 July 1849; m. 11 Apr. 1872 Elizabeth Remick,
              b. 20 May 1847 (Cornman Ms).
501.   vi.   MARTHA ABIGAIL, b. 13 Jan. 1822; m. CHARLES
              CLARK.

156. SUSANNAH HALL[6] 1758-1836 [46 Joseph[5] and Mercy Hall] was born at Falmouth ME 1 May 1758 (TRs), died there 25 Nov. 1836; married there 3 Apr. 1783 (Cumberland Co. record) GEORGE HUSTON, JR., baptized there 9 Oct. 1757, died there 21 Feb. 1829, son of George and Anne (Thompson) Huston (Hall Desc., #44; Philip H. Harris, William Huston of Falmouth, Me. [TMs, 1951, MHS], 12; Cornman Ms).

Children (**Huston**), born at Falmouth:

i.   JOSEPH, b. c1783; m. MARTHA LOW.
ii.   SARAH; m. JOSEPH LOW.
iii.   HANNAH, d.y.
iv.   ELIJAH, b. in 1789; m. POLLY RIDEOUT.
v.   MOSES, b. in 1792, d. Windham 12 June 1830, 38y;
        m. there 18 Mar. 1819 SARAH PURINTON.
vi.   FRANCES, b. in 1800; m. Portland 15 Apr. 1832
        FREEMAN HARDING.
vii.   CYNTHIA; m. CORNELIUS RHOADS.

157. ANDREW[6] 1762-1830 [46 Joseph[5] and Mercy Hall] was born at Falmouth 7 June 1762, died at North Yarmouth ME 16 June 1830; married MARY WEYMOUTH, born in 1764, died at North Yarmouth 9 Feb. 1845, 81y, daughter of James and Molly Weymouth of Gray ME (Falmouth and North Yarmouth TRs; Hall Desc., #46). Burials are in the Methodist Churchyard at West Cumberland.

In 1790 he lived at North Yarmouth, in the section now West Cumberland. He, his father and Richard Loring divided a

100-acre lot in the Gore there 16 July that year.
He was elected captain in the 6th Infantry Rgt., 2nd Brigade, on 13 June 1808, and appointed justice of the peace 28
Aug. 1817. Capt. Andrew laid out the county road from Fal-
mouth to Portland, and was a prosperous lumber trader, deal-
ing especially in ship's timbers. He built and operated
Leighton's Tavern at West Cumberland on the Gray Road, the
stage route to Lewiston (Biographical Review ... Cumberland
County, Me. [Boston, 1896], 83). In 1971, the tavern was
moved to Schooner Rocks, Cumberland Foreside, and restored
(Phyllis Sturdivant Sweetser, ed., Cumberland, Maine, in Four
Centuries [the Town, 1976], 164-5).

Children, born at North Yarmouth:

502. i.   LOVE[7], b. 20 Mar. 1787; m. NICHOLAS LOW.
503. ii.   WILLIAM, b. 30 May 1788.
      iii. JOSEPH, b. 14 Oct. 1789, lost at sea off
            George's Bank in 1815, in privateer Dash (the
            legendary Ghost Ship of Casco Bay); unm. He
            was a corporal, Capt. Watson Rand's Co., in
            1814 (MA Mil. 1812-14, 225).
      iv.   ANDREW, b. 10 Dec. 1790, also lost on the Dash
            in 1815; unm. In 1813 he served under Capt.
            Abel Atherton and Capt. James Farmer at Port-
            land harbor, and as sergeant in 1814 in Major
            John Trowbridge's cavalry (158, 164, 166).
504. v.   MERCY, b. 30 Oct. 1792; m. JOHN PETTINGILL.
505. vi.   MOSES, b. 10 Mar. 1794.
506. vii. DANIEL, b. 30 Apr. 1795.
507. viii. JAMES, b. 23 Feb. 1797.
508. ix.   NICHOLAS, b. 28 Feb. 1801.
509. x.   EZEKIEL, b. 4 June 1802.
      xi.   STEPHEN, b. 1 Sept. 1804, lost at sea.
510. xii. ROBERT, b. 29 Mar. 1808.

158. STEPHEN[6] 1764-1847 [46 Joseph[5] and Mercy Hall] was
born at Falmouth 7 May 1764, died there 2 July 1847, 83y 2m
(GS; obituary, Portland Daily Argus, 14 July); married 10
July 1796 (MH&GR, 7[1896]:213) RUTH CRAGUE, born at Windham
14 May 1758, died at Falmouth 4 Nov. 1843, 85y (GS), daughter
of Hugh and Elizabeth (Warren) Crague (Falmouth TRs; Cornman
Ms; Hall Desc., #47). In 1800 he was a farmer at Falmouth.
Burials are in the Gowen St. cemetery.

Children, born at Falmouth:

      i.   child[7], b. 1 Feb., d. 7 Feb., 1798.
511. ii.   LYDIA, b. 6 Apr. 1799; m. JEREMIAH STAPLES.
      iii. EZEKIEL, b. 15 Mar. 1800, d. 18 Jan. 1801.
512. iv.   MARTHA, b. 18 Mar. 1801; m. HENRY PRIDE.
  --   PATTY (adopted), b. in 1794, d. in 1865; m.
            Gorham in 1812 PETER INGERSOLL.

159. MARY W.[6] 1765-1815 [46 Joseph[5] and Mercy Hall] was
born at Falmouth 9 Dec. 1765, died at Gray 9 Sept. 1815; m. 5
Apr. 1792 JAMES WEYMOUTH of Gray (Gray VRs; Cornman Ms; Hall
Desc., #48).

Children (**Weymouth**), born at Gray:

i.   COMFORT, d. 13 Mar. 1832; m. Gray 5 Aug. 1819 ISAAC
     LIBBY, b. Gray 19 Jan. 1801, d. there 30 July 1833,
     son of Simeon and Elizabeth (Small) Libby (Libby
     Family, 191).
ii. MARTHA, b. Falmouth 12 Aug. 1804, d. Gray 22 July
     1855; m. there 25 Dec. 1825 DAVID LIBBY, b. there
     21 Apr. 1804, d. there 1 May 1881, son of Simeon and
     Elizabeth (Small) Libby (Libby Family, 410).
iii. MOSES; m. ---- BRACKETT.
iv. DORCAS.
v.   NANCY; m. WILLIAM B. WATTS.

160.   EZEKIEL[6] 1767-1819 [46 Joseph[5] and Mercy Hall] was
born at Falmouth 19 July 1767, died there 24 Nov. 1819; married first at Windham 2 Apr. 1795 MARTHA CRAGUE, born at
Windham 22 Oct. 1772, died at Falmouth 24 Mar. 1811, daughter
of Hugh and Elizabeth (Warren) Crague; married second at Cumberland 8 Jan. 1818 OLIVE HICKS, born at North Yarmouth 23
July 1781, died 21 Aug. 1847, daughter of Joseph and Eunice
Hicks (town VRs; Hall Desc., #49; Cornman Ms). Olive married
second 29 Feb. 1824 Capt. Eldridge Drinkwater, born 1 Mar.
1776, son of John and Susanna (Brown) Drinkwater (MH&GR,
3:265).
Ezekiel served under Capt. James Farmer in 1813, under
Capt. Abel W. Atherton in 1814, and as corporal under Capt.
Alpheus Field in 1814, defending Portland Harbor (MA Mil.
1812-4, 164, 166, 219).
His son Joseph was placed under the guardianship of his
uncle Andrew 4 Jan. 1820.

Children by Martha, born at Falmouth:

513. i.   HUGH[7], b. 27 Jan. 1796.
514. ii. JOSEPH, b. 20 May 1805.

161.   ELIZABETH[6] [Betsey] 1776-1843 [46 Joseph[5] and Mercy
Hall] was born at Falmouth 20 June 1776, died at North Yarmouth 4 Jan. 1843; married 17 Dec. 1795 JAMES WINSLOW, born
at Falmouth 5 April 1774, died at Cumberland 31 Jan. 1868,
93y, son of Samuel and Ruth (Morrell) Winslow (Cumberland and
Falmouth VRs; David Parsons Holton, Winslow Memorial [New
York, 1877-8], 2:940; Hall Desc., #54; Cornman Ms). They
lived at North Yarmouth.

Children (**Winslow**), born at North Yarmouth (in Cumberland
     VRs):

i.   LYDIA, b. 20 Aug. 1796, d. 7 Jan. 1798.
ii. MERCY L., b. 20 Dec. 1798; m. HENRY[8] LEIGHTON
     [# 955].
iii. LYDIA LEIGHTON, b. 20 Feb. 1801, d. Cumberland 20
     Feb. 1878; unm.
iv. JAMES, b. 10 July 1803, d. 22 Sept. 1815.
v.   ELIZABETH, b. 7 Aug. 1805, d. 5 Jan. 1815.
vi. AMOS ROSCOE, b. 10 Jan. 1808; m. ABIGAIL M.[8]
     LEIGHTON [# 977].

vii. ANDREW LEIGHTON, b. 12 Mar. 1810; m. 1st SARAH MOR-
RISON, dau. of Ephraim and Eunice (Hicks) Morrison
[# 142]; m. 2nd 31 Jan. 1847 MARY STUART COBB.
viii. ABIGAIL, b. 29 Oct. 1812, d. 4 Sept. 1898; m. 30 Mar.
1836 GEORGE HUSTON LOW, b. 6 May 1807, d. Falmouth
25 Mar. 1876.
ix. RUTH MORRELL, b. 22 Dec. 1814, d. 23 Sept. 1815.
x. ANN HALL, b. 6 Aug. 1816, m. 1st ELBRIDGE KING; m.
2nd int. 4 June 1847, as his 2nd wife, PETER KNIGHT,
b. Windham 7 June 1789, son of John Akers and Keziah
(Morrell) Knight. They removed to IL.
xi. BENJAMIN, b. 2 Feb. 1821, d. 22 Aug. 1825.
xii. ESTHER, b. and d. 28 Feb. 1823.

162. SARAH^6 1780-1844 [46 Joseph^5 and Mercy Hall] was born
at Falmouth 15 Aug. 1780, died there 24 Feb. 1844 (GS 1849);
married at Gray 18 Apr. 1801 WILLIAM HADLOCK, born 14 Feb.
1781, died 14 Dec. 1863 (Hall Desc., #56; Cornman Ms).
Burials are in the Blanchard Cemetery, Falmouth.

Children (**Hadlock**):

i. HANNAH, b. Cumberland 5 Nov. 1802; m. 1st 1 Mar. 1822
CYRUS HICKS [# 142].
ii. SUSAN, b. in July 1805, d. in 1877 (GS); unm.
iii. JAMES, b. Falmouth 7 July 1809, res. Westbrook; m.
22 Oct. 1837 LOVINA WASHBURN, b. 22 Oct. 1814.
v. DANIEL LEIGHTON, b. Cumberland 7 Oct. 1815; m. 1st in
Nov. 1838 EMELINE HALL, b. 1 Nov. 1816, d. 22 Aug.
1854, dau. of Greenfield and Sarah (Prince) Hall; m.
2nd MARTHA A. ROBERTS.
vi. LYDIA, b. in 1818, d. in 1849 (GS).

163. JEREMIAH^6 1793-1884 [46 Joseph^5 and Hannah Wilson]
was born at Falmouth 21 May 1793, died at Portland 1 Mar.
1884, 91y; married at Windham 30 Dec. 1818 SARAH FIELD of
that town, born 26 Feb. 1798, died at Portland 2 May 1872,
76y (Portland and Windham VRs; Cornmam Ms).
He was drafted at Falmouth for three months' service in
1814, and was in Capt. Watson Rand's Co. at Fort Sumner and
Fort Preble (MA Mil. 1812-4, 225). In 1850 he was a joiner
at Portland. He applied for bounty land 8 Jan. 1851, and
again--while living at Lisbon--on 16 Mar. 1852, receiving
warrant #48.618; he applied again 21 Mar. 1855 for additional
bounty land, and was given warrant #28.555. On 4 Apr. 1871,
aged 78 of Portland, he applied for a pension (NA-MSR
#4,557). In 1880, he was part of Edwin Boyden's household.

Children, births in Portland VRs:

515. i. GEORGE^7, b. 6 Apr. 1820.
516. ii. JOSEPH, b. 10 June 1821.
517. iii. ANN MARIA, b. 1 June 1823; m. JOHN FENHOLM.
iv. DORCAS, b. 19 Mar. 1825, d. 19 Nov. 1827.
v. HENRY H., b. 24 Feb. 1827, d. Westbrook 25 Nov.
1852, 26y (VRs); m. there 3 Aug. 1852 MARY
ELIZABETH ADAMS, b. 5 Mar. 1834, d. 21 Apr.
1855, 21y, dau. of Mark and Amanda (Hall)
Adams. No ch. He was a hotel clerk.

      vi.   CHARLES H., b. 19 Nov. 1828, d. 15 Oct. 1849;
           unm.
518. vii. ESTHER LOUISA, b. 26 Feb. 1831; m. EDWIN
           BOYDEN.
519. viii. ICHABOD WILSON, b. 16 Mar. 1833.
520. ix. ALGERNON SIDNEY, b. 16 May 1835.
      x.   WILLARD B., b. 11 June 1838, d. 17 Apr. 1843.
      xi.   MARGARET ELLEN, b. 9 Dec. 1840, d. 4 Sept.
           1842.

164. JANE[6] 1794-   [46 Joseph[5] and Hannah Wilson] was born at Falmouth 28 July 1794; married there 26 June 1816 NATHANIEL ABBOTT of Gray, perhaps son of Nathaniel and Elizabeth (Gammon) Abbott (Gray VRs; Cornman Ms).

Children (**Abbott**), order uncertain:

i.   MARY W., b. Gray 2 Nov. 1816, d. 21 Dec. (Feb.?)
       1879; m. 5 Mar. 1845 ALFRED LIBBY, b. Gray 4 Oct.
       1814, d. 25 Apr. 1897, son of Simeon and Elizabeth
       (Small) Libby (Libby Family, 191).
ii.   CYNTHIA, b. 22 Mar. 1825, d. 22 Mar. 1883; m. JOHN
       WILSON, b. 17 Sept. 1825, son of Nathaniel and
       Elizabeth (Baker) Wilson.
iii.   PERSIS, d. 29 Dec. 1891; unm.
iv.   EDWARD, d. Harpswell ME 30 Sept. 1895, 62y 7m; unm.
v.   CHARLES; m. EMELINE NASON.
vi.   JOSEPH.
vii.   MOSES.

165. ANN[6] 1797-1893 [46 Joseph[5] and Hannah Wilson] was born at Falmouth 9 Aug. 1797, died there 17 July 1893; married there 2 May 1822 HENRY HUSTON, born there 23 Apr. 1799, died there 18 Aug. 1872, son of Mark and Ednah (Knight) Huston (Huston Gen., 30; Cornman Ms; Falmouth VRs). Burials are in the Methodist Church cemetery, West Falmouth. He was a farmer.

Children (**Huston**), born at Falmouth:

i.   ELI K., b. 29 Oct. 1824, d. 20 June 1900; m. 23 Aug.
       1849 BARBARA McINTOSH COBB, b. Deering ME 29 Nov.
       1831, d. there 31 Aug. 1891, 59y 9m, dau. of Charles
       and Isabel M. (Campbell) Cobb (Isaac Cobb, Genealogy
       of the Cobb Family in New England [TMs, 1943, MHS],
       2:470).
ii.   ASA B., b. 20 Oct. 1827; m. Portland 23 Feb. 1859
       ELNORA HUSTON, b. Falmouth 2 Dec. 1841, dau. of
       Isaac and Margaret (Field) Huston. She m. 2nd
       Bradford Walker, and 3rd John Page of Quincy MA.
iii.   EBEN L., b. 9 Feb. 1841; m. Portland 16 Mar. 1870
       JULIA C. L. FOSTER.

166. DORCAS[6] 1801-1832 [46 Joseph[5] and Hannah Wilson] was born at Falmouth 2 Oct. 1801, died 24 Nov. 1832; married at Gray 22 June 1828 EBENEZER COBB LIBBY, born at Gray 19 Feb. 1800, died at Falmouth 4 Oct. 1872, son of Andrew and Sarah (Cummings) Libby.

Ebenezer married second 31 Oct. 1833 Hannah Elliot and third 20 May 1849 Mary Shaw, but had no additional children by these two wives (Libby Family, 189-90, 409; Falmouth and Gray VRs).

Children (**Libby**), born at Gray:

i.   WILSON, b. 19 May 1829; m. 1st Gray 25 Apr. 1852
       MARY A. BLAKE, d. 15 Aug. 1867; m. 2nd 23 Dec. 1869
       HATTIE A. EDWARDS of Casco, who d. 4 Sept. 1874;
       m. 3rd 3 Oct. 1878 CAROLINE E. (WHITNEY) Ramsdell of
       Falmouth.
ii.   FLORINDA, b. in 1830, d. 6 Feb. 1849.
iii.   SARAH ANN, b. 15 Nov. 1832; m. 11 Aug. 1855 ALEX-
       ANDER ROBERTSON of Poland ME, who d. 4 Oct. 1872.

167. **RACHEL**[6] 1780-1853 [48 Theodore[5] and Hannah] was born at Cherryfield ME 20 Aug. 1780, died at Steuben 26 Apr. 1853, 72y 8m (GS); married about 1800 BENJAMIN PINKHAM, born at Steuben 27 May 1779, died there 15 Apr. 1874 (GS), son of Tristram and Ann (Leighton) Pinkham [# 127] (Steuben and Cherryfield VRs; records of Leonard F. Tibbetts; Sinnett, Pinkham Gen., 16; Cornman Ms).

Children (**Pinkham**), born at Steuben:

i.   THEODORE B., b. 20 Nov. 1802, d. 11 Aug. 1830.
ii   ANDREW, b. 20 May 1804; m. HANNAH ---- . He res.
       Steuben in 1860; Hannah was not listed in 1850 or
       1860.
iii.   URIAH, b. 10 Apr. 1806; m. Harrington 10 Sept. 1838
       ANN M. DAVIS, b. 19 Apr. 1820.
iv.   SAMUEL. b. 20 Apr. 1808; m. Steuben int. 13 Dec.
       1834 SARAH S. ROYAL.
v.   BENJAMIN, JR., b. 1 Aug. 1810; m. SUSAN[8] LEIGHTON
       [# 868].
vi.   RUFUS, b. 22 Apr. 1812; m. Steuben int. 10 Apr.
       1835 MARY M. DAVIS.
vii.   REZELDA, b. 29 July 1814, d. Milbridge 11 Feb. 1899
       (VRs; 1898, 87y, GS--Evergreen Cem.); m. JOHN E.
       MITCHELL, as his second wife.
viii. JOEL, b. 5 Sept. 1816; m. LOVICIA[8] LEIGHTON [# 869].
ix.   HANNAH PLUMMER, b. 8 July 1818; unm. in 1860.
x.   LOUISA, b. 15 Nov. 1820; m. Steuben 3 Mar. 1842
       PATRICK CONNERS.
xi.   LUCY ANN HANDY, b. 4 Oct. 1822; m. JAMES W.[8] LEIGHTON
       [# 867].
xii.   JORDAN, b. 25 Dec. 1827; m. Cherryfield 26 Mar. 1853
       CATHERINE LEIGHTON, b. 29 May 1828.

168. **DOROTHY**[6] [Dolly] 1782-   [48 Theodore[5] and Hannah] was born at Cherryfield 18 June 1782; married first TRISTRAM PINKHAM, JR., born at Steuben 12 Sept. 1781, died there 26 Nov. 1825, son of Tristram and Ann (Leighton) Pinkham [# 127] (Sinnett, Pinkham Gen., 18); married second at Addison 4 Feb. 1833 JOHN C.[6] LEIGHTON, son of Samuel and Dorcas (Bunker) Leighton [# 44], by whom she had no children (town VRs; Cornman Ms).

Children (**Pinkham**), born at Steuben:

i.   SUSANNA, b. 10 May 1805, d. 22 May 1854; m. Steuben
       10 July 1828 SAMUEL DAVIS, b. in 1804, d. in 1900,
       son of Samuel and Jane (Willey) Davis [# 128].
ii.   GEORGE, b. 27 Apr. 1808.
iii.   ANNE, b. 4 Aug. 1811.
iv.   NAOMI, b, 7 Dec.1814; m. Cherryfield int. 10 May 1833
       JOSEPH A. COLSON.
v.   BETSEY, b. 8 Jan. 1822; m. Cherryfield int. 6 Nov.
       1841 LEWIS BURKE.

   169.   ELIZABETH[6] 1784-1864 [48 Theodore and Hannah] was
born at Cherryfield 7 May 1784, died there 19 Feb. 1864; married there 28 Mar. 1814 WILLIAM TUCKER, born there 3 June
1774, died 28 July 1822, probably son of Josiah and Susannah
Tucker (Cherryfield VRs; records of Leonard F. Tibbetts). He
had married first Priscilla Small, who died at Lubec 17 Nov.
1811; they had six children.

Children (**Tucker**), born at Cherryfield:

i.   URIAH, b. 23 July 1814, d. 1 Aug. 1817.
ii.   ERNEST, b. 3 June 1818, d. 15 Apr. 1820.

   170.   SUSANNAH[6] 1786-1850 [48 Theodore[5] and Hannah] was
born at Cherryfield 15 Jan. 1786, died there in Mar. 1850,
64y; married at Cherryfield int. 4 Apr. 1805 DANIEL TRACY,
born at Gouldsboro ME 16 Aug. 1769, not in the 1850 census,
son of Jonathan and Abigail (Riggs) Tracy (Cherryfield VRs;
Tracy, Hist. Address, 16, in which however Daniel is said to
have died young; Elizabeth S. Daniel and Jeanne E. Sawtelle,
Thomas Rogers, Pilgrim, and Some of His Descendants [Balti-
more, 1980], 263).

Children (**Tracy**), born at Cherryfield:

i.   ELI, b. 24 May 1808 (15 Apr. 1806, GS), d. 15 July
       1888; m. DIADAMA SMITH, b. Cherryfield in 1816, d.
       there 2 Jan. 1902, 85y 2m 5d (GS), dau. of Job, Jr.,
       and Bethia (Stevens) Smith. Burials are in Archer
       Cemetery, Upper Tunk.
ii.   AARON, b. 20 Jan. 1812, d. 27 Nov. 1823.
iii.   RICHARD, b. 22 Dec. 1815, d. 28 Jan. 1818.
iv.   MARIAN/MIRIAM, b. 20 Sept. 1818, d. Steuben 15 July
       1904; m. ---- DAVIS.
v.   SAMUEL B. MERRILL, b. 5 Feb. 1821, d. 20 Oct. 1827.
vi.   CURTIS M., b. 22 Oct. 1823, d. 21 June 1847,
       23y (GS).
vii.   JAMES SMALL, b. 24 Mar. 1826, d. 28 May 1847,
       21y (GS).

   171.   ELIZABETH[6] 1753-1846 [51 Jonnathan and Sarah] was
born at Rochester NH 18 July 1753, died at Alton 19 Feb. 1846
(GS); married at Rochester 26 Aug. 1779 (McDuffee, Rochester,
2:607) JOHN ROLLINS, born at Newington 12 Feb. 1756 (baptized
20 Feb. 1757), died at Alton 16 Dec. 1847, 91y 10m 4d, son of
Ichabod and Olive (Nutter) Rollins (Alton TRs 1:492; John R.

Rollins, Records of Families of the Name Rawlins or Rollins
[Lawrence MA, 1874], 35-6, 71-2; Barton McLain Griffin, The
History of Alton [1965], 131). Burials are in the West Alton
Cemetery.
     Rollins enlisted in Capt. James Carr's Co., Col. Nathan
Hale's 2nd NH Rgt., in 1777, and served until 11 Oct. 1782.
He remained an officer in the militia, reaching the rank of
colonel; he had 40 years of military service in all.   He
applied for a pension while of Alton, aged 59, on 21 Apr.
1818 (NA-MSR #S 45117).

     Children (Rollins):

     i.   JONATHAN, b. Rochester 14 Dec. 1779, res. Alton; m.
           1st ELIZABETH ----, b. 18 Apr. 1781, d. 21 July
           1809; m. 2nd ABIGAIL PERKINS, b. Middleton 25 Aug.
           1789.
     ii.   ANTHONY, b. Rochester 16 Sept. 1782, res. Alton and
           Rollinsford; m. Alton 18 Oct. 1803 LYDIA HEARD,
           d. Alton 12 Nov. 1850, 65y (GS).
     iii. SUSANNA, b. Rochester 15 Nov. 1785; m. WILLIAM
           EMERSON.
     iv.   SARAH, b. Rochester 5 Nov. 1788, d. Alton 22 Feb.
           1794, 5y 3m 17d.
     v.   JOHN, JR., b. Alton 20 Aug. 1791, res. New Durham and
           Middleton; m. Alton 29 May 1813 MARY PERKINS, b. 14
           Mar. 1795, d. New Durham 11 May 1863, dau. of Solo-
           mon Perkins of Middleton.
     vi.   FREDERICK, b. Alton 8 Sept. 1795, d. there 7 Mar.
           1797 (1794 in TRs).
     vii. SARAH, b. Alton 1 Oct. 1799, d. there 14 Apr. 1804.
     viii. FREDERICK B., b. Alton 1 Oct. 1799 (twin); m. 27 Jan.
           1822 ABIGAIL MILLER, b. Milton NH 9 May 1800.
     ix.   RICHARD T., b. Alton 13 Aug. 1803, res. Alton in
           1850; m. 1st 6 Oct. 1823 HANNAH MILLER.

     172.   JONATHAN[6] 1762-1848 [51 Jonathan[5] and Sarah] was
born at Rochester about 1762, buried at Alton 15 Apr. 1848
(Charles C. Mooney, Diary #3 [Ms, NHHS]); married at Rochester 28 Sept. 1786 (McDuffee, Rochester, 2:609) LUCY PLACE,
baptized at Rochester 3 May 1767, died at Alton 10 July 1853
(obituary, Morning Star of 21 Dec.), daughter of John and
Lucy (Jenness) Place. In 1790 they were listed at Rochester,
but soon after they were living at Alton Bay (Albert V.
Fisher, History of Alton, N. H. [1979], 64-5).
     As Jonathan 3rd he signed petitions in 1794 and 1796 seek-
ing incorporation of New Durham Gore, which became Alton in
1798.   On 14 June 1797 he purchased lot 7-9 from Thomas
Lauchlen (StrCD, 25:161). With Joshua Hanson, he bought 100
acres in lot 6, 2nd range, on Alton Bay from Abraham Dearborn
26 Aug. 1801, which they divided 17 Sept. (41:220-3); he sold
a portion in the Gore to Ebenezer Place, Jr., 13 Apr. 1805
(48:80).   He bought from Timothy Heard 22 Feb. 1802 50 acres
in lot 1 (46:395-7), and on 19 Nov. 1804 purchased an acre
from George Horne, Elizabeth Rawlings a witness (46:397-8).
     He was frequently chosen surveyor of lumber at town meet-
ings from 1807 to 1827.   In 1809 he was living on property of
the late Capt. Daniel Reynolds, who owned a dock, store and
farm at the Bay, and was involved in trading by gundalow on
Lake Winnipesaukee (letter from Albert Fisher 15 Feb. 1982 to

George F. Sanborn, Jr.). He was a farmer, but was living
at the town poor farm when he died. His widow lived near the
shore at Alton Bay with the Plumers.

Children, the first two born at Rochester, the rest at
   Alton, nine in all:

521. i.   JEMIMA[7], b. 31 July 1788; m. GEORGE STOCK-
             BRIDGE.
      ii.   AMOS, b. say 1791, d.y.
      iii.   ISAAC, b. in 1795, d. c1818; unm. His tax was
             abated by the town in 1817, relief voted in
             1817 and 1818, and his burial paid for 6 Mar.
             1819 (TRs).
522. iv.   HANNAH, b. in 1796; m. JOSEPH BLACKEY.
      v.   LUCY, b. in 1798, d.y.
523. vi.   JONATHAN, b. 1 Jan. 1800.
      vii.   LUCY, b. in 1803, d.y.
524. viii. LYDIA PLACE, b. 1 Jan. 1804; m. RICHARD PLUMER.

   173. LYDIA[6] 1767-1863 [51 Jonathan[5] and Sarah] was born at
Rochester 24 Apr. 1767 (Alton TRs), died at Milton NH 29
Sept. 1863 (VRs), 96y 5m 5d (GS); married first at Rochester
7 Jan. 1790 (McDuffee, Rochester, 2:595, 610) JONATHAN PLACE,
born at Rochester 29 Aug. 1764 (baptized 10 June [sic] that
year), died at Alton 1 Apr. 1807, son of John Mussett and
Elizabeth Place (Guy S. Rix, Genealogy of the Place Family
[TMs, NEHGS], 12; family register in Alton TRs 1:493); mar-
ried second at Alton 1 Feb. 1816 (TRs 1:535) STEPHEN WENT-
WORTH, born at Rochester 8 Apr. 1776, died at Milton NH 16
Dec. 1822 (GS), son of Stephen and Mary (Malcom) Wentworth
(Wentworth Gen., 2:260). Wentworth had married first 8 Nov.
1787 Olive Rollins, who died 2 May 1815 (GS), daughter of
Ichabod and Olive (Nutter) Rollins.
   In 1850 and 1860, Lydia was in the Dudley Wentworth house-
hold. Wentworth burials are in Teneriffe Mountain cemetery,
Milton. Lydia was called daughter of Amos Leighton in the
Wentworth genealogy and in the Cornman Ms.

Children (**Place**), all but the first born at Alton:

i.   JACOB, b. Rochester 25 Oct. 1791, res. Alton; m.
       HANNAH CLOUGH, dau. of Perley and Sally (Smith)
       Clough of Gilmanton.
ii.   DAVID M., b. 28 July 1793; m. 1st Milton 28 June 1833
       SUSAN TUTTLE; m. 2nd Dover 25 July 1837 JERUSHA
       SHACKLEY.
iii.   SARAH, b. 2 Sept. 1795, d. Rochester 8 Dec. 1869;
       m. MOSES ROBERTS.
iv.   LUCY J., b. 28 July 1798, d. Milton 20 June 1855,
       57y 10m 22d (GS); m. Milton 30 May 1824 DUDLEY
       WENTWORTH, b. 29 Jan. 1795, d. Milton 15 Sept. 1877,
       son of Stephen and Olive (Rollins) Wentworth.
v.   JONATHAN, b. 9 Jan. 1801, d. Farmington 30 Jan. 1880;
       m. 14 Mar. 1833 sister-in-law ABIGAIL (HENDERSON)
       Place, who d. in Oct. 1882.
vi.   JOHN D. (twin), b. 9 Jan. 1801; m. 1st TAMSEN
       WALLINGFORD; m. 2nd ABIGAIL HENDERSON.
vii.   LYDIA, b. 29 Aug. 1805, d. 13 June 1806.

174. MARY[6] [Molly] 1769-   [51 Jonathan[5] and Sarah] was
born at Rochester 30 Mar. 1769 (Alton TRs), lived at Alton in
1850, aged 81; married at Rochester 10 Nov. 1791, both of New
Durham Gore (NHGR, 5[1908]:7; McDuffee, Rochester, 2:611),
JAMES ROBERTS, born at Dover 12 Aug. 1768 (baptized 21 Aug.)
(VRs, 165), died at Alton 5 Oct. 1843 (aged 74, Morning Star
of 10 July 1844), son of Joseph and Elizabeth (Pike) Roberts
(births in Alton TRs, 1:488).
They lived in ME for a time, but soon returned to East
Alton where they remained.

Children (**Roberts**), born at Alton:

i.   NATHANIEL, b. 8 Dec. 1792; m. 1st in 1813 SARAH
       WENTWORTH, dau. of Paul and Deborah (Naylor) Went-
       worth; m. 2nd LOVE (----) Allard.
ii.   STEPHEN, b. 14 Oct. 1795, d. 8 May. 1798.
iii.   JAMES, JR., b. 24 May 1798; m. Alton 25 Dec. 1817
       MARY [Molly] WALKER.
iv.   ABIGAIL, b. 27 Mar. 1801, d. 20 Jan. 1804.
v.   JONATHAN, b. 8 May 1804, d. 20 June 1805.
vi.   MOSES, b. 8 May 180?; unm.
vii.   MARY, b. 14 Apr. 1809.

175. SARAH[6] 1772-1859 [51 Jonathan[5] and Sarah] was born at
Rochester 1 July 1772 (Alton TRs), died at Alton 16 Jan. 1859
(GS, 86y 6m 15d); married there 28 Aug. 1793 ICHABOD ROLLINS,
born at Newington NH 14 Dec. 1772 and baptized 5 Jan. 1772
[sic], died at Alton 26 Dec. 1853 (VRs), 82y (GS), son of
Ichabod and Olive (Nutter) Rollins (Rollins Gen., 19, 36,
74-5; Griffin, Alton, 129).
He was a farmer. In the 1850 census they were listed at
Alton, both aged 79, with their daughter "Sally 2nd," 46.
Family births are in Alton TRs, 1:487. Burials are in River-
side Cemetery, Alton.

Children (**Rollins**), born at Alton:

i.   JOSHUA, b. 30 Oct. 1795, res. Grantham NH; m. there
       5 Dec. 1815 ANNABEL BUCHANAN of Barnet VT, b. 29
       Nov. 1793.
ii.   STEPHEN J., b. 10 Aug. 1797, res. Alton; m. 1st 11
       Nov. 1824 ABIGAIL SEVERANCE, b. Loudon NH 22 Jan.
       1804, d. Alton 15 Feb. 1830, dau. of Jonathan and
       Miriam Severance; m. 2nd 1 Oct. 1830 her sister
       MEHITABLE SEVERANCE, b. Tuftonboro NH 15 July 1810,
       d. Alton 2 Nov. 1891.
iii.   ICHABOD, JR., b. 3 Mar. 1801, d. Alton 14 Jan. 1847,
       45y 10 m (GS); m. Alton 18 Jan. 1826 (TRs) SARAH
       [Sally] WALKER, b. Alton 20 June 1804, d. there 13
       Apr. 1866, 61y 10m (GS), dau. of Samuel and Susan
       Walker.
iv.   SARAH [Sally], b. 26 Aug. 1804, d. Alton 16 Nov.
       1862, 57y 3m (GS); unm. ("insane," 1850, 1860)
v.   ?AMOS, d.y. (listed by Griffin, but not in TRs).
vi.   CHARLES, b. 24 Feb. 1814, d. 24 Nov. 1888, 79y 9m;
       m. 25 Dec. 1835 SARAH TWOMBLEY, b. in 1818, d. 8 May
       1885.

176. HANNAH[6] 1774-1853 [51 Jonathan[5] and Sarah] was born
at Rochester 1 Feb. 1774 (Alton TRs), died at Milton NH 9
Feb. 1853, 79y 8d (GS); married JOSHUA HANSON, born at Dover
25 June 1778 (Alton TRs), died at Milton 12 Sept. 1855, 77y
2m 18d (GS). The 1850 Milton census listed Joshua, cooper,
74, and Hannah, 75. Burials are in Teneriffe Mountain Road
Cemetery. Family births are in Alton TRs, 1:490.

Children (**Hanson**), born at Alton:

i.   SARAH [Sally], b. 12 Apr. 1801, d. Milton 14 May
      1869; m. Milton 22 June 1828 JACOB WENTWORTH, b. 13
      Sept. 1802, son of Stephen and Olive (Rollins) Went-
      worth. Jacob m. 2nd 6 May 1872 Lucretia M. (Pottle)
      Gray (Wentworth Gen., 2:203).
ii.   LAVINA, b. 10 Feb. 1805; m. Milton int. 22 June 1823
      (TRs) MOSES DOWNS.
iii. HANNAH, b. 8 Jan. 1808.
iv.   MARY [Polly], b. 29 June 1811, d. 19 Nov. 1812.

177. SAMUEL[6] 1757-1844 [53 Samuel[5] and Abigail Goodwin]
was born at Rochester about 1757, died at Farmington NH 5
July 1844, 87y; married first (per Cornman Ms) ---- PLACE;
married second at Rochester 4 Oct. 1789 ABIGAIL DURGIN (Free
Will Baptist Church Records 1:124, New Durham town archives).
He was buried in the family graveyard on Silver Street. In
1850 his widow Abigail, aged 90, was living at Milton in the
Tibbetts household.
    In 1790 his household at Rochester included two sons and
two females; in 1800 at Farmington he had two sons 10-16 in
age, and two daughters under 10. He lived in the part of
Rochester set off as Farmington in 1797. He sold land to
Gilbert French 22 Mar. 1811, and deeded land in Rochester to
his brother George 4 July 1816 (StrCD, 67:119; 90:428).
    Julia Cornman placed here Samuel[5] Leighton [# 34], son of
Hatevil.

Children by a first wife, probably born at Rochester:

525. i.   ANNA[7] [Nancy], b. 4 Dec. 1775 [?]; m. NATHANIEL
            WHITEHOUSE.
526. ii.   JOHN.
527. iii. SAMUEL M. III, b. in 1787.

Child by Abigail, born at Rochester:

528. iv.   SARAH, b. say 1794; m. EDMUND TIBBETTS.

178. GEORGE[6] 1764-1843 [53 Samuel[5] and Abigail Goodwin]
was born at Rochester 4 Nov. 1764, died at Farmington 22 Dec.
1843, 79y 1m (GS); married at Portsmouth NH 17 Oct. 1787
(Farmington TRs 1:208) MARY ANN TREFFREN, born at Portsmouth
17 Feb. 1768, died at Farmington 4 Oct. 1847, 79y 7m (GS).
Burials are in a family plot on Silver Street.
    He lived on the farm homestead, held in the family for
seven generations, in the northwest parish of Rochester,
later set off as Farmington. He was at the first Farmington
town meeting 11 Mar. 1797. In 1790 his Rochester household

included one son; in 1800 at Farmington it included two sons, four daughters, and a couple over 45, probably his parents. He was deeded land by his father 4 July 1816 (StrCD, 90:428).

Children, births in Farmington TRs:

529. i.   RICHARD[7], b. 12 Oct. 1789.
530. ii.   SARAH, b. 16 June 1791; m. STEPHEN WIGGIN.
531. iii. ABIGAIL, b. 10 July 1793; m. JONATHAN CLARK.
532. iv.   JANE W., b. 28 July 1795 m. NATHANIEL CLARK.
      v.   JOSHUA W., b. 29 May 1798, d. Farmington 12
            Nov. 1825, 27y 5m (GS).
      vi.   HANNAH, b. 12 June 1800, d. Farmington 20 July
            1854, 54y 1m (GS); unm.
      vii. NANCY W., b. 16 Sept. 1802, d. Farmington 29
            July 1881, 78y 10m 13d; m. Farmington 20 Aug.
            1862 Capt. PETER Y. PEARL, b. Farmington in
            1802, d. there 5 July 1869, son of Eleazer and
            Sarah (Ellis) Pearl. No ch.
      viii. MARY S., b. 22 Sept. 1804, d. Farmington 13
            Feb. 1871, 66y (GS); unm.
      ix.   JEREMIAH W., b. 28 Aug. 1807, d. Farmington
            1876 (GS); m. Farmington 11 Aug. 1832 HANNAH
            E. AVERY of New Durham, b. in 1814, d. in 1878
            (GS). His will, made 12 Mar. 1852 and proved
            in Jan. 1877, gave his property to his wife,
            and $1 to each of his living siblings. He had
            no ch.; an adopted son George was not named in
            his will.
533. x.   JEMIMA, b. 11 Sept. 1809; m. DEXTER RICHARDSON.
534. xi.   ELIZABETH, b. 30 July 1813; m. JONATHAN
            WENTWORTH.
      xii. ?JOSEPH, b. in 1816.

179.   DOROTHY[6] [Dolly] 1752-1816 [52 David[5] and Anna Chamberlain] was born at Rochester NH 5 Aug. 1752 (Alton TRs), died at Alton 26 Sept. 1816; married at Rochester 29 Feb. 1776 (NHGR, 4[1907]:147) ROBERT WALKER, born there 10 Feb. 1753 (Alton TRs; 5 Feb. per family Bible; bapt. 25 Feb. in McDuffee, Rochester, 591), son of Joseph, Jr., and Margaret (----)(Downs) Walker (family births, Alton TRs 1:488; Walker family Bible records of descendant Olive Fitzgerald).
    Robert built a sawmill at Alton in 1785, and was a militia ensign. Descendant Leila Trefren believed Robert probably died in 1841 at the home of his son John at Ossipee.

Children (**Walker**), all but last two born at Rochester:

i.   BENJAMIN, b. 25 Sept., d. in Oct. 1776.
ii.   JOSEPH (twin), b. 25 Sept. 1776, d. in 1782.
iii. ABIGAIL, b. 17 Oct. 1777, d. 29 Mar. 1778.
iv.   ANNA, b. 30 Dec. 1779; m. JAMES HARRIMAN.
v.   JOSEPH, b. 7 June 1782; m. MARY[7] LEIGHTON [# 536].
vi.   Rev. JOHN, b. 26 Dec. 1784, d. Ossipee NH 1 June 1870;
      m. 1st in 1807 BETSEY PIPER, who d. in 1819; m. 2nd
      7 May 1820 BETSEY HEALEY, who d. 16 Nov. 1888,
      dau. of William and Lois (Ricker) Healey. He was a
      Free Baptist minister at Ossipee 1833-1870 (N. F.
      Carter, The Native Ministry of N. H. [Concord,
      1906], 673).

vii. MARY [Molly], b. 26 Dec. 1787, d. c1823, buried
      Moultonboro NH; m. New Durham 31 Oct. 1811 GEORGE
      WASHINGTON TREFREN, b. 12 Oct. 1790, d. Moultonboro
      4 Apr. 1849, son of James and Amy Trefren.
viii. ROBERT, b₇ 19 May 1790; m. Alton 13 Apr. 1817
      LYDIA G.⁷ LEIGHTON [# 540].
ix.   ELIZABETH, b. prob. Alton 7 July 1792; m. WILLIAM
      EVANS.
x.   EPHRAIM, b. Alton 11 Apr. 1795, d. Denmark ME 18 Aug.
      1871 (Bible); m. 8 Dec. 1816 MARY WOODMAN.

180. JACOB⁶ 1757-1842 [52 David⁵ and Anna Chamberlain] was
born at Rochester 12 July 1757 (baptized 31 July, NHGR
6[1909]:114), died by hanging himself at New Durham 17 Oct.
1842, 86y (TRs; 85y 3m, Morning Star); married at New Durham
11 Feb. 1781 (widow's pension application) MARY TOWNSEND,
born perhaps at Hollis ME 23 July 1761, died at New Durham 8
May 1844 (83y, Morning Star), daughter of Ebenezer Townsend
(Little, Me. Genealogies, 4:2058-9; Hiner family Bible data
and copies of letters of Jacob and of son Ephraim provided by
Charlotte Kohler).
    Jacob's military service, according to his pension applica-
tion, included two months in late 1775 under Capt. Brewster,
Col. Wingate's Rgt., at Great Island (Portsmouth), duty under
Capt. Badger in 1776, and five months that same year under
Capt. John Drew, Col. Wyman's Rgt., at Ticonderoga and Fort
Independence.
    On 24 June 1784 he was deeded land in Rochester by his
father (StrCD, 5:446). He settled at New Durham in 1788; his
household there in 1790 included six females. He bought land
at Rochester from his brother Ephraim 8 Dec. 1790 (12:375),
and then lots 4 and 5 at Ossipee 25 May 1803 (41:449). In
1814, he sold off some of his property (79:60, 265), and on
26 Feb. 1816 made over land to his son Jacob, Jr. (89:2). In
1820 and 1823, he deeded land to his brother Ephraim.
    Jacob and Mary were living with Ephraim in 1828 (his letter
to Nancy). On 10 Sept. 1832, aged 76 of New Durham, he
applied for a pension. His will, made 13 Feb. 1838 and
proved 1 Nov. 1842, named his wife and son Ephraim as co-
executors, and mentioned all eight living children. He left
the homestead to Ephraim--lot 37 and half of lot 39, second
division (StrCP, 59:18-21). His widow applied for a pension
25 Aug. 1843, aged 82 (NA-MSR #W 16136).

Children, from Hiner family Bible and New Durham VRs:

535. i.   BETSEY⁷, b. Wolfeboro NH 3 Jan. 1782; m.
            JEREMIAH EDGERLY.
536. ii.   MARY, b. 10 Mar. 1784; m. JOSEPH WALKER.
537. iii. NANCY, b. 31 May 1786; m. JOHN HINER.
538. iv.   DOROTHY, b. 28 June 1788; m. JAMES HAYES.
539. v.   JACOB, b. 6 Feb.1791.
540. vi.   LYDIA G., b. 8 Apr. 1793; m. ROBERT WALKER, JR.
      vii. RHODA, b. 11 Sept. 1795, d. 17 Nov. 1816; m. 12
            May 1816 JOHN EDGERLY, son of Andrew and Eliz-
            abeth (Tash) Edgerly. No ch.
541. viii. EPHRAIM, b.. 8 Nov. 1798.
542. ix.   HANNAH E., b. 26 Sept. 1801; m. WILLIAM
            EDGERLY.

181.   EPHRAIM[6] 1760-1834 [52 David[5] and Anna Chamberlain]
was born at Rochester 13 Feb. 1760, died at Ossipee NH 30
Nov. 1834, 74y 9m 18d (VRs); married first at Portsmouth (he
of the Gore) 17 Dec. 1780 OLIVE PERKINS, born at Rochester 16
Nov. 1762, died at Ossipee 3 Mar. 1803, daughter of Joshua
Perkins, Jr.; married second at Limington ME int. 4 Sept.
1803 MARGARET (RANDALL) Lyons (called "Miss Peggy Lyons,"
NEHGReg, 87[1933]:124), born about 1752, died at Barnstead NH
24 Feb. 1838, 76y (GS; or aged 78, sister of Elder Benjamin
Randall, at the residence of Joseph Hall, per Morning Star),
daughter of Benjamin and Margaret (Mordant) Randall. Peggy
had married first William Lyons, who died in 1801; she had no
children (Scales, Dover, 441-2).
   Ephraim purchased 21 Apr. 1780 from John Pierce of Portsmouth 150 acres in New Durham Gore, part of lot #1, first
range (StrCD, 3:521). On 24 Sept. 1781 he and Olive sold to
Timothy Davis 80 acres adjacent to the New Durham line, and
more later (5:413). On 2 May 1786, he sold to Joseph Jones
30 acres at Rochester that he had bought from his father
(12:324). He purchased 27 May 1786 130 acres at New Durham,
which he sold that day to his brother Jacob (13:50). He sold
28 acres at Rochester 7 Sept. 1790 to Joseph Peavey (12:533),
and on 30 Oct. purchased from Peavey 400 acres at Ossipee
(12:305). In 1790 he was listed at Rochester with one son
and four females.
   He was a pioneer settler at Ossipee, traveling there about
1797 by oxcart from Rochester through Wakefield into a trackless forest. He settled at what is called Leighton's Corners
(Georgia D. Merrill, History of Carroll County, N. H. [1889],
621; records of Nellie Hiday).
   His will, made 22 Jan. 1827 and proved 20 Jan. 1835, named
Jacob as principal heir and executor, and gave $25 each to
his daughters and to the children of his daughter Mehitable
Sanborn by her two husbands (StrCP, 48:385-7).

   Children by Olive, all but last born at Rochester:

543.   i.   SUSANNA[7], b. 11 Oct. 1781; m. ABRAM DRAKE and
              Rev. JOSHUA ROBERTS.
       ii.   ABIGAIL, b. 15 Oct. 1784, res. Melbourne ON,
              Canada; m. Lancaster NH 3 Nov. 1805 JONAS
              BEAMAN (A. H. Somers, History of Lancaster,
              N. H. [Concord, 1899], 191; Cornman Ms). Ch.
              Abigail, Mary, Leighton, perhaps others.
544.   iii.   JACOB, b. 30 May 1787.
545.   iv.   MEHITABLE, b. in 1789; m. ISAAC DREW and ELISHA
              SANBORN.
       v.   OLIVE, b. 15 Nov. 1794; unm. in 1835.
546.   vi.   ANNA [Nancy], b. 2 Nov. 1797; m. DANIEL KILHAM.
547.   vii.   SARAH, b. Ossipee 16 Apr. 1801; m. OLIVER
              SCATES.

182.   JONATHAN[6] 1762-1840 [52 David[5] and Anna Chamberlain]
was born at Rochester NH 12 Feb. 1762 and baptized there 13
Apr., died at Athens ME 2 Nov., 1840, 78y 6m 18d (GS); married at Rochester 20 Apr. 1784 MARY ROGERS of Lee NH, who
died about 1845.
   He bought 100 acres from Woodbury Langdon 13 June 1785, lot
2, first range, at New Durham Gore (incorporated as Alton in
1796), and purchased from James Rogers 3 Aug. 1790 half of

the 60 acres Rogers had bought of Langdon (StrCD, 8:377; 17:367-8). He bought lot 1, another 100 acres, from Langdon 29 June 1791; he sold portions of lot 1 to George Horne and to John Bennett, Jr. (17:368-9; 15:435-6; 17:57-8).

He was called Jonathan, Jr., in these deeds; on the petitions in 1794 and 1796 for establishment of a town he also signed as Jonathan, Jr., along with his uncle Jonathan and cousin Jonathan 3rd.

He erected a home in 1785 on a knoll above Cotton Brook, and set up a gristmill. Since his brother-in-law Robert Walker planned a sawmill downstream, they joined in completing that first, and then in 1790 finished the gristmill. He and Walker founded the East Alton Free Will Baptist church in 1803; its meetings were held at Jonathan's home up to Feb. 1805 (Fisher, Alton, 64-5). In 1790, his household at New Durham included two sons and a daughter.

He sold 40 acres to Ebenezer Place, Jr., 30 Apr. 1794, and on 5 Dec. 1797 sold to David Stockbridge 60 acres of lot 9, his wife Mary releasing her dower rights (48:80-1; 25:232-3). On 27 Nov. 1804 he deeded his homestead and mill to George Walker, and additional land 7 Feb. 1806; he was a resident of Athens, Kennebec County, District of Maine, when the deeds were recorded (47:206-8; 94:63-4).

On 27 Nov. 1804, also, he purchased from William True Smith of Deerfield NH (KenCD, 10:523) 100 acres in lots 83 and 86 at Athens, a new town which bordered Harmony (where his father and brother William had already settled). He sold portions of his land 28 Nov. 1808 to his son John, and on 17 May 1814 to Jonathan, Jr. (Somerset Co.Deeds, 5:538; 6:169). He mortgaged to Isaiah Dore of Athens 29 Dec. 1829 part of lot 62, and 70 acres of lot 83 and buildings, "the farm where I now live" (25:53). The 150-acre "farm he lived on," including the mortgaged portion but excepting a burying place, was sold to John Lock of Athens 18 June 1831 (27:236).

In 1810 Jonathan and his wife were at Athens with three sons and a daughter; in 1830 the household included a male 10-15, perhaps a grandson. Burials are in the Lord's Hill cemetery, Athens, for which he had donated land to the town.

Children:

548. i.   JOHN[7], b. Rochester in Feb. 1785.
549. ii.   LYDIA, b. in 1789; m. BENJAMIN FLAGG and LEVI
            EMERY.
550. iii. JONATHAN, b. in 1790.
      iv.   DAVID, b. in 1792, d. Athens 18 June 1815, 23y
            (GS); m. Mount Vernon ME, he of North Hill
            Plantation (Brighton), 10 Jan. 1815 ELEANOR
            BROWN, who d. 13 Sept. 1819, 27y (GS).
551. v.   HAZEN, b. Alton in 1797.

183. WILLIAM[6] 1764-1846 [52 David[5] and Anna Chamberlain] was born at Rochester NH 17 July 1764 (bapt. 9 Sept., NHGR, 6[1909]:115), died at Harmony ME 18 Dec. 1846, 82y (GS); married at New Durham NH 26 Nov. 1788 (5[1908]:4) MARY POTTLE, born at York ME 29 Aug. 1766 (Harmony TRs), died at Harmony 22 Nov. 1857, 91y (GS) (records of descendant Gary Rader and Harmony researcher Clara Cromwell). In 1850 Mary, 83, was living with her son Joseph. Burials are in a small private cemetery at Harmony.

In 1790, his household at Rochester included one son and three females. His father deeded to him lot 73, second division, at Rochester 20 Aug. 1794 (StrCD, 19:68), but he sold this to Ephraim Twombley 7 Jan. 1800 (33:65).

In Mar. 1800, he and his family joined with his parents in making the two-week journey to Harmony, along with their livestock--three cows, a horse, a yoke of oxen and three hogs (Cornman Ms). In the 1800 Harmony census, William was listed with his wife, three sons and three daughters.

William bought his father's homestead 1 Mar. 1809, lot 6, range 9, and then on 14 Mar. 1810 bought by mortgage from Augustine Bousquet of Philadelphia, proprietor, lot 25, center range, of 106 acres (SomCD, 7:495, 510). He took a deed from Abner Pottle to secure a debt he owed his niece Lydia Flagg (6:478).

Children, six born at Rochester, the rest at Harmony (TRs):

552. i.   DANIEL[7], b. in 1789, bp. 30 Oct. 1791 (NHGR,
            6[1909]:176).
      ii.   ELIJAH, bp. 30 Oct. 1791; d. Farmington NH 26
            May 1796, 5y 10d (Harmony TRs).
553. iii. ABIGAIL, b. 22 Feb. 1793 (bp. 22 June, 7[1910]:
            27); m. SOLOMON WATSON [# 185].
      iv.   JOHN, b. 28 May 1795 (bp. 28 May 1796, 7:28);
            d. Harmony 13 June 1817, 22y 5m 13d.
554. v.   MARY [Polly], b. 31 Dec. 1798; m. JONATHAN
            WATSON [# 185].
      vi.   MEHITABLE, b. in 1799, d. Harmony 15 Aug.
            1815, 16y 9m.
      vii. LYDIA, b. 21 Nov. 1800; m. JONATHAN GILES[7]
            LEIGHTON [# 560].
555. viii. WILLIAM CHAMBERLAIN, b. 28 Nov. 1802.
556. ix.   NANCY, b. 19 June 1805; m. JOSEPH WELCH.
      x.   JUDITH, b. 2 Dec. 1807, d. Orange MA 10
            May 1892; unm. She lived with her brother
            Benjamin.
557. xi.   JOSEPH, b. 8 June 1810.
558. xii. BENJAMIN (twin), b. 8 June 1810.
      xiii. ALFRED PERRY, b. in 1814, d. Harmony 15 Nov.
            1815, 1y 10m.

184. ELIZABETH[6] 1766-   [52 David[5] and Anna Chamberlain] was born at Rochester 2 Dec. 1766, baptized 1 Feb. 1767 (NHGR, 6[1909]:115); married at Rochester 11 Oct. 1787 (5[1908]:3) ELEAZER HODGDON. They settled at Ossipee NH.

Children (**Hodgdon**), born at Rochester:

i.   MARY, bp. 9 May 1790.
ii. NATHANIEL, bp. 19 Oct. 1794.

185. ANNA[6] [Nancy] 1770-1852 [52 David[5] and Anna Chamberlain] was born at Rochester 16 Nov. 1770 (VRs), baptized 7 July 1771 (NHGR, 6[1909]:117), died at Cambridge ME 25 June 1852 (VRs); married at Rochester 16 Nov. 1791 (5[1908]:5) JONATHAN WATSON, born at Rochester 22 Aug. 1770, died at Harmony ME 31 Jan. 1814 (town VRs; Cornman Ms).

Children (**Watson**), born at Farmington NH:

i.   SOLOMON, b. 15 July 1792; m. ABIGAIL[7] LEIGHTON
      [# 553].
ii.   JONATHAN, b. 13 Aug. 1794; m. MARY[7] LEIGHTON [# 554].
iii. EPHRAIM, b. 22 Dec. 1796; m. RACHEL[7] LEIGHTON
      [# 565].
iv.   NANCY, b. 5 Mar. 1799, d. West Needham MA 2 Dec.
      1856; m. 1st Harmony 7 Sept. 1815 BENJAMIN DREW; m.
      2nd ---- WHITCOMB.
v.   NATHANIEL, b. 21 Mar. 1801, d. Corinth ME 30 Mar.
      1866.
vi.   SILAS D., b. 8 Sept. 1803, d. Dexter ME 13 Sept.
      1889, 67y; m. Harmony 20 Apr. 1822 BETSEY BROWN, b.
      Athens 11 Feb. 1802, dau. of Robert and Elizabeth
      Brown.
vii. LOIS, b. 1 Nov. 1806, d. Cambridge ME 28 Mar. 1856.
viii. JOSEPH G., b. 24 Nov. 1808, d. Winslow ME in 1870.
ix.   JOHN B., b. 5 May 1813, d. Cambridge ME 23 Dec. 1889.

186.   DAVID[6] 1773-1854 [52 David[5] and Anna Chamberlain]
was born at Rochester 9 Nov. 1773 (1774, per Harmony TR),
died at Harmony ME 1 June 1854; married at Rochester 1 Nov.
1795 (NHGR, 5[1908]:51) ANNA [Nancy] WATSON, born at Rochester 13 Dec. 1775 (Harmony TRs), died at Harmony 2 July 1855,
81y (GS; Harmony TRs; Cornman Ms). Burials are in North Road
Cemetery, Harmony.
      On 30 May 1797 David, Jr., bought from Joseph Durgin of New
Durham half of lot 43 in the first division, Middleton NH,
and from Jonathan Leighton of Farmington on 24 Apr. 1805 part
of lot 47 (StrCD, 50:239, 240). For a time he lived at Middleton, but returned to Alton. On 14 Dec. 1805, he sold his
Middleton property to Joseph Watson (52:42-3). By 1808 he
had removed to Harmony. In 1850, he and Nancy lived there in
the household of his son Joseph.

Children, the last four births in Harmony TRs:

559. i.   NATHANIEL[7], b. Rochester in 1796.
560. ii.   JONATHAN GILES, b. Middleton 15 Dec. 1799.
561. iii. JOSEPH, b. Rochester about 1801.
562. iv.   EPHRAIM, b. 25 July 1806.
      v.   NANCY, b. 30 Aug. 1809, d. Bradford ME;
            m. JOSEPH DORE.
563. vi.   SHERBURN, b. 5 Aug. 1813.
564. vii. DAVID, b. 20 May 1816.

187.   MOSES[6] 1776-1856 [52 David[5] and Anna Chamberlain] was
born at Rochester 25 Mar. 1776 (TRs), and baptized 19 May
(NHGR, 6[1909]:118), died at Cambridge ME 4 Jan. 1856 (TRs);
married first at Wolfeboro 24 Nov. 1796 BETSEY ROGERS, born
at Rochester 22 Feb. 1778, died at Cambridge 23 Feb. 1840,
daughter of James and Rachel (Place) Rogers; married second
SUSAN (KNOWLES) Mann, who married third at Cambridge Levi
Coburn (Cornman Ms; Cambridge VRs). Burials are in the Old
Village Cemetery, Cambridge.
      He was listed at Harmony with his wife and daughter in
1800; in 1804 he was a pioneer settler at Ripley, which borders on Harmony, and was selectman there in 1817 and 1818.

They had to bring supplies from Skowhegan, 25 miles away;
Moses was said to have carried a half-bushel of corn and a
small wood stove in one trip (East Somerset County Register,
1910-11 [Auburn ME, 1912], 44). In 1834, the northern part
of Ripley was set off as the town of Cambridge.

Children by first wife Betsey:

565.   i.   RACHEL[7], b. Alton 20 Feb. 1797; m. EPHRAIM
                WATSON [# 185].
566.   ii.   SALLY, b. 13 June 1799 (Harmony TRs); m. Rev.
                FOREST HATCH, ---- ROBINSON and JOHN WOODS.
567.   iii.   SUSANNA, b. Harmony 2 June 1801; m. FOSS
                HAMILTON.
568.   iv.   ELIJAH, b. Harmony 13 July 1803.

Child by second wife Susan:

        v.   ALMIRA J., b. Cambridge in Nov. 1841, d. 3 Jan.
                1856, 14y 2m (joint burial with father).

188.   EPHRAIM[6] 1765-1849 [54 Benjamin[5] and Jane Webber] was
born at Edgecomb ME in Jan. 1765 (pension application), died
at Augusta ME 10 Dec. 1849, 86y (GS); married ESTHER ---- 23
Nov. 1789. Esther's surname has been traditionally given as
Tibbetts (Mount Vernon, Rome and Augusta VRs; Cornman Ms;
Kingsbury, Kenn. Co. Hist., 1:476-7; records of descendant
Helen VanDyke, who has gathered data on this branch of the
family). Burials are in Mount Hope cemetery, Augusta.
   In May 1776, a child of 11, he enlisted as waiter to Capt.
Henry Tibbetts, Col. Cargill's Rgt., for six months' service.
In 1790 he was listed at Washington Plantation (Mount Vernon)
with his wife and another female; in 1800, he had three sons,
a daughter, and a slave. About 1804, he removed to Augusta,
where he was shown as a farmer in 1810. Perhaps he still
owned a house in Rome; in 1810, the census-taker there noted
that he refused to provide any information.
   He and Ephraim, Jr., were at Parkman ME in 1830; on 6 Oct.
1833, aged 67 and of Parkman for the past six years, he
applied for a pension (NA-MSR #S 18937). In 1850, aged 84,
he was living with his son Ephraim at Augusta.

Children:

        i.   STEPHEN[7],b. Mt. Vernon 6 Nov. 1790; nfr.
569.   ii.   HENRY TIBBETTS, b. Mt. Vernon 4 Sept. 1796.
570.   iii.   EPHRAIM, b. Mt. Vernon 14 June 1798.
        iv.   SUSANNA K., b. Mt. Vernon 22 June 1801, d.
                Augusta 11 Mar. 1870, 67y (GS); m. ASA COOK.
        v.   ESTHER, b. 4 Apr. 1802 (Rome VRs); m. Augusta
                int. 1 Mar. 1822 WILLIAM CHAMBERLAIN. Ch.
                Ephraim d. 21 Nov. 1827, 8m 11d.
        vi.   CHARLOTTE, b. 9 May 1804 (Rome VRs); m. Augusta
                int. 5 Aug. 1825 EZRA BRADFORD, JR., b. there
                4 Feb. 1804, son of Ezra and Polly Bradford.
                Ch. Julia Ann b. Parkman 9 Dec. 1821.
        vii.   ANNA B., b. Augusta in 1808, d. there 28 Dec.
                1898, 90y (GS); m. 1st int. Parkman 29 May
                1836 FRANCIS [Frank] CONANT of Peru ME, d.

Byron ME c1853, probably son of Joseph and
Lucinda (Tufts) Conant (Frederick Odell
Conant, Conant Family in England and America
[Portland, 1887], 287); m. 2nd in 1856, as his
2nd wife, CHARLES BEARCE of Hartford ME, who
d. Livermore ME in 1887. Anna had no ch.
571.   viii. ISAAC, b. Augusta 30 July 1811.

189.   EZEKIEL[6] 1769-1857 [54 Benjamin[5] and Jane Webber] was
born probably at Edgecomb ME (in NH per 1850 census) 21 May
1768 (GS), died at Augusta 20 Sept. 1857, 89y (VRs) or 21
Aug. 1858, 89y 3m (GS); married at Mount Vernon 8 Nov. 1791
(VRs) LYDIA PEARL, born about 1774, died at Exeter ME 7 Aug.
1854, 80y 2m 24d, daughter of Simeon and Mary[5] (Leighton)
Pearl [# 36] (town VRs; Cornman Ms; records compiled by
descendant Lois Ware Thurston). They are buried in the
Atkins-Prescott cemetery at Corinna.
   In 1800, they were listed at Mount Vernon with two sons and
two daughters, and in 1810 with four sons and one daughter.
In his pension application Ezekiel stated that he served in
the War of 1812 under Capt. George Waugh; his request was
denied because he was not listed in that unit (NA-MSR).
   Ezekiel of Rome sold to George Brooks of Augusta lot 21 on
9 Mar. 1808 (KenCD, 13:154), and 100 acres to his son Silas
in lot 154 on 13 July 1817 (16:557). He is said to have been
among the first settlers of Corinna (Lilla E. Wood, A Brief
History of Corinna, Maine [Bangor, 1916], 13). They were
living at Exeter in 1850.

   Children:

572.   i.   SIMEON[7], b. Mt. Vernon 16 July 1792.
573.   ii.   SILAS, b. Mt. Vernon 24 May 1795.
       iii.   CHARLOTTE, b. Mt. Vernon 27 July 1797.
       iv.   KATE [CATY], b. 13 July 1799 (Rome VRs), prob.
              d.y.
       v.   TIMOTHY, b. Rome 24 Sept. 1801, prob. d.y.
574.   vi.   ?JOHN (not in VRs).
       vii.   EDYA, b. Rome 22 Oct. 1804, prob. d.y.
575.   vii.   HIRAM, b. Rome 26 Apr. 1807.
576.   viii. WARREN, b. in 1809.
577.   ix.   LORENZO D., b. Mt. Vernon 15 July 1811.
       xi.   ?CHARLES W., b. c1814, 36 in 1850, living next
              door to Ezekiel, with wife Hannah and ch.
              MARTHA H. b. in 1849.

190.   ISAAC[6] 1770-1855 [54 Benjamin[5] and Jane Webber] was
born probably at Edgecomb ME in Sept. 1770, died at Augusta
ME 14 May 1855, 84y 8m (VRs, GS); married at Pittston ME int.
15 Jan. 1792 (VRs) ELIZABETH [Betsey] LAWRENCE,, born at Gar-
diner ME 11 Nov. 1770, died there 3 July 1854, 83y (Gardiner
VRs; 84y in Augusta VRs), daughter of David and Elizabeth
(Eastman) Lawrence (John Lawrence, Genealogy of the Family of
John Lawrence [Boston, 1869], 149-50).
   In 1800 they were listed at Mount Vernon with four children
under 10. In 1814 he was of Pittston when he bought property
there; in 1816 he was of Mt. Vernon, buying land of James
Page of Augusta; in 1817 he was a taxpayer in Augusta.

Children, born at Mt. Vernon (TRs 2:319; last five listed in Augusta VRs also):

578. i.   LUCY[7], b. 17 Dec. 1792; m. MOSES FLANDERS.
579. ii.   DAVID, b. 4 Aug. 1794.
580. iii. EDWARD, b. 24 Sept. 1796.
581. iv.   BETSEY, b. 28 June 1799; m. PETER WAITT.
582. v.   BENJAMIN, b. 27 Mar. 1801.
      vi.   MARY C. [Polly], b. 14 Nov. 1802; m. SILAS[7]
            LEIGHTON [# 573].

191. TIMOTHY[6] 1773-1854 [54 Benjamin[5] and Jane Webber] was born probably at Edgecomb about 1773, died at Mount Vernon 16 July 1854 (VRs); said to have married MARY [Polly] DOLLOFF. His wife died 22 May 1850, but not even her first name appeared in the town records.

Timothy bought part of lot 171 at Mt. Vernon of Stephen Scribner 23 Oct. 1804 (KenCD, 9:22), and in 1817 bought part of lot 187. He served in Capt. Timothy Stevens's company in Sept. 1814 (MA Mil. 1812-1814, 279). In 1850, aged 77, he was living with Charles and Lucy Hale.

Children, born at Mt. Vernon (TRs 2:319):

      i.   LYDIA[7], b. 5 Apr. 1800; m. Mt. Vernon 18 Jan.
            1824 (VRs) VARNEY LEIGHTON, perhaps son of
            Daniel [# 197] but certainly a grandson of
            Solomon and Sarah (Varney). No known ch. In
            the Cornman Papers his mother was called
            Hannah "Blis", and he was reported to have
            settled "toward New Sharon."
583. ii.   NATHAN, b. 8 Aug. 1802.
584. iii. DAVID, b. 15 Apr. 1807.
585. iv.   GEORGE W., b. 18 Apr. 1807.
586. v.   JOHN HOVEY, b. 17 Dec. 1811.
587. vi.   LUCY, b. 12 Jan. 1815; m. CHARLES HALE.

192. LYDIA[6] 1776-1840 [54 Benjamin[5] and Jane Webber] was born probably at Edgecomb say 1776, died at Mount Vernon 3 Nov. 1840; married there int. 17 Mar. 1799 DAVID DOLLOFF, born probably at Exeter NH about 1771, died at Mount Vernon 8 Mar. 1852, son of Richard Dolloff. He married second 16 Oct. 1842 Cynthia (----) Allen, who died 22 Apr. 1845, and married third 3 Aug. 1846 Betsey (----) Gilman (records of Clayton Dolloff; Mt. Vernon TRs). Burials are in Bean Cemetery.

David was on the Mt. Vernon tax list in 1793, and bought part of lot 158 in 1795 (KenCD, 4:58). He sold this in 1810, and bought in 1811 half of lot 173--part of which he sold to Benjamin Leighton (19:139; 38:393). In 1846 he deeded his home to his son in return for support for life (149:155-7).

Child (**Dolloff**), born at Mount Vernon:

      i.   JAMES, b. 11 Dec. 1802, d. Mt. Vernon 29 Jan. 1882;
            m. 22 June 1821 ANNA TRASK, b. Brentwood NH in 1803,
            d. Mt. Vernon in 1886, dau. of Jonathan and Eliza-
            beth (Leavitt) Trask (R. D. Trask, Genealogy of the
            Trask Family [Portland, 1877], 15, 19).

193. DAVID[6] 1785-1876 [54 Benjamin[5] and Jane Webber] was born probably at Edgecomb 22 Sept. 1785, died at Mount Vernon 28 Apr. 1876, 90y 7m 6d (GS); married there 17 Oct. 1808 (int. 9 June) LYDIA ROGERS, born 17 Feb. 1787 (per Rome VRs), died at Mt. Vernon 4 Aug. 1856, 69y 6m (GS, 14 Aug.), daughter of John and Molly (Poole) Rogers (Cornman Ms).

Children, born at Mount Vernon (TRs 2:40):

588.	i.	SOPHRONIA[7], b. 11 Dec. 1808; m. EMERSON STAIN.
589.	ii.	LUCINDA, b. 25 Sept. 1810; m. JOHN HAMMOND.
590.	iii.	NATHANIEL, b. 9 Aug. 1812.
591.	iv.	ORINDA S., b. 30 Jan. 1815; m. ROBERT D. CROCKER.
592.	v.	EBENEZER, b. 27 Jan. 1817.
	vi.	MARY JANE, b. 22 Oct. 1819, d. Dixmont ME 14 Apr. 1903, 83y 5m 22d (VR); married Mt. Vernon 10 Apr. 1845 IRA GARDNER, b. c1816, d. Dixmont 20 Oct. 1905, 89y 8m 14d, son of Ansel and Anna (Stevens) Gardner. Ch. Charles d. unm.
	vii.	SYLVINA, b. 9 Apr. 1821; m. SAMUEL[7] LEIGHTON, JR. [# 610].
593.	viii.	DAVID, b. 25 Jan. 1825.
	ix.	ROXANNA S., b. 24 Sept. 1828, d. 23 Jan. 1889; m. 1st Mt. Vernon 8 Sept. 1850 ALBERT TAFT, b. Lowell MA in 1827, son of Chesley and Abigail Taft; m. 2nd WILLIAM MOORE of Lowell. A Taft ch. d. infant; Moore ch. William and Fred.

194. MOSES[6] 1760-   [55 Solomon[5] and Sarah Varney] was born probably at Rochester NH 6 Feb. 1760, died at or near Lyons, Wayne Co. NY; married at Falmouth 3 Feb. 1789 (Cumberland Co. record; Mt. Vernon TRs) MARGARET CARLL. (Julia Cornman wrote that Margaret was of Gorham ME, and the marriage was at Dover NH.)

He settled at Mt. Vernon as did his parents, and in 1790 was listed there (Washington Plantation) with his wife and daughter. They settled at Rome (West Pond), where they had a family of four sons and two daughters in 1800. They were at Rome in 1815 when Moses had to pay a judgment to William Waters; the family moved west shortly after. In the 1820 census of Lyons, Wayne Co. NY, he headed a family of wife and eight children, and in 1830 had three children at home.

Children, five born at Mt. Vernon (TRs 2:305), four at Rome (TRs 18):

	i.	SARAH[7], b. 28 Oct. 1789, d. Algansee, Hillandale Co. MI 2 Apr. 1882; m. Rome 22 Mar. 1810 SOLOMON JORDAN, d. Algansee c1854 (Cornman Ms). They settled in NY, and then MI in 1836.
	ii.	ELIZABETH, b. 13 Sept. 1792, prob. d.y.
594.	iii.	PETER, b. 30 Oct. 1794.
595.	iv.	MORDECAI, b. 25 Mar. 1796.
596.	v.	ENOCH, b. 6 Nov. 1797.
597.	vi.	JONATHAN, b. 23 May 1803.
598.	vii.	DAVID, b. 22 Nov. 1804.
	viii.	NANCY, b. 1 Jan. 1807; unm. in 1830.
599.	ix.	?SAMUEL, b. c1812 (birth not in TRs).
600.	x.	ISRAEL, b. 7 July 1813.

195. ANDREW[6] 1761-   [55 Solomon[5] and Sarah Varney] was born probably at Rochester NH 16 Aug. 1761 (Mt. Vernon record); married MARY[6] LEIGHTON, born about 1775, died 17 Apr. 1854, probably daughter of John Smithson and Sarah (Barey) Leighton [# 38].

He appeared alone in the 1790 census; in 1800 he had two sons and two daughters at Mount Vernon. He was surveyor of highways from 1797 to 1800.

His father gave him part of lot 157 on 26 Aug. 1801 (KenCD, 24:221), and 8 Apr. 1811 he sold this land and its buildings to his brother Benjamin (24:281).

In 1850 his widow Mary, 75, was living at Mt. Vernon with her sons Thomas and Andrew.

Children, born at Mt. Vernon (TRs 2:305-6):

    i.   SALLY[7], b. 18 Nov. 1789.
    ii.   EUNICE, b. 2 Oct. 1792, probably that Unice
         who d. 6 May 1817.
   iii. ANDREW, b. 22 Jan. 1795, res. Mt. Vernon in
         1850, aged 55; unm.
    iv. THOMAS, b. 10 July 1797, d. Mt. Vernon 25 Feb.
         1869 or 23 Oct. 1867 (both in VRs); unm. He
         was in Capt. Timothy Stevens company in Sept.
         1814 (MA Mil. 1812-1814, 279).

196. JOHN[6] 1766-   [55 Solomon[5] and Sarah Varney] was born probably at Edgecomb 22 May 1766 (Mount Vernon TRs); married ESTHER ---- . In 1790 he was living at Mt. Vernon (then Washington) alone; in 1800 he had a wife, four sons and a daughter. On 26 May 1806 he sold half of lot 173, 100 acres, to Simeon Lawrence of Gardiner (KenCD, 9:538). He was not in the 1810 ME census.

He and his family probably went west, and had descendants not yet identified.

Children, born at Mt. Vernon (TRs 2:306), perhaps others:

        i.   SOLOMON[7], b. 12 Jan. 1796; nfr.
601. ii.   MOSES, b. 26 Oct. 1797.
      iii. JOSEPH, b. 10 Oct. 1799; nfr.
      iv. PARTHENIA, b. 15 Dec. 1801; nfr.
602. v.   ?WILLIAM (conjectural; birth not in TRs).

197. DANIEL[6] 1770-   [55 Solomon[5] and Sarah Varney] was born probably at Edgecomb 16 Sept. 1770 (Mount Vernon TRs), died at Rome; married first 26 Feb. 1795 (Rome TRs) RUTH ---- ; married second at Rome 5 Mar. 1816 ELIZABETH ---- , who died at Mt. Vernon 24 July 1863, 82y (GS, Bean cemetery) (Cornman Ms; records of descendant Roxanne Saucier).

The marriage of an unidentified Daniel Leighton to Sarah Bliss was recorded at Thetford VT 26 Feb. 1795 (VT VRs).

In 1800 he, his wife and three sons under 10 lived at the Gore, between Mt Vernon and Readfield, which was incorporated as Rome in 1804. On 9 June 1808 he deeded land to Thomas Smith of Readfield to satisfy a court judgment (KenCD, 14:40). He was at Rome in 1830, but was not listed in the 1840 ME census.

Children by Ruth, first four in Mt Vernon TRs 2:306,
   all listed in Rome VRs 3:5:

   i.   LEVI[7], b. 21 May 1795; m. Rome 1 July 1815 Mrs.
         SALLY (----) Jewett. He served in Capt.
         Matthias Lane's company in Sept. 1814 (MA Mil.
         1812-1814, 228).
603. ii. DANIEL, b. 30 Dec. 1796 or 30 Jan. 1797 (both
         dates in VRs).
604. iii. SMITHSON, b. 17 Dec. 1798.
     iv. LOIS/LOVISA, b. 6 Jan. 1801; nfr.
     v.   WILLIAM, b. 23 Nov. 1802 [possibly # 602].
605. vi. LOVINA, b. 27 Aug. 1806; m. JOTHAM MOORE.
     vii. LOUISA (twin), b. 27 Aug. 1806; m. DAVID[7]
         LEIGHTON [# 584].
606. viii. LIBERTY, b. 4 Aug. 1808; m. ELBRIDGE OAK.

Children by Elizabeth, in Mt. Vernon TRs:

   ix.   RUTH, b. 6 Feb. 1819; m. FRANCIS THOMPSON.
   x.   LUCY, b. 24 Mar. 1820; m. Rome 28 Nov. 1842
         BRADLEY F. THING.

198.   PELATIAH[6] 1772-1842 [55 Solomon[5] and Sarah Varney]
was born probably at Edgecomb 13 Feb. 1772, died in Tazewell
County IL in 1842; married 13 Feb. 1796 (Rome record) MARY
[Polly] ---- , who died in Tazewell Co. about 1844.
   In 1800, they were listed at Mount Vernon with a son; in
1810 they were at Rome with three sons and two daughters. He
served as ensign under Capt. Matthias Lane in Sept. 1814 (MA
Mil. 1812-14, 228). He sold 25 Feb. 1815 to Eleazer Watson
of Northwood NH lot 57, near Long Pond (Rome) (KenCD,
18:587), perhaps in preparation for leaving Maine.
   A succession of crop failures, culminating in the summer-
less 1816, "eighteen-hundred-and-froze-to-death," along with
the opening of new western lands, led many families to leave
Maine for the west.
   Pelatiah was very probably the "Peltire Laton" at Delphi
Tp, Hamilton Co. OH in 1820 with two sons and two daughters,
all under 10; in 1830 he was in Switzerland Co. IN, with
three children. He next moved on to Groveland, Tazewell Co.
IL, where he had a large farm.
   Administration of his estate was given to Alanson Stockwell
5 Sept. 1842; his wife died while it was in probate (Tazewell
Co. Probate, Box 12).

   Children, three in Mt. Vernon TRs 2:304-5, next three in
   Rome VRs 19:

   i.   MARCY[7], b. 30 May 1796; d. Rome 5 Feb. 1802.
607. ii. HUMPHREY VARNEY, b. 28 Apr. 1797.
     iii. MARY, b. 23 Aug. 1798; m. in Switzerland Co.
         IN 2 July 1824 (county VRs) DAVID QUICK.
     iv. daughter, b. 12 May 1802, d. Rome 3
         Feb. 1803 ("L" on GS).
608. v.   JACOB, b. 18 Feb. 1804.
     vi. TAMSEN, b. 9 June 1807; nfr.
609. vii. ?NOAH, b. 18 June 1812 (birth not in TRs).

199. SAMUEL[6] 1774-1862 [55 Solomon[5] and Sarah Varney] was
born at Damariscotta ME 10 Feb. 1774 (Mt. Vernon record),
died at Mt. Vernon 23 Jan. 1862, 87y (VRs; 86y 11m 13d, GS);
married at Rome int. 27 Nov. 1812, certif. 5 Jan. 1813,
DOROTHEA [Dolly] FURBUSH, born at Belgrade ME 9 Mar. 1794
(Rome VRs), died at Mt. Vernon 31 Aug. 1871, 77y 6m (TRs
3:109). Their household in 1850 included Lydia Forbush, 86,
born in NH--probably Dorothea's mother. Burials are in the
Bean cemetery, Mt. Vernon. Samuel bought part of lot 159 on
24 Mar. 1817, adjacent to land owned by Andrew and Timothy.
He bought lot 38 from Daniel Wadley, and sold 60 acres of it
to John Dore of Athens 28 May 1822 (KenCD, 14:4).

Children, born at Mount Vernon (TRs 3:59):

	i.	EMILY H.[7], b. 3 Jan. 1814; m. Mt. Vernon 4 Oct. 1843 JOSEPH F. BLASLAND of Boston. No ch. Both d. Franklin MA
610.	ii.	SAMUEL, b. 17 Nov. 1816.
611.	iii.	HOSEA S., b. 25 Aug. 1819.
612.	iv.	DOROTHY F., b. 5 Aug. 1823; m. GEORGE S. WORCESTER.
	v.	SOLOMON, b. 4 June 1827, d. Winthrop ME 21 Sept. 1897 (VRs); m. Brockton MA 27 Dec. 1849 DRUSILLA DEXTER, b. 17 July 1830, d. Brockton 7 Sept. 1897, dau. of Freeman and Abigail (Harvey) Dexter of Monmouth ME. No ch. He was a joiner.

200. BENJAMIN[6] 1776-1844 [55 Solomon[5] and Sarah Varney]
was born probably at Edgecomb 12 Nov. 1776 (Mount Vernon
record), died at Lyons, Wayne Co. NY 26 Sept. 1844; married
first at Mt. Vernon 29 Oct. 1801, int Aug. 1799 (TRs), SALLY
BROWN, who died at Athens in 1814; married second at Mt. Vernon 18 Feb. 1818 SALLY CURTIS (Cornman Ms). Julia Cornman
called Sally Brown a first cousin. He was buried in Zurich
cemetery, Arcadia NY.
He sold 40 acres of lot 157 to Nathaniel Trask Perkins of
Epping NH on 1 Nov. 1813 (KenCD, 16:316). He lived at Athens
for several years, and was called "Jr." because he had an
uncle Benjamin. In 1819 he and his sons settled near Lyons
NY, at a place called West Woods. In 1830 and 1840 he was
living at Sodus.

Children by first wife, born at Mount Vernon (TRs 2:318):

	i.	SARAH[7], b. 1 Mar. 1802, d. Athens aged 14.
613.	ii.	NATHAN, b. 2 Feb. 1804.
614.	iii.	BENJAMIN, b. 11 Apr. 1806.
615.	iv.	ALVIN, b. 3 Feb. 1809.
616.	v.	GEORGE CLINTON, b. 8 July 1812.

201. MARY[6] [Molly] 1757-1850 [56 James[5] and Patience
Twombley] was born at Madbury NH in 1757, died at Barrington
NH in 1850; married there in 1783 NATHANIEL CHURCH, born in
1754, died at Barrington 18 Feb. 1826 (Cornman Ms). He
served under Capt. Peter Drown on the expedition to RI in
1778, and lost his leg in battle; he was placed on half-pay
pension (NHSP, 11:155-6).

Children (**Church**), born at Barrington:

i.   PATTY, b. in 1785; m. in 1805 JOHN NEAL.
ii.   BENJAMIN, b. in 1788, d. Barrington.
iii.   HENRY, b. in 1791, d. Barrington.
iv.   ABIGAIL, b. in 1797, d. Dover NH in 1879; m. ISAAC
        HANSON
v.   MARY, b. in 1799, d. Ossipee NH; m. ICHABOD KENNEY.
vi.   NATHANIEL, b. in 1800, d. Madbury; m. Ossipee in
        1828 FRANCES HINKLEY.
vii.   PRUDENCE, b. in 1803; m. Ossipee PATIENCE HANSON.
viii.   MOLLY L.; m. MARK THOMPSON.

202.   **SARAH**[6] 1762-1847 [56 James[5] and Patience Twombley]
was born at Barrington 5 Feb. 1762, died at Strafford 18 May
1847, 85y 3m 13d (VRS); married 17 Mar. 1789 WILLIAM BABB,
born at Barrington 17 Feb. 1765, died at Strafford 20 June
1848, son of Benjamin and Sarah (Foss) Babb (Sargent, Babbs
of New Eng., 113; Stearns, N. H. Genealogies, 3:1093; Cornman Ms) Babb was a mason.

Children (**Babb**), born at Strafford:

i.   SAMPSON, JR., b. 26 Apr. 1790, d. 20 Aug. 1865; m.
        HANNAH MILLS, b. 25 Jan. 1790, d. Strafford 12 Mar.
        1868, dau. of Samuel and Jane Mills.
ii.   WILLIAM, JR., b. 10 May 1793, d. 29 Mar. 1844; unm.
iii.   ISAAC, b. 26 Sept. 1797, d. 5 Aug. 1848; m. 28 Jan.
        1819 SALLY FOSS, b. 5 Aug. 1796, d. 5 Mar. 1851, 54y
        6m, dau. of Dr. John and Dorothy (Babb) Foss.
iv.   DENNIS, b. 10 May 1799, d. Barnstead NH 17 May 1874;
        m. 28 Nov. 1822 JUDITH WILLEY, b. 4 Jan. 1800, d. 8
        Jan. 1876.

203.   **JAMES**[6] 1768-1841 [56 James[5] and Patience Twombley]
was born at Barrington 23 Apr. 1768, died there 21 Jan. 1841;
married there 24 Nov. 1790 HANNAH BUZZELL, born 31 Mar. 1768,
died at Barrington 23 Sept. 1845, daughter of Ebenezer and
Rachel (Buzzell) Buzzell (Cornman Ms; Barrington VRs).
        He farmed the homestead he inherited from his father. He
bought from Richard Hoit of Rochester 14 Sept. 1790 part of
lot 112 in Rochester's fourth divison (StrCD, 12:245), and
more land from Samuel Small 31 Oct. 1801 (37:218).
        His will, made 6 Aug. 1839 and proved 5 Oct. 1841, gave to
Hannah life use of his property in lieu of dower, gave Israel
his properties in Barrington and Nottingham as well as the
reversion of the widow's rights, and gave his three daughters
small bequests (StrCP, 54:527-9).
        Hannah's will, made 3 Jan. 1842, was proved 4 Nov. 1845
(61:212-4).

Children, born at Barrington:

617.   i.   ISRAEL[7], b. 24 Jan. 1791.
        ii.   PATIENCE TWOMBLEY, b. 2 Feb. 1797, d. in Oct.
                1860; unm.
618.   iii.   LOIS B., b. 16 June 1800; m. DAVID BUZZELL.
619.   iv.   HARRIET, b. 19 Oct. 1803; m. SAMUEL ALLEN.

204. REUBEN[6] 1770-1842 [56 James[5] and Patience Twombley]
was born at Barrington 4 June 1770, died at Newbury VT 28
June 1842 (VRs), 72y (GS); married say 1791 MARY [Molly]
TWOMBLEY, born at Barrington 8 Sept. 1769, died at Bath NH 21
Feb. 1862, 92y 5m (GS). Burials are in the Boltonville (VT)
Cemetery.
He lived on his third of lot 143 at Barrington (later
Strafford), which he had inherited from his father; in 1800
his household there included five children.
On 3 Oct. 1800 he and his brother Isaac sold their Barrington property to Paul Tasker (StrCD, 55:22), and Reuben joined
others from Barrington in settling Sheffield VT. There he
was surveyor of highways in 1802, and tax collector in 1803,
1804 and 1807.
Perhaps losing ground financially, he moved to a rented
farm at Newbury in 1808, and in 1820 was at Bradford VT   As
his sons matured, his prosperity returned. With Reuben, Jr.,
and Jacob he purchased lot 93 at Newbury, then 100 acres of
wilderness on what was later called Leighton's Hill; he soon
purchased lot 94, an additional 100 acres, and rented another
100-acre lot. Other children bought adjacent property, until
the family holdings were 600 acres or more (Frank P. Wells,
History of Newbury, Vt. [St Johnsbury, 1902], 616; Tracy,
Reuben Leighton, 6-9).

Children:

620.	i.	REUBEN[7], b. Barrington 30 Sept. 1792.
621.	ii.	LYDIA, b. Barrington 3 May 1794; m. STEPHEN GEORGE.
622.	iii.	HANNAH, b. Barrington 7 Mar. 1796; m. ROSS C. FORD.
623.	iv.	JACOB, b. Barrington 25 Oct. 1797.
624.	v.	JONATHAN, b. Barrington 21 Dec. 1799.
	vi.	SAMUEL B., b. Sheffield 21 Oct. 1801, settled in NY. (A Samuel B. Leighton was in the 1840 NY census at York, Livingston Co., but had gone by 1850.)
	vii.	SILAS, b. Sheffield 3 Oct. 1803, removed to NY. (A Silas Leighton was in the 1840 NY census at Bennington, Geneva Co., and sold out his land there in 1844; nfr.)
625.	viii.	STEPHEN D., b. Sheffield 8 May 1806.
	ix.	SARAH H., b. Sheffield 6 Aug. 1808; m. STEPHEN BENNETT.
	x.	MARY, b. Newbury 16 June 1810, d. there 6 May 1830; unm.

205. PATIENCE[6] 1772-   [56 James[5] and Patience Twom-
bley] was born at Barrington say 1772; married at Dover NH 25
June 1796 BENJAMIN WATSON, son of William and Lucy (Otis)
Watson (Cornman Ms).

Children (**Watson**), probably born at Barrington:

i.	LILLIE; m. Barrington SOLOMON CATE.
ii.	JACOB, d. Durham NH; m. 1st ---- WILLEY; m. 2nd at Durham ---- .
iii.	CHARLOTTE; m. Barrington ---- BABB.
iv.	LUCY.

v.   CHARLES; m. Boston in 1824 NANCY GREGG.
vi.   NATHANIEL, d.y.
vii. JEREMIAH; m. HANNAH HALL.
viii ABIGAIL; m. Dover JAMES GEE.
ix.   DESDEMONA, d.y.

206. ISAAC⁶ 1774-1806 [56 James⁵ and Patience Twombley]
was born at Barrington in 1774, died at Stowe VT in 1806;
married at Nottingham NH 18 Aug. 1794 SARAH BICKFORD, who
died at Stowe in 1806.
    With his brother James, he sold his third of their Bar-
rington inheritance 3 Oct. 1800, and about 1802 settled at
Stowe VT. In 1806, he, his wife and three of their children
died of spotted fever.
    Isaac, Jr., and Sarah were raised by Daniel Moody of Stowe,
and family friends at Barrington took on the rearing of John
(Cornman Ms; William F. Whitcher, History of the Town of Haverhill, N. H. [1919], 572).

    Children:

        i.   EZEKIEL⁷, b. Nottingham in 1794, d. Stowe in
              1806.
        ii.   JAMES, b. in 1796, d. Stowe in 1806.
    626. iii. JOHN, b. Strafford NH 11 Mar. 1798.
    627. iv. ISAAC, b. Barrington 5 Dec. 1799.
        v.   HARRIET, b. Stowe in 1803, d. there in 1806.
        vi.   SARAH, b. Stowe in 1805; m. WILLARD GRIFFIN
              of St. Albans VT. Ch. Philo res. Ft. Dodge IA
              and Sunnydale KS.

207. AARON⁶ 1776-1859 [56 James⁵ and Patience Twombley]
was born at Barrington NH 11 Apr. 1776, died at Chicopee MA
11 June 1859, 83y 2m (VRs); married HANNAH WHITE of Nottingham (Cornman Ms).
    In 1797 he sold his share of the land he had inherited from
his father to his brother Stephen, Hannah releasing her dower
right. In 1800 he was listed at Barrington with wife, son
and daughter.

    Children, order and birthplace uncertain:

    628. i.   RHODA⁷, b. Barrington 11 June 1798; m. AARON
              LANG.
        ii.   CYRUS, b. in 1801, d. Nottingham in 1819.
        iii. LORENZO DOW.
        iv.   IRENE W.; m. Dover 26 July 1829 THOMAS GRAN-
              VILLE. Ch. Martha m. Dwight Moore.

208. JONATHAN⁶ 1778-1860 [56 James⁵ and Patience Twombley]
was born at Barrington 26 Apr. 1778, died at Strafford NH 5
Feb. 1860 (VRs; 81y 9m 10d per GS); married at Lee NH 13
Sept. 1801 (VRs) LOIS FOLLETT, born at Lee 18 Aug. 1779, died
at Strafford 8 May 1866 (86y 8m 20d per GS), daughter of
Joseph and Mary (Huckins) Follett (Stackpole, Durham, 2:195).
Burials are in the Babb Cemetery, Strafford.
    They removed to Sheffield VT with his brother Reuben, but

Jonathan was soon settled at Holderness NH, where he was listed on the tax list in 1810 (TRs 1:216). They also lived at Grafton NH before settling at Strafford.

Children:

629. i.   LUCINDA[7], b. Barrington 15 Dec. 1802; m. ISAAC BABB.
630. ii.   NANCY, b. Holderness 30 May 1805; m. ELIPHALET FOSS.
631. iii. ISAAC TWOMBLEY, b. Holderness 25 Nov. 1807.
632. iv.   MARY HUCKINS, b. Holderness 6 Jan. 1810; m. THOMAS G. SANBORN.
     v.   ALANSON, b. Strafford 5 Jan. 1812, d. Chelmsford MA 23 Oct. 1832 (VRs); unm.
     vi.   JOHN COLBY, b. Grafton 11 Apr. 1814, d. Strafford 29 Sept. 1816.
633. vii. JOSEPH WARREN, b. Holderness 3 June 1816.
     viii. JOHN COLBY, b. Grafton 25 Nov. 1818; m. 13 Jan. 1864 MARY A KENDALL, b. Boston 22 Oct. 1836, dau. of Joshua and Hannah Kendall. No ch. In 1900 they were living at Boston, his birth listed in Nov. 1820, hers in Oct. 1834.

209. EZEKIEL[6] 1780-1862 [56 James[5] and Patience Twombley] was born at Barrington 21 Nov. 1780, died at Ossipee NH 15 Nov. 1862; married at Barrington 10 Dec. 1805 OLIVE CATE, born at Barrington 13 Feb. 1785, died at Ossipee 6 Feb. 1878 (Cornman Ms).
He bought land at Effingham from his brother Isaac 7 Aug. 1806 (StrCD, 52:84)

Children, recorded at Ossipee:

     i.   COLBY[7], b. 12 Oct. 1808, d. Ossipee 15 July 1809.
     ii.   HANNAH, b. 20 Sept. 1811; m. 20 May 1839 GEORGE NORTON, b. Boston in 1814, son of Oliver and Bathsheba Norton [see # 634 below]. Ch. Charles W. b. 18 Dec. 1846, res. Cleveland OH.
     iii. LENORA FRANCIS, b. 27 May 1814, d. Boston 15 Aug. 1836; m. Dover 21 May 1834 GEORGE NORTON (see Emily below). No ch.
634. iv.   EMILY ANN (twin), b. 27 May 1814; m. GEORGE NORTON.
     v.   JOHN, b. 12 Mar., d. 12 Oct., 1816.
635. vi.   JAMES LYMAN, b. 19 Nov. 1817.

210. HANNAH[6] 1765-1845 [57 Isaac[5] and Anna Evans] was born at Barrington in 1765, died at Athens ME 7 May 1845, 89y (VRs); married in 1785 SAMUEL HALL, born at Dover NH 19 Mar. 1747, died at Athens 19 Apr. 1831, son of Joseph and Peniel (Bean) Hall (Stearns, N. H. Genealogies, 3:1253-4; Halls of N.E., 176).
Hall had married first at Wakefield NH 26 Aug. 1773 Bridget Gilman, born 4 Nov. 1748, daughter of Capt. Jeremy and Sarah (Kimball) Gilman; they had three children. About 1800 he left Wakefield to become Athens' first settler.

Children (**Hall**) by Hannah, born at Wakefield:

i. ANDREW, b. 10 Dec. 1786, d. Athens 29 May 1850; m.
    there 19 Jan. 1809 DOLLY COLLINS.
ii. BRIDGET GILMAN, b. 1 Sept. 1788; m. Athens 21 Nov.
    1811 JOSEPH HIGHT, JR.
iii. JEREMIAH, b. 24 Sept. 1794; m. Athens 17 Nov. 1816
    EUNICE HIGHT.
iv. JAMES, b. in Nov. 1796; m. MARTHA WEBB.
v. IRA, b. 13 Dec. 1799; m. CYNTHIA HIGHT, dau. of
    Winthrop and Mehitable (Stewart) Hight.
vi. CALVIN, b. probably Athens in 1802, d. there in
    1832; unm.

211. ANDREW[6] 1766-1826 [57 Isaac[5] and Anna Evans] was born
at Barrington in 1766, died there in Dec. 1826, 60y; married
at Strafford in 1796 (NEHGReg, 76 [1922]:36) SARAH EVANS,
born at Barrington 15 Jan. 1775, died there 14 Apr. 1872
(Cornman Ms).
Andrew Leighton, Esq., was a selectman at Barrington in
1806-1807.

Children, born at Barrington:

      i.   ANNA[7], b. in 1798; m. TIMOTHY M.[6] LEIGHTON
           [# 218].
      ii. LEVI, b. 17 Feb. 1801, d. Roxbury MA 9 July
           1836 (d. Brookline MA, 35y Morning Star); unm.
636. iii. ISAAC, b. 7 June 1803.
      iv. MARY, b. in 1805, d. Barrington 5 Jan. 1807.
      v.   TAMSEN, b. in 1807, d. Barrington 22 Apr.
           1873, 66y; unm.
      vi. ANDREW, bp. 13 Jan. 1810, d. Barrington 10 Nov.
           1811.
      vii. EDMUND EVANS, b. 19 July, d. 12 Sept., 1810.

212. REMEMBRANCE[6] 1771-1850 [57 Isaac[5] and Anna Evans] was
born at Barrington in 1771, died at Ossipee. He married at
Nottingham 4 Apr. 1799 JUDITH WHITEHOUSE (Whitehorne in the
Cornman Ms). He lived at Effingham and Ossipee.
He bought lot 13, third division, at Effingham from Simon
Nudd 30 Nov. 1801 (StrCD, 37:338). In 1850, he was 79, a
pauper, living with his son David.

Children, order and place of birth uncertain:

      i.   THOMAS[7], d. Great Falls NH, a young man.
637. ii. DAVID, b. Effingham.
638. iii. MELINDA; m. NICHOLAS OTIS.
      iv. LYDIA, b. Ossipee, d. Effingham; m. JOSEPH
           SANDERS.
      v.   LUCY, b. Ossipee, nfr.
639. vi. REMEMBRANCE, b. Effingham.
      vii. ANDREW EVANS, b. Ossipee in 1816, d. there 14
           Mar. 1870; m. 1st ---- ; m. 2nd 29 Oct. 1865
           HANNAH PEARSON, b. in 1832, dau. of John and
           Elizabeth Pearson. Ch. GEORGE N.[8] b. c1838,
           d. Ossipee 6 Nov. 1890.

213. ISAAC[6] 1775-1859 [57 Isaac[5] and Anna Evans] was born at Barrington 8 Mar. 1775, died at Effingham NH 30 Oct. 1859; married first in 1797 SARAH BUZZELL, born at Barrington 13 Dec. 1775, died at Effingham in 1831 (NH Observer of 13 Apr.), daughter of Samuel and Lydia (Evans) Buzzell; married second THEODATE (GARLAND) Dinsmore, born at Ossipee NH 23 Dec. 1793, died at Sandwich NH 11 Nov. 1876, daughter of Amos and Mary (James) Garland (James Gray Garland, Garland Genealogy {The Northern Branch} [Biddeford ME, 1897], 32; Barrington and Effingham VRs; Cornman Ms). Theodate had six Dinsmore children. In 1850 Isaac was a farmer at Effingham.

Children by Sarah, five born at Barrington, the rest at Effingham:

640.   i.   ISAAC[7], b. 22 Dec. 1798.
641.   ii.   SARAH, b. 5 Mar. 1803; m. ISAAC HANSON.
       iii. LYDIA, b. 21 Jan. 1805, d. Barrington 16 Mar.
             1864; married Barnstead 3 Sept. 1827 EBENEZER
             BUZZELL, JR., b. Barrington 19 Jan. 1800, d.
             there 22 June 1851, son of Levi and Izetta
             (Buzzell) Buzzell. They had five ch., all
             unm., 3 of them b. deaf mute (Cornman Ms).
       iv.   ANNA, b. 14 May 1807, d. 24 Oct. 1841; unm.
       v.   PHOEBE A., b. 28 Dec. 1809, d. Effingham 10
             Oct. 1893; m. 25 Jan. 1859 as 2nd wife ITHIEL
             WASHINGTON BRYANT, b. Effingham 22 Feb. 1806,
             d. there 17 Oct. 1882, son of Ithiel and
             Betsey (Evans) Bryant. No ch.
642.   vi.   LOUISA/ELIZA, b. 12 Mar. 1812; m. JOHN LEWIS.
643.   vii. KEZIAH, b. 22 Dec. 1814; m. EBENEZER TASKER.
       viii. ELIZABETH, b. 5 Jan., d. 25 Jan., 1817.

Children by Theodate, born at Effingham:

644.   ix.   GEORGE E., b. 11 Aug. 1833.
645.   x.   ELIZABETH T., b. 27 Feb. 1835; m. WILLIAM A.
             SHACKFORD.
646.   xi.   ALMIRA D., b. 26 Feb. 1837; m. ENOCH LEWIS.

214. MARK M.[6] 1780-   [58 Aaron[5] and Mary Murray] was born at Barrington NH 8 June 1780, died at Saco ME 25 July 1824; married BETSEY RAMSDELL of Biddeford ME, born 26 May 1782, died at Saco 5 Dec. 1853 (E. P. Burnham, Saco Families [Ms, Dyer Memorial Library, Saco]).

Children, born at Biddeford (first four in TRs 4:331, 346):

647.   i.   SARAH[7] [Sally], b. 19 June 1804; m. PAUL HALL.
648.   ii.   GEORGE, b. 29 Dec. 1805.
       iii. JOHN, b. 30 Oct. 1807, d. Saco 19 Aug. 1832.
       iv.   MARY, b. 20 Apr. 1810, d. 30 Aug. 1829.
       v.   BETSEY, b. 15 Oct. 1812, d. 5 Oct. 1835.
       vi.   DORCAS, b. 6 Feb. 1816, d. 15 Mar. 1852.
       vii. HENRY, b. 15 Nov. 1818, d. 19 June 1825.
       viii. ANN, b. 16 May 1820; m. in 1841 HARRISON
             CLEAVES, JR.
       ix.   OLIVE, b. 28 Feb. 1822.
       x.   LYDIA JANE, b. 3 Aug. 1824.

215.   SARAH[6] 1781-1867 [58 Aaron[5] and Mary Murray] was born
at Barrington 12 Oct. 1781, died there 6 Jan. 1867, 85y; married 2 Mar. 1806 DANIEL CLARK, born 16 May 1778, died 14 Apr.
1829, son of Daniel and Love (Drew) Clark (Cornman Ms). Both
are buried at Strafford.
Daniel had children by a first wife. His will, made 11
Apr. and proved 8 May 1829, listed his children John, Betsey
Foss and Olive; and then Sarah, Mary Ann, Timothy, Maria, and
Abiah.

Children (**Clark**):

i.   SARAH, b. 20 Mar. 1807, d. 9 Dec. 1883; m. 6 Apr.
        1871 HOWARD L. OTIS.
ii.   DANIEL, b. 13 May 1809, d. 8 Oct. 1813.
iii.   MARY ANN, b. 1 Mar. 1812, d. 15 Apr. 1884; unm.
iv.   TIMOTHY LEIGHTON, b. 16 Feb. 1815; m. PATIENCE M.[7]
        LEIGHTON [# 651].
v.   AARON LEIGHTON, b. 27 June, d. 15 Sept., 1817.
vi.   MARIA W., b. 21 Dec. 1819, d. 31 [sic] Apr. 1890;
        m. DENNIS CLARK, JR.
vii.   ABIAH W., b. 11 Jan. 1824, d. 5 Sept. 1882; m. ORSIE
        ABBOTT.

216.   WILLIAM HALE[6] 1785-1875 [58 Aaron[5] and Mary Murray]
was born at Barrington 3 Jan. 1785, died at Dover NH 23 Dec.
1875, 91y, thrown from his carriage; married 10 Mar. 1811
(Danville VRs) COMFORT WEEKS, born at Canterbury NH 29 Nov.
1792 (VRs), died at Danville VT 17 Feb. 1869, 76y 2m 18d
(VRs), daughter of Samuel, Jr., and Ruth (Eastman) Weeks (VT
VRs; Cornman Ms; Ernest A Weeks, Samuel Weeks of Danville
Vt. and His Descendants [1933]). Both are buried in Green
Cemetery, Danville.
In 1869, aged 84, he walked from Danville to Strafford (120
miles) to visit his daughter (Suncook Valley Times, Pitts-
field NH, 5 Aug. 1869, 2).

Children:

        i.   JOHN DAVIES[7], b. Wheelock VT 4 Dec. 1812, d.
                there 10 Dec. 1813.
649.   ii.   SAMUEL WEEKS, b. Wheelock 9 Sept. 1814.
650.   iii.   JEREMIAH WEEKS, b. Wheelock 23 Mar. 1817.
651.   iv.   PATIENCE MELLOWS, b. Wheelock 2 May 1820; m.
                TIMOTHY L. CLARK [# 215].
652.   v.   DANIEL M., b. Wheelock 17 May 1822.
        vi.   JONATHAN DARIUS, b. Wheelock 2 Dec. 1824, d.
                Danville 3 Sept. 1856, 32y; m. MARTHA GOULD.
                They had 2 ch: one d. infant; the other
                CHARLES[8] took the surname Gould, res. San
                Francisco CA (Cornman Ms).
653.   vii.   WILLIAM DREW, b. Lyndon VT 23 Feb. 1827.
654.   viii.   HARRISON WEEKS, b. Lyndon 25 May 1829.
        ix.   BETSEY D., b. Danville 16 May 1833, d. Straf-
                ford 6 Apr. 1883 (GS, Clark plot, Center
                Strafford Cem.); m. 20 Jan. 1858 CHARLES A. J.
                STRAW of St. Johnsbury. Ch. Estelle and
                Charles.
655.   x.   SARAH MARY, b. Danville 11 Mar. 1836; m. DAVID
                BABB and ORRIN RUSS.

Sixth Generation 149

217. JOHN[6] 1786-1875 [58 Aaron[5] and Mary Murray] was born
at Strafford NH 29 Dec. 1786, died at Little Falls NJ 10 June
1875; married in 1822 MARGARET (VanWINKLE) Terhune, born at
Spring Valley NJ 29 Jan. 1794, died in NJ 28 Aug. 1850 (Cornman Ms).

Children, born in New Jersey:

656. i.   MARIA JANE[7], b. 15 Dec. 1824; m. MARTIN E.
           DEETHS.
657. ii.   MARGARET CATHERINE, b. 25 July 1827; m.
           BURNETT BANTA.
     iii. SARAH C., b. 10 Feb. 1830, d. 28 Jan. 1883.
658. iv.   HENRIETTA, b. 6 Feb. 1835; m. CHARLES
           McCORNAE and D. H. BROWN.

218. TIMOTHY MURRAY[6] 1789-1858 [58 Aaron[5] and Mary Murray]
was born at Barrington 28 Apr. 1789, died at Northwood NH in
May 1858; married at Nottingham 14 Apr. 1816 (VRs) ANNA[?]
LEIGHTON, born at Barrington in 1798, died at Northwood in
1853, daughter of Andrew and Sarah (Evans) Leighton [# 211]
(Cornman Ms; records of descendants Albert C. Leighton and
Kathleen Crousens).
He was a mason. Burials are in a private cemetery off
Canaan Road, Barrington.

Children, order and birthplace uncertain:

659. i.   ANDREW E.[7], b. say 1816.
     ii.   EDMUND EVANS, b. in 1818, d. Strafford 26 July
           1846, 27y (Morning Star, 26 Aug.); m. Newmar-
           ket NH 18 May 1845 HANNAH CHESLEY. One ch. d.
           infant.
660. iii. SARAH ANNA, b. 15 Aug. 1821; m. GEORGE W.
           MERRILL.
     iv.   JOHN, b. in 1823, d. 17 Mar. 1849, 25y 7m; unm.
661. v.   GEORGE WASHINGTON, b. in 1825.
     vi.   DANIEL, b. in 1828, d. Barrington 22 July 1843,
           15y (Morning Star).
662. vii. TIMOTHY MURRAY, b. in 1830.
663. viii. MATTHEW THORNTON, b. 8 Aug. 1832.
     ix.   JOEL VIRGIL, b. Northwood 7 Aug. 1834, d.
           in 1854.
     x.   MARTHA JANE, b. 24 Aug. 1837, res. Newmarket
           in 1903; unm.
     xi.   MARY SUSAN, b. Northwood 28 Sept. 1840, d. 22
           Sept. 1868; m. 27 Jan. 1864 GEORGE W. MERRILL,
           widower of her sister Sarah. Ch. Mary Susan
           b. 9 July, d. 12 Oct., 1865.
     xii. VIENNA CILLY, b. in Apr. 1844, d. in 1861.

219. PATIENCE TWOMBLEY[6] 1792-1848 [58 Aaron[5] and Mary
Murray] was born at Northwood NH 22 Aug. 1792, died at Alton
NH 25 Oct. 1848; married at New Durham 26 Mar. 1820 SAMUEL
MELLOWS, born at Middleton NH 20 Oct. 1795, died at Newmarket
27 Aug. 1879, son of Samuel and Sally (Twombley) Mellows
(Cornman Ms; town VRs). They joined the Alton Free Will
Baptist church 2 Aug. 1835.

Samuel married second at New Durham 23 Nov. 1851 Elizabeth
(Thurston) Sanborn, born at Gilford about 1806, died at Farmington 19 Feb. 1871, 64y, widow of Isaac W. Sanborn.

Children (**Mellows**):

i.   AARON LEIGHTON, b. Middleton 1 Jan. 1821, d. in Feb.
        1904; m. 1st 3 Jan. 1847 LUCRETIA F. ADAMS; m. 2nd
        Deerfield NH 27 Aug. 1865 HARRIET A. JAMES. b. in
        1840, dau. of Joseph W. and Harriet (Nealey) James.
        He was a teacher, lawyer, town clerk, justice of the
        peace, and for 11 years state legislator.
ii.   HARRIET MORSE, b. Alton 4 Dec. 1822, d. Farmington
        8 Oct. 1898; m. Boston 3 Jan. 1843 GEORGE F. LEEDS.
iii.   DANIEL COLTON, b. Farmington 8 Sept. 1826, d. there
        15 May 1891, 67y 8m 7d; m. Gorham ME 14 Sept. 1851
        ADRIANNA LIBBY, b. there 29 Nov. 1835, d. 31 July
        1897, dau. of Stephen and Mary W. (Lowe) Libby
        (Libby Fam., 471).
iv.   SAMUEL BOLIVAR, b. New Durham 25 July 1830, d. Far-
        mington 11 Sept. 1858, 24y (VRs); m. New Durham 29
        July 1854 (VRs) HARRIET M. RICHARDSON, b. Moulton-
        boro NH in 1839, d. Farmington 19 Oct. 1864,
        dau. of Dexter and Jemima' (Leighton) Richardson
        [# 533]. Harriet m. 2nd 11 Aug. 1860 Daniel H.
        Plaisted.
v.   PATIENCE J., b. 9 Dec. 1833, d. 17 Jan. 1881; m. 15
        Apr. 1850 SIMON E. D. RAND, son of Simon and Betsey
        (Dame) Rand of Farmington.

220. **DANIEL**[7] 1812-1864 [60 James[6] and Sarah Seavey] was born at Farmington NH 16 Nov. 1812, died there 5 Feb. 1864 (TRs); married at New Durham NH 13 Oct. 1835 (Farmington int. 13 Sept.) ABIGAIL FURBER, born 12 July 1805, died at Farmington 5 June 1889.

She was recorded as "married out" 30 Sept. 1835, and Daniel as having removed to RI; she later rejoined the Friends with her two children (NHGR, 6[1909]:182).

Children, born at Farmington (Cornman Ms):

    i.   WILLIAM F.[8], b. 14 Aug. 1838, res. Norwich CT; m. Preston CT in 1859 NANCY HAWKINS, b. in 1833. No ch.

    ii.   JOHN, b. 27 Sept. 1844, res. Norwich CT; m. East Greenwich RI MARY F. WOOD.

221. **MARY E.**[7] 1813-1862 [61 John[6] and Mary Furber] was born at Farmington 26 Oct. 1813, died at Weare NH 30 Oct. 1862; married there 27 Feb. 1840 NATHAN C. DOW, born there 19 Feb. 1814, son of Elijah J. and Hannah (Chase) Dow.

Dow married second 7 Jan. 1864 Abigail O. Hussey, daughter of Daniel and Elizabeth (Osborn) Hussey of Henniker NH (Dow, Book of Dow, 311; Little, Weare, 821). He was a farmer and shoemaker.

Children (**Dow**), born at Weare:

    i.   LUELLA E., b. 28 Oct. 1850, d. 2 Sept. 1852.

    ii.   JOHN L., b. 6 Feb. 1854; m. 1st Weare 21 Nov. 1882 LIZZIE J. SWETT; m. 2nd 21 Sept. 1898 JESSIE SAWYER.

    iii. LUELLA E., b. 31 Jan. 1857.

222. **DAVID BREED**[7] 1821-1900 [63 Ephraim[6] and Hannah Breed] was born at Weare NH Dec. 1821, died there 3 Mar. 1900; married first at Rochester 29 July 1847 LAVINIA NUTTER, born at Rochester 21 May 1832, died at Weare 30 Aug. 1852, daughter of Jonathan, Jr., and Lucy F. (Canney) Nutter (NHGR, 2[1904]: 30); married second at Winthrop ME 31 May 1854 HANNAH M. (JONES) Farr, born 25 Dec. 1820, daughter of Reuben Jones.

David was a carpenter, and began carriage-making about 1857; his sons carried on the business. He also had a wheelwright's shop (Little, Weare, 433, 538, 634). His was a Quaker family.

Hannah Jones married first at Winthrop 4 Mar. 1846 Henry Farr; he died at West Gardiner ME 15 Aug. 1852--no children (Edith Bartlett Sumner, Descendants of Thomas Farr of Harpswell, Maine [Los Angeles, 1959], 116).

Child by first wife Lavinia, born at Weare:

    i.   CHARLES W.[8], b. 18 Oct. 1849, d. 8 Apr. 1851.

Children by second wife Hannah, born at Weare:

    ii.   CHARLES H., b. 30 Dec. 1855, res. Weare in
            1900; m. there 4 Aug. 1886 (MARY) ELLA STON-
            ING, b. there 5 Dec. 1863, dau. of Amos and
            Mary (Barrett) Stoning. Ch. INEZ ALTA[9] b.
            Weare 11 Mar. 1887. He was a carpenter and
            wheelbarrow manufacturer.
    iii.   EVERETT B., b. 31 Oct. 1857, res. Weare in
            1900; m. 13 May 1900 ESTELLE I. (BEALS) San-
            born, b. in ME 13 Mar. 1874, dau. of Isaac N.
            and Eunice J. Beals. Ch. LILLIAN ELLA[9] b. 4
            Aug. 1902. In 1900 Everett's household in-
            cluded Estelle's parents and her dau. Rosetta
            Sanborn.

223. BENJAMIN[7] 1813-1865 [66 William[6] and Mary Libby] was
born at Madbury NH in 1813, died at Concord 20 July 1865,
55y; married at Epsom NH MARY CASS, born in 1811, died at
Concord 22 June 1866, 51y (Old North Cemetery records; Cornman Ms).
He was a butcher, 39, at Concord in 1850.

Children:

    i.   JOHN W.[8], b. c1835 (1 in 1850).
    ii.   CHARLES B., b. in Mar. 1841 (12 in 1850), res.
            Epsom NH in 1900; m. 1st 17 Aug. 1862 ELIZA J.
            BICKFORD, b. Epsom in May 1844, d. 3 Mar.
            1902, 57y 9m 8d, dau. of Daniel B. and Emma J.
            (Philbrick) Bickford; m. 2nd Epsom 11 Apr.
            1903 ELLA A. (NUTTER) Roberts, b. Barnstead in
            1859, dau. of Samuel D. and Ruth (Knowles)
            Nutter.
664. iii.   JAMES GILMAN, b. Epsom 16 Apr. 1843.

224. (WILLIAM) ALEXANDER[7] 1820-1893 [66 William[6] and Mary
Libby] was born at Madbury NH 13 Mar. 1820, died at Bow NH 8 May
1893; married at Chichester NH LYDIA L. JENNESS, born 14 July
1822, died 8 May 1903. They lived at Epsom from 1847 to 1857
(Cornman Ms).
In 1850 Alexander, 29, had in his Epsom household a GIDEON
LEIGHTON, 70. In 1900 Lydia lived with her son Walter at
Manchester NH.

Children:

    i.   GEORGE W.[8], b. 13 Oct. 1842, d. 28 Nov. 1843.
    ii.   GEORGE A., b. 23 Mar. 1846, res. Manchester NH
            in 1900; m. 1st 25 Dec. 1869 AMELIA F. TANNER
            of Manchester, d. 22 May 1873; m. 2nd 18 Dec.
            1879 ROSE GOLDEN, b. Boston in July 1846. Ch.
            MAUD A.[9] b. 20 Jan. 1871, d. Concord NH 9 Dec.
            1891. In 1864 George was in a NH Inf. Rgt.
            He was a machinery manufacturer.

665.   iii.   IDA A., b. 8 Aug. 1848; m. RUFUS H. BAKER.
       iv.   ELLEN E., b. Concord 28 Dec. 1850; m. Barnstead
              23 Sept. 1871 CYRUS N. BARTON, b. 5 Mar. 1848.
              Ch. Amelia Adella b. 8 May 1878.
666.   v.   WILLIAM J., b. Epsom 9 Oct. 1855.
667.   vi.   WALTER H., b. Milford NH 18 Sept. 1857.
       vii.   CLARA A., b. 26 Sept. 1864, d. 5 May 1865.

   225.   CHARLES EDWARD[7] 1799-1885 [68 Luke Mills[6] and Elizabeth Mendum] was born at Portsmouth NH 17 Nov. 1799 (bapt. 24
Nov., NEHGReg, 82[1928]:45), died there 27 Feb. 1885, 85y;
married there 24 Oct. 1830 (83[1929]:299) FRANCES SEABURY
HALL, born 14 July 1805, died at Portsmouth 3 July 1860,
daughter of Ammi Ruhamah and Elizabeth (Seabury) Hall (Cornman Ms; Portsmouth VRs; Halls of N.E., 307).
   He was a grocer. In 1870 he was listed at Portsmouth, 70,
with daughters Fannie, 37, Kate, 29, and Emma, 22.

   Children, born at Portsmouth:

       i.   FRANCES ELIZABETH[8] [Fannie], b. 26 Dec. 1832
              (bp. 5 Feb. 1854), res. Cambridge MA; m.
              Portsmouth 24 Oct. 1872 Dr. JEREMIAH FOREST
              HALL, b. Northfield NH 2 Dec. 1816, d. Ports-
              mouth 1 Mar. 1888, son of Obadiah and Hannah
              (Forest) Hall. No ch. He had m. 1st Annette
              Livy in 1837; they had 3 ch.
              A graduate of Dartmouth Medical College in
              1837, Hall practiced medicine at Wolfeboro,
              was a surgeon in the 15th NH Rgt. during the
              Civil War, and then was a Portsmouth physician
              (Parker, Wolfeborough, 464-5).
668.   ii.   CHARLES MILLS, b. 29 Mar. 1835.
       iii.   JOSHUA JAMES, b. 4 Oct. 1837, d. Portsmouth 27
              Sept. 1864; unm. He was a Unitarian minister.
       iv.   CATHERINE HALL [Kate], b. 15 Feb. 1840, res.
              Cambridge MA; unm.
       v.   JACOB HALL, b. 2 Feb., d. 7 Oct., 1842.
       vi.   ALFRED SEABURY, b. 26 Nov. 1843, d. Washington
              DC 29 July 1863, 20y. He joined the 2nd MA
              Cav. Rgt. in 1862, and d. in service.
669.   vii.   EMELINE LINCOLN [Emma], b. 14 Aug. 1846; m.
              FREDERICK D. ALLEN.

   226.   WILLIAM M.[7] 1810-1873 [68 Luke Mills[6] and Elizabeth
Mendum] was born at Portsmouth 15 May 1810, died at Brockton
MA 23 May 1873; married at Portsmouth 28 Mar. 1832 MARIA HOP-
KINS SALT, born in NY (per 1850 census) 22 Sept. 1806, died
16 Jan. 1883 (Cornman Ms).
   He joined the US Navy 27 Sept. 1836 as an apprentice carpenter, and retired 15 Apr. 1872. He was serving as ships'
carpenter on the USS Cumberland when it was attacked and sunk
by the CSS Merrimac.

   Children:

       i.   WILLIAM HENRY[8], b. in NY 4 Jan. 1833, d. 7
              Sept. 1851.
670.   ii.   JAMES ALEXANDER, b. 22 Jan. 1835.

        iii.   OLIVE JANE, b. 15 Sept. 1836, d. 20 Oct. 1879;
               m. 5 Dec. 1865 ISAAC PARKER HALL, b. Boston
               10 July 1830, son of Jacob and Mary Ann (Hall)
               Hall (Halls of N.E., 346). No ch.

227.   JOSEPH WALTON[7] 1803-1859 [70 Mark[6] and Deborah Seavey] was born at Portsmouth 16 Mar. 1803, died there 14 Feb. 1859; married there 2 Oct. 1827 MARTHA SUMNER HART, born there 3 Sept. 1808, died there 12 Aug. 1846, daughter of George and Abigail (Pitman) Hart (Portsmouth VRs; family and Bible records of descendant Cecily Grist Greeley). He was a grocer.

Children, born at Portsmouth:

671.   i.   THOMAS[8], b. 14 Oct. 1828.
       ii.   JOSEPH, b. 30 July 1830, d. Portsmouth 27
              Sept. 1848.
       iii.   GEORGE HART, b. 22 Jan. 1832, d. 11 Jan. 1880;
              m. Boston 26 Nov. 1867 ELLEN R. (LEAVITT)
              Stewart of Bangor ME, b. in 1834, dau. of
              Edward and Rachel Leavitt. No ch. He served
              from MA during the Civil War.
672.   iv.   MARK, b. 18 Sept. 1835.
       v.   FRANKLIN, b. 31 July 1837, d. 11 Jan. 1841.
       vi.   SAMUEL, b. 1 Nov. 1839, d. 12 Sept. 1840.
       vii.   FRANKLIN ALVIN, b. 16 June 1841, lost at sea
              14 Feb. 1865; m. in 1863 ELLEN TARLTON of New
              Castle NH.
673.   viii. IVAN, b. 5 Sept. 1844.

228.   THOMAS BELL[7] 1805-1866 [70 Mark[6] and Deborah Seavey] was born at Portsmouth 2 Feb. 1805, died at Isles of Shoals ME 18 Apr. 1866; married in June 1831 ELIZA RYMES, born at Newington NH 10 Oct. 1804, died at Portsmouth 19 Nov. 1877, daughter of Christopher and Lucy E. Rymes. They are buried on Appledore Island.

Thomas Laighton was a merchant, exporter of lumber, and partner with his brother Joseph in a fishery. He edited the New Hampshire Gazette for a year, was appointed assistant postmaster and customs official, and served a term in the legislature. He was defeated in a gubernatorial election.

In 1834 he purchased for his fishery business the Isles of Shoals belonging to ME--Appledore (then Hog Island), Smuttynose, Malaga and Cedar. He was appointed keeper of the White Island light in 1839, and took his family to live there.

He gave up the lighthouse position in 1847, and built an 80-room hotel on Appledore--one of the first island resorts. The venture was very successful, setting a pattern for resort colonies which flourished well into the twentieth century. His poet-daughter Celia attracted current literary and artistic leaders such as James Russell Lowell, John G. Whittier, Nathaniel Hawthorne, Sarah Orne Jewett, Harriet B. Stowe, and Childe Hassam. He built a 40-room addition in 1859.

After his retirement in 1864, his sons enlarged the resort, and acquired the Oceanic Hotel on Star Island. Appledore is a registered national historic site because of its literary significance.

Children, born at Portsmouth:

      i.   HELEN[8], b. 21 July, d. 22 Oct., 1833.
674. ii. CELIA, b. 29 June 1836; m. LEVI L. THAXTER.
     iii. OSCAR, b. 30 June 1839, d. Portsmouth in Apr.
           1939, 99y 10m; unm. His Ninety Years at the
           Isles of Shoals (Andover MA, 1929; reprinted
           Baltimore 1988) told the story of the family
           resort business. He published his own Songs
           and Sonnets, and in 1935 edited Celia's The
           Heavenly Guest.
675. iv. CEDRIC, b. 4 Sept. 1840.

229. WILLIAM[7] 1809-1870 [70 Mark[6] and Deborah Seavey] was born at Portsmouth 7 Aug. 1809, died there 8 Sept. 1870; married 20 June 1833 MARY ANN WALKER, born at Portsmouth 27 Oct. 1812, died there 11 Mar. 1856, 42y, daughter of Paul Walker; married second MARY --- , who died at Portsmouth 26 Nov. 1874 (Portsmouth VRs; Cornman Ms, in which only one wife was listed).

    Dr. William Laighton was graduated from Harvard in 1830, and practiced as a physician at Portsmouth.

Children by first wife Mary:

676. i.   EMILY ALICE[8], b. Portsmouth 31 Dec. 1835;
          m. JOHN G. TOBEY.
677. ii. MARIANNE, b. Kennebunk ME 10 Nov. 1837; m.
          GEORGE D. DODGE.
     iii. ABIGAIL WILHELMINA, b. Portsmouth 21 Mar. 1847;
          m. Portsmouth 5 Dec. 1872 Dr. ALBION N. JOHN-
          SON of Kittery. Ch. Albion Wesley b. 18 Mar.
          1886.

230. ELIZABETH W.[7] 1812-1885 [70 Mark[6] and Deborah Seavey] was born at Portsmouth in 1812, died at Kennebunk ME 6 July 1885, 73y; married RICHARD GILPATRICK, born about 1807, died at Kennebunk 12 Aug. 1865, 58y (Cornman Ms; John Eldridge Frost, Kennebunk Record Book [TMs, 1964 MHS], 47-48).

Children (**Gilpatrick**):

i.   MARY, d. 11 May 1903; m. CHARLES C. HARVEY, b. 10
       Apr. 1832, d. 5 Oct. 1908.
ii.   WILLIAM, d. 31 Oct. 1843, aged 4.
iii.   SUSAN E., d. Kennebunk ME 16 Aug. 1896; m. her
       cousin MURRAY CHEEVER [# 232].

231. ALMIRA[7] 1816-1902 [70 Mark[6] and Deborah Seavey] was born at Portsmouth 11 Mar. 1816 (Salem MA record), died at Beverly MA 17 Dec. 1902; married MARK DENNETT of Portsmouth, born at Salem 13 Dec. 1814, died at Beverly 8 Feb. 1895, son of Mark Dennett (Salem and Beverly VRs; Cornman Ms).

    In 1850, he was a cabinet-maker at Portsmouth, his household including his wife Almira, 38, and her mother Deborah Laighton, 67.

Children (**Dennett**), the first five born at Portsmouth:

i.   MARK L., b. 26 Sept. 1842, d.y.
ii. ALBERT H., b. 10 Sept. 1843, d. infant.
iii. ALBERT H., b. 28 Mar. 1845; m. Salem 25 June 1867
     (VRs) CHARLOTTE BURRILL, b. 27 Mar. 1845, dau. of
     Josiah and Elizabeth (Wellman) Burrill. No ch.
iv. MARK, d. infant.
v.   ELLA S., b. 12 Oct. 1849; m. Salem 21 Sept. 1869
     (VRs) EDWARD A. MALOON, b. 21 Oct. 1848, son of
     William and Sarah E. (Marks) Maloon.
vi. CLARENCE, b. Beverly MA 6 Sept. 1854, d. 5 June 1878.
     He was a US Navy officer.

232.   DEBORAH[7] 1820-1892 [69 Mark[6] and Deborah Seavey] was
born at Portsmouth 6 June 1820, died 31 Jan. 1892; married at
Portsmouth Dr. JOSEPH CHEEVER (Cornman Ms).

Children (**Cheever**):

i.   ALMIRA L., b. 25 Apr 1837, d. 16 May 1894; m. EDWIN
     C. RYMES of Portsmouth.
ii. ELIZABETH W., b. 28 Nov. 1839.
iii. MARY A., b. 13 Mar. 1842; m. JOSEPH H. WYETH.
iv. MURRAY, b. 3 Feb. 1845, d. 11 Dec. 1928; m. SUSAN E.
     GILPATRICK [# 230]. No ch.
v.   JOSEPH H., b. 6 Dec. 1852, d. 16 Apr. 1884; m.
     GERTRUDE BURT.

233.   OLIVE BOURNE[7] 1807-1871 [71 James[6] and Mary Page] was
born at Portsmouth 11 July 1807, baptized 6 July [sic], died
there 9 June 1871; married there 2 Oct. 1831 (NEHGReg, 83
[1929]:25) WILLIAM SIMES, born there 9 Apr. 1806, died there
15 May 1880, son of George and Nancy (Hardy) Simes (Hurd,
Rockingham/Strafford Hist., 104; Cornman Ms).
He was a grocer. In the 1870 Portsmouth census William,
66, was listed with Olive, 62, and Mary S. Laighton, 86,
Olive's mother.

Children (**Simes**), born at Portsmouth:

i.   JAMES THOMAS, b. 21 Sept. 1834, d. Portsmouth 21
     June 1867; m. Portsmouth 28 Jan. 1864 MARY BROWN
     LIBBY, b. 17 Sept. 1841, d. Portsmouth 16 Sept.
     1867, dau. of Charles H. Brown. (Adopted by her
     aunt and uncle Capt. Daniel and Hannah Libby, she
     had been renamed Libby.)
ii. JOSEPH, b. 22 Sept. 1835, d. Boston 17 Mar. 1884;
     unm.
iii. ELLEN, b. 3 Apr. 1840, d. Portsmouth 13 Jan. 1842.
iv. ELLEN, b. 23 Feb., d. 17 Sept., 1842.
v.   WILLIAM, b. 17 Feb. 1845, res. Petersham MA; m.
     Boston 15 Feb. 1882 FRANCES SWEET NEWELL, b. 7 Apr.
     1853, dau. of James M. and Frances (Sweet) Newell.
     He was a tea importer.
vi. LAURA WOOD, b. 18 Oct. 1846, d. Portsmouth 29
     June 1849.

234.   ANN HAM[7] 1809-1887 [71 James[6] and Mary Page] was born at Portsmouth 11 Jan. 1809 (NEHGReg, 81[1927]:421), died at Montclair NJ 11 Jan. 1887; married at Portsmouth 14 Apr. 1833 (83[1929]:25) DANIEL D. BADGER, born at Badger's Island, Kittery ME 20 Oct. 1806, died at Brooklyn NY 11 Oct. 1885, son of Robert and Sarah (Beck) Badger.

He owned ironworks at Boston, New York, and Philadelphia (John C. Badger, Giles Badger and His Descendants [Manchester NH, 1909], 39).

Children (**Badger**):

i.   ANNA MARY, b. Boston 25 Jan. 1835; res. Montclair NJ; m. 27 June 1861 Dr. HENRY H. LLOYD, b. Blandford MA, d. 30 Apr. 1868, son of Marshall and Sarah (Huggins) Lloyd. He was a graduate of the NJ Medical College, and published a medical journal.

ii.   HORACE D., res. Freeport, L. I., NY; m. Brooklyn ELIZABETH BERGEN.

iii.   SARAH HELEN, d. Brooklyn in 1886; unm.

iv.   ABBIE LEIGHTON, b. Boston, d. Brooklyn c1876; m. ALEXANDER H. SEAVER.

v.   HENRY WARE, d. Brooklyn in 1902.

235.   GEORGE HOWE[7] 1809-1852 [72 John[6] and Elizabeth Howe] was born at Portsmouth 6 Sept. 1809, died there 2 Mar. 1852; married there 19 May 1833 LOUISE G. FLAGG, born there 31 Dec. 1813, died at Asheville NC 25 June 1897, daughter of Andrew and Lucy Flagg (Cornman Ms). In 1850 he was a grocer at Portsmouth.

Children, born at Portsmouth:

i.   ELIZABETH HOWE[8], b. 23 Aug. 1835, res. NYC; m. Portsmouth 29 Oct. 1863 WILLIAM S. CHASE, b. 25 July 1833, d. in July 1865.

ii.   ANNIE LOUISE, b. 11 Dec. 1837; m. Portsmouth 2 Oct. 1865 JAMES HENRY SALTER, b. 3 June 1832, d. 12 Mar. 1895 (William M. Emery, The Salters of Portsmouth, N. H. [New Bedford, 1936], 46-47).

678. iii.   LUCY ALMIRA, b. 1 Oct. 1840; m. HENRY S. LAMBERT.

iv.   GEORGE JOSHUA, b. 27 Mar. 1846; m. 1st 16 Oct. 1872 EFFIE HOGG; m. 2nd 26 Oct. 1891 BERTHA MAST. No ch.

236.   WILLIAM JAMES[7] 1812-1885 [72 John[6] and Elizabeth Howe] was born at Portsmouth 22 Jan 1812, died there 26 Jan. 1885; married there 18 May 1835 his cousin ABIGAIL BLUNT[7] LAIGHTON, born there 28 Feb. 1812, died there 1 Aug. 1878, daughter of James and Mary (Page) Laighton [# 71] (Portsmouth VRs; Cornman Ms).

He and his brother George operated a drygoods store from 1833 to 1857; he was clerk in the Navy Agent's office during the Buchanan administration (1857-1861). He served on the city council and the school committee. In 1880 his household included his daughters Mary and Abbie.

Children, born at Portsmouth:

679. i.   FRANKLIN HOWARD[8], b. 14 Apr. 1836.
      ii.   JAMES WILLIAM, b. 2 Apr., d. 19 Sept., 1841.
      iii. MARY ELLEN, b. 22 Dec. 1843, d. Portsmouth 15
            Feb. 1911; m. 11 Sept. 1867 CHARLES E. SHEDD,
            b. Albany ME 14 Oct. 1840, d. Brooklyn NY 19
            Mar. 1880, son of James P. and Mary (Proctor)
            Shedd. They removed to NYC in 1867, where he
            was a boot and shoe merchant. Ch. Mabel b. 2
            Apr. 1873, d. Portsmouth in Dec. 1950; unm.
      iv.   JOSEPHINE, b. 13 Feb. 1845, d. 2 Feb. 1846.
      v.   ABIGAIL BLUNT, b. 23 June 1849, res. Portsmouth
            with her sister Mary Shedd; unm.

237. EDWARD JOHN[7] 1814-1880 [72 John[6] and Elizabeth Howe]
was born at Portsmouth 14 July 1814, died there 17 Mar. 1880;
married at Sudbury MA 27 Nov. 1834 (VRs) HARRIET SMITH, born
there 22 Oct. 1817, died at East Cambridge MA 20 May 1859
(Boston Weekly Messenger of 1 June), daughter of Elisha and
Clarissa Smith.
    He was a fanatic spiritualist (Cornman Ms). In 1870 he was
a printer, 56, living in Eliza Penhallow's household.

Children, born at Portsmouth:

      i.   CLARISSA[8], b. say 1835, d. 24 Feb. 1836.
      ii.   CLARA OPHELIA, b. in 1836, d. Portsmouth 11
            June 1855; unm.
      iii. ADA, d. infant.
680. iv.   WASHINGTON IRVING, b. say 1840.

238. BENJAMIN DAMRELL[7] 1817-1873 [72 John[6] and Mary Dam-
rell] was born at Portsmouth 18 Mar. 1817, died there 13 Jan.
1873, 56y; married there 16 May 1841 SUSAN W. REMICK, born
there 29 Aug. 1819, buried there 12 Mar. 1907, 87y, daughter
of Joseph and Susan (Wentworth) Remick (Portsmouth VRs; Cornman Ms; Wentworth Gen., 2:255).
    Laighton served as corporal in Co. K, 16th NH Vol. Inf.
Rgt., during the Civil War. He became a farmer at Stratham
NH in 1840, and served the town as register of deeds and superintendent of schools. He refused election to the state
legislature because the duties would require long absences
from home. In 1868 the family returned to Portsmouth; he was
a clerk there in 1870.

Children, born at Stratham:

      i.   BENNETT[8], b. in 1843, d. Buffalo NY 20 Aug.
            1863; unm. He was also in Co. K, 16th Rgt.
      ii.   LAVINIA GREENLEAF, b. in 1845 (22 in 1870),
            res. Washington DC in 1903; unm. She was a
            clerk in the US pension office.
681. iii. JOHN, b. 26 Oct. 1847.
682. iv.   MARY SUSAN, b. in 1849; m. MONINA G. PORTER.
      v.   (GEORGE) RALPH, b. 31 Oct. 1858 (VRs), res.
            Portsmouth in 1900; m. 8 Dec. 1886 H. MARY
            SWAIN, b. in Mar. 1857, dau. of John D. Swain
            of Nashua NH. No ch.

239. MARY ELIZABETH[7] 1818-1878 [72 John[6] and Mary Damrell]
was born at Portsmouth 3 Oct. 1818, died there 27 Feb. 1878
(per Gen.; 16 Nov. 1880 per Cornman Ms); married 27 June
1839 SAMUEL J. DODGE, born at Portsmouth 26 Oct. 1814, died
25 May 1867 (1869 per Cornman Ms), son of Joseph and Jane
(Dennett) Dodge (Joseph T. Dodge, Genealogy of the Dodge Family [Madison WI, 1894], 233-4; Portsmouth VRs).

Children (**Dodge**), born at Portsmouth:

i.   FREDERICK LAIGHTON, b. 9 Aug. 1840, d. Detroit MI
        10 Sept. 1891; m. 27 Dec. 1873 LAURA CLEMENT,
        dau. of Major F. Clement, a Prussian Army officer.
        Capt. Dodge retired from the US Army in 1891, after
        30 yrs. service.
ii.   ALBERT LAIGHTON, b. 29 Sept. 1841, res. NY; m. 28
        June 1863 CARRIE GORDON CHAMBERLAIN, dau. of John
        and Jane Chamberlain of Cambridge MA.
iii.   SAMUEL, b. 9 Aug. 1844; m. 7 Oct. 1880 FLORENCE ANN
        BOWLES, dau. of James and Susan M. Bowles of Ports-
        mouth. He was a journalist.
iv.   WILLIAM JAMES, b. 8 June 1846, d. 20 Feb. 1889; m.
        5 Oct. 1882 LIZZIE NOONAN of Passage West, Co. Cork,
        Ireland.
v.   BENJAMIN FRANKIN, b. 20 Mar. 1850, d. 27 July 1853.
vi.   CHARLES SUMNER, b. 3 Aug. 1851; m. 27 Nov. 1872 ALICE
        M. LAMSON, dau. of Asa B. and Mary A. Lamson of
        Exeter NH.

240. OCTAVE V.[7] 1822-1866 [72 John[6] and Mary Damrell] was
born at Portsmouth 25 Jan. 1822, died at Petersburg VA 28
Feb. 1866; married first at Chicago 1 May 1854 ANNIE WIGGIN,
born at Stratham NH, died at Fulton IL 28 Jan. 1856; married
second 18 July 1857 LUCY DOROTHEA HENRY, born at Winston VA 6
Mar. 1822, died at Petersburg 26 Jan. 1898, daughter of
Edward Winston and Jane (Yuille) Henry and grand-daughter of
the patriot Patrick Henry.
In 1850 he was a printer at Portsmouth, but soon went west,
intending to seek gold in CA. Instead, he settled at Fulton
IL, where he edited and published the Fulton City Advertiser
from 1854 to 1857. Lucy Henry met Octave through her admira-
tion for his brother Albert's poetry (Cornman Ms).

Child by first wife Annie, born in IL:

i.   ALBERT[8], d. infant.

Children by second wife Lucy, born at Petersburg VA:

ii.   FAYETTE HENRY, b. 29 June 1861.
iii.   ALBERTA WINSLOW, b. 31 May 1863, res. Pawling
        NY in 1903.

241. ELLEN AUGUSTA[7] 1825-   [72 John[6] and Mary Damrell]
was born at Portsmouth 8 Oct. 1825; married first there 4
Nov. 1852 FRANCIS E. SABINE of Eastport ME; married second 21
Dec. 1865 THOMAS LEWIS, who died in 1885 (Cornman Ms).

Child (**Sabine**):

i.   WILLIAM L., b. 24 Nov. 1854, res. Portsmouth.

Child (**Lewis**):

ii.   FREDERICK DODGE, b. 20 Dec. 1867; m. in Newfoundland
      2 Aug. 1894 MARGARET CANDOW, b. 18 Jan. 1867.

242. **ALBERT**[7] 1829-1887 [72 John[6] and Mary Damrell] was
born at Portsmouth 8 Jan. 1829, died there 6 Feb. 1887, 58y;
married first there 1 Dec. 1852 (NEHGReg, 83[1929]:173) HELEN
MARR GOODRICH, born 16 Apr. 1824, died at Portsmouth 3 Feb.
1869, daughter of Jeremiah Dow and Mary Elizabeth (Nelson)
Goodrich; married second at Portsmouth 23 Oct. 1871 (83:299)
FLORENCE GOODRICH, born 5 Sep 1844, lived at Portsmouth in
1900, daughter of Moses and Ann Elizabeth (Dodge) Goodrich
(Cornman Ms).
  Albert Laighton was a bank teller; he also gained a region-
al reputation as a poet. He published a volume of poems in
1859, popular enough to merit a second edition in 1878 which
he dedicated to his cousin Celia Thaxter.

Possible child by first wife Helen, born at Portsmouth:

i.   PHILIP[8].

Children by second wife Florence, born at Portsmouth:

ii.   EDITH, b. 13 Oct. 1872.
iii. AUSTIN , b. in 1874, d. 18 June 1882 (Arthur in
      the 1880 census).
iv.   HELEN, b. 20 June 1877.

243. **SARAH RICHARD**[7] 1808-1865 [73 Samuel[6] and Mary
Fernald] was born at Portsmouth 7 May 1808, died at Bangor ME
3 Feb. 1865; married Capt. JOHN LAKE, born in 1803, died in
Panama in May 1850 (Cornman Ms).

Children (**Lake**):

i.   DAYTON W., b. in 1845, d. Brooklyn NY 26 Aug.
      1863. He served during the Civil War in Co. I,
      114th ME Vol. Inf. Rgt.
ii.   JOHN, b. 25 May 1850, d. 16 Mar. 1853.

244. **LITTLETON MILLS**[7] 1809-1885 [73 Samuel[6] and Mary Fer-
nald] was born at Portsmouth 12 Sept. 1809, died there 1 Oct.
1885, 76y; married first there 13 Jan. 1833 MARY S. HART,
born 13 Jan. 1812, died at Portsmouth 11 Mar. 1856; married
second there 24 May 1858 SARAH SMITH, born there 11 Sept.
1818 (or 9 Mar. per Gen.), died there 23 Oct. 1901, daughter
of John and Charlotte (Swasey) Smith (Portsmouth VRs; Benjamin F. Swasey, Genealogy of the Swasey Family [Cleveland OH,
1910], 340; Cornman Ms).
  Littleton was a merchant and spar-maker.

Children by Mary, born at Portsmouth:

683.   i.   EDWIN R.[8], b. 18 Nov. 1833.
       ii.   SAMUEL, b. 6 Feb. 1835, d. in KS 27 June 1884;
             m. 11 Apr. 1877 GENEVIEVE LONG, b. in 1846.
             He served in the Union Army, and was later a
             banker at Leavenworth KS.
       iii. JAMES WILLIAM, b. in Mar., d. 19 Sept., 1841.
684.   iv.   MARY WYMAN, b. 23 Feb. 1846; m. WILLIAM B.
             DOLE.

245.   **PAUL**[7] 1813-1854 [73 Samuel[6] and Mary Fernald] was
born at Portsmouth 26 June 1813, died there 20 July 1854;
married there 25 Dec. 1836 MARY WHEELER, born in 1813, died
at Columbus OH 26 Jan. 1852. A sea captain, he had completed
a voyage from Calcutta as master of the Casio shortly before
he died (Cornman Ms).

Children, born at Portsmouth:

       i.   MARY ALICE[8], b. in 1838, d. 7 May 1840.
       ii.   ANN E., b. 9 Feb., d. 9 Apr., 1840.

246.   **WILLIAM FERNALD**[7] 1815-1879 [73 Samuel[6] and Mary Fer-
nald] was born at Portsmouth 13 Nov. 1815, died at Revere MA
25 June 1879; married at Portsmouth 20 Dec. 1836 ANN L. DAL-
TON (Cornman Ms).
He enlisted in the US Navy as an apprentice carpenter in
1849, and retired as a captain in 1877.

Children, born at Portsmouth:

       i.   ALFRED STOW[8], b. 16 Aug. 1838, d. Ft. Fisher
             NC 16 Jan. 1865; m. Portsmouth 16 July 1863
             CATHERINE M. TRUNDY. No ch. He joined the US
             Navy as ensign in 1863, and died in an explo-
             sion on the fort parapet, while in charge of a
             squad trying to recover bodies.
       ii.   ALICE.
       iii. ELIZABETH HAM, b. 29 Aug. 1846, d. 14 Mar.
             1855.

247.   **MARK FERNALD**[7] 1821-1882 [73 Samuel[6] and Mary Fernald]
was born at Portsmouth 18 Mar. 1821, died 29 May 1882; married MATILDA ---- , who was born in England (Cornman Ms).

Children, said to have resided at Brooklyn NY:

       i.   GEORGE[8].
       ii.   CHARLES.
       iii. JOSEPH.
       iv.   dau., d.y.

248.   **CLARA**[7] 1831-   [73 Samuel[6] and Mary Fernald] was
born at Portsmouth 26 Feb. 1831; married at Bangor ME 26 Dec.
1855 WILLIAM HASTINGS STRICKLAND, born at Bangor 4 Feb. 1830,

died there 27 Feb. 1891, 61y, son of Hastings and Clarinda C. (Brettun) Strickland ("Rev. John Strickland and his Family," BHM, 3[1887]:11; M. V. B. Perley, History and Genealogy of the Perley Family [1906], 193; Bangor VRs).
He was a Bangor merchant, and served in the state legislature in 1876.

Children (**Strickland**), born at Bangor:

i.   FREDERICK HASTINGS, b. 9 Sept. 1856. He was aide-de-
       camp to Gov. Harris M. Plaisted.
ii.   LILLIAN MARCH, b. 31 Dec. 1860; m. ---- HILL.
iii.   WILLIAM BRETTUN, b. in Dec. 1869, d. 25 Sept. 1870.

249.   MARY ANN[7] 1800-1885 [75 John[6] and Abigail Shackford] was born at Dover NH 20 Jan. 1800, died at Wellesley MA 28 Jan. 1885; married 11 Nov. 1823 (VRs Dover, 181) JOHN ANTHONY ROLLINS, born at Somersworth NH 4 Apr. 1801, died at Wellesley 4 Sept. 1876, son of Capt. Hiram and Joanna (Wentworth) Rollins (Rollins Gen., 141; Wentworth Gen., 2:458).
Rollins was a building contractor; his work required him to reside in various states. Mary A. Rollins had a memorial stone erected marking the original Leighton home at Dover.

Children (**Rollins**):

i.   ANNA O., b. Dover 3 Oct. 1824, d. Chelsea MA 5 Dec.
       1854; unm. She was a schoolteacher at Charlestown.
ii.   AUGUSTA, b. Dover 14 Apr. 1826, res. Wellesley; unm.
iii.   Brig. Gen. HIRAM, b. Barrington NH 16 May 1827, d.
       Washington DC 19 Aug. 1868; m. Boston 13 Dec. 1853
       MARY CAROLINE [Carrie] BIGELOW, b. Boston 10 Aug.
       1831, dau. of Isaac and Harriet (Warren) Bigelow
       (NEHGReg, 87[1933]:289).
iv.   THEODORE ATKINSON, b. Barrington 4 Oct. 1829, d.
       So. Berwick ME 23 Aug. 1864; m. 8 Oct. 1855 ELLEN
       A. LORD, b. Berwick 7 Nov. 1834, d. So. Berwick 17
       Aug. 1922 (GS, So. Berwick), dau. of Hon. John P.
       Lord. No ch.
v.   PAUL WENTWORTH, b. Durhamville, Madison Co. NY
       30 Jun 1830, d. 22 Mar. 1831.
vi.   HANNAH HUNTINGTON, b. Petersburg, Rensselaer Co NY
       6 May 1832, res. Wellesley; unm.
vii.   FITZHUGH SMITH, b. Petersburg 7 May 1834, res. Newton
       MA; m. 26 July 1860 AUGUSTA LYDIA SAWYER HANSON,
       b. Dover 20 Jan. 1842, dau. of Joseph and Abigail
       (Varney) Hanson. He was a Boston merchant.
viii. EDWIN LEIGHTON, b. Petersburg 29 Nov. 1837, d.
       Wellesley 27 Nov. 1900. He res. Newtonville.

250.   RUTH[7] 1802-1885 [75 John[6] and Abigail Shackford] was born at Dover say 1802, died at Sausalito CA in 1885; married first at Dover 14 Apr. 1823 (VRs Dover, 181) JAMES M. CURTIS of Piscatabridge; married second JONATHAN LOCKE of Great Falls (Dover) NH, born at Portsmouth 20 Sept. 1802, died in CA 13 June 1878, son of Jonathan and Lydia (Hall) Locke (Arthur H. Locke, History and Genealogy of Capt. John Locke [Concord NH, nd], 253). Locke was a blacksmith; in 1849 he joined the California gold rush (Cornman Ms).

Children (**Curtis**):

i.   ALMIRA; m. Great Falls EDMUND DAVIS.
ii.   JULIA; m. ---- FRENCH.
iii. ELLEN; m. ---- FRENCH.
iv.   GEORGE.

Children (**Locke**):

v.   LYDIA HALL; m. in CA ---- DRISCO.
vi.   MARY ABBIE; unm.
vii. EDWARD A., b. in 1837, d. Dover 10 May 1878; m.
      Somersworth int. 1 Jan. 1867 EMMA H. DANIELS of
      Great Falls. No ch. He was a stonecutter.

251.   SETH[7] 1803-1830 [75 John[6] and Abigail Shackford] was
born at Dover say 1803, died 14 Feb. 1830; married 31 Mar.
1824 (NHGR, 3[1906]:94) MARTHA ANN MARY WINKLEY of Kittery.
Martha married second a Capt. Cutler, who was lost at sea.
She was identified as daughter of John and Deborah (Cain)
Winkley (Cornman Ms) and also of Francis and Martha (Brown)
Winkley (Cornman Papers).

Children:

i.   CHARLES WILLIAM[8], b. c1825, d. Portsmouth
      9 June 1854, 29y (VRs).
ii.   JANE ANN, b. Dover, d. Boston 4 Dec. 1888; m.
      Portsmouth 14 Jan. 1850 CHARLES E. MAIN.
      No ch.
iii. JOHN.

252.   JONATHAN[7] 1792-   [83 Jonathan[6] and Annah Dyer] was
born at Steuben ME 26 Nov. 1792 (TRs), died between the 1850
and 1860 censuses; married at Harrington ME 10 Nov. 1815
LYDIA STROUT, born at Cherryfield ME 27 May 1793, lived with
her son Amesbury in 1870, daughter of Benjamin and Elizabeth
Strout (town VRs).
  He was a farmer. He sold 50 acres to Warren Leighton
[# 265] on 16 Mar. 1822, half of lot 76 (WashCD, 13:371). In
1850 his Steuben household included his mother "Hannah," 79,
and in 1860 his uncle Eleazer, 60.

Children, born at Steuben:

685. i.   MARY ANN[8], b. 14 Dec. 1816; m. GEORGE SAWYER.
      ii.   JOEL, b. 20 Apr. 1818, drowned c1844; m. int.
            Steuben 22 Jan. 1840 JOANNA SAWYER, b. Mil-
            bridge 13 May 1822, d. Steuben 14 Sept. 1903
            (GS), dau. of Josiah, Jr., and Rebecca (Grin-
            dle) Sawyer. No ch. Joanna m. 2nd 7 Feb.
            1842 William Adams of Rockport--4 ch; and m.
            3rd 3 Aug. 1852 Daniel Robinson--5 ch.
686. iii. PRISCILLA, b. 20 Dec. 1819; m. WILLIAM R.
            ATWATER.
687. iv.   CLIMENA, b. 30 Jan. 1821; m. JOSIAH WALLACE.
688. v.   ORSENA [ASENATH PRATT], b. 28 Mar. 1823; m.
            DANIEL WILLEY.
689. vi.   CAROLINE, b. 19 Mar. 1825; m. STILLMAN PARRITT.

690. vii. DAVID, b. 28 Apr. 1827.
      viii. MILLBURY, b. 25 Jan. 1829, d. c1842.
691. ix.   AMESBURY (twin) b. 25 Jan. 1829.
      x.   EDWIN, b. 5 Jan. 1833, d. Steuben 30 May 1891
            (Machias Union); m. 3 Sept. 1865 MARY JANE
            WORTH of Waterville ME, b. in NS c1846 (24 in
            1870). He was a shoemaker at Steuben in 1870,
            and later res. Camden. He may have had
            another wife. Ch. IDA MAY[9] b. c1867 (3 in
            1870); m. Steuben 5 Apr. 1885 (Machias Union)
            CHARLES W. HODGKINS, b. there in 1868, son of
            Agnew H. and Elvira (Wakefield) Hodgkins.
            Charles m. 2nd Steuben 5 June 1895 Ada Wake-
            field (Johnson, Sullivan and Sorrento, 321).
692. xi.   OSGOOD E., b. 6 Sept. 1835.
693. xii. ELIZA ANN, b. 4 Feb. 1838; m. DAVID J. NASH.

253. **ANNA**[7] 1795-1859 [83 Jonathan[6] and Annah Dyer] was
born at Steuben 3 June 1795, died there 21 June 1859; married
there 19 Feb. 1814 BENJAMIN GODFREY, born 11 Dec. 1792, died
at Steuben 15 Nov. 1857, son of Ichabod and Lydia (Wakefield)
Godfrey (Steuben VRs; Cornman Ms).

Children (**Godfrey**), born at Steuben:

i.   DAVID, b. 10 June 1815, d. in 1851.
ii.   MARIA, b. 21 May 1817, d. 15 Sept. 1853; m. Steuben
      3 July 1841 HENRY D. MOORE, b. there 8 Feb. 1815,
      son of James and Molly (Dyer) Moore.
iii. JOHN KINGSLEY, b. 27 May 1819, d. 10 Sept. 1834.
iv.   LYDIA, b. 28 Apr. 1821, d. Chicago IL; m. 22 June
      1842 GEORGE GAY.
v.   ANNA LEIGHTON, b. 6 Feb. 1824; m. Cherryfield 3 Nov.
      1860 JAMES G. SANBORN.
vi.   NATHAN, b. 13 Mar. 1829; m. REBECCA DYER.
vii. WILSON, b. 13 Oct. 1831, res. Brooklyn NY; m. 15 Mar.
      1860 LOUISE M. HAWKINS of Norway.

254. **CHARITY**[7] 1796-1880 [83 Jonathan[6] and Annah Dyer] was
born at Steuben 30 Oct. 1796, died there 15 Feb. 1880; married first there int. 15 July 1827 SAMUEL NASH, born at Addison 8 Nov. 1799, died there 18 Nov. 1842, son of John and
Eunice (Merritt) Nash; married second at Steuben 25 June 1848
WILLIAM NICHOLS NASH, born 7 Apr. 1785, died at Steuben 7
June 1874, son of Isaiah and Mary (Ingersoll) Nash (Steuben
VRs; "Joseph Nash and Family," BHM, 8[1893]:155-161).
William Nash had married first Belinda Coffin, by whom he
had four children. Charity's first child, father unknown,
was adopted by his grandfather Jonathan (Cornman Ms).

Child (**Leighton**), born at Steuben:

694. i.   WOODBURY[8], b. 25 July 1816.

Children (**Nash**) by Samuel, born at Steuben:

i.   CATHERINE C , b. 13 June 1828; m. 11 Dec. 1847
      CHARLES FARROW. They went west.

ii.   REBECCA C. (twin), b. 13 June 1828, d. in Mar. 1900;
       m. Cherryfield 18 Jan. 1850 TOBIAS STROUT, b. 6
       June 1825, son of Elisha and Rebecca[9] (Leighton)
       Strout [# 385].
iii.   ANN MARIA H., b. 13 July 1830, d. 13 May 1833.
iv.   LYDIA H., b. 8 Nov. 1832, d. 24 Sept. 1855.
v.   EUNICE N., b. 13 June, d. 19 June, 1834.
vi.   ADELAIDE L., b. 1 June, d. 10 June, 1835.
vii.   JONATHAN L., b. 3 Oct. 1837; m. and went west.
viii. SUSAN ABBY, b. 13 June 1839, d. 31 Mar. 1843.

255. HENRY DYER[7] 1799-1882 [83 Jonathan[6] and Annah Dyer]
was born at Steuben 18 Apr. 1799, died there 10 Mar. 1882;
married there 28 June (Addison int. 23 June) LOVICIA WASS,
born at Addison 18 May 1805, died at Steuben 10 Feb. 1864,
daughter of John and Annie (Dyer) Wass (Steuben VRs; Cornman
Ms; Walter P. Wass, The Wass Family [1945], 9-S). Her name
was also spelled Lovisa and Lovice, but she was called
"Vici."
       H. D. was a master shipbuilder, farmer, and elder of the
Methodist church. He served in the legislature as a Whig in
1843.

Children, born at Steuben:

695.   i.   CATHERINE ALLEN[8], b. 26 July 1825; m. ALBION
              K. P. MOORE.
696.   ii.   ANN WASS, b. 9 Mar. 1827; m. GEORGE W. WAITE
              and JOHN HOLDEN.
697.   iii.   ARICSENE, b. 15 Jan. 1829; m. ELISHA C. SMALL.
       iv.   MARY SHAW, b. 21 Sept. 1831, d. Milbridge 5
              Jan. 1897; m. 27 Nov. 1853 GUILFORD PARKER
              STEVENS, b. 24 Sept. 1829, d. Milbridge 28
              Oct. 1896, son of Edward Manning and Delia
              Stevens. Their 2 ch. Fred and Anna d.y.
698.   v.   ELIZA DYER, b. 2 Sept. 1833; m. HORATIO SNOW
              CAMPBELL.
699.   vi.   ELLEN FRANCES, b. 20 Jan. 1836; m. THOMAS
              JEFFERSON CAMPBELL.
700.   vii.   FLETCHER KINGSLEY, b. 3 Mar. 1839.
701.   viii. TRUMAN W., b. 15 Aug. 1841.
       ix.   ASENATH L., b. 23 July 1843, d. 26 Sept. 1846.
       x.   CLARISSA W., b. c1846 (4 in 1850), d.y.
702.   xi.   CLARISSA W. [Clara], b. 5 Oct. 1849; m. JAMES
              PARKIN.

256. HANDY[7] 1800-1885 [83 Jonathan[6] and Annah Dyer] was
born at Steuben 21 Sept. 1800, died there 2 June 1885, 84y 8m
11d; married first there int. 21 Nov. 1826 REBECCA WASS, born
21 Nov. 1807, died at Steuben 1 July 1864, 57y 10m 25d,
daughter of John and Annie (Dyer) Wass (Wass Family, 9-S);
married second 19 July 1866 ELIZA ANN SMITH, born at Steuben
1 Jan. 1831, died there 26 Jan. 1878, daughter of Robert
Allen and Jane[7] (Leighton) Smith [# 273] (Steuben VRs; Cornman Ms). He was a merchant.
       In 1850 Handy's household included Joseph Small, 8; in 1860
it included Mary Noonan, 1, as well. The name Handy perhaps
originated with the popular Dr. Ebenezer Handy of Steuben and
Addison.

Children by Rebecca, born at Steuben:

703. i.   MARGARET WASS[8], b. 21 Sept. 1827; m. CHARLES H.
            HASKELL.
      ii.   SOPHIA JONES, b. 17 Sept. 1829, d. there 1 July
            1903; m. 11 July 1852 (JAMES) COLEMAN GOOGINS,
            b. Hancock ME 14 Feb. 1829. Ch. William P. F
            Googins b. 28 Oct. 1858; unm.
704. iii. JOHN BUCKNAM GODFREY, b. 4 Apr. 1832.
      iv.   JANE W., b. 19 Oct. 1835; m. Steuben int. 1
            Oct. 1859 GLEASON W. MOORE, b. 10 Nov. 1833,
            son of Samuel and Matilda (Wakefield) Moore
            (Wakefield Mem., 170). No ch.
      v.   HARRIET, b. in 1837, d.y.
      --   ROBERT (adopted), b. 6 Nov. 1861, res. Lowell
            MA in 1900; m. 20 Sept. 1889 SARAH FRANCES
            JORDAN, b. Ellsworth 18 Jan. 1861, dau. of
            John W. and Elizabeth (Frazier) Jordan. Ch.
            John b. Everett MA 16 Aug. 1892 (Robert's
            letter--Cornman Papers). Robert was the son
            of Eliza Smith.

257. TRYPHENA[7] 1802-1865 [83 Jonathan[6] and Annah Dyer] was
born at Steuben 19 July 1802, died at Cherryfield 20 Sept.
1865; married at Steuben int. 12 May 1822 WILLIAM BINGHAM
NASH, born at Columbia ME 25 Aug. 1796, died at Cherryfield 7
June 1874, 89y 2m, son of John and Eunice (Merritt) Nash
(BHM, 8[1893]:160; Waterhouse Gen., 2:626; town VRs).
Burials are in Pine Grove Cemetery, Cherryfield.
      Nash's will was proved 2 Dec. 1874. He was a tanner, shoe-
maker and boat builder.

Children (**Nash**), born at Cherryfield:

i.   JOHN, b. 17 Mar. 1823, d. 23 May 1849, lost on bark
       Ralph Cross; unm.
ii   HENRY LEIGHTON, b. 7 Dec. 1824, d. Cherryfield 9 Mar.
       1869; m. 7 Jan. 1856 BETSEY W. NASH, b. Addison 19
       Oct. 1826, dau. of William and Mary (Coffin) Nash.
iii.   ARTHUR RICKER, b. 18 Oct. 1826, d. Cherryfield 11
       Mar. 1885; m. Cherryfield 17 July 1852 ABIGAIL
       CATHERINE FLYNN, b. Machias 11 Apr. 1832. He was
       a druggist.
iv.   ELIZABETH MARY, b. 29 Sept. 1828, d. Steuben 16 Jan.
       1895; m. Cherryfield 19 Dec. 1873, as his 2nd wife,
       ROBERT L. MOORE.
v.   WILMOT W., b. 1 Oct. 1831, d. 21 Dec. 1861; m. CLARA
       V. (SMITH) Orcutt, dau. of William Ellis and Hannah
       (Lyon) Smith of Machias.
vi.   GEORGE M., b. 25 July 1835, d. Thibodeau LA 20 July
       1864 while a soldier; m. ALICE BOUTILLIER.
vii.   WILLIAM M., b. 13 Oct. 1837, d. Cherryfield 8 Sept.
       1921; m. 29 Nov. 1862 CAROLINE J. MOORE, b. 7 Aug.
       1839, d. 12 Dec. 1890, dau. of James W. and Susan
       Moore.
viii. ELLERY B., b. 12 Nov. 1839, d. Cherryfield 13 Jan.
       1842.
ix.   ELLERY B., b. 10 Jan. 1844, d. 17 Sept. 1890; m.
       Cherryfield 20 Apr. 1867 ANNA LAWRENCE of Machias.

258.   THOMAS[7] 1804-1863 [83 Jonathan[6] and Annah Dyer] was
born at Steuben 1 Mar. 1804, died at Belfast ME 7 Oct. 1863
(VRs); married at Steuben 7 Aug. (int. 1 July) 1828 PERSIS
TOWNSLEY DYER, born 11 Oct. 1807, died at Hyde Park MA 12
Apr. 1898, daughter of Reuben and Annie (Whitten) Dyer (Steu-
ben VRs; Cornman Ms).
A shipbuilder, he moved to Belfast in 1847.

Children, all but the last two born at Steuben:

705.   i.   CHRISTINA DYER[8], b. 20 May 1829; m. SAMUEL
             COLSON and ELIAS FULLER.
706. ii.   ALBION KEITH PARRIS, b. 10 Nov. 1830.
707. iii.   EMERY DYER, b. 25 Sept. 1832.
      iv.   STEPHEN HILL, b. 16 Sept. 1835, d. Fort
             Churchill NV 23 Nov. 1862, sergeant, 2nd CA
             Vol. Cav. Rgt.
       v.   MELVILLE, b. 8 Dec. 1838, d. Steuben 1 May
             1847.
      vi.   GEORGE EDWIN, b. 4 May 1846, d. 16 Apr. 1847.
     vii.   MARY ELLEN, b. Belfast 26 Feb. 1849, res. Hyde
             Park MA; m. Barre MA 14 Oct. 1874 DANIEL
             WESTON MASON, b. 11 Mar. 1844, son of Daniel
             and Arminda (Weston) Mason. Ch. Harold Weston
             b. Hyde Park 13 Oct. 1878 (Cornman Ms).
    viii.   GEORGE MELVILLE (twin), b. Belfast 26 Feb.
             1849, d. Portland 19 July 1930; m. there 18
             Jan. 1871 JULIA E. RANDALL, b. Westbrook 9
             Oct. 1848, d. Portland 21 Mar. 1942, dau. of
             Isaac and Ann (Estes) Randall. George was a
             carpenter.
                Ch. MABELLE FRANCES[9] b. Deering 26 Dec. 1873,
             d. 22 May 1895; m. Deering 5 Sept. 1894 EDWARD
             SYLVESTER MAGUIRE, b. Baltimore MD in 1860,
             son of Christopher and Ellen Maguire of
             Detroit MI.

259.   PERSIS TOWNSLEY[7] 1807-1884 [83 Jonathan[6] and Annah
Dyer] was born at Steuben 19 Jan. 1807, died there 12 Dec.
1884; married at Steuben 26 May 1826 OLIVER CLEAVES, born at
Kennebunk ME 12 Apr. 1801, died at Steuben 31 May 1885, son
of Nathan and Hannah (Wakefield) Cleaves (Steuben VRs; Cornman Ms).

Children (**Cleaves**), born at Steuben:

   i.   GUILFORD, b. 27 Aug. 1827, d. 18 Aug. 1895; m.
         Steuben 12 Dec. 1852 ESTHER E. ATWATER, b. in NS 15
         Aug. 1826, dau. of William and Esther (Andrews)
         Atwater.
  ii.   (BENJAMIN) FRANKLIN, b. 8 Sept. 1829, d. Addison
         8 June 1885; m. Machias ANGELINE LONGFELLOW.
 iii.   COURTNEY BABBAGE, b. 23 Aug. 1831, res. Westboro MA;
         m. Pembroke HANNAH MARDEN.
  iv.   MELISSA N., b. 3 Feb. 1834; m. 3 Feb. 1854 DAVID
         ATWATER, b. Little River NS 12 Mar. 1827, d. Steuben
         23 Sept. 1893, son of Leeman and Mary Atwater.
   v.   ANN MARIA N., b. 4 Jan. 1837; m. AMESBURY[8] LEIGHTON
         [# 691].

vi.   ALVA H., b. 22 July 1840, res. Pembroke; m. 1st SARAH
      H. ALBEE, b. E. Machias 14 July 1841; m. 2nd LOIS
      LINCOLN of Perry.
vii. EVERETT A., b. 25 Apr. 1847; m. Cherryfield 27
      June 1845 FRANCES J. COLLINS, b. 27 June 1845.

   260. IRENE[7] 1809-   [83 Jonathan[6] and Annah Dyer] was
born at Steuben 14 Jan. 1809, lived at Cherryfield; married
at Steuben 30 Oct. 1829 ISAAC SMALL, born 16 Feb. 1797, died
21 Sept. 1857, son of Elisha and Priscilla (Strout) Small
(Milliken, 4; Underhill, Small Desc., 2:176).

Children (**Small**):

i.   MARIA; m. JOHN PARKIN.
ii.   LAURA A., b. in 1832; m. JOSEPH HUTCHINSON.
iii. WINSLOW G., b. c1833; m. CLARA LAWN.
iv.   MALCOLM, b. c1835; res. in WI.

   261. ELIZABETH DYER[7] [Betsey] 1811-1878 [83 Jonathan[6] and
Annah Dyer] was born at Steuben ME 25 Jan. 1811, died at
Milltown NB 28 Dec. 1878; married 20 Apr. 1826 OLIVER GRAY
RANDALL, born at Leeds ME 12 Oct. 1809, died at Milltown 9
June 1884, son of Nathan and Susanna (Creach) Randall (Wil-
liam L. Chaffin, Robert Randall and His Descendants [NY,
1909], 160-1; Cornman Ms).

Children (**Randall**):

i.   LYDIA MARIE, b. 29 Jan. 1837, d. Calais ME 18 Aug.
      1897; unm. She was a Milltown teacher for 20 yrs.
ii.   SOPHRONIA S., b. 12 Aug. 1838, d. 12 Aug. 1839.
iii. EDWARD GRANVILLE, b. 6 Mar. 1845, d. 19 Dec. 1855.
iv.   ELLA FRANCES, b. 10 June 1848, d. 12 Sept. 1849.
v.   MARY LEONETTE, b. 29 Feb. 1854, d. 17 Sept. 1855.

   262. ALMON[7] 1818-1892 [83 Jonathan[6] and Annah Dyer] was
born at Steuben 4 Jan. 1818, died at Calais ME 14 Mar. 1892,
74y 2m 10d; married at Oak Bay NB 3 Dec. 1843 SARAH McALLIS-
TER, born in NB 16 Mar. 1815, died at Calais 27 Feb. 1886
(town VRs; Cornman Ms).
He was a ship's carpenter at Calais.

Children:

      i.   JOEL[8], b. 16 Sept. 1844, d. 15 Dec. 1845.
      ii.   ALEXANDER, b. Ledge NB 19 May 1846, d. Calais
            7 Dec. 1925, 79y 6m 15d. He was div. per
            death rec.
      iii. EMMA E., b. NB 26 Feb. 1849; m. Calais 6 Nov.
            1872 CHARLES A. McCULLOUGH, b. there in 1849,
            d. there 30 Apr. 1914, 65y 1m 8d, son of
            William and Eliza (White) McCullough. Ch.
            Mary H. b. c1874, Frank L. b. c1877, Emma b.
            c1879, and Sarah (Cornman Ms; 1880 census).
708. iv.   MARY T., b. 26 Oct. 1851; m. SAMUEL DINGLEY.
      v.   ANNA M., b. Oak Bay NB 31 May 1853, d. Auburn
            17 Jan. 1939; unm.

263. ABIGAIL[7] [Nabby] 1796-1839 [84 Mark[6] and Sally Cates]
was born at Steuben 24 Feb. 1796, died there 25 Feb. 1839;
married there 18 Oct. 1829 JAMES SMITH of Tunk Pond, born 23
Feb. 1781, died at Steuben 12 Dec. 1869, 89y (Machias Union),
son of Job and Diadama (Booth) Smith (Smith records of Arlene
Skehan; Cornman Ms; Steuben TRs).
Smith had married first Mary Jones, who died in 1828.

Children (Smith), born at Steuben:

i.   MARY A., b. 19 Aug. 1832.
ii.   JAMES, b. 1 May 1834, res. Hopedale MA; m. ANNETTE
      HALL.
iii. EDWARD KENT, b. 5 Aug. 1837, d. Steuben 17 Apr.
      1920; m. there 8 Dec. 1869 ELIZA GUPTILL, b. 14
      June 1834.

264. ELISHA[7] 1795-   [84 Mark[6] and Sally Cates] was born
at Steuben 4 Apr. 1798; married there 26 Jan. 1826 ELIZABETH
GRACE [Betsey] PARKER, born 24 Feb. 1800, daughter of William
and Polly (Grace) Parker (Steuben VRs). Both were living in
Alfred Grace's household in 1870.

Children, born at Steuben:

i.   BETHIA CATES[8], b. 31 Aug. 1827; m. Harrington
      30 Jan. (int. 21 Jan.) 1854 (VRs; NEHGReg, 91:
      [1937]387) ALFRED H. GRACE, b. Harrington 10
      July 1818. No ch. John Leighton, 49 [# 383],
      was living in their Steuben household in 1870.
ii.   FRANCIS, b. 22 Apr. 1829; not in 1850 census.

265. WARREN[7] 1800-1889 [84 Mark[6] and Sally Cates] was born
at Steuben 22 June 1800, died at Milbridge 13 Nov. 1889, 89y
4m 21d; married at Steuben 7 Nov. 1822 JOANN DYER, born 15
Oct. 1804, died at Milbridge 26 July 1883, 78y 9m 19d, daugh-
ter of Reuben and Anna (Whitten) Dyer (Steuben VRs; obituary,
BHM, 6[1890]:57; her death notice, Machias Union of 7 Aug.).
Both are buried in Evergreen Cemetery.
   In 1814, at only 14, he served as a substitute for Israel
Leighton in Capt. John Allen's company during the battle at
Pigeon Hill Cove in which a British armed barge was captured.
He was the last survivor of the action.
   Warren was a carpenter, joiner, boat builder, and community
leader. He was a land surveyor and storekeeper at Steuben,
chairman of the board of selectmen, and town treasurer. He
was justice of the peace over 50 years, from 1836 until his
death, and county commissioner from 1844 to 1856. In 1849, he
moved to Milbridge, where he was postmaster and kept a boarding house (Little, Me. Genealogies, 4:2060).
   In 1850, his household included a JOHN LEIGHTON, 14; in
1860 it included an ENOCH LEIGHTON, 23--probably the same
person.

Children, born at Steuben:

709. i.   SARAH ANN[8], b. 16 Sept. 1823; m. ISAIAH BLAIS-
            DELL.
710. ii.   GILBERT MOORE, b. 25 Aug. 1825.

711. iii. MIRIAM HANDY, b. 9 Aug. 1827; m. CHARLES PRAY.
712. iv.   PILLSBURY STEVENS, b. 11 Jan. 1830.
      v.   LINCOLN HOWE, b. 9 July 1835, d. Milbridge
            28 Jan. 1916, 80y 6m 20d; m. Charleston ME
            18 July (int. Milbridge 11 July) 1883 FANNIE
            ELLIS TIBBETTS (Fannie E. Ellis in Machias
            Union notice), b. 2 Apr. 1845, d. 10 Mar.
            1923, dau. of Hiram Tibbetts of Charleston ME.
            No ch. A ship's carpenter, he served as Mil-
            bridge tax collector, selectman, school super-
            visor and state legislator.

  266. PAMELIA[7] [Permelia] 1802-1840 [84 Mark[6] and Sally
Cates] was born at Steuben 11 Aug. 1802, died 5 Sept. 1840;
married at Steuben 2 Apr. 1826 JAMES GRACE PARKER, born 12
Mar. 1802, died at Steuben 13 Aug. 1872, 70y (Machias Union),
son of William and Polly (Grace) Parker (Steuben VRs; "Robert
Parker of Barnstable, Mass.," NEHGReg, 128[1974]:211).
  Parker married second 9 May 1841 Mary (Norton) O'Brien,
daughter of Elisha and Lucy (Wass) Norton and the widow of
Matthew O'Brien, who had three O'Brien children.

Children (Parker), born at Steuben:

i.   FREEMAN L., b. 16 Apr 1827.
ii.   SALLY, b. 26 Nov. 1829, d. 15 Nov. 1832.
iii. MARK, b. 12 May 1832, d. 12 June 1848.
iv.   BENJAMIN F., b. 24 Feb. 1834, d. 3 June 1856.
v.   DANIEL L., b. 31 Mar. 1836, d. 16 Jan. 1863; m. 24
      May 1860 NANCY (PARKER) Drisko.
vi.   ANN M., b. 25 Apr. 1838, d. 15 Aug. 1846.

  267. SEWELL[7] 1804-1860 [84 Mark[6] and Sally Cates] was born
at Steuben 28 Oct. 1804, died at Augusta ME 16 June 1860;
married first at Steuben 16 Jan. 1836 BARBARA GREEN, born 16
Jan. 1815, died at Steuben 1 Mar. 1846; married second there
27 Aug. 1847 ABIGAIL D. BRAGDON, born about 1797 (53 in
1850), died at Augusta 25 Oct. 1874, 77y (Steuben and Augusta
VRs). He is buried at Milbridge.
  In 1850 he was a ship's carpenter at Augusta. He died
intestate, and Eben Sawyer was appointed administrator 25
June 1860 (KennCP). The inventory included a house and land
at Augusta, and land at Steuben owned jointly with his
brother Warren. The widow's dower, assigned 29 Apr. 1862,
included pew 61 in the Methodist meeting house. Seth G.
Whitehouse was made guardian of Wilson 10 Mar. 1862.

Children by first wife Barbara, born at Steuben:

i.   DAVID HENRY[8], b. 24 Feb. 1837, prob. d. before
      1870; unm.
ii.   ELIZABETH ELVIRA, b. 28 May 1839, d. Augusta 21
      Jan. 1858; unm.
iii. WILSON B., b. 1 Mar. 1843, d. Augusta 25 Aug.
      1893 (VRs); m. Augusta 23 Sept. 1873 EMMA C.
      CHURCH, b. 6 Feb. 1848, d. Augusta in 1928,
      81y. No ch. He and Alden W. Philbrook were
      partners in a drygoods business. His will
      made 8 Oct. 1886 was proved 25 Sept. 1893.

268. LYDIA[7] 1806-1892 [84 Mark[6] and Sally Cates] was born
at Steuben 16 June 1806 (VRs; 1809 per GS); died at Cherryfield 3 May 1892 (GS); married first at Steuben 1 July 1827
JOHN STEWART, born 23 Apr. 1805, died 18 May 1844 (GS), son
of John and Jane (Clark) Stewart; married second 30 Sept.
1849 JONAH V. DYER; married third 14 Nov. 1859 PATRICK JAMES
KELLEY, born 15 Oct. 1811 (Steuben VRs; Cornman Ms). Burials
are in Pine Grove cemetery.

Children (**Stewart**), born at Steuben:

i.   ATKINS, b. 24 Mar. 1829, d. Steuben 5 June 1902, 83y
       2m 11d.
ii.   MATILDA MOORE, b. 2 July 1831.
iii.   PHILENA S., b. 10 June 1833.
iv.   ARTHUR L., b. 8 Dec. 1835.
v.   JOHN E., b. 18 May 1838; m. SAMANTHA[8] LEIGHTON
       [# 1059].
vi.   ABNER, b. 29 Nov. 1841, res. Columbia ME.
vii.   GEORGE L., b. 28 May 1844; m. CAROLINE[8] LEIGHTON
       [# 920].

269. NAOMI[7] 1811-1876 [84 Mark[6] and Sally Cates] was born
at Steuben 12 Dec. 1811, died there 28 Mar. 1876 (GS); married there 22 July (int. 25 May) 1832 JAMES FREEMAN CLARK,
born at Steuben 20 Apr. 1809, died there 15 Sept. 1874 (GS),
son of William and Jane (Clark) Clark and half-brother of
Lydia's husband [# 268] (Leslie Clark Johnson, Sullivan and
Sorrento Since 1760 [Ellsworth ME, 1953], 273-4; Steuben
VRs). Burials are in Smithville cemetery, Steuben.

Children (**Clark**), born at Steuben:

i.   ALBERT WILLIAM, b. 4 May 1839, res. Steuben; m.
       1 Oct. 1860 EUNICE CLEAVES, b. 10 May 1838, dau. of
       Joshua and Susan (Haskell) Cleaves.
ii.   AMANDA M., b. 3 Apr. 1841; m. ALLEN SPURLING, b.
       Gouldsboro in 1841, son of Robert and Diadama
       (Whitten) Spurling.
iii.   FRANCIS L. [Frank], b. 28 Aug. 1845; m. Steuben 4
       Mar. 1873 ROXANNA LAURA [Roxie] GRANT, b. 29 Jan.
       1856, dau. of Calvin and Susan C. (Stevens) Grant.
iv.   FREEMAN L., b. 9 Aug. 1848; m. Steuben 8 Apr. 1878
       MARY COLLINS of Cherryfield.
v.   BELINDA (twin), b. 9 Aug. 1848; m. 1st Steuben 25
       Dec. 1872 WILLIAM MILNER; m. 2nd REDMOND DAVIS.
vi.   daughter, infant in 1850 census.

270. AMY[7] 1814- [84 Mark[6] and Sally Cates] was born at
Steuben 4 Nov. 1814, lived there with her brother Freeman in
1860; married 14 Nov. 1837 JAMES KELLEY, born in Ireland 15
Sept. 1811, son of John and Esther Kelley (Cornman Ms).

Children (**Kelley**), born at Steuben:

i.   GEORGE WILLIAM, b. c1840, d. Milbridge 27 Sept. 1892,
       52y 3m; m. 1st 5 Aug. 1861 SUSAN E. CORTHELL--div.;
       m. 2nd 16 Apr. 1878 JULIA A. (HODGKINS) Ash.
ii.   LIZZIE E.

271. BELINDA NASH[7] 1818-1892 [84 Mark[6] and Sally Cates]
was born at Steuben 8 Dec. 1818, died there 25 Feb. 1892;
married 22 Feb. 1835 ALFRED S. SMITH, born at Steuben 20 Apr.
1811, died there 4 Apr. 1892, son of Justus and Polly (Allen)
Smith (Steuben VRs; Smith records of Arlene Skehan). Burials
are in Smithville cemetery.

Children (**Smith**), born at Steuben:

i.   LINDRUFF W., b. 7 July 1838, d. in action Spot-
      sylvania PA 12 May 1864; unm. He was a lieutenant
      in Co. G, 6th ME Vol. Inf. Rgt.
ii.   ROSALBRO [Rosalvo, Resolve], b. Steuben 20 Apr. 1842,
      d. there 1 June 1911; m. 25 Nov. 1865 NANCY SMITH,
      b. Steuben 14 Sept. 1841, dau. of William and
      Direxa[7] (Leighton) Smith [# 272].
iii. SAMUEL ALLEN, b. 22 Dec. 1845, d. Milbridge 9 Jan.
      1902; m. there 23 Feb. 1898 BERTHA V.[9] LEIGHTON
      [# 718].
iv.   FRANK, b. 11 Sept. 1852, d. Sullivan 28 Aug. 1930;
      m CLARA CHILCOTT of Sullivan.
v.   MARY S., b. 9 July 1854, d. Steuben 13 Jan. 1901;
      m. HENRY GUPTILL, b. Steuben 14 Sept. 1850, d. there
      13 Feb. 1931, son of Lemuel and Eliza (Archer)
      Guptill.

272. DIREXA[7] 1802-1879 [86 Alexander[6] and Mary Lawrence]
was born at Steuben 13 Feb. 1802, died there (Smithville)
16 July 1872; married there 26 Sept. 1820 WILLIAM SMITH, born
there 9 May 1798, died there 22 Sept. 1886, son of Job and
Diadama (Booth) Smith (Steuben VRs; Daniel, Thomas Rogers,
204; Johnson, Sullivan and Sorrento, 339; records of Arlene
Skehan and descendant Dawn Linden).

Children (**Smith**), born at Steuben:

i.   JOHN LAWRENCE, b. 2 May 1821, d. 14 Feb. 1907; m.
      23 Aug. 1846 CAROLINE CLEAVES, b. Kennebunk ME 8
      June 1827, d. in Nov. 1911, dau. of Joshua and Susan
      (Haskell) Cleaves.
ii.   SHERMAN, b. 12 Feb. 1823, d. 24 Feb. 1909; m. 22 Aug.
      1846 NANCY L. GUPTILL, b. Gouldsboro 10 Mar. 1830,
      d. Steuben 30 Oct. 1919, dau. of George and Eliza-
      beth (Lawrence) Guptill.
iii. JOSHUA, b. 21 Feb., d. 11 Apr., 1825.
iv.   CHARLOTTE INGALLS, b. 3 May 1826, res. Cherryfield;
      m. Palmyra ME 21 Feb. 1853 ALLISON ADAMS.
v.   ALEXANDER WESLEY, b. 6 Dec. 1828, d. 6 June 1920; m.
      1st Steuben 17 Feb. 1856 LUCRETIA SMITH, b. 7 Mar.
      1832, d. 7 May 1895, dau. of Leonard L. and Olive
      (Godfrey) Smith; m. 2nd ELIZABETH (----) Godfrey, b.
      19 Feb. 1831, d. 8 Aug. 1898.
vi.   HENRY AUGUSTUS, b. 6 June 1831, d. 18 Mar. 1914; m.
      26 Sept. 1859 EMILY O. COLE, b. Prospect Harbor 2
      June 1834, dau. of Asa and Sarah (Godfrey) Cole.
vii. MELZOR S., b. 28 Oct. 1833, d. 27 Mar. 1906; m. 1st
      17 Feb. 1856 ANN WAKEFIELD, b. 1 Dec. 1835, d. 23
      July 1873, dau. of Amasa and Jane (Dyer) Wakefield;
      m. 2nd PAULINE J. (WATTS) Smith, widow of Guilford
      Smith [# 272].

viii. FREEMAN T., b. 8 Feb. 1836; m. 1st 11 Aug. 1864 MARY
SAWYER; m. 2nd MARY DAVIS.
ix. ALONZO, b. 6 Dec. 1839, d. 29 Oct. 1912; m. Prospect
Harbor 1 Jan. 1866 ELLEN [Nellie] MOORE.
x. NANCY L., b. 14 Sept. 1841, d. in 1911; m. ROSALBRO
SMITH [# 271].
xi. CAROLINE S., b. 10 Feb. 1844; m. Milbridge 24 July
1866 SHEPLEY CLEAVES, b. 8 July 1843, son of Joshua
and Susan (Haskell) Cleaves.

273. JANE[7] 1803-1877 [86 Alexander[6] and Mary Lawrence]
was born at Steuben 28 Oct. 1803, died there 15 Aug. 1877;
married there 13 Sept. (int. 27 Aug.) 1826 ROBERT ALLEN
SMITH, born at Steuben 13 Sept. 1803, died there 16 Nov.
1863, son of Justus A. and Polly (Allen) Smith (Steuben VRs;
Johnson, Sullivan and Sorrento, 339; Smith records of Arlene
Skehan).

Children (Smith), born at Steuben:

i. EDWARD, b. 12 July, d. 21 Aug., 1827.
ii. GUILFORD P., b. 2 Nov. 1828, d. Steuben 1 May 1870,
41y; m. 4 Feb. 1855 PAULINE J. WATTS, b. 20 Oct.
1836, d. Milbridge 28 Jan. 1917, 76y, dau. of Joseph
Tupper and Hannah (Wakefield) Watts. She m. 2nd
Melzor Smith [# 271].
iii. ELIZA ANN, b. 1 Jan. 1831; m. HANDY[7] LEIGHTON
[# 256].
iv. SAMUEL, b. 13 Oct. 1833, d. 7 Aug. 1834.
v. CLARA P., b. 12 Nov. 1835; m. Gouldsboro 25 Sept.
1853 JOSEPH HARADEN.
vi. AVERILL P., b. 30 Sept. 1837, d. 25 Mar. 1914; m. 1st
Columbia 11 Nov. 1866 LUCY ALLEN; m. 2nd REBECCA
(----) Seavey. He served in 11th ME Inf. Rgt.
vii. HERMAN D., b. 1 Dec. 1840, d. 21 Apr. 1849.
viii. THEODOSIA, b. 6 May 1842, res. Dorchester MA; m. 20
Sept. 1863 (CHARLES) HERBERT HANDY.
ix. JULIA M., b. 7 May 1844, d. Harrington 30 Apr. 1915;
m. 4 July 1860 EBENEZER F. ALLEN.

274. (HORATIO) NELSON[7] 1805-1891 [86 Alexander[6] and Mary
Lawrence] was born at Steuben probably in 1806 (VRs, 18 Apr.
1805; 54 in 1860), died at Deblois ME 20 May 1891, 85y 1m 2d;
married at Steuben 26 Nov. 1828 OLIVIA JOHNSON SMITH, born at
Steuben 17 Jan. 1807, died at Annsburg 9 July 1848, daughter
of Justus and Polly (Allen) Smith; married second at Annsburg
int. 15 Feb. 1850 DELANA W. LIBBY, born about 1805 (55 in
1860), died at Deblois 17 Mar. 1889, 84y 4m 19d (Steuben and
Deblois VRs). Burials are in the Smith cemetery, Steuben.
Nelson [or H. N.] was a carpenter and joiner; about 1833 he
moved to Annsburg, incorporated as Deblois in 1852.

Children, all by first wife Olivia:

713. i. MARGUERITA WARREN[8], b. Steuben 29 Aug. 1829; m.
JOHN DORMAN.
714. ii. MELISSA, b. Steuben 2 Feb. 1832; m. JOHN
FREEMAN DORMAN.
715. iii. CALVIN S., b. Annsburg 27 June 1834.

716. iv.   EDWARD, b. Annsburg 26 May 1837.
717. v.   ANGELINE, b. Annsburg 16 Nov. 1839; m. JEREMIAH
            GOULD.
718. vi.   (WILLIAM) BARTLETT, b. Annsburg 22 Nov. 1846.

275. ABIGAIL[7] 1808-1888 [86 Alexander[6] and Mary Lawrence]
was born at Steuben 18 Apr. 1808, died at Alexander ME 13
Sept. 1888; married 16 June 1828 EZRA SMITH, born 17 Jan.
1800, died at Steuben 24 Apr. 1880, son of Allen and Margaret
(Parritt) Smith (Steuben VRs; records of Arlene Skehan).

Children (**Smith**), born at Steuben:

i.   MARGARET, b. 18 Apr. 1829, d. 21 Dec. 1847; m. THOMAS
       PERRY.
ii.   AMANDA, b. 27 Apr. 1830, d. 5 Oct. 1850.
iii.   WILMOT W., b. 13 June 1833; m. NANCY ELIZABETH PERRY.
iv.   DANIEL L., b. 30 July 1837, d. 19 Apr. 1881; m. LYDIA
       PERRY
v.   JASON, b. 13 June 1839; m. OPHELIA LYDIA McDEVITT.
vi.   EVERETT, b. 4 Aug. 1843, d. Milbridge 25 Jan. 1904;
       m. MARY HANSON.

276. ANNA[7] 1810-   [86 Alexander[6] and Mary Lawrence] was
born at Steuben 21 July 1810, lived at Toledo, Lincoln Co.
OR; married 30 Mar. 1834 WILLIAM STEVENS, born 8 Apr. 1810,
died in OR 13 Aug. 1898, son of Jonathan and Abigail Stevens.
They went west to WI, and then settled in OR (Cornman Ms).

Children (**Stevens**):

i.   JUDITH T., b. 21 Jan. 1835; m. 1st 29 Oct. 1855 Dr.
       E. T. SAVAGE; m. 2nd 30 Nov. 1865 H. W. VINCENT.
ii.   LUCY A., b. 21 Aug. 1836; m. 24 Nov. 1852 Dr. C E.
       LaDOW.
iii.   GEORGE W., b. 9 Aug. 1839; m. 1 Oct. 1862 EMMA
       PYGALL.
iv.   MARY L., b. 23 June 1843, d.y.
v.   MARY A., b. 15 Oct. 1854; unm.

277. DANIEL LAWRENCE[7] 1813-   [86 Alexander[6] and Mary
Lawrence] was born at Steuben 19 Apr. 1813, lived there in
1860; married first at Harrington 13 Feb. 1839 HANNAH
LEIGHTON; married second at Cherryfield 27 Oct. 1842 MARY
JANE LAWRENCE, born at Cherryfield 1 Dec. 1818, died at Steu-
ben 7 Apr. 1897, 77y 4m 7d, probably daughter of James Parker
and Amy (Patten) Lawrence (town VRs). He was a farmer.
   His first wife has not yet been identified. In 1850 his
Steuben household included his mother Polly, 70; in 1860 it
included JAMES[8], 22 [# 922].

Children by Mary Jane, born at Steuben:

       i.   THADDEUS[8], b. 12 Mar. 1845 (17 in 1860), res.
             in NY; m. 1st Gouldsboro 14 Aug. 1872 ADA L.
             HANDY; m. 2nd JULY MARY ---- , b. in Ireland
             c1860 (20 in 1880). No ch.
719.   ii.   JAMES P. L., b. 15 Aug. 1849.

278. CAROLINE[7] 1817-1881 [86 Alexander[6] and Mary Lawrence]
was born at Steuben 2 Sept. 1817, died there 13 Mar. 1881;
married 28 Nov. 1847 (GEORGE) STILLMAN SMITH, born 10 Dec.
1815, died at Ellsworth ME 27 Mar. 1877, 69y, son of Justus
and Polly (Allen) Smith (Steuben VRs; records of Leonard F.
Tibbetts).

Children (**Smith**), born at Steuben:

   i.   WILLIAM D., b. 27 Aug. 1848, res. Boothbay Harbor;
        m. 25 Feb. 1880 MELVINA BREWER.
   ii. HENRIETTA, b. 15 Aug. 1856; m. Gouldsboro 20 Dec.
        1873 Capt. WILLIAM H. ROSEBROOK.

279. NANCY[7] 1819-   [86 Alexander[6] and Mary Lawrence]
was born at Steuben 25 Sept. 1819; married at Windsor ME 5
June 1845 JOHN PIERCE of Cherryfield, born at Windsor 25 Apr.
1819, lived at Steuben in 1850 and 1860. Pierce had three
children by a first wife Lydia (Cornman Ms).

Children (**Pierce**), born at Steuben:

   i.   LYDIA ANN, b. 15 May 1846, res. St. Paul MN; m. ----
        STEVENS.
   ii. ALEXANDER L., b. 12 Sept. 1849; unm.
   iii. MARY JANE, b. 14 May 1854.
   iv. LUCY ANN, b. 16 Aug. 1855, d. Grand Falls MN 26
        Sept. 1888; m. Otsego MN 13 Mar. 1881 Dr. S. F.
        JOHNSON.

280. JOHN[7] 1822-1892 [86 Alexander[6] and Mary Lawrence] was
born at Steuben 9 Jan. 1822, died at Willimantic ME 12 Nov.
1892, 69y 10m; married there (Tp # 8) 11 Aug. 1847 RACHEL
STEWARD, born at Bingham ME 13 Sept. 1826, died at Willimantic 10 Apr. 1910, 88y 6m 28d, daughter of John and Mercy
(Steward) Steward (Arthur W. Steward, Ancestors and Descendants of Deacon Thomas Stewart of Canaan and Bloomfield, Me.
[TMs, nd, MHS], 61, 146-53; records of descendant Maxine
Hughes). John was not mentioned in Julia Cornman's
genealogy; his death record named his father Sandy.
    He was a farmer. Widow Rachel was in her son Alfonzo's
household in 1900. Township 8 was incorporated as Howard in
1881, and renamed Willimantic in 1883; vital records were
kept at neighboring Monson.

Children, born at No. 8:

720. i.   MARY CAROLINE[8], b. 26 May 1848; m. CHARLES N.
            FARRAR.
721. ii.   JOHN STUART, b. 6 Apr. 1851.
722. iii. ELVIRA COBURN, b. 14 Aug. 1856; m. ELLERY
            STONE.
723. iv.   ALFONZO MILTON, b. 19 Oct. 1859.
724. v.   NELLIE NEWELL, b. 1 Nov. 1862; m. WARREN
            JOHNSON.
725. vi.   OLIVE E., b. 15 Sept. 1866; m. THOMAS TRAINOR.
      vii. ABBY E., b. 3 Nov. 1869, d. 5 June 1870.

281. ZERVIAH⁷ 1802-1878 [87 Hatevil⁶ and Mary Dunbar] was born at Steuben 27 Nov. 1802, died 31 July 1878; married first 14 Sept. 1825 NATHAN PERRY, born about 1792, son of Jesse and Polly (Guptill) Perry; married second ASA BURBANK WAKEFIELD, born 25 Mar. 1807, son of Samuel and Anna (Cox) Wakefield (Wakefield Mem., 126).
Nathan Perry had five other children by a first wife Jane (records of Leonard F. Tibbetts; Steuben VRs).

Children (**Perry**), born at Steuben:

i.   ELLEN, b. 4 Feb. 1830.
ii.   ANNA L., b. 5 Oct. 1833, res. Bass Harbor; m. ---- McDONALD.
iii. HENRY M., b. 28 Sept. 1836, res. Bass Harbor.
iv.   JULIA ANN, b. 12 Dec. 1838, d. Steuben 18 Feb. 1895, 55y 2m 2d; m. 1st Steuben 26 Feb. 1855 PILLSBURY WAKEFIELD, b. 22 Dec. 1828, son of Asa Burbank and Martha (Smith) Wakefield (Daniel, Thomas Rogers, 319), and adopted a son Harlan; m. 2nd DAVID H. ELLIS.
v.   WILLIAM L., b. 14 Aug. 1843, res. Gouldsboro; m. 30 Dec. 1872 MARY L. SAWYER, b. 25 July 1847, dau. of Daniel and Maria (Moore) Sawyer.

282. LEONICE BUCKMAN⁷ 1807-1879 [87 Hatevil⁶ and Mary Dunbar] was born at Steuben 11 Sept. 1807, died 8 Apr. 1879; married 7 Feb. 1830 SAMUEL WAKEFIELD CLEAVES, born 19 Apr. 1804, died at West Gouldsboro 19 Dec. 1890, son of Nathan and Hannah (Wakefield) Cleaves (Cornman Ms; records of Leonard F. Tibbetts).

Children (**Cleaves**):

i.   ELVIRA KINGSLEY, b. 6 May 1832, d. 7 Apr. 1851.
ii.   MARY ANN, b. 17 Sept. 1834; m. W. Gouldsboro 18 Apr. 1855 JOHN A. SHAW, b. 21 Feb. 1825.
iii. JASON HILL, b. 20 Sept. 1838, d. at sea 7 Feb. 1861.
iv.   SOPHRONIA D., b. 16 Apr. 1843; m. W. Gouldsboro 25 Dec. 1880 JASON SARGENT.

283. ELEANOR SMITH⁷ 1809-1874 [87 Hatevil⁶ and Mary Dunbar] was born at Steuben 29 July 1809, died 22 Dec. 1874; married 19 Jan. 1834 ELISHA PARKER, born 19 Apr. 1804, died 15 Nov. 1874, son of William and Polly (Grace) Parker (Steuben VRs; Cornman Ms).
In 1860 her mother Mary, 79, was listed in their Parker household at Steuben.

Children (**Parker**), born at Steuben:

i.   LAURA H., b. 13 Dec. 1836; m. Steuben Capt. GEORGE PARKER.
ii.   ALFONZO, b. 18 July 1843.
iii. LUTHER, b. 5 July 1846.
iv.   IRVING, b. 14 Sept. 1849, res. Cherryfield.

284. GEORGE ULMER[7] 1811-1889 [87 Hatevil[6] and Mary Dunbar] was born at Steuben 27 Aug. 1811, died at Milbridge 1 Jan. 1889, 77y 8m 16d; married at Gouldsboro 8 Mar. 1835 (int. at Steuben 27 Jan.) LYDIA PARRAT MOORE, born at Gouldsboro 3 Dec. 1812, died at Milbridge 25 Mar. 1883, 70y 3m 23d, daughter of Nathaniel and Sarah Moore (town VRs). Burials are in Evergreen Cemetery, Milbridge. He was a ship's carpenter, 47, with his wife Lydia, 44, in 1850 at Milbridge.

Children:

726. i.   EMELINE[8], b. Steuben 30 Mar. 1836; m. SAMUEL LIBBY.
727. ii.   REBECCA M., b. Steuben 10 May 1837; m. ABIAH T. HUCKINS.
     iii. GEORGE WILLIAM, b. 16 Aug. 1838, d. in Montana; unm. (Cornman Ms).
     iv.   HENRY M., b. Milbridge 2 Sept. 1841, d. there 23 Jan. 1909, 67y 3m 21d; m. Steuben 4 Mar. 1865 JULIA H. MANSFIELD, b. Milbridge 11 June 1841 (GS), d. there 15 Oct. 1906, 65y 4m, dau. of James B. and Abigail (Brown) Mansfield. No ch.
           In an interview Capt. "Hy" Leighton, retired shipmaster, described running the Dardanelles Strait in Dec. 1876 while master of the brig Cadet, risking shelling by Turkish forts during a gale (Bangor Commercial Advertiser, 25 Nov. 1898).
728. v.   ADEN M., b. 27 July 1852.
     vi.   MARY D., b. in 1857, d. in 1865 (GS).

285. WEALTHY DYER[7] 1817-   [87 Hatevil[6] and Mary Dunbar, was born at Steuben 22 Feb. 1817; married at Sullivan 7 Jan. 1844 (int. Gouldsboro 20 May 1843) WILLARD F. HALL of Sorrento (town VRs; Johnson, Sullivan and Sorrento, 354).

Children (**Hall**):

i.   JOHN W., b. 13 Nov. 1847.
ii.   J. FLETCHER, b. 7 Feb. 1850.

286. NICHOLAS NICKELS[7] 1820-1885 [89 Israel[6] and Priscilla Strout] was born at Steuben 14 Sept. 1820, died at Milbridge 28 June 1885, 63y 10m 15d; married at Steuben 1 Jan. 1848 ELSIE HASKELL, born at Deer Isle ME 22 Feb. 1825, died at Milbridge 22 May 1915, 90y 2m 30d, daughter of Thomas and Sarah (Babbage) Haskell (Steuben and Milbridge VRs). Burials are in Evergreen Cemetery.
He was a sparmaker and shipmaster. Elsie ("Elcy" on her GS) was living with her son Augustine in 1900.

Children, born at Milbridge:

729. i.   AUGUSTINE COOMBS[8], b. 22 Mar. 1852.
     ii.   ALVAH H., b. 10 Apr. 1856, d. 20 Nov. 1858.
730. iii. ARTHUR S., b. 2 Aug. 1861.

287. MARY[7] 1819-1897 [90 Daniel[6] and Abigail Nason] was
born at Oromocto NB 28 Oct. 1819, died at Jonesport ME 28
Dec. 1896, 78y; married at Gouldsboro 17 Dec. 1839 JUSTUS
WHITE BICKFORD, born there 1 Oct. 1818, died 14 June 1899,
son of Joseph, Jr., and Betsey (Clark) Bickford (records of
Margaret Colton; town VRs; DAR Misc. Records [MHS, 1983],
2:179). Burials are in Birch Harbor cemetery.
He was a master mariner and whaler.

Children (**Bickford**), born at Gouldsboro (Prospect Harbor):

i.   LUCELIA [Lutie], b. 8 Feb. 1841, d. Steuben 17 Aug.
       1900; m. Steuben 15 Sept. 1863 ALONZO Y. STEVENS, b.
       Steuben 18 Sept. 1840, d. there 21 June 1906,
       son of Samuel and Lucinda (Leavitt) Stevens.
ii.   BETHUEL BENSON, b. 4 Apr. 1843, d. Jonesport 24 Sept.
       1908; m. SARAH E. PRESTON, b. 15 Oct. 1847, d.
       Jonesport 7 Jan. 1933.
iii.   EDNA, b. 1 Nov. 1845; m. ELWOOD ROBINSON.
iv.   JUSTUS WHITE (twin), b. 11 Nov. 1845, d. Vinal Haven
       ME 4 Nov. 1905; m. 1st in Mar. 1870 ALFARETTA CHURCH
       of Jonesport--div.; m. 2nd MARGARET FOSTER. He res.
       Portland.
v.   ARTHUR S., b. 13 Aug. 1848, d. 7 Apr. 1871.
vi.   MARY VANDELIA, b. 14 Oct. 1850, d. Gouldsboro 22 Oct.
       1938; m. there 25 Dec. 1887 SIDNEY SIMPSON ASH,
       b. 16 June 1846, d. 4 Nov. 1924.
vii.   HENRIETTA GAY ["Nettie"], b. 4 Apr. 1854, d. Troy NY
       10 Nov. 1932; m. Milbridge 5 Oct. 1884 SAMUEL CLARK
       WALLACE, b. 6 May 1832, d. 29 July 1903, son of
       William E. and Susan (Sanborn) Wallace.
viii. (ADONIRAM) JUDSON, b. 25 Sept. 1856, d. 22 June 1893;
       m. 1st Gouldsboro 31 Mar. 1888 ABBY YOUNG, b. in
       1869, d. Gouldsboro 28 July 1888; m. 2nd 15 July
       1889 MARY A. (----) Barrett.

288. THOMAS[7] 1820-1904 [90 Daniel[6] and Abigail Nason] was
born at Steuben 17 Dec. 1820, died there 9 Aug. 1904, 82y 7m
23d; married at Gouldsboro 13 Jan. 1845 DEBORAH PETTEE, born
there 14 Nov. 1824, died at Milbridge 16 Sept. 1897, daughter
of Timothy and Rachel (Tracy) Pettee (town and ME VRs).
In 1850 he was a shoemaker at Gouldsboro, and in 1860 a
fisherman at Milbridge, aged 38. In 1870, he was shown as
aged 47. He lived with his son William in 1900.

Children, born at Milbridge:

731. i.   DANIEL[8], b. 5 Dec. 1845.
732. ii.   TIMOTHY P., b, 14 Sept. 1847.
      iii.   ABBY, b. 5 Jan. 1850, d. 2 Feb. 1860.
      iv.   WILLIAM GEORGE, b. 26 Aug. 1853, d. Bangor 1
             Oct. 1925, 73y; m. Milbridge int. 14 Feb. 1876
             EMILY C. LEIGHTON, b. Steuben 24 July 1860,
             d. there 30 Dec. 1928, 68y 9m 6d, dau. of John
             and Hannah (Haycock) (Nason) Leighton [# 290].
             Ch. GRACE B. b. Lowell MA in Nov. 1881; m.
             Milbridge 20 Feb. 1903 NATHAN W. STEVENS, b.
             Steuben c1876, son of George and Martha
             (Small) Stevens.

        v.   ISABEL MARY (Mary I. in 1870), b. 20 Feb. 1855,
             d. Steuben 8 Feb. 1917; m. Milbridge 7 Feb.
             1876 EVERETT EVANS HUCKINS, b. Steuben 20 Feb.
             1853, d. Steuben 22 Dec. 1938, son of Taft and
             Mary (Evans) Huckins. Only ch. Bessie b. Mil-
             bridge 18 June 1882, d. Steuben 3 May 1918; m.
             WILLIAM HIGGINS.
       vi.   FLORINDA, b. 1 Feb. 1857, d. 1 Mar. 1898; m. 11
             July 1876 WILLIAM H. OVER, b. 14 Apr. 1846,
             res. Gouldsboro in 1900, son of Henry and
             Nancy Over. Ch. Lillian, 8 in 1880; and
             Gerald b. in Feb. 1889.
      vii.   ALICE J., b. 8 Sept. 1858, d. 8 Mar. 1860.
     viii.   THOMAS JR., b. 26 Nov. 1860, d. 14 Dec. 1874.
733.   ix.   ALICE J., b. 10 Dec. 1861.
        x.   ABIGAIL, b. 9 June 1863, res. Petit Manan Pt.;
             m. 20 Jan. 1883 JOHN McNAMARA, b. Steuben 8
             July 1846, son of John and Ruth (McCaleb)
             McNamara. No ch.
       xi.   LEONARD, b. 8 May, d. 8 Oct., 1865.
      xii.   CHARITY S., b. 4 Apr. 1866, d. 4 Nov. 1881.
     xiii.   LOTTIE, b. 15 Apr., d. 12 May, 1867.

289. ABIGAIL[7] 1823-   [90 Daniel[6] and Abigail Nason] was
born at Steuben 7 Dec. 1823; married at Gouldsboro 10 Aug.
1844 (VRs) HENRY B. CRANE, born about 1821, listed at Camden
ME in 1850, aged 29.

Children (**Crane**):

i.   ALICE J., b. c1846 (4 in 1850).
ii.   CALVIN, b. c1848 (2 in 1850).
iii.   ABIGAIL L., b. in 1850 (1/12 in 1850)

290. JOHN NASON[7] 1825-1889 [90 Daniel[6] and Abigail Nason]
was born at Steuben 5 Aug. 1825, died there 26 Aug. 1889;
married there 27 Oct. 1855 HANNAH (HAYCOCK) Nason, born in NB
18 June 1825, died at Steuben 30 June 1908, 84y, daughter of
Elliot Haycock (Steuben and ME VRs).
    Her daughter Sarah E. Nason, 10, lived with them in 1860.
John served in the Civil War 6 Apr. to 19 May 1865. From
1850 through 1880, his mother was in his household.
    In 1880 a grandson William Lovejoy, 7, was living with them
--probably Hannah's grandchild.

Children, born at Steuben:

        i.   ABIGAIL HANNAH[8] (Hannah A. in 1860), b. 17 Aug.
              1856; m. 1st Steuben 21 June 1873 NEWELL G.
              HARDISON; m. 2nd FRANK BONNEY.
       ii.   EMILY C., b. 24 July 1860; m. WILLIAM GEORGE[8]
              LEIGHTON [# 288].
      iii.   MARY L. [Lutie], b. 6 July 1863; m. Gouldsboro
              30 Dec. 1884 TRUMAN SINCLAIR of Prospect Har-
              bor. One ch. Fred.
734.   iv.   CADDIE C., b. 18 Jan. 1867; m. DANIEL SULLIVAN.

291.   ISRAEL[7] 1830-1887 [90 Daniel[6] and Abigail Nason]
was born at Steuben 15 Nov. 1830, died there 14 Oct. 1887
(Machias Union); married first at Steuben 4 Oct. 1862 ELIZA-
BETH ANN BROOKS, born 9 Sept. 1844, daughter of Solomon and
Mary (Pinkham) Brooks; married second at Cherryfield 8 Jan.
1865 HANNAH (NASON) Drinkwater, born in NB 13 Oct. 1838,
lived at Bath ME (Cornman Ms; town VRs).
     Israel lived with his brother John until his marriage. In
1870 he was a farmer, 36, at Steuben; in 1880 he was not
listed.

Child by Elizabeth, born at Steuben:

735.   i.   MARY A.[8], b. 8 Nov. 1863; m. WILLIAM H. SMALL
              and FORESTER DUNBAR.

Child by Hannah:

       ii.   CAROLINE.

292.   LEONARD H.[7] 1835-1905 [90 Daniel[6] and Abigail Nason]
was born at Steuben 4 July 1835, died there 5 Aug. 1905, 71y
1m 1d; married 28 Mar. 1874 ABBIE J. YEATON, born 28 May
1851, died at Milbridge 26 Sept. 1941, daughter of Samuel and
Lois (Dickson) Yeaton (town VRs). Burials are in Evergreen
cemetery.
     Before he joined the 30th ME Rgt. on 6 Apr. 1865, he lived
with his brother John. In 1880 he was a seaman.

Child, born at Steuben:

       i.   INEZ H.[8], b. 14 Feb. 1876, d. Steuben 15
              Dec. 1904, 30y 10m; m. Milbridge 20 Feb.
              1904 HENRY L. [Harry] DAVIS, b. Machias
              in 1878, res. Eden, son of Leroy and Naomi
              (Manchester) Davis. Only ch. Inez Eugenia b.
              Steuben 7 Dec. 1904.

293.   AMOS P.[7] 1817-1887 [91 Isaiah[6] and Mary Small] was
born at Cherryfield 26 Mar. 1817, died there 8 Mar. 1887
(GS); married at Gouldsboro 20 Oct. 1841 LOUISE T. SARGENT,
born at West Gouldsboro 2 May 1813 (51 in 1870), died at
Cherryfield 6 Sept. 1897 (GS) (town VRs). Burials are in Pine
Grove cemetery. He was a mason.

Children, born at Cherryfield:

736.   i.   SHERMAN[8], b. 14 Feb. 1843.
737.   ii.   ADONIRAM JUDSON, b. 14 Dec. 1844.
738.   iii.   MARY E., b. 2 Feb. 1849; m. GILMAN C. DYER.

294.   CYNTHIA FICKETT[7] 1814-1880 [92 Asa[6] and Loruhamah
Fickett] was born at Steuben 17 Apr. 1814, died at Milbridge
16 Sept. 1880, 66y 4m 23d (GS); married at Cherryfield int.
19 Apr. 1836 JOHN L. GRIFFIN, born at Gorham NH in 1811, died
at Milbridge 7 Jan. 1890, 78y (GS), son of Benjamin and Susan
Griffin (records of Margaret Colton; town VRs; 1850 and 1860
censuses). Burials are in Evergreen cemetery.

Children (**Griffin**):

i. CHANDLER G., b. in NH in 1837, res. Milbridge; m.
    DELIA LOOK and LIZZIE JEPSON.
ii. (GEORGE) FRANK, b. in NH in 1838, res. Boston. He
    was fire dept. captain there.
iii. ASA, b. in NH 1 June 1839, d. Gorham NH 1 Mar. 1840
    (bur. Milbridge).
iv. ALEXANDER B., b. in NH in 1841, d. Ft. Philip LA
    21 Sept. 1862, 21yd 10m (GS); unm. He served in
    Co. E, 13th ME Inf. Rgt.
v. BENJAMIN, b. in ME in 1843, d. in Africa (GS) 16 Aug.
    1862, 19y 8m.
vi. THADDEUS, b. in ME in 1845, d. 17 May 1864, 19y 6m;
    unm. He was fatally wounded in the Battle of the
    Wilderness, VA.
vii. MARY ELLEN, b. in 1847, d. Milbridge 27 Feb. 1851,
    4y 6m 1d (GS).
viii. EMMA, b. in 1848; m. Milbridge 2 Sept. 1865 (JAMES)
    WARREN COLSON.
ix. PHILEMON, b. in 1852.
x. JOHN M., b. 13 Dec. 1853, d. Milbridge 9 Oct. 1943;
    m. 1 Feb. 1873 MARY ELIZABETH FOREN, b. Cherryfield
    17 Mar. 1855, d. 4 Apr. 1938 (GS), dau. of Morris
    and Mary E. (Fickett) Foren.
xi. MARTHA MARIE, b. in 1856, res. Westerly RI; m. JOHN
    MORSE, JOHN MITCHELL and DAVID FRENCH.
xii. PHILENA [Lena], b. in 1859; m. Harrington 4 June
    1873 JOHN HASKELL.

295. JOANNA FICKETT[7] 1817-1897 [92 Asa[6] and Loruhamah
Fickett] was born at Steuben 6 May 1817, died at Milbridge 26
Feb. 1897; married at Harrington int. 10 Apr. 1836 JOHN B.
STROUT, born 10 Jan. 1808, died before 1860, son of Nathaniel
and Joanna Strout (town VRs; records of Margaret Colton).

Children (**Strout**), born at Harrington:

i. JULIETTE F., b. c1839; m. Ellsworth ME SUMNER
    FIFIELD.
ii. JOHN ALBION, b. 12 Mar. 1843, d. Milbridge 22 Oct.
    1903; m. ELLA NOONAN DOLE, b. Gouldsboro ME c1850,
    d. 14 Oct. 1889, 39y (Machias Union), dau. of David
    and Christiana B. (Haskell) Noonan. After her
    father was murdered at sea by his mate, she was
    adopted by Enoch Dole of Rowley.
iii. ISABELLE, b. 1 June 1844, d. 8 Feb. 1905; m. 1st
    EDGAR NUTTER; m. 2nd A. JACKSON[8] LEIGHTON [# 919];
    m. 3rd LEVERETT STROUT.

296. OLIVER TRAIN[7] 1819-1908 [92 Asa[6] and Loruhamah Fick-
ett] was born at Steuben 13 May 1819, died at Milbridge 7
Apr. 1908, 87y 10m 23d; married first at Harrington 29 June
1844 SUSAN HUNTLEY; married second at Harrington int. 28 Aug.
1845 ELIZABETH HALL, born about 1823 (27 in 1850), died at
Milbridge 25 Oct. 1856, 30y (Machias Union), daughter of John
and Dorcas Fernald (Willey) Hall; married third at Franklin
ME 25 Apr. 1857 CAROLINE WHITAKER, died at Harrington 29 July
1889, 60y, formerly of Columbia (Machias Union) (town VRs).

He was a mason living at Cherryfield in 1850; in 1860 he was at Harrington with only his son Frederick. (A contemporary Oliver Leighton, born in NB, lived at Calais with his wife Elizabeth Kaler.)

Children by second wife Elizabeth:

       i.   SARAH B.[8], b. c1849 (10/12 in 1850), living
            with uncle Jordan Hall in 1860, aged 12.
739.   ii. FREDERICK E., b. Milbridge 1 July 1848.
       iii. JEFFERSON A., b. Milbridge 4 Jan. 1855, d.
            Portland 3 Dec. 1932, 77y 11m 1d; m. Milbridge
            30 Oct. 1904 ELLA M. (BROWN) Sawyer, b. there
            23 Oct. 1868, d. Portland 21 July 1959, 90y,
            dau. of Haskell J. and Mary A. (Campbell)
            Brown. No ch. Ella m. 1st Milbridge 30 Nov.
            1886 Charles T. Sawyer, who d. in 1901: 3 ch.
            (her obit., Portland Press Herald).

297.   MARY B.[7] 1821-1893 [92 Asa[6] and Loruhamah Fickett] was born at Steuben 22 Sept. 1821, died at Addison 1 Aug. 1893, 81y; married first at Harrrington int. 29 Feb. 1840 SAMUEL HOOPER; married second at Harrington 23 Jan. 1859 PETER COLE; married third int. 14 Jan. 1880 LEONARD J. WHITE (town and ME VRs; Cornman Ms).
   In 1860 Peter Cole, 62, farmer, and his wife Mary, 37, were listed at Harrington; the household included George Cole, 18, and two Hooper children: Adelaide, 11, and Forest, 7. Mary had a grand-daughter Nora who married a Leighton, according to the Cornman Papers.

Children (Hooper):

    i.   (MATILDA) ADELAIDE, b. in 1849, res. Addison; m. 1st
         BYRON NORTON, son of Otis Norton; m. 2nd AARON
         COTTON, son of Seth and Eliza (Look) Cotton.
    ii. JAMES, b. in 1851, res. with Asa[6] in 1860, aged 9.
    iii. FOREST, b. c1853.
    iv. AMANDA; m. ---- FICKETT.
    v.   SARAH; m. ---- BROWN of Milbridge.

298.   HANNAH STROUT[7] 1823-1911 [92 Asa[6] and Loruhamah Fickett] was born at Steuben 4 July 1823, died at Milbridge 20 May 1911; married at Harrington int. 10 Feb. 1842 EPHRAIM STROUT, born at Harrington 13 Nov. 1817, died at Milbridge 19 Jan. 1892, 74y 2m 6d, son of Vinson and Abigail (Dinsmore) Strout (town VRs; records of Margaret Colton).

Children (Strout), born at Milbridge:

    i.   ABIGAIL, b. 18 Dec. 1842; m. Milbridge 23 Mar. 1870
         (GEORGE) WILLIAM TUCKER.
    ii. ALPHONZO, b. 2 Apr. 1844, died at sea; m. 1st Mil-
         bridge int. 6 Nov. 1866 SUSAN JORDAN; m. 2nd there
         29 Sept. 1869 LUCY J. BABBAGE; m. 3rd there 14 Feb.
         1871 SARAH ANN LEIGHTON, d. in 1872; m. 4th EMILY F.
         POMEROY (records of Leonard F. Tibbetts).
    iii. SARAH H., b. 5 July 1847, d. 3 Apr. 1915; m. 1st
         Milbridge 31 July 1865 RUFUS E. MITCHELL; m. 2nd

2 Dec. 1879 BARTLETT C. BROWN, b. 14 Sept. 1847, d.
2 Jan. 1929.

iv.   LORENZO D., b. 4 May 1849, d. Milbridge 17 Nov. 1919;
      m. MARY E. STROUT, b. 23 Feb. 1856, d. 7 May 1938,
      dau. of Obed and Clarissa (Pinkham) Strout.

v.   MEDORA, b. 19 Mar. 1853, res. Rockland ME; m. Mil-
      bridge 18 Nov. 1871 EDWARD ROSCOE.

vi.   FRANK L., b. 24 May 1857, d. Milbridge 25 Aug.
      1932; m. Milbridge 19 Nov. 1881 ADA L. STROUT, b.
      there 5 May 1862, d. there 17 Feb. 1937, dau. of
      Elbridge and Asenath (Pinkham) Strout. He was a sea
      captain.

vii. WILLIAM, b. 12 May 1859, d. of yellow fever.

viii. MARVIN P., b. 1 Jan. 1861; m. 1 Jan. 1894 ESTELLA
      STEVENS, b. 15 Sept. 1871, d. 22 Sept. 1951, dau. of
      ---- and Lucy (West) Stevens. She m. 2nd ---- SHAW.

ix.   WALTER C., b. 12 June 1864; m. 9 Aug. 1891 LUCY HALL.

299.   ISABELLE STROUT[7] 1825-1898 [92 Asa[6] and Loruhamah
Fickett] was born at Steuben 13 Apr. 1825, died at Milbridge
21 Nov. 1898, 72y 7m 8d; married at Harrington in May 1844
(int. 17 Mar.) MYRICK SMALL, born 5 May 1819, son of Larkin
and Sally (Strout) Small (town VRs; records of Margaret Colton). In 1850 Small was a ships' carpenter at Milbridge.

Children (**Small**):

i.   ELIZA A., b. in 1846, d.y.
ii.   BARTLETT, b. in 1848, d.y.
iii. IDA, b. in 1853, res. Ellsworth; m. ALVA SPENCER.
iv.   BARTON, b. in 1854; m. EMMA² LEIGHTON [# 1487].
v.   ANNA BELLE, b. Milbridge 11 Nov. 1860; m. 8 Nov.
      1879 WARREN COLSON.
vi.   WINFIELD, b. 3 Apr. 1863, d. Troy ME in 1950; m.
      SUSAN L. (STOVER) Kane. He res. Ellsworth, and
      owned Asa's family Bible.

300.   LEWIS R.[7] 1829-1893 [92 Asa[6] and Loruhamah Fickett]
was born at Milbridge 23 Feb. 1829, died at Calais 23 Mar.
1893, 64y; married at Harrington int. 7 Jan. 1851 DORCAS
WILLEY [Dolly] HALL, born at there 15 July 1836, died on
Peaks Island (Portland) 23 July 1925, 88y 10m 27d, daughter
of John and Mary (Libby) (Nash) Hall, and half-sister of
Oliver's wife [# 296] (town and ME VRs.).
He was a house carpenter. In 1860 the family lived at Milbridge, in 1870 at Robbinston, and in 1880 at Calais.

Children:

      i.   ASA[8], b. Milbridge 23 Mar. 1852, d. there 10
            Dec. 1868.
740. ii.   REDMAN JUSTUS, b. Milbridge 1 Nov. 1855.
      iii. CURTIS S., b. Milbridge 24 Jan. 1858, d. Calais
            16 Nov. 1918, 61y 9m 23d; m. 1st Harrington
            int. 15 Feb. 1877 cousin ROSANNA E. HALL, b.
            c1854, dau. of Tristram Redman and Susan Hall;
            m. 2nd Dennysville 21 Nov. 1885 ELIZABETH R.
            LYONS, b. Charlotte 8 Aug. 1862, d. Dennys-
            ville 11 June 1942, dau. of James and Eliza-

beth W. (Motz) Lyons. In 1900 he was a grocer
at Calais. Ch. ELIZABETH A.[9] b. Dennysville
18 Aug. 1886, d. Calais 9 July 1901, 14y.
   iv. SIDNEY, b. 12 Feb., d. 12 Aug., 1860.
   v.   EVERETT LINCOLN, b. 22 Oct. 1861, d. Calais 29
Oct. 1898, 37y 7d; m. there 25 Nov. 1884 MARY
M. WATSON, b. Alton NH 10 Sept. 1860, d.
Calais 20 June 1935, dau. of Enoch Jones and
Mary (Wilburn) Watson. No ch.
741. vi. HATTIE E., b. Milbridge 4 Oct. 1863; m. EUGENE
J. LADD.
   vii. LUCRETIA W., b. 4 Aug. 1865, d. Deblois 17 July
1905; m. Buctouche NB 12 Dec. 1885 (int. Calais 5 Dec.) (ERNEST) CHIPMAN CAMPBELL, b. 26
May 1862. Ch. Lewis, res. Calais.
   viii. LEWIS E., b. 7 Sept. 1867, d. Calais 14 Dec.
1878.
   ix. MARTIN B., b. in 1869, d. Calais 6 Sept. 1871.
   x.   MINNIE R., b. 12 Nov. 1870, d. Calais 3 Sept.
1871.
   xi. DORA K., b. 24 Dec. 1872, d. Calais 6 May 1873.
   xii. IDELLA MAY, b. 7 Dec. 1874, d. in Jan. 1923; m.
Marion ME 23 Sept. 1896 RALPH H. BRIDGES, b.
24 Mar. 1874, son of Charles and Lydia (Stanhope) Bridges. No ch.
742. xiii. CHARLES P., b. Calais 28 Aug. 1877.
743. xiv. EDITH EDNA, b. Calais 14 Oct. 1878; m. BEN-
JAMIN S. RANDALL.

301. ELLEN[7] 1833-1895 [92 Asa[6] and Loruhamah Fickett]
was born at Milbridge 9 Jan. 1833, died at Calais 17 Aug.
1895; married at Milbridge 21 Dec. 1850 SIMPSON S. GORDON,
born at Franklin ME 18 Jan. 1830, died at St. Stephen NB 4
Feb. 1910, son of Robert, Jr., and Theresa (Dyer) Gordon
(Franklin VRs; Cornman Ms; records of descendant Rebecca
Stark).

Children (**Gordon**), first five born at Franklin:

i.   CYRENE L., b. 20 Sept. 1851, d. Robbinston 19 Mar.
1902; m. Calais c1867 JOSHUA A. BROOKS.
ii.   MONROE R., b. 3 Jan., d. 8 Oct., 1855.
iii. ABBIE J., b. 7 Aug. 1856, d. 15 July 1918; m. 1st
NATHANIEL GORDON; m. 2nd FRANK P. GOTT.
iv.   ERASTUS P., b. 24 Mar. 1858, d. 4 Dec. 1921; res.
Minneapolis MN.
v.   FRANCES C. [Fannie], b. 13 July 1862, d. 19 Oct.
1939; m. in 1881 JOHN McADAM MURCHIE.
vi.   ALBERT B., b. 12 Apr., d. 11 Aug., 1865.

302. GEORGE F.[7] 1834-1914 [92 Asa[6] and Loruhamah Fickett]
was born at Milbridge 14 Oct. 1834, died at Milltown (Calais)
1 July 1914, after being struck by a trolleycar; married
first MARIA D. THORN, born at Sullivan 5 June 1837, died 18
Jan. 1864, daughter of Joseph and Martha (Stevens) Thorn
(Johnson, Sullivan and Sorrento, 232); married second at
Calais (both of St. Stephen NB) int. 18 Apr. 1864 ISABELLE
McELROY, born in 1834, died in 1885--div.; married third at
Calais 15 Jan. 1869 ANN M. (FOSS) Kidd, born in NB; married

fourth MARY GERTRUDE ROBB, born at Calais 4 July 1857, died
there 23 Apr. 1940, daughter of John and Mary (Hayman) Robb
(town VRs).
     A blacksmith, George was at Milbridge in 1860, St. Stephen
in 1864, Calais in 1870 (with two Foss children as well as
his own Ira and Calvin), Winslow ME in 1900, Sidney ME in
1906 (Town Register), and Vassalboro ME in 1908 (Town Register, which unusually named all four of his wives).

Children by first wife Maria, born at Milbridge:

744. i.   IRA A.[8], b. 1 Nov. 1856.
745. ii.   CALVIN D., b. 28 July 1859.
746. iii. ELMER ELLSWORTH, b. 8 July 1863.

Child by second wife Isabelle, born at St. Stephen:

      v.   ADDIE E., b. 17 Sept. 1865.

Child by fourth wife Mary, born at Calais:

747. vi.   MINA, b. 16 Mar. 1882; m. LEON HAWKES.

     303. ELEANOR M.[7] 1797-1873 [93 John [6] and Sarah Mahar] was
born at Dennysville ME 17 Feb. 1797, died at Charlotte ME 27
Aug. 1873; married at Dennysville 21 Aug. 1824 (BHM, 9[1894]:
17) JOSIAH BRIDGES of Charlotte (Pltn 3), born about 1790 (40
in 1830), died in Mar. 1891, son of John and Annie Livingston
(Hutchins) Bridges (Wilder, Pembroke Families; Cornman Ms).

Children (Bridges), born at Charlotte (VRs):

i.   ANN MARIA, b. 25 Oct. 1824; m. ---- LEACH.
ii.   MARY JANE, b. 1 Jan. 1826.
iii. ELIZABETH SARAH, b. 2 Aug. 1827.
iv.   ELIZA ANN, b. 24 May 1831, res. Newburyport MA; unm.
v.   AARON NEWELL, b. 12 Feb. 1833, res. Brentwood CA.
vi.   GEORGE C., b. 23 Mar. 1838, res. Pembroke on father's
        homestead.
vii. MARY JANE, b. 25 Oct. 1841.

     304. JOHN[7] 1801-1839 [93 John [6] and Sarah Mahar] was born
at Dennysville 31 Aug. 1801, died at Pembroke 27 Dec. 1840
(GS); married at Lubec ME 9 Aug. 1835 REBECCA[7] LEIGHTON, born
there 22 Apr. 1804, died at Pembroke 26 May 1896, 92y 2m 4d
(GS), daughter of Hatevil and Mary (Mahar) Leighton [# 95]
(town VRs; Wilder, Pembroke Families). A farmer, he lived on
lot 2, Leighton's Point.
     Adna Leighton [# 322] was named administrator of John's
estate 7 Nov. 1841 (WashCP, 10:463). Widow Rebecca managed
the farm until after 1860, when she joined her son Ezra's
household. Burials are in Clarkside Cemetery, West Pembroke.

Children, born at Pembroke:

748. i.   EZRA[8], b. 13 July 1836.
      ii.   ISAAC NEWELL, b. 25 Oct. 1837, drowned Pembroke
              25 Oct. 1862, 25y (GS).

iii.   ALMIRA B., b. in 1840, d. Pembroke 13 July
       1881, 40y 10m; unm. She res. with Ezra.

305. HATEVIL JAMES[7] 1803-1898 [93 John [6] and Sarah Mahar]
was born at Dennysville 28 Sept. 1803, died at Pembroke 6
Aug. 1898, 94y 10m 8d; married first JOANNA HERSEY, born 26
Mar. 1808, died in June 1832, daughter of Percy and Catherine
(Benner) Hersey; married second at Lubec 20 Jan. 1834 MARY
LEIGHTON, born at Lubec 27 Oct. 1811, died at Pembroke 8 Oct.
1877, 65y 11m, daughter of Hatevil and Mary (Mahar) Leighton
[# 95] (town VRs; Wilder, Pembroke Families). Burials are in
Clarkside Cemetery, West Pembroke.
A farmer, he lived on lot 6, Leighton's Point. In 1880, his
household included four grandchildren: Laura Greenlaw, 16;
Almeda Dingle, 14; a Philinda Leighton, 16; and Clarence L.
Carter, 6.

Children by Mary, born at Pembroke:

749. i.   MARY J.[8], b. 4 Mar. 1835; m. JAMES GREENLAW.
750. ii.   HATEVILLE J., b. 19 Apr. 1837.
      iii.   MARTHA ANN, b. 31 Mar. 1839, d. Pembroke 25
             Apr. 1928; m. 1st LEVI B. CARTER, b. Pembroke
             23 Feb. 1842, d. Machias 10 Jan. 1876, son of
             Samuel and Sally (Cox) Carter--div.; m. 2nd W.
             Pembroke 18 Apr. 1870 JOSIAH CROWELL, b. in NS
             in 1826, both living with her father in 1880;
             m. 3rd Pembroke int. 25 Oct. 1886 IRA C.
             CARTER, res. Mapleton ME, son of James, Jr.,
             and Joanna (Cox) Carter. Ch. Clarence Levi
             Carter b. Pembroke 12 Aug. 1873, d. Calais 21
             Mar. 1953; m. 22 Nov. 1890 Laura Estelle Hay-
             ward, b. Edmunds 7 Feb. 1874, dau. of George
             Henry and Rachel (Bridges) Hayward--div.
      iv.   EUNICE M., b. 14 Feb. 1842; m. WILLIAM DINGLE,
             b. in England. He deserted Eunice and his
             family.
      v.   JOHN F , b. 13 Sept. 1844, d. Machiasport ME 12
             June 1906, 59y; m. there 10 June 1874 (Machias
             Union) HENRIETTA [Etta] R. STEEVES, b. there
             24 Jan. 1849, d. there 14 Apr. 1939, dau. of
             Andrew and Frances (Libby) Steeves. John
             served in Co. A, 15th ME Rgt., and was a
             shoemaker.
      vi.   MARK L., b. 18 July 1847, res. CA; m. West
             Pembroke 4 July 1875 ZULEIMA P. [Lena]
             SPRAGUE, b. in 1853, d. Pembroke 4 Feb. 1879,
             22y, dau. of Capt. William C. and Mary
             Sprague. Only ch. FRANK[9] d. aged 1y.
751. vii.   JEMIMA BELL, b. 21 Mar. 1850; m. EMULUS W. S.
             CARTER.
      viii. THOMAS O., b. 1 Feb. 1853, d. Emden ME; m.
             Pembroke 7 July 1882 NANCY B. MAHAR, b. 8 Feb.
             1867, dau. of Joseph and Mary Ann (Boynton)
             Mahar of Eastport, who m. 2nd (James) Harry
             Rose and had 3 Rose ch. Ch. NEWELL W.[9], b.
             Pembroke in Sept. 1883; m. Eastport 19 Dec.
             1906 MYRA C. SPOFFORD, b. Pembroke c1886, dau.
             of Daniel P. and Lizzie (McIntosh) Spofford.

306. EDMUND[7] 1805-1891 [93 John[6] and Sarah Mahar] was born at Dennysville 12 Sept. 1805, died at Pembroke 15 Mar. 1891; married 29 Apr. 1833 MARY JANE HOLLAND, born at St. Stephen NB 3 Sept. 1808 (46 in 1860), daughter of William and Charlotte (Dustin) Holland (Pembroke VRs; Wilder, Pembroke Families).

He was a farmer and lumberman. In 1850, he and his wife "Ann" were listed at both Pembroke and Machias.

Children, born at Pembroke:

752. i.   WILLIAM HENRY[8], b. 10 Mar. 1834.
753. ii.   ISAIAH, b. 2 Apr. 1837.
      iii. CATHERINE, b. c1838 (12 in 1850), d.y.
754. iv.   CHARLOTTE ANN [Lo], b. 16 Nov. 1839; m. BENJA-
            MIN KELLEY.
755. v.   ALEXANDER, b. 10 June 1846.
756. vi.   CATHERINE, b. 5 June 1852; m. CHARLES WATT.

307. THOMAS[7] 1808-1894 [93 John[6] and Sarah Mahar] was born at Dennysville 4 Feb. 1808, died at Pembroke 17 Feb. 1894, 86y 13d; married HANNAH KELLEY, born at Trescott 1 Sept. 1813 (Pembroke VRs; 30 Apr. in Wilder, Pembroke Families), died at Pembroke 8 Jan. 1892 (Pembroke and ME TRs; Cornman Ms). He had a farm on lot 1, and operated a ferry from Leighton's Point to Lubec.

A Rebecca N., 23, listed in the 1860 census, may have been Valeria. The 1870 census included Louisa, 5, perhaps daughter of Hatevil [#317]. The town records also listed a Delia as born to him 27 Oct. 1868; she was not listed in 1870.

Children:

757. i.   AARON WHITFIELD[8], b. Trescott 6 Mar. 1834.
758. ii.   WILLIAM KELLEY, b. 6 June 1836.
      iii. VALERIA NUTTER, b. 16 May 1838, d. 7 May 1860.
      iv.   SAMANTHA KELLEY, b. 18 Jan. 1840; m. Pembroke
            7 Aug. 1859 BENJAMIN W. DUDLEY, b. there 1
            Apr. 1835, son of Henry and Abigail (Runnels)
            Dudley. He m. 2nd 18 Oct. 1863 Mary Elizabeth
            Carter, and m. 3rd Phoebe Bosworth. His
            grand-dau. Eilene m. ANDREW PERCY[10] LEIGHTON
            [# 750].
759. v.   JOHN FAIRCHILD, b. Trescott 6 Apr. 1842.
      vi.   BENJAMIN FRANKLIN, b. 8 Feb. 1844.
760. vii. ISAAC NEWELL, b. 5 July 1845.
      viii. AZOR BAKER, b. in Sept. 1850 (Oct. 1846 in 1900
            census; m. Trescott 31 Mar. 1876 SOPHRONIA
            [Phronie] SAUNDERS, b. in Dec. 1852 (1900
            census). They were at Washburn, Bayfield Co.
            WI in 1900, with dau. ETHEL[9], b. in WI in Mar.
            1882.
      ix.   LAVINA W., b. 11 Oct. 1854.

308. LUCY[7] 1810-187? [93 John[6] and Sarah Mahar] was born at Dennysville 19 Feb. 1810, died in the 1870s; married WILLIAM WILBUR, born at Pembroke 7 Sept. 1812, died there 28 Sept. 1887, son of Benjamin and Elizabeth (Blackwood) Wilbur (Wilder, Pembroke Families; records of Pamela Sparks).

William Wilbur was a master mariner. He married second 29
Jan. 1876 (Mary) Jane Ross. Although no court record has
been found to verify the crimes, Wilder stated that Wilbur
"was supposed to have been murdered by his second wife with
powdered glass cooked in his food, together with his daughters Clytie and Ruby, and her second husband [Irvin] Bennett
and a child by Bennett; she murdered in all five people over
a period of a few years."

Children (**Wilbur**), born at Pembroke:

i.   JOANNA, b. 14 Mar. 1835, liv. in 1880; unm. invalid.
ii.   JOHN LEIGHTON, b. 4 Apr. 1836, d. 23 Sept. 1899; m.
        23 Mar. 1879 ANNIE LAURA MAHAR, b. 24 Feb. 1861, d.
        2 Aug. 1936, dau. of Peter R. and Martha Ann (Cook)
        Mahar.
iii.   BENJAMIN N., b. 28 Nov. 1837, d. 11 Sept. 1897; m. 5
        July 1869 ELIZABETH MORRISON of Perry.
iv.   CHARLOTTE A., b. 2 Apr. 1840, res. Boston; m. HENRY
        VARNEY.
v.   HARRIET, b. 27 Apr. 1843, res. Londonderry NH; m.
        STEPHEN WATSON.
vi.   SARAH JANE, b. 28 Nov. 1845, d. Watertown MA in 1915;
        m. EDWIN GOULD.
vii.   CLYTIE.

309. MARY JANE[7] 1819-1899 [93 John[6] and Sarah Mahar] was
born at Dennysville 19 Oct. 1819, died at Pembroke 28 Dec.
1899, 72y 2m 7d; married there 22 Sept. 1844 JOSIAH EATON
WILBUR, born there 26 June 1821, died there 1 July 1902, 81y
5d, son of Benjamin and Elizabeth (Blackwood) Wilbur (Pembroke TRs; Wilder, Pembroke Families; records of Pamela
Sparks; Cornman Ms). He was a farmer.

Children (**Wilbur**), born at Pembroke:

i.   ORRIN SABIN, b. 15 Jan. 1847, drowned Pembroke 4 Aug.
        1885; m. 4 Dec. 1869 ALVARETTA HAYNES.
ii.   LUCY LEIGHTON, b. 28 Aug. 1848, d. Portland 5 May
        1915; m. Portland 31 July 1869 (STEPHEN) FOSTER
        CLARK.
iii.   ISRAEL L., b. 7 Feb. 1850, d. Portsmouth NH 30 Jan.
        1912; m. ESTHER SMITH.
iv.   SARAH L., b. 19 Sept. 1851, d. Pembroke 2 Apr. 1934;
        m. Capt. RAYMOND MOTZ.
v.   WILLIAM, b. 22 July 1853, d. in May 1861.
vi.   EDMUND L., b. 7 Feb. 1855, d. Pembroke 8 July 1922;
        m. MARY ELIZA CARTER.
vii.   THOMPSON DUDLEY, b. 19 Dec. 1856, d. Pembroke 26 Aug.
        1938; m. KATHERINE ANDERSON.
viii.   IRVIN P., b. 22 Sept. 1858, d. Pembroke 15 Sept.
        1861.

310. (AARON) NEWELL[7] 1823-1873 [93 John[6] and Sarah Mahar]
was born at Dennysville 18 July 1823, drowned at Pembroke 31
May 1873, 49y 10m (GS); married there 19 Nov. 1849 MARY JANE
SMITH, born there 7 Aug. 1827 (GS, 8 Aug. 1828), died there
20 Oct. 1919, 91y 2m 12d, daughter of Simeon and Rebecca
(Carter) Smith (Pembroke VRs; Wilder, Pembroke Families).

Burials are in Forest Hills Cemetery, Pembroke.
Newell was a farmer on Garnett's Head Road.

Children, born at Pembroke:

     i.   SARAH J.[8], b. 19 Mar. 1850, res. Cumberland
           Mills ME; m. Westbrook 25 Aug. 1872 GEORGE W.
           WYETH.
761. ii.   EVERETT, b. 25 Apr. 1857.
762. iii. FREDERICK, b. 14 Jan. 1862.

311. GEORGE[7] 1794-   [94 Sarah[6]] was born at Dennysville
24 March 1794, lived at Springfield ME in 1860; married at
Plantation 2 (organized as Springfield in 1834) 26 May 1815
COMFORT GUPTILL, born at Lubec about 1796 (54 in 1850), perhaps daughter of William Gubtail of Grand Manan NB (Pembroke
TRs; Wilder, Pembroke Families).
According to the Pembroke TRs he had six children. In 1850
he and Comfort were at Pembroke with his three sons, next
door to Robinson and Barbara Leighton; in 1860 they lived
next door to his son George at Springfield, with Rev. Moses
Stevens (a Free Will Baptist minister) living with them.

Children, born at Pembroke:

     i.   MARTHA HENRY[8], b. 19 Jan. 1821.
     ii.   BARBARA GUPTILL, b. 12 Apr. 1825; m. ROBINSON[8]
           LEIGHTON [# 1088].
     iii. EDWARD N. HARRIS, b. 4 Apr. 1829 (Lubec VRs),
           d. 2 Sept. 1852.
     iv.   ISAAC N., b. 24 Mar. 1832.
763. v.   GEORGE E., b. 18 Mar. 1834.

312. JAMES[7] 1800-1884 [95 Hatevil[6] and Polly Mahar] was
born at Lubec ME 16 June 1800, died at Somerville MA in Oct.
1884; married at Lubec 17 June 1827 (VRs; 27 June, Bible
record) MARY FONTAINE RUMERY, born at Eastport 16 Mar. 1803,
died at Somerville 14 Sept. 1866, daughter of Dominicus and
Mary (Fontaine) Rumery (Lubec VRs). In 1850, his Lubec
household included a niece HARRIET, 10, perhaps the same as
Catherine [# 774].
On 26 Jan. 1858, he dictated to his son James his recollections of the family history and of his own career (records of
Kingsley T. Leighton). His family Bible was owned by his
granddaughter Mary Edith.
He was first a lumberman and sawmill hand. In 1843 he
settled on a farm at Lubec Ridge, and worked as a shipwright.
He was militia captain for six years, and customs officer
during the Pierce and Buchanan administrations. He and his
wife retired to their son James's home in Somerville.

Children, born at Lubec:

764. i.   HATEVIL M.[8], b. 8 Apr. 1828.
     ii.   MARY PARMELIA, b. 27 Apr. 1829, res. Chelsea
           ME; m. Augusta 21 Jan. 1855 (VRs) CHARLES
           BLANCHARD, b. Pittston ME 20 Oct. 1834 (VRs),
           son of William J. and Lydia (Baker) Blanchard.
           Ch. Frederick and Ada.

765. iii. DOMINICUS RUMERY, b. 8 Dec. 1830.
      iv.   JAMES THOMSON G., b. 4 Apr. 1833, d. Portland
            24 Aug. 1892, 59y 4m 10d; m. 1st Cambridge MA
            6 Aug. 1859 MARTHA HELEN JENKINS (Boston
            Weekly Messenger of 10 Aug.), b. in 1834; m.
            2nd Boston 1 Jan. 1866 THERESA E. GILLESPIE,
            b. China ME in 1842, dau. of J. A. and Irene
            Gillespie (Cambridge VRs). He was a merchant.
            Ch. LORENZO[9] and GEORGE res. Chicago (Cornman
            Ms).
      v.   ELSAIDE M., b. 25 Apr. 1835; unm.
      vi.   SUSAN RUMERY, b. 28 Apr. 1837, d. New Haven CT
            9 Dec. 1907; unm.
      vii. ELLEN E., b. 15 July 1839, d. Somerville MA 12
            Sept. 1864, 25y 1m 25d (VRs); unm.

313. ISAAC[7] 1802-   [95 Hatevil[6] and Polly Mahar] was
born at Lubec 17 Jan. 1802, lived there in 1870, aged 67;
married there 23 Jan. 1827 (VRs) or 23 Dec. 1826 (Bible) ROX-
ANNA [Roxy] THAYER, born 3 June 1805 (Bible) (Lubec VRs; family Bible owned by a Mahar descendant).
He was a shipwright.

Children, born at Lubec:

      i.   AARON JACKSON[8], b. 8 June 1827 (VRs) or 9 June
            (Bible), d. infant.
      ii.   AARON, b. in Aug. 1828 (VRs) or 12 Oct. (Bible)
            1828, went west, prob. to CA (Cornman Ms); m.
            22 May 1849 ELIZA A. BRAKINS.
766. iii. JOHN T., b. 31 July 1830 (VRs) or 30 July
            (Bible).
      iv.   MARK P., b. 7 Apr. 1832 (Bible), d. in Jan.
            1850 at 18 (census mort. sch.).
      v.   KEZIAH ANN, b. 25 Apr. 1835 (VRs) or 26 July
            1833 (Bible); m. Lubec 27 July 1864 JAMES
            ROGERS. They went west (Cornman Ms).
      vi.   ISAAC M., b. 18 May 1834 (VRs) or 1835 (Bible),
            settled in CA (Cornman Ms).
      vii. ISRAEL, b. 26 July 1836 (female per 1850
            census), nfr.
767. viii. LOVINA E., b. 7 Aug. 1837 (Bible); m. CHARLES
            O. MAHAR.
768. ix.   MELISSA ABIGAIL, b. 16 Oct. 1838 (Bible); m.
            ELLERY MAHAR and JAMES KINNEY.
      x.   VELINA, b. 2 July 1840 (Bible), d.y.
769. xi.   VELINA MABEL, b. 13 Aug. 1841 (Bible); m.
            JOSIAH T. MAHAR.
770. xii. REBECCA, b. 8 Nov. 1842 (Bible); m. JAMES
            SALMON and ISRAEL ALLEN.
      xiii. ELVINA, b. 7 Apr. 1845 (Bible), d.y.
      xiv. ARIEL, b. 30 Oct. 1845 (VRs) or 9 May 1846
            (Bible), d. 30 Sept. 1864, 18y 11m.
      xv.   ELVINA ROXANNA, b. 7 Apr. 1847 (Bible) (Almira,
            21, in 1870).
      xvi. MARY J., b. 30 May 1848 (VRs), d. 30 Oct. 1864,
            15y 5m.
771. xvii. EMMA SOPHIA, b. 6 Aug. 1851 (Bible); m. ALBERT
            GODFREY.

xviii.MARK W., b. 24 Feb. 1857 (Bible; 17y in 1870);
probably m. ANNIE MOORES of Trescott. Ch.
VERNA V. WEBBER[9] d. Lubec 12 Oct. 1894,
4m 23d.

314. MARGARET[7] 1806-   [95 Hatevil[6] and Polly Mahar] was
born at Lubec 10 Jan. 1806, died at Whiting before 1844; married at Lubec 13 Nov. 1828 (VRs) HORATIO GATES ALLEN, born at
Whiting ME 6 Dec. 1800, died at Machias 6 Jan. 1871, 69y
(Machias Union), son of John and Mehitable (Crane) Allen
(Forslund, Whiting, 65). He married second Mercy (Huckins)
Leighton [# 315].
Allen was a lumberman, listed as aged 58 at Whiting in
1860. When her father's estate was distributed in 1844, Margaret's living children were named as heirs through her
right.

Children (**Allen**), born at Whiting:

i.   MARY L., b. in 1830, living in 1844, not in house-
       hold in 1850.
ii.   EDWARD H., b. 29 Nov. 1832; m. in 1856 SARAH HOAR.
iii.   KEZIAH E., b. 26 May 1835; m. in 1852 DAVID G. HOAR.
iv.   MELISSA E., b. in 1839, d. in 1842.
v.   ANN, listed as heir in 1844.

315. SAMUEL[7] 1807-   [95 Hatevil[6] and Polly Mahar] was
born at Lubec 31 Oct. 1807, died before his father's death in
1844; married at Lubec 2 Oct. 1834 MERCY HUCKINS, born about
1808 (42 in 1850), probably daughter of James and Frances
(Robinson) Huckins. He was a lumberman, and lived at Whiting
(Forslund, Whiting, 86; Wilder, Pembroke Families).
His widow married second Horatio G. Allen [# 314]. A petition by Mercy, wife of Horatio G. Allen and widow of Samuel
Leighton of Lubec, that Allen be made guardian to her children: Sophronia, Pillsbury, James Bradford, Catherine and
Sarah Jane, was granted 10 Oct. 1845 (WashCP, 13:375). In
1850 and 1860 Horatio and Mercy were listed in the Whiting
censuses with their two sets of children.

Children, born at Lubec:

772. i.   SOPHRONIA[8], b. about 1835 (15 in 1850); m.
            WILSON ANDREWS.
      ii.   PILLSBURY, b. c1836 (14 in 1850), d. Whiting
            25 Feb. 1854, 18y (GS).
773. iii. JAMES BRADFORD, b. 17 Apr. 1839 (12 in 1850).
774. iv.   CATHERINE M., b. say 1840 (not listed in 1850
            or 1860); m. BELA W. CRANE.
      v.   SARAH JANE, b. c1841 (9 in 1850); m. 1st JAMES
            B. WILBUR; m. 2nd Machias 12 May 1861 (Machias
            Union) ISRAEL P. DINSMORE, b. 17 Apr. 1838, d.
            19 June 1916, son of Alexander and Lucy (Dins-
            more) Dinsmore.
            Israel m. 2nd Mehitable (Bridges) Leighton,
            widow of James Bradford[8] Leighton [# 773]
            (Forslund, Whiting, 75).

316.   MARK[7] 1809-1881 [95 Hatevil[6] and Polly Mahar] was born at Pembroke 23 Dec. 1809, died at Lubec 31 Jan. 1881; married there 10 May 1835 ELIZA HUCKINS, born there 18 Aug. 1812, died there 18 Dec. 1884, daughter of James and Fannie (Robertson) Huckins (Lubec VRs). He was a farmer.

Children, born at Lubec (perhaps others):

775. i.   LORENA A.[8], b. Lubec 29 Mar. 1836 (1835 in VRs); m. SOLOMON CASE.
      ii.   PAMELIA, b. c1841 (9 in 1850).

317.   HATEVIL[7] 1813-1899 [95 Hatevil[6] and Polly Mahar] was born at Lubec 10 Aug. 1813, died at Pembroke 7 Apr. 1899, 85y 8m; married at Lubec 15 Dec. 1835 ELIZA ANN[7] LEIGHTON, born at Pembroke 20 Sept. 1816, died there 28 June 1905, daughter of John and Sarah (Mahar) Leighton [# 93]. (Her death record listed her husband's parents instead of her own.) He was a farmer at Pembroke (Lubec and ME VRs; Wilder, Pembroke Families; Cornman Ms, in which his wife was named Julia Ann Mooney).

Children:

      i.   ELEANOR JANE[8], b. Lubec 2 Oct. 1836, d. Pembroke 18 June 1859; unm.
776. ii.   JOSIAH L., b. Lubec 27 May 1840.
      iii.   ADVESTA LOUISE [Addie L.], b. Lubec 21 Mar. 1845, d. Pembroke 15 June 1875 (GS, Hersey Cem.); unm. She was a schoolteacher. She was perhaps the Louisa, 15, living with Thomas [# 307] in 1850.
777. iv.   (WILLIAM) ALVRA, b. Pembroke 16 Apr. 1851.

318.   KEZIAH[7] 1816-1851 [95 Hatevil[6] and Polly Mahar] was born at Lubec 12 June 1816, died there 28 July 1851; married there 5 July 1840 JAMES HUCKINS, JR., born at Eastport 27 Sept. 1810, son of James and Fannie (Robertson) Huckins (Cornman Ms).
Huckins married second Eliza --- , and had children by her (listed in the 1860 Lubec census).

Children (**Huckins**), born at Lubec:

i.   ADRIANNA [Addie], b. c1841 (8 in 1850).
ii.   CALVIN, b. c1843 (7 in 1850), res. No. Lubec; m. JULIA BARRETT.
iii.   JOSEPH, b. c1845 (5 in 1850).
iv.   PAMELIA.

319.   MARTHA[7] 1818-1904 [95 Hatevil[6] and Polly Mahar] was born at Lubec 18 Sept. 1818 (25 Feb. in Wilder, Pembroke Families), died at Perry 23 July 1904; married at Lubec 30 Mar. 1848 (int. Pembroke 8 Dec. 1847) WILLIAM HENRY BRYANT, born about 1828, son of Henry W. and Sarah Bryant, a farmer at Pembroke (Lubec VRs; Cornman Ms). He was 32 and she 29 in the 1860 Pembroke census.

Children (**Bryant**):

i.   HARTFORD W., b. c1848 (12 in 1860).
ii. ALDEN B., b. c1850 (10 in 1860).
iii. NANCY J., b. c1855 (5 in 1860).

320. AARON[7] 1822-   [95 Hatevil[6] and Polly Mahar] was
born at Lubec 8 July 1822; married there 28 Apr. 1844 ELIZA-
BETH ANN NUTTER, born about 1824 (26 in 1850). He was a
farmer (Lubec VRs; Cornman Ms).
A female, M. C., 11, was listed with him in the 1850 census; she may have been Samuel's daughter Catherine [# 774].

Children, born at Lubec:

i.   A. B.[8], male, 5 in 1850.
ii.   MARY CAROLINE [Caddie], b. 6 Feb.1846 (Eastport
      VRs), res. Eastport; m. Lubec 23 Oct. 1867
      OLIVER WORCESTER. Ch. Minnie and Winnie.
iii. ALICE M., b. c1848 (2 in 1850), d.y.
iv.   ESTHER M., b. c1849 (11 in 1860).
v.   JAMES E., b. 11 June 1851, d. New Haven CT
      7 June 18??, struck by train; m. JENNIE B.
      ---- . He res. New Haven after 1870, a cabi-
      net-maker for Yale College. 2 ch. d.y.
      (undated obit. clipping).
vi.   EMERY J., b. c1853 (7 in 1860), d. Lubec 18
      Mar. 1911, 56y; m. LAURA (TAFTS) Durand of
      Edmunds. Ch. EARL[9] b. in 1897, d. Lubec 17
      June 1904, 6y 10m.
vii. CHARLES F., b. c1857 (3 in 1860), d.y.
778. viii. ALICE, b. in Nov. 1863 (5 in 1870); m. LINCOLN
      PATTERSON.

321. JOHN M.[7] 1825-1882 [95 Hatevil[6] and Polly Mahar] was
born at Lubec say 1825, died there 16 Sept. 1882, drowned in
a squall; married there 17 Jan. 1845 ANN MARIA[7] LEIGHTON,
born at Dennysville 25 July 1818, daughter of John and Sarah
(Mahar) Leighton [# 93] (Cornman Ms; Lubec VRs).
He was a farmer at Lubec in 1850 and 1860; they were living
at Pembroke in 1870 and 1880.

Children, born at Lubec:

i.   MARY M.[8], b. c1845 (5 in 1850), d. Eastport 12
      Feb. 1924, 80y 10m 2d, as widow of a JOSEPH
      LEIGHTON. She lived with her parents in 1880,
      aged 35, with ch. CLARA J., 15, and EDDIE, 9.
ii.   BELINDA A., b. c1846 (4 in 1850).
779. ii.   MELISSA JANE, b. c1848 (2 in 1850); m. DANIEL
      McKAY.
iii. HARRIET A., b. c1849 (9/12 in 1850); m. Pem-
      broke 9 July 1872 ALVIN K. AYLWARD. Ch.
      James b. c1874; m. Pembroke 17 Nov. 1895
      Alice L. Trott, 20.
iv.   EDWARD M., b. c1855 (5 in 1860; not in 1870).
v.   CHARLOTTE R., b. c1856 (4 in 1860); m. Pembroke
      in June 1872 FREEMAN MILLS, b. c1853. Ch.
      Alice, 7 in 1880, Albert J., 5, Charles, 3.

322.   ADNA[7] 1801-1891 [96 Samuel[6] and Leah Hersey] was born at Pembroke (then Dennysville) 22 Feb. 1801, died there 26 June 1891 (GS); married there 6 Jan. 1822 AMY WOODWORTH, born at Canning NS 2 May 1805, died at Pembroke 2 Mar. 1884 (GS), daughter of William and Marcy (Pineo) Woodworth (William E. Chute, A Genealogy and History of the Chute Family in America [Salem, 1894], cclxviii; Wilder, Pembroke Families; Pembroke VRs; Cornman Ms). Burials are in Pembroke cemetery.

In 1832 Adna and his brothers Samuel and Isaiah were among those petitioning the legislature to incorporate the eastern section of Dennysville as Pembroke. Adna was a selectman most of the time from 1832 to 1858, and captain of the militia from 1828 to 1835. He inherited his father's farm, and passed it on to his son Herman.

Children, born at Pembroke:

780. i.   AMY W.[8], b. 2 Dec. 1822; m. EBENEZER FISHER.
781. ii.   LEAH REBECCA, b. 16 Jan. 1825; m. JARED NASH.
      iii. SARAH ELIZABETH, b. 28 June 1827, d. Pembroke
            2 June 1896; m. there 4 Mar. 1849 JOSEPH WIL-
            DER, JR., b. there 7 Apr. 1825, d. there 13
            July 1900, son of Joseph and Mehitable (Crane)
            Wilder. One ch., d. infant (Sidney A. and
            Gerald C. Wilder, Joseph Wilder and His Des-
            cendants, 2nd ed. [Pembroke 1902], 5).
782. iv.   ELIZA ANN, b. 2 Oct. 1830; m. JOHN C. WILDER.
      v.   ELLEN CAROLINE, b. 4 May 1833, d. 11 June 1916;
            m. Dennysville 1 Sept. 1872 JETHRO BROWN
            NUTT, b. Perry 24 May 1836, d. Lubec 1 Aug.
            1915, son of James and Sarah (Brown) Nutt. No
            ch. Brown had 4 ch. by his 1st wife Caroline
            Lincoln (Waldo Lincoln, A History of the Lin-
            coln Family [Worcester MA, 1923], 306).
783. vi.   AUGUSTUS AZOR, b. 6 Feb. 1836.
      vii. ELVINA IRENE [Irene E. in 1860], b. 17 Nov.
            1839, d. Tewksbury MA in 1911; m. Boston 19
            Oct. 1872 CHARLES SOUTHWORTH, b. Duxbury MA,
            d. 22 Nov. 1889. Ch. Herman Charles d.y.
784. viii. WILMOT ADNA, b. 15 Apr. 1842.
      ix.   CLARA ISABELLA, b. 5 Feb. 1845, d. Pembroke
            2 Dec. 1926 (GS); unm., lived with Herman.
785. x.   ARTHUR CLARENCE, b. 11 Nov. 1848.
      xi.   HERMAN CHARLES, b. 24 Apr. 1851, d. Eastport 18
            Apr. 1932, 80y 11m 25d; m. 8 Nov. 1884 SARAH
            AUGUSTA NUTT, b. Perry 16 Aug. 1864, res.
            Eastport in 1951, dau. of Jethro and Caroline
            (Lincoln) Nutt. Ch. ELLEN AUGUSTA[9] b.
            Pembroke 29 Sept. 1885; m. 18 Sept. 1909
            SEWARD BUCKNAM MATTHEWS, b. Eastport 18 May
            1887, son of Capt. Jabez and Julia (Mitchell)
            Matthews.

323.   LEAH[7] 1803-1892 [96 Samuel[6] and Leah Hersey] was born at Pembroke 7 Feb. 1803, died at Eastport 15 Feb. 1892; married first at Dennysville 7 Jan. 1819 WILLIAM LINCOLN, born 17 Feb. 1796, died 14 Oct. 1834, son of Matthew Lincoln (Bible record at NEHGS from Sarah Gardner Fisher); married second ISAAC GARDNER of Charlotte ME, born at Hingham MA 7 Apr. 1792, died at Charlotte 13 Jan. 1858, son of Warren and

Mary (Dunbar) Gardner (Wilder, Pembroke Families; Cornman Ms;
Charlotte VRs). Isaac had married first Susan Johnson--seven
children; she died at Charlotte 3 Jan. 1837.

Children (**Lincoln**):

i.   AMBROSE, b. 9 May 1820.
ii.   LEAH, b. 23 Sept. 1822; m. ---- CARTER.
iii.   ELIZABETH ANN (Eliza), b. 8 Jan. 1825, d. Woodland ME
        11 May 1918, 92y; m. 3 Oct. 1847 LUCAS W. GARDNER,
        b. Charlotte 14 Nov. 1822, d. Calais, son of Isaac
        and Susan (Johnson) Gardner.
iv.   SARAH SALOME, b. 20 Dec. 1826.
v.   ISAIAH L., b. 5 Apr. 1829; m. SARAH A. FORBES.
vi.   SUSAN, b. 16 Mar. 1832, res. Eastport; m. HIRAM
        BLANCHARD, son of David Blanchard of Charlotte. He
        owned a sardine factory.
vii.   WILLIAM G., b. 15 Jan. 1834, d. 1 Oct. 1855; unm.

Children (**Gardner**), born at Charlotte:

ix.   MARY ELLEN, b. 3 Mar. 1839, d. 4 Dec. 1866, 27y 9m.
x.   HENRIETTA ALMIRA, b. 3 July 1841.

324.   SAMUEL[7] 1805-1878 [96 Samuel[6] and Leah Hersey] was
born at Pembroke 23 Feb. 1805, died 12 June 1878 (Wilder,
Pembroke Families); married at Pembroke 23 Jan. 1829 MARTHA
ETTA FARNSWORTH, born at Norridgewock ME 15 Feb. 1808, died
in June 1883, daughter of Jonas and Maria (Gould) Farnsworth
(Moses F. Farnsworth, Farnsworth Memorial [Manti UT, 1897],
261; Cornman Ms; Pembroke VRs). He had a farm at Little
Falls. (Julia Cornman stated that he "died in the west.")

Children, born at Pembroke:

        i.   ANN MARIA[8], b. 24 Oct. 1829; m. W. Pembroke   .
                9 Feb. 1853 MYLES PHINNEY. No ch.
86.   ii.   CHARLES CARROLL, b. 11 May 1832.
        iii.   MARTHA JANE, b. 25 Sept. 1835, d. 30 May 1866;
                m. Pembroke 25 June 1860 JOSIAH S. BABCOCK.
                No ch.
        iv.   CAROLINE MARGARET, b. 5 Nov. 1834, d. 15 Sept.
                1835.
        v.   OLINDA [Linda C.], b. 16 Apr. 1836, res. IA; m.
                OLIVER S. JOHNSON of Perry, son of Oliver S.
                and Elizabeth (Hersey) Johnson. Ch. Will C.,
                Fred L., Hubert F., Olivia S. (in Wilder, Pem-
                broke Families, but see vii. below).
        vi.   JULIETTE MARGARET, b. 1 Apr. 1838, d. 29 Nov.
                1862; m. C. P. BOWLES of Lawrence MA.
        vii.   ADELAIDE LOUISA, b. 20 Dec. 1840; m. West Pem-
                broke 18 June 1859 (int. 11 June) OLIVER S.
                JOHNSON, b. 31 Jan. 1833, son of Oliver and
                Betsey Johnson (see Olinda above).
        viii.   SAMUEL ADAMS, b. 23 July 1843, d. Washington
                DC 4 Jan. 1863, in army hospital. He served
                in Co. F, 6th ME Rgt.
        ix.   LEAH HERSEY, b. 8 Mar. 1846, went west.
        x.   (MARY) HELEN, b. 27 Sept. 1848.
        xi.   PETER GILMAN, b. 29 Feb. 1852, went west.

325.   ISAIAH[7] 1807-1866 [96 Samuel[6] and Leah Hersey] was
born at Pembroke 7 Dec. 1807 (1808 in TRs), died there 25
Feb. 1866 (GS); married at Deer Island NB 4 Feb. 1834 SARAH
[Sally] HATCH, born there 10 Jan. 1818, died at Pembroke 25
Dec. 1893, 75y 11m 15d (GS), daughter of William B. and Mary
(Small) Hatch (Wilder, Pembroke Families; Pembroke VRs).
    He had a homestead at Pembroke next door to his brother
Justin, and a farm on the Steam Mill lot, Little Falls, which
was mentioned in an inventory of minor Raymond I.'s property
15 Jan. 1869 (WashCP, 23:447). In 1850 his household
included his niece Martha J., 16 [# 324].

    Children, born at Pembroke:

    i.   ELVIRA ISABELLA[8], b. 20 Mar. 1836, d. 16 June
            1838.
    ii.   WILLIAM ELDON, b. 20 May 1840, d. Pembroke 12
            Oct. 1925, 85y 4m 22d; m. there 8 Jan. 1861
            JOSEPHINE MARIA LEAVITT, b. there 23 July
            1843, d. there 14 Mar. 1912, 68y 7m, dau. of
            George Washington and Theresa (Stoddard)
            Leavitt (Emily F. Noyes, Descendants of Thomas
            Leavitt [Tilton NH, 1948], 4:115; Waterhouse
            Desc., 2:649). No ch.
                He enlisted as 1st Sgt., Co. E., 28th ME
            Inf. Rgt.; was made captain of Co. A, 1st
            Battalion, in 1863; served on the Inspector
            General's staff in 1865; and was discharged in
            1866. In 1869 he set up a factory for making
            ships' blocks and pumps; as W. E. Leighton &
            Co. he manufactured parlor organs and violin
            cases from 1880 to 1885; and in 1885-7 he was
            the first in Pembroke to can sardines. He
            operated a general store at Pembroke until
            1899.
    iii.   ELVIRA DEBORAH, b. 14 June 1842, d. Jonesport
            30 Aug. 1927; m. EDWARD EVERETT WILDER.
            No ch.
    iv.   MARY ELIZABETH [LIZZIE M.], b. 5 June 1846, d.
            Pembroke 2 Feb. 1897, 50y 7m 28d; unm.
787. v.   RAYMOND ISAIAH, b. 15 Mar. 1850.

326.   JUSTIN L.[7] 1809-1882 [96 Samuel[6] and Leah Hersey] was
born at Pembroke 22 Apr. 1809, died there 7 June 1882, 72y
(GS); married there 26 June 1831 LYDIA HERSEY, born there 5
Sept. 1810, died there 31 Mar. 1875, 65y (GS), daughter of
Isaiah and Lydia (Gardner) Hersey (Pembroke VRs; Cornman Ms;
Wilder, Pembroke Families). Burials are in the Pembroke
cemetery.
    He was a ship's carpenter, mechanic and farmer, and lived
near Little Falls. In 1870, Atwood, Henry, Lyman, Octavia
and Isaiah were still included in his household.

    Children, born at Pembroke:

    i.   LYDIA LORING[8], b. 23 Sept. 1831, d. E. Boston 5
            Apr. 1905, 73y 6m 2d; m. Lowell MA 9 Feb. 1855
            HODGSON F. BUZZELL, b. Pembroke 18 Dec. 1834,
            son of Abner F. and Betsey (Blaisdell)
            Buzzell. Ch. Ella and Nora.

    ii. (JUSTIN) ATWOOD, b. 7 June 1833, d. Pembroke
14 May 1914, 80y 11m; unm. He was a blacksmith.

788. iii. HENRY ROWLAND, b. 13 Feb. 1835.

    iv. (SAMUEL) LYMAN, b. 22 Feb. 1837, d. Pembroke 18
June 1906; m. 27 Feb. 1869 ELIZABETH KNOWLTON.
No ch. He was a seaman.

    v. (ELIZA) SOPHIA, b. 21 July 1839, d. Pembroke
13 Aug. 1872, 32y (GS); m. COLBY SHRIVER.

    vi. OCTAVIA ANGELINA, b. 28 Sept. 1842, d. in MA in
1931; unm. She had been a Pembroke schoolteacher.

    vii. ISAIAH HERSEY, b. 6 Aug. 1845, d. Pembroke 17
Aug. 1916; m. Eastport 19 Dec. 1874 LOUISA A.
(RANDALL) Wilder, b. 5 Oct. 1846, d. Pembroke
13 Dec. 1916, dau. of Charles and Elizabeth
(McDonald) Randall and widow of Edwin N. Wil-
der. No ch. He was postmaster, W. Pembroke.

    viii. ELLA MEDORA, b. 19 Oct. 1849, d. 19 July 1907;
m. Pembroke 20 Sept. 1869 JOHN LYMAN CAMPBELL,
b. there c1848, res. in MA, son of John and
Sarah L. (Hersey) Campbell. Ch. Dora, Jessie.

327.   **HATEVIL**[7] 1814-1891 [96 Samuel[6] and Tabitha LeSure]
was born at Pembroke 26 Apr. 1814, died at Lawrence MA 28
Dec. 1891 (Leighton, Gen. Sketch, 14-5); married at Pembroke
4 Jan. 1835 BARBARA WALLACE McNUTT, born on Prince Edward
Island 1 Nov. 1816, died at Lawrence 29 Dec. 1891 within an
hour of her husband (Wilder, Pembroke Families).

They were living with their daughter Lucy Dean when they
died. In 1850 he was a farmer at Pembroke, with his father,
71, living with him. In 1860, he was a brickmason at
Machias.

Children. born at West Pembroke (VRs), shown by Wilder as
born at East Machias:

789. i. HARRIET D. NEWELL[8], b. 30 Nov. 1835; m. ROSCOE
G. MITCHELL.

    ii. LUCINDA MARIA, b. 5 Sept. 1837, d. Pembroke 19
Dec. 1850, 13y (GS).

790. iii. HENRY HUDSON, b. 11 Feb. 1840.

791. iv. FRANCES O., b. 19 Dec. 1842; m. JAMES E.
HATHAWAY.

    v. FREDERICK J., b. 23 July 1845, d. Natick MA 12
Nov. 1923; m. Portland ME 16 May 1868 ALMIRA
A. PHINNEY, dau. of David and Almira
(Somersby) Phinney. No ch.

    vi. ELIZA E., b. 7 Feb. 1847, d. in 1938, 91y; m.
Boston 15 Oct. 1881 ZACHARY T. FRENCH, d. in
1935, son of Henry and Emily French (Leighton,
Gen. Sketch, 15). They res. Washington DC.
Ch. Grace Lillian b. Boston, res. Hanover NH;
m. Charles N. Bachelder of Pittsfield NH.

792. vii. GEORGE EDWARD, b. 7 Feb. 1850.

    viii. (MARIA) LUCY, b. 2 July 1852, d. in 1939, 87y;
m. 7 Oct. 1874 AUSTIN DEAN of Andover MA, b.
Frankfort ME in 1852, son of Isaac B. and Mary
A. Dean. Ch. Lena M. b. Lawrence MA, res. No.
Andover; m. James Bowers.

ix.   EVERETT, b. c1855 (5 in 1860), d. aged 13
      (Wilder).
x.   WILLIAM, b. c1857 (Willie, 3 in 1860).
xi.   AUSTIN, d. aged 4 (listed in Wilder).

328.   CHARLES HENRY[7] 1818-1893 [96 Samuel[6] and Tabitha
LeSure] was born at Pembroke 1 May 1818, died at Monmouth ME
11 Sept. 1893, 74y 6m; married at Lisbon ME 10 May 1840 SARAH
JANE McCLELLAN FARNSWORTH, born at Vassalboro ME 20 Sept.
1818 (Farnsworth Mem., 262), died at Monmouth 27 Sept. 1894,
76y 7d, daughter of Cephus and Eunice (Brown) Farnsworth
(town and ME VRs; Wilder, Pembroke Families; Cornman Ms).
Burials are at Monmouth. His death certificate recorded his
parents as Charles and Sarah (Labree) Leighton.
A farmer, he moved to Winthrop in 1848, and to Monmouth in
1855 (Henry H. Cochrane, History of Monmouth and Wales [East
Winthrop, 1894], 2:102, 787). He enlisted 10 Sept. 1862 in
Co. B, 28th ME Inf. Rgt., and was discharged 27 Dec. that
year. Sarah's will was proved 14 Jan. 1895, her son Benjamin
serving as administrator; she left her estate to be shared by
him and Charles.

Children:

793. i.   JAMES WILLIAM[8], b. Pembroke 12 Apr. 1841.
794. ii.   SUSAN O., b. Pembroke 19 Dec. 1843; m. JOHN T.
            LITTLEFIELD.
      iii. CEPHAS H., b. Pembroke 30 Nov. 1845, d. Mon-
            mouth 13 Aug. 1865, of illness contracted
            while in Co. B, 28th ME Inf. Rgt.
      iv.   BENJAMIN FARNSWORTH, b. Pembroke 1 Nov. 1847,
            d. Washington DC 5 July 1921; m. Fairfield ME
            8 Aug. 1879 SARAH FOSS, who d. in 1935, 95y.
            No ch. He was wounded during the Civil War.
            A lawyer and judge, he grad. from National
            Univ. Law School in 1875, and was dean 40 yrs
            of Howard Univ. Law School, and pres., Ameri-
            can Univ. trustees. He donated land for the
            DC Woodside ME Church and Woodside School
            (D. A. B.; Woodside Church records).
795. v.   MARCIA G., b. Pembroke 5 Oct. 1849; m. ALVIN
            BARRON and RANCE V. HAM.
      vi.   ALICE A., b. Winthrop 23 Oct. 1851, res. West
            Sumner ME; m. in Sept. 1875 JAMES BUCK. 1 ch.
796. vii. FANNIE E., b. Winthrop 18 May 1853; m. EDWARD
            BERRY.
      viii. SARAH E. [Sadie], b. Monmouth 29 Dec. 1857,
            res. Franklin MA; m. 1st ---- ; m. 2nd as a
            widow Monmouth 8 Jan. 1893 CHARLES H. UNDER-
            WOOD, b. Boston in 1841, son of William and
            Betsy Underwood of London, England. No ch.
      ix.   CORA BELLE, b. Monmouth 19 Aug. 1861, d. there
            in Dec. 1862.
      x.   CHARLES E., b. Monmouth 10 Feb. 1865, d. Wind-
            sor ME 25 July 1929.

329.   REBECCA B.[7] 1818-1891 [102 Clement[6] and Mary Wilder]
was born at Pembroke 18 Sept. 1818, died 15 Mar. 1891; married at Whiting ME in 1835 GEORGE W. CAMPBELL, born 15 Jan.

1815, died 4 Apr. 1890, son of Benjamin and Margaret Campbell
(Cornman Ms; Forslund, Whiting, 70).

Children (**Campbell**), born probably at Whiting:

i.   BENJAMIN FRANKLIN, b. 30 Oct. 1838, d. 27 June 1899;
       m. ABIGAIL WEDDLE. He served in 36th IL Inf. Rgt.
ii.   EUNICE LUCINDA, b. 15 Aug. 1840, res. Chicago; m.
       DANIEL BURNHAM.
iii.   SAMUEL ARCHIBALD, b. 7 Sept. 1843, res. Whitehall MT;
       unm.
iv.   FREEMAN L., b. 25 Feb. 1845, res. IL; m. MARIA K.
       ---- .
v.   JOSEPHINE M., b. 28 Apr. 1847, res. IL; m. HOSEA
       DeWITT.
vi.   GEORGE E., b. 29 July 1849, d. 30 Mar. 1850.
vii.   JOSEPH EDWARD, b. 25 June 1852, res. Melrose MN; m.
       ALICE CAREY STEWART. He was a physician.
viii. JAMES MELVILLE, b. 1 Aug. 1855, d. 5 Mar. 1880; m.
       MAE WOODRUTH.
ix.   LAURA MAY, b. 3 May 1858; m. JAMES E. GRANT.
x.   CHARLES R., b. 17 Jan. 1860.
xi.   HARRY A., b. 28 Dec. 1862, d. 7 Sept. 1864.

330.   ISAAC C.[7] 1828-1904 [102 Clement[6] and Mary Wilder]
was born at Trescott ME 26 May 1828, died at Machias 20 Aug.
1904, 76y 2m 23d; married there 20 Apr. 1850 (MARY) DEBORAH
VOSE, born there 2 June 1834, died there 24 Jan. 1908, daugh-
ter of Ebenezer and Mary (Baker) Vose (Machias and ME VRs;
Ellen F. Vose, Robert Vose and His Descendants [Boston,
1932], 508-9; George W. Drisko, Narrative of the Town of
Machias [1904], 570). Burials are in Court St. Cemetery,
Machias.
       In 1850 they were living with her parents, he a lumberman.
In 1870 he was a millworker; Eben Vose still lived with them.

Children, born at Machias:

797.   i.   ARABELLA[8], b. 19 Mar. 1851; m. LEVI T. LYON.
798.   ii.   CLARA ELLA, b. 10 May 1853; m. LORING F.
              LAMBERT.
       iii.   MARY IDA, b. 29 Nov., d. 1 Dec., 1855.
799.   iv.   CLARENCE LEMUEL, b. 12 Nov. 1856.
       v.   ARTHUR MELVIN, b. 1 Sept. 1858, d. in 1922
              (GS); m. ANGIE FOSS; probably m. 2nd MARY
              McFARLAND. He res. Brockton MA in 1900 alone
              with son (JOSEPH) IRVING FOSS[9] b. Snohomish WA
              21 Dec. 1893 (his mother was Mary McFarland
              on his birth record).
800.   vi.   IDA MAY, b. 14 July 1860; m. FRED M. BEVERLY.
801.   vii.   CORA EUNICE, b. 16 June 1862; m. GEORGE KANE.
       viii. (LINCOLN) ISAAC, b. 10 Mar. 1865, d. Machias 18
              Mar. 1941 (GS); m. Brookline MA 28 Aug. 1890
              JENNIE THOMAS, b. there in Sept. 1868, dau. of
              Patrick and Mary Thomas. He was a carpenter.
              Ch. ERWIN L.[9] b. 23 Dec. 1894.
       ix.   WILLIAM CLEMENT, b. 27 Mar. 1867, d. Machias 31
              Mar. 1930, 63y 2d; m. 1st there 27 Nov. 1889
              CORRIS E. MITCHELL, b. there 12 July 1869, d.
              there 21 Jan. 1915, dau. of William and Ellen

(Stuart) Mitchell; m. 2nd Bangor 28 Dec. 1918
LULU M. (DENNISON) Williams, b. Cutler ME
c1887, dau. of Orlando and Mary A. (Wright)
Dennison. No ch. He was a clothier. Lulu m.
1st 29 Nov. 1905 Gilman N. Williams of Cutler;
and m. 3rd Machias 9 June 1934 William H.
Clarke of Andover MA.
    x.   IRVING FARRELL, b. 23 Nov. 1869 (Urban, b. in
        Oct. 1869, 1880 census), d. 25 Apr. 1890; unm.
802. xi. CLINTON JOHN, b. 6 Apr. 1872.
    xii. EDITH TROWBRIDGE, b. 21 Mar. 1876, d. 8 June
        1895, 19y; unm.

331. JOSEPH HATEVIL[7] 1831-1904 [102 Clement[6] and Mary Wil-
der] was born at Trescott (as Hatevil Joseph) 30 Mar. 1831,
died at Machias 14 Mar. 1904, 72y 11m 14d; married there 2
Aug. 1851 SUSAN ADELAIDE VOSE, born there 8 May 1836, died at
Minneapolis MN 29 Apr. 1925, daughter of Ebenezer and Mary
(Baker) Vose (Vose Desc., 509-10; Machias VRs). Both are
buried in the Court St. Cemetery, Machias.
He worked in the lumber mills, and became superintendent of
the Machias Sawmills. In 1907, Susan went to MN with her son
Joseph (Cornman Ms).

Children, born at Machias:

803. i.   HORACE NEWELL[8], b. 8 Jan. 1853.
804. ii.   JOSEPHINA ERMINA, b. 21 May 1854; m. WILLIAM
           H. LYON.
805. iii. EBEN EVERETT, b. 10 Nov. 1856.
    iv.   MARY ADDIE, b. 30 Mar., d. 21 Oct., 1858.
806. v.   GEORGE ADDI, b. 29 July 1860.
807. vi.   FREDERICK ARBA, b. 5 Mar. 1864.
808. vii. JOSEPH LEROY, b. 9 Dec. 1869.
    viii. CARROLL, b. 31 July, d. 2 Aug., 1875.

332. JAMES HENRY[7] 1831-   [102 Clement[6] and Mary Wilder]
was born at Trescott 30 Mar. 1831, lived at Minneapolis MN in
1900; married first JOANNA F. BRIDGES, born in ME, d. St.
Anthony MN 4 Oct. 1856 (her obituary, Machias Union), daughter of Abraham and Ruth Bridges of Marion (Wilder, Pembroke
Families); married second MARY ---- , born in ME in Aug. 1843
(1900 census).

Child by Mary, born in MN (1900 census):

    i.   WILLIAM E.[8], b. in Aug. 1863, res. Minnea-
        polis in 1900 with ch. MYRA E.[9] b. in Sept.
        1882 and EDDIE M. b. in Nov. 1884.

333. EPHRAIM FRANKLIN[7] 1835-   [102 Clement[6] and Mary
Wilder] was born at Trescott 15 Jan. 1835, lived at Min-
neapolis MN in 1900; married JANE C. STILSON, born in IL in
Aug. 1845 (1900 census).
In 1850 he was 16, and living with his brother James at
Machias; in 1880 he was listed at Stillwater MN. In 1900 his
household included "son-in-law" George Y. Leighton, born in
IL in Feb. 1865--more probably a step-son.

Children, born in MN (1880 and 1900 censuses):

    i.   HATTIE E.[8], b. about 1867 (13 in 1880).
    ii.   JOSEPHINE L., b. about 1868 (12 in 1880).
    iii. EVELYN, b. about 1870 (10 in 1880).
    iv.   LAURA M., b. in Mar. 1875.
    v.   FRANKLIN H., b. about 1875 (5 in 1880).
    vi.   MINNIE C., b. in Apr. 1877.
    vii. BERTIE E., b. in Apr. 1886.

334. WILLIAM H.[7] 1818-1899 [105 Elijah[6] and Mary Ann
Saunders] was born at Trescott ME 29 Apr. 1818, died there 14
Aug. 1899, 81y 2m 16d; married MARGARET KELLEY, born at Trescott in Jan. 1823, died at Lubec ME 10 Sept. 1902, 78y 6m
10d, daughter of John and Rosie (Owens) Kelley (Trescott VRs;
Cornman Ms--in which the birth dates conflict with those in
the town records and with ages as given in the 1850 and 1860
censuses).
William was a ship's carpenter and a master mariner at
Trescott, and was called "Capt. Leighton." He was guardian
to his nephews James E. and Frank Leighton.

Children, born at Trescott (VRs):

        i.   WILLIAM W.[8], b. 27 Apr., d. 1 May, 1841.
809. ii.   (ARVILLA) ROBERTA, b. 18 May 1843; m. THOMAS
             M. KNIGHT.
810. iii. DAMIETTA, b. 23 May 1843; m. DANIEL LAMSON.
        iv.   MALVINA, b. 9 Apr. 1847; m. 26 Nov. 1871
             HORACE LUDGATE, b. Tower Hill NB 26 Jan. 1849.
             Ch. Verdi b. Lubec 7 Apr. 1873; m. Addie E.
             Dougherty in 1901: no ch.
        v.   (WHITMORE) WILLIAM, b. 6 July 1851, d. Trescott
             4 Nov. 1884; m. Lubec 24 Feb. 1877 MARY ETTA
             SMALL, b. c1857. Ch. MARY[9] b. c1879 (1 in
             1880), probably d.y.
        vi.   MARY LOUISE, b. 17 Apr. 1853, d. Trescott
             1 Oct. 1867 (Machias Union).
        vii. LORING FILMORE, b. 31 May 1855, d. 28 Jan.
             1886.
        viii. IDA AROLYN, b. 16 Mar. 1860; m. FRANK[8] LEIGHTON
             [# 814].
811. ix.   FRED S., b. c1875.

335. ELSAIDE[7] 1820-   [105 Elijah[6] and Mary Ann
Saunders] was born at Trescott 15 Jan. 1820, died about 1860;
married at Marion ME JACKSON BRIDGES, born in 1820 (Trescott
VRs; Cornman Ms).
In 1850, Jackson's wife was Mary J. ---- , aged 25.

Children (**Bridges**), born at Trescott, mothers uncertain:

    i.   MARY OLIVE, b. 21 June 1851.
    ii.   LYMAN R., b. 8 Dec. 1852.
    iii. LYDIA ANN, b. 3 June 1856.
    iv.   CHARLES W., b. in 1858.
    v.   dau., b. in 1860.

336. JAMES EVERETT[7] 1822-1866 [105 Elijah[6] and Mary Ann
Saunders] was born at Trescott 4 Feb. 1822, died there 12
Feb. 1866 (per widow; 13 Feb., 44y, Machias Union); married
there 3 Sept. 1845 MELINDA SIMPSON, born at Campobello NB
about 1828 (42 in 1870), died at Trescott 2 June 1874. He
was a carpenter.
He enlisted 10 Sept. 1862 in Co. C, 28th ME inf. Rgt., and
was discharged 31 Aug. 1863, after contracting a liver disease (malaria) at New Orleans.
His widow Melinda, aged 41 of Trescott, applied for a pension 4 Jan. 1869, providing dates of her marriage and James's
death. On 27 Feb. 1875, William H. Leighton [# 334] made a
pension application on behalf of minors James E. and Frank,
with an affidavit of Melinda's death (NA-MSR).
Forslund's Whiting (p. 21) mixed him with James[8] [# 773].

Children:

	i.	DANIEL[8].
812.	ii.	SAMUEL, b. Trescott 7 July 1847.
813.	iii.	WILLIAM H., b. Trescott 22 Apr. 1849.
	iv.	JAMES, b. Trescott 3 Mar., d. 6 Mar., 1851.
	v.	MARY, b. 27 Jan. 1854, not in 1860 census.
	vi.	JAMES E., b. in 1858; m. AMY ---- .
	vii.	EMMA, b. in 1860.
814.	viii.	FRANK SHERMAN, b. 15 Nov. 1864.
	ix.	?NELSON (listed in Forslund, Whiting, but not elsewhere).

337. ELEANOR[7] 1824-1851 [105 Elijah[6] and Mary Ann Saunders]
was born at Trescott 17 Mar. 1824, died there 27 Sept. 1851;
married 13 June 1850 JACOB SILVA of Cutler (Trescott VRs),
born about 1826 (34 in 1860). He was Jacob Wilson on their
marriage record. Jacob's surname was spelled Silver, Sil-
vere, Silvy, and--in the Cornman Ms--Alvin. He married
again; his wife in 1860 was Mary, 33, born in NB.
In 1850 he and Eleanor were in Elijah's household; in 1860
Jacob and his wife Mary were living there with children
Edwin, 10, Nancy born 4 Jan. 1855, and Charles E. born about
1857 (3 in 1860). A daughter Mary E. died 24 Dec. 1853.

Child (**Sylva**), born at Trescott:

i.   LEWIS EDWIN, b. 2 Aug. 1850 (Edwin in 1860).

338. (MARY) CORDELIA[7] 1831-   [105 Elijah[6] and Mary Ann
Saunders] was born at Trescott in 1831; married there 12
Sept. 1850 HENRY RICHARDSON of Whiting (Cornman Ms; records
of descendant Frank C. Morrone).

Children (**Richardson**), perhaps others:

i.   STEPHEN HENRY, b. Trescott 21 or 24 Feb. 1853, d.
      Machias 7 Dec. 1910; m. E. Machias 28 Dec. 1874
      ELVIRA JANE CATES, b Cutler 7 Apr. 1853, d. Machias
      23 Sept. 1938, dau. of Ellery and Abigail (Huntley)
      Cates.
ii.   ABRAM.

iii. DORA M., b. Trescott in 1862, d. Portland 28 Nov.
      1895, 33y 7m; m. in 1892 HENRY K. NOYES, b. Falmouth
      25 Jan. 1869, son of Frank P. and Susan (Lord) Noyes
      (Noyes Gen., 1:146).
iv. LLEWELLYN.

339. STEPHEN S.[7] 1833-1893 [105 Elijah[6] and Mary Ann
Saunders] was born at Trescott 1 Dec. 1833 (VRs), died there
31 Aug. 1893, 59y 9m; married there 2 Sept. 1861 (Machias
Union) MARIETTA SAUNDERS, born there 23 Jan. 1844, died at
Lubec 1 Mar. 1923, 80y 1m 8d, daughter of William and Mary
(Lancaster) Saunders (Trescott and ME VRs). His father was
living in their household in 1880.

Children, born at Trescott:

    i.   ALVIN A.[8], b. in Mar. 1863, res. Morse, St.
          Louis Co. MN in 1900; m. MARY SHOWERS, b. in
          Germany in Feb. 1869. In 1900 his household
          included his mother "Mary E." and sister-in-
          law Anna Showers, b. in MN in Apr. 1882.
815. ii.   MINNIE M., b. in Aug. 1864; m. GEORGE S. PERRY.
816. iii. MELVIN, b. in 1866.
    iv. JENNIE, b. in 1878.

340. ABIJAH[7] 1806-1872 [106 Samuel[6] and Jane Cochrane]
was born at Eastport 7 Sept. 1806, died there 14 May 1874,
68y; married first at Dennysville 3 Mar. 1828 HANNAH HERSEY,
born at Pembroke 22 Jan. 1806, died there 2 Sept. 1831,
daughter of Adna and Sarah[6] (Leighton) Hersey [# 94]; married
second at Lubec 25 Apr. 1832 ELIZABETH [Betsey] GOVE, born
there 8 Mar. 1808, died at Eastport 11 July 1842, daughter of
Jacob and Martha (Bacon) Gove (Gove Book, 161); married third
at Eastport 13 July 1848 (28 Nov., Cornman Ms) (LYDIA) ELIZA
PHELPS, born at Lubec 25 Oct. 1826, died at Eastport 18 Sept.
1891, 65y (town VRs; Wilder, Pembroke Families; Cornman Ms).
  Most of his children's births were posted in the Eastport
records. He moved to Eastport from Dennysville about the
time he married Elizabeth, and was a boatbuilder there in
1850, and a shipbuilder in 1870.

Children by Hannah, born at Pembroke:

    i.   SARAH JANE[8], b. 15 Feb. 1829, d. Pembroke 14
          Jan. 1854; m. JOHN GUNNISON LOWE, b. there in
          Jan. 1829, son of William Lowe. Ch. William
          E. d. 4 Feb. 1854, 5 wks. Lowe m. 2nd Caro-
          line Matilda Hersey, and 3rd Roxie Hamilton.
817. ii.   ALICE MARIE, b. 18 Oct. 1830; m. JOHN McKINLEY.

Children by Elizabeth, born at Pembroke:

818. iii. JAMES ONSVILLE, b. 18 Aug. 1833.
    iv. MELINDA ANN, b. in Mar. 1836, d. in Sept. 1841.
    v.   LUCY ELLEN, b. in Sept. 1840.

Children by Eliza, born at Eastport:

> vii.   CASSIE M., b. 11 Aug. 1850 (Amanda, 1/12 in
>   1850).
> viii. EMMA LIZZIE (Elizabeth, 17, in 1870), b. 7 Mar.
>   1853, d. 15 Mar. 1878; m. A. L. BLANCHARD.
> ix.   ANNIE L., b. 5 Mar. 1857.
> x.   JENNIE B., b. 26 Jan. 1859; m. Bangor 11 Apr.
>   1902 CHARLES F. FERRIS, b. Eastport in 1863,
>   son of John A. and Phoebe (Chaffey) Ferris.
>   He was an undertaker at Bangor.
> xi.   MARY B., b. 9 June 1861; m. Portland 15 Jan.
>   1914 ROBERT W. PETERSON, b. Plymouth MA c1843,
>   son of Lewis and Charlotte (Manter) Peterson.
>   In 1900 she had lived at Eastport with sister
>   Jennie and niece Esther Greenlaw, 14.

341. SARAH LYDIA[7] 1808-1855 [106 Samuel[6] and Jane Cochrane] was born at Eastport 30 Dec. 1808, died there 30 June 1855; married there 5 Jan. 1838 JOHN CAPEN, born at Portland ME 26 July 1801, died at Pembroke 7 Aug. 1869, son of Alexander and Jane (Kenwood) Capen (Charles Albert Capen, The Capen Family [1929], 175; Cornman Papers).
Capen was a joiner at Eastport in 1850.

Children (**Capen**), born at Eastport:

> i.   JANE MARIE [Jennie], b. 12 Aug. 1840, d. 26 Aug.
>   1869; m. GILBERT GREEN of Letete NB.
> ii.   MARY ELIZA, b. 3 Aug. 1844; m. Eastport 13 Feb. 1866
>   WILLIAM DEAN.
> iii.   CYRUS, b. 28 Dec. 1845, d. 15 May 1871; m. 28 June
>   1869 ABBIE ANN PHILBROOK of Biddeford, b. 3 Apr.
>   1849, dau. of John Marston and Ann Maria (Hazlitt)
>   Philbrook. She m. 2nd 8 Jan. 1874 Dr. George L.
>   Peaslee of Milton NH; her son Cyrus Capen was then
>   renamed Cyrus Peaslee.
> iv.   FRANK, b. 11 Sept. 1847, d. 11 June 1848.
> v.   SARAH ADELIA, b. 17 Feb. 1849; m. WILLIAM AUSTIN.
> vi.   DAVID ROSS, b. 28 Mar. 1852, d. 19 Oct. 1932; m. 6
>   July 1875 SARAH ANN DEAN, b. Pembroke 13 Nov. 1852,
>   d. Eastport 13 Nov. 1927, dau. of William and Jane
>   (Phillips) Dean.

342. SAMUEL[7] 1811-   [106 Samuel[6] and Jane Cochrane] was born at Eastport 5 June 1811; married ABIGAIL ---- , born about 1819 (31 in 1850). He was a shipmaster, 36, at Eastport in 1850. In his household was Juliette P. Ring, 39, perhaps a sister-in-law. He later lived at Boston and NYC.

Children, perhaps others:

> i.   JAMES[8], b. c1840 (10 in 1850).
> ii.   EDGAR. b. c1844 (6 in 1850).

343. GEORGE[7] 1820-1876 [106 Samuel[6] and Jane Cochrane] was born at Eastport 9 Apr. 1820, died at Lowell MA 28 Aug. 1876; married first at Eastport 25 Nov. 1844 MARY MARTHA LINCOLN,

born 4 Oct. 1819, died at Eastport 7 Dec. 1849, daughter of
Solomon and Eleanor M. (Gove) Lincoln; married second at
Eastport 25 Apr. 1852 ELIZABETH LINCOLN, born 28 July 1824,
living at Chelmsford MA in 1911, sister of Mary (Eastport
VRs; Lincoln Desc., 301-2).
In 1850 he was a seaman at Eastport with his father; he
moved to Lowell about 1860, where he worked as a carpenter.

Children by Mary, born at Eastport:

    i.   MARY MARTHA[8] (Melissa M. in 1850 census), b.
         22 Feb. 1846; m. WILLIAM JOHN WOOD.
    ii.   FREDERICK, b. in Apr. 1848, d. 15 Oct. 1849.

Children by Elizabeth:

    iii. child, b. Eastport 21 Aug., d. 27 Aug., 1853.
    iv.   SARAH CAPEN, b. Eastport 8 Dec. 1855, living in
         1911; unm.
    v.   ELLEN ELIZA, b. Eastport 1 Aug. 1858, d. there
         11 May 1860.
    vi.   LUCY JANE [Jennie], b. Lowell 17 Nov. 1861; d.
         20 Oct. 1889; unm.
    vii. ELLEN ELIZABETH, b. Lowell 10 Jan., d. 4 Aug.,
         1864.

344. ALMIRA D.[7] 1812-1886 [108 Mark[6] and Olivia Wentworth]
was born at Eastport (Perry VRs) 5 Apr. 1812, died at Perry
14 Jan. 1886; married 22 Aug. 1833 THOMAS HIBBARD, born about
1807, died at Perry 24 Dec. 1890 (Wilder, Pembroke Families;
Perry VRs; Cornman Ms). He was a farmer, 43, at Perry in
1850.

Children (**Hibbard**), born at Perry:

    i.   GEORGE L., b. 7 Feb. 1834, d. Perry 18 Mar. 1894; m.
         LUCY E. TROTT.
    ii.   OLIVIA JANE, b. 9 Aug. 1835; m. 1st Perry 27 Sept.
         1854 JACOB FOSTER GOVE, b. there 12 July 1829, d.
         there 7 Feb. 1894, son of Jacob and Martha Jane
         (Tumblesome) Gove (Gove Book, 279, 407); m. 2nd
         Rockland 10 Apr. 1905 GEORGE ROBERTS.
    iii. CLARA ALMIRA, b. 13 Sept. 1844, d. 9 May 1908; m.
         Perry 25 Oct. 1864 GEORGE EDWARD GOVE, b. Perry
         28 Dec. 1841, also son of Jacob. No ch.
    iv.   DANIEL F., b. 14 Apr. 1849; m. MATILDA JOHNSON, who
         d. 25 Sept. 1912.
    v.   ALBERT WARREN, b. 9 Dec. 1853; m. CATHERINE MARIE
         LORING.

345. SARAH RICHARD[7] 1814-   [108 Mark[6] and Olivia Went-
worth] was born at Perry 3 Apr. 1814, lived there in 1850;
married HENRY FROST, who died at Perry 9 Mar. 1871. He had
three children by a first wife Lucy (Perry VRS; Cornman Ms).

Children (**Frost**), born at Perry:

    i.   WILLIAM HENRY, b. 7 Nov. 1853; m. EMMA REYNOLDS.
    ii.   MARY OLIVIA, b. 25 July 1855; unm.

iii. SALINA, b. 7 Jan., d. 16 Jan., 1857.
iv.   ALICE J., b. 22 Jan. 1862, d. 11 Sept. 1889; m. ----
      ABBOTT of Lowell MA.

346. JOHN D.[7] 1816-1866 [108 Mark[6] and Olivia Wentworth]
was born at Perry (Eastport VRs) 10 Apr. 1816, died there 26
Apr. 1866; married first 15 Oct. 1843 LOUISA FROST, born
about 1820, died at Perry 30 Mar. 1860, 39y 6m; married second at Perry 18 Nov. 1860 SARAH O. LELAND (Perry VRs; Cornman
Ms). Three children died during one month in a diphtheria
epidemic.

Children by Louisa, born at Perry:

819. i.   SARAH ELIZA[8], b. 20 June 1844; m. ROBERT SPROUL
            and MERTON NUTT.
      ii.   HANNAH LOUISA, b. 11 Sept. 1846, d. 9 Apr.
            1850.
      iii. SILAS B. MAYBERRY, b. 18 Oct. 1848, d. 14 Apr.
            1850.
      iv.   LOUISA HANNAH, b. 8 Aug. 1852; unm.
      v.   ABBA, b. 9 Sept. 1853, d. 13 Oct. 1861, 8y.
      vi.   HELEN, b. 17 Nov. 1855, d. 11 Oct. 1861, 6y.
      vii. LAURA E., b. 28 Feb. 1858, d. 31 Mar. 1860.
      viii. DELESSIE (male), b. Mar. 1860, d. 9 Oct. 1861.

Children by Sarah, born at Perry:

      ix.   JOHN LELAND, b. 27 Sept. 1861; unm.
      x.   FRANK D., b. 17 Mar. 1863, res. Manchester NH
            in 1900; married Eastport 27 Apr. 1891 MINNIE
            HICKEY, born in ME in Apr. 1871. Ch. MAR-
            JORIE[9] b. in Aug. 1892. With them in
            1900 was sister-in-law Margaret Ribble, born
            in ME in June 1868.
      xi.   HENRY H., b. 12 Oct. 1866 (posthumous); unm.

347. EMILY[7] 1818-   [108 Mark[6] and Olivia Wentworth] was
born at Perry 15 Dec. 1818; married first JAMES MAHAR; married second ANDROS ELDRIDGE of Grand Manan NB (Perry VRs;
Cornman Papers--which contain incorrect data).
    Eldridge had five children by a first wife, born at Grand
Manan and listed in the Perry VRs.

Children (**Mahar**), born at Perry:

i.   JEFFERSON, b. 22 Mar., d. 17 Apr., 1838.
ii.   JOHN D., b. 17 May 1839, d. 26 Mar. 1850.
iii. EMILY, b. 17 Oct. 1841.
iv.   POLK, b. 1 Sept. 1844.
v.   MARK L., res. Lorain OH (Cornman Papers).

Children (**Eldridge**), born at Perry:

vi.   EUNICE OLIVIA, b. 27 Mar., d. 16 Aug., 1854.
vii. CORA ANN, b. 26 Feb. 1856.
viii. CHARLOTTE OLIVIA, b. 18 Aug. 1860, res. St. Stephen
      NB; m. NELSON BEACH.

348. THOMAS PARKER[7] 1820-1855 [108 Mark[6] and Olivia Wentworth] was born at Perry 7 Feb. 1820, died 28 Feb. 1855 (probate record); married first in May 1846 SALOME KENDALL, born at Perry 16 Mar. 1827, daughter of Benjamin and Elizabeth Kendall; married second at Perry 4 July 1848 SARAH C. KENDALL, born there 18 May 1831, sister of Salome.

Widow Sarah was made administratrix of Thomas's estate 7 Apr. 1857; an inventory taken 3 June 1858 showed no real property, and assets of $55 (WashCP, III:137; 20:435). She married second ---- TRAINOR, moved to Lowell MA, and then to Omaha NE (Cornman Ms).

Children, all by Sarah, born at Perry:

    i.   NANCY OLIVIA[8], b. 26 Feb. 1851, d. 16 June
         1852.
    ii. SAMUEL W., b. 26 Nov. 1853, d.y.
    iii. ISABELLA, d. infant.
    iv. BENTON, d. infant.
    v.   SAMUEL, probably went west with mother.

349. NANCY[7] 1823-   [108 Mark[6] and Olivia Wentworth] was born at Perry 21 May 1823, perhaps lived in IN; married DANIEL HIBBARD (Cornman Ms).

Children (**Hibbard**):

    i.   child, d.y.
    ii. CAROLINE; m. Detroit MI JOHN LEONE.

350. MARK[7] 1826-1912 [108 Mark[6] and Olivia Wentworth] was born at Perry 13 July 1826, died there 6 Oct. 1912, 86y 1m 24d; married first 18 Oct. 1849 MARIA HIBBARD, born 14 Oct. 1829, died at Perry 10 Apr. 1852; married second 4 Oct. 1852 SARAH J. HIBBARD, born at Perry 13 Apr. 1834, died there 25 Jan. 1909, 74y 9m 12d, daughter of John and Eliza (Smith) Hibbard (Perry and ME VRs; Cornman Ms).

He was a farmer and mill worker. In 1880 his daughter Jennie and her husband were in his household.

Child by Maria, born at Perry:

820. i.   JOHN H.[8], b. 14 Apr. 1850.

Children by Sarah, born at Perry:

    ii. LOVINA/LAVINIA MARIA, b. 6 Nov. 1853; m. ELMER
         SHAFF. They had 4 or 5 ch.
    iii. NANCY JANE [Jennie], b. 17 June 1855; m.
         JESSE[8] LEIGHTON [# 1096] and WILLIAM D.
         FROTHINGHAM.

351. CHARLOTTE OLIVIA[7] 1833-   [108 Mark[6] and Olivia Wentworth] was born at Perry 27 Oct. 1833, lived there in 1910; married at Perry 16 Dec. 1852 JOSHUA COGGIN GOVE, born at Lubec 3 Nov. 1826, died at Perry 19 Apr. 1902, son of Jacob and Martha Jane (Tumblesome) Gove (Gove Book, 406-7).

Joshua was a sea captain in 1853, and later a merchant at
Perry. He served as town selectman and in other posts.

Children (**Gove**), born at Perry:

i.   MARY EMMA, b. 25 Oct. 1853; m. 12 Mar. 1875 CLARENCE
      GOULDEN.
ii.   IDA ELLA, b. 19 Feb. 1856; m. 1 Oct. 1879 FRANK
      WILLIS of Rockland.
iii. FRANK LEIGHTON, b. 15 Aug. 1858, drowned in Lake Erie
      11 May 1899; m. 2 Dec. 1882 EMMA FROST, b. Perry in
      Aug. 1858, d. there 6 July 1892, dau. of Daniel D.
      and Elizabeth B. (Bulmer) Frost.
iv.   CHARLOTTE MABEL [Carlotta], b. 3 June 1861, res.
      Lorain OH; m. NEWELL GLADING.
v.   FRED FOSTER, b. 20 Aug. 1865; m. Lorain OH 5 Sept.
      1884 SARAH A. GLADING.
vi.   GEORGE EDWARD, b. 10 Sept. 1867; unm.
vii. HIRAM LEANDER, b. 15 Jan. 1871; m. Perry 2 May 1895
      LAVINIA M. [Vinnie] SELLWOOD, b. Perry c1874,
      dau. of Walter B. and Eliza (Bennett) Sellwood.

352.   GEORGE NATHANIEL[7] 1841-1893 [111 Nathaniel[6] and Mary
Getchell] was born at Milan, Ripley Co. IN 14 July 1841,
died at Chicago 30 Nov. 1893; married at Cincinnati OH 28
Nov. 1866 JULIA A. DENNISON, born in Jan. 1848, living in
1902 (data from his widow Julia--Cornman Papers).

Children, born in OH:

      i.   LELIA MAUDE[8], b. Cincinnati 21 Sept. 1867, d.
            27 Sept. 1868.
      ii.   PEARL, b. Home City OH 11 Mar., d. 16 July,
            1872.
821. iii. EDITH MYRTLE, b. Home City 19 Dec. 1874; m.
            HAROLD BROWNE.
      iv.   MARY ALICE, b. Home City 11 July 1877, d. 25
            Oct. 1878.
      v.   EVERETT HERBERT, b. Home City 30 June 1880.
822. vi.   MARIA LOUISE, b. Home City 18 May 1883; m.
            WALTER LEE.

353.   JOSEPH[7] 1843-1893 [111 Nathaniel[6] and Mary Getchell]
was born at Milan IN 14 Aug. 1843, died at Toledo OH 26 Sept.
1893, 50y 1m 12d (probate record); married at Covington KY 11
Feb. 1873 (pension file) OLIVE J. WOODWARD, born about 1853
(42 in 1895).
   He enlisted at Indianapolis 19 June 1861 in Co. I, 13th IN
Inf. Rgt. He was taken prisoner in Oct. 1861, and paroled
the next year. After returning to duty, he was wounded during the seige of Suffolk VA, and was in military hospitals
until his discharge 30 June 1864. He became a physician,
living in KY, KS, IN and from 1888 on at Toledo.
   He applied for a pension, aged 46 of Toledo, 12 June 1890,
and his widow Olive applied 22 Nov. 1895, aged 42. Her
statement named her two living children under 16 at their
father's death. Since payments to her were discontinued in
1905, she must have by then remarried or died (NA-MSR
#782-862 and #395-679).

Children (per pension record), perhaps others:

  i.   CORA M.^{8}, b. 3 Nov. 1884.
  ii.   ALICE P., b. 6 June 1893.

354. DAVID GARDINER^7 1845-   [111 Nathaniel^6 and Mary Getchell] was born at Milan IN 18 Aug. 1845, living in 1902 when he wrote to Julia Cornman; married 11 Apr. 1871 MARGARET E. RICHARDSON, born in 1847 (Cornman Papers).

Children:

  i.   LILLIAN MAY^8, b. 16 Dec. 1872; m. 11 Dec. 1892
       BENJAMIN FRANKLIN ROSER.
  ii.   ORA LEE, b. 11 Mar. 1874, d. 18 Apr. 1892; m.
       9 Dec. 1891 ALBERT H. HOVER.

355. NATHANIEL^7 1849-1902 [111 Nathaniel^6 and Mary Getchell] was born at Milan IN 2 Nov. 1849, died at Cincinnati OH 2 Nov. 1902, struck by a runaway horse; married 20 Feb. 1870 ELIZA J. CONGER, born at Aurora IN 12 Oct. 1851, daughter of George W. and Lovina J. (Dean) Conger (letter from widow Eliza in 1914--Cornman Papers). He was wounded while in the 4th OH Cav. Rgt. He was a liveryman.

  i.   EDWARD^8, b. 10 July 1871, living unm. with
       mother in 1914. He served in US Army Hospital
       Corps during Spanish-American War.
  ii.   FRANK EVERETT, b. 18 June 1875, d. 26 June
       1876.

356. SUSAN^7 1805-   [113 Thomas^6 and Mary Pearl] was born at Mount Vernon ME 7 Dec. 1805; married at Mt. Vernon 22 Feb. 1827 (int. Gardiner 7 Jan.) JAMES LAWRENCE, born 5 Feb. 1795, died at Gardiner 28 Feb. 1875, 80y 20d, son of David and Elizabeth (Eastman) Lawrence (town VRs; Lawrence Gen., 152; Cornman Ms).

Children (**Lawrence**):

  i.   ELLIS DELANO^8, b. Gardiner 15 Sept. 1828.
  ii.   JAMES WARREN, b. Gardiner 29 Nov. 1832.
  iii. VESTA LOUISE, b. 5 Mar. 1843, res. WI; m. ----
       CONDREY.

357. WARNER B.^{7} 1808-1896 [113 Thomas^6 and Mary Pearl] was born at Mount Vernon 15 May 1808, died there 2 Aug. 1896, 88y 2m 16d; married there 3 Mar. 1850 his double cousin SARAH JANE LEIGHTON, born there 8 May 1828, daughter of Joseph and Hannah (Pearl) Leighton [# 114] (Mt. Vernon VRs). Burials are in the Bean cemetery, Mt. Vernon. Sarah Jane married second CHESMAN ROBINSON (Cornman Ms).

Children, born at Mt. Vernon:

  i.   DELANO W.^{8}, b. 25 Jan. 1851, d. 18 Dec. 1863,
       12y (GS).

    ii.   JAMES WARREN, b. 14 Nov. 1854, d. 19 June 1862,
        7y 7m 4d (GS).

358. ELIZA ANN[7] 1812-1897 [113 Thomas[6] and Mary Pearl] was
born at Mount Vernon 12 Sept. 1812, died there 4 Apr. 1897,
84y 7m (GS); married there 30 Apr. 1837 NATHANIEL T. ROBIN-
SON, born 30 Apr. 1813, died at Mt. Vernon 27 Jan. 1888, 75y
(GS), son of James and Phebe Robinson (Mt. Vernon VRs; Cornman Ms). Burials are in the Bean cemetery.
    In 1850 their household at Mt. Vernon included her father
Thomas, 79, and her sister Sally Leighton, 47.

Children (**Robinson**), born at Mt Vernon:

    i.   CHARLOTTE [Lottie], b. in 1838 (12 in 1850); m. ----
         TOWLE and ---- SHERBURN.
    ii.   JAMES FRANK, m. 14 Feb. 1862 RUTH[8] LEIGHTON [# 604].
    iii. THOMAS, b. c1843 (7 in 1850), d. Mt. Vernon 20 May
         1888, 45y.

359. JOHN SMITHSON[7] 1805-1855 [114 Joseph[6] and Hannah
Pearl] was born at Mount Vernon 8 Feb. 1805, died at Augusta
21 June 1855, 50y 4m 21d (23 June, probate file); married 22
Sept. 1833 SUSAN HALEY, born at Kittery ME 10 Apr. 1810, died
at Augusta 21 Dec. 1859, 49y 9m 14d, daughter of Thomas and
Lucy Haley (town VRs).
    In 1839 he sold to his brother Benjamin half of lot 180 at
Mt. Vernon, which he had bought from his father (KennCD,
119:464).
    He was a "trader" or grocer at Augusta in 1850.
    His widow Susan was appointed administrator of his estate 4
July 1855. An inventory, made 27 July, included his home,
his store, 35 acres of land, a long "grocery list" of stock
on hand, and a still longer list of the many customers owing
him money (KennCP, 1855).

Children, born at Augusta:

823. i.   NEWBURY H.[8], b. 21 Nov. 1834.
      ii.   JULIAN MORRELL, b. in 1839, d. Augusta 25 May
          1843, 4y 11m.
824. iii. FAUSTINA, b. in 1845; m. THOMAS J. PETTIGREW.

360. JOSEPH[7] 1806-1873 [114 Joseph[6] and Hannah Pearl] was
born at Mount Vernon 30 Aug. 1806, died there 19 Feb. 1873
(GS); married there 3 Sept. 1829 POLLY McGAFFEY, born there
31 Aug. 1810, died at Augusta 14 Mar. 1894, 83y 6m 13d,
daughter of James and Sally (Bean) McGaffey (Mt. Vernon and
Augusta VRs). Burials are in Bean Cemetery.
    He was a farmer. In 1840 he and Benjamin gave bond to sup-
port their father (KennCD, 122:149). Joseph died intestate;
his son Moses was appointed administrator 24 Mar. 1873. The
probate file named widow Polly and four adult children:
Moses, Sally Brown, William, and Lydia Cole. Polly's will,
probated 11 Mar. 1895, named Moses, her executor, and the
other surviving children.

Children, born at Mt. Vernon:

     i.   JAMES MADISON[8], b. 28 Dec. 1829, d. 12 Nov.
          1892; m. MARIA AMELIA CODDING. No ch. He
          res. IL and was a captain during the Civil War
          (Cornman Ms).

825. ii. MOSES R., b. 23 June 1832.
826. iii. SALLY M., b. 16 Apr. 1834; m. EBEN M. BROWN.
     iv. WILLIAM H., b. 23 Feb. 1836, d. Mt. Vernon 5
          Dec. 1898, 63y 9m 12d; m. 1st there 22 Oct.
          1853 JANE M. TRASK, d. 1 Mar. 1876, 39y; m.
          2nd Mt. Vernon 13 Nov. 1878 MARY ANN McGAFFEY,
          b. 1 Nov. 1838, d. 25 Sept. 1901. No ch.
          In his will, made 26 Sept. 1897 and proved
          9 Jan. 1899, he left his estate, including a
          93-acre homestead, to Mrs. Lizzie Ellen Worth-
          ing. He was a bridge-building contractor for
          the NY Central RR until his retirement to Mt.
          Vernon in 1873 (Kingsbury, Hist. Kennebec
          Co., 2:496).
     v.   MARTHA, b. 19 July 1838, d. 28 Jan. 1864; m.
          Mt. Vernon int. 17 Jan. 1857 RUSSELL A.
          PORTER of Vienna. Only ch. Fred M. b. 13 Oct.
          1857, drowned Salamanca NY 27 Jan. 1882.
     vi. LYDIA ANN, b. 1 Sept. 1840, res. Mt. Vernon in
          1908 (Town Register); m. 16 May 1861 SUMNER
          COLE. Ch. Clarence J. b. 22 Sept. 1872; m.
          Edith Johnson.

361. SIMEON[7] 1809-1883 [114 Joseph[6] and Hannah Pearl] was
born at Mount Vernon 23 May 1809, died there 27 Mar. 1883,
73y 10m; married there 1 Apr. 1830 MARY [Polly] (KIMBALL)
Brown, born 29 Apr. 1799, died at Mt. Vernon 16 Feb. 1889,
89y 10m, daughter of the Rev. Jesse and Hannah (Cox) Kimball
(Leonard A. Morrison and Stephen P. Sharples, History of the
Kimball Family [1897], 1:237; Mt. Vernon vhs). Burials are
in the Bean Cemetery.
   Mary Kimball had married first 14 July 1816 Nathan Brown,
Jr., who died 2 Aug. 1827; they four children.
   Simeon was a deacon of the First Baptist church and member
of the Christian Band, an evangelical group founded at the
Bean Schoolhouse in 1818 which flourished until 1845. In the
church is a memorial window dedicated to him (George Blake,
Echoes in the Silence: History of the First Baptist Church
[1967]). He served three terms as selectman.
   Simeon's will, made 12 Mar. 1883 and proved in Apr., made
bequests to wife Mary and to grandsons George Carr and George
Wells. Mary's will, made 1 Aug. 1877 and proved 22 July
1889, made Mary E. Wells her principal heir, and also made
gifts to her four Brown children and to George Carr.

Children, born at Mt. Vernon:

827. i.   MARY ELIZABETH[8], b. 2 Dec. 1830; m. ELISHA L.
          WELLS.
828. ii. ELIZA ANN, b. 16 Feb. 1835; m. WILLIAM H. CARR.
     iii. GEORGE EDWIN, b. 3 May 1840, d. 5 Nov. 1864,
          24y 6m; unm.

362.   BENJAMIN R.[7] 1815-1886 [114 Joseph[6] and Hannah Pearl] was born at Mount Vernon 18 July 1815, died there 10 Feb. 1886, 70y 7m 7d; married there int. 21 Apr., certif. 21 May, 1844 LUCINDA BACHELDER, born at Chesterville ME 19 Aug. 1822, died at Mt. Vernon 7 June 1914, 91y 9m 19d, daughter of Moses and Lucinda (Ladd) Bachelder (VRs; Franklin C. Pierce, Batchelder-Batcheller Genealogy [Chicago, 1898], 179; Mount Vernon Town Register, 1908).

Children, all but first born at Mt. Vernon:

      i.   (CALVIN) WESLEY[8], b. Chesterville 3 Oct. 1844, d. Mt. Vernon 18 May 1914; m. there 8 Feb. 1878 AURORA ELIZA (AUSTIN) Miller, b. 28 Aug. 1841, d. Mt. Vernon 23 Mar. 1906, dau. of Benjamin and Sarah (Lord) Austin of Belgrade. No ch.

      ii. ELVIRA E., b. in 1851, res. CA; m. ----HARVEY (Town Register).

829. iii. FRANCIS B., b. 21 Mar. 1857.

      iv. EMMA E., b. in 1862, d. in 1886; m. Mt. Vernon 23 Dec. 1881 DAVID S. BROWN.

363.   THOMAS[7] 1818-1886 [114 Joseph[6] and Hannah Pearl] was born at Mount Vernon 8 Apr. 1818, died at Rochester NY 2 Feb. 1886; married 26 Nov. 1856 KATE BRINK TAYLOR, born at Oswego NY 23 Jan. 1838, died at Rochester 9 Aug. 1899, daughter of David and (Sarah) Helen (Tappan) Taylor (letter from daughter Helene--Cornman Papers).
Thomas was a bridge contractor, and founded the Leighton Bridge and Iron Works at Rochester.

Children:

      i.   THOMAS[8], b. 9 Sept. 1857, d. Rochester 3 Sept. 1864.

      ii. FRED, b. 20 Dec. 1858, d. Rochester 3 Sept. 1864.

     iii. DAVID, b. 26 Nov. 1862, d. Rochester 8 Sept. 1864.

      iv. WILLIAM, b. Rochester 10 Sept. 1865.

      v.   HELENE TAPPAN, b. Rochester 12 Jan. 1869.

364.   DELANO[7] 1824-1905 [114 Joseph[6] and Hannah Pearl] was born at Mount Vernon 16 July 1824, died at Dexter ME 13 Sept. 1905; married first ELIZA RAYMOND, born about 1841, daughter of Nathan and Mary Raymond of Fayette; married second 18 Mar. 1864 MARY C. LINNELL, born at Ripley ME 28 Dec. 1831, daughter of Ira and Elvira (Carlton) Linnell (Rachel Linnell Wynn, Descendants of Robert Linnell [Rochester NY, 1985], 132; ME VRs; Cornman Ms).
He enlisted 31 Oct. 1861 in Co. H, 14th ME Inf. Rgt., and was discharged as sergeant 17 Aug. 1865. He was wounded during this service, and received a pension (NA-MSR).
He was a farmer. They lived at Dexter; he is buried there in Mt. Pleasant cemetery. She later lived with her son George at Portsmouth.

Child by Eliza, born at Fayette:

830.   i.   EDWARD CARLETON[8], b. 3 Feb. 1862.

Children by Mary, born at Dexter:

    ii.   GEORGE EDWARD, b. 30 July 1871, d. Portland ME
        18 Mar. 1953, 81y; m. Westbrook ME 31 Dec.
        1895 MAUDE WOODBURY SWEETSER, b. Westbrook 20
        July 1876, dau. of Alfred Spear and Donazetta
        A. (Woodbury) Sweetser. No ch. (Philip Starr
        Sweetser, Seth Sweetser and His Descendants
        [Philadelphia, 1938], 169).
        After he received his BA from Tufts in 1894,
        he became a Universalist minister, serving
        Westbrook and Skowhegan ME, Newfields NH, and
        then Portsmouth for 10 years; in 1946 he re-
        tired to Portland after 23 years at Somerville
        MA (Press Herald obit., 19 Mar. 1953).
   iii.   WALTER ERVIN, b. 25 Aug. 1875, d. 3 May 1891.

365.   MARY LANE[7] 1814-1872 [115 Samuel[6] and Mary Lane] was
born at Exeter NH 27 Mar. 1814, died at Lowell MA 9 Apr.
1872; married there ORISON MELVIN, born 23 Nov. 1812, died at
Dracut MA 10 Oct. 1864, son of James and Susan Melvin (Cornman Ms).

Children (**Melvin**):

    i.   ALONZO, b. 5 Nov. 1830, d. 19 Apr. 1898; m. EMMA
      SMITH, b. 9 May 1834, d. 13 June 1913, dau. of J. P.
      and Anna (Griffin) Smith.
    ii.   MARY FRANCES, res. Leadville CO.

366.   HARRIET PEARSON[7] 1816-1897 [115 Samuel[6] and Mary
Lane] was born at Exeter NH 16 Aug. 1816, died at Lowell MA
29 June 1897; married there 2 Jan. 1838 (14 Feb., Morning
Star) LEVI BEARDSLEY STEVENS, born at Warner NH 27 May 1815,
died at Lowell 20 June 1885, son of Ichabod and Mary (Watson)
Stevens (NH and MA VRs; Cornman Ms).

Children (**Stevens**), born at Lowell:

    i.   FRANK KITTREDGE, b. 28 Sept. 1840, d. 19 Sept. 1841.
    ii.   GEORGE CLEMENT, b. 5 Sept. 1841, d. Lowell 9 Jan.
      1867; m. 1 Jan. 1860 MARINDA A. ROGERS, b. Warner
      NH 3 Mar. 1848, dau. of Benjamin and Lucinda
      (Waldron) Rogers.
   iii.   HARRIET EMILY, b. 5 Dec. 1843, d. 13 July 1844.
    iv.   LILLIE, b. 25 Apr. 1850, d. Lowell 12 Mar. 1871; unm.

367.   JOEL A.[7] 1820-1868 [115 Samuel[6] and Mary Lane] was
born at Exeter NH 17 Feb. 1820, died there 25 Sept. 1868,
49y; married first at Lowell MA 6 Oct. 1843 (VRs) EMILY BICK-
FORD; married second at Exeter 14 Nov. 1861 ELIZABETH H.
(RAND) Broughton, born at Rye NH 28 Oct. 1828, died at Exeter
23 May 1903, 73y 6m 25d, daughter of Trundy and Elizabeth H.
(Stevens) Rand (NH and MA VRs; Cornman Ms).

Joel was a printer. He was sergeant in Co. C, 6th NH Inf.
Rgt., during the Civil War.

Children, by Elizabeth, born at Exeter:

  i. EDWARD W.[8], b. 27 July 1863, d. Exeter 8 Oct.
    1891; m. 6 Nov. 1889 CARRIE F. REDMAN, b.
    Lowell MA 12 July 1860, res. there with her
    mother Roxanna in 1900. Ch. THEODORE REDMAN[9]
    b. Lynn MA 17 Dec. 1890, d. 3 Apr. 1892.
    Carrie m. 2nd Gustavus Simpson of Newport RI.
831. ii. JOHN LANE, b. 24 Aug. 1865.
  iii. MARY H., b. 20 Dec. 1867, d. 14 June 1868.

  368. **ELIZABETH A.**[7] 1805- [117 Thomas[6] and Elizabeth
Mitchell] was born at Exeter 24 July 1805; married at Palmyra
ME JOHN FOLSOM, born at Gilmanton NH 4 Apr. 1798, died at
Palmyra in 1879 or 1881, son of Joseph and Betty (Gale) Fol-
som (Folsom Fam., 1:431). In 1850 the family was listed at
Palmyra; in 1870 she and John lived there alone.

Children (**Folsom**), born at Palmyra:

i. MARIA A., b. c1830 (20 in 1850).
ii. MARTHA A., b. c1832 (18 in 1850); m. JAMES MOORE of
  Hartland.
iii. MARY E., b. c1834 (16 in 1850); m. E. S. DUTTON of
  Skowhegan.
iv. LEIGHTON JOSEPH, b. 28 July 1837, d. Old Orchard ME
  25 May 1902; m. ISABELLA MATILDA (BANGS) Kingsley.
v. CLARA S., b. c1842 (8 in 1850); m. ZIMRI BARTON.

  369. **ALBERT FRANCIS**[7] 1826-1897 [121 Joel[6] and Betsey La-
bree] was born at Bloomfield (Skowhegan) ME 5 Feb. 1826, died
there 17 Dec. 1897; married EUNICE ELLEN FOWLER, born at
Bloomfield 23 Apr. 1830, died at Norridgewock ME 2 May 1905,
75y 10d, daughter of Charles and Eunice (Emery) Fowler
(Coburn, Skowhegan, 2:659; Skowhegan VRs; Cornman Ms).
  He carried on his father's farm at Skowhegan; in 1870 his
wife was called Ellen E.

Children, born at Skowhegan:

  i. CHARLES ALBERT[8], b. 1 Oct. 1860; m. 1 Jan. 1888
    NELLIE (HIGGINS) Hilton, b. Wilton ME 14 Nov.
    1855, dau. of John Colby and Sarah (Steward)
    Higgins, who had m. 1st 24 May 1873 Albion L.
    Hilton --1 ch. (Katherine Chapin Higgins,
    Richard Higgins and His Descendants [Worcester
    MA, 1918], 442-3). Charles had no ch.
  ii. CAROLINE BOND [Carrie], b. 7 July 1868; m. 14
    Jan. 1888 Dr. JUSTIN AMES, b. Camden ME 7 Dec.
    1865. Ch. Harold Leighton Ames b. 29 Aug., d.
    16 Sept., 1893.

  370. **MARY ELIZABETH**[7] 1834-1911 [121 Joel[6] and Betsey La-
bree] was born at Bloomfield 11 Aug. 1834, died at Skowhegan
30 Nov. 1911; married 18 Oct. 1863 JAMES BUZZELL HUSSEY, born

18 Mar. 1820, died at Skowhegan, son of Timothy and Susan
(Buzzell) Hussey (VRs; Cornman Ms).
He was a tollkeeper. In 1900, widow Mary was living with
her sister Ellen.

Children (**Hussey**), born at Skowhegan:

i.   EDWIN AUGUSTUS, b. 15 Feb. 1865, d. 10 Jan. 1878.
ii.   LIZZIE THERESA, b. 10 Feb. 1871, res. Skowhegan in
      1914; unm. She was town librarian.

371.   EMILY JOSEPHINE^7 1836-   [121 Joel^6 and Betsey
Labree] was born at Bloomfield 7 Oct. 1836, lived at Fitchburg MA in 1904; married 16 July 1867 HENRY MARTIN FRANCIS,
born at Lunenburg MA 16 June 1836, died at Fitchburg 13 Oct.
1908, son of Franklin Samuel and Jane (Kimball) Francis
(Cornman Ms).

Children (**Francis**), born at Fitchburg:

i.   FREDERICK LEIGHTON, b. 5 Feb. 1870; m. 27 Sept. 1898
      LULU MAY HORTON, b. Brattleboro VT 9 Mar. 1877,
      dau. of Frank Timothy and Esther Maria (Whitney)
      Horton.
ii.   ANNIE THERESA, b. 20 Feb. 1872; m. 19 Sept. 1901
      BURTON SANDERSON FLAGG, b. Littleton MA 10 Nov.
      1873, son of Charles F. and Elizabeth Webster (Sand-
      erson) Flagg.
iii. ALBERT FRANKLIN, b. 6 Mar. 1875; m. 9 June 1898 EDITH
      MARTHA PERRY, b. Leominster MA 9 June 1877, d.
      Fitchburg 26 Mar. 1902, dau. of Charles and Jennie
      (Allen) Perry.

372.   WILLIAM^7 1776-1868 [123 Thomas^6 and Mercy Horne] was
born at Somersworth NH 13 May 1776, died at Dummer NH 31 Oct.
1868, 93y 5m 18d; married MARY AUSTIN, born about 1778, died
at Dummer 7 Sept. 1854, 76y 7m, by family tradition of Indian
birth (Stark Bicentennial Commission, History of Stark, N. H.
1774-1974 [Littleton NH, 1974], 61-2; Dummer Bicentennial
Commission, History of Dummer, N. H. [Littleton NH, 1973],
19, 87; Cornman Ms; research of David Dunlap).
   William was of Farmington in 1799, when he sold land there
to Joseph Roberts (StrCD, 32:120), but soon after was settled
at Somersworth.
   On 30 Dec. 1806, he was granted lot 229 by the proprietors
of Dummer ("Early Settlers of Dummer," NEHGReg, 127[1973]:
114); he was employed there by Beltire Daniels, agent for the
proprietors. In the spring of 1812 he moved his family there
by wagon, temporarily leaving Sarah and Phoebe with relatives
at Farmington.
   In 1810, Dummer had only seven inhabitants, and in 1813
only four households. Life was full of hardships; windows
were still kept barred against wolves and Indians. The men
farmed, cut timber, and made maple syrup; the women gathered
slippery-elm bark to trade at Portsmouth for staples.
   Dummer was incorporated in 1848 (History of Coos County,
N. H. [np, 1888], 855).

Children, birthplaces uncertain:

832. i.   MERCY[8], b. c1797; m. IRA EMERY.
833. ii.   BETSEY, b. c1799; m. DANIEL FORBUSH.
      iii. SARAH; m. 3 July 1828 ISRAEL FOSS of Barring-
            ton, b. 28 Dec. 1799, son of Dr. John and
            Dolly (Babb) Foss. He m. 1st Hannah Thompson.
      iv.   PHOEBE, b. Somersworth 29 May 1803; m. WILLIAM
            PEAVEY[7] LEIGHTON [# 498] and JOHN G. WATSON.
834. v.   JOSEPH, b. Somersworth 15 May 1807.
835. vi.   THOMAS, b. c1809.
836. vii. WILLIAM, b. 12 Sept. 1810.
      viii. NANCY, b. c1813, d. 8 Nov. 1898, 85y 5m 27d;
            m. CHARLES NEWELL.
      ix.   MARY ANN, b. in Oct. 1817, d. 2 Mar. 1835, 18y
            (GS); unm.

373. EDWARD[7] 1781-1873 [123 Thomas[6] and Mercy Horne] was
born at Somersworth 16 Apr. 1781 (Tuftonboro VRs), died at
Franklin NH 28 Mar. 1873, 93y; married first 20 Feb. 1807
(int. Farmington 14 Dec. 1805) LYDIA RAND, born at Somersworth 8 Aug. 1785 (8 Apr., Tuftonboro VRs), died at Northfield NH 6 Aug. 1812, daughter of Moses and Lydia (Wentworth)
Rand; married second 24 Apr. 1813 JUDITH RAND, born at Barnstead 16 July 1795, died at Franklin 5 Apr. 1885, daughter of
Moses and Mary R. Rand and cousin of Lydia (Runnels, Sanbornton, 2:461-2; Northfield and Franklin VRs).
   Not yet two when his father died, he was placed under the
guardianship of his stepfather Richard Hoyt of Farmington.
On reaching majority, he inherited land from his father's
estate. In 1816 he settled at Northfield, purchasing lot 189
of the original Valentine Hill grant from Jonathan Cross.
Northfield had been set off from Canterbury in 1780.
   In 1832, the part of Northfield where Edward lived was set
off as the town of Franklin; he was chairman of Franklin's
first board of selectmen, and a major landholder. The day of
his funeral, the spring mud required that his coffin be drawn
from his mansion to the cemetery by forty men (Moses T. Runnels, History of Northfield, N. H. [1881], 207-8).

Children by Lydia:

837. i.   MOSES R.[8], b. Barnstead 23 July 1808.
      ii.   IRA, b. Somersworth 27 May 1810, d. there 17
            Sept. 1811.

Children by Judith:

838. iii. LYDIA, b. Northfield 8 July 1814; m. SAMUEL
            B. BROWN.
839. iv.   THOMAS, b. Northfield 11 Mar. 1817.
      v.   JOHN S., b. Northfield 3 June 1819, d. Franklin
            19 Nov. 1821.
840. vi.   MARY A., b. Northfield 8 Nov. 1821; m. JAMES
            E. GARDNER.
841. vii. EDWARD, b. Northfield 11 Aug. 1825.
842. viii. JUDITH M., b. Northfield 8 Aug. 1827; m. WIN-
            THROP FORD and BENJAMIN SARGENT.
843. ix.   JOHN F., b. Franklin 27 May 1832.

x.   LORAIN (or LAUREN), b. Franklin 2 Jan. 1838,
      res. Janesville MN; m. 16 Oct. 1859 TIRZAH
      FRENCH, b. Columbia NH, dau. of Ovid and Sabra
      Hamilton Scott (Snow) French. Ad. ch. Lorain
      Elmer b. Redwood Falls MN 24 Jan. 1889.

374. RICHARD[7] 1787-1834 [124 Jedediah[6] and Rebecca Swain]
was born at Strafford NH 19 Feb. 1787, died at Nottingham NH
9 May 1834, 46y (VRs; Morning Star); married 6 Mar. 1817
(int. Chelsea MA 27 Dec. 1816) LOVEY WALDRON, born at Strafford 14 May 1797, died there 13 June 1860, 63y 1m, daughter
of Aaron and Hannah (Boody) Waldron (Caverly, Boody Annals,
166, 214-5).

Children, born at Nottingham:

844. i.   ZACHARIAH[8], b. 9 Mar. 1818.
      ii.   HANNAH E., b. 13 July 1822, res. Newmarket NH;
            m. in 1842 WILLIAM MEADER, b. in 1815, d. 14
            Feb. 1882, son of John and Elizabeth (Edgerly)
            Meader (Stackpole, Durham, 2:281; Granville
            Meader, comp., John Meader of Piscataqua
            [Baltimore, 1977], 2:238). Ch. Lizzie A. b.
            24 Mar. 1844, m. Hiram Mooers.
      iii. ABRAM, b. 2 Mar. 1826, d. 2 July 1827.
      iv.   JOSEPH E., b. 18 Jan. 1829, res. Pittsfield in
            1900; unm.
845. v.   ALMIRA, b. 8 May 1833; m. OLIVER GRAY.

375. JOHN ALLEN[7] 1789-1815 [124 Jedediah[6] and Rebecca
Swain] was born at Barrington 6 Jan. 1789, died at Newburyport MA 13 Jan. 1815; married at Haverhill MA 5 Nov. 1812
(int. at Newbury 30 Sept.) ELIZABETH STICKNEY, born at Haverhill 8 Jan. 1792, died probably at Plaistow NH in Aug. 1823,
daughter of Jeremiah and Elizabeth (Flanders) Stickney. She
married second at Haverhill 10 Nov. 1819 Dea. Joseph Harris;
two children (Matthew Adams Stickney, Stickney Family [Salem
MA, 1869], 484). In 1833 Jedediah Leighton remembered the
two grandchildren in his will.

Children:

      i.   WILLIAM STICKNEY[8]; unm.
      ii.   JOHN ALLEN, res. San Jose CA; m., no ch.

376. SALLY[7] 1794-1857 [124 Jedediah[6] and Rebecca Swain]
was born at Barrington 1 Sept. 1794, died at Barnstead 18
Apr. 1857; married her cousin JOHN HILL, born at Barnstead 11
May 1785, died there 14 Apr. 1845, son of William and Lucy[6]
(Leighton) Hill [# 125] (Cornman Ms; records of descendants
Lena Waldron Leighton and Alice Haubrich).

Children (**Hill**), born at Barnstead:

i.   JEDEDIAH, b. 27 Mar. 1815, d. Deerfield MI 28 Oct.
      1890; m. in MI SOPHIA CILLEY.
ii.   LUCY ANN, b. 7 July 1818, d. 13 May 1875; unm.

iii.   JOHN, b. 24 Aug. 1821, d. Strafford NH 20 Aug.
       1879; m. 24 Nov. 1859 ELIZA (SMITH) Hill [# 378].
iv.   SARAH JANE, b. 5 Mar. 1824, d. 2 Oct. 1885; m. Durham
       NH 12 Mar. 1859 JOSEPH OTIS.
v.   CHARLES W., b. 24 Oct. 1826, d. 11 Aug. 1902; m.
       CLARISSA (MUNSEY) Kinney.
vi.   MARTHA B., b. 17 Dec. 1829, d. 26 Mar. 1886; unm.
vii.   JULIA ELMA, b. 14 Sept. 1834, res. Durham NH; m. 11
       July 1867 DUDLEY P. MEADER.

377.   JAMES W.[7] 1796-1856 [124 Jedediah[6] and Rebecca Swain]
was born at Barrington 5 Oct. 1796, died at Strafford 13 Jan.
1856, 59y 3m (GS); married 10 June 1817 SARAH WINKLEY, born
at Barnstead 22 Aug. 1795, died at Farmington 20 May 1884,
88y 9m, daughter of Benjamin and Elizabeth (Pitman) Winkley
(Jeremiah P. Jewett, History of Barnstead, New Hampshire /
1772-1872 [1872], 97-8). He was called "James, Jr." because
he had an uncle James in Barrington. Burials are in Province
Road Cemetery, Bow Lake, Strafford. His will was proved in
1856 (StrCP, 68:118; 69:380). In 1850, his three daughters
were part of the household of Martha Libby at Dover.

Children, born at Strafford:

846.   i.   VARNUM HILL[8], b. 16 Dec. 1818.
       ii.   WALTER, b. 6 June 1821, d. Pittsfield NH 2 July
              1897; m. 20 Feb. 1845 SARAH A. STILES, b. 10
              Mar. 1825, d. 10 June 1901. No ch. He was a
              carpenter.
847.   iii.   JOHN JAMES, b. 21 Jan. 1824.
848.   iv.   MARY ANN, b. 5 Apr. 1827; m. JOSEPH PIPER.
849.   v.   SARAH ELIZABETH, b. 19 Nov. 1829; m. JOSEPH
              WOODMAN.
850.   vi.   HANNAH FRANCES, b. 2 Oct. 1831; m. ALPHONSO
              BOODY.

378.   HANNAH[7] 1798-1874 [124 Jedediah[6] and Rebecca Swain]
was born at Barrington 22 Nov. 1798, died at Strafford 8 Jan.
1874, 75y 1m 17d (GS); married 2 June 1818 her cousin WILLIAM
L. HILL, born at Barnstead 29 Apr. 1795, died 11 May 1849,
54y 1m 12d (GS), son of William and Lucy[6] (Leighton) Hill
[# 125] (records of Lena Waldron Leighton; Strafford VRs).
Burials are in Province Road Cemetery, Bow Lake, Strafford

Children (Hill), born at Strafford:

i.   NATHANIEL, b. in 1820. Missionary to the Sandwich
       Islands (Hawaii).
ii.   WILLIAM, b. 24 May 1822, d. 26 Feb. 1858, 35y 9m
       (GS); m. 11 Nov. 1855 ELIZA SMITH, b. 26 Sept. 1834,
       d. 11 Mar. 1905, 90y (GS), dau. of Bernard and
       Sophronia (Wallace) Smith. She m. 2nd JOHN HILL,
       JR. [# 376].

379.   THOMAS[7] 1784-1866 [126 James[6] and Abigail Horne] was
born at Farmington NH 8 June 1784, died at Milton NH 26 Mar.
1866; married first at Berwick ME in 1811 NANCY JONES, died 2
Feb. 1818; married second at Milton 28 Sept. 1824 HANNAH

JONES, born at Lebanon ME in 1795, died at Milton 7 Sept.
1852, daughter of Eliphalet and Ruth (Roberts) Jones (Cornman
Ms; records of Lewis L. Knox). Burials are in the Jones lot,
Milton cemetery.
Thomas settled at Milton in 1805, a farmer, carpenter and
machinist. On his father's death, he inherited 70 acres of
land at Milton. He operated a textile mill, manufacturing
cotton cloth, and had the first store in the area selling
domestic and West Indian fabrics (Richmond, John Hayes,
1:338).
Three of his children by Hannah were born out of wedlock.
In a codicil made to his will in 1834, his father James
referred to "Silas [Cyrus] the reputed son of my son Thomas,
and now his only son, whatever he may now be called, whether
Silas Jones or Silas Leighton, being the same he had by his
present wife," and provided to the boy the "same rights as if
he had been begotten in legal wedlock."

Children by first wife Nancy, born at Milton:

851. i.   ABIGAIL[8], b. 31 Aug. 1811; m. JEREMIAH HUSSEY.
      ii.   MARY J., b. in 1814, d. Dover in May 1853; m.
            25 July 1847 GRANVILLE W. STAPLES. They had
            2 ch.
852. iii. RHODA ANN, b. 24 Feb. 1817; m. FRANCIS LOONEY.

Children by second wife Hannah, born at Milton:

      iv.   ELMIRA VILLARS, b. 20 Dec. 1820; m. 19 Sept.
            1845 OLIVER PIERCE, b. 15 Mar. 1823, d. 24
            June 1885. No ch.
      v.   CLARA, b. in 1822, d. in 1824.
853. vi.   CYRUS K., b. 23 Sept. 1824.
854. vii. BETSEY JANE, b. 19 Aug. 1827; m. LEVI STRAW.
      viii. NANCY JONES, b. 21 June 1829, d. 13 June 1853;
            m. Lowell MA 26 July 1850 AUGUSTUS PUTNAM,
            son of Adam and Nancy Putnam. No ch.
855. ix   MARTHA AUGUSTA, b. 22 June 1831; m. LORENZO D.
            HAYES.
      x.   son, d. in Nov. 1834.

380. MARTHA[7] [Patty] 1787-1866 [126 James[6] and Abigail
Horne] was born at Barrington 15 Feb. 1787, died 1 Nov. 1866;
married at Farmington 6 Feb. 1812 (by Enos George, JP, Bar-
rington) GEORGE HAM, born at Portsmouth 20 Jan. 1788, died 10
May 1878, son of George and Rachel (Garvin) Ham (Cornman Ms).
They lived at Barrington and Strafford.

Children (**Ham**):

i.   PHEBE, b. 28 Oct. 1812, d. 23 Dec. 1853; m. GEORGE
      BREWSTER.
ii.   LEONORA, b. 23 June 1814, d. 1 June 1901; m. DARIUS
      PERKINS.
iii. MARK, b. 22 June 1816; m. 23 Jan. 1838 MARY A. WELCH,
      b. 15 Sept. 1821, d. 6 Aug. 1894.
iv.   ALBERT, b. 21 Feb. 1819, res. Dresden ME; m.
      CHARLOTTE CAVERLY.
v.   JOSEPH, b. Strafford 4 Mar. 1821, d. Roxbury MA 23
      Jan. 1907; m. 19 Oct. 1845 DOROTHY KINGMAN WATER-

HOUSE, b. Strafford 5 Dec. 1825, d. Roxbury 5 May
1899, dau. of Daniel and Lydia (Brown) Waterhouse
(Waterhouse Desc., 1:144, 2:784).
vi.   JAMES L., b. 6 Apr. 1824, res. Dresden ME; m. 1st
HELEN BLAIR; m. 2nd MARY EMERSON.
vii. GEORGE, b. 1 Sept. 1827, res. Haverhill MA.
viii. DAVID, b. 11 July 1833, res. Barrington.

381. TRUSTRUM[7] 1789-1873 [126 James[6] and Abigail Horne]
was born at Farmington 30 Nov. 1789, died at Rocester 26 Apr.
1873, 84y 4m 26d (GS); married first at Alton NH 7 Dec. 1809
(int. Farmington 4 Nov.) BETSEY PEAVEY, born at New Durham NH
25 Nov. 1790, died at Farmington 25 Jan. 1863, 72y 2m (GS),
daughter of Joseph and Abigail Peavey of Tuftonboro; married
second at Farmington 11 Nov. 1864 JANE (----) Abbott of
Manchester NH, born at New Durham about 1818 (46 in 1864),
died at Barnstead 5 June 1895, 78y (town VRs; Cornman Ms;
Merrill, Carroll County, 440). Burials are on the Leighton-
Bennett farm. His name was spelled Trustrum, not Tristram,
on all records and on his gravestone. A carpenter and stonecutter, he operated a sawmill with his brother Jedediah.
    He received a quitclaim deed from Jedediah 18 Apr. 1838 for
land left by their father, and another deed for 35 acres from
William [# 498] and Phoebe. He then rented to Hunkin Colbath
the 56-acre farm he had previously occupied.

Children, all by first wife Betsey, born at Farmington:

        i.   PHEBE[8], b. 31 Mar., d. 12 Apr., 1810 (GS).
        ii.   LEWIS, b. 17 Mar. 1812, d. 19 Apr. 1822, 10y
              (GS).
856.   iii. GEORGE, b. 8 Oct. 1813.
        iv.   ABIGAIL, b. 14 Nov. 1815, res. Moline IL; m.
              STEPHEN WALKER. Ch. Abbie m. ---- Gould, and
              George.
857.   v.   SALLY C., b. 1 Jan. 1817; m. JOSEPH QUIMBY and
              SAMUEL ALLEY.
858.   vi.   JOSEPH P., b. 15 Apr. 1820.
        vii. JOHN H., b. 5 Aug. 1823, d. Searsport ME 6 June
              1902, 79y 5m (VR); m. Farmington 26 Dec.
              1849 DRUSILLA D. MOORE, b. Searsport 20 Nov.
              1825, d. Dover NH 9 May 1895, dau. of George
              and Hope (Phelps) Moore. Their adopted ch.
              Harold M. was 13 in 1880, at Dover.
                  After 1850, they moved to Dover; he was town
              assessor there in 1857, alderman in 1869-9.
              On 24 Nov. 1865, he sold to Stephen W. Bennett
              [# 1112] "land and buildings known as the
              James Leighton farm" (StrCD, 238:204).
859.   viii. LUCINDA, b. 19 Sept. 1825; m. EDWIN A. SMITH.
860.   ix.   EMILY, b. 11 Mar. 1827; m. LEWIS W. BERRY.
        x.   ANDREW, b. 8 July 1828, d. 8 Oct. 1832, 4y 3m
              (GS; not in 1830 census).
        xi.   NANCY, b. 10 Feb., d. 20 Feb., 1830, 10d (GS).
        xii. STEPHEN, d. 19 Apr. 1834, 16 wks (GS).

382. JEDEDIAH[7] 1791-1839 [126 James[6] and Abigail Horne]
was born at Farmington NH 22 Oct. 1791, died there 22 Oct.
1839, 48y (GS); married at Farmington 24 Mar. 1811 SARAH

MURRAY, born at Barnstead 17 Jan. 1789, died at Farmington 2
Aug. 1860, 72y 5m 15d (GS), daughter of John and Rose (Canney) Murray (Farmington TRs). Sarah was called Polly on
their marriage record. Burials are on the Leighton-Bennett
farm; his is a replacement stone.

A carpenter and stonecutter, he operated a sawmill on the
Mad River with Trustrum. He bought lot 116, 3rd division, in
Farmington, sold part of it to his brother James 27 July
1829, and then repurchased it 20 Mar. 1834 (StrCD, 140:501;
174:581). In 1838 he inherited 190 acres from his father, and
quitclaimed to Trustrum his other rights in the estate.

His widow Sally was given administration of his estate 12
Nov. 1839, and her dower was set off 10 Dec. (StrCP, 50:167;
55:127-9; 56:62).

Children, born at Farmington:

      i.   MARY MURRAY[8], b. 25 June 1811, d. 17 Dec. 1898;
          m. Farmington 17 Feb. 1845 (both of Milton,
          int. Alton 13 Feb.) ELIAS SMITH EDGERLY, b.
          Alton 15 May 1820, d. Milton 2 Dec. 1850, son
          of Thomas and Hannah (Libby) Edgerly. No ch.

861. ii.   PHEBE, b. 13 Dec. 1813; m. HAZEN DUNTLEY.
     iii. MOSES CHANEY MURRAY, b. c1815, d.y.
862. iv.   MOSES CHANEY, b. 3 Feb. 1817.
     v.   DANIEL MURRAY, b. 3 May 1820, d. Farmington 21
          May 1858, 35y 18d (GS); m. Farmington int. 28
          Mar. 1841 LEAH J. FRENCH.
863. vi.   LEWIS, b. 19 Sept. 1824.
864. vii. BELINDA, b. in 1836; m. HOSEA B. KNOX.

 383. **GIDEON**[7] 1770-1846 [129 Sarah[6]] was born at Steuben ME
say 1770, died there in 1846 (26 Oct. 1826 in Cornman Ms);
married first his cousin MARTHA PINKHAM, born at Steuben 5
Dec. 1769, died there 31 Dec. 1818, daughter of Tristram,
Jr., and Ann[6] (Leighton) Pinkham [# 127]; married second at
Steuben int. 17 Apr. 1819 LUCY WAKEFIELD, born about 1785 (52
in 1850), died 20 Mar. 1861, daughter of Samuel and Ruth
(Burbank) Wakefield (Steuben VRs; Wakefield Mem., 123-4; Sin-
nett, Pinkham Gen., 19). Burials are in the Evergreen and
Pinkham Cemeteries. Lucy may have married first at Steuben 4
Sept. 1814 James Anderson.

Gideon's parentage and progeny are both partly conjectural.
On 28 Jan. 1826 heirs of Tristram Pinkham, Jr., signed a deed
quitting their rights to their brothers Richard and Thomas.
Signing in right of their mother Martha were four Leightons:
William, Hannah, Eleazer and Sally (WashCD, 16:411-3).

On 7 June 1846, the judge of probate drew up a letter of
administration to Lucy Leighton for the estate of Gideon
Leighton; it was not issued because she refused to post bond
(WashCP, 5:272). In 1860, Lucy, 70, was living at Steuben
alone, listed next to Joel Pinkham's household [# 869].

Children by Martha, born at Steuben:

      i.   WILLIAM[8], b. c1798 (52 in 1850); m. LUCY ---- ,
          born c1800 (50 in 1850). In 1850, they lived

next door to Benjamin and Susan Pinkham.
(Julia Cornman stated that a Lucy Leighton m.
30 Nov. 1828 William Leighton.)

   ii.   HANNAH.

   iii. ELEAZER, b. c1800, res. Steuben; prob. unm. In
        1850, he res. with Stillman and Caroline
        Parritt, in 1860, at 60, with Jonathan and
        Lydia Leighton, and in 1870 with Amesbury
        Leighton.

   iv.   JOHN, b. c1810, d. Steuben 22 Jan. 1887, aged
        c80 (Machias Union). John, 40, res. Steuben
        in 1850 with Charles and Margaret Haskell, and
        in 1870, 60y, with Edward Leighton, 45 (prob.
        son of Benjamin [# 134]). In his obit. he was
        nicknamed "(Uncle Gid)."

   v.   SALLY. Prob. the Miss Sally Leighton, b. c1813
        (1803 per GS, Farnsworth Cem., Sprague Falls),
        who d. Cherryfield 7 Oct. 1867, c60y (Machias
        Union). In 1850 a Sally, 37, res. Cherryfield
        with William and Lydia Small.

865. vi.   GIDEON, b. c1817 (33 in 1850).

Children by Lucy, born at Steuben:

866. vi.   MARTHA, b. 30 Jan. 1820; m. AMBROSE PINKHAM.

   vii. SOPHRONIA, b. 24 Jan. 1822; m. JAMES[7] LEIGHTON
        [# 419].

   viii. MIRIAM G., b. 12 Dec. 1823, d. Steuben 29 Nov.
        1849, 25y 11m 16d (GS); m. there 7 Dec. 1847
        ICHABOD WILLE PINKHAM. b. 20 Dec. 1824,
        son of Robert and Lydia (Fernald) Pinkham.
        Ch. Alfreda P$_8$ b. Steuben 10 Aug. 1849; m.
        James Everett[8] Leighton [# 941]. Ichabod m.
        2nd Sarah E. ---- ; they had 2 ch.

867. xi.   JAMES W., b. 1 Jan. 1826.

384. ELEAZER[7] 1780-1867 [129 Sarah[6]] was born at Steuben
about 1780, died there in 1867, 86y; married SARAH [Sallie]
STROUT, born about 1780, died in 1855, 86y.

In 1903 their daughter Susan (Leighton) Pinkham wrote to
Julia Cornman providing data on her family (copy in MHS manuscript collection); her recollections were not always consis-
tent with town records and other sources.

On 31 Oct. 1846 Eleazer purchased from David Leighton of
Harrington part of lot 50 at Pigeon Hill adjoining land of
William Leighton, 55 acres where Eleazer was then living. On
14 Apr. 1847, he mortgaged the above to Warren Leighton of
Steuben (WashCD, 61:451-2). The same 55 acres, designated as
at Pinkham's Bay, he sold to Henry Stevens 23 Feb. 1855, the
"lot I formerly lived on," adjoining the house of the late
William Leighton (83:151-2).

In 1860, Eleazer, 70, was at Unionville (Steuben) in the
household of his cousin Samuel Davis [# 128].

Children, born at Steuben:

   i.   ELMIRA[8], b. 28 Sept. 1814, d. 1834; unm.

   ii. HARRIS, b. 13 Apr. 1816, d. at sea; unm.

      iii. JOHN, b. 30 July 1818, d. at sea; unm. Perhaps
           the John, 45, who res. Steuben in 1860 with
           George West, and in 1870, 49, with Alfred and
           Bethia Grace [# 264].
868. iv. SUSAN, b. 6 Dec. 1820; m. BENJAMIN PINKHAM, JR.
      v.   SALLIE, b. in June 1822, d. 13 Aug. 1897; m.
           1st 29 June 1848 JAMES GRADY of Cherryfield,
           b. in Ireland c1805 (per 1850 census); m. 2nd
           JAMES BERRY, born in England (Cornman Ms).
           Grady ch. (perhaps others) Emily F. m. Robert
           O'Connell.
869. vi. LOVICIA, b. 20 Mar. 1825; m. JOEL PINKHAM and
           JAMES LEIGHTON [# 407].
      vii. MARY, b. in 1826; m. GIDEON[8] LEIGHTON [# 865].
870. viii. ELLEN, b. in 1828; m. DENNIS LARRY.
871. ix. LUCY, b. in 1829; m. WILLIAM GAY.
      x.   ELSIE, b. in 1832, d. before 1903.

385. **REBECCA[7]** 1780-1815 [130 Joseph[6] and Betsey Jordan]
was born at Steuben about 1780, died at Cherryfield 10 Oct.
1815 (TRs; 15 Oct. per GS); married ELISHA STROUT, born 10
June 1777, died at Cherryfield 7 Feb. 1846 (GS), son of Jeremiah and Mary (Small) Strout (town VRs).
Elisha married second Anna Ricker; they had three children.
Burials are at Cherryfield.

Children (**Strout**), born at Cherryfield:

    i.   JASON, b. 9 July 1809; m. 30 May 1842 ELIZA McCALEB.
    ii. LEONARD, b. 14 May 1811.
    iii. MARIA, b. 8 June 1813; m. 20 Feb. 1848 ANTHONY
        CHIPMAN.

386. **LUCY HOPE[7]** 1793-1871 [130 Joseph[6] and Betsey Jordan]
was born at Cherryfield ME 18 Nov. 1793, died at Minneapolis
MN 24 May 1891; married at Cherryfield int. 17 Nov. 1816
AARON LAWRENCE, born 21 Sept. 1789, died at Minneapolis 24
Sept. 1872, son of John and Jennie (Rolfe) Lawrence (records
of Leonard F. Tibbetts and Joanna Willey; Lawrence family
Bible-DAR Misc. Records, MHS; Cherryfield VRs). Burials are
in Lakewood cemetery, Minneapolis.

Children (**Lawrence**), born at Cherryfield:

    i.   REBECCA, b. 8 Jan. 1817, res. Cherryfield; m. there
        20 Sept. 1841 DAVID W. TUPPER.
    ii. SAMUEL, b. 13 Feb. 1819.
    iii. ALEXANDER, b. 3 Apr. 1821, res. Minneapolis; m.
        MARARET S. ---- .
    iv. AMOS GUPTILL, b. 23 Oct. 1823, d. in army during
        Civil War.
    v.   (WILLIAM) HARRISON, b. c1829 (21 in 1850).
    vi. FRANCIS C. [Frank], b. c1831 (19 in 1850).
    vii. CATHERINE C., b. 24 Oct. 1833, d. Cherryfield 4 Mar.
        1925; m. in Sept. 1852 SAMUEL RAY, b. 5 Sept. 1823,
        d. 24 Nov. 1898.
    viii. LEANDER, b. c1836, res. Minneapolis; m. SUSAN WILLEY.

387.   JOSEPH[7] 1794-1866 [130 Joseph[6] and Betsey Jordan]
was born at Cherryfield about 1794, died at Webster Plantation (No. 6) ME in 1866; married at Steuben 18 Mar. (int.
Cherryfield 29 Jan.) 1814 BETSEY DOWNS, born at Cherryfield 5
Oct. 1796, daughter of Allen and Annie (Willey) Downs (Steuben VRs; records of Leonard F. Tibbetts). He moved from
Steuben to Springfield, and then to Webster Plantation.
His will, probated 20 Dec. 1866, named his children and
an Elizabeth Cunningham.

Children, born at Steuben:

872.   i.   SUSAN[8], b. 11 Nov. 1816; m.MARK WORCESTER.
873.   ii.   STILLMAN WASS, b. 27 Sept. 1819.
874.   iii. ABIGAIL, b. 7 Sept. 1823; m. ISAAC WORCESTER
             and DANIEL GOULD.
875.   iv.   LEONARD STROUT, b. 27 Oct. 1825.
       v.   ELIZABETH ANN, b. 20 Nov. 1827.
       vi.   ALFRED SMITH, b. 20 June 1829, d. 8 May 1830.
876.   vii. RACHEL, b. 2 Apr. 1831; m. PARKER D. WILLEY.
877.   viii. REBECCA S., b. 16 Nov. 1833; m. PARKER DOWNS.
878.   ix.   FOSTER J., b. 2 Nov. 1835.

388.   RACHEL[7] 1797-1885 [130 Joseph[6] and Betsey Jordan]
was born at Cherryfield 20 Oct. 1797, died there 10 Apr.
1885, 89y; married there int. 25 Nov. 1830 ORREN TURU WILLEY,
born 12 July 1804, died at Cherryfield 22 Sept. 1865, 60y
(GS), son of Charles and Hannah (Guptill) Willey (Cherryfield
VRs; records of Joanna Willey). He was a farmer at Cherryfield in 1860.

Children (**Willey**), born at Cherryfield:

i.   EMILY W., b. 25 Apr. 1832, d. 23 June 1849.
ii.   BENJAMIN FRANKLIN, b. 12 Mar. 1834, d. Cherryfield
       3 Nov. 1902, 68y 9m; m. there 21 Apr. 1858 SOPHIA
       E. GUPTILL, b. there 4 Sept. 1831, dau. of Thomas H.
       and Emily Guptill.
iii.   ELIZABETH R., b. 20 June 1836, d. 15 June 1891; m.
       27 Dec. 1857 ROSCOE NASH, b. 6 May 1834.
iv.   LUCY A., b. 20 Nov. 1838, res. Harrington; m. 13 Jan.
       1861 LORENZO NASH, b. 24 Dec. 1835.
v.   GEORGE W., b. c1842 (18 in 1860).
vi.   EMELINE, b. c1853 (7 in 1860), d. 23 June 1863.

389.   EBENEZER JORDAN[7] 1801-1891 [130 Joseph[6] and Betsey
Jordan] was born at Cherryfield 7 Aug. 1801, died at Unionville (Steuben) 7 May 1891, 89y 9m; married first at Steuben
6 May 1828 DRUSILLA WILSON, born at Cherryfield 24 Oct. 1807,
died at Steuben 1 Oct. 1859, 50y (GS), daughter of Mark and
Sally (Small) Wilson (Cherryfield and Steuben VRs; Emery
Small Wilson, A Brief Account of the Wilsons ... in Cherry-
field, Me. [1892], 10, 39; Milliken, 6); married second at
Columbia 25 Oct. 1861 MIRIAM (WORCESTER) Tucker, born there
in 1805, died at Unionville 4 Apr. 1883, 78y 10m, daughter of
Moses and Hannah[6] (Leighton) Worcester [# 150] and widow of
Asa Tucker of Centerville.
Burials are in Unionville cemetery.

He and Mark Wilson were partners in Wilson and Leighton
Co., lumbering and milling wood; Emery Wilson continued in
the business.

Children by Drusilla, born at Steuben:

879.   i.   CURTIS[8], b. 9 June 1829.
       ii.   ALFRED, b. 3 Feb. 1831, d. Minneapolis MN 12
              Aug. 1888; unm.
880.   iii. GREEN, b. 15 Feb. 1833.
       iv.   HERMAN, b. c1836 (25 in 1860, b. Dec. 1839
              per 1900 census), res. Minneapolis in 1900; m.
              ANNIE W. ---- , b. in Canada in Aug. 1854. No
              ch.
       v.   ABIGAIL, b. 1 May 1838; m. MERRILL[8] LEIGHTON
              [# 911].
881.   vi.   IVORY MARK, b. 25 Oct. 1841.
882.   vii. MELISSA, b. 7 Apr. 1843; m. FOSTER J. TRACY.
883.   viii. ELBRIDGE S., b. 15 Dec. 1844.
884.   ix.   CORILLA, b. c1845 (4 in 1850); m. CHARLES
              ARCHER.

390. THOMAS[7] 1783-   [131 Robert[6] and Hannah Leighton]
was born at Falmouth ME 30 Oct. 1783, lived at Falmouth and
Westbrook; married DOROTHY [Dolly] STEWART, born about 1786
(64 in 1850), daughter of Peter and Keziah (Allen) Stewart of
Westbrook (Hall Desc., #416; Falmouth VRs; Cornman Ms).
He was a corporal in Capt. Alpheus Field's company in Sept.
1814 (MA Mil. 1812-14, 219.). In 1850 his Falmouth household
included his son Samuel and his family.

Children, born at Falmouth:

      i.   HANNAH[8].
885.   ii.   SAMUEL, b. c1810 (40 in 1850).
       iii. SUSAN, b. Falmouth 19 Dec. 1814; m. Falmouth 17
              June 1837 GEORGE FIELD. They res. Garland in
              1850, with ch. George L. 11, and Sarah A. 8.
       iv.   ROBERT, b. Westbrook 14 May 1819, d. Deering ME
              19 May 1876, 57y; m. Westbrook 19 Nov. 1845
              MARY ALLEN (Akers on int. 2 Nov.), b. c1820
              (30 in 1850). Adopted ch. William b. in
              1862, d. Portland 24 Dec. 1932, 70y 7m 6d; m.
              Addie Knight, b. Windham 30 Dec. 1860, d.
              Portland 4 Sep. 1939, dau. of Lorenzo D. and
              Mary Ann (Mayberry) Knight.
       v.   SEWARD P. (Leonard P. in Hall Desc.), b. c1824
              (26 in 1850), d. Falmouth 6 Aug. 1884, 60y; m.
              Portland 4 Oct. 1857 MAHALA R. FIELD.

391. SUSANNAH[7] 1785-1867 [131 Robert[6] and Hannah Leighton]
was born at Falmouth 25 May 1785, died at Cumberland ME 27
June 1867; married first ROBERT HALL, born 13 Oct. 1777, died
13 Apr. 1818, son of William and Elizabeth (Cox) Hall (Hall
Desc., #75, 417); married second 17 Dec. 1818 JOHN PRINCE,
born 27 May 1789, died at Cumberland 10 Oct. 1838, son of
Paul and Sarah (Southworth) Prince (Cornman Ms; town VRs).
Hall had married first Anna Hall of Addison ME.

Children (**Hall**), born at Falmouth:

i.   HANNAH, b. 22 Mar. 1810, d. 2 Aug. 1869; m. 1st AMMI
      R. WHITNEY, d. 14 Dec. 1851; m. 2nd JOHN NOYES.
ii.   LOIS, b. 5 Mar. 1812, d. 10 Mar. 1867; m. 1st LEMUEL
      GURNEY, who d. 1 Nov. 1849; m. 2nd GEORGE BABSON
      DOWNER, who d. 22 June 1870.
iii. MARY JANE, m. 1st THOMAS G. ALLEN; m. 2nd RICHARD
      DRESSER.

Children (**Prince**):

iv.   JOANNA, b. Falmouth 6 Sept. 1820, d. 16 Oct. 1853; m.
      Cumberland 3 Sept. 1840 BENJAMIN WHITEHOUSE, b.
      c1815. He m. 1st Elizabeth J. Lunt, m. 3rd Angelia
      ---- .
v.   LYDIA ANN, b. Cumberland 14 Sept. 1822, d. there 11
      July 1823.
vi.   WILLIAM LEIGHTON, b. Cumberland 14 Mar. 1825, d.
      there 2 June 1887; m. 19 Apr. 1849 SOPHRONIA GRAY
      BLANCHARD, b. Cumberland 7 Sept. 1827, d. Scarboro
      ME 13 Jan. 1914, dau. of Andrew Gray and Myra
      (Sweetser) Blanchard.

392. DANIEL[7] 1787-1860 [131 Robert[6] and Hannah Leighton]
was born at Falmouth 10 June 1787, died there 6 Sept. 1860,
73y (GS); married there 5 Jan. 1815 HANNAH COLE, born 24 Feb.
1791, died at Falmouth 7 June 1878, 87y (GS), daughter of
Ebenezer and Elizabeth (Field) Cole (Hall Desc., #418; Falmouth VRs). Burials are in the Methodist churchyard, Poplar
Ridge, West Falmouth. Hannah's widowed mother married
Daniel's father Robert.
      Daniel, Jr., served in Lt. Oliver Bray's company in Nov.
1814 (MA Mil. 1812-14, 246). In 1860, his household included
Leonard and Nancy Wilson, and Edwin and Hannah Morrill. In
1870 widow Hannah, 79, was living with her son Sewell.

Children, born at Falmouth:

886. i.   JAMES[8], b. 19 Apr. 1815.
887. ii.   (ELIZABETH) NANCY, b. 23 June 1816; m. LEONARD
            WILSON.
888. iii. SARAH ELIZABETH, b. 4 Mar. 1819; m. CHARLES A.
            WINSLOW.
889. iv.   ROBERT, b. 10 Mar. 1821.
      v.   SEWELL PRINCE, b. 2 May 1822, d. Falmouth 27
            June 1886, 64y (GS); m. 1st 28 Oct. 1861
            (SARAH) ANN MERRILL, d. Falmouth 15 Aug.
            1884, 54y; m. 2nd MINNIE SHAW. No ch.
      vi.   LOIS, b. 16 Apr. 1824, d. Falmouth 15 Oct.
            1897; m. 12 Nov. 1850 ALFRED HICKS, b. 2 Oct.
            1821, d. Falmouth 21 July 1890, son of Samuel
            and Abigail (Winslow) Hicks. No ch.
      vii. SUSAN, b. 27 June 1825, d. Falmouth 19 Feb.
            1870; m. Westbrook 19 Mar. 1866 ROBERT DYER,
            b. c1821 (49 in 1850). No ch.
890. viii. HANNAH, b. 7 July 1829; m. EDWIN MORRILL.
891. ix.   DANIEL EDWIN, b. 22 Jan. 1831.
892. x.   ABIGAIL, b. 26 Nov. 1833; m. JOHN MUNROE.
      xi.   ANDREW, b. 1 May 1836, d. 26 Jan. 1838.

393. ROBERT[7] 1791-1866 [131 Robert[6] and Hannah Leighton] was born at Falmouth 10 Dec. 1791, died at Westbrook 7 Sept. 1866, 74y; married at Cumberland 10 Sept. 1815 JOANNA PRINCE, born 14 June 1793, died at Westbrook 25 Jan. 1871, 77y, daughter of Paul and Sarah (Southworth) Prince (Hall Desc., #420; town VRs).
He was in Capt. Abel W. Atherton's company in Oct. 1813 (MA Mil. 1812-14, 165). In 1850, he was a butcher at Westbrook.

Children:

	i.	WASHINGTON[8], b. 20 Feb. 1816, drowned 9 Nov. 1832.
	ii.	HANNAH, b. 11 May 1818, d. 24 Feb. 1819.
893.	iii.	AURELIA, b. Deering 8 Sept. 1819; m. REUBEN BRACKETT and CHARLES KNIGHT.
	iv.	JOANN, b. 4 Sept. 1822, d. 22 Jan. 1899; m. 1st 23 Mar. 1845 NATHANIEL O. BRIGGS; m. 2nd 4 Mar. 1865 BYRON BURNHAM of Hopkinton NH, b. 28 Sept. 1835, son of Thomas Burnham. Ch. Daniel Briggs.
894.	v.	NELSON, b. 3 Oct. 1824.
895.	vi.	LYDIA, b. Westbrook 19 May 1826; m. JOHN DROWN and JOSEPH PORTER.
	vii.	MARY N., b. 19 Feb. 1835, d. 15 Nov. 1874; unm.

394. SARAH[7] 1797-1881 [131 Robert[6] and Hannah Leighton] was born at Falmouth 17 Sept. 1797, died there 21 July 1881; married there 30 June 1825 her cousin JOHN WEST, born perhaps at Haverhill MA 15 Feb. 1796, died at Falmouth, son of Thomas and Mary[6] (Leighton) West [# 133] (Cornman Ms; Hall Desc., #421; Falmouth VRs). He was a farmer.

Children (**West**), born at Falmouth:

i.   DANIEL, b. 27 Sept. 1825, d. in Nov. 1826.
ii.   GRANVILLE, b. 27 June 1827.
iii. LYDIA, b. 8 Dec. 1828; m. LORENZO CRESSEY.
iv.   LOIS, b. 13 Mar. 1831; m. RAY H. ELDER, JR.
v.   SARAH J., b. 10 Apr. 1833; m. GEORGE DURGIN.
vi.   HANNAH, b. 14 Aug. 1834; m. BENJAMIN CRESSEY.
vii. JAMES LEIGHTON, b. 27 May 1836; m. ADDIE E. BUCKMAN.

395. BENJAMIN[7] 1794-1853 [134 Thomas[6] and Patience Wallace] was born at Harrington ME 4 Jan. 1794, died at Milbridge 14 Mar. 1853, 59y 2m 9d (GS); married ABIGAIL BROWN, born at Harrington 9 Aug. 1799, died at Milbridge 16 May 1872, daughter of George and Mary (Strout) Brown (town VRs; Cornman Ms). Burials are in a family plot, Beaver Brook section. He was a farmer. In 1860 and 1870 Abigail and Franklin were in her son John's household. Benjamin's farm was in that part of Harrington set off to Milbridge in 1848.
Julia Cornman reported the unsupported tradition that they had 21 children, of whom only John lived to be named.

Children, born at Harrington:

896. i.   JOHN[8], b. 18 Sept. 1816.
      ii. FRANKLIN, b. c1830 (19 in 1850); unm.

396. LUCY[7] 1796-1889 [134 Thomas[6] and Patience Wallace]
was born at Harrington 11 Apr. 1796, died at Milbridge 22
Feb. 1889 (GS); married at Harrington 7 Sept. 1820 LOUIS J.
WALLACE, born there 7 Sept. 1790, died at Milbridge 25 Dec.
1870, 80y (GS), son of Col. Joseph, Jr., and Deborah (Smith)
Wallace (records of Leonard F. Tibbetts and Margaret Colton;
town VRs). Burials are in Evergreen Cemetery.

Children (**Wallace**), born at Harrington (now Milbridge):

i.   STEPHEN SMITH, b. in 1823, d. Milbridge 7 Nov. 1872
     (GS); m. there int. 2 Oct. 1854 PRISCILLA A. WAKE-
     FIELD, b. 24 Dec. 1830, d. in 1910, dau. of Daniel
     and Priscilla (Alden) Wakefield.
ii. NANCY JANE, b. in 1825 (GS-1829), d. in 1901; m. 1
     Nov. 1841 NELSON CLARK.
iii. MALCOLM, b. c1826; m. 1st Harrington int. 28 June
     1847 ELIZA A. BROWN, dau. of Thomas and Priscilla
     (Jordan) Brown; m. 2nd CHARLOTTE SARGENT, b. Goulds-
     boro 7 Nov. 1832, dau. of Samuel and Sally Sargent.
iv. GEORGE, b. in Feb. 1828, d. Galveston TX in Sept.
     1853 (GS); unm.
v.   WILLIAM E., b. 10 Mar. 1831, d. 12 Jan. 1921, 90y;
     m.1st ELIZABETH DREW; m. 2nd ELEANOR GRIFFIN.
vi. FRANCIS, b. 21 May 1835, d. Milbridge 29 May 1912; m.
     there 22 Oct. 1859 MARY D. CORTHELL, b. 17 Oct.
     1842, dau. of David and Jerusha (Drisko) Corthell
     (Corthell Gen., 85).
vii. LYDIA JANE, b. 4 Dec. 1837, d. Milbridge 25 Apr.
     1925; m. 1st JOHN HENRY REYNOLDS; m. 2nd THOMAS
     DOUGLAS.
viii. NELSON CLARK, b. 28 Apr. 1842, d. in 1928 (GS); m.
     1st Milbridge 19 Nov. 1866 LUCY H. FOSTER; m. 2nd
     ALMIRA (FOSTER) Hayford, b. 26 Oct. 1851. No ch.

397. JAMES[7] 1798-1858 [134 Thomas[6] and Patience Wallace]
was born at Harrington 11 Sept. 1798, died in the West Indies
8 Sept. 1858 (3 Sept. in probate record); married at Harrington int. 11 Nov. 1821 MARY P. [Polly] STROUT, born 17 Aug.
1798, lived at Milbridge in 1870, daughter of Solomon and
Joanna (Wallace) Strout (town VRs). James was a sea captain.
His household in 1850 included his father, aged 88. On 4
Jan. 1859, Mary P. Leighton was named administratrix of his
estate; the inventory 8 Feb. included one-eighth shares in
each of three brigs (WashCP, 21:109-11). In 1860 widow Polly
lived with her son Amos, and in 1870 with Amaziah Small.

Children, born at Harrington (Milbridge):

897. i.   SYBIL S.[8], b. 4 Feb. 1826; m. WILLIAM H. RICH.
898. ii.   DOLLY G., b. in 1828; m. JOHN T. WALLACE.
899. iii. AMOS G., b. in 1829.
      iv.   MARTHA, d.y.
900. v.   MARTHA U., b. in 1834; m. AMAZIAH R. SMALL.
      vi.   MARY A. WALLACE, b. in 1839 (21 in 1860).

398. ROBERT[7] 1800-   [134 Thomas[6] and Patience Wallace]
was born at Harrington say 1800; married JANE SMALLAGE of
Eden (Bar Harbor), born about 1798 (52 in 1850) (Cornman Ms).

Jane married second at Steuben 25 Nov. 1832 (Alfred) Thomas
Douglas. In 1850 Thomas and Jane Douglas were listed at Milbridge with three Douglas children (Alfred, Matilda and Aralinda) and Thomas Leighton, 20. Aralinda married in 1868
George B. Leighton [# 896].

Children:

    i.   OTIS[8], drowned at age 13.
901. ii.   LUCY H. W., b. in 1824; m. COURTNEY BABBAGE
           and ---- SMITH.
    iii.   JULIA, res. E. Boston; m. EZRA MURPHY.
    iv.   LOUISE, m. ---- DUMPHY. Ch. Jane, Lucy M.,
           Georgianna.
    v.   THOMAS, b. Milbridge 5 July 1830, d. Boston 25
           Oct. 1887 (VRs); m. 22 Oct. 1879 ADELE FLET-
           CHER, b. c1832, dau. of Alfred and Olive
           Fletcher. He was a seaman, US Navy. Ch.
           FRED[9] b. in 1885, res. Charlestown MA.

399. JOANNA[7] [Joan] 1802-   [134 Thomas[6] and Patience
Wallace] was born at Harrington about 1802 (48 in 1850); married first there 28 Sept. 1828 HENRY BRAY, born in Ireland,
died before 1850; married second at Harrington 10 Apr. 1853
DAVID B. STROUT, born in 1801, son of Solomon and Joanna
(Wallace) Strout (Harrington VRs; Cornman Ms). David had
married first at Harrington 27 Oct. 1819 Mary Ann McCaslin.

Children (**Bray**), born at Harrington:

    i.   CATHERINE, b. c1829 (21 in 1850), res. CA; m. Mil-
          bridge int. 2 June 1857 WILLIAM O'BRIEN of Calais.
    ii.   PALMER H., b. c1830 (20 in 1850); m. 1st 15 Jan.
          1850 SOPHIA COURIER; m. 2nd Addison int. 29 Sept.
          1852 REBECCA ROBINSON RAMSDELL.
    iii. SOPHIA, b. c1832 (18 in 1850); m. Harrington int.
          6 Apr. 1848 CHARLES AMESBURY.
    iv.   JOHN LEIGHTON, b. 12 Jan. 1836 (16 in 1850), d. in
          1892; m. 1st MARY OLIVE PERKINS; m. 2nd MARTHA
          HOLLAND or HAYLAND.
    v.   JAMES, b. c1837, drowned 16 Jan. 1858.
    vi.   MARY A., b. 15 Mar. 1842, d. 15 Sept. 1857.
    vii. WILLIAM F., b. c1843 (7 in 1850); m. Milbridge
          int. 25 Jan. 1866 MARY E. KENNEDY, b. 27 Nov. 1849,
          d. 24 Dec. 1893, dau. of James and Phebe (Cotton)
          Kennedy.

400. OTIS S.[7] 1803-1878 [134 Thomas[6] and Patience Wallace]
was born at Harrington 16 Apr. 1803, died there 16 Oct. 1878,
67y 6m; married there 28 Feb. 1825 ELIZABETH HOVEY (SEAVER)
Wallace, born at Chelsea VT 7 Feb. 1796, died 18 Oct. 1878,
77y, daughter of Dr. Richard Crafts and Christina (Slafter)
Seaver (Cornman Ms; Edmund F. Slafter, Memorial of John
Slafter [Boston, 1869], 48; Milbridge VRs). She had married
first 16 May 1813 Joseph Wallace, who died at Augusta ME 5
Apr. 1824, 32y; she had four Wallace children, born at Milbridge.
    Otis was a Milbridge farmer, 48 in 1850, 56 in 1860, 67 in
1870. His son John and wife Phebe lived with him in 1860.

Children, born at Milbridge:

902. i.   LORENA[8], b. 6 Aug. 1825; m. EPHRAIM C. PINEO.
903. ii.   LEWIS W., b. 13 Apr. 1826.
     iii. SAMANTHA ALMIRA, b. c1831; m. EPHRAIM KEITH.
           Ch. Hattie, Melvin and George (Cornman Ms).
904. iv.   ROBERT S., b. 3 June 1833.
     v.   JOHN AUGUSTUS, b. c1836 (14 in 1850); m. Mil-
           bridge int. 22 Nov. 1859 PHEBE W. GADSCOM
           (perhaps Gadcomb), b. c1845 (15 in 1860).
           Julia Cornman stated that they went west.

401.   PATIENCE[7] 1805-1879 [134 <u>Thomas[6]</u> and <u>Patience</u>
<u>Wallace</u>] was born at Harrington 5 July 1805, died at Mil-
bridge 9 June 1879, 73y 11m 9d (GS); married first at Har-
rington 18 Aug. 1825 AMOS GAY, born 21 Sept. 1801, died at
Milbridge 8 July 1849, 48y (GS), son of Jeremiah and Phebe
(Strout) Gay; married second at Milbridge 27 June 1860 WIL-
LIAM H. WALLACE (town VRs; records of Leonard F. Tibbetts and
Glenda Thayer).
Burials are in Evergreen Cemetery. In 1860 widow Patience
Gay was listed at Milbridge with four children.

Children (**Gay**), born at Milbridge:

i.   LUCY ANN, b. 25 Oct. 1826 (6 Oct. on GS), d. Mil-
       bridge 25 Apr. 1902; m. 17 Nov. 1844 WILLIAM R.
       SAWYER, b. 22 Dec. 1821. d. 16 July 1887, son of
       George and Mary (Roberts) Sawyer.
ii.   MARY JANE, b. 6 Nov. 1828, d. Milbridge 27 Jan. 1915;
       m. 1st WILLIAM WOOD; m. 2nd LEMUEL C MEANS, b. 7
       May 1825, d. 3 Jan. 1905 (GS).
iii.   MATILDA R., b. 3 Dec. 1830, d. 29 Sept. 1878; m.
       Milbridge 2 Apr. 1851 WILLIAM GODFREY, b. 8 Mar.
       1830, d. 5 Apr. 1909.
iv.   GEORGE M., b. 16 July 1833, d. at sea 26 Aug. 1848.
v.   JOEL C., b. 17 Mar. 1836, d. 22 Feb. 1923; m. 22 Mar.
       1863 ELLEN P. MANSFIELD, b. 14 July 1844, d. 28 Jan.
       1918.
vi.   PHOEBE HELEN, b. 27 May 1839, d. 3 Sept. 1840.
vii.   JAMES W., b. 6 Aug. 1841, d. 25 Sept. 1870 (GS); m.
       22 May 1863 HATTIE E. BROOKS, b. 20 Dec. 1842,
       dau. of Solomon and Lydia (Shaw) (Leavitt) Brooks.
viii. MIRANDA ELLEN, b. 9 May 1844, d. Boston 19 Oct. 1916;
       m. EDWARD B. COOK, who d. there 19 Aug. 1917.
ix.   FORESTER A., b. 16 July 1847.

402.   JOHN[7] 1794-   [135 <u>Ross[6]</u> and <u>Mary Chandler</u>] was
born at Cherryfield ME 3 Apr. 1794, lived there in 1860; married DORCAS ---- , born about 1795 (55 in 1850, 60 in 1860).
They later lived at Portland (Cherryfield TRs; Cornman Ms).

Children, born at Cherryfield:

i.   HARRIET[8] [Aretta], b. 14 Oct. 1825; m. THOMAS[7]
       LEIGHTON [# 420].
905. ii.   EZEKIEL, b. 10 Aug. 1828.
906. iii. MOSES, b. c1831.

403.   JACOB[7] 1795-1884 [135 Ross[6] and Mary Chandler] was born at Cherryfield 10 Dec. 1795, died there 27 Oct. 1884, 89y 10m (GS); married there 7 Aug. 1823 BETSEY[7] LEIGHTON, born about 1806 (45 in 1850, 54 in 1860), died there 10 Feb. 1875, 68y 4m (Machias Union), daughter of Joseph and Betsey (Jordan) Leighton [# 130] (Cherryfield VRs; records of Glenda Thayer).
He was a farmer. Burials are in Pine Grove Cemetery.

Children, born at Cherryfield:

907. i.   EVERETT T.[8], b. in 1825.
908. ii.   PILLSBURY, b. 2 July 1827.

404.   SAMUEL H.[7], 1797-1876 [135 Ross[6] and Mary Chandler] was born at Cherryfield 21 Dec. 1797, died at Bucksport ME 3 Feb. 1876, 78y; married at Gouldsboro 13 Dec. 1830 (Cherryfield int. 29 Nov.) (ELIZA) LYDIA BUNKER, born at Cherryfield about 1804 (42 in 1850), died at Bucksport 2 May 1896, 92y (town VRs; Cornman Ms).
He was a pedlar at Gouldsboro in 1850.

Children, born at Gouldsboro:

      i.   MARION[8.]
909. ii.   FRANCIS M., b. in July 1833.
      iii. JOHN W., b. 3 Oct. 1838, d. Bucksport 5 May
            1912, 75y 8m 20d; unm. He served in Co. B,
            1st ME Cav. Rgt., 1863-65. He was a civil
            engineer.
            About 1904 his sister-in-law Melissa wrote
            that he had lived for many years in KS (Corn-
            an Papers). He was probably the John W.
            Leighton at Portage, Houghton Co. MI in 1900.

405.   DANIEL[7] 1800-1870 [135 Ross[6] and Mary Chandler] was born at Cherryfield 7 June 1800, died there 5 May 1870 (GS); married there 17 July 1835 ABIGAIL [Abbie] JOY, born at St. Stephen NB 11 Nov. 1811, died at Cherryfield 2 Dec. 1874, 63y 3m 29d (GS) (Cherryfield VRs). Burials are in Sprague Falls Cemetery.
In 1870, Abigail J., 59, and her son Melvin, 17, lived with her son Truman at Cherryfield.

Children, born at Cherryfield:

      i.   TRUMAN W.[8], b. 18 Mar. 1839, d. Cherryfield 4
            Nov. 1915, 76y 7m 17d; m. there int. 15 Dec.
            1869 SARAH ELVIRA NICKELS, b. 15 Apr. 1838, d.
            Cherryfield 21 Jan. 1931, 93y 9m 7d, dau. of
            Daniel E. and Jemima (Libby) Nickels. He was
            a farmer. Ch. EDGAR D.[9] b. Cherryfield 19
            Mar. 1871, d. there 16 June 1933; m. Milbridge
            21 June 1905 SYBIL E. WILSON, b. Cherryfield
            in 1875, d. Bangor 20 June 1930, dau. of
            George and Laura (Tracy) Wilson. No ch.
910. ii.   MELVIN, b. 31 July 1854.

406. WILLIAM[7] 1803-1842 [135 Ross[6] and Mary Chandler] was
born at Cherryfield 25 June 1803, died there 9 July 1842, 37y
(GS, Willey Cemetery); married at Addison int. in Feb. 1828
MYRIAM MERRITT, born about 1800 (47 in 1850). She married
second in 1843 Obed Chapman: they were listed at Unionville
in 1850 with her two Leighton sons.
Chapman was named administrator of William's estate 8 Nov.
1843. An inventory taken 18 Nov. listed as assets a claim on
Ross Leighton's farm, and one-twelfth share in the schooner
"President", but the estate was declared insolvent 5 June
1844 (WashCP, 11:364, 538, 559).

Children, born at Cherryfield:

911. i.   MERRILL[8], b. 5 Oct. 1828.
912. ii.   GILBERT, b. c1836.

407. JAMES[7] 1805-1885 [135 Ross[6] and Mary Chandler] was
born at Cherryfield 7 Oct. 1805, died at Steuben 15 Sept.
1885, 83y; married first at Cherryfield 10 Dec. 1829 ANNA
[Annie] SMALL, born about 1799, died at Steuben 15 July 1863,
daughter of Ebenezer and Abigail[6] (Leighton) Small [# 132]
(Milliken, 4); married second LOVICIA[8] (LEIGHTON) Pinkham,
born at Steuben 20 Mar. 1825, died there 5 Feb. 1905, 80y 10m
11d, daughter of "Lezer" and Sally (Strout) Leighton [# 384].
  Lovicia married first JOEL PINKHAM [# 869], and had eight
children; one, Mary E., listed in James's household in 1870,
had probably been adopted by him (town VRs; records of Glenda
Thayer).
  In 1900, James S., Jr., and William H. were in the Milbridge household of their step-sister Dolly (Pinkham) Stull.

Children by Annie, born at Steuben:

      i.   (MARY) ABIGAIL[8], b. 21 Nov. 1830, with parents
            in 1860; unm.
      ii.   HANDY A , b. 22 Apr. 1833, d. in SC 25 Nov.
            1862 (NA-MSR; Oct. 1863 per Steuben VRs);
            unm. He enl. 4 Nov. 1862 Co. C, 11th ME Inf.
            Rgt., and d. in service.
913. iii. (LYDIA) MARGARET, b. 10 Sept. 1835; m. DANIEL
            PINKHAM.
      iv.   (JAMES) NELSON, b. 10 Jan. 1840, d. Fort Munroe
            SC 5 May 1864. He enl. with Handy in the same
            unit, and also d. in service.
      v.   WILLIAM HENRY, b. 25 Feb. 1849, d. Steuben 13
            Oct. 1931, 83y 7m 19d (as Henry H., son of
            James and Abigail); unm. In 1880, 30, he
            lived in his father's household; in 1900 he
            lived with his brother James and Dolly (Pink-
            ham) Stull.

Child by Lovicia, born at Steuben:

914. vi.   JAMES S., b. 26 Jan. 1866.

408. AARON[7] 1808-1906 [135 Ross[6] and Mary Chandler] was
born at Cherryfield 9 Mar. 1808, died at Steuben 9 Jan. 1906;
married at Cherryfield 16 Aug. 1832 BETHIA WAKEFIELD, born 30

Jan. 1812, died at Steuben 6 Aug. 1888, daughter of Lucy
Wakefield (town VRs; Cornman Ms; records of Leonard F. Tibbetts). He may have had a first wife Martha. He was a
farmer at Cherryfield in 1850, a fisherman in 1870.
According to Julia Cornman, Bethia was "Lucy Leighton's
daughter before marriage" to Gideon [# 383]. Burials are in
Sprague Falls Cemetery, Baileyville.

Children, ages from 1860 census:

    i.   ELIZABETH[8] [Lizzie], b. c1834; m. Addison
            int. 29 Sept. 1855 JAMES W. PLUMMER, b. there
            in 1831, son of John and Sally (Wass) Plummer.
            They moved away after 1860.
    ii.   CLARA M., b. c1835; m. Harrington 27 Sept. 1862
            (Machias Union) RINALDO W. PLUMMER. b. Addison
            c1834, brother of James. They too moved away.
    iii. CALEB H., b. c1838.
    iv.   THOMAS A., b. c1840.
    v.   (WILLIAM) GLEASON, b. c1842, d. 8 Sept. 1870;
            m. Addison (as Gleason W.) 25 Apr. 1869
            LEONORA [Nora] WASS, b. c1852, d. Messina,
            Sicily 3 Feb. 1875, 22y 8m 23d, dau. of
            Dimick and Phebe C. (Wass) Wass. No ch. Nora
            m. 2nd Milbridge 18 June 1873 AMAZIAH BROWN,
            son of John Sawyer and Margaret (Joy) Brown;
            he m. 2nd in 1877 Ella Wass, Nora's sister.
915. vi.   (STEPHEN) COFFIN, b. c1845.
    vii. WINFIELD SCOTT, b. c1848, d. Cherryfield 21
            Aug. 1870, 22y (GS).
    viii. MARIAM, b. c1850; m. Cherryfield int. 25 Mar.
            1869 JAMES ALBERT ATWATER, b. Steuben 15 Feb.
            1849, son of William and Priscilla[8] (Leighton)
            Atwater [# 686].
    ix.   FLORA A , b. c1853, d. 21 June 1869, 16y (GS)

409. DAVID BROWN[7] 1805-1881 [136 James[6] and Mary Brown]
was born at Harrington ME 11 Aug. 1805, died at Milbridge 25
Sept. 1881, 76y 1m 14d (GS); married at Harrington 4 Feb.
1835 ELIZA GODFREY[7] LEIGHTON, born at Steuben 28 Oct. 1815,
died at Milbridge 29 Oct. 1884, 69y, daughter of Asa and
Loruhamah (Fickett) Leighton [# 92] (town VRs; family Bible
in possession of the compiler).
In 1880, his household included Ernest[9], 9 [# 940]. On 31
Oct. 1846, he sold to Eleazer Leighton of Steuben 55 acres in
lot 50 "where Elazur now lives," on Pigeon Hill adjoining
William Leighton's lot (WashCD, 61:451).
They owned a farm at Milbridge on the Cherryfield road;
burials are in a family lot behind the farmhouse. During
summers, David sailed fishing vessels; in the winter he cut
wood, sledding the logs to Cherryfield sawmills, from which
the sawn timber was rafted to Milbridge and loaded on coastal
schooners. The homestead was left to Bill Henry and Susie.

Children, born at Milbridge:

916. i.   LYDIA L.[8], b. 13 Mar. 1836; m. ISAAC PERCY
            GRINDLE.
917. ii.   EVERLINIA K., b. 7 Dec. 1837; m. AUGUSTUS
            DONNELL.

918. iii. ABBIE MARIA, b. 2 Sept. 1839; m. ALBERT STROUT.
919. iv. (ANDREW) JACKSON, b. 29 June 1841.
      v. MARY MARVILLA, b. 25 Apr. 1843; m. LEVI C.[8]
         LEIGHTON [# 940] and HENRY C. MARTIN.
920. vi. CAROLINE L., b. 14 Mar. 1845; m. GEORGE L.
         STEWART and PIERRE CYR.
     vii. SUSANNA C., b. 25 Apr. 1847; m. WILLIAM H.[9]
          LEIGHTON [# 1480].
921. viii. ALBERT D., b. 5 Mar. 1850.
      ix. JUDSON ROY, b. 6 July 1855; m. Milbridge 28
          Aug. 1881 PHEBE S. DAVIS--div. in 1893. Ch.
          twins, d.y. Phebe m. 2nd Rockland ME 29 June
          1895 Otis G. Woodward.
       x. CHARLES, b. 30 Dec. 1858, d. 16 Oct. 1878,
          20y 9m.

410. JAMES JR.[7] 1810-1838 [136 James[6] and Mary Brown] was
born probably at Harrington say 1810, died there 13 May 1838
(per probate record); married at Harrington in 1832 (Cherryfield int. 27 June) SALLY R. SMALLAGE. She married second 3
Feb. 1840 Michael Shea.
    Widow Sally was granted administration of James's estate 7
Aug. 1838; an inventory 7 Nov. listed 50 acres of land, two
houses, one-quarter of the brig "Grand Turk," and one-eighth
of the schooner "Fame." James Walker, Jr., was made guardian
7 June 1843 of the minor children: Edwin W., Margaret and
James A.; Patrick Campbell replaced him 5 June 1844. In
1856, Albion K. P. Wallace was chosen as guardian by James A.
(WashCP, 9:422, 493; 11:322; 13:308; 20:272).

Children, born at Harrington:

       i. EDWIN W.[8].
      ii. MARGARET L.. b. c1836, lived with John and
          Deborah Gay at Milbridge, aged 14, in 1850.
922. iii. JAMES A., b. 24 Mar. 1839.

411. JOAN[7] 1807-1896 [136 James and Mary Brown] was born
probably at Harrington 19 Aug. 1807 (GS), died at Hancock ME
11 May 1896, 89y 10m 18d; married at Harrington int. 29 Sept.
1829 JOEL G. CURTIS, apparently the Jacob Curtis born at
Penobscot ME 30 Sept. 1804, died at Hancock 17 Aug. 1893, son
of Nathaniel and Polly (Grindle) Curtis (records of Elizabeth
Wescott; ME VRs). Burials are the in Brown-Curtis Cemetery
near the Ellsworth line. They were living at Ellsworth in
1830 and 1840, and at Hancock in 1850, he 43, she 41.
    Data concerning this couple are inconsistent, and need fur-
ther verification. Jacob's birth in Sedgwick records was 22
Sept. 1803, but 15 Sept. 1806 on his gravestone. Joan's
death record gave her parents as James and Joan Leighton.

Children (Curtis):

       i. ?MARY ELIZABETH, b. Blue Hill ME 17 July 1830; m.
          REUBEN GRINDLE DURGIN.
      ii. (ANN) MARIA, b. c1832, d. Hancock 27 Mar. 1924, 91y
          (GS); m. Surry 5 Oct. 1854 ISRAEL DURGIN.
     iii. CAROLINE H., b. c1833, d. 4 Aug. 1841, 8y (GS).

iv.   (JAMES) WELLINGTON, b. Ellsworth 24 Feb. 1837, d.
      Eastbrook ME 16 Dec. 1914 (GS); m. 19 June 1873
      SARAH ELLEN BUTLER.
v.   (ADOLPHUS) WASHINGTON, b. Ellsworth 4 Dec. 1839; m.
      10 May 1861 LAURA E. SCHOPPE.
vi.   MARGARET O., b. c1842, d. 28 Dec. 1844, 2y (GS).
vii. CAROLINE M., b. c1844, d. 21 Sept. 1850, 6y 6m.
viii. CALVIN H., b. c1846, d. 19 Sept. 1850, 4y 3m.
ix.   LAURA, b. c1848, d. 11 Sept. 1850, 1y 11m.
x.   EMMA R., b. Hancock 23 Feb. 1851, d. there 28 Sept.
      1894, 43y 7m 5d; m. 7 Apr. 1872 HERVEY SMITH.
xi.   ELLA F. (twin to Emma R.?); nfr.
xii. ?(FLORA) JOSEPHINE, b. c1853, d. 14 May 1878, 25y
      (GS); m. LEANDER SMITH.

412.   LOUISE CAROLINE[7] 1819-   [136 James[6] and Mary
Brown] was born probably at Harrington about 1819 (30 in
1850), perhaps resided at Haverhill MA (Cornman Ms); married
JAMES BROWN, born about 1817 (34 in 1850), son of Jesse and
Betsey (Sawyer) Brown.
He was a farmer at Hancock in 1850, his household including
James Laton, 43, perhaps his wife's cousin [# 407]. In 1870
they were at Hancock, his mother Betsey, 84, living with
them. Children's burials are in the Curtis-Brown Cemetery,
Hancock (records of Elizabeth Wescott; ME VRs).

Children (**Brown**), probably all born at Hancock:

i.   NANCY F., b. c1841, d. 2 Dec. 1876, 35y 9m (GS);
      m. JOSEPH W. GRAVES.
ii.   LUCETTA B., b. c1844 (6 in 1850), d. Hancock 11 Feb.
      1894, 47y 11m 11d (GS); m. as his 2nd wife SAMUEL T.
      DOW (Dow, Book of Dow, 128).
iii. HORACE W., b. c1846 (4 in 1850), d. in June 1864,
      17y 6m (GS), on ship from Bermuda to Fort Munroe,
      while in Co. A, 11th ME Inf. Rgt.
iv.   JESSE ALDEN, b. 6 July 1850, d. 9 Nov. 1932; m. 1st
      28 Mar. 1874 ISABEL D. YOUNG; m. 2nd Franklin ME
      14 July 1896 ALMENA (WILLEY) Leighton [# 876].
v.   WILLIAM (twin to Jesse A ?--1/12 in 1850); nfr.
vi.   CAROLINE A., b. c1853, d. 16 Oct. 1859, 5y 10m (GS).
vii. JAMES E., b. c1857, d. 26 Oct. 1881, 24y 8m 1d (GS).
viii. JOSEPH H., b. c1860 (10 in 1870), d. in 1937, 77y
      (GS); m. Surry 3 Dec. 1891 FLORA B. LUCKINS.
ix.   CADDIE A., b. c1862, d. 17 June 1865, 3y 2m (GS).
x.   FRED (twin to Caddie?--8 in 1870).

413.   HANNAH S.[7] 1828-   [136 James[6] and Mary Brown] was
born probably at Harrington about 1828 (27 in 1850, 32 in
1860), lived at Cherryfield in 1908; married first 6 Aug.
1842 GIDEON THOMPSON, born in NS 22 Sept. 1816, died before
1870 when Hannah was listed as a widow, son of John and Elizabeth (Tupper) Thompson; married second 4 Jan. 1873 ISAAC M.
PHINNEMORE, JR., born in NB about 1828, living in 1908 (Cherryfield Town Register, 1908), son of Isaac and Alice (McGouldrick) Phinnemore or Finnemore (records of Margaret Colton;
town VRs).

Children (**Thompson**), born at Cherryfield:

i.   MARY LUCRETIA, b. c1845 (5 in 1850), res. Stoneham
      MA; m. Cherryfield 18 Jan. 1865 ARTHUR B. TIBBETTS,
      b. in 1843, son of David and Mary (Tucker) Tibbetts
      [# 147].
ii.   CLARISSA, b. in 1849 (9/12 in 1850), res. Stoneham
      MA; m. ---- JOHNSON.
iii. FRED, b. c1852 (8 in 1860), res. Cambridge MA; m.
      Cherryfield 11 May 1874 CLARA E. SMALL.
iv.   ELLA, b. c1854 (6 in 1860), res. Ellsworth; m. ----
      TRIPP.
v.   ROBERT, b. c1857 (3 in 1860), res. WA
vi.   KATE L., b. c1859 (1 in 1860); m. Cherryfield 20 Jan.
      1877 JOHN MONAHAN, JR.

414. ROBERT[7] 1800-   [137 Benjamin[6] and Betsey Strout]
was born at Steuben 23 Oct. 1800, died there or at Milbridge
before 1850; married at Steuben 22 Aug. 1822 ELIZA DAVIS,
born about 1802 (48 in 1850), daughter of Samuel and Jane
(Willey) Davis (Steuben VRs; Cornman Ms).
    In 1850 widow Eliza's Unionville household included her
parents and her seven children. In 1860, she was the wife of
Harvey Archer at Harrington; in 1870 her daughters Charity
and Abby lived with them. In 1880, aged 77, she was living
with her son William.

Children, born at Steuben:

923. i.   PAMELIA[8], b. 11 Nov. 1823; m. JOHN W. DAVIS.
924. ii.   SEWELL S., b. in 1827.
      iii. ELIZABETH, d.y.
925. iv.   ELIZABETH, b. 18 July 1829; m. ROBERT DORR.
926. v.   FREEMAN, b. 5 Dec. 1831.
927. vi.   JULIA A , b. in 1833; m. FREEMAN DORR and
            WILLIAM DORR.
928. vii. CURTIS, b. 25 Dec. 1835.
929. viii. MARY J., b. in 1837; m. RICHARD DORR.
930. ix.   WILLIAM H., b. 27 June 1842.
931. x.   CHARITY, b. 17 Oct. 1844; m. CHARLES J. KING.
932. xi.   ABIGAIL DORINDA, b. 11 Sept. 1846; m. SYLVESTER
            TRACY.

415. MARY STROUT[7] [Polly] 1803-   [137 Benjamin[6] and
Betsey Strout] was born at Steuben 7 Sept. 1803; married
there 10 Nov. 1830 WILLIAM PINKHAM, born there 11 June 1806,
died there 24 Sept. 1885, son of William and Lucy (Strout)
Pinkham (Steuben VRs; Sinnett, Pinkham Gen., 16).

Children (**Pinkham**), born at Steuben:

i.   ENOCH, b. 11 Mar. 1831, d. in Aug. 1848.
ii.   ALVAH L., b. 14 Aug. 1834, d. Steuben 27 Apr. 1909;
      m. Harrington 24 Sept. 1868 MARY A. MERRITT, b. 22
      Sept. 1848, d. Steuben 3 Sept. 1912, dau. of Mark
      and Lucinda (White) Merritt.
iii. EMELINE, b. 1835.

iv.   BEULAH F., b. 1 Dec. 1836, d. Steuben 25 July 1911;
      m. 18 July 1856 GEORGE W. PINKHAM, who d. in the
      Civil War.
 v.   HENRY, b. 1 May 1841, d. 26 June 1902.
vi.   SALLY, b. c1843.

416. PERSIS[7] 1804-1890 [137 Benjamin[6] and Betsey Strout]
was born at Steuben 14 Nov. 1804 (GS-1808), died at Milbridge
in 1890 (GS); married at Cherryfield 9 Dec. 1824 NATHAN HINCK-
LEY, born 2 Oct. 1801, died at Milbridge 9 Sept. 1878 (GS),
son of Moses and Mary (Wallace) Hinckley (town VRs; records
of Margaret Colton). Burials are in Evergreen Cemetery.

Children (**Hinckley**), born at Cherryfield:

i.   MOSES, b. 2 Feb. 1824, lost at sea in Sept. 1852, 28y
       7m (GS); unm. He was a sea captain.
ii.   LEONARD, b. 12 June 1826; unm.
iii.   MARY E., b. c1827, d. Milbridge 30 Oct. 1837, 10y.
iv.   ELIAS, b. c1831, lost at sea with Moses in Sept.
       1852, 22y 8m (GS); unm.
v.   JOEL, b. 7 May 1833, d. Milbridge 14 Oct. 1921, 88y
       5m 7d; m. ALMIRA D. STROUT, b. in 1838, d. in 1925
       (GS).
vi.   ALBION, b. 26 June 1836, d. Milbridge 26 June 1898;
       m. HANNAH EVANS, b. in 1845, d. in 1929 (GS).
vii.   CELIA, b. c1838; m. IRA SHAW.
viii. ELIZABETH, b. c1840; m. Milbridge int. 16 Sept. 1864
       ISAAC McCOLLUM.
ix.   HANDY, b. 10 Aug. 1843, d. Milbridge in 1929 (GS);
       m. Milbridge 30 Aug. 1875 (THERESA) ANTOINETTE SAW-
       YER, b. 8 Nov. 1846, d. 31 Dec. 1911 (GS).
x.   ANGELINA, b. 8 Mar. 1848, d. 8 Mar. 1911, 63y 0m 0d
       (GS); m. Cherryfield 17 Feb. 1868 WILLIAM SHAW.

417. ALICE W.[7] [Elsie] 1808-1879 [137 Benjamin[6] and Betsey
Strout] was born at Steuben about 1808 (42 in 1850), died at
Milbridge 17 May 1871, 62y (GS); married at Harrington (as
Elsie) int. 10 Dec. 1831 LEVI CALVIN CORTHELL, born at Harrington about 1809, died at Milbridge 20 Jan. 1860 (GS), son
of Charles and Elizabeth (Lovett) Corthell (town VRs; Corthell Gen., 65-6; records of Margaret Colton). Burials are
in the Wallace Cemetery. He was a sea captain at Milbridge
in 1850.

Children (**Corthell**), born at Milbridge (census record):

i.   ANGELINE B., b. c1834; m. Milbridge 29 May 1864
       JOHN P. SMALL, d. in 1928.
ii.   LEVI L., b. c1835, d. Para, Peru, 9 Feb. 1856, 21y
       1m (GS); unm. He was a sailor.
iii.   NAPOLEON B., b. c1837; m. Milbridge 10 June 1864
       HANNAH HUTCHINS, dau. of John and Mary Catherine
       (Rich) Hutchins.
iv.   BENJAMIN A , b. 8 Dec. 1841, d. Milbridge 29 Aug.
       1907; m. 1st there 3 Aug. 1867 MARY ELIZABETH
       WALLACE, b. there 10 Nov. 1849, d. 31 Mar. 1879,
       dau. of Robert and Ann (Nash) wallace; m. 2nd in FL
       MARY J. NIX, who m. 2nd Abner Wallace.

418. JOSHUA M.[7] 1808-1892 [137 Benjamin[6] and Betsey Strout]
was born at Steuben 10 June 1808, died at Milbridge 30 May
1892, 83y 11m 20d; married at Machias 8 Dec. 1834 (Steuben
int. 28 Nov.) BETSEY STANHOPE, born at Steuben 25 July 1816,
died at Milbridge 21 Dec. 1897, 81y 5m 5d, daughter of Rodol-
phus and Mary (Brown) Stanhope (town VRs). Burials are in
Evergreen Cemetery.
A farmer and fisherman, Joshua lived on land originally
granted to Thomas[5] Leighton [# 42] on Pigeon Hill Bay, part
of which is still (1988) family-owned. Joshua's father and
brother had farms adjoining his.

Children, born at Steuben:

933.	i.	BENJAMIN FRANKLIN[8], b. 30 Nov. 1835.
934.	ii.	AMANDA M., b. 27 Nov. 1838; m. WILLIAM F. DAVIS and WILLIAM H.[8] LEIGHTON [# 930].
935.	iii.	HARRIET J., b. 11 June 1840; m. ALBERT H. TUCKER and GEORGE PIERCE.
	iv.	PERSIS A., b. 29 Oct. 1843; m. 4 Jan. 1867 NICHOLAS BROWN, b. 25 Dec. 1841. No ch.
	v.	EBENEZER, b. c1844 (6 in 1850). He served in the 20th ME Inf. Rgt. in the Civil War.
	vi.	THOMAS, b. c1846 (4 in 1850).
	vii.	ELSIE C., b. 12 Jan. 1847; m. 2 Oct. 1870 WILLIAM H. MARDEN, b. So. Canton ME in 1845, son of Charles W. and Eliza H. Marden. Ch. Betsey L. res. Newburgh NY (Cornman Ms).
936.	viii.	LEONARD D. H., b. 8 Oct. 1851.
937.	ix.	FRED J., b. 25 Nov. 1860.
938.	x.	ARTHUR, b. c1865 (5 in 1870).

419. JAMES P.[7] 1813-1897 [137 Benjamin[6] and Betsey Strout]
was born at Steuben 18 Apr. 1813 (30 in 1850), died at Mil-
bridge 29 Sept. 1897; married 28 Nov. 1839 SOPHRONIA[8]
LEIGHTON, born at Steuben 24 June 1822, died at Milbridge 10
Feb. 1899, 77y, daughter of Gideon and Lucy (Wakefield)
Leighton [# 383] (town VRs; records of Joanna Willey).
Burials are in Evergreen Cemetery. She was usually called
Sophrona.
Capt. James was a master of fishing vessels. On Sophrona's
death certificate, her father's name was later altered from
Gideon to William.

Children, born at Milbridge:

	i.	BENJAMIN F [8], b. c1840 (10 in 1850), not in 1860 census.
939.	ii.	PHILENA H., b. 27 Nov. 1841; m. BARNARD PINKHAM.
940.	iii.	LEVI C , b. 23 Mar. 1843.
941.	iv.	(JAMES) EVERETT, b. 2 Jan. 1845.
942.	v.	MARY A., b. 8 June 1847; m. LEANDER MARTIN.
	vi.	?SOPHIA N., b. c1847 (3 in 1850).
	vii.	LORENZO D., b. 2 Nov. 1850, d. Milbridge 22 Nov. 1931; m. Milbridge int. 16 Jan. 1892 IDA A. HUNTLEY, b. 4 July 1869, dau. of John and Dolly A. (Munson) Huntley of Wesley--div. in 1894. No ch. He was a sailor. Ida m. 2nd Andrew J. Grover.

viii. NAPOLEON C., b. 12 Apr. 1854, d. Milbridge 2
      Oct. 1885, 31y 5m 20d; m. there 16 July 1882
      LAURA A. STROUT, b. there 23 Feb. 1863, d.
      there 25 May 1906, 43y 2m 2d, dau. of Ezra S.
      and Sarah[8] (Leighton) Strout [# 1070]. Ch.
      AVERY N.[9] b. Milbridge 24 Apr. 1885, res.
      Somersworth NH in 1905 (Cornman[8]Ms). Laura m.
      2nd 29 Aug. 1896 Nathan Everett[8] Leighton
      [# 896].

943. ix. MOSES H., b. 22 July 1857.
      x.   AMOS G., b. 17 Mar. 1860, d. Milbridge 2 Oct.
           1866, 5y 9m 19d (GS).
944. xi. WILLARD HENRY, b. 1 July 1862.
      xii. ALICE JANE, b. 25 Sept. 1864, d. Milbridge 20
           Oct. 1865, 1y 15d (GS).

420. THOMAS[7] 1814-1890 [137 Benjamin[6] and Betsey Strout]
was born at Steuben 2 Mar. 1814 (VRs; 1815 per GS; aged 40 in
1860, 42 in 1870), died at Cherryfield 4 Aug. 1890 (GS); married there 22 May 1848 HARRIET[8] LEIGHTON, born at Steuben 14
Oct. 1828 (1825 per GS), died at Cherryfield 11 Apr. 1880,
daughter of John and Dorcas (----) Leighton [# 402] (town
VRs, Cornman Ms). Burials are in the Willey Cemetery at
Cherryfield.
    In 1850, his brother Edward was living with them. On 3 May
1861 Thomas enlisted in Co. G, 6th ME Inf. Rgt. In 1880 his
son Nathan S. and his family lived with him at Steuben.
    His wife was recorded variously, as Aretta, Iretta, and
Nettie; her name may have been Harrietta. The marriage
record showed Harriet.

Children, born at Steuben:

945. i.   ROBERT L.[8], b. 4 June 1850.
946. ii.   (NATHAN) SHAW, b. 31 May 1853.
      iii. ANGELINE, b. 18 Apr. 1855; m. 1st 25 Jan. 1878
            CHARLES J. LOW, b. 25 Mar. 1849, son of Daniel
            Jr. and Tryphena (Dorr) Low--prob. div.; ch.
            Mary G. b. July 1880, David M. b. Feb. 1883,
            Drusilla b. Mar. 1890, Frank b. Dec. 1893,
            Austin N. b. Dec. 1896. In 1900 and 1910 her
            Steuben household was headed by JAMES CORNEIL,
            b. in Apr. 1864, son of Thomas and Emily Cor-
            neil; she and James perhaps married.
      iv.   BETHIA [Bitha], b. c1856 (Bertha, 4 in 1860),
            not in 1870 census.
      v.   (CHARLES) HENRY, b. 16 Nov. 1858, 21 in 1880.
      vi.   ELIZABETH [Lizzie], b. 2 June 1864, d. Steuben
            5 Dec. 1919; m. W. Gouldsboro 28 Feb. 1888
            AMMI C. BUNKER, b. there 25 Feb. 1858, d.
            Steuben 19 May 1929, son of Enoch Nahum and
            Mary (Crabtree) Bunker (Moran, Bunker Gen,
            1:76). Ch. Thomas Enoch b. Gouldsboro 8 Mar.
            1895, res. Searsport; unm. Bunker had m. 1st
            W. Sullivan Millie Ashley, who d. c1887; they
            had one ch.
      vii. EDWARD [Eddie], b. c1868, d. Bangor 16 Oct.
            1936, 68y; unm.
      viii. PHENA, b. c1868 (2 in 1870), not in 1880
            census.

421. JOHN[7] 1775-1854 [138 Pelatiah[6] and Elizabeth Allen]
was born at Falmouth ME 4 June 1775, died at Cumberland ME 19
Nov. 1854; married first at Windham ME 22 Sept. 1796 (MH&GR,
7[1896]:213) LEONICE SAWYER, born in May 1772, died at Cumberland 2 Apr. 1850, daughter of Jonathan Sawyer; married
second at Gray 25 Jan. 1852 ELIZABETH [Betsey] (THOMPSON)
Delano, who died 10 Oct. 1862, widow of Amaziah Delano (Joel
Andrew Delano, American House of Delano [New York, 1899],
230; Falmouth and Cumberland TRs; Hall Desc., #153; Cornman
Ms). In 1800 he was listed as a farmer at North Yarmouth,
but soon settled at Cumberland. In 1850 he was at Cumberland
in the household of William Hall [# 978].

Children by Leonice:

947. i.   ELIZABETH[8] [Betsey], b. Cumberland 4 Jan. 1797;
            m. DANIEL ALLEN.
948. ii.   MARY, b. Cumberland c1799; m. SAMUEL COBB.
949. iii. CLARISSA, b. No. Yarmouth 20 Apr. 1800; m.
            OTIS ALLEN.
950. iv.   ESTHER, b. Cumberland say 1802; m. ELLIOT MAX-
            FIELD and BENJAMIN SAWYER.
951. v.   JAMES HICKS, b. 27 May 1804.
      vi.   PETER, b. say 1806, d.y.
952. vii. ISAAC SAWYER, b. Cumberland 19 June 1808.
      viii. WILLIAM, b. Cumberland c1812, lost at sea; m.
            MARY KNIGHT, who m. 2nd John Stillwell.

422. THOMAS[7] 1777-1830 [138 Pelatiah[6] and Elizabeth Allen]
was born at Falmouth 14 Feb. 1777, died at Windham ME 25 Nov.
1830; married at Windham 3 Mar. 1806 DORCAS ALLEN, born at
Westbrook 18 Mar. 1784, died at Windham 11 Oct. 1833, daughter of Joseph and Mary (Baker) Allen of Windham (Hall Desc.,
#154; town VRs; Cornman Ms.).
He served from Windham in Capt. Nathan Gould's company,
Sept. 1814 (MA Mil. 1812-14, 211).

Children, born at Windham:

953. i.   ANDREW ALLEN[8], b. 12 Aug. 1806.
      ii.   MARY ALLEN, b. 24 May 1810, d. 8 May 1837; unm.
954. iii. SUSAN ALLEN, b. 16 Apr. 1812; m. HENRY SENTER.

423. ROBERT[7] 1779-1851 [138 Pelatiah[6] and Elizabeth Allen]
was born at Falmouth 20 June 1779, died there 7 Mar. 1851;
married there 17 Jan. 1802 TABITHA FOWLER, born 25 July 1780,
died at Falmouth 17 Feb. 1860, 79y 7m, daughter of Moses
Fowler (town VRs; Hall Desc., #155). Burials are in Poplar
Ridge Cemetery, West Falmouth.
He was a farmer in what became Westbrook. He served in
Capt. Abel W. Atherton's company at Portland Sept. to Nov.
1813 (MA Mil. 1812-14, 166). In 1850 Tabitha, 70, was living
at Cumberland with her son Moses.

Children, born at Falmouth:

      i.   ?EDWARD[8], b. c1802.
955. ii.   HENRY[8], b. 20 June 1803.

956.   iii. LEWIS, b. 1 Apr. 1805.
957.   iv.   LOUISA, b. 12 Dec. 1806; m. ISAAC SKILLINGS.
       v.   JOAN, b. 9 Nov. 1808, d. 30 Nov. 1811 (GS).
       vi.   ELBRIDGE, b. 8 Feb. 1812; perhaps m. ----
             BARTLETT (but unm. in Cornman Ms).
958.   vi.   JOANNA, b. 9 Feb. 1814; m. WILLIAM THOMPSON.
959.   vii. HARRIET, b. 20 May 1816; m. JOHN H. OXNARD.
960.   viii. MOSES WASHINGTON, b. 14 Feb. 1818.
       ix.   ALFRED, b. 19 Feb. 1821, drowned in Duck Pond
             9 Aug. 1839, 18y.

424. CHESLEY[7] 1781-   [138 Pelatiah[6] and Elizabeth Allen]
was born at Falmouth in 1781, lived at Turner ME in 1850,
aged 66; married first at Hebron ME 26 Apr. 1810 (VRs) RUTH
CUSHMAN, born at Hebron in Feb. 1791, daughter of Gideon and
Ruth (Shaw) Cushman (Henry W. Cushman, Genealogy of the Cush-
mans [Boston, 1855, 162); married second LUCY ---- , born
about 1793 (57 in 1850) (Hall Desc., #156; Hartford VRs).
    He, then of Hartford ME, sold 21 acres of land at Falmouth
to George Leighton 9 July 1817 (CumbCD, 78:300). He served
from Hartford in Lt. Cyrus Thompson's company at Portland in
Sept. 1814 (MA Mil. 1812-14, 225).

Children, born at Hartford, two perhaps by second wife:

       i.   MARY CUSHMAN[8] [Polly], b. 22 Oct. 1811, res.
             Hartford in 1850, pauper; unm.
       ii.   JOSEPH SHAW, b. 22 July 1813.
       iii. ALVIN, b. 13 Oct. 1815.
       iv.   CLARISSA, b. 13 Apr. 1818.
       v.   LEWIS F., b. 28 July 1820, d. Buckfield ME 18
             June 1900, 79y 10m 22d; m. MARGARET A. BRAD-
             BURY, b. c1822--div. In 1850 he was without
             a family at Hebron ME.
       vi.   SARAH [Sally], b. in 1822; m. ANSON MERRILL.
       vii. HANNAH, b. c1824, d. Hartford 7 July 1912, 88y;
             unm. She lived in the Hartford almshouse in
             1900.
       viii. SOLOMON, b. c1825 (18 in 1850), d. Hartford 28
             July 1892, 67y; unm.
       ix.   CHARLOTTE, b. c1828 (22 in 1850).
       x.   PELATIAH, b. c1830 (14 in 1850), d. Washington
             DC 7 Dec. 1862; unm. He served in Co. F, 17th
             ME Inf. Rgt.
       xi.   SUSAN, b. c1838 (12 in 1850).

425. DORCAS[7] 1783-1833 [138 Pelatiah[6] and Elizabeth Allen]
was born at Falmouth in 1783, died at North Yarmouth 16 Mar.
1833; married there int. 10 Aug. 1814 GEORGE JOHNSON, born
there 7 Oct. 1790, son of Nathan and Mary Johnson (town VRs;
Cornman Ms; Hall Desc., #160).

Children (**Johnson**), born at North Yarmouth:

       i.   MARY ANN, b. 9 Apr. 1815.
       ii.   BETSEY, b. 11 May 1817.
       iii. CHARLOTTE, b. 1 June 1819; m. ---- REED.
       iv.   AMOS OSGOOD, b. 12 July 1821, drowned at sea.

v.   NATHAN, b. 3 July 1823, res. Gloucester MA.
vi.   DORCAS, b. 4 Dec. 1825, d. 27 Mar. 1826.
vii. GEORGE WASHINGTON, b. 24 Apr. 1828; res. Manchester
      NH.

426.   CHARLOTTE[7] 1785-1839 [138 Pelatiah[6] and Elizabeth
Allen] was born at Falmouth in 1785, died in 1839; married 5
June 1806 JOHN MARSHALL LINCOLN, born in 1781, died in 1849,
son of Urbanus and Lydia (Barnes) Lincoln (Hall Desc., #157;
George L. Davenport, Genealogies of the Families of Cohasset,
Mass. [Cohasset MA, 1909], 249; letter of Dr. J. A. Tobey--
Cornman Papers; Cornman Ms). Lincoln married second Ruth L.
Tower, born in 1798 and died in 1859.

Children (Lincoln):

i.   ELIZABETH [Betsey], b. 12 Nov. 1806.
ii.   HANNAH.
iii. CORNELIUS, b. 9 Jan. 1809, d. at sea in 1883; m. 2
      Dec. 1830 HANNAH BEAL, dau. of Christopher and
      Hannah (Lambert) Beal.
iv.   LYDIA, b. 16 Jan. 1811; m. 1 July 1832 ANDREW MORSE.
v.   EUNICE.
vi.   JOHN MARSHALL, b. 3 Mar. 1814, d. in 1871; m. 10 Nov.
      1833 ABIGAIL LINCOLN.
vii. SARAH, b. 30 Mar. 1816; m. 17 Oct. 1833 MELZAR GROCE.

427.   GEORGE[7] 1787-1866 [138 Pelatiah[6] and Elizabeth Allen]
was born at Falmouth 11 Oct. 1787, died there 28 Mar. 1866,
78y 5m 17d (GS); married at Windham 7 Apr. 1814 ABIGAIL MAYB-
ERRY, born there 6 Nov. 1792, died at Falmouth 31 Mar. 1879,
86y 5m (1880, 86y, GS), daughter of Richard and Miriam
(Thompson) Mayberry (Nathan Gould, Descendants of William
Mayberry of Windham [TMs, nd, MHS], 111; Falmouth and Windham
VRs; Hall Desc., #159; Cornman Ms; records of descendant Ruth
L. Froeberg).
      George was a farmer. At 70, he lived at Belfast in 1850
with his brother-in-law Job Shaw. In 1870, Abigail, 78,
lived with her son Cyrus. Burials are in the Universalist
Cemetery, West Cumberland.

Children, born at Falmouth:

961. i.   JOSEPH MAYBERRY[8], b. 16 Aug. 1814.
      ii.   ABIGAIL, b. 14 Mar., d. 17 Apr., 1816.
962. iii. GEORGE WASHINGTON, b. 4 May 1818.
963. iv.   HANNAH, b. 8 July 1821; m. THOMAS HICKS and
            HENDRIK SMART.
964. v.   AMOS, b. 20 Aug. 1823.
      vi.   MARIA, b. 13 Oct. 1825; m. JAMES[8] LEIGHTON
            [# 886].
      vii. RUFUS (twin), b. 13 Oct. 1825, d. 20 Aug. 1826.
965. viii. ALBERT, b. 7 Mar. 1829.
966. ix.   ADDISON GREENLEAF, b. 25 May 1831.
      x.   JULIA ANN, b. 18 Apr. 1834, d. 25 Feb. 1901; m.
            HUGH WOODBURY LARRABEE, res. in IL. Ch. Sarah
            Stella.
967. xi.   CYRUS CUMMINGS, b. 22 Feb. 1837.

428.   DOROTHY[7] 1790-   [138 Pelatiah[6] and Elizabeth Allen] was born at Falmouth about 1790; married at Falmouth 5 Oct. 1809 (TRs) JOB SHAW of Hartford ME (Hartford VRs; Cornman Ms). They lived at Hartford in 1810 and 1820, at Waldo in 1830, and in 1850 at Belfast, he 68 and she 64.
Job and Dorothy Shaw of Hartford on 20 Mar. 1819 quitclaimed to her brothers George and Ezekiel Leighton "all land in Falmouth which Pelatiah father of Dorothy died seized of" (CumbCD, 81:421).

Children (**Shaw**), born at Hartford:

i.   PELATIAH LEIGHTON, b. 11 Feb. 1810.
ii.   NATHANIEL, b. 4 Nov. 1811.
iii. DOROTHY, b. 17 Mar. 1814.
iv.   EUNICE, b. 21 Mar. 1816.
v.   HANNAH, b. 3 Apr. 1818.
vi.   ELIZABETH, b. 7 Apr. 1820.
vii. EBENEZER, b. 9 Oct. 1821.
viii. ALPHEUS, b. 8 Feb. 1824.
ix.   MARY, b. c1828 (21 in 1850).
x.   SAMUEL, b. c1833 (17 in 1850).

429.   EZEKIEL[7] 1794-1872 [138 Pelatiah[6] and Elizabeth Allen] was born at Falmouth 9 May 1794, died there 6 Jan. 1872; married 13 Nov. 1817 (as Ezekiel, Jr., in Windham int. 18 Oct.) MARY CHUTE MAYBERRY, born at Windham 6 Apr. 1800, died at Falmouth 30 May 1881 (GS, 31 May 1879), daughter of Richard and Miriam (Thompson) Mayberry (Gould, Mayberry Desc., 111; Hall Desc., #161; Falmouth TRs). Burials are in Poplar Ridge Cemetery, West Falmouth.
He was a farmer at Cumberland; in 1860 and 1870, his household included his son Charles.

Children, born at Falmouth:

i.   MIRIAM MAYBERRY[8], b. 27 Apr. 1818; m. ISAAC SAWYER[8] LEIGHTON [# 952].
ii.   CHARITY, b. 3 Dec. 1819, d. 12 Sept. 1835.
968. iii. ELIZABETH, b. 11 Sept. 1821; m. JOSEPH HICKS.
iv.   MARY, b. 13 Nov. 1823, d. 12 May 1853; unm.
v.   LEONARD, b. 29 Nov. 1825, d. Cumberland 8 Feb. 1900, 74y; m. BETSEY BARBARA (FIELD) Hicks, b. Portland 1 Mar. 1818, a. Cumberland 4 Feb. 1900, dau. of James and Polly S. (Lowe) Field and widow of John Hicks. No ch. Living with them in 1860 at Cumberland were James Hicks, 20, and Adrianna Hicks, 17.
vi.   DANIEL MAYBERRY, b. 27 Nov. 1827, d. Boston 3 Sept. 1903 (VRs); m. c1852 AMELIA SMITH, b. in Canada in Jan. 1833. In 1900, they ran a boarding-house in Boston.
vii. EMILY JANE, b. 20 Mar. 1830, res. No. Deering; m. 25 Feb. 1861 ELBRIDGE MITCHELL, b. Freeport 25 Apr. 1820.
viii. EZEKIEL, b. 26 Oct. 1832, d. 11 Apr. 1837.
ix.   CHARLES HENRY, b. 24 Feb. 1836, d. Falmouth 20 Jan. 1909, 73y; m. 1st 3 Sept. 1863 MARY ELIZABETH LIBBY, b. 26 Dec. 1843, dau. of Arthur and Nancy Ann (Cobb) Libby (Libby Fam.,

457); m. 2nd 25 Oct. 1898 NANCY A. JOHNSON, b.
18 Aug. 1840 (1834-1911, GS). Ch. MARY^9, d.
aged 12. He served in the Civil War 1861-65,
and was discharged injured. He res. Falmouth
in 1900, with his wife (called Mary A.) and
"grandson" Leroy Winslow, b. in Dec. 1887.

430. NATHANIEL C.^{7} 1779-1849 [139 Jedediah^6 and Eunice
Gerrish] was born at Falmouth 21 July 1779, died there 22
Aug. 1849; married DORCAS [Dolly] WILSON, born 22 Nov. 1778,
died at Falmouth 22 Nov. 1866, daughter of Ichabod Wilson
(Falmouth VRs: records of Barbara Clark Brown; Hall Desc.,
#162). He was a lieutenant in Maj. John Trowbridge's cavalry
detachment in 1814 (MA Mil. 1812-14, 158). In 1850 widow
Dolly, 71, was living in Daniel Shaw's household.

Children, born at Falmouth:

969. i.   LAVINA^8, b. 22 Nov. 1800; m. DANIEL SHAW, JR.
970. ii.   EUNICE, b. 7 Feb. 1802; m. JOSHUA GOWER.
971. iii. JANE, b. 20 Oct. 1805; m. ISAIAH DAVIS.
972. iv.   JEDEDIAH, JR., b. 16 May. 1808.
973. v.   ICHABOD WILSON, b. 22 Mar. 1811.
      vi.   LUCY ANN, b. 1 Mar. 1820, d. 31 Aug. 1832.

431. MARY^7 1781-   [139 Jedediah^6 and Eunice Gerrish]
was born at Falmouth say 1781, lived at Westbrook; married at
Falmouth NATHANIEL HALE, born 23 May 1783 (Hall Desc., #163;
Cornman Ms).

Children (**Hale**):

i.   MARY, b. in 1806; m. ASA^7 LEIGHTON [# 457].
ii.   JOSEPH; m. SALLY PRIDE of Pride's Corner, Westbrook.
iii. LORENZO; m. LOUISA PRIDE.

432. LOIS^7 1784-1877 [139 Jedediah^6 and Eunice Gerrish]
was born at Falmouth 17 Sept. 1784, died there 6 Apr. 1877,
82y 6m; married there 19 Nov. 1812 CYRUS WILSON, born 18 Aug.
1789, died there 14 July 1873, son of Nathaniel and Sarah
(Pride) Wilson (Falmouth and Cumberland TRs; Hall Desc.,
#164; records of Toni Packard).

Children (**Wilson**), born at Cumberland:

i.   CAROLINE, b. 11 Feb. 1813, d. Falmouth 16 Sept. 1831;
      unm.
ii.   MARY, b. 31 Dec. 1814, d. 27 June 1902; m. BENJAMIN
      F. DOUGHTY.
iii. ALMIRA, b. 26 Jan. 1816, d. Cumberland 8 Feb. 1905;
      unm.
iv.   ELBRIDGE, b. 9 Dec. 1817, d. 29 Jan. 1879; unm.
v.   JOSEPH, b. 4 May 1820, d. 9 Dec. 1879; unm.
vi.   CHARLES NEWELL, b. 3 July 1822, d. 9 Feb. 1896; m.
      29 Nov. 1849 MARTHA MOUNTFORT.
vii. WILLIAM HENRY, b. 1 Dec. 1824; m. MAHALA CUMMINGS
      WILSON.

viii. HANNAH, b. 5 Dec. 1826; m. JAMES NOYES[8]LEIGHTON
      [# 1124].
  ix. CORNELIUS, b. 14 Feb. 1829, d. 13 Jan. 1898; m. JULIA
      CUMMINGS WILSON.
   x. NATHANIEL LEIGHTON, b. 11 Apr. 1832; m. 1st SARAH
      SHAW; m. 2nd 10 Apr. 1897 ANNIE M. SHAW, b. in 1844,
      dau. of James and Hannah (Wilson) Shaw
  xi. (MIRANDA) AUGUSTA, b. 17 Dec. 1834; m. ELI RUSSELL.
 xii. (LORENZO) HALE, b. 3 June 1837; m. 15 Jan. 1879
      SARAH FRANCES MORRISON, b. 29 Oct. 1856.

433. PETER[7] 1785-1848 [139 Jedediah[6] and Eunice Gerrish]
was born at Falmouth 18 Feb. 1785, died there 28 June 1848;
married there 29 Jan. 1806 RACHEL WINSLOW, born there 22 May
1788, died at Portland 7 Oct. 1865, 77y (VRs), daughter of
Hezekiah and Phoebe (Doughty) Winslow (Hall Desc., #165;
David Parsons Holton, Winslow Memorial [N. Y., 1888], 2:841,
937; Falmouth TRs). Burials are in Poplar Ridge Cemetery,
West Falmouth.

Children, born at Falmouth:

974.   i. JOEL[8], b. 17 June 1807.
      ii. AMOS, b. 22 Feb., d. 5 Mar., 1809.
975. iii. LOUISE, b. 17 Feb. 1810; m. THOMAS NEWMAN.
976. iv. ADAM W., b. 30 Dec. 1812.
977.   v. ABIGAIL M., b. 13 June 1814; m. AMOS R.
          WINSLOW.
978. vi. EMELINE, b. 6 Sept. 1818; m. WILLIAM S. HALL.
     vii. EUNICE, b. 11 Aug. 1821; m. ANDREW[8] LEIGHTON
          [# 503].

434. GEORGE[7] 1789-1868 [139 Jedediah[6] and Eunice Gerrish]
was born at Falmouth 20 Sept. 1789, died there 6 Nov. 1868,
79y (GS); married first 28 Feb. 1812 SUSANNA BAKER, born 18
Aug. 1793, died 22 Aug. 1855 (GS), daughter of William and
Lydia Baker; married second 17 Apr. 1856 THANKFULL (HALL)
(Lovering) Tubbs, born at Falmouth 19 Aug. 1800, daughter of
Timothy and Abigail (Austin) Hall (Hall Desc., #166, 555;
Falmouth TRs). Burials are in a private lot at Falmouth
behind the former Horace Soule home.
   George served in Major John Trowbridge's cavalry detachment
in Sept. 1814 as a dispatch rider (MA Mil. 1812-14, 158). To
distinguish him from his uncle [# 427], he was known as
George, Jr. He later commanded a militia battalion of
cavalry, and thus was usually called Major George.
   In 1880, Thankfull, 79, was living at Falmouth with her
step-son Lorenzo.

Children by Susanna, born at Falmouth:

979.   i. WILLIAM B.[8], b. 6 July 1813.
980. ii. MARIA, b. in Oct. 1815; m. ELIAS P. MARSTON.
981. iii. GEORGE W., b. 4 Oct. 1817.
982. iv. LEONARD, b. 23 Mar. 1820.
983.   v. LORENZO H., b. 26 Feb. 1822.
      vi. CHARLES D., b. 27 July 1827, d. 7 Dec. 1828.

435. JOSIAH L.[7] 1792-1866 [139 Jedediah[6] and Eunice Ger-rish] was born at Falmouth 14 Apr. 1792, died there 18 Jan. 1866; married first 15 June 1815 ANNA WILSON, born 23 Apr. 1795, died 19 Oct. 1849, 54y (GS), daughter of Nathaniel and Sarah (Pride) Wilson; married second 20 Oct. 1850 CYNTHIA PURINTON, born about 1800 (60 in 1860), died in Sept. 1878 (Falmouth VRs; Hall Desc., #167). Burials are in a private lot behind the former Horace Soule home.

Josiah was 78 at death according to his gravestone; the death notice in the Morning Star of 29 Aug. 1866 stated he died at 73. He was a farmer at North Falmouth.

Children by Anna, born at Falmouth:

984. i.   ROYAL[8], b. 19 Oct. 1816.
     ii.   SARAH JANE, b. 24 Apr. 1818, res. Portland; m. 17 Dec. 1843 LINDSEY FRYE, b. 8 June 1814, d. Deering 5 July 1884, son of John and Abigail (Blanchard) Frye. No ch.
     iii. HORATIO G., b. 23 Feb. 1823, d. 26 Sept. 1846, 26y (GS; 23y 7m per Morning Star); unm.
     iv.   JASON, b. 3 Dec. 1828, d. Westbrook 5 Apr. 1894; m. Portland 23 Dec. 1856 MARTHA HALE, b. Westbrook 8 Spr. 1835, d. there 14 Jan. 1901, dau. of Josiah and Martha (Roberts) Hale. Ch. WALTER LENWOOD[9] b. Westbrook 2 Feb. 1858; m. Falmouth 14 Aug. 1884 JENNIE L. PACKARD, b. 22 Oct. 1860, d. Westbrook 21 Jan. 1901, dau. of Nathaniel and Adelaide (Sherman) Packard: ch. ETHEL PACKARD[10] b. in MA 22 July 1887.
     v.   CYNTHIA H., b. 13 Feb. 1831, d. Portland 4 Dec. 1922, 91y 9m 22d; unm.
985. vi.   NATHANIEL WILSON, b. 11 June 1833.
986. vii. RANDALL, b. 8 Aug. 1838.

436. EUNICE[7] 1794-1843 [139 Jedediah[6] and Eunice Gerrish] was born at Falmouth say 1794, died at Peru ME 8 Oct. 1843 (VRs); married at Falmouth 9 Apr. 1822 (int. Cumberland 4 Apr.) JOSIAH GERRISH, born at Falmouth 1 Dec. 1793, died at Peru 6 July 1867 (GS), son of Nathaniel and Alice (Abbott) Gerrish. Burials are in the Knight-Waite Cemetery, Peru (Hollis Turner, History of Peru, Me. 1789-1911 [Augusta ME, nd], 122; Hall Desc., #168; Peru VRs; records of Evelyn K. Arsenault).

Josiah married second at Falmouth 25 Dec. 1844 Hannah May-berry, daughter of Richard and Miriam (Thompson) Mayberry (Mayberry Desc., 111).

Children (**Gerrish**), born at Falmouth:

i.   MARTHA ANN, b. 21 Nov. 1824, d. Peru 7 July 1867 (GS); m. there 24 May 1851 JOHN KNIGHT, b. there 13 July 1818, d. there 26 Apr. 1896, son of Amos and Lucy (Knight) Knight. He m. 2nd 9 Jan. 1868 Mary Shaw.
ii.   LORANA, b. 15 Dec. 1830, d. Peru 4 Oct. 1891; m. Falmouth 13 Sept. 1852 JOSIAH HALL, b. Wrentham MA 4 May 1824, son of George and Hannah (Smith) Hall.

iii.   CAROLINE W., b. in 1833, d. Peru 28 Dec. 1865; unm.
iv.   EPHRAIM MARSTON, b. in 1835, d. Peru 10 Aug. 1879;
       m. there 30 Sept. 1866 ANNETTE E. KNIGHT.
v.   EUNICE, d. Peru, aged 12.

437.   JONATHAN[7] 1823-1865 [139 Jedediah[6] and Mary Marston]
was born at Falmouth about 1823 (26 in 1850), died there 13
Oct. 1866, 43y (Morning Star of 31 Jan. 1866; died in 1865,
42y, GS); married at Falmouth 4 Dec. 1850 MARY ANN TINKHAM,
born at Hartford ME 4 Nov. 1827, died at Falmouth 17 Nov.
1909, 84y 13d, daughter of Ephraim and Martha (Noyes) Tinkham
(Falmouth VRs; Hall Desc., #169). Burials are in Poplar
Ridge Cemetery, West Falmouth.
    He was a farmer. In 1860, his household included his
mother Mary, 77. In 1870 his widow, 45, headed a household
at Gray including three Leighton children. She may have married second at Gray 1 Aug. 1867 Samuel S. Farwell.

Children, born at Falmouth:

987. i.   MARTHA JANE[8] [Jennie], b. 28 Aug. 1851; m.
            CORNELIUS B. ROSS.
      ii.   MARY, d. 24 Oct. 1853, 3m 23d (GS).
      iii. CELIA H., b. 2 June 1855, d. Gray 2 Feb. 1902,
            46y 8m; unm.
      iv.   FRANK N., b. 9 Jan. 1858, d. Gray 16 Feb. 1901,
            43y 2m 7d; unm.
      v.   ANNIE E., b. c1863 (31 in 1894); m. Mechanic
            Falls 7 July 1894 JOHN E. BERRY, b. Paris ME
            in 1858, son of Elijah S. and Merinda Berry.

438.   ADELINE[7] 1824-   [139 Jedediah[6] and Mary Marston]
was born at Falmouth 17 Dec. 1824, lived at Everett MA in
1902; married 2 Oct. 1842 JOSEPH H. KEEN, born at Hebron ME
27 Oct. 1818, lived at Poland ME, son of Nathaniel and Lydia
(Hutchinson) Keen (Cornman Ms; Hall Desc., #170).

Children (**Keen**):

i.   MARY ANN, b. Falmouth 20 July 1843; m. JOHN F. WELCH.
ii.   BETSEY M., b. Hebron 25 Oct. 1846; m. CYRENIUS W.
        CROCKER.
iii.   JEDEDIAH LEIGHTON, b. Falmouth 29 Nov. 1848.
iv.   CLARA A., b. Falmouth 4 Dec. 1852.
v.   ROYAL H., b. Hebron 17 Apr. 1857.
vi.   SARAH F., b. Poland 15 June 1859.
vii.   LUTHER B., b. Poland 3 June 1862.

439.   EBENEZER[7] 1781-1869 [141 Hatevil[6] and Lucy Staples]
was born at Falmouth 14 July 1781, died at Westbrook 20 Jan.
1869; married at Windham 3 July 1807 HANNAH HAWKES, born
there 23 Apr. 1786, died at Westbrook 17 Sept. 1878, daughter
of Amos and Deborah (Flint) Hawkes (Ethel F. Smith, Adam
Hawkes of Saugus, Mass. [1980], 194; Hall Desc., #182).
Hannah's family were Quakers.
    Soon after his marriage, he bought a number of lots at
Windham, and between 1820 and 1830 built up large holdings at
Westbrook (Biog. Rev. ... Cumberland Co., 70).

Children:

988. i.   LUCY[8], b. Westbrook 17 Sept. 1808; m. JAMES
            LAMB.
989. ii.   ALVIN, b. 9 Dec. 1810.
      iii. EMILY JANE, b. 19 Jan. 1816; m. Westbrook 27
            Dec. 1840 GEORGE WILLIAM COBB, b. there 28
            Oct. 1817, res. Stroudwater section, son of
            William and Lepha (Cobb) Cobb (Cobb Fam.,
            2:462, 552). He was a butcher. Ch. George
            Randall b. Westbrook 15 May 1842; m. FANNIE
            A.[8] LEIGHTON [# 446].
      iv.   HOLMAN, b. 31 Oct. 1821, d. Westbrook 14 July
            1884; unm. He was a carpenter, living with
            his parents in 1860.
      v.   ELVIRA D., b. 23 Nov. 1826; m. Lyman ME
            int. 25 May 1849 (NEHGReg, 97[1943]:234)
            JESSE KIMBALL, b. c1822 (28 in 1850), son of
            Jesse and Ruth (Lyman) Kimball. Ch. Eliza
            Minerva m. Simon Dennett.

440. ISAAC[7] 1783-1862 [141 Hatevil[6] and Lucy Staples] was
born at Falmouth 19 Aug. 1783, died there 4 July 1862, 79y
10m 15d (GS); married at Paris ME 10 Oct. 1811 (Falmouth int.
6 Oct.) MINERVA SHAW, born 8 Aug. 1790, died at Portland 28
Aug. 1863, 73y (GS; VRs), daughter of Solomon and Anna (Hay-
ward) Shaw of Paris (Hall Desc., #183; Cornman Ms). Burials
are in the Brook Street Cemetery.
     Isaac was deeded a 64-acre lot by his father 2 Apr. 1806
(CumbCD, 48:466). In 1810 he was commissioned lieutenant of
militia, and served under Major Weeks in the 2nd Brigade in
the War of 1812 as captain of an artillery company, receiving
his commission 4 May 1813 (MA Mil. 1812-14, 154; NA-MSR). In
1850 Capt. Isaac's Falmouth household included Dorothy, 70,
and George F., 30 [# 515].

Children, born at Falmouth:

990. i.   MINERVA ANN[8], b. 7 Nov. 1812; m. BRADFORD
            RAYMOND.
991. ii.   LAVINA SHAW, b. 31 Mar. 1815; m. JAMES HICKS.
992. iii. LORENZO SHAW, b. 10 Mar. 1817.
      iv.   CHARLES HENRY, b. 31 Oct. 1820, d. at sea,
            returning from Matanzas, Cuba, on bark Oxford.
      v.   LUCY JANE, b. 5 Jan. 1834, d. 8 Jan. 1919; m.
            Westbrook 24 Nov. 1859 ORLANDO B. CRAM, b. 13
            Mar. 1833, res. with Isaac in 1860. Ch.
            Henry L. b. Portland 7 Feb. 1871; m. 24 Sept.
            1895 Bertha Greenough, b. 25 Apr. 1870.

441. DANIEL[7] 1785-1872 [141 Hatevil[6] and Lucy Staples]
was born at Falmouth 3 May 1785, died there 26 May 1872, 87y
(GS); married first there 14 Feb. 1807 MARY STAPLES, born 7
Mar. 1786, died at Falmouth 17 Feb. 1850, 64y (GS), daughter
of Joseph and Miriam Staples; married second 27 Oct. 1850
SUSAN (MORSE) Marston, b. 4 Feb. 1804. Burials are in Brook
Street Cemetery (Hall Desc., #184; Falmouth TRs).
     He was a master carpenter. He served under Capt. Alpheus
Field in 1814 (MA Mil. 1812-14, 219). In 1850 Daniel and his

children Mary and Franklin were living with Daniel Jr. at
Falmouth. Susan had married first Simeon Marston, who died
at Gray in 1846; they had four children (Marston Gen., 170).

Children by Mary, born at Falmouth:

	i.	HATEVIL[8], b. 3 Dec. 1809, d. 16 Sept. 1849, 42y (GS); unm.
993.	ii.	SILAS, b. 8 Apr. 1810.
994.	iii.	JOSEPH, b. 28 Apr. 1812.
995.	iv.	LUCY ANN, b. 9 Apr. 1814; m. OLIVER HARDY.
996.	v.	DANIEL, b. 8 Sept. 1816.
	vi.	JEREMIAH, b. 8 Dec. 1818, d. 8 Sept. 1819.
	vii.	MARY, b. 30 Nov. 1820, d. 20 Sept. 1859, 38y (GS); unm.
997.	viii.	JAMES GOWEN, b. 11 Mar. 1823.
	ix.	OCTAVIA, b. 31 Mar. 1825, d. 5 June 1901; m. 2 May 1849 BENJAMIN DONNELL, b. 10 Oct. 1809, d. Falmouth 10 Mar. 1865 (town VRs; Cornman Ms). A stonecutter, he and Octavia res. Falmouth in 1850 next door to Daniel Jr. with his son Samuel C., aged 6 [#1573].
	x.	FRANKLIN, b. 20 Sept. 1827, d. Falmouth 17 Oct. 1869, 42y (GS); m. Portland 3 June 1861 PHOEBE E. (MORSE) Pinkham, born in Dec. 1812, d. in 1882. No ch. He was a shoemaker.

442. ICHABOD[7] 1787-1813 [141 Hatevil[6] and Lucy Staples]
was born at Falmouth 25 Oct. 1787, died at Norway ME 20 Dec.
1813; married at Falmouth 12 Dec. 1811 LYDIA CLARIDGE, born
there 6 Dec. 1793, died at Bangor ME 19 Sept. 1870, daughter
of William and Ursula (Baker) Claridge [# 144] (Hall Desc.,
#185; town VRs).
Widow Lydia accompanied her sons to Bangor; she was living
with Ansel there in 1850, aged 58.

Children:

998.	i.	ANSEL[8], b. Falmouth 2 Mar. 1812.
999.	ii.	ICHABOD ELBRIDGE, b. Norway 25 Oct. 1813.

443. SILAS[7] 1791-1878 [141 Hatevil[6] and Lucy Staples]
was born at Falmouth 20 June 1791, died there 7 June 1878
(TRs; in 1876, 87y, on GS); married at Falmouth 17 Dec. 1812
(Silas Jr. on Windham int. 21 Nov.) ABIGAIL ROBERTS, born at
Somersworth NH 20 Sept. 1791, died at Falmouth 18 Apr. 1855,
63y 7m (GS), daughter of James and Martha (Goodwin) Roberts
(Hall Desc., #186; Falmouth VRs). Burials are in Brook
Street Cemetery.
Silas Jr. (uncle Silas [# 145] was living in town) was a
house carpenter. Later called Squire Leighton for his
responsible positions, he was justice of the peace over 40
years, from 1819 to 1861, and state legislator in 1827-8. He
was a major in the militia, and marshal for the 1860 census.
He constructed the Blackstrap Monument, a 40-foot tower on
Blackstrap Mountain, for Dependence Furbish and Charles
Doughty, but it failed to become a tourist attraction (Port-
land Scrapbook, MHS). In 1860, he was living with his son
Granville at Falmouth.

Children, born at Falmouth:

   i.   LOUISE ROBERTS[8], b. 23 Aug. 1813; m. JOEL[8]
           LEIGHTON [# 974].
   ii.   JULIA ANN, b. 26 Feb. 1816; m. ADAM W.[8]
           LEIGHTON [# 976].
   iii. LUCINDA, b. 20 Sept. 1818, d. in Feb. 1885; m.
           29 Apr. 1843 PHILIP RUSSELL, son of Joseph
           and Priscilla (Shaw) Russell. No ch.
   iv.   CORDELIA, b. 27 Mar. 1821, d. 1 Oct. 1871; m.
           Falmouth 23 Feb. 1847 WILLIAM RUSSELL, b.
           c1820 (40 in 1860), son of Joseph and Pris-
           cilla (Shaw) Russell. He was a farmer at
           Cumberland in 1850. Ch. Edwin O. b. c1848,
           res. Cumberland Foreside.
1000. v.   JAMES EDWIN, b. 22 Aug. 1823.
1001. vi.   GRANVILLE ROBERTS, b. 25 Jan. 1826.
       vii. MINERVA SHAW, b. 11 Jan. 1829; m. ALBERT[8]
           LEIGHTON [# 1004].
1002. viii. LUCY GOWEN, b. 19 Jan. 1835; m. THOMAS J.
           PEARSON.

444.   JUDITH[7] 1792-1862 [143 David[6] and Lucy Baker] was
born at Falmouth 28 Mar. 1792, died there 25 May 1862 (GS);
married there 12 Oct. 1816 WILLIAM J. ELDER, born 2 Aug. 1790
(60 in 1850), died at Falmouth 28 May 1855 (GS), probably son
of William and Keziah Elder (Cornman Ms; Hall Desc., #203).
Burials are in Brook Road Cemetery.
They lived with her brother Thaddeus at Falmouth in 1850.
Elder was a quarry rock-blaster.

Children (**Elder**), born at Falmouth:

   i.   LUTHER B., b. 12 July 1819 (GS-1817), d. Falmouth
           9 Oct. 1884 (GS); m. MARY JANE GRAFFAM, b. 20 Feb.
           1820, d. 30 Jan. 1910 (GS).
   ii.   LEVI LEIGHTON, b. 20 Sept. 1820, d. 5 Apr. 1887; m.
           28 Dec. 1858 MARY E. REYNOLDS.
   iii. DAVID L., b. c1827, d. Falmouth 19 May 1829, 1y 7m
           (GS).
   iv.   LEONARD P., b. c1833, d. Falmouth 19 Jan. 1851, 17y
           4m (GS).
   v.   FRANCES, res. Chicago; m. ---- WILKINSON of Bidde-
           ford.
   vi.   LUCY, res. Chicago; m. ---- .
   vii. ALMIRA, res Chicago; unm. in 1902.

445.   LEVI[7] 1793-1874 [143 David[6] and Lucy Baker] was born
at Falmouth 23 June 1793, died there 23 Oct. 1874, 81y; married there 9 Dec. 1820 HANNAH ELLIOT, born 14 Oct. 1799, died
at Falmouth 29 or 30 Dec. 1880, 81y, daughter of Jacob and
Ann (Baker) Elliot (Falmouth TRs; Hall Desc., #203).
He was a musician in Capt. William Haskell's artillery company in 1814, serving at Ft. Scammel (MA Mil. 1812-14, 153).
He was a farmer. In 1860, aged 66, he had two Merrill children in his home; in 1870, aged 77, he lived with his son
Albert.

Children, born at Falmouth:

1003. i.   FRANCES IRENE[8], b. 13 July 1821; m. REUBEN
            MERRILL.
1004. ii. ALBERT, b. 26 Apr. 1825.

446. THADDEUS[7] 1794-1860 [143 David[6] and Lucy Baker] was
born at Falmouth 14 Nov. 1794, died there 5 June 1860; married in Aug. 1820 ABIGAIL WINSLOW ELLIOT, born at Windham 28
May 1801, died at Falmouth 12 Jan. 1860, daughter of David
Pettingill and Submit (Hall) Elliot (Hall Desc., #204; Holton, Winslow Mem., 2:932).
He was a farmer, grocer and carpenter, and served as town
constable. He was a musician in Capt. Isaac Leighton's
artillery company in 1814 (MA Mil. 1812-14, 154). In 1850
his children were living with Adrial [# 452] at Biddeford.

Children, born at Falmouth:

       i.   KERWIN WATERS[8], b. 15 Aug. 1822, d. Portland
             19 Aug. 1889, 68y (VRs); m. Westbrook 1 Aug.
             1847 HARRIET E. KNIGHT, b. in 1820, d. Port-
             land 24 Feb. 1886, 66y (VRs), dau. of Major
             Daniel and Polly (Dale) Knight. He was a
             granite cutter. One ch., d. infant.
       ii.   ROWENA HILL, b. 23 Oct. 1823; m. JEDEDIAH[8]
             LEIGHTON [# 972].
1005. iii. LEVI ELLIOT, b. 12 June 1824.
1006. iv.   DAVID HENRY, b. 10 May 1826.
       v.   ANGELINA, b. 7 July 1828, d. there 12 July
             1875, 43y; unm.
       vi.   ELLEN MIRANDA, b. 16 Aug. 1831, d. Portland 19
             Jan. 1917, 83y; unm., res. Haverhill MA.
       vii. LOUISE E., b. 27 Mar. 1834, d. in Dec. 1889;
             m. GEORGE LOUGEE, b. in France. No ch.
       viii. LUCY, b. 16 Apr. 1839, d. Falmouth 5 Aug.
             1897; m. Westbrook 25 July 1858 JOHN C.
             WALDEN, d. Falmouth 26 June 1888 (GS, Brook
             St. Cem.). One ch., d. infant.
       ix.   FRANCES A. [Fannie], b. c1846 (14 in 1860); m.
             1st 24 Nov. 1864 GEORGE RANDALL COBB, b.
             Westbrook 15 May 1842, d. there 2 Oct. 1868,
             son of George W. and Emily[9] (Leighton) Cobb
             [# 439]; m. 2nd 15 Feb. 1876 ELIAS MILTON
             JACOBS of Stroudwater. Ch. Lillian M. Cobb
             b. 13 Feb. 1865.

447. EPHRAIM[7] 1798-1878 [143 David[6] and Lucy Baker] was
born at Falmouth 14 June 1798, died there 21 May 1878, 79y
11m 7d; married first at Westbrook 28 Mar. 1826 SOPHIA COBB,
born at Deering 2 June 1803, died at Falmouth 2 May 1849, 46y
11m (GS), daughter of Jonathan and Abigail (Nason) Cobb (Cobb
Family, 2:394; Hall Desc., #206); married second 9 June 1850
HANNAH (HARMON) Manchester, born 29 June 1806, died at Falmouth 27 Dec. 1878, 72y 5m (GS). Burials are in Brook St.
Cemetery.
He was a farmer. In 1860 his household included his Manchester step-daughters Lucretia B., 24, and Martha E., 13.

Children by first wife Sophia:

    i.   EMILY C [8], b. c1827 (23 in 1850), res. Lewis-
         ton ME; m. 28 Dec. 1848 ALFRED DUNHAM, b.
         c1822. They lived with Daniel and Matilda
         Dunham at Falmouth in 1850. Ch. Evelina b.
         c1849.
1007. ii.   MELVIN A., b. Westbrook 24 Jan. 1839.

448. THANKFUL H.[7] 1800-1886 [143 David[6] and Lucy Baker]
was born at Falmouth 31 Aug. 1800, died there 25 July 1886,
86y; married there 18 Apr. 1828 JAMES COBB III, born there in
1800, died at Deering 15 July 1852, 52y, son of Jonathan and
Abigail (Nason) Cobb (Cobb Fam., 2:394, 471; Hall Desc.,
#207). They lived at Westbrook and West Falmouth; her sister
Ursula lived with them. Burials are in Brook St. Cemetery.

Children (**Cobb**):

    i.   HARRIET F., b. Westbrook 8 Jan. 1829, d. 8 Dec. 1848,
         19y 11m (GS); unm.
    ii. EVELINA L., b. 12 Dec. 1837, d. 12 Dec. 1848, 12y
         (GS).

449.   EDWARD GILMAN[7] 1793-1850 [144 Paul[6] and Phoebe
Gilman] was born at Falmouth 21 July 1793, died there 22 Feb.
1850, 56y (GS); married first 21 June 1818 HANNAH D. HICKS,
born 9 Mar. 1793, died at Falmouth 30 Sept. 1824 (GS), daughter of James and Abigail[6] (Leighton) Hicks [# 142]; married
second JANE TITCOMB HALL, born 7 Dec. 1805, died 3 Feb. 1867,
62y 2m (GS), daughter of Solomon and Sarah (Brown) (Titcomb)
Hall (Hall Desc., #208; Falmouth TRs). Burials are in Brook
Street Cemetery.
    He was a musician in Capt. Isaac Leighton's artillery com-
pany in 1814 (MA Mil. 1812-14, 154). In 1860, his widow's
household included her three children, and also Eliza J.[8]
[# 1011], daughter of Timothy Leighton.

Children by Hannah, born at Falmouth:

1008. i.   JAMES HICKS[8], b. 8 Feb. 1819.
      ii.   RUFUS, b. 2 Feb., d. 8 Oct., 1821.
1009. iii. ANDREW HICKS, b. 11 June 1822.
      iv.   SUMNER, b. 2 Apr., d. 3 May, 1824.

Children by Jane, born at Falmouth:

    v.   HANNAH HICKS, b. 3 May 1829, d. Falmouth 14
          Feb. 1905, 76y 9m; unm., lived with Alfred.
    vi.   RUEL SHAW, b. 26 June 1833, d. Falmouth 11
          Mar. 1857, 23y 8m (GS); unm.
    vii. ALFRED LOT, b. 6 Mar. 1847, d. Falmouth 25
          Apr. 1905, 58y; unm.

450.   TIMOTHY[7] 1800-1860 [144 Paul[6] and Phoebe Gilman] was
born at Falmouth 28 Nov. 1800, died at Portland about 1860;
married at Portland 6 Oct. 1842 MARY JANE (GILMAN) Cole (Hall
Desc., #212). She had three Cole children.

A Timothy Leighton was sentenced to four months in jail for
larceny (Portland Daily Argus, 24 Jan. 1845).

Children:

1010. i.   WILLIAM, b. say 1843.
1011. i.   ELIZA J.[8], b. Falmouth 20 May 1845; m. AUGUS-
            TUS ABBOTT and WILLIAM BERRY.

451. HENRY [7] [Harry] 1806-   [144 Paul[6] and Phoebe
Gilman] was born at Falmouth 3 Sept. 1806, lived at Windham
in 1870; married first at Windham 3 Sept. 1829 ANN [Nancy]
HANSCOM, born at Windham 20 Jan. 1806, died there 27 Feb.
1856, daughter of Aaron and Rebecca (Akers) Hanscom; married
second at Windham 25 Dec. 1866 SARAH (----) Tyler. He was
a farmer, house carpenter and joiner (Windham VRs; Hall
Desc., #214).

Children by Ann, born at Windham:

1012. i.   AARON HANSCOM[8], b. 7 Nov. 1830.
       ii.   JOEL, b. 9 Dec. 1831, d. Portland 29 Jan.
             1903, 68y; m. 1 Feb. 1859 MARY SUSAN[9]
             LEIGHTON, b. 20 May 1842, d. Westbrook 18
             Mar. 1893, dau. of Joseph and Jane (Walker)
             Leighton [# 994]. Adopted ch. Jenny E.
             b. c1866.
       iii. CORNELIUS S. BRACKETT, b. 5 Feb. 1833, d. 20
             Oct. 1835.
       iv.   ADRIAL NASON, b. 25 Nov. 1835, d. 5 Feb. 1841.
       v.   CORNELIUS S. BRACKETT, b. 20 Mar. 1836, d. 2
             Mar. 1861; unm. He lived with Isaac Cobb in
             1860.
       vi.   PHOEBE ANN, b. 20 July 1837, d. 29 Jan. 1838.
1013. vii. PHOEBE ANN, b. 23 Nov. 1839; m. CHARLES A.
             DALTON.
1014. viii. ADRIAL NASON, b. 23 Jan. 1842.
       ix.   CHARLES HENRY, b. 7 Oct. 1844, d. 5 Sept.
             1845.
1015. x.   EMILY JANE, b. 8 Nov. 1846; m. JOHN S. IRISH.
1016. xi.   APPHIA NASON, b. 5 Sept. 1847; m. CHARLES F.
             TITCOMB.
       xii. REBECCA ELLEN [Nellie], b. 24 Jan. 1850; m.
             EUGENE BRYANT, b. 14 May 1848, son of Rufus
             and Lucy Ann (Howard) Bryant (G. T. Ridlon,
             Saco Valley Settlements and Families [Port-
             land, 1895, reprint 1984], 532). Ch. Persis.

452. ADRIAL NASON[7] 1809-1884 [144 Paul[6] and Phoebe Gilman]
was born at Falmouth 18 Apr. 1809, died at Deering ME 11 June
1884, 75y 1m 23d; married at Quincy MA 1 Jan. 1834 RHODA
WELLMAN PACKARD, born at Quincy 13 Sept. 1812, died at Deering 8 Nov. 1904, 92y 1m 25d, daughter of Samuel and Rhoda
(Wellman) Packard (Hall Desc., #215; Cornman Ms; town VRs).
Burials are in Evergreen Cemetery, Portland.
    He owned a granite-cutting business, with operations at
Quincy, Boston, Lowell and Cohasset MA, and Auburn NY. In
1860, his household included his nephew Andrew [# 1009] and
his grandson Enoch Hathaway.

Children:

      i.   ELIZA ANN[8], b. Quincy 10 July 1835, d. 21 Nov.
           1839.
1017. ii.   EMILY JANE, b. Hallowell ME 28 Apr. 1836; m.
           JAMES B. HATHAWAY.
1018. iii. RHODA ELIZABETH, b. Milford MA 3 Nov. 1838; m.
           WESLEY P. DUTTON.
1019. iv.   GEORGE WARREN, b. Quincy 13 Nov. 1840.
      v.   EDWIN AUGUSTUS, b. Quincy 20 Mar. 1844, d.
           Portland 10 Jan. 1934, 89y (obit.); m. 1 Jan.
           1867 CARRIE ELIZABETH HARDY, b. 11 Aug. 1847,
           d. Portland 18 Dec. 1928, 81y 3m 27d, dau. of
           Benjamin Hardy. Ch. FLORENCE LOUISE[9] b. 23
           Mar. 1878; unm. in 1934.

453. ANN GILMAN[7] 1812-1885 [[144 Paul[6] and Phoebe Gilman]
was born at Falmouth 1 May 1812, died at Brownton MN 9 May
1885; married at Milton MA 6 Oct. 1835 (VRs) SAMUEL BLAKE
BROWN, born at Andover NH 6 Oct. 1811, died at Brownton 27
Dec. 1891, son of Samuel and Rebecca (Felton) Brown (Hall
Desc., #216; records of descendant Elinor Clow).
They lived at Auburn NY, moved west to Dixon IL, and in
Apr. 1858 established a town named for them in McLeod Co. MN.
From 1862 to 1864 they lived at St. Paul, to escape the Sioux
uprising. He served in Co. B, 4th MN Vol. Inf. Rgt., in
1864-65.

Children (**Brown**):

    i.   HENRIETTA BRYANT, b. Milton MA 24 June 1836; m.
        LOCKHART OCOLOCK.
    ii.   ALONZO LEIGHTON, b. Auburn NY 9 Nov. 1838, res.
        Brownton; m. BEDINA EVENA [Di] SAVAGE.
    iii. CHARLES HENRY, b. Falmouth ME 20 Sept. 1841, d. Cor-
        inth ME 26 June 1862. He was a Civil War soldier.
    iv.   ALFRED AUGUSTUS, b. Auburn 27 May 1844, d. in MN 30
        Jan. 1871; m. 11 Jan. 1870 KITTIE BENNETT.
    v.   ANDREW J., b. Auburn 25 Dec. 1845, d. Frisco Springs
        AR 21 Sept. 1888.
    vi.   EMMA FRANCES, b. Auburn 27 May 1848, d. Clark Fork ID
        in May 1913; m. Auburn 9 May 1864 EDWARD SIDNEY
        LLOYD, b. 9 June 1836.
    vii. HORACE EUGENE, b. Auburn 15 May 1850, d. there 12
        Apr. 1853.
    viii. MARTHA ANNA, b. Auburn in Apr. 1854, d. in May 1914;
        m. MOSES WHITCOMB.

454. ELEANOR[7] 1792-   [145 Silas[6] and Bethane White] was
born at Falmouth in 1792, died at Boston; married JEREMIAH
PENNELL, JR., born in 1790, died at Skowhegan ME 1 May 1863
(pension file), 73y, son of Jeremiah and Priscilla (Thompson)
Pennell (Charles N. Sinnett, The Pennell Genealogy [TMs, nd,
MHS], 48-9; Hall Desc., #219). He married second at Athens
ME 19 Jan. 1834 Eliza Merrill, who in turn married second 25
Oct. 1854 Siba Russell (pension record).
    Jeremiah enlisted in Capt. Lemuel Bradford's Co. of rifle-
men in Feb. 1813, and was pensioned for a disability (NA-
MSR). He was a shoemaker.

Children (**Pennell**):

i.   SUMNER, b. Westbrook 21 Jan. 1812, res. Boston; m.
      EUNICE CURRIER of Lyman ME, dau. of Deacon John
      Currier.
ii.   WILLIAM LLOYD, b. 21 Sep. 1815, d. 9 Dec. 1876; m.
      Portland 18 Sept. 1838 JANE B. FOGG, b. Freeport ME
      24 Oct. 1821, dau. of Enos and Experience (Higgins)
      Fogg. He was an engineer at Boston.
iii. MARY ANN, b. Minot ME 26 Oct. 1817; m. 27 June 1840
      JEROME BONAPARTE VEAZIE, b. Boston 18 May 1818, d.
      29 May 1867. He was a mason at So. Boston.
iv.   FRANCES E., b. Westbrook 31 Jan. 1821, d. 5 June
      1847; m. GEORGE RODNEY COOPER of Hamden CT.
v.   EMILY JANE, b. Portland 23 Jan. 1822; m. Gray 22 Oct.
      1845 MOSES TRUE, b. No. Yarmouth in Oct. 1821.
vi.   DAVID SPEAR, b. in 1824, d. Yarmouth 15 Apr. 1861
      (GS--Brook St., Falmouth); unm. He was a music
      teacher at Boston.
vii. ELIAS LEIGHTON, b. in 1826, rem. to CA c1850; nfr.
viii. EUNICE, b. in 1830, d. in 1846.

455. SARAH[7] 1793-   [145 Silas[6] and Bethane White] was
born at Falmouth 31 Aug. 1793; married SAMUEL GOULD PENNELL,
born in Oct. 1789, died at Hartland ME 6 July 1876, son of
Jeremiah and Priscilla (Thompson) Pennell (Sinnett, Pennell
Gen., 48-9; Hall Desc., #218).
      Samuel was a pensioner of the War of 1812. They lived in
Oxford County--at Sumner in 1820, at Buxton in 1840, and at
Brighton in 1850 when he was a shoemaker, 61, with Sarah, 56,
with a household including Jason, 19, Joseph, 15, and also
Enoch and Abigail Ford.

Children (**Pennell**):

i.   CHARLES HENRY, b. 3 Aug. 1811, went to sea; nfr.
ii.   BETHANA, b. 21 Apr. 1813, d. New Vineyard ME in Jan.
      1863; m. BENJAMIN JORDAN.
iii. SAMUEL, b. 26 Sept. 1815, went to sea; nfr.
iv.   GREENLEAF, b. 8 Dec. 1817.
v.   MARY, b. 4 July 1820; m. in 1840 SAMUEL PENNELL
      YOUNG, b. in 1818, son of Samuel and Mary (Pennell)
      Young.
vi.   Rev. SILAS LEIGHTON, b. 18 July 1824, res. Palmyra
      ME.
vii. PRISCILLA, b. 10 Mar. 1826, d. in 1833.
viii. ABIGAIL S., b. 27 Sept. 1827; m. 4 July 1847 ENOCH
      LINCOLN FORD.
ix.   JASON, b. 29 May 1832.
x.   JOSEPH LEAVITT, b. 24 Aug. 1835, res. CA; m. ---- .

456. ELIAS HALL[7] 1799-1891 [145 Silas[6] and Bethane White]
was born at Falmouth 9 May 1799 (GS, 9 Mar.), died at Auburn
ME 22 Dec. 1891 (GS); married at Gray int. 6 Jan. 1828
LUCINDA FRANK, born 12 Mar. 1809, died at Auburn 30 Jan.
1881, 70y 10m 18d (GS), daughter of James, Jr., and Sally
(Pennell) Frank (Hall Desc., #219; town VRs). Burials are in
a family plot on Washington Street, Auburn.

Elias moved from Falmouth to Poland in 1833, and then to Minot (now Auburn); in 1850 he was a farmer at Danville (which became part of Auburn in 1867). He served in Co. B, 25th ME Inf. Rgt., in 1862.

Children:

     i.   GRANVILLE HALL[8], b. Poland 11 Aug. 1829; m. ---- FIELDS.

     ii. SARAH HATCH, b. Falmouth 20 June 1831, d. Auburn 11 Nov. 1853, 23y 5m (GS); m. ALLEN CLARY FORD, a Lewiston stonecutter. Ch. James res. Danville.

     iii. ALVAH LIBBY, b. Poland 16 Apr. 1833, d. Auburn 6 Jan. 1842, 9y 9m (GS).

     iv. CYRUS HENRY, b. Poland 16 Apr. 1833, d. Auburn 22 Oct. 1853, 19y 9m (GS).

     v.   BETSEY ANN, b. Danville 6 Mar. 1837; m. Danville 5 Nov. 1854 (as Ann) ALLEN CLARY FORD, who had 1st m. her sister Sarah.

     vi. HANNAH HANSON, b. Danville 1 May 1839; unm.

     vii. ALPHEUS FRANK, b. Danville 25 Mar. 1841, d. 14 May 1843, 3y 1m (GS).

     viii. ALPHEUS FRANK, b. Danville 26 Dec. 1843, d. Auburn 1 Dec. 1853, 10y 11m (GS).

     ix. MATILDA NEWCOMB, b. 6 Jan. 1845, d. Auburn 27 Sept. 1847, 1y 8m (GS).

1020. x.   ALVAH, b. Danville 25 June 1847.

     xi. NICHOLAS (twin), b. 25 June 1847, d. Auburn 9 Apr. 1866, 18y 9m 15d (GS). He served in the Civil War.

     xii. LOUISE FREEMAN, b. Auburn 3 Oct. 1853; m. Auburn 3 July 1873 BENJAMIN L. WARE.

457. ASA[7] 1801-1873 [145 Silas[6] and Bethane White] was born at Falmouth 17 July 1801, died there 30 Dec. 1873, 72y (30 Sept., 73y, GS); married first at Cumberland 25 Nov. 1827 (int. Westbrook 7 July) MARY HALE, born about 1806, died at Falmouth 3 Sept. 1832, 26y (GS), daughter of Nathaniel and Mary (Leighton) Hale [# 431]; married second 28 Aug. 1835 ELIZA ANN HICKS, born about 1812, died at Falmouth 11 Oct. 1857, 45y (GS), daughter of Nathaniel and Sarah (Twombley) Hicks (Cornman Ms; town VRs; Hall Desc., #220). Burials are in the Brook Street Cemetery.

He lived on the homestead of his grandfather George. In 1850 his household included his father Silas, 78, and two sons of Joseph [# 514].

Children by Mary, born at Falmouth:

1021. i.   HALE[8], b. 2 Sept. 1828.

     ii.   CARPENTER, b. 1 Apr. 1830, went to CA.

1022. iii. MARY HALE, b. 16 Aug. 1832; m. ANSEL NEAL.

Children by Eliza, born at Falmouth:

     iv. BETHANA, b. 5 Feb. 1837, res. Boston in 1900 (census) with Etta and Edwin Naylor [# 1022] and 3 other sisters; unm.

    v.   LAVINA, b. 19 Dec. 1838, res. Boston in 1900;
         unm.
    vi. REBECCA, b. 3 Feb. 1842, res. Boston in 1900;
         unm.
1023. vii. LEANDER, b. 12 Sept. 1845.
    viii. JULIETTE (called Hannah in 1850), b. 12 July
          1850, res. Boston in 1900; unm.
    ix. ELLEN, b. 21 May 1852; m. 28 Jan. 1891 EDWARD
         L. BABBAGE, b. Falmouth in 1854. No ch.
    x.   EMMA J., b. 25 May 1854, res. Mt. Holly VT in
         1902; m. 30 Apr. 1890 JOHN LYFORD SPAULDING,
         JR., son of John L. and Susan Spaulding.
         No ch.

458. STATIRA[7] 1805-   [145 Silas[6] and Bethane White] was
born at Falmouth 2 Nov. 1805; married at Gray 27 May 1827 JOB
YOUNG FOSTER, born at Gray 23 Dec. 1803, died there, son of
Jacob and Mary (Young) Foster (Franklin C. Pierce, Foster
Genealogy [Chicago, 1899], 345; Hall Desc., #222).

Children (**Foster**):

    i.   NICHOLAS L., b. 2 Jan. 1828; m. MARY S. FOSTER.
    ii. JULIA ANN, b. Madison ME 1 Apr. 1830, res. Dry Mills
         ME; m. 16 Nov. 1848 JOB A. SPENSER, b. 26 Apr. 1823.
    iii. MARY, b. Madison 10 Mar. 1832; m. WILLIAM JACKSON.
    iv. JAMES L., b. Madison 19 Apr. 1834; unm.
    v.   THOMAS, b. Gray 20 Nov. 1837; unm.

459. MOSES[7] 1790-1875 [146 Isaac[6] and Mary Worcester] was
born at Columbia ME 19 Oct. 1790, died there 17 Jan. 1875,
84y (GS); married there int. 8 Apr. 1813 PRUDENCE ALLEN, born
there about 1794 (66 in 1860), died at Columbia Falls 15 May
1871, 77y (GS), daughter of Gideon and Susan (Rideout) Allen
(Leighton, Autobiography, 11ff; MH&GR, 9[1898]:221-3; Columbia VRs). Burials are in Epping Cemetery.
Moses settled in the wilderness of Epping, a district of
Columbia, lumbered along the St. John River during the War of
1812, and rafted logs from Fredericton to Saint John NB. He
served in Capt. Holmes Nash's militia company.
He later moved his family to the Gideon Allen homestead,
opening there a general store in which his son Levi became a
partner. In 1860 Moses and Prudence were living with William
Ingersoll.

Children, born at Columbia:

1024. i.   LOVICIA S.[8], b. 6 Apr. 1816; m. DANIEL
            SINCLAIR.
1025. ii.   LEVI, b. 18 Sept. 1818.
1026. iii. JASON CLAPP, b. 14 May 1820.
      iv.   WARREN, d. infant.
1027. v.   ASA G., b. 6 Apr. 1825.
1028. vi.   OTIS M., b. 7 July 1827.
1029. vii. CYRENE BANCROFT, b. 1 May 1830; m. WILLIAM H.
            INGERSOLL.
1030. viii. SOPHIA A., b. 8 July 1831; m. OBADIAH ALLEN.
1031. ix.   PRUDENCE, b. 8 May 1833; m. DAVID WASS.

     x.   MARY A. D., b. 9 Mar. 1837, d. Columbia 16
            Feb. 1906, 68y 11m 7d; m. Columbia int. 16
            Oct. 1859 ENOCH AUBURN LOW, d. 21 Dec. 1886,
            50y 3m (GS). No ch.
1032. x.   SUSANNA, b. c1842; m. ZENUS TABBUTT.

460. SAMUEL[7] 1792-1876 [146 Isaac[6] and Mary Worcester] was born at Columbia 22 Sept. 1792, died there 5 Aug. 1876; married first at Jonesport 29 Oct. 1814 MARY ANN WARD, born at Columbia in 1793, died there 26 Nov. 1838 (GS), daughter of John and Rebecca (Lovett) Ward; married second at Columbia int. 26 Nov. 1842 ELIZABETH [Betsey] (WARD) Hamlin, born about 1806, sister to Mary Ann and widow of Isaac G. Hamlin (Leighton, Autobiography, 11ff; town VRs). Burials are in Epping Cemetery, Columbia. In 1850, he was a farmer, his household including four Hamlin step-children.

Children by Mary Ann, born at Columbia:

     i.   CATHERINE B.[8], b. c1823 (27 in 1850), d. in MN
            71y; m. there ---- (Cornman Papers).
     ii.   VIENNA, b. c1825 (25 in 1850), res. Milbridge
            in 1870, 45; unm.
1033. iii. (BENJAMIN CAMPBELL) COFFIN, b. 29 June 1825.
1034. iv. ALPHEUS BILLINGS, b. in 1826.
1035. v.   (NATHANIEL) GREEN, b. in 1828.
     vi.   AMBROSE, b. c1832 (18 in 1850); unm.
     vii. LUCRETIA, b. c1835 (15 in 1850), res. MN; m.
            in ME LEWIS HILLMAN DORMAN, b. in 1834,
            son of Israel and Joanna (Kingsley) Dorman.

Children by Betsey, born at Columbia:

     viii. HANNIBAL HAMLIN, b. c1843 (16 in 1860), d.
            Fredericksburg VA 13 May 1863, 19y 9m. He
            enl. 29 Apr. 1861 as corporal, Co. G, 6th ME
            Inf. Rgt., and was killed in action.
1036. ix. MARY ANN, b. c1845 (14 in 1860); m. ROBERT W.
            BUCKNAM.
     x.   CHARLES P., b. in Apr. 1847, res. Haverhill MA
            in 1900 (census) with 2nd wife Ellen J. --- ,
            b. in NH in May 1847.
     xi.   FREDERICK S., b. in 1849, d. 29 June 1863,
            13y 10m (GS).

461. LEVI W.[7] 1795-1874 [146 Isaac[6] and Mary Worcester] was born at Columbia 11 Feb. 1795, died there 11 Aug. 1874; married first at Steuben ME 21 Mar. 1822 (Columbia int. 18 Dec. 1821) LEONICE COFFIN, born at Columbia 24 Nov. 1801, died there 15 Jan. 1830, 29y (GS), daughter of Elisha and Ruth (Cates) Coffin ("Sketches in Columbia," MH&GR, 9[1898]: 84ff); married second there 31 Jan. 1832 MARY L. WHITTEN, born at Lubec about 1812, died at Columbia 11 Mar. 1835, 23y (GS); married third at Cherryfield 26 June 1835 ELIZABETH [Betsey] SMALL, born there 29 Apr. 1815, died at Addison 27 May 1894, 80y 7m (GS), daughter of James and Priscilla (Worcester) Small (Underhill, Small Desc., 1:17-8). Burials are in Epping Cemetery, Columbia.

Levi was a stone mason. On 5 June 1833 Levi was appointed
guardian of his children by Leonice, probably because she had
left property to them (WashCP, 8:244).

Children by Leonice, born at Columbia:

    i.   ALBION KEITH PARRIS[8], b. 6 Apr. 1823, d. Ban-
        gor ME 7 Apr. 1892; m. Columbia 16 Aug. 1849
        MARY C. ROBINSON, b. Cherryfield in 1822, d.
        Bangor 10 Sept. 1906, dau. of Rev. Nathaniel
        S. and Mary (Ward) Robinson of Dover ME. No
        ch. He first taught school at Addison, and
        later owned Leighton Bros., a boot and shoe
        store at Bangor. He served in the Civil War.
        Burials are in Mt. Hope Cemetery, Bangor.

    ii.   (GILBERT) LAFAYETTE, b. 28 July 1825, d. Ban-
        gor 16 May 1894; unm. He was a business
        partner with Albion.

1037. iii. RUTH ANN, b. 29 Oct. 1827; m. JASON CROWELL.
1038. iv. JOHN WILSON, b. 6 June 1829.

Children by Mary, born at Columbia:

    v.   FRANCIS G. [Frank], b. 27 Mar. 1836, d. Colum-
        bia 10 Aug. 1873 (GS); m. Harrington 4 July
        1866 SARAH A. ALLEN, b. Centerville ME 15
        Oct. 1839, d. Columbia Falls 28 Mar. 1930,
        90y 5m 15d, dau. of Henry and Leah (Jacobs)
        Allen. No ch.
        He served in Co. C, 6th ME Inf. Rgt. and in
        the 2nd ME Cav. Rgt. 1861-65.

    vi.   LEONICE A., b. 6 June 1833, d. Columbia 20
        Jan. 1894; m. Harrington 5 Apr. 1873 HORATIO
        R. BRIDGHAM. No ch.

    vii. GEORGE N., b. c1835 (25 in 1860), d. Yorktown
        VA 8 May 1862, 27y, of wounds; unm. He was
        sergeant, Co. G, 6th ME Inf. Rgt.

Children by Betsey, born at Columbia:

    viii. CLARISSA M. [Clara], b. 7 Mar. 1839, d. Colum-
        bia 7 Mar. 1861, 22y 6m; unm.

    ix.   MARGARET S. [Maggie], b. 11 Mar. 1841, d. 7
        June 1871; unm.

    x.   STEPHEN SILSBY, b. 29 June 1843, d. Columbia
        22 May 1906; m. there 30 Nov. 1865 IRENE T.
        INGERSOLL, b. there 16 June 1846, d. there 2
        Sept. 1927, dau. of Fonze Green Hill and Lucy
        Corthell (Worcester) Ingersoll (Lillian D.
        Avery, Genealogy of the Ingersoll Family in
        America [NY, 1926], 52).
        Stephen served in the 6th and 15th ME Inf.
        Rgts., and was postmaster of Epping Village.
        Ch. HARVEY G.[9] b. Columbia 9 July 1870, d.
        Bangor in 1928; m. Columbia 31 Dec. 1891
        HATTIE E. PHIPPS, b. there in Dec. 1866:
        their ch. NONA[10] b. Charlotte 23 Oct. 1899,
        d. infant.

1039. xi. JAMES H., b. in June 1848 (12 in 1860).

462. LOVICIA[7] [Lovicey] 1797-1872 [146 Isaac[6] and Mary
Worcester] was born at Columbia 26 May 1797, died at Aurora
ME 25 July 1872, 75y 1m 29d; married first at New Charlestown
(now Charleston) ME 18 May 1817 (Bible record; Columbia int.
30 Mar.) STEPHEN OSGOOD, born at Orono ME 30 Mar. 1786, died
at Columbia 12 Feb. 1834, 48y (GS, Epping Cemetery, Columbia), son of Joseph and Sarah (Tibbetts) Osgood (Ira Osgood,
Descendants of John, Christopher and William Osgood [Salem
MA, 1894], 138; "Henry Tibbetts of Dover," NEHGReg,
99[1945]:115); married second at Columbia 17 Sept. 1835
Deacon SAMUEL SILSBY, JR., born at Acworth NH 3 Apr. 1785,
died at Aurora 14 June 1871, 86y, son of Samuel Silsby of
Charleston (Columbia VRs; Osgood Bible and other family
records of descendant Barbara Acton).

Children (**Osgood**), all but two born at Columbia:

i.   MARY, b. 6 Feb. 1818, d. Bradley ME 2 June 1901, 83y
      4m; m. Holden ME 28 Apr. 1836 (Bible) THOMAS ROWE,
      b. Eddington ME 3 Feb. 1812, d. Holden 11 Feb. 1867
      (Bible).
ii.   JOSEPH W., b. 14 Nov. 1819, d. Sheldonville MA 14 May
      1904, res. Pawtucket RI; m. 1st 9 Jan. 1842 ELVIRA
      METCALF, d. 13 Aug. 1852; m. 2nd Ellsworth ME 22
      Feb. 1854 HANNAH MORGAN, who d. 15 June 1885.
iii. STEPHEN B., b. 17 Feb. 1822, d. Chicago 22 June 1908;
      m. HANNAH E. CASE, b. Kenduskeag ME, d. Hudson WI 28
      Dec. 1896, dau. of Dr. Isaac Case. Stephen res.
      Ellsworth and Hudson.
iv.   BENJAMIN SILSBY, b. 11 May 1824, d. 18 July 1825.
v.   BENJAMIN SILSBY, b. Addison 9 Oct. 1825, d. St. Paul
      MN in Mar. 1915; m. 1st 2 Mar. 1852 LUCINDA SILSBY,
      b. Aurora 23 Dec. 1824, d. in Jan. 1901, dau. of
      Benjamin and Polly (Morse) Silsby; m. 2nd ELLA S.
      BROWN of Dalton MA.
vi.   JAMES BLAKE, b. Addison 1 Jan. 1828, d. Washington DC
      24 Mar. 1902; m. CORNELIA A. UPHAM. He was a War
      Dept. auditor.
vii. SARAH TIBBETTS, b. 23 Jan. 1831, d. Minneapolis MN 2
      Dec. 1903; m. 1st Bangor 25 July 1856 GEORGE RICH;
      m. 2nd Columbia 15 July 1861 STEPHEN JAMES McCASLIN,
      who had m. 1st MARY JANE[9] LEIGHTON [# 472].
viii. LOVICEY S., b. 2 May 1833, d. Aurora 10 Nov. 1851;
      unm.

Children (**Silsby**), born at Aurora:

ix.   GEORGE SELDON, b. 10 Aug. 1836, d. Coldwater KS 7
      July 1930; m. Winterport ME 18 Mar. 1857 MARY SHAW
      RICH, b. 2 July 1837, d. 30 Dec. 1898.
x.   CHARLES PAYSON, b. 22 Oct. 1838, d. in 1911; m. 1st
      Alfred ME 27 Nov. 1859 OLIVE TRAFTON; m. 2nd Blue
      Hill ME 4 Sept. 1864 FANNIE H. SANDS.

463. DANIEL R.[7] 1799-1871 [146 Isaac[6] and Mary Worcester]
was born at Columbia 18 Aug. 1799, died at Addison 16 Dec.
1871, 72y 3m 28d (GS); married first at Columbia int. 27 Apr.
1823 ABIGAIL WASS [Nabby] INGERSOLL, born 24 Jan. 1805, died
at Columbia 15 May 1842, 37y 3m 2d, daughter of William, Jr.,
and Susanna Shaw (Wass) Ingersoll (Avery, Ingersoll Family,

32; Columbia VRs); married second HARRIET ANN McALLISTER,
born at Oak Bay NB 14 Feb. 1813, died at Columbia 27 June
1857; married third there 8 Jan. 1869 HANNAH H.
(WORCESTER) Look, born there 24 June 1802, died there 13 June 1880,
daughter of Moses, Jr., and Hannah[6] (Leighton) Worcester
[# 150] and widow of Moses Look (town VRs; records of Leonard
F. Tibbetts). In 1870 he was listed at Addison, his household including a stepson Leon Look. Burials are in Epping
Cemetery. Daniel was a farmer at Columbia.

Children by Abigail, born at Columbia:

1040. i.   WILLIAM HILLMAN[8], b. 13 Dec. 1823.
1041. ii.   ISAAC L., b. 11 Jan. 1826.
       iii. ELI I., b. 15 Feb. 1828, d. 13 May 1832, 4y 2m
             28d (GS).
1042. iv.   MELISSA NASH, b. in 1830; m. JOSEPH WORCESTER.
1043. v.   FONZE G. H., b. 18 Sept. 1832.
1044. vi.   AUGUSTA ANN, b. in 1837; m. SIDNEY AUSTIN.
       vii. WARREN GILBERT, b. 30 Oct. 1839, d. Baton
             Rouge LA 22 Jan. 1863, 22y 2m 23d (GS); unm.
             He was in Co. D, 22nd ME Inf. Rgt.

Children by Harriet, born at Columbia:

       ix.   CELESTIA, d. before 1850.
       x.   ELI ALFRED (A. E. on GS), b. c1844 (6 in
             1850), drowned in May 1868 during river log
             drive; unm. He was in Co. D, 22nd ME Inf.
             Rgt., 1862-63.
1045. xi.   MARY ABIGAIL, b. 28 Jan. 1847; m. STEPHEN
             YOUNG.

464. HARRISON THATCHER[7] 1801-1900 [146 Isaac[6] and Mary
Worcester] was born at Columbia 21 Nov. 1801 (death record),
died there 30 Aug. 1900, 98y 9m 9d; married there 29 Dec.
1825 OLIVE D. CONLEY of Dixmont ME, born in NB 29 Dec. 1804,
died at Columbia 23 May 1891, 71y (Columbia and ME VRs).
   He was called Harrison T., Thatcher and H. T. He was a
farmer at Columbia; in 1860 a Conley niece and nephew were in
his household. At the age of 94, he was interviewed concerning his recollections of day-to-day life in the past (Boston
Sunday Globe, 8 Dec. 1895).

Children, born at Columbia:

       i.   PHILANDER W.[8], b. 2 Jan. 1827, res. CA in 1850
             as cook in a mining camp (NEHGReg, 91[1937]:
             328), and in 1880 res. Seattle WA.
1046. ii.   JOHN CALVIN, b. 13 Apr. 1829.
1047. iii. ELIZABETH CHRISTINE, b. 18 Feb. 1831; m.
             JONATHAN PINEO.
1048. iv.   HARRISON B., b. 19 Aug. 1835.
1049. v.   JOTHAM S., b. 10 Feb. 1841.
       vi.   DIREXA JANE, b. 25 Dec. 1843, d. 22 Jan. 1875;
             m. Columbia 28 Nov. 1866 Capt. LUTHER A.
             DYER, b. Addison in 1838, son of Luther P.
             and Delana A. (Look) Dyer. They res. Stone-
             ham MA and Seattle WA. Ch. Luther Harrison
             b. 3 Sept. 1867, served in US Navy.

465.   AARON[7] 1804-1884 [146 Isaac[6] and Mary Worcester] was born at Columbia 14 Jan. 1804, died at Bangor 11 Nov. 1884, 80y 10m; married at Addison 3 Jan. 1830 his cousin ELIZA ANN WORCESTER, born there 27 Oct. 1808, died at Columbia 19 Nov. 1879, daughter of John and Mary (Fernald) Worcester (Columbia VRs; records of Leonard Tibbetts).
In 1870 he was a farmer at Columbia. Burials are in Epping Cemetery there.

Children, born at Columbia:

	i.	MARY EMILY[8], b. 18 Nov. 1830, d. 16 Jan. 1841.
	ii.	WEALTHEA A., b. 11 Aug. 1832, d. Columbia 4 Feb. 1907, 74y 5m 15d; unm. She lived with her brother Hollis.
1050.	iii.	JAMES L., b. 3 Jan. 1835.
1051.	iv.	SAMANTHA L., b. 28 Feb. 1838; m. JOHN E. STEWART.
1052.	v.	HOLLIS J., b. 20 July 1847.
	vi.	SELDEN B., b. 20 Oct. 1849 (Oct. 1853 per 1900 census), res. Minneapolis MN in 1900; m. 6 Jan. 1880 EMMA CHADBOURNE (Cornman Ms), b. in ME in Jan. 1858, perhaps dau. of Benjamin and Emily (Chadbourne) Chadbourne. Ch. HENRY MELLIN[9] [Harry] b. Bangor 23 Jan. 1883.

466.   SARAH[7] [Sally] 1806-1883 [146 Isaac[6] and Mary Worcester] was born at Columbia 28 Apr. 1806, died there 22 Jan. 1882, 77y; married there 12 June 1827 JUSTUS SMITH TUCKER, born there 25 Mar. 1800, died there 19 Jan. 1882, 83y, son of Samuel and Esther[6] (Leighton) Tucker [# 147] (town VRs).
His first name was often spelled Justice. In 1860 they were living with their son Francis. The Machias Union stated that he died 20 Jan., and she two days after.

Children (**Tucker**), born at Columbia:

i.   JUSTUS, JR., b. in 1824, d. Addison 14 Sept. 1869, 45y; m. Columbia 1 Oct. 1848 PERMELIA WORCESTER, dau. of Amos and Sally (Ward) Worcester.
ii.   ELIZA ANN, b. 25 Oct. 1828; m. 1st Columbia 14 Dec. 1845 AARON WASS, b. 7 May 1826, d. 7 June 1848, son of Levi and Amy (Knowles) Wass (Wass Fam., 83); m. 2nd 25 Nov. 1852 ENOCH LINCOLN TABBUTT, b. 3 May 1829, d. 16 Apr. 1884, son of William Tabbutt.
iii. FRANCIS MERRIAM, b. 29 Aug. 1838, d. 3 May 1871; m. Columbia 2 Mar. 1860 SARAH J. HAMLIN, dau. of Isaac G. and Betsey (Ward) Hamlin.

467.   MARY ANN[7] [Annie] 1812-1896 [146 Isaac[6] and Mary Worcester] was born at Columbia 13 Oct. 1812, died at Columbia Falls 11 May 1896 (VRs, as Ann), 83y 5m; married first at Columbia 17 Dec. 1829 JUSTUS RAMSDELL, born about 1802, died 13 July 1836, 34y, son of Nathaniel and Hepsibah (Norton) Ramsdell; married second at Columbia int. 9 Mar. 1839 FRANCIS ALLEN, born in 1811, died 30 Apr. 1878, son of Robert and Sarah (Ingersoll) (Ingersoll) Allen (Columbia VRs; records of descendant Theodora Sawyer).

Children (**Ramsdell**), born at Columbia:

i.   CORDELIA WILSON, b. 23 Feb. 1833, d. Columbia Falls
      20 Feb. 1904; m. Columbia 1 Apr. 1856 BENJAMIN C.
      PINEO, b. 9 July 1832, d. 31 Aug. 1881, son of
      Gamaliel and Charlotte (Chamberlain) Pineo.
ii.   AMANDA M., b. 28 Dec. 1836, d. 3 Feb. 1851.

Children (**Allen**), born at Columbia:

iii. SARAH F., b. 5 Jan. 1840; m. Columbia 29 Sept. 1859
      JEROME P. WASS, d. 1 May 1886, son of Enoch and
      Clarissa (Davis) Wass.
iv.   (MARY) EMILY, b. 11 Jan. 1842; m. Columbia 30 Oct.
      1860 AUGUSTUS SPRINGER WHITE, b. Columbia Falls 1
      Sept. 1831, d. 1931, son of Ichabod and Parmelia
      White.

468.   ENOCH[7] 1794-1853 [148 Thomas Parritt[6] and Miriam
Worcester] was born at Columbia about 1794 (56 in 1850), died
at sea 11 Feb. 1853 (GS); married at Indian River int. 19
Mar. 1829 SUSANNA EMERSON, born at Jefferson ME 9 Dec. 1802,
died at Addison 8 Aug. 1885, 84y (GS), daughter of Eusebius
and Margaret (Lennan) Emerson (town VRs; records of Leonard
Tibbetts and Darryl Lamson). Burials are in the Indian River
Cemetery, Addison.
On 7 Mar. 1820, he bought from the Commonwealth of Massa-
chusetts lot 3 of 100 acres on Moore Island, Addison (WashCD,
14: 265-6); he lived in the Addison portion of the Indian
River settlement. He died of cholera during a voyage around
Cape Horn to CA. Widow Susan administered his estate, inven-
toried 12 June 1855 (WashCP, 19:229-30; 20:182).

Children, born at Addison:

1053.   i.   EMERY WADE[8], b. 9 Apr. 1830.
        ii.   CHARLOTTE, b. c1832, d. 25 Oct. 1842, 9y (GS).
1054.   iii. LYMAN PAGE, b. 9 Apr. 1834.
        iv.   THERESA, b. c1835, d. 24 Oct. 1846, 11y (GS).
1055.   v.   LANGDON S., b. in June 1838.
        vi.   JOSEPH EMERSON, b. 9 Apr. 1839, d. Cold Harbor
              VA 2 June 1864, killed in action. He enl. as
              corporal, 9th ME Inf. Rgt., in 1861, and re-
              enl. as a sergeant in 1864.
1056.   vii. SUSANNA E., b. 1 June 1841; m. NATHANIEL
              BRADFORD.
1057.   viii. HELEN THERESA, b. 1 June 1846; m. ALMON
              CROWLEY.

469.   ELI FORBES[7] 1796-1862 [148 Thomas Parritt[6] and Miriam
Worcester] was born at Columbia 28 May 1796 (29 May 1895,
Springfield VRs), died at Eastport ME 10 June 1862 (Spring-
field VRs), 67y (GS); married first at Steuben 11 Dec. 1820
(Jonesboro int. 1 Dec.) SARAH DYER [Sally] McKENZIE, born at
Addison 9 Jan. 1802 (9 May 1804, Springfield VRs), died at
Springfield 14 Sept. 1857, 55y (GS), daughter of John and
Susanna (Knowles) McKenzie; married second at Springfield 3
July 1859 DORCAS (----) Mallett, born about 1801 (59 in

1860). Burials are in Old Springfield Corner Cemetery (Leona
T. Brown and Frances S. Webster, Days Before Yesterday in
Springfield, Maine, 1834-1984 [1984], 107, 140; town VRs).
He was a farmer and shoemaker. He settled at Springfield
17 July 1838 (town record); the town was incorporated in
1834. Son Holley, 21, lived with them in 1850; in 1860 Eli
and Dorcas were there by themselves.

Children, all by Sally, born at Addison:

1058. i.   JULIA B.^{8}, b. 10 July 1822; m. SAMUEL TUCKER.
1059. ii.   NANCY L., b. 31 Aug. 1825; m. JEDEDIAH
             MERRILL, JR.
       iii. HOLLEY EMERSON, b. 27 Dec. 1829, d. at sea 7
             June 1854 of tuberculosis (Springfield TRs),
             25y; unm. He was said to have been buried
             secretly in Boston Common to avoid quarantine
             restrictions.

470.   ROBERT BARTON^7 1798-1865 [148 Thomas Parritt^6 and
Miriam Worcester] was born at Columbia about 1798 (52 in
1850), died at Addison in 1865, 75y (GS); married first at
Columbia int. 29 Dec. 1820 MARGARET [Peggy] BARFIELD, born
about 1801, died at Addison 19 Mar. 1828 of childbed, daughter of Richard and Jane (Dorr) Barfield; married second at
Addison int. 14 Aug. 1828 ELIZABETH A. [Eliza] DYER, born
about 1806, died at Addison 15 Mar. 1845, 39y (GS), daughter
of Lemuel and Elizabeth (Leach) Dyer; married third at Addison int. 9 Aug. 1846 OLIVETTE [Olly] (DRISKO) Rogers, born at
Addison about 1804 (56 in 1860), died before 1870, daughter
of John and Phebe (Parker) Drisko and widow of Joseph Prince
Rogers (Columbia and Addison VRs). Burials are in Hall's
Hill Cemetery.
Robert was a lumberman and fisherman at Addison. On 15
July 1829, he sold to his brother Enoch the 100-acre lot "on
which I have been residing, called Hall's Hill lot" (WashCD,
20:24). Six Rogers stepchildren were living in his household
in 1850.

Children by Peggy, born at Addison:

1060. i.   ENOCH 2ND^8, b. c1822.
1061. ii.   MIRIAM, b. in 1824; m. LORENZO SMITH and
             GEORGE McNAUGHTON.
1062. iii. JANE BARFIELD, b. in 1826; m. LEVI B. SAWYER.
1063. iv.   MARGARET, b. 19 Mar. 1828; m. RICHARD B. DORR.

Children by Eliza, born at Addison:

1064. v.   LUTHER P., b. in Feb. 1830.
1065. vi.   LEMUEL DYER, b. 7 Oct. 1832.
1066. vii. (GEORGE) ULMER, b. in 1835.
       viii. ANNA B., b. 28 Mar. 1837, d. Bridgeport CT 20
             Feb. 1926; m. Addison 20 Aug. 1854 STILLMAN
             McKENZIE EMERSON, b. there 23 Dec. 1831, d.
             Bridgeport 1 Nov. 1908, son of Eusebius and
             Susanna K. (McKenzie) Emerson. Ch. Estella
             M. b. Jonesport 22 Aug. 1856, d. 21 Aug.
             1888; m. George R. Wilson of Pawtucket RI.

1067. ix.   ELVIRA C., b. 7 Feb. 1839; m. ALVIN J. STEELE.
1068. x.   SUSANNA E., b. in 1841; m. JAMES E. BAGLEY.
       xi.   ROBERT BARTON, JR., b. in 1843, d. Memphis TN
             23 Oct. 1863; unm. He was in Co. H, 12th ME
             Inf. Rgt.

471. LUCY[7] 1801-1880 [148 Thomas Parritt[6] and Miriam Worcester] was born at Addison in 1801, died at St. Martin s Island MI in 1880 (Machias Union of 27 July); married first JOHN DRISKO 4TH, born about 1801, drowned at Indian River 21 Nov. 1834, son of John and Phebe (Parker) Drisko; married second at Addison int. 12 Feb. 1839 JOHN S. BURNS, born in Ireland in 1803 (naturalized at Machias 8 Oct. 1856), died at Jaffa, Palestine, 23 Oct. 1866 (Leonard F. Tibbetts and Darryl B. Lamson, Early Families of Jonesport, Maine [Brewer, 1984], 40, 83).

The Palestine Colony: In 1862 the Rev. George J. Adams came to Addison and made it the home base of his Church of the Messiah. He preached that the coming of the Messiah was imminent, but that first the Old Testament prophecies must be fulfilled, that the children of Judah--the Jews--must be returned to Palestine. He sought converts to be the children of Ephraim, foretold as those who would prepare the way for the Jews.

Adams, a former actor, alcoholic and cast-out Mormon, built up congregations in MA, NH and ME; of them the Indian River followers were the most enthusiastic, accepting his call to labor for God in Palestine. Adams and Abraham McKenzie made a voyage to scout out the land in 1865, and brought back glowing reports of fertile land and the welcoming attitude of the Turks.

Despite the warnings, pity or ridicule of their neighbors, Adams's followers sold their farms, homes, livestock, shops and mills, and bought or gathered the tools, seeds, provisions--even prefabricated buildings--needed for their new lives as farmers, traders, and craftsmen in a strange land.

Improbable as it seems, on 10 Aug. 1866 the Nellie Chapin set sail from Jonesport to carry the Palestine Emigration Society to the Holy Land--156 Yankee men, women and children, two-thirds of them from Addison and Jonesport. At Jaffa the Adams Colony soon disintegrated in disillusion, suffering and disgrace. In less than a year, only twenty remained; some had died of disease, but most had somehow made their way back to the United States. Mark Twain described the colony's plight in Innocents Abroad.

Of the group, 22 were in the family of "Gram Burns," the Lucy above, and thirteen more were Leighton relatives. Each is noted in this book. Leonard F. Tibbetts has traced the descendants of the Jaffa colonists.

The Adams Colony has been the subject of several studies, particularly Peter Amann's "Prophet in Zion: The Saga of George J. Adams," (New England Quarterly, 37[Dec. 1964]: 477-500); and Reed M. Holmes's The Forerunners. The Tragic Story of 156 Down East Americans ... [Independence MO, 1981]. Mr. Holmes set forth his thesis that the Adams group paved the way for the Zionist movement and the creation of the Israeli nation in "George Adams and the Forerunners," Maine Historical Society Quarterly, 21[Summer 1981]:19-49.

Children (**Drisko**), born at Addison:

i.   LORENZO, b. c1822, d.y.
ii.   ALBION K., b. in 1842, d. Addison 5 June 1858; unm.
        He was a tailor, and a cripple.
iii.   PHEBE PARKER, b. 26 July 1827, d. Jaffa 29 Nov. 1866;
        m. Addison int. 15 Dec. 1849 ABRAHAM LINCOLN NORTON,
        b. Jonesport 20 Jan. 1823, d. there 29 Aug. 1881,
        son of Jeremiah Beal and Hannah (Sawyer) Norton. He
        was a ships' carpenter. They took 4 ch. to Jaffa.
        He m. 2nd Addison 1 Mar. 1873 Henrietta Bernice
        (Lord) Cole.
iv.   PRISCILLA ANN, b. in 1828, d. St. Martin's Island MI
        6 Apr. 1902; m. 1st ACKLEY EZRA NORTON, b. Jonesport
        in 1828, d. Chelsea MA 1 Jan. 1871, son of Phineas
        Manwarren and Frances Etta (Beal) Norton; m. 2nd in
        MI ALBERT BARTMAN of Germany. Norton, a sea cap-
        tain, took his wife and 5 ch. to Jaffa.
v.   GEORGE ALVIN, b. 23 Nov. 1830, d. Misery Bay (near
        Escanaba) MI 28 July 1905; m. Addison 3 Dec. 1852
        ELIZABETH C. SKINNER, b. Jonesport in 1834, d. in MI
        in 1920, dau. of Justin and Rachel (Cummings)
        Skinner. They went to Jaffa, taking a dau.
vi.   JOHN A., b. in 1834, d. Escanaba MI in the 1890s; m.
        1st Addison 5 Jan. 1862 CHARLOTTE L. PARKER, b.
        Jonesport in 1841, d. c1868, dau. of James and Mary
        (Farley) Parker; m. 2nd CALCILDA A. BLUNT, b. Jones-
        port in 1847, res. Schofield WI in 1893, dau. of
        Thomas P. and Ann (Farley) Blunt. No ch. John took
        his first wife "Cassie" to Jaffa.

Children (**Burns**), born at Addison:

vii.   JAMES EVERETT, b. in 1840, d. St. Martin's Island MI
        in 1880s; unm. He went to Jaffa with his mother.
viii.   LUCY M., b. in Mar. 1842, d. Addison 2 May 1850 (GS).
ix.   CHARLES E., b. 17 Mar. 1849, d. Chicago 29 Sept.
        1911; m. in MI CATHERINE COFFEY, b. MI in 1851, d.
        there in 1913, dau. of Edward and Mary (Mulligan)
        Coffey. He too went to Jaffa with his mother.

472. NAHUM H.[7] 1803-1867 [148 Thomas Parritt[6] and Miriam
Worcester] was born at Columbia in 1803 (47 in 1850), died at
Addison 13 Mar. 1867, 64y (GS); married first at Addison int.
6 Feb. 1828 PHOEBE PARKER DRISKO, born at Addison in 1806,
died there 29 June 1849, 42y 9m (GS), daughter of John and
Phebe (Parker) Drisko; married second at Addison 9 Apr. 1860
ABIGAIL [Nabby] (COFFIN) (Tucker) Crowley, born at Addison in
1791, daughter of Matthew and Jane (Wass) Coffin (Leighton,
Columbia Sketch, 22). Nabby had married first Isaac Tucker,
son of Samuel and Esther[6] (Leighton) Tucker [# 147], and
second James Crowley (town VRs; records of Darryl Lamson and
descendant Leonard F. Tibbetts). Burials are in Indian River
Cemetery.

Children, all by Phoebe, born at Addison:

        i.   MARY JANE[8], b. in Sept. 1828, d. Columbia 18
                Oct. 1889; m. Columbia int. 2 Aug. 1847 JAMES
                MUNROE McCASLIN, b. there 12 June 1822,

        d. 6 Jan. 1907, son of Alexander and Abigail
        (Knowles) McCaslin. No ch. He m. 2nd Sarah
        T. (Osgood) Rich [# 462].
    ii. ABITHA D., b. in 1830; m. URIAH WASS[8] LEIGHTON
        [# 1076].
    iii. HARRIS S., b. 1 May 1832, d. Addison 18 Aug.
        1921, 89y 3m 17d; m. there 9 Oct. 1852 ELVINA
        A.[8] LEIGHTON, b. there 9 Dec. 1835, d. there
        8 Sept. 1919, dau. of John C. and Eunice B.
        (Wright) Leighton [# 473]. No ch.
        A sea captain, he was listed at Jonesport in
        1900 and 1910.
    iv. AVERY W., b. 3 June 1834, d. Staten Island NY
        10 Dec. 1853, 19y 6m 7d (GS), of smallpox.
1069. v. JASON DRISKO, b. 3 Nov. 1835.
    vi. JAMES PARKER, b. in 1837, not in 1860 census.
1070. vii. SARAH A., b. 17 July 1839; m. EZRA S. STROUT.
1071. viii. REBECCA DRISKO, b. 16 Nov. 1840; m. DAVID JOY.
1072. ix. LUCY W., b. in 1842; m. CHARLES W. TRACY.
1073. x. LAURA DRISKO, b. 8 Jan. 1844; m. JOHN HENRY
        FOSTER.
    xi. PORTER, b. in 1845, not in 1850 census.
    xii. NAHUM, JR., b. c1846 (4 in 1850, 33 in 1880),
        res. Milbridge in 1905 with Laura; unm.
1074. xiii. PHEBE PARKER, b. 29 June 1849; m. WARREN
        FOSTER.

473. JOHN C.[7] 1805-1873 [148 Thomas Parritt[6] and Miriam
Worcester] was born at Columbia 27 Jan. 1805, died at Addison
15 Feb. 1873 (GS); married at Addison 10 Jan. 1829 EUNICE B.
WRIGHT, born at Addison 14 Apr. 1809, died there 25 Jan.
1875, 65y 9m (GS), daughter of John and Catherine (Ayers)
(Crowley) Wright (Addison VRs; records of Darryl Lamson,
Leonard F. Tibbetts, and descendant Genevieve Ireland).
Burials are in Indian River Cemetery, Addison. He was a
fisherman and seaman. John's middle initial probably stands
for Coffin.

Children, born at Addison:

1075. i.   LOWELL WILLIAM[8], b. 11 Dec. 1828.
1076. ii. URIAH WASS, b. 10 Aug. 1830.
1077. iii. REBECCA DRISKO, b. 9 June 1833; m. EPHRAIM
           WHITNEY.
      iv. ELVINA A., b. 9 Dec. 1835; m. HARRIS S.[8]
           LEIGHTON [# 472].
      v.   JOHN WRIGHT, b. 12 July 1837, d. 23 Feb. 1854,
           16y 7m 13d (GS).
1078. vi. ISAAC WILLIS, b. 29 Dec. 1839.
1079. vii. GEORGE P., b. 4 Jan. 1842.
1080. viii. DANIEL WEBSTER, b. 18 Mar. 1844.
1081. ix. (PRISCILLA) JANE, b. 30 Apr. 1846; m. GEORGE
           WELLINGTON WHITE.
      x.   (HORACE) ALFRED, b. 6 May 1849, d. Jonesboro
           11 May 1928, 77y; m. there 1 Apr. 1877
           CALISTA E. FARNSWORTH, b. there 10 Jan. 1860,
           d. there 7 Sept. 1935, dau. of Ephraim and
           Margaret (Hatch) Farnsworth.
             In 1850 and 1860 he was listed as Alfred H.,
           a quarryman. Ch. ETHEL EUNICE[9] b. Jonesboro

3 Feb. 1878, d. 1 Mar. 1908; m. Machias 15
Oct. 1898 CHARLES PENNELL SMITH, b. Whitney-
ville ME 24 Mar. 1869, son of Asa Kingman and
Hannah (Pennell) Smith.

474.   CURTIS M.[7] 1807-1864 [148 Thomas Parritt[6] and Miriam
Worcester] was born at Addison in 1807, killed in VA during
the Battle of the Wilderness 6 May 1862; married at Addison
int. 3 Aug. 1830 PHILENA EMERSON, born at Jefferson ME 26 May
1811, died at Addison in June 1852, daughter of Eusebius and
Margaret (Lennan) (Bryant) Emerson (records of Darryl Lamson
and Leonard F. Tibbetts).
    He was a sea captain. He enlisted in 1863 in Co. H, 1st ME
Heavy Artillery Rgt.

Children, born at Addison:

	i.	EMELINE[8], b. in 1831 (19 in 1850); unm.
1082.	ii.	LUCY DRISKO, b. 21 Dec. 1833; m. BENJAMIN KELLEY ROGERS.
1083.	iii.	HARRIET NEWELL, b. 22 Dec. 1835; m. REUBEN CHANDLER.
1084.	iv.	ARTHUR, b. 16 Feb. 1837.
	v.	ELVIRA J., b. in Apr. 1840, d. Jonesport 8 May 1914, 74y; unm. and long bed-ridden. Ch. Edwin W. Look, b. Addison 6 June 1866, d. there 17 July 1952, 86y, was raised by Austin and Emily Look.
	vi.	(JAMES) CURTIS, b. in 1841, d. Gettysburg PA in July 1863. He enl. 2 Nov. 1861.
	vii.	AUGUSTA J., b. 19 Mar. 1844, d. Addison 16 Sept. 1921, 77y; m. there 19 Dec. 1863 PORTER B. LOOK, b. there in Nov. 1842, d. Machias 2 Feb. 1922, son of Thomas and Mary (Look) Look. Ch. Nellie Eva b. 12 Sept. 1864.
	viii.	EDGAR, b. in Mar. 1850, nfr.
1085.	ix.	(IRA) BOARDMAN, b. 21 May 1852.

475.   BARNABAS BEAL[7] [Barney] 1814-1892 [148 Thomas Par-
ritt[6] and Miriam Worcester] was born at Addison in 1814, died
at Cottage City MA 2 Apr. 1892; married first at Centerville
ME int. 7 May 1839 MARY WASS STEVENS, born about 1817 (33 in
1850), died at Jaffa, Palestine, 30 Oct. 1866, daughter of
Edmund and Sophia (Wass) Stevens; married second at Cottage
City 2 May 1889 MARY JANE (SYLVIA) (Smith) Look, born at
Edgartown MA in 1844, adopted daughter of Francis and Jane S.
Sylvia (Addison VRs; records of Leonard F. Tibbetts). Mary
Jane had married first Roland Smith, and second Daniel M.
Look of Tisbury. Barnabas is buried at Edgartown.
    He was a ships' carpenter. He served in Co. D, 22nd ME
Inf. Rgt., in 1862-63. In 1866 he and his family were part
of the Palestine Emigration Society [see # 471]; his first
wife died in Palestine.
    He returned and settled at Cottage City, now Oak Bluffs,
founded in the 1860s as a Methodist summer colony on Martha's
Vineyard and later enlarged as a retirement community, especially for mariners. His widow Mary Jane made application
for a pension 4 May 1892.

Children by first wife, born at Addison:

  i.   CHARLOTTE L.^{8}, b. 27 Feb. 1841, d. 1 Mar. 1855
         (GS, Hall's Hill), burned to death.
1086. ii.   ELI A., b. 10 June 1843.
      iii. FRANCES M., b. c1846 (4 in 1850), res. W.
            Haven CT in 1916; m. 1st HIRAM HATCH; m. 2nd
            ORRIN PAUL. Ch. Hiram Hatch, Jr. (Cornman
            Ms).
1087. iv.   MARY SOPHIA, b. c1848 (2 in 1850); m. JOHN E.
            SANDEFORD.
       v.   EDMUND WELLINGTON, b. 19 Jan. 1852, d. 22
            Sept. 1853, 20m 3d (GS, Hall's Hill).

476. MOSES WORCESTER^7 1817-1890 [148 Thomas Parritt^6 and
Miriam Worcester] was born at Addison 23 Feb. 1817 (on GS),
died at Cottage City (now Oak Bluffs) MA in 1890; married at
Jonesport 31 July 1851 NANCY N. SKINNER, born at Jonesport in
1836 (24 in 1860), daughter of Justin and Rachel (Cummings)
Skinner (Tibbetts, Jonesport Families, 44). Nancy married
second 6 Aug. 1892 Hiram Luce of Oak Bluffs.
  Moses was a stone and brick mason. He, his wife and son
also took part in the Jaffa expedition [#471]. After their
return, they settled at Escanaba MI with relatives, but soon
returned east to live at Cottage City. In 1880 his son Melville and his family lived there with them.

Children, born at Addison:

  i.   MELVILLE JAMES^8 (James M. in 1860), b. in
         1852; m. in MA ANNA$_9$P. ---- , b. c1854 (26 in
         1880). Ch. CLARANA^9 b. c1878.
  ii.   MIRIAM, b. in 1860, d.y.

477. DORCAS^7 1791-   [149 Phineas^6 and Annie Worcester]
was born at Columbia ME 14 Sept. 1791, lived at Eastport;
married there 25 May 1810 WILLIAM SWAIN (Cornman Ms).

Children (**Swain**):

  i.   SARAH; m. ---- TUCKER.
  ii.   WILLIAM J.; m. LOUISA JOY.
  iii.   WALTER.
  iv.   OTIS; m. ---- GARDNER.

478. HOLLAND^7 1798-1842 [149 Phineas^6 and Annie Worcester]
was born at Columbia 2 Apr. 1798, drowned in the Pembroke
River in 1842; married 24 Aug. 1819 JANE KATHERINE ROBINSON
of Pembroke. He was a carpenter, and lived at Bailey's Mistake, a cove below West Quoddy Head, Lubec (Pembroke VRs;
Wilder, Pembroke Families).

Children, born at Lubec:

  i.   WORCESTER^8, b. 20 Feb. 1821, d. Chelsea MA
         28 Nov. 1856, 33y (VRs); m. 1st ELIZABETH S.
         REYNOLDS, b. c1821, d. Pembroke 2 Dec. 1847,

26y (GS); m. 2nd 20 Nov. 1849 MARY ANN
CROSIER, b. c1823 (27 in 1850). He was a
carpenter at Eastport in 1850. Ch. ANGELIA[9]
b. Charlestown MA 22 June 1852.
1088.   ii.   ROBINSON, b, 9 Oct. 1823.
        iii. ANNIE, b. 10 July 1826; nfr..
        iv.   HANNAH, b. 5 Dec. 1828; m. Pembroke 30 Dec.
              1848 ELISHA D. CUSHING, b. there 29 Dec.
              1827, d. in WI, son of Solomon and Pamelia
              (Davidson) Cushing (per Wilder).
        v.   ?ALONZO.
        vi.   PHINEAS, d. in July 1835.
1089.   vii. CHARLES E., b. 6 Dec. 1835.

479.   SABRINA[7] [Sabra] 1804-1880 [149 Phineas[6] and Annie
Worcester] was born at Columbia 17 Mar. 1804, died at Lubec
18 Mar. 1880; married 6 Oct. 1825 JAMES BLISS BRAWN, born at
Fredericton NB 17 Feb. 1801, died at Lubec 8 Feb. 1888, son
of William and Mary (Rideout) Brawn (Cornman Ms; records of
descendant Katherine Acker).

Children (**Brawn**), born at Lubec:

i.   LYDIA ANN, b. 19 July 1826; m. OTIS JOHNSON.
ii.   ELIZABETH J., b. 18 Feb. 1829, res. Lubec; m. Grand
       Manan EDWARD KING.
iii.   AMOS WORCESTER, b. in 1831, d. Rockland ME in Mar.
       1877; m. in 1861 MARY J. EAMES of NS. No ch.
iv.   DANIEL THAYER, b. 30 Oct. 1837, d. Lubec 23 Nov.
       1908; m. Lubec 12 Aug. 1872 MARY CHARLOTTE NUTTER,
       b. Lubec 6 May 1854. A shipmaster, he served in the
       US Navy during the Civil War.
v.   CAROLINE O., b. in 1840, d. 25 Dec. 1880; m. Lubec
       7 Nov. 1857 WILLIAM H. ALLEN, b. Lubec 17 Mar. 1835.
vi.   SUSAN E., b. in 1844 (16 in 1860), d. 16 Mar. 1891;
       m. Lubec 4 Apr. 1867 JAMES GUPTILL.
vii.   STEPHEN J., d. Lubec in 1850, aged 3.

480.   ALFRED CARPENTER[7] 1814-1885 [149 Phineas[6] and Annie
Babcock] was born at Perry 6 Apr. 1814 (Eastport VRs), died
there 26 Mar. 1885; married 25 Dec. 1838 JANET MORRIS, born
at Ayrshire, Scotland, 3 Oct. 1818, died at Perry 18 July
1906, daughter of James and Margaret (Moody) Morris (Perry
VRs; records of descendant Patricia Leighton).
       He was a millwright and farmer. Janet (Janette, Jeanette)
was living at Gainesville FL in 1888 with her son Alfred, and
in 1900 lived with Addie in IL.

Children, born at Perry:

        i.   RUFUS MERRITT[8], b. 6 Aug. 1840, d. Perry 9
              Dec. 1864; m. ---- .
1090.   ii.   JAMES MORRIS, b. 28 June 1842.
1091.   iii. ALFRED WALLACE, b. 26 Oct. 1844.
1092.   iv.   GEORGE FRANKLIN, b. 22 July 1846.
        v.   ADRIANNA, b. 19 Sept. 1848, d. 5 Feb. 1857.
        vi.   CHARLES A., b. 3 Oct. 1850, d. Perry 15 July
              1931; m. West Pembroke 3 Oct. 1876 LYDIA E.

WHEELER, b. Eastport 8 Aug. 1852, d. Perry 16
Apr. 1923, 70y 8m 8d, dau. of Nicholas and
Frances (Coffin) Wheeler. No ch. He was a
farmer at Perry.
1093.   vii.   ADRIANNA [Addie], b. 16 Aug. 1857; m.
RENALVIN OUTHOUSE.
viii.   SILAS M., b. 7 Nov. 1858, d. 28 Nov. 1863.

481.   JACOB[7] 1818-1884 [149 Phineas[6] and Annie Babcock] was
born at Perry 30 Sept. 1818, died at Machiasport in 1884;
married first at Machias 18 Aug. 1845 (VRs) SARAH E. SMALL of
Machiasport, born about 1827 (23 in 1850); married second at
Machias 28 Oct. 1863 ALMEDA WHITNEY of Jonesport (Amanda in
Machias Union) born in MA about 1811 (59 in 1870).
A ships' carpenter, he and his family were in the Machiasport household of David Trafton in 1850. His second wife was
listed as Almeda Barker in the Cornman Ms.

Children by Sarah:

i.   FRANCIS W.[8], b. c1846 (4 in 1850, 27 in
1870), d. Chelsea MA in 1885; m. Machiasport ---- . He was a mariner.
1094.   ii.   SUSAN, b. c1849 (2 in 1850); m. GILBERT S.
SANBORN.
iii.   ARTHUR, b. in 1850 (1/12 in census; not shown
in the Cornman Ms or in the 1860 census).

482.   ISAAC[7] 1820-1876 [149 Phineas[6] and Annie Babcock]
was born at Perry 25 Nov. 1820, died at Machiasport in 1876;
married at Machias 6 Feb. 1852 CHARLOTTE A. (MARSTON) Ames,
born at Machiasport 22 Mar. 1825, daughter of Elisha and
Mehitable (Phinney) Marston (Machias VRs; Cornman Ms). She
had married first Charles C. Ames (Marston Gen., 145).
Isaac was a ships' carpenter at Machiasport in 1860; his
household included four Ames children.

Children, born at Machiasport:

1095.   i.   (FRANCES) ALBERTA[8] [Bertha], b. c1854; m.
WALTER DOUGHTY.
ii.   ANNIE BABCOCK, b. c1870 (1/12 in 1870), res.
Somerville MA.

483.   OLIVER PERRY[7] 1823-1886 [149 Phineas[6] and Annie Bab-
cock] was born at Perry 13 Mar. 1823 (Eastport VRs), died at
East Boston MA 20 Oct. 1886, 63y (VRs); married at Eastport 2
Nov. 1856 KATHERINE W. PORTER of Cooper, born at Charlotte ME
27 Mar. 1830, daughter of Hugh and Jane (Coates) Porter (town
VRs; Cornman Ms).
Oliver, a carpenter, lived at Pembroke ME and at Medford
and Dorchester MA. In 1900 his widow was living with Grace
and Maxwell Stark.

Children:

i.   MELVIN P., b. Medford MA 13 Sept. 1857, d. 26
Oct. 1884, 27y 1m 13d.

ii.   GRACE A., b. Medford in 1861; m. 20 Sept. 1888
      WESLEY MAXWELL STARK, b. NS in 1860, son of
      Joshua and Margaret Stark. W. Maxwell was a
      printer at Boston in 1900, and she a music
      teacher.

484.   ANNIE[7] 1825-   [149 Phineas[6] and Annie Babcock] was
born at Perry 16 Dec. 1825, lived at Eastport in 1903 with
her son Andrew; married 19 Dec. 1846 JOHN J. BENNER, born 25
Jan. 1825, died 10 Nov. 1895, son of John and Mary Ann (Whitney) Benner (Eastport VRs; Cornman Ms).
      In 1880 at Jonesboro a Nina M. Leighton, aged 6, was listed
in their household.

Children (**Benner**):

i.   ST CLAIR, b. Dennysville 13 Dec. 1848; m. in 1868
       ---- .
ii.   ADELAIDE P., b. 13 Dec. 1852, d. 4 Feb. 1887; m. Add-
       son 5 Nov. 1877 JOHN SEAVEY, JR.
iii.   ANDREW MELVIN, b. Pembroke 14 July 1854, res. East-
       port; m. ---- .
iv.   (CHARLES) EDGAR, b. Columbia 14 July 1854; m. 1st
       Machias 14 June 1873 (Machias Union) MARY E. LAM-
       BERT; m. 2nd Addison 8 Aug. 1880 ELIZA A. KELLEY,
       dau. of Samuel M. Kelley.
v.   CLARA ELLA, b. Perry 20 Feb. 1857; m. in 1882 ---- .
vi.   (ANNA) BERNICE, b. 19 Sept. 1864; m. in 1887 ---- .
vii.   FLORENCE J., b. 20 June 1865, d. 15 June 1892; m.
       Jonesboro 21 Dec. 1882 EDWARD ABBOTT of Pittston ME
       (Machias Union).

485.   ANDREW JACKSON[7] 1829-1888 [149 Phineas[6] and Annie
Babcock] was born at Perry 13 Dec. 1829, died there 30 Nov.
1888; married at Perry 23 Oct. 1851 SOPHIA GLEASON JOHNSON,
born at Perry 29 Mar. 1829, died at Machias 13 Sept. 1864,
35y 15d (Machias Union), daughter of Oliver Shedd and Betsey
(Hersey) Johnson (Perry VRs; Wilder, Pembroke Families). In
1860 they were living at Whitneyville.

Children:

1096.   i.   JESSE GLEASON[8], b. Perry 2 Nov. 1852.
1097.   ii.   SAMUEL JOHNSON, b. 17 Jan. 1858.
1098.   iii.   FREDERICK HILL, b. Pembroke 28 Nov. 1859.

486.   JOHN EMERSON[7] 1796-1874 [152 Stephen[6] and Polly Emer-
son] was born at Strafford NH (then Barrington) 15 Jan. 1796,
died at Pittsfield NH 7 Nov. 1874; married at Strafford 28
Jan. 1830 (Nottingham int. 28 Dec. 1829) SARAH F. LUCY, born
at Nottingham 29 Dec. 1806, died at Pittsfield 15 Mar. 1877,
daughter of John and Lydia (Davis) Lucy (D. Hamilton Hurd,
History of Merrimack and Belknap Counties, N. H. [Philadel-
phia, 1885], 258; Cornman Ms; town VRs). Burials are in
Floral Park Cemetery, Pittsfield.
      He was a farmer at Strafford and then at Gilmanton, where
the family was listed in 1850.

Children, the first five born at Strafford (VRs):

1099. i.   ANDREW STEPHEN^8, b. 2 Jan. 1831.
1100. ii. LEVI ALVIN, b. 28 July 1832.
       iii. LYDIA ABIGAIL, b. 4 May 1834, d. 2 Mar. 1835.
1101. iv. MARIA JANE, b. 10 Feb. 1836; m. DARIUS SANDERS
            and WILLIAM TRUE SANDERS.
       v.   ABBIE MARY [Mary A.], b. 9 June 1838, d. in
            1926; m. 25 Nov. 1864 HIRAM ELLIOT LOCKE, b.
            Loudon NH 11 Nov. 1836, d. in 1926, son of
            Reuben and Eliza (Shaw) Locke. No ch. Hiram
            served in Co. E, 13th NH Inf. Rgt., and then
            became a carriage painter at Pittsfield NH
            (Locke Gen., 361).
       vi. ADELAIDE SARAH [Addie], b. Gilmanton 4 May
            1843, d. Pittsfield 6 Oct. 1868; m. 4 Mar.
            1865 ALFRED$_8$WARDWELL of Andover NH, who m.
            2nd DORA S.^{8} LEIGHTON [# 1108]. Ch. HARRY
            ALFRED WARDWELL b. Pittsfield 6 Feb. 1867,
            drowned Haverhill MA 14 June 1889; unm

487. GIDEON^7 1799-1857 [152 Stephen^6 and Polly Emerson]
was born at Strafford NH 24 June 1799, died at Newburyport MA
18 Apr. 1857, 57y 10m; married at Newburyport 13 Nov. 1827
HANNAH TAPPAN, born there 24 Dec. 1804, died there 3 Dec.
1878, probably daughter of John and Sally Tappan (Newburyport
VRs; Cornman Ms).

Children, born at Newburyport:

1102. i.   EUNICE^8, b. 6 Oct. 1828; m. WILLIAM LITTLE.
1103. ii. MARY ESTHER, b. 7 July 1830; m. NATHANIEL G.
            PIERCE.
1104. iii. ANDREW JACKSON, b. 20 Aug. 1833.

488. SARAH^7 [Sally] 1802-1883 [152 Stephen^6 and Polly
Emerson] was born at Strafford 13 Nov. 1802, died in Aug
1883; married at Dover 6 June 1827 HENRY FOLSOM, born at
Wolfeboro NH in 1803, died at Great Falls (Walpole) NH 2 Oct.
1847, son of Jacob and Eleanor (Smart) Folsom (Folsom Fam.,
1:435; Cornman Ms).

Children (**Folsom**), born at Great Falls:

i.   GEORGE GILMAN, b. 24 Dec. 1827, d. Berwick ME 8 Jan.
      1879; m. 1st 1 Jan. 1850 NANCY JANE LITTLEFIELD, b.
      Lebanon ME, d. No. Waterboro ME 27 July 1896,
      dau. of George Littlefield--div.; m. 2nd MARIA F.
      JONES.
ii.   CHARLES H., b. 10 July 1836, d. Berwick 29 June 1902;
      m. 6 Mar. 1870 ELIZA A. MOORE, b. Springvale ME 10
      Jan. 1842, dau. of Joshua and Sarah Moore.
iii. OLIVE ANN, b. 2 Apr. 1841, d. 2 Dec. 1848.

489. HANNAH^7 1804-1850 [152 Stephen^6 and Polly Emerson]
was born at Strafford 15 Nov. 1804, died at Worthington OH 20
Aug. 1850; married 7 Dec. 1825 EBENEZER FOSS, born at Barrington NH 30 Mar. 1801, died at Kankakee IL 22 July 1893,

son of Samuel and Sarah (Horne) Foss (George S. Rix, Foss
Family in America [Concord NH, 1914], 66; records of descen-
dants William Bonser and Blanche Bennett). They settled in
Ohio; he later went on to Iroquois County IL.

Children (Foss):

i.   SAMUEL, b. in 1826, res. Kinton OH; m. 22 Aug. 1850
        OLIVE TOPLIFF.
ii.   JUSTIN O., b. 20 Feb. 1827, res. Indianapolis IN; m.
        20 Feb. 1857 ELLEN DRAGGS.
iii.   LONZETTA S., b. Jefferson OH 17 Mar. 1829; m. 1 Jan.
        1860 ---- SIMPKINS.
iv.   FRANCIS MARION, b. Columbus OH 30 Nov. 1843, d. Gar-
        field KS; m. 1st 25 Dec. 1866 ELIZABETH MILBURY,
        b. Smith Tp, Peterborough, Ont. 5 Apr. 1850, d.
        Scottsville KS 1 May 1877, dau. of John Thomas and
        Dinah (Ivison) Milbury; m. 2nd Stark Co. IL 18 May
        1880 JOANNA DEAO, dau. of Eli and Mary Ann (Simmer-
        man) Deao.
v.   JOSEPHINE V., b. Dana IL 19 Sept. 1849; m. JOHN
        BURRISS.

490. MARY E.[7] 1806-1866 [152 Stephen[6] and Polly Emerson]
was born at Strafford 15 Oct. 1806, died at Boston 4 Nov.
1866; married 29 Apr. 1832 LUTHER BRADFORD SAMPSON, born at
Dover 24 Nov. 1809 (or at Readfield ME 12 Dec. 1808 according
to Stearns), died at Rochester NH 24 May 1884, son of Dr.
Nehemiah and Bathsheba (Baker) Sampson (Stearns, N. H.
Genealogies, 2:961; letter from Luther, Jr.--Cornman Papers).
He may have married again.
   He was a cotton-mill supervisor and lived at Somersworth,
Dover, and Saco ME.

Children (Sampson):

i.   JOHN CALVIN, b. Dover 1 Dec. 1839, killed in action
        at Petersburg VA 30 July 1864; unm. He served in US
        Navy in 1861-2, enl. in 1862 as sergeant, 9th NH
        Inf. Rgt. He was promoted to captain.
ii.   LUTHER BRADFORD, JR., b. Great Falls 1 Sept. 1841,
        res. Somersworth; m. Horseheads NY 10 Mar. 1864
        SUSAN E. PATTERSON, b. Milford PA 18 June 1846, dau.
        of Virgil and Elizabeth W. (Wainwright) Patterson.
        He served in the 8th PA Inf. Rgt. 1861-4, and was
        promoted from private to captain. He owned the
        Rochester Carpet Co.
iii.   HELEN AMANDA, b. 9 May 1843, res. Little Rock IL in
        1903; m. 29 Sept. 1863 Capt. JAMES BLAISDELL, b. 19
        July 1835, d. 4 June 1897.
iv.   ANDREW LEIGHTON, b. Berwick ME 21 Mar. 1845, d. Roch-
        ester NH 11 Sept. 1875; m. in 1873 NETTIE DOYLE, b.
        in NS. He served in US Navy 1861-2.

491. ANDREW[7] 1808-1881 [152 Stephen[6] and Polly Emerson]
was born at Strafford 7 Apr. 1808, died at Lowell MA 7 Dec.
1881 (VRs); married first at Pittsfield NH 12 July 1835 MARY
ANN LANGLEY, born at Deerfield NH in 1815, died at Lowell 8
May 1857, daughter of James, Jr., and Mary (Morse) Langley;

married second 13 Oct. 1858 MARY J. B. WHITE, born at Methuen
MA 19 Apr. 1835, daughter of Fairfield and Rebecca (Stephens)
White (Cornman Ms). Andrew operated a fabric bleaching mill
at Lowell. His widow married second in Feb. 1883 Dr. Joseph
Roberts Hayes, who died at Methuen 26 July 1894 (Richmond,
John Hayes, 1:348).

Children, all by first wife, born at Lowell (VRs):

      i.   ANDREW STEPHEN[8], b. 14 May 1836, d. 29 May
             1838.
     ii.   ANDREW M., b. 6 July, d. 13 Oct., 1840,
             2m 16d.
1105. iii.   WALTER HENRY, b. 14 Sept. 1841.
     iv.   MARY A. MORSE, b. 5 Feb. 1844, d. Concord NH
             20 Apr. 1887; m. Lowell 20 Oct. 1871 BARKER
             GREENWOOD, son of Joseph and Alice Greenwood
             of England. No ch.
      v.   ALFRED AUGUSTUS, b. 1 June 1846, d. 15 Aug.
             1847, 1y 2m 15d.
     vi.   SOPHIA DEAN, b. 9 July 1848, d. 21 Aug. 1849,
             1y 11m 11d.
1106. vii.   JULIA ELLEN, b. 4 Jan. 1852; m. DANIEL CORN-
             MAN. She compiled a manuscript Leighton
             genealogy. See Introduction.

492. STEPHEN[7] 1813-1896 [152 Stephen[6] and Deborah Willey]
was born at Strafford 18 Apr. 1813, died there 11 Aug. 1896,
83y 3m 4d (GS); married at Strafford 24 Oct. 1833 SUSAN MONT-
GOMERY, born at Barrington 5 Oct. 1812, died at Strafford 1
Dec. 1898, 86y 26d (GS) (Strafford VRs; Cornman Ms). Burials
are in a family cemetery near Willey Pond, Strafford
He served as selectman in 1848, 1863 and 1864, and as state
legislator in 1850.

Children, born at Strafford:

      i.   JOHN STEPHEN[8], b. 16 Jan. 1834, d. 14 Mar.
             1919, 85y 1m 26d (GS); m. 1 Jan. 1870 ANN
             FURBER of Farmington. No ch.
1107. ii.   ABBIE JANE, b. 24 Apr. 1836; m. EDWARD WHIT-
             NEY.
1108. iii.   DORA SOPHRONIA, b. 15 Feb. 1842; m. ALFRED
             WARDWELL.

493. LEVI WASHINGTON[7] 1796-1857 [153 Joseph[6] and Hannah
Babb] was born at Farmington NH 4 Feb. 1796 (TRs), died there
2 Jan. 1857, 60y 11m (GS); married there 11 Mar. 1821 (int. 6
Nov. 1820) TAMSEN A. CHAMBERLAIN of New Durham, born 14 July
1798, died at Farmington 9 Mar. 1868, 69y 7m 24d (GS) (Hurd,
Rockingham/Strafford Cos., 637; Stearns, N. H. Genealogies,
2:692; records of descendant Lewis L. Knox). Burials are on
the Joseph Leighton farm off Ten Rod Road, Farmington. His
household in 1850 included Samuel R. Leighton, 8--perhaps the
son of Joseph and Clarinda [# 1442].
    Levi served as private under Capt. Andrew Pierce 24 May to
7 June 1814 (NH Mil. Hist., 2:116, 203), and on 16 Nov. 1820
was commissioned captain of the 8th Co., 2nd NH Militia Rgt.
(Knox family papers include the signed commission).

In 1837 he was executor of his father's will, and took over
the homestead farm. His own will, made 1 Aug. 1855 and
proved in Feb. 1857, left the farm to his son John, who later
sold it to Stephen Bennett (StrCP, 68:166; 70:79; 71:1).

Children, born at Farmington (TRs):

1109. i.   HANNAH BABB[8], b. 21 Mar. 1822; m. JOHN COLBATH
             and JOHN KILROY.
       ii.   MARY CHAMBERLAIN, b. 1 Aug. 1824, d. 4 Aug.
             1850, 26y 3d (GS); unm.
1110. iii. JOHN WARREN, b. 8 Feb. 1826.
       iv.   LEVI WOODBURY, b. 5 Mar. 1830, d. 9 Aug. 1888,
             58y 5m 3d (GS); m. Farmington int. 6 Jan.
             1855 SOPHIA AVERILL, b. Mt. Vernon NH 17 Dec.
             1832, d. 29 Apr. 1922, 88y 4m 12d (GS),
             dau. of Bernard and Harriet (Richardson)
             Averill. No ch.
1111. v.   TAMSEN ABIGAIL, b. 16 July 1834; m. EDWIN P.
             MOONEY.
1112. vi.   EMILY MARY, b. 23 July 1840; m. STEPHEN W.
             BENNETT.

494. ABIGAIL EMMONS[7] 1799-1881 [153 Joseph[6] and Hannah
Babb] was born at Farmington 28 Jan. 1799, died there 6 May
1881; married 21 July 1816 MARK DEMERITT, born at Farmington
6 June 1792, died there 22 Oct. 1875 (Hurd, Rockingham/
Strafford Cos., 637) or 3 Nov. 1876 (Sargent, Babbs of New
Eng., 161; Stearns, N. H. Genealogies, 4:1832), son of Paul
and Betsey (Davis) Demeritt. He was a justice of the peace,
selectman and state legislator (Scales, Strafford Co., 488).

Children (**Demeritt**), born at Farmington (VRs):

i.   CHARLES M., b. 2 Feb. 1818, d. Rochester 24 June
       1897; m. MARY ANN LANG of Brookfield.
ii.   HANNAH M., b. 19 Jan. 1820, d. Rochester 22 Oct.
       1875 (or 2 Dec. 1892, Stearns, 1:88); m. there 14
       Apr. 1842 JOHN FRANK BICKFORD, b. there 22 Dec.
       1814, d. there 10 Feb. 1901, son of John and Love
       (Brown) Bickford (Catherine Bickford Fahnestock,
       Three Hundred Fifty Years of Bickfords in New
       Hampshire [1971], 374-75).
iii.   JOHN F , b. 27 Mar. 1822, d. Farmington 14 June 1904,
       82y 2m 14d.
iv.   SAMUEL G., b. 29 Aug. 1826, d. 10 May 1840.
v.   MARTHA E., b. 18 Jan. 1829; m. 9 Apr. 1848 WILLIAM
       WENTWORTH, b. Farmington 10 Nov. 1820, res. Roches-
       ter, son of William and Huldah (Hussey) Wentworth
       (Wentworth Gen., 2:566).
vi.   JOSEPH LEIGHTON, b. 22 May 1831.
vii.   PAUL J., b. 28 Mar. 1833, d. 3 June 1898. He was a
       merchant in MA.
viii. LOIS G., b. 22 July 1835, res. Rochester; m. there 21
       June 1860 WILLIAM HENDERSON, b. 2 Apr. 1837.
ix.   EMILY A , b. 9 Mar. 1838, res. Ossipee NH; m. in Jan.
       1862 EDWIN PAYSON HODSDON of St. Louis MO, son of
       Ebenezer and Catherine (Tuttle) Hodsdon (Stearns,
       N. H. Genealogies, 4:1975-6).

495. SALLY[7] 1793-1839 [154 Andrew[6] and Margaret Babb] was
born at Strafford in 1793, died there 19 Mar. 1839, 46y (GS);
married at Pittsfield NH 17 Nov. 1814 ANDREW NEAL HILL, born
at Strafford 12 May 1787, died at Gilmanton NH 2 Apr. 1858,
son of Andrew and Judith (Gerrish) Hill (W. B. Lapham, John
Hill of Dover [Augusta ME, 1889], 14-5; Sargent, Babbs of New
Eng., 161; Cornman Ms). Burials are in the Ridge Cemetery,
Center Strafford.

Children (Hill), born at Strafford:

i.   Dr. LEVI GERRISH, b. 7 July 1812, d. 23 Feb. 1898; m.
        30 July 1837 ABIGAIL BURNHAM SHACKFORD, d. 25 Oct.
        1895, dau. of Samuel Shackford of Barrington.
ii.   ANDREW LEIGHTON, b in 1814, d. in 1891; m. in 1842
        ANN FRANCIS. He res. Norfolk VA.
iii.   HANNAH ABIGAIL, b. 24 June 1818, d. Cambridge MA 8
        Dec. 1892; m. 12 Nov. 1840 JOHN HUCKINS, b. Straf-
        ford 12 Mar. 1815, d. there 8 Dec. 1889, son of
        Joseph and Hannah B. (Waldron) Huckins (NEHGReg,
        68[1914]:253). No ch.
iv.   MARY MARGARET, b. 27 Aug. 1822, d. 25 Dec. 1880; m.
        29 Mar. 1840 ALFRED TASKER, b. 9 Mar. 1817, d. 11
        Nov. 1886.

496. HANNAH E.[7] 1800-1844 [154 Andrew[6] and Margaret Babb]
was born at Strafford 16 Oct. 1800, died at Norfolk VA 21
Nov. 1844; married 22 Sept. 1825 Dr. AARON BUZZELL, born at
Parsonsfield ME 10 Mar. 1802, died at Norfolk in 1847, 45y,
son of Rev. John and Anna (Buzzell) Buzzell (Buzzell-Orr
Families, 1:2, 8; Cornman Ms). He practiced medicine at
Strafford and Norfolk.

Children (Buzzell):

i.   Dr. ANDREW JAMES, b. in 1831, d. in 1865 while an
        army surgeon; m. SARAH WENDELL, b. in 1832, dau. of
        Oliver and Veanie Wendell (J. W. Dearborn, History
        of Parsonsfield, Me. [Portland, 1888], 146).
ii.   ANN MARGARET.

497. ANDREW DYER[7] 1812-1884 [154 Andrew[6] and Margaret
Babb] was born at Strafford 18 Sept. 1812, died at Belmont NH
23 Jan. 1884; married (as Capt. Andrew) at Upper Gilmanton
(now Belmont) 1 Oct. 1834 (Morning Star) MARY JANE HACKETT,
born at Gilmanton NH 2 Mar. 1809, died at Laconia NH 16 Jan.
1899, daughter of Allen and Mary (Young) Hackett (NEHGReg,
33[1879]:9; Cornman Ms). He was selectman at Strafford in
1841-2.

Children, born at Strafford:

        i.   OLIVE AMANDA[8], b. 15 July 1835, d. Gilmanton
                12 June 1857; unm. She was a Boston teacher.
1113.   ii.   ANNA, b. 3 Feb. 1837; m. WILLIAM L. SWAINE.
        iii.   MARY DYER, b. 10 Dec. 1840, d. Belmont NH 16
                May 1884.
        iv.   ELLEN MARGARET, b. 21 May 1843, d. 21 May
                1862.

498. WILLIAM PEAVEY[7] 1801-1849 [155 Levi[6] and Sally Pea-
vey] was born at Farmington NH about 1801, died there 29 Mar.
1849; married first at Farmington 16 Jan. 1823 (int. 29 Dec.
1822) ABIGAIL TITCOMB[7] LEIGHTON, born at Strafford 22 Nov.
1805, died at Farmington 7 Mar. 1826, daughter of Andrew and
Margaret (Babb) Leighton [# 154]; married second at Farmington 7 May 1827 PHOEBE[8] LEIGHTON, born 29 May 1803, died at
Dover 4 June 1879, daughter of William and Mary (Austin)
Leighton [# 372] (town VRs; Cornman Ms; research of David
Dunlap).
    William bought from Lemuel Rand in 1833 the Daniel Horne
homestead, and sold it to Trustrum Leighton 18 Apr. 1838
(StrCD, 157:526). He lived on the family homestead until it
was sold to his cousin Levi W. Leighton 17 Feb. 1840
(185:360). He did not appear on the Farmington tax rolls
from 1842 to 1846; in 1846 and 1847 he paid a poll tax only.
    In an unusual contract, Phoebe agreed 2 Dec. 1841, in
return for $300, furniture for one bedroom and half the fam-
ily crockery, not to call on William for support for her or
her children. At Dover on 16 Oct. 1847 she acknowledged
receipt of the payment, and the "dissolution of our matrimo-
nial contract" (Farmington TRs).
    In 1843 Phoebe was a knitting-mill worker at Cocheco Mills,
Dover; in 1850 she appeared there with daughters Abbie Mansur, Hannah and Phoebe E. She married second 8 Nov. 1871, as
his second wife, JOHN N. WATSON, who died at Dover 23 Dec.
1875, 83y.

Child by Abigail, born at Farmington:

     i.   SARAH JANE[8], b. 24 July 1824, d. Strafford 26
           May 1880 (GS); m. there 3 Oct. 1841 NEHEMIAH
           FOSS, b. 11 July 1818, d. 19 Dec. 1903 (GS).
           Ch. Charles E. b. Strafford 24 Feb. 1845, d.
           20 May 1876; m. Sarah J. ---- , b. 6 Apr.
           1848, d. 17 Aug. 1878. Burials are in a
           private cemetery on Route 126.

Children by Phoebe, born at Farmington:

     ii.   ABIGAIL TITCOMB, b. 11 Jan. 1828, d. Placer
           Co. CA 9 Aug. 1855; m. Dover 1 Nov. 1845
           HORACE MANSUR, d. in CA. He went to CA
           c1849, returned for his family in 1852. Ch.
           James C b. in Jan. 1847; unm.
     iii. LEVI DURGIN, b. 31 Dec. 1829, d. 14 Mar. 1830.
     iv.   MARY ANN, b. 24 Jan. 1831, d. 6 Apr. 1842.
1114. v.   HANNAH EMMONS, b. 15 June 1833; m. EDWARD
           LITTLEFIELD.
     vi.   EMMA PHOEBE [Phoebe E.], b. 9 Mar. 1837, d.
           Dover 7 Aug. 1919; m. 1st Barrington 15
           Jan. 1859 CHARLES NEAL; m. 2nd 24 Oct. 1889
           STEPHEN P. JENNESS, b. Somersworth 25 Oct.
           1840, d. 11 Jan. 1897, son of John and
           Abigail Jenness. No ch.

499. MARY RICHARDSON[7] [Polly] 1802-1848 [155 Levi[6] and
Sally Peavey] was born at Farmington about 1802, died 4 May
1848, 45y; married at Farmington 27 May 1821 JOHN HOYT, born

Daniel and Jane (Wentworth) Hoyt or Hoit.
Hoyt married second 31 July 1848 Louise Cates (Hoyt Fam.,
116; Wentworth Gen., 2:3).

Children (**Hoyt**):

i.   WILLIAM.
ii.   GEORGE.
iii. MARY, res. Boston.
iv.   LEVI, res. Barrington; m. twice.
v.   WENTWORTH.

500. MARIA TITCOMB[7] 1808-1889 [155 Levi[6] and Sally Peavey]
was born at Farmington 4 Sept. 1808, died there 21 Dec. 1889;
married there 13 Dec. 1832 LEVI M. PINKHAM, born 17 May 1808,
died at Farmington 20 Oct. 1875, son of Dodavah and Mary
(Wells) Pinkham (Sinnett, Pinkham Gen., 252; Cornman Ms).

Children (**Pinkham**), born at Farmington:

i.   MARY ANN, res. Farmington; m. HENRY JENKINS.
ii.   LEVI L., b. 14 May 1835, d. Farmington 30 Mar. 1899,
      63y 10m; m. 1st ISABELLA MOORE; m. 2nd AUGUSTA
      COOPER.
iii. MARTHA JANE, b. 21 July 1843, res. New Durham; m. 30
      Aug. 1863 SAMUEL EVANS, b. New Durham 21 May 1843.

501. MARTHA ABIGAIL[7] 1822-1921 [155 Levi[6] and Sally Pea-
vey] was born at Farmington 13 Jan. 1822, died at Dover 17
Mar. 1921, 99y 2m 4d; married 8 Sept. 1843, as his second
wife, CHARLES CLARK, born 26 Nov. 1821, died at Rochester 18
Mar. 1895 (NH VRs; Cornman Ms).

Children (**Clark**), born at Rochester:

i.   JOSEPH LEIGHTON, b. 2 Oct. 1845, res. Dover; m. HELEN
      ESTES of Rochester.
ii.   MARTHA SUSAN, b. 6 June 1847, d. 19 Feb. 1849.
iii. MARTHA SUSAN, b. 11 Dec. 1852, res. Swampscott MA; m.
      JOHN LEAVITT of Somersworth.
iv.   CHARLES W., b. 5 Feb. 1855, res. Portland ME; m. EVA
      L. LORD, dau. of John Lord of Acton ME.
v.   GEORGE E., b. 21 Jan. 1858, res. Dover; m. EUNICE
      GRANT of Epsom.
vi.   MARY A , b. 9 Jan. 1860, d. 26 June 1887; unm.

502. LOVE[7] [Lovey] 1787-1867 [157 Andrew[6] and Mary Wey-
mouth] was born at Falmouth ME 20 Mar. 1787, died 11 Mar.
1867; married at Gray ME 31 Mar. 1803 NICHOLAS LOW, JR., born
at Cape Ann MA 25 Nov. 1777, died at Gray 24 Oct. 1854, son
of Nicholas and Martha (Sanders) Low (Gray VRs; records of
descendant Susan Leach).

Children (**Low**), born at Gray:

i.   MARY W., b. 5 Sept. 1804, d. 23 Mar. 1881; m. 13 Dec.

1881, son of Joseph and Mercy (Whitney) Libby.
ii.   ABIGAIL, b. 27 Mar. 1806.
iii. ANDREW, b. 8 July 1807, d. 24 Jan. 1874; m. 27 Nov.
      1832 EUNICE CORNING.
iv.   WILLIAM, b. 19 May 1809.
v.   MERCY, b. 13 Dec. 1813, d. 20 Sept. 1814.
vi.   DANIEL, b. 28 May 1821, d. 28 Mar. 1899; m. 17 Oct.
      1847 LUCY HUTCHINGS.
vii. CAROLINE, b. 20 Oct. 1825, d. 9 Feb. 1840.
viii. SAMUEL, b. 25 Mar. 1830, d. 2 May 1839.

503.   WILLIAM[7] 1788-1840 [157 Andrew[6] and Mary Weymouth]
was born at Falmouth ME 30 May 1788, died at Cumberland ME 3
Oct. 1840, 52y (GS); married first at North Yarmouth ME 25
Dec. 1813 PATIENCE PETTINGILL, born at Windham ME in 1791,
died at Cumberland 12 May 1826 (TRs; 1827, 35y per GS), prob-
ably daughter of Moses and Catherine (Elliot) Pettingill
(Charles H. Pope and Charles I. Pattingill, A Pattingall
Genealogy [Boston, 1906], 104); married second at Windham
MARY ANN FIELD, born there 12 May 1800, died 28 Sept. 1877,
77y 4m (GS), daughter of William and Anna (Manchester) Field
(Frederick C Pierce, Field Genealogy [Chicago, 1901], 2:991;
Hall Desc., #423; Cornman Ms; Cumberland VRs).
  In May 1841, William's brother Moses was appointed guardian
of the seven minor children. In 1860 widow Mary was in Silas
Russell's household with Patience, Elias and Anna.

Children by Patience, born at Cumberland:

      i.   CATHERINE[8], b. 5 Nov. 1814, d. 13 Dec. 1818.
      ii.   JOSEPH, b. 20 Oct. 1816.
      iii. WILLIAM, b. 1 July 1819, d. Mobile AL; m.
            twice--3 ch. by 1st wife d.y., scarlet fever,
            3 ch. by 2nd wife (Cornman Ms).
      iv.   MOSES, b. 16 Sept. 1821, drowned at sea.
      v.   ZELINDA, b. 8 Dec. 1823, d. 29 July 1826.
      vi.   PATIENCE P., b. 20 Mar. 1826, d. Portland 3
            Jan. 1892, 65y 10m (GS); unm.

Children by Mary Ann, born at Cumberland:

      vii. ANDREW, b. 8 Jan. 1829, d. Cumberland 11 Feb.
            1890; m. 1 Jan. 1852 EUNICE LEIGHTON, b.
            Falmouth 11 Aug. 1821, d. Portland 20 Aug.
            1910, dau. of Peter and Rachel (Winslow)
            Leighton [# 433]. He was a butcher and pro-
            visions merchant. An adopted ch. Annie
            Florence b. Portland 9 June 1863; m. 18 Oct.
            1881 George M. Palmer.
      viii. CATHERINE, b. 19 May 1831, d. Everett MA 31
            Jan. 1899; m. 10 Nov. 1851 PETER M. GOFF of
            Catskill NY, b. Charlestown MA in 1829,
            son of Isaac Goff. Ch. William and Everett.
      ix.   ELIAS FIELD, b. 2 Mar. 1833, d. Harpswell ME
            9 Dec. 1912, 78y 9m 7d (ME VRs; GS); unm. He
            enl. in Co. B, 25th ME Inf. Rgt., in 1862.
1115. x.   MARY SUSAN BRACKETT, b. 9 Apr. 1835; m. SILAS
            RUSSELL.
      xi.   ANNA FIELD, b. 26 Feb. 1837, d. Gorham 13 Mar.
            1915, 78y 15d (VRs; GS); unm.

504. MERCY[7] 1792-1830 [157 Andrew[6] and Mary Weymouth] was born at Falmouth 30 Oct. 1792, died there 30 July 1830, 37y (GS, Methodist Churchyard, as Pattangall); married at Windham 10 Dec. 1815 JOHN PETTINGILL, born at Windham say 1786, son of Moses and Catherine (Elliott) Pettingill (Pope, Pattingall Gen., 176; Hall Desc., #426; records of Susan Leach; Cornman Ms). He served in the US Army from 1812 to 1817.

Children (**Pettingill**), born at Cumberland:

i.	MARY, b. 5 June 1816; m. JAMES MORRISON, JR.	
1116.	ii.	ANDREW, b. 10 Dec. 1818.
	iii.	CATHERINE, b. 12 June 1820.
	iv.	MARTHA; prob. m. Capt. GEORGE HALL of St. Andrews NB.
	v.	PRUDENCE.
	vi.	FRANCES.

505. MOSES[7] 1794-1876 [157 Andrew[6] and Mary Weymouth] was born at Falmouth 10 May 1794, died at Cumberland 12 June 1876, 82y 3m; married first at North Yarmouth 20 May 1819 LOEMMA PEARSON, born there 21 Oct. 1798, died at Cumberland 5 Apr. 1827, 28y 6m (VRs; GS), daughter of Jonathan and Mehitable Pearson; married second 10 Aug. 1830 HANNAH (PEARSON) Rideout, born in 1801, died 23 Oct. 1886, 85y 7m 3d, sister of Loemma. Hannah had married first at Cumberland 20 Nov. 1823 William Rideout, Jr. (records of Nellie Leighton; town VRs; Hall Desc., #427). Burials are in Poplar Ridge Cemetery, West Falmouth.

Moses was a farmer and teacher, and was state legislator for two years.

Children by Loemma, born at Cumberland:

1117.	i.	ALVIN[8], b. 21 Sept. 1821.
	ii.	AUGUSTA, b. 9 Dec. 1823; m. CHARLES JORDAN[8] LEIGHTON [# 1122].
1118.	iii.	GARDNER, b. 15 Aug. 1825.

Children by Hannah, born at Cumberland:

1119.	iv.	LOEMMA PEARSON, b. 13 May 1831; m. NATHANIEL WILSON.
1120.	v.	JONATHAN BRADBURY, b. 21 June 1834.
	vi.	HARRIET ELIZABETH, b. 14 Mar. 1836, d. Cumberland 8 Feb. 1904; m. 5 May 1877 ALBERT MOUNTFORT, b. 7 Dec. 1845. Ch. Albert b. and d. 10 July 1878; 2 adopted ch. Bertie Deering (1887-1894) and Alton Oscar, b. Lewiston 3 Apr. 1889.
	vii.	GEORGE OLIVER, b. 24 Jan. 1840, d. 21 July 1848, 8y 6m.
1121.	viii.	(PATRICK) HENRY, b. 19 Mar. 1841.
	ix.	MOSES WEYMOUTH, b. 12 Feb. 1843, d. 8 Sept. 1863, 20y 6m 26d. He served in 25th ME Rgt.

506. DANIEL[7] 1795-1840 [157 Andrew[6] and Mary Weymouth] was born at Falmouth 30 Apr. 1795, died at Cumberland 26 Sept. 1840, 45y; married first at Gray 28 Feb. 1822 SALLY DYER, born there 12 May 1801, died at Cumberland 23 Mar. 1826, 25y;

married second at Westbrook 7 Aug. 1838 ELIZA C. (LIBBY)
Small, born at Gray in Sept. 1812, daughter of David and Mary
(Cobb) Libby (town VRs; Cornman Ms; Libby Fam., 190; Hall
Desc., #428). Eliza had married first Nathaniel Small of
Windham, and then third at Cumberland 22 Feb. 1849 Ephraim
Morrison [# 142].
Daniel was probably the private under Capt. Watson Rand in
1814 (MA Mil. 1812-14, 225). He was later called "Captain,"
maybe a militia rank. He was of Gray 12 Dec. 1822 when he
sold a lot at Cumberland to John Brackett (CumbCD, 104:110).

Children by Sally, born at Cumberland:

    i.   MARY FRANCES[8], b. 25 July 1822; m. Westbrook
        26 Mar. 1845 ISAAC A. BRAGDON.
    ii.   ELEANOR J. [Ellen], b. 5 Apr. 1825; m. Cumber-
        land THOMAS H. A. PRINCE of Portland.

Child by Eliza:

    iii. DANIEL, res. in CA.

507. JAMES[7] 1797-1844 [157 Andrew[6] and Mary Weymouth] was
born at Cumberland ME 23 Feb. 1797, died there 12 Apr. 1844,
47y; married at North Yarmouth 14 Feb. 1819 PRUDENCE BLAN-
CHARD, born at Cumberland 4 Jan. 1800, died there 25 Oct.
1874, 73y, daughter of Beza and Prudence (Rideout) Blanchard
(town VRs; Hall Desc., #429; Cornman Ms). Burials are in
Poplar Ridge Cemetery, West Falmouth.
James settled on a 300-acre farm at Pittsfield ME about
1823, and next engaged in lumbering and operating a sawmill
on the upper Stillwater River, at Orono ME. Returning to
Cumberland, he purchased a gristmill which he operated until
his death (Biog. Rev. ... Cumberland Co., 83). In 1850 and
1860 his widow Prudence and daughter Roxanna were living with
his son Charles at Cumberland.

Children:

1122. i.   CHARLES JORDAN[8], b. Cumberland 7 June 1820.
       ii.   CHRISTINE LORING, b. Cumberland 1 May 1822, d.
           there (as Christianna) 14 July 1844; unm.
1123. iii. ANDREW, b. Pittsfield 28 Feb. 1824.
1124. iv. JAMES NOYES, b. Pittsfield 27 Feb. 1826.
1125. v.   ENOS, b. Pittsfield 21 Aug. 1828.
1126. vi. JOSEPH, b. Pittsfield 11 Jan. 1831.
1127. vii. LOEMMA PEARSON, b. Pittsfield 19 Mar. 1833; m.
           JOHN HULIT.
1128. viii. FRANCES JANE, b. Orono 4 Nov. 1835; m. GEORGE
           W. SNELL.
1129. ix. ROXANNA ADAMS, b. Cumberland 6 June 1839; m.
           HOLLIS R. MOUNTFORT.
       x.   MARGARET LORING, b. Cumberland 7 Feb. 1843, d.
           3 Apr. 1844, 14m.

508. NICHOLAS[7] 1801-1873 [157 Andrew[6] and Mary Weymouth]
was born at Falmouth 28 Feb. 1801, died there 5 Nov. 1873,
73y (GS); married 9 May 1822 DEBORAH M. WHITNEY, born about
1818 (32 in 1850), died at Falmouth 11 Apr. 1870, 52y (Hall

Desc., #430; town VRs; Cornman Ms). Burials are in Poplar
Ridge Cemetery, West Falmouth. He was a farmer.

Children, born at Falmouth:

   i.   WILLIAM[8], b. 23 May, d. 24 May, 1843.
  ii.   ELIZABETH CHRISTIANA, b. 7 July 1844, d. (at
         Auburn, in Daily Argus of 30 Oct.) 18 Oct.
         1845, 1y 3m 11d.
 iii.   HENRY COFFIN, b. 1 Aug. 1846, d. 18 Apr. 1847.
  iv.   (NATHANIEL WINFIELD) SCOTT, b. 28 Aug. 1847,
         d. Waverly MA 8 Jan. 1898, 50y (GS); m. Port-
         land 28 Nov. 1870 SADIE L. WYMAN. No ch.
         (They also had a church wedding 1 Jan. 1871.)
         His obituary in the New York Times 19 Jan.
         1898 called him the "Landseer of the United
         States." They are buried in the Universalist
         Churchyard, Falmouth.
         Scott got his start in horse-trading at 14,
         and by the age of 17 had saved enough to set
         up in Portland as a painter, and to study
         under Harrison Bird Brown. Although he did
         landscapes, he was famed for paintings of
         horses. They are in many museum collections,
         and command high auction prices.
         From 1880 on, he had a studio at Boston, and
         lived at Revere House, rendezvous for horse
         owners and trainers. His lithographs for
         Currier and Ives had wide popular appeal.
         The last year of his life was spent in an
         insane asylum.
         See Sherwood E. Bain's biographical article
         in Antiques, Mar. 1979, 544ff.
   v.   BENJAMIN WHITNEY, b. 22 June 1850, d. in 1922
         (GS); m. Westbrook 19 Aug. 1884 ANNA L.
         LIBBY, b. in NH in Mar. 1864. In 1900, they
         lived at Dover MA.

   509.   **EZEKIEL**[7] 1802-1878 [157 Andrew[6] and Mary Weymouth]
was born at Falmouth 4 June 1802, died at Cumberland 30 Apr.
1878, 75y 11m; married 25 Dec. 1834 LUCY ANN HULIT, born at
Cumberland 28 Sept. 1816, died there 11 Aug. 1906, 89y 10m,
daughter of Capt. Jonathan and Hannah (Buckman) Hulit or
Hulet (Hall Desc., #431; town VRS). He was a farmer.
Burials are in the Universalist Churchyard, West Cumberland.
   His widow Lucy was living with Edward and Lorania Hall in
1880 and 1900.

Children, born at Cumberland:

1130. i.   CAROLINE W.[8], b. 7 Dec. 1835; m. HOMER BLAN-
          CHARD and WILLIAM BLANCHARD.
     ii.   HANNAH B., b. 5 Jan. 1838, d. 20 July 1857,
          19y 6m (VRs; 13 July on GS); unm.
1131. iii.   LORANIA, b. 30 June 1840; m. EDWARD HALL.

   510.   **ROBERT**[7] 1808-1861 [157 Andrew[6] and Mary Weymouth]
was born at Cumberland 29 Mar. 1808, died there 3 Oct. 1861,
53y 6m (GS); married at New Gloucester ME 17 June 1832 (VRs)

CYNTHIA MORSE, born there 29 June 1813, died at Cumberland 4
Sept. 1878, 65y (GS), daughter of Enoch and Eunice (Russell)
Morse (town VRs; Hall Desc., #433; Cornman Ms).
He was a miller and butcher at West Cumberland. Burials
are in the Universalist Churchyard there.

Children, probably born at Cumberland:

      i.   MARY MATILDA[8], b. 2 Feb. 1833, d. in 1900; m.
             1st RUFUS MORRISON of Cumberland, who d. in
             1879 (GS); m. 2nd BENJAMIN KIDDER. No ch.
      ii.   STEPHEN HENRY, b. 16 Nov. 1834, d. 8 May 1847,
             12y 6m (GS).
1132. iii.   CHARLES WENDALL, b. 11 Mar. 1836.
1133. iv.   GEORGE WOODWARD, b. 29 Oct. 1838.
1134. v.   OLIVE JANE, b. 24 Oct. 1840; m. AMOS WINSLOW.
1135. vi.   ALTHEA CAROLINE, b. 10 Mar. 1842; m. NATHAN
             SHAW.
1136. vii.   ENOCH O. MORSE, b. 16 Sept. 1844.
1137. viii. ROBERT NELSON, b. 17 Apr. 1846.
      ix.   CYNTHIA ELLEN, b. 24 June, d. 24 Sept., 1848,
             3m (20 Sept. 1847, GS).
      x.   FLORENCE J. E., d. 14 Apr. 1849, 5 wks (GS).
      xi.   ERVIN MILLEGEVILLE, b. in 1851 (9 in 1860),
             res. Evansville IN; m. LOUISE ---- .
      xii.   WILLIS J., d. 12 Feb. 1853, 5m.
      xiii. MELISSA, b. 2 Dec. 1857, d. 18 Aug. 1858,
             8m 11d (GS).

511. LYDIA[7] 1799-1880 [158 Stephen[6] and Ruth Crague] was
born at Falmouth 6 Apr. 1799, died there 10 Apr. 1880, 81y
(GS); married there 3 Jan. 1826 JEREMIAH STAPLES, born 25
June 1794, died at Falmouth 2 May 1840, 46y (GS), son of
Joseph and Miriam Staples (Falmouth VRs; Cornman Ms).
Burials are in Gowen Street Cemetery.

Children (**Staples**), born at Falmouth:

i.   STEPHEN, b. 13 Oct. 1826.
ii.   JOSEPH, b. 26 Jan. 1829.
iii. MARTHA ANN, b. 13 Feb. 1831; m. LEVI ELLIOT[8] LEIGHTON
     [# 1005].
iv.   MIRIAM, b. 14 Nov. 1833, d. 21 Aug. 1867, 33y (GS);
     unm.
v.   LUCY C., b. 11 Dec. 1835, d. 10 Sept. 1836, 10m (GS).
vi.   JEREMIAH, b. 25 Aug. 1838, d. 29 Jan. 1872, 33y 5m
     (GS).

512. MARTHA[7] 1801-1874 [158 Stephen[6] and Ruth Crague] was
born at Falmouth 18 Mar. 1801, died at Westbrook in July
1874; married at Falmouth 22 Nov. 1822 HENRY PRIDE, born in
1799, died at Westbrook 15 Oct. 1853, son of Henry and Nancy
(Brackett) Pride (VRs; Hall Desc., #435; Cornman Ms).

Children (**Pride**), born at Westbrook:

i.   MARY ANN, b. 2 Apr. 1823, d. Westbrook 4 Mar. 1909;
     m. WILLIAM GOWEN.

ii.   DWINAL, b. 31 May 1825, d. Westbrook 7 Apr. 1915;
      m. 2 Oct. 1854 SARAH SMALL LIBBY, b. Lagrange ME 24
      May 1835, d. Westbrook 2 Feb. 1901, dau. of Bryant
      and Elizabeth (Waterhouse) Libby.
iii. LYDIA STAPLES, b. 19 Feb. 1828; m. CHARLES PRATT.

513. HUGH[7] 1796-1868 [160 Ezekiel[6] and Martha Crague] was
born at Falmouth 27 Jan. 1796, died there 8 Dec. 1868, 72y;
married there 9 June 1826 MIRIAM HUSTON, born there 15 Sept.
1803, died there 7 Dec. 1886, daughter of Mark and Edna
(Knight) Huston (Harris, William Huston, 30; Falmouth VRs;
Hall Desc., #441). He was a farmer. In 1860, his son Mark
and his family were in Hugh's household.

Children, born at Falmouth:

1138.   i.   MARTHA B.[8], b. 2 Nov. 1826; m. ELISHA HIGGINS.
        ii.   FRANCES ELLEN, b. 20 Nov. 1828, d. 13 Aug.
              1829.
1139.   iii. PHOEBE ANN, b. 24 Sept. 1830; m. BENJAMIN
              BAILEY.
1140.   iv.   MARK LYMAN, b. 24 Feb. 1833.
        v.   SOPHRONIA, b. 5 May 1835, d. Portland 20 Mar.
              1921; unm.
        vi.   HELEN, b. 14 Aug. 1838, d. 4 Jan. 1850.
        vii. OREN B. (twin), b. 14 Aug. 1838, d. 10 Feb.
              1868.
        viii. MARCELLUS, b. 1 Jan. 1844, d. Falmouth 31 Jan.
              1903, 57y 8m; unm.

514. JOSEPH[7] 1805-1838 [160 Ezekiel[6] and Martha Crague]
was born at Falmouth 20 May 1805, died there 19 Sept. 1838;
married at North Yarmouth 24 Dec. 1826 (int. Westbrook 18
Nov.) EUNICE HICKS, born at Windham ME 4 Nov. 1802, died at
Falmouth 12 Jan. 1885, daughter of Nathaniel and Sarah (Twombley) Hicks (Hall Desc., #442; town VRs; Cornman Ms).
   His uncle Andrew [# 157] was made his guardian in 1820. On
9 May 1827, Lydia Baker, widow of Josiah, deeded to Joseph
and his brother Hugh her dower rights in land their father
Ezekiel had purchased ("land in Westbrook Joseph now lives
on"), but in which Lydia had a life use (CumbCD, 109:306).
On 10 Jan. 1831 Hugh quitclaimed to his brother Joseph his
share of their father's homestead (160:215).

Children, born at Falmouth:

        i.   SARAH MATILDA[8], b. 15 Aug. 1827, d. 19 Aug.
              1829.
        ii.   EZEKIEL NATHANIEL, b. 12 July 1829, d. Port-
              land 26 Feb. 1909, 79y 7m 24d; m. Windham
              int. 13 June 1857 OCTAVIA M. LEGROW, b.
              Windham 20 Aug. 1831, d. Portland 29 Jan.
              1918, dau. of Ephraim and Lydia (Purinton)
              Legrow. No ch. He lived with Asa [# 457] in
              1850, and became a Portland merchant.
        iii. WILLIAM SILLS, b. 29 Aug. 1831, d. Fairfax
              Courthouse VA 6 May 1864; unm. He was said
              to have served in the Confederate Army; no
              record of him is in NA-MSR files.

iv.   JOSEPH WARREN, b. 4 Oct. 1836, d. Toledo OH 26
       Feb. 1891; mar., no ch. A guard at Toledo
       almshouse, he d. after being attacked by an
       escaped convict (obit., MHS scrapbook).

515. GEORGE F.[7] 1820-1896 [163 Jeremiah[6] and Sarah Field]
was born at Pownal ME 6 Apr. 1820, died at Deering 9 May
1896, 76y 1m 3d; married at Portland ME 5 July 1853 HANNAH
COLLINS DAVIS, born at Deering 5 Feb. 1833, died at Portland
24 Nov. 1920, 67y 9m 19d, daughter of Isaiah H. and Jane[6]
(Leighton) Davis [# 971] (town VRs). Burials are in Evergreen Cemetery.
In 1850 George was living at Falmouth with Isaac Leighton
'[# 440].

Children, born at Westbrook:

    i.   EMMA J.[8], b. 7 Apr. 1854, d. 27 July 1875,
           21y; unm.
    ii.   HATTIE FRANCES, b. 10 May 1857, d. 17 Sept.
           1862.
    iii.   GEORGIANNA S., b. 26 Feb. 1867; m. 15 Oct.
           1895 CHARLES HENRY CLIFFORD, b. Newfield ME
           28 June 1869. Ch. Marion b. Deering 7 May
           1896.

516. JOSEPH[7] 1821-1882 [163 Jeremiah[6] and Sarah Field] was
born at Portland 10 June 1821, died at Mount Vernon ME 19
July 1882, 61y 1m 9d (GS); married first 5 Mar. 1846 (int.
Westbrook 8 Feb.) ELIAZABETH ANN BODGE, born at Windham 22
Mar. 1827, died at Amesbury MA in Dec. 1890, daughter of Wil-
liam and Mary W. (Walker) Bodge--divorced (town and ME VRs;
George Harvey, The Bodge Family of Mass., N. H., and Me.
[TMs, 1982, MHS], 46); married second SUSAN P. RAND, born at
New Sharon about 1828, died at Mt. Vernon 5 Jan. 1911, 82y
11m 1d, daughter of Reuben and Sophia (Norris) Rand.
Susan had had a previous husband. In 1880 Joseph and Susan
had in their Mt. Vernon household son John A., 13, and daugh-
ter Mary E., 10--perhaps his step-children.
Joseph's estate was administered to Daniel Thing 23 Apr.
1883; named as heirs were widow Susan, Elfreda McKenzie of
Bridgewater MA, and Charles H. and Elizabeth, both of Boston.
Susan married third at Mount Vernon 27 Feb. 1895 GEORGE
LAWTON, born at Fall River MA about 1845, son of Josiah and
Susan (Dodson) Lawton.

Children by Elizabeth:

    i.   CHARLES H.[8], b. Lewiston 13 Feb. 1854; m. 1st
           5 Sept. 1882 ALICE F. BROWN, b. c1857, dau. of
           William R. and Jane Brown of Quincy MA; m. 2nd
           30 Aug. 1884 ESTELLE MADDOCKS, b. Belfast
           c1864, dau. of Charles E. and Lucy (Kilton)
           Maddocks; m. 3rd Randolph ME 25 Sept. 1901
           ALICE M. DERRY, b. there c1863, dau. of Chris-
           topher H. and Julia A. (Gaston) Derry. No ch.
           (his letter about 1904, Cornman Papers). He
           was an engineer.

ii.   ELIZABETH M., b. Lewiston c1859; m. 3 Oct. 1883
      (ANTHONY) SMITH McLEAN, b. in NS c1850, son of
      Anthony and Jennie McLean. He was a carriage-
      maker.
iii. ELFREDA, b. c1865; perhaps m. 1st ----McKENZIE
      or HECTOR McKINNEY; m. 2nd ---- THORPE; m.
      3rd Auburn 2 Oct. 1928 ERNEST GROVES, b.
      Brunswick c1870, son of George and Lucy A.
      (Lake) Groves.

517. ANN MARIA[7] 1823-   [163 Jeremiah[6] and Sarah Field]
was born at Portland 1 June 1823; married JOHN FENHOLN, a
German immigrant (Cornman Ms). In 1850, he was listed at
Portland as John Fenno.

Children (**Fenholn**):

i.   SARAH, b. in 1846.
ii.   EVELINE, b. in 1848.

518. ESTHER LOUISA[7] 1831-1893 [163 Jeremiah[6] and Sarah
Field] was born at Portland 26 Feb. 1831, died there 19 Dec.
1893; married there 17 Nov. 1856 EDWIN BOYDEN of Springfield
MA, born about 1833 (47 in 1880) (Portland and ME VRs; not
named in Cornman Ms). He was a Portland grocer.

Child (**Boyden**), perhaps others:

i.   ADDIE, b. in 1871 (9 in 1880).

519. ICHABOD WILSON[7] 1833-1892 [163 Jeremiah[6] and Sarah
Field] was born at Portland 16 Mar. 1833, died at Boston 11
Mar. 1892, 59y; married first at Portland 16 Nov. 1859 SARAH
F. BACON, born at Windham 9 Jan. 1830, died 5 Feb. 1875,
daughter of John and Eunice Knight (Pennell) Bacon; married
second at Portland 22 Dec. 1876 NANCY P. SKILLINGS, born 25
Feb. 1828 (MH&GR, 2[1891]:173), died 13 Mar. 1901, 73y 1m,
daughter of Simeon and Nancy (Adams) Skillings (town and ME
VRs). Sinnett's Pennell Genealogy (p. 88) misnamed both
Ichabod and Sarah. In 1880 Ichabod was at Portland with his
sister Esther, but without a wife.
  Sometimes called Wilson, he built and operated a sawmill at
Little Falls, Gorham, which he sold in 1864; and had a store
there destroyed by fire in 1864 (Hugh D. McLellan, History of
Gorham, Me. [Portland, 1880, reprint 1903], 278, 311).

Children, both by Sarah, born at Portland:

i.   WALTER ERNEST[8], b. 1 Nov. 1861; nfr. He was a
      seaman.
ii.   HATTIE FRANCES, b. 11 Feb. 1866, d. 16 Jan.
      1868, 1y 11m.
iii. ADDIE MARIA, b. 26 May 1871.

520. ALGERNON SIDNEY[7] 1835-   [163 Jeremiah[6] and Sarah
Field] was born at Portland 16 May 1835, lived in MA; married

at Westbrook 27 June 1856 SUSAN PARKHURST KIMBALL, born at
Lowell MA 27 Apr. 1834 (VRs), daughter of Phineas Parkhurst
and Mary Kimball (Cornman Ms).

Children:

    i.   ALGERNON[8], d. Fall River MA 22 Mar. 1868.
    ii. EUGENE PRITCHARD, b. Boston in Feb. 1860,
        res. Cambridge in 1900; m. 5 Oct. 1898 JENNIE
        EDITH HEARTZ, b. Charlottetown PEI in May
        1879, dau. of James J[9] and Margaret (Ames)
        Heartz   Ch. LEROY H. b. in Oct. 1899, res.
        Dorchester MA.
    iii. BARTON R., b. New Bedford MA 15 Feb. 1871, d.
        15 Nov. 1875.
    iv. IDA S., b. Westbrook ME, res. Boston; m. 19
        Aug. 1903 LUTHER S. PHELPS, b. Shirley MA in
        1860, son of Stuart and Priscilla (Winslow)
        Phelps.

521. JEMIMA[7] 1788-1855 [172 Jonathan[6] and Lucy Place] was
born at Alton NH 31 July 1788 (TRs), died there 15 Aug. 1855,
67y (GS); married at New Durham 28 Mar. 1811 (VRs) Capt.
GEORGE STOCKBRIDGE, born at Stratham NH 29 Apr. 1786, died at
Alton 27 May 1859, 73y (GS), son of Israel and Hannah (Thurston) Stockbridge (Alton TRs; Bible and other records of
descendant George F. Sanborn, Jr.; NEHGReg, 135[1981]:227-8;
Stearns, N. H. Genealogies, 1:267; Cornman Ms).
No record of his military service has been found; he may
have been called "captain" because he operated large boats or
gundalows on the lake. George, cooper, 65, and Jemima, 63,
were listed at Alton in 1850. Burials are in the Riverside
Cemetery, Alton.

Children (**Stockbridge**), born at Alton (TRs):

    i.   CAROLINE, d. infant (Cornman Ms).
    ii. ADELINE, b. 17 May 1814, d. Alton 22 Sept. 1884; m.
        Alton 31 Dec. 1837 cousin WILLIAM GRAY STOCKBRIDGE,
        b. there 26 May 1814, son of John and Abigail (Gray)
        Stockbridge.
    iii. HORACE NASON, b. 26 Aug. 1816, d. Boston 1 Nov. 1883;
        m. Alton 1 Aug. 1836 LUCY F. COLOMY, b. Farmington
        c1814, d. there 17 Aug. 1884, 69y 8m 15d..
    iv. ISAAC LEIGHTON, b. 21 Mar. 1819, d. Alton 16 May
        1901; m. Alton 8 Sept. 1839 MATILDA C. LUCY, b.
        Jackson NH 23 Apr. 1821, d. Alton 10 Aug. 1882, dau.
        of John Tuttle and Joanna (Elkins) Lucy. He was a
        stonemason and cooper.
    v.   SOPHRONIA DURKEE, b. 1 Oct. 1821, d. Meredith 5 Feb.
        1916; m. Alton 22 Feb. 1847 Dr. GEORGE SANBORN, b.
        Gilford NH 27 Oct. 1820, d. Meredith 10 Nov. 1888,
        son of Samuel Gilman and Sarah (Mason) Sanborn. He
        received an MD degree from Dartmouth in 1850.
    vi. LUCY JANE, b. 3 June 1825, d. Alton 26 May 1911; m.
        New Durham 11 July 1844 HIRAM P. HORNE of Dover NH,
        who d. in ME 9 Nov. 1891. They res. Milton and
        Alton NH, and York ME.

522. HANNAH[7] 1796-1884 [172 Jonathan[6] and Lucy Place] was
born at Alton 30 June 1796, died there 11 Oct. 1884 (GS), 88y
4m 17d; married at Alton 7 May 1819 JOSEPH BLACKEY, born perhaps at Moultonboro about 1786 (64 in 1850), died at Alton 11
Apr. 1859, 74y, probably son of Mark Blackey (Alton TRs;
records of George F. Sanborn Jr.; Cornman Ms). Burials are
in Riverside Cemetery, Alton.
    Joseph, a farmer, lived at Alton and Center Harbor. His
name appeared in Alton records as Blakeley, and his children
and descendants used that spelling of the surname.

Children (**Blackey/Blakeley**):

i.   ELBRIDGE, b. in 1820, d. infant.
ii.   JONATHAN LEIGHTON, b. Center Harbor 12 Sept. 1822
       (GS-1821; 27 in 1850), d. Alton 6 Sept. 1906 (VRs);
       m. 27 Mar. 1853 HANNAH (FOLSOM) Piper, b. Gilford NH
       22 Feb. 1826, d. 7 Apr. 1909, dau. of Nathaniel and
       Hannah (Folsom) Folsom and widow of Joshua Piper
       (Folsom Fam. 1:300). She had 3 Piper ch., and was a
       long-time invalid. He was a pedlar in 1850.
iii.   CASPER, b. c1824, d. infant.
iv.   ELBRIDGE, b. c1826, d. in 1854; unm.
v.   ROSILLA, b. 12 Jan. 1828 (1 Jan. 1827 per GS), d.
       Laconia NH 9 Oct. 1906; unm.

523. JONATHAN[7] 1800-1855 [172 Jonathan[6] and Lucy Place]
was born at Alton 1 Jan. 1800, died at Moultonboro NH 28 July
1855; married there int. 17 Jan. 1824 (TRs 1:201) NANCY
BLACKEY, born at Alton 1 Jan. 1801, died at Center Harbor NH
6 Mar. 1885, 84y 2m 5d, daughter of George Blackey (records
of George F. Sanborn, Jr.; town VRs; Cornman Ms).
    He is buried at Center Harbor, and she in Bean Cemetery,
Moultonboro. He was a cooper.

Children, born at Moultonboro:

i.   JOHN B.[8], b. 6 Oct. 1824, d. ("single") Moul-
       tonboro 6 June 1891, 66y; m. 1st JANE ---- ;
       m. 2nd Meredith NH 26 Jan. 1867 CATHERINE
       GILMAN. A blacksmith, he lived at Center
       Harbor and at Moultonboro. He served in Co.
       G, 12th NH Inf. Rgt., 1862-4, and was fully
       disabled in action at Chancellorsville VA
       (NA-MSR 30,711). No ch.
1141. ii.   CALVIN, b. 27 Mar. 1826.
1142. iii. ALONZO, b. 10 Nov. 1828.
iv.   DELANO, b. 18 Nov. 1832, d. Moultonboro 7 Nov.
       1898, 65y 10m 19d; unm. He was a sergeant in
       Co. H, 4th NH Inf. Rgt.
v.   JAMES PLACE, b. 21 Jan. 1834, d. 1 Feb. 1842.
1143. vi.   MARY ANN, b. 26 Feb. 1842; m. TRISTRAM
       GLIDDEN.

524. LYDIA PLACE[7] 1804-1894 [173 Jonathan[6] and Lucy Place]
was born at Alton 1 Jan. 1804 (43 in 1850), died at Laconia
NH 13 Jan. 1894, 87y; married at Alton 24 June 1827 RICHARD
PLUMER, born at Farmington NH 15 Mar. 1800, died at Laconia

13 Feb. 1895, 94y 10m 29d, son of Joseph and Sarah (Roberts)
Plumer (Alton TRs; NH VRs; records of George F. Sanborn, Jr.;
Cornman Ms).
   Plumer was a farmer and stonemason. In 1850 his Alton
household included his father Joseph, 83, and his mother-in-
law Lucy Leighton, 83. Burials are in Riverside Cemetery,
Alton.

Children (**Plumer**), born at Alton:

i.   MARY E., b. 5 Sept. 1828, d. Alton 17 July 1866, 37y
       10m 12d (GS); unm.
ii.   CHARLES H., b. 9 Apr. 1831, d. 25 Jan. 1887; m. Alton
       29 Dec. 1855 MARY ANN PHILBRICK.
iii.   RICHARD BELKNAP, b. 21 June 1833, d. Laconia 4
       Sept. 1912; m. 1st MARY WIGGIN [# 530]; m. 2nd Gil-
       ford 4 Feb. 1872 MARY A (LOVERING) Lane. They res.
       Tilton NH.
iv.   THOMAS, b. 1 Aug. 1835, d. Alton 8 Jan. 1864, 28y 5m
       8d (GS).
v.   LYDIA ELLEN, b. 9 Oct. 1838, d. Concord NH (as Ellen
       L.) 21 Apr. 1923; m. 13 Nov. 1861 DANIEL PAYSON of
       Windsor VT.
vi.   LUCY M., b. 9 Nov. 1841, res. Plainfield NJ and
       Brooklyn NY; m. SIDNEY E. FLOWERS.

525.   NANCY ANNA[7] 1775-1865 [177 Samuel[6]] was born at
Rochester NH 4 Dec. 1775, died at Farmington NH 24 Sept
1865; married at Rochester 12 Nov. 1794 NATHANIEL WHITEHOUSE,
born 6 Oct. 1768, died at Farmington 21 Apr. 1851, son of
Turner Whitehouse (town VRs; Cornman Ms). He was a farmer at
Middleton and Farmington.

Child (**Whitehouse**), born at Middleton:

i.   GEORGE LEIGHTON, b. 6 Jan. 1797, d. Farmington 19
       Nov. 1887, 90y 10m 13d (VR); m. Rochester in June
       1822 LIBERTY DAME, b. there 11 Mar. 1802, d. Farm-
       ington 17 Nov. 1885, dau. of Paul Dame. George
       served in the War of 1812, was a civil engineer,
       militia captain and judge, and served in the state
       legislature in 1830 and again in 1856-7 (Hurd,
       Rockingham/Strafford Cos., 628).

526.   JOHN[7] 1780-1830 [177 Samuel[6] and Abigail Durgin] was
born at Farmington NH say 1780, died at Corinth ME about 1830
(Cornman Ms); married at Farmington int. 24 Dec. 1802 ANNA
[Nancy] WIGGIN, who perhaps died at Corinna ME 2 Dec. 1867.
   Julia Cornman's manuscript listed 13 children, some surely
belonging to Hiram and Annie, others probably to John
[# 577]. Town records provide some clarification, but more
data are needed to identify this family group fully.

Possible children:

i.   ?SUSAN[8], b. c1804; probably m. Corinna 1 May
       1831 JESSE CARSON.
1144. ii.   JOHN LANGDON, b. Farmington 2 Apr. 1810.
       iii.   NATHANIEL, d. Brimstead Center; unm.

            iv. ?ANNIE; m. c1833 HIRAM[8] LEIGHTON [# 574].
1145. v.   AMOS COFFIN, b. 12 Nov. 1816.
1146. vi. JOSHUA WIGGIN, b. Tuftonboro 4 Mar. 1822.

527. **SAMUEL M.** III[7] 1787-1858 [177 Samuel[6] and Abigail
Durgin] was born at Farmington about 1787 (64 in 1850), died
at Exeter ME 23 July 1858; married at Farmington 28 Feb.
1811 MARTHA ANN FRENCH, born in NH about 1793 (57 in 1850), died
at Exeter 18 July 1854, 60y 10m (18 June, GS) (Tuftonboro,
Farmington and Exeter VRs; Cornman Ms; records of descendant
Helen Lord). Burials are at Exeter Mills.
A farmer, blacksmith and millwright, he moved from Tuftonboro NH to Exeter in 1825.

Children, births recorded in Exeter TRs:

1147. i.   IRA A.[8], b. Farmington 18 July 1811.
1148. ii.   LYMAN, b. Tuftonboro 26 Mar. 1813.
1149. iii.   MARY, b. Tuftonboro 10 Sept. 1816; m. WILLIAM
              WADLEIGH.
1150. iv.   ALVIN, b. Tuftonboro 10 Mar. 1819.
       v.   ENOCH, b. Farmington 26 Mar. 1822, d. Exeter
              18 Mar. 1849, 26y 7m; unm.
1151. vi.   ELIZABETH W. [Lizzie], b. Exeter 26 Feb. 1825;
              m. JOSEPH R. FOLSOM and ALCOTT HERSEY.
1152. vii.   MARTHA ANN, b. 19 Aug. 1827; m. GEORGE JOSE.
       viii. JAMES HENRY, b. Exeter 14 Jan. 1828.
       ix.   LOENZA, b. Exeter 9 Apr. 1830, d. there 7 Mar.
              1904 (6 May, GS); m. Exeter 29 Dec. 1850
              JACOB EASTMAN, b. 24 Apr. 1826, d. 16 Dec.
              1912, son of Hazen and Abigail Eastman. No
              ch. He was guardian of Lyman's children.
1153. x.   SAMUEL, b. Exeter 29 Aug. 1832.
       xi.   SIMON FRENCH, b. Exeter 13 Sept. 1835, d.
              Augusta (state hosp.) 17 Feb. 1892, 56y 5m;
              m. Bangor 6 Dec. 1856 SARAH M. COLE of Wind-
              sor ME, b. in 1835, d. 5 Apr. 1899, dau. of
              John and Nancy Cole. He owned a boarding-
              house at Hampden. Ch. MYRTLE ESTELLE[9]
              [Myrtie] b. E. Hampden 20 Aug. 1868, res.
              Seattle WA; m. 15 Apr. 1890 FRED G. DRAKE of
              Newton, b. in 1858, son of James H. and Ann
              Drake.

528. **SARAH**[7] 1794-   [177 Samuel[6] and Abigail Durgin] was
born at Farmington about 1794 (56 in 1850); married there 20
June 1813 EDMUND TIBBETTS, born at Rochester NH 16 July 1784,
died at Milton NH 11 June 1868, 84y (NEHGReg, 99[1945]:147;
Cornman Ms). In 1850 "Edwart Tebbets," farmer, was listed at
Milton with his wife, sons Ebenezer and Seth, and his mother
Abigail, 90.

Children (**Tibbetts**), order uncertain:

    i.   EBENEZER, b. c1820 (30 in 1850); unm.
    ii.   IRENA.
    iii.   MARY.
    iv.   ABIGAIL; m. Milton ---- WAKEMAN.

v.   LIBERTY; m. THOMAS DAVIS.
vi.   ERI; m. 1st New Durham ELVIRA COLBATH; m. 2nd
      ELIZA PINKHAM.
vii. SETH, b. c1834 (16 in 1850).

529. RICHARD[7] 1789-1863 [178 George[6] and Mary Ann Treffen]
was born at Farmington NH (then Rochester) 12 Oct. 1789, died
there 1 Sept. 1863, 75y (GS); married there 17 Dec. 1815
RACHEL KIMBALL, born at New Durham 11 Aug. 1795, died at Farmington 7 June 1873, 77y 10m (GS), daughter of Daniel and
Sarah (Jones) Kimball (NH VRs; Morrison, Kimball Family
1:232; Cornman Ms). Burials are in the Silver Street Cemetery, Farmington.
    He served in Capt. Andrew Pierce's company in 1814, and was
state legislator in 1858.
    His will written 26 Apr. 1862 was proved 6 Oct. 1863; in it
his son Samuel was named executor. Use of the 80-acre homestead farm in Farmington and Milton was given during her
lifetime to his widow Rachel, and thereafter to Samuel's wife
Elizabeth. The sons Joseph and George were each given $5
(StrCP, 75:2).

    Children, born at Farmington (TRs):

    1154. i.   JOSEPH J.[8], b. 29 Apr. 1816.
    1155. ii.   SAMUEL J., b. 7 May 1819.
           iii. GEORGE F., b. 3 Oct. 1827, d. 2 Nov. 1829, 2y
                 2m (GS).
    1156. iv.   GEORGE F., b. 18 Jan. 1830.
           v.   DANIEL K., b. 7 July 1839, d. 4 Aug. 1843, 4y
                 1m (Morning Star).

530. SARAH[7] 1791-1871 [178 George[6] and Mary Ann Treffen]
was born at Farmington 16 June 1791, died there 12 Aug. 1871;
married at New Durham 2 Nov. 1820 STEPHEN M. WIGGIN, born at
Alton NH 20 Apr. 1776, died 28 Nov. 1844 (Cornman Ms).

    Children (**Wiggin**):

    i.   MARY J., b. Alton 20 Aug. 1821, d. 28 Sept. 1851; m.
          RICHARD PLUMER, res. Stoneham MA, son of Richard and
          Lydia (Leighton) Plumer [# 524].
    ii.   GEORGE L., b. 21 Jan. 1826, d. 16 Mar. 1876; m.
          SARAH WINGATE.
    iii. LEWIS R., b. Moultonboro NH 9 Mar. 1829, d. 31 Dec.
          1896; m. 1st CORDELIA DeCATER of Wolfeboro NH; m.
          2nd MARTHA TANNER.
    iv.   SUSAN, b. 24 Jan. 1832, d. Farmington 31 Oct. 1903,
          71y 9m 7d; m. 9 June 1853 JOSHUA P. RICHARDSON, b.
          Derry NH 20 Oct. 1828, d. Farmington 4 July 1869.

531. ABIGAIL[7] 1793-1872 [178 George[6] and Mary Ann Treffen]
was born at Farmington 10 July 1793, died at Dover NH in
1872; married at Farmington 12 Apr. 1815 JONATHAN CLARK, born
at New Durham in 1789, died at Middleton NH 17 Nov. 1843, son
of Samuel and Abigail (Hanson) Clark (Cornman Ms).

Children (**Clark**):

i.   ELMIRA, res. CA; m. Rev. DAVID LORD.
ii. EMILY, d. aged 21; unm.
iii. JOHN, b. in 1821, d. Dover in 1892; m. 1st FRANCES
     CUTLER of Charlestown MA; m. 2nd ANNIE HODGKINS of
     Portland ME.
iv. ZELIA W., d. Concord NH; unm., insane.
v.   EDWIN, d. Dover; unm.
vi. MARY ANN, d.y., Dover.
vii. RACHEL, insane.
viii. MARTIN, res. MA; m. Dover SARAH M. ROLLINS, b.
     Moultonboro 10 Mar. 1834, dau. of Eliphalet and
     Margaret (Murray) Rollins (Rollins Gen., 107).

532.   JANE W.[7] 1795-1825 [178 George[6] and Mary Ann Treffen]
was born at Farmington 28 July 1795, died 1 June 1825; mar-
ried at Farmington 9 Feb. 1815 NATHANIEL CLARK, born at New
Durham in 1794, son of Samuel and Abigail (Hanson) Clark.
Nathaniel and Jane settled at St. Johnsbury VT about 1819.
He married second about 1827 Lydia Chesley (Cornman Ms).

Children (**Clark**):

i.   BETSEY, b. 24 Aug. 1815, res. Kingston NH; m. ----
     CHASE.
ii. EUNICE, b. 29 Sept. 1817.
iii. JAMES, b. St. Johnsbury 14 July 1821, d. Five Islands
     NS c1856; m. in Colchester Co. NS MARY JANE STEELE,
     dau. of William and Isabella (O'Leary) Steele.
iv. FREDERICK L., b. 7 Apr. 1823.

533.   JEMIMA[7] 1809-1885 [178 George[6] and Mary Ann Treffen]
was born at Farmington 11 Sept. 1809, died there 24 Apr.
1885; married DEXTER RICHARDSON, born at Moultonboro NH 13
Aug. 1817 (VRs), died at Farmington 14 Dec. 1855 (VRs; in
1854, 48y, GS), son of Jonathan and Sarah (Freese) Richardson
(Cornman Ms). Burials are in the Silver Street Cemetery,
Farmington.

Children (**Richardson**):

i.   HARRIET M., b. c1839, d. Farmington 19 Oct. 1864, 25y
     (GS); m. 1st New Durham 29 Jul. 1854 SAMUEL BOLIVAR
     MELLOWS, b. 25 July 1830, d. 19 May 1858, son of
     Samuel and Patience[6] (Leighton) Mellows [# 219]; m.
     2nd 11 Aug. 1860 DANIEL H. PLAISTED.
ii. CHARLES BARTLETT, b. Moultonboro 1 Aug. 1844, d. 3
     Feb. 1878; m. Farmington 12 Nov. 1865 CHARLOTTE
     JANE HAYES, b. Alton NH 17 Nov. 1843, d. Laconia NH
     23 May 1916, dau. of Daniel and Patience Horne
     (Evans) Hayes (Richmond, John Hayes, 2:651).

534.   ELIZABETH[7] 1813-   [178 George[6] and Mary Ann
Treffen] was born at Farmington 30 July 1813, lived at Ossi-
pee NH; married 29 Apr. 1839 JONATHAN WENTWORTH, son of
Stephen and Sally (Cottle) Wentworth (Wentworth Gen., 1:550).

Children (**Wentworth**):

i.   SARAH FRANCIS, b. 31 Oct. 1841; m. 25 Nov. 1857
       FRANCIS K. BROWN of Ossipee.
ii.   GEORGE LEIGHTON, b. 28 Aug. 1849; m. 5 Feb. 1875
       LUELLA J. HAYNES of Epping NH.
iii.   MARY LEIGHTON, b. 12 Apr. 1854.

535. **BETSEY**[7] 1782-1836 [180 Jacob[6] and Mary Townsend] was
born at Wolfeboro NH 3 Jan. 1782, died at Alton 7 Sept. 1836;
married 23 Apr. 1801 (Free Will Baptist records 1:133, in New
Durham Town Archives) JEREMIAH EDGERLY, born at New Durham NH
13 May 1776 (or 1778), died at Alexandria NH 8 Mar. 1852, son
of Caleb and Abiah (Cilley) Edgerly (NEHGReg, 15 [1861]:338;
Stackpole, Durham, 2:174; Norman Edgerly Ms, NEHGS Collections; family records of Elaine Kohler Miller; Alton TRs;
Cornman Ms). In 1843 he moved to Alexandria to live with his
son Jere.

Children (**Edgerly**), all but first born at Alton:

i.   JEREMIAH WARD [Jere], b. New Durham 5 July 1802, res.
       Alexandria; m. Alton 15 May 1825 ELEANOR LOCKE
       ALLARD, dau. of Job Allard of Rochester. No ch.
ii.   WALTER COOPER, b. 4 June 1804, res. Newport ME; m.
       ANNA CHESLEY STONE, b. Bangor ME 19 Feb. 1807,
       dau. of David Stone.
iii.   BETSEY LEIGHTON, b. 23 June 1809, d. Farmington NH 28
       Mar. 1898, 88y 9m 5d; m. 9 Dec. 1835 LEWIS FREEMAN
       JONES, b. New Durham 2 Sept. 1813, d. Farmington 14
       Feb. 1887.
iv.   MARY TOWNSEND, b. 17 Oct. 1811, d. Farmington 3 Apr.
       1906, 94y 5m 16d; m. 16 Mar. 1829 SOLOMON GRAY, b.
       Farmington 21 Dec. 1808, d. there 28 Aug. 1875.
v.   HIRAM WENTWORTH, b. 8 Sept. 1814, d. New Durham 21
       Sept. 1900; m. 1st 3 Jan. 1838 JOANNA RANDALL; m.
       2nd 24 July 1850 HARRIET YEATON; m. 3rd 29 Dec. 1875
       SARAH (EVANS) Twombley.
vi.   Rev. DAVID LEIGHTON, b. 18 Apr. 1818, d. New Durham
       2 Sept. 1891; m. 1st Alton 17 Nov. 1836 OLIVE PLACE,
       b. in 1817, d. New Durham 22 Apr. 1848; m. 2nd
       Dover 22 July 1851 ALMIRA B. CHAMBERLAIN, b. in
       1832, d. New Durham 18 Feb. 1869; m. 3rd there 27
       Sept. 1870 ATTILA JANE WINSLOW, who d. there 23 Mar.
       1888.
       David was ordained 30 Nov. 1850 as a Free Will
       Baptist minister (Carter, N. H. Native Ministry
       [Concord, 1906], 17-8).

536. **MARY**[7] [Polly] 1784-1849 [180 Jacob[6] and Mary Town-
send] was born at New Durham 10 Mar. 1784, died 16 Aug. 1849;
married (as Molly) 28 Nov. 1805 JOSEPH WALKER, born at
Rochester 7 June 1782 (Alton TRs), died 5 Jan. 1868, son of
Robert and Dorothy[6] (Leighton) Walker [# 179] (Cornman Ms;
records of Elaine Kohler Miller).
    They settled at Exeter ME about 1824. Joseph had a second
wife Lovina; in 1850 they were listed at Emden ME, he 58, his
wife 55.

i.   ISAAC, b. 3 Sept. 1806; m. ABIGAIL HALL of Exeter,
        who d. in Oct. 1900.
ii.   BENJAMIN, b. 28 Feb. 1808, d. 20 Aug. 1883; m. MARY
        OSGOOD, b. Exeter 11 Sept. 1808, dau. of Joseph and
        Nancy (Wilkins) Osgood (Osgood Desc., 392).
iii.   JACOB L., b. 28 Apr. 1810, d. New Durham 11 May 1812.
iv.   ABIGAIL, b. 15 July 1812, d. 18 Jan. 1883; m. JOHN
        KIMBALL of Exeter.
v.   JESSE W., b. 22 July 1814, d. New Durham 25 Dec.
        1816.
vi.   LORINDA, b. 17 May 1816, res. Exeter; m. there 15
        Feb. 1835 JOSEPH RICH, b. 9 Mar. 1809, d. 15 Nov.
        1892.
vii.   MARY H., b. 21 Sept. 1818, d. New Durham 22 July
        1819.
viii.   RHODA, b. 28 May 1820, d. 22 Sept. 1875; m. Exeter
        JOHN OSGOOD, b. there 10 Nov. 1810, d. there 25
        Oct. 1865, son of Joseph and Nancy (Wilkins) Osgood
        (Osgood Desc., 393).
ix.   DOROTHY, b. 15 Nov. 1822, d. 6 Feb. 1842; unm.
x.   JOSEPH, b. 13 Oct. 1825, d. 26 Apr. 1888; m. Garland
        ME 22 Jan. 1851 SARAH SKINNER.

537.   NANCY[7] 1786-1842 [180 Jacob[6] and Mary Townsend] was
born at New Durham 31 May 1786, died at White Pigeon MI 28
May 1842; married at Middleton NH 26 Feb. 1813 JOHN LAVIN
HINER, born 3 Apr. 1790, died at Marengo IL 14 Dec. 1873. He
married second 5 May 1844 Elizabeth Laws.
    John Hiner was a storekeeper at Middleton Corner NH. In
1820 he purchased land at Moreland Tp, Northampton Co. PA,
and settled his family at Mauch Chunk (now Jim Thorpe). In
1837-8 they went to White Pigeon MI; he had moved on by 1865
to Marengo, near Galena, IL (family and Hiner Bible records
of descendant Elaine Kohler Miller; Cornman Ms; town VRs).

    Children (**Hiner**):

i.   HENRY [Harry], b. 16 Dec. 1813, d. 19 Feb. 1842; m.
        White Pigeon SARAH ANN ROBINSON, dau. of Moses and
        Elizabeth Robinson.
ii.   JAMES, b. 8 Feb. 1819, d. 7 Dec. 1869; m. White
        Pigeon 24 Apr. 1841 MARIETTA BROWN.
iii.   SABRINA, b. 17 Apr. 1823, d. 6 Apr. 1835.
iv.   JOHN L., b. 6 Mar. 1826, d. Ontario WI in 1910; m.
        Geneva WI 24 Feb. 1855 SUSAN P. HATCH, b. in 1835,
        d. in 1894.
v.   CHARLOTTE, b. 8 Nov. 1827, d. 31 Oct. 1913; m. White
        Pigeon 8 Nov. 1845 JACKSON KOHLER, res. Portage WI.
vi.   JACOB, b. 30 Jan. 1830; m. CHARLOTTE ---- , b. 27
        Sept. 1838.

538.   DOROTHY[7] [Dolly] 1788-1885 [180 Jacob[6] and Mary Town-
send] was born at New Durham 28 June 1788, died at Milton NH
26 Apr. 1885, 96y 9m 28d; married at New Durham 7 Mar. 1811
JAMES HAYES, born at Rochester NH 9 June 1786, died at Milton
8 Oct. 1866, son of Daniel and Eunice (Pinkham) Hayes (Rich-

mond, John Hayes, 1:304, 498; Cornman Ms; town VRs). Burials
are in the Hayes Cemetery, Milton. James was a pensioner of
the War of 1812.

Children (**Hayes**), born at Milton:

i.   NANCY LEIGHTON, b. 3 Mar. 1812, d. Milton 12 Apr.
       1895, 83y 1m; m. 1st 28 Aug. 1836 THOMAS HAZELTINE
       BARTLETT; m. 2nd NATHANIEL BAKER.
ii.   AMASA T., b. 1 Jan. 1814; m. MARY TOWNSEND[8] LEIGHTON
       [# 539].
iii.   EPHRAIM L., b. 20 June 1816, res. Natick MA; m.
       ELMIRA P. TOWNE, b. Danvers MA in 1822.
iv.   ELIZABETH PEARL [Betsey], b. 11 Dec. 1818, d. 11 May
       1898, res. Boston; m. 2 Apr. 1840 WILLIAM TOWNE,
       JR., b. 28 Dec. 1811, d. Milton 16 Dec. 1879.
v.   ASA H., b. 22 Feb. 1821, d. Milton 24 Dec. 1897, 76y
       10m 22d; unm.
vi.   MARIA LOUISA, b. 9 July 1823, d. 20 Apr. 1859; m.
       Milton 13 Apr. 1854 CHARLES A. FURBER.
vii.   MARY A. (twin), b. 9 July 1823, d. 24 Nov. 1838,
       15y 4m 15d.
viii. JACOB; unm.

539.   JACOB[7] 1791-1870 [180 Jacob[6] and Mary Townsend] was
born at New Durham 6 Feb. 1791, died at Milton NH 22 Dec.
1870; married first 20 Feb. 1812 SOPHIA TASH EDGERLY, born 23
Feb. 1792, died at Exeter ME 1 Mar. 1854 (28 Feb., 62y, in
Morning Star,), daughter of Andrew and Elizabeth (Tash) Edgerly; married second MARY [Polly] (----) Glidden.
    Jacob served under Capt. Reuben Hayes in 1814, and was pen-
sioned for this service. "Jacob juner" sold to Reuben Hayes
8 Dec. 1818 60 acres in lot 39, second division, "purchased
of my honored father" (StrCD, 108;628). In 1822 he took his
family to Exeter, and in 1850 owned the farm next to that of
his son Alfred. After Sophia's death, he returned to Milton
(Little, Me. Genealogies, 4:2058-9).

Children, all by Sophia:

1157. i.   ALFRED COGSWELL[8], b. New Durham 28 Dec. 1812.
1158. ii.   JOHN EDGERLY, b. New Durham 6 Jan. 1816.
1159. iii.   RHODA ELIZABETH, b. 26 Apr. 1818; m. SETH
              MORSE.
       iv.   MARY TOWNSEND, b. Exeter 28 Feb. 1823, d.
              Farmington 11 Mar. 1894, 70y; m. 8 Apr. 1858
              GEORGE BLAKE, b. Milton 1 Jan. 1814, d. there
              in Dec. 1880, son of James and Dorothy[7]
              (Leighton) Hayes [# 538]. Born Amasa T.
              Hayes, he had the Mass. General Court change
              his name to George Blake (Richmond, John
              Hayes, 2:248). Ch. Eva Anna b. Milton 18
              Dec. 1858; m. 17 Oct. 1883 Alfred C Varney.
       v.   JACOB, JR., b. Exeter 26 Jan. 1826, d. 21 Oct.
              1827.
1160. vi.   FRANCIS FISHER [Frank], b. Exeter 11 July
              1828.
1161. vii.   CHARLES WESLEY, b. Exeter 15 Mar. 1831.
1162. viii. SOPHIA ANNIE, b. Exeter 4 Mar. 1833; m. IRA A.
              QUINT.

540. LYDIA G.[7] 1793-1871 [180 Jacob[6] and Mary Townsend] was born at New Durham 8 Apr. 1793, died at Exeter ME 6 Oct. 1871; married at Alton NH 13 Apr. 1817 (TRs) ROBERT WALKER, JR., born at Alton 19 May[6] 1790, died at Exeter 20 Mar. 1863, son of Robert and Dorothy[6] (Leighton) Walker [# 179].
They settled at Exeter in the winter of 1827-1828 (town VRs; Cornman Ms).

Children (**Walker**):

  i.   JOHN M., b. Alton 8 Nov. 1818, d. 2 June 1890; m.
        PHOEBE M. MORSE, d. 9 May 1848.
  ii.   LOIS M., b. Alton in Sept. 1822, res. Bradford ME; m.
        2 Apr. 1851 GEORGE M. TREAT, b. 22 Mar. 1822, d.
        28 Oct. 1883.
  iii. NANCY E., b. Corinna ME 10 July 1834, d. 9 Dec. 1900;
        m. 3 Dec. 1856 THOMAS N. SMITH, b. 23 Apr. 1822, d.
        Bangor 28 Oct. 1903.

541. EPHRAIM[7] 1798-1847 [180 Jacob[6] and Mary Townsend] was born at New Durham 8 Nov. 1798, died there 18 May 1847 (at age 47 in Morning Star), thrown from his horse; married at Alton 7 June 1817 NANCY FAITH EDGERLY, born there 23 Sept. 1796, died at Dover NH 4 Nov. 1882, daughter of Andrew and Elizabeth (Tash) Edgerly (NEHGReg, 15[1861]:338; Scales, Strafford Co., 548; Cornman Ms; records of Elaine Kohler Miller, including Ephraim's letters to his sister Nancy Hiner). In 1850 widow Nancy was listed at Alton, 53, with Caroline, 10, and Jonathan Edgerly, 72. She died at the Steele home.
As a young man, Ephraim purchased from his father 3 Oct. 1820 land in New Durham's second division near Merrymeeting Pond (StrCD, 112:244) and cleared the wilderness for farming. On 3 Nov. 1823, he purchased another 40 acres, half of lot 39, from his father, and sold the land to Reuben Hayes (127:295; 123:313). (Hayes had already bought the other half of lot 39 from Jacob, Jr.)
Ephraim and Nancy were baptized in 1832 at the East Alton Free Will Baptist Church; in 1837 he was a member of the church committee.
When his estate was administered in 1847, guardians were appointed for Caroline and Mary. By the time Nancy's dower was set off in 1848, Nahala had purchased his brother William's share (StrCP, 50:330; 62:233; 63:246-7).

Children, born at New Durham:

1163. i.   NAHALA DAVIS[8], b. 27 Nov. 1818.
1164. ii.   EVERETT WARREN, b. 16 May 1820.
1165. iii. WILLIAM ALLEN, b. 13 Aug. 1821.
       iv.   HIRAM, b. 12 Dec. 1822, d. 28 Feb. 1824.
       v.   CAROLINE ALICIA, b. 6 Feb. 1840, d. Dover 28
           Mar. 1925; m. 9 Dec. 1885 THOMAS M. STEELE,
           b. New Durham 11 Nov. 1833, d. Dover 1 July
           1917, 83y 7m 20d, son of David Steele. No
           ch. He had m. 1st 2 Nov. 1853 Mary E. Drew,
           and 2nd Deborah Jane Varney.
       vi.   MARY E. FRANCES, b. 24 Dec. 1844, d. 3 Oct.
           1849.

542. HANNAH E.[7] 1801-1887 [180 Jacob[6] and Mary Townsend]
was born at New Durham 26 Sept. 1801, died at Exeter ME 22
Jan. 1887; married at Alton 23 Apr. 1820 WILLIAM EDGERLY,
born at New Durham 30 July 1798, died at Exeter 25 Mar. 1863,
son of Andrew and Elizabeth (Tash) Edgerly (NEHGReg, 15
[1861]:338; town VRs; Cornman Ms).
They settled at Exeter in 1825.

Children (**Edgerly**), the first two born at New Durham, the
rest at Exeter:

i.   FREEBORN, b. 4 Jan. 1821, d. Exeter 18 June 1900; m.
      Bradford ME 31 May 1846 SARAH STROUT, b. Limington
      ME 19 Feb. 1826, d. Exeter 27 Oct. 1887, dau. of
      Rev. James, Jr., and Lydia (Sanborn) Strout (Robert
      Taylor, Strout Family [TMs, MHS], 91).
ii.   MARTHA, b. 31 Jan. 1823, d. 8 July 1824.
iii. WILLIAM, b. 1 Aug. 1825, d. 27 July 1824.
iv.   (NANCY) MARIA, b. 10 Feb. 1828, d. Somerville MA 23
      Apr. 1910, 82y; m. Exeter 10 Feb. 1853 JAMES ALBERT
      STROUT, b. Limington in 1826, d. Somerville 16 Aug.
      1894, brother of Sarah (Taylor, Strout Fam., 91).
v.   HANNAH LOUISE, b. 16 Jan. 1831, d. 1 Jan. 1870; m. 21
      Sept. 1858 JOHN LIBBY.
vi.   EPHRAIM VanBUREN, b. 6 Dec. 1833; m. 6 June 1857
      EMMA HURD.
vii. LEVI WOODBURY, b. 23 Dec. 1835; m. 30 Apr. 1867
      CELESTA BEALE.
viii. CLARISSA ANN, b. 1 Nov. 1839; m. 26 Apr. 1862 JUDSON
      BARKER.
ix.   EXELONA FREDOLINA, b. 22 Apr. 1840, d. 20 Aug. 1847.
x.   WILLIAM FRANKLIN, b. 16 Sept. 1842; m. 25 July 1863
      CISTIE BILLINGS.

543. SUSANNA[7] 1781-1855 1781-1855 [181 Ephraim[6] and Olive
Perkins] was born at Rochester NH 11 Oct. 1781, died probably
at Ossipee 8 Mar. 1855; married first at Tamworth NH ABRAHAM
DRAKE, born at Effingham NH 20 Nov. 1773, died there 3 May
1813, son of Weare and Anna (Taylor) Drake (Alice S. Thompson, The Drake Family of N. H. [Concord, 1962], 85; Harold M.
Taylor, Family History of Anthony Taylor [np, 1935], 103);
married second 18 Oct. 1813 Rev. JOSHUA ROBERTS, born 18 Feb.
1767, died 23 Mar. 1839, son of Joshua and Ruth (Smith) Roberts of Kennebunk ME (Dearborn, Parsonsfield, 403).

Child (**Drake**), born at Effingham NH:

i.   GEORGE WASHINGTON, b. 14 Dec. 1799, d. Portsmouth 27
      May 1857; m. Effingham 18 Oct. 1821 SUSAN BARKER,
      b. 21 May 1802, d. Portsmouth 7 Nov. 1891, dau. of
      Simeon and Hannah (Rundlett) Barker.

Children (**Roberts**), born at Kennebunk ME:

ii.   ABRAHAM D., b. 30 Aug. 1814, d. Porter ME 7 Sept.
      1860; m. 14 Sept. 1837 ALMIRA RIDLON, b. Buxton ME
      26 Oct. 1820.
iii. JOSHUA S., b. 16 Mar. 1816, d. 6 Mar. 1853; m. 24
      Dec. 1837 ELIZA B. RICE, b. Buxton 16 Sept. 1819.

iv.   SALLY J., b. 11 Oct. 1818, d. 14 July 1902; m. 3 Nov.
      1836 FRANCIS S. RICE, b. 24 Dec. 1807, d. Saco ME
      5 Apr. 1876.
 v.   SUSANNA O., b. 1 May 1822, d. 22 Dec. 1893.
vi.   JACOB L., b. 14 June, d. 20 Aug., 1824.

544.   JACOB[7] 1787-1875 [181 Ephraim[6] and Olive Perkins]
was born at Rochester NH 30 May 1787, died at Ossipee NH 24
Apr. 1875; married 19 Dec. 1806 SARAH WENTWORTH, born at
Dover 21 June 1785, died at Ossipee 12 Aug. 1862, daughter of
Drisco and Anna (Wentworth) Wentworth (Wentworth Gen.,
1:498-9; 2:199-201; Ossipee VRs).
He was with his parents when they settled at Ossipee, was
the first to clear land in the red oak forest between Ossipee
and Newfield, and accumulated extensive land at Leighton's
Corner (Merrill, Carroll Co. Hist., 461). He was justice of
the peace, and a pillar of the Free Will Baptist Church--
which he built beginning in 1804 on land that he had donated
(Minnie I. Leighton, The Early Settlers' Meeting House at
Leighton's Corner [np, 1933]). The church is now owned by
the Ossipee Historical Society.

Children, born at Ossipee:

1166.   i.   EPHRAIM[8], b. 8 Sept. 1807.
        ii.   WILLIAM, b. 4 Jan. 1809, d. 15 May 1811.
        iii.   JOHN, b. 5 June 1809, d. 15 Jan. 1813.
        iv.   JOHN W., b. 18 Apr. 1813, d. 22 Mar. 1815.
1167.   v.   CHARLES, b. 7 Aug. 1815.
1168.   vi.   ELIZABETH WENTWORTH, b. 25 July 1817; m.
               ISRAEL LEIGHTON SANDERS.
1169.   vii.   JACOB M., b. 24 Sept. 1819.
1170.   viii. LEONARD WENTWORTH, b. 12 Sept. 1822.
1171.   ix.   ELVIRA M., b. 3 Mar. 1825; m. BENJAMIN SMITH,
               SAMUEL F. ALLEN, GUSTAVUS ADDITON, ---- COOK,
               AND ---- PARSONS.
        x.   BENJAMIN, b. 28 Nov. 1826, d. 18 Mar. 1828.
        xi.   SUSAN, b. 29 Sept. 1829, d. 30 Jan. 1830.

545.   MEHITABLE[7] 1789-1822 [181 Ephraim[6] and Olive Perkins]
was born at Rochester in 1789, died in ME in 1822; married
first at Wolfeboro NH int. 26 Oct. 1806 ISAAC DREW, JR.
(Parker, Wolfeborough [The Town, 1901], 360); married second
about 1820 ELISHA SANBORN, born at Wakefield NH 10 July 1770,
died at Athens ME 1 June 1851, son of Joseph and Anna (Philbrick) (Marston) Sanborn. Elisha had married first Sarah
Fellows, who died in Aug. 1820 leaving eight children; he
married third Sarah Philbrick of Harmony, and fourth Winifred
Blish of Sebec (Sanborn Family, 174).

Children (**Drew**), perhaps others:

  i.   ABRAM.
 ii.   SARAH.
iii.   OLIVE, b. 22 Nov. 1811, d. Saco ME 22 Sept. 1879; m.
        in 1829 OLIVER DYER, b. Biddeford 7 Apr. 1806, d.
        Saco 13 June 1872 (Saco VRs; letter from Dr. Emerson
        Baker, the York Institute Museum). No ch.
        Oliver had been both merchant and councilman at

Boston; he retired to Saco, and was mayor there in
1871. Olive left their estate to the town for what
is now the Dyer Memorial Library.

Child (**Sanborn**):

iv.   SUSAN, b. 15 Mar. 1821; m. JOSIAH GERRISH of Acton.

546. ANNA[7] [Nancy] 1797-1843 [181 Ephraim[6] and Olive Per-
kins] was born at Ossipee NH 2 Nov. 1797, died at Alfred ME
28 Apr. 1843, 46y (GS); married at Alfred 3 Dec. 1818 DANIEL
KILHAM, born there 2 Sept. 1779, died there 22 Oct. 1842
(GS), son of John Frost and Mehitable (Babson) Kilham (Cornman Ms; records of Nellie Hiday). Burials are in the Alfred
Congregational Church cemetery.

Children (**Kilham**), born at Alfred (baptisms from Alfred
church records):

i.   REBECCA DYER, b. 6 Jan. 1819 (bp. 2 May), d. Sanford
       ME 22 July 1893; m. 24 Feb. 1842 SALTER EMERY of
       Melrose MA, b. 22 Aug. 1818, d. 27 Apr. 1892,
       son of Thomas and Betsey (Emery) Emery.
ii.   JOHN, b. 16 Apr. 1820, d. 16 Sept. 1823.
iii.   AUSTIN (twin), b. 16 Apr. 1820, d. 7 May 1821.
iv.   JOHN AUSTIN, b. 25 Feb. 1824 (bp. 13 June), d. in VA
       23 May 1864 during the Battle of the Wilderness; m.
       in 1848 CAROLINE BROWN.
v.   EPHRAIM LEIGHTON, b. 25 Sept. 1826, d. 31 Aug. 1832.
vi.   OLIVE PERKINS (twin), b. 25 Sept. 1826 (bp. 20 May
       1827), d. Melrose MA 26 Mar. 1891; m. 27 Oct. 1844
       as his 2nd wife DENNIS HATCH, b. 21 Sept. 1808, d.
       Waterloo IA 7 Apr. 1870, son of Henry and Eunice
       (Thompson) Hatch.
vii.   ELIZABETH LOVETT, b. 22 Jan. 1833, d. 21 Apr. 1839.
viii. DANIEL TAPPAN, b. 15 Feb. 1835, d. 21 Apr. 1839.
ix.   SARAH LEIGHTON, b. 25 June 1836; m. 1st 2 Jan. 1859
       JOHN L. TRIPP, b. 4 Aug. 1834, d. Portsmouth NH,
       son of Robert and Betsey (Linscott) Tripp; m. 2nd 25
       June 1877 JOSEPH L. MARTIN, b. in 1806, d. Ports-
       mouth 26 June 1887, son of Abraham and Mary (Cole)
       Martin.
x.   ALBERT DODGE, b. 6 Nov. 1840 (bp. 7 Nov.), d. Boston
       22 Nov. 1888; m. 24 June 1860 RUTH LITTLEFIELD,
       dau. of Moses and Ruth (Littlefield) Littlefield.

547. SARAH[7] [Sally] 1801-1883 [181 Ephraim[6] and Olive Per-
kins] was born at Ossipee 16 Apr. 1801, died at Boston 1 Nov.
1883; married in Sept. 1819 OLIVER SCATES, born at Milton NH
21 Apr. 1800, died at Ossipee 26 May 1846, son of Dodovah and
Lydia (Hanson) (Manning) Scates (Stearns, N. H. Genealogies,
4:1942-3; Merrill, Carroll Co. Hist., 621).

Children (**Scates**), born at Ossipee:

i.   DODOVAH, b. 21 Jan. 1821, d. 16 Sept. 1882; m. 1st
       LUCY DUNBAR STUDLEY, b. Scituate MA 4 Oct. 1821
       (VRs), dau. of Lewis, Jr., and Emily Studley; m.
       2nd ---- .

ii.   ABIGAIL, b. 28 Apr. 1823; m. SAMUEL N. HOWE, b.
      Canterbury NH in Oct. 1820, d. in Jan. 1902.
iii. SALLY, b. 4 Aug. 1825, d. 1 Sept. 1826.
iv.   CLARK SWETT, b. 13 Sept. 1827, d. Ossipee 16 Jan.
      1904; m. there 24 Nov. 1853 HARRIET O. CHADBORN, b.
      Effingham 20 Mar. 1828, d. Ossipee 26 Aug. 1900,
      dau. of Oliver and Mary (Tarr) Chadborn (or of Rev.
      Levi and Martha (Hodsdon) Chadbourne, per Chadbourne
      Family Assn.)
v.   MARIA, b. 22 Mar. 1830; m. 1st 1 Dec. 1854 CHARLES
      AUGUSTUS TOWLE, b. Canaan NH 14 June 1833, d. 19
      Aug. 1870, son of Col. Isaac and Rebecca (Locke)
      Towle; m. 2nd Ossipee 1 Oct. 1873 JOEL H. SANDERS
      b. 30 June 1827, d. 6 Mar. 1889.
vi.   SARAH, b. 14 Oct. 1833; m. CHARLES P. KNOWLTON, b.
      Ashland MA 28 Sept. 1833.
vii. ALICE, b. 28 Mar. 1835; m. Somersworth 4 July 1853
      HARRISON B. DAVID.
viii. HANNAH ELIZABETH [Annie], b. 17 Oct. 1837, res. Med-
      ford MA; m. 17 Oct. 1859 JOHN W. FISK of Winchester.
ix.   JOHN, b. 28 Apr. 1841, res. So. Hanson MA; m. 1st
      in May 1867 ISABELLA C. STUART, b. So. Boston 22
      Feb. 1843; m. 2nd Mrs. LUCY (----) Holmes of
      Falmouth ME.

548.   JOHN L.[7] 1785-1840 [182 Jonathan[6] and Mary Rogers]
was born at Rochester or New Durham NH in Feb. 1785, died at
Bradford ME 24 Nov. 1840, 55y (GS, Mills Cemetery); married
at Wolfeboro NH 3 Mar. 1808 (TRs) SABRINA SHAW, born at Lee
NH 22 July 1788, died at Diamond Bluff WI 6 Jan. 1881, 92y 6m
(GS), daughter of George and Elizabeth (Townsend) Shaw (family records of descendant Isabel Wiggins; Henrietta Farwell,
Shaw Records [Bethel ME, 1904], 284-5).
      He went with his parents from Alton NH to Athens ME in
1805, and was listed there in 1810 with a son and daughter
under 10. He sold to Benjamin Flagg 28 Oct. 1813 80 acres
from lots 83 and 86, which he had purchased from his father
(SomCD, 7:38). In 1820, his Athens household included a
daughter 10-16, two sons and two daughters all under 10, and
an extra adult female. About 1826, the family settled at
Bradford; he was selectman there in 1831.
      His widow, 62, lived with her son Leonard at Bradford in
1850 and (as Salina) in 1860. She was still in his household
in WI in 1870 and 1880.

Children, born at Athens:

         i.   SOPHRONIA[8], b. in Mar. 1808, d. c1824, 17y.
1172.   ii. FREEMAN, b. 15 Apr. 1811.
         iii. ADORA, b. in 1812, d. infant.
         iv. MATILDA, b. 8 Jan. 1814, d. Diamond Bluff WI
              18 Mar. 1906; m. Bradford 26 Nov. 1837 ENOCH
              L. QUIMBY, b. Sandwich NH 10 Oct. 1814, d.
              Diamond Bluff 23 Dec. 1890, son of John Smith
              and Nancy (Marston) Quimby (Henry Cole Quin-
              by, Quinby (Quimby) Family [NY, 1915], 2:
              297-8). In 1850 they were listed at Sandwich
              with his nephew George and niece Louisa; soon
              after they went to IL, and in 1854 to Diamond
              Bluff.

Matilda's letters to her niece Eliza Graves
in 1897, 1901 and 1905 gave detailed family
data on three Leighton and Shaw generations.
   v.   BENJAMIN, b. about 1816, d. infant.
  vi. LEONARD T., b. 7 Dec. 1818, d. Diamond Bluff
        14 Apr. 1897 (GS); m. MARY (----) Richard-
        son, b. in NY in 1835. In 1870, he was unm.,
        a farmer at Oak Groves, Pierce Co. WI; in
        1880 he and Mary were at Spring Brook Tp,
        Dunn Co. WI with 5 Richardson children. In
        1897 Matilda wrote that Leonard's wife and
        daughters were at Rice Lake WI, and planning
        to move to Seattle.
 vii. MARY J., b. 17 July 1820, d. 14 Mar. 1889; m.
        ---- YOUNG.
1173. viii. JOHN W., b. 21 Dec. 1822.

549. LYDIA[7] 1789-1861 [182 Jonathan[6] and Mary Rogers] was
born at New Durham Gore (the later Alton) in 1789, died at
Skowhegan ME 6 Dec. 1861; married first at Athens ME in 1815
Dr. BENJAMIN FLAGG, born at Grafton MA 25 Apr. 1784, died at
Athens 1 Jan. 1816 (GS, Lord's Hill), son of Samuel and Lydia
(Rockwood) Flagg (Charles A. Flagg, Descendants of Eleazer
Flagg [Boston, 1903], 35); married second in 1819 LEVI EMERY
of Bloomfield (Skowhegan), born at Townsend (Boothbay) ME 3
Nov. 1762, son of Zachariah and Sarah Emery (Rufus Emery,
Descendants of John and Anthony Emery [Salem MA, 1896], 323).
    Benjamin Flagg had studied medicine at Worcester, married
first Lydia Harrington in 1806, had a son Benjamin, Jr., per-
haps divorced his first wife, and settled at Athens in 1806.
Administration of his estate was granted to his widow Lydia
10 Feb. 1816 (SomCP, 1:480).

Child (**Flagg**), born at Athens:

   i.   SARAH BENJAMIN, b. 2 Mar. 1816, d. Skowhegan 19 Dec.
       1896; m. in 1839 EPHRAIM BIGELOW.

Child (**Emery**), born at Skowhegan (perhaps others):

  ii. ELEANOR LEIGHTON, b. 16 Sept. 1820, d. Skowhegan 25
       Sept. 1892; m. 15 Apr. 1845 ELEAZER COBURN, b.
       Bloomfield 9 Feb. 1820, d. Skowhegan 10 Mar. 1850,
       son of Eleazer and Mary (Weston) Coburn (George A.
       and Silas R. Coburn, Descendants of Edward Colburn/
       Coburn [1913], 96).

550. JONATHAN[7] 1790-1815 [182 Jonathan[6] and Mary Rogers]
was born at Alton NH about 1790, died at Athens ME 6 Aug.
1815 (GS, Lord's Hill); married at Cornville ME int. 9 Jan.
1814 (VRs) NANCY FOWLER.
    His widow was granted administration of his estate 5 Feb.
1816; the inventory included about 70 acres in lot 86, which
had been deeded to Jonathan, Jr., by his father (SomCP,
1:479; 2:5).
    Nancy married second Avery Ricker; about 1849 they joined
her son at Sheboygan Falls WI.

Child, born at Athens:

1174. i.   JONATHAN[8], b. 31 May 1815.

551. HAZEN[7] 1797-1869 [182 Jonathan[6] and Mary Rogers] was
born at Alton NH about 1797, died at Upton MA 3 May 1869, 71y
8m 17d; probably married first a widow ELEANOR ---- ; married
second in Nov. 1824 OLIVE LORD, daughter of James Lord; married third at Upton int. 19 May 1838 LYDIA SADLER ALDRICH,
born at Upton 26 Apr. 1817, daughter of Clark and Polly
(Wood) Aldrich (Upton VRs; letter in Cornman Papers from
granddaughter C. Millie Leighton).
     Hazen and his wife were in Athens in 1820 with two sons
under 10; in 1830 their household included a son under 5,
another 10-15, a daughter 5-10, and a male 16-18. He lived
for some time at "an unincorporated place called No. 3, 2nd
range, Bingham Purchase" (probably now Thorndike), and while
there, on 10 July 1824, sold to his father half of lot 62 in
Athens "that I bought of Joshua Hall" (SomCD, 14:278).
     He was of Athens again when he quit-claimed lot 84 at Wel-
lington 18 Nov. 1828, and when he sold 200 acres in No. 3,
"the lot which I have occupied," 15 June 1829 (23:11, 143).
On 26 Feb. 1834 he deeded part of lot 63, 100 acres and
buildings, to his brother Jonathan of Bloomfield [# 550] and
to his son David of Athens (35:245), Olive releasing her
dower right.
     C. Millie Leighton stated that Hazen's first wife had a
daughter who was married to a Locke, but otherwise she had no
knowledge of the children born in ME.
     Hazen apparently was divorced from Olive. She was among
the twelve heirs of James Lord of Athens who on 27 Jan. 1842
quitclaimed their rights to Alvah Lord (54:55-6); she was
listed as Olive Leighton of Solon, singlewoman, late wife of
Hazen Leighton. Before 1840 Hazen had removed to MA.
     A Hazen Leighton descended from William[1] of Kittery died at
Harmony 12 July 1827.

Children, by a probable first wife, born at Athens:

        i.   DAVID[8], b. c1815, probably the David who m. 4
              June 1835 JUDITH VEAZIE WENTWORTH, b. Orring-
              ton ME 6 May 1818, d. there 22 Jan. 1885, 66y
              8m 16d (GS, N. Orrington), dau. of Ephraim and
              Hannah (Rich) Wentworth (Wentworth Gen. 2:
              427). He lived at Levant with wife and son in
              1850 and 1860, and probably d. there.
              Ch. CHARLES WELLINGTON[9] b. Athens 31 Mar.
              1837, d. So. Orrington 17 May 1905; m. 1st 18
              June 1861 (SARAH) JANE BOYNTON, b. 19 May
              1838, d. 9 Nov. 1892 (GS); m. 2nd So. Orring-
              ton 11 Feb. 1902 widow DOROTHY W. (TRIPPIT)
              Berry, b. Meddybemps ME c1840, dau. of George
              and Mary A. (Ward) Trippit.
1175. ii.   ASA, b. 19 July 1819.

Children by Olive, born at Athens:

1176. iii.   MARIA, b. 23 Nov. 1830; m. BRYCE M. STEWARD.

iv.   LEVI, b. c1830 (30 in 1860); m. Cornville 24
      Oct. 1855 (VRs) ADELINE HUTCHINS of Welling-
      ton, b. c1832 (28 in 1860). He was listed
      alone at Athens in 1860.

Children by Lydia, born at Upton (VRs):

     v.   AMELIA RAWSON, b. 11 Mar. 1839; m. 1st ---- ;
            m. 2nd ---- CLARK.
1177. vi.   (EMILY) ADELAIDE, b. 5 Apr. 1841; m. ALBERT
            S. DRAKE.
1178. vii. LYMAN A., b. 25 Nov. 1843.
    viii. HAZEN, b. 1 Apr. 1846, res. Northboro MA
            in 1900 (census); m. Upton 20 Nov. 1867 LYDIA
            S. BAKER, b. there in Nov. 1843 (per census),
            dau. of Nathan and Sybil (Leland) Baker.
    ix.   MARY JANE, b. 3 Dec. 1849.
    x.   GEORGE H., b. in 1852; m. 10 Dec. 1875 MARY$_9$
            SOUTHARD, b. Richmond ME. Ch. ELLA ALICIA^9 b.
            5 Mar. 1874; m. 25 July 1892 (ME VRs) BENJAMIN
            F. CAMERON, b. in NS in 1872, son of Hugh and
            Edith Cameron.

552. DANIEL^7 1789-1816 [183 William^6 and Mary Pottle] was
baptized at Rochester NH 30 Oct. 1791 (born 5 Sept. 1789, per
Harmony (ME) town record), died at Harmony 10 Sept. 1816, 27y
5d; married there 30 Sept. 1813 Mrs. SARAH (----) Doore
(Harmony VRs).

Children, born at Harmony:

    i.   MARY^8, b. 26 Sept. 1814.
    ii.   MEHITABLE, b. 8 Nov. 1816 (posthumous).

553. ABIGAIL^7 1793-   [183 William^6 and Mary Pottle] was
born at Rochester NH 22 Feb. 1793 (Harmony record); married
at Harmony 23 Mar. 1815 SOLOMON WATSON, born at Farmington 16
July 1792, died at Harmony 16 Oct. 1868, son of Jonathan and
Anna$_6$ (Leighton) Watson [# 185] (Harmony TRs; Cornman Ms).

Children (**Watson**), born at Harmony:

    i.   MAHALA, b. 17 Dec. 1815, d. Harmony 19 July 1890,
            74y 7m (GS, Libby Cemetery); m. RICHARD LORD BROWN.
    ii.   MATILDA, b. 25 Dec. 1817; m. JOSEPH MAGOON, b. St.
            Albans ME 7 Feb. 1818.
    iii.   ALFRED, b. 21 Feb. 1820; m. ABIGAIL PEASE.
    iv.   SOLOMON, b. 23 May 1822; m. ACHSAH JOHNSON.
    v.   JULIA ANN, b. 7 Nov. 1824; m. DAVID PEASE and
            CHARLES^8 LEIGHTON [# 1194].
    vi.   MARY, b. 15 Feb. 1827; m. ALBERT PERRY.
    vii.   CORODONE, b. 16 Nov. 1838 (male, 40 in 1880); m.
            ---- BACHELOR.

554. MARY^7 [Polly] 1798-   [183 William^6 and Mary Pot-
tle] was born at Rochester NH 31 Dec. 1798 (Cambridge ME
record); married at Harmony ME 2 May 1816 JONATHAN WATSON,
born at Farmington 13 Aug. 1794, died at Cambridge ME 29 Aug.

1853, son of Jonathan and Anna[6] (Leighton) Watson [# 185]
(Cambridge VRs; Cornman Ms). They were pioneer settlers at
Cambridge.

Children (**Watson**), in Cambridge VRs:

i.   LEONARD RUSSELL, b. 15 Sept. 1816.
ii.   MARY, b. 29 Sept. 1818, d. 19 July 1823.
iii. JONATHAN, JR., b. 18 Mar. 1821.
iv.   MARY, b. 23 Aug. 1823.
v.   ABIGAIL, b. 11 Dec. 1825.
vi.   WILLIAM, b. 29 [sic] Feb. 1827.
vii. JOSEPHINE, b. 25 Feb. 1830.
viii. GEORGE RILEY, b. 8 May 1832.
ix.   SARAH [Sally], b. 11 Aug. 1834.
x.   ALURA, b. 23 May 1837.
xi.   MARQUIS LAFAYETTE, b. 3 Aug. 1841.

555. WILLIAM CHAMBERLAIN[7] 1802-1860 [183 William[6] and Mary
Pottle] was born at Harmony ME 28 Nov. 1802, died at New
Salem MA 25 Nov. 1860, 57y 11m 25d (VRs); married first at
Harmony 8 Apr. 1823 RELIEF J. BROWN, born at Brewer ME 5 June
1805, lived at Biddeford ME in 1850, daughter of Frank Brown
of Athens; married second POLLY TRAFTON, born about 1819;
married third 14 Dec. 1854 CAROLINE GILES, born at Shutesbury
VT about 1802, daughter of James and Mary Giles (Harmony TRs;
Cornman Ms).
He and Relief were apparently divorced; she was listed at
Biddeford in 1850, with John H., 19, Aaron F., 14, George H.,
10, and 10 boarders.
In 1850 he was a Harmony farmer, listed with wife Polly,
31, and his youngest five children (including those also
listed with Relief). He lived later at Marlboro NH, and in
1854 was of Orange MA.

Children by Relief, born at Harmony:

i.   RELIEF H.[8], b. 28 Jan. 1826; m. 11 Jan. 1844
      NATHAN GLENWOOD.
ii.   HARRIET, b. 28 Jan. 1826, not with a parent in
      in 1850.
1179. iii. JOHN HARRISON, b. 29 Apr. 1831.
1180. iv.   (AARON) FRANKLIN, b. 15 Mar. 1837.
      v.   GEORGE, b. in 1840, lost at sea 14 Dec. 1863
            on the Weehawken.

Children by Polly:

vi.   MARY, d. Harmony 18 June 1850, 8y.
vii. LAURA, b. c1845 (5 in 1850), res. E. Westmore-
      land NH; m. ---- BROWN.
viii. WILLIAM HENRY, b. c1847 (3 in 1850), d. Pt.
      Comfort VA in Mar. 1863, a Union soldier.

556. NANCY[7] 1805-   [183 William[6] and Mary Pottle] was
born at Harmony 19 June 1805, lived at Carmel ME in 1880;
married JOSEPH WELCH, born at York ME 20 July 1786, died at
Newburgh ME 5 Sept. 1873 (GS, Hill Cemetery). He had five or

more children by a first wife, and lived at Wellington, Harmony, Hampden and Newburgh (Harmony VRs; records of descendant Kathy Emerson).

Children (**Welch**), born at Harmony:

i. ANN, b. 31 Jan. 1835.
ii. LYDIA, b. 2 July 1837, d. W. Hampden ME 1 Aug. 1926
    (GS, Oak Grove Cem., Bangor); m. c1859 JOHN M. EMER-
    SON, b. Hampden 4 Mar. 1834, d. Bangor 11 Sept.
    1916, son of Justus Sanford and Emily J. (Stanley)
    Emerson.

557. JOSEPH 2ND[7] 1810-1895 [183 William[6] and Mary Pottle]
was born at Harmony 8 June 1810, died there 8 Mar. 1895, 84y
9m (GS); married at Athens ELVIRA GRANT, born at Pownal ME 28
Nov. 1815, died at Harmony 12 Jan. 1898, 82y 1m 15d, daughter
of William and Susannah (Blackstone) Grant (town and ME VRs;
Cornman Ms). Burials are in North Road Cemetery.
    In Clara Cromwell's records of Harmony families (Ms Collec-
tions, MHS), she reported repeatedly that Joseph's marriage
to Elvira took place 6 Apr. 1846. In one place, she listed
their intentions as filed 15 Dec. 1833, but later lined
through the date. The Athens town records no longer exist.
    He was referred to as Joseph 2nd because of his older
cousin [# 561], and later was designated Capt. Joseph, perhaps for militia service. In 1850 his mother Mary, 83, lived
with him.
    He later went west to IL, and then to a farm at Parsons,
near Topeka KS, but he returned to Harmony.

Children, born at Harmony:

1181. i.   ORRIN PULLEN[8], b. 21 Nov. 1834.
1182. ii.   WAYLAND, b. 14 June 1837.
      iii. OCTAVIA, b. 26 Mar., d. 16 Apr., 1839, 3 wks.
      iv.   CHANDLER, b. 12 Mar. 1840, d. 18 Mar. 1841.
      v.   MARY W., b. 27 Dec. 1842, d. 27 Oct. 1856, 14y
            10m (GS; 26 Oct. in Morning Star), burned to
            death.
      vi.   EDGAR M., b. 15 Dec. 1847, d. 15 Aug. 1850, 2y
            8m (GS).
1183. vii. ELLEN M., b. 12 Sept. 1851; m. MORTIMER
            PINGREE.
1184. viii. ETTA F., b. 4 June 1856; m. HERBERT BARTLETT.
      ix.   WILLARD JOSEPH, b. 6 Oct. 1860, d. Skowhegan
            17 Mar. 1939, 78y 5m 11d; m. Harmony 25 Dec.
            1886 ALICE M. COLLINS, b. there 6 Mar. 1859,
            d. Skowhegan 3 Mar. 1948, dau. of Jacob and
            Naomi (Perkins) Collins. In 1900 a nephew
            Clifton McSorley res. with them.
            Ch. ROY H.[9] b. Harmony 20 Aug. 1887, d.
            Skowhegan in 1961 (GS); m. Athens 28 June
            1911 LIZZIE M. TURNER, b. there 5 July 1893,
            d. Skowhegan in 1964, dau. of Frank P.[10] and
            Lillian (Turner) Turner: ch. ORRIN W.[10] b.
            Harmony 2 Feb. 1924, d. Skowhegan 8 Oct.
            1950 in a sawmill accident; unm.

558.   BENJAMIN[7] 1810-1892 [183 William[6] and Mary Pottle]
was born at Harmony 8 June 1810, died at Orange MA 10 Oct.
1892, 82y 3m 2d; married SUSAN SAVAGE, born at Anson ME 27
Dec. 1811 (Harmony VRs), died at Orange 1 Oct. 1886, 73y 10m
8d, daughter of John and Betsey Savage.
  Called Benjamin Esq., he was a farmer, teacher and surveyor
of timber. In 1850 his Harmony household included his sister
Judith, 42, and his nephew Sherburn, 16. He and Susan
settled at Orange, where Hoyt and Emily Howard joined them
(Harmony VRs; letter from Emily in 1914, and from Carrie Lord
Andrews in 1915-Cornman Papers).

  Children, born at Harmony:

      i.   CAROLINE AUGUSTA[8], b. 17 Nov. 1833, d. Harmony
             11 Aug. 1838.
      ii.   FRANCES M., b. 14 July 1836, not in household
             in 1850.
      iv.   EMILY FRANCES, b. in 1842 (7 in 1850), d.
             Orange 18 Oct. 1864; m. Vernon VT 22 May 1859
             HOYT E. HOWARD, b. Wendell MA 19 Mar. 1838,
             res. Springfield MA in 1914, son of Artemas
             and Susanna (Ward) Hoyt. No ch.
1185. v.   EDWIN MARCELLUS, b. 13 Aug. 1848.

559.   NATHANIEL[7] 1796-1863 [186 David[6] and Nancy Watson]
was born at Middleton NH 6 Aug. 1796 (TRs), died at Harmony
ME 23 May 1863, 66y (GS); married at Clinton ME 21 Sept. 1819
(VRs; Harmony int. 15 Aug.) SUSANNA LEWIS, born at Phillips-
burg (now Hollis) ME 14 Mar. 1802, died at Harmony 27 May
1850, 48y 2m (GS; 26 May in Morning Star).
  A farmer, he purchased 14 Mar. 1818 from Augustine Bousquet
of Philadelphia, proprietors' agent, 106 acres in lot 25 of
Harmony's center range (SomCD, 7:521-2). Susanna's will,
proved in July 1850, left her estate to her husband, except
for $1 each to her daughters and to a granddaughter (SomCP,
22:336). In 1860, Nathaniel, gent., 62, was living at Harmony
with Dennis and Addie Cookson.

  Children, born at Harmony (VRs):

1186. i.   LUCINDA[8], b. 22 June 1820; m. WILLIAM B.
             PERKINS.
      ii.   SOPHRONIA, b. 18 Aug. 1822; res. Moro ME; m.
             Harmony 12 Nov. 1845 GEORGE W. BARTON of
             No. 7, range 5 (near Moro).
1187. iii. MELINDA, b. 15 Feb. 1825; m. CHARLES PERKINS.
1188. iv.   DIANA, b. 11 Nov. 1827; m. FREEMAN QUIMBY and
             JOHN HIGHT.
1189. v.   LEWIS T., b. 4 Sept. 1831.
1190. vi.   ABIGAIL B., b. 15 June 1834; m. JOTHAM BOWKER.
1191. vii. ANN M., b. 11 June 1836; m. JAMES WHITEHOUSE.
      viii. (FRANCES) ADELINE [Addie], b. 19 Mar. 1837, d.
             Harmony in Jan. 1894; m. 1st DENNIS COOKSON,
             b. in NH c1835, d. 15 Aug. 1863 in Civil War;
             m. 2nd JOHN TAYLOR of Auburn ME. Cookson ch.
             Liston, 5, Alice, 3 (1860 Harmony census).
      ix.   ?SUSIE, adult, unm. in 1850, when named in
             mother's will. Not in 1850 census.

560.   JONATHAN GILES[7] 1798-1883 [186 David[6] and Nancy Watson] was born at Middleton NH 15 Dec. 1798 (VRs), died at Harmony ME 31 Dec. 1883, 84y (1884, GS); married first there 12 Sept. 1819 LYDIA[8] LEIGHTON, born there 21 Nov. 1800, died there 30 Apr. 1835, daughter of William and Mary (Pottle) Leighton [# 183]; married second at Wellington ME 1 Nov. 1835 (Harmony int. 18 Oct.) LYDIA (DREW) Smith, born at Harmony 9 Apr. 1808, died at Athens 15 Nov. 1894, 86y 7m 7d (GS), daughter of Reuben and Sally (Page) Drew (Harmony VRs; Cornman Ms). Burials are in North Road Cemetery, Harmony.
    Jonathan was living at Wellington in 1850, but was at Athens in 1860 and 1880. Lydia Drew had married first Joseph Smith, and had three Smith children at Wellington: Ambrose, Asa and Lydia P.--the latter was in Jonathan's household in 1850, aged 15.

Children by first wife, born at Harmony:

1192.	i.	IRENE DEARBORN[8], b. 3 Aug. 1821; m. ISAIAH CHADBOURNE.
1193.	ii.	SABRINA, b. 9 Dec. 1822; m. ISAIAH DORE, JR.
1194.	iii.	CHARLES, b. 23 Apr. 1825.
1195.	iv.	PARMELIA, b. 1 Aug. 1827; m. CALVIN DORE.
	v.	SHERBURN, b. 22 Nov. 1833; d. Harmony 14 June 1920; m. 15 Sept. 1854 (int. Gardiner 14 Oct.) ABBIE WEBB, b. Harmony 4 Aug. 1833, d. there 18 Feb. 1914, dau. of Benjamin and Harriet (Rhoades) Webb. Adopted ch. Hattie b. in 1869, d. 16 Nov. 1875, 6y 7m.

Children by second wife, all but two born at Harmony:

1196.	vi.	HIRAM, b. 14 Apr. 1837.
1197.	vii.	ALBERT D., b. 28 Jan. 1840.
1198.	viii.	HARRIET NEWELL, b. 30 June 1842; m. JOHN HOYT and NELSON TOWLE.
1199.	ix.	LEONARD HATHAWAY, b. 18 Sept. 1844.
1200.	x.	MARY E., b. 19 May 1849; m. DAVID DAVIS.
1201.	xi.	JOSEPH, b. Wellington 6 Aug. 1850.
	xii.	JOSEPHINE (twin), b. Wellington 6 Aug. 1850, d. Harmony 13 Oct. 1858, 8y 2m (GS).

561.   JOSEPH[7] 1801-   [186 David[6] and Nancy Watson] was born at Middleton NH (Harmony record) about 1801 (49 in 1850), died in the Black Hills SD (Cornman Ms); married at Harmony 25 Oct. 1821 BETSEY E. WRAY, born 9 Nov. 1801, lived at Hudson ME in 1870, 67, with Almira Goodwin (Harmony TRs).
    In 1850 his household at Harmony, next door to his brother Nathaniel's, included his parents.

Children, born at Harmony:

1202.	i.	LEVI[8], b. 3 Nov. 1823.
	ii.	MEHITABLE, b. 18 Oct. 1825 (23 in 1850).
1203.	iii.	JOSEPH, b. 23 Feb. 1828.
	iv.	ANGELINE, b. 23 Jan. 1830.
1204.	v.	WARREN CHARLES, b. 25 Aug. 1832.
	vi.	LOREN B., b. 11 Dec. 1835 (14 in 1850).
	vii.	ALMIRA, b. 28 Mar. 1838, res. Hudson in 1870; m. ---- GOODWIN.

562. EPHRAIM[7] 1806-   [186 David[6] and Nancy Watson] was
born at Harmony ME 25 July 1806; married at Shapleigh ME in
1831 (Athens int. 29 May) JUDITH WILLEY of Athens, who was
born at Shapleigh (records of descendant Theron M. Clement;
Cornman Ms).

Child, born at Harmony (perhaps others):

1205. i.   ALEXANDER[8], b. 1 Aug. 1831.

563. SHERBURN[7] 1813-1862 [186 David[6] and Nancy Watson] was
born at Harmony 5 Aug. 1813, died at Athens 14 June 1862, 49y
10m 10d (GS); married first at Harmony 8 May 1836 LOVINA LIT-
TLEFIELD, who died at Athens 18 Nov. 1840, 28y (GS); married
second at Harmony int. 11 Apr. 1841 MARY (?DEALING) Tibbetts,
born in NH about 1803, died at Athens 6 Dec. 1881, 78y 9m 17d
(GS). Mary was the widow of William Tibbetts, Jr., who had
died at Athens 17 Sept. 1840, 33y (Harmony VRs; Cornman Ms).
Burials are in Mount Rest Cemetery, Athens.
    In 1850 Sherburn was a farmer at Harmony, his household
including Flavilla, 19, and three Tibbetts step-children:
William, 18, Nelson, 14, and Martha, 11. In 1860 his home
was at Athens. His will was proved 2 Sept. 1862, with his
son Chandler as executor (SomCP, 33:120). Chandler owned the
family Bible.

Children by second wife Mary, born at Harmony:

    i.   CHANDLER[8], b. 19 Nov. 1841, d. Harmony 31 Mar.
          1895, 53y 3m 12d (GS); m. ELLA M. DeLATE, b.
          9 May 1849, d. 28 Jan. 1903 (GS; VRs).
    ii.   GEORGE, b. in 1844, d. Harmony 14 July 1846,
          2y 5m 5d (GS; Morning Star).
    iii. MARILLA MARY, b. 3 Sept. 1848, res. Bangor; m.
          3 Sept. 1870 JAMES AUGUSTUS BOARDMAN, b.
          Skowhegan 19 Dec. 1847, son of James M. and
          Eliza Harriet (Lawrence) Boardman. Ch.
          Harold Sherburn b. 31 Mar. 1874 (Samuel Lane
          Boardman, A Family Memorial [np, nd], 45.).

564. DAVID[7] 1816-1862 [186 David[6] and Nancy Watson] was
born at Harmony 20 May 1816, died at Waterville ME 8 Sept.
1862, 45y 4m; married at Harmony int. 29 Aug. 1840 LAURA
EVANS, born about 1817, died at Waterville 8 Mar. 1897, 79y
9m (town and ME VRs). Burials are in Pine Grove Cemetery,
Waterville. They were listed at Waterville in 1850.

Children, born at Waterville:

    i.   HELEN JOSEPHINE[8], b. c1844, d. Waterville 5
          Feb. 1848, 3y 3m.
1206. ii.   CLARENCE A., b. in Feb. 1849.

565. RACHEL[7] 1797-1874 [187 Moses[6] and Betsey Rogers] was
born at Alton NH 20 Feb. 1797, died at Cambridge ME 7 Mar.
1874; married in 1818 EPHRAIM WATSON, born 22 Dec. 1795, died
at Cambridge 16 Feb. 1847, son of Jonathan and Nancy[7]
(Leighton) Watson [# 185] (town VRs; Cornman Ms).

He was a farmer, and a pioneer settler in the part of
Ripley which became Cambridge in 1854.

Children (**Watson**), in Ripley and Cambridge VRs:

i.   NANCY, b. 19 Sept. 1818, d. Raymond ME 23 Jan. 1886;
        m. 1st LEONARD WATSON; m. 2nd -;-- TICKEY of Lewis-
        ton; m. 3rd 11 Aug. 1867 GEORGE⁷ LEIGHTON of Cam-
        bridge [# 585]; m. 4th ---- KNIGHT of Raymond.
ii.   HAZEN, b. 14 June 1820, d. 30 Dec. 1847.
iii.   EPHRAIM, JR., b. 9 Sept. 1822, d. 6 Dec. 1841.
iv.   HIRAM, b. 21 Dec. 1824, d. Guilford ME 22 June 1878;
        m. BETSEY DAVIS.
v.   FRANCES P. [Fannie], b. 27 Oct. 1827, d. 6 Feb. 1912;
        m. DAVID HOOPER.
vi.   ALMIRA, b. 18 July 1829; m. 21 June 1856 BENJAMIN
        W. MITCHELL.
vii.   NELSON, b. 27 Dec. 1831, d. Cambridge 23 Apr. 1902,
        69y 3m 27d; m FANNY HATCH [# 566].
viii.   JEFFERSON, b. 29 Sept. 1833, d. Dexter ME 5 May 1905;
        m. DELCINIA ROGERS and ELVIRA ALLEN.
ix.   MADISON, b. 27 Mar. 1836, d. Cambridge 10 Nov. 1848.
x.   ELVIRA, b. 6 Dec. 1838, d. Cambridge 16 Aug. 1849.

566. SALLY⁷ 1799-1884 [187 Moses⁶ and Betsey Rogers] was
born at Harmony ME 13 June 1799, died at Dexter ME 20 Feb.
1884; married first Rev. FOREST HATCH, born at Wells ME 11
Nov. 1796 (Cambridge record), died at Cambridge 3 May 1834,
son of Elias and Lucy (Chadbourne) Hatch; married second ----
ROBINSON; married third JOHN WOODS (town VRs; Cornman Ms).
Hatch was ordained a Baptist minister in 1827.

Children (**Hatch**), born at Cambridge:

i.   BETSEY R., b. 16 Mar. 1818, m. Cambridge ROYAL GRANT.
ii.   ELIAS SELDEN, b. 10 Oct. 1820, d. 3 Sept. 1821.
ii.   ELIAS SELDEN, b. 14 June 1822, d. in Mar. 1887; m.
        LOIS JANE LEAVITT.
iii.   FANNY NEWELL, b. 20 May 1826, res. Wellington; m.
        NELSON WATSON [# 565].
iv.   JACOB FOREST, b. 27 Dec. 1830, d. Dexter 4 Jan. 1915;
        m. MARTHA HARRIS.

567. SUSANNA⁷ 1801-1853 [187 Moses⁶ and Betsey Rogers] was
born at Harmony 2 June 1801, died at Cambridge ME 21 Jan.
1853; married FOSS HAMILTON, born at Coxhall (now Lyman) ME
21 Feb. 1797 (Cambridge record), died at Cambridge 6 Mar.
1854, son of Elijah and Mary (Gould) Hamilton (town VRs;
records of Joseph Odiorne and Elizabeth Rhoton; Cornman Ms).
They were listed at Ripley in 1830, and Cambridge in 1850.

Children (**Hamilton**), births recorded at Cambridge:

i.   MOSES LEIGHTON, b. 20 Oct. 1819; m. ELIZA ANN
        PACKARD, b. 20 Mar. 1822.
ii.   AARON, b. 28 June 1821; m. SALLY J. PERRY.
iii.   ALANSON, b. 7 Nov. 1825, res. in MA
iv.   EPHRAIM W., b. 27 Dec. 1828, d. 26 May 1831.
v.   SUSANNA, b. 17 Dec. 1831; m. SETH GORDON of Bangor.

vi.   EPHRAIM WATSON, b. 10 Nov. 1834.
vii.   SHERBURN ROBINSON, b. 25 Aug. 1836; unm.
viii. LOANTHA, b. 24 Dec. 1837, d. 24 Apr. 1853.
ix.   NEWMAN DAVIS, b. 21 June 1839, res. in MA; m. 24 Apr.
       1860 MARY JANE BUCKLEY, b. perhaps Manchester,
       England, in 1842, d. Beaver Dam NB 2 Dec. 1906,
       dau. of Sydney and Sarah Buckley. She m. 2nd
       Israel Smith.
x.   ELDULLA CAROLINE, b. 28 Aug. 1842; unm.
xi.   RACHEL WATSON, b. 7 Jan., d. 14 Jan., 1844.
xii.   BETSEY ANN, b. 29 Mar. 1845, res. in MA.

568.   ELIJAH[7] 1803-1864 [187 Moses[6] and Betsey Rogers]
was born at Harmony 13 July 1803, died at Cambridge 22 May
1864, 59y (VRs); married in June 1822 ISABEL McNELLY, born at
Clinton ME 23 July 1803, daughter of Michael and Susan
(Pushor) McNelly (town VRs; Cornman Ms). He was a farmer.

Children:

       i.   LUCY ROGERS[8], b. Ripley 17 Sept. 1822, d.
             Cambridge 11 May 1857; unm.
1207. ii.   (ELIJAH) FISHER, b. Cambridge 11 July 1842.

569.   HENRY TIBBETTS[7] 1796-   [188 Ephraim[6] and Esther]
was born at Mount Vernon ME 4 Sept. 1796, died in NY between
1850 and 1855; married first ---- ; married second AMANDA
(----) [?Bowen], born in NY about 1814.
He had settled at Portville, Cattaraugus Co. NY by 1820. In
1850 he was a farmer there, 52, with his wife Amanda, 36,
born in NY. In the state census of 1855, widow Amanda's
household included her stepson Solomon, an Abigail Bowen, 15,
and her four Leighton children.

Children by first wife, born in NY:

1208. i.   HENRY TIBBETTS[8], b. 1 Apr. 1830.
       ii.   ELBRIDGE, b. c1833 (17 in 1850).
       iii. SOLOMON, b. c1835 (15 in 1850).

Children by Amanda, born in NY:

       iv.   ESTHER, b. c1841 (9 in 1850, 13 in 1855).
       v.   WALTER, b. c1843 (7 in 1850).
       vi.   GEORGE, b. c1849 (1 in 1850).
       vii. ANN, b. c1852 (3 in 1855).

570.   EPHRAIM[7] 1798-1876 [188 Ephraim[6] and Esther] was born
at Mount Vernon 14 Jun, 1798, died at Augusta ME 28 Dec.
1876, 76y 6m; married at Mt. Vernon 17 Nov. 1820 HANNAH
BRAINARD, born there 10 June 1793, died at Augusta 20 Apr.
1870, 75y, daughter of Nathaniel and Roxanna (Austin) Brainard (Lucy A. Brainard, Genealogy of the Brainard-Brainerd
Family in America [Hartford, Conn., 1908], 1:126; Augusta
VRs). Burials are in Mt. Hope Cemetery, Augusta.
    Ephraim was a taxpayer at Augusta in 1822, but settled at
Parkman ME about 1826. They returned to Augusta about 1837,

where in 1850 he was a farmer, 50, his household including
his wife Hannah, 53, their children, his father Ephraim Sr.,
84, and a boy George, 5.
They had removed to NY about 1841, and then to IA, near
Wellman, about 1843. They retired to ME.

Children, births listed in Parkman TRs:

      i.   LAURA ANN[8], b. Mt. Vernon 30 July 1822, d.
              Augusta 1 Apr. 1915; m Augusta 10 Nov. 1844
              NATHANIEL NASON, b. 18 June 1814, d. 22 Feb.
              1900. No ch. He had m. 1st Augusta int.
              2 July 1837 Sarah Dureen.
1209. ii.   HENRY MARTIN, b. Parkman 20 Nov. 1824.
      iii.   ROXANNA BRAINARD, b. Parkman 30 Dec. 1827, d.
              Augusta 27 Dec. 1898, 70y 11m 27d (GS); m.
              there 9 Jan. 1855 SAMUEL GREENLEAF [Green]
              CUMMINGS, son of Samuel Cummings. No ch.
      iv.   ROSELLA CLOUGH (twin), b. Parkman 30 Dec.
              1827, d. Augusta 30 Nov. 1907; m. there (as
              Rosilla) 26 Oct. 1851 THOMAS CONANT, b. Top-
              sham ME 30 Mar. 1809, son of Joseph and
              Lucinda (Tufts) Conant (Conant Family, 377,
              475). Ch. William Henry b. Wayne ME 7 Sept.
              1855, res. Augusta; m. Wayne 9 June 1882 KATE
              McKINNON, b. New Canada NS 3 Sept. 1861, dau.
              of Laughlin and Effie McKinnon.
      v.   OWEN OAKS, b. 22 Nov. 1828, d. 31 Mar. 1839.
1210. vi.   ESTHER C., b. 1 May 1831; m. JOHN P. ANKERLOO.
      vii.   ABIGAIL ROBINSON, b. 13 Dec. 1833; m. Augusta
              int. 11 May 1881 WILLIAM E. LOWELL, b. No.
              Monmouth ME in 1825, son of William, Jr., and
              Jemima (Maxim) Lowell. No ch. He had m. 1st
              Augusta 17 Dec. 1853 Hannah Caton; m. 2nd
              there int. 2 July 1855 Mary H. Cogswell.
      viii. SULLIVAN AUGUSTUS, b. 13 Nov. 1836, d Augusta
              25 May 1848, 11y 6m.

571. ISAAC[7] 1811-1881 [188 Ephraim[6] and Esther] was born at
Augusta ME 30 July 1811 (1812 per Parkman VRs), died at Wellman, Washington Co. IA 17 Aug. 1881; married 4 July 1837
(Parkman int. 19 June) PAMELIA [Permelia] LANCASTER, born at
Corinna ME 4 Oct. 1816 (1814 in family records), died at
Wellman 2 May 1891, daughter of Elihu and Sarah (Tuck) Lancaster (town VRs; records concerning Isaac and his descendants compiled by Helen VanDyke).
He learned brickmasonry as a youth. After his marriage he
settled briefly in Cattaraugus Co. NY, and then became a
pioneer settler at Lime Creek Tp, Washington Co. IA, where he
was a farmer and stock-raiser (Portrait and Biographical
Album of Washington County, Iowa [Chicago, 1887], 418-9).

Children, the last four born in Washington Co. IA:

1211. i.   CHARLOTTE BRADFORD[8], b. 30 Apr. 1837 (Parkman
              VRs); m. ELNATHAN W. CARPENTER.
1212. ii.   STEPHEN TIBBETTS, b. Parkman 6 Feb. 1839.
1213. iii.   MARIAM JORDAN, b Cattaraugus Co. NY 20 Mar.
              1842; m. THOMAS JEFFERSON ALLEN.

        iv.   LYMAN C., b. Washington Co. IA 4 Sept. 1847,
              d. there 18 Feb. 1852.
        v.   ALICE JANE, b. 24 May 1852, d. Keota IA 23
              July 1934; m. DANIEL W. WOLFE. No ch.
        vi.   EZRA L., d. infant 7 July 1853.
1214.   vii. DELPHINA ANN, b. 17 Oct. 1856; m. ALLEN N.
              McELWAIN.

572. SIMEON[7] 1792-1869 [189 Ezekiel[6] and Lydia Pearl] was
born at Mount Vernon ME 16 July 1792 (Rome VRs), died at
Augusta 9 Apr. 1869; married at Augusta 20 June 1826 ELIZA-
BETH [Betsey] LeBARON, born at Rome 17 Aug. 1806, died at
Augusta 21 Dec. 1890, 85y, daughter of James and Rhoda
(Tracy) LeBaron (Mary L. Stockwell, Descendants of Francis
LeBaron [Boston, 1904], 179-80; Rome and Augusta VRs; records
of descendant Lois W. Thurston).
Simeon served under Capt. George Waugh in 1814 (MA Mil.
1812-1814, 279). He and his brother Silas bought land at the
Gore (Readfield) from Thomas Winthrop 7 Nov. 1818; he sold
his share to Neal Bean 5 Jan. 1820 (KenCD, 34:240), and was
on the 1820 Augusta taxlist. He was at Mt. Vernon in 1830,
at Exeter in 1840, and in 1850 he was a farmer at Readfield,
57, with Betsey, 42, and six children.
He received bounty land warrant #19325 for his militia service, for 40 acres in 1850, and 120 acres in 1855, but probably sold the rights. His widow applied for a pension in
1871 and 1878 (NA-MSR #8833). In 1880, she was living with
her son Aaron at Augusta.

Children, births listed in Exeter ME VRs:

1215.   i.   JAMES C.[8], b. 20 Feb. 1827.
1216.   ii.   SILAS FREDERIC, b. 24 Jan. 1829.
1217.   iii. LYDIA, b. 5 Sept. 1832; m. NATHANIEL CHURCH.
1218.   iv.   AARON, b. 1 Nov. 1834.
        v.   IRA, b. 29 Apr. 1842, not in 1850 census.
        vi.   FRANCIS H., b. 26 May 1846.
1219.   vii. (ELIZABETH) JANE [Jennie], b. 5 Aug. 1847; m.
              CHARLES E. NASON.

573. SILAS[7] 1795-1868 [189 Ezekiel[6] and Lydia Pearl] was
born at Mount Vernon 24 May 1795, died at Augusta 27 May
1868, 74y; married there 5 Apr. 1821 MARY [Polly] LEIGHTON,
born at Gardiner ME 11 Nov. 1802, died at Augusta 28 Feb.
1867, 65y 3m, daughter of Isaac and Betsey (Lawrence)
Leighton [# 190] (town VRs). Burials are in Coombs' Mills
Cemetery, Augusta.
He served under Capt. Timothy L. Stevens in 1814 (MA Mil.
1812-1814, 279). In 1830 he lived at Readfield, and in 1850
was a farmer at Augusta, with his wife, son Charles, and John
Pearl, 57. His estate was administered by Charles Titcomb in
July 1868 (KenCP); his "only son" Charles received the homestead, which included 78 acres at Augusta and Manchester.

Children, born at Augusta (Cornman Ms):

1220.   i.   CHARLES[8], b. c1822 (28 in 1850).
        ii.   EDWARD, d. in CA.
        iii. GEORGE, res. CA.

574. HIRAM[7] 1807-1868 [189 Ezekiel[6] and Lydia Pearl] was born at Rome 26 Apr. 1807, died at Augusta 5 Mar. 1868 (VRs; 5 Jan., 60y 10m per GS); married first at Corinna ME 11 Mar. 1833 (int. Exeter 22 Jan.) ANNA[8] LEIGHTON, probably daughter of John and Anna (Wiggin) Leighton [# 526]; married second at Corinna 27 Mar. 1845 NANCY ANN SANBORN, born at Athens ME 5 Aug. 1824, died at Bangor ME 23 Mar. 1903, daughter of Elisha and Sarah (Philbrick) Sanborn (Sanborn Gen., 174; town VRs; Cornman Ms).

In 1850, he was a millman at Exeter, with Nancy and their children. In 1870, widow Nancy and five children were in the Augusta household of Moses and Abigail Morrill. She lived at Bangor in 1892.

Child by Anna, born at Corinna:

    i.   LYDIA ANN[8], b. 10 June 1837; m. Augusta 31 Jan. 1854 SANFORD M. BEAN, b. Readfield c1831, (23 in 1854), son of Josiah Pierce and Ellen Amelia (Pratt) Bean (Bernie Bean, John Bean of Exeter [3rd ed., 1977], 294).

Children by Nancy:

            ii.   FRANCES E. [or FRANCIS], b. c1846 (4 in 1850).
1221. iii. (TIMOTHY) ANDREW, b. Levant in 1847.
            iv.   CYRUS P., b. c1849 (6/12 in 1850), d. Augusta 26 Apr. 1864, 14y 5m 6d (GS, Coombs' Mills).
1222.   v.   JOSEPH, b. Exeter 31 Dec. 1851.
            vi.   NAOMI E., b. c1856 (14 in 1870); perhaps m. 21 Apr. 1876 CLARENCE F. RAYNES of Bangor.
          vii.   WILLIAM, b. c1858 (12 in 1870).
     viii.   JULIUS, b. c1861 (9 in 1870); m. Dexter 27 Nov. 1884 FLORILLA BIGELOW.

575. WARREN[7] 1809-1881 [189 Ezekiel[6] and Lydia Pearl] was born in ME in 1809, died at Corinna 18 Sept. 1881, 72y 1m 7d (GS); married HANNAH ROGERS, born at Ripley ME about 1818, died at Corinna 5 Oct. 1888, 70y (GS).

Although his birth record has not been found, he was almost certainly a son of Ezekiel; in 1850 he was a farmer at Corinna living next door to Lorenzo [# 576], his household including Ruth Rodgers, 40, and in 1860 he was a millman there. Burials are in Nutter Cemetery, Corinna.

Children, born at Corinna (VRs):

    i.   (CHARLES) NELSON, b. c1842, d. 16 June 1870, 28y (GS).
1223. ii.   STILLMAN A., b. 17 Feb. 1844.
       iii.   ELLEN M., b. 27 Dec. 1846; m. Corinna 17 Feb. 1863 MELVIN J. PERRY.
       iv.   ELIZA M., b. 12 Oct. 1851.

576. LORENZO D.[7] 1811-1896 [189 Ezekiel[6] and Lydia Pearl] was born at Mount Vernon 15 July 1811, died at Corinna 2 Feb. 1896, 84y 6m 17d; married at Exeter 23 June 1839 (10 July in Morning Star) PHOEBE ANN NUTT, born at Perry 7 Dec. 1821, died at Corinna 29 May 1900, 78y 5m 22d, daughter of John

Glidden and Susan (Nudstrom) Nutt (town and ME VRs). (Her death record showed Atkinson IL as her birthplace.)
He was a farmer at Corinna in 1850, and a millman there in 1860. Burials are in Nutter Cemetery, Corinna.

Children, born at Corinna:

      i.   LEWIS FRANKLIN[8], b. 17 Mar. 1840, d. Baton
             Rouge LA 21 June 1863, 22y 3m 2d (GS), while
             cpl., Co. A, 22nd ME Inf. Rgt.
      ii.   CHARLES HENRY, b. 1 Sept. 1844, d. Corinna 12
             Aug. 1863, 18y 11m 11d (GS). He also served
             in Co A, 22nd ME Inf. Rgt.
1224. iii. ELLEN SUSAN, b. 16 May 1849; m. CHARLES T.
             TEWKSBURY.
1225. iv.   MERRILL D., b. 12 Aug. 1856.

577. JOHN[7] - [?189 Ezekiel[6] and Lydia Pearl] married ANNA ---- (Cornman Ms). He is a shadowy figure, and was not listed in town records other than as father of five children. John was listed at Corinna in 1830, and in 1840 lived there next to Lorenzo and Warren Leighton; he was not listed in 1850.
Julia Cornman placed him as a son of Ezekiel, but this page of her manuscript was not clear and had many erasures.

Children, born at Corinna (VRs):

      i.   ELIZABETH[8], b. 10 Oct. 1827, d. 11 Nov. 1860,
             33y.
      ii.   MARY ANN, b. 17 Jan. 1829.
      iii. CAROLINE, b. 20 Mar. 1833, d. Farmington NH
             8 Nov. 1869, 35y.
      iv.   EMELINE (twin), b. 20 Mar. 1833.
1226. v.   ABIGAIL, b. 4 Dec. 1835; m. HIRAM PAIGE.

578. LUCY[7] 1792-1869 [190 Isaac[6] and Betsey Lawrence] was born at Mount Vernon 17 Dec. 1792, died at Marietta OH 12 Sept. 1869, 77y 8m; married at Pittston ME 27 Dec. 1812 (1842 in published VRs) MOSES FLANDERS, born at Wiscasset ME 14 July 1783, died at Marietta 5 Aug. 1852, 69y 22d, son of Enoch and Anna (Crocker) Flanders (Edith Flanders Dunbar, The Flanders Family [Rutland VT, 1935], 216). They settled in OH in 1813.

Children (**Flanders**), born at or near Marietta:

      i.   MOSES, d. Shelbyville IL in 1902; m. 5 Jan. 1844
             LUCINDA CHAPMAN, b. in 1828, dau. of Simeon Chapman.
      ii.   AARON, b. 29 Jan. 1827, d. Marietta 3 Dec. 1896; m.
             1st CHRISTIANNA DABOLD; m. 2nd SARAH DABOLD.
      iii. NEHEMIAH, b. in Mar. 1834, d. Warrensburg MO 15 Sept.
             1915; m. 23 Sept. 1853 JANE STEWART.

579. DAVID[7] 1794-1864 [190 Isaac[6] and Betsey Lawrence] was born at Mount Vernon 4 Aug. 1794, died at Augusta 4 July 1864, 69y 11m; married there 21 May 1818 CELIA WINSLOW BURDEN, born at New Vineyard ME 3 May 1800, died at Augusta 18

Feb. 1892, 91y 9m 15d, daughter of James S. and Celia (Winslow) Burden (Lawrence Fam., 149-50; town and ME VRs). Burials are in the Coombs Mills Cemetery, Augusta. He served under Capt. George Waugh in 1814 (MA Mil. 1812-1814, 279). He was a taxpayer at Augusta in 1818, and a farmer there in 1850. Celia's name was Birding on the marriage record, and elsewhere Burdine and Barden.

Children, born probably at Augusta:

      i.   HANNAH S.[8], b. c1819, d. Augusta 6 Jan. 1882, 62y 9m (GS); m. DAVID ATKINS. They settled in TX, Julia Cornman noted. Ch. Lida A. b. 6 June 1856, d. 4 June 1927 (GS).

      ii.   LUCY F., res. Vienna ME; m. HARRIS CHAMBERLAIN.

1227. iii. EDWARD, b. 18 Sept. 1821.
1228. iv. WILLIAM A., b. in Aug. 1827.
1229. v.   HORACE P., b. 21 May 1840.
      vi. ?ELIZA J. (Lawrence Gen.; not in 1850 census).

580.   EDWARD[7] 1796-1826 [190 Isaac[6] and Betsey Lawrence] was born at Gardiner ME 24 Sept. 1796 (Mt. Vernon TRs). He was probably the Edward who died at Gouldlsboro ME 4 Feb. 1826; and who had married first 3 May 1818 HANNAH BARNEY SMITH, born at Taunton MA 23 July 1789, daughter of Ebenezer and Betsey (Cobb) Smith; and married second at Gouldsboro 6 Aug. 1820 MARY A. SMITH, born at Taunton 11 May 1799, sister of Hannah ("Gen. David Cobb," BHM, 4[1888]:6-7). Mary married second at Gouldsboro 8 Mar. 1828 (TRs) Philip Bunnell of New Portland, and removed to Phillips ME.
Edward Leighton was a trader, and was chosen as selectman at Gouldsboro in 1823. His probate inventory listed 117 acres at Gouldsboro, and shares in a saw mill, grist mill, and schooners and sloops; reference was made to his three small children, and to a fourth expected (research of Wade descendant Edith Eastman).

Children by wife Mary, born at Gouldsboro:

      i.   CAROLINE ELIZABETH[8], b. 29 Dec. 1821; m. W. G. ---- .
      ii.   EDWARD AUGUSTUS, b. 9 Feb. 1824.
1230. ii. MARY ELLEN, b. 15 May 1825; m. JAMES N. WADE.

581.   BETSEY[7] 1799-1858 [190 Isaac[6] and Betsey Lawrence] was born at Gardiner 28 June 1799, died there 4 Apr. 1858, 59y 9m; married there 23 Feb. 1832 Capt. PETER WAITT, JR., born at Danvers MA 22 Jan. 1774, died at Gardiner 11 Dec. 1836, 63y, son of Peter and Margaret Waitt. He had married first at Marblehead MA 22 Nov. 1795 Elizabeth Wilson--they had thirteen children (Deloraine P. Corey, The Waite Family of Malden MA [Malden, 1913], 40-1; Gardiner VRs).

Children (**Waitt**), born at South Gardiner:

i.   RACHEL S., b. 22 Apr. 1833; m. Gardiner 23 Nov. 1856 GEORGE WILKINSON.
ii.   EMILY F., b. 11 Oct. 1835, d. 16 June 1854, 18y 8m.

582. BENJAMIN S.[7] [Peleg] 1801-1863 [190 Isaac[6] and <u>Betsey Lawrence</u>] was born at Mount Vernon 27 Mar. 1801, died at <u>Belgrade ME</u> 24 Sept. 1863; married at Augusta int. 23 July 1825 LUCY LUCE of Readfield, born in 1805, died at Belgrade 6 Apr. 1869 (town VRs; Cornman Ms).
In 1850 he was a farmer at Belgrade, with six children at home. On 2 Nov. 1864, Benjamin Eldred was appointed administrator of his estate, insolvent after the 70-acre farm and homestead had been sold (KenCP).

Children, the first six births in Mt. Vernon TRs:

	i.	CAROLINE E.[8], b. 26 Aug. 1826.
	ii.	RICHARD, b. c1827, res. Belgrade Depot; m. ---- WELLMAN.
1231.	iii.	SAMUEL H., b. 24 June 1828.
	iv.	LOUISA [Hannah], b. 8 Sept. 1830.
	v.	MARY C., b. 10 Mar. 1833; m. 29 Apr. 1857 WILLIAM D. ALEXANDER, b. c1829, son of John Alexander of Belgrade (Kingsbury, <u>Kennebec County</u>, 2:1018). Ch. Jane, Frank and Frank William.
	vi.	ISAAC, b. 26 Mar. 1835, d. Belgrade 5 Oct. 1850, 15y 6m.
	vii.	MARIA, b. c1838 (12 in 1850).
	viii.	SALOME P., b. Belgrade 24 Oct. 1841.
	ix.	FLORENCE T., b. Belgrade 17 July 1847; m. there int. 31 July 1865 DAVID McCONNELL.

583. NATHAN[7] 1802-1876 [191 Timothy[6]] was born at Mount Vernon 2 Aug. 1802, died at Augusta 31 Mar. 1876, 73y 8m; married at Hallowell ME 25 Dec. 1828 (Augusta int. 29 Nov.) MIRANDA BLUNT, born at Mt. Vernon 16 May 1805, died at Redding CA 19 Apr. 1886, daughter of Andrew and Merideth (Monk) Blunt (town VRs; Cornman Ms).
He was a taxpayer at Augusta in 1828. In 1880, Miranda was living there with her son Harvey.

Children, born at Augusta (also listed at Mt. Vernon):

1232.	i.	HENRY MARTIN[8], b. 22 Oct. 1829.
	ii.	HANNAH ELIZABETH (twin), b. 22 Oct. 1829, d. Redding CA 26 May 1913; unm.
	iii.	MARTHA W., b. 28 Sept. 1831, d. 15 Oct. 1832.
	iv.	MARY M., b. 24 Nov. 1833, d. 2 Nov. 1849.
	v.	HORACE F., b. 23 July 1835, d. 21 Sept. 1844.
	vi.	HARVEY N., b. 14 Aug. 1839, res. in FL; m. 1st Augusta 18 June 1865 LIZZIE A. FLETCHER, b. 30 Aug. 1847, d. 18 May 1912, dau. of Joseph and Lydia (Neal) Fletcher; m. 2nd 11 June 1913 LENA P. WALCH, b. Wurtenburg, Germany, 16 Oct. 1870, dau. of Chrystopher and Christine (Knittel) Walch. No ch. Adopted ch. Burton Fletcher b. in Feb. 1877. Harvey served in Co. B, 3rd ME Inf. Rgt., and was a pensioner. He settled in KS, lived in CA 27 yrs., and retired to Zephyrhills FL (NA-MSR). In 1900 he, Lizzie and Burton were living at Buckeye, Shasta Co. CA.

vii. HARRISON A., b. 4 June 1841, d. 15 Apr. 1847.
1233. viii. HAMPTON W., b. 7 Mar. 1844.
ix.   HARRIET V. [Hattie], b. 27 Jan. 1846, d. 23
      May 1878; m. Augusta 1 Apr. 1871 WILLIAM
      MOSHIER. No ch.

584. DAVID[7] 1805-1888 [191 Timothy[6]] was born at Mount
Vernon 15 Apr. 1805, died at Cambridge ME 20 July 1888, 84y
(GS); married at Parkman int. 10 June 1832 LOUISA[7] LEIGHTON,
born at Rome 27 Sept. 1806, died at Cambridge 26 June 1889,
83y (GS), daughter of Daniel and Ruth[6] Leighton [# 197] (town
VRs; records of Leighton A. Nutting and Ethelyn Howard).
Burials are in the Village Cemetery, Cambridge.

Children, listed in Cambridge VRs:

        i.   HANNAH[8], b. Monmouth 17 Dec. 1832, d. 9 Apr.
             1892, 59y; m. BENSON ARNO.
        ii. MARTHA R., b. 15 Oct. 1834; m. Sangerville ME
             int. 30 Dec. 1856 WILLARD B. GOFF, b. 22 July
             1833, res. Auburn in 1872, son of William and
             Louisa (Read) Goff.
        iii. BETSEY P., b. 14 Apr. 1837, d. 11 Mar. 1878;
             m. JOHN T. PACKARD, b. Parkman ME 3 Feb.
             1828, son of Silvanus and Mary (Washburn)
             Packard, who had m. 1st Irene Cole of Cam-
             bridge (Charles Packard Wright, Descendants
             of Samuel Packard [nd], MHS, 154).
1234.   v.   HELEN LOUISA, b. 7 Jan. 1839; m. HORATIO
             NUTTING.
1235.   v.   JAMES SULLIVAN, b. 6 Sept. 1841.

585. GEORGE W.[7] 1807-1868 [191 Timothy[6]] was born at Mount
Vernon 18 Apr. 1807, died at Cambridge 21 July 1868, 61y;
married first BETSEY CARLL (or CLARK), born about 1817 (33 in
1850); married second at Cambridge 11 Aug. 1867 NANCY WATSON
[# 565] (town VRs; Cornman Ms).
He was a taxpayer at Augusta in 1844, and a farmer there in
1850. Julia Cornman said he had four or five children who
died young.
His estate was administered 6 Oct. 1868 (SomCP, 23:428-9);
no children were listed as heirs.

Children by Betsey:

        i.   OLIVE P.[8] b. Mt Vernon 21 Feb. 1841, not in
             1850 census.
        ii. GEORGE, b. c1847 (3 in 1850).

586. JOHN HOVEY[7] 1811-1870 [191 Timothy[6]] was born at
Mount Vernon 17 Dec. 1811, died there 4 Dec. 1870, 60y; mar-
ried at Belgrade 11 Mar. 1838 (Mt. Vernon int. 18 Feb.) NANCY
BUTTERFIELD, born at Farmington ME in 1814, died at Mt. Ver-
non 4 Apr. 1892, 77y 7m 28d (Mt. Vernon and Belgrade VRs;
Cornman Ms).
Burials are in Taylor Yard, Mt. Vernon. He was a farmer.

Children, born at Mount Vernon:

1236. i.   LUCY JANE[8], b. 1 Aug. 1837; m. SAMUEL STAIN,
            JR.
1237. ii. TIMOTHY, b. 29 Jan. 1839.
       iii. MARTHA ANN, b. 16 Aug. 1840.
       iv. MERINDA, b. c1842 (8 in 1850), d. 6 Jan. 1863,
            20y 10m (GS).
       v.   LEANDER P., b. 8 Nov. 1843, d. 17 July 1863,
            19y 3m (GS), while serving in the army.
       vi. CHARLES W., b. 6 July 1845, d. Mt. Vernon 27
            Mar. 1877, 31y 8m; unm.
       vii. EDWIN W., b. 1 Nov. 1847, res. Readfield ME;
            m. ---- . No ch.

587. LUCY[7] 1815-   [191 Timothy[6]] was born at Mount
Vernon 12 Jan. 1815; married at Rome 30 Dec. 1838 CHARLES D.
HALE of Kingsbury ME, born about 1815, lived at Belgrade
Mills (letter from Mrs. Charles C. Hale in 1914--Cornman
Papers). In 1850 Charles, 35, and Lucy, 33, lived at Mt.
Vernon between the homes of John H. and Warren Leighton;
their household included her father Timothy, 77.

Children (**Hale**):

i.   CHARLES C , b. 27 May 1847 (3 in 1850, but b. in 1857
      per wife), d. Cambridge ME 30 Jan. 1895; m. ---- .
ii.   ELDESTA [Dusty], b. c1849 (1 in 1850); m. ----
      CHANDLER.
iii. GEORGIA.

588. SOPHRONIA[7] 1808-1885 [193 David[6] and Lydia Rogers]
was born at Mount Vernon 11 Dec. 1808, died there 8 Mar. 1885
(or 1889); married there int. 20 May 1829 EMERSON STAIN, born
there 22 Oct. 1806, died there 24 Oct. 1873, son of Emerson
and Rebecca (Carr) Stain (Mt. Vernon VRs; Cornman Ms).

Children (**Stain**), born at Mt. Vernon:

i.   DAVID, b. 20 Jan. 1830; m. MARY ROBBINS.
ii.   JAMES FRANKLIN, b. 10 Nov. 1831; m. MARY ---- .
iii. (DORENDA) CAROLINE, b. 12 Oct. 1833; m. BENJAMIN
      WELLS, son of Stephen Wells.

589. LUCINDA[7] 1810-1866 [193 David[6] and Lydia Rogers] was
born at Mount Vernon 25 Sept. 1810, died 9 Aug. 1866; married
at Rome 20 Aug. 1831 JOHN HAMMONS (Rome VRs; Cornman Ms).

Children (**Hammons**), born at Rome:

i.   IRA, bp. 26 Dec. 1831.
ii.   ?MATILDA, res. Rome; m. ---- VARNUM.
iii. ?ELLEN.
iv.   MARY M., bp. 8 Oct. 1835.
v.   HENRY F., bp. 8 Sept. 1837.
vi.   JAMES B., bp. 6 May 1839.
vii. JOHN, bp. 17 Nov. 1841.
viii. JULIANA, bp. 6 Aug. 1843.

590. NATHANIEL[7] 1812-1891 [193 David[6] and Lydia Rogers]
was born at Mount Vernon 9 Aug. 1812, died there 24 Mar. 1891
(20 Mar., 78y per GS); married at Rome 30 Nov. 1837 MARY L.
FOLSOM, born 8 May 1819, died at Mt. Vernon 21 June 1891,
72y, daughter of Peter Sanborn, Jr., and Mary (Lane) Folsom
(Mt. Vernon VRs; Folsom Fam., 1:364; Chapman, Lane Gen.,
1:24). Burials are in Bean Cemetery. He was a Mt. Vernon
farmer.

Children, born at Mt. Vernon:

	i.	CHARLOTTE ORINTHA[8], b. 7 Nov. 1839, d. 9 Sept. 1841, 22m.
	ii.	JOHN HENRY, b. 1 May 1841, d. 21 May 1847, 6y.
	iii.	PETER LORILLARD, b. 18 Feb. 1843, d. 19 May 1847, 4y 3m.
1238.	iv.	ROSCOE GREEN, b. 10 Apr. 1845.
1239.	v.	EDWARD EVERETT, b. 12 May 1847.
1240.	vi.	(NATHANIEL) COREY, b. 25 Feb. 1850.
	vii.	MARIETTA, b. 2 Jan. 1856; m. Mt. Vernon 28 Nov. 1878 MARION F. EATON of Vienna, b. in Oct. 1844, listed at Vienna in 1880 and 1900. Ch. Alton W. b. in 1879, Fritz R. b. in Apr. 1884.

591. ORINDA S.[7] 1815-1901 [193 David[6] and Lydia Rogers]
was born at Mount Vernon 30 Jan. 1815, died at Dixmont ME 25
May 1901; married at Mt. Vernon 27 Mar. 1838 ROBERT DAVIS
CROCKER, born at Barre MA 7 Aug. 1812, died at Dixmont 18
July 1895, son of Nathaniel and Lydia (Goddard) Crocker
(records of descendant Frances DeMars; town VRs; Cornman Ms).

Children (**Crocker**), born at Dixmont:

i.   HENRY DAVIS, d. infant.
ii.   LEWIS NELSON, b. 18 May 1840, d. Dixmont 30 Nov.
      1919; m. there 22 Aug. 1861 VESTA J. BEAN, b. Dix-
      mont 24 Dec. 1842, d. Detroit ME 8 Apr. 1913, dau.
      of James Madison and Betsey Jane (Plummer) Bean.
iii. ALBERT DAVIS, b. 4 June 1842, d. Dixmont 10 Jan.
      1923; m. 6 Mar. 1872 ABBIE B. WRIGHT, b. 8 Oct.
      1843, d. Jackson ME 26 June 1923, dau. of J. H. and
      Dorothy Wright.
iv.   MARY FRANCES, b. 2 Sept. 1844, d. 14 Apr. 1920; m. 1
      Jan. 1866 ASHLEY CLARY THORNDIKE, b. 5 June 1839, d.
      Millinocket ME 14 Apr. 1920. She owned grandfather
      David's family Bible (Cornman Ms).
v.   EMMA CARRIE, b. 19 Sept. 1849, d. Jackson 29 June
      1924; m. 16 June 1867 EVERETT EDWARD MORTON, b.
      Jackson 21 Dec. 1844, d. there 10 Oct. 1921,
      son of Alonzo and Mary (Croxford) Morton.

592. EBENEZER CARL[7] 1817-1919 [193 David[6] and Lydia
Rogers] was born at Mount Vernon 27 Jan. 1817, died there 21
Dec. 1919, 102y 10m 24d; married there 17 Dec. 1850 LUCY ANN
CARR, born at Vienna ME 14 July 1832, died at Mt. Vernon 10
May 1896, 83y 9m 26d, daughter of Stephen and Betsey (Soper)
Carr (Mt. Vernon and ME VRs; his letter in 1907--Cornman
Papers). Burials are in Bean Cemetery.

Eben was a merchant, owner and operator of the Mount Vernon
House. He was interviewed for an article in the Portland
Sunday Telegram 11 Feb. 1917; he was at that time the oldest
voter in ME.

Children, born at Mt. Vernon (VRs):

      i.   IDA ELDORA[8], b. 28 May 1854, d. 31 Mar. 1856
            or 29 June 1857 (both dates in VRs).
1241. ii.   ALICE BETSEY, b. 11 Nov. 1857; m. WILLIAM M.
            TYLER.

593. DAVID[7] 1825-1858 [193 David[6] and Lydia Rogers] was
born at Mount Vernon 25 Jan. 1825, died there 22 Sept. 1858,
33y 8m; married PHILSA HEATH, who died 28 Apr. 1876, daughter
of Gilman and Lydia Heath (Mt. Vernon VRs; Cornman Ms).
Burials are in Bean Cemetery.

Child, mother unknown, born at Mt. Vernon:

1242. i.   DAVID FRANKLIN[8], b. 5 Oct. 1843.

Children by Philsa, born at Mt. Vernon:

     ii.   IDA ELDORA, d. at 10m 5d.
    iii.   IDA ELDORA, d. 29 June 1851, 16y 3d.
     iv.   PHILSA A., d. 29 June 1857.

594. PETER[7] 1794-   [194 Moses[6] and Margaret Carll] was
born at Mount Vernon 30 Oct. 1794 (30 Nov. in Rome VRs),
lived at Wakesha, Kalamazoo Co. MI; married first at Williamson, Wayne Co. NY 24 Feb. 1825 SALOME S. SHIRTLIFF (Wayne
Sentinel of 9 Mar.); married second before 1850 FANNY ---- ,
born in CT about 1791 (59 in 1850).
He served under Capt. Matthias Lane in 1814 (MA Mil. 1812-
1814, 228). Like his parents he settled in Wayne Co.; in
1830 he and his wife were living at Marion NY with a son and
two daughters, all under 5, and in 1840 they were at Sodus
with a son 15-20 and four females. In 1850 he was a farmer
at Williamson with his wife Fanny.

Children by Salome, born at Wayne Co. NY:

      i.   NATHAN[8], b. c1826 (under 5 in 1830).
     ii.   LUCY W., b. c1827 (23 in 1850); m. Sodus 2
           Feb. 1848 (Co. VRs) MYRON NICHOLS, b. c1825,
           son of Thomas and Elizabeth Nichols. Ch.
           Salome b. Sodus in 1850, perhaps others.
    iii.   MARY [Polly], b. c1830 (20 in 1850); m. Sodus
           15 Mar. 1849 DANIEL D. PULVER, b. c1827. Ch.
           Francis b. Sodus in 1850, perhaps others.

595. MORDECAI[7] 1796-1846 [194 Moses[6] and Margaret Carll]
was born at Mount Vernon 25 Mar. 1796, died at Sturgis MI 5
Apr. 1846; married in NY VESTA C. CONANT, born 5 Jan. 1799,
daughter of Sylvanus and Eleanor (Spooner) Conant of Medina
NY (Conant Fam., 260; Cornman Ms).

He served under Capt. Matthias Lane in Sept. 1814, and then
under Capt. John Gould in Nov. (MA Mil. 1812-14, 228, 283).
He went to Wayne Co. NY with his parents, and then later
settled in MI.

Children, born in Wayne Co.:

1243. i.   EMILY[8], b. 25 June 1825; m. JAMES WREN.
       ii.   PORTER, b. 31 Mar. 1828, d. Sturgis 15 Mar.
             1899; unm.
       iii. (WILLIAM) SPENCER, b. 25 Apr. 1832, d. 22 May
             1873, res. Denver CO; m. 18 Nov. 1858 HELEN
             S. HATCH, b. LeRoy NY 30 Sept. 1840, res.
             Toledo OH, dau. of Harvey and Sarepta (Lyman)
             Hatch (Ruth A Hatch-Hale, Genealogy and
             History of the Hatch Family [Salt Lake City,
             1928], 392). No ch.

596. ENOCH[7] 1797-1856 [194 Moses[6] and Margaret Carll] was
born at Mount Vernon 6 Nov. 1797, died at Lima, LaGrange Co.
IN in Nov. 1856; married in NY PHOEBE COWAN, born at Providence RI 29 Oct. 1799, died at Lima 1 Nov. 1859, daughter of
David and Esther Cowan (Cornman Ms).
He went to Wayne Co. NY with his parents, and about 1835
settled in IN. In 1850, his LaGrange Co. household included
his seven living children.

Children, six born in Wayne Co., the last three at Lima:

       i.   ANDREW[8], b. 1 Aug. 1825, d. 12 June 1832.
       ii.   DAVID, b. 24 Nov. 1826, d. 20 Oct. 1897; m.
             ELIZABETH FLEMMING, adopted dau. of Elder A
             Flemming. No ch. She m. 2nd at Sturgis MI
             ---- PEARSON.
       iii. MARINUS, b. 23 Oct. 1828, d. 30 Sept. 1852.
       iv.   EMERY, b. 23 Sept. 1830, d. 24 Aug. 1832.
1244. v.   NELSON, b. 1 May 1832.
1245. vi.   ELISHA, b. 16 June 1834.
1246. vii. WILLIAM WALLACE, b. 15 Apr. 1836.
       viii. NANCY, b. 17 Sept. 1840, d. 9 Jan. 1913; unm.
       ix.   JOHN COWAN, b. 29 June 1842, d. 29 Mar. 1903;
             unm.

597. JONATHAN[7] 1803-1881 [194 Moses[6] and Margaret Carll]
was born at Rome ME 23 May 1803, died at Geneva NY 14 Feb.
1881 (Geneva Gazette of 18 Feb.); married ANN BRADLEY, born
in CT in 1811 (GS; 69 in 1880), died in 1901 (GS), daughter
of Lewis and Sarah (Waterbury) Bradley of Marion NY (Cornman
Ms; Lewis H. Clark, History of the Churches of Sodus, N. Y.
[1876], 36).
He was a merchant in 1860, aged 54; his Sodus household
included an Elizabeth Wilcox, born in CT in 1790. A year
before his death, the couple moved to Geneva, where he had a
shop selling "Yankee Notions." Burials are in Pleasantview
Cemetery, Williamson.
In a letter written in 1902 his Sodus neighbor Mary A.
Clark stated he had settled at Sodus in 1856, and that his
children lived at Geneva (Cornman Papers).

Children, probably born at Williamson:

i. PHILO W.[8], b. in 1836 (GS), d. Sodus 25
Aug. 1862. He enl. in 1861 in Co. K, 44th NY
Inf. Rgt., and was disch. with tuberculosis
in 1862 at Philadelphia (NA-MSR).

ii. CAROLINE A , b. in 1838, d. in 1854 (GS).

iii. LEWIS B., b. c1840 (19 in 1860, 24 in 1864),
d. Hawkeye IA 8 Jan. 1881; m. HANNAH ADAMS,
b. NY in June 1843, res. alone Eden Tp NY in
1900, widow He was bur. at Bethel, Fayette
Co. IA. He served in Co. B, 9th NY Heavy
Artillery Rgt, in 1864-65 (NA-MSR).

iv. ?ELIZABETH, b. in 1841, d. 1919; m. ---- VanWIE
(GS).

v. ANN ELIZA, b. c1846 (14 in 1860).

vi. ALICE A., b. 23 Oct. 1849; m. Sodus 25 Feb.
1873 FREDERICK VanHUBEN of Geneva, b. in
Switzerland c1851. Ch. Herbert, aged 1 in
the 1875 census.

598. DAVID[7] 1804-1891 [194 Moses[6] and Margaret Carll] was
born at Rome ME 22 Nov. 1804, died at Sodus, Wayne Co. NY 4
Apr. 1891 (VRs), 84y 4m (GS); married in Jan. 1836 JULIA ANN
DANFORTH, born 23 May 1815, died at Sodus 24 Feb. 1888, 72y
9m (GS), daughter of William and Cynthia (Noble) Danforth
(Lucius M. Boltwood, Family of Thomas Noble [Hartford CT,
1878], 432); letters of son Charles and of Mary Clark--
Cornman Papers). He had no children, but adopted his wife's
nephew.
In 1840 they were listed at Marion NY. He was an elder of
the Sodus Presbyterian Church, and owned a dry-goods store.
He enlisted in the 98th NY Inf. Rgt., but was soon discharged
for disability.

Child, adopted, used Leighton surname:

-- CHARLES ADELBERT, b. Sodus in 1850, res. NYC;
m. in 1876 CORNELIA T. GOLDING. He was a
broker. Ch. Kate Golding d. in 1879.

599. SAMUEL[7] 1812-1875 [?194 Moses[6] and Margaret Carll]
was born in ME in 1812 (38 in 1850), died at Otsego, Allegan
Co. MI 2 Feb. 1875, 64y 4m 8d (MI VRs); married HANNAH ---- ,
born in NY about 1817 (32 in 1850), died at Otsego 16 May
1873, 56y 2m 10d (county VRs).
In 1840 a Samuel B. Leighton was listed at York, Livingston
Co. NY. In 1850, Samuel was at Otsego, his household including Royal Sherwood, 39, who was born in NY.
Placing Samuel as a son of Moses is conjectural. A page of
a letter in the Cornman Papers from a Carll relative advised
Mrs. Cornman to write to Amos Leighton to see if "he or some
of his family can give you some records of Israel & Daniel
Leighton. I think Daniel was Amos Leighton's Grandfather, &
son of Solomon. Amos' father was Samuel."
Samuel was certainly a grandson of Solomon, and very likely
a son of Moses.

Children:

    i.   RUTH[8], b. in NY c1842 (8 in 1850).
    ii.   AMOS, b. in NY in Sept. 1844, res. Otsego in
            1880 and 1900; m. Plainwell MI in 1870 CHAR-
            LOTTE [Lottie] HEALEY, b. in Canada in Sept.
            1852. Ch. PEARL[9] b. in MI in 1879.
    iii. MARY J., b. in NY c1847 (3 in 1850); m. Otsego
            4 Apr. 1866 (co. record) JOHN HOGLE, 24.
    iv.   ALICE ADELIA, b. Otsego 22 Dec. 1853; m. Casco
            Tp, Allegan Co. 8 Feb. 1880 (co. record)
            CLARENCE EVERETT FOWLER.

600. ISRAEL[7] 1813-1891 [194 Moses[6] and Margaret Carll] was born at Rome ME 7 July 1813, died at Holland, Isabella Co. MI 19 May 1891; married at Lyons, Wayne Co. NY 5 May 1842 SUSAN OWENS, born at Lyons 22 July 1817, died at Wakeshima, Kalamazoo Co. MI 2 Dec. 1870, daughter of Hugh and Abigail Owens; married second JEANIE ---- , born in NY about 1827 (53 in 1880). His household in 1880 included a step-daughter Emily Steinburg, 23, her husband Waite, 37, and their child Clara B. Steinburg, 4.
He was first a schoolteacher, and then a stone mason and contractor at Sodus NY. He left NY about 1853, first settling at Lima IN, and then becoming a farmer in MI. He died while living with his son Charles (History of Allegon County, Mich. [1907], 291; Cornman Ms; data from Charles--Cornman Papers; records of Henry F. Thomas).

Children by Susan:

1247. i.   CHARLES H.[8], b. Sodus 30 Aug. 1843.
1248. ii.   NELSON EWANS, b. Sodus 2 Mar. 1848.
       iii. ANDREW, b. Lima IN 1 Mar. 1854, res. Rose Hill
              NC; m. 1 July 1903 FRANCES DORANG, b. 27 May
              1884, dau. of James and Sue (Hallen) Dorang.
              He was an ordained minister.

601. MOSES[7] 1797-   [?196 John[6] and Esther] was born at Mount Vernon 26 Oct. 1797. He was very probably the Moses Leighton listed in Switzerland Co. IN in 1830, with a wife, a son under 5, another between 5 and 10, and a daughter under 5. In 1850, he was living in Woodford Co. IL, 52, with his wife SALOME ---- , 50, born in ME, their five children, and an Amanda Smith, 6. In each census he lived near Humphrey [# 607], suggesting a close relationship.
Switzerland County was settled by natives of NJ, of some southern states and of Switzerland; it was far from the typical migration routes of New Englanders. Other Leightons appeared in records there, such as Cyrus W. who married in Switzerland Co. 14 Feb. 1824 Elizabeth Newbold; they must also stem from Solomon Leighton of Mt. Vernon.

Children, born in IN:

    i.   JOSEPH[8], b. c1825 (25 in 1850).
    ii.   HIRAM, b. c1828 (22 in 1850); m. in Tazewell
            Co. IL 13 Jan. 1839 ANNA BELL SHOBER, b. in
            VA say 1825 (25 in 1850, 31 in 1860)--div.

No ch. In 1850 he res. alone in Woodford Co.
Hiram probably m. 2nd 5 Mar. 1852 ELIZABETH
AYRES. Annabell m. 2nd 26 Apr. 1849 Lewis E.
McKinney, who d. Pekin IL 20 Feb. 1851; she
m. 3rd Thomas McKinney (co. records).
iii. CYNTHIA, b. c1831 (19 in 1850).
iv. FRANCES, b. c1832 (18 in 1850).
v. son [Sardina?], b. c1834 (16 in 1850).

602. WILLIAM[7] 1800-   [? 196 John[6] and Esther] was born
say in 1800, lived in Switzerland Co. IN, died in IL; married
ELIZABETH (----) Webber, born 7 June 1793, died 14 Aug.
1857, 64y 3m 7d (GS, Sheeta Cemetery, Wyoming IL). Elizabeth
had married first ---- Webber: two children James and Philip;
she married third Joseph Ackley: son Joseph.
      William's parentage like Moses's is conjectural, although
he too is almost certainly a grandson of Solomon of Mount
Vernon ME. Family tradition has called him a son of Jacob
[# 608], but he must have been of Jacob's generation instead.
The death certificates of his sons listed the parents as
unknown.
      Theda (Leighton) Chapman compiled a genealogy of William's
descendants for circulation within the family; it did not
cite sources--nor many place names. Her work has been further
documented for some family groups by (Comilla) Jean Leighton
[# 2270]; other information has been derived from censuses.

Children, born in Switzerland Co. IN:

1249. i.   JOHN[8], b. 2 Feb. 1827.
1250. ii. WILLIAM, b. in 1829.

603. DANIEL[7] 1796-   [197 Daniel[6] and Ruth] was born at
Mount Vernon 30 Dec. 1796 or 30 Jan. 1797 (both in VRs); mar-
ried POLLY ---- .
      He served under Capt. Matthias Lane from Rome in 1814 (MA
Mil. 1812-14, 228). He was probably the Daniel listed at
Sangerville ME in 1830.

Children, listed in Parkman TRs 2:91:

i.   RUEL, b. 5 Dec. 1831.
ii. POLLY JANE, b. 28 Aug. 1833.

604. SMITHSON[7] 1798-   [197 Daniel[6] and Ruth] was born
at Mount Vernon 17 Dec. 1798, lived in Waldo Co. ME in 1850;
married at Mt. Vernon 5 Dec. 1822 (Rome int. 9 Nov.) ELIZA M.
ZALLOLLEY, born at Mt. Vernon 6 Jan. 1801 (VRs; 17 May 1805
per Cornman Ms), lived in MI, 76, with her son Leander in
1880 (town VRs). Births were listed in both Mt. Vernon and
Parkman records. He was a farmer, living at Rome in 1823,
Mt. Vernon in 1830, Parkman in 1840, and in 1850 at Frankfort
as a ships' carpenter.

Children, all but the first born at Mt. Vernon:

i.   JANE MARIAH[8], b. Rome 29 July 1823.
ii. FRANCES AUGUSTA, b. 30 Aug. 1826.

1251. iii. CAROLINE EMERY, b. 29 Dec. 1828; m. HEMAN A.
             FOWLER.
       iv.   ELIZABETH ANN, b. 1 Jan. 1831.
       v.   FRANKLIN PORTER [Frank], b. 9 Jan. 1834, res.
             Port Huron, St. Clair Co. MI in 1880; m. EMMA
             ---- , b. in NH c1840. Ch. FRANK⁹ b. in
             MI c1871.
       vi.   RUTH ISABELLA, b. 23 Dec. 1835; m. Mt. Vernon
             14 Feb. 1862 (JAMES) FRANK ROBINSON, b. 23
             Sept. 1835, d. Mt. Vernon 4 May 1898, son of
             Nathaniel and Eliza (Leighton) Robinson
             [# 358].
1252. vii. LEANDER A , b. in Aug. 1840.

   605. LOVINA⁷ 1804-1898 [197 Daniel⁶ and Ruth] was born at
Rome 27 Aug. 1804, died 15 Jan. 1898; married at Mt. Vernon
23 Jan. 1823 JOTHAM MOORE, born at York ME 15 Jan. 1800, died
at Parkman ME 9 Nov. 1871, son of David and Dorcas (Moore)
Moore (town VRs; records of descendant Roxanna Saucier).
He was a Mt. Vernon farmer, but by 1840 the family had
settled at Parkman.
Burials are in North Dexter.

Children (**Moore**), ten born at Mt. Vernon, last four at
   Parkman (VRs):

i.   son, b. 15 Feb. 1824, d.y.
ii.   ROBERT, b. 27 Feb. 1825, d. 25 Feb. 1828.
iii.   SAMUEL JUDSON, b. 7 Feb. 1827; m. 1st Parkman MARY
       TYLER, who d. 3 June 1859, 26y 3m 12d; m. 2nd 3 July
       1860 MARY WEYMOUTH.
iv.   JOHN COLBY, b. 20 Oct. 1828, d. Thomaston ME 11 Apr.
       1894; m. Parkman 5 Apr. 1858 REBECCA PACKARD, b.
       Parkman 3 Dec. 1837, d. Abbott ME 10 Apr. 1904,
       dau. of James and Lydia (Harris) Packard.
v.   LUCINDA CATHERINE, b. 22 Jan. 1831, d. Parkman 23
       Aug. 1906; m. ALFRED AUSTIN.
vi.   JOTHAM BICKFORD, b. 16 Feb. 1833.
vii.   CHARLOTTE DAVIS, b. 4 Feb. 1835, d.y.
viii. OLIVE JANE, b. 4 Feb. 1835 (twin), d. in 1859; m.
       JOHN HARLOW.
ix.   ROBERT M., b. 9 Jan. 1837.
x.   WILLIAM H., b. 11 Sept. 1838, d. 18 Sept. 1908; m.
       ARVILLA TREFEATHERING.
xi.   GAYLAN HARRISON, b. 11 Jan. 1841; m. Parkman 7 Sept.
       1862 SUSAN D. W. HOLBROOK--div.
xii.   CHARLES, b. 4 Mar. 1844.
xiii. JANE, b. 22 Aug. 1846, d. 11 June 1865.
xiv.   GEORGE, b. 30 Aug. 1849.

   606. LIBERTY⁷ 1808-1893 [197 Daniel⁶ and Ruth] was born at
Rome 4 Aug. 1808, died 5 May 1893; married at Sangerville ME
in June 1832 ELBRIDGE OAK, born at Sangerville 18 Aug. 1813,
died at Flora, Clay Co. IL 12 Feb. 1889, son of Solomon and
Susanna (Clark) Elbridge (town VRs; Henry L. Oak, Family
Register/Nathaniel Oak of Marlborough, Mass. [1906], 42).
They settled in IL about 1848.

Children (**Oak**):

i.   CYRUS, b. Parkman 21 Jan. 1835.
ii.   MARSHALL, b. Parkman 27 Oct. 1836.
iii. JOHN.
iv.   SUSAN.
v.   ABIGAIL.

607. HUMPHREY VARNEY[7] 1797-1880 [198 Pelatiah[6] and Mary]
was born at Mount Vernon 29 Apr. 1797, died at Corydon, Wayne
Co. IA, 28 Dec. 1880, 84y (co. record); married in Switzer-
land Co. IN 6 Apr. 1821 FRANCES [Fannie] BROUY, born at Cul-
pepper Courthouse VA 1 July 1806, died at Howard, Wayne Co.
IA 15 June 1881, 75y 11m 12d (co. record), daughter of Elisha
Brouy or Broy. An unlikely family tradition held that she
was a doctor and medical school graduate. Burials are in
Medicineville Cemetery, Howard.
Humphrey went west with his parents, and in 1830 was listed
in Switzerland Co. IN with a wife, son and two daughters.
The family then settled in Tazewell County IL; in 1840 his
household there included a slave. By 1850 he was settled at
Metamora, Woodford Co. IL.
About 1854 he moved on to IA, and tried to establish a town
at Medicineville. His speculation failed when he was unable
to sell off lots. In 1856, he owned a store at now-vanished
Somerset, Mercer Co MO, near the IA line. With his son John,
he obtained rights to "construct and vend Johnson's Improved
Folding Beadstids," and set up shop at Centerville. On 30
May 1859 he sold a Medicineville lot to his son-in-law Wil-
liam Prince--a lot his son Jacob inherited from the Princes
in 1899 (records of descendants Billie Leighton Flora, Sharon
Thorne, Dale Ginn and Kathy Gardner).
In 1860 and 1870, he lived at Howard Tp; in 1880 his house-
hold at Wright Tp included Rachel and her Dewey children.

Children:

1253. i.   PELATIAH[8], b. in IN 19 Aug. 1823.
       ii.   OLIVE, b. in IN c1825 (25 in 1850).
1254. iii. JACOB, b. Metamora IL 1 July 1831.
1255. iv.   WILLIAM, b. in IL c1833 (17 in 1850).
1256. v.   JOHN BROY, b. in IL 14 Dec. 1835.
1257. vi.   RACHEL J., b. in IL c1837; m. ANDREW DEWEY and
             JOHN STINE.
1258. vii. HUMPHREY VARNEY, b. in IL 21 Nov. 1839.
1259. viii. FRANCES EVELYN, b. in IL 17 Aug. 1842; m.
             WILLIAM PRINCE.
       ix.   THOMAS, b. in IL c1843 (7 in 1850).

608. JACOB[7] 1804-1835 [198 Pelatiah[6] and Mary] was born at
Rome ME 18 Feb. 1804, died in Tazewell County IL 17 Nov. 1835
(probate record); married at Vevay, Switzerland Co. IN 1 June
1826 (co. record) CHRISTINA J. PETERS, born in PA 8 Mar.
1808, died at Groveland IL 8 July 1890, 82y 4m 0d (GS, Groveland Cemetery), daughter of John Peters. She married second
in Tazewell Co. 9 Jan. 1839 Kezer Hancock.
Jacob went west to IN with his father; in 1830, he was
listed in Switzerland Co. IN with two sons under 5. He moved
his family to IL about 1831, where he owned a farm adjacent

to his father's. His widow was named administratrix of his
estate, but declined in favor of her father-in-law Pelatiah
(Tazewell Co. probate records; records of Helen Price
Joiner). In 1850 Kezer Hancock's household included Christina, 40, and her four Leighton sons.

Children:

         i.   NOAH, b. in IN in 1829, d. Eureka, Woodford
              Co. IL 29 Apr. 1905; m. per death record.
1260.   ii.   DAVID, b. in IN 12 Apr. 1830.
1261. iii.   ANDREW J., b. in IL 29 Nov. 1832.
1262.   iv.   SILAS WASHINGTON, b. in IL 4 June 1833.

   609.   NOAH REUBEN[7] 1812-1893 [?198 Pelatiah[6] and Mary]
was born in ME 18 June 1812, died at Wheeler's Grove IA 21
July 1893; married in Tazewell Co. IL 16 Apr. 1835 (county
record) AMANDA ANN EWING, born near Russellville, Logan Co.
KY 6 May 1812, died at Wheeler's Grove 13 Apr. 1884, daughter
of Robartus and Mary Ewing. Burials are in Buckner Cemetery,
Montgomery Co. IA
   The 1840 census listed him in Wayne Co. IL; in 1850, he was
at Metamora, Woodford Co. IL, farming land near Humphrey's.
The next year he settled at Sugar Creek, Logan Co. IL, on the
Chris Ewing farm, and in 1865 at Wheeler's Grove, Pottawattamie Co. IA
   Although no proof has yet been found, it is a reasonable
conjecture that he, Humphrey and Jacob were either brothers
or first cousins (Bible and family records of descendants
Lynette Strickland and Olive Thompson; letter and records
from Sidnah in 1907-Cornman Papers)

   Children, birthplaces uncertain:

         i.   ROBERT EWING[8], b. 29 Mar. 1836, d. 19 Oct.
              1840.
        ii.   WILLIAM L. D., b. 21 July 1838, d. 1 Oct.
              1840.
       iii.   MARY MAHALA, b. IL 17 Oct. 1840, d. Glendale
              CA 27 Jan. 1927, res. Delta CO in 1907; m.
              GILES H. COWLEY.
        iv.   (RICHARD) BAXTER, b. IL 24 Sept. 1842, d.
              Helena AR 11 Aug. 1863, of yellow fever,
              serving in Co. F , 106th IL Inf. Rgt.
1263.   v.   MARTHA ELEANOR, b. IL 2 Jan. 1845; m. SAMUEL
              CALDWELL ALSWORTH.
1264.   vi.   FRANCES ELIZA, b. near Peoria IL 14 Apr. 1847;
              m. PETER G. CONKLE.
       vii.   TALITHA JANE, b. IL 20 Apr. 1849, d. 12 May
              1855.
1265. viii. SIDNAH ROBINSON, b. Logan Co. IL 10 July 1851.
        ix.   JAMES WHITTIER (twin), b. 10 July, d. 31 Aug.,
              1851

   610.   SAMUEL[7] 1816-1897 [199 Samuel[6] and Dorothea Furbush]
was born at Mount Vernon ME 17 Nov. 1816 (1813 in Parkman
records), died at Parkman ME 14 Nov. 1897, 80y 11m 27d; married at Mt. Vernon 4 Dec. 1847 SYLVINA LEIGHTON, born there
9 Apr. 1822, died at Parkman 11 Nov. 1901, 79y 7m 2d (suicide

by hanging), daughter of David and Lydia (Rogers) Leighton
[# 193] (town and ME VRs). Burials are in the Bean Cemetery,
Mt. Vernon.
In 1841 he bought a 100-acre farm at Parkman. He was chosen
selectman for two terms (Biographical Review ... Somerset,
Piscataquis, Hancock, Washington and Aroostook Counties [Bos-
ton, 1898], 686-7; letter from Lizzie Ring Leighton--Cornman
Papers). His wife was sometimes listed as Sylvania. In 1900
she was living with her son J. Blasland.

Children, born at Parkman:

1266. i.   FREDERICK^8, b. 29 Mar. 1849.
       ii.   LYDIA ELDORA, b. 12 Mar. 1852, d. Parkman 14
             July 1854, 2y 4m (GS).
1267. iii. (JOSEPH) BLASLAND, b. 8 July 1855.
1268. iv.   IRA GARDNER, b. 23 Apr. 1857.

611. HOSEA S.^{7} 1819-1898 [199 Samuel^6 and Dorothea Fur-
bush] was born at Mount Vernon 25 Aug. 1819 (20 July in Parkman VRs), died at New Sharon ME 21 Jan. 1898, 78y 4m 27d;
married first at Mt. Vernon 23 Apr. 1842 MARY F. PAGE, born
at New Sharon 28 Mar. 1823 (5 Apr. in Parkman VRs), died
there 28 Mar. 1894, 70y, 11m 13d, daughter of Nathan and Ruth
(Elliot) Page; married second there 14 Feb. 1895 widow ALICE
R. (GRAY) Sanders, born at Embden ME 9 Feb. 1839, died at New
Sharon 18 Nov. 1928, 89y 9m 9d, daughter of Aaron and
Patience (Colcott) Gray (town and ME VRs; Cornman Ms).
He at various times lived on the Pacific coast, had a grain
and flour business at Boston, and had a store and farm at
Dexter ME.

Children, by Mary:

       i.   CHESTER^8, d. in WA.
1269. ii.   DANIEL, b. say 1848.

612. DOROTHY F.^{7} 1823-1897 [199 Samuel^6 and Dorothea Fur-
bush] was born at Mount Vernon 5 Aug. 1823, died there 21
Oct. 1897; married there 7 June 1846 GEORGE SULLIVAN WORCES-
TER, born at Thornton NH 18 May 1825, died at Mt. Vernon, son
of Noah and Nancy (Fogg) Worcester (Sarah Alice Worcester,
Descendants of Rev. William Worcester [Boston, 1914], 167;
Whitten, Samuel Fogg, #931; town VRs). In 1850 Lucy J.
Leighton [# 1236] lived with them.

Children (Worcester), born at Mt. Vernon:

       i.   (GEORGE) JEROME, b. 4 Mar. 1847; m. EMMA B. VARNUM.
       ii.   EMILY B., b. 7 June 1849.
       iii. FRED, d.y.

613. NATHAN^7 1804-1883 [200 Benjamin^6 and Sally Brown] was
born at Mount Vernon 2 Feb. 1804, died at Williamston, Ingham
Co. MI 8 Aug. 1883; married first 1 Jan. 1826 ABIGAIL CARLL,
born 27 Aug. 1803, died at Williamston 23 Mar. 1875, daughter
of Benjamin and Molly (Fields) Carll; married second widow
AMANDA (----) Julian, who died in 1891.

Nathan went with his parents to Wayne Co. NY, and lived
there at Lyons and Huron. About 1854, he became a pioneer
settler at Williamston on a 175-acre farm. He was town sup-
ervisor, treasurer, justice of the peace and school inspector
(Portrait and Biographical Record of Kalamazoo, Allegan and
Van Buren Counties, Mich. [Chicago, 1892], 535; Portrait and
Biographical History of Ingham and Livingston Counties, Mich.
[Chicago, 1891], 631; Cornman Ms).

Children by Abigail:

  i. SARAH LORILLA[8], b. 22 Oct. 1827, d. William-
      ston 11 July 1891; m. Cherry Valley NY 21
      Sept. 1857 MERRITT CHAPELL, who d. William-
      ston in Sept. 1888, son of Henry and Amy
      Chapell. No ch.
  ii. SUSAN, b. Lyons 19 Feb. 1829, d. Conway MI 28
      Mar. 1908; m. 23 Sept. 1848 WILLIAM H. SHOW-
      ERMAN, b. Huron 12 Sept. 1825, d. Conway 10
      Apr. 1889.
  iii. SYRENA, b. 11 Dec. 1830, d. 14 Aug. 1843.
  iv. MARY L. CODRISKEY, b. Huron 28 Dec. 1832, d.
      Bath MI 16 Sept. 1904; m. 1st TRUMAN CASE of
      Alton NY; m. 2nd SHERBURN D. WATSON.
  v. HIRAM, b. Huron 9 May 1835, d. 25 Oct. 1847.
1270. vi. STEPHEN PHILBRICK, b. Huron 19 Jan. 1837.
1271. vii. NATHAN, b. Huron 26 July 1839.
  viii. ABIGAIL JANE, b. Huron 21 Nov. 1841; m. 16
      Feb. 1868 SILAS E. VANNETER, b. Trenton NJ
      17 Feb. 1838, son of John S. and Catherine
      (Schermerhorn) Vanneter.
  ix. JAMES, b. Huron 10 Aug. 1844, d. in 1845, 1y.
  x. CLARISSA, b. Huron 2 Mar. 1846, res. San Jose
      CA; m. 1st 23 Mar. 1866 JAMES ESPEY, b. Dor-
      setshire, England, 1 Oct. 1845, d. 7 July
      1888, son of Malachi and Charlotte (Larkman)
      Espey; m. 2nd ----GAGE.
1272. xi. NANCY FAIRCHILD, b. Huron 6 Jan. 1849; m.
      SCOTT WALDO and BENJAMIN CARLL.

614. BENJAMIN[7] 1806-1882 [200 Benjamin[6] and Sally Brown]
was born at Mount Vernon ME 11 Apr. 1806, died at Sodus,
Wayne Co. NY 4 Jan. 1882, 75y 8m 24d (GS); married first FAN-
NIE DENNIS, born 20 May 1816, died at Sodus 1 Mar. 1845, 28y
9m 10d (GS), daughter of Moses and Rhoda (Spring) Dennis;
married second CHLOE B. BAKER, born 19 Sept. 1817, died at
Sodus 2 Sept. 1846, 28y 11m 13d (GS), daughter of Amasa and
Ellizabeth Baker; married third SOPHRONIA WHITING, born at
Bridgewater NY 23 Dec. 1807, died at Sodus 26 July 1891 (GS),
daughter of Samuel and Zilpah Whiting (Cornman Ms). Burials
are in Zurich Cemetery, Arcadia NY. He was a farmer.

Children by Fannie, born at Sodus:

1273. i. RHODA RELIANCE[8], b. 15 June 1837; m. GILBERT
      SHAW.
  ii. ANDREW J., b. 11 May 1842, killed in Battle of
      the Wilderness VA 5 May 1864, serving in Co.
      D, 111th NY Inf. Rgt.; unm.

Child by Chloe, born at Sodus:

    iii. CHLOE BERTHEMA, b. 11 May 1846, d. Sodus 13
          Apr. 1871; m. IRA SEBRING. Ch. Ira b. 30
          Mar. 1871.

Child by Sophronia, born at Sodus:

    iv.   FRANCES JOSEPHINE, b. 25 Sept. 1848, d. Sodus
          14 Sept. 1863, 14y 11m 20d.

615. ALVIN[7] 1809-1888 [200 Benjamin[6] and Sally Brown] was
born at Mount Vernon 3 Feb. 1809, died at Eaton Rapids, Eaton
Co. MI 26 July 1888, 79y 5m 23d; married first at Sodus NY 19
Apr. 1833 AURILLA ALDEN, born in NY 21 Dec. 1809, died at
Eaton Rapids 19 Mar. 1856, daughter of Edward E. and Malinda
Alden; married second 12 Nov. 1856 SARAH (----) Hill, widow
of William Hill (Cornman Ms). His first wife was sometimes
called Aurelia.
     Alvin went to Wayne Co. NY as a boy with his parents, and
became a farmer at Sodus. About 1850, he took his family to
MI, where he at first settled at Hamlin Tp, Eaton Co. (Por-
trait and Biographical Album of Barry and Eaton Counties,
Mich. [Chicago, 1891], 690).

Children by Aurilla, born at Sodus NY:

    1274. i.   ALDEN[8], b. 20 Jan. 1834.
           ii.   GEORGE JAPHET, b. 8 Jan. 1836, killed in
                 action Ft. Hudson LA 27 May 1863; unm. He
                 was 1st sgt., 6th MI Heavy Artillery Rgt.
    1275. iii. FRANKLIN S., b. 8 Dec. 1838.
    1276. iv.   SARAH, b. 8 Dec. 1841; m. LUCIUS GIDDINGS.
    1277. v.   MARY MELINDA, b. 13 Apr. 1843; m. GILBERT B.
                 HOGLE.
           vi.   URANA, b. 4 July 1846, d. Eaton Rapids 26
                 Apr. 1910; m. WILLIAM P. BROWN, res. Ellen-
                 dale ND. No ch.

616. GEORGE CLINTON[7] 1812-1902 [200 Benjamin[6] and Sally
Brown] was born at Mount Vernon 8 July 1812, died at Otsego,
Allegan Co. MI 17 Nov. 1902; married in Wayne Co. NY 31 Oct.
1837 ROXELDA DENNIS, born about 1812 (38 in 1850), died at
Otsego 7 Sept. 1867, daughter of Joseph and Hannah Dennis;
married second about 1868 widow EMILY (TRESCOTT) Lawton, born
at East Sheffield MA 1 Oct. 1822, died at Otsego 2 Aug. 1904.
     He was taken to NY by his parents as a child, and in 1850
was listed as a mason at Sodus. In 1851, he took his family
to Eaton Co. MI (Cornman Ms).

Child, born at Lyons NY:

    i.   JAMES ALVIN[8], b. 27 Aug. 1842, d. Otsego MI
          8 Oct. 1875, 33y 1m 12d (MI VRs); unm.

617. ISRAEL[7] 1791-1866 [203 James[6] and Hannah Buzzell] was
born at Barrington NH 24 Jan. 1791, died there 3 Jan. 1866;
married 28 Nov. 1813 MARY BUZZELL, born at Effingham NH 29

Dec. 1789, died at Barrington 7 Dec. 1858, daughter of John
and Elizabeth (Randall) Buzzell (Cornman Ms; town VRs).
In his will, made 4 Apr. 1865, he left $1 to John, $50 and
movables to Mary Elizabeth, and his house and land to James
T., the executor (StrCP, 80:45).

Children, born at Barrington:

1278. i.   JOHN BUZZELL[8], b. 24 Aug. 1826.
1279. ii.   JAMES TWOMBLEY, b. 22 Apr. 1829.
       iii. MARY ELIZABETH, b. 24 Nov. 1831; m. 19 Oct.
             1863, as his 3rd wife, JOSEPH ALBERT CATES,
             b. Barrington 28 Dec. 1825. Ch. Anna Vina b.
             there 28 May 1865.

618. LOIS B.[7] 1800-1878 [203 James[6] and Hannah Buzzell]
was born at Barrington 16 June 1800, died 9 Oct. 1878; married 20 Feb. 1825 (int. 5 Dec. 1824) DAVID BUZZELL, born 17
Aug. 1797, died 5 July 1875, probably son of Solomon Buzzell
(Waterhouse Desc., 1:562; Cornman Ms).

Children (**Buzzell**), born at Barrington:

i.   LYDIA OLIVE, b. 8 May 1826, d. Strafford NH 30 Dec.
       1916; m. 20 Sept. 1848 JOSEPH GARLAND, b. Strafford
       5 Oct. 1821, d. there 26 Jan. 1897, son of Nathaniel
       and Lydia (Caverno) Garland (Garland Gen., 109).
       She was also called Olive L.
ii.   ISRAEL L., b. 9 May 1829, d. 9 Nov. 1871; m. 1 Mar.
       1854 SARAH ELIZABETH DOW.
iii.   SOLOMON, b. 30 May 1833; m. 31 May 1862 SUSAN E.
       ALLEN, b. 18 Dec. 1830.
iv.   DAVID O., b. 7 July 1839; m. 20 Oct. 1863 MARTHA A
       NEAL, b. in 1842, d. 16 Nov. 1902.

619. HARRIET[7] 1803-1886 [203 James[6] and Hannah Buzzell]
was born at Barrington 19 Oct. 1803, died there in June 1886;
married 21 Sept. 1823 SAMUEL ALLEN, born at Lee NH 26 May
1801 (town VRs; Cornman Ms).

Children (**Allen**), born at Barrington:

i.   MARY L., b. 2 Feb. 1824; m. LORENZO TASKER of North-
       wood.
ii.   JAMES L., b. 8 Mar. 1826, d. Rochester 18 Oct. 1898;
       m. MARY A. HOYT, b. 25 July 1827, dau. of Benjamin
       and Mahala Hoyt of Barrington.
iii.   HIRAM, b. 5 Nov. 1828.

620. REUBEN[7] 1792-1843 [204 Reuben[6] and Mary Twombley] was
born at Barrington 30 Sept. 1792, died at Newbury VT 25 Feb.
1843, 52; married in 1814 MARY [Polly] SARGENT, born at
Strafford in 1794, died at Newbury 29 Sept. 1878, 84y, daughter of Joseph and Susan Sargent (Tracy, Reuben Leighton, 9;
Wells, Newbury Hist., 616). Like his father he settled at
Newbury; he cleared his own farm on Leighton's Hill, which
was inherited by his son Lorenzo.

Children, born at Newbury:

1280. i.   LORENZO DOW[8], b. 26 Mar. 1815.
1281. ii.   ROSWELL, b. 22 Oct. 1818.
1282. iii. MARY ANN, b. 29 Apr. 1820; m. JOHN WALLACE.
1283. iv.   SUSAN, b. say 1823; m. WILLIAM WALLACE, JR.
1284. v.   CHARLES, b. 27 Oct. 1825.
       vi.   JOHN LOVEJOY, b. 6 Sept. 1827, d. Newbury 25
             Nov. 1910; m. there 8 Aug. 1849 MARY JANE
             LINDSEY, b. there 3 Dec. 1829, d. there 10
             Mar. 1910, dau. of Hardy and Letitia (Ger-
             ould) Lindsey. Ch. CHARLES WESLEY[9] b.
             Newbury 5 July 1853, d. there 21 Jan. 1895,
             drowned during ice harvest; m. 27 Nov. 1878
             ERMINA HOLT of Derby VT.

   621. LYDIA[7] 1794-1883 [204 Reuben[6] and Mary Twombley] was
born at Barrington 3 May 1794, died 9 Mar. 1883; married at
Bradford VT 10 Mar. 1822 STEPHEN GEORGE, born at Newbury 8
June 1793, died 2 Oct. 1867 (VT VRs; Tracy, Reuben Leighton,
9; Cornman Ms).

Children (**George**), the first three born at Bradford, the
rest at Newbury:

i.   REUBEN L., b. 4 Feb. 1823, d. 26 Aug. 1886; m. MEHIT-
       ABLE CHAMBERLAIN, b. 11 Sept. 1822, d. 7 Jan. 1889,
       dau. of Blanchard and Susanna Chamberlain.
ii.   SAMUEL L., b. 30 July 1824.
iii.   GIDEON, b. 7 May 1826.
iv.   STEPHEN L., b. 16 Apr. 1828.
v.   JOHN S., b. 29 Aug. 1830, d. in Feb. 1901; m. MARY
       JANE WOOD, b. Springfield VT 7 Oct. 1833, d. 20 July
       1897, dau. of George and Mary Wood.
vi.   JAMES W., b. 13 Aug. 1832, d. 1 Aug. 1892; m. 9 Mar.
       1856 DIADAMA BUTTERFIELD, b. 18 Oct. 1836, dau. of
       Welby Butterfield of Topsham VT.
vii.   ALPHONZO W., b. 4 Feb. 1836.

   622. HANNAH[7] 1796-1880 [204 Reuben[6] and Mary Twombley] was
born at Barrington 7 Mar. 1796, died at Lowell MA 8 Nov.
1880; married ROSS C. FORD of Newbury VT, son of Seth Ford
(Tracy, Reuben Leighton, 9; Cornman Ms).

Children (**Ford**):

i.   HAZEN, b. 26 Apr. 1815, d. 6 Dec. 1894; m. 25 Mar.
       1841 CHRISTINE WALLACE, dau. of William Wallace.
       They res. Newbury and Barnet VT.
ii.   ROSS, b. 11 Jan. 1817, d. 1 June 1885; m. Tunbridge
       VT in Feb. 1841 DEBORAH NOYES.
iii.   SETH, b. 29 Aug. 1818; m. AMANDA PADDLEFORD. He was a
       stage driver and horse dealer.
iv.   DAN YOUNG, b. 13 Sept. 1820, d. 25 Sept. 1905; m. 1st
       17 Sept. 1838 CHARLOTTE WOODBURY, d. 14 Feb. 1870;
       m. 2nd Lyndon VT AVA B. MORGAN.
v.   EMILY S., b. 18 Dec. 1822, d. 3 Dec. 1889; m. 5 Oct.
       1843 JAMES Y. PRESCOTT, b. Newbury 21 Dec. 1820, d.
       21 Apr. 1884.

vi.   JANE S., b. 3 Apr. 1825, d. in Jan. 1864; m. Monroe
      VT AUSTIN PADDLEFORD.
vii. MARY S., b. 26 Mar. 1828, d. 7 Aug. 1854; m. Lowell
      MA ---- SHERMAN.
viii. ELIZA V., b. 26 Sept. 1832; m. EDWARD TAPLIN.
ix.   HANNAH H., b. 3 May 1835, d. in NE 11 Jan. 1887;
      m. DANIEL SIMPSON BARTLETT, b. Litchfield NH 8 Nov.
      1835, d. Grinnell IA 28 June 1912, son of Nathan and
      Fannie (Jones) Bartlett. Daniel m. 2nd Kate Wal-
      lace, dau. of John and Mary^8 (Leighton) Wallace
      [# 1282].
x.   LUCIA A., b. 26 July 1837, res. Dennison TX; m. 1st
      JOSEPH ALLEN CHAMBERLAIN; m. 2nd ---- LEVY.
xi.   HELEN H., b. 22 June 1842; m. 18 Nov. 1857 HENRY N.
      NILES.

623. JACOB^7 1797-1867 [204 Reuben^6 and Mary Twombley] was
born at Barrington NH 25 Oct. 1797, died at Corinth VT 31
Mar. 1867; married there 30 June 1822 SALOME BOWERS, born
about 1803, died at Bradford VT 12 May 1862, 59y (VT VRs;
Tracy, Reuben Leighton, 9; Cornman Ms). Burials are in Upper
Plains Cemetery, Bradford.

Children:

      i.   MARTHA^8, b. Newbury 7 Oct. 1823, res. Madison
            WI; m. Bradford VT 7 May 1843 JOSEPH W. WIN-
            SHIP, son of Charles Winship.
      ii.   FREDERICK PLUMMER, b. Newbury 22 Aug. 1824;
            unm.
      iii. WILLIAM, b. Newbury 21 Feb. 1826; m. Salem NY
            JANE ---- . They had 2 daus.: 1 res. TX,
            mar.; and FRANCES^9, res. Salem.
1285. iv.   ANN B., b. Newbury 24 Nov. 1829; m. ----
            PHILLIPS.
      v.   EMILY JANE [Emma], b. say 1833, res. Pueblo
            CO; m. 1st Bradford 22 Dec. 1857 CHARLES
            HEATH (div.); m. 2nd at Pueblo J. [Jack]
            WILLIS. Ch. Luther Heath and others.
1286. vi.   MARY ELIZABETH, b. Bath NH 10 Jan. 1835 (11
            Jan. 1834 in Newbury VRs); m. HARRY B.
            STEVENS.
      vii. JAMES A., b. Bradford VT 2 Mar. 1839, d. dur-
            ing Civil War; m. Bradford MARY WELLS.
            No ch.

624. JONATHAN^7 1799-   [204 Reuben^6 and Mary Twombley]
was born at Barrington 21 Dec. 1799, lived at Newburyport MA;
married SARAH ---- (Tracy, Reuben Leighton, 9; Newburyport
VRs).

Possible children:

      i.   SARAH P.^{8}; m. Newburyport 21 Mar. 1844
            JOSEPH N. JACQUES of Haverhill MA.
      ii.   DOLLY S., b. c1829; m. Newburyport 12 Oct.
            1848 JAMES HENRY HALL, b. 21 Nov. 1822,
            son of Joseph and Nancy (Hickey) Hall.

625. STEPHEN D.[7] 1806-1870 [204 Reuben[6] and Mary Twombley] was born at Sheffield VT 8 May 1806, died at Woodsville (a village at Haverhill) NH 4 Sept. 1870; married at Newbury VT 5 Mar. 1829 SARAH D. CARBEE, born at Bath NH 15 July 1807, died at Woodsville 5 Feb. 1885, 77y, daughter of Joel and Louisa (Downes) Carbee (town VRs; Tracy, Reuben Leighton, 9; Whicher, Haverhill NH, 572; Hamilton Childs, ed., Gazeteer of Grafton County, N. H., 1709-1886 [Syracuse NY, 1886], 1:367; 2:142). Stephen moved from Newbury to Bath, and on 11 Jan. 1842 sold off his Newbury land.

Children, first seven born at Newbury, the rest at Bath:

1287.	i.	GEORGE W.[8], b. 27 May 1829.
	ii.	ELIZABETH (twin), b. 27 May 1829, d. Bath 15 May 1844.
1288.	iii.	ANDREW J., b. 28 May 1831.
	iv.	JOEL C. (twin), b. 28 May 1831, res. Newhall CA in 1892; m. 1st ---- , 2 ch. d.y.; m. 2nd Carrie ---- , no ch. He went west, a miner.
1289.	v.	STEPHEN L., b. 24 Apr. 1833.
1290.	vi.	SARAH A., b. 9 Sept. 1835; m. DAVID FORSYTH.
1291.	vii.	LOIS CARBEE, b. 14 June 1837; m. MICHAEL M. STEVENS.
	viii.	JOHN H. C., b. 16 July 1840, d. Bath in 1849.
1292.	ix.	(LYDIA) JANE, b. 17 Dec. 1843; m. WILLIAM MORSE.
	x.	CHARLES W., b. 11 Nov. 1845, res. Greenfield MA in 1900; m. 15 Apr. 1874 LUELLA M. WOODS, b. in Feb. 1845, dau. of William and Martha (Minot) Woods. He res. Pasadena CA after 1900 (his report--Cornman Papers).
1293.	xi.	ALBERT HENRY, b. 17 May 1847.
	xii.	MARY ELIZABETH, b. 16 Oct. 1849, d. Bath 15 May 1871; unm.

626. JOHN[7] 1798-1889 [206 Isaac[6] and Sarah Bickford] was born at Strafford NH 11 Mar. 1798, died at Dover NH 15 May 1889; married first 23 May 1823 PHEBE BUZZELL, born at Strafford 18 Oct. 1799, died at Dover 21 Dec. 1860, daughter of John and Lydia (Buzzell) Buzzell; married second at Dover 25 Jan. 1862 LAVINA S. HUSSEY, born at Rochester in 1812, died at Dover 29 Oct. 1892, 81y, daughter of Joseph and Betsey (Horne) Hussey (E. H. Hussey, History of the Richard Hussey Family [TMs, 1954, MHS], 102; Cornman Ms).
He was for a time a farmer at Ossipee. In 1842, he lived at Eaton NH; in 1850 he was a mechanic at Dover.

Children, all by Phebe, all but first born at Ossipee:

i.	SARAH JANE[8], b. Barrington 20 June 1824, d. Lowell MA 31 May 1842, 18y (Morning Star); unm.
ii.	MARY ANN, b. 11 Dec. 1827, d. Dover 30 Sept. 1861; unm.
iii.	JOHN BUZZELL, b. 23 Feb. 1829, d. Dover 21 Aug. 1847.
iv.	LYDIA SUSAN, b. 18 July 1831, d. Dover 16 Dec. 1847.

1294.   v.   HANNAH FRANCES, b. 27 Feb. 1833; m. JOHN HENRY
              BUZZELL.
        vi.   ISAAC, b. 20 Sept. 1835, d. Ossipee 6 Jan.
              1838.
        vii. LENORA ADELINE, b. 11 Oct. 1837, d. Dover 5
              Nov. 1890; m. 1st 27 Nov. 1856 SAMUEL P.
              LELAND, b. Dover in 1834; m. 2nd JONATHAN A.
              HANSON. Ch. William Hanson b. Dover.

    627.   ISAAC[7] 1799-1870 [206 Isaac[6] and Sarah Bickford] was
born at Barrington NH 5 Dec. 1799, died at Hyde Park VT 7
Sept. 1870; married first at Stowe VT 24 Sept. 1820 (VRs)
NANCY BRIGHAM, born at Swanzey NH 31 Oct. 1799, died at Hyde
Park 23 Sept. 1845, 46y; married second at Wolcott VT 5 Jan.
1846 MARTHA (WRIGHT) Chamberlain, born at Northfield VT 1
Oct. 1808, lived at Mapleton MN in 1903 (Cornman Ms; records
of descendant Nellie Hiday; VT VRs).
    A farmer and shoemaker, he lived at Hyde Park and Stowe VT.

Children by Nancy, born at Hyde Park VT:

        i.   SARAH ANN[8], b. 4 Nov. 1822, d. Hyde Park 24
              24 July 1826.
        ii.   HANNAH MARIE, b. 9 Apr. 1824, d. Johnson VT 13
              13 Feb. 1854; m. Hyde Park 16 Feb. 1847 LOA
              W. JONES, b. Johnson in 1822, d. Hyde Park 10
              Sept. 1899. Ch. Samuel Harrison b. Johnson
              23 Aug. 1848.
1295.   iii. LOTT BRIGHAM, b. 9 June 1826.
        iv.   DANIEL MOODY, b. 23 Aug. 1828, d. Hyde Park
              25 July 1838.
1296.   v.   ASA WALLACE, b. 8 Dec. 1829.
        vi.   KEZIAH MADORA, b. 1 Jan. 1832, d. Hyde Park 18
              Dec. 1851, 20y.
1297.   vii. ARIEL HUNTON, b. 29 Sept. 1834.
1298.   viii. LUCIUS NOYES, b. 8 Apr. 1836.
1299.   ix.   HEALEY CADY, b. 2 Aug. 1838.
        x.   WILLIAM HALE, b. 20 Apr. 1841; m. Stowe VT 13
              Sept. 1864 (LUCY) ADELINE [Addie] CHAMBER-
              LAIN, b. there 21 Feb. 1840. He was a farmer
              at Burns, LaCrosse Co. MI in 1870, and then a
              hotel-keeper in MN. He res. Clark WA in 1900
              with wife Lucy A., and Centralia WA in 1903
              (Cornman Ms). No ch.
1300.   xi.   AURELIA, b. 15 June 1843; m. CHARLES MORSE and
              LLOYD COLBY.

Children by Martha, born at Hyde Park VT:

1301.   xii. ELLEN ANNETTE, b. 4 July 1847; m. EDGAR R.
              BENTLEY.
1302.   xiii. JANE SARAH, b. 26 Apr. 1851; m. JOHN SPRAGUE

    628.   RHODA[7] 1798-   [207 Aaron[6] and Hannah White] was
born at Barrington NH 11 June 1798, died at Springfield MA;
married at Nottingham NH 29 Mar. 1818 AARON LANG, born there
14 Sept. 1797, died in 1859, son of Thomas and Mary (Simpson)
Lang (Moore, Lang Fam., 57). They lived at Chicopee MA

Children (**Lang**):

i.   CYRUS, b. 18 June 1822, d. Springfield 9 Nov. 1882;
      m. 10 June 1848 ANN M. GAYLORD, d. East Orange NJ
      2 Sept. 1901.
ii.   ADA.
iii. HANNAH.
iv.   MELVINA.
v.   ANN.

629. LUCINDA[7] 1802-1840 [208 Jonathan[6] and Lois Follett]
was born at Barrington 15 Dec. 1802, died there 27 Aug. 1840;
married at Strafford 5 Feb. 1826 ISAAC BABB, born at Dover 1
Dec. 1795, died there 31 Dec. 1864, son of William and Esther
(Hodgdon) Babb (Cornman Ms; Sargent, Babbs of New Eng., 148).
Isaac had married first about 1816 Mary Hayes, who died 16
Jan. 1817; and married second about 1818 Margaret Hayes, who
died 6 Mar. 1825 leaving four children (Richmond, John Hayes,
1:223; Cornman Ms). He married fourth at Barrington 10 Nov.
1841 Martha Cater, and married fifth at Dover 15 Feb. 1846
Lydia Grant. He is buried at Barrington.
    His children by Lucinda were placed under the guardianship
of his half-brother William Babb 7 Sept. 1847, and were
brought up in various families (StrCP, 50:335).

Children (**Babb**), born at Barrington:

i.   MARIA ELIZABETH, b. 27 June 1827, d. Madbury 3 Nov.
      1904; m. 1 May 1854 CHARLES H. CATER, b. Barrington
      7 May 1831, d. Madbury 12 Sept. 1904, son of Joel
      and Annie (Babb) Cater.
ii.   MARGARET HANNAH, b. 19 May 1830, d. Dover in May
      1900; m. Dover 10 Nov. 1881 GEORGE F. CANNEY, b. in
      1834, d. Charlestown MA 19 Apr. 1914, son of Isaac
      and Betsey (Cater) Canney. George had m. 1st
      Margaret Cheswell.
iii. (ISAAC) FREEMAN, b. 9 Dec 1834, d. Dover 10 Dec.
      1895, 60y 1d; m. 7 Dec. 1858 MARY H. MORSE, b.
      Randolph VT 20 July 1835, d. 8 July 1902, dau. of
      Jacob and Alice (Goodale) Morse.
iv.   MARY ESTHER, b. 1 Nov. 1838, d. Dover 1 Jan. 1900; m.
      15 Mar. 1864 GEORGE W. RUSSELL, b. in 1838, d. in
      battle Boydton VA in 1862, while a sergeant, Co. K,
      5th NH Inf. Rgt.
v.   JOHN ALLISON, b. 5 Mar. 1840, d. 16 May 1867; m.
      Dover 4 Jan. 1866 MARY BICKFORD. He served in Co.
      K, 11th NH Rgt., during the Civil War.

630. NANCY[7] 1805-1862 [208 Jonathan[6] and Lois Follett] was
born at Holderness NH 30 May 1805, died at Strafford NH 3
Aug. 1862; married there 10 Jan. 1828 ELIPHALET FOSS, born at
Strafford 7 Mar. 1801, died 24 Sept. 1884 (Richmond, John
Hayes, 1:204; Cornman Ms). Foss married second 9 Sept. 1864
Cynthia D. Rand.

Children (**Foss**), born at Strafford:

i.   ELIZA JANE, b. 11 May 1829; m. Strafford 15 May 1850
      Capt. JOHN GILMAN HOLMES, b. there 18 Nov. 1823,

son of William and Phoebe (Hayes) Holmes.
ii.   HANNAH A., b. 30 Apr. 1837, d. Jacksonville FL 29
      June 1897; m. 1 May 1864 GEORGE F. NUTTER.
iii. NANCY LEIGHTON, b. 20 Feb. 1841; m. 15 May 1860
      WARREN H. PERKINS, b. Strafford 8 Sept. 1832.

631. ISAAC TWOMBLEY[7] 1807-1878 [208 Jonathan[6] and Lois
Follett] was born at Holderness NH 25 Nov. 1807, died at
Hartford VT 11 Feb. 1878 (VRs); married first JEMIMA WOOD of
Lebanon NH, daughter of Capt. John Wood; married second at
Hartford 30 Mar. 1864 SARAH ESTABROOKS, born at Lebanon NH 22
June 1822, daughter of Aaron and Sarah (Gusher) Estabrooks
(Cornman Ms; William Booth Estabrook, Genealogy of the Esta-
brook Family [Ithaca NY, 1891], 77). In 1900, widow Sarah
was in her son Joseph's household, as were Martha and Henry.

Children, all by Jemima, all but first born at Hartford:

      i.   JOHN WOOD[8], b. Lebanon NH 1 Dec. 1831, d.
            Malone NY 30 Jan. 1893; m. there MARY
            ANGENETTE HARDY.
      ii.   BENJAMIN CUTTER, b. 11 July 1833, d. 1 July
            1850.
1303. iii. ELLEN FRANCES, b. 9 Aug. 1836; m. WILLIAM H.
            CHILD.
      iv.   MARTHA JANE, b. 4 Oct. 1837; m. Royalton VT 24
            Dec. 1874 (VRs) ORANGE NORTON BARTLETT, b. 5
            July 1819, d. Royalton 20 Aug. 1890, son of
            Orange N. Norton. No ch.
      v.   HENRY CLAY, b. 8 June 1839, res. Hartford in
            1900; unm.
1304. vi.   EDWIN THOMAS, b. 15 Aug. 1841.
      vii. JOSEPH WARREN, b. 13 Oct. 1846, res. Hartford
            in 1900 (census); m. MARY A. (KENDALL)
            Leighton, b. Boston 22 Oct. 1836, dau. of
            Joshua and Hannah Kendall. She had m. 1st in
            1864 John Colby Leighton [# 208].

632. MARY HUCKINS[7] 1810-1894 [208 Jonathan[6] and Lois Fol-
lett] was born at Holderness NH 6 Jan. 1810, died at Wells
River VT; married 28 Nov. 1829 (1828 per Gen.) THOMAS GEORGE
SANBORN, born at Enfield NH 9 Mar. 1805, died at Wells River
5 Apr. 1880, son of Benjamin and Betsey (Rand) Sanborn (Corn-
man Ms; Sanborn Gen., 496).
He was a stonemason, and served as justice of the peace at
Thetford VT.

Children (**Sanborn**):

i.   MINERVA E., b. Lebanon NH 28 Dec. 1830, res. Preston
      IA; m. Wells River 28 Oct. 1866 SAMUEL PAGE.
ii.   MARCELLA J., b. Lebanon 7 Sept. 1832, d. 12 Nov.
      1892; m. Thetford VT 29 Sept. 1855 NEWTON J. HOWARD.
iii. ALANSON LEIGHTON, b. Springfield NH 19 Apr. 1834, d.
      Norfolk VA 11 July 1863, shot by a "secessionist."
      He was a lieutenant in a VT Rgt. Unm.
iv.   THOMAS DARWIN, b. Grafton NH 31 Dec. 1836, res. Thet-
      ford; m. 2 Nov. 1865 FRANCES E. SPAULDING.

v.   MARY M., b. Thetford 28 Oct. 1838, d. in NE; m. 6
      Dec. 1857 Dr. HARLEY P. MATHEWSON of Jefferson IN,
      who grad. from Dartmouth Med. Col. in 1862.
vi.   LOUISA W., b. Thetford 19 Apr. 1841, d. 22 Sept.
      1892; m. 26 Nov. 1864 ELIPHALET J. FOSS of Boston,
      b. 24 Feb. 1840.
vii. JOHN C., b. Thetford 13 Oct. 1850, res. Orange CA.

633. JOSEPH WARREN[7] 1816-1861 [208 Jonathan[6] and Lois
Follett] was born at Holderness NH 3 June 1816, died at Boston 18 Mar. 1861, 44y (VRs), by suicide; married 1 Feb. 1838
MARY PRESCOTT LAWRENCE, born at Groton MA 7 Feb. 1816 (Cambridge VRs), died at West Medford MA 21 Jan. 1898, daughter
of John and Margaret (Gregg) Lawrence (town VRs; Cornman Ms).

Children:

1305. i.   HARRIET JOSEPHINE[8] [Hattie], b. Groton MA 5
             Apr. 1839; m. AUSTIN C. DEWEY.
       ii.   GEORGE NORTON, b. Boston 10 June 1841, d.
             there 5 July 1844 (Cambridge VRs).
       iii. (JAMES) HENRY, b. Boston 13 Dec. 1842, res.
             Somerville MA in 1900 (census); m. Boston 7
             Sept. 1870 (VRs) (SUSAN) ANNA GILSON, b. Cam-
             bridge 27 July 1845, d. Somerville 22 Jan.
             1915, dau. of Henry T. and Mary S. (Bailey)
             Gilson. No ch.
       iv.   GEORGIANNA, b. Boston 10 Mar. 1848; m. there
             4 Dec. 1865 WILLIAM W. WINKLEY of Barrington
             NH, b. 18 Mar. 1835, son of James A. and
             Hannah Winkley. Ch. William H. b. Somerville
             MA 25 July 1872; m. Grace Decker.

634. EMILY ANN[7] 1814-1882 [209 Ezekiel[6] and Olive Cate]
was born at Dover NH 27 May 1814, died at Boston 25 Apr.
1882; married at Boston (both of West Newton) 14 Nov. 1859
(VRs) GEORGE NORTON, born at Boston in 1814, son of Oliver
and Bathsheba Norton.
He had married first Lenora F. and second Hannah E.,
Emily's sisters (Cornman Ms).

Children (Norton), born at Boston:

i.   LILLIAN FRANCES, b. 7 Oct. 1860.
ii.   GEORGIANNA LEIGHTON [Georgie], b. 29 Nov. 1863, liv-
      ing in 1903; unm.
iii. MARY GERTRUDE, b. 18 May 1872, d. 11 June 1896; unm.
      She was principal, Cleveland (OH) School of Art.

635. JAMES LYMAN[7] 1817-1861 [209 Ezekiel[6] and Olive Cate]
was born at Ossipee NH 19 Nov. 1817, died there 25 Apr. 1861,
43y (VRs); married at Dover 5 Mar. 1839 (Morning Star) AMANDA
M. DELAND, born about 1817 (33 in 1850), died at North Conway
NH 27 Feb. 1892, 78y 10m 8d (buried at Kearsage NH), daughter
of David Deland (Cornman Ms).
In 1850, James's Ossipee household included his parents and
his sister Emily A.

Children, per 1850 census, born at Ossipee:

    i.   OLIVE JOSEPHINE[8], b. c1839 (11 in 1850).
    ii.   LEONORA FRANCES, b. c1842 (8 in 1850).
1306. iii. GEORGE NORTON, b. in Mar. 1847.

636. ISAAC[7] 1803-1836 [211 Andrew[6] and Sarah Evans] was
born at Barrington NH 7 June 1803, died there 22 Jan. 1836
(33y, Morning Star); married 29 Mar. 1831 MARIA SUSAN CATE,
born in 1807, died in 1845 (Cornman Ms). Widow Maria was
made administratrix of his estate 2 May 1836 (StrCP, 50:48;
51:116).

Only child, born at Barrington:

1307. i.   ELIZA C.[8], b. 26 Aug. 1831; m. MOSES OTIS.

637. DAVID[7] 1801-   [212 Remembrance[6] and Judith White-
house] was born at Effingham about 1801 (49 in 1850), lived
at Ossipee; married DORCAS WELCH, born about 1802 (48 in
1850 (Cornman Ms).
He was a farmer at Ossipee in 1850; his household included
his father Remembrance, 79, Mary Welch, 77, and Abigail
Welch, 70, the two latter born in MA.

Children:

1308. i.   ABIGAIL[8], b. c1831 (19 in 1850); m. REUBEN
          MAYBERRY.
    ii.   BARZILLAI W., b. 31 Dec. 1833, d. Philadelphia
          6 Jan. 1863, in military hosp.; unm.
    iii. EMILY B., b. 12 May 1835, d. 14 May 1862; m.
          Ossipee 2 Oct. 1859 ISAAC CHADBOURNE, b. Eff-
          ingham 6 Jan. 1829, d. Bridgton ME 16 Jul.
          1906, son of Oliver Chadbourne (Chadbourne
          Family Assn. records). He m. 2nd Ossipee 17
          Mar. 1864 Hannah E. Leighton (iv. below), and
          m. 3rd Elizabeth ---- .
    iv.   HANNAH E., b. c1837 (13 in 1850); m. ISAAC
          CHADBOURNE (see iii).
    v.   DAVID, b. 5 Mar. 1841, d. Ossipee 25 Aug.
          1865; unm.
    vi.   THOMAS, d. Effingham 14 Nov. 1848.

638. MELINDA[7] 1804-   [212 Remembrance[6] and Judith White-
house] was born at Effingham or Ossipee say 1804, died at
Manchester NH; married at Strafford 2 June 1831 NICHOLAS OTIS
of Sheffield VT, probably son of Joseph and Elizabeth (Berry)
Otis of Strafford NH (Cornman Ms). They were living at Farmington in 1850.

Children (**Otis**):

    i.   DYER LEIGHTON, res. Barnstead Center NH; m. 21 Nov.
          1858 MARY M. HOWE.
    ii.   HARRISON G., d. 1 May 1901; m. MARY MORRILL.
    iii. HIRAM, b. 30 Nov. 1841; m. 25 Feb. 1869 SARAH A.
          PITMAN, b. Barnstead 30 Aug. 1846.

639. REMEMBRANCE[7] 1806-   [212 Remembrance[6] and Judith
Whitehouse] was born probably at Effingham NH about 1806 (74
in 1880), died at Biddeford ME; married first PRISCILLA FEN-
DERSON of Parsonsfield ME; married second OLIVE A. WILSON,
born at Biddeford in 1819, died at Saco ME 31 Oct. 1892, 73y
4m, daughter of Benjamin and Leah (Rolfe) Wilson (Biddeford
and Saco VRs).
They were living at Biddeford in 1850, he a sawyer, 38, and
Priscilla 36. In 1880, he was living with his sons John and
Charles at Biddeford.

Children, probably by Priscilla, listed in Biddeford VRs:

	i.	CHARLES H.[8], b. Saco 13 Mar. 1835, d. there
		23 Mar. 1902; m. 1st MARY E. ---- , b. 3 Aug.
		1835, d. 15 Feb. 1890; m. 2nd 4 Aug. 1894
		MARY (CHICK) Lowell, b. in Nov. 1834, d. 22
		Nov. 1906. No ch.
	ii.	MARY C., b. 21 July 1836 (12 in 1850).
	iii.	PRISCILLA, b. 23 Sept. 1838, d. 3 June 1849.
	iv.	JOHN B., b. 3 June 1841, d. 25 July 1842.
1309.	v.	JOHN, b. 3 Aug. 1843 (11 in 1850).
	vi.	HARRISON, b. 3 June 1846, d. 21 Sept. 1847.
	vii.	ADELINE, b. 13 July 1848 (1 in 1850).
1310.	viii.	HARRISON G., b. 18 May 1849 (1/12 in 1850).
	ix.	PRISCILLA, b. 22 Oct. 1853 (1854 per VRs),
		d. 12 June 1854.
	x.	LAURA (twin), b. 22 Oct. 1853, d. 11 July
		1854.
	xi.	MARIA S., b. 18 May, d. 16 Nov., 1856.

640. ISAAC[7] 1798-1872 [213 Isaac[6] and Sarah Buzzell] was
born at Barrington NH 22 Dec. 1798, died at Effingham NH 21
Dec. 1872; married 22 Oct. 1840 MERCY CHICK, born at Parsonsfield ME 13 Apr. 1809, died at Effingham 15 Dec. 1893, daughter of John and Mercy (Granville) Chick (Cornman Ms). In 1850
he was a farmer at Effingham.

Children, born at Effingham:

1311.	i.	CHARLES H.[8], b. 13 July 1841.
	ii.	SARAH ANN, b. 20 Aug. 1843, d. 24 Apr. 1853.
1312.	iii.	ELIZA JENNIE, b. 21 Nov. 1845; m. FRANK B.
		PINNEY.
	iv.	MARIA FRANCES, b. 23 Feb. 1848, res. Revere
		MA; m. 1 Jan. 1876 DANIEL PARKER DEMERITT,
		b. Effingham 27 Feb. 1849, d. there 20 Oct.
		1906, son of Daniel and Ann (Andrews) Demer-
		itt. Ch. Allen Atwood b. 6 Sept. 1879; m. 20
		Oct. 1908 Agnes Strupenny.
	v.	JOHN A., b. 24 Dec. 1850, d. Haverhill MA
		25 Oct. 1875.
	vi.	SARAH ANN, b. 26 Oct. 1853, res. Freedom NH.
1313.	vii.	ELLA MARY, b. 18 Nov. 1856; m. GEORGE C.
		LEAVITT.

641. SARAH[7] 1803-1882 [213 Isaac[6] and Sarah Buzzell] was
born at Effingham NH 5 Mar. 1803, died 4 Sept. 1882; married
ISAAC HANSON of Ossipee NH (Cornman Ms).

Children (**Hanson**), born at Ossipee:

i.   PHOEBE, b. in 1840, res. Laconia NH; m. 1st WOODBURY
     WHITEHOUSE; m. 2nd STEPHEN AVERY of Laconia, son of
     Caleb and Lucinda (Willey) Avery.
ii. JOHN (twin), b in 1840, d. Ossipee in 1908.
iii. DENANCY [?].
iv. JAMES (twin).

642. **LOUISA**[7] 1812-1890 [213 Isaac[6] and Sarah Buzzell] was
born at Effingham NH 12 Mar. 1812, died at Farmington 7 May
1890, 78y 1m 26d (VRs); married in 1831 JOHN LEWIS of Ossipee, born in 1802, son of John and Sarah Lewis (Cornman Ms).
They lived at Ossipee, Effingham and Farmington.

Children (**Lewis**):

i.   ELIZABETH, b. in 1832, d. in 1856; m. in 1854 WILLIAM
      H. LOCKE of Dover. No ch.
ii.   ANN CAROLINE, b. Ossipee 3 Sept. 1836, d. Farmington
      4 June 1923, 86y 9m 1d; m. 24 June 1858 IRA ELKINS,
      b. Farmington 3 Nov. 1832, son of John C and Achsah
      (Varney) Elkins.
iii. JOHN E., b. Ossipee in 1839, d. Farmington 10 Oct.
      1888, 49y 11m 10d (TRs); m. in 1860 NELLIE DYER. No
      ch. She m. again.
iv.   LOUISA, b. Effingham in 1843, d. Farmington in 1867.
v.   JENNIE M., b. Effingham in 1845, res. Providence RI;
      m. JOSEPH BARNEY. No ch.
vi.   GEORGE M., b. in 1847, d. 14 Oct. 1919, 72y 2m 3d;
      m. in 1879 ANNIE MERROW.
vii. CHARLES, b. in 1850, res. Somersworth NH; unm.
viii. HENRY, b. in 1854, d. Farmington in 1879; m. there
      in 1878 HATTIE BURNS.

643. **KEZIAH**[7] 1814-1879 [213 Isaac[6] and Sarah Buzzell] was
born at Effingham NH 22 Dec. 1814, died 31 May 1879; married
2 June 1842 EBENEZER TASKER, born at Bartlett NH 15 Dec.
1820, died at Berwick ME 22 Sept. 1875, son of Eben and Polly
(Hosmer) Tasker (Cornman Ms).

Children (**Tasker**):

i.   ANDREW J., b. Bartlett 4 Sept., d. 16 Oct., 1843.
ii.   JOHN HOOPER, b. Bartlett 4 Sept. 1845, d. Newburyport
      MA 6 Apr. 1912; m. 10 Sept. 1873 SARAH F. WOODMAN,
      dau. of William B. and Eunice W. (Brown) Woodman.
iii. SARAH FRANCES, b. Bartlett 14 Jan. 1848; res. Man-
      chester NH.
iv.   MARY ELIZA, b. Jackson NH 23 Nov. 1850; m. 9 Sept.
      1872 HOMER E. SLACK.
v.   LYDIA GREENLEAF, b. Jackson 21 Oct. 1852, d. Berwick
      ME 29 Sept. 1877; m. 15 Dec. 1875 JOSEPH T. LOCKE.
vi.   EBEN WILLIS, b. Bartlett 22 Apr. 1854, d. 14 June
      1860.
vii. IDA A., b. Bartlett 13 Nov. 1857, d. 14 Sept. 1907;
      m. 15 Oct. 1881 WILLIAM KIMBALL NICHOLAS of Peter-
      boro NH, b. 13 Jan. 1853, son of Thomas Symonds and
      Susan M. (Carter) Nicholas.

644.   GEORGE E.[7] 1833-1900 [213 Isaac[6] and Theodate Gar-
land] was born at Effingham 11 Aug. 1833, died at Haverhill
MA 15 Apr. 1900, 66y 8m 4d (VRs); married 14 Mar. 1859 SUSAN
JANE MOULTON, born at Madison NH 19 Dec. 1839, died at Haver-
hill 18 Mar. 1899, daughter of John and Mehitable (Glidden)
Moulton (Cornman Ms). He was a carpenter.

Children, born at Effingham (VRs):

1314. i.   GEORGE H.[8], b. 25 Apr. 1860.
        ii.   CHARLES N., b. 25 Nov. 1861, d. 14 July 1910;
              m. 14 Feb. 1896 ALMIRA BLANCHARD, b. in MA in
              Oct. 1867. They res. Haverhill in 1900,
              without children.
        iii. WILLIAM H., b. 18 Feb. 1863, d. Haverhill 14
              Mar. 1902, 39y 24d (VRs); m. 15 Jan. 1885
              NETTIE H. LITTLE, b. in NH in Dec. 1862. No
              ch. In 1900 he was a shoe manufacturer at
              Haverhill, with sister-in-law Emma and nephew
              Urban in his household.
        iv.   EMMA J., b. 3 June 1864; m. 23 Dec. 1911 FRANK
              T. A. MEADER of Boston, born 17 Nov. 1859,
              son of Bartlett Dexter and Hattie E. (Morris)
              Meader. No ch.
        v.   SEWELL K., b. 23 Oct. 1865, res. Haverhill in
              1900; m. 13 June 1884 SUSAN A. JONES of Not-
              tingham NH, b. NH in Aug. 1856, dau. of Miles
              and Jane (Watson) Jones. No ch.

645.   ELIZABETH FRANCES[7] 1835-1911 [213 Isaac[6] and Theodate
Garland] was born at Effingham 27 Feb. 1835, died at Utica NY
10 Sept. 1911; married at Portland ME 14 Aug. 1855 WILLIAM
ALBERT SHACKFORD, born at Poland ME 14 July 1829, died at
Utica 12 Nov. 1913, son of Joshua and Nancy (Thompson) Shack-
ford (Cornman Ms).
He was a millwright and pattern-maker.

Children (**Shackford**), born at Lewiston ME:

i.   GEORGE ALBERT, b. 30 Jan. 1860, res. Utica; m. there
      11 Mar. 1882 BELLE RANSOM, b. Deerfield NY 22 Sept.
      1863, dau. of William and Elizabeth (Lyons) Ransom.
ii.   FRANK SHERMAN, b. 1 Nov. 1864, d. Lewiston 3 May
      1868.

646.   ALMIRA D.[7] 1837-   [213 Isaac[6] and Theodate Gar-
land] was born at Effingham 26 Feb. 1837, lived at Haverhill
MA; married 16 Aug. 1868 ENOCH LEWIS of Center Sandwich NH,
who died in 1880 (town VRs; Cornman Ms).

Child (**Lewis**), born at Sandwich NH:

i.   HERMAN E., b. 12 Nov. 1870; m. 9 Sept. 1896 CARRIE L.
      STORER, b. Haverhill MA, dau. of Joshua Storer.

647.   SARAH[7] 1804-1864 [214 Mark[6] and Betsey Randall] was
born at Biddeford ME 13 June 1804, died at Portland ME 22
Feb. 1864; married there 4 Oct. 1827 PAUL HALL, born 3 Mar.

1802, died at Falmouth ME 28 Oct. 1839, son of Silas and Hannah (Neal) Hall (Hall Desc.; Cornman Ms).

Children (**Hall**):

i.   CHARLES CARROLL PIERCE, b. 8 Mar. 1829, drowned in
        Saco River 24 July 1840.
ii.   JOHN HENRY, b. 13 July 1835; m. MARY FRANCES PLUMMER.

648.   GEORGE[7] 1805-1858 [214 Mark[6] and Betsey Randall] was
born at Biddeford ME 29 Dec. 1805, died at Saco 26 Dec. 1858,
53y; married first at Biddeford 15 Dec. 1829 OLIVE B. WARREN,
born 3 Nov. 1808, died at Biddeford 6 May 1833, daughter of
Benjamin W. Warren of Salmon Falls; married second 26 Dec.
1833 HANNAH S. FOWLER, born 2 Dec. 1812, died at Biddeford 1
July 1880 (29 June, 68y, per GS) (E. P. Burnham, Saco Families [TMs, Dyer Memorial Library]; Biddeford VRs). Burials
are in Laurel Hill Cemetery, Saco.

Children by Olive, born at Biddeford:

i.   MARY JANE[8], b. 9 July 1830, d. Wakefield MA 14
        Feb. 1872, 41y 6m; m. CHARLES G. STAPLES,
        born 6 May 1828, d. Saco 7 Sept. 1867. She
        was included in The Poets of Maine (George
        Bancroft Griffith, comp. [Portland, 1888],
        443) under her maiden name.
ii.   SARAH E., b. 29 July 1832, d. 29 Sept. 1851,
        19y 2m; unm.
iii.   GEORGE E., b. in 1833, d. 20 Nov. 1833, 7m
        20d.

Children by Hannah, born at Biddeford:

iv.   GEORGE H., b. 8 Apr., d. 20 Nov., 1835.
v.   GEORGE H., b. 10 Sept. 1836, d. Saco 4 Feb.
        1856, 19y 5m.
vi.   EMILY, b. 10 Nov. 1840, d. 26 June 1853,
        12y 7m.

649.   SAMUEL WEEKS[7] 1814-1864 [216 William Hale[6] and Comfort Weeks] was born at Danville VT 9 Sept. 1814, died in VA
5 May 1864, killed in the Battle of the Wilderness; married
first at Danville 30 July 1837 CYNTHIA J. HEATH, born about
1817, died at Danville 7 Dec. 1861, 44y 4m 24d, daughter of
Simeon and Susan Heath; married second at Danville 25 Dec.
1861 SIBIL (SCALES) Way, born at Lunenburg VT about 1823 (42
in 1865), died 8 Feb. 1899, daughter of I. Scales and widow
of Lyman Way (Danville VRs; Cornman Ms).
     Samuel lived at Barnstead, Pittsfield and Danville, and was
a farmer and shoemaker. He was nearly fifty when he enlisted
23 Dec. 1863 as a private in Co. H, 4th VT Inf. Rgt.
     In 1865 his widow Sibil filed for a pension, listing in her
declaration three Leighton children under 16, and her three
minor Way children: William, 13, Jane, 11, and Sylvia. She
had no children by Samuel (NA-MSR pension #46164).

Children by Cynthia, most born at Danville:

i.   SYLVIA JANE[8], b. 16 June 1838, d. 1 Oct. 1839.
1315.   ii.   ALMEDA JANE, b. 20 Aug. 1839; m. OTIS F. HILL.
1316.   iii.   ELSA JANE WHITE [Elsie], b. 2 Nov. 1841; m.
                JOHN DORWAY.
          iv.   SYLVIA P. F., b. 9 Aug. 1843 (16 July in
                Barnstead VRs), d. 14 Jan. 1845.
           v.   WILLIAM H. H., b. 16 July 1847.
1317.   vi.   ROSINA, b. 18 Sept. 1849; m. JOHN BIRCK.
         vii.   son, b. Strafford 28 Mar. 1852.
        viii.   OLIVE E., b. Pittsfield 2 June 1853.
          ix.   HENRY, b. in 1856, d. in Apr. 1863.
           x.   EMEZETTA V. [Carrie], b. Danville 4 Sept.
                1858, res. Lyndon VT; m. Danville 19 Jan.
                1880 GEORGE WILLIAM HEATH.
          xi.   OTIS FRANKLIN [Frank], b. Danville 24 Aug.
                1860; m. there 27 Aug. 1891 MARY A. FINN, b.
                Fall River MA c1873. Ch. SAMUEL WEEKS[9] b.
                Pittsfield NH 1 Dec. 1892, d. Old Orchard
                Beach ME in Mar. 1974, 81y (obit. named no
                survivors).

650.   JEREMIAH WEEKS[7] [Jerry] 1817-1894 [216 William Hale[6]
and Comfort Weeks] was born at Barnstead NH 23 Mar. 1817
(VRs), died at St. Johnsbury VT in Nov. 1894, 80y (VRs); married first at Danville 6 Feb. 1842 JULIA ANN TICE, born about
1822, died at Danville 4 Aug. 1851; married second there 15
Aug. 1852 MARTHA HARRIS; married third Mrs. C. L. Dow (VT
VRs; Cornman Ms).

Children by Julia, probably all born at St. Johnsbury:

i.   SARAH MARY[8], born about 1842; m. Concord VT 8
       Mar. 1866 (aged 25) DANIEL P. WILCOMB.
ii.   SUSAN W., b. 22 Aug. 1843, d. 7 Nov. 1854, 11y
       (Danville VRs).
iii.   CYNTHIA E., b. about 1845; m. (aged 20) St.
       Johnsbury 24 June 1865 FRANCIS M. WARREN.
iv.   COMFORT, b. say 1847, res. Concord VT; m.
       CHARLES DODGE.
v.   CHARLOTTE H., b. say 1849, d. Lunenburg VT 10
       Dec. 1908, 58y 7m 18d; m. St. Johnsbury 3
       Feb. 1872 CHARLES A CARR. No ch.
vi.   JULIA, b. about 1850, d. Concord VT 27 Jan.
       1881, 32y 9m 10d; m. (both aged 21) St.
       Johnsbury 8 Sept. 1871 ALFRED J. DODGE.
       Ch. Julia.

Children by Martha, born at St. Johnsbury:

1318.   vii.   ABBIE J., b. say 1853; m. (ROMANZO) EDWARD
                BALCH.
        viii.   MARTHA, b. about 1860; d. St. Johsbury 7 May
                1864, 3y 9m 10d.
          ix.   MARTHA E., b. 31 July 1865, res. CA; m. GEORGE
                SMITH of St. Johnsbury. Ch. Marsha, Julia.

651.   PATIENCE MELLOW[7] 1820-1905 [216 William Hale[6] and
Comfort Weeks] was born at Barnstead NH 2 May 1820, died at
Strafford NH 18 May 1905; married there 27 June 1844 TIMOTHY

LEIGHTON CLARK, born 16 Feb. 1815, died at Strafford 4 Jan. 1892 (or 1882), son of Daniel, Jr., and Sarah[6] (Leighton) Clark [# 215] (Cornman Ms; records of descendant Kathleen Crousen). Burials are in Strafford Center Cemetery.

Children (**Clark**), born at Strafford:

i.   SARAH JANE, b. 3 Sept. 1845, d. in 1919.
ii.   GEORGE E., b. 11 Dec. 1846, res. Framingham MA; m.
      29 May 1872 ABBIE F. CUTTING.
iii. JOHN W., b. 3 Sept. 1849, d. Storm Lake IA 13 Oct.
      1881; m. 1st 17 Dec. 1870 SARAH E. HOBBS, d. 25 July
      1878; m. 2nd 27 Jan. 1880 HANNAH M. BUCKHOLDER.
iv.   CALISTA A. (twin), b. 3 Sept. 1849, d. Dover NH in
      1907; m. 22 Jan. 1877 SIDNEY A HAWKINS.
v.   CHARLES PALMER, b. 22 Feb. 1855; m. Cherokee IA 29
      Aug. 1876 KATIE MILLERICK.

652. DANIEL M.[7] 1822-1897 [216 William Hale[6] and Comfort Weeks] was born at Wheelock VT 17 May 1822, died at Dover NH 27 Jan. 1897, 74y 8m 10d; married first at Danville VT 11 Jan. 1845 THERESA [Thurza] POPPY, born at Sutton VT 20 Sept. 1828, died at Dover 14 Mar. 1885, daughter of John Coffrey Poppy; married second 27 Nov. 1886 MARTHA A. (WIGGIN) Roberts, born at Somersworth NH 15 Mar. 1836, died at Concord (state hosp.) 13 Oct. 1922, 86y 6m 28d, daughter of Dudley and Mehitable (Lord) Wiggin (NH VRs; Cornman Ms; her pension application: NA-MSR #223-196). Martha had married first John Roberts.

He enlisted 13 Aug. 1862 in Co. C, 11h NH Inf. Rgt., was wounded at Petersburg VA, captured and held prisoner for six months, and discharged 19 May 1865. He was destitute in 1890, aged 68, living at Somersworth NH.

His widow Martha applied for her own pension 11 Aug. 1897, pointing out that all their former property had been sold for non-payment of taxes and that she was completely dependent upon town aid.

Children by Thurza, first five born at Danville:

         i.   COMFORT E.[8], b. 18 Nov. 1846, d. 14 Mar. 1847.
         ii.   ROSETTA FISHER, b. 9 Dec. 1847; m. 14 July
               1886 ALDEN B. COOK, b. Dover 21 Sept. 1832.
               No ch.
         iii. CELIA ANN TAYLOR, b. 20 Dec. 1849, res. Lynn
               MA; m. ARCHIBALD H. DOLBEAR.
1319.   iv.   BETSEY JANE, b. 8 Nov. 1851; m. WINTHROP S.
               COLEMAN.
         v.   AARON ORLANDO, b. 20 May 1854, d. 27 Oct.
               1874, killed on railroad.
         vi.   ELLEN ELIZABETH CATHERINE, b. 1 Mar. 1856.
         vii. IDA A., b. Pittsfield NH 14 July 1858, d.
               Dover 3 Jan. 1903; m. JAMES L. GARSIDE. No
               ch.
         viii. ELIZABETH M., b. 5 Apr. 1862, res. Cambridge
               MA; m. CHARLES W. WOOD. Ch. Florence, per-
               haps others.
         ix.   CORA B., b. 13 Mar., d. 25 Apr., 1868.

653.   WILLIAM DREW[7] 1827-1900 [216 William Hale[6] and Comfort Weeks] was born at Lyndon VT 23 Feb. 1827 (1823 in VRs;
Apr. 1826 per 1900 census), died at Groton VT 8 June 1900,
74y (VRs); married first 24 Feb. 1853 MARTHA H. THOMPSON,
born at Gilmanton NH 6 Nov. 1836; married second 27 Dec. 1864
LUCINDA H. NASON, born 16 Nov. 1836, died 12 July 1898,
daughter of John and Mary (Pike) Nason; married third at Groton 31 Mar. 1899 (he aged 73) SYLVINA ANNIS, born in Apr.
1829 (per 1900 census) (Cornman Ms; VT VRs).

Children by Martha:

    i.   HARRISON L.[8], b. Danville 24 Nov. 1852, d. 15
            Mar. 1854.
    ii.   ELIZABETH E., b. 7 Sept. 1855, res Sea Cliff,
            L.I. NY; m. 1st ---- TREADWELL; m. 2nd JOHN
            DONCOURT.
    iii. CHARLES H., b. 24 Nov. 1859.

Child by Lucinda, born at Haverhill NH:

1320. iv. ANNA B., b. 27 Feb. 1869; m. ONSLOW D. PERRY.

654.   HARRISON WEEKS[7] [Harry] 1829-1906 [216 William Hale[6]
and Comfort Weeks] was born at Lyndon VT 25 May 1829 (25 Mar.
in Danville VRs), died at Danville VT 8 Jan. 1906, 77y 5m
14d; married first there 8 Dec. 1853 MARY B. GOULD, born at
Walden VT in 1833, died there 17 Nov. 1857, daughter of H. K.
and Mary Gould; married second MARY ---- , born in May 1843,
lived at Danville in 1900 (Danville VRs; Cornman Ms).

Child by first wife, born at Danville:

    i.   HIRAM K.[8], b. 7 Apr. 1856, res. Dover NH in
            1900; m. 1st St. Johnsbury VT 31 Dec. 1881
            EMMA S. DURGIN; m. 2nd 3 Apr. 1889 RUTH A.
            MILLS, b. Canada 11 Jan. 1853. No ch.

Children by second wife, born at Danville:

    ii.   MARY B., d. 14 Aug. 1862, 3y 1m 8d.
1321. iii. FREDERICK, b. in June 1864.
    iv.   GEORGE J. B., b. 25 July 1868 (1870 per 1900
            census), res. Dover; unm.
    v.   FRANCES M. [Fannie], b. 4 Aug. 1872; m.
            Danville 19 Nov. 1890 ELMER GREEN. Ch. Mary.
    vi.   HERBERT [Bertie], b. 17 Oct. 1875, res. Dover;
            unm.

655.   SARAH MARY[7] 1836-1909 [216 William Hale[6] and Comfort
Weeks] was born at Danville VT 11 Mar. 1836, died at Dover NH
6 Apr. 1909; married first at Strafford NH 28 Aug. 1858 DAVID
H. BABB, born there 5 Aug. 1834, died 15 July 1861, 27y
(hanged himself), son of Joel and Charlotte (Babb) Babb (Sar-
gent, Babbs of New Eng., 165); married second at Danville 19
Aug. 1865 ORRIN B. RUSS, born 9 Mar. 1836 (Cornman Ms; VT and
NH VRs).

Children (**Babb**):

i.   JOHN DAVID, b. Dover 25 July 1857, d. in 1936 (estate
     adm. 7 July); m. 1st 1 May 1879 JENNIE S. ROBERTS,
     d. 20 Dec. 1893, dau. of Charles and Emeline (Per-
     kins) Roberts, b. 12 Dec. 1861; m. 2nd 2 Aug. 1901
     LIZZIE A HENDERSON, b. 30 Apr. 1862, d. 24 Oct.
     1926, dau. of Charles and Elizabeth (Chesley)
     Henderson. No ch.
ii. CHARLES F., b. 20 July, d. 25 Aug., 1859.
iii. ABBY C , b. 18 Nov. 1861, d. 16 July 1901.

Children (**Russ**):

iv. GEORGE B., b. Dover 10 June 1866; m. 28 May 1892
     LUCY W. GOULD.
v.   FRANK E., b. St. Johnsbury VT 1 Mar. 1868; m. 10 Mar.
     1887 KATIE M. DOWNING, b. Concord NH 22 Feb. 1868.
     He served in 1st NH Vol. Rgt. during the Spanish-
     American War.
vi. CORA E. M., b. 3 May 1872, d. 18 Mar. 1879.
vii. COMFORT W., b. 2 Dec. 1873, d. 14 Feb. 1874.

656. MARIA JANE[7] 1824-1900 [217 John[6] and Margaret Van-
Winkle] was born in NJ 15 Dec. 1824, died 28 Apr. 1900; mar-
ried 12 Nov. 1848 MARTIN E. DEETHS, born 5 June 1808, died in
Sept. 1887 (Cornman Ms).

Children (**Deeths**), born in NJ:

i.   LEIGHTON, b. 11 Jan., d. 16 June, 1850.
ii. MARGARET, b. 10 Dec. 1852; m. 22 Dec. 1875 GARRET
     MARINER, b. in Oct. 1847, d. in Nov. 1876.
iii. HENRIETTA, b. 20 Feb. 1855.
iv. SARAH, b. 17 Apr. 1859.
v.   KATHERINE B., b. 1 May 1862, d. 30 May 1883.

657. MARGARET CATHERINE[7] 1827-   [217 John[6] and Margaret
VanWinkle] was born in NJ 25 July 1827, lived at Paterson NJ;
married at Passaic NJ 28 Mar. 1850 BURNETT [Barney] BANTA,
born at New York NY 22 July 1825, died 24 Apr. 1890, son of
John and Polly (Westervelt) Banta (Theodore H. Banta, Banta
Genealogy [NY, 1893], 200; Cornman Ms). They lived at Paterson, Bergen Co. NJ.

Children (**Banta**), born in NJ:

i.   MARGARET LOUISE, b. 9 Feb. 1851; m. 19 Oct. 1874
     FREDERICK HENRY GELDERMAN, b. in Prussia.
ii. MARY ELIZABETH, b. 25 Nov. 1852, d. 19 June 1860.
iii. JULIA, b. 22 July 1855.
iv. HENRIETTA L., b. 8 Sept. 1858; m. 22 Nov. 1882
     CHARLES GUSLAND BURR, b. 1 June 1857, d. 12 Apr.
     1892.
v.   HENRY E. MILFORD, b. 25 July, d. 26 Sept., 1861.
vi. WILLIAM, b. 19 July 1865, d. 30 July 1866.
vii. FRANK, b. 23 Mar. 1868, d. 2 Dec. 1874.

658. HENRIETTA[7] 1835-   [217 John[6] and Margaret Van-
Winkle] was born in NJ 6 Feb. 1835; married first 30 Apr.
1856 CHARLES McCORNAE, born 11 Oct. 1833, died 5 Sept. 1864;
married second 29 May 1867 D. H. BROWN, born 5 June 1830,
died 19 Nov. 1896 (Cornman Ms).

Children (**McCornae**):

i.   JOHN L., b. 1 May 1857, d. 31 July 1858.
ii.   CLARA, b. 21 Apr. 1859, d. 23 Feb. 1861.
iii. ELMER E., b. 18 Aug. 1861; m. 14 June 1887 MARGARET
      MARSHALL, b. in Apr. 1864.

Children (**Brown**):

iv.   CHARLES, b. 29 Sept. 1868.
v.   HARRY, b. 1 May 1870, d. 21 June 1871.
vi.   KITTIE B., b. 28 Sept. 1873; m. in Dec. 1898 JOHN
      NIGHTINGALE, b. in Nov. 1865.

659. ANDREW E.[7] 1816-1853 [218 Timothy[6] and Anna Leighton]
was born in NH about 1816, died at Deerfield NH 4 Feb. 1853;
married about 1849 SARAH A. TILTON, who died in 1855, daughter of Samuel and Deborah (Batchelder) Tilton of Deerfield
(Pierce, Batchelder-Batchellor Gen. 154; Cornman Ms). He was
a shoemaker.

Child, born at Deerfield:

1322. i.   WASHINGTON T.[8], b. 30 Oct. 1850.

660. SARAH ANNA[7] 1821-1861 [218 Timothy[6] and Anna Leigh-
ton] was born 15 Aug. 1821, died 2 Jan. 1861; married at Boston 31 Jan. 1846 GEORGE W. MERRILL, born 8 June 1821, lived
at Natick MA, son of Winthrop and Martha Merrill (Cornman
Ms). George married second Sarah's sister Mary.

Children (**Merrill**):

i.   FLORA A., b. 5 Dec. 1847.
ii.   ABBIE N., b. 10 Dec. 1850.
iii. AMY S., b. 10 Feb., d. 1 Oct., 1856.

661. GEORGE WASHINGTON[7] 1825-1863 [218 Timothy[6] and Anna
Leighton] was born in 1825, died at Northwood NH 27 May 1863;
married there 10 Nov. 1851 NANCY JANE SHAW, born 28 Jan.
1830, died 21 Mar. 1896, daughter of John and Betsey Shaw.
Widow Nancy married second 19 Apr. 1866 William H. Gilpatrick
(Cornman Ms).

Children:

i.   AURETTA[8], b. 28 June 1852, d. 5 May 1854.
ii.   ANNA J., b. Nottingham 10 July 1855, d. 10
      Oct. 1858.
iii. GEORGE HERBERT, b. Nottingham 11 May 1857,
      res. there in 1900; m. 17 Dec. 1882 ELIZA A.
      ROBINSON, b. Nottingham in Jan. 1856, dau. of

Clark and Ann P. Robinson. Ch. RALPH R.[9]
b. Nottingham 10 Oct. 1899.
iv.   IRVING, b. Northwood 7 Sept. 1860, d. Haver-
      hill MA 7 Apr. 1933; m. 18 Jan. 1887 FLORA A.
      CLOUGH, b. 6 Apr. 1852. They res. Hampstead
      NH in 1900.

662.   TIMOTHY MURRAY[7] 1830-1857 [218 Timothy[6] and Anna
Leighton] was born at Barrington NH 24 Apr. 1830 (Bible),
died at Northwood NH 18 Dec. 1857, 27y 8m (GS, Canaan Rd.,
Barrington); married at Nottingham 28 June 1852 (VRs) MARY
ANN DAVIS, born there 10 July 1829, daughter of Solomon and
Hannah (Hall) Davis (Northwood VRs; family Bible records from
Mrs. David Prugh; records of Ernestine Leavitt; Cornman Ms).
He was a blacksmith.
     His widow married second Eben K. Gerrish of Deerfield;
Stackpole's Durham (2:110) stated that Mary Ann m. 3rd ----
Davis, probably an error.

Children, born at Northwood:

i.   FRANK D.[8], b. 24 Jan. 1853, d. 27 Apr. 1854
      (Bible).
ii.   EMMA HARRIET, b. 13 Dec. 1855, d. 6 Jan. 1856
      (Bible; VRs).
iii. CHARLES TIMOTHY, b. 15 Mar. 1857, d. Notting-
      ham 21 Sept. 1937, 80y; m. there 19 June 1895
      CORA BELL WOODMAN, b. Laconia NH 15 Jan. 1865
      (records of dau.). In 1870 he res. with his
      mother and Eben Gerrish. Ch. ERNESTINE[9]
      b. Northwood 1 Nov. 1896, res. Nottingham in
      1978; m. DUDLEY LEAVITT. No ch.

663.   MATTHEW THORNTON[7] 1832-1861 [218 Timothy[6] and Anna
Leighton] was born at Barrington NH 8 Aug. 1832, died at
Auburn NH 18 Sept. 1861; married first at Nottingham 6 Jan.
1854 HARRIET A. ALLEN of Georgetown MA, born at Deerfield in
1834, died in 1855; married second at Deerfield 29 Jan. 1856
HANNAH E. (CATE) James, born at Deerfield 8 June 1836, died
at Goffstown NH 22 May 1863, 26y 11m 14d (VRs).
     Hannah had married first at Epsom NH 5 June 1853 William E.
James; they had one child (Cornman Ms).
     Matthew was a shoemaker at Deerfield in 1850. He was
buried at Auburn; Hannah was buried at Manchester NH.

Child by Harriet, born at Northwood (VRs):

i.   ABBIE FRANCES[8], b. 6 Sept. 1854, d. 5 Mar.
      1855, 6m.

Children by Hannah:

ii.   (JOSEPH) CARROLL, b. Deerfield 25 Sept. 1856,
      d. Lowell MA 31 Mar. 1881, 24y 6m 7d; m. Low-
      ell 1 Oct. 1877 MARY E. HARPER, b. there 24
      Apr. 1856, dau. of James and Eliza (Thorpe)
      Harper. He was known both as Joseph and
      Carroll until he changed his name legally to

WILLIAM H.   Ch. JAMES HARPER[9] b. Lowell 12
Sept. 1878, res. there in 1900 with grandmother Eliza Harper; m. EDITH HILL.

1323.   iii.   FRANK EDMUND, b. Auburn 9 Jan. 1858 (VRs).
        iv.   WASHINGTON T., b. Auburn in 1859 (9/12 in 1860
              census).
        v.   ANNA B., b. 17 Mar., d. 26 July, 1861.

EIGHTH GENERATION

664. JAMES GILMAN[8] 1838-   [223 Benjamin7 and Mary Cass]
was born at Epsom NH 16 Apr. 1838, lived at Concord; married
at Alexandria NH 1 May 1857 NELLIE AMELIA HILL, born there 10
Jan. 1843 (Cornman Ms; Dover VRs).
The family was at Concord in 1880, he 42 and she 38; in
1900 he and Nellie were there with no children at home.

Children:

1323.	i.	IDA LUELLA[9], b. 2 Mar. 1858; m. HENRY SHACKFORD and JOHN TIBEAU.
1324.	ii.	BENJAMIN BYRON, b. 17 Dec. 1861.
1325.	iii.	OSCAR GILMAN, b. Concord 7 Feb. 1863.
	iv.	HATTIE EVA, b. in 1865, d. Concord 13 Mar. 1883; unm.
	v.	daughter, b. Concord 9 Jan. 1872, not in 1880 census.
	vi.	JAMES HARRY, b. Concord 24 Sept. 1873, res. Lowell MA; m. Bristol NH 10 Jan. 1900 ISABEL YATES JONES, b. 27 Jan. 1872, dau. of Abraham G. Jones. He was Harry J., 6, in 1880.

665. IDA A.[8] 1848-   [224 William7 and Lydia Jenness] was
born at Epsom NH 8 Aug. 1848, lived at Baltimore MD; married
3 July 1872 RUFUS H. BAKER, born 17 Oct. 1845 (Cornman Ms).

Children (**Baker**):

i.   PERCY C , b. 30 May 1873, d. 29 Dec. 1891.
ii. LEONORA, b. 9 June 1878.

666. WILLIAM IRVING[8] 1855-   [224 William7 and Lydia
Jenness] was born at Epsom NH 9 Oct. 1855, lived at Concord;
married at Plymouth NH 11 Feb. 1880 MARY ELDORA CONNELL of
Plymouth, born in Feb. 1859 (per 1900 census) (Cornman Ms;
Concord VRs).
He was a carriage-painter, and assistant postmaster at Con-
cord. He and Mary were living there in 1900 with their three
children.

Children, born at Concord:

i.   CORA ELDORA[9], b. 31 July 1880.
ii. JOHN CONNELL, b. 26 Aug. 1882.
iii. MAUDE ELEANOR, b. 2 July 1895.

667. WALTER H.[8] 1857-1903 [224 William[7] and Lydia Jenness] was born at Milford NH 18 Sept. 1857, died at Concord (state hosp.) 15 Dec. 1903; married at Contacook NH 28 May 1882 ELIZA [Lizzie] HOLMES, born at Johnston VT 5 July 1855 (29 in 1891).

He was listed at Manchester NH in 1900, with two children and his mother in his household but no wife (Cornman Ms; Manchester VRs).

Children, born at Manchester NH:

i.	EVA M.[9], b. 14 Jan. 1883, d. 16 June 1902; unm.
ii.	WILLIAM A., b. 29 June 1886, d. Manchester 18 Sept. 1890.
iii.	HOWARD H., b. 12 Nov. 1891.

668. CHARLES MILLS[8] 1835-1900 [225 Charles[7] and Frances Hall] was born at Portsmouth NH 29 Mar. 1835, died there 26 Mar. 1900; married first there 27 Oct. 1864 MARIA LOUISE PEN-HALLOW, born 21 Nov. 1844, died at Portsmouth 20 Aug. 1865; married second there 4 Dec. 1866 FLORENCE SULLIVAN PEDUZZI, born there 1 Sept. 1843, lived at NYC, daughter of Dominic and Mary Emily (Sullivan) Peduzzi (Portsmouth VRs; NEHGReg, 83[1929]:299; Cornman Ms).

He was a grocer at Portsmouth. In 1880 his household included Mary Peduzzi, 75; in 1900 his widow was living at Portsmouth with her son Paul.

Children, all by Florence, born at Portsmouth:

	i.	PAUL DeBLOIS[9], b. 8 Sept. 1868, lived at NYC in 1903 and later at Stamford CT (Cornman Ms).
	ii.	FLORENCE MARION, b. 4 Dec. 1870. She was medical examiner for NY Life Ins. Co. and an MIT graduate per Cornman Ms, but is not in their records.
	iii.	EMILY SULLIVAN, b. 31 Dec. 1871, d. Portsmouth 3 Aug. 1892, 20y.
1326.	iv.	ALBERT PARKER, b. 25 Sept. 1875.

669. EMELINE LINCOLN[8] 1846-1910 [225 Charles[7] and Frances Hall] was born at Portsmouth 14 Aug. 1846 (bapt. 7 June 1863, NEHGReg 83 [1929]:295), died at Cambridge MA 26 Mar. 1910; married at Portsmouth 26 Dec. 1878 (83:259) FREDERICK DeFOREST ALLEN, born 25 May 1844, died at Cambridge 4 Aug. 1897, son of George Nelson and Mary Caroline (Rudd) Allen (Cornman Ms). He was professor of classical philology at Harvard.

Children (**Allen**):

i.	BARBARA FRANCES, b. 12 Jan. 1880, d. 3 Jan. 1886.
ii.	ARTHUR FREDERICK, b. 4 Oct. 1886.
iii.	MARGARET, b. 31 Dec. 1888.

670. JAMES ALEXANDER[8] 1835- [226 William[7] and Maria Salt] was born at Portsmouth 22 Jan. 1835, lived at Boston; married at Portsmouth 2 Nov. 1858 ANNIE BACHELDER, born 30 June 1831 (Cornman Ms).

Children:

    i.   GERTRUDE^9, b. 13 Sept. 1859.
    ii.   WILLIAM B., b. Brookline MA 20 Sept. 1862, res.
        Boston in 1900 (census); m. 2 June 1897 FLO-
        RENCE EMMA BEAN of Somerville MA, b. in Aug.
        1870, dau. of James H. and Harriet Bean. Ch.
        HENRY BEAN^{10} b. and d. 18 Aug. 1899.

671. THOMAS^8 1828-1882 [227 Joseph^7 and Martha Hart] was
born at Portsmouth 14 Oct. 1828, died in 1882; married 20
Sept. 1849 MARTHA J. PRAY, born in Jan. 1830 (1900 census).
He was a grocer at Portsmouth in 1850, and later a carpenter.
During the Civil War he served three years in a MA regiment
(Cornman Ms). In 1900 widow Martha lived at Portsmouth with
her brother Albert M. Pray.

Children, born at Portsmouth:

    i.   CHARLES^9, b. say 1850, d. Somerville MA 12 Dec.
        1907.
    ii.   ANNIE, b. in 1852, res. Kittery ME; m. Ports-
        mouth 18 Aug. 1872 WILLIAM A. GARLAND, b. New-
        ington NH 14 Aug. 1846, son of Leonard S. and
        Almira (Whitcomb) Garland. One ch. d.y.
        (Garland Gen., 168).

672. MARK^8 1835-1908 [227 Joseph^7 and Martha Hart] was
born at Portsmouth NH 18 Sept. 1835, died 11 Mar. 1908; mar-
ried at Wolfeboro NH 26 Jan. 1857 ESTHER A HOME, born 26
Oct. 1832, daughter of James and Eunice (Fogg) Home (Whitten,
Samuel Fogg, 1:710; Cornman Ms).
Mark Laighton was a building contractor, and then a fire
insurance appraiser and adjuster. In 1900, his household at
Somerville MA included his daughter and her husband.

Child, born at Charlestown MA (VRs):

    i.   ABIGAIL STETSON^9, b. 28 Mar. 1860, d. 12 Mar.
        1935; m. 18 June 1890 WILMER BRACKETT CLARK,
        b. Farmington NH 24 Nov. 1854, d. in 1917,
        son of Brackett Weeks and Abigail Amanda
        (Wentworth) Clark. No ch. He was a jeweler
        at Boston.

673. IVAN^8 1844-1889 [227 Joseph^7 and Martha Hart] was
born at Portsmouth 5 Sept. 1844, died 14 Sept. 1889; married
at Portsmouth 24 Feb. 1868 ELLEN CORNELIA [Nellie] WOOD-
WORTH, born there 21 Feb. 1845, daughter of James and Ellen
M. (King) Woodworth (records of descendant Cecily Grist
Greeley, including family Bible of Joseph^7; Portsmouth and
Somerville VRs; Cornman Ms).
Ivan Laighton enlisted at Biddeford ME in Co. A, 10th ME
Inf. Rgt. After being a machinist at the naval yard, in 1873
he began a 16-year career on the Somerville police force. In
1880, his Somerville MA household included his mother-in-law
Ellen M. Woodworth. Nellie lived there in 1900 with Everett,
Herbert and Alice.

Children, born at Somerville MA:

    i.   EVERETT W.^{9}, b. 18 May 1869, d. Somerville 29
            May 1955; m. RUTH BRYANT. No ch. Freight
            clerk, B & M RR.
1327. ii.   HERBERT IVAN, b. 30 Jan. 1873.

674. CELIA^8 1836-1894 [228 Thomas^7 and Eliza Rymes] was
born at Portsmouth 29 June 1836, died at Appledore Island,
Isles of Shoals ME 26 Aug. 1894; married there 30 Sept. 1851
LEVI LINCOLN THAXTER, born at Watertown MA 2 Feb. 1824, died
at Kittery ME 31 May 1884, son of Levi and Lucy (White) Thaxter.
    Celia Thaxter was a widely-read poet; she and Levi attract-
ed to her father's Appledore House the literary and artistic
great of the period. From 1860, when her first poem was published, she won critical acclaim for her nature poetry and
essays, and her work still appears in anthologies. Best
known are her Poems (1872), Drift-weed (1879), An Island
Garden (1874), and her volumes of poetry for children.
    Levi was graduated from Harvard in 1843 (classmate of James
Russell Lowell), and from Harvard Law School. During a visit
to the Isles of Shoals he was requested to stay on as tutor
to Thomas Laighton's children; he and Celia were married
before her sixteenth birthday. They settled at Newtonville
MA in 1856. She left Levi in 1872, returning to Appledore to
nurse her mother. After 1880 she made her home at Kittery--
spending each summer on Appledore Island.
    For Celia's biography, see D.A.B 18:397-8; her granddaugh-
ter Rosamund Thaxter's Sandpiper: the Life and Letters of
Celia Thaxter [1962], and--for a feminist viewpoint--Jane E.
Vallier's Poet on Demand [Camden ME, 1982].

    Children (**Thaxter**):

    i.   KARL, b. Appledore ME in 1852, d. Worcester MA in
           1912. He was mentally retarded from birth.
    ii.   JOHN, b. Newburyport MA 29 Nov. 1854; m. Worcester
           MA 1 June 1887 MARY GERTRUDE STODDARD.
    iii. ROLAND, b. Newtonville 28 Aug. 1858, d. Boston 22
           Apr. 1932; m. Cambridge MA 15 June 1887 MABEL GRAY
           FREEMAN. He was a botany professor at Harvard.

675. CEDRIC^8 1840-1899 [228 Thomas^7 and Eliza Rymes] was
born at Portsmouth NH 4 Sept. 1840, died at Medford MA in
1899; married JULIA STOWELL, born in Feb. 1860, lived at
Isles of Shoals in 1900 (ME census), daughter of Everett and
Abby (Cory) Stowell (Cornman Ms). He was partner with his
brother Oscar in operating the resort hotels on Appledore and
Star Islands. In 1900, Julia was listed also at Cambridge MA
with her three daughters.

    Children:

        i.   RUTH STOWELL^9, b. Boston 17 June 1883. She was
             a music teacher and professional violinist.
        ii.   MARGARET, b. in Mar. 1885; m. Manila, Philip-
             pine Islands, 29 Jan. 1907 EDWARD W. FORBES.
        iii. BARBARA, b. in Nov. 1891; m. WILLIAM DURANT.

676.   EMILY ALICE[8] [Emma] 1835-   [229 William[7] and Mary
Walker] was born at Portsmouth 31 Dec. 1835; married there 17
May 1855 (Bible, 18 May) JOHN GOODWIN TOBEY, born at Eliot ME
27 Jan. 1834, son of William and Polly (Goodwin) Tobey (fam-
ily Bible of Dr. James A. Tobey, NEHGReg, 127[1973]:131-2;
Rufus Babcock Tobey and Charles H. Pope, Tobey (Tobie, Toby)
Genealogy [Boston, 1905], 308; Cornman Ms).
They lived at Worcester, and then at Portsmouth, where he
was a real estate broker.

Children (**Tobey**):

i.   CLARENCE, b. 16 Apr., d. 19 June, 1858.
ii.   RUFUS TOLMAN, b. 12 July 1859, d. 23 Feb. 1946.
iii.   WILLIAM LAIGHTON, b. Worcester 4 Nov. 1861 (Bible,
       14 Nov. 1860), res. Winthrop MA; m. Boston 1 Dec.
       1898 MARGARET S. (CAMPBELL) Frazer, dau. of Henry D.
       and Agnes Campbell, b. Calais ME in 1862.
iv.   daughter, d. Worcester 2 July 1872.
v.   JOHN GOODWIN JR., b. Worcester 10 Nov. 1873. He was
       a lawyer.
vi.   ROSA B., b. 24 June 1876.
vii.   FRED CHAMBERLAIN, b. 12 Jan. 1878.

677.   MARIANNE[8] 1837-   [229 William[7] and Mary Walker]
was born at Kennebunk ME 10 Nov. 1837; married at Portsmouth
NH 22 Dec. 1864 (NEHGReg, 83[1929]:299) GEORGE D. DODGE, born
at Hampton Falls NH 4 May 1836, son of George Hubbard and
Mary (Keeley) Dodge (Dodge Family, 1:365-6).
Before his marriage, George owned a bookshop at Savannah
GA   After the war began he was drafted into the Confederate
Army, but made a dramatic escape to the north.
He was one of the first to establish a summer residence at
Hampton Beach.
The Dodge genealogy stated they had four sons and two
daughters, but did not name them.

Children (**Dodge**):

i.   GEORGE HUBBARD, b. 1 Apr. 1866; m. MINNIE E. PIERCE.
ii.   MINNIE GERTRUE, b. 1 May 1867.
iii.   RALPH MORTIMER, b. 24 Dec. 1877.
iv.   WALLACE D. C., b. 29 Nov. 1879.

678.   LUCY ALMIRA[8] 1840-   [235 George[7] and Louise Flagg]
was born at Portsmouth 1 Oct. 1840; married there 29 June
1865 HENRY S. LAMBERT, born 24 May 1843. In 1903 they lived
at Asheville NC (Cornman Ms). He was an acting master in the
US Navy, 1862-65.

Children (**Lambert**):

i.   WILLIAM HOFFMAN, b. 19 Nov. 1866, d. 30 May 1899.
ii.   HARRY CLIFFORD, b. 31 Jan. 1870, d. 8 Sept. 1871.
iii.   GEORGE HERMAN, b. 27 Sept. 1873; m. Chicago IL 12
       Mar. 1901 JULIA M. GIBSON, d. 12 Oct. 1901.
iv.   ELIZABETH CHASE, b. 10 July 1882.

679. FRANKLIN HOWARD[8] 1836-1901 [236 William[7] and Abigail Leighton] was born at Portsmouth 14 Apr. 1836, died at Chiloquin OR 16 May 1901; married there 12 Oct. 1873 SARAH ELIZABETH KENNEY, born at Muscatine IA 20 Aug. 1846, daughter of Samuel and Maria Ann (Porter) Kenney or Kinney (Cornman Ms).

He settled at Umatilla OR in 1860 as a merchant, moved to Salem in 1875, then to Astoria, and in 1886 to a farm at Seaside, where they were living in 1900 (census).

Children, born in OR:

    i.   ALBERT LYMAN[9], b. W. Chiloquin 15 Nov. 1874, d. Seaside 2 Oct. 1904.

    ii.   WILLIAM JAMES, b. Astoria 25 Mar. 1877.

    iii. FRANKLIN HOWARD, b. Astoria 20 Apr. 1879; m. 15 Sept. 1903 NELLIE STANLEY, dau. of Samuel and Mary Ann (Conroy) Stanley.

    iv.   BENNETT, b. Seaside 28 Apr. 1882; m. 21 Dec. 1909 MYRTLE ST CLAIR.

    v.   HUGH LLOYD, b. Seaside 6 Dec. 1887, d. in 1888.

680. WASHINGTON IRVING[8] 1840- [237 Edward[7] and Harriet Smith] was born at Portsmouth say 1840, died before 1880; married at Portsmouth 11 Jan. 1867 ARABELLA EMERY LYNN, born there 16 Mar. 1845 (Nov. 1844 per gen.), died there a widow 23 Mar. 1897, daughter of Andrew and Eliza Mary Perkins (Emery) Lynn (Emery Desc., 262; Cornman Ms).

In 1880 "Isabella" Laighton was listed at Portsmouth with her two sons.

Children, born at Portsmouth:

    i.   FREDERICK SMITH, b. 6 May 1869 (12 in 1880; T. SMITH, b. 1868, per gen.), d. Boston 15 Mar. 1894.

    ii.   WASHINGTON IRVING, b. 20 Oct. 1872 (1871 per gen.), d. W. Newton MA 18 Apr. 1893; unm. He was a telegraph inspector.

681. JOHN[8] 1847- [238 Benjamin[7] and Susan Remick] was born at Stratham NH 26 Oct. 1847; married at Portsmouth 12 Apr. 1880 MARY EMILY HALEY, who was born 9 Mar. 1850. He was a Portsmouth grocer (Portsmouth VRs; Cornman Ms).

Children, born at Portsmouth:

    i.   PHILIP DAMRELL[9], b. 4 Dec. 1885, d. Portsmouth in Sept. 1910.

    ii.   RUTH BEAL, b. 15 July 1888.

    iii. REMICK HALEY, b. 28 Aug. 1892.

682. MARY SUSAN[8] 1849- [238 Benjamin[7] and Susan Remick] was born probably at Stratham NH in 1849; married at Portsmouth 3 Aug. 1880 MONINA G. PORTER, born 20 Aug. 1849, died en route from military assignment in the Phillipines, son of Adm. William D. Porter (Portsmouth VRs; Cornman Ms).

Children (**Porter**), born at Portsmouth:

i.   EDNA PAULDING, b. 17 June 1881.
ii.   BENNETT LAIGHTON, b. 9 Aug. 1883.

683.   EDWIN R.[8] 1833-   [244 Littleton[7] and Mary Hart]
was born at Portsmouth 18 Nov. 1833, lived at New Haven CT;
married first ELVIRA --- ; married second 10 Sept. 1867 ELIZA
TIGHE, born at London, England, in 1844 (26 in 1870) (Cornman
Ms; Portsmouth VRs).
In 1880 their Portsmouth household included George Tighe,
19.   Edwin was a naval yard clerk, but was later employed in
CT by the New York, New Haven and Hartford RR.

Children by Elvira, born at Portsmouth:

i.   LEONARD MARCH[9], b. 23 May 1859 (as Leo M.),
       res. New Haven; m. ISABELLE WOOD of Ports-
       mouth. Ch. EDWARD HENRY[10] b. 1 Apr. 1892.
ii.   EDWIN HENRY CLARE, b. 11 Oct. 1862.

684.   MARY WYMAN[8] 1846-   [244 Littleton[7] and Mary Hart]
was born at Portsmouth 23 Feb. 1846, lived at Los Angeles CA;
married at Portsmouth 9 June 1869 WILLIAM B. DOLE of Bangor
ME, born 26 June 1841, died in CA 23 Oct. 1897, son of Albert
and Miriam Dole (Cornman Ms).   They settled at Pomona CA in
1882, where he became a bank president.

Children (**Dole**), born at Bangor:

i.   ARTHUR McDONALD, b. 17 Dec. 1874, d. Pomona 23 Oct.
       1897.
ii.   EDITH LAIGHTON, b. 4 Nov. 1881, d. Pomona 26 Aug.
       1882.

685.   MARY ANN[8] 1816-   [252 Jonathan[7] and Lydia Strout]
was born at Steuben ME 14 Dec. 1816, died before 1860; married there 8 Oct. 1834 GEORGE B. SAWYER, born 11 Feb. 1812,
died 16 July 1899, son of Josiah Jr. and Rebecca (Grindle)
Sawyer.   He married second Jane McEachern (Steuben and ME
VRs; Sawyer Index, 36).
He was a ships' carpenter at Milbridge in 1850 with his
wife Mary; in the 1860 and 1870 censuses there, his wife was
Jane.   He and Jane had four children.

Children (**Sawyer**):

i.   DAVID, b. 24 Oct. 1834, d. in July 1895 (GS, Ever-
       green Cemetery); m. HENRIETTA ---- .
ii.   MARY A., b c1838 (12 in 1850).
iii.   PHEBE E., b. c1840 (9 in 1850); m. HARRISON B.[8]
       LEIGHTON [# 1048].

686.   PRISCILLA[8] 1819-1890 [252 Jonathan[7] and Lydia Strout]
was born at Steuben 20 Dec. 1819, died there 19 Nov. 1890;
married there 13 Sept. 1837 WILLIAM R. ATWATER, born in NS 20
May 1811, son of David A. and Melissa Atwater (Steuben VRs;

data from Caroline Dunbar--Cornman Papers).
Priscilla's husband was called Hiram Atwood by Katherine
Richmond (John Hayes, 2:706).

Children (**Atwater**), born at Steuben:

i.   CAROLINE LEIGHTON, b. 9 Nov. 1840; m. Steuben 6 Nov.
      1858 JOHN YEATON DUNBAR, b. there 21 Oct. 1831, res.
      Dyer's Bay, son of Peter and Catherine (Yeaton)
      Dunbar.
ii.   LYMAN, b. 13 Mar. 1843, lost at sea in 1852.
iii. MARY JANE, b. 12 July 1846, res. Searsport ME and
      Lynn MA; m. 1st 2 May 1863 NATHAN D. YEATON, b.
      Steuben 27 May 1837; m. 2nd ALEXANDER SWEETSER.
iv.   DAVID, b. 14 Mar. 1847, res. Lynn MA; m. CARRIE ROSS
      of Rockland ME, b. 18 Mar. 1854, d. Steuben 10 Mar.
      1918.
v.   JAMES ALBERT, b. 15 Feb. 1849, res. Lynn MA; m. (as
      Albert J. in Machias Union) Cherryfield int. 25
      Mar. 1869 MARIAM LEIGHTON [# 408]. He div. her
      after she left him to go to CA
vi.   ASENATH W., b. 19 Dec. 1851, d. Steuben 17 Aug. 1889;
      m. Lynn MA GEORGE WRIGHT.
vii. LYDIA, b. 22 Feb. 1854, res. Portland ME; m. WILLIAM
      HOPKINS of Southwest Harbor, Mt. Desert Island.
viii. LAURA S., b. 11 Jan. 1856, d. Rochester NH 29 Nov.
      1930, 75y 10m 15d; m. 1st Lynn MA WALTER JONES; m.
      2nd Springvale ME HENRY HANSON; m. 3rd Rochester NH
      31 Dec. 1913 GEORGE GASTON HAYES.
ix.   CHARLES F., b. 27 Jan 1858, res. Jonesport ME; m.
      Steuben 11 July 1891 RUTH DRISKO of Columbia.
x.   ANNIE BELLE, b. 5 May 1860, d. Steuben 17 May 1906;
      m. there 25 Apr. 1879 JOSEPH STANLEY JR., b. 1 Mar.
      1836, son of Joseph and Hannah (Gilley) Stanley of
      Cranberry Isles ME.

687. CLIMENA[8] 1821-1893 [252 Jonathan[7] and Lydia Strout]
was born at Steuben 30 Jan. 1821, died at Milbridge ME 6 July
1893, 71y 6m (town VRs; GS); married first at Milbridge 20
Feb. 1840 JOSIAH WALLACE, born at Cape Elizabeth ME in Oct.
1796, died at Milbridge 12 Aug. 1884, 88y 10m (GS), son of
Josiah Jr. and Sally (Roberts) Wallace; married second LEVI
P. STROUT, born at Milbridge 17 Apr. 1826, died there 11 Aug.
1910, son of Lewis and Lydia (Smith) Strout (records of Margaret Colton; town VRs).
    Burials are in Evergreen Cemetery. Josiah married first
Sally Sawyer; they had three children. Levi had a first wife
Mary who died in 1881.

Children (**Wallace**), born at Milbridge:

i.   WILBUR L., b. in 1841, d. serving in Civil War.
ii.   CLAUDIUS, b. in 1842, also d. serving in Civil War.
iii. SARAH, b. 12 Oct. 1844, d. 5 Aug. 1883, 38y 9m 23d;
      m. 19 Apr. 1864 WILLIAM EMERY PINKHAM, b. Milbridge
      8 Mar. 1839, d. there 17 Nov. 1913, 74y, son of
      Robert and Ann (Perry) (Cole) Pinkham. He m. 2nd
      19 Oct. 1884 Martha E. Mitchell (Sinnett, Pinkham
      Gen., 82).

iv.   EDWIN L., b. 24 Sept. 1847, d. Milbridge 6 Apr. 1912;
       m. 1st 24 Aug. 1878 EMMA G. SAWYER, b. 19 June 1855,
       d. 7 Jan. 1882, 26y 6m 19d (GS), dau. of Joseph W.
       and Mary Jane (Wallace) Sawyer; m. 2nd Milbridge 19
       July 1884 JEANETTE SAWYER, b. 7 Sept. 1852, d. 27
       Jan. 1899, 46y 4m 20d (GS), dau. of Daniel Look and
       Mariah A (Moore) Sawyer; m. 3rd Milbridge 25 Mar.
       1900 MARGARET (HAYLAND) Sawyer, b. Cherryfield in
       1856, d. in 1938.
v.   ROSINA S., b. in 1859, d. in 1922; m. 1st 14 July
       1880 NAHUM YOUNG; m. 2nd 5 Feb. 1893 EVERETT W.
       MITCHELL.

    688. ORSENA[8] [Asenath Pratt] 1823-1901 [252 Jonathan[7] and
Lydia Strout] was born at Steuben 28 Mar. 1823, died at Cherryfield 28 Feb. 1901, 77y 11m 2d; married there 13 Aug. 1843
DANIEL WILLEY, born there 4 Apr. 1814, died there 15 July
1900, son of Charles and Hannah (Guptill) Willey (town VRs;
records of Joanna Willey).   Orsena called herself Asenath
Pratt Leighton.

    Children (Willey), born at Cherryfield:

i.   MELBOURNE HOYT, b. 18 Sept. 1846, d. Cherryfield in
       1915; m. 1st there 25 Sept. 1866 MARTHA W. BURNHAM
       of St. George ME; m. 2nd there 25 Oct. 1883 (MARTHA)
       EMMA CLEAVES; m. 3rd there 4 Sept. 1901 SELEDA B.
       SPROUL.
ii.   AUGUSTA LOUISA, b. 26 May 1848, d. 4 Aug. 1850.
iii.   ARTHUR NASH, b. 6 Feb. 1850, d. 26 Oct. 1907; m.
       Cherryfield 9 Jan. 1884 ISADORE E. (GARNETT)
       Stickney.
iv.   EVERETT ELWYN, b. 8 Oct. 1853, d. 17 Apr. 1873.
v.   HATTIE, b. 29 Nov. 1853; m. 16 Jan. 1878 EDWARD
       RICKER WINGATE.
vi.   HAROLD, b. 7 Nov. 1856, d. 25 Aug. 1879.

    689. CAROLINE[8] 1825-   [252 Jonathan[7] and Lydia Strout]
was born at Steuben 19 Mar. 1825; married there int. 7 Nov.
1846 STILLMAN PARRITT, born at Harrington 20 Feb. 1818, son
of Samuel and Rhoda (Joy) Parritt (town VRs).

    Children (Parritt), born at Harrington:

i.   HENRIETTA, b. 1 Apr. 1849; m. Harrington 26 Aug. 1871
       (Machias Union) SIMEON STROUT, son of John Strout.
ii.   EUNICE C., b. 22 July 1853, res. Steuben; m. JOSEPH
       STROUT, son of David Strout of Harrington.
iii.   LORANA H., b. 9 Feb. 1856, res. Poland Springs ME; m.
       Steuben 15 May 1878 (Machias Union) EDWIN A. STROUT,
       brother of Joseph.

    690. DAVID[8] 1827-1899 [252 Jonathan[7] and Lydia Strout]
was born at Steuben 28 Apr. 1827, died at Calais ME 25 Jan.
1899, 71y 8m 25d; married at Calais 29 Nov. 1855 ABIGAIL
SPOONER, born in NB about 1832 (36 in 1870, 48 in 1880),
lived at Calais in 1899 (town VRs).
    He was a carpenter.

Children, born at Calais:

    i.   HERBERT W.[9], b. 7 Nov. 1856 (Albert W., 13 in
        1870), d. Lewiston ME 6 Mar. 1935; m. 1st
        ELIZABETH E. SEARS of Eastport; m. 2nd JENNIE
        ANDERSON, b. 1891, d. 1965 (GS). Burials are
        in Evergreen Cemetery, Auburn. He was a car-
        penter. Ch. FREDERICK WALLACE[10] b. Calais 17
        Mar. 1881.
    ii.   EMMA M., b. c1859 (21 in 1880; Mary E. in
        1870), res. Haverhill MA; m. ---- LOOK.
1328. iii. JOEL JONATHAN, b. 12 July 1860.
    iv.   HATTIE M., b. c1872 (8 in 1880).

691. AMESBURY[8] 1831-1903 [252 Jonathan[7] and Lydia Strout]
was born at Steuben 25 Jan. 1831 (29 in 1860, 38 in 1870;
1829 per VRs), died at Camden ME 23 Mar. 1903, 72y 2m 26d;
married at Steuben 25 Dec. 1854 ANN MARIA N. CLEAVES, born
there 4 Jan. 1837, died at Camden 1 June 1913, 76y 4m 28d,
daughter of Oliver and Persis Townley (Leighton) Cleaves
[# 259] (town VRs; Cornman Ms).
Amesbury was a seaman and then ship captain, sailing from
NYC to foreign ports, and surviving several shipwrecks--one
with a cargo of corn on Hens and Chickens Ledge in Buzzard's
Bay.
After twenty years at sea, he became a ships' carpenter at
Milbridge. In 1901, he and Annie made their home at Camden
with Wendell.

Children, born at Steuben:

    i.   LUELLA[9], b. 12 Oct. 1855; m. CHARLES[9] LEIGHTON
        [# 1490].
1329. ii.   ADELBERT CLEAVES, b. 17 Feb. 1859.
    iii. LEONETTA C. [Nettie], b. 7 Oct. 1860, d. 11
        Oct. 1864, 4y.
    iv.   MARY M., b. 26 Jan. 1864, d. in 1866.
    v.   LINWOOD L., d. Steuben 23 July 1867, 18m
        (Machias Union).
    vi.   CAROLINE PARRITT [Carrie], b. 23 May 1867, d.
        at sea in 1892; m. Cherryfield 13 Dec. 1890
        JOHN W. STOVER, d. at sea in 1891. Ch. Ralph
        Leighton b. Milbridge in Oct. 1891, res.
        with Amesbury in 1900.
1330. vii. LEONETTA RANDALL [Nettie], b. 22 Nov. 1869; m.
        WILLIAM D. UPTON.
1331. viii. WENDELL SCOTT, b. 27 June 1872.

692. OSGOOD E.[8] 1835-1901 [252 Jonathan[7] and Lydia Strout]
was born at Steuben 6 Sept. 1835, died at Milbridge 18 Aug.
1901, 65y, by suicide; married perhaps third 26 Mar. 1879
INEZ ELLA HARNDEN, born at Steuben about 1857 (36 in 1893),
lived at Westport ME in 1908, daughter of Charles A and
Clara P. (Parritt) Harnden--div. She married second Asahel
E. Gove at Bath ME 4 Nov. 1893; they had no children (Gove
Book, 273).
Osgood was said to have had three wives. In 1860 he lived
with his parents; in 1900 he was living alone at Milbridge.

Child by Inez, born at Steuben (perhaps others):

    i.   RALPH F.^{9}, b. c1887; m. Rockland 25 Dec. 1908
          WINIFRED A. CLARK, who m. 2nd Rockland 31$_{10}$Jan.
          1916 Harold L. Karl. Ch. NEIL FREDERICK^{10} b.
          Portland 30 July 1909.

693. ELIZA ANN^8 1838-   [252 Jonathan^7 and Lydia Strout]
was born at Steuben 4 Feb. 1838; married there 13 Oct. 1857
(Machias Union) DAVID JONES NASH, born 7 Feb. 1836 (Steuben
and Harrington VRs; Cornman Ms). (The newspaper named them
Shaw Nash and Ellen Leighton, but the Steuben intentions 25
Sept. gave their correct names.)

Children (**Nash**), born at Harrington:

    i.   MABEL, b. in 1855, d. Harrington 21 Jan. 1856.
    ii.   BYRON, b. 14 Sept. 1859, d. Harrington 28 June 1873,
          14y (Machias Union.
    iii. MABEL V., b. 21 Apr. 1865, res. in OH; m. ---- KING
          (Harrington Town Register).
    iv.   DANA I., b. 7 Jan. 1869; m. ELLA^9 LEIGHTON [# 694].

694. WOODBURY^8 1816-1885 [254 Charity^7] was born at
Steuben 25 July 1816, died at Harrington 9 Dec. 1885; married
at Cherryfield 5 Apr. 1843 (Harrington int. 21 Feb.) EMMA
LAWRENCE, born at Addison 11 Aug. 1822, died at Harrington 16
Oct. 1913, 91y 2m 5d, daughter of James P. and Mary Blake
(Alline) Lawrence (town and ME VRs; Cornman Ms).
Woodbury was raised as a son by his grandfather Jonathan.
He was a ships' carpenter and boat builder at Harrington.
Widow Emma was living at Harrington in 1900 with her son
Herbert, and was there in 1910 with her daughter Annie.

Children, born at Harrington:

1332. i.   CHARLES E.^{9}, b. 3 Feb. 1845.
1333. ii.   MARY M., b. 19 Jan. 1847; m. GEORGE H. COFFIN.
1334. iii.   REBECCA C., b. 30 Nov. 1848; m. ISAAC BOYNTON.
1335. iv.   HERBERT N., b. 2 May 1851.
      v.   ANNIE B., b. 1 Jan. 1853, d. Harrington 1 Apr.
              1939; unm. She res. Hyde Park MA in 1900 with
              sister Flora, and at Harrington in 1910.
      vi.   WILLIS L., b. 15 Sept. 1855, d. 8 Sept. 1856.
      vii.   HARRIET B., b. 30 Dec. 1857, d. 6 June 1860,
              2y 6m.
1336. viii.   FLORA B., b. 11 Feb. 1860; m. PHINEAS FRIEND.
      ix.   ELLA G., b. 25 Mar. 1863; m. DANA I. NASH, b.
              Harrington 7 Jan. 1869, res. So. Middleton MA,
              son of David J. and Eliza Ann^8 (Leighton) Nash
              [# 693]. Ch. Jessie N. and Byron.

695. CATHERINE ALLEN^8 1825-1866 [255 Henry D.^{7} and Lovicia
Wass] was born at Steuben 26 July 1825, died at Belfast ME 2
Mar. 1866; married at Steuben 7 Jan. 1844 ALBION K. P. MOORE,
born at Steuben 18 May 1821, died there 15 Jan. 1892, son of
Samuel and Matilda (Wakefield) Moore (Wakefield Mem., 130;
records of Margaret Colton; town VRs).

Children (**Moore**), born at Steuben:

i.   LOIS J., b. 20 Sept. 1845, d. Steuben 8 Aug. 1879; m.
      1 Oct. 1864 CHARLES GILBERT CLEAVES, b. 29 July
      1840, d. Steuben 29 Apr. 1885, son of Joshua and
      Susan (Haskell) Cleaves.
ii.   ANNETTE W., b. 17 Jan. 1847, res. Portland ME; m.
      GEORGE D. LORING.
iii. CHARLES A , b. 13 Nov. 1849; m. Steuben 31 Dec. 1872
      ADA L. TABBUTT, dau. of Stillman and Juliette
      (Smith) Tabbutt.
iv.   MARTHA M., b. 6 Apr. 1851, res. Brockton MA; m.
      MILLARD AVERY of Ellsworth.
v.   EBENEZER S., b. 29 Dec. 1854, d. 11 Nov. 1856.
vi.   KATE B., b. 8 Jan. 1859; m. 1st Milbridge int. 11
      Oct. 1880 THOMAS E. STROUT, d. at sea; m. 2nd
      Milbridge int. 12 June 1881 Capt. JAMES W. BROWN.
vii. HARRY T. (twin), b. 8 Jan., d. 18 Jan., 1859.
viii. FLORENCE MAY, b. 29 Apr. 1864, d. Orono ME in 1945;
      m. FREDERICK SMITH WALLACE, son of Charles A and
      Susan Wallace.

696. ANN WASS[8] 1827-1908 [255 Henry D.[7] and Lovicia Wass]
was born at Steuben 9 Mar. 1827, died at Teck ID 7 Aug. 1908;
married first at Steuben 25 July 1847 GEORGE W. WAITE of Halifax NS, born 18 June 1828, died at Milbridge ME 15 Sept.
1866, son of John and Abiah Dean (Hall) Waite; married second
JOHN D. HOLDEN of Omro WI (town VRs; Cornman Ms).
She took her family west to WI, and later lived in Idaho
with her son Henry.

Children (**Waite**):

i.   JULIA A , b. Steuben 1 Oct. 1851, d. 21 Oct. 1857.
ii.   EMILY MORSE, b. Steuben 8 Sept. 1852; m. Omro WI 5
      Apr. 1874 FREDERICK M. BUNKER.
iii. HENRY, b. Steuben 3 June 1854, d. Teck ID 20 Apr.
      1910; m. Oshkosh WI 24 June 1883 CATHERINE A.
      TEASLEE.
iv.   ROBERT SHAW, b. Milbridge 6 May 1857, d. Omro WI 5
      Oct. 1880; unm.
v.   ELIZA CAMPBELL. b. Milbridge 10 Aug. 1858; m. Omro WI
      17 Aug. 1880 ANDREW LARRABEE.
vi.   GEORGIA ANN WASS, b. Milbridge 10 Mar. 1864, d. Omro
      5 Sept. 1871.

697. ARICSENE[8] 1829-1894 [255 Henry D.[7] and Lovicia Wass]
was born at Steuben 15 Jan. 1829, died at Cherryfield ME 26
Apr. 1894, 65y 5m; married at Steuben 22 Oct. 1852, as his
second wife, (ELISHA) COFFIN SMALL, born at Cherryfield 17
Feb. 1821, died there 17 July 1906, son of Joseph and Betsey
(Tucker) Small (town and ME VRs; Cornman Ms).

Children (**Small**), born at Cherryfield:

i.   CELIA A., b. 2 Sept. 1853, d. 8 Oct. 1896, 43y; m.
      Cherryfield 15 June 1882 ALVAH F. FARNSWORTH, b.
      Beddington c1857, d. Bangor 28 Feb. 1923, son of Eri
      Coffin and Elizabeth (Pettingall) Farnsworth.

ii.   MILTON T., b. 30 Aug. 1855; m. Ducktown TN in Oct.
       1892 HARRIET STUART, b. 1 Mar. 1870, dau. of Joseph
       and Jane (Witt) Stuart.
iii.   ELIZABETH T., b. 22 Feb. 1857, res. Columbia Falls
       ME; m. 16 Sept. 1886 ELMER SMALL, b. Cherryfield
       30 Sept. 1861, son of Winslow G. and Clara (Lawn)
       Small.
iv.   WALTER W., b. 19 June 1860.
v.   MABEL P., b. 5 Sept. 1867.

698.   ELIZA DYER[8] 1833-1910 [255 Henry D.[7] and Lovicia
Wass] was born at Steuben 2 Sept. 1833, died at Westboro WI 6
Nov. 1910; married at Steuben 19 Aug. 1855 (Machias Union)
Major HORATIO SNOW CAMPBELL, born at Cherryfield 1 Oct. 1828,
died at Medford WI 19 Apr. 1886, son of James Archibald and
Thirza (Fickett) Campbell. He had a first wife Lydia Jane
(records of Leonard F Tibbetts; Cornman Ms).

Children (**Campbell**):

i.   PERLEY MORRIS, b. Butte des Morts, Winnebago Co. WI
       13 May 1856; unm.
ii.   ALICE MOORE, b. Butte des Morts 31 Dec. 1857, res.
       Seattle WA; m. Medford WI 5 Jan. 1886 THOMAS
       FARRELL.
iii.   ELMER ELLSWORTH, b. Oshkosh WI 19 Sept. 1865, d.
       Westboro WI in 1917; m. Mt. Pleasant PA 10 Apr. 1890
       ELLA A FITZ, b. England 16 July 1863, dau. of John
       and Mary Ann (James) Fitz.

699.   ELLEN FRANCES[8] 1836-1900 [255 Henry D.[7] and Lovicia
Wass] was born at Steuben 20 Jan. 1836, died at Fargo ND 5
Sept. 1900; married at Cherryfield ME 20 Aug. 1858 (THOMAS)
JEFFERSON CAMPBELL, born at Cherryfield 8 Oct. 1834, died at
Oshkosh WI 20 Jan. 1905, son of James Archibald and Thirza
(Fickett) Campbell (Cornman Ms; daughter Nellie Love's letter
in 1920--Cornman Papers). They lived at Omro WI.

Children (**Campbell**), born at Omro WI:

i.   NELLIE, b. 8 Dec. 1859, d. 12 Dec. 1863.
ii.   MARTHA LEWIS, 17 June 1861.
iii.   MERRITT LATHROP, b. 26 Mar. 1864, res. Neenah WI;
       m. 26 Mar. 1899 STELLA JOSLYN.
iv.   NELLIE MAY, b. 30 Oct. 1867, res. Fargo ND; m. 26
       June 1893 ANDREW ALEXANDER LOVE.
v.   SARAH [Sadie], b. 18 Jan. 1872.
vi.   HARRY, b. 12 Mar. 1874; m. Jamestown NY 25 Dec. 1896
       JESSIE A. CLARK, b. 3 June 1877, dau. of Harrison W.
       and Julia (Felton) Clark.
vii.   daughter, b. 25 May, d. 12 June, 1880.

700.   FLETCHER KINGSLEY[8] 1839-1911 [255 Henry D.[7] and
Lovicia Wass] was born at Steuben 3 Mar. 1839, died at Edgewood PA 21 Mar. 1911; married at Sullivan ME 16 Apr. 1864
MARY ADELAIDE JOHNSON, born at East Sullivan 9 Jan. 1845,
died at Braddock PA 7 Dec. 1933, daughter of Stephen Jr. and

Charlotte (Martin) Johnson (records of granddaughter (Mary) Adelaide Remington Williams; Steuben and Sullivan VRs; Cornman Ms).

Fletcher built a shingle mill which he had operated for several years before he was 22 years old. He enlisted as sergeant, Co. C, 11th ME Inf. Rgt., 4 Nov. 1861, and served during the Peninsular Campaign. After his marriage, he lived in NY, and in 1871 built and operated a stave and lumber mill at Confluence, Somerset Co. PA. In 1879 he settled at Braddock, where he opened a plumbing business, and served the borough as school director and burgess. In 1896 he retired to Edgewood Park (J. W. Jordan, Genealogical Memoirs of Pennsylvania [1908], 3:177).

His widow, "Aunt Mary," was a summer visitor at Sullivan, and presented to the East Sullivan Union Church a sterling silver communion service in memory of her father, a long-time deacon there (Johnson, Sullivan and Sorrento, 380).

Children:

	i.	JULIA ANN[9], b. Steuben 7 June 1865, d. Braddock 3 Apr. 1903; unm. She was a schoolteacher.
1337.	ii.	HENRY STEPHEN, b. Harristown NY 11 Mar. 1867.
1338.	iii.	ANNIE GODFREY, b. Hammonton NY 20 Jan. 1869; m. ALEXANDER M. STEVENSON.
	iv.	CHARLOTTE JOHNSON, b. Confluence PA 29 Jan. 1873, d. Braddock 16 July 1903; m. 10 June 1897 Dr. WILLIAM ALEXANDER CLEMENTSON, b. Fayette City PA 20 Dec. 1873, d. 16 Feb. 1912, son of George H. Clementson. No ch. He grad. from Jefferson Med. Col., Philadelphia PA
1339.	v.	FRANK KINGSLEY, b. Confluence 4 Oct. 1876.
	vi.	ELLA CAROLINE, b. Braddock 29 Nov. 1880, d. there 16 Apr. 1882.
1340.	vii.	EMMA LEONA, b. Braddock 14 Feb. 1884; m. PAUL REMINGTON.

701. TRUMAN W.[8] 1841-   [255 Henry D.[7] and Lovicia Wass] was born at Steuben 15 Aug. 1841, lived in WI; married at East Machias 25 May 1878 EMMA (SHUTE) Morrison (both of Machiasport, Machias Union), born in NY about 1848 (1880 census), lived at Omro WI.

In 1870 he was a blacksmith at Embarron, Waupaca Co. WI, with his wife "Emily B.," 23; they were at Green Lake WI in 1880. In 1900 he lived alone at Fairview OR.

Children, born in WI:

	i.	ETTA[9], b. c1859 (11 in 1870), res. Cape Horn WA in 1914, (then aged 48, her letter--Cornman Papers).
	ii.	LOUISA, b. c1867 (13 in 1880).
	iii.	JOHN W., b. c1868 (11 in 1880).
	iv.	ROBERT W., b. c1878 (2 in 1880).

702. CLARISSA WASS [8] [Clara] 1849-   [255 Henry D.[7] and Lovicia Wass] was born at Steuben 5 Oct. 1849; married 2 June 1869 JAMES LEWIS PARKIN of Fairfield ME, born at Salisbury NB (town VRs; Cornman Ms). They lived at Milbridge in 1880.

Children (**Parkin**):

i.   WINIFRED, b. 10 June 1870.
ii.   ELLA MORSE. b. 27 Dec. 1872.
iii. JOHN HENRY, b. 3 Jan. 1875; m. in Feb. 1905 ELLA
      LOUISE WELLS.
iv.   BERTHA S., b. 29 Apr. 1876; m. 9 June 1898 HERBERT O.
      BROWN.
v.   ROBERT WAITE, b. 15 Feb. 1881, d. Fairfield 31 Mar.
      1901; unm.
vi.   MARY STEVENS, b. 9 June 1883; m. Fairfield 10 Feb.
      1914 ALVA BERNARD CANHAM, b. No. Vasselboro c1882,
      son of Fred and Catherine (Cavanaugh) Canham.

703.   MARGARET W.[8] 1827-1886 [256 Handy[7] and Rebecca Wass]
was born at Steuben 21 Sept. 1827, died there 28 Dec. 1886,
59y; married 29 Dec. 1844 Capt. CHARLES HENRY HASKELL, born
at Rochester MA 6 Mar. 1803, died at Steuben 25 Dec. 1896,
son of Zebulon and Susanna (Sherman) Haskell (Steuben VRs;
Ira J. Haskell, Chronology of the Haskell Family [Lynn MA,
1943], 157; Mary L. Holman, Descendants of William Sherman of
Marshfield, Mass. [1936], 140).

Children (**Haskell**), born at Steuben:

i.   REBECCA L., b. 6 June 1846, d. Gouldsboro ME 5 Apr.
      1876; m. there EUGENE HANDY.
ii.   HATTIE H., b. 16 Oct. 1849, d. 8 Dec. 1864.
iii. LUCY ANN, b. 6 Jan. 1853, d. 12 Mar. 1885; m. Capt.
      GEORGE NEWELL, b. in England.
iv.   CHARLES H., b. 23 July 1855; m. 31 May 1888 NELLIE R.
      CUMMINGS, b. 2 June 1866.
v.   GEORGE W., b. 10 Sept. 1857, res. Steuben in 1932;
      unm.

704.   JOHN BUCKNAM GODFREY[8] 1832-1900 [256 Handy[7] and
Rebecca Wass] was born at Steuben 4 Apr. 1832, died there 20
May 1900; married first there 17 Oct. 1856 ABBY S. DRISKO,
born at Addison ME 13 Oct. 1835, died at Steuben 21 June
1886, daughter of Caleb Haskell and Hannah C (Cole) Drisko
(town and ME VRs; Cornman Ms); married second at Steuben 2
Oct. 1887 HATTIE A. RAY (Machias Union).
John was often called Bucknam; he was a farmer at Steuben
in 1860, and a lumberman there in 1870. Abby's death date
appeared twice in the Machias Union, as 20 May and 20 June.

Children, born at Steuben:

i.   FRANCES A.[9] [Fannie], b. 21 Oct. 1858; m.
      Cherryfield ME 16 Mar. 1881 CHARLES SMITH of
      Eden (Bar Harbor).
ii.   HATTIE H., b. c1868 (2 in 1870), res. West
      Sullivan.
iii. MAUD, b. 10 July 1873, d. 6 June 1875.

705.   CHRISTINA DYER[8] 1829-1902 [258 Thomas[7] and Persis
Dyer] was born at Steuben 20 May 1829, died at Wakefield MA
19 Feb. 1902; married first at Milford MA 17 Dec. 1848 SAMUEL

COLSON, born at Searsport ME 17 Feb. 1815, died at Matanza, Cuba, 20 July 1873, son of Elias and Lorena Etta Colson; married second 19 Aug. 1882 ELIAS FULLER, died at Wakefield 5 Oct. 1894 (Cornman Ms; town and MA VRs).
In 1850, Samuel, a ship captain, and his wife Christina lived at Belfast with her parents.

Children (**Colson**), all but first born at Belfast:

i.   EMERY LEIGHTON, b. East Boston 12 Dec. 1851; m. 11 Sept. 1879 ALICE M. HOWARD of Milford MA, b. 22 July 1857, dau. of Alden Emery and Maria Elizabeth (Bright) Howard.

ii.   AMOS ROBERTS, b. 26 Oct. 1854, d. there 19 May 1856, 6m 24d (VRs).

iii. FRED, b. 4 Sept., d. 21 Sept., 1855, 17d.

iv. SAMUEL E., b. 13 Nov. 1858, d. 16 Mar. 1860.

v.   SAMUEL G., b. 8 Aug. 1861, res. Wakefield MA; m. Brooklyn NY in Oct. 1898 GERTRUDE E. BURRILL, b. 22 Apr. 1867.

vi. ALONZO BLANCHARD, b. 23 July 1863, d. Chelsea MA 23 Jan. 1879.

706. ALBION KEITH PARRIS[8] 1830-1907 [258 Thomas[7] and Persis Dyer] was born at Steuben 7 Nov. 1830, died at Portland ME 29 May 1907, 76y 6m 22d; married at East Boston (Leonard F. Tibbetts notes), int. at Addison 18 Aug. 1853, DEBORAH CURTIS WASS, born at Addison 14 Aug. 1835, died at Portland 7 Dec. 1901, 66y, daughter of Chipman and Mary L. (Curtis) Wass (town and ME VRs; Cornman Ms; Wilder, Pembroke Families). He and many other men were named for Albion King Parris, Maine's second governor (1822-27).
They settled first at Pembroke ME, where he was a ship caulker in 1860. About 1863 they removed to Portland where he set up A. K. P. Leighton & Co., a ship-building company; he was a shipwright at Deering in 1880 and Portland in 1900.

Children, born at Pembroke:

1341. i.   EVELYN WILDER[9], b. 11 June 1854; m. ALBERT T. COBB.

1342. ii. STEPHEN HILL, b. 9 Nov. 1862

707. EMERY DYER[8] 1832- [258 Thomas[7] and Persis Dyer] was born at Steuben 25 Sept. 1832 (Feb. 1836 per 1900 census), lived at Boston in 1900; married first at Boston 27 Sept. 1857 ROXANNA BURG, born at Boston 5 Oct. 1838, died at East Boston 5 Aug. 1883, 45y 9m (VRs), daughter of Andrew A. and Eliza Anna (Williams) Burg; married second at Wilmington DE 28 Oct. 1884 SARA T. SYNETTE, born in MA in Apr. 1850, lived at Boston in 1900, daughter of William J. and Rachel Sewall (Williams) Synette (Boston VRs; Cornman Ms).
Emery made his first voyage at 14, to Cuba, and learned the shipbuilding trade at his father's yard at Belfast. At 20 he took employment at James E. Simpson's drydocks at East Boston; a year later he was partner in Foster and Leighton, ship repairers, and by 1872 was sole owner of the firm. He made investments in ships and their cargoes, holding shares in as

many as 27 vessels (Biographical Sketches of Representative
Citizens of Massachusetts [Boston, 1903], 559-60).
Emery and Sara adopted Harry W., born in MA in Jan. 1892
(1900 census), son of George Synette.

Children by Roxanne, born at East Boston:

i.   PERSIS[9], b. in 1860, d. Middleboro MA in Aug.
        1868.
ii.   GERTRUDE, b. 8 Aug. 1863, d. 27 Aug. 1864.
iii.   FRANK BURG, b. in 1865, d. Middleboro in Aug.
        1868.
iv.   ANNIE F., b. in Aug. 1867, d. Boston 1 May
        1868, 9m.
v.   EMERY LORING, b. 6 Mar., d. 21 Aug., 1869, 5m
        15d.
vi.   MILDRED, b. in Feb. 1871, d. 9 Jan. 1876, 4y
        11m.
vii.   THOMAS FOSTER, b. 8 Nov. 1874, d. 30 Mar. 1875,
        4m 22d.

708.   MARY T.[8] 1851-1890 [262 Almon[7] and Sarah McAllister]
was born at Calais ME 26 Oct. 1851, died 23 June 1890; mar-
ried 26 Oct. 1878 (int. 16 Oct., MH&GR, 2[1891]:125) SAMUEL
DINGLEY, born at Gorham ME 29 Sept. 1832, lived at Marshfield
MA and Standish ME, son of Jacob and Deborah (Libby) Dingley
(town VRs; Cornman Ms).
Dingley had married first 25 Dec. 1861 Lucretia A. Files of
Gorham, who died 26 Oct. 1876; they had four children.

Children (**Dingley**):

i.   ANDREW LIBBY, b. 21 Nov. 1879, res. Gardiner ME.
ii.   DONALD LEIGHTON, b. 19 May (or 14 Mar.) 1884.

709.   SARAH ANN[8] 1823-   [265 Warren[7] and Joan Dyer] was
born at Steuben ME 16 Sept. 1823; married at Ellsworth ME 30
Dec. 1848 ISAIAH BLAISDELL of Franklin (Cornman Ms).

Children (**Blaisdell**):

i.   FREDERICK, res. Ellsworth; m. FLORENCE KINGSBURY.
ii.   WALTER, res. Bangor; m. MARY HOLT.

710.   GILBERT MOORE[8] 1825-1896 [265 Warren[7] and Joanna
Dyer] was born at Steuben 25 Aug. 1825, died at Milbridge 12
May 1896, 70y 8m 13d; married perhaps at Freeman ME 21 Apr.
1848 MARY S. WHITNEY, born at Freeman 2 Feb. 1826, died at
Milbridge 12 Dec. 1894, 68y 10m, daughter of Isaac and Elizabeth (Parlin) Whitney (town and ME VRs; GS; Cornman Ms).
Burials are in Evergreen Cemetery, Milbridge.
    G. M. Leighton was a shipmaster and builder, who owned sev-
eral packets and freighters in the coastal trade. He held
various town offices. Later he was a steamship captain for
the Ward Line, on the New York-Cuba run.
    In 1860 his household was at Steuben; by 1870 he had
settled at Milbridge. His household there in 1880 included
his son's family and his niece Lizzie L., 20 [# 1345].

Children, born at Steuben:

1343. i.   CHARLES P.^{9}, b. 27 Feb. 1849.
1344. ii.   EMMA TERESA, b. 25 Sept. 1851; m. CHARLES J.
             BROWN.
      iii.   BERTHA VILENA, b. 2 Jan. 1855, d. Milbridge 3
             Dec. 1929; m. 1st 14 July 1884 ADEN M.^{8} LEIGH-
             TON [# 728]; m. 2nd Steuben 23 Feb. 1898 SAM-
             UEL ALLEN SMITH, b. there 23 Dec. 1846, d.
             Milbridge 23 Jan. 1902, son of Alfred and
             Belinda (Leighton) Smith [# 271]. No ch.
      iv.   son, b. and d. in 1862 (GS).

711. MIRIAM HANDY^8 1827-1889 [265 Warren^7 and Joanna Dyer]
was born at Steuben 9 Aug. 1827, died at Milbridge 29 Sept.
1889 (60y per GS); married there int. 13 July 1853 CHARLES F.
PRAY of Augusta ME, born 3 July 1832, died at Milbridge 3
Nov. 1887, 56y 4m (town VRs; Cornman Ms).
He was a watchmaker and jeweler; they lived in Warren's
household in 1860.

Children (**Pray**):

i.   EDITH.
ii.   MARCIA, b. c1860 (10 in 1870); m. BION C WHITNEY.
iii.   WARREN L., b. Milbridge 19 Oct. 1863, d. there 21
       Jan. 1921, run down by auto; m. 12 Jan. 1898 EFFIE
       D. SAWYER, b. in 1873, dau. of Gustavus and Frances
       (Fickett) Sawyer. He was a selectman

712. PILLSBURY STEVENS^8 1830-1870 [265 Warren^7 and Joanna
Dyer] was born at Steuben 11 Jan. 1830, died at Milbridge 2
Jan. 1870, 40y (GS); married at Steuben 26 July 1852 (24 July
by Rev. Enoch M. Fowler, NEHGReg, 91[1937]:387; 1853 per VRs;
Milbridge int. 21 July 1852) ISABELLA R. STROUT, born 10 Feb.
1835, died at Milbridge 10 Feb. 1865, 30y (Milbridge and
Steuben VRs). Burials are in Evergreen Cemetery, Milbride.
He was a farmer at Steuben in 1860, and at Milbridge in
1870. His orphaned children were cared for by other families
after his death; Annie and Isabella were with their uncle
Lincoln in 1870, and Lizzie with her uncle Gilbert.

Children, born at Steuben:

       i.   ANNA T.^{9} [Annie], b. 26 Aug. 1854, d. Addison
               ME 12 June 1881, 26y 10m; m. Milbridge 3 Oct.
               1874 (Machias Union) PHILANDER P. KNOWLES, b.
               Addison c1846 (14 in 1860), d. Helena MT 17
               Apr. 1930, son of Leander A. and Mary Ann
               (Plummer) Knowles.
1345. ii.   ELIZABETH L. [Lizzie], b. 29 Feb. 1860; m.
               FRANK SAWYER NASH.
       iii.   ELLA UPTON, b. 26 Jan. 1862, res. Dixon IL; m.
               5 Oct. 1893 DeWITT CLINTON OWEN. She was
               adopted in 1865 by Warren and Harriet Hunter
               (WashCP, L 1227). Ch. Florence Elizabeth
               b. Dixon 20 June 1901.
       iv.   ISABELLA F. [Belle], b. 22 Mar. 1864, d. Mil-
               bridge 24 Apr. 1883 (19y, GS); unm.

713.   MARGUERITA WARREN[8] 1829-   [274 H. Nelson[7] and
Olivia Smith] was born at Steuben ME 29 Aug. 1829, lived at
Plaistow NH; married at Annsburg (Deblois) ME 25 Oct. 1851
JOHN DORMAN, born at Jonesboro ME 17 Mar. 1827, adopted son
of Benjamin and Eliza (Weston) Dorman of Beddington (Beddington VRs; records of Margaret Colton; Cornman Ms). Her name
often was spelled Margaret. They were listed at Beddington
in 1880.

Children (**Dorman**), born at Beddington:

i.   HORATIO NELSON, b. 8 Sept. 1852, d. 27 Apr. 1872.
ii.   OLIVIA L., b. 21 Apr. 1854; m. WILLIAM BROWN.
iii.   GEORGE C., b. 28 Jan. 1856; m. 18 Oct. 1884 EMELINE
       RICHARDSON of Aurora ME.
iv.   LEVERETT B., b. 29 May 1859; m. ELLA LINSCOTT
       APPLETON.
v.   ERASTUS ELMER, b. 12 May 1861; m. IDA CLARK, b. in
       1857, d. in 1929.
vi.   IZORA P., b. 23 July 1865; m. OSCAR DEARBORN.

714. MELISSA[8] 1832-   [274 H. Nelson[7] and Olivia Smith]
was born at Steuben ME 2 Feb. 1832, lived at Olympia WA; married at Columbia ME 14 Oct. 1852 (JOHN) FREEMAN DORMAN, born
at Beddington ME 26 May 1830, died at Kingston MN 15 Nov.
1888, son of Nathaniel and Phoebe (Schoppe) Dorman (Beddington VRs; records of Margaret McKay; George W. Drisko, Life of
Hannah Weston [Machias ME, 1903], 107; Cornman Ms).

Children (**Dorman**):

i.   ANDREW HERBERT, b. Beddington 10 Mar. 1854; m. CORA
       McCOLLEY.
ii.   PHOEBE ALICE, b. Beddington 10 Nov. 1855; m. MASON
       COLBY GRIFFIN, b. Annsburg 28 May 1848, d. in CA in
       Jan. 1922.
iii.   ALONZO SMALL, b. Cherryfield 21 June 1858, res. WA;
       unm.
iv.   MINNESOTA [Minnie], b. in MN 3 May 1866; m. 1st in
       1888 GEORGE LOW; m. 2nd in 1902 ELIAS EAKLE.

715.   CALVIN SMITH[8] 1834-1916 [274 H. Nelson[7] and Olivia
Smith] was born at Annsburg (Deblois) 22 June 1834, died
there 1 Mar. 1916 (VRs; GS, 23 Feb.); married first there 21
Nov. 1858 ELLEN JANE SHOREY, born there 31 Mar. 1839, died
there 7 Mar. 1861, 21y 11m (GS), daughter of John and Wealthy
Shorey; married second 29 June 1862 ANNIE C. TORREY, born at
Plymouth ME 15 Mar. 1837, died at Deblois 24 Apr. 1909, 72y
1m 13d, daughter of Fanuel Sandford and Abigail (Collins)
Torrey (Frederick C Torrey, Torrey Families [Lakehurst NJ,
1929], 2:267; Deblois VRs). Burials are at Deblois.
   He was a farmer at Deblois. He served as town treasurer
from 1877 to 1909; his account book has been preserved at the
Narragaugus Historical Society, Cherryfield.

Child by Ellen, born at Deblois:

i.   ADDIE L.[9], b. 22 June 1858, d. 17 Oct. 1863, 5y
       (name uncertain, perhaps male).

Children by Annie, born at Deblois:

     ii.   PERCY, b. and d. 14 June 1863.
     iii. ANGELINE, b. 13 June 1864, d. 29 Sept. 1865.
1346. iv.   JOSIAH GOULD, b. 3 Sept. 1865.
     v.   ABBIE T., b. 29 Feb. 1868; m. Ellsworth 21 Dec.
           1898 FRANK L. JELLISON of Surry, b. Waltham MA
           c1863, son of Benjamin and Jane E. Jellison.
           Ch. Howard L. b. 23 Sept. 1899.
     vi.   WILLIAM S., b. 16 Oct. 1871; m. 6 Sept. 1905
           EDITH L. MacARTHUR.
     vii. MELISSA E., b. 8 July 1876; m. 14 Aug. 1902
           LESLIE L. PRESCOTT.

716. EDWARD[8] 1836-1906 [274 H. Nelson[7] and Olivia Smith]
was born at Steuben 26 May 1836, died at Seattle WA 10 Jan.
1906; married first at Deblois 27 Nov. 1859 EMMA A. SHOREY,
born there 30 June 1841, died there 3 Sept. 1870, daughter of
John and Wealthy Shorey; married second at Minneapolis MN 5
July 1878 ELIZABETH JOSEPHINE RICKETSON, born at Peru NY 10
July 1854, died at Seattle 26 Feb. 1913, daughter of Ezra
King and Marinda (Wescott) Ricketson (Deblois VRs; records of
Arlene Skehan; Mrs. G. W. Edes, William Ricketson and His
Descendants [1932], 2:376-7).

Edward was a logger and lumberman at Deblois, and a seaman
in 1870. He took his children to MN, and was living at Rock
Creek, Pine Co., in 1880. He became a millwright, settled at
Seattle in 1889.

Children by Emma, born at Deblois:

     i.   WINFIELD E.[9], b. 2 May 1861, d. Deblois 4 Apr.
          1870.
     ii.   ADDIE ESTELLE, b. 12 Aug. 1864, res. Dryden WA;
          m. JOHN WALTON.
     iii. GEORGIANNA, b. 24 Sept. 1869, res. Duluth MN;
          m. ---- SCANLON.

Children by Elizabeth, born in MN:

     iv.   CLARA MAY, b. Rush City MN 1 June 1879, res.
          Vancouver BC; m. 1st 3 Mar. 1894 WALTER WILSON
          --div. 1896; m. 2nd 11 Sept. 1897 CHARLES
          RICHARD HOOPER of San Francisco; m. 3rd A L.
          SILVEY. Wilson was a dancing master, Hooper a
          civil engineer. Ch.: Clyde Edward Wilson, b.
          18 Nov. 1895.
     v.   GENEVIEVE, b. Rush City 18 Jan. 1882, res.
          Morris IL; m. 1st 2 Nov. 1899 HARRY C. MIFFORD
          of Tacoma WA--div.; m. 2nd Dr. WILLIAM JOHN
          FERGUSON, b. Wilmington IL 22 Sept. 1870,
          son of Jeremiah Holland and Mary Jane (Huston)
          Ferguson, a dentist at Morris. She had no ch.
     vi.   EDWARD CHARLES, b. Rock Creek MN 17 Oct. 1885,
          res. Seattle; m. there 4 Oct. 1908 MAY LULU
          SHACKLEFORD, b. Beloit Co. KS 1 Nov. 1885,
          dau. of William F. and Cassandra (Swisher)
          Shackleford. Ch. FRANCES ELIZABETH[10] b.
          Seattle 1 May 1913. A mechanical engineer, he
          managed Central Heating Co., Seattle.

717. ANGELINE[8] 1839-1929 [275 H. Nelson[7] and Olivia Smith]
was born at Deblois ME 16 Nov. 1839, died at Minneapolis MN
13 Jan. 1929, while living with her daughter Mabel; married
at Deblois 26 July 1857 JEREMIAH GOULD, born at Steuben 26
June 1837, died at Fair Haven, Stearns Co. MN, son of Pearson
and Sophia Gould (records of Arlene Skehan and of descendant
Earl L. Grinols; Cornman Ms).
They settled at Minneapolis MN in 1863, lived in 1865 at
Lake Sylvia, Wright Co., returned to Minneapolis, and then
settled at Fair Haven in 1902.

Children (**Gould**):

i.   SARAH E. [Sadie], b. Cold Harbor ME 25 Feb. 1858,
      d. Seattle WA 3 Aug. 1937; m. Minneapolis 3 Apr.
      1875 HORACE E. LIBBY, b. Deblois 10 Apr. 1850, res.
      Kingston MN, son of Edmund and Mary (Pineo) Libby
      (Libby Family, 507).
ii.   ANNIE EVELYN, b. Cold Harbor 11 Mar. 1860, d. Fair
      Haven 1 Jan. 1908; m. 1st CECIL PARTRIDGE; m. 2nd
      HENRY DOBLE.
iii. ANGELINA ETTA [Angie], b. Lake Sylvia 18 July 1866,
      d. Bemidji, Beltrami Co. MN; m. Fair Haven 18 July
      1884 ERNEST ELLSWORTH GRINOLS, son of Ernest and
      Isabelle (Cooper) Grinols.
iv.   WALTER AUGUSTUS, b. Lake Sylvia 30 Apr. 1867, res.
      Bemidji; m. ELSIE GRINOLS, sister to Ernest.
v.   MABELLA MILDRED [Mabel], b. Minneapolis 1 May 1874,
      d. 5 Aug. 1956; m. Fair Haven 2 Jan. 1895 WILLIAM
      W. THAYER, res. McNaughton WI.

718. (WILLIAM) BARTLETT[8] [Bart] 1846-1917 [274 H. Nelson[7]
and Olivia Smith] was born at Annsburg (Deblois) 22 Nov.
1846, died there 18 Oct. 1917, 70y 10m 28d; married first at
Cherryfield ME 9 June 1866 ADELAIDE F. WILSON, born 7 Dec.
1848, died at Deblois 27 Nov. 1893, daughter of Henry and
Sophia (Hutchinson) Wilson of Deblois; married second at
Cherryfield 23 July 1898 MARY E.[9] LEIGHTON, born there 12
Dec. 1856, died at Beddington 21 Feb. 1934, 77y 2m 9d, daughter of Pillsbury and Mary (Phinnemore) Leighton [# 908] (town
and ME VRs). In 1870 he and his family were in his father's
household; he and Mary lived at Deblois in 1900. Bartlett
was a house carpenter, and owned a hotel at Deblois.

Children, all by Adelaide, born at Deblois:

i.   ERMINA H.[9] [Mina], b. 11 Apr. 1867, res. Ells-
      worth Falls ME; m. Ellsworth 13 Dec. 1890
      CHARLES S. COTTLE, b. there 8 Mar. 1867, d. in
      1937, son of Moses H. and Hannah H. (Grindle)
      Cottle. Ch. William Bartlett b. 1 May 1891.
ii.   ANGIE B., b. 23 Oct. 1869, res. So. Beddington
      ME; m. Deblois 23 Oct. 1888 FRANK G. FARNS-
      WORTH, b. 13 Mar. 1861, son of Leonard J. and
      Nancy J. (Wilson) Farnsworth. No ch. Angie
      was Bernice on the 1870 census, and Agnes B.
      on her intentions of marriage.
iii. LUCRETIA S. [Cretia], b. 2 May 1872; m. JAMES
      H. AVERY, b. 13 Mar. 1861. Ch. Mildred L.
      b. 2 Mar. 1902.

719.   JAMES P. L.[8] 1849-1911 [277 Daniel[7] and Mary Jane
Lawrence] was born at Steuben 15 Aug. 1849, died at Boston
aboard ship in 1911; married there 22 Nov. 1888 (Milbridge
VRs) ROSE E. WORKMAN, born at Cherryfield 2 Apr. 1863, daughter of Edmund Stevens and Harriet S. (Tracy) Workman.
    Rosa was not listed in the 1900 census, but James and Doris
were in the Cherryfield Register in 1905.

Child, born at Steuben:

    i.   DORIS CATHERINE WORKMAN[9], b. 26 Dec. 1892 d.
           Portland 16 Mar. 1981; m. Jonesport 25 Sept.
           1914 LLOYD DODGE NUGENT, b. Lubec 15 July
           1892, d. 9 Dec. 1961, son of Charles N. and
           Belle (Bangs) Nugent. Ch. Barbara. Lloyd was
           a pharmacist.

720.   MARY CAROLINE[8] 1848-1924 [280 John[7] and Rachel Steward was born at Monson ME 26 May 1848, died at Dexter ME 14
Nov. 1924; married at Monson 13 Mar. 1869 CHARLES WILLIAM
FARRAR, born at Bradford ME in 1841, died at Dexter 21 Sept.
1913, 72y 8m 27d, son of John W. and Elizabeth (Day) Farrar
(records of Maxine Hughes; Dexter VRs; Farwell, Shaw Records,
146). He served in Co. E., 22nd ME Inf. Rgt., 1861-65.

Children (**Farrar**), born at Dexter:

    i.   MATTIE NORA, b. 6 Oct. 1872.
    ii.   LIZZIE MAY, b. 16 Dec. 1875.
    iii.   ERNEST CHARLES, b. 24 Apr. 1879.

721.   JOHN STUART[8] 1851-1918 [280 John[7] and Rachel Steward]
was born at Monson ME 6 Apr. 1851, died at Sonora, Tuolumne
Co. CA 14 Dec. 1918; married there 27 Apr. 1884 LIZZIE MAY
SHAW, born at Jeffersonville CA 16 Aug. 1862, died 9 Mar.
1929, daughter of Benjamin G. and Louisa J. (Foster) Shaw
(records of Maureen Baker; his 1906 letter--Cornman Papers).
    John's middle name was also given as Steward. He went west
to Sonora CA about 1879, and had farms and ranches at Sali-
das, at Stent in 1897, Twp 6, Tuolumne Co. in 1900 (census),
and Stockton in 1906.

Children, born in CA:

            i.   FRED WILBUR[9], b. Arcata, Humboldt Co., 23 Jan.
                   1885, d. Sonora 22 June 1979; m. Sonora 28
                   Dec. 1909 EDNA BEATRICE HALES. No ch.
    1347.   ii.   ROY STEWART, b. Springfield CA 15 Sept. 1887.
    1348.   iii.   ETHEL LOUISE, b. Sonora 20 July 1889; m. ELMER
                   D. DUNBAR.
            iv.   ARTHUR HARRISON, b. Sonora 21 Apr. 1891, d. 16
                   Oct. 1920; unm.
            v.   CARRIE ALMA [Callie], b. Sonora 20 May 1894, d.
                   Sacramento CA 28 Jan. 1954; m. Eureka CA 12
                   Sept. 1927 HARRY LISCOM, d. in 1928. No ch.
            vi.   CLARENCE ALBERT (twin), b. Sonora 20 May 1894,
                   d. there 10 Mar. 1949; m. 1st CELIA GONDALFO;
                   m. 2nd MAY CARLEY. No ch.

vii.   twins who d.
viii.   soon after birth.
ix.   RACHEL J. SHAW, b. Stent 13 Dec. 1899, d.
       Sacramento in Aug. 1968; m. San Francisco 26
       June 1924 (CHARLES) RAYMOND [Ray] HARRY, b. 13
       May 1898, d. San Francisco 13 Mar. 1957. He
       was a grocer. Ch. Merton Leighton b. Sonora
       CA 23 July 1928; m. 1st 19 Dec. 1949 Mabel
       Stewart--div. in 1954; m. 2nd Doris Brown--
       div. in 1965.

722.   ELVIRA COBURN STEWARD[8] 1856-1933 [280 John[7] and
Rachel Steward] was born at Monson 14 Aug. 1856, died at
Dover ME 26 Nov. 1933; married at Monson 25 July 1877 ELLERY
LEONARD STONE, born at Ripley ME 8 Aug. 1858, died at West
Garland ME 4 May 1921, son of Leonard and Violet (Leavitt)
Stone (Bible and other records of Joanne Prescott; town and
ME VRs). He was a farmer; his name was given in the family
Bible as both Ellery L. and Leonard E.

Children (**Stone**):

i.   CORYDON W. [Corry], b. Monson 6 Mar. 1878, d. there
       12 Oct. 1886.
ii.   STANLEY W., b. Monson 20 July 1880, d. Dover ME 17
       Jan. 1939; unm.
iii.   MILDRED VIOLET, b. Monson 4 Aug. 1887, d. Bangor ME
       14 Apr. 1963, res. Guilford; m. 1st W. Garland 23
       Oct. 1907 ALMOND GRANT; m. 2nd there 30 June 1919
       PAUL PERIN, b. in Italy 11 Oct. 1892, a druggist.
       One ch. Beatrice V. Grant.
iv.   LEONARD JOHN, b. Willimantic ME 26 Oct. 1892, d.
       Dexter ME 8 Nov. 1966; m. Garland 9 Nov. 1919 CLARA
       LOUISE BUTTERS, b. Exeter ME 1 Oct. 1891, d. Bangor
       28 May 1969, dau. of Henry and Ida (Leathers)
       Butters.

723.   ALFONZO MILTON[8] 1859-1933 [280 John[7] and Rachel
Steward] was born at Monson 19 Oct. 1859, died at Willimantic
ME 31 Aug. 1933; married at Monson 11 Feb. 1890 IDA BELLE
JOHNSTON, born at No. 8 (Willimantic) 9 Feb. 1867, died 28
Mar. 1950, daughter of James and Melinda (Wade) Johnston
(town VRs; records of descendant Maxine Hughes; his letter in
1915--Cornman Papers).
     In 1900 they were at Willimantic, with his mother in their
household. He was a farmer. His descendants have held
reunions at Willimantic as recently as 1986.

Children, born at Willimantic:

1349. i.   CLYDE LENDALL[9], b. 11 Sept. 1890.
1350. ii.   CLIFFORD ALTON, b. 27 June 1892.
1351. iii.   VERDELL ADELBERT, b. 5 Apr. 1894.
1352. iv.   VANCE VERNE, b. 7 Oct. 1895.
1353. v.   GUY ELSCOTT, b. 11 Feb. 1898.
1354. vi.   RODNEY JOHN, b. 31 July 1900.
      vii.   PERCY WILMONT, b. 13 Aug. 1902, d. Monson 16
             Apr. 1949; m. 30 June 1943 MARY (FROST) Jones,
             widow of Urban Jones. No ch.

1355. viii. LYNWOOD LEE, b. 26 Sept. 1905.
       ix. IVAN WADE, b. 31 Aug. 1908, d. Topsham ME 21
            Dec. 1983; m. 1st 24 Nov. 1932 MAE O. BANNIST-
            ER of Moncton NB; m. 2nd 2 Feb. 1947 RUTH
            MEISTER. No ch.

724. **NELLIE NEWELL**[8] 1862-1907 [280 John[7] and Rachel Stew-
ard] was born at No. 8 (Monson) 1 Nov. 1862, died there 7
June 1907; married 30 Oct. 1881 WARREN T. JOHNSON of Dexter,
born in Mar. 1860, son of Loren and Lydia Johnson (records of
Maxine Hughes).
In 1900 they were living at Monson.

Children (**Johnson**):

i.   NINA E., b. in Sept. 1883.
ii.   MAUD EVA, b. in Oct. 1885.
iii. WALTER L., b. in June 1891.
iv.   MAURICE E., b. Monson 3 Sept. 1893.
v.   GUY L., b. Monson 30 Jan. 1898.

725. **OLIVE EMILY**[8] 1866-   [280 John[7] and Rachel Steward]
was born at No. 8 (Monson) 15 Sept. 1866; married at Monson 4
July 1885 THOMAS TRAINOR of Windsor, PEI, son of John and
Elizabeth (Fitzsimmons) (McEwen) Trainor (records of Maxine
Hughes; St. Lawrence Parish Register, Morell PEI).

Children (**Trainor**):

i.   DELIA AGNES, b. Willimantic 14 Feb. 1886.
ii.   MICHAEL JAMES, b. Morell 16 Apr. 1888 (bp. 21 Apr.).
iii. WILLIAM VINCENT, b. Morell 4 Nov. 1890 (bp. 24 Nov.).
iv.   HERBERT SYLVESTER, b. Morell 20 Aug. 1892 (bp. 21
      Aug.); m. there 10 Aug. 1915 MARY ETHEL DUFFY.
v.   THOMAS ALPHONSO, b. Morell 6 May 1894 (bp. 13 May).
vi.   MARY JANE, b. Morell 9 Aug. 1895 (bp. 11 Aug.).
vii. PATRICK RAYMOND, b. Morell 16 July 1897 (bp. 18
      July).
viii. JOSEPH HENRY, b. Morell 19 June 1899 (bp. 2 July);
      m. there 25 Nov. 1942 WINNIFRED DUFFY.
ix.   STEPHEN LOUIS.

726. **EMELINE**[8] 1836-1897 [284 George[7] and Lydia Moore] was
born at Steuben ME 30 Mar. 1836, died at Gouldsboro 29 June
1897, 61y 2m 29d; married there 30 Oct. 1859 SAMUEL W. LIBBY,
born there 30 Apr. 1830, died there 11 July 1910, 80y 2m 11d,
son of Daniel and Mary A (Whitaker) Libby (Gouldsboro, Steuben and ME VRs; records of Margaret Colton; Cornman Ms). The
Libby genealogy (p. 472) named her Emeline Nason.

Children (**Libby**), born at Gouldsboro:

i.   FRANK S., b. 17 Sept. 1864; m. 16 Oct. 1897 LIZZIE A.
      JOY, b. in 1871, d. 19 Jan. 1942 (GS), dau. of
      Robert and Sarah (Campbell) Joy. No ch.
ii.   DANIEL G., b. 14 Dec. 1870.

727. REBECCA M.[8] 1837-   [284 George[7] and Lydia Moore]
was born at Steuben 10 May 1837, lived at No. Lubec ME; married at Milbridge ME 16 Mar. 1856 (Machias Union) ABIAH F
HUCKINS, born about 1832 (28 in 1860), son of James and
Joanna Huckins of Lubec (Cornman Ms). In 1860 he was a carpenter at Lubec; he and Rebecca lived with his parents.

Children (**Huckins**), order uncertain:

  i.   ADA F., b. c1857 (3 in 1860).
  i.   ANNA L., b. Lubec 13 Oct. 1858 (VRs).
  ii.   GEORGE W.
  iii. ERNEST C., b. c1865 (30 in 1895); m. Lubec 5 Dec.
        1895 (VRs) MARY F. REYNOLDS.
  iv.   JAMES.
  v.   MABEL C ; m. Lubec before 1892 LEWIS LANCASTER.

728. ADEN M.[8] 1852-   [284 George[7] and Lydia Moore]
was born at Milbridge ME 27 July 1852, died at San Francisco
CA; probably married first IDA LOUISE RAY, born at Harrington
about 1857 (23 in 1880), died at Brooklyn NY 21 Aug. 1921 (ME
VRs), daughter of John and Evelyn (Willey) Ray; married second at Milbridge 14 July 1884 BERTHA V.[9] LEIGHTON, born there
2 Jan. 1855, died there 3 Dec. 1929, daughter of Gilbert and
Mary (Whitney) Leighton [# 718]--divorced (town and ME VRs;
Cornman Ms). He was a sea captain.
  Julia Cornman stated that he never married. In 1880 Ida
Leighton was at Harrington with her son Harris, 9, living
with her parents. Perhaps she and Aden did not marry, or if
so were divorced. Ida later married Ira Benjamin Strout (GS,
1855-1914); her gravestone shows her as his wife, born in
1853, died in 1921. Bertha married second at Milbridge 23
Feb.1898 Samuel Smith [# 271] of Steuben; they were living at
Milbridge in 1900.

Probable child by Ida:

  i.   HARRIS[9], b. c1874 (6 in 1880).

729. AUGUSTINE COOMBS[8] 1852-1937 [286 Nicholas[7] and Elsie
Haskell] was born at Steuben 22 Mar. 1852, died at Milbridge
12 Jan. 1937; married first at Eastport ME 2 May 1873 LUDIAN-
NIA BROWN, born at Deer Isle; married second at Steuben 20
Sept. 1880 EVA JANET (GUPTILL) Crane, born at Franklin ME 15
July 1859, died at Milbridge 2 July 1935, 73y 11m 2d, daugh-
ter of George W. and Matilda (Pattingill) Guptill (town and
ME VRs; Cornman Ms; Milbridge Town Register, 1905). Burials
are in Evergreen Cemetery, Milbridge.
  He was a merchant and accountant, and served as mayor of
Milbridge. In 1880 he and his son were living with his
father at Milbridge; in 1900 his mother Elsie lived with him.

Child by Ludiannia, born at Milbridge:

  i.   FRANK S.[9], b. 22 May 1874, res. Eden (Bar Har-
        bor); m. there 28 Oct. 1899 MYRTLE F. [Myrtie]
        GRANT, b. Sandy Point ME in Dec. 1876, dau. of
        James and Nellie (Carlisle) Grant--div. in
        1909. He was a printer.

Children by Eva, born at Milbridge:

ii.   ARNOLD, b. 10 Aug. 1881, d. Milbridge in 1971
      (GS), 90y, suicide; m. there 17 May 1913
      LUCRETIA DYER STROUT, b. there in 1886, d.
      there in 1981, 95y (GS), dau. of Judson and
      Adrianna S. (Martin) Strout. No ch. He was
      a dentist.
iii. CHARLES G., b. 14 Dec. 1882, res. Nashua NH.
      He was a printer.
iv.   (MARY) OLIVE, b. 15 Apr. 1887, d. 11 Aug. 1969;
      m. Milbridge 24 Apr. 1916 (ARTHUR) ALLAN WAL-
      LACE, b. San Francisco c1886, son of George M.
      and Ada E. (Brown) Wallace.
v.   NELLIE W., b. 4 Aug. 1889, d. 11 Dec. 1891 (b.
      1891, d. 1892 per GS).
vi.   GERTRUDE W., b. 24 May 1900.

730. ARTHUR S.[8] 1861-1921 [286 Nicholas[7] and Elsie Has-
kell] was born at Steuben 2 Aug. 1861, died at Milbridge 29
Aug. 1921, 60y 29d; married at Steuben 16 Nov. 1886 EDITH
LOTTIE DYER, born at Milbridge 31 Jan. 1863, died there 25
Sept. 1937, 74y 7m 24d, daughter of Austin and Mary (Ray)
Dyer (town VRs; Milbridge Register 1905). Burials are in
Evergreen Cemetery, Wallace lot. He was a tailor.

Children, born at Milbridge:

i.   AUSTIN N.[9], b. in May 1888, m. 1st Lubec 14 May
      1913 BERTHA FISHER, b. Machias c1891, dau. of
      George W. and Jessie (Skinner) Fisher; m. 2nd
      10 Nov. 1956 EFFIE DELILA (LOOK) Spear. Ch.
      MARGUERITE CHARLOTTE[10] b. Milbridge 15 Feb.
      1914. Effie had m. 1st 31 [sic] Apr. 1928
      John R. Spear.
ii.   daughter, b. 8 Nov. 1897, d. infant.
iii. CHARLOTTE M., b. 1 Dec. 1898; unm.

731. DANIEL[8] 1845-1917 [288 Thomas[7] and Deborah Pettee]
was born at Steuben 5 Dec. 1845, died at Milbridge 19 Aug.
1917, 71y 8m 24d; married at Prospect Harbor 11 June 1874 ADA
E. HANDY PETTEE, born at Birch Harbor in Mar. 1859, died at
Milbridge 30 Oct. 1915, 54y, daughter of William and Elmira
(Lindsey) Pettee (town VRs; Milbridge Town Register 1905).
He was a fisherman, and lived at Petit Manan Point. In 1880
his household included his niece IDELLA[9], aged 1 [# 733].

Children, born at Milbridge:

i.   FLORA E.[9], b. 24 Feb. 1876, d. 1 Apr. 1898; m.
      1st Steuben ME 27 May 1893 HENRY RANDALL, b.
      Columbia c1872, son of George and Celestia
      (Ames) Randall; m. 2nd 18 May 1896 LUTHER
      PINKHAM, b. in 1876, son of William H. and
      Lydia (Brooks) Pinkham.
ii.   LAURA P., b. 30 Mar. 1880; m. FRED J.[8] LEIGHTON
      [# 937] and ARTHUR GOMES.
1356. iii. DAVID H., b. in Jan. 1883.
1357. iv.   HOLLIS, b. in Oct. 1887.

vi.   CLARA C , b   12 Feb. 1898; m. So. Gouldsboro
      17 Oct. 1924 CLARENCE WOOD LEWIS, b. Eastport
      c1886, son of George E. and Lucy (Prince)
      Lewis. He was div. from a first wife.
vii. son [?ALVERNE], b. 25 Apr., d. 23 Sept., 1900.
viii. ADELBERT (twin), b. 25 Apr., d. 20 Oct., 1900.

732. TIMOTHY P.[8] 1847-1924 [288 Thomas[7] and Deborah Pet-
tee] was born at Milbridge ME 14 Sept. 1847, died a widower
at Portland ME 22 Feb. 1924; married first at Steuben 19 Aug.
1873 MARY F. OVER, b. Steuben 19 Jan. 1853, daughter of Henry
and Nancy Over--probably divorced, since she married second
Brewer Spurling; married second at Milbridge int. 28 May 1887
EMMA E. COLSON, died there 18 Dec. 1890, 31y; married third
at Steuben 8 Nov. 1891 (Machias Union) CADDIE SULLIVAN of
Steuben (Gouldsboro Town Register, 1911; town and ME VRs).
     In 1900 he was at Nashua NH with his wife HALLIE A. ---- ,
born in VT in Aug. 1846, and his two sons. In 1911 the two
sons lived with their mother Mary Spurling at Gouldsboro.

Children by Mary, born at Steuben:

1358. i.   HENRY O.[9], b. 19 Sept. 1875.
1359. ii. NEWELL P., b. 31 May 1877.

733. ALICE J.[8] 1861-   [288 Thomas[7] and Deborah Pettee]
was born at Milbridge 10 Dec. 1861; married at Gouldsboro in
1882 (certif. issued 30 Sept.) WILSON G. LINDSAY, born in
Aug. 1856. They lived alone at Steuben in 1900.

Child (**Leighton**):

i.   IDELLA[9], b. Milbridge 19 Mar. 1879; m. 1st
     there 4 July 1897 JOSEPH W. MITCHELL, b.
     there 18 Aug. 1875, son of Nathaniel Pinkham
     and Nancy Y. (Beals) Mitchell--div.; m. 2nd
     Steuben 16 June 1900 IRA COLEWELL, b. there
     c1872, son of Hiram and Elizabeth (Pyne)
     Colewell--div.; m. 3rd (as Delia) at Bar Har-
     bor 27 Feb. 1903 WILLIAM P. LUCKINS, b. Surry
     c1879, son of Willard and Nancy Luckins.

734. CADDIE C.[8] 1867-1893 [290 John Nason[7] and Hannah Hay-
cock] was born at Steuben ME 18 Jan. 1867, died there 9 May
1893, 26y 4m 21d; married there 30 Aug. 1885 DANIEL SULLIVAN,
born at Cork, Ireland, 12 Mar. 1849, died at Sailors' Snug
Harbor, Staten Island NY 3 Aug. 1914, son of John and Mary
Sullivan (records of Norman Sullivan; Steuben VRs).
     He was a seaman.

Children (**Sullivan**), born at Steuben:

i.   JOHN THOMAS, b. 26 Mar. 1887, d. Day's Ferry,
     Woolwich ME 14 July 1966; m. 1st ---- ; m. 2nd
     Levina ---- .

ii.   LEONARD LEIGHTON, b. 15 May 1889, d. Portland 27
       Sept. 1950; m. 1st Boothbay Harbor ME 26 Dec. 1911
       ELIZABETH MARY SPOFFORD; m. 2nd JUANITA ---- .

735.   MARY ANN[8] 1863-1898 [291 Israel[7] and Elizabeth
Brooks] was born at Steuben 8 Nov. 1863, died there 26 July
1898, 34y 8m 21d; married first at Cherryfield 5 July 1879
(Machias Union) WILLIAM H. SMALL, born at Steuben 13 Mar.
1859, son of Warren T. and Eliza (Tracy) Small; married second at Steuben 30 Aug. 1883 FORESTER DUNBAR, born 13 Dec.
1861, died there 1 July 1932, son of John Yeaton and Caroline
(Atwater) Dunbar. He married second Martha (Johnson) Hackett
of Sullivan ME (Steuben VRs; records of Leonard F. Tibbetts).

Children (**Dunbar**), born at Steuben, perhaps five in all:

i.   HENRY E., b. 30 Apr. 1885, d. 12 Apr. 1938.
ii.   JOSIE, b. 10 Sept. 1889, d. Steuben 20 Oct. 1986 (her
      obit.); m CHARLES A. SAWYER.

736.   SHERMAN[8] 1843-1921 [293 Amos[7] and Louise Sargeant]
was born at Cherryfield ME 14 Feb. 1843, died at Omro WI 4
June 1921; married first at Steuben 4 Mar. 1866 FLORA L. WIL-
SON, born there 6 Nov. 1848, died at Cherryfield 21 July
1866, 17y 8m (Machias Union; GS), daughter of Emery Small and
Deborah Sylvester (Wilson) Wilson (Wilsons of Cherryfield,
10); married second 3 June 1870 HARRIET [Hattie] BUNKER, born
in ME 24 Sept. 1843, daughter of Francis and Shuah (Ham)
Bunker.
He was a lumberman. He was buried at Forest Home Cemetery,
Milwaukee. The Wilson genealogy and the Cornman Ms stated
that he had no children, but the 1880 and 1900 censuses for
Omro, Winnebago Co. WI listed him with wife Harriet, son
Leslie, and mother-in-law Shuah Bunker.

Child by Hattie, born in WI:

i.   LESLIE SHERMAN[9], b. in Jan. 1879, res. Neenah,
      WI per family tradition.

737.   ADONIRAM JUDSON[8] 1844-1906 [293 Amos[7] and Louise
Sargeant] was born at Cherryfield 14 Dec. 1844, died at Ever-
ett MA 8 June 1906 (Bible); married at Steuben 9 Apr. 1870
MARIA MOORE GODFREY, born 22 Apr. 1845, died 19 May 1911
(Bible), daughter of James and Almira (Yeaton) Godfrey [# 85]
(records of Edgar L. Leighton Jr., including Godfrey/Lamson
family Bible; Cornman Ms).
In 1870, they lived with his father at Cherryfield. He
became a residential building contractor, living at Chelsea
MA in 1880, and at Everett in 1900. He was a deacon of the
Universalist Church.

Children, born in MA:

i.   HARRIET LOUISA[9], b. 31 Jan. 1871, d. Everett
      c1938; unm. She is buried in Woodlawn Ceme-
      tery, Everett.

ii.   MAHLON KINSMAN, b. 11 Nov. 1873, d. Everett in
      1928, 55y; unm. Harriet lived with him in the
      house their father built. He was corporate
      clerk of R. H. Stearns Co., and was called an
      intimate of Pres. Coolidge.
1360. iii. EDGAR LAWSON, b. 15 Dec. 1880.

738. MARY ELIZA[8] 1849-1934 [293 Amos[7] and Louise Sargeant]
was born at Cherryfield 2 Feb. 1849, died at Newtonville MA
in 1934; married at Addison ME 2 Jan. 1875 GILMAN COLSON
DYER, born there 29 May 1845, died at Harrington ME 3 Oct.
1909, son of Luther C and Delana A. Dyer (town VRs; records
of Leighton Gorham Harris).

Child (**Dyer**), born at Boston:

i.   MARY LOUISA, b. 14 Dec. 1885, d. Newton MA in 1971;
      m. GORHAM WALLER HARRIS, b. in 1885, d. Newtonville
      in 1951, son of Joseph and Mary Waller (Patterson)
      Harris.

739. FREDERICK EDWIN[8] 1848-1906 [296 Oliver[7] and Elizabeth Hall] was born at Milbridge ME 1 July 1848, died at
Steuben 26 Nov. 1906, 57y 4m; married at Dennysville 22 Sept.
1871 (MARY) ETTA PRESTON, born at Plantation 14 (near Dennysville) 22 Aug. 1854, died at Milbridge 10 Sept. 1927, 72y
10d, daughter of Nathan Clifford and Mary J. (Dodge) Preston
(town and ME VRs; Cornman Ms). Burials are in Evergreen Cemetery, Milbridge.
    In 1880 they were living at No. 14, and at Steuben in 1900,
his brother Jefferson part of their household each time.

Children:

1361. i.   CHLOE LOUISE[9], b. Milbridge 28 Dec. 1873; m.
            RICHARD GASTON.
1362. ii.   FREDERICK EDWARD, b. Harrington 3 June 1876.
      iii. ANNIE ELIZABETH [Lizzie], b. Milbridge 24 Oct.
            1878, d. Steuben 16 Jan. 1899, 20y 2m 23d,
            unm.
1363. iv.   NATHAN LEONARD, b. Princeton ME 2 May 1882.
      v.   VIOLA MAY, b. Princeton 27 May 1885; m. Belfast
            16 May 1944 (as his 2nd wife) LaFOREST ALLEN-
            WOOD, b. Belmont ME c1886, son of Noah and
            Angeline (Hatch) Allenwood.
      vi.   LOWELL RAYMOND, b. Beddington 5 Mar. 1892, d.
            Harrington 24 May 1897 (5y 2m in VRs; GS has
            7y 2m 19d).

740. REDMAN JUSTUS[8] 1855-1883 [300 Lewis[7] and Dorcas Hall]
was born at Milbridge 1 Nov. 1855, died at Calais 30 Nov.
1883; married at Addison 9 Feb. 1882 (MARTHA) ELLEN[9] [Nellie]
(LEIGHTON) Barker [# 1607], born in 1846, lived at Rockland,
daughter of Enoch 2nd and Caroline (Crowley) Leighton. She
had married first 6 Mar. 1869 CHARLES WILLIAM BARKER (town
VRs), and married third WALTER HARTWELL. Redman (sometimes
written Redmond) was a barber at Jonesport.

Children, born at Jonesport:

1364. i.   ALBERTA[9], b. 23 May 1882; m. MAYNARD DAMON.
1365. ii.   MARTIN REDMAN, b. in Feb. 1884.

741. HATTIE EMMA[8] 1863-1915 [300 Lewis[7] and Dorcas Hall]
was born at Milbridge 4 Oct. 1863, died at Westbrook ME 26
July 1915, lived at Limerick ME; married at Calais 29 Sept.
1886 EUGENE JENNESS LADD, born at Deerfield NH 18 Aug. 1865,
died at Westbrook 31 May 1948, son of Rev. Enoch and Hannah
Margaret (Rand) Ladd (town and ME VRs; records of Ione Ladd
Barton). Ladd, a papermaker, married second Agnes Kelley.

Children (**Ladd**), born at Westbrook:

i.   DANA LEWIS, b. 16 Apr. 1890, d. 28 Aug. 1954.
ii.   CLARA MARGARET, b. 20 Dec. 1895, d. 1 Aug. 1897.
iii.   ENOCH EUGENE, b. 8 Feb. 1899, d. in France 8 Jan.
       1919 while serving in WW I.
iv.   IONE DELLA, b. 12 Aug. 1902, d. Westbrook 11 Mar.
       1988; m. 28 Sept. 1927 GEORGE HAROLD BARTON, d. in
       1977 (her obit.). They owned Barton's Greenhouse
       (later Barton's Florists).

742. CHARLES P.[8] 1877-1904 [300 Lewis[7] and Dorcas Hall]
was born at Calais ME 28 Aug. 1877, died at Westbrook ME 18
July 1904, 27y 1m; married at Saint John NB 13 Oct. 1896
BESSIE M. McDOUGALL, born at St. George NB in Mar. 1878 (1900
census), daughter of Peter and Lucinda (Cogswell) McDougall
(town and ME VRs; records of Ione Barton). In 1900, they
were living at Marlboro MA, where he was a shoemaker.

Children, probably four in all:

i.   EDITH V.[9], b. Calais 15 Apr. 1897.
ii.   FLORENCE, b. in MA in June 1899, res. with
       cousin Albert Cogswell in 1900.
iii.   DORCAS, b. Calais 28 June, d. there 14 July,
       1904, 14d.

743. EDITH EDNA[8] 1878-1930 [300 Lewis[7] and Dorcas Hall]
was born at Calais 14 Oct. 1878, died at Peaks Island (Portland) 30 Oct. 1930, 78y 16d; married at Harrington ME 3 Oct.
1903 (Portland int. 29 Sept.) BENJAMIN STRAFFORD RANDALL,
born 21 Feb. 1872, son of Alonzo and Abbie (Mitchell) Randall
(records of Ione Ladd Barton). She resided at the Hebron
Sanitarium.

Children (**Randall**):

i.   FLORA DORCAS, b. Westbrook 24 Sept. 1904.
ii.   ROBERTA MAE, b. Portland 31 July 1909.

744. IRA ABIJAH[8] 1856-1936 [302 George[7] and Maria Thorn]
was born at Calais ME 1 Nov. 1856, died at Winter Harbor ME 9
Mar. 1936, 79y 4m 8d; married first in 1879 HENRIETTA T.
[Etta] GETCHELL, born at Saint John NB 25 Apr. 1859, died at

Winter Harbor 1 Mar. 1917, 57y 10m 6d, daughter of John W.
and Catherine (McDonald) Getchell; married second at Calais
10 July 1918 FRANCES ADELAIDE McBEAN, born at Ledge NB about
1861, daughter of William and Sarah B. (Thornton) McBean
(Calais and ME VRs; Cornman Ms).
Ira lived for a time at Providence RI. In 1900 he was a
barber, living with his wife at Calais

Children by Etta, born at Calais:

1366. i.   LEE O.^{9}, b. 21 June 1880.
1367. ii.   ROY GORDON, b. 22 Aug. 1882.
      iii. GUY E., b. 19 Apr. 1885; m. Providence RI 21
            Apr. 1913 GERTRUDE W. COOKE, b. 16 May 1894,
            dau. of Charles Wesley and Minnie (White)
            Cooke.

745. CALVIN D.^{8} 1859-1921 [302 George^7 and Maria Thorn]
was born at Milbridge 28 July 1859, died at Calais 28 Nov.
1921, 62y 3m; married there 16 Nov. 1886 AMANDA [Mandy] FRYE,
born at Canterbury NB 25 Dec. 1863, daughter of John and Lizzie (Haman) Frye (Calais and ME VRs; Cornman Ms). He was a
millwright, living in the Milltown section of Calais.

Children, born at Calais:

1368. i.   HARRY G.^{9}, b. 19 Aug. 1887.
      ii.   CHESTER N., b. 19 Apr. 1892, d. 25 Mar. 1893.
      iii. RALPH N., b. 25 Feb. 1894.
      iv.   HELEN L., b. 18 Apr. 1896; m. Calais 5 May 1915
            PERCY SPRAGUE, b. Milltown NB c1893 (22 in
            1915), son of John and Margaret (Ray) Sprague.
1369. v.   ERNEST E., b. 17 July 1898.
      vi.   (MARY) EDITH, b. 2 Apr. 1901; m. Lewiston ME 14
            Nov. 1921 FRED ROY, b. in Canada c1888,
            son of George and Mary (King) Roy.
      vii. GLADYS P., b. 23 Dec. 1903, d. Calais 6 Feb.
            1922, 18y 1m 12d.
      viii. MABEL DORIS, b. 26 Oct. 1906, d. Orland ME 29
            Aug. 1976, 69y; m. 1st ---- KIDDER; m. 2nd
            Bucksport ME 22 May 1933 as his second wife
            SHIRLEY J. BOWDEN, b. Orland c1890 (43 in
            1933), son of John C and Carrie (Hutchins)
            Bowden. Mabel was buried in Oak Grove Ceme-
            tery, Orland, and left no direct survivors
            (her obit.).

746. ELMER ELLSWORTH^8 1863-1938 [302 George^7 and Maria
Thorn] was born at Milbridge 8 July 1863, died at Bangor ME
(hosp.) 23 Oct. 1938, 75y 3m 16d; married first at Calais 13
Dec. 1882 ALICE MAUD SEARS, born at Baileyville ME 13 Apr.
1865, died there 26 May 1931, 66y 1m 13d, daughter of Thomas
and Alice (Blair) Sears; married second at Baileyville 4 Jan.
1932 widow JANE (KNIGHT) Larrabee, born at Alexander ME 1
July 1868, died at Baileyville 14 May 1932, daughter of Paul
and Lavina R. Knight (town and ME VRs). Burials are at Alexander.
    Elmer lived at Baileyville, where he was a blacksmith and
farmer.

Children by Alice, born at Baileyville:

1370. i. HENRIETTA MAE^9 [Etta], b. 14 June 1884; m.
          DAVID MacDONALD JR.
1371. ii. WILLIAM IRA, b. 8 Oct. 1886.
      iii. MABEL, b. 4 Nov., d. 29 Dec., 1888.
1372. iv. ERNEST NORMAN, b. 14 Sept. 1890.
      v.   (ELMER) HOWARD, b. 14 Nov. 1892, res. Princeton
           ME; m. Woodland 24 Dec. 1915 EMMA EDGERLY, b.
           Princeton c1894, dau. of Samuel and Julia
           (White) Edgerly.
           He was a farmer. Ch. CLARENCE ARTHUR^{10} b.
           Princeton 11 Sept. 1916; m. Calais 12 Nov.
           1938 INA EVELYN HATT, b. Baileyville c1921,
           res. Pawtucket RI in 1988, dau. of Eugene and
           Nellie (Robb) Hatt.
      vi. RALPH MILFORD, b. 13 Nov. 1895; m. Eastport 4
           Sept. 1920 ETTA M. WENTWORTH, b. Eastport
           c1896 (24 in 1920), dau. of George C. and
           Linnie B. Wentworth. She was div. from a 1st
           husband.
      vii. FRED ALTON, b. 12 Feb., d. 26 Feb., 1898 (or b.
           27 Jan., d. 9 Feb., 1899, per Eastport VRs).
      viii. BLANCH HELEN, b. 5 Nov. 1900, d. Lubec 20 Oct.
           1980; m. St. Stephen NB 12 June 1925 (East-
           port VRs) MURRAY PRESCOTT EMERY.
      ix. RAYMOND CLARENCE, b. 17 Oct. 1903, res. Solon
           and Perry ME; m. 14 June 1928 HELENA MARY$_{10}$
           URQUHART of Eastport. Ch. JANET M.^{10} b.
           c1932; m. Eastport 11 Mar. 1950 FRED HUNTING-
           TON, b. Calais c1929, son of Herbert and Ida
           (Carr) Huntington.
      x.   ARTHUR EUGENE, b. 23 Nov. 1905, res. Paradise
           CA in 1974.

747. MINA^8 1882-1936 [302 George^7 and Mary Roff] was born
at Calais 16 Mar. 1882, died at Stockton Springs ME 24 Feb.
1936; married at Augusta ME (as "Minor" Leighton) 11 Mar.
1900 LEON ROBERT HAWKES, born at Vassalboro ME in June 1879,
son of George B. and Fostina F (Crawford) Hawkes.
    They lived at Baileyville and Vassalboro (town and ME VRs;
Vassalboro Town Register, 1906; records of descendant Susan
Cook).

Children (Hawkes):

i.   LEONICE MARGUERITE, b. Vassalboro 14 June 1901.
ii.   ELLEN GERTRUDE, b. Winslow 6 May 1903.
iii. FAUSTINA I., b. in 1905.
iv.   ARRIETTA M., b. Vassalboro 10 Feb. 1906, d. Penobscot
      22 Aug. 1926.
v.   son, b. New Gloucester 19 Sept. 1907.
vi.   HOLLIS DONOVAN, b. Vassalboro 2 Oct. 1908; m. 27 July
      1933 HAZEL MURCH.
vii. DOROTHY, b. Baileyville 6 Aug. 1910.
viii. HARRY E., b. Baileyville 2 Oct. 1914; m. 20 Apr. 1935
      ADELAIDE GAMBLE.
ix.   child, b. Baileyville 2 Mar. 1916.

748. EZRA WOODBURY[8] 1836-1915 [304 John[7] and Rebecca Leighton] was born at Pembroke ME 13 July 1836, died there 8 Apr. 1915, 78y 9m 6d; married there 2 May 1869 (Lubec int. 22 Apr.) ADA MARDENA [Addie] HUCKINS, born at Lubec 18 Apr. 1851, died at Pembroke 8 June 1936, daughter of William and Mary J. (Knights) Huckins (Pembroke VRs; Wilder, Pembroke Families). Burials are in Clarkside Cemetery.

His mother and sister Elmira were in his household in 1870 and 1880. He owned his father's farm, lot 2, and built a large house there. He served as town selectman.

Children, born at Pembroke:

    i.   LORENZO SABINE[9], b. 13 Nov. 1870, d. 9 Mar. 1877, 6y 3m 27d (GS).
1373. ii.   ALBERT WOODBURY, b. 28 Nov. 1877.
1374. ii.   (LELIA) MABEL, b. 7 Nov. 1889; m. BENJAMIN W. CLARK.

749. MARY JANE[8] 1835-   [305 Hatevil[7] and Mary Leighton] was born at Pembroke ME 4 Mar. 1835; married JAMES GREENLAW from England, a miner, who deserted her. She lived with her daughter Martha Ashley (Wilder, Pembroke Families; Cornman Ms). In 1860, James lived at Tp 7, R 2, with a Lucy, 16.

Children (**Greenlaw**):

    i.   MARTHA JANE; m. LEANDER ASHLEY.
    ii.   LAURA, b. c1864, res. with grandfather in 1880.

750. HATEVILLE JAMES[8] 1837-1909 [305 Hatevil[7] and Mary Leighton] was born at Pembroke 19 Apr. 1837, died there 19 Aug. 1909, 72y 4m; married there 4 Sept. 1859 MARY ANN MAHAR, born probably at Marion ME 20 June 1836, died at Pembroke 15 Oct. 1898, 62y 3m 25d, daughter of Edmund and Deborah (Jones) Mahar (Wilder, Pembroke Families; Pembroke VRs). Burials are in Clarkside Cemetery.

A farmer, he developed land purchased from his father. In 1860 he was a lumberman.

Children, born at Pembroke:

    i.   ODION[9], b. 30 July 1860, d. Pembroke 10 Mar. 1930, 69y 7m 11d; unm. He was a farmer.
    ii.   CAROLINE, b. 25 Apr. 1862, d. 7 Nov. 1863, 1y 6m 12d (GS).
    iii.   MARINER, b. 29 Dec. 1864, d. Calais 16 May 1942; m. there 14 Dec. 1911 DELIA E. DODGE, b. in NS c1881, d. Pembroke in 1966 (GS), dau. of Frank and Laura (Ward) Dodge. He owned his father's farm. Ch. ANDREW PERCY[10] b. 13 Nov. 1912, d Calais (hosp.) 15 Apr. 1989 (obit.); m. Pembroke 24 Dec. 1938 EILENE B. DUDLEY, b. there c1915, dau. of Herbert and Emma (Little) Dudley [# 307]. No ch.
    iv.   LOUISA {?CAROLINE], b. 29 Oct. 1868, d. Leicester MA, struck by car; m. FRED LAMB. No ch. She res. Worcester in 1900 with half-brother George Mahar.

vi.   EVA L., b. in May 1870, d. 28 Oct. 1876,
      6y 5m 10d (GS).
vii. AUSTIN, b. 10 May 1874, d. Pembroke 9 Sept.
      1930, 56y 3m 29d; unm., res. Auburn MA.
--   LILLA M. (adopted), b. 21 Mar. 1883, d. in
      1969; m. Pembroke 7 Dec. 1901 JOHN B. MAHAR,
      b. there about 1877, son of Howard and Sedalia
      (Norwood) Mahar.

751. JEMIMA BELL[8] 1850-1934 [305 Hatevil[7] and Mary Leigh-
ton] was born at Pembroke 21 Mar. 1850, died at North Andover
MA 15 Sept. 1934; married at Pembroke 9 Aug. 1868 EMULUS WES-
TON SELDEN CARTER, born 1 May 1844, died at Pembroke 19 Mar.
1883, son of James and Joanna (Cox) Carter (Pembroke VRs;
Wilder, Pembroke Families; GS, Clarkside Cemetery).

Children (**Carter**), born at Pembroke:

i.   MARY JANE, b. 5 June 1869, res. N. Andover; m. EDMUND
      DUNN.
ii.   KEZIAH S., b. 11 Oct. 1876; m. ALBERT[9] W. LEIGHTON
      [# 1373].
iii. ROSETTA M. (twin), b. 11 Oct. 1876; m. FRED DUNN.
iv.   ANNETTE O. [Nettie], b. 24 Sept. 1877, d. Boston 22
      Aug. 1934; unm.

752. WILLIAM HENRY[8] 1834-1917 [306 Edmund[7] and Mary Hol-
land] was born at Pembroke 10 Mar. 1834 (1836 in pension
application), died at Proctor PA 10 Jan. 1917, 83y 10m 10d;
married first at Pembroke 14 June 1855 (VRs; 1854 in Wilder)
LOUISA L. WILCOX, born at Shivaree NS 13 Oct. 1831, died near
the end of 1870 (Wilder, Pembroke Families; Pembroke VRs;
pension file); married second at Cascade Tp PA in 1877 NANCY
SHIRES, born at Kellyburg PA 13 Dec. 1863, died at Hillsgrove
PA 30 Nov. 1932, daughter of George Shires.
    He farmed lot 36 near his father; in 1860 he was a seaman
at Trescott, with a boy Freeman Leighton, 8, in his household. He enlisted in the US Navy 26 Oct. 1863, and was discharged 6 Jan. 1865. He was boatswain's mate on the USS Flag
near his brother Isaiah's ship when he died, and served also
on the Sea Foam and the Princeton.
    In the spring of 1872 he left for PA, leaving his children
in ME, and settled in Wyoming Co. (affidavit of cousin Jemima
[#751]) as a farmer. He applied there for a pension (#16961
NA-MSR); his widow applied also in 1917.

Children by Louisa, born at Pembroke:

      i.   JOHN[9], b. 18 Aug. 1855.
      ii.   LOUISA L., b. 2 May 1858.
1375. iii. EDWARD E., b. 11 Apr. 1862.
      iv.   WILLIAM H., b. 17 July 1864.

Children by Nancy, listed in pension application:

      v.   MAGGIE, b. 11 May 1877.
      vi.   GEORGE, b. 9 Apr. 1879.

753.   ISAIAH[8] 1837-1864 [306 Edmund[7] and Mary Holland] was
born at Pembroke 2 Apr. 1837, drowned at Charleston SC 9 June
1864; married at Pembroke 13 Aug. 1856 LOVICIA ANN [Visa]
TROTT, born at Perry ME about 1832 (28 in 1860), died there
20 Jan. 1865. Her name was spelled Lovice and Lovicey.
   Isaiah was a mariner at Perry in 1860. He enlisted in the
US Navy under the alias of Joseph Mahar, and was serving as
captain of the maintop on the gunboat Neipsic, part of the
fleet blockading Charleston SC, when he died. "Whilst lower-
ing a boat from the ship, the forward fall got unhooked, and
the after fall got foul, the boat swung broadside against
wind and wave, the ship being under way at the time, surged
round and the boat was capsized."
   Edmund was made guardian of his grandchildren 8 June 1865,
and secured a pension for them (NA-MSR #C854).

   Children, born at Perry:

         i.   SARAH A [9], b. 1 Dec. 1858.
   1376. ii.   CLARENCE HERBERT, b. 27 Apr. 1861.

   754.   CHARLOTTE ANN[8] [Lo] 1839-1892 [306 Edmund[7] and Mary
Holland] was born at Pembroke 16 Nov. 1839, drowned there 30
Apr. 1892, capsized in the Falls; married there 19 Sept. 1856
BENJAMIN KELLY, born at Trescott 15 May 1825 (Pembroke TRs).
   An untraced Charlotte Leighton married at Portland 27 Sept.
1883 Sewell Mahar.

   Children (**Kelly**), born at Pembroke:

   i   ADA, b. 28 Sept. 1860.
   ii.   WILLIAM EDMUND, b. 29 Sept. 1862.
   iii. ISAIAH, b. 30 Apr. 1865.
   iv.   LIZZIE JANE, b. 10 Dec. 1869.
   v.   HOWARD SCOTT, b. 26 Mar. 1870.
   vi.   GEORGE, b. 8 Nov. 1877.

   755.   ALEXANDER[8] [Sandy] 1846-   [306 Edmund[7] and Mary
Holland] was born at Pembroke 10 June 1846, lived at Lubec in
1919; married first at Pembroke 8 July 1868 HANNAH J. MATZ;
married second at South Lubec 15 Dec. 1869 ELVIRA A. HILTON,
born at Milbridge 1 June 1850, died at Lubec 11 Apr. 1896,
45y 11m 23d, daughter of Winslow and Rosella (Owen) Hilton;
married third at Lubec 27 Aug. 1898 ELIZA J. TRECARTIN, born
at Lubec about 1866 (32 in 1898), died there 30 Aug. 1906,
40y 6m, daughter of Thomas and Eunice (Tinker) Trecartin
(Pembroke and Lubec VRs; Wilder, Pembroke Families; data from
son Oscar--Cornman Papers).

   Children, all by Elvira, born at West Pembroke except last
      three born at Lubec:

         i.   INA MAUDE[9], b. 15 Nov. 1870; m. ---- ATWOOD.
   1377. ii.   GEORGE DALLAS, b. 22 Sept. 1872.
         iii. BERTHA BLANCH, b. 13 Sept. 1874; m. Lubec 18
                  Dec. 1893 JOHN McBRIDE, b. Eastport c1866 (27
                  in 1893), son of John and Jane (Hill) McBride.
                  Ch. Glen b. Lubec 13 Sept. 1897.

iv. AMY WINIFRED, b. 22 May 1877; m. 1st Lubec 9
June 1897 GEORGE T. MOSES, son of Fred and
Helen (Carey) Moses of Grand Manan; m. 2nd
Lubec 11 Jan. 1919 GEORGE WILLIAM DAVIS, b.
Jonesport 18 Jan. 1871, son of Daniel Richardson and Mary Augusta (Beal) Davis. Davis had
m. 1st 6 Dec. 1890 Minerva Ripley--div.; and
m. 2nd in 1900 Josephine Taylor.
v. OSCAR BELMONT, b. 23 Sept. 1878, d. aged 3.
vi. CLARENCE HERBERT, b. 9 Aug. 1880; m. 1st Lubec
18 Aug. 1902 FLORA M. MATHEWS, b. c1883 (19 in
1902); m. 2nd Lubec 18 Aug. 1917 SUSIE M.
DAVIS, b. Calais c1897, dau. of George and
Minerva (Ripley) Davis [iv above].
1378. vii. ALONZO BELMONT, b. 14 Jan. 1882.
viii. ESTELLA MAY, b. 8 Apr. 1884.
ix. OSCAR, b. 21 Jan. 1886 (23 Jan. per VRs); unm.
in 1915.
x. FANNY DELEMARIE, b. 19 Nov. 1887, d. 7 Sept.
1888, 9m.

756. CATHERINE[8] [Kate] 1852-1884 [306 Edmund[7] and Mary
Holland] was born at Pembroke 5 June 1852, died in 1884; married CHARLES WATT of Grand Manan, NB, born about 1849 (31 in
1880) (Pembroke TRs).

Children (**Watt**), born at Pembroke:

i. CHARLES, b. 23 Sept. 1868.
ii. NELLIE PATTEN, b. in 1870; d. 3 Sept. 1894, 23y 11m
10d; unm.
iii. NELSON ALLEN, b. 2 June 1872.
iv. MARY J., b. c1875 (5 in 1880).
v. ROBERT, b. c1880 (4/12 in 1880).

757. AARON WHITFIELD[8] 1834-1906 [307 Thomas[7] and Hannah
Kelley] was born at Trescott (Pembroke VRs) 6 Mar. 1834, died
at Lubec 21 Dec. 1906, 73y; married at Lubec 21 Mar. 1853
ANNA LEIGHTON, born at Lubec 25 Apr. 1820, died there 28
Aug. 1899, 79y, daughter of Hatevil and Mary (Mahar) Leighton
[# 95] (Wilder, Pembroke Families; Pembroke and Lubec VRs).
He was sometimes called Whitfield.

Children, born at Pembroke:

i. LORETTA[9], b. 28 Jan. 1855; m. Pembroke 17 June
1877 THOMAS A. ASHBY, b. England c1850,
son of Alfred Ashby.
ii. LORENZO S., b. 7 Mar. 1857, d. 7 July 1860.
1379. iii. JOSIAH WOODBURY, b. 15 Feb. 1862.
1380. iv. (JAMES) HOWARD, b. 7 Aug. 1863.

758. WILLIAM KELLEY[8] 1836-1862 [307 Thomas[7] and Hannah
Kelley] was born at Trescott 6 June 1836, drowned at the
falls there 5 Oct. 1862 with Isaac N. [# 304]; married 9 Dec.
1859 ELIZABETH KINNEY, born 8 July 1841, daughter of Alfred
and Rebecca Kinney (Pembroke and Lubec VRs; Wilder, Pembroke
Families). He was a farmer at Lubec in 1860.

Children, born at Lubec:

    i.   ABBY JANE[9], b. 12 Dec. 1859, d. Lubec 30 Sept.
        1864 (Machias Union had Abel J., grandchild
        of Alfred and Rebecca Kinney, aged 4).
    ii.   CLARISSA, b. 23 Nov. 1862 (posthumous).

759. JOHN FAIRCHILD[8] 1842-   [307 Thomas[7] and Hannah
Kelley] was born at Trescott 6 Apr. 1842 (VRs), lived at
Duluth MN in 1922; married say 1866 HENRIETTA ----, born in
ME in Jan. 1846 (per 1900 census).
In 1861 he enlisted in Co. A, 15th ME Inf. Rgt., in 1864
re-enlisted in the same company in TX, and was discharged at
Augusta ME in 1866. He had received pistol wounds in 1864 in
LA, and been a prisoner for a year.
In 1868, he enlisted in Co. L, 3rd Artillery Rgt. of the
regular army, and was given a disability discharge in FL in
1870. His occupation listed as soldier, he, his wife and son
were in the household of James Wilson at Trescott in 1870.
Although he was listed at Trescott in 1880, his pension
application that year stated he was aged 37, of Whiting. The
1900 census and a medical report in 1904 showed him living at
Washburn, Bayfield County WI; pension files showed him at
Duluth in 1922 (NA MSR-- #499556).

Children, born probably at Trescott:

1381. i.   WILLIAM JUDSON[9], b. in May 1867.
      ii.   CASSANDRA [?], b. c1871 (9 in 1880).
      iii. SAMANTHA, b. c1875 (5 in 1880).
      iv.   WILLARD, b. in Jan. 1878 (3 in 1880), res. WI
          with parents in 1900.
      v.   LORIA, b. in 1880 (3/12 in 1880).
      vi.   JANE, b. in May 1882 (per 1900 census).

760. ISAAC NEWELL[8] 1844-1917 [307 Thomas[7] and Hannah
Kelley] was born at Pembroke 5 July 1844, died there 18 Mar.
1917, 70y 7m 24d; married there 24 Feb. 1869 LAURA S.
[Louisa] DUNN, born there 18 Feb. 1849, died there 9 Feb.
1925, 76y 11m 22d, daughter of George C. and Eliza A. (Holland) Dunn (Pembroke and ME VRs; Wilder, Pembroke Families;
records of Lettie Blackwood).
He was a farmer and brickmason, and lived on Leighton
Point, the fourth generation on lot #1. He served in Co. H,
9th ME Inf. Rgt. Burials are in Clarkside Cemetery.

Children, born at Pembroke:

    i.   BENJAMIN F [9], b. 5 July 1870, d. 4 Feb. 1891
        (GS); unm.
1382. ii.   ABBIE JANE, b. 21 July 1875; m. CLAUDE PEACOCK.
      iii. CORA MAY, b. 1 Aug. 1877, d. Eastport in 1973;
         m. JOHN HENDERSON of Eastport. No ch.
1383. iv.   BERTHA ELIZA, b. 26 Jan. 1880; m. JESSE HILTON.
1384. v.   ELLA, b. 5 Jan. 1884; m. JOSIAH J. WILBUR.
1385. vi.   ALICE, b. 28 Oct. 1885; m. BURTON NEWMAN.
      vii. WILLIAM L., b. 28 Feb. 1887, d. in 1889 (2y 25d
         per GS).

viii. JESSIE BERNICE, b. 28 June 1889, d. in 1967;
     m. Eastport 12 June 1916 FRED LEROY MARSHALL,
     b. Pembroke c1891, son of Byron B. and Lydia
     A. (Wilder) Marshall. No ch.

761.   EVERETT HERSEY[8] 1857-1902 [310 Aaron[7] and Mary Smith]
was born at Pembroke 25 Apr. 1857, died there 12 Dec. 1902,
45y 7m 21d; married there 26 June 1880 EMMA SOPHILIA MAHAR,
born there 1 Oct. 1859, died there 26 Mar. 1942, daughter of
Peter Ryland and Martha Ann (Cook) Mahar (Pembroke and ME
VRs; Wilder, Pembroke Families).
He lived on Leighton Point, on lot #5 of his grandfather
John's original holding, and was a farmer and sailor.
Burials are in Clarkside Cemetery.

Children, born at Pembroke:

       i.   JESSIE MAY[9], b. 29 Sept. 1882, d. 12 Aug. 1883,
             4y 10m (GS).
       ii.   MYRTIE IVA, b. 15 May 1884, d. 24 Mar. 1908,
             23y 10m 9d; unm.
1386. iii. ARTHUR ROBIE, b. 21 Mar. 1886.
       iv.   NETTIE EMMA, b. 29 Nov. 1888; m. Pembroke 1
             Jan. 1918 HARLAND W. BROWN, b. W. Pembroke
             c1887 (31 in 1918), son of Allen H. and Bessie
             M. (Hersey) Brown.
       v.   WALTER WYETH, b. 17 Sept. 1891, d. Pembroke 3
             Sept. 1920, 28y 11m 17d; unm.
       vi.   ALBERTA EMMA, b. 1 Oct. 1895, moved away; mar.,
             1 ch. (ROBERTA ERMINA, 1900 census.)
1387. vii. LLOYD EVERETT, b. 13 May 1900.
       viii. VELMA MAUDE, b. 29 June 1902, d. at 15y.

762.   FREDERICK[8] 1862-1922 [310 Aaron[7] and Mary Smith] was
born at Pembroke 14 Jan. 1862, died there 11 Apr. 1922, 60y
2m 25d; married first there 2 Feb. 1884 WINNIE CHRISTIE
MAHAR, born in 1864, died at Eastport 3 Apr. 1910, daughter
of Peter Ryland and Martha Ann (Cook) Mahar--divorced; married second at Pembroke 2 Apr. 1889 ELIZABETH C. [Lizzie]
CLARK, born at Perry 26 Apr. 1866, died at Pembroke 18 Apr.
1939, 72y 11m 22d, daughter of Andrew and Elizabeth Ann (Loring) Clark (Pembroke and ME VRs; letter from wife Elizabeth--
Cornman Papers).
In 1900 his mother was in his Pembroke household. Burials
are in Forest Hills Cemetery.

Children by Lizzie, born at Pembroke:

       i.   GRACE LILLIAN[9], b. in Feb. 1890; m. ----
             KINGSBURY.
       ii.   RALPH EDWIN, b. 11 Sept. 1895; d. in 1918,
             while serving in Co. B, 25th Marine Battalion.
1388. iii. WILLIAM PRESCOTT, b. 3 Apr. 1898.

763.   GEORGE E.[8] 1834-1895 [311 George[7] and Comfort Gup-
till] was born at Pembroke 18 Mar. 1834, died there 12 Jan.
1895, 60y; married first there 11 Dec. 1854 BELINDA COGGINS

of Lubec, born 25 Aug. 1833, died at Pembroke 7 July 1872;
married second 4 Jan. 1874 HATTIE W. KNOWLTON, born at Pembroke in Dec. 1857, died at Deer Island ME 17 Jan. 1935 (Pembroke and ME VRs; Wilder, Pembroke Families; Cornman Papers).
George Goggins filed 6 June 1856 an accounting as guardian of
Belinda Leighton (WashCP 20:249).
In 1860, the household was at Springfield ME, including
WILLIS A [9], 13 [# 1088], and at Pembroke in later censuses.
His farm was on Old Hersey Road.

Children by Belinda, born at Pembroke:

1389. i.   MARTHA J.[9], b. c1855 (14 in 1870); m. ?ISAAC E.
             TAYLOR and REUBEN FLANDERS.
       ii.   WILLIAM J., b c1857 (3 in 1860), prob. d.y.
       iii. ADDIE C., b. c1858 (2 in 1860), prob. d.y.
       iv.   THERESA, b. c1860 (10 in 1870).
       v.   ADA A., b. Pembroke 28 Apr. 1864.
       vi.   WILLIAM W., b. c1866 (14 in 1880); m. Rochester
             NH 19 Oct. 1888 (VRs) NELLIE F. HORNE, b.
             Rochester, dau. of Parker and Mary Ann Horne.
       vii. EDWARD E., b. c1868, d. Rochester NH 4 Nov.
             1900, 32y 11m 3d; m. there 3 Apr. 1891 ANGIE
             HUSSEY, b. there 29 July 1869, d. 23 July
             1891, dau. of Silas and Rosina A (Hussey)
             Hussey (Stearns, N. H. Genealogies, 4:1921;
             Richmond, John Hayes, 1:280). No ch.
       viii. EVA E., b. c1869 (8/12 in 1870), d. Rochester
             10 Apr. 1903, 32y 5m; m. there 6 Nov. 1888
             (both of Newton Junction) GEORGE S. HOYT, b.
             c1863, son of Seth and Eliza (Cadeaux) Hoyt.
       ix.   GEORGE H., b. in Mar. 1872, res. Haverhill MA
             in 1900; m. LOUISA ---- , b. in MA in Jan.
             1874.

Children by Hattie, born at Pembroke:

       x.   JESSE H., b. c1875 (5 in 1880), res. Rochester
             NH and Haverhill MA (Cornman Papers).
       xi.   MAUD MARION, b. c1877 (3 in 1880), res. Deer
             Island NB; m. 1st W. Pembroke 31 Dec. 1895
             JOHN E. MINER, b. c1865 (30 in 1895); m. 2nd
             Eastport 5 Dec. 1908 JAMES W. DOUGHTY, b. Deer
             Island c1887 (21 in 1908), son of Fred and
             Effie Doughty.
       xii. IVAN R., b. 29 Jan. 1879; m. Pembroke 25 Dec.
             1901 RACHEL E. LOWE, b. there c1881, d. in
             1951 (GS), dau. of William and Adeline W.
             (Owen) Lowe. Ch. MELVIN THEODORE[10] b. 14 Jan.
             1906, d. Bangor 22 June 1989; m. Dover-Fox-
             croft 27 Mar. 1926 ROVENA C HILLMAN, b. there
             c1903, dau. of William and Elizabeth (Paul)
             Hillman. No ch. Melvin and Rovena were both
             teachers; he was a principal at Brewer.
1390. xiii. ISAAC H., b. 24 May 1880 (1882 in delayed birth
             record).
       xiv. ARTHUR C , b. 7 Oct. 1882, res. FL; m. Eastport
             14 Mar. 1919 CORA E. (FARLEY) Pettigrew, b.
             Dennysville ME c 1884 (35 in 1919).
1391. xv.   FRANK D., b. in July 1886.
1392. xvi. (DELWIN) FRANCIS, b. 8 June 1890.

xvii. XIMENA, b. 14 Jan. 1892; m. Pembroke 13 Apr.
     1908 HOWARD B. WALLACE, b. Deer Island NB
     c1884, son of Burnham and Bertie (McNeill)
     Wallace.
xviii.NELLIE, b. 29 Oct. 1893; m. LINDSAY WALLACE.

764. HATEVIL M.[8] 1828-   [312 James[7] and Mary Rumery]
was born at Lubec ME 8 Apr. 1828, lived at Boston in 1903;
married first at Augusta ME int. 28 Oct. 1853 (VRs, which
listed the marriage as 30 Oct. 1854) LUCY T. BLANCHARD, born
at Hallowell ME 26 Feb. 1830, daughter of William J. and
Lydia (Baker) Blanchard of Pittston; married second or third
at Boston 23 Mar. 1870 (VRs) MARY P. WEBBER, born there in
1835 (Cambridge VRs), daughter of Alonzo J. and Mary Webber
(town VRs; Cornman Ms). In 1903 his niece Mary Edith wrote
that she thought he had two wives named Blanchard (Cornman
Papers).
   He lived at Chelsea ME, then as "Hartwell" was at New Haven
CT in 1870, and in 1903 was reported living at Boston in an
"old folks' home."

Children by Lucy, born at Pittston:

      i.   CHARLES T.[9], b. 22 Oct. 1854, d. 13 Sept. 1856.
     ii.   JAMES W., b. 13 May 1856.
1393. iii.   ADELBERT RUSSELL, b. say 1859.

765. DOMINICUS RUMERY[8] 1830-1913 [312 James[7] and Mary Rum-
ery] was born at Lubec 8 Dec. 1830, died at New Haven CT 14
Jan. 1913; married first at Lubec 15 Apr. 1853 HANNAH RING
WINSLOW, born there 8 June 1834, died at New Haven 12 Dec.
1896, daughter of Capt. Jacob Snow and Elizabeth (Clark) Winslow (Winslow Memorial 2:appendix 168); married second 11
June 1901 SARAH BURR (STURGES) Morton of Fairfield CT, born
16 Dec. 1845. Sarah had married first in 1872 William E.
Morton of Portland ME; he died in 1895 (Lubec VRs; letters
from widow Sarah and sister-in-law Mary Edith in 1914--
Cornman Papers; family records of Kingsley Leighton Jr.)
   Dominicus was first a fisherman and carpenter, but in 1852
he left Lubec, carrying a character reference signed by the
selectmen. He was employed in locomotive construction at
Somerville MA, and became a manufacturer, settling at New
Haven about 1868. He invented, patented and built the
Leighton Parlor Sleeping Car, which was sold to railroads
trying to break the Pullman monopoly.

Children:

1394. i.   ALTON WINSLOW[9], b. Portland ME 3 Apr. 1857.
     ii.   ALMA, b. 24 May 1859, d. NYC 11 June 1925; m.
            24 Aug. 1903 ARTHUR HARMOUNT GRAVES, b. New
            Haven 22 Jan. 1879, d. Meriden CT 31 Dec
            1931, son of Joseph Alvin and Mary F (Har-
            mount) Graves. No ch.
            Yale AB 1900, PhD 1907, he was prof. of
            botany and curator of Brooklyn Botanical Gar-
            den. He m. 2nd Helen Tiffany--1 dau.
            Alma, a trained kindergarten teacher, con-
            ducted "Miss Leighton's School" at New Haven.

1395. iii. FREDERICK LINCOLN, b. Somerville MA 1 Apr.
              1866.
       iv.   FRANK BACON, b. New Haven 22 July, d. 11 Sept.,
             1871.

766. JOHN T.[8] 1830-1882 [313 Isaac[7] and Roxana Thayer] was
born at Lubec ME 30 July 1830, drowned there 16 Sept. 1882
when his boat capsized in a squall; married there 17 July
1853 ANNA MARIA ROBINSON, born about 1833 (24 in 1860, 37 in
1870, 47 in 1880), died at Augusta ME 4 Jan. 1895, 61y (Lubec
VRs; family Bible; Cornman Ms).
   John was a seaman, and lived at Strait Bay, Lubec, next to
his father. In 1880, his household included his daughter
Annie's son "Walter H.," 2. About 1880, his wife entered the
state insane hospital at Augusta, where she spent the rest of
her life.

Children, born at Lubec:

       i.   SARAH J.[9], b. c1855 (5 in 1860), d. Lubec 11
             Oct. 1884; m. Lubec 21 Aug. 1880 LEANDER
             HUCKINS. No ch.
1396. ii.   ANNIE A., b. c1856 (4 in 1860).
       iii. ALEXANDER, b. c1858 (2 in 1860), not in 1870
             census.
       iv.   ISAAC, b. in 1860, d. Lubec 15 Dec. 1864, 4y.
       v.   ISAIAH, b. 19 Apr., d. 10 Dec., 1864.
       vi.   JOHN, b. 14 Apr. 1867, not in 1870 census.
1397. vii. GEORGE M., b. 27 Apr. 1869 (10 in 1880).

767. LOVINA[8] 1837-   [313 Isaac[7] and Roxana Thayer] was
born at Lubec 7 Aug. 1837 (Bible); married there 14 Feb. 1864
CHARLES OTIS MAHAR of Lubec, born in July 1842. Her name
appeared as Malvinia on the marriage record, Levina Isabel on
Hannah's birth record, but family papers show Lovina (Lubec
VRs; Wilder, Pembroke Families; obituary of Vesta). In 1900
their Lubec household included "son" Wilbur McFadden born in
Mar. 1895 and "daughter" Alberta McFadden born in Sept. 1896.

Children (**Mahar**), born at Lubec:

i.   HARRY, b. in Sept. 1866 (1900 census).
ii.   ADRIEL M., b. c1868 (Milton E., 12, in 1880); m.
       Lubec 29 Nov. 1906, at 38, MYRTLE GLIDDEN of Calais,
       20.
iii.   BELINDA, b. c1868 (Malinda, 2 in 1870); m. JAMES
       BRADLEY.
iv.   (AARON) JACKSON, b. in Nov. 1868; unm.
v.   MARY M., b. c1870 (10 in 1880).
vi.   VESTA JANE, b. 16 May 1872; m. (JAMES) HOWARD[10]
       LEIGHTON [# 1380].
vii.   LILLIAN [Lillie], b. 27 Jan. 1875; m. 1st ---- LORD;
       m. 2nd HENRY W. STEWART.
viii. CHARLES LAFAYETTE, b. in Nov. 1879.
ix.   HANNAH ELIZABETH, b. 30 July 1879; m. Lubec 19 Sept.
       1907 MAYNARD GLIDDEN of Calais, b. c1879.
x.   FRED, b. c1880 (28 in 1907), res. Pembroke; m. Lubec
       22 July 1907 GRACE OWEN, b. c1886.

768. MELISSA ABIGAIL[8] 1838-1904 [313 Isaac[7] and Roxana
Thayer] was born at Lubec 16 Oct. 1838 (Bible), died there 6
Feb. 1904; married first at Pembroke ME 7 July 1857 (WILLIAM)
ELLERY MAHAR; married second JAMES KINNEY (records of descen-
dant Glenata Hettrick; town VRs).

Children (**Mahar**), born at Lubec:

i.   ADA EUDORA, b. 20 Mar. 1860; d. Lubec 15 Jan. 1944;
      m. Trescott 23 May 1882 HENRY FRANKLIN WILCOX, b.
      there 6 June 1850, d. Lubec 17 Nov. 1923, son of
      Andrew Jr. and Sarah Ann (Owen) Wilcox.
ii.   JENNIE ALMA, b. 20 Mar. 1863.
iii. ADDIE V., b. c1865, d. Lubec 4 Jan. 1898, 34y; unm.
iv.   WILLIAM ELLERY [Will], b. 5 Mar. 1868, d. Lubec 31
      July 1958; m. there 15 Dec. 1891 ETHEL C, BYERS of
      St. George NB.

769. VELINA M.[8] [Vena] 1841-1930 [313 Isaac[7] and Roxana
Thayer] was born at Lubec 13 Aug. 1841 (Bible), died there 25
Sept. 1930, 89y 1m 12d; married there int. 22 Aug. 1870
JOSIAH TROTT MAHAR, born at Pembroke about 1840 (40 in 1880),
died at West Lubec 7 Dec. 1898, 63y, son of Joseph and
Rebecca (Trott) Mahar (Lubec VRs; records of Capt. Alfred
Kelley).
They raised her sister Annie's children. Velina was listed
as Margaret, 38, in 1880.

Children (**Mahar**), born at Lubec:

i.   EDITH A., b. c1872 (8 in 1880); m. ROBERT ARCHER.
ii.   (WILLIAM) ELLERY, b. c1873 (6 in 1880); m. Lubec 24
      Mar. 1915 (her 2nd mar.) NELLIE THOMPSON, who was b.
      c1887.
iii. COLON HARVEY, b. 8 Apr. 1876; m. Lubec 28 Jan. 1898
      MAGGIE ROBINSON.

770. REBECCA[8] 1842-1907 [313 Isaac[7] and Roxana Thayer]
was born at Lubec 8 Nov. 1842, died at Bangor ME 9 July 1907;
married first at Lubec 3 July 1865 JAMES SALMON; married second there 25 Jan. 1876 ISRAEL ALLEN, born about 1832 (37 in
1870), died about 1911, son of Samuel and Jane (Thornton)
Allen (Lubec and ME VRs; records of Alfred Kelley). Her two
Salmon children died young.
Israel Allen, a Lubec fisherman, had married first about
1863 Anna Maria Tucker; their son George was born in 1866.

Children (**Allen**), born at Lubec:

i.   ROSCOE SAMUEL, b. 17 June 1878, d. Lubec in May 1967;
      m. Lubec 1 July 1905 ANNIE MARIA WALLACE.
ii.   CECILIA, b. 18 Oct. 1883; m. 1st ARTHUR DENNISON; m.
      2nd GORDON STURKS.

771. EMMA SOPHIA[8] 1851-   [313 Isaac[7] and Roxanna
Thayer] was born at Lubec 6 Aug. 1851 (27 in 1880); married
there 21 Aug. 1873 ALBERT H. GODFREY, born about 1838 (Lubec
VRs). He had four children by a first wife.

Children (**Godfrey**), born at Lubec:

i.   RENA H., b. c1874 (6 in 1880).
ii.   CLARA, b. c1876 (4 in 1880).

772. SOPHRONIA[8] 1835-   [315 Samuel[7] and Marcia Huckins]
was born at Lubec about 1835 (45 in 1880); married in 1852
WILSON ANDREWS, born in NB about 1830 (30 in 1860), died at
Whiting 14 Oct. 1874 (Forslund, Whiting, 66--data in part
questionable). In 1860 their Whiting home was next door to
that of Horatio G. Allen. In 1880 she and Mabel lived at
Whiting in Otis Malone's household.

Children (**Andrews**), born at Whiting:

i.   WILLIS H., b. 14 Aug., d. 18 Sept., 1854.
ii.   IDA J., b. 1 Apr. 1856.
iii. LUELLA, b. 7 Feb. 1858.
iv.   FANNY, b. 14 Jan. 1859.
v.   ALFRETTA, b. 11 July 18?? (not in censuses).
vi.   ?MABEL WINNIFRED, b. 29 Oct. 1874.

773. JAMES BRADFORD[8] 1839-1865 [315 Samuel[7] and Marcia
Huckins] was born at West Lubec 17 Apr. 1839, died at Whiting
ME 30 May 1865, 27y (GS); married about 1862 MEHITABLE ALLEN
BRIDGES, born at Whiting 30 June 1844 (Wilder, Pembroke Families). Forslund's History of Whiting (p. 86) combined him
with James Everett[7] [# 336], making him into one James with
two wives.
    James was a lumberman and saw-mill hand. He served in the
28th ME Inf. Rgt. He is buried in the Village Cemetery at
Whiting. Widow Mehitable married second Israel P. Dinsmore,
the widower of James's sister SARAH J.[8] (LEIGHTON) Wilbur
[# 315], and had four Dinsmore children.

Child, born at Whiting:

1398. i.   WILLIS HERBERT[9], b. 19 Apr. 1864.

774. CATHERINE A.[8] [Katie] 1840-1904 [315 Samuel[7] and
Marcia Huckins] was born at Lubec say 1840, died at Whiting
23 Feb. 1904; married at Lubec 26 Mar. 1855 BELA W. CRANE,
born at Whiting 6 Feb. 1834, died there 3 Jan. 1908, son of
John and Mehitable (Wilder) Crane (ME VRs; Forslund, Whiting,
71).

Children (**Crane**), born at Whiting:

i.   ELLEN MARIA [Nellie], b. 12 Oct. 1860.
ii.   LILLIE E., b. 23 Oct. 1863, d. 17 June 1945; m. OSCAR
      DINSMORE, b. 9 Jan. 1858, d. 19 Oct. 1939, son of
      Alexander and Lucy Dinsmore.
iii. JESSE B., b. 27 Feb. 1865; m. 1st EDNA V. FOSS; m.
      2nd 4 July 1900 PHILENA B. CROSBY.
iv.   FRED H., b. 5 June 1868; m. ANNA CRANE.

775. LORENA A.[8] 1836-   [316 Mark[7] and Eliza Huckins]
was born at Lubec 29 Mar. 1836; married there 3 Jan. 1858
SOLOMON T. CASE, born 20 Dec. 1833, died at Lubec 5 Aug.
1903, son of William and Mary (Ramsdell) Case (Lubec VRs;
Cornman Ms).

Children (**Case**), born at Lubec:

i.   IRVING, b. 19 Feb. 1865; m. 1 May 1899 MARY DAVIS, b.
      1872. He was the postmaster at Lubec.
ii.   (MARY) ESTHER, b. 11 Jan. 1867; m. Eastport 23 Jan.
      1892 JOHN MOHOLLAND, b. in 1871.
iii. CHARLES HERMAN, b. 26 July 1870; m. 18 Dec. 1897
      MARGARET LAMSON.
iv.   ANNIE, b. 20 Jan. 1876; unm. She was a teacher at
      Haverhill MA.

776. JOSIAH LIVINGSTON[8] 1840-1928 [317 Hatevil[7] and Eliza
Leighton] was born at Lubec 27 May 1840, died at Newport RI 9
Apr. 1928; married 10 Nov. 1867 JANE EUPHEMIA YOUNG, born at
Pennfield NB 8 Sept. 1845, died at Newport 5 Oct. 1897,
daughter of John Bailey and Priscilla Paul (Hawkins) Young
(Wilder, Pembroke Families; Pembroke TRs; Cornman Ms). He
was a ships' carpenter at Pembroke in 1870 and 1880.

Children, born at Pembroke:

1399. i.   ERNEST ALVA[9], b. 17 Feb. 1869.
      ii.   CHARLES BAILEY, b. 2 Mar. 1871, d. E. Orange NJ
            in June 1929; m. 6 Jan. 1897 LILLIAN VORHEES
            of Newark. He res. Elizabeth NJ, employed by
            Public Service Co. Ch. CHARLES BAILEY JR.[10]
            b. 11 Dec. 1908.
      iii. ALICE ELEANOR, b. 25 Dec. 1874, res. Newport.
1400. iv.   HAROLD LIVINGSTON, b. 4 July 1877.

777. (WILLIAM) ALVRA[8] 1851-1929 [317 Hatevil[7] and Eliza
Leighton] was born at Lubec 16 Apr. 1851, died at Pembroke 10
May 1929, 78y; married first at Eastport 21 Dec. 1875 SARAH
E. BRIDGES, born at Meddybemps ME 12 Oct. 1839, died at Char-
lotte ME 27 Dec. 1928, daughter of John and Mary (Prescott)
Bridges--divorced; married second at Pembroke 30 June 1905
JESSIE M. KENDRICK, born at Campobello NB 10 May 1878, died
at Pembroke in 1959 (GS), daughter of Alonzo and Mary
(McBride) Kendrick (town VRs; records of daughter Lillian).
Burials are in the Hersey Cemetery.
      A farmer and fisherman, Alvra lived on the family home-
stead. In 1900 his mother was in his household. His marriage and death records showed him as Alvin, and his gravestone as Alvera. (Oddly, Wilder's Pembroke Families listed
Humboldt Co. CA for Jessie's birth, and Eureka CA for the
marriage.)

Child by Jessie, born at Pembroke:

1401. i.   LILLIAN MAY[9], b. 10 June 1907; m. MASON D.
            SHAW.

778.   ALICE[8] 1863-   [320 Aaron[7] and Elizabeth Nutter]
was born in Nov. 1863, lived at South Brewer ME; married LIN-
COLN PATTERSON, born in Oct. 1860 (Cornman Ms). They were
living at Lubec in 1900.

Children (**Patterson**):

i.   BLANCHE, b. in Sept. 1885.
ii.   NORMAN, b. in Apr. 1889.
iii.   MABEL, b. in Feb. 1891.
iv.   EVA, b. in June 1896.
v.   ERMA, b. in Sept. 1898.

779.   MELISSA   J.[8] 1848-   [321 John[7] and Ann Maria
Leighton] was born at Lubec about 1848 (2 in 1850), lived at
New Haven CT in 1903; married at Pembroke 10 Aug. 1876 DANIEL
McKAY, born about 1856 (24 in 1880, Pembroke) (Cornman Ms).
Melissa was listed as Jane, 12, in 1860, and as Melvina J.,
34, in 1880.

Children (**McKay**):

i.   EDWARD J. (John, 3 in 1880).
ii.   ALICE M., b. c1880 (3/12 in 1880).
iii.   WILBUR.
iv.   CHARLES.

780.   AMY WOODWORTH[8] 1822-1880 [321 Adna[7] and Amy Wood-
worth] was born at Pembroke 2 Dec. 1822, died at Canton NY 21
July 1880; married at Charlotte ME 27 Sept. 1841 Rev. EBEN-
EZER FISHER JR., DD, born at Charlotte 6 Feb. 1815, died at
Canton 21 Feb. 1879, son of Ebenezer Fisher.
Graduate of St. Lawrence Univ., Fisher was a Universalist
pastor, and a founder and president of Canton Theological
School (Cornman Ms).

Children (**Fisher**):

i.   EBENEZER EVERETT M.D., b. Addison ME 5 Sept. 1844;
       m. ---- . He was a physician at Old Mission MI.
ii.   AMY W., b. Salem MA 29 Apr. 1850, d. 31 Aug. 1887;
       m. IRVING S. BIGELOW of Weymouth MA.
iii.   NELLIE ESTELLA, b. So. Dedham MA 24 Feb. 1855, d.
       Canton 4 Feb. 1861.

781.   LEAH REBECCA[8] 1825-1894 [322 Adna[7] and Amy Woodworth]
was born at Pembroke 16 Jan. 1825, died at Addison 15 Jan.
1894, 68y 11m 29d; married at Pembroke 3 Nov. 1844 JARED COF-
FIN NASH, born at Addison 12 Mar. 1816, died at Columbia ME 2
Aug. 1876, 59y 5m, son of William J. and Mary (Coffin) Nash
("Joseph Nash Family," BHM 8[1893]:59; town VRs).

Children (**Nash**), born at Addison Point:

i   AUGUSTUS J. [or JARED A.], b. 2 June 1846, d. Addison
       13 Apr. 1901; m. Columbia 7 Dec. 1867 JULIA A.
       CURTIS, res. Somerville MA.

ii.   Capt. ROSWELL FISHER, b. 6 Feb. 1849, d. 5 Aug. 1876,
       27y 7m; m. MARY ANN AUSTIN, b. Addison 18 Oct. 1850.
iii.   WILMOT LEIGHTON [Willie], b. 6 June 1858, d. 13 June
       1864, 6y 7d.

782. ELIZA ANN[8] 1830-1882 [322 Adna[7] and Amy Woodworth]
was born at Pembroke 2 Oct. 1830, died there 3 June 1882;
married there 20 July 1850 Capt. JOHN CRANE WILDER, born
there 30 Sept. 1827, died there 15 Feb. 1903, son of Joseph
and Mehitable (Crane) Wilder. He married second 28 Apr. 1887
Harriet Thomas (Townsend) Hersey: no children (letter from
son Sidney--Cornman Papers; Wilder Desc., 6; Waterhouse
Desc., 2:650; Pembroke VRs)

Child (**Wilder**), born at West Pembroke:

i.   SIDNEY AUGUSTUS, b. 27 Jan. 1852; m. 13 Feb. 1870
       CAROLINE AUGUSTA LEAVITT, b. Pembroke 9 June 1852,
       d. 14 May 1910, dau. of George Washington and
       Theresa Ruth (Stoddard) Leavitt. City editor of the
       Eastport Sentinel, Sidney compiled a Wilder gen-
       ealogy and a manuscript on Pembroke families.

783. AUGUSTUS AZOR[8] 1836-1907 [322 Adna[7] and Amy Wood-
worth] was born at Pembroke 6 Feb. 1836, died at Old Mission
MI 8 Oct. 1907; married first at Canton NY 16 Jan. 1866 MARY
WALLACE, born 30 May 1854, died at Middleton NY 30 May 1876,
daughter of Orson and Elizabeth (Webster) Wallace; married
second ABBIE L CURTIS, born at Dalton WI 30 May 1854, daughter of Henry and Lucena (Higbee) Curtis (Cornman Ms).
He served two years during the Civil War in the 60th NY
Inf. Rgt. He received a degree from St. Lawrence Univ. at
Canton, and was ordained pastor of the Middleton NY Univer-
salist Church. In 1880 and 1900 he and Abbie were living at
Peninsula Tp, Traverse Co. MI. (The Cornman Ms contained an
incredible number of May 30 dates.).

Children by Abbie, born at Old Mission MI

1402. i.   WILMOT AUGUSTUS[9], b. 28 Mar. 1878.
      ii. CURTIS ARTHUR, b. 3 Nov. 1884.
      iii. LENA AMY, b. 2 July 1889, d.y.

784. WILMOT ADNA[8] 1842-1907 [322 Adna[7] and Amy Woodworth]
was born at Pembroke 15 Apr. 1842, died at Canton NY 2 May
1907; married there 24 Dec. 1884 ISADORA BARBARA WALLACE,
born there 7 Apr. 1860, daughter of Orson and Elizabeth (Webster) Wallace (Cornman Ms).
He was a store clerk at Pembroke in 1870, and later joined
his brother at Canton.

Children, born at Canton:

i.   HERBERT WALLACE[9], b. 9 Oct. 1886, d. 16 May
       1970, 83y. Graduate of St. Lawrence Univ. in
       1911, he was a high school physics teacher and
       farmer (obit.).

1403. ii.   ROY FISHER, b. 3 Dec. 1888.
       iii. daughter, b. 17 June 1897, d. infant.
       iv.   EVERETT WILTON, b. 19 Feb. 1902, res. Canton
             in 1970.

785. ARTHUR CLARENCE[8] 1848-1921 [322 Adna[7] and Amy Wood-worth] was born at Pembroke 11 Nov. 1848, died at Chagrin Falls OH (ME VRs) 19 July 1924, 75y 8m 8d; married 25 Nov. 1876 FLORA ELLEN SPRAGUE, born at Pembroke 22 July 1855, died at Cleveland OH 23 Feb. 1936, daughter of George Washington and Mary Elizabeth (Bosworth) Sprague (Pembroke VRs; Cornman Ms; Wilder, Pembroke Families). He was a farmer. Burials are in Clarkside Cemetery, Pembroke. He and Flora lived with John and Blanche Ewen in their old age.

Children, born at Pembroke:

    i.   BLANCHE FLORA[9], b. 26 Aug. 1877; m. Pembroke
          10 Mar. 1899 JOHN C. EWEN of Franklin ME, b.
          in Scotland c1875 (24 in 1899), son of Charles
          and Isabel (Warenden) Ewen.
    ii.   HERBERT A., b. 6 Sept., d. 11 Sept., 1881.

786. CHARLES CARROLL[8] 1832-1863 [324 Samuel[7] and Martha Farnsworth] was born at Pembroke 11 May 1832, killed in action at Rappahannock Station VA 7 Nov. 1863, 31y; married at Pembroke 1 Aug. 1859 CECELIA B. BABCOCK, born at Eastport 10 Mar. 1838. died at Presque Isle ME 2 Nov. 1909, 71y 7m 22d, daughter of Enoch and Mary (Bowman) Babcock (town and ME VRs; Cornman Ms; Wilder, Pembroke Families).
He was a seaman at Pembroke in 1860, and enlisted 9 Sept. 1864 as corporal, Co. F., 6th ME Inf. ᵖgt. He was buried at Dennysville. In 1870, Cecelia and her children were living with her mother at Pembroke.

Children, born at Pembroke:

    i.   SARAH D.[9], b. 22 July 1861.
    ii.   CHARLES B., b. 12 Oct. 1863, d. Presque Isle
          19 Nov. 1881, 19y 1m; unm.

787. RAYMOND ISAIAH[8] 1850--1916 [325 Isaiah[7] and Sarah Hatch] was born at Pembroke 15 Mar. 1850, died there 18 Nov. 1916, 66y 8m 3d; married 27 Nov. 1872 ADELINE F. [Addie] DAY, born at Belfast ME 29 Jan. 1851, died at Pembroke 30 May 1914, daughter of George W. and Sarah (Thompson) Day (Wilder, Pembroke Families; Pembroke and ME VRs). Burials are in Forest Hills Cemetery.
He joined with his brother William Elden Leighton in the manufacture of ship pumps and blocks and then of parlor organs; he was also an agent for the Singer Sewing Machine Co. In 1885 he was appointed postmaster for West Pembroke.

Children, born at Pembroke:

    i.   EMMA DAY[9], b. 26 May 1877; m. 1st Pembroke 10
          Oct. 1899 GEORGE A. HARMON, b. Machiasport
          c1874 (25 in 1899), a druggist at Jonesport,

son of Alvin B. and Sarah N. (Phinney) Harmon;
m. 2nd Jonesport 5 Jan. 1929 EDGAR A. WORCES-
TER, b. Columbia c1878, son of Joseph and
Evelyn (Allen) Worcester.
ii.   FLORENCE L. DAY [Flossie], b. 17 Mar. 1882; m.
W. Pembroke 3 Jan. 1903 JOHN BOYNTON, b. Pem-
broke c1878 (24 in 1903), son of Robert and
Diane (Owen) Boynton.

788.   HENRY ROWLAND[8] [Roland] 1835-1917 [327 Justin[7] and
Lydia Hersey] was born at Pembroke 13 Feb. 1835, died there
21 Jan. 1917, 82y; married about 1877 MARIA ELIZABETH LYONS,
born at Edmunds ME 2 Apr. 1845, died at Pembroke 2 Mar. 1917,
71y 11m, daughter of Stephen and Augusta (Morang) Lyons
(Cornman Ms; Pembroke and ME VRs). Roland was a seaman.

Children, born at Pembroke:

i.   MILFORD L.[9], b. 21 Jan., d. 27 July, 1878.
ii.   STEPHEN J., b. 16 July 1879 (Edmunds VRs), d.
Bangor 1 Apr. 1938, 56y 8m 15d; unm.

789.   HARRIET NEWELL[8] 1835-1910 [327 Hatevil[7] and Barbara
McNutt] was born at Pembroke 30 Nov. 1835, died 15 Oct.
1910; married at Machiasport 11 Jan. 1860 ROSCOE G. MITCHELL
of Machias (Leighton, Gen. Sketch, 14; Cornman Ms). Mitchell
was a master builder.

Children (**Mitchell**):

i.   SIDNEY ALBERT.
ii.   INA EDITH.
iii. GEORGE EVERETT, b. c1868; m. Perry 12 Dec. 1894
ADELLA[9] LEIGHTON [# 1090].
iv.   FRED WILLIAM.
v.   MYRTLE BARBARA [Myrtie].

790.   HENRY HUDSON[8] 1840-1915 [327 Hatevil[7] and Barbara
McNutt] was born at Pembroke 11 Feb. 1840, died in MA in
1915; married before the Civil War ANNIE LAURIE CLIFFORD,
born in Jan. 1836 (1900 census) (Leighton, Gen. Sketch. 14;
Cornman Ms).
He was wounded while serving in the Civil War. In 1870 he
was a harnessmaker at Norridgewock ME. They were listed at
Boston in 1880, he 41, Anna 40, and was listed then also at
Manchester NH, 42 and 39, with George H., 9. In 1900 they
were at Hyde Park MA with his son's family.

Child, born at Norridgewock ME:

1404. i.   GEORGE HENRY[9], b. 29 June 1872.

791.   FRANCES O.[8] [Fannie] 1842-1929 [327 Hatevil[7] and Barbara McNutt] was born at Pembroke 19 Dec. 1842, died at Concord NH (state hosp.) 1 Nov. 1929, 90y 11m (VRs) in 1901;
married first at Machiasport ME 12 Sept. 1863 (Machias Union)

JAMES E. HATHEWAY, son of James E. and Hannah (Penniman) Hatheway (Cornman Ms); married second --- RICHARDS. She died a widow, resident of Fremont NH, and was buried in Center Cemetery, Sandown NH.

Children (**Hatheway**):

i.   WILLIAM E.
ii. JULIA; m. WILLIAM EDWARD BARKER.

792. GEORGE EDWARD[8] 1850-1938 [327 Hatevil[7] and Barbara McNutt] was born at Pembroke 7 Feb. 1850, died at Miami FL 8 Feb. 1938, 89y; married at Boston 12 Dec. 1872 HARRIET WIL-LIAM LEATHERBEE, born there 12 Feb. 1849, died at Brookline MA 29 Oct. 1923, daughter of James William and Caroline Cleaper (Drew) Leatherbee.
George was a building contractor, first at Portland ME and then at Boston, where he and Isaac F. Woodbury were partners. Among their projects were the old Harvard Medical School, the new Old South Church, the Boston Public Library, the north wing of the State House, and the Christian Science Church. He was also president of a match company and commodore of the Winthrop Yacht Club. He lived at Roxbury Highlands (Leighton, Gen. Sketch, 15-16).

Children:

i.   WALTER LEATHERBEE[9], b. Roxbury MA 4 Nov. 1876, d. St. Petersburg FL 10 Jan. 1951; m. Newton Center 15 Nov. 1912 HELEN PROSSER FIELD, b. 10 Dec. 1883, dau. of George Addison and Harriet Wilcox (Prosser) Field. No ch.
He was graduated from Harvard, AB 1901 and MA 1902, and from the Univ. of Virginia, Ph.D. in 1908. He was for years the Latin department master at the Boston English High School.
He was a councilor of NEHGS, and compiler of the Leighton Genealogical Sketch, which he published in 1940.
ii. FRED CLEAPER. b. 21 May 1879, d. Boston 5 Dec. 1888.
1405. iii. CHARLES EDWARD, b. Boston 20 Sept. 1880.
1406. iv. STANLEY WINTHROP, b. Winthrop MA 22 Aug. 1887.
v.   ROBERT, d. infant.

793. JAMES W.[8] 1841-1884 [328 Charles[7] and Sarah Farns-worth] was born at Pembroke 12 Apr. 1841, died at Auburn ME 23 July 1884; married first at Auburn (he of Lisbon) 4 Sept. 1866 MARY E. [Abbie] SMITH of Rumford, who died 27 Jan. 1874 (GS); married second at Auburn 12 June 1875 MARY (ABBOTT) Berry of Lewiston ME, born about 1851 (29 in 1880), died at Monmouth 24 Dec. 1880 (GS) (town VRs; Wilder, Pembroke Fami-lies). Burials are at Monmouth.
He served in the 1st ME Cav. Rgt. and in the 1st Div., DC Vol. Cav. Rgt., during the Civil War.
In 1880 he lived at Auburn, 37; his stepson Forest Berry, 12, was in the household.

Children by Mary:

  i.   WILLIAM HENRY[9], b. Lisbon Falls ME in Apr. 1876
       (per 1900 census); m. 1st 17 Aug. 1897 MARY A.
       (----) Williams, b. Belgrade in Nov. 1872
       (per 1900 census), dau. of Robert and Sarah E.
       ---- ; m. 2nd Lynn MA 8 Oct. 1906 VERNA M.
       WITHAM, b. Norway ME c1885, dau. of Josiah and
       Mary J. (Crockett) Witham--div.; m. 3rd Lewis-
       ton ME 16 June 1912 ELSIE INGA FOY of Auburn,
       b. Jay ME c1887 (25 in 1912), dau. of Fred and
       Anna (Laplante) Foy. He was a barber. Verna
       m. 2nd in 1918 William H. Callahan.
 ii.   CORA B., b. c1877 (3 in 1880), d. Auburn 14
       Jan. 1878.
iii.   ALICE M., b. c1879 (1 in 1880).

794. SUSAN O.[8] 1843-1908 [328 Charles[7] and Sarah Farns-
worth] was born at Pembroke 19 Dec. 1843, died at Monmouth ME
16 Jan. 1908, 64y 29d; married there 4 Sept. 1863 JOHN T.
LITTLEFIELD, born at Kennebunk ME 17 July 1831, died at Biddeford ME 29 May 1899, 68y 10m 12d, son of Theodore and Ruth
(Huff) Littlefield (town VRs; Cornman Ms; John E Frost, Biddeford Record Book [1968] MHS 1:75).
Burials are in Biddeford. They were listed there in 1880.

Children (**Littlefield**):

  i.   ELLA, b. in Dec. 1863, not in 1880 census.
 ii.   ALVARETTA, b. c1864 (16 in 1880), d. in 1934 (GS).
iii.   MAUD, b. 6 Dec. 1866; m. Biddeford 2 May 1891 JAMES
       E. DAVIS, son of Hiram and Hannah (Childs) Davis.
 iv.   FRANK, b. 21 Oct. 1876; m. EMMA BAKER (RICHARDS)
       Lyman of Rochester.

795. MARCIA G.[8] 1849-   [328 Charles[7] and Sarah Farns-
worth] was born at Pembroke 5 Oct. 1849; married first in
Jan. 1872 ALVIN J. BARRON of Lewiston; married second RANSHAR
V. [Rance] HAM of Moscow ME, born about 1845 (35 in 1880)
(Wilder, Pembroke Families).
In 1880 the Ham household at Moscow included Marcia's sis-
ter Sadie E., 22, her son Alvin Barron Jr. and the three Ham
children; Edith was listed as Sadie E. Ham, aged 1.

Child (**Barron**):

  i.   ALVIN J. JR., b. c1870 (10 in 1880).

Children (**Ham**):

  i.   JOHN H., b. c1873 (7 in 1880).
 ii.   LIZZIE H., b. c1876 (4 in 1880).
iii.   EDITH A , b. Moscow c1879 (21 in 1900); m. Winthrop
       ME 4 Aug. 1900 MAURICE GREELEY, b. Somerville ME
       c1872 (28 in 1900).

796. FANNIE E.[8] 1853-   [328 Charles[7] and Sarah Farns-
worth] was born at Winthrop ME 18 May 1853; married EDWARD

BERRY of Bingham, born in May 1859, perhaps son of Isaac C and Cynthia Berry (Cornman Ms). They lived at Moscow ME in 1900.

Children (**Berry**):

i.   ELEANOR, b. in July 1885.
ii.   JOHN, b. in Dec. 1896; m. DORA ---- .
iii. ALICE, b. in June 1888.
iv.   JENNIE, b. in June 1888 (twin).
v.   SUSAN, b. in June 1889.
vi.   NELLIE, b. in Mar. 1891.
vii   BENJAMIN, b. in Oct. 1892.

797.   ARABELLA[8] 1851-   [330 Isaac[7] and Mary Vose] was born at Machias ME 19 Mar. 1851; married there 8 Jan. 1870 LEVI T. LYON. They lived at Brookline MA (Vose Desc., 508-9; Cornman Ms; Machias VRs).

Children (**Lyon**), born at Brookline:

i.   ERNEST LEIGHTON, b. 27 Nov. 1870; m. in June 1899
      GRACE CHAPIN.
ii.   MARY LAURA, b. 16 Jan. 1873; m. Brookline 26 Sept.
      1893 JAMES PARKER BOYDEN, b. So. Walpole MA 17 June
      1867, son of Elbridge P. and Mary Elizabeth (Boyden)
      Boyden.
iii. HENRIETTA BAKER [Nettie], b. 26 May 1879; m. Brook-
      line 29 Nov. 1899 SELDEN ROBERT ALLEN, b. NYC 4 Dec.
      1875, son of Jeremiah and Sarah E. (Finnegan) Allen.

798.   CLARA ELLA[8] 1853-   [330 Isaac[7] and Mary Vose] was born at Machias 10 May 1853; married 7 Aug. 1872 LORING F. LAMBERT of Machiasport, born about 1850 (30 in 1880) (Vose Desc., 509; Cornman Ms). They lived at Machias in 1880.

Children (**Lambert**):

i.   ADELAIDE, b. 26 Oct. 1876.
ii.   BERTHA M., b. 20 Nov. 1881; m. E. Boston 14 Sept.
      1899 FREDERICK ALBERT HUSSEY.
iii. HAROLD, b. Calais ME 19 July 1889.
iv.   ?CARROLL.

799.   CLARENCE LEMUEL[8] 1856-   [330 Isaac[7] and Mary Vose] was born at Machias 12 Nov. 1856; married there 17 Sept. 1894 MABEL G. THAXTER, born at Machias 3 July 1869, died 4 June 1903, daughter of Marshall and Mary (Davis) Thaxter (Vose Desc., 509; Machias VRs). In 1900 he was a millwright at Machias.

Children, born at Machias:

i.   HAZEL THAXTER[9], b. 3 July 1895.
ii.   MERLE EDWIN THAXTER, b. 4 June 1903, probably
      d. infant.

800.   IDA MAY[8] 1860-   [330 Isaac[7] and Mary Vose] was
born at Machias 14 July 1860; married there 20 June 1880
(Machias Union) FRED MUNSON BEVERLY, born at Whiting in Feb.
1863, son of John and Drusilla (West) Beverly (Vose Desc.,
509). They lived at Lubec in 1900.

Children (Beverly), born at Calais:

i   MARJORIE LOUISE, b. 4 Oct. 1890; m. 5 June 1913
        ROBERT RUTHERFORD DRUMMOND, b. Bangor 29 Jan. 1883,
        son of Franklin Hayden and Charlotte Catherine
        (Chalmers) Drummond (Josiah H. Drummond, Descen-
        dants of Alexander Drummond [Brattleboro VT, 1942],
        64). He was professor of German, Univ. of Maine.
ii.   (CORA) MILDRED, b. 13 May 1892.
iii.   VERNE CURTIS, b. 15 June 1894, d. a widower Bangor 5
        Nov. 1987. Grad. of Univ. of Maine in 1920, he was
        for 33 yrs Aroostook Co. extension agent (obit.).
        No ch. He res. Veazie.
iv.   GLADYS EDITH, b. 23 Feb. 1896, res. Wakefield MA in
        1987; m. 24 Oct. 1925 ROLAND PACKARD.

801.   CORA EUNICE[8] 1862-   [330 Isaac[7] and Mary Vose] was
born at Machias 16 June 1862; married there 23 June 1886
GEORGE W. KANE, born in Sept. 1860 (Vose Desc., 509).

Children (Kane), born at Machias:

i.   HOWARD FRANCIS, b. 14 May 1887. He graduated from
        Bowdoin College in 1909.
ii.   AGNES N., b. 10 Oct. 1888, d. 5 May 1890.
iii.   ELSIE MAY, b. 5 July 1900.

802.   CLINTON JOHN[8] 1872-1948 [330 Isaac[7] and Mary Vose]
was born at Machias 6 Apr. 1872, died there 22 July 1948, 70y
3m 16d (per VRs; 1942 per GS); married there 4 Nov. 1896
JOSEPHINE [Josie] McCABE, born at Machias 22 Dec. 1871), died
there 27 Nov. 1946, daughter of James and Susan (Whitney)
McCabe (Vose Desc., 509; Machias VRs). Burials are in the
Court St Cemetery.
He was a carpenter in 1900, living with his parents; in
1930 he was a Machias merchant.

Children, born at Machias:

i.   ELSIE MAY[9], b. 5 July, d. 8 July, 1900.
ii.   MADELINE ALICE, b. 29 Apr. 1902; m. 1st Machias
        7 Aug. 1930 HARRY BERNARD CAMBRIDGE, b.
        Edmunds ME c1904 (26 in 1930), son of Harry B.
        and Emily (Ward) Cambridge; m. 2nd Ellsworth
        ME 15 June 1947 widower JAMES HENRY KILTON, b.
        Machias c1896, son of Ira K. and Linda B.
        (Blythen) Kilton.

803.   HORACE NEWELL[8] 1853-1927 [331 Joseph[7] and Susan Vose]
was born at Machias 8 Jan. 1853, died at Minneapolis MN 8
Nov. 1927; married at Machias 19 May 1874 SARAH LONGFELLOW

HEATON, born there 7 Feb. 1852, daughter of Isaac and Lydia Goodhue (Longfellow) Heaton (Vose Desc., 509-10).
He went to Minneapolis as a carpenter in 1876. In 1881 he formed with his brother Eben the contracting firm of H. N. Leighton & Co., which built the Guaranty Loan Building in 1890 and other structures. In 1891 he formed H. N. Leighton Printing Co. with Eben and Willliam H. Lyon. He was elected Republican alderman from 1898 to 1902 (Drisko, Machias, 573; Cornman Ms).

Children, all but the first born at Minneapolis:

i.   MABELLE ERMINA^9, b. Machias 28 July 1875.
ii.   ADDIE L., b. 7 June 1879 (b. in ME per 1880 census).
iii.   MAUDE ALICE, b. 30 June 1882.
iv.   ELIZABETH AMELIA [Lizzie], b. 14 Apr. 1884, d. 3 Nov. 1906; unm.
v.   LEWIS LEROY, b. 28 Sept. 1886.
vi.   GEORGE EVERETT, b. 20 June 1888; m. 4 June 1913 GARNETT STONE.
vii.   SARAH LYDIA, b. 30 Jan. 1891; m. 11 Jan. 1911 JOHN H. ZARFOS.

804.   JOSEPHINE ERMINA^8 1854-1901 [331 Joseph^7 and Susan Vose] was born at Machias 21 May 1854, died there 12 Dec. 1901; married there 3 July 1869 WILLIAM HENRY LYON, son of William Penniman and Sarah (Getchell) Lyon (Vose Desc., 510; Cornman Ms).
After his wife's death, he married again and settled at Minneapolis, joining his brother-in-law's printing firm.

Children (**Lyon**):

i.   WILLIAM HENRY, b. Machias 14 Feb. 1871; m. MILDRED ROGERS.
ii.   HORACE CARROLL, b. Machias 24 Jan. 1872, d. Minneapolis in Aug. 1892.
iii.   LELIA ETHEL, b. Minneapolis 29 Apr., d. in Aug., 1886.

805.   EBEN EVERETT^8 1856-1921 [331 Joseph^7 and Susan Vose] was born at Machias 10 Nov. 1856, died at Minneapolis MN 10 Mar. 1921; married there 19 July 1879 MARY E. CUSHING of Wesley ME (Machias Union), born in Oct. 1856 (1900 census; Vose Desc., 510; Drisko, Machias, 573; Cornman Ms). He joined his brother in the Leighton Bros. Printing Co.

Children, born at Minneapolis:

i.   ETHEL LOUISA^9, b. 7 June 1880; m. PHILIP BELLIN. Ch. Philip Leighton b. 31 Aug. 1901.
ii.   INA ADELAIDE [Addie], b. 31 Aug. 1882.
iii.   JOSEPH LEROY, b. 7 July, d. 10 July, 1884.
iv.   SUSAN CUSHING, b. 25 Jan. 1888, d. 30 Mar. 1889.
v.   RUTH MARY, b. 27 May 1892.
vi.   VERA JOSEPHINE, b. 13 Oct. 1896.

806. GEORGE ADDI[8] 1860-   [331 Joseph[7] and Susan Vose] was born at Machias 29 July 1860, lived at Minneapolis MN in 1900; married there 6 Dec. 1884 HERMINA ANTOINETTE [Minnie] BAER, born in WI in July 1860, died at Minneapolis 27 Dec. 1921 (Vose Desc., 510; Cornman Ms). At 19, George was living there with his brother Horace in 1880.

Children, born at Minneapolis (MN VRs):

    i.   HORACE ADDI[9], b. 16 Sept. 1887.
    ii. RALPH ARBA, b. 27 May 1889.
    iii. CLARENCE ARTHUR, b. 29 Aug. 1891.
    iv. JOSEPHINE ALICE, b. 19 Jan. 1897.

807. FREDERICK ARBA[8] 1864-   [331 Joseph[7] and Susan Vose] was born at Machias 5 March 1864, lived at Minneapolis MN; married at Mobil MN 28 Nov. 1900 SARAH O'HERON, born 11 Oct. 1874, daughter of John and Rosa (Mullen) O'Heron (Vose Desc., 510; Cornman Ms).

Children, born at Minneapolis (VRs):

    i.   JOHN JOSEPH[9], b. and d. 24 Oct. 1901.
    ii. SUSAN ROSANNA, b. 22 May 1903.
    iii. BERNICE MARIE, b. 30 May 1905.
    iv. GLADYS EVELYN, b. 8 July 1908.

808. JOSEPH LEROY[8] [Roy] 1869-   [331 Joseph[7] and Susan Vose] was born at Machias 9 Dec. 1869, lived at Minneapolis MN; married at Machias 16 Jan. 1895 ANNIE W. McEACHERN of NS, born at Machias 8 June 1873, died there 30 Nov. 1962, daughter of Archibald and Miriam (Smith) McEachern (Vose Desc., 510; Machias VRs; Cornman Ms).
A carpenter and building contractor, Roy appeared in the 1900 Machias census as Leroy J. His daughter Adelaide had the family Bible of her grandparents Joseph and Susan.

Children, born at Machias:

    i.   MARION BLANCHE[9], b. 26 Aug. 1896.
    ii. SELDEN LYON, b. 18 June 1898.
    iii. (MIRIAM) ADELAIDE, b. 25 July 1901; m. in MN
         EDWARD J. QUINN.

809. (ARVILLA) ROBERTA[8] [Bertie] 1843-   [334 William[7] and Margaret Kelley] was born at Trescott ME 18 May 1842 (VRs; 30 May 1843 in Cornman Ms); married at Lubec 28 Aug. 1864 THOMAS A. KNIGHT of Houlton, born in May 1839, son of Artson Knight (Cornman Ms). They lived at Lubec in 1900, her brother Fred with them.

Children (**Knight**):

    i.   EVELINA [Vina], b. c1867 (13 in 1880 Lubec census).
    ii. THOMAS H. [?Hallie], b. c1869 (11 in 1880).
    iii. MOODY, b. c1870 (10 in 1880); m. 17 Nov. 1898 SUSIE
         MORRISON, b. c1876.

iv. HARRY, b. c1873 (7 in 1880); m. 14 Apr. 1894 LOTTIE
     B. SMITH, dau. of I. B. and Lottie (Towle) Smith.
v.   FREDERICK T., b. in Aug. 1875; m. 2 Dec. 1901
     LILLIE COLLAMORE.
vi. (LORING) WHITMORE, b. c1879 (1 in 1880).
vii BLANCHE, b. 22 Feb. 1883.

810. DAMIETTA[8] 1845-   [334 William[7] and Margaret Kelley] was born at Trescott 23 May 1845 (VRs), lived at Lubec; married DANIEL LAMSON, born at Lubec 19 Nov. 1844, son of John Alcott and Mary Ann (Ford) Lamson (William J. Lamson, Descendants of William Lamson of Ipswich, Mass. [1917], 327; Lubec VRs; Cornman Ms). They lived at Lubec in 1870 and 1880.

Children (**Lamson**):

i.   INA, b. 25 Dec. 1866.
ii.   THOMAS, b. Lubec c1867; m. 1 Jan. 1896 EMILY FAUNEY.
iii. HENRY, b. 5 May 1869.
iv.   FREDERICK, b. 8 Apr. 1870.
v.   MARGARET M., b. 8 Aug. 1871; m. Lubec 1 Aug. 1903
      JOHN W. PEABODY, b. in 1879, son of Charles and Mary
      (Moreland) Peabody.
vi.   SARAH, b. 31 May 1873.
vii. IDA ARDELLA [Della], b. 13 Aug. 1877.

811. FRED S.[8] 1875-   [334 William[7] and Margaret Kelley] was born at Trescott about 1875 (5 in 1880 census), lived at Baileyville in 1926; married first at Lubec 8 Jan. 1898 ESTHER CRANE, born at Whiting about 1879 (19 in 1898), daughter of Hayden and Alice (Wilcox) Crane; married second at Calais 9 Oct. 1926 widow NINA B. (CLARK) Frost, born at Pembroke about 1882 (44 in 1926), daughter of George E. and Alice (Knight) Clark (Wilder, Pembroke Families; town and ME VRs). Nina had married first in 1899 Aaron Frost
     Fred's marriage record clearly showed Margaret Kelley as his mother, though she would have been 53 at his birth in 1875. He may have been adopted. Fred was a mill nightwatchman at Baileyville in 1910.

Children by Esther, born at Whiting:

i.   CECIL VICTOR[9], b. 28 Oct. 1898; m. 25 Sept.
      1925 HELEN RYAN of Baileyville. Both were
      teachers in 1926. Ch. JOHN FREDERICK[10]
      b. Calais 23 June 1926.
ii.   ARTHUR W., b. 27 Jan. 1900.
iii. MAUD, d. Lubec 24 Sept. 1901, 4m (VRs).

812. SAMUEL[8] 1847-   [336 James[7] and Malinda Simpson] was born at Trescott ME 7 July 1847, lived at Sterling MA in 1900; married at Lubec 1 Apr. 1871 (Machias Union) ABBIE S. MYERS, born there in Mar. 1843 (but 27 in 1880) (records of Hazel Wells; Cornman Ms).
     In 1880 the family was listed at Castle Hill Plantation, Aroostock Co.; in 1900 Samuel and Abbie lived at Sterling, with Guy and Lizzie in their household.

Children by Abbie:

    i.   JOHN[9], b. c1878 (2 in 1880).
    ii.   LEROY, b. c1880 (5/12 in 1880).
    iii. GUY, b. in Aug. 1881 (1900 census).
    iv.   ELIZABETH L. [Lizzie], b. Parkman ME 7 Nov.
          1883 (VRs).

813. WILLIAM HENRY[8] 1849-1910 [336 James[7] and Malinda
Simpson] was born at Trescott 22 Apr. 1849, died at Kingman
ME 22 Nov. 1910, 62y 7m; married about 1872 NANCY SAPPHIRE
BRITTEN, born at Cherryfield 25 Jan. 1853, died at Lincoln ME
26 Sept. 1937, 84y 8m 1d. They are buried at Danforth (town
and ME VRs; records of Hazel Wells).
He was a woodsman and log-driver at Lubec in 1880 and at
Danforth in 1900. He served in Co. B., US Coast Guard.

Children:

1407. i.   MARY E.[9], b. Cherryfield 12 Dec. 1872; m.
              MELVIN LANCASTER.
1408. ii.   EMMA, b. Cherryfield 8 Nov. 1874; m. C WESLEY
              COFFIN.
      iii. JAMES EVERETT, b. 15 Nov. 1877, d. Philippines
              1 Nov. 1900; unm. He served in the Spanish-
              American War, and is buried in the Presidio
              National Cemetery.
1409. iv.   ROBERT A., b. Trescott 18 Sept. 1879.
1410. v.   LEWIS K., b. Trescott 8 May 1881.
      vi.   ORVILLE, b. Trescott 17 Aug. 1883, d. Kingman
              25 Oct. 1906, 23y; unm.
1411. vii. IRVING, b. Trescott 10 May 1886.
1412. viii. EUGENE SIMPSON, b. Prentiss 14 Oct. 1890.

814. FRANK SHERMAN[8] 1865-1916 [336 James[7] and Malinda
Simpson] was born at Lubec 15 Nov. 1864, died at Bangor ME 4
Feb. 1916, 52y 2m 18d; married first at Lubec 5 July 1885 IDA
AROLYN[8] LEIGHTON, born at Trescott 16 Mar. 1864, died at
Sterling MA, daughter of William and Margaret (Kelley)
Leighton [# 334]; married second at Lubec 24 Oct. 1909 AMANDA
C. (McFADDEN) (----) Brown, born at Trescott about 1862 (47
in 1909) (town and ME VRs; records of Hazel Wells and descen-
dant Cindy Reynolds).
In 1900 his household at Lubec included his aunt (and moth-
er-in-law) Margaret (Kelley) Leighton; he was a truckman. In
1910 he was a shoe-merchant at Lubec.

Children:

1413. i.   FRANK GERALD[9], b. Trescott 3 Dec. 1897.
  --   CORA [Edna D.] (adopted), b. Trescott 8 Aug.
              1890, d. Lewiston ME 2 Apr. 1963 (obit.); m.
              1st ---- WILES--div.; m. 2nd Columbia Falls ME
              29 May 1912 WILLARD M. DONOVAN--div.; m. 3rd
              Winterport 8 Aug. 1914 ANDREW S. BRENNER, b.
              Scotland c1872, son of John and Isabella
              (Sinclair) Brenner; m. 4th a HENRY LEIGHTON.
              Cora called herself Edna after her adoption.

815.   MINNIE M.[8] 1864-   [339 Stephen[7] and Marietta
Saunders] was born at Trescott in Aug. 1864 (per 1900 census,
which also listed her as born in Canada); married GEORGE S.
PERRY, born in Apr. 1860. They lived at Machias in 1900.

Children (**Perry**), born at Machias:

i.   HARRY B., b. in Feb. 1885.
ii.   WALDO D., b. in Jan. 1888.
iii. NETTIE M., b. in Nov. 1896.
iv.   EDITH G., b. in Aug. 1898.

816.   MELVIN[8] 1866-   [339 Stephen[7] and Marietta Saun-
ders] was born at Trescott in Apr. 1866 (per 1900 census);
married at East Machias 17 Oct. 1894 (VRs; 19 Oct. in Whiting
VRs) ANNETTE F. [Nettie] McLAUGHLIN, born at Whiting 13 Sept.
1873, died at Belmont NH in 1944, daughter of Truman and Mary
McLaughlin (Forslund, Whiting, 86; Trescott and Whiting VRs).
He was a farmer at Trescott in 1900 and 1910.

Children, all but first and last born at Trescott:

1414. i.   JESSE SENNETT[9], b. Whiting 2 Apr. 1895.
1415. ii.   MYRA V., b. 20 July 1897; m. HARRY GILPATRICK.
      iii. TERESA A., b. 1 Mar. 1899.
1416. iv.   HARLAND M., b. 22 July 1903.
      v.   AZOR B., b. 21 Apr. 1905.
      vi.   CHRISTINE, b. Lubec 10 Feb. 1918, d. in Feb.
            1981 (obit); m. Lubec 7 May 1938 WELLINGTON
            HUNTLEY.

817.   ALICE MARIA[8] 1830-1876 [340 Abijah[7] and Hannah Her-
sey] was born at Pembroke ME 18 Oct. 1830, died at Dennysville 16 May 1876; married there 21 Apr. 1864 JOHN McKINLEY
(Dennysville VRs).

Children (**McKinley**), born at Dennysville:

i.   FRANK, b. 9 Oct. 1866, d. 12 Oct. 1867.
ii.   NELLIE, b. 7 Mar. 1868, d. 3 June 1869.
iii. WILLIAM, b. 6 Oct. 1869.
iv.   EDWIN, b. 29 Mar. 1871.
v.   HARRY, b. 25 Apr. 1874.

818.   JAMES ONSVILLE[8] 1833-1879 [340 Abijah[7] and Hannah
Hersey] was born at Pembroke 18 Aug. 1833, died at Ferndale,
Humboldt Co. CA 4 July 1879, 45y (Eastport VRs); married at
Eastport 12 May 1859 EULALIA TREAT, born at Prospect ME 6
Feb. 1837, daughter of Upham Stowers and Sarah (Sanborn)
Treat (John Harvey Treat, The Treat Family [Salem MA, 1893],
356, 433). In 1860 he was a boat-builder at Eastport; in
1880 Eulalia and her son Fred were living at Ferndale, and in
1900 she was living alone at Pacific, Humboldt Co.

Children:

i.   FREDERICK AUSTIN[9], b. Eastport 8 June 1862, d.
      there 18 July 1867, 5y 1m 10d.

ii.   son, b. and d. Eastport 3 Feb. 1869.
iii. FREDERICK H., b. c1876 (4 in 1880).

819.   SARAH ELIZA[8] 1844-1925 [346 John[7] and Louisa Frost]
was born at Perry ME 20 June 1844, died there 29 Oct. 1925,
81y 3m 29d; married first 7 Apr. 1866 ROBERT H. SPROUL; married second (FREDERICK) MERTON NUTT, born at Perry 16 Feb.
1845, died there 14 Apr. 1906, son of James and Sarah (Brown)
Nutt (her letter in 1904--Cornman Papers; Perry and ME VRs).

Children (**Sproul**):

i.   MATILDA; m. ERNEST CLARK.
ii.   ERNEST G., b. c1868; m. Perry 27 July 1894 ALICE L.
      CROSBY, dau. of James E. and Ella (Shaughnessy)
      Crosby of Lubec.

820.   JOHN H.[8] 1850-1884 [350 Mark[7] and Maria Hibbard] was
born at Perry 14 Apr. 1850, died 5 Feb. 1884; married HELEN
M. GOODWIN, born about 1856 (24 in 1880), daughter of John
and Mary Goodwin.
John was listed at Perry in 1870 and 1880; later he lived
at Saint John NB and in MA (Cornman Ms; Perry VRs). In 1891,
Mark and Mary were living with Helen's parents at Saint John
(NB census).

Children, born at Perry:

i.   LESLIE M.[9], b. 14 Feb. 1879.
ii.   MARK F., b. 27 May 1881.
iii. MARY MARIA, b. 8 Apr. 1883.
iv.   GERTRUDE, b. 4 Aug. 1885.

821.   EDITH MYRTLE[8] 1874-   [352 George[7] and Julia Den-
nison] was born at Home City OH 19 Dec. 1874; married 9 Jan.
1895 HAROLD [Harry] BROWN, born at Cincinnati, son of Pearson
and Jennie Brown (mother's letter--Cornman Papers).

Children (**Brown**), born at Home City:

i.   HAROLD LEIGHTON, b. 4 Mar. 1898.
ii.   GEORGE PEARSON, b. 30 Dec. 1902.

822.   MARIA LOUISE[8] 1883-   [352 George[7] and Julia Den-
nison] was born at Home City OH 18 May 1883; married WALTER
LEE of Cincinnati, son of Thomas and Willamena Lee (mother
Julia's letter--Cornman Papers).

Children (**Lee**), born at Home City:

i.   MARY LOUISE, b. 14 Aug. 1906.
ii.   MARGARET DENNISON, b. 1 Jan. 1909.

823.   NEWBURY H.[8] 1834-   [359 John Smithson[7] and Susan
Haley] was born at Augusta ME 21 Nov. 1834, lived at Lowell
MA; married 24 Dec. 1861 MARY HELEN CROSS, born in Nov. 1839

(1900 census), daughter of Gershom and Mary (Smart) Cross (Cornman Ms).
In 1900 widow Mary was living at Lowell in her son Edward's home.

Children, born at Lowell:

       i.   NEWBURY^9, d. Lowell 5 Aug. 1867 (Augusta VRs).
1417. ii.   EDWARD NEWBURY, b. 14 Jan. 1869.

824. FAUSTINA^8 1845-   [359 John Smithson^7 and Susan Haley] was born at Augusta in 1845, lived at Kittery ME; married 4 Oct. 1863 THOMAS JACKSON PETTIGREW of Newburyport MA, son of Thomas and Mary Ann (Weeks) Pettigrew (Cornman Ms).

Children (**Pettigrew**), born at Kittery:

i.   HENRY JACKSON, b. 11 Sept. 1864, d. 1 Sept. 1865.
ii.   SUSAN EVELYN, b. 6 Sept. 1866. She became a nun,
       order of St. Margaret.
iii.   EMMA FAUSTINA, b. 12 Nov. 1867, d. 19 May 1878.
iv.   AUGUSTA MARIA, b. 6 May 1869, res. Waltham MA; m. 9
       Aug. 1896 D. KERFORT SHUTE.
v.   THOMAS LEIGHTON, b. 18 July 1876, d. 6 Sept. 1877.
vi.   PEARL EDNA, b. 23 June 1880, res. Kittery; m. WILLARD
       CALEB CHICK.

825. MOSES RIGGS^8 1832-1907 [360 Joseph^7 and Polly McGaffey] was born at Mount Vernon ME 23 June 1832, died there 26 Feb. 1907, 74y 8m 4d; married at Augusta ME 18 June 1868 CHARLOTTE ANGELINE DAVIS, born at Mt. Vernon 18 June 1842, died there 25 Jan. 1929, daughter of Capt. Samuel Brigham and Mary (Stain) Davis (Mt. Vernon and Augusta VRs; records of descendant Henry C Leighton; Cornman Ms). Burials are in the Bean Cemetery.
He was self-educated, and as a youth taught school. He joined his uncle Thomas in his bridge-construction business, drawing contracts and supervising work sites. In 1880 he retired to Augusta, and served two terms there as mayor. In 1900, his household was at Augusta, but soon after he and Charlotte returned to Mt. Vernon, living on the Samuel Davis homestead, his wife's birthplace. His son was appointed administrator of his estate 25 Mar. 1907.

Children, born at Mount Vernon:

       i.   HILTON C.^{9}, b. 7 Dec. 1869, d. 6 Mar. 1870, 3m.
1418. ii.   RALPH WEBSTER, b. 28 June 1875.

826. SALLY M.^{8} 1834-1901 [360 Joseph Jr.^{7} and Polly McGaffey] was born at Mount Vernon 16 Apr. 1834, died 13 Oct. 1901; married at Mt. Vernon 10 Dec. 1854 EBENEZER M. BROWN (Mt. Vernon VRs; Cornman Ms).

Children (**Brown**), born at Mt. Vernon:

i.   JULIA ANNETTE, b. 9 Apr. 1855, d. 1 July 1903.
ii.   ELLEN ALBERTA, b. 12 June 1858.

iii.   ALICE MAY, b. 4 July 1860; m. Mt. Vernon 17 Sept.
       1887 HENRY A. MOOERS.
iv.   MARTHA, b. 18 Nov. 1864, res. Groveland MA; m. 8 Aug.
       1888 WALTER GREENOUGH.

827.   MARY ELIZABETH[8] 1830-1918 [361 Simeon[7] and Mary Kim-
ball] was born at Mount Vernon 2 Dec. 1830, died 30 Oct.
1918; married at Mt. Vernon 15 Nov. 1852 ELISHA L. WELLS,
born in 1831, lived at Mt. Vernon in 1908 (Mt. Vernon VRs;
Cornman Ms; Mount Vernon Town Register, 1908).

Children (**Wells**), born at Mt. Vernon:

i.   ADA LADORA, b. 27 June 1853; m. ---- THOMS.
ii.   GEORGE OSBORN, b. 24 June 1860; m. EMMA A. SWIFT,
       b. in 1879.

828.   ELIZA ANN[8] 1835-1878 [361 Simeon[7] and Mary Kimball]
was born at Mount Vernon 16 Feb. 1835, died in 1878; married
at Mt. Vernon 20 Oct. 1855 WILLIAM H. CARR, born 29 May 1826,
son of Dearborn and Eliza (Smith) Carr (Mt. Vernon VRs; Cornman Ms).

Children (**Carr**):

i.   HARTWELL; unm.
ii.   GEORGE EDWIN, b. Fayette ME c1864, res. Boston; m.
       Mt. Vernon 8 Nov. 1894 ANNETTE G. [Nettie] DOLLOFF,
       dau. of J. William and Hannah (Raymond) Dolloff.

829.   FRANCIS B.[8] 1857-1937 [362 Benjamin[7] and Lucinda
Bachelder] was born at Mount Vernon 21 Mar. 1857, died there
12 Oct. 1937, 80y 6m 21d; married there 18 Dec. 1886 MARY
ETTA JOHNSON, born at Cape Elizabeth ME 11 Dec. 1864, died at
Augusta (hosp.) 7 May 1921, 56y 4m 27d, daughter of Edwin L.
and Amelia Johnson (Mt. Vernon VRs; Mt. Vernon Town Register,
1908). Burials are in the Bean Cemetery.
       F. B. Leighton was a farmer.

Children, born at Mount Vernon:

i.   IDA EMMA[9], b. 28 Nov. 1887, d. Winthrop ME 30
                   Mar. 1918, 30y 4m; unm.
1419. ii.   EDWIN WESLEY, b. 31 Aug. 1889.
      iii. GEORGE F., b. 15 Nov. 1897, d. 19 Dec. 1901,
                   4y 1m 4d (Georgie, female, on 1900 census).

830.   EDWARD CARLETON[8] 1862-1942 [364 Delano[7] and Eliza
Raymond] was born at Fayette ME 3 Feb. 1862, died at Winthrop
ME 4 Oct. 1942; married first ELLA M. ---- ; married second
at Wayne ME 22 July 1900 CORA A. (WELLS) Dalton of Madison
ME, born at Solon ME 2 Mar. 1869 (36 in 1900), died at Port-
land 23 June 1932, 68y 2m 28d, daughter of Horace and Sarah
(Maynard) Wells (ME VRs; Cornman Ms; obituary of son Leslie).
       He was a cooper or barrel manufacturer and in 1937 a dealer
in lumber at Mt. Vernon.

Possible child by Ella:

  i.   RUBIE J.[9], b. in 1886, d. Foxboro MA 18 Mar.
       1887, 1y 10d (VRs).

Children by Cora:

  ii.   LLOYD JENNINGS, b. Mt. Vernon 17 June 1901.
  iii. (LESLIE) MAYNARD, b. Mt. Vernon 8 Oct. 1903, d.
       Winthrop ME 17 Aug. 1983, 79y (obit.); m.
       there 17 Oct. 1941 MADELINE ALBEE RILEY, b.
       Attleboro MA in 1905, d. in 1971, dau. of
       Raymond C. and Martha C. (Bragg) Riley.
       L. Maynard owned Leighton Lumber Co.; he ret.
       in 1967 but became pres., Commnity Service
       Tel. Co. He collected antique autos. Ch.
       NATALIE[10] res. New Fairfield CT; m. ----
       WEISE.
  iv.   ANN L., b. Winthrop ME 15 July 1905.
  v.   LEONA, b. 27 July 1906.
  vi.   SARAH, res. St. Petersburg FL in 1983; m. ----
       THOMAS.

831. JOHN LANE[8] 1865-   [367 Joel[7] and Elizabeth Rand]
was born at Exeter NH 24 Aug. 1865, lived at Lowell MA; married first ANASTASIA M. [Anne] LYNCH, born at Dracut MA 30
June 1865, died at Lowell 2 Feb. 1910; married second NELLIE
FLYNN, daughter of John and Mary (Brooks) Flynn (Cornman Ms).
   In 1900 he worked for Railroad Express; his wife was listed
as Mary A. Leighton.

Children by Anastasia, all but the first born at Lowell:

       i.   JOHN L.[9], b. Exeter 30 June, d. 22 Sept., 1886.
1420. ii.   ELIZABETH MARY, b. 5 Aug. 1887; m. JOHN OWENS.
      iii. JOEL THOMAS, b. 25 Dec. 1889, d. 28 July 1908.
      iv.   JOHN G., b. 15 Oct. 1892.
      v.   THOMAS, b. 4 Nov. 1905.

832. MERCY[8] 1797-   [372 William[7] and Mary Austin] was
born probably at Somersworth NH about 1797 (52 in 1850, 63 in
1860); married about 1831 IRA EMERY (Stark Hist., 37). In
1860 she was living with her parents at Dummer NH.

Children (**Emery**), order uncertain:

  i.   LUCY.
  ii.   JANE.
  iii. NATHANIEL; m. 1st SARAH BLAKE; m. 2nd MARY JANE
       DAMON; m. 3rd ---- HUNTOON; m. 4th ROSETTA ROBERTS.
  iv.   ELIZABETH; m. WILLIAM WOODWARD. No ch.
  v.   ?LEVI, b. in 1836 (14 in 1850).

833. BETSEY[8] [Lizzie] 1799-1861 [372 William[7] and Mary
Austin] was born at Somersworth about 1799, died 7 Dec. 1861;
married at Stark NH in 1833 DANIEL FORBUSH, born at Ware MA
26 July 1791, died at Dummer NH 26 July 1859, son of James

and Eunice (Brown) Forbush (Frederick C. Pierce, Forbes and
Forbush Gen. [1892], 70; Dummer Hist., 48; records of Mary
Newton).
Daniel had married first at Stark NANCY GRAPES, who died in
1831; they had seven children. In 1849, Lizzie was living
with her brother William.

Children (Forbush), born at Dummer:

  i.   JAMES HENRY, b. 9 Oct. 1836, res. Crystal NH; m. 1st
       BETSEY D. NICHOLS; m. 2nd MARY A. HORN.
  ii.   NANCY, b. 25 May 1837, res. Crystal; m. Chelsea MA
       JOHN N. HOWLAND.
  iii. (WILLIAM) HARRISON, b. 5 Jan. 1841; m. 4 July 1862
       IDA GREEN.

834. JOSEPH[8] 1807-1850 [372 William[7] and Mary Austin] was
born at Somersworth NH 15 May 1807 (1808 per GS), died at
Stark NH 27 Jan. 1890, 82y 8m 1d; married first there 27 Apr.
1835 HARRIET ROWELL, born there 13 Apr. 1815 (1817 per GS),
died at Dummer 17 Nov. 1869, 53y, daughter of Edward and Abi-
gail (Smith) Rowell; married second 9 Apr. 1871 HARRIET
SCALES, born in ME about 1852 (20 in 1872), lived at Chesterville ME in 1921, daughter of Enoch and Ruth Scales of Wilton
ME (Henry Hardon, Families of Coos County N. H. [mss, 1930,
NHHS]; Stark Hist., 61; town VRs). Burials are in the West
Dummer Hill Cemetery.
When Dummer was organized in 1849, Joseph was on the first
board of selectmen (Hist. Coos Co., 859). He owned most of
Phillips Brook valley, where he built a sawmill. In 1850 and
1860 his home was at Dummer.
The history of Stark (pp. 222-4) described a mysterious be-
witching in his home, which only years later was revealed as
caused by his children Jim and Abigail.

Children by first wife Harriet, born at Dummer:

        i.   TRUSTRUM[9], b. in Aug. 1839, d. Dummer 25
              Nov. 1842 (GS).
        ii.   GEORGE, b. in Feb. 1841, d. in accident 15 May
              1862, 21y 9m (GS).
1421. iii. JOHN, b. 11 June 1843.
1422. iv. EDWARD FRANK, b. 7 Oct. 1845.
1423. v.   BARKER BURBANK, b. 6 Jan. 1848.
1424. vi. JAMES MONROE, b. 15 June 1850.
       vii. JOSEPH MASON (twin), b. 15 June 1850, d. Dummer
              19 Oct. 1851.
1425. viii. ABIGAIL, b. 15 May 1853; m. HENRY WALKER.

Children by second wife Harriet, born at West Milan:

        ix.   CAROLINE M. [Carrie], b. 7 Mar. 1872; m. 1st
              WALTER E. BICKFORD, b. W. Milan 21 Dec. 1865,
              son of John M. and Catherine (Forbush) Bick-
              ford; m. 2nd Gardiner ME 20 Jan. 1924 (VRs)
              JOSEPH F ARSENAULT, b. Augusta ME in 1890,
              son of Benoit and Mary Rose (Arsenault)
              Arsenault (Pierce, (Forbes/Forbush, 70). Ch.
              Harold Bickford res. Augusta in 1930.

    x.   S. BARKER, b. 26 Jan. 1874 (Cyrus, 6, in 1880).
    xi. dau. (twin), b. and d. 26 Jan. 1874.
    xii. ZOA [Zoey], b. 29 Sept. 1882; m. 1st Farmington
         ME 20 Apr. 1902 (VRs) JAMES BUTTERFIELD, b.
         Chesterville ME in 1865, son of William and
         Weighty (Whittier) Butterfield--div.; m. 2nd
         W. Farmington ME 13 June 1928 ARTHUR A. OAKES,
         b. Chesterville c1886, son of Alfred R. Oakes.

    835. THOMAS[8] 1809-   [372 William[7] and Mary Austin] was
born at Dummer NH about 1809, not listed in the 1850 census;
married 13 Sept. 1829 MARINDA GRAPES, born in VT about 1812
(38 in 1850). He lived at Dummer (Harnden, Coos County Families).

    Children, born at Dummer:

    1426. i.   WILLIAM[9], b. 27 Jan. 1830.
    1427. ii.   THOMAS, b. 1 June 1833.
          iii. CHESTER, b. c1849 (7/12 in 1850).

    836. WILLIAM[8] 1810-1897 [372 William[7] and Mary Austin] was
born at Dummer 12 Sept. 1810 (38 in 1850), died at Stark 20
July 1897; married first MARY ANN ---- , born in Sept. 1817,
died 2 Mar. 1835 (GS); married second NANCY NEWELL, born at
Andover MA 11 May 1813, died at Stark 8 Nov. 1898, daughter
of Charles and Hannah C. (Shattuck) Newell (town VRs; Hardon,
Coos County). Burials are at West Dummer.
He was a railroad brakeman in 1850.

    Children by Nancy:

    i.   MARY ANN[9], b. in 1838, d. infant.
    ii.   HANNAH (twin). d. 10 Nov. 1838, 10d (GS).
    x.   HANNAH ANNA, b. 26 Mar. 1841, d. in 1901; m.
          DANIEL COLE, b. in 1838, d. in 1911 (GS).
    xi.   CHARLES, b. in Jan. 1843, d. 6 Aug. 1927; m.
          27 Nov. 1864 CAROLINE F. BICKFORD, b. Dummer
          2 Oct. 1848, d. 4 Nov. 1907, dau. of John M.
          and Catherine (Forbush) Bickford. Only ch.
          MABEL H.[10] b. Dummer in Oct. 1878, d. 19
          Apr. 1888.

    837. MOSES R.[8] 1808-1885 [373 Edward[7] and Lydia Rand] was
born at Barnstead NH (Tuftonboro per death record) 23 July
1808, died at Sanbornton 28 Oct. 1885; married first there 4
Oct. 1835 MARY [Polly] SMITH, born there 15 Oct. 1812, died
there 28 June 1872, daughter of Elisha and Polly (Hoyt)
Smith; married second at Gilmanton NH 6 May 1873 LYDIA (RAND-
LETT) Ladd, born there 28 Oct. 1815, died 23 Mar. 1902,
daughter of Josiah and Betsey (Potter) Randlett (Runnels,
Sanbornton, 2:461-2, 499; Odiorne, Rundlett-Randlett, 304;
Mary E. Hanaford, Meredith, N. H., Annals and Genealogies
[Concord, NH, 1932], 115-6; Cornman Ms).
    In 1836, he settled as a farmer at Sanbornton Bay. Lydia
had married first 28 Oct. 1835 Daniel Gale Ladd of Belmont
NH; they had two children.

Children by Mary, born at Sanbornton:

     i.   LYDIA[9], b. 8 Sept. 1836, res. Laconia; m. 30
          July 1857 COLLAMER J. SMITH of Concord NH, b.
          in VT. Ch. Carrie Augusta b. Concord 30 June
          1858, d.y.
     ii.   SAMUEL WALLACE, b. 4 July 1838, d. Annapolis MD
          16 Sept. 1863, 25y 2m; unm. He was corporal,
          Co. I, 1st NH Cav. Rgt.
1428. iii. IRA B., b. 16 May 1840.
     iv.   WESLEY, b. 1 Feb. 1842, d. Gettysburg PA 2 July
          1863, 21y 5m, killed in action in Co. H,
          12th NH Inf. Rgt.
     v.   FREEMAN, b. 16 Nov. 1845, d. Laconia 27 Oct.
          1866, 21y; unm.
1429. vi.   EDWARD, b. 15 Dec. 1847.
1430. vii. ADELINE, b. 9 Nov. 1849; m. FRANK MORRILL and
          ALPHEUS BEAN.
1431. viii. JOEL, b. 13 June 1858.

838. LYDIA[8] 1814-   [373 Edward[7] and Judith Rand] was
born at Northfield NH 8 July 1814, died about 1907; married
at Northfield 16 Nov. 1837 SAMUEL BUTLER BROWN, born there 11
Nov. 1813, died there 18 Aug. 1871 (Cross, Northfield, 207-8;
Cornman Ms).
Widow Lydia lived at West Newton MA with her daughter Mary
Morrill.

Children (**Brown**), born at Northfield:

     i.   ANNA M., b. 31 Dec. 1838, d. Bridgeport CT 22 Dec.
          1910; m. 17 Dec. 1866 JOSEPH C LYFORD, b. North-
          field 8 July 1830, res. Wilton IA and elected mayor
          there.
     ii.   ALBERT, b. 21 Aug. 1840; m. ELLEN ELIZABETH[9] LEIGHTON
          [# 1432].
     iii. LAURA, b. 14 Nov. 1843, d. 18 Oct. 1857.
     iv.   MARY C., b. 17 June 1847; m. 22 Nov. 1871 JOHN B.
          MORRILL, b. Thornton NH 13 Dec. 1844, d. W. Newton
          MA 24 Aug. 1881, son of John and Catherine (Heague)
          Morrill.
     v.   LYMAN, b. 24 July 1849, res. Fairbury NE; m. Wilton
          IA in Apr. 1878 LIZZIE DAVIS. He was a grain
          dealer.

839. THOMAS[8] 1817-1874 [373 Edward[7] and Judith Rand] was
born at Northfield NH 11 Mar. 1817, died at Canterbury NH 24
Aug. 1874; married 1 Jan. 1844 ELIZA ANN SANBORN, born 17
Dec. 1824, died at Canterbury 25 Dec. 1891, daughter of Ben-
jamin and Hannah (Clough) Sanborn (Sanborn Gen., 452; Cornman
Ms). He settled on an intervale along the Merrimack River at
Canterbury, where he was a farmer and a specialist in treat-
ing horses.

Child, born at Franklin NH:

1432. i.   ELLEN ELIZABETH[9], b. 12 July 1848; m. ALBERT
          BROWN [# 838].

840.   MARY A.[8] 1821-1901 [373 Edward[7] and Judith Rand] was born at Franklin NH 8 Nov. 1821, died at Concord NH 26 Mar. 1901, 74y 4m 20d; married in 1850 JAMES EDWARD GARDNER, born at Newburyport MA 7 Jun 1808 (VRs), died at Franklin NH 16 May 1883, son of Robert and Lydia (Burley) Gardner (town VRs; Cornman Ms).

They lived at Lowell MA; in 1900 the widow Mary lived at Concord with her daughter Susie.

Children (**Gardner**), born at Lowell:

i.   ADELINE, b. 3 Oct. 1852, d. 3 Oct. 1855.
ii.   ANNA M., b. in Aug. 1855, d. 5 Apr. 1860.
iii.   LAURA A., b. 20 Nov. 1857, d. 6 Dec. 1858.
iv.   EDWIN L., b. in Mar. 1861, d. 10 Apr. 1862.
v.   SUSAN [Susie], b. 7 Dec. 1864, res. Concord NH; m.
        GEORGE IRVING FOSTER, b. Bangor ME 7 June 1863. He
        was manager, Ford Foundry Co.

841.   EDWARD[8] 1825-1891 [373 Edward[7] and Judith Rand] was born at Northfield NH 11 Aug. 1825, died at Osage City KS 14 Jan. 1891; married 28 Mar. 1851 SARAH E. KENT, born 27 Sept. 1828, lived with her daughter Leonia in OK in 1915. In 1870 Edward was a farmer at Marcellon, Columbia County WI.

Leroy named Leonia and Minnie as his only siblings (his letter in 1915--Cornman Papers); the Cornman Ms listed also Adrianna, Mercy, Arthur and Agnes, perhaps younger children who died young.

Children, born at Marcellon:

1433. i.   (EDWARD) LEROY[9], b. 28 Sept. 1860.
      ii.   (SARAH) LEONIA, b. c1863 (7 in 1870), res.
            Woodward OK in 1915; m. ---- HASTINGS.
      iii. MINNIE MAY, b. c1869 (1 in 1870), res. Cheney
            OK in 1915; m. ---- DISHEN.

842.   JUDITH M.[8] 1827-1904 [373 Edward[7] and Judith Rand] was born at Northfield NH 8 Aug. 1827, died at Evanston IL 26 May 1904; married first at Sanbornton NH 8 Jan. 1851 as his second wife WINTHROP H. FORD, born there 22 Jan. 1816, died at Concord NH 22 Feb. 1874, son of William and Elizabeth (Hilton) Ford (Runnels, Sanbornton, 2:284); married second 8 May 1893 BENJAMIN C. SARGENT, born at Concord 27 Sept. 1825, died 29 Dec. 1904, son of Challis and Sarah Sargent (Cornman Ms). Ford was a partner in the Ford Bros. foundry business at Concord.

Children (**Ford**), born at Concord:

i.   EMMA AUGUSTA, b. 21 June 1852, d. Lowell MA 19 Aug.
        1907; m. 25 Sept. 1873 FREDERICK GEORGE TILTON, b.
        Tilton NH 7 Feb. 1849, res. Lockeford CA, son of
        Jeremiah Carter and Emily (Morrell) Tilton.
ii.   JOSEPH HILTON, b. 21 May 1854, res. Concord; m. 12
        Nov. 1876 ANNA WATKINS of Scranton PA.
iii.   ABBIE FRANCES, b. 22 Aug. 1856, d. 5 May 1857.

iv.   CLARA BELLE, b. 1 Aug. 1858; m. 30 Aug. 1877 FRED
       CUMMINGS JENNEY, b. Concord 12 Sept. 1848, d. Toledo
       OH 27 May 1914, son of Chauncey Perry and Lucia
       (Cummings) Jenney.
v.   EDWARD LEIGHTON, b. 13 Mar. 1863, res. Toledo; m. 18
       Feb. 1890 HENRIETTA LOUISE BRADLEY, b. in 1871, dau.
       of Hiram and Hannah Elizabeth (Foster) Bradley.

843. JOHN F.[8] 1832-1903 [373 Edward[7] and Judith Rand] was
born at Northfield NH 27 May 1832, died at Franklin 9 Nov.
1903; married first at Sanbornton NH 27 Aug. 1857 MARY ANN
HANNAFORD, born 19 Sept. 1839, died at Franklin 5 June 1886,
daughter of John A and Mary H. (Park) Hannaford; married
second 9 Feb. 1888 EMMA C. COLBY, born at Bow NH 29 Dec.
1852, daughter of Leonard L. and Mary A (Page) Colby of Canterbury NH (Cornman Ms; Cross, Northfield, 208; Northfield
and Franklin VRs). A farmer, he owned the family homestead
at Franklin, which had formerly been part of Northfield. His
two youngest children were in his household in 1900.

Children by Mary Ann, born at Franklin:

       i.   MARIA F.[9], b. 13 June 1858, d. Franklin 30 July
              1881; unm
1434. ii.   NELLIE A , b. 9 Sept. 1860; m. BENJAMIN F
              KIMBALL.
1435. iii.   GEORGE E., b. 15 Oct. 1864.

Children by Emma, born at Franklin:

       iv.   LEONARD C , b. 13 June 1889; m. 20 Aug. 1912
              HENRIETTA M. RODD, b. Penacook NH, d. Franklin
              3 June 1913, dau. of Samuel and Ida B.
              (Williams) Rodd. Ch. BARBARA RODD[10] b.
              Franklin 3 June 1913.
       v.   MARY EMMA, b. 12 Mar. 1895.

844. ZACHARIAH[8] 1818-1898 [374 Richard[7] and Lovey Waldron]
was born at Nottingham NH 9 Mar. 1818, died at Epsom NH 9 May
1897; married 9 Aug. 1840 MISHEL STRAW BARTLETT, born at
Northwood NH 18 Apr. 1812, died at Epsom 31 July 1888, daughter of John and Ruth (Elkins) Bartlett. Her name was also
spelled Mischal (Cornman Ms; town and NH VRs).

Children, born at Strafford NH:

       i.   RICHARD[9], b. 27 Mar., d. in Apr., 1841.
       ii.   JAMES W., b. 31 Mar. 1842, d. Philadelphia PA
              13 Nov. 1864, en route home from caring for
              sick and wounded soldiers.
       iii.   TRIPHENA L. [Phena], b. 2 Sept. 1847, d. Epsom
              29 June 1915; m. there 31 Dec. 1873 CHARLES B.
              MARDEN, b. there 9 Aug. 1850, d. there 31 May
              1874, son of Philip C. and Louisa (Buswell)
              Marden (Getchell, Marden Fam., 391). No ch.
1436. iv.   ALBERT RICHARD, b. 8 Dec. 1849.
1437. v.   JOHN FRANK, b. 6 May 1853.
       vi.   HORACE G., b. 23 Apr. 1857, res. Epsom in 1900;
              unm.

845. ALMIRA[8] 1833-   [374 Richard[7] and Lovey Waldron]
was born probably at Nottingham 8 May 1833; married at Pittsfield NH 6 Sept. 1856 OLIVER J. GRAY, born 26 Feb. 1832, died
11 July 1893 (Cornman Ms).
     She and her daughters were living at Pittsfield in 1903
(Town Register).

Children (**Gray**), born at Northwood (VRs):

i.   ANNIE L., b. 12 Apr. 1862; m. F. H. HARTWELL.
ii.   LIZZIE E., b. 25 Dec. 1864.

846. VARNUM HILL[8] 1818-1902 [377 James[7] and Sarah Winkley]
was born at Strafford NH 16 Dec. 1818, died at Farmington NH
23 Apr. 1902, 83y 4m 7d; married first 14 Oct. 1841 DOROTHY
WOODMAN JONES, born at Middleton NH 28 Mar. 1818, died there
5 May 1865, daughter of Samuel and Mary (Woodman) Jones; married second at Lowell MA 20 May 1866 ELVIRA HAMBLET BUMFORD,
born at Lowell 1 Apr. 1837, died at Farmington 21 May 1895,
58y 1m 20d, daughter of David and Dorcas (Horne) Bumford
(Cornman Ms; Jewett, Barnstead, 98).
     They lived at Middleton, where he was a carpenter. In 1900
he was living with his son Charles.

Children by Dorothy, born at Middleton:

1438. i.   CHARLES HENRY[9], b. 21 Apr. 1842.
      ii.   JAMES SAMUEL, b. 15 May 1844, d. Lawrence MA 26
            Dec. 1869; m. 16 July 1866 EMMA H. WENTWORTH,
            dau. of Bartholomew Wentworth of So. Berwick
            ME. No ch. He was also called Daniel Samuel.
      iii. MARY ELIZABETH, b. 28 Dec. 1846, d. Middleton
            5 Nov. 1864.
1439. iv.   (SARAH) FRANCES, b. 14 Apr. 1853; m. CYRUS
            YORK.
      v.   WALTER VARNUM, b. 22 June 1855, d. Middleton
            26 Nov. 1864.

847. JOHN JAMES[8] 1824-1898 [377 James[7] and Sarah Winkley]
was born at Strafford NH 21 Jan. 1824, died at Worcester MA 2
Nov. 1898; married first 20 Dec. 1846 MARY E. CLARK, born at
Manchester NH 12 Oct. 1826, died there 15 Apr. 1849, 22y
(Morning Star), daughter of Elder Mayhew Clark; married second 26 July 1851 DEBORAH BUTLER AMBROSE, born at Starks ME 30
Oct. 1833, daughter of Dr. Jonathan and Mehitable (Carr)
Ambrose (William Collins Hatch, History of the Town of Industry, Me. [Farmington ME, 1893], 499; Cornman Ms).
     He was a machinist, and lived at Lawrence MA where he
served as selectman in 1888-9.
     In 1900 widow Deborah's household at Lawrence included the
family of her son Seymour.

Children, all by second wife Deborah:

i.   MARY ELIZABETH[9], b. Salmon Falls NH 10 July
      1852; m. Lawrence 14 Nov. 1878 JOHN E.
      POWERS. No ch.
ii.   JOHN AMBROSE, b. Salmon Falls 13 Dec. 1854,
      d. Worcester 10 Apr. 1886.

1440. iii. EMMA FRANCES, b. Strafford 16 Aug. 1859; m.
            ANSON L. GRIFFIN.
      iv.   SEYMOUR JAMES, b. Middleton 27 Jan. 1863; m.
            15 July 1885 LUCY D. CHAPMAN.

848. MARY ANN[8] 1827-   [377 James[7] and Sarah Winkley]
was born at Strafford NH 5 Apr. 1827; married 22 Sept. 1850
JOSEPH PIPER, born 25 Jan. 1824, died at Strafford 5 Oct.
1887, son of Joseph and Judith (Hill) Piper (Cornman Ms).

Children (**Piper**), born at Strafford:

i.   MARY ELIZABETH, b. 26 July 1851, d. 9 Apr. 1852.
ii.   JOHN FRANKLIN, b. 2 Feb. 1853; m. 18 Sept. 1878 MARY
      E. CANNEY, dau. of Charles N. Canney.
iii. BENJAMIN WINKLEY, b. 19 Aug. 1855, d. Northwood NH
      12 Aug. 1886; m. MARY E. DUNCAN, b. 15 Aug. 1858.
iv.   JOSEPH JAMES, b. 12 Aug. 1859, d. Strafford 24 July
      1890.
v.   CLARA EMMA, b. 15 Oct. 1864.

849. SARAH ELIZABETH[8] 1829-1903 [377 James[7] and Sarah
Winkley] was born at Strafford NH Nov. 1829, died there 12
Apr. 1903, 73y 4m (GS); married 30 June 1851 JOSEPH J. WOOD-
MAN, born at Sanbornton NH 4 Aug. 1826, died at Strafford 23
May 1898, 71y 9m 19d (GS), son of Joshua and Almira (Johnson)
Woodman (Cornman Ms; Strafford VRs). Burials are in Caverly
Hill Cemetery, Bow Lake.

Children (**Woodman**), born at Strafford:

i.   WALTER L., b. 13 Jan. 1852, d. Strafford 24 Oct.
      1895; m. Dover 17 Nov. 1881 LAURA E. FOSS.
ii.   JAMES J., b. 30 July 1854; m. 23 Sept. 1882 AGGIE S.
      GORE, dau. of Dennis Gore.
iii. SARAH A., b. 3 Oct. 1856, d. Strafford 5 Aug. 1882.
iv.   JOHN A., b. 7 Aug. 1859; m. Lynn MA 5 Oct. 1882
      FANNIE E. (CUSHING) Fawcett.
v.   MANSON B., b. 20 July 1862; m. 5 Jan. 1902 FLORENCE
      L. HATCH, b. 15 June 1882.

850. HANNAH FRANCES[8] 1831-1869 [377 James[7] and Sarah Wink-
ley] was born at Strafford 2 Oct. 1831, died 15 Apr. 1869;
married 16 Nov. 1856 ALPHONSO H. BOODY, born 28 Mar. 1829,
died 12 July 1901, son of Zechariah and Abigail (Watson)
Boody (Caverly, Boody Annals, 250; Cornman Ms). He married
second 7 Nov. 1869 Mrs. Rosetta J. Foye.

Children (**Boody**):

i.   EVERETT S., b. 1 Nov. 1858; m. 1st 25 Jan. 1885 GRACE
      D. EDMONDS; m. 2nd 25 Dec. 1894 LOUISE A. HUSSEY.
ii.   FRED EUGENE, b. 30 Oct. 1860, res. Epsom NH; m. 19
      July 1890 ROSALIE DEMERITT, b. in 1869, d. 10 June
      1892.
iii. FRANK A , b. 11 Sept., d. 2 Oct., 1863.

851. ABIGAIL[8] 1811-1867 [379 Thomas[7] and Nancy Jones] was born at Milton NH 31 Aug. 1811, died at Farmington NH 27 Nov. 1867; married there 17 June 1827 JEREMIAH HUSSEY, born there 1 Aug. 1801, died there 27 Sept. 1864, son of Micajah and Olive (Hanson) Hussey (Hussey Fam., 105; Cornman Ms; Farmington TRs). Burials are in the Hussey Cemetery, Barrington. Jeremy was a stonecutter.

Children (**Hussey**), born at Farmington:

i.   THOMAS L., b. 24 Nov. 1827, d. 7 Sept. 1864; m. MARY McDUFFEE. No ch.
ii.   MICAJAH J., b. 15 Apr. 1830, d. 20 Jan. 1863; m. 1st Lowell MA 13 Sept. 1849 SARAH DORRETY, b. in Ireland in 1826, dau. of James and Mary Dorrety; perhaps m. 2nd ELIZABETH NUTE.
iii.   JAMES FRANKLIN, b. 2 July 1832, d. Farmington 30 Sept. 1921, 89y 2m 28d; m. Somersworth 21 Nov. 1860 SARAH A. EDGERLY.
iv.   NANCY J., b. 20 Nov. 1834, d. 2 Dec. 1866; m. Milton J. LEIGHTON DUNTLEY [# 861].
v.   STEPHEN A , b. 3 Mar. 1837; unm.
vi.   CHARLES E., b. 12 Feb. 1840, d. 25 Aug. 1868; unm.
vii.   JOHN D., b. 12 May 1842, d. 18 Feb. 1865; unm.
viii.   WILLIAM E., b. 23 Dec. 1844; m. Rochester NH 19 Mar. 1865 ANNIE CLARK.
ix.   (MARY) ELLEN, b. 29 May 1847, d. in 1889; m. (per Cornman Ms) ALBERT JOHNSON or (per gen.) CHARLES HOWARD of Rochester.
x.   ROSINA H., b. 23 Mar. 1850, d. 24 Mar. 1878; m. JAMES HOWELL of Ossipee.
xi.   FRANCES, b. 18 Dec. 1852, d. 24 July 1886; m. HENRY STUMKE of Boston.
xii.   ESTELLE, b. 25 Oct. 1857, d. 6 July 1878; unm.

852. RHODA ANN[8] 1817-1896 [379 Thomas[7] and Nancy Jones] was born at Milton 24 Feb. 1817, died 22 June 1896; married 22 Feb. 1847 FRANCIS C LOONEY, born at Manchester, England, 28 June 1802, died 24 June 1854.
As a youth Francis had emigrated from England to Milton in 1820 (Cornman Ms).

Children (**Looney**):

i.   EDWIN F , b. 14 Apr. 1848, d. 5 July 1865.
ii.   CHARLES H., b. 11 July 1849, d. Milton 22 Apr. 1902; m. 28 Sept. 1871 EMILY E. WELLS, b. 28 Sept. 1854

853. CYRUS K.[8] 1824-1872 [379 Thomas[7] and Hannah Jones] was born at Milton 23 Sept. 1824, died there 22 July 1872; married 18 Mar. 1846 SOPHIA MARTIN HAYES, born at Rochester 22 Apr. 1824, died at Milton 20 May 1905, 81y 28d, daughter of George and Lydia (Jones) Hayes (Richmond, John Hayes, 1:28, 338; town, NH and ME VRs; Cornman Ms).
In 1850 Cyrus was a farmer at Milton, listed next door to his father.
His widow Sophia was living at Milton with her son Edwin in 1900.

Children, born at Milton:

i.   GEORGE J.^{9}, d. 20 Jan. 1847.
ii. FRANK H., b. in 1849 (2 in 1850), d. in 1891.
iii. ANNIE L., b. in 1852, d. in 1879; m. ORRIN
     VARNEY.
iv. CARLA [or CORA], b. 6 Nov. 1854, d. in 1897; m.
     AUGUSTUS CALUMY.
v.   JAMES A , b. 15 Apr. 1858, d. Lebanon ME 3 Mar.
     1923, 64y 10m 27d; m. 25 Feb. 1877 ELIZABETH
     E. [Lizzie] (MORSE) Hall, b. Newton MA in
     1856, d. Lebanon 1 May 1927, dau. of Joseph
     and Mary C Morse. They removed from Milton
     to Lebanon in 1908. Ch. ETTA M.^{10} b. c1874
     (6 in 1880, Milton census).
vi. LYDIA H., b. 22 Dec. 1863, d. 9 Jan. 1864, 18d.
vii. EDWIN L., b. 6 July 1865; m. CARRIE REMICK, who
     was b. in July 1872.

854. BETSEY JANE^8 1827-   [379 Thomas^7 and Nancy Jones]
was born at Milton NH 19 Aug. 1827, lived at Hyde Park MA;
married at Warner NH 26 July 1850 LEVI H. STRAW, born 10 Nov.
1828, died at Grafton NH 18 Nov. 1875, son of Steven and Marion Straw (Cornman Ms).

Children (**Straw**):

i.   FRANK LEIGHTON, b. 11 July 1851, res. Hyde Park; m.
     17 Sept. 1880 LILLA BELLE ESTABROOK.
ii. WILLIAM RICHARDSON, b. 29 Nov. 1854, res. Hyde Park.
iii. MARY HELEN (twin), b. 29 Nov. 1854.
iv. ANTOINETTE McKIM, b. 14 Dec. 1864.

855. MARTHA AUGUSTA^8 1831-1873 [379 Thomas^7 and Nancy
Jones] was born at Milton 22 June 1831, died at Rochester NH
14 Aug. 1873, 43y 2m; married at Farmington 29 Mar. 1849
(TRs) Capt. LORENZO DOW HAYES, born at Rochester 24 May 1822,
died there 27 Feb. 1871, son of George and Lydia (Jones)
Hayes (Richmond, John Hayes, 538-9; Cornman Ms).
Lorenzo Hayes was a captain of militia and a shoe manufac-
turer at Rochester.

Children (**Hayes**), the first three born at Milton, the
    rest at Rochester:

i.   EUGENE AUGUSTUS, b. 18 Nov. 1850, d. 17 June 1924; m.
     1st Rochester 29 Aug. 1877 LUCIE J. SEVERANCE, b. 24
     May 1850, d. 22 Feb. 1888, dau. of Levi and Sarah
     Severance; m. 2nd Warren ME 3 Jan. 1891 ADELIA LOIS
     TEAGUE, b. 11 May 1864, d. 13 Apr. 1892, dau. of
     James Teague. About 1890 he was supt. of a shoe
     factory at Warren.
ii. KIRK BYRON, b. 11 Nov. 1852, res. NY; m. 5 Apr. 1880
     JENNIE YOUNG.
iii. FRED, b. 28 Nov. 1854, d. 20 Aug. 1904; m. 20 Oct.
     1887 LISETTA D. [LIZETTE] ROOS, b. 24 Aug. 1852, d.
     Boston 18 Jan. 1912. He res. Winthrop MA.
iv. ANNIE, b. 29 Sept. 1858, d. in 1859, 5m 5d.

v.   LILLIAN J., b. 19 May 1861, d. 15 May 1931, 69y; m.
     Milton 15 Jan. 1889 FRED B. WENTWORTH, b. 3 Aug.
     1864, son of Simon and Frances J. (Cook) Wentworth.
vi. FRANK ROSCOE, d. 11 Aug. 1869, 3y 12d.

856. GEORGE[8] 1813-1890 [381 Trustrum[7] and Betsey Peavey]
was born at Farmington NH 8 Oct. 1813, died at Rochester 26
Mar. 1890; married first at Farmington 22 Apr. 1838 EMILY W.
ROBERTS, born there 26 Dec. 1815, died at Dover NH 16 Dec.
1855, daughter of Ephraim and Hannah (Roberts) Roberts (Henry
W. Hardon, Roberts Family [mss, NHHS], 1:184; NHGR, 6[1909]:
25); married second at Farmington int. 10 July 1856 LYDIA A.
PINKHAM, born at Tuftonboro NH 12 Apr. 1834, died at Dover 27
Apr. 1919 (South Berwick [ME] VRs), 85y 15d, daughter of
Daniel and Sophia (Drew) Pinkham (Sinnett, Pinkham Gen., 35;
Farmington TRs).
Burials are in the Pinkham Cemetery west of Dover Point
Road, Dover. Emily was a Quaker until she "married out."
The family was listed at Dover in 1850, including Susanna
Roberts, 78; they were at Rochester in 1880.

Children by Emily, all but the last born at Farmington:

1441. i.   AMASA ROBERTS[9], b. 12 Sept. 1838.
      ii.   HANNAH ELIZABETH, b. 14 Nov. 1841, res. Dover;
            unm.
      iii. LUCETTA ROBERTS [Etta], b. 3 Sept. 1843, d. No.
            Berwick ME 26 May 1921, 77y 10m 23d; unm. She
            res. Dover.
      iv.   GEORGE HENRY, b. 9 Sept. 1845, d. Haverhill MA
            13 Sept. 1900; m. in Apr. 1874 ANNA MAUDE FUR-
            BER, b. Wolfeboro NH 18 July 1848, d. Haver-
            hill 27 Jan. 1895. No ch.
      v.   ELIZA ELLEN, b. 14 Mar., d. 23 Nov., 1849, 8m
            9d (GS).
      vi.   MARY EMMA, b. Dover 6 Dec. 1852, d. No. Berwick
            21 Jan. 1926, 73y 1m 15d; unm.

Children by Lydia, born at Farmington:

      vii. CHARLES A., b. 30 Mar. 1857, d. Dover 2 Jan.
            1866, 8y 9m.
      viii. FLORA H., b. 3 Aug. 1859; m. EDWARD EVERETT
            TAYLOR GERRISH, b. York ME 16 Dec. 1858, son
            of Dr. Christopher Prentice and Hattie A.
            (Hill) Gerrish (Charles N. Sinnett, Gerrish
            Genealogy [Tms, nd, MHS], 10). No ch.
      ix.   FOREST L., b. 23 July 1862, d. So. Berwick 28
            Nov. 1923, 61y; m. ---- . No ch.
      x.   CHARLES A., b. 11 May 1873, d. Rochester 2 July
            1903; m. ---- . No ch.
      xi.   ANNA, b. 18 Apr. 1865, d. Dover 19 Apr. 1880,
            15y (GS).

857. SALLY C.[8] 1817-   [381 Trustrum[7] and Betsey Peavey]
was born at Farmington 1 Jan. 1817, lived at Haverhill MA;
married first 15 June 1835 JOSEPH C. QUIMBY of Dover, born 6
Oct. 1813, died 6 Mar. 1863, 50y 5m; married second SAMUEL
ALLEY (Cornman Ms).

Children (**Quimby**):

i.   ANDREW L., b. 24 Sept. 1838, d. Dover 6 July 1892,
     54y 9m 11d; m. MARY SHEPHERD.
ii. JOHN, b. 8 July 1841, d. Dover 20 Jan. 1872; m. CLARA
     HUTCHINGS.

858. JOSEPH P.[8] 1820-1854 [381 Trustrum[7] and Betsey Pea-
vey] was born at Farmington 15 Apr. 1820, died there 15 Oct.
1854; married there 15 May 1839 (int. 26 Apr.) CLARINDA C
VARNEY, born at Middleton NH 25 Apr. 1817, died at Dover NH
21 Dec. 1893, daughter of John and Bethana Varney (Cornman
Ms; Farmington TRs).

Children, born at Farmington:

	i.	STEPHEN W.[9], b. 29 June 1840; m. MARTHA BERRY.
1442.	ii.	SAMUEL R., b. 27 Oct. 1841.
	iii.	FRANCES JANE, b. 9 Nov. 1843; m. GEORGE WILLIAMS.
	iv.	MARY EMILY, b. 11 Feb. 1846, d. 14 Sept. 1847.
1443.	v.	MARY AUGUSTA, b. 2 Nov. 1848; m. THEODORE S. APPLEBEE.
1444.	vi.	JAMES W., b. 6 Sept. 1850.
	vii.	ABBIE E., b. 5 July 1852, d. Dover; m. THOMAS CHASE of Haverhill. No ch.
1445.	viii.	CLARA B., b. 10 Sept. 1854; m. TYLER PROCTOR and GEORGE ABBOTT.

859. LUCINDA[8] 1825-1895 [381 Trustrum[7] and Betsey Peavey]
was born at Farmington 19 Sept. 1825, died at Rochester 17
Feb. 1895; married 2 Sept. 1848 EDWIN A SMITH, who died at
Rochester 2 Dec. 1887 (Cornman Ms).
Her illegitimate daughter by Ichabod Hayes was attributed
to the wrong mother in Richmond's John Hayes (277-8).

Child (**Leighton**):

i.   ELLA J.[9], b. 4 July 1844; m. 30 Dec. 1890
     ABEDNEGO DREW, b. Barrington 19 May 1839, d.
     Rochester 9 Nov. 1900.

Children (**Smith**):

ii. TRISTRAM A., b. 11 Apr. 1858; unm.
iii. FRANK M., b. 29 Mar. 1861; m. 1st JULIA SULLIVAN, d.
     1892; m. 2nd JOSIE MURPHY.

860. EMILY MARIA[8] 1827-   [381 Trustrum[7] and Betsey
Peavey] was born at Farmington 11 Mar. 1827, lived at Rochester NH; married at Farmington 17 June 1848 LEWIS N. BERRY,
born at Alton NH 7 Mar. 1824, died at Milton NH 5 June 1863
(Cornman Ms).

Children (**Berry**):

i.   JAMES F , b. 15 July 1854, d. 4 Apr. 1855.
ii. JANETTE E., b. 24 July 1857, d. 20 Mar. 1897; unm.

861. PHEBE[8] 1813-1871 [382 Jedediah[7] and Sally Murray] was
born at Farmington 13 Dec. 1813, died at Milton NH 28 Nov.
1871; married at Farmington 18 Oct. 1829 HAZEN DUNTLEY of
Sandwich NH, born 25 Feb. 1805, died at Milton 15 Oct. 1884
(Cornman Ms; Farmington and Milton VRs; records of Lewis L.
Knox). In 1840 and 1850 Duntley was a blacksmith at Milton.
He served from 1861 to 1864 in the 1st NH Vol. Cav. Rgt.

Children (**Duntley**):

i.   EMILY P., b. 13 Mar. 1830, d. 4 Dec. 1897; m. 3 Dec.
        1847 HANSON DOWNS.
ii.   LORENZO D., b. 13 Feb. 1832; m. 10 Mar. 1855 SUSAN E.
        DEARBORN, b. 1 Oct. 1833.
iii.   (JEDEDIAH) LEIGHTON, b. 27 Oct. 1834; m. Milton 28
        Nov. 1860 NANCY J. HUSSEY, b. Farmington 16 Nov.
        1834, d. 2 Dec. 1866, dau. of Jeremiah and Abigail[8]
        (Leighton) Hussey [# 851].
iv.   JOSEPH, b. 5 Mar. 1837, d. 13 Nov. 1838.
v.   MARY J., b. 5 Aug. 1839; m. 15 June 1888 HAMILTON
        REYNOLDS.
vi.   IRA N., b. 16 Mar. 1842; m. 18 Apr. 1867 SARAH A.
        HODGMAN.
vii.   AMOS C , b. 18 Mar. 1844; m. 3 Nov. 1867 MARY A
        SAWYER.
viii.   LORANA, b. 7 Mar. 1846, d. 11 Jan. 1911, 64y 10m 4d;
        m. 30 Mar. 1867 JOHN L. CARSON.
ix.   BETHANA (twin), b. 7 Mar. 1846; m. 27 Jan. 1866 JOHN
        P. PINKHAM.
x.   ELZENA, b. 3 Dec. 1848, d. 5 Sept. 1849.
xi.   PHEBE A., b. 3 Oct. 1851; m. 10 Sept. 1874 ALBERT
        NUTTER.

862. MOSES CHENEY[8] 1817-1876 [382 Jedediah[7] and Sarah
Murray] was born at Farmington 3 Feb. 1817, died there 1 Apr.
1876; married there 28 Oct. 1838 HANNAH E. TANNER, born 29
Dec. 1822, died 3 Aug. 1906, 86y 7m 5d, daughter of John and
Mary (Thompson) Tanner (Farmington TRs; records of descendant
Lewis L. Knox). Burials are in Pine Grove Cemetery.
     He was a carpenter, sometimes called Cheney. He bought
considerable land at Farmington between 1847 and 1862 (StrCD
201:189; 202:205; 222:453-4; 223:23). He deeded property to
his son John 18 Nov. 1874, and to his son Mark 14 June 1875
(256:523; 258:20).
     His estate was inventoried 6 June 1876, and an accounting
given in Apr. 1877 (StrCP 83:182; 87:92); his widow Hannah
received her share 3 Jan. 1877 (StrCD 261:166).

Children, born at Farmington:

        i.   CHARLES H.[9], b. 26 Oct. 1839, d. infant.
        ii.   JAMES BARTLETT, b. 9 Oct. 1842, d. 14 Sept.
                1846.
        iii.   GEORGE EDWIN [Ed], b. 6 Jan. 1845, d. Farming-
                ton 30 Mar. 1907, 63y 2m 24d; m. 26 Dec. 1867
                CLARA S. SMITH, b. Farmington 5 Dec. 1850, d.
                there 16 Sept. 1930, 79y 9m 11d, dau. of
                George K. and Hannah (Colomy) Smith. No ch.
1446. iv.   CHARLES HENRY, b. 3 Nov. 1846.
1447. v.   JOHN WOODBURY [Wood], b. 10 Aug. 1848.

vi.   JAMES FRANCIS [Frank], b. 20 Jan. 1850, d.
      Farmington 22 May 1884; m. Rochester 29 Mar.
      1871 CLARA F. [Carrie] WILLEY, dau. of William
      H. Willey of Milton NH. No ch.
vii. MARK F., b. 5 Feb. 1852, d. Farmington 3 July
      1911, 59y 5m; m. 28 Nov. 1906 FANNIE M. LORD
      of Lebanon ME.
viii. CLARA A., b. 29 Aug. 1853, d. 25 Nov. 1916, 63y
      2m 8d; m. Rochester 21 Dec. 1874 SIMON T.
      SMITH, b. there 20 Aug. 1850, d. 3 June 1936,
      son of James F. and Sarah E. Smith. No ch.
ix.   WILBUR SMITH, b. 16 June 1855, d. 21 Mar. 1928,
      72y 9m 15d (GS). He lived alone at Pepperell
      MA in 1900.
1448. x.   (AUGUSTUS) FREEMONT, b. 7 Dec. 1856.

863.   LEWIS L.[8] 1824-1891 [382 Jedediah[7] and Sarah Murray]
was born at Farmington 19 Sept. 1824, died at Dover (hosp.)
11 Feb. 1891; married at Lebanon ME 4 July 1848 (VRs) LUCINDA
JANE JONES, born there 4 Apr. 1826, died at Milton NH 15 June
1911, daughter of Thomas and Hannah (Hayes) Jones (Richmond,
John Hayes, 1:211, 277-8; Cornman Ms.
Lewis was a shoemaker at Milton. His will made in July
1890 left his Milton homestead to his widow (StrCP 107:178).
Burials are in Silver Street Cemetery, Milton. Lucinda was
in Adelbert's Milton household in 1910, aged 87.

Children:

1449. i.   MARILLA M.[9], b. Lebanon ME 18 July 1849; m.
            ROBERT L. KNIGHT and JEREMIAH MAHONEY.
      ii.   LUELLA F., b. Milton 4 Mar. 1850; m. 1st 23
            June 1872 GEORGE W. WHITEHOUSE, b. in 1844,
            son of Stephen and Lucinda Whitehouse; m. 2nd
            15 May 1882 GEORGE W. LEATHERS, res. Alton Bay
            in 1907. She had no ch.
1450. iii. ADELBERT O., b. Milton 24 July 1852.

864.   BELINDA[8] 1836-1882 [382 Jedediah[7] and Sarah Murray]
was born at Farmington about 1836, died 20 Mar. 1882; married
HOSEA B. KNOX, born about 1830, died 2 Oct. 1895 (Cornman
Ms). In 1850 Belinda, 16, was living with her brother Lewis.
Hosea and his family were listed at Milton in 1860. He
served in the Civil War.

Children (**Knox**):

i.   CLARA, b. 13 Feb. 1854, d. 1 Oct. 1873.
ii.   EMMA, b. 19 Oct. 1856; m. 12 Nov. 1877 JAMES H.
      RINES.
iii. SADIE, b. 12 Nov. 1860.
iv.   FRANK, b. 25 Dec. 1862; m. 25 June 1896 LAURA A.
      STEWART.
v.   FOREST, b. 8 Jan. 1871.

865.   GIDEON[8] 1817-1867 [? 383 Gideon[7] and Martha Pinkham]
was born at Steuben ME in 1817 (1807 per GS; 33 in 1850),
died at Cherryfield ME 8 Dec. 1867 (GS); married at Steuben

18 Dec. 1842 MARY[8] LEIGHTON, born in 1828, died at Ellsworth ME 11 Jan. 1911, daughter of Eleazer and Sallie (Strout) Leighton [# 384] (town and ME VRs). His household was at Cherryfield in 1850 and 1860; widow Mary was listed in the Cherryfield Register in 1908.

No Gideon was listed among the heirs of Martha (Pinkham) Leighton [# 127] in 1826, perhaps because he was a minor. The John mentioned as Martha's son might have been commonly known as Gideon. Although the relationship is not clear in the records, Gideon[8] was almost without a doubt a son of the first Gideon.

Children, born at Cherryfield:

1451. i.   EMMA N.[9], b. in 1843; m. FRED GOOGINS and LEWIS
            BURKE.
1452. ii.   JASON L., b. in 1845.
      iii. HARRIS E., b. c1850 (10 in 1860).

866. MARTHA[8] 1820-   [383 Gideon[7] and Lucy Wakefield] was born at Steuben 30 Jan. 1820, lived at Rockland ME in 1903 (Cherryfield Town Register); married 2 Apr. 1848 AMBROSE PINKHAM, born 24 Nov. 1822, lived at Rockland, son of Robert and Lydia (Fernald) Pinkham (Cornman Ms; Sinnett, Pinkham Gen., 19). They were living at Steuben in 1860, he 36, a seaman, and she 35.

Children (**Pinkham**):

i.   ALONZO, b. c1849 (11 in 1860); unm.
ii.   MARIAM, b. c1851 (9 in 1860).
iii. LABEN H., b. c1853 (7 in 1860).
iv.   SIMEON, b. c1855 (5 in 1860).

867. JAMES W.[8] 1826-1899 [383 Gideon[7] and Lucy Wakefield] was born at Steuben 1 Jan. 1826, died there 28 Oct. 1899, 74y 9m 27d; married there int. 12 Oct. 1846 LUCY ANN PINKHAM, born 4 Oct. 1822, died at Milbridge 30 Jan. 1906, 83y 3m 27d (GS), daughter of Benjamin and Rachel[6] (Leighton) Pinkham [# 167] (Steuben VRs; records of Jeannette Leighton). He was a seaman.

Children, born at Steuben:

1453. i.   MILLARD F [9], b. 7 Nov. 1848.
      ii.   GEORGE W., b. 12 Nov. 1855; m. Steuben 16
            Mar. 1890 SARAH E. PINKHAM. He was a sea
            captain.
      iii. ELI D., b. 15 June 1856; m. Steuben 9 Nov. 1889
            BERTHA HARNDEN, b. Gouldsboro in 1868,
            dau. of Joseph and Clara (Smith) Harnden.
1454. iv.   ANDREW P., b. 10 May 1858.

868. SUSAN[8] 1819-1910 [384 Eleazer[7] and Sallie Strout] was born at Steuben 6 Dec. 1819, died there 24 Jan. 1910, 91y 1m 8d (VRs; 24 Nov. per GS); married at Steuben int. 7 Aug. 1835 BENJAMIN PINKHAM JR., born there 1 Aug. 1810, died there 2 July 1892, 83y 10m (GS), son of Benjamin and Rachel[6] (Leigh-

ton) Pinkham [# 167] (Steuben VRs; Sinnett, Pinkham Gen., 17;
her letter of 17 Oct. 1903, MHS mss collections). Burials
are in Pinkham Cemetery, Pinkham's Bay.

Children (**Pinkham**), born at Steuben:

i   ALFRED T., b. 6 Dec. 1838.
ii.   ELVIRA, b. 17 Feb. 1841; m. Steuben 5 Oct. 1861
      JOSIAH PINKHAM, b. 1 Apr. 1837, son of Richard and
      Priscilla (Pinkham) Pinkham.
iii. HARRIS E., b. 28 Apr. 1843; m. HANNAH CLARA CONNORS.
iv.   LORINDA, b. 15 Apr. 1846, d. 1 Feb. 1933; m. JOHN
      COLEWELL.
v.   GILBERT, b. 20 Nov. 1847; m. JENNIE LIBBY.
vi.   JOHN E., b. 25 Nov. 1849, d. 20 Nov. 1876.
vii. JAMES EVERETT, b. 30 Aug. 1853, d. 1 Nov. 1933; m.
      ABBIE ELLA GAY, dau. of William and Lucy^8 (Leighton)
      Gay [# 871].
viii. SARAH E., b. 4 Apr. 1854, d. in 1856.
ix.   ELLEN S., b. 4 May 1856; m. GEORGE^9 LEIGHTON [# 928].
x.   LENORA, b. 9 Jan. 1859, d. Steuben 31 Aug. 1929; m.
      ---- LINDSAY.
xi.   ADA, b. 22 Feb. 1865.

869. LOVICIA^8 [Lovice] 1825-1905 [384 Eleazer^7 and Sallie
Strout] was born at Steuben 20 Mar. 1825, died there 5 Feb.
1905, 81y; married first there 19 Oct. 1841 JOEL PINKHAM,
born there 5 Sept. 1816, died there 2 Sept. 1911, son of Benjamin and Rachel$_7$ (Leighton) Pinkham [# 167]; married second
about 1865 JAMES^7 LEIGHTON [# 407] (Steuben VRs; her letter
in 1903--Cornman Papers; records of Margaret Colton). In
1860 Joel, 40, and Lovisi, 38, were listed at Steuben; they
apparently were later divorced.
She was said to have had three children who died during a
diptheria epidemic in 1863. In 1880, she and James Leighton
were listed at Steuben, along with her Pinkham daughters
Lovina, 24, and Mary Ella, 19.

Children (**Pinkham**), born at Steuben:

i.   JULIA ANN, b. 7 Mar. 1842; m. STEPHEN RIDER.
ii.   ALMIRA, b. 19 Mar. 1845; m. BENJAMIN F^8 LEIGHTON
      [# 933] and CHARLES MOORE.
iii. DOLLY, b. 25 Nov. 1846; m. in NJ 23 Feb. 1866 BENJA-
      MIN STULL.
iv.   EMILY FRANCIS, b. 25 Mar. 1850; perhaps m. 4 July
      1873 GUILFORD YOUNG.
v.   EMERY, b. 4 Dec. 1851, lost at sea.
vi.   LOVINA, b. 13 Nov. 1853, d. Steuben 28 Apr. 1930; m.
      in 1884 GEORGE GUPTILL PENDLETON, b. Gouldsboro 5
      Feb. 1858, d. 14 Dec. 1895, son of Samuel C. and
      Ruth Rice (Tracy) Pendleton (Everett H. Pendleton,
      Brian Pendleton and his Descendants [np, 1910],
      709.). He had m. 1st in 1880 Margaret Joy.
vii. JOSEPH IRA, b. 18 July 1857, d. Steuben 9 Sept. 1919;
      m. MARY ---- . In 1860 he was Ira, aged 4.
viii. MARY ELLA, b. 22 July 1860; m. Steuben 2 Sept. 1897
      JAMES PINKHAM, b. there about 1858, son of Isaac W.
      and Bethia (West) Pinkham.

870.   ELLEN[8] 1828-   [384 Eleazer and Sallie Strout] was
born at Steuben in 1828, died before 1903; married DENNIS
LARRY of Cherryfield, born in Ireland about 1822 (Cornman Ms;
letter of sister Susan Pinkham).
In 1870, they were listed at Cherryfield with six children.

Children (**Larry**), born at Cherryfield:

i.   MARY E., b. c1853.
ii.   MARGARET, b. c1855.
iii. NANCY, b. c1857.
iv.   JOHN, b. c1859.
v.   KATIE, not in 1870 census.
vi.   DENNIS JR., b. c1867.
vii. MATTIE, b. c1870 (5/12 in census).

871.   LUCY[8] 1829-   [384 Eleazer[7] and Sallie Strout] was
born at Steuben about 1829; married 23 Nov. 1850 WILLIAM GAY
of Machias, born in 1825, son of Lemuel and Mary Gay (Cornman
Ms). In 1860 William, 33, and Lucy, 29, were listed at
Machias.

Children (**Gay**):

i.   LAURA, b. c1851 (9 in 1860).
ii.   CHARLES, b. c1854 (6 in 1860).
iii. GEORGE, b. c1856 (4 in 1860).
iv.   ABBIE ELLA, b. Machias 2 May 1858; m. JAMES E. PINK-
      HAM [# 868].
v.   EMILY.
vi.   HATTIE.
vii. LUCRETIA.

872.   SUSAN[8] 1816-   [387 Joseph[7] and Betsey Downs] was
born at Steuben ME 11 Nov. 1816; married at Springfield ME 14
Nov. 1837 MARK WORCESTER, born at Columbia ME in Mar. 1816,
died at Springfield 26 Oct. 1902, 86y 6m 29d, son of Isaac
and Lydia (Tucker) Worcester (ME VRs; Cornman Ms; records of
Leonard F. Tibbetts).
In 1840 Mark's family was listed at Cherryfield; in 1850,
they were at Tp 7, Range 3 (Prentiss), Penobscot Co.

Children (**Worcester**):

i.   JULIETTE, b. Cherryfield c1838 (12 in 1850).
ii.   MARK, b. Cherryfield in Dec. 1840, not in 1850
      census.
iii. THOMAS, b. c1842 (8 in 1850); m. 20 Sept. 1863 ANNA
      CARVER of Lincoln ME.
iv.   ELIZABETH, b. Webster Pltn c1845 (5 in 1850), d.
      Springfield 13 Mar. 1919; m. 6 Aug. 1865 CHARLES
      DOWNS.
v.   ROBERT S., b. Springfield c1847 (3 in 1850), d. Pren-
      tiss 11 Feb. 1923, 75y 1m 26d; m. EMMA LAMB, b.
      Prentiss c1852, d. 15 July 1922, 69y 6m 29d, dau. of
      Joseph and Sarah J. (Treadwell) Lamb.
vi.   LYDIA, b. c1849 (1 in 1850).

873. STILLMAN WASS[8] 1819-1899 [387 Joseph[7] and Betsey Downs] was born at Steuben ME 27 Sept. 1819, died at Caribou ME 11 July 1899, 80y 9m 20d; married at Springfield ME 25 Dec. 1843 THERESA E. WALTON, born at Burke VT in Jan. 1828 (1900 census), lived at Caribou in 1900 with her daughter Samantha Crockett (town and ME VRs; records of Leonard F. Tibbetts; Cornman Ms). He was buried at Webster Plantation. He left Cherryfield in 1839 to settle at Springfield. About 1843 he and James Austin were the first settlers at Tp 6 (later named Webster Plantation), where he had a 325-acre lot (History of Penobscot County, Maine [Cleveland, 1882], 2:510-11). In 1850 and 1860 his family was at Carroll (Tp 6, range 2); in 1870 he was listed as "Solomon" at Prentiss (Tp 7 Range 3), and in 1880 (as Leyhton) at Webster Plantation. (In 1860 he was listed as 44, his wife "Sarah" as 33.) He had ten children, of whom eight were living in 1880.

Children:

	i.	MARY T.[9], b. Prentiss 3 Sept. 1845; m. Springfield 23 Sept. 1866 HIRAM A. COOPER.
1455.	ii.	ALFRED STEPHEN, b. 9 Dec. 1847.
	iii.	LUTHER W., b. 25 Mar. 1850, res. Dassell MN; m. Springfield ME int. 14 Oct. 1872 HARRIET H. [Hattie] BARTLETT, b. c1852. Ch. MINNIE[10] b. in MN c1879. In 1874 he owned the first wagon shop at Dassell. In 1881 he started a hardware business with J. M. Johnson; in 1887 he formed Osterland & Leighton, general merchants. He also owned a 325-acre farm there (History of Meeker County, Minn. [1888], 318).
	iv.	HANNAH, b. c1853 (7 in 1860; Anna, 14, in 1870).
	v.	JOHN R., b. c 1855 (5 in 1860, not listed in 1870).
	vi.	CATHERINE A., b. c1855 (5 in 1860, not listed in 1870).
1456.	vii.	SAMANTHA, b. Webster in Jan. 1857; m. HARLAND P. CROCKETT.
	vii.	HENRY PARKINS, b. Prentiss c1860 (20 in 1880), res. MA; m. 1st Springfield 6 Jan. 1884 ELIZA BOYINGTON; m. 2nd 22 Apr. 1891 FLOSSIE McEACHERN, b. PEI c1868 (23 in 1891), dau. of Daniel and Mary McEachern.
	viii.	ROSE V. [Rosie], b. c1863 (17 in 1880), res. in MA.
	xi.	LILLIAN I., b. c1866 (14 in 1880; "Sally," 4, in 1870).
	xii.	ARONA [?], b. Webster Pltn 10 July 1870, d. there 25 Mar. 1893, 22y 5m 18d. Female.

874. ABIGAIL[8] 1823-1901 [387 Joseph[7] and Betsey Downs] was born at Steuben 7 Sept. 1823, died at Springfield 4 Mar. 1901, 78y 8m 28d; married first ISAAC WORCESTER JR., born at Columbia ME in 1815, died at Springfield 11 Jan. 1861, 44y 7m 10d (GS), son of Isaac and Lydia (Tucker) Worcester; married second 16 Mar. 1867 DANIEL GOULD (records of descendant Sharon Cimpher and of Leonard F. Tibbetts; Springfield VRs).

Isaac Worcester was a farmer at Webster Plantation and Springfield. Burials are at Springfield.

Children (**Worcester**):

i.   MARY, b. in 1842, d.y.
ii.   FREEMAN, b. Webster Pltn in 1843, d. Springfield 2
      July 1895, 52y; m. 24 Jan. 1867 MARY ANN (DOWNS)
      Tucker, b. Steuben 18 Oct. 1833, d. Springfield 6
      Mar. 1908, 75y 4m 19d, dau. of Ichabod and Susan
      (Worcester) Downs and widow of Seward Tucker, who
      had d. in the army 14 Aug. 1864 without ch.
iii. ROXIE, b. c1844 (16 in 1860), m. Webster Pltn 4 July
      1860 GEORGE TUCKER, son of Isaac Tucker.
iv.   ANN M., b. c1846 (14 in 1860), d. Springfield 25 Aug.
      1872, 26y 11m 8d (GS).
v.   ELI LEIGHTON, b. c1848 (12 in 1860); m. Springfield
      2 Sept. 1871 CELESTIA BOYINGTON of Prentiss.
vi.   ISAAC, b. c1850, d.y.
vii. ALBERT, b. c1851 (9 in 1860); m. Springfield 31 Mar.
      1872 MELVINA DAVIS.
viii. SEWELL, b. c1854 (6 in 1860).
ix.   ABIGAIL ELLINE, b. Springfield 7 Aug. 1856, d. there
      12 Apr. 1943, 86y 8m 5d; m. there int. 23 June 1874
      JOHN C. LYONS.
x.   FRANKLIN, b. c1859 (1 in 1860).

875.   LEONARD STROUT[8] 1825-1886 [387 Joseph[7] and Betsey
Downs] was born at Steuben 27 Oct. 1825 (VRs; at Cherryfield
per pension application), died at Webster Plantation 12 May
1886; married first 26 Feb. 1852 CORDELIA SCAMMON, born at
Franklin ME 2 July 1833, daughter of Daniel and Lucy Wilson
(Guptill) Scammon; married second at Cherryfield 14 Aug. 1855
ELSIE PHILLIPS, born at Columbia, died at Springfield 15 Feb.
1869 (1870 per pension affidavit); married third at Hancock
ME 28 Apr. 1873 (pension file) RACHEL JOHNSON, born at Deer
Island NB about 1831, died at Springfield 8 Dec. 1896, 65y
(town and ME VRs).
   He enlisted 2 Sept. 1861 in Co. D, 11th ME Inf. Rgt., re-
enlisted 4 Jan. 1864 in SC, and was discharged 17 Feb. 1865.
His arm and elbow were shattered by gunshot at Deep Botton VA
16 Aug. 1864; he was also hospitalized for malaria and for a
rupture.
   Leonard, 60, Rachel, 44, and Benjamin, 4, were listed at
Franklin in 1880. He applied for a pension 21 Jan. 1865,
aged 43, and further on 12 Oct. 1881, aged 63 of Cherryfield.
He included affidavits stating that his wife Elsie had died
destitute and was buried by the town, and that his children
(not named) had been put out as town charges. He was of
Springfield when he died. His widow Rachel applied for a
pension 19 July 1890 and 30 Mar. 1893, naming her son Bennie
(NA MSR #43,956).

Children by Elsie:

1457. i.   STILLMAN F.[9], b. c1852 (19 in 1870).
       ii.   MARTHA E., b. Prentiss 11 Mar. 1858.
       iii. ANNA E., b. Prentiss 15 Sept. 1859.
1458. iii. FRANK H., b. Springfield 17 Nov. 1868.

Child by Rachel, born at Springfield:

1459.   iii. BENJAMIN, b. 25 Mar. 1876.

876. RACHEL[8] 1831-   [387 Joseph[7] and Betsey Downs] was
born at Steuben 2 Apr. 1831; married 4 May 1851 PARKER D.
WILLEY, born at Cherryfield 1 Oct. 1831, died there 23 May
1898, son of William G. and Mary (Davis) (Downs) Willey.
   Parker married second 4 Apr. 1877 Medora Farnsworth (town
and ME VRs; records of Vicki Jordan Smith; Cornman Ms).

Children (**Willey**), born at Cherryfield:

i.   ALMENA J., b. 2 Apr. 1854; m. 1st STILLMAN[9] LEIGHTON
       [# 1457]; m. 2nd JESSE A. BROWN [# 412].
ii.   (ADA) MINNIE, b. 3 Jan. 1858 (?16 in 1880); m.
       EVERETT[8] LEIGHTON [# 1616].
iii.   EDGAR, b. c1860, not in 1870 census.
iv.   FLORA A., b. c1861; perhaps m. ADELBERT GRANT.
v.   BENJAMIN C., b. c1866, d. 22 Nov. 1910; m. 9 Oct.
       1887 BEULAH MERRITT.
vi.   WARREN L., b. c1868 (12 in 1880, Cherryfield).
vii.   ERNEST L., b. c1869; m. 18 Oct. 1910 CARRIE JORDAN.
viii. ROSE MAY, b. 25 Apr. 1875; m. WILLIAM SCOTT.
ix.   WILLIAM (twin), b. 25 Apr., d. in Nov., 1875.

877. REBECCA S.[8] 1833-   [387 Joseph[7] and Betsey Downs]
was born at Steuben 16 Nov. 1833; married at Springfield 15
Nov. 1852 PARKER DOWNS JR. of Webster Plantation, born in
1834, son of Parker and Betsey (Smith) Downs (Cornman Ms).
   Parker had been raised by his step-father Isaac Tucker. In
1860 he and Rebecca were living at Prentiss.

Children (**Downs**), perhaps others:

i.   IRA, b. c1853 (7 in 1860).
ii.   LEONARD, b. c1856 (4 in 1860).
iii.   ELIZABETH, b. c1858 (2 in 1860).

878. FOSTER J.[8] 1835-1911 [387 Joseph[7] and Betsey Downs]
was born at Cherryfield (death record) 2 Nov. 1835, died at
Webster Plantation 12 June 1911, 75y 7m 10d; married first
ELIZABETH ----, born about 1833 (27 in 1860); married second
MARY J. STANLEY, born at Prentiss in 1850, died at Bangor ME
(hosp.; as of Prentiss) 9 Mar. 1917, daughter of Thomas and
Ruth (Spencer) Stanley--divorced; married third at Prentiss
25 Sept. 1893 MARTHA A. (EATON) Richardson, born there 18
Sept. 1850, died at Bangor 12 Feb. 1941, daughter of Isaac M.
and Lucy (Stanley) Eaton and divorced wife of Charles
Richardson (ME VRs).
   He enlisted 22 Apr. 1864 in Co. I, 11th ME Inf. Rgt. In
1860 he was listed at Tp 6 Range 3 (later Webster Plantation); in 1880 and 1890 he was living at Springfield, and in
1900 again at Webster Plantation.

Child by Elizabeth, born at Tp 6:

i.   ELIZA F.[9], b. in 1860 (1/12 in census).

Children by Mary:

ii.   IDA VIOLA, b. Webster Pltn c1873 (7 in 1880);
       m. Prentiss 18 Dec. 1895 JAMES COFFEY, b. in
       York Co. NB c1853 (42 in 1895), res. Drew
       Pltn, son of James and Catherine (Scarlet)
       Coffey; m. 2nd Caribou ME 11 May 1929 GEORGE
       E. SPARKS, b. there c1876, son of Nathan and
       Mary E. Sparks.
ii.   MATTIE E., b. Springfield c1881 (18 in 1900);
       m. 1st Prentiss 6 Oct. 1900 GEORGE RICHARDSON
       of Springfield, b. Prentiss c1876 (24 in
       1900), son of Charles and Martha (Eaton)
       Richardson; m. 2nd Prentiss 29 Aug. 1926
       JAMES T. JIPSON, b. Burlington ME c1888, son
       of Wesley and Nancy (Davis) Jipson.

879. CURTIS[8] 1829-1895 [389 Ebenezer[7] and Drusilla Wilson]
was born at Steuben 9 June 1829 (9 Apr. 1819, GS), died there
28 May 1895, 65y 11m; married at Franklin ME 28 Aug. 1851
SARAH G. [Sally] SCAMMON, born there 26 Aug. 1835, died at
Steuben 7 June 1928, 92y 9m 11d, daughter of Daniel and Lucy
Wilson (Guptill) Scammon (town VRs; Cornman Ms; records of
Jeannette Leighton). Burials are in Unionville Cemetery,
Steuben.

Children, born at Steuben:

         i.   ARICZENE, b. 20 Oct. 1853, d. 18 Dec. 1861.
1460.   ii.   MILFORD, b. 2 Feb. 1855.
         iii. DANIEL LIVINGSTON, b. 7 Feb. 1857, d. Union-
               ville 21 Apr. 1891.
         iv.   EBENEZER LIVINGSTON (twin), b. 7 Feb. 1857,
               res. Minneapolis MN; unm.
1461.   v.   HOLLIS J., b. 4 Apr. 1859.
         vi.   VONALMER, b. 14 June 1861, d. 9 Oct. 1863.
         vii. MINNIE M., b. 19 June 1872, d. 30 Aug. 1873.
1462.   viii. ALFRED J., b. 29 Nov. 1874.

880. GREEN[8] 1834-1896 [389 Ebenezer[7] and Drusilla Wilson]
was born at Steuben 15 Feb. 1834, died there 10 Dec. 1896,
65y 10m; married there 7 Aug. 1856 ARETHUSA T. FARNSWORTH,
born at Jonesboro ME 26 Aug. 1835, daughter of Joshua and
Louise (Worcester) Farnsworth (town and ME VRs).
     He served in Co. C, 20th ME Inf. Rgt., and volunteered for
an additional year in the 1st ME Sharpshooters Rgt.
     A lumberman, he lived at Columbia ME in 1870, and then at
Cherryfield in 1880 and 1890. His widow was living at Steuben in 1900 with Morris and Reuben Higgins. Burials are in
Unionville Cemetery.

Children:

1463.   i.   CHARLES S.[9], b. 28 June 1857.
1464.   ii.   HERVEY H., b. Columbia 11 June 1858.
1465.   iii. GEORGE H., b. 31 Mar. 1862.
         iii. WILLIS M., b. Columbia 24 Apr. 1864.
         v.   LUCY C., b. c1868, d. Steuben 1 Apr. 1891,
               22y 11m 17d (Machias Union).

        vi.   KITTY, b. 14 Apr. 1868; m. GEORGE HIGGINS.
              Ch. Reuben b. 26 Oct. 1881.
1466.   vii. MINNIE C., b. Steuben 17 Sept. 1872; m.
              CHARLES W. TRACY.

881. IVORY MARK[8] 1841-1923 [389 Ebenezer[7] and Drusilla
Wilson] was born at Steuben 25 Oct. 1841, died there 4 Aug.
1923; married 28 Oct. 1865 ELIZA-ANN (TRACY) Small, born at
Cherryfield 7 Dec. 1838, died at Steuben 22 Aug. 1916, 77y 8m
15d, daughter of Eli and Diadama (Smith) Tracy and widow of
Warren Small (town VRs; records of Jeannette Leighton and
Arlene Skehan; Cornman Ms).
He was a lumberman. In 1870 his household included his
step-daughter Lucy A. Small, 14. Burials are in Unionville
Cemetery, Steuben.

Children, born at Unionville (Steuben):

        i.   LILLIAN[9], b. 15 Sept. 1868; m. WILLIAM[9]
              LEIGHTON [# 1589].
1467.   ii.   ELMER E., b. 4 May 1870.
1467a. iii. EUDORA [Dora], b. 26 Jan. 1874; m. DAVID C.
              SMITH.
        iv.   MINNIE MAUD, b. 13 Mar. 1876, d. Milbridge 13
              Nov. 1938; m. 1st Sullivan 23 May 1895 EDWARD
              RAYMOND NOYES, b. Cutler 30 Dec. 1873, res.
              Winter Harbor, son of Edward and Mary A.
              (Ward) Noyes (Johnson, Sullivan and Sorrento,
              121; Noyes Gen., 1:30)--div.; m. 2nd Winter
              Harbor 22 Dec. 1908 HAROLD SUMNER, b. Goulds-
              boro c1875, son of Benjamin F. and Sarah
              Sumner. Ch. Darrell Leighton Noyes b.
              Steuben 22 Oct. 1896; m. Mary Welch of Phila-
              delphia. Edward Noyes m. 2nd Flora Davis of
              Rockport ME.
        v.   MABEL PARKER, b. 20 Mar. 1879, d. Bangor ME 19
              Mar. 1956; m. Cherryfield 22 Aug. 1914 HER-
              BERT MONAGHAN, b. Ellsworth ME 6 July 1881,
              d. Bangor 12 Jan. 1976, son of Charles and
              Catherine (Doyle) Monaghan.

882. MELISSA[8] 1843-1897 [389 Ebenezer[7] and Drusilla Wil-
son] was born at Steuben 7 Apr. 1843, died at Bangor 4 July
1897; married at Steuben 12 July 1860 FOSTER JACOB TRACY,
born at Cherryfield 9 Apr. 1840, died at Sherman ME 22 Oct.
1909, 70y 6m 13d, son of Eli and Diadama (Smith) Tracy (town
and ME VRs; Daniel, Thomas Rogers, 320, 375; records of
Arlene Skehan; Cornman Ms).

Children (Tracy):

i.   ROSE, b. 14 Oct. 1861; m. HUGH LOVE of St. Stephen
       NB.
ii.   ALICE, b. 30 Aug. 1864; m. THEODORE STONE.
iii.   VELORA, b. 3 Feb. 1867, d. 12 Dec. 1955; m. FRANK
       YORKSIE.
iv.   MADISON, b. 24 July 1869; m. HELEN STONE.
v.   MAUD, b. 15 Nov. 1871; m. WILLIAM COREY.

vi.   ALFRED LESLIE, b. St. Stephen NB 8 Nov. 1875, d.
       Bangor ME 28 Jan. 1960; m. Staceyville Pltn ME 25
       Dec. 1893 CARRIE VESTA ARCHER, b. Cherryfield ME 5
       Mar. 1872, d$_8$ there 10 Mar. 1910, dau. of Charles H.
       and Corrilla^8 (Leighton) Archer [# 884].
vii.   BURDETTE, b. 7 Nov. 1878, d. 18 Aug. 1959; m. ----
       TRACY.
viii. THEODORE, b. 19 July 1882, d.y.

883. ELBRIDGE S.^{8} 1844-1922 [389 Ebenezer^7 and Drusilla
Wilson] was born at Steuben 15 Dec. 1844, died at Bangor ME
in 1922, 75y; married at Steuben 6 Dec. 1874 EVESTA [Vesta]
TUCKER, born there 19 Sept. 1856, died at Sullivan ME 5 Apr.
1932, 74y 6m 16d, daughter of Abram and Jerusha (Grant)
Tucker (town and ME VRs; Cornman Ms; records of Jeannette
Leighton). Burials are in Unionville.
    From 1903 on he was a patient at the state mental hospital.
He had been a lumberman.

Children, born at Steuben:

1468. i.   DRUSILLA^9, b. 25 Apr. 1876; m. MATTHEW
             MITCHELL and JOHN O'BRIEN.
1469. ii.   GERTRUDE, b. 9 Dec. 1878; m. WILFRED H.
             GORDON.
1470. iii. EVERETT T., b. 6 June 1881.
       iv.   VIDA MOORE, b. 25 Nov. 1886.
1471. v.   ALVIN W., b. 2 Aug. 1888.
1472. vi.   RALPH CLIFTON, b. 29 Mar. 1895.
1473. vii. JUSTIN S., b. 23 Apr. 1897.

884. CORRILLA^8 1845-1910 [389 Ebenezer^7 and Drusilla Wil-
son] was born at Steuben in 1845, died there 7 Mar. 1910, 64y
4m 23d; married 18 Nov. 1867 CHARLES HENRY ARCHER, born at
Steuben 14 Oct. 1848, died at Cherryfield 23 Dec. 1927, 79y
2m 9d, son of Eliakim and Jane (Barfield) Archer (town and ME
VRs; Cornman Ms). Her name was also spelled Corella and Car-
rella.

Children (**Archer**), born at Cherryfield:

i.   CARRIE VESTA, b. 5 Mar. 1872; m. ALFRED LESLIE TRACY
       [# 882].
ii.   FRANCES [Fannie] (twin), b. 5 Mar. 1872, d. 27 Jan.
       1954; m. ELMER E. SAWYER, b. 25 Feb. 1863, d. Mil-
       bridge ME 2 Jan. 1917, son of Joseph W. and Mary
       Jane (Wallace) Sawyer.
iii.   FRANK, drowned Friendship ME 4 July 1903.
iv.   BERTHA, b. c1879; m. in CA 31 Dec. 1906 THOMAS N.
       WILSON of Worcester MA.

885. SAMUEL^8 1810-   [390 Thomas^7 and Dorothy Stewart]
was born at Falmouth about 1810 (50 in 1860); married ELIZA-
BETH JOHNSON, born at Falmouth about 1816 (34 in 1850), died
at Cumberland 3 Oct. 1858, 42y (GS, Methodist Churchyard,
West Cumberland; town VRs; Cornman Ms).
    In 1850, they were living in his father's Falmouth house-
hold; in 1860 they were listed at Cumberland.

He enlisted in Oct. 1861 in Co. B, 12th ME Inf. Rgt, re-
enlisted in Co. G., 15th ME Rgt., and was discharged in Oct.
1866.

Children:

    i.   CHARLES HENRY[9], b. Falmouth 28 Apr. 1838, d.
            Portland (as widower) 12 Mar. 1913; perhaps
            m. Westbrook int. 19 Apr. 1867 LOUISA G.
            SCHWARTZ (but unm. in Cornman Ms). He served
            in Co. G, 15th ME Inf. Rgt., 1861-1863. He
            was a Portland wood-dealer. [See # 1572]
    ii.   GEORGE LYMAN, not in 1850 or 1860 censuses.
    iii. SARAH ANN, not in 1850 or 1860 censuses.
    iv.   SUSAN, not in 1850 or 1860 censuses.
    v.   MARY ELIZABETH, b. c1844 (6 in 1850); m. Wind-
            ham 6 Mar. 1862 SAMUEL LIBBY, b. 2 Mar. 1838,
            son of James and Mary (Libby) Libby (Libby
            Family, 459). Only ch. Louisa May b. Cumber-
            land 23 Jan. 1863.
1474. vi.   ROSELLA, b. Cumberland 26 Oct. 1854; m. FRANK
            D. HIGGINS.

886.   JAMES[8] 1815-1875 [392 Daniel[7] and Hannah Cole] was
born at Falmouth 19 Apr. 1815, died at Portland 29 Apr. 1875,
60y; married at Falmouth 9 Mar. 1849 MARIA[8] LEIGHTON, born
there 13 Oct. 1825, died at Eastport ME 2 Jan. 1905, daughter
of George and Abigail (Mayberry) Leighton [# 427] (town and
ME VRs; records of Toni Packard). Burials are in Evergreen
Cemetery.
   In 1850 he was a Falmouth shoemaker. In 1860 he and his
family were included in Robert and Susan Dyer's household; he
was then a merchant.

Children, born at Falmouth:

    i.   MARY JANE[9], b. 2 June 1847, d. 29 Oct. 1869;
            m. EDWARD BURNELL. Ch. Jennie Maria b. in
            June 1869, d. 4 May 1911; m. Ramsey Crook.
1475. ii.   HUBBARD CHANDLER, b. 19 Feb. 1849.
    iii. ALONZO, b. 8 Dec. 1851, d. Eastport 17 May
            1917, 65y 5m (VR); m. Boston 23 Feb. 1888
            JULIA EVELYN SMITH, b. Eastport 19 Oct. 1862,
            d. there 17 July 1940, dau. of Samuel Coombs
            and Sarah Jane (Dockerly) Smith. No ch. He
            was a tailor at Eastport in 1900, but had
            previously lived at Boston.

887.   (ELIZABETH) NANCY[8] 1816-1892 [392 Daniel[7] and Hannah
Cole] was born at Falmouth 23 June 1816, died there 16 Jan.
1892, 75y 6m 23d; married there 5 Jan. 1839 LEONARD WILSON,
born 5 May 1817, died at Cumberland 28 Oct. 1901, son of
Nathaniel and Elizabeth (Baker) Wilson (town and ME VRs;
Cornman Ms). Burials are in the Methodist Churchyard, West
Falmouth.
   In 1860 Nancy and her family were living at Falmouth with
her parents, but without Leonard present.

Children (**Wilson**), born at Falmouth:

i.   DANIEL, b. 25 May 1839; m. ABIGAIL ANN[9] LEIGHTON
      [# 961].
ii.   ALTHEA S., b. 3 Jan. 1841, d. 15 Nov. 1928; m. 11
      Sept. 1860 GEORGE L. MARSTON, b. 2 Nov. 1836,
      son of Elias P. and Maria[8] (Leighton) Marston
      [# 980].
iii. NATHANIEL J., b. 16 Mar. 1843, d. 24 Sept. 1919; m.
      6 Apr. 1867 MARGARET ANN PIERCE, b. 12 Aug. 1851,
      d. 19 Oct. 1918.
iv.   HANNAH ELIZABETH, b. 2 June 1846, d. 23 May 1927; m.
      Cumberland 17 Jan. 1866 ROYAL LINCOLN ABBOTT, b. 2
      May 1842, d. 21 Jan. 1917.

888.   SARAH ELIZABETH[8] 1819-1871 [392 Daniel[7] and Hannah
Cole] was born at Falmouth 4 Mar. 1819, died there 16 Nov.
1871; married there 9 Nov. 1837 CHARLES W. WINSLOW, born
there 18 Apr. 1817, died there 5 Aug. 1880 (records of Nellie
Smith Leighton: Cornman Ms; Falmouth VRs).

Children (**Winslow**), born at Falmouth:

i.   JASON L., b. 13 Feb. 1838, d. 17 Nov. 1869; m. HANNAH
      L. SNELL, b. 2 Sept. 1840, d. 4 Sept. 1868, dau. of
      Joseph Hutchinson and Sarah (Barton) Snell.
ii.   MARY ELLEN, b. 11 Jan. 1840, d. 15 Nov. 1928; m. 28
      Apr. 1860 WILLIAM H. SNELL, b. 18 Mar. 1836, d. 27
      Mar. 1925, brother of Hannah.
iii. SARAH EMELINE, b. 13 Feb. 1842, d. 13 Feb. 1913; m.
      13 Sept. 1862 ALBERT S. LEGROW, b. 24 Feb. 1840, d.
      10 Feb. 1899.
iv.   ADELAIDE V., b. 10 Aug. 1845, d. 3 July 1868; unm.
v.   LOIS H., b. 10 Aug. 1847, d. 17 Sept. 1871; unm.
vi.   CHARLES E., b. 24 Feb. 1849, d. Falmouth 16 Jan.
      1893; m. 4 Jan. 1873 ELLA F. NEWTON, b. 5 Sept.
      1856, d. in Sept. 1925.
vii. SEWELL PRINCE, b. 11 Feb. 1854, d. 18 Sept. 1916; m.
      18 Oct. 1882 LULU SYMONDS, b. 12 Feb. 1860, d. 19
      Feb. 1897.
viii. WALTER HERBERT, b. 6 Feb. 1856, d. 1 May 1915; m. 12
      Oct. 1881 MARY C. DRESSER, b. in Oct. 1854.
ix.   WILLIAM EVERETT, b. 3 Mar. 1859; m. 10 Aug. 1881
      DORCAS E. MERRILL, b. 15 Jan. 1859, dau. of Fenrick
      and Julia A (Hall) Merrill.
x.   LEON MUNROE, b. 9 Feb. 1866; m. 27 Feb. 1887 MINNIE
      RICHARDS, b. 22 Apr. 1866.

889.   ROBERT[8] 1821-1893 [392 Daniel[7] and Hannah Cole] was
born at Falmouth 10 Mar. 1821, died there 15 May 1893, 72y
2m; married there 8 Dec. 1847 LUCY G. LEIGHTON, born there
29 June 1827, died there 28 Dec. 1902, daughter of Jedediah
and Mary (Marston) (Noyes) Leighton [# 139] (Falmouth and ME
VRs; Cornman Ms). Burials are in the Methodist Churchyard,
West Falmouth.
     He was a farmer. In 1870 his parents were living in his
Falmouth household. In 1900 his widow Lucy lived with her
son James.

Children, born at Falmouth:

  i. CELIA[9], b. 22 Sept. 1848, d. 4 Apr. 1850 (GS).
  ii. ROBERT WILLIS, b. 23 Aug. 1851, d. 15 Mar.
    1854, 2y 10m 20d (GS).
  iii. WILLIE, b. 9 Mar. 1854, d. 15 Sept. 1857,
    3y 6m 9d (GS).
  iv. MARY ELLA, b. 13 Jan. 1856, d. Portland 21 May
    1920, 64y 4m 8d (VRs); m. Falmouth 13 Jan.
    1874 WILLIAM WALLACE LIBBY, b. Gray ME 28
    Mar. 1846, d. Falmouth 18 Jan. 1918, 71y 7m
    20d, son of Alfred and Mary W. (Abbott) Libby
    (Libby Family, 191). No ch.
  v. JAMES MONROE, b. 3 Oct. 1860, d. Cumberland
    22 Nov. 1930; m. Portland 2 July 1885 ADDIE
    MAY WINSLOW, b. 4 Aug. 1862, dau. of Sumner
    and Mary S. (Knight) Winslow. No ch.
    The old family homestead on Hurricane Rd.,
    with its house built about 1810, was sold by
    the widow Addie about 1966, when she was aged
    104.

890. **HANNAH**[8] 1829-1904 [392 Daniel[7] and Hannah Cole] was born at Falmouth 7 July 1829, died there 8 July 1904; married there 5 Apr. 1849 EDWIN MORRILL, born at Cumberland 29 Aug. 1827, died 16 Mar. 1909, son of Josiah and Sarah Morrill (Falmouth VRs; Cornman Ms).

Children (**Morrill**), born at Falmouth:

  i. ALPHONZO B., b. 19 Sept. 1849, d. in Aug. 1875; unm.
  ii. THEODORE, b. 19 Dec. 1850, d. 7 July 1911; m. 23 Jan.
    1879 LIZZIE M. PARKER, b. 22 Feb. 1860, d. in July
    1951.
  iii. EMMA, b. 4 July 1853, d. 23 Mar. 1872; unm.
  iv. IRVING, b. 27 Mar. 1855; m. 7 Mar. 1881 ANNIE E.
    BLACK, b. 19 May 1866.

891. **DANIEL EDWIN**[8] 1831-1899 [392 Daniel[7] and Hannah Cole] was born at Falmouth 22 Jan. 1831, died there 28 Feb. 1899; married 7 Dec. 1865 REBECCA JANE[9] LEIGHTON, born 17 Feb. 1847, died 3 Oct. 1925 (GS), daughter of Joseph Mayberry and Maria (Sawyer) Leighton [# 961] (Falmouth VRs). Burials are in the Methodist Churchyard, West Falmouth. In 1900, widow Rebecca was living with her daughter.

Child, born at Falmouth:

1476. i. ANNIE MARIA[9], b. 15 Dec. 1870; m. WILLIAM H.
    PEARSON.

892. **ABIGAIL**[8] 1833-1881 [392 Daniel[7] and Hannah Cole] was born at Falmouth 26 Nov. 1833, died at Portland 3 Dec. 1881; married 17 Apr. 1854 JOHN MUNROE, born at Tarsi, Scotland, 17 Apr. 1816, died at Portland 10 June 1865 (Cornman Ms; Portland and Falmouth VRs).

Children (**Munroe**), born at Falmouth:

i.   JOHN G., b. 13 Nov. 1855; m. 19 Nov. 1889 HELEN
       ISABEL BAILEY, b. 11 Sept. 1862.
ii.   ROBERT EDWIN, b. 18 June 1858.
iii.   ABBIE FLORENCE, b. 8 Sept. 1860.

893. AURELIA[8] 1819-1884 [393 Robert[7] and Joanna Prince]
was born at Deering ME 8 Sept. 1819, died there 19 Jan. 1884;
married first at Westbrook 24 Mar. 1842 REUBEN G. BRACKETT,
born there 2 Mar. 1820, son of Reuben and Elizabeth (Morrill)
Brackett (Herbert I. Brackett, Brackett Genealogy [Washington
DC, 1907], 166); married second at Deering 4 July 1853
CHARLES LEWIS KNIGHT, born at Westbrook 24 Oct. 1824, died at
Deering 22 Jan. 1897, son of Abner and Eunice (Huston) Knight
(town VRs; Cornman Ms).
    Her name was Arvilla on the marriage record, Orilla on the
intentions.

Child (**Brackett**):

i.   ELLEN H., b. 6 May 1843, res. Los Angeles; m. 1 Jan.
       1863 ALEXANDER COBB.

Children (**Knight**):

ii.   JOHN F., b. 8 Feb. 1855; m. MARY L. ROBERTS.
iii.   WILLIAM EDGAR, b. 24 Mar. 1858; m. 4 Nov. 1887 ELLEN
       DORCAS BAKER.
iv.   MARY E., b. 11 Oct. 1864; m. 2 Jan. 1895 JAMES F
       ALLEN, b. Falmouth 19 Sept. 1866, son of William and
       Emily F. (Libby) Allen.

894. NELSON[8] 1824-1894 [393 Robert[7] and Joanna Prince] was
born at Falmouth 3 Oct. 1824, died at Deering (Portland) 4
Feb. 1894, 69y; married first at Wolfeboro NH 2 July 1849
MARY E. FROST, born there 2 Nov. 1826, died at Westbrook 2
Mar. 1868, 41y 4m; married second at Westbrook 24 Oct. 1870
ANNIE M. BLADES (town VRs; Cornman Ms). Burials are in Evergreen Cemetery.
    In 1850 he was a butcher at Westbrook; his household then
included Lydia Frost, 16. Deering was set off from Falmouth
and Westbrook in 1871, but merged into Portland in 1889.

Children by Mary, born at Westbrook:

1477. i.   NELSON[9], b. 10 Dec. 1849.
1478. ii.   ARLESTA, b. 18 May 1851.
       iii.   ELLEN ROSALIE, b. 7 Oct. 1852; m. 1st NATHAN-
              IEL HARNDEN; m. 2nd Standish ME 27 Nov. 1878
              WILLIAM D. STEVENS, b. c1845, son of Daniel
              and Ann Stevens. Ch. Blanch May Harnden
              b. c1875.
       iv.   G.F. KING, b. 2 Sept. 1861, d. 12 May 1862.

Child by Annie:

       v.   MARY E., b. 9 Mar. 1873, d. 7 Nov. 1879, 6y.

895. LYDIA[8] 1826-   [393 Robert[7] and Joanna Prince] was
born at Westbrook 19 May 1826, lived at Biddeford ME; married
first 25 June 1842 JOHN M. DROWN, born in VT about 1823; married second JOSEPH PORTER (Cornman Ms). In 1850 the Drown
household was listed at Portland.

Children (**Drown**):

i.   WASHINGTON, b. c1847 (3 in 1850).
ii.   HARRIET GENEVIEVE, b. c1848 (2 in 1850); m. ----
      ALLEN.
iii. EMMA.
iv.   FRANK.

896. JOHN[8] 1816-1896 [395 Benjamin[7] and Abigail Brown] was
born at Steuben 18 Sept. 1816, died at Milbridge 10 Sept.
1896, 79y 11m 18d (VRs; GS, 79y 10m 8d); married at Harrington 5 Nov. 1840 SUSAN BROWN, born there 3 Feb. 1821, died at
Milbridge 16 May 1892, 71y 3m 13d, daughter of Simeon and
Isabella (Strout) Brown (town VRs). Burials are in a family
lot in the Beaver Brook section.
Capt. John lived in the part of Harrington called Cherryfield Harbor, which in 1848 was set off and organized as the
town of Milbridge.
He had a farm, was a master mariner, and owned shares in
several coastal ships. The brig J. Leighton, for one, was
owned by John, his sons, his father-in-law and others, and
sailed under his son William H. in 1870, and under John's
command in 1875.

Children, born at Milbridge:

       i.   GEORGE BROWN[9], b. 25 Feb. 1842, d. Milbridge
              13 Dec. 1869; m. there 17 May 1868 ARALINDA
              DOUGLAS, b. there 11 July 1840, d. there 6
              Nov. 1907, dau. of (Alfred) Thomas and Jane
              (Smallage) (Leighton) Douglas [# 398]. No
              ch.
1479. ii.   WARREN WALLACE, b. 14 Jan. 1845.
1480. iii.   WILLIAM HENRY, b. 7 June 1847.
       iv.   EUDORA E., b. 18 Dec. 1851, d. 15 June 1854,
              2y 5m 27d (GS).
       vi.   FRANCIS, b. 7 June 1854, d. Milbridge 9 July
              1903, 49y 1m 2d; m. there int. 7 July 1880
              LAURA E. WHITTAKER, b. 20 Sept. 1858,
              dau. of Elisha and Elizabeth (Douglas)
              Whittaker. Ch. SUSAN F[10] b. 8 July 1881,
              d. 29 Aug. 1894. Frank was a master mariner.
              Laura m. 2nd Harrington 3 Mar. 1906 Leverett
              Strout, b. c1843, d. Milbridge in July 1927,
              son of Joseph W. and Sybil (Whitten) Strout.
       vii.   EVERETT NATHAN, b. 31 May 1858, d. Milbridge
              28 June 1941, 83y 1m 27d; m. Harrington (as
              Nathan E.) 29 Aug. 1896 LAURA J. (STROUT)
              Leighton, b. Milbridge 23 Mar. 1863, d. there
              25 May 1906, dau. of Ezra and Sarah[8]
              (Leighton) Strout [# 1070] and widow of NAPO-
              LEON[8] LEIGHTON [# 419]. Everett had no ch.
1481. viii. CLARA, b. 24 May 1863; m. EDWARD M. STANLEY.

897. SYBIL S.[8] 1826-1899 [397 James[7] and Mary Strout] was
born at Milbridge 4 Feb. 1826, died there 17 Apr. 1899; married at Harrington 28 Sept. 1845 Capt. WILLIAM H. RICH, born
7 Sept. 1825, lost at sea 12 May 1868, son of Samuel and Hannah (Brown) Rich. Rich died while master of the brig M. E.
Miller (records of Margaret Colton; Cornman Ms; town VRs).
Burials are in Evergreen Cemetery, Milbridge.

Children (**Rich**), born at Milbridge:

i.   FRED W., b 25 Feb. 1847, d. Havana, Cuba, 28 Aug.
        1874; m. GEORGIANNA [Georgie] FOSTER, b. 11 Mar.
        1857, d. Milbridge 22 Oct. 1921, dau. of James and
        Elizabeth (Ray) Foster.
ii.   FRANCIS F., b. 15 July 1848, d. 24 June 1851.
iii.   HELEN GEORGIA [Nellie], b. 22 Jan. 1852, d. Milbridge
        in 1935; m. JASON[8] LEIGHTON [# 1069].
iv.   JAMES S., b. 21 July 1854, lost at sea near Havana 28
        Aug. 1874; unm.
v.   WILLIAM H., b. 3 Aug. 1862, d. Milbridge 7 June 1954;
        m. 1st IZELLE CAMPBELL; m. 2nd NELLIE M. SAWYER,
        dau. of William R. and Lucy A (Gay) Sawyer; m. 3rd
        CAROLINE KNOWLES, b. 10 Dec. 1880, d. Milbridge 31
        May 1947. No ch.
vi.   FRANK B., b. 6 Apr. 1867, d. 23 Oct. 1947; unm. Res.
        Everett, MA.

898. DOLLY G.[8] 1828-1883 [397 James[7] and Mary Strout] was
born at Milbridge in 1828, died there 7 Oct. 1883 (GS); mar-
ried there 5 Apr. 1849 JOHN THORNDIKE WALLACE, born there 18
Oct. 1828, died there 14 Mar. 1889, 60y 4m 23d (GS), son of
John T. and Lucy A (Upton) Wallace (Milbridge VRs; Cornman
Ms; records of Margaret Colton). Burials are in Evergreen
Cemetery. Wallace married second Dorcas (Field) Corvalko.

Children (**Wallace**), born at Milbridge:

i.   EFFIE J., b. 4 Nov. 1850, d. Milbridge 9 Dec. 1935;
        m. there 5 Nov. 1879 FRANCIS W. [Frank] SAWYER, b.
        10 June 1853, d. there 14 Dec. 1921.
ii.   EDMUND U., b. c1853; unm.
iii.   FOSTER E., b. 2 Oct. 1854, d. Milbridge 5 Feb. 1904;
        m. 12 Jan. 1880 ADELAIDE S. [Addie] ROBERTS, b. 28
        June 1855, dau. of Sylvester and Joanna (Hutchings)
        Roberts of Milbridge.
iv.   AUGUSTUS H., b. c1856, d. Bar Harbor 1930 (GS); m.
        Milbridge 24 Oct. 1880 HELEN C. SAWYER, b. in NC in
        1856, d. in 1905 (GS), dau. of Franklin and Susan C.
        (Wood) Sawyer.
v.   (MARY) LETITIA, b. 21 Apr. 1858, d. Milbridge 1 June
        1924 (GS, Letitia E.); m. ALVIN E. DRESSER, b. 31
        Mar. 1857, d. there 5 Nov. 1935.
vi.   ELMER E., b. in 1860; unm.
vii.   HARRIET B., b. in 1862, d. in 1932 (GS); m. 17 Aug.
        1886 HENRY H. GRAY, b. in 1853, d. in 1935 (GS).
viii.   ALBION K. P., b. c1863, d. Milbridge in 1945 (GS); m.
        6 Jan. 1887 IDA M. SMITH, b. in 1865.
ix.   ADELBERT, b. c1865; m. 20 Dec. 1887 MARY MERRITT.
x.   JOHN T., b. in 1868, d. Milbridge 5 Mar. 1939; unm.

899. AMOS G.[8] 1829-1869 [397 James[7] and Mary Strout] was
born at Milbridge in 1829, died there 26 June 1869 (Machias
Union); married there 15 Jan. 1856 MARY NORTON, born about
1839 (21 in 1860, 32 in 1870), daughter of Barnabas and Abigail (Colson) Norton.
    He was a sailor. In 1860 he, Mary and his mother-in-law
Abigail were living at Milbridge with Amaziah Small; in 1870
widow Mary and her son were in the Elbridge household. She
was called Mary Sprague and Norton by Julia Cornman; she may
have married second a man named Sprague.

    Child, born at Milbridge:

    i.   AMOS SPRAGUE[9], b. c1861 (9 in 1870). Julia
          Cornman wrote that he res. Bangor and had ch.
          JAMES[10] who went west.

900. MARTHA U.[8] 1834-   [397 James[7] and Mary Strout] was
born at Milbridge in 1834; married there 8 Aug. 1855 AMAZIAH
R. SMALL, born 13 Dec. 1829, died at Milbridge 1 Nov. 1898,
son of James and Priscilla (Worcester) Small (Underhill,
Small Desc., 2:178; Milbridge and ME VRs; records of Margaret
Colton). Burials are in Evergreen Cemetery. In 1870, her
mother was living in their household.

    Children (**Small**), born at Milbridge:

    i.   PRISCILLA MARY [Prissie], b. 8 May 1859, d. Hartford
          CT in Mar. 1935; m. Columbia Falls 28 Sept. 1881
          ALBERT RUFUS WALLACE, b. 12 Apr. 1855, d. Milbridge
          16 May 1896 (GS), son of Samuel Clark and Harriet
          (Sanborn) Wallace.
    ii.   FANNIE M., b. 22 Nov. 1860, d. 10 Dec. 1881, 21y 18d;
          unm.
    iii. EDWARD D., b. 26 Mar. 1863, d. Hartford CT 27 Mar.
          1926; m. 1st IDA PARKER, d. Milbridge 24 June 1895;
          m. 2nd Boston c1896 MARGARET [Nellie] MARSHALL, b.
          Milbridge 27 Oct. 1879, d. there 25 Apr. 1970,
          dau. of James and Ellen (Whelan) Marshall.

901. LUCY H.[8] 1824-   [398 Robert[7] and Jane Smallage]
was born at Milbridge in 1824; married first 8 Mar. 1845
COURTNEY BABBAGE, born at Swans Island ME about 1823 (27 in
1850), son of Courtney and Mercy (Joyce) Babbage or Babbidge;
married second at Charlestown MA ---- SMITH (Cornman Ms).
    In 1850 the Babbage household was at Milbridge, where
Courtney was a ships' carpenter.

    Children (**Babbage**), born at Milbridge:

    i.   CHARLES M., b. c1846 (4 in 1850).
    ii.   ELIZA A , b. c1848 (2 in 1850).

902. LORENA[8] 1825-1911 [400 Otis[7] and Elizabeth Seaver]
was born at Milbridge 6 Aug. 1825, died at Columbia Falls ME
9 May 1911, 85y 5m 16d; married at Columbia 27 Nov. 1846 EPH-
RAIM CHAMBERLAIN PINEO, born in NH in 1816, died at Columbia

Falls 31 Jan. 1897, 80y 1m 3d, son of Gamaliel and Charlotte
D. (Chamberlain) Pineo (town VRs; Cornman Ms).
Their sons Benjamin and James dropped the surname Pineo,
and called themselves Leighton.

Children (**Pineo**), born at Columbia:

i.   BENJAMIN LEIGHTON, b. in 1848 (11 in 1860); m. LIDA
      TABBUTT.
ii.   OTIS E., b. in 1849 (10 in 1860), res. in MA; m.
      Columbia 29 May 1877 HATTIE A. WESTERN of Jonesboro.
iii. EPHRAIM R., b. c1853 (7 in 1860).
iv.   JAMES LEIGHTON, b. in 1860 (2/12 in census).

903.   LEWIS W.[8] 1826-1906 [400 Otis[7] and Elizabeth Seaver]
was born at Milbridge 13 Apr. 1826, died at Cherryfield 31
Dec. 1906, 80y 8m 18d; married at Milbridge int. 14 Apr. 1851
REBECCA JANE RANDALL, born at Harrington 6 Oct. 1832, died at
Milbridge 20 Oct. 1911, 79y 14d, daughter of Stillman and
Catherine (Dixon) Randall (records of Margaret Colton; town
and ME VRs).
He was a seaman. In 1900 Rebecca was living at Harrington
with Everett and Dora Webb.

Children, born at Milbridge:

1482. i.   BENJAMIN F.[9], b. 12 Aug. 1853.
       ii.   CORETTA [Cora], b. c1856 (14 in 1870), res.
             Milbridge in 1914; m. there 27 Dec. 1873
             LUTHER W. LOOK of Addison, b. c1852 (28 in
             1880, Harrington). Ch. Leander b. c1874,
             Charles b. c1877, Aloma b. c1879.
1483. iii. OTIS S., b. 14 Dec. 1857.
       iv.   ELDORA E. [Dora], b. in Aug. 1859, res.
             Springfield MA in 1914; m. Cherryfield 4 Feb.
             1884 EVERETT C. WEBB, b. in June 1860. Ch.
             Hervey b. Aug. 1884, Georgia M. b. Sept.
             1890.
       v.   ALICE J. [Allie], b. c1862 (18 in 1880), d. 14
             Oct. 1884, 22y; m. GILBERT H.[9] LEIGHTON
             [# 1502].
       vi.   JOSEPH L., b. in Apr. 1865 (per 1900 census),
             res. No. Andover MA in 1900 and 1915; m.
             NELLIE J. RINE, b. in MA in July 1865.
       vii. CHRISTIANA [Chrissie], b. c1867 (13 in 1880),
             d. Milbridge 30 Apr. 1886, 19y.
1484. viii. GEORGE B., b. 11 Feb. 1870.
       ix.   JOHN A (twin), b. 11 Feb. 1870, res. Mil-
             bridge in 1915; m. Ellsworth ME 14 Sept. 1901
             PEARL EDNA McPIKE, b. Topsfield ME 19 Apr.
             1883, d. Milbridge 17 May 1939, dau. of
             Richard and Amelia J. B. (Patten) McPike of
             Eden. A seaman, John had perhaps lived for
             a time in KS.
       x.   SAMUEL EDWARD IRA, b. 14 Apr. 1872, d. Trenton
             ME 11 Dec. 1943, 71y 7m 27d; m. Eden 14 Dec.
             1898 ALICE MAY BUNKER, b. there 25 Dec. 1874,
             dau. of Aaron S. and Arletta Ann (Mayo) Bunk-
             er (Moran, Bunker Gen., 1:54). Ch. (EUDORA)

ETTA^{10} b. 6 Feb. 1903; m. Bar Harbor 6 Feb.
1924 MAURICE CARLTON KING, b. there c1902,
son of George H. and Lizzie M. (Haynes) King.
ix. ADELLA M., b. c1875 (5 in 1880), d. Franklin;
m. Harrington 29 Dec. 1894 JOHN B. COOK, b.
there in 1856 (38 in 1894), son of Nathaniel
and Louisa M. (Colson) Cook. Cook was div.
from a 1st wife.

904. ROBERT S.^{8} 1833-1911 [400 Otis^7 and Elizabeth Seaver]
was born at Milbridge 3 June 1833, died there 24 July 1911,
78y; married there 12 June 1857 SOPHRONIA B. STROUT, born at
Harrington 23 Oct. 1837, died at Milbridge 6 Oct. 1912, 75y
11m 20d, daughter of James and Mehitable (Brown) Strout (town
and ME VRs; Cornman Ms). He was a mariner as well as being a
farmer.

Children, born at Milbridge:

            i.   JAMES P.^{9}, b. 8 Feb. 1859, not in 1860 census.
1485.   ii.   WILLIAM H., b. 2 Apr. 1862.
1486.   iii.   ROBERT McCLELLAN, b. 22 Dec. 1863.
1487.   iv.   EMMA FOSTINA, b. 16 Dec. 1865; m. BURTON
                 SMALL.
            v.   HATTIE GENETTE, b. 27 Dec. 1867, res. Groton
                 MA; m. Milbridge 4 Jan. 1887 JOHN A. FRYE of
                 Gardner MA
           vi.   ELIZABETH HOVEY [Lizzie], b. 18 Mar. 1872,
                 res. Gardner MA; m. Milbridge 7 Jan. 1891
                 WALTER L. WORMER of Grand Manan NB. No ch.
          vii.   MARY, b. 30 June 1875, d. 5 June 1896.
         viii.   LEMUEL JAMES (twin), b. 30 June 1875, d. Mil-
                 bridge 14 Sept. 1934; unm.
1488.   ix.   EDNA G., b. 18 Nov. 1879; m. FRANK McINERNEY

905. EZEKIEL^8 1828-   [402 John^7 and Dorcas] was born at
Cherryfield 10 Aug. 1828, died about 1870; married at Steuben
5 Nov. 1860 (Machias Union) LUCRETIA CATES, born probably at
Cutler ME in Aug. 1841, died perhaps in WA in 1905, daughter
of Ambrose and Deborah (Small) Cates (town VRs; Cornman Ms).
In 1870 Lucretia, 35, and Emma, 6, were in the household of
Alonzo and Abitha Cook; she was a servant there in 1880. She
married second at Milbridge 30 June 1886 Jacob Oliver Wilson;
they moved to Seattle.

Children:

            i.   (CLARA) EMMA^9, b. Cherryfield in 1862, d.
                 Columbia Falls 7 Jan. 1902, 39y 7m 2d; unm.
           ii.   MELVILLE, b. Columbia in 1865, d. Milbridge
                 26 Mar. 1892, 27y 2m 22d. He was a seaman.

906. MOSES^8 1831-1883 [402 John^7 and Dorcas] was born at
Cherryfield about 1831 (27 in 1860, 39 in 1870), died at
Unionville (Steuben) 10 Nov. 1883; married (ELIZABETH) JANE
MORSE, born in NB 17 Apr. 1837 (1842 per GS), died at Cherry-
field 15 Apr. 1884 (Machias Union), daughter of Asa and Han-
nah Morse (town VRs; records of Jeannette (Smith) Leighton

and Margaret Colton; Cornman Ms). Burials are in the Tracy
plot, Unionville Cemetery. He served during the Civil War
in Co. I, 13th ME Inf. Rgt.

Children, born at Unionville:

    i.   EMILY[9], b. 17 Apr. 1857, d. there 9 May 1926;
          m Cherryfield 12 Apr. 1872 ALBERT S. WILSON,
          b. there 8 Mar. 1848, d. Bangor (hosp.) 11
          Aug. 1917, son of William R. and Mary T.
          (Small) Wilson (Wilsons of Cherryfield, 12).
          Ch. Melvin b. 15 May 1874, d. 14 Oct. 1920;
          unm.
    ii.   MOSES KELLEY, b. in Jan. 1859, d. Unionville
          21 Oct. 1879, 20y 9m (Machias Union); unm.
1489. iii. WILLIAM, b. 21 May 1866.
    iv. MELVINA, b. c1877 (3 in 1880).
    v.   JEANNETTE, b. 26 Mar., d. 7 May, 1883.

907. EVERETT T.[8] 1823-1865 [403 Jacob[7] and Betsey Leigh-
ton] was born at Cherryfield about 1823 (37 in 1860), died at
Natchez MS 9 July 1864; married at Cherryfield 23 Feb. 1856
CYRENE WILLEY, born at Cherryfield 8 Dec. 1838, died there 28
Oct. 1905, daughter of Samuel and Hannah Willey. Cyrene married second at Cherryfield 10 Apr. 1871 John Campbell, who
died 5 Oct. 1914: three Campbell children (town VRs; records
of Margaret Colton).
   Everett served in Co I, 13th ME Inf. Rgt., in the Civil
War. Taken ill at Alexandria LA in May 1864, he was sent to
the hospital at Natchez by steamer and died there.
   Cyrene applied for a pension for herself and for her four
children 1 Dec. 1864 (NA-MSR #62.170). She was given administration of Everett's estate 5 July 1865 (WashCP, 21:29);
on 13 Apr. 1871 James A Milliken was appointed guardian of
the children.

Children, born at Cherryfield:

    i.   HORACE M.[9] [Hod], b. 8 May 1856, d. Cherry-
          field 7 July 1919, 62y 1m 29d; m. there 6
          Mar. 1880 (Machias Union) SUSAN M. FARNS-
          WORTH, b. Beddington ME 7 Aug. 1856 (Drisko,
          Hannah Weston, 128; Aug. 1858 in 1900
          census), d. Cherryfield 13 June 1929, dau.
          of Leonard and Nancy (Wilson) Farnsworth.
          Ch. LUCRETIA J.[10] [Cretia] b. 23 Apr.
          1881; m. 3 July 1903 GOWEN WHITTAKER, b.
          Gouldsboro c1882, son of Hiram and Ophelia
          (Fernald) Whittaker. In 1910 Horace had an
          adopted son Everett L. Crocker, 19.
    ii.   LAURA ETTA, b. 14 Apr. 1857; m. 1st Milbridge
          28 Sept. 1883 HENRY S. STEVENS; m. 2nd Har-
          rington 18 Nov. 1893 FRANK A. DORR, b Cher-
          ryfield in May 1871, son of Richard W. and
          Mary[8] (Leighton) Dorr [# 929].
    iii. ELIZABETH F. [Lizzie], b. 8 Feb. 1859; m.
          Cherryfield 23 Apr. 1874 ALFONSO WILLEY,
          b. there 27 Apr. 1853, son of Horatio Balch
          and Betsey Ann (Archer) Willey.
    iv.   JOSEPHINE ISABEL, b. 15 Mar. 1860.

908. PILLSBURY[8] 1827-1896 [403 Jacob[7] and Betsey Leighton]
was born at Cherryfield 2 July 1827, died there 18 Feb. 1896,
69y 7m 14d; married there 11 Nov. 1853 MARY C. PHINNEMORE,
born at Musquash NB 15 Dec. 1835, died at Cherryfield 4 Dec.
1920, 84y 11m, daughter of Isaac and Alice (McGouldrick)
Phinnemore or Finnemore (Cherryfield VRs; records of Margaret
Colton and Glenda Thayer). Burials are in the Pine Grove
Cemetery.
Pillsbury had a lumber business with his son Alvin. In
1870 his father Jacob, 74, lived with him. He died from a
fall on the ice; in 1900 and 1910 his widow was living with
her son Harry.

Children, born at Cherryfield:

1490. i.   CHARLES H.[9], b. in May 1858.
       ii.   MARY E., b. in 1858; m. WILLIAM BARTLETT[8]
             LEIGHTON [# 718].
       iii. LESTER J., b. c1859 (7/12 in 1860), d. while
             a young man.
1491. iv.   ALVIN PILLSBURY, b. 5 July 1862.
1492. v.   HARRY GARFIELD, b. 21 Dec. 1880.

909. FRANCIS M.[8] 1833-1900 [404 Samuel[7] and Lydia Bunker]
was born at Gouldsboro ME in July 1833 (38 in 1871); died in
MA 17 Mar. 1900; married first MARIA WOODS; married second at
Brandon VT 31 May 1872 MELISSA OLIVIA EDDY, born at Bristol
VT 15 Jan. 1838, died in 1921, daughter of Samuel and Clar-
issa (Eastman) Eddy (Ruth S. D. Eddy, Eddy Family in America
[Boston, 1930], 614). Melissa married second Col. Benjamin
Tucker (her letter--Cornman Papers).
Frank was a harness-maker. His two children by his first
wife became estranged from their father and step-mother.

Children by first wife Maria:

       i.   FRANK W.,[9] b. in 1852; res. Paris ME in 1880.
       ii.   FRED, b. in 1854, res. Lawrence MA, a bank
             cashier.

Children by second wife Melissa:

       iii. FLORA C., b. Chelsea MA 28 Nov. 1878, res. NYC
             in 1905; m. 1st 13 Feb. 1897 FRANK J. MURPHY,
             b. Boston in 1874 (23 in 1897), son of Thomas
             and Mary E. Murphy; m. 2nd Brandon VT 11 Aug.
             1905 HENRY G. SPRECKEL.
       iv.   ANNA MAUD, b. Arlington MA 10 Sept. 1879, d. 8
             Oct. 1882.

910. MELVIN[8] 1854-   [405 Daniel[7] and Abigail Joy] was
born at Cherryfield 31 July 1854, lived at Portland ME in
1921; married first at Milbridge 3 Feb. 1889 ELIZABETH JANE
[Lizzie] FRANCIS, born there about 1872 (21 in 1893), daughter of Joseph and Susan (Jordan) Francis--divorced; married
second at Cherryfield 18 July 1891 (Surry int. 6 July) (CORA)
LOUISA ANDERSON, born at Blue Hill ME 1 Dec. 1870, died at
Newton MA 6 Oct. 1954, daughter of Charles and Augusta (Clau-
son) Anderson (her obituary, Portland Press Herald 8 Oct.;

Oct.; town and ME VRs; records of Margaret Colton).
Melvin was a carpenter. In 1900 he lived at Eden (Bar Har-
bor); he moved to Portland in 1917. He had lived also at
Hancock and Orono. Lizzie married second at Bar Harbor 13
May 1893 John W. Kelley. Melvin's second wife was called
Louise C. in her obituary. Burials are in the Forest City
Cemetery, Portland.

Child by first wife Lizzie, born at Milbridge:

    i.   FRANK ELMER[9], b. 14 June 1889, res. Bangor; m.
           there 25 Apr. 1912 EDITH M. THOMAS, b.
           Lagrange ME c1887, dau. of Franklin and Clara
           (Lyshaw) Thomas.

Children by second wife Louisa:

    ii.   MILDRED ESTELLE, b. Surrey 15 Jan. 1892, res.
           Braintree MA in 1954; m. Portland 15 Sept.
           1921 ALTON S. COUSINS of Oakland, b. Portland
           c1896 (25 in 1921), son of Reuben A. and
           Grace (Saunders) Cousins.
    iii. RALPH M., b. Hancock 26 Jan. 1893, res.
           Auburndale MA in 1954.
    iv.   LESTER H., b. Hancock 2 Feb. 1894, res. Port-
           land; m. Jonesport 9 Oct. 1916 VIOLA BEAL, b.
           there c1895, dau. of Henry E. and Lottie C.
           (Gould) Beal. Lester was a druggist. Ch.
           CHARLOTTE LOUISE[10] b. Portland 24 Jan. 1923;
           m. Blue Hill 5 Apr. 1942 IRA HUNTLEY of
           Portland.

911. MERRILL[8] 1828-1914 [406 William[7] and Myriam Merritt]
was born at Cherryfield 5 Oct. 1828, died at Steuben 4 Dec.
1914, 86y 2m; married 15 July 1860 ABIGAIL F. LEIGHTON, born
1 May 1838, died before her husband, daughter of Ebenezer and
Drusilla (Wilson) Leighton [# 389] (town and ME VRs; records
of Margaret Colton and Jeanette Leighton).
He was a lumberman, 22, in 1850, in the household of his
step-father Obed Chapman. In 1880 he was a Steuben farmer.
Burials are in the Unionville Cemetery, Steuben.

Children, born at Cherryfield:

    i.   JEFFERSON[9], b. 19 May 1861, d. 29 Jan. 1865,
           3y 5m 11d.
    ii.   FRANCIS O., b. 16 Dec. 1863, d. 27 Sept. 1865,
           1y 9m 9d.
    iii. ALCORA E. [Cora], b. 23 Apr. 1867, d. Deblois
           ME 15 July 1886; m. Steuben 3 June 1885 JERE-
           MIAH TORREY, b. Beddington ME 6 Feb. 1864,
           son of Sumner and Abigail (Oakes) Torrey. No
           ch. He m. 2nd 20 Aug. 1837 Lillian McDevitt;
           one ch. (Torrey Families, 354).
1493. v.   ARVILLA E., b. 21 Jan. 1872; m. ELMER TRACY.

912. GILBERT[8] 1836-   [406 William[7] and Myriam Merritt]
was born at Cherryfield about 1836 (14 in 1850), lived at
Bangor in 1900; married at Steuben 4 July 1858 (Machias

Union) HANNAH MORSE, born 10 Apr. 1843, died at South Portland in Sept. 1928, daughter of Asa and Hannah Morse (town
and ME VRs).
He was living with his mother Miriam and stepfather Obed
Chapman in 1870. In 1880 his Cherryfield household included
a nephew Perley Morse, 5.

Children:

```
          i.    MARY ANN⁹, b. in 1859 (per 1880 census).
          ii.   TRYPHENA, d. 25 Aug. 1863, 3m.
          iii.  ALZADA A [Sadie], b. Cherryfield in Dec.
                1864, d. Portland 29 Aug. 1907, 43y; unm.
1494.     iv.   CLIFTON COFFIN, b. Cherryfield in Jan. 1866.
          v.    IRENE M., b. Cherryfield in Apr. 1868, res.
                Portland in 1914. Ch. VIOLET H. b.
                Ellsworth Falls in 1896; m. Portland 1 June
                1914 GEORGE E. CHRISTY, b. Gorham ME in 1895,
                son of George E. and Mattie J. (Taylor)
                Christy.
          vi.   NELLIE E., b. in July 1870; m. Cherryfield 2
                Dec. 1891 IRVING WEBBER of Ellsworth Falls.
1495.     vii.  FRANK, b. in May 1873.
```

913. (LYDIA) MARGARET⁸ 1835-1922 [407 James⁷ and Anna
Small] was born at Steuben 10 Sept. 1835, died there 22 Jan.
1922; married there 14 Aug. 1854 DANIEL BEAN PINKHAM, born
there 10 Dec. 1829, died there 1 Nov. 1894, 65y, son of
Richard and Elizabeth (West) Pinkham (Sinnett, Pinkham Gen.,
18; Cornman Ms; records of Margaret Colton and Leonard F.
Tibbetts; Steuben VRs).
Daniel was a seaman and then a farmer at Steuben. His
birthdate is given variously; that used above was provided in
a letter from his widow (Cornman Papers). She was listed as
Margret in 1860, and Lydia M. in 1870 and 1880.

Children (**Pinkham**), born at Steuben:

```
i.     child, b. 27 Sept. 1854, d. infant.
ii.    GLEASON W., b. 20 Feb. 1856, d. Steuben 30 Nov. 1934;
       m. there 17 Mar. 1876 ELLA RHODA BROOKE, b. 28 Aug.
       1861, dau. of Solomon and Lydia (Shaw) (Leavitt)
       Brooke.
iii.   ELIZA ANN, b. 6 Jan. 1859, d. 15 Nov. 1864.
iv.    LAURA E., b. 6 June 1861; m. CROSBY STEVENS.
v.     EUNICE O., b. 12 Dec. 1863; m. GEORGE M. SPAULDING.
vi.    SHERMAN D., b. c1868 (12 in 1880).
vii.   ARTHUR L., b. in 1870, d. 29 May 1897, 27y.
viii.  LYDIA M., b. c1873 (7 in 1880).
ix.    GEORGE A , b. 1 Dec. 1875, d. 9 Dec. 1895, 20y.
```

914. JAMES S.⁸ 1866-1938 [407 James⁷ and Lovicia Leighton]
was born at Unionville (Steuben) 26 Jan. 1866, died at Waltham MA 28 Apr. 1938 (Columbia VRs), 72y 3m 2d; married at
Steuben 14 Sept. 1906 widow ALZENA [Eliza] (SPRAGUE) Lindsey.
born at Cherryfield 1 May 1882, died at Columbia ME 15 Dec.
1937, 55y 7m 14d, daughter of James and Clara (Randall)
Sprague (Steuben, Columbia and ME VRs). In 1900 James was
single, living with Dolly (Pinkham) Stull [# 869].

Children:

     i.   CLARA M.^{9}, b. Columbia 21 June 1907.
     ii. RODNEY, b. Milbridge 5 Feb. 1911, res.
          Franklin.
     iii. LOVICIA JANE, b. Columbia c1912 (17 in 1929);
          m. Harrington 9 Nov. 1929 ERWIN CARTER, b.
          Columbia in 1905, son of Charles V. and Annie
          (Wass) Carter--div.; m. 2nd Milbridge 18 Apr.
          1955 JOHN LESLIE HODGKINS, b. c1911, son of
          Orrin and Mertie E. (Higgins) Hodgkins.
1496. iv. EDWIN M., b. Columbia 29 Aug. 1914.
      v.   CLAIR, b. Columbia 21 June 1917, d. there 25
           Oct. 1918, 11y 4m 4d.
      vi. STEPHEN, b. Harrington 14 Nov. 1919.
1497. vii. LLOYD D., b. Columbia 27 Jan. 1921.

915.   COFFIN STEPHEN^8 1845-1928 [408 Aaron^7 and Bethia
Wakefield] was born at Cherryfield 17 Apr. 1845, died at
Arlington MA 14 Feb. 1928; married at Addison 25 Dec. 1866
(Machias Union) JULIA E. DRISKO, born there 13 Jan. 1846,
died 24 Aug. 1915, daughter of Benjamin Franklin and Nancy
(Plummer) Drisko (town and ME VRs; Cornman Ms). Burials are
in Church Hill Cemetery, Addison.
     He served from 29 Oct. 1861 to 18 Nov. 1864 in Co. G, 11th
ME Inf. Rgt., and received gunshot wounds in his left leg and
right hand. He was sometimes called Stephen C. Leighton. In
1900 his household was at Cambridge MA

Children, born at Addison:

     i.   GERTRUDE MAY^9 [Gertie], b. 5 Jan. 1868, d.
          Addison 13 Sept. 1883.
     ii. WALSTEIN H., b. in June 1870, res. Arlington
          and in 1900 Cambridge MA; m. Columbia Falls
          14 Oct. 1897 GERTRUDE F. PETERSON, b. there
          in Dec. 1870, dau. of Pelham B. and Amelia
          (Crowley) Peterson. He was a carpenter. Ch.
          GLADYS P.^{10} b. Columbia Falls 11 Aug. 1899.
     iii. BLANCHE, b. in July 1872; m. LEVERETT DUNBAR,
          b. in ME in Jan. 1873. Both were living with
          Coffin in 1900. Ch. Marion b. Cambridge in
          Apr. 1895.
     iv. WINIFRED SCOTT, b. 6 Feb. 1874, d. Cambridge
          24 Mar. 1900, 26y 1m 18d (Addison VRs).
     v.   HOLLAND P., b. in Aug. 1877.
     vi. BERNARD F., b. in Mar. 1881.

916.   LYDIA L.^{8} 1836-1896 [409 David^7 and Eliza Leighton]
was born at Milbridge 13 Mar. 1836, died at No. Blue Hill ME
2 Sept. 1896, 60y 6m; married 24 Mar. 1856 (ISAAC) PERRY
GRINDLE, born at Penobscot ME 21 Sept. 1811, died at No. Blue
Hill 21 Feb. 1908, 98y, son of James and Mary (Harriman)
Grindle.
     He had married first 24 Mar. 1836 Eliza Ann Osgood, who
died 20 Aug. 1855; they had eight children (records of Elizabeth Wescott; town VRs). Burials are in Seaside Cemetery,
Blue Hill.

Children (**Grindle**), born at Blue Hill:

i.   ELIZA ANN, b. 1 Aug. 1858, d. Ellsworth 17 Apr.
      1954, 96y 8m 16d; m. 20 Oct. 1879 OBED TYLER
      HINCKLEY, b. Blue Hill 25 Mar. 1842, d. in 1916,
      son of Obed and Louisa (Cushing) Hinckley.
ii.   FREEMAN SPARKS, b. 7 Apr. 1860, d. Blue Hill 14 Mar.
      1943; m. 1st 10 Sept. 1881 RACHEL A. WEBBER--div.;
      m. 2nd MARY GERRISH, b. in 1865, d. in 1934 (GS).

917.   EVERLINIA K.[8] [Evelyn] 1837-   [409 David[7] and
Eliza Leighton] was born at Milbridge 7 Dec. 1837, lived at
Franklin ME; married at Milbridge 10 Nov. 1855 AUGUSTUS C.
[Gus] DONNELL, born about 1832 (38 in 1870), not listed in
1880 (town and ME VRs; Cornman Ms).
He was a farmer at Franklin.

Children (**Donnell**), born at Franklin:

i.   HENRY A., b. c1859 (21 in 1880); m. LILLIE LIBBY.
ii.   FREDERICK I., b. c1861 (19 in 1880); m. ESTHER HAVEY.
iii. CARRIE E., b. c1863 (17 in 1880); m. LORENZO BRAGDON.
iv.   GENEVA F. [Jennie], b. c1865 (15 in 1880); m. LORING
      WENTWORTH.
v.   LILLIAN, b. c1867 (13 in 1880); m. FRANK WENTWORTH.
vi.   L. CARLTON, b. c1869 (11 in 1880); m. Franklin 30
      Nov. 1899 MAIDIE L. GERRISH, b. there in 1869,
      dau. of Follett and Maria (Blaisdell) Gerrish.
vii. CLIFTON DAVID (twin), b. c1869; m. Franklin 30 May
      1918 AGNES G. (BUNKER) Fraser, b. there in 1876,
      dau. of Lafayette A. and Sarah (Snider) Bunker. She
      and a 1st husband were divorced.
viii. FLORA, b. c1872 (8 in 1880); m. Franklin 22 June 1895
      HOWARD W. HOOPER, b. there in 1872, son of Thomas H.
      and Lucretia (Abbott) Hooper.
ix.   PERCY W., b. c1874 (6 in 1880); m. MYRTLE RUTTER.
x.   INEZ E., b. c1876 (4 in 1880); m. 14 Jan. 1905 GEORGE
      WELCH.
xi.   GRACE S., b. c1878 (2 in 1880); m. Franklin 17 Oct.
      1904 HARRY L. HARDISON, b. there in 1881, son of
      Willard L. and Annie (Springer) Hardison.
xii. LIZZIE J., d.y.

918.   ABBIE MARIA[8] 1839-1913 [409 David[7] and Eliza Leigh-
ton] was born at Milbridge 2 Sept. 1839, died there 5 Mar.
1913; married there 14 Oct. 1859 ALBERT A. STROUT, born at
Harrington 6 Oct. 1826, died at Milbridge 12 Oct. 1915, son
of Joseph and Ruth (Cates) Strout (Milbridge VRs). Burials
are in Evergreen Cemetery.
      Albert had married first Mary Ann Strout (GS, 1824-1851),
daughter of Barnard and Abigail (Fickett) Strout, and had
married second at Columbia 14 Aug. 1852 Irene R. Grace, who
had died 18 May 1857.
      In 1860 Albert, 34, carpenter, and "Martha A.," 21, were
listed at Milbridge; his son Irving, 2, and his mother Ruth
were in the household.

Children (**Strout**), born at Milbridge:

i.   HELEN ROWENA, b. 26 Aug. 1862, d. So. Portland 19
      Aug. 1951; m. Milbridge 22 Oct. 1879 EMERY WILSON
      STROUT, b. there 29 Apr. 1852, d. Portland 6 Apr.
      1919, son of William and Martha (Lowe) Strout.
ii   SYDNEY E., b. 16 Oct. 1865, d. Milbridge 21 Oct.
      1920; m. there ADA D. STROUT, b. in 1852, d. in
      1942.
iii. GERTRUDE A., b. 15 Jan. 1871, d. Milbridge 1 May
      1906, 35y 3m 16d; m. there 19 Oct. 1890 WILLIAM A.
      SAWYER of Jonesport, b. Milbridge 13 Jan. 1867, d.
      at sea 2 Feb. 1902, 35y 21d, son of George W. and
      Mary Elizabeth (Kelley) Sawyer.

919.   (ANDREW) JACKSON[8] [Jack] 1841-1889 [409 David[7] and
Eliza Leighton] was born at Milbridge 29 June 1841, died
there 5 Oct. 1889, 48y 3m; married first there 1 Nov. 1863
ELIZABETH CORTHELL, born there about 1848, died before 1870,
daughter of Joseph and Hannah (Dyer) (Warren) Corthell; mar-
ried second there 1 Jan. 1871 ISABELLA (STROUT) Nutter, born
1 June 1844, died Milbridge 8 Feb. 1905, 60y 7m 7d, daughter
of John and Joanna[7] (Leighton) Strout [# 295] (Milbridge
VRs). Burials are in Evergreen Cemetery.
   Jack served from 10 Sept. 1862 to 31 Aug. 1863 in Co. C,
28th ME Inf. Rgt. He was a mariner and then a sea captain.
In 1870, he and Elizabeth were living with her parents.
   Isabella Strout had married first at Milbridge 24 Nov. 1860
Edwin Nutter. She married third there 5 Dec. 1901 Leverett
Strout, born about 1843, died in July 1927 (GS), son of
Joseph W. and Sybil (Whitten) Strout. (Leverett had married
first Abitha J. Wallace, and married third 3 Mar. 1906 Laura
E. (Whitaker) Leighton, widow of Francis [# 896]).

Children by Elizabeth, born at Milbridge:

      i.   NETTIE[9], b. 17 Apr. 1866; m. Milbridge 10 June
            1883 (Machias Union, Anthony D. and Nellie)
            ARTHUR D. McKENNEY, b. Monson ME in May 1862,
            d. Milbridge 6 July 1907, 44y, son of Charles
            and Lydia (Goodwin) McKenney. In 1905 he was
            a stonecutter at Milbridge. Ch. Ralph b. in
            Jan. 1886 and Harmon b. in Nov. 1888 (1900
            census).
1498. ii.   HARMON CURTIS, b. 30 Sept. 1867.

920.   CAROLINE[8] [Caddie] 1845-1878 [409 David[7] and Eliza
Leighton] was born at Milbridge 14 Mar. 1845, died 13 Sept.
1878, 33y 6m (GS); married first at Gouldsboro 4 July 1865
(Machias Union), GEORGE L. STEWART, born 28 May 1844, son of
John and Lydia[7] (Leighton) Stewart [# 268]; married second
PIERRE T. CYR (town VRs; family records of compiler). She
and her Cyr children are buried in the family graveyard at
Milbridge. She and Pierre lived at Lynn MA.

Children (**Stewart**):

i.   WILLIAM H., b. 16 Apr. 1868, d. 31 Oct. 1939, 71y;
      m. MARION ---- and others. He res. Malden MA.
ii.   DANIEL.

Children (**Cyr**):

iii. FRANK, d. Milbridge at 19m (GS).
iv.   LESTER, d. Milbridge at 3y (GS).

921. ALBERT D.[8] 1850-1904 [409 David[7] and Eliza Leighton]
was born at Milbridge 5 Mar. 1850, died there 24 Dec. 1904,
54y 9m 21d; married there 25 Apr. 1876 FLORENCE SAWYER, born
1 July 1851, died at Milbridge 15 Aug. 1908, 57y 1m, daughter
of Charles and Caroline (Fickett) Sawyer (Milbridge VRs; Milbridge Town Register, 1905). Burials are in Evergreen Cemetery. He was a building contractor, she a teacher.

Children, born at Milbridge:

1499. i.   ELIZA G.[9], b. 9 May 1877; m. HARVEY E.
             CRIMMIN.
        ii.   ARTHUR A , b. 5 June 1879, res. Milbridge in
             1905; m. OLIVE KINGSLEY of Hope RI.
        iii. RALPH S., b. 6 Sept. 1881.
        iv.   MARK C., b. 3 Mar. 1884, d. Waterville ME 7
             Dec. 1931, 47y 9m 4d; m. MARIA CLARK, b.
             Smithfield 29 Nov. 1897, d. 22 June 1930, 35y
             6m 23d, dau. of Fred H. and Nancy Clark.
        v.   IDA M., b. 15 Jan. 1886, res. Malden MA in
             1905; m. CLEMENT V. COTHRELL of Taunton MA.
        vi.   EVA F., b. 14 Nov. 1887, died in 1948 (GS);
             unm. She was a teacher at Brockton MA.
        vii. DAVID B., b. 26 Feb. 1890, d. 5 Nov. 1893.

922. JAMES A.[8] 1839-1898 [410 James[7] and Sally Smallage]
was born at Steuben 24 Mar. 1839, lost at sea 27 Nov. 1898;
married at Milbridge 5 May 1875 MARY ASENATH FOSTER, born
there 26 Apr. 1858, died there 2 Nov. 1932, 74y 6m 7d, daughter of Joseph and Asenath (Baker) Foster (Milbridge and ME
VRs). Burials are in Evergreen Cemetery.
    In 1860 he was a seaman, 22, in the Steuben household of
Daniel [# 277]. He served in the US Navy 26 Aug. 1861 to 27
Aug. 1862 as a seaman on the John Adams, and then in Co. I,
20th ME Inf. Rgt. until 4 Jan. 1865 (NA-MSR); he was a pensioner. He became a master mariner.
    He may have married first at Milbridge 15 Oct. 1862 Lydia
H. Mansfield, born there in 1843, daughter of James B. and
Abigail (Brown) Mansfield. He was not listed in the 1870 ME
census.

Children by Mary, born at Milbridge:

1500. i.   JOSEPH FOSTER[9], b. 15 Mar. 1876.
        ii.   ETHEL A., b. in Oct. 1878; m. Milbridge 22
             Feb. 1902 FRANK M. GRAY, b. c1874, son of
             Charles W. and Mary M. (Warren) Gray of
             Portland.
        iii. MARGARET, b. in Oct. 1889; m. Milbridge 12
             Aug. 1914 ARTHUR EDWARD MONTAGUE TREMAINE of
             Winthrop MA, b. Halifax NS in 1879, son of
             Richard W. and Lenora W. (Harrington)
             Tremaine.
1501. iv.   JAMES EDWIN, b. 26 July 1893.

923.   PAMELIA[8] [Parmelia] 1823-1911 [414 Robert[7] and Eliza
Davis] was born at Steuben 11 Nov. 1823, died there 26 June
1911, 88y 11m; married there 18 Aug. 1843 JOHN W. DAVIS, born
there 29 Aug. 1823, died there 30 Apr. 1910, 86y 8m 1d, son
of Richard and Abigail (Downs) Davis (Milbridge and ME VRs;
Cornman Ms--which listed the first three children only).

Children (**Davis**):

i.   ABIGAIL, res. Milbridge.
ii.   SEWELL O., b. Milbridge 9 Jan. 1845; m. MARIA
      McKINNEY, b. Columbia 17 Nov. 1846, d. Steuben 15
      July 1904, dau. of Owen McKinney.
iii. ORRIN, b. Steuben, res. Milbridge; m. 1st MARY PINK-
      HAM; m. 2nd SARAH CONNORS.
iv.   WILLIAM Y., b. Steuben c1863 (7 in 1870), d. there 16
      July 1906, 44y; m. ASENATH YOUNG.
v.   ADA S., b. 30 July 1865; m. MOSES[8] LEIGHTON [# 943].

924.   SEWELL S.[8] 1827-1901 [414 Robert[7] and Eliza Davis]
was born at Steuben in Oct. 1827 (in 1900 census; aged 48 in
1870), died at Harrington 2 July 1901; married int. 20 Nov.
1851 SOPHRONIA OAKES, born at Carmel ME about 1837, died at
Harrington 19 Feb. 1900, 63y 10m 23d (VRs; GS, 18 Feb., 63y
11m 6d), daughter of Levi and Mary (Graves) Oakes (ME VRs;
Oak, Family Register, 36). Burials are in the William Frye
Cemetery.
   In 1860 they lived at Cherryfield; in 1870 he was a farmer
at Harrington.

Children:

i.   DIANA[9], b. c1854 (6 in 1860); m. Harrington
      int. 2 Sept. 1872 CURTIS ROBINSON. Ch.
      Guilford d. Harrington 10 Sept. 1900, 24y.
1502. ii. GILBERT HATHAWAY, b. in Sept. 1856.

925.   ELIZABETH[8] [Betsey] 1829-   [414 Robert[7] and Eliza
Davis] was born at Steuben 18 July 1829, lived at Cherryfield; married 3 Oct. 1844 ROBERT DORR, born 30 Jan. 1829,
died 6 Aug. 1891, son of John and Mary (Willey) Dorr (town
VRs; Cornman Ms).

Children (**Dorr**), born at Cherryfield:

i.   CHARLES W., b. 16 Feb. 1851 (11 in 1860), m. Cherry-
      field int. 3 Apr. 1871 SARAH TIBBETTS of Epping, b.
      in 1853, dau. of Henry and Mary Ann Tibbetts.
ii.   MARY ADELINE, b. 16 Apr. 1853; m. RUEL B. OAKES.
iii. ESTHER, b. 8 May 1856; m. ALMON TORREY.
iv.   (JULIA) EVA, b. c1859 (1 in 1860); m. EDMUND J.
      TENAN.
v.   CYNETTE E., b. c1863 (7 in 1870).
vi.   HENRY MELVIN, b. c1867 (3 in 1870); m. ELIZA TENAN.
vii. MILLARD F , b. c1871 (24 in 1895); m. 23 Mar. 1895
      CLARA C. KELTON, b. Harrington in 1880, dau. of
      Carter and Ada (Davis) Kelton.

926. FREEMAN[8] 1831-1901 [414 Robert[7] and Eliza Davis] was born at Steuben 5 Dec. 1831, died at there 11 Oct. 1901; married in 1854 MARIA DAVIS, born at Cherryfield 3 Sept. 1837, died at Steuben 15 Feb. 1911, 75y 5m 12d, daughter of Charles and Maria (Tracy) Davis (town VRs; Cornman Ms).
Freeman, 35, Maria, 24, and Angeline, 2, were listed at Steuben in 1860.

Children, born at Steuben (Unionville):

	i.	ANGELINE[9], b. 26 Aug. 1858, d.y.
1503.	ii.	ABIGAIL ANN, b. 9 Aug. 1863; m. NOAH PETTEE.
	iii.	CLARA, b. 23 Mar. 1865; m. HERVEY[9] LEIGHTON [# 1464].
1504.	iv.	WINFIELD, b. 30 Mar. 1871.

927. JULIA A.[8] 1833- [414 Robert[7] and Eliza Davis] was born at Steuben in 1833, died at Cherryfield in 1897; married first in 1852 FREEMAN DORR; married second in 1854 WILLIAM DORR, born about 1833 (37 in 1870, Cherryfield) (Cornman Ms).

Children (**Dorr**), by William:

i. JAMES A., b. c1854 (6 in 1860); m. CHARITY HART.
ii. GILBERT, b. c1856 (4 in 1860; Sherburn H., 14 in 1870); unm.
iii. ELMIRA A., b. c1859 (1 in 1860); m. CHARLES WILLEY.
iv. EVERETT CURTIS, b. c1862 (8 in 1870); m. ALICE HART.
v. JOHN B. H., b. c1866 (4 in 1870); unm.
vi. ELIZABETH L., b. c1869 (1 in 1870).

928. CURTIS M.[8] 1835-1923 [414 Robert[7] and Eliza Davis] was born at Steuben 24 Dec. 1836 (GS), died at Milbridge 19 Dec. 1923, 86y 11m 25d; married at Cherryfield 22 Sept. 1862 (Machias Union) MARY A. McALPIN of Calais, born 31 May 1842, died at Milbridge 15 Mar. 1901, 58y 9m 15d (Cornman Ms; ME VRs; their birth dates vary in censuses, in the Cornman Ms and on gravestone inscriptions). Burials are in Evergreen Cemetery.
Curtis was a farmer and later a fisherman. He served in Co. H., 18th ME Inf. Rgt., and in the 1st ME Heavy Artillery Rgt. 2 Aug. 1862 to 6 June 1865; he lost his index finger in battle (NA-MSR).

Children, born at Steuben:

	i.	GEORGE C.[9], b. 10 Apr. 1863, d. Steuben in 1947 (GS); m. there 16 Mar. 1896 ELLEN S. PINKHAM, b. there 4 May 1856, d. there 25 Dec. 1938, dau. of Benjamin and Susan[8] (Leighton) Pinkham [# 868]. No ch. Both lived with her mother in 1900, Steuben.
	ii.	ELDORA S., b. in 1866 (4 in 1870); m. ANDREW P.[9] LEIGHTON [# 1554].
	iii.	ULYSSES G., b. 28 July 1867, d. Steuben 22 June 1937; unm.
1505.	iv.	ALMER, b. 10 Aug. 1870.
1506.	v.	FLORILLA, b. 6 Sept. 1874; m. REUBEN MARTIN and JOHN PELLUM.

vi.   EVERARD G., b. 26 Feb. 1875. d. Bangor (hosp.)
      14 Oct. 1939, 64y 7m 18d (1938-GS); m. Mil-
      bridge 17 Dec. 1901 ETTA M. BRITTON, b. there
      22 Jan. 1880, d. Machiasport 28 Mar. 1963,
      dau. of George and Alice (Cates) Britton. No
      ch. He was a fisherman.
1507. vii. (GERTRUDE) EDITH., b. 30 July 1878; m. GEORGE
      JOY.

929. MARY JANE[8] 1839-   [414 Robert[7] and Eliza Davis]
was born about 1839 (21 in 1860); married at Cherryfield 25
Apr. 1857 RICHARD W. DORR (Cornman Ms). In 1880, Richard,
45, lived at Cherryfield with his wife Mary J., 40.

Children (**Dorr**), born at Cherryfield:

i.   ETTA, not in 1880 census.
ii.   (AZEL) SNOW; m. ELLA MORSE.
iii. SOPHRONIA, b. c1865 (15 in 1880); m. HORACE WILLEY.
iv.   FRANK NASH, b. Cherryfield c1871 (22 in 1893); m.
      Harrington 18 Nov. 1893 LAURA[9] (LEIGHTON) Stevens
      [# 907].
v.   ABBIE, res. Marshfield; m. ---- ROBINSON.

930. WILLIAM H.[8] 1842-1917 [414 Robert[7] and Eliza Davis]
was born at Steuben 27 June 1842 (GS, 1841), died at Gouldsboro 10 June 1917, 75y 11m 14d; married at Steuben 19 Mar.
1868 AMANDA M.[8] (LEIGHTON) DAVIS, born there 27 Nov. 1838,
died there 27 July 1915, 76y 8m, daughter of Joshua M. and
Betsey (Stanhope) Leighton [# 418]. Burials are in Union
Church Cemetery, Steuben.
Amanda married first in 1860 WILLIAM FREEMAN DAVIS [# 934],
and had two Davis children (Steuben and ME VRs; Cornman Ms).
William was a farmer at Steuben. He served as corporal,
Co. G, 6th ME Inf. Rgt. 29 Apr. 1861 to 28 June 1864, and
received an ankle injury (NA-MSR).
In 1870 their household included Hannah Leighton, 74, and
the two Davis children; in 1880 his mother Eliza Archer was
in their home; and in 1900 their granddaughter Amanda R.
Spurling lived with them.

Children, born at Steuben:

1508. i.   BENJAMIN FRANKLIN[9], b. 18 Aug. 1870.
      ii.   ETHEL MELISSA, b. 19 Oct. 1872, res. Franklin;
            m. 1st Steuben 9 Sept. 1890 (Machias Union)
            JAMES L. COLEWELL, b. Steuben c1860, son of
            Hiram and Elizabeth (Pyne) Colewell; m. 2nd
            30 Dec. 1899 GEORGE C. GORDON, b. Franklin in
            June 1867, son of Philip Carpenter and Ann
            (Newman) Gordon. Ethel had no ch.

931. CHARITY S.[8] 1844-1900 [414 Robert[7] and Eliza Davis]
was born at Steuben 17 Oct. 1844, died there (as daughter of
Justin Archer and Charity Leighton) 20 Dec. 1900; married 6
July 1861 CHARLES J. KING of Jonesboro, born 2 Jan. 1840,
lived at Cherryfield in 1880, son of Charles G. and Nancy
(Archer) King (Steuben VRs; Cornman Ms).

In 1860, Charity, 16, was living at Harrington with her mother and step-father Harvey Archer.

Children (**King**):

i.   MILLARD EDGAR, b Cherryfield 14 Aug. 1862.
ii.   ARVIDA, b. Great Pond (Hancock).
iii. LIDA ELBERTA, b. Cherryfield.
iv.   AVA MABEL, b. 1 May 1868 (14 in 1880); m. MELZOR
      WILLEY.
v.   WILLIAM D., b. Great Pond in 1874 (7 in 1880), d. 17
      Feb. 1888.
vi.   PEARL, b. 14 Feb. 1878 (Perley, 4 in 1880).

932.   ABIGAIL DORINDA[8] 1846-1928 [414 Robert and Eliza Davis] was born at Steuben 11 Sept. 1846, died there 3 Feb. 1929, 82y 4m 23d; married at Calais 16 Sept. 1865 (Machias Union) SYLVESTER WHITAKER TRACY, born at Gouldsboro ME 24 July 1836, died at Steuben 4 Jan. 1916, son of Eri and Hannah (Ash) Tracy (town and ME VRs; records of Margaret Colton).

Children (**Tracy**), born at Steuben:

i.   CORA E., b. 23 Sept. 1866, d. in 1951; m. 1st 21 May
      1884 GEORGE NUTTER, b. Gouldsboro 20 May 1835, d.
      Steuben 2 Dec. 1921; m. 2nd 24 Dec. 1932 HENRY
      FRAZIER, b. Ellsworth in 1867, d. there in 1953.
ii.   MERRILL B., b. 13 Aug. 1871, d. Steuben 15 Jan. 1932;
      m. 2 Nov. 1911 LILLIAN[9] LEIGHTON [# 943].
iii. ARTHUR E., b. 20 Aug. 1879, d. Portland 5 Jan. 1963;
      m. 27 Oct. 1904 ALIDA HARRIS, b. Eastport 29 Oct.
      1884, d. there 13 June 1943.

933.   BENJAMIN FRANKLIN[8] 1835-1867 [418 Joshua[7] and Betsey Stanhope] was born at Steuben 30 Nov. 1835, died at Milbridge 14 Sept. 1867, 31y 9m 14d (GS, Evergreen Cemetery). He had a son by ALMIRA PINKHAM; she was born at Steuben 19 May 1845, daughter of Joel and Lovicia[8] (Leighton) Pinkham [# 869], and married Charles Moore of Cherryfield.
      Julia Cornman stated Benjamin never married, but a Benjamin F. Leighton married 12 July 1861 Rachel O. Drew of Lawrence MA, born at Machias in 1841, daughter of Hilary M. and Jane E. Drew.
      He enlisted, aged 28, 15 July 1861 in Co. G, 6th ME Inf. Rgt., and re-enlisted 4 Mar. 1864 in Co. H, 1st ME Cavalry Rgt. He was wounded 24 June 1864, discharged for disability, and was a pensioner (NA-MSR #62.154).

Child by Almira, born at Steuben:

i.   BENJAMIN F[9], b. 20 June 1865.

934.   AMANDA M.[8] 1838-1915 [418 Joshua[7] and Betsey Stanhope] was born at Steuben 27 Nov. 1838, died there 27 July 1915, 76y 8m; married first there int. 1 May 1860 WILLIAM FREEMAN DAVIS, born there 10 May 1839, killed in battle 5 May 1864, son of Richard and Abigail (Downs) Davis; married second 19 Mar. 1868 WILLIAM H.[8] LEIGHTON [# 930].

Children (**Davis**), born at Steuben:

i.   PHEBE H., b. 9 Feb. 1861; m. EDWARD SPURLING of
     Gouldsboro.
ii. WILLIAM FREEMAN, b. 20 Oct. 1864, d. 19 Nov. 1939;
     m. LILLIAN JOY of Gouldsboro.

935. HARRIET J.[8] 1840-1898 [418 Joshua[7] and Betsey Stan-
hope] was born at Steuben 11 June 1840, died at Sullivan ME 8
June 1898; married first ALBERT H. TUCKER, born at Springfield ME 17 Nov. 1835, died at Sullivan 23 Nov. 1902, 68y 6m,
son of David Tucker; married second at Seal Harbor ME 21 May
1898 GEORGE E. PIERCE, born at Mt. Desert about 1846, son of
Ezekiel and Sarah (Keefe) Pierce (ME VRs; Cornman Ms).

Children (**Tucker**):

i.   JOSIE, b. 8 Dec. 1864, res. Sullivan; m. 1st ISAAC
     FREEMAN; m. 2nd GEORGE PREBLE.
ii. BESSIE E., b. 8 Dec. 1871, res. Bangor; m. Steuben
     30 May 1890 ROBERT WORCESTER.

936. LEONARD DORMAN HINCKLEY[8] 1851-1928 [418 Joshua[7] and
Betsey Stanhope] was born at Steuben 8 Oct. 1851, died there
5 Dec. 1928, 78y 1m 27d; married first there MARY A. PINK-
HAM, born 10 Apr. 1858, died Milbridge 27 June 1887, 29y 2m
17d, daughter of George Pinkham; married second 17 Nov. 1888
MATILDA J. [Tid] (WORKMAN) Yeaton, born at Steuben 27 Sept.
1850, died 3 July 1903, 52y 9m 6d, daughter of Solomon and
Nancy (Dunbar) Workman; married third at Steuben 1 Jan. 1905
DAISY FERNALD, born at Gouldsboro in July 1876, daughter of
William H. and Lydia E. (Hamilton) Fernald (Steuben and ME
VRs; records of Margaret Colton). Burials are in Evergreen
Cemetery.
     Leonard was a fisherman. Matilda had married first at
Steuben 29 Aug. 1874 Edwin M. Yeaton who died at sea; in 1900
Leonard's household contained three Yeaton step-children.
Widow Daisy married second 19 June 1938 Harvard E. Crowley of
Gouldsboro.

Child by Mary, born at Steuben:

1509. i.   ELSIE C.[9], b. 2 July 1876; m. FRANK FAULKNER.

Child by Matilda, born at Steuben:

1510. ii. JASPER L., b. 7 Jan. 1891.

937. FREDERICK JOSHUA[8] 1862-1934 [418 Joshua[7] and Betsey
Stanhope] was born at Steuben 25 Nov. 1860, died at Milbridge
30 Jan. 1934, 73y 2m 5d; married there 26 Dec 1897 LAURA P.[9]
LEIGHTON, born there 30 Mar. 1880, died at Ellsworth (hosp.),
daughter of Daniel and Ada (Pettee) Leighton [# 731] (Milbridge VRs; records of descendant Donald Leighton).
     Fred was a fisherman. After his death, his son bought from
his mother and sister their shares of the family farm. Laura
married second ARTHUR GOMES and lived at Lucerne ME.

1511.   i.   BETSEY[9], b. 1 July 1898; m. ORA RHOADES and
              HERMAN SAWYER.
1512.   ii.   JOSEPH STROUT, b. 24 Mar. 1900.

938.   ARTHUR[8] 1865-   [418 Joshua[7] and Betsey Stanhope]
was born at Steuben about 1865 (5 in 1870); married ALDANA
DUNHAM, born at Swan's Island about 1870 (31 in 1901), daughter of Frederick and Abigail (Stanley) Dunham--divorced.
    Aldana was living at Stonington in 1900 with her cousin
Augustus Dunham; the two children were listed with their
grandfather Frederick Dunham at Deer Isle. She married second at Stonington 20 Oct. 1901 AUGUSTUS DUNHAM, born at Deer
Isle about 1875, son of Obadiah and Sarah W. (Gross) Dunham.

Children:

        i.   EVA P., b. Rockland ME 22 Dec. 1892.
        ii.   LINNIE A., b. Deer Isle 9 Feb. 1896; m.
              Swans Island 28 Oct. 1913 WALTER J. STANLEY,
              b. there c1888, son of George W. and Ina
              (Holbrook) Stanley.

939.   PHILENA H.[8] 1841-1899 [419 James[7] and Sophronia
Leighton] was born at Milbridge 27 Nov. 1841, died there 6
Apr. 1899, 58y 4m 9d; married at Cherryfield 17 Nov. 1867
(named in the Machias Union Pamelia H.) BARNARD G. PINKHAM,
born 16 Dec. 1830, died at Milbridge 22 Mar. 1912, son of
Barnard and Millie (Walker) Pinkham (town VRs; records of
Margaret Colton).
    Burials are in Evergreen Cemetery.

Children (**Pinkham**), born at Cherryfield:

        i.   ALICE J., b. 30 May 1868, d. Milbridge 22 Mar. 1928;
              m. 23 Dec. 1894 JOSEPH B. STROUT, b. 24 July 1864
              (GS, 2 July 1867), d. Milbridge 10 Apr. 1924,
              son of Elbridge and Basmuth (Pinkham) Strout.
        ii.   JAMES B., b. 24 Feb. 1880, d. Milbridge 19 July 1956;
              m. ELLA M. MORRISON, b. 20 Dec. 1893, d. Milbridge
              16 June 1943.

940.   LEVI C.[8] 1843-1871 [419 James[7] and Sophronia Leigh-
ton] was born at Milbridge 23 Mar. 1843, died there 6 June
1871, 28y (GS); married there 24 Feb. 1866 MARY MARVILLA[8]
LEIGHTON, born there 25 Apr. 1843, died there 11 May 1899,
56y 19d, daughter of David and Eliza Godfrey[7] (Leighton)
Leighton [# 409].
    Mary married second at Milbridge 10 May 1875 HENRY C. MAR-
TIN, born at Sullivan in 1833, died at Milbridge 26 Apr.
1905, son of Daniel and Marion Martin (Milbridge VRs). Her
name also appeared as Marvilla M.
    Levi enlisted in Co. A, 13th ME Inf. Rgt., on 20 Nov. 1861.
In 1870, he was a seaman at Milbridge.

Child, born at Milbridge:

i.   ERNEST J.[9], b. 22 Sept. 1870, d. Sailors' Snug
      Harbor, Staten Island NY 24 Sept. 1954; unm.
      A sailor until retirement in 1940, in 1880 he
      was living with his grandfather David. He
      named as heirs three cousins: Freeman Grindle
      of Ellsworth [# 916], Frances Donaldson of
      Rowayton CT [# 944], and Vera L. Roberts of
      Milbridge [# 1516] (letter from SSH).

941. (JAMES) EVERETT[8] 1845-1891 [419 James[7] and Sophronia
Leighton] was born at Milbridge 2 Jan. 1845, drowned 2 July
1891; married at Steuben 12 Jan. 1865 (he 24, she 16) ALFREDA
PINKHAM, born there 10 Aug. 1849, died at Milbridge 19 Apr.
1886, daughter of Ichabod and Miriam[8] (Leighton) Pinkham
[# 383] (Sinnett, Pinkham Gen., 19; town VRs; records of
Leonard Tibbetts).
In 1870 and 1880 Everett was a seaman at Milbridge.

Children:

i.   EFFIE A.[9], b. Steuben 15 July 1866, d. Mil-
      bridge 18 Jan. 1892; married there 21 Dec.
      1887 GEORGE CROCKER, b. Bangor c1863, d. Mil-
      bridge in June 1903, 40y. Ch. Everett b.
      Milbridge in 1892; m. 27 Sept. 1913 Leonora
      Wakefield, b. Sullivan 25 Oct. 18955, d. 8
      Dec. 1969, dau. of Rodney and Abbie Wake-
      field. Leonora m. 2nd Earl Strout.
1513. ii.   AMOS GAY, b. Milbridge 26 Apr. 1870.
iii. MARION [Mamie], b. c1874 (6 in 1880), d.
      Augusta 21 Dec. 1942; unm.
iv.   ELLA, b. Milbridge in Aug. 1875, d. Bangor
      (hosp.) 18 May 1906; unm.
v.   MELVIN, b. c1877 (3 in 1880).
1514. vi.   CLARA M. [Carrie], b. Milbridge 19 June 1880;
      m. NEWELL H. WALLACE.
vii. EVERETT EUGENE, b. Milbridge 17 Mar. 1882.

942. MARY A.[8] 1847-1928 [419 James[7] and Sophronia Leigh-
ton] was born at Milbridge 8 June 1847, died there 5 Jan.
1928; married at Gouldsboro 13 Sept. 1874 (Machias Union)
LEANDER E. MARTIN, born 16 Oct. 1845, died at Milbridge 11
July 1930 (17 July GS), son of Philip and Lucy (Read) Martin
(Milbridge VRs; Johnson, Sullivan and Sorrento, 345).
Burials are in Evergreen Cemetery.

Children (**Martin**), born at Milbridge:

i.   SOPHRONIA, b. 9 Sept. 1875, d. Milbridge 5 Sept.
      1960; m. 25 Dec. 1895 ARTHUR A. SARGENT, b. 14 May
      1865, d. Milbridge 24 Oct. 1940.
ii.   FLORA E., b. in 1876, d. Milbridge 11 Dec. 1895;
      unm.

943. MOSES H.[8] 1857-1929 [419 James[7] and Sophronia
Leighton] was born at Milbridge 22 July 1857, died there 10
June 1929 (10 July per GS); married there int. 7 May 1888 ADA

STEVENS DAVIS, born at Steuben 30 July 1865, died at Mil-
bridge 8 Jan. 1926, daughter of John W. and Pamelia[8]
(Leighton) Davis [# 923] (Milbridge VRs). Burials are in
Evergreen Cemetery. He was a carpenter.

Children, born at Milbridge:

    i.   LILLIAN M.[9], b. 27 July 1888, d. Nashua NH 25
        June 1984, 94y; m. Milbridge 2 Nov. 1912
        MERRILL B. TRACY, b. Steuben 13 Aug. 1872, d.
        there 15 Jan. 1932, son of Sylvester and
        Abigail[8] (Leighton) Tracy [# 932] (her obit.,
        from Steuben). Ch. Morris A. b. Steuben 3
        Feb. 1913, res. Nashua; m. 1st 3 Nov. 1935
        Evelyn Rice--div.; m. 2nd Mona B. Kimball.
    ii.   LUCY HELEN, b. 18 May 1892, d. Ellsworth
        (hosp.) 29 Aug. 1984, 92y; m. Milbridge 3
        Oct. 1908 JESSE R. PHINNEY.

944. WILLARD HENRY[8] 1862-1922 [419 James[7] and Sophronia
Leighton] was born at Steuben 1 July 1863, died at Milbridge
1 Aug. 1922, 60y 1m; married there 16 Oct. 1883 LAURA BROWN
HINCKLEY, born 26 Jan. 1865, died at Milbridge 9 Aug. 1942,
daughter of Albion and Hannah (Evans) Hinckley [# 416] (Milbridge VRs; records of Joanna Nash Willey).
    Burials are in Evergreen Cemetery; all his children are
listed on the monument. He was a mariner and fisherman.

Children, born at Milbridge:

    i.   COLIN HERBERT[9], b. in Apr. 1884 (1900 census),
        d. in 1936 (GS); m. ADA MASON.
    ii.   IRVING HINCKLEY, b. 4 Sept. 1887, d. 9 May
        1955 (GS); m. MARGARET ---- . He res. Balti-
        more MD in 1954.
    iii. CHARLOTTE ALFREDA [Lottie], b. 10 Feb. 1890;
        m. ARTHUR CARR.
    iv.   MELVINIA DIXON [Vena], b. 12 Mar. 1892; m.
        Bangor 28 Aug. 1920 ALBERT D. BARTLETT, b.
        Forest City c1898, son of Frank W. and Ada M.
        (Robinson) Bartlett.
1515. v.   HAZEL, b. 19 July 1893; m. NATHANIEL NOYES.
    vi.   son, b. 16 Sept., d. 17 Sept., 1894.
    vii. son, b. and d. 9 Mar. 1896.
    viii. EFFIE ALMIRA, b. 20 Jan. 1897, d. Cherryfield
        in 1975 (GS, Pine Grove Cem.); m. 17 Jan.
        1920 FRANK NASH.
    ix.   FRANCES S. [Fannie], b. 27 June 1898, d.
        Rowayton CT 7 Oct. 1984 (BDN obit.); m. JOHN
        J. DONALDSON.
    x.   KATHERINE PYNE [Kate], b. 2 June 1900, d. Ban-
        gor (hosp.) 14 May 1945; m. Bar Harbor 20
        Jan. 1923 PAUL SANFORD RICHARDS, b. c1895,
        son of Fred S. and Mary (Sanford) Richards.
    xi.   daughter, b. 10 June 1901.
    xii. HANNAH SOPHRONIA, b. 7 May 1902, res. Bar
        Harbor in 1975; m. there 23 Aug. 1936 IRVING
        L. CUNNINGHAM, b. there c1906, son of Arthur
        and Josie (Richardson) Cunningham.

xiii. JAMES ALBION, b. 24 May 1903, d. Milbridge 26
      Nov. 1947; m. BERNICE ---- .
1516. xiv. VERA THERESA, b. 14 May 1907; m. CLAIR
      ROBERTS.
      xv. CORA BURNHAM, b. 26 June 1908; m. 1st Bar Har-
      bor 28 Nov. 1927 PHELPS A. CLARK, b. Hancock
      c1906, son of Walter P. and Etta (Jellison)
      Clark; m. 2nd 9 Nov. 1946 WARREN A. RAND.
      xvi. son, stillborn 7 May 1910.

945. ROBERT L.[8] 1850-   [420 <u>Thomas</u>[7] and <u>Harriet Leigh-</u>
<u>ton</u>] was born at Steuben 4 June 1850, lived at Cherryfield in
1910; married at Steuben int. 1 Apr. 1872 SARAH BARBER, born
at Cherryfield about 1849, died there 23 Feb. 1904, 53y,
daughter of John and Patience Barber (town and ME VRs). He
was a farmer at Cherryfield.

Children, born at Cherryfield:

    i.   CHARLES A.[9], b. in Nov. 1873, d. Cherryfield
        in Oct. 1903, 28y; m. there 28 Nov. 1900
        LAURA M. GRANT, b. there in 1879, d. there
        30 Dec. 1900, 21y 3m 9d, dau. of Adelbert and
        Flora A. (Willey) Grant. No ch.
    ii.   LILLIAN E., b. 25 Oct. 1879; m. WINFIELD[9]
        LEIGHTON [# 1504].
    iii. BERTHA M., b. in Mar. 1883; m. Cherryfield 26
        July 1902 WILLIAM E. DRISCOLL, b. there
        c1881, son of John and Lydia (Young)
        Driscoll. Ch. Cora E. and Ernest C.
    iv.   FRANK R., b. 25 Feb. 1886, d. Lewiston ME
        (hosp.) 6 May 1932. 45y 2m 11d; m. ELLA ----.
        He res. New Gloucester, and was farm manager,
        Pownal State School (obit.).
1517. v.   HARRY MELVIN, b. 7 Feb. 1891.
1518. vi.   FRED W., b. 27 Jan. 1892.

946. (NATHAN) SHAW[8] 1853-   [420 <u>Thomas</u>[7] and <u>Harriet</u>
<u>Leighton</u>] was born at Steuben 31 May 1853; married ELIZA
---- , born about 1854 (26 in 1880). In 1880 they lived in
his father's household at Steuben with three children.

Children, per 1880 census:

    i.   JOHN[9], b. c1876 (4 in 1880).
    ii.   MINNIE, b. c1878 (2 in 1880).
    iii. SUSIE, b. c1879 (10/12 in 1880).

947. ELIZABETH[8] [Betsey] 1797-1822 [421 <u>John</u>[7] and <u>Leonice</u>
<u>Sawyer</u>] was born at Cumberland ME 4 Jan. 1797, died 8 Oct.
1822; married at North Yarmouth 17 Oct. 1814 DANIEL ALLEN,
born at Windham 10 Apr. 1793, died 9 May 1855, 63y, son of
Joseph and Mary (Baker) Allen. Daniel married second 15 Mar.
1823 Mary Fenley, who died in 1876, 77y (town VRs; Allen
records of Leroy Bailey; Cornman Ms). Burials are at Gray.
    Allen was a farmer and licensed Free Baptist preacher.

Children (**Allen**), born at Windham:

i.   MARY ANN, b. 5 Dec. 1815, d. Lynn MA 24 Mar. 1875; m.
     23 Sept. 1838 JOHN PRAY, b. Shapleigh ME 1 Feb.
     1804, d. 11 Feb. 1857. Pray was a machinist.
     Burials are at Shapleigh.
ii. DAVID, b. 15 Mar. 1818, d. 7 Sept. 1844.
iii. LEONICE, b. 23 June 1820, d. Malden MA 27 Jan. 1910;
     m. 14 Aug. 1845 ANSEL LEWIS LIBBY, b. Limington ME
     in Apr. 1823, d. Portsmouth OH in Sept. 1870, son of
     Daniel and Dorcas (McDonald) Libby (Libby Family,
     525).
iv. PETER LEIGHTON, b. 8 Oct. 1822, d. 17 June 1897; m. 3
     July 1846 CLARISSA (ALLEN) Illsley, b. Cumberland 13
     Apr. 1824, d. 4 Nov. 1891, dau. of Elijah and Olive
     (Illsley) Allen. He made carriages and sleighs.

948.   MARY[8] 1799-1864 [421 John[7] and Leonice Sawyer] was
born at Cumberland about 1799, died at Windham 1 Apr. 1864;
married at Falmouth 17 Oct. 1814 SAMUEL COBB, born there in
1790, died at Windham 18 Apr. 1870, son of Ephraim and Sarah
(Parke) Cobb (Cobb Family, 2:392, 463; Cornman Ms).

Children (**Cobb**), born at Windham:

i.   JOHN LEIGHTON, b. 18 Mar. 1816; m. CATHERINE LIBBY,
      dau. of Isaac and Sally (Humphrey) Libby.
ii.   SARAH MARIE, b. 2 Apr. 1817; m. Windham 23 Oct. 1834
      EPHRAIM COBB, b. there 26 Feb. 1808, d. there 11
      Dec. 1875, son of Peter and Sally (Hodge) Cobb.
iii. NANCY ANN, b. say 1818; m. 28 Feb. 1836 ARTHUR LIBBY,
      b. 12 Jan. 1812, d. Windham 22 June 1880, son of
      William and Hannah (Gould) Libby.
iv.   ESTHER MAXFIELD, b. c1820, d. 9 Aug. 1868, 48y; m.
      1st Gorham ME int. 12 Apr. 1846 JAMES WESCOTT JR.;
      m. 2nd ---- DYER.
v.   HULDAH EXPERIENCE; m. JAMES ELLIOT.
vi.   SAMUEL MORRISON, b. 22 Feb. 1826, d. Windham 13 Aug.
      1896, 68y 5m; m. there 18 June 1848 LUCINDA LIBBY,
      b. 14 Mar. 1825, d. 3 Apr. 1886, 61y, dau. of Isaac
      and Sally (Humphrey) Libby.
vii. MARY ANN.
viii. ISAAC, d. infant.
ix.   ELLIOT ALPHONZO, d. infant.
x.   DORCAS ELLEN, b. 13 Aug. 1831; m. AARON[8] LEIGHTON
      [# 1012].

949.   CLARISSA[8] 1800-1883 [421 John[7] and Leonice Sawyer]
was born at North Yarmouth ME 20 Apr. 1800, died in 1883;
married at North Yarmouth 9 Oct. 1817 OTIS ALLEN, born at
Windham in 1797, died at Gray 30 Mar. 1873, 76y 8m, son of
Joseph and Mary (Baker) Allen (Allen records of Leroy Bailey;
town VRs). Burials are at Gray. He was a farmer, and served
at Portland from Aug. to Nov. 1814, in the War of 1812.

Children (**Allen**), born at Windham:

i.   MARY JANE, d. 22 Nov. 1838, 16y.
ii. BETSEY, d. 12 Feb. 1838, 12y.

iii. CYNTHIA A., d. 20 Oct. 1842, 13y.
iv.   ALVIN, d. 23 Nov. 1858, 22y 2m 7d.
v.   HULDAH, res. So. Windham; m. JOHN DOLLEY.
vi.   ALFRED R., d. 6 May 1855; m. 12 June 1847 SALOME
      LIBBY, b. 16 Mar. 1814, d. 24 Mar. 1902, 78y.
      dau. of William and Hannah (Gould) Libby.
vii. WILLIAM, d. a soldier of yellow fever; m. ---- .
      He served in the 1st, 10th and 30th ME Rgts.
viii. SARAH, b. in 1832, d. Cumberland Mills 4 Sept. 1911;
      m. 1st AMASA WENTWORTH; m. 2nd ALVIN FRANK.
ix.   CHARLES B., b. in 1841, d. in 1905; m. 31 Oct. 1863
      CYNTHIA DOUGHTY, b. in 1847, d. 27 Jan. 1900, 52y
      9m, dau. of George W. Doughty.
x.   LEVINA, res. Westbrook; m. BENJAMIN ELWELL.
xi.   ALONZO PORTER, b. 16 May 1844, d. Portland 28 Nov.
      1908; m. 1st GEORGIA CAROLINE ALLEN; m. 2nd RACHEL
      H. DOLE, d. 6 Mar. 1871, 21y 10m 7d.

950. ESTHER[8] 1802-   [421 John[7] and Leonice Sawyer] was
born at Cumberland ME say 1802; married first there 4 Jan.
1822 ELLIOT MAXFIELD, born at North Yarmouth 1 Nov. 1798, son
of Robert and Tabitha (Clough) Maxfield; married second at
North Yarmouth 2 Sept. 1849 BENJAMIN SAWYER of New Gloucester, born about 1795 (Cornman Ms; No. Yarmouth VRs).
In 1850, the Sawyer household included Melissa Sawyer, 6.

Children (**Maxfield**):

i.   ROBERT C., res. North Yarmouth; m. there 28 Nov. 1850
      HARRIET A. PAINE of Pownal.
ii.   ALLEN.
iii. ELIZABETH; m. 1st ---- WHITNEY; m. 2nd ---- SPEAR.
iv.   FRANCES, res. North Yarmouth.

951. JAMES HICKS[8] 1804-1884 [421 John[7] and Leonice Sawyer]
was born at Cumberland 27 May 1804, died at Gray ME 4 Feb.
1884, 86y (GS); married at Gray 24 Apr. 1827 ANN MARIA
DOUGHTY, born there in Apr. 1803, died there 11 Nov. 1873,
70y 7m (GS), daughter of Joshua and Ann (Tobey) Doughty
(Cornman Ms; church census for 1846 by A. L. Lincoln, in
George T. Hill, History, Records and Recollections of Gray,
Me. [np, 1978] MHS, 366; Nelson, Gray Families, 4). Burials
are in South Gray Cemetery.

Children, born at Gray:

1519. i.   ANN HUNTRESS[9], b. 7 May 1827; m. THOMAS M.
            FOWLER.
1520. ii.   HULDAH D., b. c1828 (18 in 1846); m. JOSEPH P.
            KING.
1521. iii. JAMES EDWIN, b. 22 Jan. 1831.
      iv.   WILLIAM HENRY, b. 18 Oct. 1834, d. Gray 24
            Mar. 1918, 83y 5m 6d; unm.
      v.   EUNICE G., b. c1837 (9 in 1846); m. Falmouth
            14 Jan. 1860 JAMES S. DOLE of Westbrook.
1522. vi.   LOUISA B., b. c1839 (7 in 1846); m. ANDREW G.
            LORING.

1523.   vii.   JOSHUA D., b. c1841 (5 in 1846).
         viii.   HENRIETTA C., b. c1844 (1 1/2 in 1846); m.
                 Gray int. 6 Nov. 1863 LEWIS A. SIMPSON.

952.   ISAAC SAWYER[8] 1808-1866 [421 John[7] and Leonice Saw-
yer] was born at Cumberland 19 June 1808, died there 30 Jan.
1866, 57y[8] (GS); married first MARTHA FIELD; married second
MIRIAM M.[8] LEIGHTON, born at Falmouth 27 Apr. 1818, died at
Portland 23 Dec. 1901, 83y 7m 26d, daughter of Ezekiel and
Mary (Mayberry) Leighton [# 429] (Cornman Ms; town and ME
VRs). Burials are in the Methodist churchyard, West Cumber-
land.
    He was a farmer. In 1850 he and Miriam lived next door to
Jedediah[6] Leighton [# 139].

    Child by Martha, born at Cumberland:

         i.   CHARLES H.[9], b. c1836 (14 in 1850), res.
                Auburn; m. and had 3 ch. (Cornman Ms).

    Children by Miriam, born at Cumberland:

         ii.   WILLIAM HORACE, b. in Aug. 1842; d. W. Cumber-
                land 23 Sept. 1861, 19y.
         iii.   SOPHRONIA AMELIA, b. 20 Apr. 1856; m. 1st
                CHARLES AMBROSE WALTON of Castine; m. 2nd
                CHARLES BLAKE of Westbrook. Ch. Charles Wil-
                liam Walton b. c1878; William Walton Blake.
                In 1880 she and son Charles res. Falmouth.

953.   ANDREW ALLEN[8] 1806-   [422 Thomas[7] and Dorcas
Allen] was born at Windham ME 12 Aug. 1806, lived there in
1880; married there 1 Nov. 1834 MARGARET M. HAWKES, born in
1813 (37 in 1850), daughter of Benjamin and Tamsin (Cobb)
Hawkes (Smith, Adam Hawkes, 393; Windham VRs). Andrew was a
farmer.

    Children, born at Windham:

1524.   i.   EMILY JANE[9], b. c1840 (20 in 1860); m. ALLEN
                PRIDE and ALBERT BODGE.
1525.   ii.   BENJAMIN T., b. 6 Apr. 1845.

954.   SUSAN A.[8] 1812-1905 [422 Thomas[7] and Dorcas Allen]
was born at Windham 16 Apr. 1812, died there 5 Mar. 1905;
married there 15 Oct. 1835 HENRY FARNSWORTH SENTER, born
about 1815 (35 in 1850), died there 17 Apr. 1886, son of Asa
and Fannie (Farnsworth) Senter (Dole, Windham in the Past,
579; Cornman Ms). In 1850 they lived at Windham next door to
his parents.

    Children (Senter), born at Windham:

         i.   HENRIETTA [Etta], b. c1837 (13 in 1850), d. in 1879;
                unm.
         ii.   CHARLES P., b. Windham 19 Apr. 1838; m. 19 Aug. 1890
                MARY MELVINA (WATERHOUSE) Libby, b. Lowell MA 20

June 1847, d. Windham 11 May 1895, dau. of Prentiss
M. and Sarah J. (Rounds) Waterhouse. No ch. She
had had 5 ch. by James Henry Libby (Waterhouse
Desc., 3:1298).
iii. ALBION, b. c1840, d. Westbrook 14 Apr. 1908, 68y 8m
15d; m ANNETTE LIBBY.
iv. ANDREW, d.y.
v. FANNIE E., b. c1844 (6 in 1850), d. in 1888; m. T. E.
HANSON. No ch.
vi. ALFONZO, b. c1846 (4 in 1850); m. ELIZABETH WEBB, b.
Windham 3 Sept. 1834, dau. of Stephen and Tabitha
(Reed) Webb. No ch.
vii. JOHN G., b. c1849 (8/12 in 1850); m. Windham 14 Mar.
1874 ALBINA C. HALL, b. there 6 June 1852, dau. of
William F. and Lavina (Fogg) Hall (Whitten, Samuel
Fogg, 1:686).
viii. WILLIAM H.; m. EMILY M. WHITCOMB.
ix. GEORGE H., b. c1853, d. Windham 30 July 1908, 55y 4m
1d; m. ----.

955. HENRY[8] 1803-   [423 Robert[7] and Tabitha Fowler] was
born at Falmouth 20 June 1803, lived at Bangor ME; married
first MARY WINSLOW, born at North Yarmouth 10 Dec. 1798,
daughter of James and Elizabeth[6] (Leighton) Winslow [# 161];
perhaps married second at Bangor 31 May 1857 LYDIA JANE PAGE
(Cornman Ms).
He was a tallow chandler at Bangor in 1850.

Children by Mary:

i.   CHARLES S.[9], b. c1829 (21 in 1850).
ii.   AMANDA M., b. c1830 (20 in 1850).
iii. GEORGE WINSLOW, b. c1841 (9 in 1850), res.
      Bangor in 1892. He and Charles owned G. W. &
      C S. Leighton, provisions (city dir.).

956. LEWIS[8] 1805-1876 [423 Robert[7] and Tabitha Fowler] was
born at Falmouth 1 Apr. 1805, died at Freeport ME 10 Dec.
1876; married MARTHA PREBLE OXNARD, born at Portland 12 Dec.
1805, died at Freeport 18 Feb. 1890 (town VRs; Cornman Ms).
In 1850 he was a ships' carpenter at Westbrook, and in 1870
a farmer at Freeport. He went west to Lansing MI in 1856,
but did not settle there.

Children:

1526. i.   LEWIS FREDERICK[9], b. in Oct. 1831.
1527. ii.   ANN MARIA, b. Durham c1835; m. WILLIAM H.
            LOW.
1528. iii. ROBERT FOWLER, b. Durham 23 Jan. 1839.
      iv.   CLARA MARTHA, b. Durham 3 Nov. 1841; m.
            WILLIAM McLAUGHLIN. No ch.
      v.   (JULIA) ROSETTA, b. Durham c1843 (7 in 1850),
            res. Boston; m. FRANK CASEY. No ch.
1529. vi.   HATTIE L., b. Portland c1846 (4 in 1850); m.
            JOSEPH C CAREY.
      vii. JOHN HENRY, lost at sea.

957. LOUISA[8] 1806-1891 [423 Robert[7] and Tabitha Fowler]
was born at Falmouth 12 Dec. 1806, died at Gray 24 Dec. 1891;
married at Cumberland 7 Jan. 1831 ISAAC SKILLINGS, born there
17 Aug. 1795, died at Gray 3 Mar. 1879, son of Benjamin and
Mary (March) Skillings (Cumberland and Gray TRs; Cornman Ms).

Children (**Skillings**), born at Gray (in Cumberland TRs):

i.   HARRIET, b. 15 Sept. 1832; unm.
ii.   BENJAMIN FRANKLIN, b. 4 May 1839, d. Gray 31 Mar.
      1907; m. 24 June 1866 ELLEN D. LIBBY, b. Gray 23
      Jan. 1842, d. there 30 Mar. 1907, dau. of William
      and Deborah (Brown) Libby.

958. JOANNA[8] 1814-1897; [423 Robert[7] and Tabitha Fowler]
was born at Falmouth 9 Feb. 1814, died at Gray 22 Feb. 1897;
married at Gray 8 July 1847 WILLIAM THOMPSON, born 21 Sept.
1821, son of Joseph and Priscilla (Mountfort) Thompson (Cornman Ms; town VRs).

Children (**Thompson**), born at Gray:

i.   WILLIAM A., b. 7 Sept. 1847, res. So. Windham; m. 10
      Dec. 1871 CLARA P. STEVENS, b. Windham 7 Sept. 1850,
      dau. of Isaac and Hannah (Sawyer) Stevens of Brain-
      tree MA.
ii.   JOHN H., b. 16 Oct. 1848, res. E. Weymouth MA; m. 30
      Nov. 1876 MARTHA J. CARTLAND, b. Windham 1 May 1849,
      d. 8 Feb. 1914, dau. of John and Nancy (Milliken)
      CARTLAND.
iii. MARY A , b. in May 1850, d. in 1885; m. 1 May 1870
      CHARLES L. VARNEY, b. Windham 27 Jan. 1843, son of
      Timothy and Peace (Varney) Varney.
iv.   SUMNER, b. 22 Feb. 1853; m. in 1877 ETTA (BURRITT)
      Bates, who d. in Feb. 1912, dau. of Albert and
      Miranda Burritt.

959. HARRIET[8] 1816-   [423 Robert[7] and Tabitha Fowler]
was born at Falmouth 20 May 1816, lived at Freeport; married
at Falmouth 26 Mar. 1836 (int. Durham 14 Feb.) JOHN H. OXNARD
of Durham, born in 1808 (town VRs; Cornman Ms).
     In 1850 Oxnard was a sailor at Freeport; in 1860 he was a
shipmaster there, his household including an Edward Leighton,
58; in 1870 his household included a Drusilla M. Leighton,
40. John was a brother-in-law of Lewis Leighton [# 956].

Children (**Oxnard**), born probably at Durham:

i.   EDWARD PREBLE, b. c1837 (mariner, 23, in 1860).
ii.   ALFRED F., b. c1839 (mariner, 21, in 1860).
iii. JOHN THOMAS, b. c1845 (15 in 1860), res. Haverhill
      MA.
--   EMMA J. (adopted), b. Freeport 21 Nov. 1848; m. HENRY
      THAYER of Gray.

960. MOSES WASHINGTON[8] 1818-1884 [423 Robert[7] and Tabitha
Fowler] was born at Falmouth ME 14 Apr. 1818, died there 30
June 1884, 66y; married at Gray 21 Nov. 1844 MARY MERRILL

THOMPSON, born there 3 Oct. 1819, died at Falmouth 6 June
1913, 93y 8m 3d, daughter of Capt. Joseph and Priscilla
(Mountfort) Thompson (Falmouth and Gray VRs; records of Toni
Packard). Burials are in the Methodist Churchyard, Poplar
Ridge, West Falmouth.
He was a farmer. In 1850 his Falmouth household included
his parents. In 1864 he enrolled in Co. B, 25th ME Inf. Rgt.

Children, born at Falmouth:

1530.   i.   HENRY THOMPSON^9, b. 10 Sept. 1845.
        ii.   PRISCILLA BLANCHARD, b. 22 Jan. 1849; m.
              ALFRED S.^{9} LEIGHTON [# 1532].
1531.   iii. HOLLIS FRANKLIN, b. 27 June 1854.

961.   JOSEPH MAYBERRY^8 1814-1898 [427 George^7 and Abigail
Mayberry] was born at Falmouth 16 Aug. 1814, died at Deering
ME 28 Mar. 1898, 53y 7m 2d; married 24 Feb. 1836 MARIA
SAWYER, born at Westbrook 28 Mar. 1815, died at Falmouth 4
Oct. 1889, daughter of Alfred Sawyer (town VRs).
He was a farmer at Falmouth. In 1850 his household in-
cluded Ezekiel [# 509], and in 1870 Daniel and Abigail Wilson
were in his home. Burials are in the Universalist Cemetery,
West Cumberland. Maria had been left an orphan and adopted
into a family surnamed Frank (Cornman Ms).

Children, born at Falmouth:

        i.   ABIGAIL ANN^9, b. 22 Aug. 1838, d. 6 Mar. 1923;
              m. 14 Oct. 1864 DANIEL WILSON, b. 25 May
              1839,$_8$d. 14 May 1891, son of Leonard and
              Nancy^8 (Leighton) Wilson [# 887]. Ch. Emma
              May b. 1 May 1869; m. 31 Mar. 1887 Augustus
              D. Black--no ch.
        ii.   RUFUS M., b. 20 Dec. 1839, d. Portland 24 June
              1917, 77y; m. 24 Jan. 1872 MARY A. ROBERTS,
              b. Saco 4 June 1848, d. 2 Feb. 1930, 83y 28d,
              dau. of Hezekiah and Julia (Skillings)
              Roberts. No ch.
1532.   iii. ALFRED S., b. 7 May 1843.
        iv.   REBECCA JANE, b. 17 Feb. 1847; m. DANIEL E.^{8}
              LEIGHTON [# 891].
        iv.   ALVERADO, b. 27 Sept. 1853, d. Portland 18
              June 1940, 87y (his obit.); m. 25 Dec. 1881
              SARAH S. BABBIDGE, b. No. Haven ME 18 Feb.
              1856, d. Portland in 1923, 66y, dau. of James
              and Olive (Parker) Babbidge. They$_0$res. Port-
              land in 1900. Ch. ESTHER PERKINS^{10} b. Fal-
              mouth 28 Mar. 1886, res. Portland in 1940;
              unm.

962.   GEORGE WASHINGTON^8 1818-1897 [427 George^7 and Abigail
Mayberry] was born at Falmouth 4 May 1818, died there 20 May
1897, 79y 15d; married first there 11 June 1848 RUTH C.
NOYES, born there 7 Nov. 1824, died there 5 Apr. 1877, 52y 4m
29d, daughter of Reuben and Susan W. (Locke) Noyes (Henry E.
Noyes and Harriette E. Noyes, Genealogical Record of Some of
the Noyes Descendants of James, Nicholas and Peter Noyes
[Boston, 1904], 1:101; Locke Gen., 77, 165; Falmouth VRs);

married second OLIVE HODGDON, who died at Falmouth 11 June 1892, 66y, daughter of Daniel and Marion Hodgdon. He was a Falmouth farmer. Burials are in Pine Grove Cemetery, Falmouth Foreside.

Children by Ruth, born at Falmouth:

    i.   ABBIE SUSAN^9, b. in 1853, d. 15 July 1874, 21y 5m (GS).
    ii.   HERBERT G., b. 8 Feb. 1857, d. 22 July 1873, 16y 5m 14d (called George H. in censuses).

963. HANNAH^8 1821-   [427 George^7 and Abigail Mayberry] was born at Falmouth 8 July 1821, lived at Augusta; married first at Falmouth 19 Aug. 1841 THOMAS HICKS, born about 1814 (36 in 1850), lost at sea, son of George and Hannah (Allen) Hicks; married second at Augusta 6 June 1858 HENDRICK SMART, born at Vassalboro ME about 1812 (42 in 1854), son of Levi Smart.
Smart married first Avis W. ---- , who died 14 Feb. 1854, 38y, and married second 14 Nov. 1854 Rachel (Merrill) Hallowell, who died 4 Feb. 1858, 41y (Augusta VRs; Cornman Ms).

Children (**Hicks**):

    i.   ELIZABETH ELLEN, b. c1842 (8 in 1850); m. IRVING DUNHAM.
    ii.   GEORGE, b. c1844 (6 in 1850).
    iii. REUBEN, b. c1847 (3 in 1850).
    iv. LUCY, b. c1848 (2 in 1850).

Children (**Smart**);

    v.   GEORGE W., res. Medford MA
    vi.   IDA, d. Augusta 7 Apr. 1881, 22y.

964. AMOS^8 1823-1901 [427 George^7 and Abigail Mayberry] was born at Falmouth 20 Aug. 1823, died there 30 Jan. 1901, 77y 5m 10d; married there 4 July 1850 SARAH PRINCE NOYES, born there 8 July 1828, died there 14 Sept. 1900, 72y 2m 6d, daughter of Nathaniel and Susan (Noyes) Noyes (Noyes Desc., 1:101; Falmouth VRs). Burials are in Pine Grove Cemetery, Falmouth Foreside.
He was a Falmouth farmer in 1850; in 1860 Mary A Noyes, 24, was in his household. In 1879 he was called a tin pedlar; in 1880 the Portland directory listed his firm Tenney & Leighton, stamped and japanned ware, at Fore St., Portland.

Children, born at Falmouth:

    i.   HOWARD W.^{9}, b. c1851 (8 in 1860), d. Falmouth 28 Nov. 1876, 25y; m. there int. 9 June 1873 (MARIE) ESTELLE WYMAN, b. Fairfield ME c1859, dau. of David and Harriet Wyman--div. No ch. She m. 2nd Portland 25 Oct. 1893 Stanislaus M. Hamwell.
1533. ii.   EDGAR BARTON, b. 8 Dec. 1866.
    iii. EDWARD A. (twin), b. 8 Dec. 1866, d. 6 Aug. 1882 (GS).

965. ALBERT[8] 1829-1865 [427 George[7] and Abigail Mayberry]
was born at Falmouth 7 Mar. 1829, died there 12 Sept. 1865,
36y (GS); married at Portland 27 Nov. 1859 (ANNA) SALOME BEAN
HUSTON, born at Falmouth 11 Mar. 1843, died at South Portland
22 Dec. 1922, daughter of Isaac and Margaret (Field) Huston
(Harris, William Huston, 43-4; town VRs; Cornman Ms)
    In 1860 they were living at Falmouth with his brother
George, and had a month-old child. Widow Salome married second ---- Preble, and third Caleb Hunt of Taunton MA, but had
no children by them. She died at the home of her granddaughter Ella Talbot.

Children, born at Falmouth:

1534. i.   SCOTT DYER[9], b. 30 May 1861.
       ii.   ELIZABETH ELLEN, b. c1863, d. So. Portland; m.
             10 Dec. 1883 GEORGE OLIVER LEEMAN, b. Wool-
             wich ME c1859, d. Everett MA in 1894, son of
             George L. and Laura J. Leeman. He was an
             iron-worker. Ch. Ella Leighton b. Hyde Park
             MA 19 June 1883; m. So. Portland 6 May 1902
             Frederick William Talbot, b. Gray 2 May 1873,
             d. So. Portland 12 May 1937.
       iii. ADELAIDE, d.y.
       iv.   ?LORETTA.
       --   ALBERT LELAND (adopted, kept surname Keith).

966. ADDISON GREENLEAF[8] 1831-1906 [427 George[7] and Abigail
Mayberry] was born at Falmouth 25 May 1831, died there 2 Mar.
1906 (Westbrook VRs; GS, 74y); married at Portland 3 July
1859 (VRs; 1857 per family Bible) SARAH WARREN DeCRENEY, born
there 23 Feb. 1838, died at Falmouth 23 Feb. 1923 (Portland
VRs), 85y, daughter of Louis Jules and Nancy (Warren) DeCreney (town and ME VRs; Bible and other family records of
descendant Ruth L. Froeberg). Burials are in a family plot
off Brook Road, Falmouth.
    He was a farmer at Falmouth. In 1860 they were living with
his parents on Blackstrap Road. In 1900 he was living alone
at Portland, and his wife was living at Falmouth with three
of her sons.
    Clifford and Ora owned a music store on Congress St.; Arno
and Warren had their offices on the second floor. Warren,
Leon and Arno were also accomplished musicians.

Children, born at Falmouth:

1535. i.   LOUVILLE GREENLEAF[9], b. 30 Oct. 1859.
       ii.   EUGENE FREDERICK, b. 22 Nov. 1861, d. Falmouth
             19 Aug. 1877, 15y 9m.
1536. iii. HARRIET WARREN, b. 7 Nov. 1864; m. EDWIN W.
             HULIT.
1537. iv.   VIRGIL LOUIS, b. 11 Feb. 1867.
       v.   ORA LLEWELLYN, b. 29 May 1869, d. 27 Nov.
             1898, 29y 6m (GS), lost on steamer Portland.
       vi.   WARREN DeCRENEY, b. 29 Sept. 1872, d. New
             Haven CT 7 Aug. 1964, 91y 11m; unm. He was
             an optometrist and owned the family Bible.
       vii. NELLY D., b. 21 Jan. 1873, not listed in
             1880).

1538.   vii.   LEON PERCY, b. 25 Nov. 1874.
1539.   viii   ARNO LESLIE, b. 19 Nov. 1877.
        ix.   CLIFFORD EUGENE, b. 7 July 1882, d. Portland
               22 Nov. 1933, 51y; m. 10 Mar. 1930 MARY
               CURRAN. No ch. He was a musician and music
               teacher.

967. CYRUS CUMMINGS[8] 1837-1901 [427 George[7] and Abigail
Mayberry] was born at Falmouth 22 Feb. 1837, died there 1
Nov. 1901, 64y 8m 9d; married there 3 July 1861 MARGARET REED
STUBBS, born at Cumberland 4 July 1842, died at Falmouth 17
Mar. 1916, 73y 8m 13d, daughter of Edward and Eliza M. (Day)
Stubbs (town and ME VRs; Cornman Ms). Burials are in the
Universalist Churchyard, West Cumberland.
He was a Falmouth farmer. In 1870 his mother Abigail, 78,
was in his household.

Children, born at Falmouth:

1540.   i.   WILLIS HOWARD[9], b. 12 Aug. 1862.
1541.   ii.   CLARA S., b. 15 Dec. 1864; m. FREDERICK L.
               MERRILL.
        iii.   CORA BELLE, b. 7 May 1867; m. Falmouth 28 Nov.
               1895 THOMAS BOWEN LOOK, b. Addison ME 5 Oct.
               1862, son of Jonas W. and Lucy Ann (Chandler)
               Look. No ch. He was a sea captain.
        iv.   EVA GERTRUDE, b. 27 May 1869; m. Falmouth 22
               Jan. 1890 FREDERICK E. MOULTON of Gorham, b.
               19 Jan. 1869. Ch. Onsville J. and Merton.
1542.   v.   EDWARD JAMES, b. 15 Oct. 1872.

968. ELIZABETH[8] 1821-1904 [429 Ezekiel[7] and Mary Mayberry]
was born at Falmouth 11 Sept. 1821, died at Portland 10 July
1904, 83y; married JOSEPH HICKS, born at Falmouth 17 Oct.
1819, died there 10 Dec. 1880, son of George and Hannah
(Allen) Hicks (Hall Desc. #1094; Cornman Ms). Burials are in
the Methodist Churchyard, West Cumberland. They were listed
at Cumberland in 1850.

Children (**Hicks**), born at Cumberland (VRs):

i.   ANSON NEWELL, b. 9 Aug. 1844.
ii.   MARY ELIZABETH, b. 9 Apr. 1845; m. LEANDER[8] LEIGHTON
        [# 1023].
iii.   JOHN H., b. 15 Dec. 1847, d. 6 Apr. 1887; unm.
iv.   ERVIN E., b. 7 July 1858; m. 3 June 1882 FLORENCE
        NOYES.

969. LAVINA[8] 1800-1870 [430 Nathaniel[7] and Dolly Wilson]
was born at Falmouth 22 Nov. 1800, died 14 May 1870; married
5 Oct. 1820 DANIEL SHAW JR., born 14 Dec. 1795, died 19 Mar.
1878 (Cornman Ms).

Children (**Shaw**), born at Cumberland:

i.   ELIZABETH, b. 5 May 1823; m. 5 Nov. 1859 ISRAEL
        MORRILL, b. 8 May 1817. No ch.
ii.   JOANNA, b. 20 July 1825, d. in Feb. 1842; unm.

iii. NATHANIEL L., b. 20 Apr. 1828, d. in 1904; m. 4 Jan.
     1854 REBECCA F. HAWKES, b. 15 Feb. 1835, dau. of
     Daniel L. and Abigail A (Pennell) Hawkes (Smith,
     Adam Hawkes, 198).
iv. MARTHA, b. 19 Mar. 1831, d. Westbrook 2 Aug. 1904; m.
     Windham 25 Dec. 1851 THOMAS C. HAWKES, b. Windham 26
     Apr. 1828, d. Westbrook 24 July 1906, son of Isaiah
     and Rebecca (Cobb) Hawkes (Smith, Adam Hawkes, 398).
v.   JASON G., b. 8 Oct. 1834; m. 27 Aug. 1865 MINERVA
     COBB.
vi. LUCY E., b. in July 1837, d. in Feb. 1842.
vii. DANIEL BRADBURY, b. in May 1840, d. in Oct. 1842.
viii. DANIEL B., b. 30 Apr. 1844, res. So. Windham; m. 1st
     22 Jan. 1862 LOUISA CLOUDMAN, b. in Nov. 1841, d. 19
     Oct. 1884; m. 2nd in June 1901 ELLA GILMAN.

970. EUNICE[8] 1802-   [430 Nathaniel[7] and Dolly Wilson]
was born at Falmouth 7 Feb. 1802; married JOSHUA GOWER JR.,
born at New Gloucester 6 June 1802, died 9 Mar. 1876, son of
Joshua and Sarah Gower (Cornman Ms; New Gloucester VRs).
They were listed at Westbrook in 1850.

Children (**Gower**):

i.   JANE LEWIS, b. 2 May 1826, res. Portland; m. WILLIAM
      QUIMBY.
ii.   JASON, b. in 1828, d. infant.
iii. AMELIA H., b. 5 Mar. 1830, d. 13 Aug. 1899; m. JOSHUA
      ROBERTS of Westbrook, b. 2 Feb. 1814. No ch.
iv.   RUTH WILSON, b. 5 Mar. 1832; m. 5 July 1857 WILLIAM
      BABB, b. 5 Mar. 1827, d. Westbrook 25 Feb. 1899,
      son of Lemuel and Eliza (Jones) Babb.
v.   HANNAH NOYES, b. 24 May 1834, res. Westbrook
      (Harriet, 17, in 1850).
vi.   SARAH E., b. 10 Sept. 1836, res. Portland; m. 5 Dec.
      1859 Rev. EDWIN S. ELDER, b. 12 Dec. 1837.
vii. LUCY A , b. in Dec. 1838, d. in Feb. 1840.
viii. JASON M., b. 12 June 1840; res. Westbrook.
ix.   CHARLES DAVIS, b. 3 Jan., d. in July, 1843, 6m.
x.   ANSEL L., b. 13 July 1844; m. 1 May 1878 CAROLINE
      MARTIN.

971. JANE[8] 1805-1867 [430 Nathaniel[7] and Dolly Wilson] was
born at Falmouth 20 Oct. 1805, died at Westbrook 19 Jan.
1867; married there 12 Apr. 1830 ISAIAH HACKER DAVIS, born 2
Aug. 1809, died 21 Mar. 1878, son of Gardner and Dorcas (Goddard) Davis (town VRs; records of descendant Evelyn Cobb;
Cornman Ms). Burials are in Evergreen Cemetery.

Children (**Davis**), born at Westbrook:

i.   HENRY HARPER, b. 14 Sept. 1831, d. 11 Dec. 1901,
      struck by train; unm.
ii.   HANNAH COLLINS, b. 5 Feb. 1833; m. GEORGE F.[7]
      LEIGHTON [# 515].
iii. ZERUAH PAGE [Vida], b. 18 Apr. 1835, d. Falmouth 18
      Feb. 1931; m. JOHN E. [Jake] FOBES, drowned in 1899.
iv.   NATHANIEL LEIGHTON, b. 20 Apr., d. 19 Nov., 1839.
v.   CHARLES R., d.infant.

vi.   FRANCES HELEN [Ellie], b. 19 Mar. 1844, d. Falmouth
      7 Nov. 1922; m. in 1865 FRANCIS ORMAN JONATHAN
      PRIDE, b. Westbrook 4 Dec. 1838, d. Falmouth 16 Jan.
      1911, 73y, son of Thomas and Charlotte Pride.
vii. CHARLES HAMLIN, b. 17 July 1846, d. 19 Jan. 1926; m.
      17 Mar. 1881 HELEN AUGUSTA HOLMAN, b. 17 May 1847,
      d. 2 Dec. 1909, dau. of Amasa and Apphia (Powers)
      Holman of Dixfield.

972.   JEDEDIAH JR.[8] 1808-1892 [430 Nathaniel[7] and Dolly
Wilson] was born at Falmouth 16 May 1808, died there 2 Mar.
1892, 83y 9m; married first there 16 Apr. 1830 (Westbrook
int. 3 Jan.) EMMA JANE DAVIS, born at Falmouth in 1806, died
there 3 Apr. 1847, 41y (GS), daughter of Gardner and Dorcas
(Goddard) Davis; married second 26 Nov. 1847 ROWENA HILL[8]
LEIGHTON, born there 23 Oct. 1823, died there 30 Sept. 1906,
82y 11m, daughter of Thaddeus and Abigail (Elliot) Leighton
[# 446] (records of Nellie Smith Leighton; town and ME VRs;
Cornman Ms). Burials are in the Packard Cemetery, Pride's
Corner, Westbrook.

Called "junior" because his grandfather was still living,
he was later known as "captain," perhaps a militia rank. He
was a farmer at Falmouth, in the portion which became part of
Westbrook.

In 1850 and 1860 his young children lived with their grandmother Dolly; in 1870 his household included his mother-in-
law Abigail.

Children by first wife Emma, born at Westbrook:

        i.   GARDNER DAVIS[9], b. 31 Jan. 1832; m. 24 Nov.
             1853 SARAH F. GRAY, b. c1832, dau. of Jere-
             miah Gray. They rem. to PA, and thence west.
             Ch. GARDNER DAVIS[10], and probably others.
1543.   ii. LUCY ANN, b. 22 Oct. 1834; m. EDWARD COBB.
        iii. EMILY JANE, b. 18 Aug. 1837, d. 12 Mar. 1928;
             m. 2 June (or 12 Nov.) 1870 ANSEL DYER WASS,
             b. in Feb. 1831, d. 24 Jan. 1899, son of Otis
             and Melinda (Dyer) Wass (Wass Fam., 64). He
             was brevet Brig. Gen. of the 6th and 19th ME
             Inf. Rgts. Ch. Ansel Stanley b. Boston 30
             May 1873; m. St. Louis MO in 1909 Minnie
             Alwilda Grover.
        iv. DORCAS DAVIS, b. 17 Sept. 1838, d. 3 Feb.
             1919; m. 2 June 1870 CHARLES COBB JR., b.
             Westbrook 8 Dec. 1838, d. 19 Sept. 1914,
             son of Charles and Isabella (Campbell) Cobb
             (Cobb Fam., 2:471). Ch. Hattie Mae b. 4 Aug.
             1871; m. 31 Dec. 1910 Fred Barker Libby, b.
             30 Mar. 1863, d. 15 Dec. 1914.
        v.   LOIS WILSON, b. 8 Mar. 1841, d. 9 June 1913;
             m. 16 Feb. 1865 WILLIAM BOLTON, b. Westbrook
             12 Oct. 1841, d. 31 Dec. 1908. No ch.
        vi. ELIZABETH LAMBERT, b. 22 June 1845; m. Boston
             28 Nov. 1866 GORHAM R. WHITNEY, b. Falmouth
             26 Sept. 1840, son of Ammi P. and Hannah
             Whitney. Ch. George Milton b. 23 Sept. 1869;
             m. Mary Elizabeth Whitney.

Children by second wife Rowena, born at Falmouth:

1544.   vii.   ISAIAH DAVIS, b. 17 May 1848.
1545.   viii. NATHANIEL, b. 15 Apr. 1851.
        ix.   FREDERICK HENRY, b. 1 Aug. 1852, drowned Port-
               land 21 Aug. 1892, 39y 1m 4d; unm.
1546.   x.   ANGIE ELLA, b. 30 Oct. 1854; m. ALMON MARSTON.
        xi.   CHARLES W., b. 13 Oct. 1863, d. Portland 1
               Feb. 1909, 45y; m. W. Falmouth 12 Apr. 1892
               MARY ELIZABETH WINSLOW, b. Deering 27 Sept.
               1864, d. Portland 24 Feb. 1938, 75y 4m 27d,
               dau. of Andrew and Mary Elizabeth (Knight)
               Winslow. He was a butcher.   Ch. WINIFRED
               ADELAIDE[10] b. 6 June 1895, d. Portland 7
               Sept. 1933, 38y 3m 1d; m. RALPH McMILLAN.

973.   ICHABOD WILSON[8] 1811-1907 [430 Nathaniel[7] and Dolly
Wilson] was born at Falmouth 22 Mar. 1811, died at South
Portland 18 Jan. 1907, 95y 10m; married 23 Mar. 1836 EMILY
JANE SMALL, born at Gray 2 June 1817, died at South Portland
3 Aug. 1908, 91y 2m 1d, daughter of George and Sallie (Wescott) Small (town VRs; records of Barbara Brown; Cornman Ms).
    He had a grocery store at Little Falls, South Windham, in
1838, and also operated a sawmill.   In 1858 he became superintendent of the Cumberland-Oxford Canal (McLellan, Gorham,
278, 311).   At the start of the Civil War he established a
wholesale flour and grain business at Portland (newspaper
article [MHS scrapbook] 26 Mar. 1904, marking his 93rd birthday).   In their old age he and Emily lived with their son
Ervin.

    Children:

        i.   NATHANIEL BRADBURY[9], b. Falmouth 7 Apr. 1837,
               d. Westbrook 14 Oct. 1838.
1547.   ii.   (ICHABOD) MELVILLE, b. Falmouth 24 Jan. 1839.
1548.   iii.   ORLANDO, b. Gorham 22 Dec. 1840.
        iv.   SARAH FRANCES, b. Gorham 22 June 1843, d. So.
               Portland 1 Sept. 1925; m. 14 May 1863 CHARLES
               PERRY BRACKETT, b. 8 Apr. 1838, son of
               Willard and Olive (Low) Brackett.   No ch.
        v.   child, b. Gorham 10 Feb. 1845, d. infant.
1549.   vi.   ERVIN SMALL, b. Gorham 9 Feb. 1848.
1550.   vii.   ALPHEUS SHAW, b. 16 Oct. 1855.

974.   JOEL[8] 1807-1884 [433 Peter[7] and Rachel Winslow] was
born at Falmouth 17 June 1807, died there 28 Dec. 1884, 77y
6m; married there 22 Feb. 1836 LOUISE ROBERTS[8] LEIGHTON, born
there 23 Aug. 1813, died there 25 Mar. 1881, 67y, daughter of
Silas and Abigail (Roberts) Leighton [# 443] (Falmouth VRs;
Cornman Ms).   Burials are in Poplar Ridge Cemetery, Methodist
Churchyard, West Falmouth.
    He was listed as a farmer at Cumberland in 1850, and at
Falmouth in 1860 and after.

    Children, born at Falmouth:

1551.   i.   JULIA[9], b. 5 Oct. 1841; m. BENJAMIN S. HUSTON.
        ii.   OSROE, b. 7 July 1845, d. 11 June 1855, 10y.

1552. iii. ABIGAIL, b. 28 Mar. 1848; m. RICHARD ROBERTS.
       iv.   LUCINDA R., b. 28 July 1851, d. 14 June 1861,
             10y (GS).
1553. v.   ROLAND, b. 10 July 1853.

975. LOUISE[8] 1810-1897 [433 Peter[7] and Rachel Winslow] was
born at Falmouth 17 Feb. 1810, died at Portland 17 Dec. 1897;
married 16 Dec. 1832 THOMAS NEWMAN of Portland, born at Falmouth 25 May 1812 (Cornman Ms).

Children (**Newman**):

i.   CHARLES HENRY, b. 15 Oct. 1834, d.y.
ii.   MARY CAROLINE, b. 21 Sept. 1836; m. JONATHAN B.[8]
      LEIGHTON [# 1120].
iii. SARAH LOUISE, b. 29 July 1840; m. 9 Oct. 1861 TURNER
      O. CAREY.
iv.   CHARLES HENRY, b. 15 Apr. 1849, d. 14 Dec. 1870; unm.

976. ADAM W.[8] 1812-1866 [433 Peter[7] and Rachel Winslow]
was born at Falmouth 30 Dec. 1812, died at Portland 5 Mar.[8]
1866, 54y; married at Falmouth 17 June 1837 JULIA ANN[8]
LEIGHTON, born at Falmouth 20 Feb. 1816, died at Portland 21
Dec. 1898, 82y 10m, daughter of Silas and Abigail (Roberts)
Leighton [# 443] (town VRs; Cornman Ms). Burials are in the
Methodist Cemetery, West Falmouth. He was a farmer at Falmouth; in 1850 and 1860 his mother Rachel was with him.
He moved to Portland, where he operated a grocery store for
the four years before his death (Little, ME Genealogies,
1:659; 4:2057). Widow Julia lived with her son Wendell.

Children, born at Falmouth:

1554. i.   BYRON[9], born 29 Sept. 1839.
1555. ii.   WENDELL, born 6 Oct. 1842.
1556. iii. WILBUR FISKE, b. 16 Apr. 1845.
1557. iv.   ADAM PHILLIP, b. 6 Apr. 1851.
1558. v.   AMBROSE PETER, b. 20 July 1853.
       vi.   ?OLIVIA, b. c1856 (4 in 1860).

977. ABIGAIL M.[8] 1814-   [433 Peter[7] and Rachel Winslow]
was born at Falmouth 13 June 1814; married 29 Oct. 1834 AMOS
ROSCOE WINSLOW, born at Cumberland ME 10 Jan. 1808, died at
West Cumberland 25 Apr. 1892, son of James and Elizabeth[6]
(Leighton) Winslow [# 161] (Winslow Mem., 940; Cumberland
VRs; Cornman Ms).

Children (**Winslow**), born at Cumberland:

i.   RACHEL SUSAN, b. 12 July 1835, res. Portland.
ii.   AMOS ROSCOE JR., b. 12 July 1837; m. OLIVE JANE[8]
      LEIGHTON [# 1134].
iii. ELIZABETH JANE, b. 8 Apr. 1839; m. 7 Sept. 1371
      ELBRIDGE W. KNIGHT.
iv.   EUNICE ELLEN, b. 13 May 1841, d. Weston MA 24 Dec.
      1915, 71y 7m 11d; m. SIDNEY WOOD WASHBURN, b. W.
      Falmouth in May 1837, d. Waltham MA 9 Feb. 1887, 49y
      9m, son of Otis and Rachel Washburn.

v.   RUTH ETTA, b. 18 Apr. 1843, d. 21 Nov. 1865.
vi. ORLANDO JASPER, b. 4 Apr. 1845, d. Portland 5 Apr.
     1893; m. 17 Mar. 1868 ELLA JANE HUSTON, b. 15 Mar.
     1851, d. Portland 15 Jan. 1919, dau. of Nathan Lord
     and Mary Ann (Knight) Huston.
vii. SOPHRONIA LORD, b. 8 Feb. 1849; m. CHARLES A.
     ROBINSON.
viii. NEAL DOW, b. 11 June 1852

978. EMELINE[8] [Emmie] 1818-1864 [433 Peter[7] and Rachel
Winslow] was born at Falmouth 6 Sept. 1818, died at Portland
1 Mar. 1864; married 6 June 1838 WILLIAM SIDNEY HALL, born 13
Dec. 1813, died at Morris Plains NJ 6 Nov. 1881, son of
Greenfield and Sarah (Prince) Hall (town VRs; Cornman Ms),
In 1850 their household at Cumberland included John[7]
Leighton, 76 [# 421]. Hall married second Hattie Eaton.

Children (Hall), born at Cumberland:

i.   ADAM LEIGHTON, b. 26 July 1838, d. 4 Sept. 1846,
     8y 4m.
ii. SARAH EMELINE, b. 1 Aug. 1844 m. 3 July 1861 BENJAMIN
     BISHOP.
iii. HORATIO COLEMAN, b. 15 Mar. 1849, d. Jersey City NJ
     19 Jan. 1890; m. 1st in 1877 SUSIE ---- ; m. 2nd
     Nyack NY EMMA CONKLIN.
iv. JULIA FRANCES, b. 2 Sept. 1851; m. 20 Feb. 1872 LEROY
     S. SANBORN. He was the Portland city auditor.

979. WILLIAM B.[8] 1813-1902 [434 George[7] and Susanna Baker]
was born at Falmouth 6 July 1813, died there 10 June 1902,
88y 11m; married there 9 Dec. 1837 ABIGAIL K. HUSTON, born
there 28 Dec. 1811, died there 26 Sept. 1902, 90y 8m 28d,
daughter of Mark and Edna (Knight) Huston (Falmouth VRs).
  He was a farmer, and in 1850 lived next door to his parents. His household in 1870 included his nephew Frank, 14
[# 981]. He and Abbie were listed in Horace's household in
1900.

Children, born at Falmouth:

       i.   LORINDA[9], b. 12 Oct. 1838; m. Cumberland 11
            Jan. 1866 (VRs) OTIS ALLEN MOUNTFORD. No ch.
1559. ii. EDNA M., b. 28 Oct. 1844; m. WINSLOW LUFKIN.
       iii. HORACE, b. 5 June 1849, d. Falmouth 15 Apr.
            1920, 70y 10m 10d; m. 1st ---- ; m. 2nd Fal-
            mouth (as a widower) 3 July 1909 widow GRACE
            E. (STACY) Stickney, b. Bangor NY c1875, dau.
            of Frank and Adelaide (Barlow) Stacy. She m.
            3rd W. Falmouth 21 Aug. 1924 Frank H. Field.

980. MARIA[8] 1815-1866 [434 George[7] and Susanna Baker] was
born at Falmouth in Oct. 1815, died there 19 Nov. 1866; married there 21 Apr. 1833 ELIAS P. MARSTON, born at West Falmouth 25 Sept. 1809, died at Pownal ME 12 July 1884, son of
Benjamin and Anna (Hobbs) Marston (Marston Gen., 212, 216-8;
town VRs; Cornman Ms).
  Marston was a farmer and church deacon.

Children (**Marston**), born at Pownal:

i.   HENRIETTA, b. 29 Apr. 1834; unm.
ii.   GEORGE LYMAN, b. 20 Nov. 1836, res. Deering; m. 11
      Sept. 1860 ALTHEA S. WILSON [# 887].
iii. CHARLES AUGUSTUS, b. 22 Mar. 1840, res. Pownal; m. 17
      Oct. 1865 MARY STUBBS.
iv.   ALMON, b. 29 Nov. 1841; m. ANGIE ELLA^9 LEIGHTON
      [# 1546].
v.   JAMES T., b. 28 Feb. 1846, res. Haverhill MA; m. 29
      July 1874 PAMELIA D. WRIGHT.
vi.   ELIAS CONVERSE, b. 29 May 1848, d. 12 May 1852.
vii. son, b. 29 May, d. 2 June, 1850.
viii. ELIAS CONVERSE, b. 5 June 1852, res. Pownal; m. 23
      Mar. 1873 MARY N. RYDER.

981. GEORGE W.^{8} 1817-1863 [434 George^7 and Susanna Baker]
was born at Pownal ME 4 Oct. 1817, died there 11 Aug. 1863;
married 28 Oct. 1845 SOPHRONIA WILSON, born in June 1822,
died 14 June 1860, daughter of Nathaniel and Elizabeth
(Baker) Wilson (Pownal VRs; Cornman Ms).
A house carpenter, George and his wife were listed in his
brother Lorenzo's household in 1850.

Children, born at Pownal:

i.   HENRIETTA M.^{9}, b. 29 June 1847; m. 1 Jan. 1872
      HARLAN B. TRUE. No ch.
ii.   (ASBURY) WESLEY, b. 12 Sept. 1849, d. Portland
      25 July 1900, 51y 9m; m. 9 Oct. 1888 MARY A.
      STACY, b. Kezar Falls ME c1912, d. Portland
      5 Feb. 1930, 18y, dau. of George and Sarah
      (Guptill) Stacy. No ch.
iii. FRANK L., b. 21 Aug. 1856, d. Portland 18 Oct.
      1938, 83y 1m 27d; unm.

982. LEONARD^8 1820-1897 [434 George^7 and Susanna Baker]
was born at Falmouth 23 Mar. 1820, died at South Boston MA 20
Apr. 1897; married first at Portland 13 Apr. 1848 CAROLINE P.
TRUNDY, born at Pittston ME about 1824, died 12 Jan. 1855,
31y 3m 12d, daughter of William and Harriet (Carleton) Trundy
of Wiscasset; married second at Boston 1 Feb. 1857 LUCY M.
DODGE, born in MA 25 Oct. 1834, died at South Boston, daughter of Ephraim Dodge (Cornman Ms).
In 1880 Leonard was a ships' carpenter at South Boston. In
1900 Lucy was living with Sheridan and Helen Bisbee.

Children by Lucy, born at Boston:

1560. i.   CORA E.^{9}, b. 26 Nov. 1858; m. JOHN E. DODGE.
1561. ii. HELEN DODGE, b. 15 Dec. 1871; m. SHERIDAN
            BISBEE.

983. LORENZO H.^{8} 1822-1902 [434 George^7 and Susanna Baker]
was born at Falmouth 26 Feb. 1822, died there 20 Dec. 1902,
80y; married about 1848 LUCY G. [Ruby] RUSSELL, born at Falmouth in Sept. 1829 (per 1900 census), died there 2 Oct.
1900, 71y 25d, daughter of Joseph R. and Lucy W. Russell

(Cornman Ms; town VRs). Burials are in the Methodist Churchyard, Poplar Ridge, West Falmouth.
He was a farmer at Pownal in 1850 and 1860, and at Falmouth
in 1870 and after.

Children, probably born at Pownal:

1562.   i.   JOSEPH R.^{9}, b. 5 June 1849.
        ii.   HARRIET G., b. 8 Apr. 1851; m. NATHANIEL^9
              LEIGHTON [# 1545].
        iii. CLINTON, b. 29 Apr. 1853, d. 23 Mar. 1855.
        iv.   FREDERICK C., b. 13 Aug. 1855, d. 20 Aug.
              1857.
1563.   v.   ADA F., b. 10 Mar. 1859; m. CLARENCE M.
              MORRILL.
        vi.   LENA C., b. 20 Dec. 1860, d. Portland 11 Dec.
              1937, 76y 11m 21d; m. 10 Jan. 1894 FREDERICK
              A. LANE, b. Sherbrook PQ 21 Oct. 1865,
              son of Edmund G. and Marie (Dixon) Lane.
              No ch.
        vii. GEORGE W., b. 15 Oct. 1863, d. Portland 26
              Dec. 1935, 71y 2m 11d, a widower.
        viii. RALPH C , b. 5 Apr. 1867, d. Falmouth 4 Dec.
              1937, 70y 7m 29d; unm. He owned the family
              homestead.
1564.   ix.   ALICE GERTRUDE, b. 20 Jan. 1870; m. ALBION
              WILSON SHAW.

984.   ROYAL^8 1816-1902 [435 Josiah^7 and Anna Wilson] was
born at Falmouth 19 Oct. 1816, died at Portland 26 Jan. 1902,
86y 3m 7d; married first at Westbrook 15 Feb. 1859 ADELAIDE
W. (PRIDE) Mansfield, who died 13 June 1864; married second
at Portland 17 Jan. 1866 HULDAH HAWKES, born at Windham 24
May 1824, died at Portland 2 May 1903, 77y 11m 18d, daughter
of Benjamin and Ruth (Roberts) Hawkes (town and ME VRs;
Smith, Adam Hawkes, 385; Cornman Ms).
Royal was a grocer at Woodfords Village. Huldah founded
the Casco St. Seminary for Young Ladies about 1856, and operated it for ten years. In 1881 she became a Quaker (Falmouth
Monthly Meeting, Book 2, 1865-1917, MHS), and was a leader in
the Society of Friends. In 1889 she went to Palestine as
superintendent and matron of the Ramallah Mission near Jerus-
alem; when she returned in 1891 she lectured in the US for
two years on the Mission's work. In 1893 she returned to Palestine for three more years.

Child by Adelaide:

        i.   ADDIE IDELLA^9, born 24 Mar. 1864; m. in Sept.
              1900 PETER F. PORTER. Ch. Frances Hope b. 6
              Sept. 1901, perhaps others.

Child by Huldah, born at Portland:

        ii.   FREDERICK ERNEST, b. in June 1867; unm.

985.   NATHANIEL WILSON^8 1833-1899 [435 Josiah^7 and Anna
Wilson] was born at Falmouth 11 June 1833, died at Brooklyn
NY 12 Aug. 1899; married first at Portland 27 June 1861 MARY

ELIZABETH PURINTON, born 9 Oct. 1835, died at Brooklyn 18 May 1882, daughter of George Hussey and Harriet (Loring) Purinton (Charles H. Pope, Loring Genealogy [Cambridge MA, 1917], 130); married second 19 Nov. 1884 HELEN HUDSON, born 12 Nov. 1855, died 26 Dec. 1898 (letter from daughter Hattie in 1904--Cornman Papers).

Nathaniel was graduated from Bowdoin Medical College in 1857, and from New York Medical College in 1858; he set up his practice at Brooklyn, where he resided for 40 years. He was a surgeon with the 72nd and 173rd NY Vol. Inf. Rgts. from June 1861 to Nov. 1864, with brevet rank of lieutenant colonel. He was president of the Union Board of US Pension Examiners (Bowdoin College General Catalog).

Children by Mary, born at Brooklyn:

    i.   HATTIE[9], b. 14 Aug. 1863; m. 24 Oct. 1889
           GEORGE R. COMINGS, b. 2 June 1860. Ch. Lois
           Leighton b. Brooklyn 22 July 1898.
    ii.   MELVILLE HENRY, b. 10 Oct. 1865; m. 23 June
           1897 ELLA LATHAM, b. Noank CT 7 July 1868,
           dau. of James and Mary E. Latham. Ch.
           WILSON[10] b. 30 Nov. 1900 (Melville's letter-
           Cornman Papers).
   --   CHARLES WILLARD (adopted in 1875), b. 20 Dec.
           1871; m. 25 May 1895 Adelaide White.

Child by Helen, born at Brooklyn:

    iii. OLIVE WINIFRED, b. 13 Nov. 1888.

986. RANDALL[8] 1838-1927 [435 Josiah[7] and Anna Wilson] was born at Falmouth 8 Aug. 1838, died at Portland 8 May 1927, 89y 3m; married 1 Jan. 1860 MARY ELLEN KILBOURN, born at Scarborough ME 29 Nov. 1837, died at Portland 2 Dec. 1921, daughter of John and Mary (Libby) Kilbourn (Cornman Ms; town and ME VRs).

He was a grocer at Deering, formerly part of Westbrook.

Children, born at Deering:

    i.   HERBERT AUGUSTUS[9], b. 10 Aug. 1862, d. Bow-
           doinham ME 13 Aug. 1924, 78y 11m 2d; m. 11
           July 1884 MARY TWING. No ch. A watchmaker
           and jeweler, he became a pioneer in making
           ice cream in 1886. In 1899 he opened a shop
           on Congress Square, incorporated in 1900 as
           Deering Ice Cream Co. of New England; he sold
           out soon for health reasons (his letter to
           Charles E. Stickney, pres., Deering Ice
           Cream Co., 3 Mar. 1924).
    ii.   SCOTT KILBOURN, b. 27 July 1866, d. Deering 22
           Nov. 1895, 30y 3m 28d; m. 30 May 1891 HATTIE
           E. DAMON, b. in Apr. 1863, res. Norwell MA in
           1900 with mother Rosella and ch. HELEN
           LOUISE[10] b. 6 July 1894.
    iii. MABEL K., b. 24 July 1870, d. Deering 29 Nov.
           1895, 26y 4m; unm.
    iv.   AVA, b. 25 Nov. 1880.

987. **MARTHA JANE**[8] 1851-1931 [437 Jonathan[7] and Mary Tinkham] was born at Falmouth 28 Aug. 1851, died at Portland 15 May 1931, 78y 8m 17d; married 7 Jan. 1868 CORNELIUS BUTLER ROSS, born at Gray 29 July 1848, died at Falmouth 4 June 1925, son of Joseph and Almira (Cobb) Ross (Cornman Ms; Falmouth and ME VRs).

Children (**Ross**):

i.   IDELLA MAY [Della], b. Portland 17 Nov. 1869; m. 1st 1 May 1889 BENJAMIN F. O'BRIEN, b. in NS 14 May 1850, d. 8 Mar. 1896; m. 2nd 2 Oct. 1901 JOHN MARSTON, b. Falmouth 16 Jan. 1876.
ii.   INEZ GRACE, b. Portland 28 May 1877; m. ELMER F HUSTON [# 1551].
iii. EUGENE WOODBURY, b. Falmouth 31 Dec. 1882; m. EVA M. HAVENER.

988. **LUCY**[8] 1808-1897 [439 Ebenezer[7] and Hannah Hawkes] was born at Westbrook (then Falmouth) 17 Sept. 1808, died 29 Feb. 1897; married at Westbrook int. 20 Apr. 1834 JAMES LAMB, born in 1787, died in 1865 (Cornman Ms).

Children (**Lamb**), born at Westbrook:

i.   EMILY J., b. 27 Feb. 1834; m. 4 June 1877 HORATIO DANIELS.
ii.   WILLIAM WARREN, b. 27 Feb. 1837, res. Cumberland Mills; m. in 1862 SUSAN SMITH of Lovell ME.
iii. MARY ELLEN, b. 27 Apr. 1841, d. No. Windham 12 Jan. 1943, "nearly 102" (obit.); m. 6 Feb. 1867 BENJAMIN WEBBER of NS.
iv.   MERRITT, b. 18 Feb. 1843; m. OLIVE SMITH.
v.   ANNIE R., b. c1845; m. Westbrook 20 May 1878 WINFIELD S. SWETT.
vi.   JOHN WILSON, b. 10 Mar. 1849.

989. **ALVIN**[8] 1810-1884 [439 Ebenezer[7] and Hannah Hawkes] was born at Westbrook 9 Dec. 1810 (Bible), died at Cumberland Mills (Westbrook) 14 Feb. 1884, 73y; married there 2 Feb. 1836 HANNAH L. SAWYER, born there 15 June 1816, died there 5 Jan. 1892, 75y 6m 20d, daughter of Jonathan and Ann (Cobb) Sawyer (Alvin's Bible data from Dr. Dwight Leighton; Biographical Review of ... Cumberland County, 70; town VRs). Burials are in Saccarappa Cemetery, Westbrook. He was a stone mason and brick manufacturer.

Children, born at Westbrook:

i.   PHILENA[9], b. 30 Apr. 1837, d. Westbrook 31 Jan. 1906; m. there 15 Dec. 1859 GEORGE BARBOUR, b. there 4 Oct. 1823, d. there 16 Mar. 1918, son of David and Mary (Brackett) Barbour. Ch. Ella May b. 2 June 1869, d. Gorham 10 June 1944; m. Willis H. Sawyer--no ch. (Brackett Gen., 187).
1565. ii.   (SUMNER) SEWELL, b. 3 Apr. 1839.
1566. iii. GEORGE WILLIAM, b. 23 Jan. 1841.

1567.   iv.   HANNAH A , b. 7 Nov. 1842; m. WILLIAM BACON.
1568.   v.   ELVIRA K., b. 4 May 1848; m. ELVIN O. SWETT.
1569.   vi.   EBENEZER JR., b. 27 Mar. 1850.
1570.   vii. FRANCIS L., b. 19 July 1852.
        viii. MARY L., b. and d. 20 May 1855 (Bible).
1571.   ix.   CHARLES H., b. 27 Nov. 1858.

990. MINERVA ANN[8] 1812-1882 [440 Isaac[7] and Minerva Shaw]
was born at Falmouth 7 Nov. 1812, died at Lyman ME 23 July
1882; married at Falmouth 18 Nov. 1834 (Lyman int. 25 Oct.)
BRADFORD RAYMOND, born at Lyman in 1809, died in 1869, son of
John and Polly (Smith) Raymond (Samuel Raymond, Genealogies
of the Raymond Families of New England [N. Y., 1886], 164;
Cornman Ms).
He was listed as a farmer at Lyman in 1850.

Children (**Raymond**), born at Lyman:

i.   MELVILLE B., b. in 1835; m. in 1859 MARY HENRY of
       Springfield IL.
ii.   MARY A., b. in 1837; m. in 1864 MELVILLE CRAM of
       Deering.
iii.   CHARLES E., b. in 1843, d. aged 1 wk.
vi.   ALICE M., b. in 1846, not in 1850 census.
v.   ABBY, b. c1847 (3 in 1850; perhaps same as Alice),
       res. Alfred ME.
vi.   JOHN W., b. in 1849, res. Waterboro ME; m. 1 Dec.
       1871 MARCELLA LOWE.
vii.   CHARLES E., b. in 1853, res. Alfred; m. HANNAH EDWARD
       of Lyman.
viii. LEIGHTON (twin), b. in 1853, d. in 1869.

991. LAVINA SHAW[8] 1815-1874 [440 Isaac[7] and Minerva Shaw]
was born at Falmouth 31 Mar. 1815, died at Danville ME 25
Mar. 1874; married at Falmouth 28 Feb. 1838 JAMES HICKS, born
at Falmouth 23 Apr. 1811, died at Auburn ME 25 May 1893, 82y
1m 2d, son of Samuel and Abigail (Winslow) Hicks (Hicks
Ancestry, 8; Falmouth and Danville TRs).

Children (**Hicks**), born at Danville:

i.   CHARLES H., b. 29 Mar. 1839, d. in 1905; m. 1st JULIA
       L. LOVEJOY; m. 2nd 16 Jan. 1883 ABBY L. BLAIR, b. 26
       Apr. 1856.
ii.   DORA L. [Dolly], b. 10 June 1844; unm.

992. LORENZO SHAW[8] 1817-1881 [440 Isaac[7] and Minerva Shaw]
was born at Falmouth 10 Mar. 1817, died at Portland 16 May
1881, 64y; married Falmouth 18 May 1841 MARGARET A. BROWN,
born at Westbrook 26 June 1816, died there 3 Sept. 1883,
daughter of Samuel and Dorcas (Jordan) Brown (Tristram F.
Jordan, Jordan Memorial [1882], 407; town VRs; Cornman Ms).
He was a machinist and stationary engineer.

Child, born at Portland:

1572.   i.   CHARLES HENRY[9], b. 12 Nov. 1842.

993.   SILAS[8] 1810-1893 [441 Daniel[7] and Mary Staples] was born at Norway ME 8 Apr. 1810, died at Gray ME 3 Apr. 1893, 82y 11m 25d; married 11 Dec. 1836 APPHIA S. LIBBY, born at Gray 19 Sept. 1816, died there 6 Apr. 1893 (three days after her husband), 76y 6m 24d, daughter of Andrew and Susan Libby (town VRs; Cornman Ms). Burials are in the South Gray Cemetery.
He was a house carpenter and joiner, listed at Falmouth in 1840, Westbrook in 1850, and then at Gray.

Children:

	i.	MARY SUSAN[9], b. 15 Nov. 1837, d. 23 Oct. 1842 (GS) 4y 9m.
	ii.	CHARLES WESLEY, b. 11 July 1840, d. Gray 26 Feb. 1841.
1573.	iii.	ELLA MARIA, b. 19 Apr. 1845; m. SAMUEL C DONNELL [# 441].
	iv.	LUCRETIA H., b. 15 Jan. 1847; m. WILLIAM OLIVER of Bath.
	v.	LEWIS F., b. 7 Nov. 1857, d. 29 Mar. 1864.
	vi.	CAROLINE B. [Callie], b. 21 May 1862; m. 1st 3 Dec. 1887 JOHN C. PECK, b. 12 Feb. 1847, d. 23 Sept. 1896; m. 2nd 7 June 1899 PERCIVAL B. ROLFE, b. Portland 5 Sept. 1853, son of Samuel and Mary (Wilson) Rolfe.

994.   JOSEPH[8] 1812-1885 [441 Daniel[7] and Mary Staples] was born at Norway ME 28 Apr. 1812, died at Falmouth 3 Apr. 1885; married 22 Mar. 1836 JANE WALKER, born at Falmouth in 1814, died there 8 Oct. 1868, 54y 8m (GS) (town VRs; Cornman Ms). Burials are at Pride's Corner, Westbrook.
In 1850, Joseph was a stonecutter at Westbrook, his household including Mary Walker, 64, and Susan Briggs, 20.

Children, born at Westbrook:

1574.	i.	OLIVER H.[9], b. 21 Mar. 1837.
	ii.	LYDIA E., b. c1839 (11 in 1850); m. 1st 16 Apr. 1856 CHARLES M. KNAPP of Portland; m. 2nd JOHN MASON. No ch.
	iii.	MARY SUSAN, b. 20 May 1842; m. JOEL[8] LEIGHTON [# 451].
	iv.	GEORGE WESLEY, b. 9 Oct. 1845, drowned 23 Aug. 1862, 18y.
	v.	LUCY ANN, b. 24 May 1848; m. Westbrook 9 June 1866 CHARLES E. BANGS of Standish. Ch. Nellie m. Herbert Small.
	vi.	ADELAIDE, b. in 1853 (44 in 1897); m. 1st ---- ; m. 2nd ---- TOBEY; m. 3rd Farmington ME 19 May 1897 as his third wife FRANCIS Y. LOCKE, b. Temple ME in 1837, son of Francis Y. and Isabel (Fields) Locke.

995.   LUCY ANN[8] 1814-1893 [441 Daniel[7] and Mary Staples] was born at Falmouth 9 Apr. 1814, died there 5 Sept. 1893; married 4 Oct. 1834 OLIVER HARDY, born at Windham ME 15 Feb. 1811, died at Falmouth 3 Feb. 1890, son of Thomas and Priscilla Hardy (town VRs; Cornman Ms). Burials are at Pride's Corner, Falmouth. In 1850 their household at Falmouth included John Mountfort, 15, and Albina Manchester, 9.

Children (**Hardy**), born at Falmouth:

i.   ELENORA M., b. in 1837, d. 28 Jan. 1859, 22y (GS).
ii.   GEORGE F., b. in 1843, d. 8 July 1863, 19y 10m (GS).

996. DANIEL[8] 1816-1899 [441 Daniel[7] and Mary Staples] was born at Falmouth 8 Sept. 1816, died at Gray ME 15 Aug. 1899, 82y 11m 8d; perhaps married first MARION SWETT; married at Westbrook 30 Nov. 1852 DEBORAH C. (HODGKINS) Cobb, born at Raymond ME 30 July 1825, died there 11 Nov. 1904, 79y 3m 22d, daughter of Ebenezer and Mary (Webb) Hodgkins. Deborah had married first 30 Nov. 1843 Samuel S. Cobb (Cornman Ms; Cobb Family, 2:457).

In 1850 Daniel 3d, 34, a farmer, lived at Falmouth; his father, 85, lived with him. In 1870 he was living with two children and no wife at Falmouth; in 1880 he was listed at Casco with his daughter Clara Foster.

An OLIVE, daughter of Daniel and Marion (Swett) Leighton, died single 17 June 1892.

Children by Deborah, born at Deering:

1575. i.   CLARA[9], b. 26 Nov. 1853; m. EDWARD FOSTER.
      ii.   FRANKLIN, b. c1859 (11 in 1870), d. 27 Nov.
            1898, lost on steamer Portland; m. ---- .

997. JAMES GOWEN[8] 1823-1894 [441 Daniel[7] and Mary Staples] was born at Falmouth 11 Mar. 1823, died at Yarmouth ME 3 Dec. 1894, 72y 6m; married first at Falmouth 6 May 1852 ELIZABETH A. BRYANT of Portland, who died 19 Nov. 1862; married second at Falmouth 2 Apr. 1865 HANNAH SUSAN (PEARSON) Leighton, born at Portland 26 Mar. 1834, died at Falmouth 21 Dec. 1902, 68y 9m, daughter of Edwin and Prudentia (Hanscom) Pearson (town VRs; Cornman Ms). She had married first 3 July 1856 JAMES EDWIN[8] LEIGHTON [# 1000].

In 1840 James enlisted in the US Army, and served in FL during the Seminole War. He was a machinist boarding at Portland in 1850, and was at Falmouth with his parents in 1860. He enlisted 3 Mar. 1864 in Co. F, 20th ME Inf. Rgt., and was discharged wounded (NA-MSR). He lived at Westbrook in 1880, and moved to Yarmouth in 1887. In 1900 his widow Hannah was listed at Yarmouth with her daughters Mary and Nellie.

Children by Elizabeth, born at Portland:

i.   FRANK B.[9], b. 1 Mar., d. 1 July, 1853, 8m 16d.
ii.   ABBY L., b. c1857 (23 in 1880); unm. She
      lived with Granville [# 1001] in 1860.

Children by Hannah, born at West Falmouth:

ii.   MARY ELLEN, b. 1 Dec. 1865, d. Falmouth 23
      June 1903, 37y 6m 21d; unm.

1576. iii. IRVIN MATHIAS, b. 16 Nov. 1869.
       iv. NELLIE BEATRICE, b. 20 Jan. 1873, d. Falmouth
            18 Mar. 1936, 62y 2m 3d.; unm.

998. ANSEL[8] 1812-1877 [442 Ichabod[7] and Lydia Claridge]
was born at Falmouth 2 Mar. 1812, died at Bangor 8 Dec. 1877,
65y 9m 6d; married at Bangor 28 Nov. 1836 ELEANOR WILSON
SAUNDERS, born at Prospect ME 16 Jan. 1811, died at Bangor 4
Feb. 1899, 88y 19d, daughter of John and Martha Saunders
(Cornman Ms; Bangor VRs). Burials are in Mt. Hope Cemetery,
Bangor.
Ansel [Anson, Ancil] was apprenticed as a boy to a tin-
plate manufacturer at Westbrook. In 1832 he moved to Bangor
as a tin plater, forming Leighton & Wing Co. After Wing
left, Ansel's brother Ichabod joined the firm. They later
formed Leighton, Davenport & Co., gas-fitters (History of
Penobscot County, Maine, 2:774-5). In 1850 his household
included his brother Ichabod's family.
His will, proved in Dec. 1877, named his wife and the three
living children. His widow lived with her son Horace.

    Children, born at Bangor:

        i.   MARY JANE[9], b. 15 Dec. 1837; m. 13 Sept. 1859
              GEORGE SUMNER CHALMERS. Ch. George Leighton
              b. 31 Mar. 1861; m. 12 Nov. 1895 Elmira A
              Moore.
        ii.   LYDIA MARIA, b. 29 July 1839; m. 23 June 1864
              MANLY GREENLEAF TRASK. He joined the family
              business. Ch. Mattie Louise b. 11 Sept.
              1866.
        iii. MARTHA LOUISE, b. 19 Mar. 1842, d. Bangor 20
              Aug. 1864, 22y 5m.
        iv.   HORACE WILSON, b. 5 June 1846, d. Bar Harbor
              ME 7 May 1904, 57y 11m 2d; m. 27 Dec. 1893
              ALICE MAUD NORTON, b. Bangor 9 Feb. 1858, d.
              there 5 Nov. 1921, 63y 8m, dau. of Robert L.
              and Marion (McGrath) Norton. No ch. He car-
              ried on the family business.

999. ICHABOD ELBRIDGE[8] 1813-1881 [442 Ichabod[7] and Lydia
Claridge] was born at Norway ME 25 Oct. 1813, died at Bangor
25 Nov. 1881, 68y 1m; married there 9 Jan. 1845 SOPHIA LORD
ROGERS, born in 1814, died at Bangor 31 July 1851 (Bangor and
ME VRs; Cornman Ms). Burials are in Mt. Hope Cemetery.
Ichabod worked with his brother as a tinsmith at Bangor.
In 1867 he established there Brown & Leighton, a meat market.

    Child, born at Bangor:

        i.   ALBERT HENRY[9], b. 24 Oct. 1845, d. Bangor 22
              July 1887, 40y 9m; m. there 17 Apr. 1884
              GEORGIE ETTA LORD of Lowell MA, b. 9 Nov.
              1861, who m. 2nd Benjamin E. Sproul. Ch.
              ARLINE[10] b. 4 Aug. 1885; m. Bangor 15 June
              1910 BENNETT R. CONNELL, b. Woodstock NB
              c1884, son of Charles W. and Maggie B.
              (Cowan) Connell. In 1892 Albert operated
              Getchell, Leighton & Co. (city directory).

1000. JAMES EDWIN[8] 1833-1856 [443 Silas[7] and Abigail Roberts] was born at Falmouth 22 Aug. 1833, died at West Falmouth 14 Oct. 1856, 33y; married there 3 July 1856 HANNAH SUSAN PEARSON, born at Portland 26 Mar. 1834, died at Falmouth 21 Dec. 1902, 68y 9m, daughter of Edwin and Prudentia (Hanscom) Pearson. She married second James Gowen[8] Leighton [# 997].

Child, born at Falmouth:

1577. i.   ABIGAIL R.[9], b. 6 Aug. 1856; m. HERBERT M. PELTON.

1001. GRANVILLE ROBERTS[8] 1826-1881 [443 Silas[7] and Abigail Roberts] was born at West Falmouth 25 Jan. 1826, died there 8 May 1881; married at Cumberland 31 May 1855 CLIMENA REBECCA PRATT, born at Poland ME in 1829 (GS, 1826), died at Falmouth 2 July 1872 (Falmouth and ME VRs; Cornman Ms). Burials are in the Universalist Cemetery, West Cumberland. In 1860 and 1870 they were living in his father's household.

Children, born at West Falmouth:

    i.   ABBY[9], b. c1857 (3 in 1860, not in 1870 census).
    ii.   EVA[9], b. c1861 (9 in 1870).
    iii. JAMES EDWIN, b. 25 Aug. 1865, d. Portland 5 Oct. 1920, 55y 1m 10d; m. there 3 Aug. 1886 LUCINDA M. CROCKER, b. Machiasport in Aug. 1867 (per 1900 census). He joined Co. B, 1st ME Rgt., in 1898. Ch. CLYMENA PRATT[10] b. in June 1888; m. 21 May 1917 LEROY SHAW TUCKER, b. c1883, son of Harden and Rita (Blake) Tucker.
1578. iv.   GRANVILLE WILBUR, b. 5 Mar. 1868.

1002. LUCY GOWEN[8] 1835-1900 [443 Silas[7] and Abigail Roberts] was born at West Falmouth 19 Jan. 1835, died at Falmouth 12 Dec. 1900 (GS, 1890), 65y 10m 21d; married 23 Feb. 1857 THOMAS JOSIAH PEARSON, born at Windham 11 Feb. 1832, died at Falmouth 27 July 1914, 82y 5m 16d, son of Edwin L. and Prudentia (Hanscom) Pearson (town and ME VRs; Cornman Ms). Burials are at Pride's Corner, Westbrook.

Children (**Pearson**), born at Falmouth:

    i.   ADA J., b. 11 Dec. 1858, d. 24 Aug. 1862.
    ii.   JAMES H., b. 16 Feb. 1859, d. 15 Aug. 1861.
    iii. WILFRED, b. 5 Jan. 1861, d. 23 Aug. 1862.
    iv.   FREDERICK CLARENCE, b. 20 Apr. 1863, d. 16 Feb. 1897; m. 24 Sept. 1885 HATTIE M. BACHELDER, b. 12 Feb. 1867.
    v.   WILLARD HERBERT, b. 1 Jan. 1865; m. ANNIE M.[9] LEIGHTON [# 1476].
    vi.   CORDELIA RUSSELL, b. 9 Mar. 1867; m. LOUVILLE GREENLEAF[9] LEIGHTON [# 1535].
    vii. ANNIE ISABEL, b. 23 Feb. 1869; m. ROLAND[9] LEIGHTON [# 1551].

viii. GRACE VIOLA, b. 30 Apr. 1871; m. 18 Nov. 1896 CHARLES
R. DRESSER, b. 16 June 1870, res. Falmouth.
ix.   HATTIE A , b. 23 May 1873, d. Falmouth 1 Sept. 1877.
x.   MINNIE ADA, b. 23 May 1876, res. CA; m. ALBERT S.
MORSE.
xi.   HATTIE A., b. 13 July 1877.
xii. EDWIN FOREST, b. 7 July 1880.

1003. FRANCES IRENE[8] 1821-1854 [445 Levi[7] and Hannah
Elliot] was born at Falmouth 13 July 1821, died there 4 Dec.
1854; married REUBEN DEERING MERRILL, born there 21 Sept.
1821, died there 5 Apr. 1857, son of Isaac and Elizabeth
(Merrill) Merrill (Samuel Merrill, A Merrill Memorial, An
Account of the Descendants of Nathaniel Merrill [Cambridge
MA, nd, MHS], 2:623; Cornman Ms). Burials are off Brook
Road, Falmouth.
Merrill was a carpenter. In 1860 the orphans Ellen and
Charles were listed with their grandparents Levi and Hannah
Leighton.

Children (**Merrill**), born at Falmouth:

i.   ELLEN M., b. 3 Oct. 1846, d. 5 Dec. 1864.
ii. ORETTA MAUD, b. 14 Oct. 1851, d. 10 Mar. 1852 (GS).
iii. CHARLES VINAL, b. 4 July 1852; m. 7 Oct. 1874 SUSAN
MORRELL COBB, dau. of Otis Cobb.

1004. ALBERT[8] 1825-1892 [445 Levi[7] and Hannah Elliot] was
born at Falmouth 26 Apr. 1825, died at West Falmouth 11 July
1892, 67y 2m 15d; married 28 Oct. 1852 MINERVA SHAW[8]
LEIGHTON, born at West Falmouth 11 Jan. 1829, died there 18
July 1911, 82y, daughter of Silas and Abigail (Roberts)
Leighton [# 443] (Falmouth VRs).
He was a farmer at Falmouth. His widow was living with her
son Granville in 1900.

Children, born at West Falmouth:

1579. i.   CARLETON FOREST[9], b. 24 Aug. 1853.
      ii. GRANVILLE WILLIS (twin), b. 24 Aug. 1853, d.
           Falmouth in 1929 (as George Willis); unm.
      iii. FRANCES ESTELLA [Fannie], b. 1 Feb. 1862, d.
           W. Falmouth 19 Jan. 1933, 70y 11m 15d; unm.

1005. LEVI ELLIOT[8] 1824-1893 [446 Thaddeus[7] and Abigail
Elliott] was born at Falmouth 12 June 1824, died there 20
Apr. 1893, 68y; married 6 July 1852 MARTHA ANN STAPLES, born
13 Feb. 1831, died at Highland Lake, Falmouth, 4 Dec. 1903,
daughter of Jeremiah and Lydia[7] (Leighton) Staples [# 511]
(Falmouth VRs). She was accidentally shot by her nephew Carroll Bailey. Burials are in the Pine Grove Cemetery, Falmouth Foreside.
Levi was a granite cutter. In 1900, his widow and daughters Lydia and Mame were living with her son Willis.

Children, born at Falmouth:

      i.   GEORGIANNA^9, b. 15 Apr. 1853, d. 26 May 1861.
1580. ii. FRANK WILLIS, b. 10 Sept. 1854.
     iii. LYDIA ELLA, b. 27 July 1856, d. 14 Nov. 1903;
         unm.
     iv. LEVI ELLIOT JR., b. 8 Sept. 1858, d. Portland
         7 Apr. 1920, 60y 7m; m. 1 Apr. 1890 ANNIE
         LORD HUTCHINS, b. 6 Mar. 1872, res. San Fran-
         cisco. He was a granite works foreman. Ch.
         BERNARD ELLIOT^{10} b. Portland 26 Nov. 1891.
1581. v. GEORGIANNA, b. 19 Oct. 1860; m. CLARENCE W.
         BAILEY.
     vi. WILLIS HARPER, b. 28 Mar. 1862; res. Falmouth
         in 1900; unm.
     vii. MARY A [Mame], b. 15 Aug. 1864, d. Westbrook
         4 Oct. 1914, 50y 1m 19d; unm.

1006. **DAVID HENRY**^{8} 1826-1892 [446 Thaddeus^7 and Abigail
Elliott] was born at Falmouth 10 May 1826, died at Portland 2
May 1892, 63y 3m; married at Falmouth 29 Apr. 1852 APPHIA J.
HANSCOM, born at Windham ME about 1827, died at Portland 24
Mar. 1880, 53y (Falmouth and Portland VRs; Cornman Ms).
Burials are in Forest City Cemetery, South Portland.
David was a Portland stonecutter; in 1860 his household
there included Charles W., 24 [probably # 1132]. He enlisted
in Co. I, 1st ME inf. Rgt., 3 May 1861, re-enlisted 31 Aug.
1864, and was discharged for insanity 17 Jan. 1865. He was
awarded a pension (NA-MSR #527,470); an examination in 1892
showed him paralyzed, near death.
Apphia, called the daughter of Aaron and Rebecca (Akers)
Hanscom, was in fact their granddaughter. According to
the research of Robert Hanscom, she was a daughter of Edwin
Pearson and Prudentia Hanscom, born before they were married.

Children, born at Portland:

      i.   ELLEN REBECCA^9, b. 29 Apr. 1853; m. 1st Port-
         land int. 30 Aug. 1868 EDWIN M. LEAVITT; m.
         2nd in 1876 GEORGE L. RAMSEY. Ch. Edwin
         Leavitt Jr. b. 1871, and George Ramsey.
     ii. EMILY LOUISE, b. 25 May 1857, d. Portland 23
         July 1902, 44y 2m; m. there 24 Nov. 1886
         SAMUEL BARBRICK.

1007. **MELVIN A.**^{8} 1839-   [447 Ephraim^7 and Sophia Cobb]
was born at Westbrook 24 Jan. 1839. Julia Cornman stated
that he "had 4 children in Lewiston" (Cornman Ms), and that
he "left his wife and ch. and no one knows where he went"
(Cornman Papers).
Jean York, while researching her family, found a Melville
Leighton in Lewiston with four children who also had left his
family and disappeared. In 1870 Melville and his wife Ann
were listed at Lewiston with their four children.
It is very likely that Melvin was the Melville who married
Ann York, born about 1836, died at Auburn ME 23 Dec. 1921,
daughter of Alfred and Eunice (Walker) York. Ann married
second at Lewiston int. 18 Apr. 1872 Henry C. Seimans (town
and ME VRs).

Children of Melville by Ann:

        i.   IDA^9, b. in VT c1859.
        ii.   ETTA (twin), b. in VT c1859.
1582.   iii. EDMUND H., b. Elnore VT 8 Aug. 1860.
        iv.   GEORGE H., b. in ME c1865, res. Lewiston
              with Henry and Ann Seimans in 1880.

   1008.   JAMES HICKS^8 1819-1905 [449 Edward^7 and Hannah
Hicks] was born at Falmouth 8 Feb. 1819, died there 14 Oct.
1905, 86y 8m; married 18 Jan. 1845 REBECCA G. KNIGHT, born at
Deering 9 July 1811, died there 1 Dec. 1898, 87y, daughter of
Simeon and Lucy (Grant) Knight (Tibbetts, Knight Desc., 124;
town and ME VRs; Cornman Ms).
   He was a stonecutter at Westbrook in 1850, and lived at
Deering in 1880 and at Portland in 1900.

   Children, born at Portland:

        i.   ABBIE A ^{8}, b. 30 May 1844, res. with father at
              Portland in 1900; m. 28 May 1872 STEWART
              HALL, b. 25 July 1845. Ch. Charles S. b.
              9 July 1873; m. Minnie Batchelor and Annie
              McDonald.
1583.   ii.   NATHANIEL HALE, b. 15 Oct. 1847.

   1009.   ANDREW HICKS^8 1822-1903 [449 Edward^7 and Hannah
Hicks] was born at Falmouth 11 June 1822, died at Portland 17
Mar. 1903, 81y 9m 6d; married at Quincy MA 24 Dec. 1845 ABBIE
MORRILL [Abba] WHEELER, born 19 Aug. 1821, died at Deering 30
Aug. 1896, 75y 10d, daughter of David and Priscilla (Hardy)
Wheeler (Cornman Ms; town and ME VRs).
   He was a Portland stonecutter and marble worker. In 1860
they shared a house with Adrial [# 452]; in 1900 he lived
with his son-in-law Walter Brown.

   Children, born at Portland:

        i.   IDA LEONARD^9, b. 10 Feb. 1849, d. Otisfield ME
              26 Nov. 1875, 26y; m. 9 Dec. 1874 ALBION H.
              NUTTING, b. 6 Apr. 1836. No ch.
        ii.   ELLEN OLIVER, b. 8 June 1852; m. 10 June 1872
              WALTER H. BROWN of Portland. No ch.
        iii. WALTER E., b. 7 Mar. 1857, d. 2 Apr. 1859.
        iv.   HATTIE SUSAN, b. 3 May, d. 28 Oct., 1861.
        v.   HERBERT ANDREW, b. 1 Feb., d. 3 Sept., 1865.

   1010.   WILLIAM W.^{8} 1843-1907 [450 Timothy^7 and Mary Jane
Gilman] was born at Falmouth say 1843 (33 in 1877, 37 in
1880, 45 in 1892), died at Togus Veterans Hospital 1 Feb.
1907 (pension file); married first in July 1869 MARY JANE
ALLEN, born at Monmouth ME in 1847 (Cornman Ms; 36 in 1880),
died in 1886; married second at Boston 14 Mar. 1887 MAUD
KEENAN, born at Greene ME about 1865, died at Brunswick ME 15
Oct. 1908, 35y, daughter of George and Melinda (Crowell)
Keenan; married third 8 Mar. 1892 SARAH (ANDERSON) Beers,
born at PEI about 1871 (21 in 1892), daughter of John and Ann
(Calhoun) Anderson (town and ME VRs; Cornman Ms).

William enlisted in Co. B, 12th ME Inf. Rgt. 14 Oct. 1861, re-enlisted in Co. D 1 Jan. 1864, and was discharged at Savannah GA 8 Apr. 1866. He was awarded an invalid pension for a wound in the right eye at the Battle of Winchester VA in Sept. 1864, and for rheumatism contracted near Baton Rouge in 1863 (NA-MSR #194-248).

He was a farmer, a leather worker at Durham in 1880, a fisherman in 1887, and then a carpenter at Portland. He filed pension affidavits from Lisbon Falls in 1878, Augusta in 1890, and Portland in 1894.

Children by Mary Jane, born at Durham:

1584. i. ALFRED DONNELL^9, b. in Apr. 1870.
ii. CORA E., b. c1878 (1 in 1880); m. 1st at Harpswell ME 3 Nov. 1903 CHARLES E. WILLIAMS, b. Phippsburg c1879, son of Aaron and Ella (Leavitt) Williams--div.; m. 2nd Pittsfield 12 May 1907 JAMES RUSSELL, b. in Canada c1880, son of Herman and Julia (Moulton) Russell.

1011. ELIZA JANE^8 1848-1923 [450 Timothy^7 and Mary Jane Gilman] was born at Falmouth 20 May 1848, died at Portland 24 Jan. 1923, 75y 8m 4d; married first 10 July 1864 AUGUSTUS ABBOTT, born in 1840--divorced; married second in Sept. 1878 WILLIAM HENRY BERRY, born at Poland ME 28 June 1857, died 29 Jan. 1942, son of Wilson and Annie (Wilbur) Berry (ME VRs; Cornman Ms; records of descendant Elizabeth Moody). Burials are in Pine Grove Cemetery, Falmouth. In 1900 William and Eliza Berry lived at Poland.

Children (**Abbott**), born at Falmouth:

i. IDA M., b. 20 Feb. 1865; m. 1st in 1879 FRANK BERRY (brother of William H.); m. 2nd 12 Jan. 1886 JAMES W. BABBIDGE, b. 9 Sept. 1858.
ii. (MARY) ALICE, b. 16 Dec. 1866, d. Gorham ME 18 Dec. 1946; m. 29 Dec. 1887 IVORY DEARBORN.
iii. WILLIAM A., b. 20 Apr. 1869; m. MAGGIE McDONALD.
iv. CHARLES, b. 20 July 1871.
v. ALFRED L., b. 18 Nov. 1873; m. DELLA CHAPLIN.

Children (**Berry**):

vi. ANNA ELIZA, b. Deering 20 Apr. 1879, d. Brookline MA 9 May 1961; m. 1st Portland 18 Feb. 1894 SIMON CLIN-TON [Samuel] MOODY, b. S. Portland 26 Aug. 1853, d. Westbrook 2 Apr. 1941, son of Sewall and Mary Ann (Hunnewell) Moody--div.; m. 2nd Portland 23 June 1912 JOHN FREDERICK GOODE of Boston.
vii. HERBERT L. [Bertie], b. Poland 4 May 1881; m. Fairfield ME 29 Dec. 1900 ELLA WHEELER, b. Winslow c1882, dau. of Wellington E. and Mary Louise (Simpson) Wheeler.
viii. GRACE B., b. 2 Aug. 1882, d. 3 Aug. 1934; m. JOHN NOYES.
ix. MAUD A., b. 2 Dec. 1885; m. 20 June 1900 CHARLES L. CURTIS.

1012. AARON HANSCOM[8] 1830-1913 [451 Henry[7] and Ann Hanscom] was born at Westbrook ME 7 Nov. 1830, died at Windham 25 Sept. 1913, 82y 10m 8d; married at Windham 22 July 1854 DORCAS ELLEN COBB, born there about 1837, died there 26 Apr. 1905, 68y 1m 4d, daughter of Samuel and Mary[8] (Leighton) Cobb [# 948] (Cobb Family, 2:463; Windham VRs; Cornman Ms).
A Windham farmer, he lived next door to his father-in-law

Children, born at Windham:

1585.	i.	CHARLES H.[9], b. 17 Jan. 1855.	
	ii.	JAMES E., b. 8 Mar. 1857, not in 1860 census.	
1586.	iii.	LIONEL E., b. 14 May 1859.	
	iv.	LONA, b. 8 Sept. 1860, d. 14 May 1868.	
	v.	FRED, b. 22 Mar. 1866, d. 9 Apr. 1867.	
	vi.	FRED W., b. c1870, d. Windham 25 Jan. 1907, 37y 5m 5d; unm.	

1013. PHOEBE ANN[8] 1839-1875 [451 Henry[7] and Ann Hanscom] was born at Windham 23 Nov. 1839, died 28 May 1875; married at Windham 3 July 1862 CHARLES A. DALTON (Cornman Ms).

Children (**Dalton**):

i.   CHARLES, d. infant.
ii. ANNIE L., d. 13 Aug. 1901; m. in Sept. 1883 CHARLES B. EATON, d. 22 Nov. 1902.
iii. ELLEN; m. JOHN COTTON.

1014. ADRIAL NASON[8] 1842-1902 [451 Henry[7] and Ann Hanscom] was born at Windham 23 Jan. 1842, died at Dayton ME 28 Feb. 1902, 60y 1m 5d; married first at Windham 11 Mar. 1867 ELIZABETH (HARRIS) Eastman of Windham; married second at Portland 22 Jan. 1872 ABBIE E. WHITNEY, born about 1858 (22 in 1880), died at Portland 24 May 1881; married third MARY DELPHINA (CYR) LaRiviere, born at Westbury PQ 19 Apr. 1842, died at Biddeford ME 6 May 1930, 88y 17d, daughter of Prospere and Amelia (Biron) Cyr (town VRs; Cornman Ms). He was buried at St. Joseph's Cemetery, Biddeford.
Adrial enlisted 15 July 1861 in Co. H, 20th ME Inf. Rgt, served also in Co. K, 2nd ME, was discharged disabled in Nov. 1863, and was pensioned. In 1890 he lived at Biddeford; in 1900 he was listed at Dayton, his household including Mary's grandchildren Arthur Brady, born at Biddeford in Apr. 1887, and Clara Brady, born in MA in Mar. 1890, and his stepson Oliver LaRiviere.

Children by Abbie:

1587.	i.	FRANK ADRIAL[9], b. Portland 24 Mar. 1875.	
	ii.	ABBIE E., d. Cape Elizabeth 25 May 1881.	

1015. EMILY JANE[8] 1846-   [451 Henry[7] and Ann Hanscom] was born at Windham 8 Nov. 1846; married there 22 Apr. 1865 JOHN S. IRISH, born 7 Feb. 1835, son of Isaac and Lois Irish (town VRs; Cornman Ms). In 1904 he was a farmer at Woodfords (now Portland).

Children (**Irish**), born at Windham:

i. CORA E., b. 10 May 1868; m. 21 May 1887 ROBINSON
    PRATT, b. 26 Oct. 1859.
ii. FRANK P., b. 24 June 1878; m. 4 Oct. 1899 CHARLOTTE
    E. CASWELL, b. 9 May 1879.
iii. WALTER I., b. 24 Apr., d. 13 Sept., 1883.

1016. APPHIA NASON[8] 1847-   [451 Henry[7] and Ann Hanscom]
was born at Windham 5 Sept. 1847; married 5 Mar. 1869 CHARLES
F. TITCOMB, born 21 Aug. 1846 (Cornman Ms).

Children (**Titcomb**):

i.   MARY PEARSON, b. 21 June 1871.
ii. CHARLES WILLIAM, b. 27 Feb. 1874.
iii. GRACE, b. 10 Dec. 1875.
iv. EMELINE GERTRUDE, b. 11 June 1878, d. 31 Oct. 1883.
v.   APPHIA ISABELLA, b. 6 Dec. 1880.

1017. EMILY JANE[8] 1836-   [452 Adrial[7] and Rhoda Pack-
ard] was born at Hallowell ME 28 Apr. 1836; married at Cape
Elizabeth ME 3 July 1858 JAMES BRIGHTMAN HATHAWAY, son of
William and Susan (Brightman) Hathaway (M. E. Jones, Genealogy of Jones-Hathaway-Richards-Gooding [TMs, 1934, MHS],
105; Cornman Ms).

Children (**Hathaway**):

i.   NELLIE SMITH, b. Cambridgeport MA 30 June 1860; m.
      Fall River MA 23 Dec. 1880 BENJAMIN STRAWBRIDGE.
ii.   JAMES EDWIN; m. IDA CARR.
iii. SUSAN EMERSON, b. c1868, d. Fall River 14 Feb. 1872.
iv.   HARRY, d.y.
v.   HARRY DUANE, b. in Aug. 1872; m. LULA FREELOVE.
vi.   ADRIAL WARREN, res. Fall River; m. ALICE PORTER.
vii. BENJAMIN FRANKLIN; unm.

1018. RHODA ELIZABETH[8] 1838-   [452 Adrial[7] and Rhoda
Packard] was born at Milford MA 3 Nov. 1838, lived at Chelms-
ford MA; married (as Elizabeth R.) 17 Aug. 1857 WESLEY PARKER
DUTTON, born at North Chelmsford 4 Jan. 1826, died at Medford
MA 21 July 1898, son of Parker Dutton (Cornman Ms). He was a
contractor.

Children (**Dutton**):

i.   CARRIE ISABELLE, b. 28 Nov. 1858.
ii. FRANK PARKER, b. 1 Apr. 1861, d. 29 Jan. 1902. He
     served in Co. E, 5th MA Rgt., Spanish-American War,
iii. GEORGE ELMER, b. 6 Aug. 1864; m. 11 Nov. 1891 EMILY
     M. JACOBS, b. 24 Sept. 1866.
iv. JOHN WESLEY, b. 31 Oct. 1866, d. 18 Sept. 1875.

1019. GEORGE WARREN[8] 1840-1900 [452 Adrial[7] and Rhoda
Packard] was born at Quincy MA 13 Nov. 1840, died at Deering
(Portland) 27 Nov. 1900; married there 19 June 1870 ALEXINA

FISHER [Zena] DRINKWATER, born at Yarmouth ME 7 Sept. 1841
(death record), died at Deering 27 Dec. 1932, 96y 3m 20d,
daughter of Nicholas and Mary (White) Drinkwater (Portland
VRs; Cornman Ms; records of descendant Mae Miller Federhen).
He settled at Deering, where he owned a monumental-granite
business. In 1900 his household included his mother Rhoda.
Burials are in Evergreen Cemetery.

Children, in Portland VRs:

1588. i.   ZENA MAY^9, b. Quincy MA 9 Sept. 1870; m.
             FRANCIS T. MILLER.
       ii.   WILLIAM ELSTON, b. 9 May 1872, d. Kirkwood MO
             9 Nov. 1952; married St. Louis MO 26 Nov.
             1910 VIRGINIA EDWARDS, dau. of Charles and
             Elizabeth (Treadway) Edwards. No ch.
             Grad. of Bowdoin, BA 1895, and Harvard, MD
             1900, he practiced at St. Louis, was on the
             faculty of St. Louis Univ., and was pres.,
             Barnard Mem. Hosp. He joined the Royal Army
             Med. Corps in 1915 (BEF), and then served in
             the US Army Med. Corps 1917-19 (obit., Port-
             land Sunday Telegram, 15 Nov. 1952).
1589. iii. IDA LEORA, b. 4 Feb. 1877; m. HENRY ROBBINS.
       iv.   DORA VanSCHORN, b. 19 Oct. 1880; m. Portland
             18 Apr. 1911 WILLIAM LAMB WISH, b. there
             c1885, son of Joseph H. and Harriet H.
             (Harmon) Wish. Ch. Elizabeth Leighton Wish.

   1020. ALVAH^8 1847-1906 [456 Elias^7 and Lucinda Frank] was
born at Danville (now Auburn) ME 25 June 1847, died there 3
Mar. 1906, 58y 8m 8d; married at Auburn 1 Jan. 1868 DELORA
ANN MOWER, born at Auburn 4 Aug. 1851, died there 19 June
1919, 69y 10m 15d, daughter of William and Hannah Mower of
Turner ME (Auburn VRs). He served in Co. A, 30th ME Inf.
Rgt., 1863-65. He was a barber and hairdresser.

Children, born at Auburn:

1590. i.   LEON^9, b. 4 Sept. 1873.
       ii.   LILLA L., b. c1876 (4 in 1880).
       iii. MILDRED E., b. c1878 (2 in 1880); m. Auburn 31
             Aug. 1895 OLIVER FRANK PAUL, b. c1866,
             son of Oliver P. and Fannie (Oliver) Paul.
       iv.   ERLON CHESTER, b. in Sept. 1884; m. Portland
             11 July 1921 widow MARGERY (KINMOND) Jordan,
             b. there in 1881, d. there 26 July 1944, dau.
             of George T. and Bridget (Donahue) Kinmond.
       v.   LOLA MAY, b. in Jan. 1886; m. Auburn 16 Jan.
             1906 ELMER PERRY SARGENT, b. Portland c1885,
             son of Oliver P. and Annie (Morton) Sargent.
       vi.   ERMA EUDORA, b. in Feb. 1889; m. Auburn 16 May
             1906 CHESTER LINWOOD FRANCIS, b. Lewiston in
             1889, son of Frank E. and Alice M. (Rogers)
             Francis.

   1021. HALE^8 1828-1906 [457 Asa^7 and Mary Hale] was born at
West Falmouth 2 Sept. 1828, died there 26 May 1906, 78y 8m
25d; married there 28 Jan. 1852 BETSEY JANE MOODY, born at

Minot ME 15 Oct. 1830, died at Falmouth 6 Mar. 1907, daughter of John and Jane (Maxim) Moody (Falmouth and Portland VRs; Cornman Ms). Burials are a in private cemetery off Brook Road.
Hale lived on the farm purchased by his pioneer great-grandfather George, but also had a granite business.

Children, born at Falmouth:

    i.   HORACE^9, b. 14 Nov. 1852, d. Falmouth 24 Mar.
        1878, 25y 4m 10d (GS).
    ii. EDITH JANE, b. 30 Dec. 1854, d. Portland 7 May
        1922, 67y 4m 7d; unm.
    iii. MOODY, b. 5 Aug. 1859, res. Revere MA in 1900;
        m. Falmouth 23 Jan. 1889 widow EMMA (ALLEN)
        Russell, b. in Sept. 1859, dau. of David and
        Cordelia (Morrill) Allen. No ch. He was
        superintendent of police, Nantasket MA.
    iv. JEROME CARPENTER, b. 10 Jan. 1864, d. Portland
        19 Oct. 1930, 66y 9m 9d; m. 19 Sept. 1888
        ELIZABETH P. HALL, b. Falmouth 27 Feb. 1864,
        d. Portland 24 Apr. 1941, dau. of Capt. Alvin
        and Julia (Hutchinson) Hall. No ch. He was
        a stone-cutter.
1591. v.   GERTRUDE, b. 31 Oct. 1867; m. ARTHUR BODKIN.

1022. MARY HALE^8 1832-   [457 Asa^7 and Mary Hale]
was born at West Falmouth 16 Aug. 1832; married at Portland int. 24 Mar. 1856 ANSEL NEAL (Cornman Ms).

Child (**Leighton**):

    i.   ETTA^9, b. 5 Mar. 1855, res. Boston in 1900; m.
        18 Oct. 1884 EDWIN NAYLOR, b. W. Chelmsford
        MA c1854, son of John M. and Mary M. Naylor.

Children (**Neal**):

    ii. GEORGE, res. Burlington VT.
    iii. CHARLES.

1023. LEANDER^8 1845-1916 [457 Asa^7 and Mary Hale] was born at West Falmouth 12 Sept. 1845, died at Portland 11 Aug. 1916, 70y; married at Cumberland 1 Dec. 1872 (28 Feb., Gray VRs) MARY ELIZABETH [Lizzie] HICKS, born at Cumberland 9 Apr. 1845, died at Portland 6 Sept. 1920, 74y, daughter of Joseph and Elizabeth^8 (Leighton) Hicks [# 968] (town VRs). He was a stonecutter. In 1900 his mother-in-law lived with them.

Children, born at Portland:

    i.   CLARA ALBERTINA^9, b. 12 Nov. 1880, d. Portland
        8 Oct. 1933; m. there 12 Apr. 1924 NORMAN
        WILLIAM ANDERSON, b. Freeport in 1894, son of
        William C. and Annie L. (Morrell) Anderson.
        No ch. (obit., Portland Press Herald).
    ii. HAROLD LEROY, b. 14 Nov. 1887, res. Boston in
        1933.

1024. LOVICIA S.[8] [Lovicy] 1816-1854 [459 Moses[7] and Prudence Allen] was born at Columbia ME 6 Apr. 1816, died there 27 Oct. 1854; married there int. 23 Feb. 1835 her cousin DANIEL A. SINCLAIR, born at Robbinston ME 16 Aug. 1805, died at Columbia Falls 25 Aug. 1886, 81y 2m, son of Thomas and Martha (Allen) Sinclair (records of Darryl Lamson and Leonard F. Tibbetts; Columbia VRs).

Daniel married second at Columbia 4 Aug. 1855 Deborah (Small) Cates. Burials are in Epping Cemetery.

Children (**Sinclair**), born at Columbia:

i.   CHARLES, b. in Sept. 1836, d. Columbia Falls 12 Nov. 1864, 26y 2m (GS); unm. Co. D, 22nd ME Inf. Rgt.
ii.   THOMAS JEFFERSON, b. 29 Apr. 1838, d. Columbia Falls 10 July 1900; m. 25 Mar. 1860 MARGARET A. CUMMINGS, b. 6 Dec. 1839, d. Columbia Falls 4 Aug. 1886, dau. of Ichabod and Catherine W. (Skinner) Cummings.
iii. ANNA JERUSHA, b. 2 Dec. 1839, res. Sandwich MA; unm.
iv.   ISORA THELMA, b. 5 May 1841, res. Salem MA; unm.
v.   AMANDA HATHAWAY, b. 4 Feb. 1843, res. Salem MA.
vi.   ALMON ROSWELL, b. in 1845, drowned aged about 24.
vii. GEORGE LEMUEL, b. 13 Feb. 1848, res. Salem MA; m. 30 Sept. 1886 Rosa B. Rogers.

1025. LEVI 2ND[8] 1818-1912 [459 Moses[7] and Prudence Allen] was born at Columbia 18 Sept. 1818, died at Columbia Falls 7 Oct. 1912, 94y 19d; married at Columbia 7 May 1846 LUCY C. (WASS) Tibbetts, born there 17 June 1821, died at Columbia Falls 30 Dec. 1914, daughter of Levi and Emma (Knowles) Wass (Wass Family, 83). He was called "Second" because he had an uncle Levi living. Lucy had married first in 1841 John C Tibbetts, who was drowned in the Machias River 7 May 1843; they had a child who died young, and Ernvesta A , born 27 June 1842 and raised by Levi as his own.

Levi apprenticed as a carpenter at an Addison shipyard until his right hand was permanently injured by an axe. He then studied at Washington Academy, East Machias, and was a teacher from 1842 to 1849. He opened a store at Epping Lower Corner, a village at Columbia, in 1848, and took his brother Jason as partner in 1854. In 1871 he sold the store to Jason.

Levi entered politics as a Democrat in 1850, and was state representative in 1854-5. He was justice of the peace from 1854 to his death, town treasurer for 21 years, and school supervisor.

In 1872 he set up L. Leighton & Son, a mercantile and shipbuilding business at Columbia Falls. He was a pioneer in canning blueberries, owned a lumber company, and was the proprietor of Leighton House, a hotel.

At 72, he published the Autobiography of Levi Leighton [Portland, 1890], "the simple record of a well-spent life," with chapters on his philosophy of government, education and religion.

His career is well-documented, in Biographical Review ... Somerset, Piscataquis, Hancock, Washington and Aroostook Counties [Boston 1898], 535-7; in a lengthy obituary in the Bangor Daily News, 9 Oct. 1912; and in his "Sketches in Columbia, Maine," [MH&GR 9(1895):84-94].

Child, born at Columbia:

1592. i.   HORACE MANN[9]. b. 14 Apr. 1850.

1026. JASON CLAPP[8] 1820-1881 [459 Moses[7] and Prudence
Allen] was born at Columbia 14 May 1820, died there 21 July
1881, accidentally drowned in his well; married at Columbia
by brother Levi 19 Dec. 1857 his cousin JANE WHITNEY WORCES-
TER. born there 14 Jan. 1840, died at Harrington ME 3 Apr.
1911, daughter of Leonard and Love M. (Corthell) Worcester
(Jason's obituary, Machias Union, 26 July and 2 Aug. 1881;
Columbia VRs; Cornman Ms).
Jane married second at Milbridge 14 Feb. 1883 Christopher
W. McCaslin (Machias Union).
Jason was partner with his brother Levi in a general store
at Epping Corner, and then continued the business on his own
after 1871. He was called Esquire. Burials are in Epping
Cemetery.

Children, born at Columbia:

        i.   LORENZO DOW[9], b. 25 July 1859, d. 11 Aug.
               1860, 1y 18d (GS).
1593. ii.   ALBERT B., b. 15 May 1863.
      iii.   GEORGE H., b. 10 Dec. 1867, res. Haverhill MA
               after 1900; m. 1st Columbia 9 May 1889 CHAR-
               LOTTE E. [Lottie] PHIPPS, b. there 17 Feb.
               1872, d. there 16 May 1900, dau. of Stephen
               E. and Evelina P. (Smith) Phipps; m. 2nd 31
               July 1902 CLARA L. DAY, b. c1873, dau. of
               Norris P. and Eliza (Hersey) Day of Lowell
               MA. Ch. LAFOREST H.[10] b. in Oct. 1890.
       iv.   JANE ATWOOD [Jennie], b. 10 May 1875, res.
               Haverhill MA; m. 1st Portland 10 May 1917
               WILLIAM O. ALDEN, b. c1859, son of William
               and Elizabeth (Emery) Alden; m. 2nd Portland
               27 Nov. 1924 EDWARD JAMES DEVINE, b. there
               c1876, son of Bernard and Bridget O. (Haney)
               Devine and a druggist.

1027. ASA GREEN[8] 1825-1872 [459 Moses[7] and Prudence Allen]
was born at Columbia 6 Apr. 1825, died there 6 Jan. 1872, 47y
8m; married there int. 14 Aug. 1850 (Centerville int. 7 July)
(MARY) MARIA ALLEN, born at Centerville ME 1 June 1830, died
at Columbia 8 Nov. 1884, 54y 5m 7d, daughter of Obadiah and
Mary (Mansfield) Allen (Columbia VRs; Cornman Ms; records of
descendant Lillian Bergman). Burials are in Epping Cemetery.
Asa was a farmer and lumberman.

Children, born at Columbia:

        i.   ELLEN M.[9] (Nell), b. c1851 (9 in 1860), res.
               Somerville MA; m. Columbia 18 Aug. 1873
               CHARLES HODGDON of Salem MA. Ch. Harry and
               Charles.
1594. ii.   EDGAR HARVEY, b. 14 Apr. 1853.
      iii.   WILLIE L., b. 28 Jan. 1858, d. 28 May 1865,
               7y 5m 18d (GS).

1595. iv.   MILLICENT E., b. 6 Jan. 1862; m. RUSSELL M.
            SMITH.
1596. v.   ALBRO B., b. 25 Apr. 1868.

1028. OTIS M.[8] 1827-1881 [459 Moses[7] and Prudence Allen]
was born at Columbia 7 July 1827, died there 21 Feb. 1881;
married there first by brother Levi 5 Dec. 1857 ELIZABETH M.
TABBUTT, born at Addison ME 15 Apr. 1826, died at Columbia 5
March 1866, 40y 1m 15d (GS), daughter of Charles and Isabella
(Merritt) Tabbutt; married second also by Levi 2 Mar. 1872
SALOME W. CUMMINGS, born at Jonesport about 1836 (44 in
1880), buried at Marshville (Harrington), daughter of Ichabod
and Catherine (Skinner) Cummings.
Salome married second at Harrington int. 24 May 1883 Wil-
liam Henry Ramsdell, and married third in 1895 Thomas B.
Mitchell (town and ME VRs; records of Leonard F. Tibbetts;
Cornman Ms).
Otis was a farmer at Columbia; "Saloma," 31, was his house-
keeper there in 1870. Burials are in Epping Cemetery. Julia
Cornman stated he had no children, but two sons are listed in
the 1880 census. Everett may have been the son of George
Ulmer[8] [# 1066].

Possible children:

i.   EVERETT U.[9], b. c1859 (1 in 1860, 21 in 1880).
ii.   LESTER, b. c1875 (5 in 1880).

1029. CYRENE BANCROFT[8] 1830-   [459 Moses[7] and Prudence
Allen] was born at Columbia 30 Mar. 1830; married there 13
May 1852 WILLIAM HEZEKIAH INGERSOLL, born there 19 Apr. 1831,
lived at Columbia Falls, son of William Jr. and Susanna Shaw
(Wass) Ingersoll (Lillian D. Avery, Genealogy of the Inger-
soll Family in American [New York, 1926], 53; records of
Leonard F. Tibbetts; Columbia VRs).
They lived on her father's homestead.

Children (**Ingersoll**), born at Columbia:

i.   LENORA HARRIS, b. 25 Dec. 1853, d. Columbia 18 Dec.
      1888; m. Columbia Falls 20 Dec. 1872 LEMONT JEFFER-
      SON NORTON, son of Abram Thatcher and Eliza E.
      Norton. He m. 2nd 25 Dec. 1889 Laura Merritt.
ii.   SELMER V. LORENS, b. 23 Apr. 1859; m. Columbia 31
      July 1880 CLARA IDELLA ROCKWELL, b. 6 May 1862,
      dau. of Jared Ingersoll and Lydia Catherine
      Rockwell.
iii. WILLIAM EDWIN, b. 25 Aug. 1865; m. LEVONIA E. GRANT,
      dau. of John and Mabel Eldora (Tibbetts) Grant.

1030. SOPHIA A.[8] 1831-1898 [459 Moses[7] and Prudence Allen]
was born at Columbia 8 July 1831, died at Somesville, Mount
Desert Island, 25 Apr. 1898, 66y 9m 17d; married at Columbia
30 Oct. 1853 her cousin OBADIAH W. ALLEN JR., born 12 Apr.
1829, died at Somesville 9 June 1915, 86y, son of Obadiah and
Mary (Mansfield) Allen (Columbia and Mount Desert VRs:
records of Leonard F. Tibbetts). Burials are in Brookside
Cemetery, Somesville.

Children (**Allen**):

i.   INEZ R., b. Columbia 27 Oct. 1854, d. Mt. Desert 3
      Feb. 1875, 20y 4m; unm.
ii.   PRUDENCE L. [Dencie], b. Columbia 18 July 1858, d.
      Mt. Desert 30 May 1927; m. 10 Feb. 1878 ISAAC SOMES,
      b. 11 July 1846, son of David and Sally Somes.
iii. MELVILLE L., b. Columbia 27 Jan. 1862, d. Mt. Desert
      19 Nov. 1939, 77y; m. 6 May 1888 EMMA A. HOLMES, b.
      Cranberry Isles 20 Aug. 1859, dau. of Leonard and
      Mary A Holmes.
iv.   ANDREW W., b. c1870, d. 6 Feb. 1875, 4y 8m (GS).

1031. PRUDENCE[8] [Dency] 1833-1916 [459 Moses[7] and Prudence
Allen] was born at Columbia 8 May 1833, died there 13 May
1916, 83y 5d; married there 4 July 1855 DAVID FREEMAN WASS,
born there 4 Oct. 1834, died at Fort Monroe VA 16 Nov. 1862,
28y 1m 13d, son of Levi and Emma (Knowles) Wass (Wass Family,
84; ME VRs; Cornman Ms; records of Leonard F. Tibbetts).
Burials are in Epping Cemetery.
He died while serving in Co. D, 22nd ME Inf. Rgt.; his
widow was awarded a pension. In 1890 Dency was living with
Mary Phipps at Minneapolis, but she then returned to live at
Columbia with Della Tabbutt.

Children (**Wass**), born at Columbia:

i.   MARY LOUISE, b. 22 Jan. 1857, res. Minneapolis; m.
      Columbia 1 Jan. 1881 CHARLES W. PHIPPS, b. Cooper
      ME 4 Oct. 1845, son of William and Eliza Phipps.
ii.   FRANCES MADELLA [Della], b. 20 Apr. 1859, d. 12 Dec.
      1949; m. 4 Feb. 1882 CHARLES HERBERT TABBUTT, b.
      Columbia Falls 27 Dec. 1858, d. 23 Jan. 1936,
      son of Andrew Jackson and Victoria S. (Allen)
      Tabbutt.

1032. SUSANNA T.[8] 1842-1876 [459 Moses[7] and Prudence
Allen] was born at Columbia about 1842 (8 in 1850), died at
Cape Elizabeth ME 1 Sept. 1876; married at Addison 7 July
1859 ZENUS WILDER TABBUTT, born there 30 Jan. 1834, died in
1905 (GS, Woodbine Cemetery, Ellsworth), son of Charles and
Isabella (Merritt) Tabbutt (town VRs; records of Leonard F.
Tibbetts).
Zenus, a sea captain, lived at No. Lamoine. Susanna was
not included in her brother Levi's outline of the family
(MH&GR 9[1898]:221).

Children (**Tabbutt**):

i.   LESLIE H., b. Columbia in Apr. 1861, d. there 27 Feb.
      1868, 6y 10m (GS, Epping Cem.).
ii.   ALFRED W., b. Columbia in Feb. 1864, d. there 17 Mar.
      1868, 4y 1m (GS, Epping Cem.).
iii. IDA, b. c1865; m. GEORGE STURGIS, son of Dr. John
      Sturgis of Portland.
iv.   EVA S., b. Harrington 3 June 1866, d. Corea 2 Aug.
      1899; m. Addison 2 Aug. 1889 JOHN W. STINSON.

1033. (BENJAMIN CAMPBELL) COFFIN[8] 1825-   [460 Samuel[7] and Mary Ann Ward] was born at Columbia 29 June 1825, died at Cape Town, South Africa; married at Beddington ME int. 11 Apr. 1848 LOUISA C. DORMAN, born there 15 Mar. 1827, died in Nov. 1852, daughter of Israel and Joanna (Kingsley) Dorman (records of Leonard F. Tibbetts; town VRs).

In 1850 Coffin was a lumberman at Annsburg (now Deblois); his household included his brother N. Green Leighton, 21.

Children, born at Deblois:

    i.   HARRIET E.[9], b. 30 Oct. 1848.
    ii.   ALVAH MALCOLM, b. 30 Nov. 1850, d.y.

1034. ALPHEUS BILLINGS[8] 1827-1897 [460 Samuel[7] and Mary Ann Ward] was born at Columbia 15 Dec. 1827 (Deblois VRs), died at Fair Haven MN in 1897; married at Deblois ME int. Jan. 1853 IRENE L. GOULD, born 22 May 1826, died at Fair Haven in 1910, daughter of Pearson and Sophia Gould of Beddington ME (Cornman Ms; Deblois VRs). In 1860 they lived at Deblois; in 1880 they were listed at Southside, Wright Co. MN, and in 1900 widow Irene lived there with Melbourne.

Children:

    i.   MELBOURNE[9], b. Deblois 17 Aug. 1853, res.
        South Side, Wright Co. MN in 1900; m. AGNES
        ---- , b. in MN in Dec. 1870. In 1900 his
        mother-in-law Winfret Hobert, b. in Ireland
        in Mar. 1830, was living with them. Son
        WINFRED[10] b. in MN in Feb. 1898.
1597. ii.   (HENRY) ALVA, b. Deblois 9 Sept. 1856 (Alva H.
        in 1880 census).
    iii. ANDREW H., b. Deblois c1859 (6/12 in 1860).
    iv.   JENNIE E., b. in MN c1869 (11 in 1880).
    v.   ABBY A., b. in MN c1870 (10 in 1880).

1035. (NATHANIEL) GREEN[8] 1828-1896 [460 Samuel[7] and Mary Ann Ward] was born at Columbia in 1828, died at Unionville (Steuben) 10 Dec. 1896; married first at Beddington ME 12 Sept. 1852 (MARY) EMELINE DORMAN, born there 9 Aug. 1829, daughter of Israel and Joanne (Kingsley) Dorman; married second AUBINE (LIBBY) Johnson, born at Machiasport about 1865, daughter of John F and Mary E. (Cole) Libby (Libby Fam., 317; records of Leonard F. Tibbetts; Cornman Ms).

He served in Co. C, 1st ME Sharpshooters Rgt., from 12 Oct. 1864 to 22 June 1865. He settled in MN, and was listed there in 1880 with his wife Aubine. He was said to have had eleven children.

Children by Emeline:

    i.   GEORGE[9], b. in MN c1866 (14 in 1880).
    ii.   JENNIE, b. in MN c1873 (7 in 1880).

1036. MARY ANN[8] 1845-   [460 Samuel[7] and Mary Ann Ward] was born at Columbia about 1845 (14 in 1860), lived at Hannibal MO in 1900 with her son Edgar; married at Columbia 24

Feb. 1866 ROBERT WILLIAM BUCKNAM, born there 2 Aug. 1837, died there 6 July 1878, son of John and Sarah (Little) Bucknam (Ann Theobald Chaplin, A Bucknam-Buckman Genealogy [Baltimore, 1988], 141-42; Leighton, Autobiography, 11; Columbia VRs). He had married first in 1862 Nancy H. Stiles, who died 25 Dec. 1863 without children. In 1880 widow Mary was listed with her children at Harrington ME; her sister Vienna lived with her. She went to MO with Edgar, and lived for a time at St. Louis.

Charles Henry Pope (in A History of the Dorchester Pope Family [Boston, 1888], 237) stated that Thomas Richardson Pope of Brighton MA married at Cambridge int. 8 Oct. 1844 Nancy Ward Leighton, 1817-1887, daughter of Samuel and Betsey (Ward) Leighton of Columbia. The Cornman Ms repeated this inaccurate statement.

Children (**Bucknam**), born at Columbia:

i.   SARAH LEIGHTON, b. and d. in 1867.
ii.   JOHN CHARLES, b. 4 July 1870.
iii. JOSEPH H., b. 11 Feb. 1875, d. 4 Sep. 1899.
iv.   EDGAR H., b. 20 Jan. 1877

1037. **RUTH ANN**[8] 1827-1881 [461 Levi[7] and Leonice Coffin] was born at Columbia 29 Oct. 1827, died 29 Dec. 1881; married before 1850 JASON A CROWELL (Cornman Ms). In 1880 they were listed at Bangor ME, he 55, she 49.

Children (**Crowell**):

i.   FRANK L.
ii.   HARRIET L. [Hattie], b. c1855 (25 in 1880).
iii. GEORGE A., b. c1862 (18 in 1880).
iv.   RUTH, b. Bangor 10 Aug. 1868 (VRs).

1038. **JOHN WILSON**[8] 1830-1911 [461 Levi[7] and Leonice Coffin] was born at Columbia ME 6 June 1830, died at Columbia Falls 6 Feb. 1911, 81y 1m; married at Columbia 19 Oct. 1865 (MARTHA) AUGUSTA SIMMONS, born at Stockton Springs ME 16 June 1843, died at Columbia Falls 25 Feb. 1918, daughter of George and Lydia (Smith) Simmons (Cornman Ms; Columbia and ME VRs).

Often called Wilson, he was a farmer at Columbia Falls, which was set off from Columbia in 1863, and later a sailor of Columbia in 1870. Burials are in Epping Cemetery.

Children, born at Columbia Falls:

1598. i.   GEORGE NELSON[9], b. 12 Sept. 1868.
       ii.   RALPH WILSON, b. 19 Mar. 1872, d. Columbia 27
             Aug. 1947, 75y 5m 8d; unm.
1599. iii. RUTH MAY, b. 3 July 1875; m. JOHN D. HATHAWAY.

1039. **(JAMES) HENRY**[8] 1848-1905 [461 Levi[7] and Betsey Small] was born at Columbia in June 1848, died at Addison ME 12 Mar. 1905, 57y 9m; married first at Addison 25 May 1872 ADA L. WASS, born there 24 Feb. 1853, died there 7 Oct. 1897, daughter of Edward F. and Louise L. (Wass) Wass; married second there 1 Mar. 1879 MILLIE G. RYMER, born there 15 Dec.

1858, died there 31 Aug. 1934, 75y, daughter of Francis and Emily R. (Gale) Aymer (Addison VRs; Cornman Ms)

Millie married second (as Mattie) 10 Oct. 1916 Henry S. Kane, born about 1858, son of Perley and Sarah (Fogg) Kane of Brooklin ME (Whitten, Samuel Fogg, 1:1677). Burials are in Church Hill Cemetery. James served in Co. B, ME State Guard Inf. Rgt., in 1864. Often called Henry J., he was a house painter, and lived at Addison Point.

Child by Millie, born at Addison:

    i.   CLIFTON HENRY^9, b. 2 Dec. 1880, res. Pitts-
        burgh PA in 1903.

1040. WILLIAM HILLMAN^8 1823-1871 [463 Daniel^7 and Abigail Ingersoll] was born at Columbia 13 Dec. 1823, died there 30 May 1871, 47y 5m 17d; married there int. 17 Aug. 1850 CAROLINE W. (CROWLEY) Leighton, born at Addison 18 Dec. 1822, died at Harrington ME 29 July 1889, 66y 7m 11d, daughter of Flourence and Mercy (Look) Crowley and widow of ENOCH^8 LEIGHTON 2ND [# 1060] (records of Leonard F. Tibbetts and Darryl Lamson; Columbia VRs).

He was a farmer and butcher at Columbia, and was sometimes called Hillman. Burials are in Epping Cemetery. In 1860 his household included MARTHA ELLEN^9, 13, his step-daughter.

Children, born at Columbia:

    i.   (ENOCH) ABNER^9, b. 28 Aug. 1851, d. 16 Sept.
        1875, 24y 22d (GS, as E. Abner); unm.
    ii.   ASAPH H., b. 9 Apr. 1853, d. Columbia 4 Mar.
        1917, 63y 10m 25d; m. there 12 Mar. 1887
        FLORA B. LOOK, b. Addison 10 Apr. 1863, d.
        Columbia 15 Jan. 1938, 74y 8m 21d, dau. of
        Moses W. and Christianna P. (Look) Look.
        No ch.
1600. iii. FRANCES C. [Fannie], b. 20 Aug. 1856; m.
        EVERETT C. GRANT.
1601. iv. LESLIE F., b. 30 May 1861.
    v.   ETTA G., b. 2 Feb. 1865, d. 4 Sept. 1869,
        4y 7m 2d (GS).

1041. ISAAC L.^{8} 1826-1903 [463 Daniel^7 and Abigail Ingersoll] was born at Columbia 11 Jan. 1826, died at Foxboro MA 24 Feb. 1903, 77y 1m 3d; married at Calais ME 10 Aug. 1855 (VRs) LYDIA YOUNG, born at Oak Bay NB 1 Mar. 1835, died at Foxboro 6 June 1910, 75y 3m 5d, daughter of William and Mary (McAllister) Young (records of Darryl Lamson; Columbia VRs; Cornman Ms).

In 1860 Isaac was a Columbia farmer, and later was listed as a pedlar. He settled in MN about 1870, but in 1880 was living at Cherryfield ME. In 1900 his household at Foxboro included his daughter Mary.

Children, all but the last born at Columbia:

    i.   child^9, b. 15 Sept., d. 21 Sept., 1856.
    ii.   ESTELLE GERTRUDE [Stella], b. 25 May 1859, d.
        Foxboro MA 22 Oct. 1891; m. 1st at Columbia

24 July 1878 CHARLES H. CARVER, b. 25 Dec.
1854, d. Woods Hole MA 12 Oct. 1878; m. 2nd
at Foxboro 8 Apr. 1891 EVERETT E. SMITH, b.
22 Jan. 1870. No ch.

1602. iii. CARRIE ELLA, b. 15 Oct. 1860; m. GEORGE A
             SMITH.
        iv. ALFONZO WENTWORTH, b. 10 Sept., d. 27 Sept.,
             1864, 17d.
1603.   v. ROSWELL GILBERT, b. 2 July 1866.
        vi. MARY HARRIET, b. Cosmo MN 12 June 1872, d.
             Boston 22 Sept. 1965. She was a nurse at
             Washington DC.

1042. MELISSA ANN NASH[8] 1830-1870 [463 Daniel[7] and Abigail
Ingersoll] was born at Columbia about 1830 (30 in 1860), died
19 May 1870, 40y 1m; married at Columbia 27 Apr. 1850 JOSEPH
WORCESTER JR., born about 1823 (37 in 1860), son of Joseph
and Abigail (Nash) Worcester (Columbia VRs; Cornman Ms).

Child (**Worcester**), born at Columbia (perhaps others):

i.   AMANDA MELISSA, b. about 1856 (4 in 1860, as
     Melissa), d. Columbia Falls in 1890, 35y; m. Colum-
     bia int. 31 May 1880 GEORGE M. DORR, b. c1857,
     son of Donald W. and Cynthia (Magee) Dorr.

1043. FONZE GREEN HILL[8] 1832-1899 [463 Daniel[7] and Abigail
Ingersoll] was born at Columbia 18 Sept. 1832, died there 3
Oct. 1899, 67y 16d; married there 26 June 1869 GENETTA ALLI-
SON WORCESTER, born there 27 June 1848, died there 4 July
1913, 65y 5m 7d, daughter of Moses and Diadama (Smith) Worcester (Columbia VRs; records of Leonard Tibbetts; Cornman
Ms). Burials are in Epping Cemetery. In 1910 Genetta was
living with her son Eathiel.
He was named for his uncle F. G. H. Ingersoll. He enlisted
15 July 1861 as corporal, Co. G, 6th ME Inf. Rgt., and was
discharged 15 Aug. 1864; he took part in numerous battles,
and was wounded at Rappahannock Station VA in 1863. He was
pensioned for his service.

Children, born at Columbia:

i.   WENTWORTH A [9], b. 14 Mar. 1870, d. Machias 23
     July 1942, 72y; m. 1st Jonesport 12 Mar. 1900
     EDITH M. [Nettie] RICHARDSON, b. there in
     Oct. 1861, d. there 24 Feb. 1901, 29y 4m 3d,
     dau. of Jonathan and Mary Jane (Kelley)
     Richardson; m. 2nd Columbia 26 Oct. 1904
     MARCIA A. COFFIN, b. there in 1877, dau. of
     George W. and Addie L. (Smith) Coffin; m. 3rd
     Columbia 24 Sept. 1925 EDITH I. (FOLLMER)
     Drisko, b. Rosindale MA 26 Nov. 1892, d.
     Greeley 1 Jan. 1951, dau. of William and
     Eunice A. (Parnell) Folsom. No ch. Went-
     worth conducted a blueberry business at
     Columbia.
ii. ETTA CLYDE, b. 27 Mar. 1872, res. Wesley ME;
     m. Columbia 1 Feb. 1899 ORRIN ELIJAH DAY,

                    b. Wesley 19 Feb. 1869, son of J. Millard and
                    Josephine (Guptail) Day. He m. 2nd HATTIE
                    E. (STEWART) Carey, dau. of John and Saman-
                    tha⁸ (Leighton) Stewart [# 1051]. No ch.
          iii.   ROY C., b. 20 Nov. 1874, d. in 1944 (GS), res.
                    Boston; probably unm.
1604.   iv.   EATHIEL W., b. 23 Feb. 1876.
1605.   v.   RONIE D., b. 24 Nov. 1878; m. RALPH E. WORCES-
                    TER.
          vi.   ALTON C , b. 3 Apr. 1885, d. West Grafton MA
                    10 Apr. 1959; m. in May 1922 BLANCHE ROBBINS
          vii.   SUSIE RENA, b. 31 Dec. 1887; m. Columbia 21
                    Sept. 1910 CHARLES C. DRISKO, b. Columbia
                    Falls c1881, son of Edwin I. and Hattie
                    (Donovan) Drisko. Ch. Genetta Leighton
                    Drisko b. in 1912, d. in 1956.

   1044. (AUGUSTA) ANN⁸ 1837-1867 [463 Daniel and Abigail
Ingersoll] was born at Columbia about 1837 (Ann A., 13 in
1860), died at Addison 9 Sept. 1867, 30y 10m 26d (GS; Machias
Union); married there 7 Nov. 1860 H. SIDNEY AUSTIN, born
there 4 May 1839, died at Staten Island NY (Sailors' Snug
Harbor) 4 Apr. 1918, 78y, son of Moses Carleton and Mary J.
(Small) Austin (Addison VRs; Cornman Ms; records of Leonard
F. Tibbetts). She was called Amanda A. on her gravestone.
Her daughter was raised by her uncle John Austin. Burials
are in Church Hill Cemetery, Addison.
   Sidney was a mariner and shipmaster for 27 years. He mar-
ried second 2 Aug. 1872 Isabel S. [Belle] (Madden) Wallace,
and had a son Harry Barton; married third a Mrs. Lunt; and
married fourth Maria C. Fisher.

   Child (**Austin**), born at Cherryfield:

   i.   CORA ELLA, b. in 1865, d. Springfield MA 18 Jan.
            1921; m. Addison 2 June 1892 BURTON LUTHER TIBBETTS,
            b. there 30 Dec. 1863, d. W. Jonesport 4 Sept. 1907,
            son of Luther Ingersoll and Cordelia Wilson (Worces-
            ter) Tibbetts.

   1045. MARY ABIGAIL⁸ [Abbie] 1847-1880 [463 Daniel⁷ and
Harriet McAllister] was born at Columbia 28 Jan. 1847, died
at Oak Bay NB 17 Nov. 1880; married there 17 Oct. 1867
STEPHEN HILL YOUNG, born there 30 Mar. 1843, died there 16
Apr. 1901, son of William and Mary (McAllister) Young
(records of M. W. Chase).
   Young married second Ada Blanche Hazen. He was a farmer.

   Children (**Young**), born at Oak Bay:

   i.   INEZ HATTIE, b. 2 Nov. 1868, d. at 4y.
   ii.   MARY EMMA, b. 2 May 1870, d. Brookline MA 30 Nov.
            1915; m. Somerville MA 5 Aug. 1896 FRANK HERBERT
            GORDON, b. St. John NB 25 Sept. 1873, d. Somerville
            27 Feb. 1945, son of James Henry and Eleanor (Clark)
            Gordon.
   iii.   ROY LEIGHTON, b. 3 Mar. 1872, d. Vancouver BC 6 Sept.
            1939; m. Somerville 30 Oct. 1930 ANNA BELLE STANLEY.

iv.   EDITH BLANCHE, b. 14 Dec. 1875, d. Chamcook NB 5 Feb.
      1938; m. Oak Bay 25 Jan. 1899 EDWARD F. DOUGHERTY.
 v.   SUSANNA HARRISON, b. 20 Oct. 1877, d. Bocabec NB 4
      Jan. 1955; m. Oak Bay 10 Apr. 1901 JOHN S. BROWN-
      RIGG.

1046. JOHN CALVIN[8] 1829-1911 [464 Harrison[7] and Olive Con-
ley] was born at Columbia 13 Apr. 1829, died at Oakdale MA 4
Nov. 1911; married first 13 Apr. 1865 SUSANNA T. JACOBS, born
about 1838 (27 in 1865), died at Portland ME 16 May 1871,
32y; married second at Portland 8 July 1874 HANNAH D. ROB-
BINS, born at Eastport ME in June 1835, died at Portland 27
June 1903, 68y 1d, daughter of Jonathan B. and Mary E.
(Aymer) Robbins (Cornman Ms; Portland VRs).
     Julia Cornman called Susanna "Lucy Therese" Jacobs, but she
was named Susanna on their Milbridge intentions 19 Mar. 1865
(and he was there named Calvin).

Child by Susanna, born at Columbia:

      i.   HELEN[9] [Nellie], b. 16 June 1866 (13 in 1880).

Child by Hannah, born at Portland:

      ii.   MARY WOODBURY, b. 14 May 1876; m. Portland 9
            Sept. 1904 HENRY L. ORTER, b. Bridgeport CT
            c1863, son of Leonard and Jane (Hart) Orter.

1047. ELIZABETH CHRISTINE[8] [Lizzie] 1831-1896 [464 Harri-
son[7] and Olive Conley] was born at Columbia 18 Feb. 1831,
died at Stoneham MA 16 Mar. 1896; married at Columbia int. 9
July 1849 JONATHAN PINEO, born there about 1822, died at
Stoneham, son of Gamaliel and Charlotte D. (Chamberlain)
Pineo. He was pensioned for his service as sergeant, 1st ME
Heavy Artillery Rgt. (Columbia VRs; Cornman Ms).

Children (**Pineo**):

      i.   PHILANDER L., b. Columbia 28 July 1850, res. Augusta
            MT.
      ii.   HARVEY U., b. Addison in 1859, d. Stoneham.

1048. HARRISON BURBANK[8] [Harry] [464 Harrison[7] and Olive
Conley] was born at Columbia 19 Aug. 1835, lived at Medford
MA in 1900 (census) with his son; married at Calais 11 Oct.
1855 PHOEBE B. SAWYER, born in Jan. 1842 (per 1900 census),
daughter of George and Mary Ann[8] (Leighton) Sawyer [# 685]
(town VRs; Cornman Ms). He was a "tin man" at Milbridge in
1860, and a tin plater at Columbia in 1870.

Children:

      i.   FRANCES EMMA[9] [Fannie], b. c1858 (2 in 1860).
      ii.   HARLAN R., b. Milbridge in Jan. 1866, res.
            Malden MA; m. Bangor ME 20 Aug. 1891 LAURA C.
            BEAL, b. in July 1867, dau. of Henry W. Beal.

1049.   JOTHAM S.[8] 1841-1893 [464 Harrison[7] and Olive Con-
ley] was born at Columbia 10 Feb. 1841, died at Olympia WA 3
Aug. 1893; married first at Centerville ME 10 Feb. 1865
RACHEL ETTA ALLEN, born 17 Feb. 1847, died at Centerville 17
Feb. 1869, 22y (GS), daughter of Henry and Leah (Jacobs)
Allen; married second at Ellsworth ME 29 Apr. 1870 LUCRETIA
M. WILLEY, born at Steuben ME 5 Sept. 1850, died at Olympia 2
Apr. 1910, daughter of Samuel and Lydia (Morse) Willey (Corn-
man Ms; ME VRs). Rachel was buried at Centerville.
    Jotham enlisted 1 Mar. 1865 in the 12th ME Inf. Rgt. He
was living at Cherryfield at the time of his marriage to
Lucretia, and the same year moved west to WA, where he was
settled at Olympia in 1881.

Child by Rachel, born at Columbia:

  i. MABEL E.[9], b. 26 Oct. 1866, res. Boise ID;
    m Columbia 25 Aug. 1897 as his 2nd wife
    LUTHER H. HOLLIS, b. Brockton MA about 1836,
    d. 24 Feb. 1901, c65y, son of Royal and Sarah
    A. (Hayden) Hollis. No ch.

Children by Lucretia, born at Oakland WA:

1606. ii. CHARLES E., b. 1 May 1871.
  iii. BERTHA D., b. 2 Jan. 1877, res. Olympia; m.
    24 Feb. 1902 FRANK R. SWAN, b. Haldam KS 25
    July 1874, son of Robert and Ella (Loring)
    Swan.

1050.   JAMES L.[8] 1835-   [465 Aaron[7] and Eliza Worcester]
was born at Columbia 3 Jan. 1835, lived at Belmont NH in
1900; married first at Columbia int. 3 Nov. 1873 MARY E.
BASELEY of Lowell MA; married second there 3 Jan. 1875 CHAR-
LOTTE ELLEN [Nellie C] FOLSOM, born at Gilmanton NH 1 June
1846, daughter of Samuel Dudley and Eunice (Folsom) Foster of
Laconia NH (Folsom Family, 1:396; Cornman Ms). He was a
carpenter.

Children by Charlotte (Belmont VRs):

1607. i. MARTHA A.[9] [Mattie], b. 12 Feb. 1877; m.
    AUSTIN CURRIER.
  ii. CARRIE B., b. 3 June 1880, res. E. Boston; m.
    ---- PENNIMAN.
  iii. FLORENCE N. (twin), b. in 1880.

1051.   SAMANTHA L.[8] 1838-   [465 Aaron[7] and Eliza Worces-
ter] was born at Columbia 28 Feb. 1838; married there 20 Dec.
1865 JOHN E. STEWART, born there 18 May 1838, son of John and
Lydia (Leighton) Stewart [# 268] (Cornman Ms; Columbia VRs).

Children (**Stewart**), born at Columbia:

  i. HATTIE E., b. 7 June 1867, res. Brockton MA; m. 1st
    WILLARD CAREY of Cooper ME, d. Brockton 19 Aug.
    1902; m. 2nd ORRIN DAY of Wesley [# 1043].
  ii. MARCIA E., b. 29 July 1868, res. West Bridgewater MA;
    m FRANK HATCH of Castine.

1052. HOLLIS J.[8] 1847-1923 [465 Aaron[7] and Eliza Worces-
ter] was born at Columbia 20 July 1847, died there 5 Apr.
1923, 75y 8m 16d; married at Beddington 15 June 1872 SARAH A.
LONGFELLOW, born there 23 May 1854, died at Columbia in Feb.
1928, daughter of David and Laura (Jenkins) Longfellow (town
VRs; Cornman Ms). Burials are in Epping Cemetery.
He was a farmer and painter. Julia Cornman stated he was
in Central America for three years.

Children, born at Columbia:

    i.   LAURA E.[9], b. 7 Nov. 1873, d. 16 Oct. 1890,
        17y (GS).
    ii.   WILLARD C , b. 17 June 1884, d. 3 May 1894.

1053. EMERY WADE[8] 1830-1907 [468 Enoch[7] and Susanna Emer-
son] was born at Addison ME 9 Apr. 1830, died there 22 Nov.
1903, 73y 9m 13d; married first there 25 Dec. 1852 MERCENA
[Mercy] LENNAN, born at Hampden ME 15 Sept. 1832, died at
Addison 17 Dec. 1878, daughter of Rev. Bryant Lennan Jr.;
married second at Columbia 18 Jan. 1881 (Machias Union) CARO-
LINE SUSAN [Carrie] FARNSWORTH, born at Jonesport 4 Nov
1855, died at Auburn ME (nursing home) 8 July 1936, 80y,
daughter of Holley Emerson and Almena Kittredge (Cummings)
Farnsworth (letter from Carrie--Cornman Papers; Cornman Ms;
Tibbetts, Jonesport Families, 89). He and Carrie adopted
Orel L., born 1 Nov. 1884, who was living at Brunswick ME in
1905. Burials are in Hall's Hill Cemetery, Addison.
He was a farmer and butcher at Indian River village.

Children by Mercy, born at Addison:

    i.   OSCAR ENOCH[9], b. 3 Nov. 1853, d. there 28 June
        1882, 29y; m. there 3 Nov. 1877 (Machias
        Union) VIOLETTA MORTON [Lettie] TIBBETTS, b.
        there 20 Dec. 1857, d. Newton MA 21 June
        1910, 52y 6m 1d, dau. of Luther Ingersoll and
        Cordelia Wilson (Worcester) Tibbetts. Ch.
        OSCAR ENOCH[10] JR. b. 14 Feb. 1880; m. 12 Aug.
        1903 HELEN G. SARGENT of Methen MA, b. 16
        Dec. 1880, dau. of Walter S. and Agnes G.
        (Jackson) Sargent: no ch.
        Widow Lettie m. 2nd Columbia Falls 5 Dec.
        1883 Capt. Thomas C. Drisko: 2 ch.
    ii.   EVA [Effie], b. 1 May 1859, d. 23 June 1864.
    iii. HOWARD M., b. 13 Feb. 1865, d. 25 Dec. 1887;
        unm.
    iv.   ETHEL M., b. 13 Sept. 1868, d. 19 Nov. 1892,
        24y 2m 6d; unm.
    v.   WINFRED A , b. 19 Mar. 1870, d. 5 May 1882.

Children by Carrie, born at Addison:

    vi.   dau., b. and d. in Nov. 1889.
    vii. son, b. and d. in May 1893.

1054. LYMAN PAGE[8] 1834-1908 [468 Enoch[7] and Susanna Emer-
son] was born at Addison 9 Apr. 1834, died at Lynn MA 31 Dec.
1908, 74y 8m 22d; married at Addison 1 Feb. 1862 MELVINA L.

ATKINS, born at Canaan ME in July 1840 (1900 census), died at
Lynn 28 Apr. 1911 (Cornman Ms; Addison and Lynn VRs).
    Lyman enlisted as a corporal in Co. D, 1st ME Cavalry Rgt.,
1 Oct. 1861, re-enlisted 1 Feb. 1864, and was discharged disabled 27 Mar. 1865. He had been injured during a raid on
Richmond VA in Mar. 1864, and in Aug. was shot in the jaw.
    In 1870 he was a farmer at Addison. He was pensioned and
his widow also received a pension, for which she applied in
1909, aged 68, of Lynn (NA-MSR #72-320, 675.753).

    Children, born at Addison:

        i.   ALICE MAY^9, b. 19 June 1862, d. 5 Sept. 1897;
              unm.
        ii.   CORA E., b. 8 June 1866, d. 11 Aug. 1891; m.
              Lynn 18 Sept. 1889 CARROLL A. DWINALL, b. 26
              June 1867.

    1055. LANGDON S.^{8} 1838-1900 [468 Enoch^7 and Susanna Emer-
son] was born at Addison in June 1838, died at Escanaba MI 19
Nov. 1900, 62y 5m 20d, killed in railroad accident; married
at Addison 29 Nov. 1860 MATILDA J. DRISKO, born at Jonesport
in Apr. 1842, died at Escanaba about 1920, daughter of
Timothy and Rachel (Cummings) (Skinner) Driscoll (records of
Darryl Lamson; Addison VRs).
    He was a seaman at Addison in 1870, and in 1890 had settled
in Delta County, MI, where he was a contractor for concrete
sidewalks. In 1900 his Escanaba household included his "sister" Christiana E. (Drisko) Emerson, born in ME in Apr. 1857,
widow of George M. Emerson.

    Children, born at Addison:

        i.   BYRON ALTON^9, b. in Feb. 1864, d. Rochester MI
              about 1918 (Mayo Clinic); m. Escanaba 10 Jan.
              1894 HARRIET VanVALKENBURG, b. in June 1874,
              dau. of Peter and Mary (Eastman) VanValken-
              burg. No ch.
        ii.   MILDRED CHRISTIANA [Millie], b. in 1870, d.
              Manistique MI in 1924; m. LOVEATUS PLUMMER
              NORTON, b. Addison in 1861, d. Manistique in
              1932, son of Ackley and Priscilla (Drisko)
              Norton [# 471]. Ch. Alton A , Perry, Alice
              and Ethel.

    1056. SUSANNA E.^{8} 1841-1913 [468 Enoch^7 and Susanna Emer-
son] was born at Addison 1 June 1841, died there 23 Jan.
1913; married there 27 Oct. 1859 NATHANIEL BRADFORD, born at
Plymouth MA 27 Apr. 1830, died at Addison 11 Feb. 1875, 44y,
son of David and Betsey (Briggs) Bradford (records of Leonard
F. Tibbetts; Cornman Ms; Addison VRs).
    Bradford was a sea captain. In 1860 his Addison household
included his mother-in-law Susanna.

    Children (**Bradford**), born at Addison:

        i.   MARY EVA, b. 3 Apr. 1862, d. in 1914; m Addison 20
              Oct. 1879 ORLANDO S. CROWLEY, b. there 23 Nov. 1856,

d. Staten Island NY (Sailors' Snug Harbor) 24 Aug. 1955, 98y 9m 1d, son of William D. and Frances S. (Yeaton) Crowley.

ii.   FREDERICK LELAND, b. 16 Jan. 1864, d. Addison 30 July 1949; m. MARGARET ELIZABETH REILLY, b. 26 Jan. 1876, d. 7 Mar. 1960.

iii. FRANK ATWOOD, b. 30 Nov. 1867, d. Addison 8 Nov. 1951; m. Jonesport 25 Oct. 1890 TRYPHENA ETTA [Phena] SMITH, b. 8 Oct. 1868, d. Addison 11 July 1960, dau. of Samuel and Lydia (Alley) Smith.

1057.   HELEN THERESA[8] [Ellen] 1846-   [468 Enoch[7] and Susanna Emerson] was born at Addison 1 June 1846, died at Lynn MA about 1915; married at Addison 17 Jan. 1867 ALTON LIBBY CROWLEY, born there in 1843, lost at sea with his crew of five 16 Sept. 1888, son of Matthew Coffin and Elizabeth Ann (Crowley) Crowley (Addison VRs; Waterhouse Gen., 3:1252; Cornman Ms).

Children (**Crowley**):

i.   IDA MABEL, b. Jonesport 19 Nov. 1867, res. NYC; m. Lynn MA 23 Dec. 1889 JAMES FRANCIS [Frank] GIBBS.
ii.   (MARIE) MAUD, b. in 1872, res. Lynn; m. HARRY CLEVE-LAND of Lynn.
iii. CHARLES MERRILL, b. in 1874, res. Lynn.

1058.   JULIA B.[8] 1822-1899 [469 Eli[7] and Sarah McKenzie] was born at Indian River (Addison) 10 July 1822, died at Webster Plantation 14 Aug. 1899, 77y 1m 4d; married at Springfield ME 15 Feb. 1846 SAMUEL TUCKER 3RD, born at Cherryfield 6 Feb. 1822, died at Webster Plantation 28 Feb. 1907, 85y 22d, son of Samuel Jr. and Annice (Smith) Tucker (records of Leonard Tibbetts and Darryl Lamson; town VRs).
In 1850 Tucker was a farmer at Springfield; he had settled at Webster Plantation by 1860.

Children (**Tucker**):

i.   AARON, b. Prentiss ME 16 Apr. 1847, d. while in the army 21 Apr. 1864; unm.
ii.   HARRIET MARY [Hattie], b. Springfield 15 Jan. 1848, d. Webster Pltn. 19 Apr. 1935, 87y 3m 4d.
iii, CALISTA D., b. Webster Pltn 2 Nov. 1850, d. Spring-field 20 Sept. 1865, 14y 10m (GS).
vi.   LYDIA, b. c1853 (7 in 1860), not in 1870 census.
v.   HOLLEY LESTER, b. Webster Pltn 26 June 1859, d. Bangor (hosp.) 24 July 1916; m. 16 Nov. 1884 MABEL KIMBALL, b. 25 Sept. 1867, d. Lincoln ME 29 Jan. 1951, 83y, dau. of George and Roxanna (Stevens) Kimball. Mabel m. 2nd 1 July 1919 Leroy Tucker.

1059.   NANCY L.[8] 1825-1901 [469 Eli[7] and Sarah McKenzie] was born at Addison 31 Aug. 1825, died at Topsfield ME 4 Oct. 1901; married in June 1842 JEREMIAH MERRILL, born at Sumner ME 12 May 1823, died at Topsfield 25 Aug. 1898, 73y 3m 3d, son of Jeremiah and Priscilla (Atwood) Merrill (town VRs; records of descendant Kay Soucie).

In 1850 their Springfield household included Merrill's mother Priscilla, 65. He was a farmer.

Children (**Merrill**), born at Topsfield:

i.   CHARLES FORBES, b. 30 Mar. 1843, d. Northwood IA 23 May 1902; m. Lee ME 3 Sept. 1866 GERTRUDE BURKE, b. Lee 26 Dec. 1845, d. Minneapolis MN 6 May 1931, dau. of James and Rachel (Getchell) Burke.

ii.   CLINTON, b. 2 Mar. 1846, d. in accident 8 Sept. 1852.

iii. WINFIELD SCOTT, b. 26 Feb. 1848, d. in VA 4 Aug. 1864 as a result of wounds suffered during the Battle of the Wilderness.

iv.   ALICIA LILLIAN, b. Topsfield 30 Apr. 1850, d. Old Town ME 28 May 1914; m. JOHN D. F. WHITE.

v.   GRACE EMMA, b. 3 June 1855, d. Machias ME 4 Apr. 1900; m. PELHAM NOYES.

vi.   SARAH ETTA, b. 14 Sept. 1857. d. 5 Apr. 1859.

vii. EVELYN ATWOOD, b. 22 Aug. 1862, d. in Jan. 1940; m. FLORA SPOONER. They res. Auburn.

viii. PHINEAS LESTER [Finnie], b. 27 Nov. 1865; m. BERTHA BAILEY, who d. Norwalk CT 17 Sept. 1934.

ix.   MINNIE LURA (twin), b. 27 Nov. 1865; m. EPHRAIM PRAY, who d. in Jan. 1920.

x.   JERRY TAUNTON, b. 10 Aug. 1868, d. Newark NJ 22 Dec. 1934; m. ANNIE FORBES.

1060. ENOCH 2ND[8] 1822-   [470 Robert[7] and Peggy Barfield] was born at Addison about 1822, died at sea before 1850; married at Addison 9 Mar. 1845 CAROLINE W. CROWLEY, born at Addison 18 Dec. 1822, died at Harrington ME 29 July 1889 (Machias Union), daughter of Flourence and Mercy (Look) Crowley. She married second WILLIAM HILLMAN[8] LEIGHTON 17 Aug. 1850 [# 1040] (Addison VRs).
Enoch was presumed dead after he failed to return from a voyage. In 1850 widow Caroline and her daughter lived at Addison with her parents.

Child, born at Addison:

1608. i.   MARTHA ELLEN[9], b. in 1846; m. CHARLES WILLIAM BARKER, REDMAN JUSTUS[8] LEIGHTON [# 740] and WALTER HARTWELL.

1061. MIRIAM[8] 1824-1869 [470 Robert[7] and Peggy Barfield] was born at Addison about 1824, drowned there 29 Apr. 1869 (Machias Union); married first at Addison 4 Feb. 1846 LORENZO SMITH, born at Jonesboro 9 Aug. 1825, died about 1847, son of Moses and Mary (Carleton) Smith; married second about 1849 GEORGE McNAUGHTON, born at Edinburgh, Scotland, 22 Mar. 1826, died at Addison 17 Sept. 1903. In 1860 George and Miriam were living at Addison with her father and step-mother.
George was a tanner, and served in Co. K, 30th ME Inf. Rgt., during the Civil War. Although they apparently lived in MA and MN, they returned to ME. George married second 24 June 1870 Sarah Jane (McDonald) Grover (Cornman Ms; Addison VRs; records of Leonard F. Tibbetts).

Children (**McNaughton**):

i. EUDORA [Dora], b. in 1850, d. Indian River with her
    mother 29 Apr. 1869, both drowned crossing a stream
    while straw-berrying.
ii. GEORGE ENOCH, b. Stoneham MA 26 Feb. 1852, d. Abbott
    ME 17 Mar. 1935; m. SARAH ----. A stonecutter, he
    res. Hancock ME.
iii. JANE, b. in 1854, res. Quincy MA; m. JOHN COYLE.
iv. MARY, b. Minneapolis MN (per census) in 1856, d.
    Indian River in 1870s.
v. JAMES, b Addison 11 Mar. 1860, d. Bangor (hosp.) 9
    Apr. 1942; m. 2 Mar. 1901 ELIZABETH DYER. He res.
    Tremont ME.
vi. CORA MAUD, b. Addison in 1864, res. Malden MA; m.
    ALBERT Van HORN.

1062. JANE BARFIELD[8] 1826-1876 [470 Robert[7] and Peggy Bar-
field] was born at Addison in 1826, died at Jonesport 21 July
1876, 50y; married at Addison int. 27 May 1846 LEVI BAGLEY
SAWYER, born at Jonesport 24 Mar. 1826, died there 14 May
1891, son of Daniel Jordan and Mary (Bagley) Sawyer (town
VRs; Tibbetts, Jonesport Families, 161).
    In 1850 he was a Jonesport sailor, with Elvira Leighton[9],
aged 11 [# 474], in his household. He was later a merchant
and sea captain.

Children (**Sawyer**), born at Jonesport:

i. FRANCESCA T., b. 31 May 1847, d. 11 Jan. 1938, 90y
    8m 15d; m. Lancaster NB in 1866 THOMAS A. DRISKO, b.
    Jonesport 28 July 1841, d. in 1904, son of Jeremiah
    and Jane (Huntley) Drisko.
ii. IDA MAE, b. in Nov. 1854, res Cedar Rapids IA and
    Hastings NE; m. Jonesport 8 Sept. 1878 LUTHER HOW-
    LAND, b. in NY in Nov. 1838. He was a dry goods
    merchant.

1063. MARGARET[8] 1828-1905 [470 Robert[7] and Peggy Barfield]
was born at Addison 19 Mar. 1828, died at Columbia 16 June
1905 (GS, 9 June), 78y 2m 22d; married there 9 July 1848
RICHARD BARFIELD DORR, born there 25 Feb. 1815, died there 3
Dec. 1910 (GS), son of Jonathan and Judith (Worcester) Dorr
(town VRs; Cornman Ms; records of Leonard Tibbetts).
    Richard Dorr was a farmer at Columbia. Burials are in
Epping Cemetery.

Children (**Dorr**), born at Columbia:

i. ELIZA JANE, b. 4 Nov. 1849, d. Columbia 3 Dec. 1878,
    29y; m. Columbia Falls 22 Mar. 1871 JOSHUA L. KIN-
    CAID, b Columbia in Dec. 1842, d. there 16 Mar.
    1883, son of Samuel and Eunice (Dorr) Kincaid. He
    m. 1st Cherryfield 17 May 1864 ISABELLA HANNA, who
    d. 15 Feb. 1870; and m. 3rd Sevina Dorr (iv below).
ii. ALICE E., b. in 1851, d. Jonesport 17 Sept. 1904; m.
    3 Apr. 1874 ALMON TORREY, b. in 1852. He m. 2nd
    Phebe (Davis) Wilcox.

iii.   HARRIET E., b. 26 Aug. 1853, d. Belfast ME 12 July
       1913, 59y 10m 16d; m. 1st Columbia 31 Dec. 1870 MIL-
       LARD FILLMORE TENNEY, b. there in 1851, d. c1880; m.
       2nd GEORGE ELLIS BAGLEY [# 1068].
iv.   SEVIA ALVIRA [Zevia] (Olivia in 1860), b. in Feb.
       1858, res. Cherryfield; m. 1st 2 June 1880
       JOSHUA L. KINCAID, her sister's widower; m. 2nd
       Columbia int. 24 Feb. 1885 GILBERT L. HILL, b.
       Cherryfield in Oct. 1835, son of Rufus and Mary M.
       Hill.
v.   JULIA E., b. 6 Mar. 1863, d. in 1939; m. there 29
       Jan. 1883 WILLIAM JASPER WORCESTER, b. 7 Jan. 1861,
       d. 22 Mar. 1939, son of Moses and Diadama (Smith)
       Worcester. No ch.

1064.   LUTHER P.[8] 1830-1905 [470 Robert[7] and Elizabeth
Dyer] was born at Addison in Feb. 1830, died there 6 Aug.
1905, 75y; married there 12 May 1851 CAROLINE S. KELLEY, born
at Addison 4 Feb. 1831, died at Calais ME 16 July 1915, 84y
5m 4d, daughter of Samuel M. and Belinda Nash (Merritt) Kelley (records of Leonard Tibbetts; town and ME VRs). Burials
are in the William Gray Cemetery, Addison.
Luther was a seaman and then a ships' carpenter. In 1900
their son William lived with them.

Children, all but one born at Addison (Indian River):

i.   SAMUEL KELLEY[9], b. 5 Feb. 1852, d. Addison 27
       Jan. 1928, 75y 11m 21d; m. there 29 June 1884
       GERTRUDE B. LOOK, b. there 22 Nov. 1866, d.
       there 23 July 1963, dau. of Moses Worcester
       and Mary Elizabeth (Farnsworth) Look. No ch.
ii.   BELINDA ANN [Annie B.], b. 25 Aug. 1856, d.
       Calais 29 Mar. 1941; m. JAMES ALBERT HATT, b.
       2 June 1853, d. Calais 13 May 1918, son of
       Jesse and Dorothy (Holmes) Hatt. No ch.
iii.   LEMUEL H., b. c1859 (21 in 1880), d. 28 Aug.
       1885.
iv.   WILLIAM HARRIS, b. c1862, d. Addison 11 Aug.
       1910, 47y 10m; unm. He was a seaman.
1609. v.   GEORGE A., b. in Oct. 1864.
1610. vi.   LULA C., b. 18 Apr. 1866; m. GEORGE AUSTIN
       and JOHN P. WASS.
1611. vii.   ELIZABETH A., b. 18 May 1868; m. GEORGE
       DAUPHINEE and LESLIE A. TIBBETTS.
1612. viii. DELIA C., b. St. George NB 24 May 1870; m.
       FRANK N. BECKETT.

1065.   LEMUEL DYER[8] 1832-1873 [470 Robert[7] and Elizabeth
Dyer] was born at Addison 7 Oct. 1832, died in TX in Mar.
1873, killed in an accident aboard his ship; married 4 Dec.
1852 CALISTA W. THOMPSON, born at Addison 5 Dec. 1833, died
at Milbridge ME 20 June 1908, daughter of John and Miriam V.
(Norton) Thompson. Calista married second at Cherryfield 29
May 1892 John S. Campbell (Cornman Ms; town and ME VRs).
Burials are in Evergreen Cemetery, Milbridge; Lemuel's stone
there has the dates 1831-1872.
He was a sea captain. He appeared in the Columbia 1860
census as Samuel.

Children:

i.   ELLINGTON[9], b. Jonesport 28 May 1853, d. in a
      subway accident, Boston; m. 2nd Milbridge 30
      Dec. 1903 his cousin NELLIE A THOMPSON, b.
      Columbia Falls 1 Dec. 1871, d. S. Duxbury MA
      10 Sept. 1942, dau. of Ira G. and Cecilia A
      Thompson. No ch. He was a sea captain, and
      then a US Navy training officer.

1613. ii.   ELIZABETH [Eliza], b. Addison 4 Mar. 1856; m.
             ALGERNON MARTIN.
1614. iii. CAROLINE MAY, b. Addison 19 May 1858; m.
             FRANKLIN P. LACKEE.
1615. iv.   EDWARD S., b. 11 July 1862.
1616. v.   GEORGE B., b. Jonesport 1 Jan. 1865.
       vi.   ERNEST J., d.y.

1066. (GEORGE) ULMER[8] 1835-1871 [470 Robert[7] and Elizabeth
Dyer] was born at Addison about 1835, died at sea in Dec.
1871; married first at Addison 2 Nov. 1857 SARAH ESTHER
PARKER, born at Jonesport in 1837, died about 1862, daughter
of James and Mary (Farley) Parker; married second at Lubec ME
28 Jan. 1864 LUCINDA ELLIS, born in 1842, died about 1865;
married third at St. Stephen NB 12 Mar. 1867 ESTHER ANN
CLARK, born about 1850, lived at Milwaukee WI. Widow Esther
married second in 1875 Voranus Coffin Lynch (Cornman Ms; town
VRs; records of Leonard F. Tibbetts).
Ulmer enlisted in Co. D, 2nd ME Sharpshooters Rgt., 25 Dec.
1863. He was serving as first mate when he died of yellow
fever (obituary, Portland Press Herald 17 Jan. 1872).
He was probably named for George Ulmer (1755-1825), major
general, sheriff, and legislator.

Children by Sarah:

i.   ?MARY[9], d. Milbridge 16 Oct. 1864, 7y 4m 12d.
1617. ii.   EVERETT U., b. Centerville ME 13 May 1859.
       iii. LUTHER, b. c1862, res. Saint John NB.

1067. ELVIRA C.[8] 1839-1927 [470 Robert[7] and Elizabeth
Dyer] was born at Addison 7 Feb. 1839, died at Haverhill MA
12 Mar. 1927, 88y (84y 1m 5d per VRs) ; married at Addison 24
May 1856 (Machias Union) ALVIN J. STEELE, born there in July
1835, died at Boothbay Harbor ME 9 Feb. 1908, son of Josiah
Drisko and Belinda (Tucker) Steele (town and ME VRs; records
of descendant William Ives; Tibbetts, Jonesport Families,
108; Cornman Ms).
Steele was a seaman at Machias in 1870, and was listed at
Eastport in 1900.

Children (**Steele**):

i.   MARY ELIZABETH, b. Addison in 1858, res. Haverhill in
      1927; m. Haverhill AI CRAIG.
ii.   ELVIRA E, b. in 1863; m. Columbia Falls 12 Dec. 1896
      GEORGE A. SAWYER, b. Jonesport in Sept. 1863, son of
      J. H. and Ronie (Hinckley) Sawyer (Fred E. Sawyer,
      Genealogical Index of the Sawyer Families of
      New England [np, 1983], 41).

iii.   LILLIAN B. [Lilla], b. Jonesport 7 Feb. 1864, d.
       Boothbay Harbor 27 May 1918; m. Jonesport 14 Mar.
       1885 EBENEZER JUDSON [Eben] KELLEY, b. there 19 Oct.
       1855, d Chelsea MA 12 June 1931, son of William
       Henry and Eunice Drisko (Sawyer) Kelley.
iv.   WALLACE NEWBURY, b. in Dec. 1865, res. Eastport; m.
       ANNIE LANG.
v.   EUDORA M., b. in May 1870.
vi.   FANNIE M., b. in June 1873, d. Boothbay Harbor 4 May
       1953; m. Lynn MA 5 May 1892 HARVEY McFADDEN JOY, b.
       Jonesport in Oct. 1865, d. Portland 11 Nov. 1939,
       son of Uriah C. and Mary Ann (Barker) Joy.
vii.   MILLARD L., b. in Oct. 1876, drowned Boothbay Harbor
       after 1900; unm.
viii. MARK A , b. in 1879.

1068.   SUSANNA ESTHER[8] 1841-1898 [470 Robert[7] and Elizabeth
Dyer] was born at Addison in 1841, died at Jonesport 5 Dec.
1898; married about 1859 JAMES EUGENE BAGLEY 3RD, born at
Jonesport 28 July 1829, died there 19 Dec. 1903, son of James
Jr. and Rachel Brown (Kelley) Bagley (Tibbetts, (Jonesport
Families, 15; records of descendant Darryl Lamson).
    James Bagley was a carpenter and shoemaker. They lived at
Jonesport.

Children (**Bagley**), born at Jonesport:

i.   DAVID WILLIAM, b. 1 Oct. 1860, d. 1 June 1866.
ii.   GEORGE ELLIS, b. 21 Jan. 1863, d. Cambridge MA 13
       May 1956; m. 1st Columbia Falls 5 May 1882 HARRIET
       E. (DORR) Tenney [# 1063]; m. 2nd c1916 MARGARET
       (WORCESTER) Williams.
iii.   VINAL CHANDLER, b. 1 Feb. 1866, d. Portland 4 July
       1929; m. Jonesport 15 Jan. 1886 ANNETTE E. COFFIN,
       b. there 27 May 1866, d. 18 Dec. 1931, dau. of
       George Stillman and Laura Augusta (Gardner) Coffin.
       He was a sea captain.
iv.   CORDELIA ABIGAIL, b. 15 Dec. 1868, d. Jonesport 7
       Feb. 1948; m. there 28 May 1887 CHARLES H. DUDLEY,
       b. Eastport 17 July 1854, d. Jonesport 2 May 1929.
v.   JAMES MILTON, b. 17 Mar. 1871, d. Ellsworth ME 28
       June 1962; m. Jonesport 1 June 1897 his cousin
       ESTHER ELMENA BAGLEY, b. Centerville ME 6 July 1871,
       d. Ellsworth 6 Aug. 1962, dau. of Richard and Soph-
       ronia (Allen) Bagley.
vi.   ELMER BURTON [Bertie], b. 3 Jan. 1875, d. Jonesport
       11 Mar. 1929; m. 1st there 5 Oct. 1901 LENA RACHEL
       DONOVAN, b. there in Mar. 1883, d. there 24 Apr.
       1907, dau. of Edward Mansfield and Lucinda D.
       (Smith) Donovan; m. 2nd GERTRUDE LAURA KELLEY, b.
       there 23 May 1881, d. 30 Mar. 1965, dau. of George
       Washington and Laura Ann (Kelley) Kelley.
vii.   LAURA MAY, b. 2 Apr. 1877, d. Addison 6 Nov. 1955; m.
       1st Jonesport 28 Feb. 1894 BYRON ATWOOD DONOVAN, b.
       there 31 July 1868, d. there 21 July 1894, son of
       Daniel Rogers and Olive A. (Kelley) Donovan; m. 2nd
       there 11 Mar. 1897 WILLIAM LEWIS GUPTILL, b. Addison
       19 May 1867, d. there 8 Mar. 1922, son of Nehemiah
       A. and Isabella (Smith) Guptill.

viii. FRANK LEROY, b. 12 Feb. 1881, d. Jonesport 11 Apr.
       1848; m. there 15 June 1907 ELVA MAE GRIFFIN, b. 5
       Nov. 1885, d. 5 May 1960, dau. of James and F. Ella
       (Glidden) Griffin.
ix.   HARVEY EUGENE, b. 25 Mar. 1884, d. Jonesport 4 Sept.
       1958; m. there 5 Oct. 1911 LEILA BELL MITCHELL, b.
       there 7 Feb. 1891, dau. of David Carroll and Mary
       Maude (Kelley) Mitchell.

1069. JASON DRISKO[8] 1835-1917 [472 Nahum[7] and Phoebe
Drisko] was born at Addison 3 Nov. 1835, died at Milbridge 9
Feb. 1917, 74y 3m 6d; married first at Jonesport 20 Oct. 1860
(Machias Union) MARY ELIZA DRISKO, born at Addison 14 May
1842, died at sea 7 Aug. 1868, 26y, daughter of Edmund C. and
Hannah W. (Allen) Drisko; married second at Milbridge 13 Oct.
1880 HELEN GEORGIA RICH, born there 22 Jan. 1852, died there
30 Oct.1935, daughter of William H. and Sybil S.[8] (Leighton)
Rich [# 897] (town VRs; Cornman Ms; records of Leonard F.
Tibbetts).
Records of Capt. Jason's voyages, ships and cargoes are
preserved in the manuscript collection, MHS. His first wife
died of yellow fever on the Raven as they were returning from
Cuba to NY.

Children by Mary:

            i.   AVERY D.[9], b. NYC 10 May, d. 18 July, 1861.
1618.   ii.   CARRIE C., b. Addison 30 Sept. 1862; m. ORRIN
                 P. SWANTON.
1619.   iii.   LUCRETIA SMALL, b. Milbridge 11 Oct. 1864; m.
                 A. LINCOLN WALLACE.

1070. SARAH A.[8] 1839-1900 [472 Nahum[7] and Phoebe Drisko]
was born at Addison 17 July 1839, died at Milbridge 3 Feb.
1900, 60y 6m; married about 1860 EZRA S. STROUT, born at Milbridge 2 Feb. 1835, died there 13 Oct. 1905, 70y 8m 11d, son
of Lewis and Lydia (Smith) Strout (Cornman Ms; records of
Leonard F. Tibbetts; town VRs). Burials are in Evergreen
Cemetery.

Children (**Strout**), born at Milbridge:

i.   CORA M. LEIGHTON, b. 29 May 1861, d. 7 Feb. 1896
       (VRs; 1886 GS); m. there 6 Feb. 1879 LEWIS PINKHAM,
       b. 5 Aug. 1858, d. there 11 Sept. 1923, son of David
       and Louise (Strout) Pinkham.
ii.   LAURA J., b. 23 Feb. 1863; m. 1st NAPOLEON[8] LEIGHTON
       [# 419]; m. 2nd NATHAN E.[9] LEIGHTON [# 896].
iii.   ARVILLA M., b. 5 Sept. 1864, d. Milbridge 25 Dec.
       1892, 27y 3m; m. Harrington 25 Dec. 1880 HERBERT O.
       STROUT, b. 19 May 1859.
iv.   MARTHA ROWENA, b. 13 Mar. 1867; m. DARIUS DICKEY JOY
       [# 1071].
v.   AVERY, d. in 1868, aged 5m (GS).
vi.   LENA [Linnie], b. 5 Mar. 1869, d. 31 Oct. 1924; m. in
       Aug. 1886 FRED NEAL of Waltham MA
vii.   GEORGE V., b. 9 Nov. 1870, d. Milbridge 28 Feb. 1935;
       m. 1st in 1891 FLORENCE STROUT--div.; m. 2nd 16 Oct.
       1915 MARY EAKINS.

viii. WILLIAM, b. in May, d. in Dec., 1873, 7m.
ix.   WILLIAM, b. 25 May 1876, d. Milbridge 21 Mar. 1892,
      15y 10m.

1071.   REBECCA DRISKO[8] 1840-1913 [472 Nahum[7] and Phoebe
Drisko] was born at Addison 16 Nov. 1840, died at North Haven
ME 11 Jan. 1913, 72y 1m 26d; married at Milbridge 29 Sept.
1857 DAVID BERIAH JOY, born at Addison 11 Aug. 1837, died
there 15 Oct. 1912, son of Beriah S. and Phebe (Cox) Joy
(Darryl Lamson, Families of Laura Bagley Donovan Guptill
[rev. edition, 1982, MHS], 49-51). Burials are in Joyville
Cemetery, South Addison.
Their household included David's niece Mary Etta, whose
mother Mary (Joy) Carver had died giving birth.

Children (**Joy**), born at Addison:

i.   PHEBE L., b. 29 Jan. 1862, d. Columbia 12 Aug. 1877,
      15y 5m.
ii.   DARIUS DICKEY, b. 14 Apr. 1864, d. Addison 12 Mar.
      1943; m. there 12 Mar. 1887 MARTHA R. STROUT, b. 13
      Mar. 1877, d. there 7 Mar. 1933, dau. of Ezra and
      Sarah[8] (Leighton) Strout [# 1070].
iii. VIOLA L., b. 28 Mar. 1866, d. 11 Oct. 1883.
iv.   DAVID E., b. 20 Nov. 1867, d. Arlington MA 29 Nov.
      1959, 92y; m. 1 Jan. 1894 MARY E. BURNS, b. Machias
      15 Apr. 1871, d. Addison 11 Apr. 1946, dau. of John
      W. and Julia (Flaherty) Burns.
v.   MARGARET B., b. in Apr. 1871, d. Machias 3 Jan. 1925;
      m. in 1893 WILLIAM E. WASS, b. in Oct. 1862, d. 7
      June 1930, son of Edwin R. and Elizabeth (Burns)
      Wass.
vi.   (HARRIS) WEBSTER, b. 4 Aug. 1876, d. Jonesboro 27
      Oct. 1955, 78y; m. FLORA M. BEAL, b. Addison 30 June
      1880, d. Jonesport 8 Dec. 1961, dau. of Darius
      Dickey and Sabrina E. (Sawyer) Beal.
vii. SUSAN E., b. 9 Feb. 1878, d. in Mar. 1981, 103y; m.
      EMERY WOOSTER, b. in 1884, d. in 1968.

1072.   LUCY W.[8] 1842-1912 [472 Nahum[7] and Phoebe Drisko]
was born at Addison about 1842 (38 in 1880), died at Corea
(Gouldsboro) 17 Mar. 1912; married at Jonesport 20 Jan. 1865
CHARLES WILLIAM TRACY, born at Gouldsboro 12 Mar. 1833, died
there 16 Aug. 1896, 63y 5m 4d, son of Eri and Hannah (Ashe)
Tracy (town VRs; records of Virgilia Tracy).

Children (**Tracy**), born at Gouldsboro:

i.   ASENATH E.[9], b. 1 Jan., d. 1 Nov., 1866.
ii.   JASON L., b. 6 Aug. 1868; unm.
iii. ELLA B., b. 19 Feb. 1870, res. CA
iv.   JOHN HANDY, b. 22 May 1872, d. Bucksport ME 17 Oct.
      1954; m. 14 Oct. 1896 ALICE BELLE BUNKER, b. 2 July
      1878, d. in 1976, dau. of Uriah G. and Hannah
      (Cleaves) Bunker.
v.   HATTIE J., b. 7 Nov. 1874, d. 2 Sept. 1954; m. JOHN
      D. TRACY.
vi.   CARRIE E., b. 10 Sept. 1877, res. Sullivan; m. 1st
      GEORGE L. RICE; m. 2nd FRED SMITH.

1073. **LAURA DRISKO**[8] 1844-1916 [472 Nahum[7] and Phoebe Drisko] was born at Addison 8 Jan. 1844, died at Milbridge 20 Jan. 1916; married there 20 Jan. 1866 JOHN HENRY FOSTER, born there 21 Jan. 1841, died there in 1890, son of William Godfrey and Catherine Campbell (Ray) Foster (Cornman Ms; records of Leonard F. Tibbetts).

Children (**Foster**):

i.   KATIE CAMPBELL, b. Milbridge 23 Nov. 1866, d. 3 Apr. 1880.
ii.   HANNAH F., b. Columbia 8 Mar. 1872, res. Boston; m. ---- KEENAN (Milbridge Town Register, 1905).
iii. RAYMOND LEIGHTON, b. Milbridge 16 June 1886.

1074. **PHEBE PARKER**[8] 1849-1923 [472 Nahum[7] and Phoebe Drisko] was born at Addison 29 June 1849, died at Milbridge 2 Feb. 1923, 73y 9m 4d; married at Columbia 31 May 1873 WARREN FOSTER, born at Milbridge 24 Apr. 1846, died there in 1908, son of William Godfrey and Catherine Campbell (Ray) Foster (Frederick C. Pierce, Foster Genealogy [Chicago, 1899], 690-93; Cornman Ms; records of Margaret Colton). He was a sea captain.

Children (**Foster**):

i.   MARY, b. Columbia 1 May 1874, d. Milbridge 21 Dec. 1958; m. ELIAS BURTON GRIFFIN, son of John W. and Ida (Bracey) Griffin.
ii.   MARGARET DYER, b. Columbia Falls 8 May 1880, d. Milbridge 21 Oct. 1950; unm.

1075. **LOWELL WILLIAM**[8] 1828-1907 [473 John[7] and Eunice Wright] was born at Addison 11 Dec. 1828, died at Jonesport 22 Feb. 1907, 78y 2m 22d; married first at Portland 26 Sept. 1855 CAROLINE S. YORK, born there 22 Feb. 1829, died at Addison 19 Feb. 1872, 43y; married second 13 June 1874 PAMELIA MABEL YOUNG, born at Calais 4 Nov. 1843, died at Beals Island 9 Dec. 1925, 82y 2m 5d, daughter of Jacob Young. Pamelia married second about 1908 Capt. John A. Beal (Tibbetts, Jonesport Families, 74; Cornman Ms; Addison and ME VRs).
    He was a farmer and sea captain at Indian River. He was listed as William L. in 1870; in 1900 he and Pamelia lived with his son George. Burials are in Indian River Cemetery.

Children by Caroline, born at Addison:

i.   FRED LOWELL[9], b. in 1856, d. in 1860 (GS).
ii.   WILLIAM HARRISON, b. 20 June 1858, d. Jonesport 11 Aug. 1910; m. Addison 28 May 1892 LOUISA ESTELLE [Lula] DONOVAN, b Addison 6 Aug. 1869, d. Providence RI 25 July 1952, dau. of Charles and Salome Wass (Tabbutt) Donovan. No ch. He was retired from the Providence Fire Dept. Lula m. 2nd Providence 1 Feb. 1912 Harold Bellows [Harry] Crosby.
iii. JOHN WRIGHT (twin), b. 20 June 1858, d. in 1878 (GS).

iv.   ALICE M., b. say 1860, d. aged 6m (GS).
v.   GEORGE A., b. 10 Mar. 1863, d. Bangor 6 Nov.
       1935; m. Jonesport 11 Apr. 1895 ESTHER C.
       COUSINS, b. Addison 6 Aug. 1869, dau. of
       George M. and Emeline A (Merritt) Cousins.
       He was a butcher, constable, deputy sheriff,
       and insurance agent at Addison. His widow
       was called Gertrude. Ch. CAROLYN M.[10] b.
       Addison 23 Oct. 1895; m. Machias 21 July 1919
       GORDON C McCABE, b. there c1895, son of
       Harry C. and Addie C. (Jack) McCabe.
vi.   MABEL, b. 10 Dec. 1865, d. in 1867, 18m (GS).
1620. vii. CHARLES WEBSTER, b. 10 Apr. 1868.

1076.   URIAH WASS[8] 1830-1910 [473 John[7] and Eunice Wright]
was born at Addison 10 Aug. 1830, died there 11 Aug. 1910,
79y 5m 19d; married first there 19 Aug. 1852 ABITHA D.[8]
LEIGHTON, born there in 1830, died at Jaffa, Lebanon, 6 Dec.
1885, daughter of Nahum H. and Phoebe (Drisko) Leighton
[# 472]; married second at Addison 9 May 1874 ANNA S. DYER,
born at Addison in Dec. 1847, died there 11 Aug. 1906, 57y
9m, daughter of Silas Briggs and Julia A. (Ingersoll) Dyer
(Addison VRs; records of Leonard F. Tibbetts).
    Uriah was a fisherman at Indian River. He and Abitha
became part of the Palestine Emigration Society in 1866 (see
471 for historical note). Two of their children died of
unsanitary conditions at Jaffa.
    Abitha refused to return with Uriah from Palestine; he
later divorced her for desertion.

Children by Abitha, born at Addison:

i.   IDELLA W.[9], b. in 1854, d. Palestine in 1867.
ii.   JAMES AVERY, b. 2 Oct. 1856, d. Addison 6 May
       1858, 19m 1d (GS).
1621. iii. RALPH I., b. 18 Aug. 1859.
iv.   FLORA L., b. in 1865, d. Palestine in Nov.
       1866.

1077.   REBECCA DRISKO[8] 1832-1921 [473 John[7] and Eunice
Wright] was born at Addison 9 June 1833, died at Jonesboro 3
Sept. 1921, 88y 2m 25d; married there int. 31 Mar. 1857 EPH-
RAIM WHITNEY, born there 14 July 1835, died there in May
1904, son of Gustavus Fellows and Hannah (Libby) Whitney
(Cornman Ms; records of Leonard F. Tibbetts and of descendant
Jo-Ann Scheleen; ME VRs). He was superintendent of a granite
quarry.

Children (**Whitney**), born at Jonesboro:

i.   ESTELLA HANNAH, b. in 1857; m. HORACE COLLIER NOYES,
       b. in Nov. 1854, son of George W. and Elmira (Farns-
       worth) Noyes. He had a 2nd wife.
ii.   (GEORGE) EDWARD, b. in 1860, d. Jonesboro in 1879,
       19y (GS).
iii.   MARY EDITH [Mame], b. in Dec. 1862; m. WILLIAM E.
       RONEY of Vinal Haven ME, b. in Aug. 1858.

iv. FRANK SEAVEY, b. 22 Mar. 1864, d. Portland 13 June
     1947; m. 27 Nov. 1895 JOSEPHINE LOUISE OCKINGTON,
     b. Stratford NH 10 Apr. 1870, d. Portland 5 July
     1951, dau. of Benjamin Brooks and Rhoda Ann (Wright)
     Ockington. They res. Stratford, then moved to Port-
     land c1910.
 v. GEORGE MASON, b. 30 Apr. 1879; m. EVA B. WHITE.

1078. ISAAC WILLIS[8] 1839-1916 [473 John[7] and Eunice
Wright] was born at Addison 29 Dec. 1839, died at Portland 31
Dec. 1916, 77y; married at Addison 7 Jan. 1868 ANTOINETTE R.
[Nettie] CROWLEY, born there 27 Apr. 1850, died at Portland
15 May 1922, 72y, daughter of Joel S. and Harriet C (McKen-
zie) Crowley (Addison and Portland VRs; records of grandson
Joel). Burials are in Evergreen Cemetery.
  He served in Co. H, 9th ME Inf. Rgt., 21 Sept. 1861 to 13
July 1865, was wounded in the knee, and was a pensioner. He
was a merchant at Addison, and later lived at Portland.

Children, born at Addison:

1622. i.   JOEL CROWLEY[9], b. 19 June 1872.
       ii. LETITIA [Lettie], b. 16 July 1875, d. Augusta
            (state hosp.) in Feb. 1956; m. Portland 7
            Jan. 1902 CLIFTON CHESLEY POOLER, b. Portland
            in May 1875, d. in 1956, son of James J. and
            Ida (Elder) Pooler. No ch.

1079. GEORGE P.[8] 1842-1923 [473 John[7] and Eunice Wright]
was born at Addison 4 Jan. 1842, died at Bangor 17 Nov. 1923,
82y 10m 13d; married at Addison 11 Feb. 1871 SOPHRONIA JANE
DOBBIN, born at Jonesport 19 Jan. 1847, died there 20 Feb.
1921, 74y 1m 1d, daughter of George Washington and Eliza
Green (Norton) Dobbin (Addison and Jonesport VRs; Darryl B.
Lamson, Lamson Family of Jonesport, Maine [Baltimore, 1978],
53; records of Leonard F Tibbetts; Cornman Ms).
  He served in Co. A, 1st ME Sharpshooters Rgt., in the Civil
War. He was a lobsterman and then sea captain at Jonesport;
in 1910 he was a farmer there. He was listed as Patrick in
the 1850 census, but George P. in other records.

Children:

       i.   NELLIE B.[9], b. Addison 22 Nov. 1871, d. Calais
            (hosp.) 4 Feb. 1924; m. Jonesport 26 Mar.
            1895 MILLARD HENRY [Mill] EMERSON, b. Addison
            1 Aug. 1875, d. there 26 Mar. 1957, son of
            Eugene and Josephine M. (Rogers) Emerson.
            Ch. Carroll Eugene b. 15 Feb. 1896, d. 10
            June 1958; m. Effie White. Millard m. 2nd
            Stella Norton.
1623. ii. WALDO, b. 15 Oct. 1874.
1624. iii. LESTER, b. 1 Nov. 1875.
       iv. HARRY L., b. Jonesport 6 Aug. 1879, d. there
            2 Oct. 1939; m. there 2 Sept. 1914 JENNIE
            ELIZABETH HINCKLEY, b. there 15 Oct. 1882, d.
            15 Apr. 1959, dau. of Charles S. and Alice M.
            (Kelley) Hinckley. No ch. He was a railroad
            mail clerk.

1080. (DANIEL) WEBSTER[8] [Webb] 1844-1906 [473 John[7] and Eunice Wright] was born at Addison 18 Mar. 1844, died at New York NY 13 Nov. 1906; married at Addison 7 Mar. 1874 LOUISA MARIA TABBUTT, born at Steuben 7 Apr. 1851, died at Bar Harbor in Mar. 1928, 76y 10m 26d, daughter of Hiram and Almira D. (Moore) Tabbutt (records of Leonard F. Tibbetts; town and ME VRs). Burials are in Tabbutt Cemetery, Addison. He was a master mariner.

Children, born at Addison (Indian River):

1625.   i.   HIRAM TABBUTT[9], b. 18 Oct. 1877.
1626.   ii.   MABEL MOORE, b. 5 Sept. 1879; m CLARENCE DOW.
1627.   iii. ALMIRA D., b. 5 Aug. 1884; m. HORACE PREBLE.

1081. (PRISCILLA) JANE[8] 1846-1913 [473 John[7] and Eunice Wright] was born at Addison 30 Apr. 1846, died probably at Hudson ME in Feb. 1913; married (as Jane P.) at Calais 30 June 1871 (Machias Union; int. 31 May at Tp 7) GEORGE WELLINGTON WHITE, born at Topsfield 1 May 1851, died at Hudson 8 May 1919, son of (George) Stillman and Mary E. (Howe) White (Topsfield VRS; records of descendants Genevieve Ireland and Janet I. Delory; Cornman Ms).
George was a Bangor & Aroostook Rail Road worker.

Children (**White**):

i.   HORACE W., b. prob. Addison 21 Jan. 1872; m. MARIAH
      NOBLE.
ii.   MAUD ESTELLA, b. prob. Addison 21 Apr. 1874; m. HARRY
      NOBLE.
iii. CLIFTON WILLIE, b. Addison 7 Jan. 1876, d. Livermore
      Falls ME 24 Apr. 1956, 80y; m. 1st Caribou ME 23
      June 1906 LILLIAN GERTRUDE PETERSON, b. Woodland ME
      3 July 1884, d. Caribou 1 May 1916, dau. of Evalde
      Gothard and Judith (Olson) Peterson--div. in 1912;
      m. 2nd ---- .
iv.   GEORGE W., b. Topsfield 15 May 1887; m. LYDIA BLAKE.
v.   HERMAN, b. Topsfield 1 Dec. 1890, d. Hudson in Apr.
      1912; unm.

1082. LUCY DRISKO[8] 1833-1921 [474 Curtis[7] and Philena Emerson] was born at Addison 21 Dec. 1833, died at Jonesport 8 Jan. 1921, 88y 16d; married at Addison 12 Apr. 1851 BENJAMIN KELLEY ROGERS, born at Jonesport 14 June 1829, died there 21 Sept. 1879, 50y 3m 17d, son of Joseph Prince and Olivette (Drisko) Rogers (Tibbetts, Jonesport Families, 143; Jonesport Town Register, 1905; Cornman Ms).
Benjamin and Lucy were among those emigrating to Palestine in 1866 [# 471].

Children (**Rogers**):

i.   ELEANORA P. [Nora], b. Addison 13 Oct. 1851, d.
      Jonesport 15 Feb. 1915, 63y 4m; m. there 29 Jan.
      1870 WARREN ENNIS CROWLEY, b. in 1846, d. at sea,
      son of Matthew Coffin and Elizabeth Ann (Crowley)
      Crowley.

ii. THERESA L., b. Addison 8 July 1854, d. 23 Feb. 1946;
     m. Jonesport 21 June 1873 ABRAM BILLINGS KELLEY, b.
     there 12 Oct. 1836, d. there 24 Jan. 1909, son of
     Aaron and Rebecca Sawyer (Norton) Kelley. No ch.
iii. BRADFORD, b. c1858, d. Boston before 1900.
iv. ARTHUR R., b. Jonesport 15 Nov. 1860, d. there 24
     Nov. 1945; m. there 27 June 1885 AMANDA CORDELIA
     DAVIS, b. in June 1863, d. in 1949, dau. of David M.
     and Eliza F. (White) Davis. He was a building
     contractor.
v.   GEORGE, b. c1863, d. Jaffa, Palestine, 8 Oct. 1866.
vi. ALTON V., b. Jaffa 9 June 1867, d. Ellsworth ME 31
     July 1957; m. 1st Jonesport 24 Sept. 1890 JULIA A.
     SAWYER, b. in June 1875, d. in 1966, dau. of Eben J.
     and Philena Augusta (Kelley) Sawyer--div.; m. 2nd
     SARA T. AUSTIN, b. Addison 20 Apr. 1880, d. 17 Aug.
     1944, dau. of Junius Noble and Elizabeth M.
     (Thompson) Austin.
vii. CLIFTON M. [Kip], b. Jonesport 15 June 1870, d.
     Bangor 25 Mar. 1947; m. GENEVA MAY FRENCH, b. Jones-
     port 17 Oct. 1873, d. 11 July 1935, dau. of Lorenzo
     D. and Adrianna N. (Johnson) French. He was a book-
     keeper

1083. HARRIET NEWELL[8] 1835-1908 [474 Curtis[7] and Philena
Emerson] was born at Addison 22 Dec. 1835, died there 13 June
1908; married there 14 June 1855 REUBEN CHANDLER, born there
11 May 1835, died there 6 June 1918, son of Christopher and
Sarah (Drisko) Chandler (Addison VRs; Cornman Ms; records of
Leonard F. Tibbetts).

Children (**Chandler**), born at Addison:

i.   ELLA J., b. 14 Mar. 1856, d. Northfield ME 6 June
     1886; m. in Aug. 1876 FRED THOMAS of Boston. No ch.
ii. EMELINE AUGUSTA [Emma], b. 14 Feb. 1858, d. Addison
     10 Apr. 1942; m. there 25 Sept. 1880 EUGENE EVERETT
     SMALL, b. Milbridge in July 1844, d. Addison 4 Dec.
     1914, son of Timothy and Rhoda (Whitten) Small.
iii. MELVINA, b. 21 Aug. 1860, d. 11 Dec. 1871.
iv. ELIZABETH, b. 15 Feb. 1863, d. 25 Dec. 1871.
v.   CURTIS M., b. 12 May 1868, d. 29 Jan. 1872.
vi. JOSEPHINE L., b. 22 Nov. 1871, d. 3 Nov. 1887.
vii. ESTELLA M., b. 19 May 1875, d. Addison 31 Mar. 1917;
     m. JOHN W. DAVIS, son of Henry and Lydia (Alley)
     Davis.

1084. ARTHUR[8] 1837-1909 [474 Curtis[7] and Philena Emerson]
was born at Addison 16 Feb. 1837, died at Bay de Noc, Delta
Co. MI 3 Mar. 1909, 74y 15d; married first at Jonesport 19
Dec. 1864 LOIS MANSFIELD DONOVAN, born there in Sept. 1845,
died in Delta Co. MI about Nov. 1889, daughter of Jeremiah
and Esther (Rogers) Donovan; married second at Escanaba MI 7
Oct. 1891 ADELINE (FONTAINE) Ansell, born in MI in 1868, died
at Newberry, Luce Co. MI 27 Feb. 1940, daughter of John Fontaine (Tibbetts, Jonesport Families, 76; records of Darryl
Lamson; Cornman Ms). He was a farmer at Addison in 1870, and
was later a boat engineer in MI.

Children by Lois (perhaps two others):

1628. i.   MINA H.⁹, b. Jonesport in July 1867; m. GEORGE
             BARTLEY.
       ii.   ADELAIDE E., b. Jonesport in Sept. 1870, d.
             Escanaba MI 3 Nov. 1941; m. in 1891 CHARLES
             J. DADY, b. in IL in Nov. 1866, d. Escananba
             14 May 1929. He was a railroad engineer.
             Ch. Robert Charles b. 28 June 1896, d. 26
             June 1930; m. Mae Ridings.
       iii. LOIS, b. in MI in Nov. 1889 (Lou in the 1900
             census).

Children by Adeline, born in MI:

       iv.   PHILENA [Lena], b. Escanaba 29 Oct. 1892; m.
             1st there 6 Nov. 1912 CYRUS ONSLEY, son of
             Price and Nancy (Crain) Onsley; m. 2nd there
             8 Feb. 1918 CLAUDE DeSHERMAN, son of Caesar
             and Mary (Lator) DeSherman.
       v.   (ARTHUR) CURTIS, b. Bay de Noc 1 May 1894.
       vi.   ROY, b. 15 Mar. 1896.
       vii. GEORGE B., b. 6 Mar. 1898.

1085. (IRA) BOARDMAN⁸ 1851-1914 [474 Curtis⁷ and Philena
Emerson] was born at Addison 22 May 1851, died at Escanaba MI
3 Apr. 1914; married at Jonesboro 13 Oct. 1872 ELIZABETH A
[Lizzie] TUPPER, born at Roque Bluffs ME 19 Jan. 1857, died
at Escanaba 19 July 1943, daughter of James Pierpont Schoppe
and Delia W. (Cates) Tupper (town VRs; records of Leonard F.
Tibbetts; Cornman Ms).
     In 1870 they lived with her parents at Jonesboro. In 1880
they were still listed at Jonesboro, but soon afterward they
settled in MI, where he was a marine engineer. In 1900 they
were at Escanaba (he as Irwin B., born in Apr. 1855), with
their sons Fred and Herbert.

Children:

       i.   CURTIS J.⁹, b. Jonesboro in 1873, d.y. in MI.
1629. ii.   FRED H., b. Jonesboro in Apr. 1879.
       iii. HERBERT A , b. Escanaba in Nov. 1882, d. there
             12 Sept. 1965; m. there 9 Nov. 1906 LUCILLE
             ROEMER, dau. of John Roemer. No ch.
       iv.   JOHN, b. in MI, not in 1900 census.

1086. ELI A.⁸ 1843-1914 [475 Barnabas⁷ and Mary Stevens]
was born at Addison 10 June 1843, died at Oak Bluffs MA 6
Mar. 1914; married 5 Sept. 1870 EDITH ROBBINS, born at Hyan-
nis MA 26 Oct. 1849, died 3 Feb. 1933, daughter of Timothy
and Emily Robbins (records of Leonard F. Tibbetts; MA VRs:
Cornman Ms).
     He served in Co. D, 22nd ME Inf. Rgt., 10 Sept. 1862 to 14
Aug. 1863.
     He was a carpenter and then a building contractor in MA,
and by 1880 had joined his father at Oak Bluffs (then Cottage
City). After fifteen years on the police force, he became
chief of police there.

Children:

    i.   MAUD ESTELLE[9], b. Taunton MA 17 Mar. 1872; m.
          21 Nov. 1900 FREDERICK WARREN SMITH, b.
          Edgarton MA 15 Jan. 1866, son of George A
          and Lucy P. Smith.
    ii.   AUGUSTUS WELLINGTON, b. Somerville MA 28 Jan.
          1877, d. 17 June 1899; unm.

1087. MARY SOPHIA[8] 1848-   [475 Barnabas[7] and Mary Ste-
vens] was born at Addison in 1848, lived at Cottage City MA
in 1903; married JOHN E. SANDEFORD (Cornman Ms; records of
Leonard F. Tibbetts).

Children (**Sandeford**):

    i.   GERTRUDE MAY; m. 19 Oct. 1898 RAY ALTON BUNKER.
    ii.   ESTELLE LOUISE; m. 14 Oct. 1903 ROGER C. NORRIS.
    iii. JOHN.

1088. ROBINSON[8] 1823-   [478 Holland[7] and Jane Robinson]
was born at Lubec 9 Oct. 1823; married BARBARA GUPTAIL[8]
LEIGHTON, born 12 Apr. 1825, died 9 Dec. 1853, daughter of
George and Comfort (Guptill) Leighton [# 311] (Lubec VRs;
Wilder, Pembroke Families). In 1850 they were living at
Pembroke.

Child, born at Pembroke:

    i.   WILLIS A [9], b. in 1845 (in military record,
          but aged 3 in 1850), d. Annapolis MD 12 Apr.
          1864. He enl. in Co. C, 4th ME Inf. Rgt., 31
          Aug. 1863, aged 18, deserted 11 Oct. 1863 and
          was taken prisoner (NA-MSR).
          His great-grandfather George was given
          admin. of his estate 15 Dec. 1865 (WashCP
          22:399-400).

1089. CHARLES E.[8] 1835-1911 [478 Holland[7] and Jane Robin-
son] was born at Lubec 6 Dec. 1835, died there 7 May 1911,
76y; married 15 June 1855 ELIZABETH A FLYNN, born at Picton
NS in Nov. 1832 (per 1900 census, but listed as 56 in 1891),
died at Lubec 22 Jan. 1916, daughter of James Flynn (records
of descendant Alfred Kelley, NB research of Glenata Hettrick;
ME VRs; NB censuses of 1861 thru 1891). Burials are in the
Lamson Cemetery, Lubec.
    He settled at Grand Manan NB at or before his marriage, and
was a fisherman and millwright there in 1891. Living with
him in 1861 was a Henry Leighton, 17.
    According to Julia Cornman he was a sailmaker at East Bos-
ton in 1903, but in 1910 he and his wife were at Lubec, living with Stephen and Ardella Huntley.

Children, born at Grand Manan NB:

    i.   ELIZA F.[9], b. c1855 (6 in 1861); m. Grand
          Manan 10 Oct. 1874 JOHN N. FOSTER, b. there

29 Oct. 1849.   Ch. Louise Reed res. Boothbay
Harbor.
1630.   ii.   GEORGE MARINER, b. 3 July 1859.
1631.   iii.   WILLIAM L., b. c1860 (1 in 1871).
1632.   iv.   ALDEN J., b. 8 Sept. 1864.
        v.   LYNN; m. AUSTIN LEVI, b. Grand Manan in
               1864 (17 in 1881), res. British Columbia.
               Ch. Grey (per Erroll Leighton).
1633.   vii.   CHARLES E., b. 2 Feb. 1869.
1634.   vi.   ARDELLA, b. 6 June 1870; m. STEPHEN HUNTLEY.

1090.   JAMES MORRIS[8] 1842-1907 [480 Alfred[7] and Janet
Morris] was born at Perry ME 28 June 1842, died at Portland
(hosp.) 13 Dec. 1907, 65y 5m 15d; married at Boston 22 Sept.
1870 (Machias Union) MARY ELIZABETH OUTHOUSE, born at Compton
IL 24 July 1846, died in MA 23 Dec. 1914 (Perry VRs), daughter of James and Elizabeth Outhouse (town and ME VRs; Wilder,
Pembroke Families; Cornman Ms).
   He served in the US Navy 16 Oct. 1862 to 10 Feb. 1864, and
was on the frigate Chesapeake while it was part of the squa-
dron blockading Mobile (NA-MSR). He lived at Perry, where he
was a carpenter and landsman. Burial is in the Hillside Cemetery, Eastport.

Children, born at Perry:

   i.   ADELLA IRENE[9] [Ada], b. 15 Aug. 1871, res.
          Milltown (Calais) ME; m. Perry 12 Sept. 1894
          GEORGE EVERETT MITCHELL, born Sharon ME
          c1868 (21 in 1894), son of Roscoe G. and
          Harriet W.[8] (Leighton) Mitchell [# 789]. She
          was a music teacher, he a builder and archi-
          tect. Ch. Marion b. Roxbury MA 21 Dec. 1895.
   ii.   LUELLA, b. 31 Oct. 1876, res. Germantown PA;
          m. 29 June 1904 HUGH LESLEY. She was a
          nurse.
   iii.   JAMES ALFRED, b. 25 June 1879, d. Eastport 24
          Mar. 1936, 57y 1m 29d; m. there 28 Oct. 1908
          MARY LOUISE WALLACE, b. in Canada in 1883,
          dau. of J. L. and Madeline (McDonald) Wal-
          lace. He operated a mill and adjoining store
          (Bangor Weekly Commercial, 14 Feb. 1918).
   iv.   CHARLES WILLIAM WALLACE [Willie], b. 23 Apr.
          1882, res. Marion IA (per Wilder). In 1903
          he was a sailor on the Old Dominion Line's
          Hamilton, and was said to have worked on the
          Panama Canal.

1091.   ALFRED WALLACE[8] 1844-   [480 Alfred[7] and Janet Mor-
ris] was born at Perry 26 Oct. 1844, lived at Jacksonville FL
in 1903; married 16 Nov. 1870 TERESA O. POTTLE, born at Perry
4 Apr. 1848, daughter of Simon and Elizabeth Pottle (Cornman
Ms; records of descendant Patricia Leighton). In 1880 he was
listed at Perry as Wallace A.

Children, born at Perry:

1635.   i.   EDWIN RUFUS[9], b. 23 Sept. 1871.
1636.   ii.   WALLACE LEROY, b. 28 Sept. 1878.

1092. GEORGE FRANKLIN[8] 1846-1914 [4P0 Alfred[7] and Janet Morris] was born at Perry 22 July 1846, died there 20 June 1914, 67y 10m 10d; married there 5 Feb. 1878 CORA MARIA LORING, born there 4 Mar. 1852, died at Elgin IL 29 May 1926, 73y 2m 20d, daughter of John and Elizabeth (Trott) Loring (Pope, Loring Gen., 145; Perry VRs; Cornman Ms). A millwright, he lived at Perry and Eastport.

Children, born at Perry:

    i.   EDGAR LORING[9], b. 17 Nov. 1879, drowned
           Perry 28 July 1896.
    ii.   ELIZABETH JANET [Bessie], b. 13 Apr. 1884,
           res. Minneapolis MN; m. DAVID OUTHOUSE.
    iii. CATHERINE F. [Kate], b. 14 June 1886, res.
           Minneapolis.
    iv.   CHURCH, b. 30 May 1888, res. in midwest.

1093. ADRIANNA[8] [Addie] 1857-   [480 Alfred[7] and Janet Morris] was born at Perry 16 Aug. 1857, lived at Lilly Lake, Kane Co. IL; married in IL 27 Sept. 1878 RENALVIN OUTHOUSE, born in Apr. 1853, died in 1893 (Cornman Ms).
In 1900 her mother Janet was living in the Outhouse household at Lilly Lake.

Children (**Outhouse**), born in IL:

    i.   FREDERICK, b. 29 Jan. 1879.
    ii.   LAURA, b. in 1881.
    iii. MYRTLE, b. in 1883.
    iv.   MARY, b. in 1885.

1094. SUSAN[8] 1849-1887 [481 Jacob[7] and Sarah Small] was born at Machiasport about 1849 (2 in 1850, 32 in 1880), died there in 1887; married there 4 May 1867 (Machias Union) GILBERT S. SANBORN, born at Machias 12 Apr. 1844, son of James L. and Pamelia A. (Small) Sanborn (Machias VRs: Sanborn Gen., 239).
Sanborn was a sea captain, living at Machiasport in 1880.

Children (**Sanborn**), born at Machiasport:

    i.   INEZ M., b. c1866 (14 in 1880).
    ii.   BERTIE (son), b. c1871 (9 in 1880).
    iii. ABBIE E., b. 8 Apr. 1874.
    iv.   JAMES M., b. 22 Nov. 1876.
    v.   ARNOLD, b. c1879 (1 in 1880).

1095. FRANCES ALBERTA[8] [Fannie] 1852-   [481 Isaac[7] and Charlotte Marston] was born at Machiasport ME in 1852, lived at Somervile MA in 1903; married 13 Feb. 1875 WALTER HEWEY DOUGHTY, born at Topsham ME 3 Aug. 1849, son of Samuel Bond and Mary Starbird (Wilson) Doughty (Charles W. Sinnett, James Wilson and Descendants [TMs, nd, MHS], 31; Cornman Ms).
Doughty was an inventor and manufacturer of rubber-goods at Providence RI. His wife was called Bertha as well as Fannie.

Children (**Doughty**), born at Malden MA:

i.   ROBERT S., b. in 1878.
ii.   ISAAC ROLAND, b. in 1882.

1096. JESSE GLEASON[8] 1852-   [485 Andrew[7] and Sophia
Johnson] was born at Perry ME 2 Nov. 1852, lived there in
1908; married first NANCY JANE[8] [Jennie] LEIGHTON, born at
Perry 17 June 1855, lived at So. Paris ME in 1908, daughter
of Mark and Sarah (Hibbard) Leighton [# 350]--divorced; married second at Boston 28 Apr. 1891 (Machias Union) ETTA H.
FOSS of Marshfield ME.
He was a carpenter at Perry in 1880, lived at Roslindale MA
in 1904 (Wesley's marriage record), and was again at Perry in
1908. Jennie married second at South Paris ME 26 July 1890
WILLIAM D. FROTHINGHAM; their son William L. was born there
13 Jan. 1893 (VRs).

Children by Jennie:

     i.   LENA MAY[9], b. Perry 18 July 1878; m. Bangor 17
            Apr. 1908 ARTHUR M. COX, b. there c1884,
            son of Thomas and Annie (Buckley) Cox.
1637. ii.   WESLEY E., b. Perry 21 May 1880.
     iii.   son, b. Manchester NH 8 Dec. 1884.

Children by Etta:

     iv.   JAMES MADISON, b. 19 Oct. 1891.
     v.   ETHEL ELIZABETH, b. 9 Sept. 1897.

1097. SAMUEL JOHNSON[8] 1858-1936 [485 Andrew[7] and Sophia
Johnson] was born at Perry 17 Jan. 1858, died at Eastport 16
Feb. 1936, 78y 1m; married first at Eastport 21 May 1879
ANNIE COOK of Perry; married second at So. Robbinston 14 Feb.
1882 (JENNIE) MAUD GOVE [as Amanda J.] born at Perry 4 Aug.
1860, died there 24 Sept. 1894, 34y 1m 20d, daughter of John
Tumbleson and Thursa (Potter) Gove; married third at Robbin-
ston 11 Feb. 1896 her sister ELLA G. GOVE, born at Perry 27
Mar. 1871, died at Eastport 20 Jan. 1919, 47y 9m 27d (Gove
Book, 408; Perry and ME VRs; Cornman Ms).
He was a house carpenter at Perry, and in 1897 a millman.

Children by Jennie Maud, born at Perry:

     i.   MABEL SOPHIA[9], b. 17 May 1883, res. Perry; m.
            8 Jan. 1903 CHARLES HENRY ADAMS, b. Deer
            Island NB in 1875, son of Charles H. and
            Jemima (Elliot) Adams.
     ii.   MAY PLAISTED (Maria in 1900), b. 12 July 1885;
            m. Eastport 10 Nov. 1917 LEWIS CHESTER ARM-
            STRONG, b. Perry in 1868, son of John Jr. and
            Amy (Monroe) Armstrong.
     iii.   THURSA EVELYN [Theresa], b. 30 Nov. 1887; m.
            Pembroke 25 Sept. 1909 JOHN GIBSON RICKER, b.
            Perry c1889, son of G. P. and Laura (Gibson)
            Ricker.
     iv.   NINA GRACE, b. 12 Oct. 1891.

Children by Ella:

    v.   ELLERY GOVE, b. Perry 27 Dec. 1897; m. 10 May
           1921 JANE G. PATCH, b. Eastport c1900, dau.
           of Simeon and Ella (Parker) Patch--div. in
           1926. Ch. DENAIDER[10] b. Eastport in 1921.
           Jane m. 2nd 2 Mar. 1931 Harry Mitchell.
    vi.   NADINE ALYS, b. Perry 4 July 1903; m. Calais
           17 Oct. 1929 ARTHUR EUGENE LAWRENCE, b. East-
           port in 1902, son of William H. and Ada
           Lawrence.
1638. vii. SAMUEL JOHN, b. Eastport 22 Apr. 1906.

1098. FREDERICK HILL[8] 1859-   [485 Andrew[7] and Sophia
Johnson] was born at Pembroke 28 Nov. 1859, lived at Framingham MA in 1900; married 29 Nov. 1882 MARY ELIZABETH McDONALD
of Saxonville MA (listed as E. M. in census), born 5 Jan.
1864 (Cornman Ms).

Children:

    i.   JAMES ANDREWS, b. 12 Mar. 1885, d. 23 July
           1889.
    ii.   EDITH GENEVIEVE, b. Framingham in Sept. 1887;
           m. 4 Sept. 1906 BURTON L. BROWNE, b. Kenne-
           bunk ME in 1880, son of John F and Susan J.
           (Butland) Browne.

1099. ANDREW STEPHEN[8] 1831-1921 [486 John[7] and Sarah Lucy]
was born at Strafford NH 2 Jan. 1831, died at Bloomingburgh
NY 6 Aug. 1921; married first at Gilmanton NH SARAH F. GRIF-
FIN, born there 20 Sept. 1836, died there 16 Oct. 1865, 31y
(GS), daughter of Richard and Linda (Hutchinson) Griffin;
married second at Haverhill MA 3 Feb. 1870 SARAH JANE (CARD)
Parker, born at Exeter NH 18 Dec. 1851, died at Pittsfield NH
19 Aug. 1894 (records of descendant Donald Leighton; Pittsfield VRs; Cornman Ms). Burials are at Floral Park Cemetery,
Pittsfield, except for his first wife who is buried with her
parents at Gilmanton.
    He was a shoemaker at Gilmanton in 1850, at Haverhill in
1880, at Pittsfield in 1900, and at Gilmanton in 1908 (Town
Register). He was living with his daughter Addie when he
died.

Children by first wife:

1639. i.   CLARENCE JOHN[9], b. Gilmanton 9 Mar. 1855.
      ii.   ARDELLA A., b. Gilmanton 11 Mar. 1859, d.
           there 5 Nov. 1869, 10y 8m.
      iii. ANDREW DYER, b. Gilmanton 3 Oct. 1861, res.
           Lynn MA in 1900; m. 1st 3 Mar. 1884 HARRIET
           STONE; m. 2nd 24 Oct. 1894 LAURA A. HIGGINS,
           b. in Canada in Dec. 1864. Ch. MARY[10] b. 12
           Mar. 1885, not in 1900 census. Laura's dau.
           Lizzie b. in Sept. 1880, m. William Warren.
1640. iv.   EUGENE FOREST, b. Pittsfield 13 Aug. 1863.
1641. v.   SARAH EVA, b. Pittsfield 6 Oct. 1865; m. ELMER
           DUSTIN.

Children by second wife, born at Pittsfield:

vi. ARTHUR, b. and d. 25 Sept. 1871.
1642. vii. ADDIE MARION, b. 17 Nov. 1873; m. WALLACE B. GRIFFIN.
viii. CARRIE PARKER, b. 13 Jan. 1877, d. Pittsfield 3 July 1961; m. 1st Hampton NH 24 June 1893 JAMES AUGUSTUS BONSER of Rochester NH; m. 2nd HAZEN TUTTLE. Ch. Millard Parker Bonser b. Pittsfield 5 July 1894, d. 18 Dec. 1900. Carrie and her son res. with her brother Andrew in 1900.

1100. LEVI ALVIN[8] 1832-1862 [486 John[7] and Sarah Lucy] was born at Strafford 28 July 1832, died in battle at Fair Oaks VA 1 June 1862; married at Gilmanton 28 June 1855 (or 27 Jan. 1856) ELIZA J. GRIFFIN, born at Epsom NH in 1835, lived at Northwood NH (Cornman Ms; Northwood VRs).
He enlisted 4 Sept. 1861 as sergeant in Co. C, 5th NH Vol. Inf. Rgt.

Children, born at Northwood:

i. ROSCOE SELDEN[9], b. 27 Jan. 1858, res. Brooklyn NY (Cornman Ms); m. in 1879 LUCY N. HARTWELL of Bridgewater MA, b. c1856, dau. of Charles Hartwell. Ch. FLORENCE[10] b. c1879. In 1880 Lucy, 24, res. Middleboro MA with her father, as did her dau. Florence.
ii. HENRY LEVI, b. 29 May 1859, d. 4 Dec. 1887; m. 17 Dec. 1881 JULIA A. LALLY, b. Epping NH 10 July 1860, lived at Lynn MA in 1900 with her mother Kate Lally. No ch.

1101. MARIA JANE[8] 1836-1923 [486 John[7] and Sarah Lucy] was born at Strafford 10 Feb. 1836, died 20 June 1923; married first at Pittsfield 13 Oct. 1857 DARIUS W. SANDERS, born 6 Mar. 1831, died at Pittsfield 28 Apr. 1874; married second 27 Nov. 1884 WILLIAM TRUE SANDERS, born at Chicopee MA in 1842, died 9 Mar. 1890 (Cornman Ms). Burials are in Floral Park Cemetery, Pittsfield.

Children (**Sanders**), by first husband, born at Pittsfield:

i. GEORGE CASPER, b. 13 May 1862, d. 26 Mar. 1895.
ii. FANNIE S., b. 19 Dec. 1864 (GS, 1863), d. 10 Feb. 1870.

1102. EUNICE[8] 1828-   [487 Gideon[7] and Hannah Tappan] was born at Newburyport MA 6 Oct. 1828 (VRs); married there 9 June 1848 WILLIAM ALFRED LITTLE, born there 4 June 1822, died 29 Nov. 1897, son of Joshua and Ann (Tappan) Little (Newburyport VRs; George T. Little, Descendants of George Little [Auburn ME, 1882], 496).
A cordwainer, he had married first in 1844 Abigail C Bragdon, who died 4 Nov. 1847 after bearing three children.

Children (**Little**), born at Newburyport:

i.   EDWARD WARREN, b. 9 Aug. 1850, d. 9 Dec. 1851.
ii. GIDEON LEIGHTON, b. 11 Oct. 1852, d. 11 Aug. 1894; m.
     24 June 1877 MARY E. WALCH.
iii. MARY ALBA, b. 20 Dec. 1854.
iv. WILLIAM ALFRED, b. 29 July 1859.
v.   EDWARD WARREN, b. 27 Feb. 1871.

1103. MARY ESTHER[8] 1830-1858 [487 Gideon[7] and Hannah Tap-
pan] was born at Newburyport 7 July 1830, died there 13 Oct.
1858; married there 10 May 1849 NATHANIEL G. PIERCE, born
there 27 Jan. 1827, died there 14 Oct. 1855, son of Henry and
Thankful (Foot) Pierce (Newburyport VRs; Cornman Ms). He was
a mariner.

Children (**Pierce**), born at Newburyport:

i.   RUFUS L., b. 2 Oct. 1849; m. 4 Mar. 1873 ELIZA D.
     PEARSON, b. 30 Sept. 1849.
ii. HANNAH ELIZABETH, b. 4 Sept. 1851; m. 13 Nov. 1877
     GEORGE PAGE, d. 28 May 1884.
iii. NATHANIEL, b. 13 Aug. 1853, d. in Dec. 1854.
iv. MARY, b. 3 Aug. 1854, d. in May 1858.

1104. ANDREW JACKSON[8] 1833-   [487 Gideon[7] and Hannah
Tappan] was born at Newburyport 20 Aug. 1833, lived there in
1900; married ELIZA J. PARKER, born in NS about 1842 (1900
census) (Cornman Ms). His household in 1900 included several
Adams and Page relatives.

Children (in Cornman Ms):

i.   HENRY EMERSON[9], b. 12 June 1867; m. 11 May
     1890 BERTHA MATTERSON. No ch. in 1903.
ii. MARY E., b. 11 July 1868, d. in Oct. 1874.

1105. WALTER HENRY[8] 1841-1896 [491 Andrew[7] and Mary Lang-
ley] was born at Lowell MA 14 Sept. 1841, died at Augusta ME
30 Nov. 1896, 56y; married first at Lowell 21 Nov. 1865
FRANCES MARIA FRENCH, born there 24 Sept. 1845, died 5 Sept.
1872, daughter of Amos Binney and Sarah (Dearborn) French;
married second 12 Feb. 1887 SARAH STEPHENSON, born 25 Dec.
1855, who lived with her father Gen. Luther Stephenson at
Hingham MA in 1900 (George Oakes Jaquith and Georgetta
Jaquith Walker, Jaquith Family in America [NEHGS, Boston,
1982], 97; Cornman Ms).
Walter was a physician. In 1880 his three children were
listed at Lowell in Amos French's household. In 1900 Walter
was listed at Lowell with his children Amos and Frances.

Children by Frances, born at Lowell:

i.   WALTER FRENCH[9], b. 27 Sept. 1866; m. MAY
     DUNLAP, b. Lowell 3 May 1865. Ch. WALTER F.
     JR.[10] b. 4 May 1893. In 1900 he res. Lowell
     with his bros. Amos and Frank, while May and
     her son lived with her sister Daizella Brown.

     ii.   AMOS B., b. 6 Dec. 1867.
     iii. FRANCES M., b. 6 Apr. 1870.

Child by Sarah (1900 Hingham census):

     iv.   LUTHER STEPHENSON, b. Milwaukee WI in May
           1887.

1106. JULIA ELLEN[8] 1852-1921 [491 Andrew[7] and Mary Langley] was born at Lowell MA 4 Jan. 1852, died at Washington DC in Jan. 1921; married 8 Oct. 1877 DANIEL CORNMAN, born at Carlisle PA 8 Feb. 1852, died at Washington 5 Feb. 1924, son of Ephraim and Barbara Cornman. Both are buried in Arlington National Cemetery.
Julia was graduated from Salem (MA) Normal School in 1872, and was a teacher at Lowell before her marriage. She and her husband lived at or near various US army posts; she lived mainly at So. Weymouth MA while he was outside the US. About 1902 she became determined to compile a Leighton genealogy, and engaged in extensive correspondence and travel until after her husband's retirement. Her research and its results are described in the Introduction.
Daniel was a career army officer, graduating from the US Military Academy at West Point in 1873, and retiring as colonel in 1915. He served in the Indian campaigns, and then in Cuba, the Phillipines, and Mexico (USMA Archives).

Children (**Cornman**):

     i.   LEIGHTON RANDOLPH, b. Vancouver WA 23 Sept. 1878,
         res. San Diego CA in 1925. He was a physician, who
         graduated from Columbia College of Physicians and
         Surgeons in 1903.
     ii.   DANIEL ROBERTS, b. Boise ID 21 July 1881, res. in DC
         in 1925.

1107. ABBIE JANE[8] 1836-   [492 Stephen[7] and Susan Montgomery] was born at Strafford NH 24 Apr. 1836, lived there with her brother John in 1900; married at Lawrence MA 24 Nov. 1859 EDWARD P. WHITNEY, born at Thorndike ME 24 Mar. 1834, died 8 Mar. 1872, son of P. Luther and Lydia Whitney (Cornman Ms).

Children (**Whitney**):

     i.   EDWARD L., b. 20 Dec. 1860; m. 14 Sept. 1889 ANNIE
         SNOW, b. 29 Aug. 1861.
     ii.   CHARLES H., b. 9 Feb., d. 29 June, 1863.
     iii. JOHN S., b. 17 June 1865, d. 5 Jan. 1866.
     iv.   WALTER H., b. 23 Apr. 1870, d. 21 Mar. 1871.

1108. DORA SOPHRONIA[8] 1842-1881 [492 Stephen[7] and Susan Montgomery] was born at Strafford 15 Feb. 1842, died 3 Mar. 1881; married at Haverhill MA 26 Aug. 1869 (VRs) ALFRED WARDWELL of Andover MA, son of Simon and Eliza D. Wardwell (Cornman Ms). He was a shoemaker.
Wardwell had married first ABBIE SARAH[8] LEIGHTON [# 486].
Dora was listed as Deborah in the 1850 census.

Children (**Wardwell**):

i.   ADDIE L., b. 26 Aug. 1870.
ii. WALTER, b. in 1872, d. in 1878.
iii. FRANK H., b. in Nov. 1876.

1109. **HANNAH BABB**[8] 1822-1904 [493 Levi[7] and Tamsen Chamberlain] was born at Farmington NH 21 Mar. 1822, died there 23 Apr. 1904, 82y 1m 2d; married first there 19 Mar. 1842 JOHN H. COLBATH, died 14 Dec. 1844; married second 27 Mar. 1850 JOHN P. KILROY (Cornman Ms). According to Julia Cornman, Hannah's Kilroy children took the Leighton surname.

Children (**Colbath**), born at Farmington:

i.   FRANCIS W., b. 3 July 1843; m. ELLEN A. BOODY, b. New Durham 3 Jan. 1847, dau. of Col. Zechariah and Joan (Runnels) Boody.
ii. SUSAN, b. 14 Dec. 1844, d. 9 Aug. 1869; m. 1st JOHN AVERILL, d. in Civil War; m. 2nd GEORGE WASHINGTON PICKERING.

Children (**Kilroy**), born at Farmington:

iii. MARY C., b. 24 Aug. 1851, d. 24 Feb. 1936, 84y 6m; m. 29 May 1870 JOHN M. BOODY, b. 14 June 1844, d. 3 Aug. 1893.
iv. LUELLA F., b. 21 Apr. 1853, d. 28 Dec. 1888, 35y 8m 7d; m. 7 Nov. 1873 JOHN H. BARKER, b. c1840, son of John and Emily Barker.
v.   (EMMA) JOSEPHINE, b. 15 Sept. 1854; m. 7 Oct. 1873 WILLIAM A. DIXON, b. Eliot ME c1850, son of George M. and Maria S. Dixon.

1110. **JOHN WARREN**[8] 1826-1880 [493 Levi[7] and Tamsen Chamberlain] was born at Farmington 8 Feb. 1826, died there 20 Aug. 1880; married at Dover NH 29 Apr. 1847 (VRs) SUSAN C BENNETT, born at Farmington 7 Aug. 1822, died there 8 Sept. 1899, 77y 1m 1d, daughter of William and Mary (Wingate) Bennett (Farmington VRs; Cornman Ms). Burials are in Pine Grove Cemetery.

Children, born at Farmington:

i.   JOHN B.[9], b. 26 Nov. 1848, d. Farmington 6 Jan. 1925, 76y 1m 10d; m. there 16 Nov. 1880 SUSAN I. BERRY, b. Barnstead in Jan. 1861, d. in 1931 (GS), dau. of Plummer G. and Abbie A. (French) Berry. No ch.
ii. ARABELLA MARY, b. 29 May 1851, d. Farmington 5 Apr. 1918, 66y 10m 7d; m. there 27 Jan. 1868 HENRY C. NUTTER, b. there c1846, son of Richard and Asenath (Drown) Nutter. No ch.
iii. CHARLES WARREN, b. 14 May 1854, d. Farmington 1 Dec. 1932, 78y 6m 17d; m. Alton NELLIE A. FULLER, b. c1857, d. in 1950 (GS), dau. of William W. and Aurelia Fuller. No ch.

1111. TAMSEN ABIGAIL[8] 1834-1920 [493 Levi[7] and Tamsen Chamberlain] was born at Farmington 16 July 1834, died there 8 Apr. 1920, 85y 8m 22d; married at Pittsfield NH 25 Nov. 1857 (Joseph Mooney, Diary #13, Ms, NHHS) EDWIN P. MOONEY, born at Farmington 29 Dec. 1831, died there 14 May 1878, son of John H. and Lavinia (Chamberlain) Mooney (Stearns, NH Genealogies, 2:692; Cornman Ms; letter from Frank Mooney-- Cornman Papers).

Child (**Mooney**):

i.   FRANK E., b. Alton 20 May 1859, d. Farmington 25 July 1934, 75y 2m 5d (VRs); m. 27 June 1883 ANNA B. BEN- NETT. He owned F E. Mooney Co., building supplies.

1112. EMILY MARIA[8] 1840-   [493 Levi[7] and Tamsen Cham- berlain] was born at Farmington 23 July 1840; married there int. 19 Apr. 1858 STEPHEN W. BENNETT, born there 5 Aug. 1831, died 2 Apr. 1901, son of William and Mary (Wingate) Bennett (Cornman Ms; Farmington VRs).   He purchased the Leighton homestead from John H.[9] Leighton [# 381].

Children (**Bennett**), born at Farmington:

i.   MARY E., b. 12 Aug. 1858; m. AUGUSTUS FREEMONT
      LEIGHTON [# 1448].
ii.   GEORGE W., b. 24 Sept. 1860; m. 15 Oct. 1887 EMMA A
      COLBATH, b. Natick MA 14 Feb. 1847, d. Farmington
      12 Feb. 1895, 47y 11m 30d, dau. of Freeman C. and
      Urana (Beal) Colbath.
iii. STEPHEN W., b. 5 Sept. 1864, d. by suicide 1 Mar.
      1864, 25y 1m 27d.
iv.   ELLEN F , b. 20 May 1868, d. 12 Nov. 1885.
v.   JOSEPH L., b. 22 Apr. 1872.
vi.   JOHN L., b. 15 Aug. 1874, d. Farmington 25 Oct. 1911,
      37y 2m 10d.
vii. PARKER D., b. 10 Sept. 1877; m. GRACE[10] LEIGHTON
      [# 1442]
viii. CLARA P. (twin), b. 10 Sept. 1877; m. in Dec. 1896
      EUGENE C. HOWARD.

1113. ANNA[8] 1837-1900 [497 Andrew[7] and Mary Hackett] was born at Strafford NH 3 Feb. 1837, died at Laconia NH 17 Jan. 1900; married 12 Mar. 1857 WILLIAM L. SWAINE, born in 1827, died at Laconia 11 Sept. 1901, son of Gorham and Mary (Rand- lett) Swaine (Cornman Ms).

Children (**Swaine**):

i.   GERTRUDE, b. 4 Oct. 1858, res. Boston; m. there 30
      Jan. 1889 THOMAS H. MATTHEWS.
ii.   CHARLES WILLIAM, b. 23 Nov. 1862.

1114. HANNAH EMMONS[8] 1833-1930 [498 William[7] and Phoebe Leighton] was born at Farmington 15 June 1833, died at High- land Park, Wayne County MI 20 Aug. 1930; married at Dover NH 17 Aug. 1852 (Dover Gazette) EDWARD E. LITTLEFIELD, born at

Wells ME 24 Oct. 1828, died at Dover 17 Nov. 1905, 76y 24d,
son of Ralph and Olive (Eades) Littlefield (Waterhouse Gen.,
2:1099; records of David Dunlap). Burials are in Pine Hill
Cemetery, Dover.
Edward was a supervisor in the Cocheco Mill. His widow
lived with their granddaughter (Martha) Estelle (Patterson)
Chapman.

Children (**Littlefield**), born at Dover:

 i.   CHARLES ALBERT, b. 21 Jan. 1853, d. Dorchester MA 1
       June 1904; m. Dover 7 Nov. 1878 LIZETTA [Etta]
       LINCOLN.
 ii.   EDWARD AUGUSTUS, b. 29 July 1855, d. West Somerville
       MA 19 Nov. 1923; m. Dover 16 Oct. 1886 ROSA MORSE
       SMITH.
 iii. ESTELLA ABIGAIL, b. 3 Feb. 1859, d. Dover 28 July
       1876.
 iv.   MARY EMILY, b. 8 Feb. 1863, d. Dover 7 Nov. 1927; m.
       1st there 16 Oct. 1886 ROBERT PATTERSON; m. 2nd
       there 7 Sept. 1898 CHARLES HODSDON.
 v.   MARTHA W., b. 10 Apr. 1866, d. 10 Nov. 1872.

1115.   MARY SUSAN BRACKETT[8] 1835-   [503 William[7] and
Mary Field] was born at Cumberland 9 Apr. 1835, lived there
in 1903; married there 2 Feb. 1855 SILAS RUSSELL, born there
2 Feb. 1834, son of John and Lucinda (Fogg) Russell (records
of descendant William L. Russell; Cornman Ms; town VRs).
Silas's household at Cumberland in 1860 included his wife's
siblings Patience, 33, Elias, 27, and Anna F , 23, and her
mother Mary Leighton, 64. He was sometimes listed as Cyrus.

Children (**Russell**), born at Cumberland:

 i.   NELLIE, b. 19 Nov. 1859, res. Gray; m. 14 Dec. 1879
       ARTHUR FOSTER.
 ii.   LUCINDA, b. 14 Jan. 1861, d. Deering 9 June 1900; m.
       10 Apr. 1881 WADSWORTH VERRILL of New Gloucester ME.
 iii. EDGAR L., b. 9 Sept. 1863; unm.
 iv.   BERTHA G., b. 16 Sept. 1864, res. Portland; m. 20
       July 1893 GEORGE E. HAM of Rochester NH.
 v.   WILLIAM LEIGHTON, b. 9 May 1865, d. Gray 9 Oct. 1920;
       m. Gray 20 Dec. 1888 JULIA MERRILL, b. there 3 Apr.
       1866, d. in 1951, dau. of John and Martha Ann
       (Merrow) Merrill.
 vi.   MINNIE GERTRUDE, b. 16 Dec. 1869, d. 11 Aug. 1872.
 vii. FANNIE C., b. 14 Mar. 1871; m. in Dec. 1891 CHRISTO-
       PHER PERHAM of Portland.
 viii. JOHN M., b. 10 Oct. 1873.
 ix.   GRACE M., b. 2 Aug. 1875; m. 16 Nov. 1898 CHARLES D.
       GUSTIN of Deering, b. in 1870, son of Darius and
       S. M. (Foss) Gustin.
 x.   MARY A [Mamie], b. 2 Sept. 1877, res. Portland; m.
       24 June 1898 GRANVILLE P. STEVENS.

1116.   ANDREW[8] 1818-1887 [504 John Pettingill and Mercy[7]
Leighton] was born at Cumberland 10 Dec. 1818, died at Glou-
cester MA 26 June 1887; married first there 27 July 1846 ANN
MARIA KEMP, born in 1827, daughter of John and Maria Kemp of

Salem MA; married second 7 Feb. 1880 ELIZABETH B. JOYCE, born
at Newburyport MA in Feb. 1849, lived at Gloucester in 1900,
daughter of John and Mary (Butler) Joyce of Newfoundland
(Pattingall Gen., 176; Gloucester VRs; records of Susan
Leach).
Andrew took his mother's surname. He was a mariner and
then a sea captain. In 1880 his Gloucester household
included his Baker granddaughters Jennie, 11, and Lillian, 9.

Children by Ann, probably born at Gloucester:

    i.   BENJAMIN^9, b. Gloucester 30 Aug. 1847.
    ii.   AUGUSTUS H., b. Gloucester 4 Oct. 1849.
    iii. MARY E., b. c1870 (10 in 1880).
    iv.   ANDREW, b. c1872 (8 in 1880).
    v.   MABEL, b. c1876; m. 1st 7 Apr. 1896 PERCY
        HALL, b. Gloucester c1875, son of Frederick
        T. Hall--div.; m. 2nd Portland 8 July 1913
        JOHN HARVEY MacDONALD, b. Lewis PEI c1887,
        son of Alfred and Elizabeth (Stewart) Mac-
        Donald (ME VRs).
    vi.   ALICE BLANCH, b. in Dec. 1879, res. with widow
        Elizabeth in 1900.

    1117. ALVIN S.^{8} 1821-1905 [505 Moses^7 and Loemma Pearson]
was born at Cumberland 21 Sept. 1821, died there 1 Jan.
1905, 83y 3m 11d; married first at Portland 24 May 1852 ANN-
MARIA STORER MERRILL, born about 1828, died at New Gloucester
ME (Portland VRs) 31 Jan. 1855, 27y, daughter of Benjamin and
Ruth (Merrill) Merrill (Merrill Desc. 2:625; GS, Pine Grove
Cemetery, Falmouth Foreside); married second LUCY JANE PEN-
LEY, born at Danville ME 6 Jan. 1821, died at Cumberland 21
Mar. 1902, 81y 2m 14d, daughter of John and Desire (Dingley)
Penley (obituary, Portland Press Herald, 22 Mar.; Robert
Penley, Penley Family in England and America [Ontario, 1958],
45; town VRs). Alvin was a house carpenter.

Children by Ann-Maria, born at Portland:

    i.   PRESTON MERRILL^9, b. 7 Mar. 1853, d. Cumber-
        land Center 29 Mar. 1933, 80y 16d; unm. He
        was a florist.
    ii.   ANNIE M., b. say 1853, res. Bradentown FL in
        1933; m. Gray int. 15 Dec. 1885 LEWIS W.
        WHITNEY.

Children by Lucy, born at Portland:

    iii. ALVIN PENLEY, b. 17 Nov. 1857, went west.
        He grad. from Colby College in 1882.
    iv.   dau., b. 23 May 1860, d.y.
    v.   MOSES W., b. 6 Jan. 1862, d. Cumberland 10
        July 1932, 70y 6m 4d; unm. He was a farmer.

    1118. GARDNER S.^{8} 1825-1902 [505 Moses^7 and Loemma Pear-
son] was born at Cumberland 15 Aug. 1825, died at North Yarmouth ME 1 Oct. 1902, 77y 1m 16d; married at Cumberland 18
May 1848 MINERVA WHITNEY, born at Gray 29 Apr. 1828, died at

North Yarmouth 21 Dec. 1903, 70y 7m, daughter of Alexander
and Barbara (Winslow) Whitney (their obituaries; records of
Nellie Smith Leighton and Toni Packard; town VRs). Burials
are in Walnut Hill Cemetery.
He purchased a farm at North Yarmouth in Dec. 1848, on
which they lived all their lives. He served in Co. B, 25th
ME Inf. Rgt., 29 Sep 1862 to 10 July 1863.

Children, born at North Yarmouth:

1643. i.   GEORGE AUGUSTUS[9], b. 31 Mar. 1849.
1644. ii.   EMILY FRANCES, b. 25 Jan. 1851; m. GEORGE P.
             SKILLIN.
1645. iii. GARDNER JR., b. 21 Aug. 1855.
       iv.   (BARBARA) ELLEN, b. 4 May 1857, d. N. Yarmouth
             2 May 1911, 53y 11m 27d; unm.
       v.   SIDNEY LAMONT, b. 29 Feb. 1868, d. N. Yarmouth
             19 Apr. 1927, 59y 1m 21d; unm. He farmed the
             family homestead.
       vi.   ALICE MINERVA, b. 11 May 1875, d. N. Yarmouth
             4 Sept. 1944, 69y 3m 23d; unm.

1119. LOEMMA PEARSON[8] 1831-1924 [505 Moses[7] and Hannah
Pearson] was born at Cumberland 13 May 1831, died at Gray 8
Mar. 1924, 72y 9m 23d; married at Cumberland 7 Nov. 1850
NATHANIEL BAKER WILSON, born 26 July 1827, died at Cumberland
26 June 1896, 68y 11d, son of Nathaniel and Elizabeth (Baker)
Wilson (town VRs). Burials are in the Methodist Churchyard,
West Cumberland. He was a merchant.

Children (**Wilson**), born at Cumberland:

i.   GEORGE N., b. 24 Jan. 1851; m. 1st 23 June 1876 EMILY
       A. SANBORN; m. 2nd CARRIE RUSSELL.
ii.   ALVAH L., b. 28 Feb. 1854; m. 25 May 1875 ELLA J.
       WINSLOW.
iii.   ARNIE H., b. 8 May 1860, d. 8 Oct. 1861, 17m (GS).
iv.   HERMAN M., b. 29 Jan. 1865, d. in 1932; m. 24 Sept.
       1888 HARRIET MOUNTFORT, b. Cumberland 9 June 1867,
       d. 31 Mar. 1902, dau. of Hollis R. and Roxanna
       (Leighton) Mountfort [# 1129].
v.   SCOTT, b. 12 Jan. 1870; m. So. Windham 24 Dec. 1895
       ELIZABETH MARIE BODGE, b. there 17 Apr. 1871, dau.
       of John Jackson and Martha Marie (Webb) Bodge
       (George Harvey, The Bodge Family of Mass., N. H. and
       Me. [TMs, 1982, MHS], 45). Grad. of Penn. Law
       School in 1893, Scott became Assoc. Justice, Maine
       Supreme Court.

1120. JONATHAN BRADBURY[8] 1834-1920 [505 Moses[7] and Hannah
Pearson] was born at Cumberland 21 June 1834, died at Portland 26 Dec. 1920, 86y 6m 4d; married at Portland 25 Sept.
1862 (MARY) CAROLINE NEWMAN, born there 21 Sept. 1836, died
there 23 Mar. 1890, 53y 6m, daughter of Thomas and Louise[8]
(Leighton) Newman [# 970] (Cornman Ms: town and ME VRs;
records of Nellie Smith Leighton, including newspaper
articles; his obituary in Daily Argus, 27 Dec. 1920).
Burials are in Evergreen Cemetery.

Jonathan's middle name was Bradbury on his birth and death record, although other sources give it as Bradford. He enlisted in Co. B, 25th ME Inf. Rgt. in Oct. 1861, and served throughout the war, being promoted to sergeant. He became a successful building contractor. In 1900 he was living with his son Ashton.

Children, born at Portland:

1646.	i.	HOWARD NEWMAN[9], b. 11 June 1863.
1647.	ii.	ASHTON LaFOREST, b. 27 Dec. 1865.
1648.	iii.	MINNIE LOUISE, b. 14 Apr. 1868; m. PERRY E. SIMMONS.
	iv.	ISSIE MAY, b. 28 Apr. 1878; m. Portland 23 Nov. 1905 PERCY T. FARNUM, b. Boston c1877, son of Aaron V. and Annie M. (Harrison) Farnum. (She was Mary E. at birth, and Jessie M. in 1880.)

1121. (PATRICK) HENRY[8] 1841-1909 [505 Moses[7] and Hannah Pearson] was born at Cumberland 19 Mar. 1841, died there 5 July 1909, 68y 3m 16d; married first at Portland 22 Nov. 1864 SARAH AUGUSTA CLOUGH, born at Cumberland 14 Nov. 1844, died there 2 Aug. 1867, 22y 8m 18d, daughter of Joseph and Mary Clough; married second at Portland 21 June 1876 NELLIE PHIN-NEY, born at Gorham ME 5 Feb. 1852, died at Cumberland 12 Apr. 1924, 72y 2m 7d, daughter of Alexander and Ann Maria (Rounds) Phinney (records of descendant Toni Packard; town and ME VRs; Cornman Ms). Burials are in the Methodist Churchyard, West Cumberland.
He had his name changed from Patrick to Henry P. by court action. He served in Co. C, 6th ME Inf. Rgt., in 1861, was discharged for disability, and re-enlisted in 1862 in Co. B, 25th ME Inf. Rgt. In 1880 his household included his mother; in 1900 his mother-in-law and his three younger children were living with him.

Child by Sarah, born at West Cumberland:

1649.	i.	EMMA W.[9], b. 8 June 1866; m. FRED A. BURNELL.

Children by Nellie, born at West Cumberland:

	ii.	PERCY AUGUSTUS, b. 8 Jan. 1877, d. Springfield MA; probably unm.
	iii.	LINWOOD FREEMAN, b. 25 Feb. 1878, d. Cumberland 16 Apr. 1932; m. Cumberland Center 6 Nov. 1901 MAUD WINIFRED FARWELL, b. there 6 Nov. 1874, d. Portland (hosp.) 5 Dec. 1945, 71y,, dau. of Simeon L. and Sarah (Greeley) Farwell. No ch. He was a poultry dealer.
1650.	iv.	FANNIE AUGUSTA, b. 4 Dec. 1881; m. PERLEY N. PACKARD.

1122. CHARLES JORDAN[8] 1820-1883 [507 James[7] and Prudence Blanchard] was born at Cumberland 7 June 1820, died there 10 July 1883, 63y; married there 8 July 1845 AUGUSTA[8] LEIGHTON, born there 8 Dec. 1823, died there 16 Jan. 1891, daughter of

Moses and Loemma (Pearson) Leighton [# 505] (Cornman Ms; town VRs; records of Toni Packard). Burials are in the Methodist Churchyard, West Cumberland.

His mother and some of his siblings were in his household in 1850 and 1860.

Children, born at Cumberland:

	i.	WILLIAM AUGUSTINE[9], b. 31 Aug. 1847, d. 2 Dec. 1860.
1651.	ii.	HERBERT BLANCHARD, b. 18 June 1848.
	iii.	MARGARET ELLEN, b. 21 Feb. 1850, d. 4 July 1863.
	iv.	GEORGE RANDALL, b. 2 Aug. 1852, d. Cumberland 30 Dec. 1920, 68y 4m 28d; unm.
	v.	son, b. and d. 8 Jan. 1858 (GS).
	vi.	WILLIS HOWARD, b. 15 Nov. 1860, d. New Gloucester ME 26 Feb. 1938; m. Cumberland 1 Jan. 1884 IDA FARWELL, who d. there 2 May 1943. Ch. ROY O.[10] b. W. Cumberland 2 June 1884, d. 18 Sept. 1885.
	vii.	EMMA, b. 7 Aug. 1862, d. 9 May 1863 (GS).

1123. ANDREW[8] 1824-1900 [507 James[7] and Prudence Blanchard] was born at Pittsfield ME 28 Feb. 1824, died at Yarmouth ME 27 Apr. 1900, 76y 1m 17d; married at Cumberland 16 Jan. 1851 RUTH ETTA PURVIS, born there 20 Aug. 1829, died at Yarmouth 15 June 1914, 85y 6m 5d, daughter of Adam and Ruth (Tibbetts) Purvis (town and ME VRs; records of Nellie (Smith) Leighton; Cornman Ms). Burials are in Riverside Cemetery, Yarmouth.

Andrew bought a Yarmouth farm in 1847 which he later enlarged. He enlisted in Co. E, 17th ME Inf. Rgt., 18 Aug. 1862, and was transferred sick 1 Dec. 1863 to the Veterans Reserve Corp. He was a farmer and dealer in hay and produce. In 1869-1870 he represented Yarmouth in the state legislature (Biog. Rev, Cumberland Co., 83-4).

Children, born at Yarmouth:

	i.	FREDERICK WILTON[9], b. 23 Mar. 1852, d. there 4 Oct. 1905, 53y 10m 29d; unm.
	ii.	ELLA FLORENCE, b. 24 July 1853, d. 23 Mar. 1878; unm.
	iii.	MARY ETTA, b. 5 June 1856, d. in Mar. 1942 (obit.); unm.
1652.	iv.	HATTIE FLORENCE, b. 10 July 1860; m. JOHN E. BAKER.

1124. JAMES NOYES[8] 1826-1917 [507 James[7] and Prudence Blanchard] was born at Pittsfield ME 27 Feb. 1826, died at West Cumberland 30 Dec. 1917, 91y 10m 3d; married 8 Mar. 1855 HANNAH WILSON, born at Cumberland 5 Dec. 1827, died there 23 Jan. 1899, 71y 1m 18d, daughter of Cyrus and Lois (Leighton)[7] Wilson [# 432] (town and ME VRs; Cornman Ms).

He was a sailor in 1850, living with his brother Charles, but became a farmer at Portland, and then about 1867 had a farm at West Cumberland.

Children, born at Portland:

    i.   OSCAR WEBSTER[9], b. 20 Nov. 1855, d. W. Cum-
          berland 1 Dec. 1933, 78y; unm.
    ii.   EVA WILSON, b. 6 Dec. 1859, d. W. Cumberland
          in Feb. 1946, 86y; unm.
    iii. EMMA WALTON, b. 6 Feb., d. 6 Aug., 1862.
    iv.   HANNAH, res. with Oscar in 1933; unm.

1125. ENOS[8] 1828-1905 [507 James[7] and Prudence Blanchard]
was born at Pittsfield ME 21 Aug. 1828, died at West Cumberland 30 Mar. 1905, 76y 7m; married at Gray 2 Oct. 1850 DIANA
GILBERT, born at Livermore ME 17 July 1829, lost at sea 27
Nov. 1898 on steamer Portland, daughter of Caleb and Bathsheba (Leavitt) Gilbert (obituary 6 Dec.; Noyes, Leavitt
Desc., 2:50; town and ME VRs; Cornman Ms).
Enos was a farmer at Cumberland; in 1900 Flora and Charles
were still living in his household.

Children, born at West Cumberland:

1653. i.   EUGENE MELVILLE[9], b. 3 Oct. 1850.
1654. ii.   ARABELLA STOWE, b. 6 Nov. 1852; m. SEWELL
             MOUNTFORT.
1655. iii. FRANKLIN BARRETT, b. 17 Nov. 1856.
       iv.   FLORA ADELAIDE, b. 1 Jan. 1860; d. Westbrook
             11 Nov. 1921, 61y 10m 10d; unm.
       v.   FREDERICK LEWIS, b. 7 Jan. 1862; res. West-
             brook in 1900; unm.
1656. vi.   EDWARD CLINTON, b. 17 Oct. 1864.
1657. vii. CHARLES EVERETT, b. 25 July 1868.

1126. JOSEPH[8] 1831-   [507 James[7] and Prudence Blan-
chard] was born at Pittsfield ME 11 Jan. 1831 (1833 in cen-
suses), lived at Dent Tp, San Joaquin Co. CA in 1900; married
GEORGIE ETTA DORSEY, born in MO in Nov. 1850.
He lived for a time in MO, but had settled in CA by 1870.
In 1880 his household at Dent Tp included his brother-in-law
George N. Dorsey.

Children, born in CA (from 1880 and 1900 censuses):

    i.   JAMES NELSON[9], b. in July 1870, res. Dent Tp
          in 1900; m. FLORENCE ---- , b. in CA in Oct.
          1872. Twins LOLA[10] and LULU b. in Aug. 1896.
    ii.   CYNTHIA PRUDENCE, b. c1873 (7 in 1880).
    iii. JOE ELLA, b. c1878 (2 in 1880).
    iv.   BERTHA, b. in June 1883.
    v.   JOSEPH R., b. in Sept. 1895.

1127. LOEMMA PEARSON[8] 1833-1862 [507 James[7] and Prudence
Blanchard] was born at Pittsfield ME 19 Mar. 1833, died at
Yarmouth 1 Jan. 1862, 28y 9m; married at Cumberland 9 Feb.
1854 JOHN HULIT, born at Cumberland 20 Nov. 1825, son of
Jonathan and Hannah Hulit (or Hulet) (Cumberland VRs; Cornman
Ms). Burials are in the Methodist Churchyard, West Cumber-
land.

Children (**Hulit**), born at Cumberland:

i.   ELLA AUGUSTA, b. 30 Nov. 1856, d. Westbrook ME 20
        Nov. 1892; m. Gray 22 June 1884 GEORGE WILLIAM
        INGERSOLL, b. Windham 19 Dec. 1852, son of Abram A.
        and Olive L. (Frank) Ingersoll (Avery, Ingersoll
        Family, 118).
ii.   HARRIET E., b. 19 Dec. 1859, d. 19 Mar. 1862, 3y 3m
        15d.
iii.   EMMA H., b. 9 May 1861, d. 20 Apr. 1862, 11m 14d.

1128.   FRANCES JANE[8] 1835-1861 [507 James[7] and Prudence
Blanchard] was born at Orono ME 4 Nov. 1835, died at Portland
17 Aug. 1861, 37y 9m; married GEORGE WASHINGTON SNELL, who
died 17 Nov. 1890, 56y (GS) (Cornman Ms).

Children (**Snell**), born at Portland:

i.   ADA C., b. in June 1855, d. 18 Feb. 1863, 8y 8m.
ii.   FREDERICK W., b. in Jan. 1859, d. 4 Oct. 1862, 3y
        10m.

1129.   ROXANNA ADAMS[8] 1839-1884 [507 James[7] and Prudence
Blanchard] was born at Cumberland 6 June 1839, died there 18
Nov. 1884 (GS); married 26 Dec. 1863 HOLLIS RANDALL MOUNT-
FORT, born there 7 Nov. 1836, died in 1925 (GS), son of Sam-
uel and Nancy Mountfort (Cumberland VRs; Cornman Ms; obituary
of son Charles). Burials are in the Methodist Churchyard,
West Cumberland.
Hollis was a lieutenant in the Union Army.

Children (**Mountfort**), born at Cumberland:

i.   ADA FRANCES, b. 29 May 1865; m. HENRY LAWRENCE.
ii.   HARRIET MARGARET, b. 9 June 1867; m. HERMAN WILSON
        [# 1119].
iii.   CHARLES RANDALL, b. 6 Dec. 1868, d. 17 July 1955.
iv.   WALTER HENRY, b. 8 Jan. 1873, res. W. Cumberland in
        1955.
v.   GEORGE EVERETT, b. 20 June 1876, res. Portland in
        1955.

1130.   CAROLINE W.[8] 1835-1895 [509 Ezekiel[7] and Lucy Hulit]
was born at Cumberland 7 Dec. 1835, died there 1 Dec. 1895;
married first there 4 July 1858 HOMER ERWIN BLANCHARD, born
there 2 June 1831, died at Fredericksburg VA 1 Dec. 1862,
while serving in the army, son of Sewell and Jane (Libby)
Blanchard; married second 15 Jan. 1867, as his second wife,
WILLIAM SAVAGE BLANCHARD, born at Cumberland 25 Jan. 1826,
died there 15 Feb. 1891, 71y 21d, son of Andrew Gray and Myra
(Sweetser) Blanchard (Cumberland and ME VRs; Cornman Ms).

Child (**Blanchard**) by Homer, born at Cumberland:

i.   WALTER E. JR., b. 31 Dec. 1858; m. 3 Oct. 1886 AGNES
        TIBBETTS of Bristol.

Child (**Blanchard**) by William, born at Cumberland:

ii.   ANNA VICTORIA, b. 31 July 1870; m. 31 Mar. 1896 RALPH
      S. PORTER, b. Cumberland in 1874, son of Sylvanus S.
      and S. F. (Jordan) Porter.

1131. LORANIA[8] 1840-1902 [509 Ezekiel[7] and Lucy Hulit] was
born at Cumberland 30 June 1840, died there 20 Aug. 1902, 62y
1m 19d; married there 10 Apr. 1871 EDWARD T. HALL, born there
24 May 1846, died there 24 Oct. 1914, 68y 5m, son of Cushman
and Mary S. (Thayer) Hall (Cumberland and ME VRs; Cornman
Ms). Burials are in the Methodist Churchyard, West Cumberland. He was a farmer. Her mother Lucy lived with them.

Children (**Hall**), born at West Cumberland:

i.   GEORGE FRANK, b. 21 Oct. 1871, d. 7 June 1915, 43y 7m
      12d; unm.
ii.   son, b. 2 Apr., d. 16 Apr., 1874, 14d.
iii. FLORENCE MAY, b. 11 Feb. 1876, d. 6 Nov. 1910, 34y
      8m; unm.
iv.   CARRIE BLANCHARD, b. 11 Mar. 1881.

1132. CHARLES WENDALL[8] 1836-1923 [510 Robert[7] and Cynthia
Morse] was born at Cumberland ME 11 Mar. 1836, died at Port-
land 9 July 1923, 87y 3m 27d; married there 16 Dec. 1862
SARAH LEWIS COBB, born at Deering 10 Aug. 1841, died at Port-
land 23 Oct. 1916, 75y, daughter of Charles and Isabella
McIntosh (Campbell) Cobb (town and ME VRs; Cornman Ms).
  He lived at Cumberland in 1870, and Deering in 1880, as a
market worker.

Children, born at Deering:

i.   ISABELLA COBB[9] [Belle], b. 17 Apr. 1864, d.
       Cape Elizabeth 29 July 1931; m. Freeport ME
       16 Sept. 1885 HARRY MONROE CUSHING, b. there
       14 Nov. 1860, d. Portland 31 Jan. 1942, son
       of Charles and Martha (Campbell) (Brewer)
       Cushing. Ch. Helen Gertrude b. Portland 15
       Oct. 1890.
ii.   (ELIAS) WILSON, b. 4 July 1867, res. Somer-
       ville MA in 1900; m. Portland 8 Apr. 1891
       BERTHA MAY NEWCOMB, b. Berwick ME 3 Feb.
       1874, dau. of Frank E. and Mary Augusta
       (Libby) Newcomb. No ch.
iii.   LENA MAY, b. 20 Jan. 1870; m. Portland 7 Mar.
       1904 JOSEPH HENRY EWING, b. there 7 Dec.
       1867, son of William and Ann Elizabeth (Lee)
       Ewing.
iv.   ETHEL VIOLA, b. 4 Dec. 1882.

1133. GEORGE WOODWARD[8] 1838-   [510 Robert[7] and Cynthia
Morse] was born at West Cumberland 29 Oct. 1838, lived at
Evansville IN; married 19 Mar. 1864 CAROLINE M. [Carrie]
STEVENS, born in ME about 1844 (36 in 1880) (Cornman Ms).
  In 1880, his household was at Madison, Dubois Co. IN.

Children:

   i.   OLA[9], b. in ME c1865 (15 in 1880), later
          res. Cumberland Mills ME.
   ii.   LILLIAN B., b. in ME c1867 (13 in 1880).
  iii. WILBUR, b. in ME c1869 (11 in 1880).
   iv. FLORA C., b. in IN c1871 (9 in 1880).
    v. GEORGE W., b. in IN c1875 (5 in 1880).
   vi. JASPER, d. Indianapolis; not in 1880 census.

1134. OLIVE JANE[8] 1840-   [510 Robert[7] and Cynthia
Morse] was born at West Cumberland 24 Oct. 1840; married 27
Aug. 1857 AMOS ROSCOE WINSLOW, born at Cumberland 12 July
1837, son of Amos and Abigail[8] (Leighton) Winslow [# 977].
They lived at Cape Elizabeth ME in 1903 (Cornman Ms; Cumber-
land VRs).

Children (**Winslow**), born at Cumberland:

   i.   FANNIE, b. 26 Jan. 1858; m. 10 July 1876 EDWARD R.
          FILES, b. Portland 17 Dec. 1855.
   ii.   OLA, b. 1 June 1860, d. 6 Oct. 1861.
  iii. FRANK, b. 13 Apr. 1862, d. 25 Aug. 1864.
   iv. ERNEST, b. 25 Aug. 1867, d. 18 May 1875.
    v. INA, b. 8 Dec. 1869; m. 9 Jan. 1898 EUGENE WILBUR
          WHEELER, b. New Ipswich NH 5 Dec. 1864.

1135. ALTHEA CAROLINE[8] 1842-1887 [510 Robert[7] and Cynthia
Morse] was born at Cumberland 10 Mar. 1842, died 27 Nov.
1887; married 19 Mar. 1864 NELSON M. SHAW, born at Cumberland
1 Sept. 1836, son of John and Martha Shaw (Cornman Ms; Cumberland VRs).

Children (**Shaw**), born at Cumberland:

   i.   HOWARD L., b. 22 Oct. 1865; m. in Apr. 1889 ALICE
          BRADFORD, b. Friendship ME 25 July 1868.
   ii.   JOHN M., b. 4 Feb. 1867; m. 10 Oct. 1891 MINNIE
          CHASE, b. No. Yarmouth ME 29 July 1872.
  iii. HERBERT N., b. 30 Oct. 1868, d. 26 Feb. 1905, struck
          by a train; unm.
   iv. EMMA D., b. 7 Apr. 1871.
    v. ANGIE M., b. 17 Aug. 1872, d. 31 Oct. 1895.
   vi. ETHEL C., b. 23 Nov. 1875.
  vii. MARTHA A., b. 21 Nov. 1880.

1136. ENOCH O. MORSE[8] 1844-1926 [510 Robert[7] and Cynthia
Morse] was born at Cumberland 16 Sept. 1844, died at Falmouth
8 Apr. 1926, 80y 6m 18d; married at Portland 4 Sept. 1882
LILLIAN [Lily] BRACKLEY, born at Kingfield ME 29 Aug. 1864,
not listed with Enoch in 1900, daughter of Howard and Matilda
(Packard) Brackley (town VRs; Cornman Ms).

Children:

1658. i.   MAUD L.[9], b. Portland 12 Dec. 1883; m. LOUIS
             KING.
1659. ii.   MARK SAMUEL, b. Springfield MA 13 Dec. 1885.

1137. ROBERT NELSON[8] 1846-1902 [510 Robert[7] and Cynthia Morse] was born at West Cumberland 17 Apr. 1846, died there 7 Jan. 1902, 55y 8m; married at Gray 17 Dec. 1876 ELLEN EMELINE WHITNEY, born there 9 Feb. 1852, died at Portland 19 Sept. 1927, daughter of James and Emeline (Stubbs) Whitney (town VRs; Cornman Ms). Burials are in the Methodist Churchyard, West Cumberland.

Children, born at Cumberland:

1660.   i.   ARTHUR N.[9], b. 11 Oct. 1877.
        ii.   FLORENCE MAY, b. 1 Sept. 1879, res. in NB; m.
              Perth NB 25 Sept. 1912 PHILIP J. BRITT.
        iii. EVERETT J., b. 20 Sept. 1880, d. Portland
              (hosp.) 12 June 1896, 15y 8m 23d.
1661.   iv.   EDWIN W., b. 22 June 1882.
1662.   v.   PERLEY ROBERT, b. 12 Feb. 1884.
        vi.   SCOTT TRUE, b. 27 Nov. 1885.
        vii. MABEL C., b. 23 Oct. 1887; m. 9 Mar. 1910
              ROGER H. GUTHRIE. Ch. Margaret E.
        viii. TILLIE E., b. 11 Apr. 1890, d. Portland 26
              Sept. 1965; m. W. Falmouth 28 May 1912 JOHN
              F. FARMER, b. Farmington ME c1887, son of
              Edwin H. and Georgia A. (Perkins) Farmer.
              Ch. Georgie E.

1138. MARTHA[8] 1826-1857 [513 Hugh[7] and Miriam Huston] was born at Falmouth 2 Nov. 1826, died 2 Sept. 1857; married 2 Aug. 1850 ELISHA HIGGINS, born at Falmouth 9 Feb. 1823, died there 26 Mar. 1892, 69y 1m, son of Elisha and Lucy (Sawyer) Higgins (town VRs; Cornman Ms; Higgins Desc., 297, 419).
Elisha was a farmer. He married second at Biddeford ME 10 May 1859 Olive Dearborn, daughter of Joseph and Tamar (Woodman) Dearborn: three children.

Children (**Higgins**), born at Deering:

i.   JENNIE S., b. 12 June 1851, d. 2 May 1852.
ii.   FLORENCE, b. 29 Dec. 1853.
iii. FLORINA MORRILL [Rena], b. 26 Dec. 1854, d. 12 Sept.
      1882.
iv.   MARTHA; m. FRED A. COBURN.

1139. PHOEBE ANN[8] 1830-1899 [513 Hugh[7] and Miriam Huston] was born at Falmouth 24 Sept. 1830, died 12 Aug. 1899; married at Westbrook 29 June 1857 BENJAMIN F. BAILEY of Deering (town VRs; Cornman Ms.)

Children (**Bailey**):

i.   WARREN B., b. 16 Sept. 1859; m. HALLIE KENNEY.
ii.   HELEN I., b. 13 Sept. 1862; m. 6 Nov. 1890 JOHN G.
      MONROE, b. Portland 13 Nov. 1856.

1140. MARK LYMAN[8] 1833-1869 [513 Hugh[7] and Miriam Huston] was born at Falmouth 24 Feb. 1833, died there 21 Oct. 1869; married at Westbrook ME 1 Aug. 1858 EUNICE McINTOSH COBB,

born there 26 Apr. 1836, died 5 Mar. 1883, 46y, daughter of
Charles and Isabel McIntosh (Campbell) Cobb (Cobb Family,
2:470; Falmouth and Westbrook VRs; Cornman Ms).
Mark enlisted 29 Sept. 1862 in Co. I, 25th ME Inf. Rgt. He
was a farmer and blacksmith.

Children, born at Falmouth:

      i.   ELI HUSTON[9], b. 24 Nov. 1859, d. Falmouth 20
            Sept. 1884, 25y; m. ALMEDA LIBBY. No ch.
     ii.   EDWARD MILTON, b. 6 Dec. 1862, d. in 1908; m.
            7 June 1900 MARY GILLIS. He res. Cheyenne
            WY. Ch. ELEANOR[10] b. there in 1901, d. in
            1920.
1663. iii. JENNIE ISABEL, b. 17 Dec. 1865; m. FRANK
            MOUNTFORT.
     iv.   SUMNER CHARLES, b. 27 Nov. 1867, d. Portland
            2 Feb. 1942 in an auto accident; unm.

1141. CALVIN B.[8] 1826-1878 [523 Jonathan[7] and Nancy
Blackey] was born at Center Harbor NH 27 Mar. 1826, died at
Concord NH 6 Apr. 1878, 52y 10d; married at Concord 26 July
1850 SARAH DAVIS SALTMARSH, born at Hookset NH 29 Mar. 1830,
died at Concord 22 June 1872, 42y, daughter of Aaron and
Joanna (George) Saltmarsh (Cornman Ms; records of Old North
Cemetery, Concord). Calvin served in Col. Caleb Cushing's MA
Rgt. during the Mexican War.

Children, born at Concord:

1664. i.   GEORGIANNA[9], b. 5 Dec. 1851; m. EBENEZER D.
            GREEN.
     ii.   ADDIE, b. 18 Jan. 1854, d. 14 Sept. 1918, 64y
            7m 20d; unm.
1665. iii. FRED, b. 25 Oct. 1857.
     iv.   CHARLES H., b. 18 Oct. 1859; m. 1st 6 June
            1884 ADDIE F. ROWELL, b. Lebanon ME 1 June
            1860, d. Concord 18 June 1890, dau. of Horace
            N. and Caroline M. (Bachelder) Rowell; m. 2nd
            26 Nov. 1901 CARRIE CHAPMAN.
     v.   SARAH L., b. 8 Feb. 1862, d. 27 June 1863.
     vi.   HARRY, b. 10 June 1864, res. Concord in 1900;
            m. Northam NH 24 Dec. 1890 ELIZA CAROLINE
            RODD, b. PEI 17 Nov. 1864, dau. of James Yeo
            and Thurza (Lyle) Rodd.
     vii. FRANK A., b. 15 June, d. 31 July, 1867.
     viii. MAUDE, b. 12 Sept. 1868, d. 17 Jan. 1930, 62y
            4m 5d; unm.

1142. ALONZO[8] 1828-1910 [523 Jonathan[7] and Nancy Blackey]
was born at Moultonboro 10 Nov. 1828, died at Center Harbor
NH 17 Jan. 1910; married at Moultonboro 27 Mar. 1855 SARAH A.
GLIDDEN, born at Brome PQ 27 Mar. 1840, daughter of Andrew
and Sally (Fall) Glidden (George W. Chamberlain and Lucius G.
Strong, Descendants of Charles Glidden [Boston, 1925], 282;
Cornman Ms).
He was an engineer on steamships at Alton Bay and Center
Harbor for 20 years; the family was listed at Moultonboro
in 1900, including son George and his family.

Children, born at Moultonboro:

1666. i.   JAMES PLACE^9, b. 20 Mar. 1856.
1667. ii.   ELNORA, b. 14 May 1858; m. GIDEON MORE.
       iii. ELIZABETH, b. 27 May 1860, d. 17 Jan. 1862.
       iv.   ELIZABETH, b. in 1862, d. in 1864.
1668. v.   WILLIAM E., b. 10 Apr. 1865.
       vi.   GEORGE W., b. 24 Apr. 1866, res. Center Har-
             bor; m. 12 Nov. 1887 ELIZABETH M. HANSON
             (Mary E. in 1900), b. 24 Nov. 1864, dau. of
             George O. and Amelia R. (Flanders) Hanson.
             Ch. CHARLES A.^{10} b. Center Harbor 25 Jan.
             1893.
       vii. SARAH L., b. 8 May 1869, d. 28 Jan. 1870.
       viii. ARTHUR L., b. 8 July, d. 19 July, 1874.
       ix.   OTIS MOORE, b. 8 Sept. 1883, d. 27 Jan. 1884.

1143. MARY ANN^8 1842-1898 [523 Jonathan^7 and Nancy
Blackey] was born at Moultonboro 26 Feb. 1842, died there 24
Nov. 1898, 56y 8m 29d; married at Sandwich NH 3 Sept. 1859
TRISTRAM GLIDDEN, born at Brome PQ 3 Sept. 1835, died at
Moultonboro in 1910, son of Andrew and Sally (Fall) Glidden
(Cornman Ms).
Glidden served in the 5th NH Inf. Rgt. during the Civil
War. His will was proved 11 Jan. 1911.

Children (**Glidden**), born at Moultonboro:

i.   EDWARD G., b. 3 Feb. 1864, res. Somerville MA; m.
      GRACE W. BREWSTER.
ii.   HARRY, b. 22 Jan. 1867, d. 22 June 1872, 5y 8m.
iii. ANNIE, b. 23 Mar. 1884.

1144. JOHN LANGDON^8 1810-1884 [526 John^7 and Anna Wiggin]
was born at Farmington NH 2 Apr. 1810, died at Garland ME 24
Jan. 1884; married at Dexter ME 21 Apr. 1837 AURILLA RUSSELL,
born at Bloomfield (Skowhegan) ME 19 July 1810, died at Garland 26 May 1879 (town and ME VRs; Cornman Ms).
They lived at Silvers Mills (Dexter) and then at Garland,
where he was a farmer in 1850. Aurilla's will, made 22 May
1879, mentioned all her living children but Stephen.

Children, all but one born at Garland:

       i.   STEPHEN F.^{9}, b. Silvers Mills 5 Mar. 1838, d.
             Garland 4 Jan. 1904, 69y 9m 29d; m. Bangor ME
             10 Jan. 1885 ABBIE RICHARDS, b. Great Works
             (Old Town) ME 14 Nov. 1844, d. E. Bangor 16
             Jan. 1917, 72y 2m 2d, dau. of George W. and
             Mary A. (Parker) Richards. No ch. He res.
             Dexter.
1669. ii.   JOHN LANGDON, b. 28 May 1843.
       iii. HENRIETTA [Etta], b. 27 Apr. 1845, d. Dexter
             12 Apr. 1929, 84y 1m 15d; unm. She lived
             with Charles at Garland.
       iv.   CHARLES A., b. 19 Nov. 1847, d. Dexter 2 Nov.
             1929, 87y 11m 13d; unm.
1670. v.   SARAH A., b. 25 May 1850; m. CHARLES S. YOUNG.
       vi.   PRESTON, b. c1854 (6 in 1860), d.y.

1145. AMOS COFFIN[8] 1816-1894 [526 John[7] and Anna Wiggin] was born at Farmington NH 12 Nov. 1816, died at Bangor ME 5 Dec. 1894, 77y 23d; married at Dexter ME 4 May 1845 ANN TIB-BETTS, born about 1818 (32 in 1850), died at Bangor (Cornman Ms; Bangor and Dexter VRs).
He was a farmer at Dexter in 1850, but was soon settled at Bangor as a joiner and carpenter. He served in the Civil War (GAR marker, Oak Grove Cemetery).

Children, born at Dexter:

    i.   HENRY M.[9], b. 21 Jan. 1846, d. Bangor 10 Apr.
         1914, 68y; unm.
    ii. GEORGE B., b. 23 Nov. 1847, d. 3 Nov. 1856.
    iii. WALTER, b. 25 Nov. 1851, d. 18 Nov. 1852.
    iv. CHARLES P., b. 5 Dec. 1854, d. Bangor 28 Jan.
         1918, 64y (GS, Mount Hope Cemetery); unm.

1146. JOSHUA WIGGIN[8] 1822-1913 [526 John[7] and Anna Wiggin] was born at Tuftonboro NH (death record) 4 Mar. 1822, died at Hollis ME 12 Dec. 1913, 91y 8m 14d; married at Dexter ME 9 Dec. 1852 LAURA AGNES ADDITON, born at Leeds ME 19 Nov. 1831, died at Dexter 11 Aug. 1891, daughter of David and Matilda (Preston) Additon (Daniel, Thomas Rogers, 198; ME VRs; Cornman Ms). Burials are at Dexter.
He was a butcher and grocer at Dexter. In 1900 he was living at Franklin NH in the Bradeen household.

Children, born at Dexter:

    i.   STANFORD MELVILLE[9], b. 10 Sept. 1853, d.
         Dexter 4 Nov. 1930; m. there 8 Nov. 1885
         LAURA A. HASKELL, b. Garland 10 Sept. 1852,
         d. Dexter 6 Aug. 1930, dau. of Jacob and Mary
         (Bates) Haskell. Ch. BERTHA MARY[10] b. 25
         June 1887. He was a grocer 25 yrs., then in
         1898 Dexter mgr., Waterville Trust Co., and
         later Bangor mgr,, Merrill Trust Co.
    ii. EMMA ADELLE, b. 5 Oct. 1856, d. Gardiner ME
         17 July 1933; m. Dexter 5 Dec. 1889 Rev.
         ALLAN W. BRADEEN, b. Mexico ME 24 Feb. 1855,
         d. 13 May 1915, son of Isaac and Philena
         (Billington) Bradeen. He was a graduate of
         Bates College in 1888 and a Free Will Baptist
         pastor. Ch. Leroy S. b. in RI 18 Jan. 1891.
    iii. IDA MAY, b. 11 Mar. 1853; m. 11 Mar. 1886
         FREDERICK WILLIAM COPELAND, b. N. Easton MA
         in 1848, d. there in 1899. Ch. Oakes b. 14
         Nov. 1891, d. Watertown MA 18 Feb. 1902.
    iv. EDITH, b. 2 May 1871, d. 9 Apr. 1876, 4y 11m.

1147. IRA A.[8] 1811-1902 [527 Samuel[7] and Martha French] was born at Farmington NH 18 July 1811 (Exeter ME VRs; 1813 on GS), died at Pittsfield ME 17 Nov. 1902, 89y 4m 1d; married at Exeter 5 Nov. 1837 EUNICE G. TIBBETTS, born there 4 Apr. 1817, died at Pittsfield 27 Jan. 1899, 83y 9m 28d, daughter of Henry and Mary (Crane) Tibbetts (Exeter and ME VRs; Cornman Ms; records of Helen Lord and Evarts Leighton). Burials are in the Pittsfield Cemetery.

He was a farmer at Pittsfield. In 1850 the family was
listed at Corinth; in 1900 he was living at Pittsfield with
his son Clarence.

Children:

1671. i.   ALONZO TRUE[9], b. Exeter 17 July 1838.
1672. ii.   CHARLES HENRY, b. Exeter 22 Mar. 1840.
       iii. CYRUS P., b. Exeter 2 Jan. 1843, d. in Libby
             Prison in 1864; unm. He served in the 2nd ME
             Cav. Rgt.
       iv.   ROSCOE G., b. Exeter c1846 (14 in 1860), d.
             Peaks Island (Portland) 14 Dec. 1917, 70y 8m
             10d; m. FLORA BOSWELL, b. Skowhegan 11 June
             1852, d. Portland 30 June 1932, 80y 12d,
             dau. of Henry Boswell. He was a harness
             maker at Skowhegan in 1870, and later owned
             Leighton Mfg. Co., Portland harness-makers.
1673. v.   FREDERICK JOSEPH, b. Corinth 2 Jan. 1851.
       vi.   JOHN B., b. 2 Feb. 1854, res. Brockton MA in
             1900; m. 28 Dec. 1898 FLORA H. CUSHMAN, b. in
             MA in Feb. 1865.
1674. vii. (CLARENCE) EUGENE, b. Corinth 18 Feb. 1857.
       viii. IRA A., b. 8 Mar. 1859, res. Boulder MT; m. 29
             Dec. 1886 CORA M. HARTWELL, b. Kansas City
             MO, dau. of Jacob and Susan Hartwell. After
             grad. Univ. of MI, MD in 1885, he practiced
             medicine at Boulder (J. Miller, History of
             Montana [1894], 2:414). They may have
             adopted a dau.

1148. LYMAN[8] 1813-1867 [527 Samuel[7] and Martha French]
was born at Tuftonboro NH 26 Mar. 1813 (Exeter TRs), died at
Exeter ME 5 Dec. 1867, 53y 8m; married at Exeter Mills 12
Nov. 1837 NANCY TIBBETTS, born 7 June 1816, died at Corinth
ME 18 Feb. 1905, 88y 8m 11d, daughter of Joseph and Sarah
(Crane) Tibbetts (Exeter TRs; records of Evarts Leighton;
Cornman Ms). Burials are in Exeter Mills Cemetery.
     He was a blacksmith at Exeter Mills. After his death, his
youngest children, Lyman, Helen and Josephine, were placed
under the guardianship of their uncle Jacob Eastman.

Children, born at Exeter:

1675. i.   ELBRIDGE[9], b. 12 Mar. 1838.
       ii.   SARAH ELIZABETH, b. 6 Feb. 1840, d. 20 Oct.
             1848, 8y 8m.
       iii. HENRIETTA, b. 27 Jan. 1842, d. 20 Oct. 1848.
       iv.   GEORGE A., b. in 1844, d. 3 Nov. 1848, 4y 11m.
       v.   EUGENE, b. in 1846, d. 22 Oct. 1848, 2y 3m.
       vi.   LYMAN JR., b. 11 Oct. 1848, d. Exeter in May
             1929; m. 27 Jan. 1871 MARIA OSGOOD, b. there
             11 Feb. 1852, d. 30 May 1941, dau. of John W.
             and Rhoda (Walker) Osgood. No ch. He was a
             blacksmith.
1676. vii. HELEN M., b. 15 Sept. 1851; m. GEORGE PIO.
1677. viii. JOSEPHINE, b. 10 Aug. 1853; m. EUGENE
             PRESCOTT.

1149. MARY[8] 1816-1857 [527 Samuel[7] and Martha French] was born at Tuftonboro NH 10 Sept. 1816 (Exeter VRs), died at Exeter ME 10 Apr. 1857, 40y 5m (GS); married there in 1838 WILLIAM W. WADLEIGH of Corinna, born about 1817, died 8 Dec. 1874, 57y (town VRs; Cornman Ms). Burials are in Exeter Mills Cemetery.

Children (**Wadleigh**):

    i.   MALVINA, b. Corinth ME 17 Aug. 1841, res. Salem MA;
          m. WINFIELD MITCHELL.
    ii.   MARGARETTA [Etta], b. 9 Sept. 1842, d. Exeter 6 Mar.
          1863; m. CHARLES WHITNEY.
    iii. WINFIELD, res. Hampden ME; m. 1st ELIZABETH [Lizzie]
          MILLER; m. 2nd VILLA FRIZZELL.
    iv.   ELLA, b. 31 July 1847, res. Dorchester MA; m. LOREN
          D. ROBINSON of Exeter, son of Joseph Jr. and Cynthia
          (Pease) Robinson.
    v.   WYMAN, b. 22 Feb. 1849, res. Hampden; m. GRACE BROWN.
    vi.   ROBERT, b. 18 Mar. 1857, d. Bangor ME in July 1901.

1150. ALVIN[8] 1819-1872 [527 Samuel[7] and Martha French] was born at Tuftonboro NH 10 Mar. 1819 (Exeter VRs), died at Bangor ME 23 Apr. 1872, 53y 1m; married at Winthrop ME 30 Oct. 1844 LYDIA ORCUTT, born there 19 Apr. 1812, died at Bangor 16 Jan. 1897, daughter of Leonard and Charity (Reynolds) Orcutt (Everett S. Stackpole, History of Winthrop, Maine [The Town, 1925], 526; Exeter and ME VRs). Burials are in the Mt. Hope Cemetery, Bangor.
He was a farmer at Exeter in 1850, but soon moved to Bangor where he was a truckman and mariner. His widow lived with Leonard.

Children:

    1678. i.   LEONARD LEROY[9], b. 22 Jan. 1849.
          ii.   VIOLETTA MOORE [Lettie], b. 13 July 1853, d.
                Bangor 29 Mar. 1871 (GS, Exeter Mills.)

1151. ELIZABETH W.[8] [Lizzie] 1825-   [527 Samuel[7] and Martha French] was born at Exeter ME 26 Feb. 1825; married first 5 Mar. 1846 JOSEPH ROBINSON FOLSOM, born at Exeter 22 Dec. 1819, died at St. Johnsbury VT 9 Nov. 1855, son of James and Mary (Butters) Folsom; married second ALCOTT HERSEY (Folsom Family, 1:503; Cornman Ms).
She had no Hersey children.

Children (**Folsom**), born at Exeter:

    i.   WILBUR A., b. 9 May 1847, res. Stetson ME; m. 18 June
          1869 ABBIE M. HOUSTON.
    ii.   FRANK E., b. 25 Mar. 1849; m. 1st 20 June 1876 ELLA
          D. HOLT, d. 2 May 1899; m. 2nd 22 July 1906 CALLIE
          H. (STEVENS) Prescott, dau. of Austin Stevens.
    iii. ELIZABETH EMMA [Lizzie], b. 11 Apr. 1853, d. Exeter
          6 July 1875; m. 1 Dec. 1872 CHARLES VERNON BARKER,
          son of Noah Barker. She was raised by her aunt
          Loenza Eastman.

1152. MARTHA ANN[8] 1827-   [527 Samuel[7] and Martha French] was born at Exeter 19 Aug. 1827, lived at Bangor; married at Exeter 26 Dec. 1850 GEORGE M. JOSE, born 3 Jan. 1826, died at Bangor 10 July 1895 (Cornman Ms; Exeter and ME VRs). Burials are in Mt. Hope Cemetery, Bangor.

Children (**Jose**):

i.   ADA I., b. 19 Apr. 1852, d. Bangor 29 Apr. 1943; m. CHARLES W. WINCHESTER.
ii.   (GEORGE) WALTER, b. E. Hampden 7 May 1854, d. Bangor 12 Sept. 1916, 59y 4m 5d; unm.

1153. SAMUEL[8] 1832-1912 [527 Samuel[7] and Martha French] was born at Exeter 29 Aug. 1832 (1833-GS), died there 27 Oct. 1912 (GS-1911), 78y 2m 3d; married there 11 Nov. 1855 ELLEN MARY CALL, born at Dresden ME 24 Nov. 1838, died at Exeter 30 Apr. 1902, 64y 5m 6d, daughter of Philip and Catherine (Turner) Call (Exeter and ME VRs; records of Helen Lord; Cornman Ms). Burials are at Exeter Mills. He was a farmer at Exeter.

Children, born at Exeter Mills:

	i.	EDWIN W.[9], b. 24 Aug. 1857, d. Bangor 20 May 1939, 82y; unm.
1679.	ii.	ERNEST L., b. 24 Mar. 1871.
	iii.	KATHERINE MABEL [Katie], b. 23 Mar. 1873, d. Exeter 15 Sept. 1944; m. 4 Feb. 1902 FREDERICK L. CRANE, b. Kenduskeag ME 13 Mar. 1877, d. Exeter 28 Oct. 1943, son of George M. and Jenny (Oakman) Crane. Adopted ch. George H. b. Boston 12 Apr. 1912, d. E. Corinth 12 May 1982.

1154. JOSEPH J.[8] 1816-1891 [529 Richard[7] and Rachel Kimball] was born at Farmington NH 29 Apr. 1816, died there 9 Dec. 1891, 75y 7m 10d; married at Rochester NH 5 Jan. 1840 (Farmington int. 17 Nov. 1839) ALMIRA LEGROW (Farmington TRs; Cornman Ms). He may have married again.
He was buried in the Silver St. Cemetery; the children are buried in the Legrow Cemetery, Rochester.

Children, born at Farmington:

	i.	MARY ELLEN[9], b. in 1842, d. 15 Aug. 1842, 3m.
	ii.	BENJAMIN F., d. in 1843, 26d (GS).
	iii.	JAMES F., b. in 1845, d. 18 Oct. 1845, 21d.
1680.	iv.	JOSEPH HENRY, b. in 1846.
	v.	DAVID EDWIN, b. say 1848; m. ADDIE CHAMBERS. Ch. FRANK[10].
	vi.	LIZZIE; m. FRANK TAPPAN and ---- BLUM.
	vii.	FRANK; unm.
	viii.	ELMIRA, b. 6 Feb. 1852, d. Boston 9 Apr. 1854.

1155. SAMUEL J.[8] 1819-1894 [529 Richard[7] and Rachel Kimball] was born at Farmington 7 May 1819, died there 27 Dec. 1894, 75y 7m 8d; married there 14 Apr. 1844 MARY ELIZABETH

SHERBURNE, born at Portsmouth NH 16 Mar. 1825, died at Farmington 14 Mar. 1909, 83y 11m 26d, daughter of Daniel and
Jane (Colbath) Sherburne (town VRs; Cornman Ms).
They are buried in Pine Grove Cemetery. In 1880 their
household included Henry and his family; in 1900 widow Mary
lived with her son Henry.

Children, born at Farmington:

    i.   (CHARLES) HENRY^9, b. 24 Sept. 1848, d. Farm-
         ington 14 July 1931; m. Pittsfield 3 Sept.
         1869 GEORGIA M. RHINES, b. New Durham NH 4
         Dec. 1851, d. Farmington 20 May 1936, dau. of
         Samuel and Charlotte (Evans) Rhines. He was
         Henry C., a shoeworker, 31, in 1880. Ch.
         ELIZABETH M.^{10} b. 3 June 1872, d. 17 Nov.
         1912; m. 2 Dec. 1890 JAMES F. AVERY, b.
         Rochester c1864, son of Azariah and Susan E.
         Avery--no ch.
    ii. MARY H., b. 20 Sept. 1850; unm.
1681. iii. ELIZABETH M., b. 23 Sept. 1852; m. J. CLINTON
         CURTIS.
    iv. CLEMENT PERCY, b. 15 Oct. 1867, d. 7 Apr.
         1870, 2y 2m 6d (GS).

1156. GEORGE F.^{8} 1830-1887 [529 Richard^7 and Rachel Kim-
ball] was born at Farmington 18 Jan. 1830, died at New Durham
NH 6 Jan. 1887; married first ELLEN SAMPSON of Pittston ME;
married second at Marblehead MA 1 Sept. 1866 MARGARET SAND-
WICH, born in NS 17 Mar. 1840, died at Farmington 19 May
1913, 73y 2m 2d, daughter of James and Mary Sandwich (town
VRs; Cornman Ms; records of Marion Wentworth).
In 1880 the family was listed at Farmington, including Mary
and the Adamses.

Child by Ellen:

    i.   son^9, d. Farmington 16 May 1859, infant
         (GS, Silver St. Cem.).

Children by Margaret:

    ii. MARY, b. in MA 5 Jan. 1868; m. Farmington 24
         Dec. 1914 MANFRED TIBBETTS.
1682. iii. RACHEL K., b. Marblehead 4 July 1869; m. FRANK
         A. ADAMS.
    iv. GEORGE F., b. in MA 3 Feb. 1871; m. Farmington
         28 June 1924 MARY AGNES ORDWAY.
    v.   ELIZABETH, b. Farmington 8 July 1874, d. in
         1965; m. 1st there 31 July 1894 WINTHROP C.
         ARMSTRONG, b. Alton in 1873, son of Charles
         M. and Alice E. Armstrong; m. 2nd 31 Dec.
         1902 FRED N. TIBBETTS. Ch. Emma V. Armstrong
         b. 18 Mar. 1896; m. 26 July 1917 Fred O.
         Tibbetts.
1683. vi. JOHN H. (twin), b. Farmington 8 July 1874.
1684. vii. MARGARET E. [Nellie], b. in MA 13 Nov. 1877;
         m. ARTHUR WARE.

1157. ALFRED COGSWELL[8] 1812-1894 [539 Jacob[7] and Sophia Edgerly] was born at New Durham NH 28 Dec. 1812, died at Exeter ME 29 Aug. 1894, 81y 8m 1d; married first there 10 Aug. 1834 DORCAS LeBARON, born at Rome ME in May 1809, daughter of James and Rhoda (Tracy) LeBaron (Stockwell, LeBaron Desc., 77); married second ESTHER PRATT, born at Bloomfield (now Skowhegan) about 1821, died at Corinna ME 10 Oct. 1901, 80y 28d, daughter of Asa and Clarissa (Burrill) Pratt (ME VRs; Cornman Ms; Little, Me. Genealogies, 4:2059).
Alfred was a farmer at Exeter, and was reported to have had eleven children.

Children, first seven named in Exeter VRs:

	i.	ALBINA STANHOPE[9], b. 8 May 1835; m. 13 Aug. 1857 CHARLES LABREE of Foxcroft ME. They had 2 daus.
1685.	ii.	GEORGE PEMBROKE, b. 12 June 1837.
1686.	iii.	(ASA) GANCELO, b. 8 Mar. 1839.
1687.	iv.	WILLIAM ALLEN, b. 28 Sept. 1840.
	v.	MARY ANNA, b. 1 Apr. 1843, d. 14 Nov. 1869; unm.
	vi.	GILMAN ORLANDO, b. 26 Dec. 1844, d. 3 Oct. 1863.
	vii.	EDWIN TAYLOR, b. 6 Apr. 1847, d. 31 Dec. 1850.
1688.	viii.	LLEWELLYN MORSE, b. 9 Oct. 1850.
	ix.	EDWIN, b. 20 Oct., d. 23 Dec., 1851.

1158. JOHN EDGERLY[8] 1816-1877 [539 Jacob[7] and Sophia Edgerly] was born at New Durham NH 6 Jan. 1816, died at Orrington ME 16 June 1877; married at Exeter ME 15 Apr. 1841 MATILDA GERRISH BUTTERS, born there about 1819, daughter of Daniel and Catherine (Gerrish) Butters (town VRs; Orrington Town Register, 1907; Cornman Ms).
He moved from Exeter to Garland, where he was listed as a farmer in 1850 and 1860; he then settled with his family on a farm at Orrington.
His will, made 3 Apr. 1877, made bequests to wife Matilda, his daughters Etta A., Augusta Preble and Ella Rogers, and his grandchild Minnie.

Children:

1689.	i.	AUGUSTA C.[9], b. Exeter 29 Mar. 1842; m. EDWIN PREBLE.
	ii.	HENRIETTA A. [Etta], b. 11 Aug. 1844, d. Brewer ME 29 Oct. 1916, 72y 2m 18d; unm.
	iii.	ALVRA W., b. 13 Sept. 1847, d. 27 Mar. 1876; m. Orrington 26 Nov. 1868 MARY E. FOWLER. He was a corporal, Co. H, 31st ME Inf. Rgt.
	iv.	ELLA S., b. 11 May 1853, res. Brewer; m. 14 Oct. 1873 WESTON H. ROGERS.

1159. RHODA ELIZABETH[8] 1818-1885 [539 Jacob[7] and Sophia Edgerly] was born at New Durham 26 Apr. 1818, died at Corinna ME 25 Aug. 1885; married at Corinna 26 July 1840 SETH MORSE, born 8 July 1818, died at Corinna 8 Aug. 1887, son of Philip and Lovina Morse (Corinna VRs; Cornman Ms). He was a farmer at Corinna.

Children (**Morse**), born at Corinna:

i.   SOPHIA D., b. 6 Nov. 1841, d. 7 Dec. 1872.
ii.   MILES LLEWELLYN, b. 3 Oct. 1842, d. 22 Mar. 1844.
iii. FRANCES ELLA, b. 7 Aug. 1845; m. Dr. HOBART A. RICH-
      ARDSON of Benton ME.
iv.   PHOEBE M., b. 16 May 1849.
v.   ADDIE S., b. 20 Apr. 1854, res. Charlestown MA; m.
      H. WATSON GRANT, b. 29 July 1850.

1160. FRANCIS FISHER[8] 1828-1898 [539 Jacob[7] and Sophia
Edgerly] was born at Exeter ME 11 July 1828, died at Farmington NH 15 Oct. 1898, 70y 3m 4d; married at Lebanon ME 4 Jan.
1852 (VRs) ELIZABETH ANN WATSON, born at Farmington 28 Oct.
1836, lived with her son Frank at Lynn MA in 1900 (Cornman
Ms; Farmington VRs). Frank served in Co. C, 13th NH Inf.
Rgt., during the Civil War. He was a painter and paper-
hanger by trade.

Children, born at Farmington:

i.   FRANK ELLWIN[9], b. 16 July 1854, res. Lynn MA
      in 1900; m. Farmington 6 June 1878 NETTIE M.
      YOUNG, b. Newport ME c1858.
ii.   CHARLES, b. 16 Nov. 1855, res. Lynn MA; m. 11
      May 1887 GRACE E. PAUL, b. 19 Sept. 1861.
      Ch. CHARLES and LESLIE both d. infant. He
      was an attorney and court clerk at Lynn.

1161. CHARLES WESLEY[8] 1831-1875 [539 Jacob[7] and Sophia
Edgerly] was born at Exeter ME 15 Mar. 1831, died at Corinna
ME 10 June 1875; married at Exeter 15 Jan. 1852 HANNAH S.
HILL, born there 8 Mar. 1833, lived at Corinna in 1903,
daughter of Nathaniel and Elizabeth (Stevens) Hill. She married second 6 May 1876 Ivory S. Barker (Cornman Ms; Exeter
and Corinna VRs). Charles and his brother Frank were probably the sawyers listed at Orono ME in 1850. In 1860 Charles
was a farmer at Exeter.

Children:

i.   CHARLES FRANK[9], b. Orono 14 July 1853, d. 3
      June 1862.
ii.   LESLIE MORSE, b. W. Garland 6 Oct. 1855, d.
      16 June 1862.
1690. iii. ANGIE, b. Corinna 17 Oct. 1856; m. CHARLES M.
      GRIFFIN.
iv.   FLORA, b. Exeter 24 Feb. 1858, d. 28 May 1862.

1162. SOPHIA ANNIE[8] 1833-1914 [539 Jacob[7] and Sophia
Edgerly] was born at Exeter ME 11 Mar. 1833, died 19 July
1914, 80y; married 19 Sept. 1864 IRA A. QUINT, born 22 Sept.
1833 (Cornman Ms). They lived at Farmington NH.

Children (**Quint**):

i.   CARRIE MAY, b. 28 May 1867; m. 1st 2 Sept. 1883
      ERRILL MONTAGUE EDGERLY; m. 2nd ALONZO OTIS.

ii.   ANNIE MAUD, b. 26 Oct. 1870, d. 2 Oct. 1878.
iii.   ADELAIDE MORSE, b. Milton NH 16 Oct. 1873; m. 11 Jan.
       1904 WILLIAM HARRY RICKER, b. Wolfeboro in 1873.

1163. NAHALA DAVIS[8] 1818-1862 [541 Ephraim[7] and Nancy
Edgerly] was born at New Durham NH 27 Nov. 1818, died at
White Sulphur Springs VA 14 Nov. 1862; married at Lowell MA
10 Oct. 1841 (VRs) SARAH ANNE EDGERLY, born at Alton NH 1
Feb. 1816, died at Farmington NH 30 Mar. 1862, 46y, daughter
of Jonathan and Sarah Whitehouse (Edgerly) Edgerly (McDuffee,
Rochester, 1:223-4; Norman Edgerly, Edgerly Genealogy [Ms,
NEHGS]; records of Marion Wentworth; Cornman Ms).
    In 1850, "N. D." was a shoemaker at Alton. He enlisted in
Co. H, 9th NH Inf. Rgt., 30 July 1862, was mustered out sick
13 Aug. 1862, and died en route to hospital.
    Family accounts stated that he was ordered by a brutal sur-
geon to march 75 miles to Washington. After walking 31 miles
in one day, he was stopped by rain. He was provided with a
shelter tent and a man to watch him, but the watcher deserted
his post; Nahala was found dead on the bare ground in the
morning, and buried there.
    Parker W. Horne was made guardian of the two orphans, and
applied for their pension in 1863 (NA-MSR #29143).

Children, born at Alton:

1691. i.   EPHRAIM H.[9], b. 20 Nov. 1848.
1692. ii.   CHARLES WARREN, b. 9 June 1852.

1164. EVERETT WARREN[8] 1820-1863 [541 Ephraim[7] and Nancy
Edgerly] was born at New Durham NH 16 May 1820, died at Far-
mington 14 Mar. 1863; married at Lowell MA 27 Mar. 1846 (VRs)
ALICE OLIVE EDGERLY, born at New Durham 16 Mar. 1823, died at
Farmington 16 Feb. 1908, 84y 11m, daughter of Jonathan and
Sarah Whitehouse (Edgerly) Edgerly (Scales, Strafford Co.,
548; Cornman Ms).
    In 1850 Everett was listed as a farmer at Alton with his
wife "Ellis." He enlisted 15 Aug. 1862 in Co. C, 13th NH
Inf. Rgt., was discharged with jaundice 25 Feb. 1863, and
died soon after.
    In Sept. 1862 his widow Alice applied for a pension (NA-
MSR #8278). In 1880 and 1900 she lived with her daughter
Clara at Farmington; in 1907 she was a dressmaker (Farmington
Town Register).

Children:

        i.   SARAH LOUISA[9], b. New Durham 30 Oct. 1847, d.
              there 21 June 1848.
        ii.   AMOS EDGAR, b. New Durham 14 Mar. 1849, res.
              Berwick ME in 1900; m. 1 Nov. 1871 CLARA EVA
              RAND of Portsmouth. No ch. He was cashier,
              Somersworth National Bank.
        iii. CLARA ELIZABETH, b. Alton 27 Jan., d. 22 Feb.,
              1851.
        iv.   ALICE ADAH, b. Alton 3 Oct., d. 19 Nov., 1852.
        v.   WARREN EVERETT, b. Alton 11 May 1854, d. in
              Apr. 1917; m. 1st 24 Oct. 1899 MARANTHA MUL-
              LOY, b. Lewiston ME 15 Aug. 1852, d. there

22 Apr. 1917, 63y 8m 7d (buried Berwick),
dau. of Ernest and Ellen J. (Young) Mulloy;
m. 2nd A. L. (----) Seavey; m. 3rd in 1925
widow MABELLE Rand. A shoe-pattern manufacturer, he lived at Auburn, and was buried at
Berwick. No ch.

   vi.   ADRIANNA, b. Alton 11 Oct. 1856, d. Farmington
          12 Feb. 1857.
  vii. ISORA ALMA, b. Farmington 20 Jan. 1859.
 viii. CLARA BELL, b. Farmington 19 June 1860, d.
          there 20 Feb. 1911, 50y 8m 12d; m. there 6
          Oct. 1884 CHARLES F. DAVIS, b. Saco ME (as
          Charles Phillips) in 1849, d. in 1917,
          adopted son of Amaziah and Harriet (Emmons)
          Davis. Ch. Earle R. b. in Mar. 1886.

1165. WILLIAM ALLEN[8] 1821-1899 [541 Ephraim[7] and Nancy
Edgerly] was born at New Durham NH 13 Aug. 1821, died at
Brighton MA 24 June 1899; married 16 Aug. 1848 ELIZABETH M.
STANTON, born at Strafford NH 13 Aug. 1821, lived at Natick
MA in 1900, daughter of Ezra F. Stanton (records of Marion
Wentworth).

Children, born at Natick:

    i.   GEORGE WILLIAM[9], b. 9 Mar. 1853; m. 30 June
          1890 IDA MAY PORTER. No ch.
    ii. FRANK LUCIUS, b. 15 Aug. 1854, d. 21 Sept.
          1856, 1y 1m 6d.
1693. iii. JENNIE EDITH, b. 9 Jan. 1863; m. Rev. AMASA
          C. FAY.

1166. EPHRAIM[8] 1807-1883 [544 Jacob[7] and Sarah Wentworth]
was born at Ossipee NH 8 Sept. 1807, died at Newfield ME 24
Mar. 1883; married at Eaton NH 4 Jan. 1827 RACHEL MANSON,
born at Limerick ME 17 Jan. 1809, died at Wakefield NH 2 Nov.
1889, daughter of John and Sarah (Small) Manson (Wentworth
Gen., 2:199-201; Newfield research of Ruth Ayers; records of
Nellie Hiday). They are buried at Ossipee.
A farmer and cooper, he settled at Newfield about 1846.

Children:

1694. i.   JOHN M.[9], b. Effingham 12 Apr. 1827.
1695. ii. JACOB, b. Ossipee 12 Oct. 1828.
1696. iii. SARAH ANN, b. Eaton 29 Aug. 1830; m. JOSEPH
          MORRILL WOODMAN.
    iv. CHARLES HENRY, b. Ossipee 6 Feb. 1833, d. 16
          Oct. 1903; m. LUCENA ----- , b. in NY in Nov.
          1840. They res. Nq_0 Adams MA in 1880 and
          1900. Ch. ELLA R.[10] b. in MA in Mar. 1875.
1697. v.   WALLACE WASHINGTON, b. Ossipee 25 Dec. 1836.
    vi. LEWIS, b. 25 Dec. 1838, d. Ossipee 1 June
          1864; m. LILLIAN E. GLIDDEN of Springfield
          MA. He contracted a fatal illness while
          serving in Co. C, 5th ME Inf. Rgt.
   vii. EDWIN GEORGE, b. 19 July 1842, d. Ossipee 4
          May 1864 of a service disability; unm. He
          served in Co. A, 2nd NH Inf. Rgt.

1698.   viii. ELIZABETH M., b. Wakefield 13 Apr. 1845; m.
              ASA FREEMAN HORNE.

1167. CHARLES[8] 1815-1857 [544 Jacob[7] and Sarah Wentworth]
was born at Ossipee 7 Aug. 1815, died there 1 Apr. 1857, 41y;
married there 24 Oct. 1838 his second cousin SARAH [Sally]
WENTWORTH, born 17 July 1820, lived with her son Albert at
Ossipee in 1904, daughter of Mark and Anna Wentworth. She
married second at Wolfeboro NH 21 Apr. 1861 Benjamin R. Lyons
(Cornman Ms; Wentworth Gen., 2:199-203; records of Nellie
Hiday).
   He farmed his grandfather's homestead at Leighton's Corner.
In 1880 his widow Sarah was living with her son Albert.

   Children, born at Ossipee:

        i.   OLIVE J.[9], b. 8 July 1839, d. 6 Nov. 1861;
              unm.
1699.   ii.   ALBERT WEEKS, b. 12 Mar. 1843.
1700.   iii. GEORGE HENRY, b. 22 Apr. 1848.
        iv.   CHARLES BYRON, b. 25 Mar. 1855, d. Ossipee 10
              Oct. 1898; m. 15 June 1880 ALICE ADELINA
              GRAVES, b. Ipswich MA 20 Jan. 1856, d.
              Ossipee 1 June 1921, dau. of Calvin and
              Joanna (Bean) Graves. No ch. He was town
              selectman at Ossipee in 1894.

1168. ELIZABETH WENTWORTH[8] 1817-1909 [544 Jacob[7] and Sarah
Wentworth] was born at Ossipee 25 July 1817, died there 14
July 1909; married there 19 Mar. 1846 ISRAEL LEIGHTON SAN-
DERS, born there 5 June 1820, died there 2 Mar. 1908, son of
John and Elizabeth (Buzzell) Sanders (letter from grand-
daughter Miriam Tucker--Cornman Papers; Wentworth Gen.,
2:199-201). They lived at Leighton's Corner.

   Children (**Sanders**), born at Ossipee:

i.   HARRIET, b. 6 Dec. 1847, d. Ossipee 3 Aug. 1895; unm.
ii.   ELVIRA, b. 12 Aug. 1849, res. Gloucester MA.
iii.   SARAH ELIZABETH, b. 12 Feb. 1852, res. Hyde Park MA;
       m. 19 May 1875 CHARLES H. TUCKER.
iv.   FRANCENA ISRAELETTE, b. 17 Nov. 1855; m. Hyde Park MA
       20 Oct. 1886 WILLIS ALLEN DELANO of Portland ME, b.
       Augusta 28 Sept. 1861, son of Charles S. and Julia
       (Marston) Delano (Delano, House of Delano, 270).
v.   CHARLES LEIGHTON, b. 2 May 1859, res. Somerville MA;
       m. 25 Dec. 1885 CLARA S. WENTWORTH, b. Wakefield NH,
       who d. 24 Dec. 1913, dau. of Benjamin and Mary A.
       (Roberts) Wentworth.

1169. JACOB M.[8] 1819-1873 [544 Jacob[7] and Sarah Wentworth]
was born at Ossipee 24 Sept. 1819, died at Boston 26 Mar.
1873, 53y 6m 30d;; married at Exeter NH 13 June 1848 ADELINE
A. HUNNEWELL of Exeter, born about 1823 (Wentworth Gen.,
2:200; Cornman Ms).
   He became a physician, practicing at Wakefield NH, at Acton
ME in 1850, and then at Newfield ME.
   In 1862 he was appointed surgeon in the 168th NY Inf. Rgt.

Children:

  i. EDWARD^9, b. Ossipee 29 July 1850, res. Exeter
     and NYC; mar. ---- , 2 ch. (Cornman Ms).
  ii. MARGARET, b. Newfield in 1853, res. NYC; unm.
     She was a high school teacher.

1170. LEONARD WENTWORTH^8 1822-1895 [544 Jacob^7 and Sarah
Wentworth] was born at Ossipee 12 Sept. 1822, died at Shap-
leigh ME 5 Nov. 1895, 72y 1m 23d; married first at Portland
ME 1 May 1850 ISABELLA GRAHAM HOOLE, born in ME about 1830
(20 in 1850); married second at Shapleigh 22 Oct. 1866 HANNAH
MOULTON LITTLEFIELD, born there in 1834, daughter of John and
Sarah (Garland) Littlefield (Wentworth Gen., 2:200; Bowdoin
College General Catalog; Cornman Ms).
  He attended Bowdoin Medical School in 1847-8, and set up
his practice at Durham NH after his marriage. He enlisted in
Co. D, 11th ME Inf. Rgt, 19 Oct. 1861. He practiced medicine
at Shapleigh from 1869 until shortly before his death.

Children by Isabella:

  i. JOSEPH EDWARD^9, b. Waverly NY 8 Feb. 1852;
     m. 1st 23 Sept. 1887 EVELYN M. HURD, dau. of
     William and Mary of Great Falls NH; m. 2nd
     EVA A. JOSSELYN of Camden ME, b. in Sept.
     1874, dau. of James A. and Bessie B. (Good-
     rich) Josselyn. Joseph and Eva were listed
     with her father at Boston in 1900. A sales-
     man, Joseph lived at Shapleigh.
  ii. FLORENCE ISABELLA, b. 10 June 1857, d.y.

1171. ELVIRA M.^{8} 1825- [544 Jacob^7 and Sarah Went-
worth] was born at Ossipee 3 Mar. 1825, lived at Saco ME;
married first 6 Aug. 1845 BENJAMIN BENEIGH SMITH, born at
Ossipee, died in Sept. 1859; married second 8 Dec. 1860 SAM-
UEL F. ALLEN, died in July 1862; married third in June 1864
GUSTAVE ADDITON of Falmouth; married fourth ---- COOK; married fifth ---- PARSONS (Wentworth Gen., 2:201; Cornman Ms).

Children (**Smith**):

  i. JAMES EDWIN [GEORGE F.], b. 6 Feb. 1847, d. 2 Nov.
     1872; m. 9 Jan. 1869 SUSIE A. SENNETT.
  ii. BETSEY E., b. 8 Sept. 1851, d. 19 Sept. 1859.
  iii. ANN AUGUSTA, b. 13 June 1853; m. in Mar. 1873 JAMES
     DICKEY of Cumberland, and res. Saco.

1172. FREEMAN^8 1811-1890 [548 John^7 and Sabrina Shaw] was
born at Athens ME 15 Apr. 1811, died at Spring Bluff (now
Winthrop Harbor), Lake County IL 2 Aug. 1890; married at
Bradford ME 4 July 1837 ELIZA ANN DAVIS, born at Penobscot ME
7 May 1818, died at Diamond Bluff, Pierce County WI 7 July
1897, daughter of Dr. Isaac and Sarah (Swett) Davis (Farwell,
Shaw Records, 284-5; obituary, Palmyra [WI] Enterprise, 6
Aug. 1890; family papers and letters of his sister Matilda
and daughter Eliza, now owned by descendants Isabel Wiggins
and Anabel Robertson). Burials are at Palmyra.

They went west from Bradford in 1842, first to OH, then to Fulton, Rock Co. WI in 1844, and to Palmyra in 1856. He was a farmer. He died at the home of his daughter Minnie.

Children:

1701. i.   CHARLES MELVILLE^9, b. Bradford ME 21 Nov. 1838.
       ii.   ALBINA ANN, b. Bradford 7 May 1841, d. White-water, Jefferson Co. WI 11 May 1887; m. there 2 Oct. 1861 WILLIAM WIGHT, b. in PA. No ch.
       iii. (LOUISA) MATILDA, b. Zanesville OH 9 Sept. 1843, d. Manitou CO 3 Apr. 1891; m. Palmyra 16 Dec. 1866 CHARLES RICH, b. Exeter ME 14 Jan. 1837.
1702. iv.   ELLEN MARIA, b. Fulton 13 Oct. 1845; m. SETH S. MORTON.
       v.   dau., b. Fulton 30 Oct., d. 30 Nov., 1847.
1703. vi.   ELIZA ADELINE, b. Fulton 5 Nov. 1849; m. H. THEODORE GRAVES.
       vii. CAROLINE EMMA [Carrie], b. Fulton 27 May 1851, d. Palmyra 4 May 1872; unm.
1704. viii. MARY JANE [Minnie], b. Palmyra 19 Dec. 1857; m. ELIJAH DANIELS.

1173. JOHN W.^{8} 1822-1901 [548 John^7 and Sabrina Shaw] was born at Athens ME 21 Dec. 1822, died at Seattle WA 2 Aug. 1901, 79y 7m 17d; married in ME ELLEN F. ---- , born about 1835 (25 in 1860), died 31 Aug. 1897 (copy of their obituaries sent by Matilda Quimby to her niece Eliza). In 1860 they were at Bradford ME. In 1870 they settled in Republic Co. KS, and about 1890 moved on to Seattle, where they were listed in 1900 in Walter Wood's household.

Children:

       i.   EDMUND W.^{9}, b. c1856 (4 in 1860; not in obit.)
1705. ii.   GEORGE M., b. Bradford in 1859.
       iii. LEONARD T., b. KS in Apr. 1878, res. Nome, Alaska, in 1901.
       iv.   CORA A.; m. ---- ATWELL.
       v.   MABEL A., res. Seattle in 1901; m. ---- MOHLER.
       vi.   LETTA M., res. Seattle; m. in Jan. 1897 WALTER H. WOOD.

1174. JONATHAN^8 1815-1897 [550 Jonathan^7 and Nancy Fowler] was born at Athens ME 31 May 1815, died at Sheboygan Falls WI 19 Oct. 1897; married at Bingham ME 11 Mar. 1839 ELIZABETH C. LITTLEFIELD, born at Bloomfield (Skowhegan) ME 2 Oct. 1822, died at Sheboygan Falls 19 Mar. 1913, daughter of Aurin Z. and Betsey (Littlefield) Littlefield (Portrait and Biographical Record of Sheboygan County, Wisc. [Chicago, 1894], 394-5; Carl Zillier, History of Sheboygan County [1912], 2:128-9; records of descendant Arvid Leighton). Burials are in the Sheboygan Falls Cemetery.
       His uncle John, as guardian, apprenticed him to a carpenter and joiner. For four years Jonathan was a lumberman on the Penobscot River. He joined Co. A, 1st Rgt., 8th Light Inf.

Div., serving as ensign in 1838, and as lieutenant in 1840 to
1842 (Coburn, Skowhegan, 593).
The young couple went west to Milwaukee in June 1843, where
he drove the pilings for the first pier at Sheboygan. The
next year they settled at Sheboygan Falls, where he and his
father-in-law built the first sawmill, Littlefield & Leighton
Mills. He sold the mill in 1854, and built another on his
130-acre farm which lay on both banks of the river.
   In 1864 he went to Montana in the gold rush, staying seven
years in the Bannock area; in 1870 Elizabeth, 48, was listed
at Sheboygan as a farmer, with four children at home.
   Isabelle was administrix of her mother's estate, and in
1915 sold the land to Walter J. Kohler, president of the Kohler Co. (clipping, Sheboygan County News).

   Children, all but first born at Sheboygan:

             i.   FRANCES E.[9], b. prob. Skowhegan ME c1842; d.
                  Long Beach CA c1933; m. RICHARD MELVIN GIF-
                  FORD, d. c1922. They res. Omro MN, and in
                  1911 Canby MN. Adopted ch. Arthur res. Long
                  Beach; m. Lydia R. ---- .
   1706.   ii.   GEORGE H., b. 20 June 1845.
   1707.   iii.   CHARLES AUGUSTUS, b. 16 Aug. 1847.
            iv.   CHARLOTTE E., b. c1852 (18 in 1870); m. Rev.
                  LUCIUS J. DINSMORE, b. c1851, d. Chicago 9
                  Dec. 1906, 55y, son of Rev. Alvin and Elvira
                  (Dunn) Dinsmore. Both attended Lombard Col.
                  (now Meadville Theol. School); Lucius became
                  a pastor in MN, WI and finally at Chicago's
                  Third Universalist Church (Universalist
                  Register [1908], 12). Only ch. Nina B. d.
                  Chesaning, Saginaw Co. MI, probate 15 May
                  1967; m. ---- Gilbert: no ch.
             v.   ISABELLE [Belle], b. 15 Apr. 1854, d. She-
                  boygan Falls 10 Dec. 1941; unm. She was a
                  school teacher.
            vi.   ARTHUR J., b. 1 June 1857, d. Sheboygan 9 Dec.
                  1921; m. 1st SADIE (----) Trask; m. 2nd 11
                  Nov. 1918 ANNA DITTMAN . He was publisher of
                  the Pewaukee [WI] Times in 1897, and later
                  res. Chilton, Calumet Co. WI.
           vii.   ALICE, d. aged 2y.
          viii.   child, d. infant.

   1175. ASA[8] 1819-1883 [551 Hazen[7]] was born at Athens 19
July 1819, died in Canada 14 Dec. 1883; married JUDITH BLAKE
of Rumney NH (letter from Katie Wheelock Leighton--Cornman
Papers). He was a farmer, and justice of the peace at So.
Durham, PQ.

   Children, born in Quebec Province:

             i.   HAZEN[9], b. 4 Sept. 1845, d. 4 Aug. 1873 (or
                  1893); m. KATIE WHEELOCK, b. Greenwich NY
                  3 Jan. 1850. He was a banker.
            ii.   ABIGAIL, d. in 1894; m. Hatley PQ 3 May 1862
                  (both of Durham Tp) EDWIN WAKEFIELD (records,
                  Free Will Baptist Ch., St Francis Dist.;
                  brother Hazen witnessed the marriage).

    iii.   FANNIE ELEANOR, d. in 1872; m. CHARLES E.
           BATES.

1176. MARIA[8] 1830-1915 [551 Hazen[7] and Olive Lord] was
born at Athens 23 Nov. 1830 (GS), died there 3 July 1915, 84y
7m 9d (GS); married BRYCE M. STEWARD, born 4 Nov. 1818 (GS),
died 29 Dec. 1882, 70y 1m 25d (town and ME VRs). Burials are
in Mount Rest Cemetery, Athens.

Children (**Steward**), born at Athens:

i.   LEVI L., b. 19 Nov. 1851, d. Solon ME 24 Nov. 1902,
         51y 5d (GS); unm.
ii.   ANDREW S., b. 14 Oct. 1853, d. Solon 19 Aug. 1894,
         40y 10m 5d (GS).

1177. EMILY ADELAIDE[8] 1841-1886 [551 Hazen[7] and Lydia Ald-
rich] was born at Upton MA 5 Apr. 1841, died at Westboro MA
25 Apr. 1886; married at Upton 15 Aug. 1859 ALBERT STONE
DRAKE, born at Shrewsbury MA 19 Mar. 1826, died at Milford MA
19 July 1876, son of Jonathan H. and Ann Bruce (Stone) Drake
(town VRs; Drake Fam., 126). He had four children by his
first wife Laura Pierce.

Children (**Drake**), born at Upton:

i.   ANNIE B., b. 27 July 1860, res. Worcester MA.
ii.   ROSA B., b. 21 June 1863, d. Upton 24 Feb. 1872.
iii.   LOTTIE LYDIA, b. 24 Apr. 1868; m. Upton 4 Sept. 1889
         GEORGE E. HILL.

1178. LYMAN A.[8] 1843-   [551 Hazen[7] and Lydia Aldrich]
was born at Upton MA 28 Nov. 1843, lived at Worcester MA in
1900; married in 1866 CAROLINE S. [Carrie] CLARK, born in CT
in July 1846, daughter of Ollin Clark (Upton VRs; Biographical Review of Worcester County, Mass. [1899], 2:774-5; letter
from his daughter C. Millie--Cornman Papers).
    He served in Co. B, 25th MA Inf. Rgt., from 1861 until
discharged disabled; he then re-enlisted in 1863 in Co. D,
3rd MA Heavy Artillery Rgt., and was discharged in Sept. 1865
as sergeant. Settling at Clinton MA in 1861, he started as a
carpenter, and developed a building firm, contracting to construct industrial and residential structures in MA and CT
    In 1892 he formed the Clinton Wall Trunk Mfg. Co., which
manufactured builders' supplies such as doors and sashes as
well as trunks. In 1880 he lived at Clinton; in 1900 he was
living on Leighton Ave. at Worcester, near his son Albert.

Children, born at Upton:

i.   CARRIE AMELIA[9] [C. Millie], b. 30 Jan. 1868.
ii.   CLARENCE HAZEN, b. 1 Apr. 1870, not in 1880
         census.
iii.   ALBERT E., b. in Mar. 1872 (1900 census); m.
         CAROLINE E. [Carrie] MACK, b. in Nov. 1874.
         Ch. EUGENE L.[10] b. in Jan. 1899.
iv.   MARY E., b. c1877 (3 in 1880).
v.   (CHARLES) FRANK, b. in Nov. 1878.

1179. JOHN HARRISON[8] 1831-1912 [555 William[7] and Relief Brown] was born at Harmony ME 29 Apr. 1831, died at Anoka MN in 1912; married first in 1852 NANCY M. HEATH, born in 1831 (49 in 1880), died in 1887, 56y; married second in 1891 ETTA T. WHITE, born in WI in Mar. 1853 (Cornman Ms).
    Like his father he moved to MA. Later he settled in MN, appearing at Minneapolis in the 1880 and 1900 censuses.

Children by Nancy:

1708. i.   FRED H.[9], b. So. Orange MA 27 May 1855.
        ii.   GEORGE W., b. Athol MA in 1857, d. New Salem
              MA 8 Sept. 1859, 2y 3m 8d (VRs).

1180. (AARON) FRANKLIN[8] [Frank] 1836-   [555 William[7] and Relief Brown] was born at Harmony ME 15 Mar. 1836, lived at Keene NH in 1880; married first 10 Aug. 1857 ELVIRA WOODWARD of Warwick MA, born in 1832, died at Marlboro NH 10 May 1868, daughter of Augustus and Lutheria Woodward; married second at Marlboro in 1870 RUTH E. UNDERWOOD, born at Orange MA 2 Feb. 1853, died at Bowdoinham ME 1 Feb. 1912, 58y 11m 28d, daughter of Lyman and Elvira (Phinney) Underwood (family records of Joyce Sanborn; Marlboro VRs; Cornman Ms).
    Frank lived at Malden and other MA towns, at Marlboro, and in 1880 was listed with Ruth and their children at Keene. After he deserted her, Ruth took her children to ME and raised them there at Bowdoinham.

Children by Elvira:

1709. i.   FLORA J.[9], b. Norwich MA in Oct. 1859; m.
              OREN ROBY.
1710. ii.   IDA L., b. New Salem MA 28 June 1862; m.
              WILLIAM H. LAWRENCE.
        iii. WILLIAM A , b. Ervin MA 1 July 1864, res.
              Acton MA in 1900; m. LILLIAN ---- , b. in
              Canada in Apr. 1862.
        iv.   HERBERT U., b. Marlboro NH 13 Jan., d.
              Jaffrey NH in July, 1868.
        v.   HENRY O. (twin), b. Marlboro 13 Jan. 1868,
              res. E. Brookfield. He was adopted, and
              renamed Frank Fisher.

Children by Ruth, first two born at Marlboro:

        vi.   CHARLES C., b. 9 July 1872, d. Bowdoinham ME
              4 July 1909, 36y 11m 26d; m. 13 Aug. 1894
              GERTRUDE GILFORD, b. in MA in May 1873. In
              1900 they were listed at Acton MA.
              Ch. ANNIE A [10] b. W. Gardiner ME 7 Apr.
              1897, but not in 1900 census.
1711. vii. (FLORENCE) MELIENE [Marlie], b. 28 Sept. 1877;
              m. GEORGE CHADWICK.
1712. viii. HARLIE, b. Keene NH 7 May 1879.

1181. ORRIN PULLEN[8] [O. P.] 1834-1908 [557 Joseph[7] and Elvira Grant] was born at Harmony ME 21 Nov. 1834, died at Tecumseh, Shawnee County KS 15 Mar. 1908, 73y (county VRs); married at Pana IL 2 Oct. 1864 (LENA) SULTANA TOMLINSON, born in Franklin County KY 22 Aug. 1848, daughter of Alva and Eliza (Broughn) Tomlinson.

Orrin settled on the Ohio River at Pana IL, and established a saw mill there. His construction of gunboats for the Union Army resulted in a Confederate raid across the KY border, in which his mill was completely burned. He rebuilt it, but went bankrupt after the war ended.

The family next settled on a 160-acre farm outside Tecumseh KS, overlooking the Oregon Trail, purchased in 1870 (Shawnee Co. Deeds 23:168). About ten years later, Sultana left her husband and disappeared somewhere in South America. O. P. Leilghton died after being crushed by a horse in a stall.

Descendant J. Gary Rader has provided extensive data on this family, based on family papers, the family Bible given Orrin by his mother Elvira, and interviews in 1970-71 with Dr. Orrin L. Leighton.

Children, two born at Pana, the rest at Tecumseh (dates from family Bible):

	i.	CLARA ELVIRA^9, b. 13 Mar. 1866, d. 19 Mar. 1869.
1713.	ii.	WILLARD JOSEPH, b. 8 Mar. 1868.
1714.	iii.	(MARY) ETTA, b. 18 Dec. 1870; m. JOHN A. MITCHELL.
1715.	iv.	CHARLES WAYLAND, b. 19 June 1873.
	v.	LENA, b. 27 Dec. 1875, d. 8 Jan. 1876.
	vi.	ORRIN LLEWELLYN, b. 20 Feb. 1877, d. Joplin MO 30 May 1976, 96y 6m; unm. He was a physician at Kansas City KS (his genealogical notes to Clara Cromwell--Mss Collections, MHS.)
1716.	vii.	EMMA, b. 4 Sept. 1879; m. EDWIN MILLER.

1182. WAYLAND^8 1837-1902 [557 Joseph^7 and Elvira Grant] was born at Harmony ME 14 June 1837, died at Pasadena CA 25 Mar. 1902; married 13 Nov. 1859 MARY ANGELENE EMERY, born at Athens ME 26 Sept. 1835, died at Skowhegan ME 24 Apr. 1927, 91y 6m 28d, daughter of Zachariah and Abigail (Cole) Emery (Cornman Ms; town and ME VRs). They are buried in Mount Rest Cemetery, Athens.

He lived at Harmony until 1884, when he settled at Athens. He was a merchant there in 1900. After his death, his widow lived with her daughter Della. In 1917, a stained-glass window was placed in the Union Church in Wayland's memory.

Children, born at Harmony:

	i.	IDELLA^9 [Della], b. 1 Nov. 1863, res. Skowhegan; m. 25 Dec. 1881 DARIUS H. BARTLETT, b. Harmony 3 Mar. 1838, son of Cyrus and Sarah Ann (Butler) Bartlett. No ch.
	ii.	ESTELLA (twin), b. 1 Nov. 1863, d. 13 Jan. 1878, 14y 2m 13d (GS).

1183. ELLEN M.^{8} 1851-1882 [557 Joseph^7 and Elvira Grant] was born at Harmony 12 Sept. 1851, died there 12 Aug. 1882, 30y 11m (GS); married in 1868 MORTIMER PINGREE, born at Parkman ME in 1845, died at Maxwell City NM 1 July 1908, 65y 1m

(GS), son of Parkman and Mary (Barker) Pingree. He had a second wife (Harmony records of Clara Cromwell; Cornman Ms). Burials are in the Crossroads Cemetery, Harmony.

Children (**Pingree**), born at Harmony:

i.   BERTRAND M., b. 4 July 1869, d. 18 Apr. 1874 (GS).
ii.   EMMA BELLE, b. 3 Dec. 1873, d. Wellington ME 22 Apr.
      1896, 22y (GS, North Rd Cem., Harmony); m. FRED
      LIBBY.
iii. CARRIE GAGE, b. 17 May 1877, res. Long Beach CA; m.
      HARRY A. ROLLINS of Parkman, d. Buckeye AZ 12 Mar.
      1911, son of Edward and Abbie (Willard) Rollins.
iv.   NELLIE M., b. 16 Feb. 1880 (Mary in 1880 census), d.
      23 Apr. 1912; m. in 1896 GEORGE McSORLEY of Guilford
      ME, son of Andrew McSorley.

1184.   ETTA FRANCES[8] 1856-1915 [557 Joseph[7] and Elvira Grant] was born at Harmony 4 June 1856, died there 4 Apr. 1915, 58y 10m 2d; married 18 Oct. 1873 HERBERT O. BARTLETT, born at Harmony 2 Mar. 1854, died there 20 Nov. 1899, 45y 8m 18d, son of Stedman and Silvinia (Soule) Bartlett (Harmony records of Clara Cromwell; Cornman Ms; town and ME VRs). Burials are in Chadbourne Cemetery, Harmony.
He owned a woolen mill at Harmony, continued by his son as the Harmony Yarn Mill. In 1911 Etta was living at Harmony with her daughters (Harmony Town Register, 1911-1912).

Children (**Bartlett**), born at Harmony:

i.   BERNICE H., b. 6 June 1878, d. in 1942 (GS); m. 12
      June 1914 GEORGE H. PRATT, b. Newport ME 28 Mar.
      1880, son of Isaiah and Hattie M. (Herson) Pratt.
ii.   HARRY ASHTON, b. 2 Aug. 1883, d. in 1947 (GS); m. 14
      Oct. 1913 LULU N. HASKELL, b. Lincoln ME 8 May 1887,
      dau. of Samuel and Georgia A (Welans) Haskell.

1185.   EDWIN MARCELLUS[8] 1848-1871 [558 Benjamin[7] and Susan Savage] was born at Harmony 13 Aug. 1848, died at Greenfield MA 23 Apr. 1871; married 19 Apr. 1868 JOSEPHINE A. WILLIAMS of Hubbardston MA, daughter of John M. and Abbie F. Williams. Josephine married second George Jenness (Cornman Ms).

Child, born at Orange MA (VRs):

1717. i.   EDWIN MARCELLUS JR.[9], b. 25 Nov. 1870.

1186.   LUCINDA[8] 1820-1855 [559 Nathaniel[7] and Susan Lewis] was born at Harmony 22 June 1820, died at Pittsfield ME say 1855; married at Harmony int. 16 Oct. 1840 WILLIAM B. PER-KINS, born about 1815 (35 in 1850) (Cornman Ms). In 1850, they lived at Harmony, next door to her father.

Children (**Perkins**):

i.   HENRY, b. c1841 (9 in 1850).
ii.   ROSCOE, b. c1843 (7 in 1850).

iii. ?NATHANIEL, b. c1846, d. 8 Feb. 1912, 65y.
iv.   CLARENCE, b. c1849 (1 in 1850).

1187. MELINDA[8] 1825-1848 [559 Nathaniel[7] and Susan Lewis]
was born at Harmony 15 Feb. 1825, died there in 1848 (GS);
married 21 Aug. 1842 CHARLES PERKINS (Cornman Ms).

Possible children (**Perkins**):

i.   LAURA; m. MARINER HAYDEN. Perhaps the Laura with
      Nathaniel[7], 6 in 1850.
ii.   SUSAN ANN (named in grandmother Susan's will).

1188. DIANA[8] 1827-1894 [559 Nathaniel[7] and Susan Lewis]
was born at Harmony 11 Nov. 1827, died at Athens ME 18 Jan.
1894, 66y; married first at Harmony 30 Oct. 1845 FREEMAN
QUIMBY, who died of typhus in 1847; married second JOHN G.
HIGHT, born at Athens 3 Feb. 1826, died there 8 Apr. 1907,
81y, son of Thomas A. and Sarah (Horn) Hight (Truslow, Hight
Families, 27; town VRs; Cornman Ms).

Child (**Quimby**):

i.   FREEMAN, b. c1847, res. Hoquiam WA.

Children (**Hight**), born at Athens:

ii.   ANN, b. c1849, d. Skowhegan in 1886; m. RICHARD W.
      BROWN, d. in 1868.
iii. JOHN L., b. c1853, d. Athens 8 Dec. 1895, 42y 11m 7d;
      m. ROSE M. FARMER.
iv.   CARRIE L., b. 6 Feb. 1857, d. Athens 3 Apr. 1879
      (GS); unm. She was a schoolteacher.
v.   FRANK, b. c1859, d. infant (GS).
vi.   GEORGE C., b. 18 Nov. 1868, d. Gardiner ME 10 June
      1950; unm. A graduate of Bates College, he was a
      district school superintendent.

1189. LEWIS T.[8] 1831-   [559 Nathaniel[7] and Susan Lewis]
was born at Harmony 4 Sept. 1831, died in Canada (Cornman
Ms); married 30 Sept. 1849 MARY W. LOCKE, born at Athens 22
Aug. 1828, died at Solon 7 July 1914, 85y 10m 13d, daughter
of George and Margaret (Bradbury) Locke (Locke Gen., 187,
355; Cornman Ms).
   Lewis and Mary were living with his father in 1850; in 1860
Mary, occupation "lady," headed a household in Harmony with
her five children. She married second 12 June 1867 William
Garrett, who died 12 Sept. 1885, 63y; they had two children.
   In 1870 the Garrett household at Hartland ME included Flav-
illa and Lewis T. Leighton. Widow Mary Garrett later lived
with her daughter Katy M., wife of Eliphalet P. Cooley of
Solon (Katy's letter about her half-siblings in 1915--Cornman
Papers). Burials are in Mount Rest Cemetery, Athens.

Children, born at Athens:

i.   AUGUSTA C.[9], b. 28 May 1850; m. 10 Sept. 1869
      ALPHONZO COOKSON.

         ii.   (CARRIE) ALMEDA, b. 7 June 1852, d. 11 Mar.
               1918, 65y 9m 4d (GS); m. 20 Sept. 1869
               ASA JUDKINS. They res. Winthrop ME in 1915.
        iii.   FLAVILLA, b. 7 Dec. 1853, d. 8 Sept. 1855.
         iv.   FLAVILLA, b. 18 Aug. 1855, d. 25 May 1876, 21y
               (GS); unm.
          v.   CHARLES F., b. 10 Oct. 1857, d. 5 Sept. 1859.
 1718.   vi.   LEWIS T., b. 10 Aug 1859.

   1190.   ABIGAIL B.[8] [Abbie] 1834-   [559 Nathaniel[7] and
Susan Lewis] was born at Harmony 15 June 1834, lived at
Pittsfield ME; married at Harmony 26 Aug. 1850 JOTHAM BOWKER,
born at China ME about 1831, killed during the Battle of the
Wilderness VA 4 May 1864. He had been discharged as dis-
abled, but re-enlisted at Ellsworth ME (NA-MSR; Cornman Ms).

   Children (**Bowker**):

   i.   SUSAN, b. 11 Apr. 1852, d. in Oct. 1924.
   ii.   CLARA, b. 17 Nov. 1854.
   iii.   NINETTA, b. 22 Feb. 1859.
   iv.   ABBIE LOUISE, b. 24 Feb. 1863.

   1191.   ANN M.[8] 1836-1901 [559 Nathaniel[7] and Susan Lewis]
was born at Harmony 11 June 1836, died 16 May 1901, 63y 1m 5d
(GS); married at Athens int. 29 Nov. 1858 JAMES WHITEHOUSE,
born at Brighton ME 2 June 1839, died at Athens 15 Nov. 1884,
45y 5m 13d, son of Ivory and Sally (Goodwin) Whitehouse
(Cornman Ms; Athens records of Elaine Prince). Burials are
in Mount Rest Cemetery.

   Children (**Whitehouse**):

   i.   ALWILDA A., b. in 1857, d. 28 Jan. 1875, 17y (GS).
   ii.   CORA E., b. 30 Sept. 1859, d. 7 Aug. 1861, 1y 10m
          (GS).
   iii.   NELLIE M., b. in 1864, d. 16 Nov. 1881, 17y 5m (GS).
   iv.   ETTA M., b. 4 May 1868
   v.   ADDIE F., b. 28 Jan. 1871, d. 4 Oct. 1896 (25y 8m 7d
          in VR; 24y 8m 19d on GS); unm.
   vi.   SUSIE, b. in 1876.

   1192.   IRENE DEARBORN[8] 1821-1891 [560 Jonathan[7] and Lydia
Leighton] was born at Harmony 3 Aug. 1821, died 27 Jan.
1891; married ISAIAH CHADBOURNE, born at Harmony in Aug.
1813, died there 26 Jan. 1899, 85y 10m, son of Isaiah and
Rosamund (Hatch) Chadbourne.
   Isaiah married first Sylvia Hatch (Harmony VRs; letter from
son Loren--Cornman Papers). Burials are in the Chadbourne
Cemetery, Harmony.

   Children (**Chadbourne**), born at Harmony:

   i.   LOREN, b. 5 Aug. 1848, d. Harmony in 1915 (GS); m.
          Cambridge ME 11 Dec. 1868 VESTA A. STAFFORD, d. 14
          Aug. 1938, 89y 11m 2d.
   ii.   JOHN P., b. in 1855, d. Harmony 18 Feb. 1895, 40y;
          unm.

1193. SABRINA[8] 1822-1921 [560 Jonathan[7] and Lydia Leighton] was born at Harmony 9 Dec. 1822, died there 4 Feb. 1921; married 12 July 1845 ISAIAH DORE JR., born at Harmony 13 Dec. 1821, died there 2 Sept. 1879, son of Isaiah and Eleanor (Stafford) Dore (Harmony VRs; Cornman Ms). Burials are in Chadbourne Cemetery.

Isaiah was a Harmony farmer; in 1850 his father, 63, lived with them. Sabrina lived with her daughter Ella at Shirley ME in 1914.

Children (**Dore**), born at Harmony:

i.   ORRIN, b. 4 Apr. 1846, d. Harmony 27 Mar. 1928 (GS);
      m. HARRIET M. ---- .
ii.   IRA, b. 11 Feb. 1854, d. Harmony 27 Apr. 1940 (GS).
iii. ELLA, b. 3 Oct. 1868, res. Shirley; m. 23 May 1899
      JOHN HENRY CHURCH.

1194. CHARLES E.[8] 1825-1912 [560 Jonathan[7] and Lydia Leighton] was born at Harmony 3 Apr. 1825, died there 12 July 1912, 87y 3m 9d; married first there 30 Nov. 1845 MALINDA (BROWN) Lombard, born at Livermore ME 14 July 1811, died at Harmony 25 Jan. 1892, 80y 6m (GS), daughter of John and Mary (Gammon) Brown and widow of Henry Lombard of Harrison ME; married second at Harmony 25 Dec. 1892 JULIA ANN (WATSON) Pease, born at Cambridge ME 7 Nov. 1824, died at Harmony 13 Mar. 1906, 81y 4m 6d, daughter of Solomon and Abigail[7] (Leighton) Watson [# 553] and widow of David Pease (Harmony VRs; Cornman Ms).   Burials are at North Road, Harmony.

Charles was a Harmony farmer. In 1850, his household included his Lombard step-children Frances E., 19, and William H., 8. He served in Co. A, 9th ME Inf. Rgt., from 29 Sept. 1864 to 30 June 1865. His daughter Clara was at home in 1870.

Children by Malinda, born at Harmony:

1719. i.   CHARLES EDWIN[9], b. 7 Mar. 1847.
       ii.   MELISSA A., b. 29 Mar. 1849, d. 7 Aug. 1850.
1720. iii. CLARA A., b. 19 June 1851; m. HOVEY FRENCH.
       iv.   WILLIAM, b. in 1858, d. 7 Aug. 1859, 10m.

1195. PAMELIA[8] [Parmelia] 1827-1861 [560 Jonathan[7] and Lydia Leighton] was born at Harmony 1 Aug. 1827, died there 3 Oct. 1861; married there 17 Apr. 1851 CALVIN DORE, born 31 March 1826, died at Harmony 6 Feb. 1870, son of Isaiah and Eleanor (Stafford) Dore (Harmony VRs; Cornman Ms).

Children (**Dore**), born at Harmony:

i.   WARREN, b. c1852 (8 in 1860)
ii.   ROSETTA, b. 18 Apr. 1857, d. 19 Oct. 1937; m. Harmony
      10 May 1875 WALLACE B. HUNTRESS, b. there 22 Feb.
      1853, res. Ripley ME, son of Leonard R. and Frances
      Ellen (Lombard) Huntress (Henry Winthrop Hardon,
      George Huntress of Bloody Point and Some of His
      Descendants [TMs, NYC, 1981], 2:53). No ch.

1196. HIRAM[8] 1837-   [560 Jonathan[7] and Lydia Drew] was born at Harmony 14 Apr. 1837, lived at Petersham MA in 1900; married 11 June 1861 (LAURA) MARIA DORE, born at Athens ME 30 Oct. 1838, died at Athol MA 10 Nov. 1909, daughter of Silas and Laura (Mayo) Dore (letter from Eva Jeffreys--Cornman Papers; Walter H. Dore, History of the Dore Family [np, 1908], 18; Harmony records of Clara Cromwell; Cornman Ms).

He was listed at Petersham in 1880; in 1900 his household there included his brother Albert, as well as his children Edwin and Bertha.

Children:

    i.   LAURA A.[9], b. Athens 1 May 1863, d. Petersham
            6 Feb. 1886; unm.
    ii.   EDWIN HIRAM, b. Athens 30 Oct. 1865, unable to
            walk from birth.
   iii. EVA JOSEPHINE, b. Athens 14 Feb. 1868, d. in
            1928; m. 11 June 1896 THOMAS R. JEFFREYS, b.
            Farmington ME 12 July 1850, d. in 1934,
            son of John and Ann (Bryant) Jeffreys. No
            ch. They res. W. Somerville MA, and are
            buried at Athens.
    iv.   RILLA BELLE, b. Athens 17 Feb. 1872; m. HARRY
            F. [9] LEIGHTON [# 1199].
    v.   BERTHA MABEL, b. Petersham 28 Sept. 1874; unm.

1197. ALBERT D.[8] 1840-1907 [560 Jonathan[7] and Lydia Drew] was born at Harmony 28 Jan. 1840, died at Petersham MA in 1907; married LUCY WEBB, born about 1840, died at Harmony 7 Oct. 1875, 35y (VRs), daughter of Benjamin and Harriet (Rhoades) Webb (Cornman Ms).

He was a grocer at Athens in 1870, but after his wife died he joined his brother Hiram at Petersham.

Child, born at Harmony:

1721. i.   PERLEY L.[9], b. in Oct. 1872.

1198. HARRIET NEWELL[8] 1842-   [560 Jonathan[7] and Lydia Drew] was born at Harmony 30 June 1842, lived at Skowhegan ME in 1910; married first 29 Nov. 1861 JOHN HOYT, born at Vienna ME, died in 1882; married second at Skowhegan 26 May 1910 as his third wife NELSON S. TOWLE, born about 1840, son of William and Sarah (McCrillis) Towle (ME VRs; Cornman Ms).

Children (**Hoyt**):

    i.   ALBERT H., b. 12 Mar. 1863.
    ii.   ADRITH, b. 15 July 1874.

1199. LEONARD HATHAWAY[8] 1844-1930 [560 Jonathan[7] and Lydia Drew] was born at Harmony 18 Sept. 1844, died at Athens 17 Dec. 1930, 86y 3m 1d; married at Athens 3 Nov. 1866 MARY ANN MARBLE, born at Harmony 11 Apr. 1850, died at Athens 15 Jan. 1922, 71y 9m 4d, daughter of Frederick and Abbie (Corson) Marble (Harmony and ME VRs; Cornman Ms).

He was a farmer at Harmony in 1870, and at St. Albans ME in
1880. They moved to Petersham MA in 1887, and then to Walpole MA, where in 1900 he, Mary and Harry were in the town
almshouse. In 1911 they were living at Cambridge ME (Town
Register). Both are buried at Harmony.

Children, born at Athens:

1722.   i.   WILLARD CARR[8], b. 11 Apr. 1870.
        ii.   JOSEPHINE MAUD, b. 6 Jan. 1872; m. 1st 11 Oct.
              1890 ORRIN W. WATSON, b. West Mills (Indus-
              try) ME 18 May 1870, son of Sidney and Mary
              D. (Ladd) Watson; m. 2nd 27 Feb. 1923
              CHARLES[10] LEIGHTON [# 2072]--div. They res.
              Boston c1911. Ch. Helen Mary Watson b.
              W. Somerville MA 19 Mar. 1897.
        iii. HARRY FREDERICK, b. 13 Jan. 1875, res. Phila-
              delphia in 1910; m. 1 Oct. 1906 RILLA BELLE[9]
              LEIGHTON, b. Athens 13 Feb. 1872, dau. of
              Hiram and (Laura) Maria (Dore) Leighton
              [# 1196]. They also res. Roxborough and
              Somerville MA, and Braddock PA   He was a
              veterinarian.

1200. MARY E.[8] 1849-1948 [560 Jonathan[7] and Lydia Drew]
was born at Harmony 19 May 1849, died in 1948 (GS); married
at Athens 3 Nov. 1866 DAVID DAVIS, born at Harmony in 1842,
died at Cornville ME 5 Feb. 1907, son of Luther and Mary
(Smith) Davis (ME VRs; Cornman Ms; Cornville Town Register,
1912).
In 1850, she was listed as Sylvina, aged 1. Davis served
in Co. C, 13th ME Inf. Rgt., and in Co. K, 30th ME (GS).
Both are buried in Mount Rest Cemetery, Athens.

Children (**Davis**), perhaps others:

i.   CLARENCE LELAND, res. Roxbury MA in 1912.
ii.   JENNIE E., b. in 1872, d. in 1892; m. J. EDWARD
      CLEVELAND, b. in 1865, d. in 1928 (GS).
iii. WALTER E., b. c1890 (18 yrs. after Jennie), res.
      Roxbury in 1912.

1201. JOSEPH[8] 1850-1924 [560 Jonathan[7] and Lydia Drew] was
born at Wellington ME 6 Aug. 1850, died at Harmony 31 Jan.
1924, 73y 4m 15d; married first 8 Oct. 1874 ALBERTA M.
[Bertie] MARBLE, born at Harmony in 1857 (23 in 1880), died
there 10 July 1913, 55y, daughter of Josiah and Julia (Dyer)
Marble--divorced in 1894; married second at Athens 26 May
1895 SARAH M. [Sadie] YORK, born there 7 July 1865, died
there 12 Apr. 1930, 64y 9m 5d, daughter of Eben and Jane
(Potter) York (Harmony and Me VRs; Cornman Ms). Burials are
in Mount Rest Cemetery, Athens.
He was a farmer. In 1880 he and Alberta were living with
her parents at Harmony. After their divorce she married second at Harmony 1 Oct. 1894 Henry H. Lawrence.
In 1900, Joseph's household at Athens included his step-son
Frank York, born in Nov. 1888; the family lived at Harmony in
1911 (Harmony Town Register 1911-1912).

Children by Alberta, born at Harmony:

      i.   MARTHA M.^{9} [Mattie], b. 30 Apr. 1884 (GS), d.
            Harmony 29 May 1904, 20y 29d (VRs); unm.
1723. ii.   LEON D. H., b. 29 Sept. 1890.

1202. LEVI^8 1823-   [561 Joseph^7 and Betsey Wray] was
born at Harmony 3 Nov. 1823; married first LYDIA ---- , born
about 1825 (25 in 1850); married second MARGARETTA (----)
[?Sterling], born in England in Apr. 1846.
In 1860 he was a merchant at Harmony. In 1880 he and Mar-
garetta were listed at Dodge Center MN, his household includ-
ing Fred, 22, and Sterling step-children Harrison A., born in
IL in Dec. 1868, and Fannie, b. in IL about 1871. His widow
Margaretta was living at Dodge Center in 1900 with her son
Harrison and her daughter Alice.

Children by Lydia, probably born at Harmony:

      i.   FRANCES^9, b. c1845 (5 in 1850), d.y.
      ii.   LLEWELLYN, b. c1848 (1 in 1850), d. 5 Aug.
            1850, 2y (GS, North Rd. Cemetery, Harmony),
1724. iii. FREDERICK E., b. in Oct. 1857.
      iv.   FRANCES, b. c1863, d. 1 Aug. 1870, 6y 7m (GS).

Child by Margaretta, born in MN:

      v.   ALICE, b. in May 1883.

1203. JOSEPH^8 1828-1887 [561 Joseph^7 and Betsey Wray] was
born at Harmony ME 23 Feb. 1828, died 1 Nov. 1887, 60y 8m
(GS); married MARTHA S. BRADEEN, born about 1835, died 1 Oct.
1888, 53y 9m (GS). (On her son George's death record she was
named Martha Pendexter.) Burials are in Gilead Cemetery.
They lived at Hudson ME; in 1870 his mother Betsey, 67, was
listed with them. They later lived at Gilead ME.

Children:

      i.   CHARLES A.^{9}, b. c1855 (15 in 1870), d. Gilead
            8 Feb. 1895, 38y (1896, GS); unm.
1725. ii.   JOHN ADAMS, b. 17 Dec. 1857.
1726. iii. GEORGE EDWARD, b. 2 Nov. 1860.
      iv.   ALICE, b. c1866 (4 in 1870), d. Shelburne 18
            May 1891, 24y (GS).
      v.   HOWARD, b. c1871 (9 in 1880), d. in 1896 (GS).
      vi.   CELIA EVELYN, b. c1878 (2 in 1880); m. Raymond
            ME 23 May 1896 CHARLES HENRY COLE of Shel-
            burne, b. there c1869, son of Charles and
            Ellen (Stinchfield) Cole.

1204. WARREN CHARLES^8 1833-1922 [561 Joseph^7 and Betsey
Wray] was born at Harmony 25 Aug. 1833 (at Garland 15 Aug.,
per pension file; Aug. 1841 in 1900 census), died at Bangor
ME 26 Apr. 1922, 90y 8m 11d; married ELIZA O. KNOX, born at
Bradford (or Corinna) ME 30 Dec. 1832, died at Bangor 24
Sept. 1914, daughter of J. H. and M. B. (Champion) Knox (town
and ME VRs).

They were living at Harmony in 1860, where he was a shoe-
maker. He was enrolled 29 Aug. 1862 in Co. D, 20th ME Inf.
Rgt., and transferred to the 16th Rgt., Volunteer Reserve
Corps 11 Sept. 1863, after suffering sunstroke at Falmouth
VA. He understood that transfer to be a discharge, and left
for home 17 Feb. 1864. His application for a pension was
rejected 1 Oct. 1897 because he was recorded as a deserter
(NA-MSR #1002,793).
     In 1880 he and Eliza were living at Old Town ME; he was at
Kenduskeag in 1898 (pension file). In 1900, Warren was
listed as a boarder at Old Town, but he and Eliza were also
listed at Bangor, living with George Williamson.

Children, perhaps others:

    i.   DORA M.^{9}, b. Harmony 17 Oct. 1862; m. 1st
             Bangor 3 July 1886 STEPHEN McKINNON; m. 2nd
             Bangor 27 Feb. 1901 JOHN F. TODD, b. Dedham
             ME in 1857, son of Benjamin P. and Martha
             (Parsons) Todd.
    ii.   ETTA, b. c1870 (10 in 1880).
    iii. ROSE B., b. Des Moines IA (Harmony VRs) 16
             Apr. 1872 (7 in 1880).

1205. ALEXANDER^8 1831-   [562 Ephraim^7 and Judith
Willey] was born at Harmony 1 Aug. 1831, lived at Levant ME
in 1900; married 16 Nov. 1856 LORENDA J. GARLAND, born at
Newburgh 30 Apr. 1831, died a widow at Bangor 14 Mar. 1905,
73y 10m 14d, daughter of Joseph and Mary (Brackett) Garland
(Garland Gen., 96; records of Theron Clement; ME VRs).
     In 1860 they were at Greenfield ME, sharing a house with
William and Lovina Garland, and in 1870 in their own home
there: in 1880 they were listed at Tp 32 (near Greenfield),
and in 1900 at Levant. He was a farmer. His wife was also
called Lucinda and Lorinda.

Children, probably all born at Greenfield:

         i.   FLORA^9, b. c1858 (Floraetta, 12 in 1870).
1727. ii. ADELIA JANE, b. 1 Apr. 1860; m. HOWARD WESTON.
1728. iii. MARILLA J., b. in Mar. 1865; m. EARL MANN.
         iv. HORACE, b. c1868 (2 in 1870).
1729. v.   WILLIAM ALBERT, b. 13 July 1875.

1206. CLARENCE ASHLEY^8 1849-1915 [564 David^7 and Laura
Evans] was born at Waterville ME in Feb. 1849, died there 12
Feb. 1915, 66y 8d; married at Port Clyde ME int. 26 Dec. 1876
OCTAVIA MASTERS JORDAN, born at Bath ME 17 Mar. 1850, died at
Thomaston 25 Aug. 1935, daughter of George and Betsey (Mas-
ters) Jordan (town and ME VRs).
     Col. Leighton in 1893 purchased the Hathaway Shirt Co. in
Waterville, control of which at his death went to his son.
He was buried at Thomaston.

Child, born at Portland:

    i.   EDWARD KAVANAUGH^9 [Ned], b. 18 Sept. 1878, d.
             Belleair FL 20 Feb. 1953; m. Rockland ME 18
             Aug. 1903 WINIFRED LOUISE SPEAR, b. there 21

Jan. 1880, d. 8 Sept. 1953, dau. of Fred R.
and Clara L. (Furbush) Spear. No ch.
Grad. of Bowdoin in 1901, he was pres. and
treas., Hathaway Shirt Co. He sold his
interest in 1932 but continued as board
chairman until his death. He res. Rockland;
he d. while on vacation (obit.; alumni file,
Bowdoin College).

1207. (ELIJAH) FISHER[8] 1842-1923 [568 Elijah[7] and Isabel
McNally] was born at Cambridge ME 11 July 1842, died there 23
Aug. 1923, 81y 1m 12d; married there 5 Jan. 1863 LOUISA
FRANCES ROGERS, born there 20 July 1846, died there 30 Aug.
1919, 73y 1m 10d, daughter of Gardner and Elvira (Little-
field) Rogers (town and ME VRs; records of Regina Turgeon
Leighton). Burials are in the Village Cemetery, Cambridge.
Fisher was a farmer at Cambridge. In 1880 his mother Isa-
bel, 76, was in his household.

Children, born at Cambridge:

	i.	LUCY BELL[9], b. 19 Oct. 1866, d. 28 July 1870.
1730.	ii.	JAMES LOREN, b. 27 July 1868.
	iii.	LOIS, b. 2 June, d. 28 July, 1870.
	iv.	LUCY ELLEN, b. 11 July 1871, d. Hartland ME 11 June 1957; m. Dexter 7 Jan. 1903 DANIEL C. PACKARD, d. Cambridge 31 Dec. 1936, son of John T. and Irene (Cole) Packard. No ch.
	v.	IRA, b. 11 June 1874, d. 5 Feb. 1876.
1731.	vi.	ELIJAH, b. 7 Aug. 1877.
	vii.	LENA FRANCES, b. 5 Jan. 1887, d. Hartland 4 Feb. 1981, 94y; unm. (BDN obit.)

1208. HENRY TIBBETTS[8] 1830-1915 [569 Henry[7]] was born at
Portville, Cattaraugus Co. NY 1 Apr. 1830, died at Ransom,
Ness Co. KS 15 Feb. 1915, 84y 10m 14d; married 28 Sept. 1852
EMELINA BARLOW, born at Portville 13 Apr. 1832, died at Ransom 11 Feb. 1915, daughter of Jonathan and Olive (Geer) Barlow (George Barlow, Ancestry and Descendants of Jonathan Barlow and Plain Rogers [Brooklyn NY, 1891], 143-4; clipping of
their joint obituary). On his death certificate his father's
name was shown as Solomon.
He was a farmer. In 1853, they settled in OH. He served
as sergeant, Co. H, 129th OH Inf. Rgt., in 1863. They moved
on to Marshall MO in 1868, McPherson Co. KS in 1874, and
finally to Ness Co. in 1886.
Their obituary listed their children, and included as sur-
vivors Mrs. John Sunley of Ransom and Mrs. H. S. Haag of
Corning CA.

Children, all but last born in OH:

	i.	MARY ADELL[9], b. 25 June 1853, d. in OH 16 May 1856.
1732.	ii.	FRANKLIN, b. 18 Apr. 1855.
	iii.	FLORENCE JANE, b. 6 July 1858; unm. in 1886.
1733.	iv.	MARIAM, b. 11 Sept. 1862; m. NEWTON GIFFIN.
	v.	LAURA OLIVE, b. in MO 20 Sept. 1874, d. in KS 13 Apr. 1876.

1209. HENRY MARTIN[8] 1824-1903 [570 Ephraim[7] and Hannah
Brainard] was born at Parkman ME 20 Nov. 1824, died at
Augusta ME 22 Nov. 1902, 78y 1d; married there 16 June 1856
MARTHA HAMLIN PAGE, born there 20 Sept. 1825, died there 1
Apr. 1915, 89y 6m 12d, daughter of Levi and Mary Craig (Ham-
lin) Page (town VRs; Kingsbury, Kennebec County, 1:476-7;
H Franklin Andrews, Hamlin Family [Exira IA, 1902], 899;
records of Helen Van Dyke). Burials are in the Forest Grove
Cemetery.
He joined the CA gold rush in 1850, and ran a profitable
livery stable. He was kicked on the hip by a wild horse, and
had to use a cane thereafter. He returned to Augusta, married and built a large house on Coombs Mill Road (now renamed
Leighton Road). He had an extensive farm, where he had an
orchard of over 300 trees and raised cattle and sheep.

Children, born at Augusta:

    i.   SUSAN HAMLIN[9], b. 6 May 1857, d. Augusta 30
          May 1902; married there 14 June 1888 ROSCOE
          E. PENNEY, b. in May 1862. In 1900 they
          lived at Augusta without ch.
   ii.   CHARLES SULLIVAN, b. 13 June 1862, d. Manches-
          ter ME 21 July 1908, 46y, suicide by gunshot.

1210. ESTHER C.[8] 1831-   [570 Ephraim[7] and Hannah Brain-
ard] was born at Parkman 1 May 1831; married at Augusta 27
June 1855 JOHN P. ANKERLOO. His name was spelled Ancarloo on
his marriage record, but also appeared in other records as
Ankaloo and Ancholov (town VRs; Cornman Ms).
He was a dyer, born in Sweden. In 1859 the Bangor city
directory listed Ankerloo & Leighton Co., a dye-house. He
sold his dyeshop, and went to Manchester NH where he joined
Amoskeag Mills.

Children (**Ankerloo**), per Cornman Ms:

    i.   ETTA, res. Manchester; m. WILL GILMAN.
   ii.   JOHN.

1211. CHARLOTTE BRADFORD[8] 1837-1908 [571 Isaac[7] and Pamelia Lancaster] was born at Augusta ME 30 Apr. 1837, died at
Chadron NE 6 Aug. 1908; married at Dayton, Washington Co. IA
8 June 1856 (county VRs) ELNATHAN W. CARPENTER (Cornman Ms).

Children (**Carpenter**):

    i.   STEPHEN WINCHESTER.
   ii.   MARY MARIE; m. ---- HAMILTON.

1212. STEPHEN TIBBETTS[8] 1839-1914 [571 Isaac[7] and Pamelia
Lancaster] was born at Parkman 6 Feb. 1839, died at Iowa City
IA 15 Apr. 1914; married in Washington Co. IA 12 Nov. 1873
JANE WELLMAN, born at Newport IN 22 Aug. 1853, died at Iowa
City 11 Jan. 1936, daughter of Joseph and Lucy (McDonald)
Wellman (records of descendants Helen Van Dyke and Golda L.
Jenkinson).

As a child he went to IA with his family, and settled at Wellman, named for his wife's father. He served from 24 Sept. 1861 to 17 July 1865 in Co. C, 11th IA Inf. Rgt., taking part in battles at Shiloh, Vicksburg, and Atlanta, and in Sherman's march through Georgia. He became a farmer and stock-raiser. In 1879 he took up 160 acres in SD, but did not settle there (Portrait and Biographical Album of Washington County, Iowa [Chicago, 1887], 419; George W. Kingsbury, History of Dakota Territory [Chicago, 1915], 5:996; Washington Co. VRs).

Children, born at Wellman:

      i.   ELMER ALLEN^9, b. 8 Nov. 1874, d. Iowa City 1 Feb. 1948; m. Evans IA 2 Jan. 1902 ISABELLE MARTIN, b. Durham, England, 1 Oct. 1875, d. 10 Aug. 1926, dau. of Walter and Louise Martin. They adopted a ch. Dudley Orin. Elmer was a teacher and merchant, listed at Des Moines in 1900.

1734.   ii.   ESTHER INEZ, b. 31 Oct. 1876; m. LEONARD J. SMITH.

1735. iii. WALTER LANE, b. 10 Dec. 1877.
1736.   iv. WILBUR STEPHEN, b. 8 May 1881.
1737.   v. ISAAC WELLMAN, b. 16 July 1885.
1738.   vi. MORRIS MORGAN, b. 4 Aug. 1887.
1739. vii. GOLDA ERA, b. 23 Jan. 1890; m. HARRY ROGERS JENKINSON.
1403. viii. LEWIS LANCASTER, b. 15 July 1892.

1213. MARIAM JORDAN^8 1842-1907 [571 Isaac^7 and Pamelia Lancaster] was born in Cattaraugus Co. NY 20 (or 30) Mar. 1842, died at Wellman IA 6 Mar. 1907; married at Dayton Mills IA 1 Jan. 1861 THOMAS JEFFERSON ALLEN, born in Franklin Co. IN 8 Nov. 1836, died at Wellman 6 Apr. 1923 (records of descendant Helen Van Dyke).

Children (**Allen**), born in Washington Co. IA:

      i. SEREPTA, d.y.
     ii. CLARA BELLE, b. Dayton Mills 10 June 1864, d. Wellman 22 Jan. 1950; m. 1st 27 Feb. 1883 JOHN POLAND, d. 1 Aug. 1883; m. 2nd 7 Mar. 1888 NORTON HENRY MESSENGER, b. Green Tp IA 22 Apr. 1855, d. Poweshiek Co. IA 28 July 1936, son of William H. and Laura Abigail (Thayer) Messenger.
   iii. BERTHA MAY, b. 13 Dec. 1866, d. 27 Sept. 1932; m. 20 Mar. 1889 WILLIAM L. ROMINE.
    iv. ALICE ANNETTE, b. 19 Mar. 1869, d. 13 Dec. 1932; m. 19 June 1895 J. E. TURNIPSEED.
     v. ADA ESTELLE, b. 25 Nov. 1871, d. 9 Jan. 1947; m. 17 Oct. 1894 WILLIAM M. McKINLEY.
    vi. ERNEST LEIGHTON, b. 24 July 1874, d. 8 July 1950.
   vii. GEORGIA, d.y.
  viii. JOHN EVERETT, b. 8 June 1881, d. 8 Feb. 1963; m. 1st CLARA BICKFORD; m. 2nd MAUD MIRES.
    ix. THOMAS GLEN, b. 29 Nov. 1884, d. 11 June 1952; m. 22 Oct. 1906 EMMA MAE PERRIN, b. 29 Mar. 1887, d. 13 Aug. 1941.

1214. DELPHINA ANN[8] 1856-1919 [571 Isaac[7] and Pamelia Lancaster] was born in Washington Co. IA 17 Oct. 1856, died 22 Sept. 1919; married at Wellman IA 29 Sept. 1887 ALLEN NICHOLS McELWAIN, born at Davenport IA 19 July 1856, died at Ainsworth IA 7 Dec. 1940 (records of Helen Van Dyke).

Children (**McElwain**):

i.   ETHEL MAE, b. 7 Feb. 1882; m. 26 Nov. 1913 GEORGE
        FRANCIS TROTTER, b. 5 Oct. 1881, d. 1 Nov. 1966.
ii.   HOWARD LEIGHTON, b. 24 July 1895; m. in Sept. 1941
        MARY SCOTT TRANCIN.

1215. JAMES C.[8] 1827-1905 [572 Simeon[7] and Elizabeth LeBaron] was born at Exeter ME 20 Feb. 1827, died at Easton MA 16 June 1905; married first at Augusta ME 3 Nov. 1851 ELIZA[8] LEIGHTON, born about 1822, died at Augusta 5 Dec. 1860, daughter of David and Celia (Burden) Leighton [# 579]; married second at Boston 19 Dec. 1861 HANNAH HALLAN, born in NY in June 1834 (1900 Easton census), daughter of William and Mary Hallan (records of Lois Ware Thurston; town VRs). He served in the Union army during the Civil War.

Adopted child:

--   GEORGE FRANK, b[9] So. Easton MA in July 1884;
        m. 1st ELLA B. LEIGHTON [# 1218]--div.; m.
        2nd Augusta 15 Feb. 1919 ALICE G. WHITEHOUSE,
        b. Pittsfield in 1901, dau. of Arthur White-
        house. Ch. Raymond Edward b. 11 Aug. 1920,
        and Clarence George b. 20 Oct. 1921.
        Alice m. 2nd Augusta 13 May 1923 Fred A.
        Groves

1216. SILAS FREDERIC[8] 1829-1876 [572 Simeon[7] and Elizabeth LeBaron] was born at Exeter 24 Jan. 1829, died at West Gardiner ME 30 Mar. 1876, 47y; married at Augusta 3 Aug. 1851 (Bible) AMANDA MARY FRANCES BEAN, born at Readfield ME 15 Apr. 1833, died at West Gardiner 10 July 1910, 77y 2m 25d, daughter of Joshua O. and Abigail M. (Chesley) Bean (town VRs; records of descendant Lois Ware Thurston, including his family Bible). Burials are at Hallowell ME.

He enlisted 30 Apr. 1861 in Co. E, 3rd ME Inf. Rgt., and served at the battle of Bull Run; he was wounded in the arm at Gettysburg in 1863, and was hospitalized until his discharge 28 June 1864. He re-enlisted 20 Sept. 1864 in Co. A, 9th ME Inf. Rgt., and was discharged disabled 26 June 1865 (NA-MSR).

He bought a home at Hallowell in 1866, and in 1868 he and Amanda moved to a house Amanda had purchased at West Gardiner. He died intestate; Amanda was granted administration 24 Apr. 1876.

Amanda married second at West Gardiner 4 Nov. 1876 as his third wife Benjamin F. Haines, who died 10 July 1879. She then married third at Gardiner 28 Aug. 1880 Sanford Brann; after they were divorced in 1885, she resumed the name Leighton. In 1900 she was living at Litchfield with her daughter Eva.

Children:

1741.   i.   EVA ESMERILDA^9, b. Augusta 4 Mar. 1853; m.
               FORREST T. HARRIMAN.
         ii.   WILLIAM C., b. Augusta 22 July, d. 5 Oct.,
               1854.
1742.   iii. FLORA GENEVA, b. W. Gardiner 21 July 1857; m.
               GEORGE W. SPEAR.
         iv.   EUGENE P., b. Manchester (Bible) 24 Nov. 1860,
               d. Augusta 13 July 1861, 9m (VRs).
         v.   HERBERT L., b. Hallowell 6 June 1867, d. there
               14 Aug. 1868, 10m.
1743.   vi.   ALBERT LeBARRON, b. W. Gardiner 28 Oct. 1869.

1217. LYDIA^8 1832-1861 [572 Simeon^7 and Elizabeth LeBaron]
was born at Exeter 5 Sept. 1832, died at Augusta 2 Apr. 1861,
29y 7m; married there 10 Mar. 1855 NATHANIEL G. CHURCH, born
at Canaan ME about 1825, died at Augusta 9 Aug. 1863, 38y,
son of Randall Church (Augusta VRs; Cornman Ms).
   Church had married first 18 June 1848 Margaret Powers, and
married third 26 Oct. 1861 Mrs. Hannah M. Haines.

Child (**Church**), born at Augusta:

i.   LYDIA JANE, b. 17 Nov. 1857, res. Pasadena CA; m.
      Belgrade 11 Mar. 1876 FRANK EVERETT CLEMENT, b.
      there 22 Jan. 1855, son of Harrison G. and Sally W.
      (Perry) Clement (Percival Wood Clement, Ancestors
      and Descendants of Robert Clements [Philadelphia,
      1927], 2:741).

1218. AARON^8 1834-1918 [572 Simeon^7 and Elizabeth LeBaron]
was born at Parkman (per death record) 1 Nov. 1834, died at
Augusta 28 Nov. 1918, 88y 27d; married first at Gardiner 17
Dec. 1863 ELIZABETH J. [Lizzie] WILKINSON, born at West Gar-
diner about 1841, died at Augusta 17 Oct. 1868, daughter of
S. G. and Betsey Wilkinson; married second at Augusta 18
Sept. 1878 RUTH FOSS, born at Rome ME 19 Dec. 1857, died at
Augusta 7 June 1913, daughter of Eben and Dorcas (Clement)
Foss (town VRs; records of Lois Ware Thurston). Burials are
in Mt. Pleasant Cemetery.
   His birth was listed in Exeter records as 1 Nov. 1830; he
was 34 at Augusta in 1870 and 45 in 1880. The 1900 Augusta
census showed him as born in Nov. 1825. His mother Betsey,
73, lived with him in 1880.
   He served 14 June 1861 to 2 Dec. 1862 in Co. I, 3rd ME Inf.
Rgt., and was listed as a pensioner at Augusta on the 1890
census schedule.

Children by Lizzie:

1744.   i.   LEWIS M.^{9}, b. Augusta 17 Nov. 1867.
1745.   ii.   HERBERT E., b. Gardiner c1868.

Children by Ruth, born at Augusta:

         iii. FRANK, b. c1879 (11/12 in 1880; b. in Jan.
               1880 per 1900 census).

iv. ARTHUR H., b. 27 Aug. 1881; m. Augusta 29 Nov.
     1911 MYRTLE (STRATTON) Doyle, b. Sidney ME
     c1877, dau. of Charles A and Georgia E.
     (Barrows) Stratton. Ch. MELVIN ARTHUR[10] b.
     12 Apr., d. 29 Apr., 1913. Myrtle had m. 1st
     Augusta 5 May 1893 George A. Doyle.
v.   IDA MAE, b. in Jan. 1884; m. 1st Augusta 27
     June 1906 BERNARD G. PIERCE, b. Greenwood ME
     c1877, son of Isaac N. and Mary (Emerson)
     Pierson--div.; m. 2nd Augusta 28 Apr. 1914
     FRANK E. PAGE, b. Wiscasset c1886, son of
     Jerry H. and Gussie (Cookson) Page.
vi. ELLA BESSIE, b. 20 June 1885; m. 1st Augusta 9
     Dec. 1903 GEORGE FRANK LEIGHTON, adopted son
     of James Leighton [# 1215]--div. in 1907; m.
     2nd Augusta 2 Nov. 1907 FRED W. LEVIER, b.
     Oswego NY c1881, son of James P. and Emma E.
     (Guernsey) Levier; m. 3rd Sidney 21 July 1914
     FRED H. ROBINSON, b. Monmouth ME c1888, son
     of Edwin and Hattie (Daggett) Robinson--div.;
     m. 4th Augusta 11 Oct. 1919 ERNEST ESTES, b.
     Durham ME c1886, son of Alva and Mary M.
     (Curtis) Estes. Ch. by George Leighton: ROSE
     M.[10] b. Augusta 4 Feb. 1906; m. 8 Oct. 1929
     DONALD PETTINGILL.
vii. LULA A , b. 24 June 1889; m. Augusta 23 Dec.
     1911 GEORGE H. YOUNG, b. Waterville c1886,
     son of George and Georgianna (Cowin) Young.
viii. WILBUR BURLEIGH, b. 5 July 1892, d. 25 Sept.
     1918 (GS). He served in the US Army during
     World War I.

1219. (ELIZABETH) JANE[8] [Jennie] 1847-1910 [572 Simeon[7]
and Elizabeth LeBaron] was born at Augusta 5 Aug. 1847, died
there 16 Oct. 1910; married there 16 Aug. 1873 CHARLES EDWARD
NASON, baptized there 18 Oct. 1835, son of Apphia Nason
(Augusta and ME VRs).

Children (**Nason**), born at Augusta:

i.   GEORGIA H., b. 22 Feb., d. 13 Aug., 1876.
ii. BESSIE M., b. about 1882 (21 in 1903); m. Augusta 25
     Feb. 1903 CHARLES S. HILL, b. Westport ME c1880,
     son of Stephen H. and Erma (Whitten) Hill.

1220. CHARLES[8] 1822-1884 [573 Silas[7] and Mary Leighton]
was born at Augusta about 1822 (28 in 1850), died there 22
Apr. 1884, 63y 8m; married there 29 Sept. 1866 CAROLINE A.
WADE, born about 1846, died at Augusta 14 Mar. 1875, 29y 1m
(GS) (Cornman Ms; Augusta VRs). Burials are in Coombs Mill
Cemetery, North Augusta
He was a farmer, with a 75-acre homestead at Augusta and
Manchester on the Mt. Vernon Road. His will, made 24 June
1873, was proved in June 1884, with Samuel Titcomb serving as
executor; it named his wife and two children. (Julia Cornman
stated he had three blind children.)

Children, born at Augusta:

i.   LELIA L.^{9} [Lettie], born c1868 (2 in 1870).
ii. DERWOOD A., b. in 1869, d. Augusta 11 Jan.
     1894, 24y 11m 23d.

1221. (TIMOTHY) ANDREW^8 1847-1930 [574 Hiram^7 and Nancy
Sanborn] was born at Levant or Exeter in 1847, died at Bangor
13 Sept. 1930, 83y 13d; married first at Augusta 5 June 1871
SUSAN H. JACKSON, born at Rome about 1857 (23 in 1880); mar-
ried second 15 Feb. 1893 ABBIE E. ROLLINS, born at Augusta 5
Dec. 1842, died at Vassalboro ME 24 June. 1927, 83y 6m 19d,
daughter of Valentine and Mary A (Holt) Rollins (town and ME
VRs). His children's marriage records listed him as born at
Oakland ME, and her at Rome.
Timothy A , 34, was listed at Augusta in 1880 with his wife
Susie and his five children. He was a carpenter, sometimes
called T. Andrew; on his death record he was named Andrew
Timothy, recently of Albion ME. In 1900 he and Abbie joined
the Society of Friends at Vassalboro, but a year later
resigned (NEHGReg, 69[1915]:318).

Children by Susie:

i.   SUSIE E.^{9}, b. c1874 (6 in 1880); perhaps m.
      Augusta 12 Mar. 1890 WILLIAM J. LATER.
ii.   FRED A , b. c1876 (4 in 1880).
iii. ALVIN J., b. c1877 (3 in 1880).
iv.   (GYNETH) FRANK, b. c1879 (1 in 1880), res.
      Rockport ME; m. (as Frank E.) Camden ME 8
      Aug. 1910 ANNIE A. MILLER, b. there c1893,
      dau. of G. W. and Lilla M. (Prescott) Miller.
v.   SADIE MABEL, b. Augusta 19 May 1881; m. Camden
      ME 25 Jan. 1898 FRED W. GRAY, b. there c1874,
      son of A. H. and Addie (Knight) Gray.

1222. JOSEPH W.^{8} 1851-1916 [574 Hiram^7 and Nancy Sanborn]
was born at Exeter ME 31 Dec. 1851, died at Sangerville ME 24
Feb. 1916, 65y 1m 24d; married at Dexter ME 23 Dec. 1875
LAURA A. SILVER, born at Garland ME in Feb. 1855, lived at
Sangerville in 1943, daughter of Ezra S. and Deborah Silver
(town VRs). In 1900 they lived at Sangerville.

Child, born at Augusta:

i.   NORRIS SILVER^9, b. 29 Sept. 1885; m. Guilford
      ME 27 Nov. 1912 FLORA JANE STEEVES, b. Salis-
      bury NB c1890, dau. of Cyril and Mary (Hay-
      ward)$_{10}$Steeves of Sangerville. Ch. MARGARET
      LAWS^{10} b. Sangerville 10 Sept. 1912; m.
      Guilford 27 Aug. 1936 KENNETH R. BADGER, b.
      Parkman c1911, son of Ray A and Inez M.
      (Coombs) Badger.

1223. STILLMAN A.^{8} 1844-1900 [575 Warren^7 and Hannah
Rogers] was born at Corinna ME 17 Feb. 1844, died there 7
July 1900, 56y 5m; married there 14 Sept. 1867 PRUDENCE J.
[Prudie] CANNEY, born at Exeter ME in Sept. 1844, died at
Corinna 18 Oct. 1907, 62y, daughter of William and Charlotte
(Hill) Canney (Corinna VRs). Burials are in Nutter Cemetery.

He was a farmer at Sangerville in 1870, and at Corinna in
1880. In 1900 he and Prudie were inmates of the Corinna
almshouse.

Children, born at Corinna:

i.   ALICE MABEL[9], b. in 1870, d. Corinna 3 Feb.
      1881, 11y 1m 21d (GS).
ii.   FRANK W., b. in 1873 (5 in 1880), d. Corinna
      15 Sept. 1912, 38y 11m 24d, by suicide; unm.

1224.   (ELLEN) SUSAN[8] 1849-1935 [576 Lorenzo[7] and Phoebe
Nutt] was born at Corinna 16 May 1849, died there 1 June 1935
(GS); married at Dexter 31 Jan. 1866 CHARLES T. TEWKSBURY,
born 1 Dec. 1841, died 22 Feb. 1922 (GS; town VRs). Burials
are in Nutter Cemetery, Corinna.
Tewkesbury served during the Civil War in the US Navy and
in Co. C, 9th ME Inf. Rgt.

Children (**Tewksbury**), born at Corinna:

i.   LEWIS EVERETT, b. 8 Jan. 1869.
ii.   CHARLES LORENZO, b. 12 Dec. 1872.
iii. ELEANOR EDITH PEARL, b. 13 Oct. 1876.
iv.   MAURICE PORTER, b. 22 June 1881.
v.   MILDRED ELZARA, b. 26 Sept. 1890.

1225.   MERRILL D.[8] 1856-1922 [576 Lorenzo[7] and Phoebe Nutt]
was born at Corinna 12 Aug. 1856, died there 6 Apr. 1922, 65y
7m 24d; married there 25 Dec. 1879 HELENA E. [Lena] HOWARD,
born at Linneaus, Newfoundland, 27 June 1862, died at Sangerville ME 24 Apr. 1930, 67y 9m 28d (GS) (town and ME VRs).
Burials are in Nutter Cemetery, Corinna.

Children, born at Corinna:

i.   ERNEST B.[9], b. 23 Aug. 1881, d. Houlton ME 18
      July 1929, 47y 10m 26d; m. 1st RUTH S.
      DEGRASSE, b. Houlton 15 July 1884, d. there
      20 Sept. 1916, 32y 2m 5d, dau. of Woodman and
      Alice (Sealey) Degrasse; m. 2nd Dover ME 27
      Nov. 1918 ANNA G. DONOVAN, b. Houlton c1891,
      dau. of B. A. and Mary (Milton) Donovan. Ch.
      MERRILL WOODMAN[10] b. Houlton 1 Oct. 1911.
      Ernest was a druggist.
ii.   EDNA MORRELL, b. in Apr. 1883 (per 1900 cen-
      sus); m. Guilford ME 9 June 1920 JOHN GILLEN,
      b. Glenville CT c1880 (40 in 1920), son of
      Owen and Bedelia (Commody) Gillen.

1226.   ABIGAIL[8] [Abbie] 1835-   [577 John[7] and Anna] was
born at Corinna ME 4 Dec. 1835; married 9 Feb. 1865 HIRAM
PAIGE of Pittsfield ME, born 26 Jan. 1833, son of Nathan and
Sarah Ann (Lang) Paige (town VRs; Cornman Ms).
They were Quakers. They lived with their son Herbert at
Pittsfield in 1908 (Town Register); Hiram was an invalid at
the time.

Children (**Paige**):

i.   CHARLES FRANKLIN, b. 12 Nov. 1865, d. 24 Nov. 1894;
      m. 31 Dec. 1892 VONA HAM of Gilmanton NH.
ii.   HERBERT MARDEN, b. Pittsfield 13 Oct. 1867; m. SARAH
      LUELLA BUTMAN, b. Bradford ME in June 1870. He was
      a Pittsfield merchant.
iii. ANNIE LEIGHTON, b. 24 Feb. 1871; unm.
iv.   MYRTLAND LANG, b. 11 Mar. 1873, res. Danvers MA; m.
      25 Apr. 1894 ETTA MAY CHURCHILL.
v.   JESSIE GERTRUDE, b. 17 Aug. 1875; res. Lynn MA; m.
      GEORGE E. THORNELL.

1227.   EDWARD[8] 1821-1894 [579 David[6] and Celia Burden] was
born at Augusta 18 Sept. 1821, died there 18 Apr. 1894, 73y
7m 18d; married first there 3 Nov. 1851 SOPHIA H. CARLTON of
Readfield, died 8 Jan. 1867, 45y 3m (GS); married second
there 24 Oct. 1869 LAURA A. COTTLE, born at Manchester about
1850 (20 in 1870 and 42 in 1894), died at Augusta in 1927--
divorced in 1892 (Augusta VRs). Burials are in Coombs Mills
Cemetery.
    He was a farmer at Augusta. Laura married second at
Augusta 12 Nov. 1894 William M. Ware.

Children by Sophia, born at Augusta:

1746. i.   WILLARD ALLEN[9], b. in Aug. 1852.
       ii.   MARY, b. c1856 (14 in 1870), not in the 1880
             census.
       iii. PHILENDA, b. 25 Dec. 1858, d. Old Town ME (as
             Lynn Carlton) 24 June 1940; unm.

Children by Laura, born at Augusta:

       iv.   MARTELLA M., b. c1871 (9 in 1880).
       v.   GEORGE B., b. in 1876 (4 in 1880), d. Augusta
             27 Dec. 1892, 16y 5m 15d.

1228.   WILLIAM A.[8] 1827-   [579 David[7] and Celia Burden]
was born at Augusta in Aug. 1827, lived at Portland OR; married at Augusta 1 July 1857 JULIA B. HANSCOM, born in Oct.
1839, daughter of Joseph and Martha Hanscom of Hallowell ME
(Augusta VRs). In 1900 they were living at Portland with his
son Eugene.

Child born at Augusta:

1747. i.   EUGENE A [9], b. in Dec. 1858.

1229.   HORACE P.[8] 1840-1927 [579 David[7] and Celia Burden]
was born at Augusta 21 May 1840, died there 21 Feb. 1927, 86y
9m; married first at Augusta 28 July 1864 ARVILLA M. SCRIB-
NER, born in 1846, died at Augusta 16 Nov. 1872, 26y 6m,
daughter of Samuel and Mary (Pierce) Scribner; married second
there 2 Oct. 1891 CLOTHILDE RUSSELL, born about 1860, died 30
Mar. 1948, 89y 2m (GS), daughter of John and Harriet (McCobb)
Russell of Jefferson ME (Augusta and ME VRs; Cornman Ms).
Burials are in Coombs Mills Cemetery.

574   A Leighton Genealogy

Horace was a farmer at Augusta. In 1870 his mother Celia, 70, was in his household. In 1900 Horace's wife Clothilde was listed as Maria, born in Jan. 1860.

Children by Arvilla, born at Augusta:

   i.   MAURICE EVERETT[9], b. 26 Jan. 1865, d. New Sharon ME 3 May 1946, 81y 3m 7d; m. in CA (per Cornman Ms) AUGUSTA ECKWALL, b. 16 Feb. 1865, d. 22 Jan. 1911 (GS). His widow was given as Helen on his death record.

   ii. LILLIAN A., b. 12 Nov. 1867; m. 16 Nov. 1886 CHARLES B. PHILBRICK, b. Augusta in 1865, son of James M. and Frances Philbrick. Ch. Clarence b. 14 Nov. 1891.

1230.   MARY ELLEN[8] 1825-1880 [580 Edward[7] and Mary Smith] was born at Gouldsboro ME 15 May 1825, died at Augusta 23 Aug. 1880, 54y; married there 7 Jan. 1846 JAMES NEWELL WADE, born there 4 Feb. 1818, died there 2 Nov. 1902, son of James and Keziah Wade (Augusta VRs; records of descendant Edith Eastman).
Wade married second 1 May 1883 Jane McFarland.

Children (**Wade**), born at Augusta:

   i.   CHARLES H., b. 18 Nov. 1846, d. at sea 4 Mar. 1870, lost off Cape Horn.
   ii. JAMES E., b. 26 Mar. 1849, d. 10 Dec. 1917; m. 8 May 1871 AMANDA SARAH JAQUITH, b. Palermo ME 10 May 1847, dau. of Luke and Sarah (Worthen) Jaquith (Jaquith Family, 566).
   iii. GEORGE F., b. 21 June 1851; m. 7 Sept. 1872 ABBIE L. PERKINS.
   iv. HIRAM, b. 20 Aug. 1854, d. 1 Oct. 1869, 15y.
   v.   (MARY) HELEN, b. 26 July 1858.
   vi. JOHN KNOX, b. 3 Dec. 1861, d. Cheyenne WY 17 May 1892; m. there 20 Sept. 1887 KATE BRISTOL, b. Guilford CT 27 May 1865, d. Columbia SC 9 Oct. 1940, dau. of Samuel Allen and Ellen Maria (Lee) Bristol.
   vii. ADELINE ANNIE [Addie], b. 20 Jan. 1864; m. 12 Nov. 1888 EUGENE M. CHASE.

1231.   SAMUEL H.[8] 1828-1899 [582 Benjamin[7] and Lucy Luce] was born at Mount Vernon ME 24 June 1828, died at Avon ME 25 Jan. 1899, 70y 6m 25d; married first LYDIA E. WELLMAN, born about 1838 (32 in 1870), died at Belgrade 15 Feb. 1872; married second in Nov. 1872 (Belgrade int. 14 Oct.) SARAH ANN LITTLE, born 8 May 1842, died 4 Feb. 1877, daughter of Henry Wood and Eliza (Wildes) Little (Little Desc., 361); married third MARCIA A. BEAN, born at Jay ME in Aug. 1841 (per 1900 census), died at Avon ME 5 Apr. 1923, 81y (1928, GS), daughter of Dudley and Elvira (Douglas) Bean (town and ME VRs). Burials are in Greenwood Cemetery, Phillips.
He was a farmer at Belgrade in 1870, and in 1880 was living at Brunswick ME. In 1900 Marcia was living at Avon with her "son-in-law" Charles H.

Child by Lydia, born at Belgrade:

1748.   i.   FRANK HERBERT[9], b. 22 Nov. 1858.

Child by Sarah, born at Brunswick:

       ii.   (CHARLES) HENRY, b. in Jan. 1877 (per 1900
              census), res. Avon; m. W. Kennebunk 26 May
              1926 GRACE M. (NOBLE) Langley, b. there
              c1884, d. Portland 27 Jan. 1948 (GS, Avon),
              dau. of Fremont and Isabel (Richardson)
              Noble--div.

1232.   HENRY MARTIN[8] 1829-1905 [583 Nathan[7] and Miranda
Blunt] was born at Augusta ME 22 Oct. 1829 (Mt. Vernon VRs),
died at Waterville ME 5 Oct. 1905, 75y 11m 17d; married in
1853 ANNIE E. KINNEY, born at Galway, Ireland, 15 May 1835,
died at Sidney ME 22 Mar. 1905, 69y 10m 7d, daughter of Patrick R. and Mary (Tracy) Kinney (town VRs; Cornman Ms).
Burials are in Coombs Mills Cemetery, Augusta.
       He was a farmer at Sidney ME (Belgrade-Sidney Town Regis-
ter, 1904).   In 1900 their household there included two
Leighton grandchildren: NATHALIE[10] born in Feb. 1892, and
HENRY H. born in June 1893.

Children, dates and places uncertain:

       i.   GEORGE[9].
       ii.   MARY L., b. 9 June 1856, d. 27 Oct. 1890 (GS);
             m. ---- CROWELL.
       iii. LIZZIE.
       iv.   HARRIET M. [Hattie], b. c1858, d. 9 Mar. 1879,
             21y (GS).
       v.   WILLIAM N., b. c1861 (19 in 1880).
       vi.   ELLA F., b. c1866 (14 in 1880), res. Augusta;
             m. ---- REYNOLDS.
       vii. EDITH M., b. c1872 (8 in 1880); m. Sidney 29
             June 1892 CHARLES W. HAMMOND, b. there c1864,
             son of S. C. and Emily (Reynolds) Hammond.
       viii FREDERICK A., b. in May 1873, res. Lewiston in
             1900, Lisbon Falls in 1904. He was a barber.
       ix.   HERBERT M., b. Sidney 4 May 1875; m. 1st 19
             Aug. 1902 ABBIE M. MITCHELL, b. Sidney in
             1883; m. 2nd ALICE J. McAULEY, who was b.
             Lancaster Ont., Canada.
             In 1904 he was an engineer at Manchester NH.
             Ch. by Alice: VIVIAN M.[10] b. Augusta 5 Mar.
             1910.

1233.   HAMPTON W.[8] 1844-1909 [583 Nathan[7] and Miranda
Blunt] was born at Augusta 7 Mar. 1844, died at Long Beach CA
5 Sept. 1909; married at Winthrop ME 28 Mar. 1885 HELENA
THOMPSON PRESCOTT, born 9 Apr. 1851, lived at Long Beach,
daughter of John Calvin and Almira A (Thompson) Prescott
(town VRs; Cornman Ms).
       Hampton served in Co. G, 19th ME Inf. Rgt., and was wounded
at Gettysburg.
       In 1900, they were living at Riverside CA.

Children, perhaps others:

    i.   EDNA M.^{9}, b. Winthrop 17 July 1887.
    ii.   HAMPTON R., b. Trinidad CO 26 Oct. 1890; m.
        4 Dec. 1911 RUTH CRONK.

1234. HELEN LOUISA^8 1839-1919 [584 David^7 and Louisa
Leighton] was born at Cambridge ME 7 Jan. 1839, died at Guilford ME 24 Jan. 1919 (GS); married 8 Dec. 1863 HORATIO NELSON
NUTTING, born at Parkman ME 24 Mar. 1838, died at Redwood
City CA 30 Nov. 1882, son of Jesse and Betsey (Thurston) Nutting (Thurston Gen. 190; Helen's letter--Cornman Papers;
records of descendant Leighton A. Nutting). Burials are at
Guilford.
Horatio graduated from Colby College in 1863, and became a
teacher and later an attorney. He was school superintendent
and district attorney of San Mateo Co., editor of the Times
and Gazette, and mayor of Redwood City from 1874 to 1876.
Widow Helen returned to ME.

Children (**Nutting**), born at Redwood City:

    i.   LESTER CARROLL, b. 9 Sept. 1873, d. W. Roxbury MA in
        1930; m. Boston 18 Aug. 1895 FLORENCE JEANETTE
        BEARSE, b. Chatham MA 12 May 1872, d. W. Roxbury 14
        Dec. 1928, dau. of Stephen Fifield and Rebecca
        (Jackson) (Smith) Bearse.
    ii.   JESSE, b. in 1879, d. in 1960 (GS); m. IDA N. SAN-
        BORN, b. Willimantic ME 4 Mar. 1880, d. Dover-
        Foxcroft (hosp.) 7 Nov. 1925, dau. of Charles A.
        and Rose (Harrington) Sanborn--div.

1235. JAMES SULLIVAN^8 1841-1936 [584 David^7 and Louisa
Leighton] was born at Cambridge 6 Sept. 1841, died at Harmony
1 Sept. 1936, 94y 11m 25d; married first at Cambridge 30 June
1867 ELVIRA E. WATSON, born there 30 June 1850 (Bible), died
there 24 Aug. 1874, 22y 1m 24d (GS), daughter of Hiram and
Betsey (Davis) Watson; married second there 12 Nov. 1873 EVA
ANN COLE, born there 6 Mar. 1857, died there 20 Apr. 1931,
76y 1m 14d, daughter of Daniel and Angenette (Lowell) Cole
(letter and Bible records from son Fred P.--Cornman Papers;
Cambridge and ME VRs; records of Ethelyn P. Howard; Cambridge
Town Register 1911-1912). Burials are in Village Cemetery
#2, Cambridge.
He was a farmer. In 1870 he, Elvira and Fred were listed
at Cambridge with his parents.

Children by Elvira, born at Cambridge:

    i.   FRED PERLEY^9, b. 27 Nov. 1868, d. Sangerville
        16 July 1918, 49y 7m 19d; m. there 22 June
        1895 ALMEDA E. DAVIS, b. there 21 July 1872,
        dau. of George W. and Philena (Carle) Davis.
        Ch. GEORGE SULLIVAN^{10} b. Sangerville 20 June
        1896.
    ii.   (LEROY) SELVIN, b. 2 Sept. 1870, d. Parkman 29
        June 1935; m. Cambridge 3 Nov. 1899 ANNELLA
        M. [Annie] PARKER, b. Parkman in Oct. 1881,

dau. of Henry W$_{10}$and Emma (Brown) Parker.
Ch. HENRY JAMES^{10} b. 31 Aug. 1901, d. Parkman
17 May 1943; m. Dexter 1 Jan. 1920 LILLIAN
PEARL HAYDEN, b. Exeter ME c1898, dau. of
Edward and Minnie (Hoyt) Hayden: no ch.
Lillian m. 2nd William Howard Packard (Wight,
Packard Desc., 201).

Children by Eva, born at Cambridge:

iii.   ELVIRA E., b. 22 Aug. 1874, d. 5 Feb. 1962;
       m. 1st Cambridge 19 Nov. 1900 HARRY H.
       HARRIS, b. Parkman 7 Dec. 1869, d. Cambridge
       16 July 1932, son of Thomas J. and Lizzie M.
       (Allen) Harris; m. 2nd 14 Oct. 1939 FRED
       PALMER, who d. in July 1946. No ch. Harris
       was a jeweler at Hartland (Cambridge Town
       Register, 1911-1912).
iv.   VINAL SULLIVAN, b. 12 Feb. 1878, d. 21 May
       1962; m. Cambridge 6 May 1916 ANNIE E.
       (GOULD) Perkins, b. there 29 Sept. 1877, d.
       Dover-Foxcroft 13 June 1923, dau. of Joshua
       and Mary (Lyshaw) Gould. No ch. She had m.
       1st 2 Jan. 1912 Carroll E. Perkins.
v.   ALBERT H., b. 7 May 1873, d. 27 June 1962; m.
       Cambridge 13 July 1907 ALBINA G. [Bina]
       STEVENS, b. Garland 21 Nov. 1880, d. 20 Jan.
       1972, dau. of Daniel and Hadassah (Moulton)
       Stevens. No ch. Bina was divorced from a
       1st husband.
1749. vi.   MABEL EDNA, b. 1 Sept. 1880; m. HENRY TURNER,
       CLARENCE HAMILTON and RUPERT PACKARD.

1236.   LUCY JANE^8 1837-   [586 John^7 and Nancy Butter-
field] was born at Mount Vernon ME 1 Aug. 1837; married at
Readfield 20 May 1861 (Mt. Vernon int. 21 Feb. 1860) SAMUEL
STAIN JR., born at Mt. Vernon in 1831, son of Samuel and Han-
nah Stain (Cornman Ms).
   In 1850, Lucy was listed as part of George Worcester's
household. Stain married second before 1880 Divona Currier.
He was a farmer.

Children (**Stain**):

i.   Samuel, b. in 1866, d. in 1871.
ii.   Archer [Archie], b. in 1877.

1237.   TIMOTHY^8 1839-1931 [586 John^7 and Nancy Butterfield]
was born at Mount Vernon ME 29 Jan. 1839, died at Denver CO
25 July 1931; married at Mt. Vernon 14 Nov. 1867 SARAH E.
HUNTOON, born at Hallowell ME 20 Apr. 1846, died at Readfield
ME 3 May 1910, 64y 14d, daughter of Edwin and Caroline (Hep-
worth) Huntoon (town VRs; Cornman Ms). Burials are at Readfield Corner.
   Timothy served from 10 Sept. 1862 to 25 Aug. 1863 in Co. C,
21st ME Inf. Rgt. He was a farmer at Mt. Vernon; in 1880 his
household there included his mother Nancy, 60, and in 1900
his son Fred.

Children, born at Mt. Vernon:

    i.   BERTRAM EDWIN[9], b. 19 Apr. 1869, d. Lewiston
        ME 14 Sept. 1920, 51y; m. Hallowell 29 Apr.
        1893 LILLIAN M. DIXON, b. Boothbay in Jan.
        1870, dau. of John and Diana (Frost) Dixon.
        He was a carpenter at Sanford in 1900, and a
        merchant at Readfield in 1908. Lillian m.
        2nd 16 Dec. 1925 Fred D. Elliott.
   ii. FRED MARTIN, b. 13 Apr. 1875, res. Readfield;
        m. Mt. Vernon 30 June 1904 LUCIE M. PHIL-
        BRICK, b. there c1884, d. Readfield 13 Oct.
        1910, dau. of Maurice and Della L. (Carson)
        Philbrick. Ch. FREDA CAROLINE[10] b. Readfield
        26 Dec. 1906. He was a merchant.

1238. ROSCOE GREEN[8] 1845-1872 [590 Nathaniel[7] and Mary
Folsom] was born at Mount Vernon 10 Apr. 1845, died there
(Augusta VRs) 23 July 1872, 27y 3m 13d; married at Readfield
13 Oct. 1868 ELDORA C. [Dora] ROBINSON, who was appointed
administratrix of his estate 12 Aug. 1872.

Children, born at Readfield:

    i.   MYRTLE[9], b. in 1870, d. before her father.
   ii. MARCIA E., b. in Sept. 1871.

1239. EDWARD EVERETT[8] 1847-   [590 Nathaniel[7] and Mary
Folsom] was born at Mount Vernon ME 13 May 1847, lived at
Southboro MA in 1880; married at Ashland MA 16 Nov. 1869 ELLA
ANNETTE PARKER, born there 16 Dec. 1850, lived there with
Lester and Daisy in 1900, daughter of Josiah and Caroline
(Peck) Parker (Theodore Parker, (John Parker of Lexington
[Worcester MA, 1893], 298, 407; Cornman Ms).
    Edward was a carpenter, and had lived previously at Stone-
ham and Foxboro MA.

Children:

    i.   EDWARD P.[9], b. Ashland 1 Dec. 1870, res.
        Worcester MA in 1900; m. ANNIE ---- , b. in
        MA in May 1869. Ch. IVA B.[10] b. in MA 4
        Mar. 1892.
   ii. LESTER LISLE, b. Mt. Vernon 7 Nov. 1872.
  iii. DAISY G., b. Southville 21 Feb. 1881.

1240. (NATHANIEL) COREY[8] 1850-1897 [590 Nathaniel[7] and
Mary Folsom] was born at Mount Vernon 25 Feb. 1850 (VRs; 1853
in death record), died at Farmington ME 15 May 1897, 44y 2m
20d, killed in construction accident; married at Mt. Vernon
25 Dec. 1876 ELLA SAMANTHA EATON, born in July 1852, lived at
Mt. Vernon in 1908 (Town Register), daughter of Azor Webster
and Adeline (Brown) Eaton of Vienna (Cornman Ms; records of
descendant Ray Kendall).
    N. Corey was a mason and farmer. His will, made 30 Mar.
1894 and proved 28 June 1897, named his wife Ella executrix
and sole heir.

Children, born at Vienna ME:

    i.   LIZZIE MAY[9], b. 26 Sept. 1881; m. Mt. Vernon
           21 Nov. 1910 LOU M. PHILBRICK, b. there
           c1878, son of Maurice and Ella (Carson)
           Philbrick.
1750. ii.   DOLL CECIL (twin), b. 26 Sept. 1881; m. MORRIS
           J. KENDALL.

1241. ALICE BETSEY[8] 1857-   [592 Ebenezer[7] and Lucy Ann
Carr] was born at Mount Vernon 11 Nov. 1857; married there 14
Nov. 1874 WILLIAM M. TYLER, born at Vienna ME 9 July 1849,
died at Mount Vernon 19 Jan. 1905, son of James and Eliza
(Morton) Tyler (town VRs; Cornman Ms).

Children (**Tyler**), born at Mt. Vernon:

    i.   JARVIS LARUE, b. 15 May 1875; m. 21 Jan. 1903 ELSIE
         PIERCE, b. Farmington ME 29 Dec. 1877, dau. of
         Charles and Ella (Crowell) Pierce.
   ii.   LORA ALICE, b. 20 Sept. 1877, d. Montreal PQ 28 July
         1904; unm.

1242. DAVID FRANKLIN[8] [Frank] 1843-   [593 David[7]] was
born at Cambridge ME 5 Oct. 1843; married first at Abbot ME 6
Mar. 1865 (4 Mar. in Cambridge VRs) widow JEMIMA S. (COLE)
Martin, daughter of Solomon and Asenath Cole of Abbot; mar-
ried second at Cambridge 31 Aug. 1870 an ELLEN M. LEIGHTON
(VRs).

Child by Ellen, born at Cambridge:

    i.   GEORGE FRANK[9], b. 3 Jan. 1871, d. Dayton ME 26
         May 1950, 77y; m. Dexter 2 Oct. 1904 MYRTIE
         ESTELLE MERRYMAN, b. Dexter 17 Apr. 1879, d.
         in 1956, dau. of David and Lizzie (Rand)
         Merryman.

1243. EMILY[8] 1825-1905 [595 Mordecai[7] and Vesta Conant]
was born 25 in Wayne Co. NY June 1825, died at Sturgis MI 7
Feb. 1905; married 3 Feb. 1848 JAMES WREN, born 24 Dec. 1817,
died at Sturgis 8 Jan. 1900, son of Joseph and Mary Wren of
England (Cornman Ms.)

Children (**Wren**):

    i.   JAMES, b. 8 Aug. 1849.
   ii.   RANSOM L., b. in Oct. 1850; unm.
  iii.   HELEN, b. 27 Nov. 1853, d. 26 Apr. 1900; m. 23 Oct.
         1879 WILLIAM FARROW.
   iv.   CARRIE, b. 16 July 1860, d. 31 Oct. 1897; unm.

1244. NELSON[8] 1832-1863 [596 Enoch[7] and Phoebe Cowan] was
born in Orleans County NY 1 May 1832, died at Murfreesboro TN
28 Apr. 1863 while serving in Co. G, 88th IN Inf. Rgt.; married at Van Buren, Lagrange Co. IN 1 Jan. 1853 CHARLOTTE E.
DALTON, born at Geneva NY 15 Aug. 1832, died at Middlebury IN

27 Dec. 1912, daughter of John and Catherine Dalton of Albany NY (Cornman Ms).
Widow Charlotte filed for a pension at Lima 3 Mar. 1864 (NA-MSR W-125376), and the children's guardian filed 9 Mar. 1868 (WC-17-501); the applications included birthdates for the children. Charlotte married second at White Pigeon MI 9 Dec. 1867 Addison Parker of Fawn River MI, who was born in Genessee Co. NY about 1845; she married third in Lagrange Co. 3 Dec. 1879 William Bycroft.

Children, born at Scott, Lagrange Co.:

1751. i.   HENRIETTA^9, b. 25 Oct. 1853; m. JOHN PAGE.
        ii.   LOUIS EDWARD, b. 15 Aug. 1856, d. 25 Jan. 1912.
1752. iii. ANDREW JACKSON, b. 26 May 1857.
1753. iv.   JOHN JAY, b. 18 Aug. 1859.
        v.   IDA M., b. 25 Apr. 1862, d. 26 Dec. 1863.

1245. ELISHA^8 1834-   [596 Enoch^7 and Phoebe Cowan] was born in Orleans Co. NY 16 June 1834, lived in CA in 1900; married 1 May 1863 MARY J. (LINDRUM) [?Hurd], born in LA 22 Sept. 1838, died in CA 28 July 1913 (Cornman Ms).
He went to California in 1854. In 1880 his household at Pasadena, San Mateo Co., included a stepson George Hurd, 18. In 1900 he and his wife Mary were at Tp 5, San Mateo Co..

Children, born in California:

        i.   MARY ORPHA^9, b. 18 May 1864.
        ii.   EMILY ALICE, b. 7 Aug. 1866.
        iii. JESSIE FLORENCE, b. 16 July 1870; m. WILLIAM LINNON CRANDALL, son of William Osborne Crandall. Ch. Walter Leighton and Kenneth Osborne.

1246. WILLIAM WALLACE^8 1836-   [596 Enoch^7 and Phoebe Cowan] was born at Lima IN 15 Apr. 1836; married 6 Apr. 1865 JULIA MARIA STEVENS, born in IN 29 Jan. 1835, died 3 Feb. 1910, daughter of Jonathan and Sophia (Slater) Stevens (Cornman Ms). In 1880 they lived at Rock Creek, Bartholomew Co. IN; his age was given as 30. They were not listed in the 1900 IN census.

Children, born in IN:

        i.   FAY ERMINA^9, b. 6 Oct. 1873, d. 13 Oct. 1912; m. Mt. Grove MO 26 May 1911 AUSTIN FUERST, b. 19 Oct. 1876, son of Albert and Sarah V. Fuerst. Ch. Margaret Leighton b. 8 Sept. 1912.
        ii.   LINNIE, b. c1875 (5 in 1880).
        iii. MONTY L., b. c1878 (2 in 1880).

1247. CHARLES H.^{8} 1843-   [600 Israel^7 and Susan Owens] was born at Sodus, Wayne Co. NY 30 Aug. 1843, lived at Rutland, Isabella Co. MI in 1880 and 1900; married at Wakesha MI 8 Sept. 1867 MARGARET (Maggie) MARTIN, born at Bayham in

Canada 22 Apr. 1843, daughter of Thomas and Margaret (Camp) Martin (Cornman Ms; his letter-Cornman Papers).
His parents moved to a farm at Wakesha, Kalamazoo Co. MI when he was 10; in 1872 he was settled on his own farm at Rutland, Isabella Co. He was justice of peace, town clerk, school inspector and singing instructor (Isaac A. Fancher, History of Isabella County, Mich. [1911], 654).

Children, born in MI:

1754.   i.   HERBERT J.^{9}, b. Wakesha 3 Dec. 1868.
        ii.   RAYMOND, b. Wakesha 17 Sept. 1871; m. Belding
              MI 24 June 1908 INEZ REYNOLDS, b. Lincoln MI
              24 Jan. 1884, dau. of John and Comfort
              (Jewell) Reynolds.
        iii. WILBUR W., b. Rutland 19 Apr. 1874, d. there
              12 Mar. 1889.

1248.   NELSON EWANS^8 1848-   [600 Israel^7 and Susan Owens] was born at Sodus NY 2 Mar. 1848, lived at Hopkins Station MI in 1900; married 2 Oct. 1878 FRANCES MARY BUTLER, born in NY 12 Sept. 1849, daughter of John and Honore Butler (Cornman Ms).
He was taken to Wakesha MI in 1852 by his parents. After receiving his MD degree from Long Island (NY) Medical College in 1881, he practiced as a physician at Hopkins Station MI (Henry F. Thomas, History of Allegan County, Mich. [1907], 291).

Child, born at Hopkins Station:

        i.   BRUCE R.^{9}, b. 25 Mar. 1883, res. Kalamazoo.
              He received an MD degree from Western Reserve
              Univ., Cleveland, in 1912.

1249.   JOHN G.^{8} 1827-1918 [602 William^7 and Elizabeth] was born in Switzerland Co. IN 2 Feb. 1827, died at Richmond IN 14 Apr. 1918, 90y 2m 8d (VRs); married MARY JANE CROSS, born at Terre Haute IN 19 July 1838, died at Hoopston IL 8 Jan. 1878, 39y 5m 20d (records of Theda Leighton Chapman).
They lived near Castleton, Wyoming Co. IL. He settled at Uniontown KS after his wife died, but in 1880 was listed at Grant City, Vermilion Co. IL, and in 1900 at Benton MI.
His death record noted that he was born in IN, but did not name his parents. In 1860 the Stark Co. IL census listed John as aged 32 and born in OH.

Children, born in IL:

1755.   i.   CHARLES ALBERT^9, b. Wyoming Co. 29 Jan. 1856.
1756.   ii.   FRANCIS WILLIAM, b. Wyoming Co. 10 Feb. 1857.
1757.   iii. MILES EDWIN, b. Wyoming Co. 8 Mar. 1861.
        iv.   ELMER JOHN, b. Wyoming Co. 17 June 1863, d.
              Richmond IN 10 June 1931, 67y; m. FLORENCE
              (----) Moffett, b. in IN in Aug. 1878.
              They were at Benton Harbor in 1900, his step-
              son Asa Moffett, b. in IN in Mar. 1893, list-
              ed with them.

v. EDMUND ULYSSES, b. Wyoming Co. 9 June 1865, d.
Kingfisher OK[10] 3 Feb. 1947, 81y; m. ---- .
Ch. GEORGE[10], ELMER, JOHN, ZELLA, CLARENCE,
MERLE and PAULINE.

vi. MARY JANE, d. infant.

vii. KATIE E., b. c1869 (11 in 1880).

viii. ANNA LAURA, b. c1871 (9 in 1880), d. Hoopston
IL in 1879 (GS).

ix. FLORENCE, b. c1874 (6 in 1880).

1250. WILLIAM M.[8] 1829-1891 [602 William[7] and Elizabeth]
was born in Switzerland Co. IN about 1829 (31 in 1860), died
in Sanborn Co. SD 22 Aug. 1891, 62y 5m; married first at Tou-
lon, Stark Co. IL 12 Mar. 1857 MATILDA DAMON, born in 1846,
died probably at Hoopston in 1875; married second at Wyoming,
Stark Co. 22 Aug. 1875 LUCINDA REDDING, born in OH about
1849, died in 1929 (GS, Woonsocket) (records of Theda
Leighton Chapman and C. Jean Leighton).
Consent was given by J. B. Damon of Northampton, Peoria
Co., 7 Mar. 1857 for Matilda to marry; she was then only 11
years old (Stark Co. records).
He and Lucinda settled in Vermilion Co. IL in 1877; in 1880
their home was there was at Grant. They then settled at
Alpena SD. They are buried in the Eventide Cemetery at Woon-
socket SD.

Children by Matilda, born in Stark Co. IL:

i. IDA FRANCES[9], b. 24 Dec. 1857, d. 2 Sept.
1882; m. 29 Sept. 1878 WILLIAM AULT. Only
ch. Jessie d. 29 Sept. 1955; m. 1st Oscar
Lynch; m. 2nd Matthew Smith.

ii. CLARA ELIZABETH, b. 19 Sept. 1861, d. 7 Jan.
1881, 20y.

1758. iii. REUBEN ARIZONA, b. 15 Apr. 1863.
1759. iv. WILLIAM SHERMAN, b. 16 Apr. 1865.
1760. v. GEORGE DELBERT, b. 29 June 1867.
1761. vi. HERBERT ALONZO, b. in Oct. 1871.

Children by Lucinda:

vii. EVA MATILDA, b. Stark Co. 20 Feb. 1876, d. 27
Sept. 1878.

viii. ALTON AMBROSE, b. Vermilion Co. 18 Sept. 1880,
d. infant.

ix. JAMES ARTHUR, b. Vermilion Co. 1 June 1882, d.
there 4 May 1940; m. 1 Apr. 1910 GUSTA
SALTER who d. in Jan. 1963. Ch. HOMER
GILMER[10] and LYLE.

x. FREDERICK WALTER, b. Vermilion Co. 10
Nov. 1885, d. in CA in 1954; m. VERA ISABEL
---- . They lived near Los Angeles. Ch.
EVELYN[10].

1251. CAROLINE EMERY[8] 1828-   [604 Smithson[7] and Eliza
Zallolley] was born at Parkman ME 29 Dec. 1828; married at
Fairfield int. 25 Sept. 1848 HEMAN A. FOWLER, born in Waldo
Co. ME in 1824, lived at Casco, Allegan Co. MI, son of George

and Sarah (Ward) Fowler (Portrait and Biographical Record of Kalamazoo, Allegan and Van Buren Counties, Mich. [Chicago, 1892], 395).
Fowler was a merchant at Lewiston ME, and settled at Otsego MI in 1853. In 1862 he took up 160 acres of forest wilderness at Casco.

Children (Fowler), said to have been seven in all:

    i.   LLEWELLYN.
    ii. CLARENCE.
    iii. LILLIE; m. WILLIS BAKER.
    iv. ARTHUR.
    v.   ADDIE; m. M. BOWER.

1252. LEANDER A.[8] 1840-   [604 Smithson[7] and Eliza Zallolley] was born perhaps at Parkman ME in Aug. 1840; married in MI SARAH T. ---- , born there in Sept. 1849. In 1880 and 1900 they were listed at South Haven, Van Buren Co..

Children, born in MI (perhaps others):

    i.   ZELIA[9], b. c1865 (15 in 1880).
    ii. ADRIANNA R., b. in Mar. 1880.

1253. PELATIAH[8] 1823-1892 [607 Humphrey[7] and Frances Broy] was born in Switzerland Co. IN 19 Aug. 1823, died at Howard Tp, Wayne Co. IA 22 Sept. 1892, 64y 1m 3d (GS); married in Switzerland Co. (VRs) 28 Jan. 1849 MARY EWING TRUSCOTT, born in Edwards Co. IL 5 June 1829, died at Howard Tp 30 June 1916, daughter of William and Martha (Ewing) Truscott. Burials are in Medicineville, near Howard.
His will dated 9 Jan. 1890 was proved 12′ Oct. 1894 (Wayne Co. probate records). It named his wife and living children: James, Humphrey, Martha Ginn, Rose Pettit, Silas and Rachel.
He was listed as a farmer in IL censuses, 1840 and 1850; he then settled at Howard IA., where he took up 129 acres 16 Apr. 1856 (Wayne Co. land records 185:78). With his brother John he secured a permit to manufacture and sell "Johnson's Improved Folding Bedstids." He and Mary settled at York Tp (Powersville), Putnam County MO, across the state line from Wayne Co. IA
Billie L. Flora and Sharon Thorne have done extensive research on this branch of the family; Kathy Gardner has searched newspaper and court records.

Children:

1762. i.   JAMES H.[9], b. Woodford Co. IL 28 Mar. 1850.
      ii.   MARY JANE, b. 3 Feb. 1852; m. Putnam Co. MO
            1 Apr. 1869 (co. rec.) GEORGE S. WARD.
1763. iii. HUMPHREY VARNEY, b. Wayne Co. IA 20 Mar. 1855.
      iv.   WILLIAM M., b. Wayne Co. 23 Jan. 1858, d.
            there 26 Apr. 1865, 7y 3m 3d.
1764. v.   MARTHA FRANCES, b. Wayne Co. 25 Feb. 1861;
            m. GEORGE L. GINN.
      vi.   ROSE EMMA, b. Putnam Co. MO 23 Aug. 1865; m.
            SOLOMON PETIT.
1765. vii. SILAS, b. Putnam Co. 23 Mar. 1867.

viii. RACHEL LOUISA [Lid], b. Putnam Co. 23 Nov.
1870, d. 18 June 1918; m. WILLIS REUBEN
HALEY. Ch. Mary Z.

1254. JACOB[8] 1831-1899 [607 Humphrey[7] and Frances Broy]
was born at Metamora, Woodford Co. IL 1 July 1831 (GS), died
at Allerton, Wayne Co. IA 6 June 1899 (GS); married first in
Wayne Co. 8 Nov. 1855 (court rec.) NANCY JANE HARDING, born
in IN 3 Sept. 1840 (GS), died at Howard 18 Sept. 1874 (GS),
daughter of Samuel Perry and Mary (Rigen) Harding; married
second at Mendota MO 27 Feb. 1877 (pension rec.) LAURA M.
ANDERSON, born in IA 3 Dec. 1847 (GS), died Minot ND 18 Jan.
1939, 91y 1m 15d (VRs), daughter of James and ----(Probasco)
Anderson. Burials are in the Kilbourne-Rankin-Brown Cemetery
(records of Billie L. Flora and Sharon Thorne).
Jacob was drafted 6 Oct. 1864 into Co. F, 16th IA Inf.
Rgt. and discharged 19 July 1865. He was a farmer, and owner
of Maple Grove stock farm at Warren Tp, Wayne Co. IA.
He applied for a disability pension 8 Mar. 1883, then aged
52, of Allerton (NA-MSR #XC 2671-206), claiming general
debility, and a "broken and shattered constitution." His
widow Laura of Allerton filed for her pension 26 June 1899
(NA-MSR #701 563).

Children by Nancy (besides several who died in infancy):

1766.   i.   SAMUEL HUMPHREY[9], b. St. John's, Putnam Co.
MO, 1 Sept. 1856.
1767.   ii.   (WILLIAM) DAVID, b. Warren Tp, Wayne Co. IA 27
Jan. 1859.
1768.   iii. MARY ELIZABETH, b. in IA 2 Mar. 1863; m. ELIAS
JOHNSON.
--   (KALIDA) ELTON, step-son, b. c1862, res. Minot
ND; m. BELLE LOCKMAN. He received an LLB.
from the Univ. of IA in 1886, and was an
attorney and real estate agent. Ch. Roy,
William and Inez.
Ella (Leighton) Miller, when interviewed by
Billie Flora in Mar. 1986, stated Elton was
the son of Laura Anderson, and was named
Leighton although not legally adopted.

1255. WILLIAM[8] 1833-1886 [607 Humphrey[7] and Frances Broy]
was born in Woodford Co. IL in 1833 (17 in 1850), died prob-
ably at Florence CO 23 Jan. 1886; married in Putnam Co. MO
(VRs) 8 Nov. 1857 NANCY ELLEN GARRETT, born at Newmarket IN
18 July 1839, lived at Hesperus, LaPlata Co. CO in 1902.
Nancy married second at Halfrock MO 16 Nov. 1890 (VRs) James
M. Lyon (research by Billie Flora and Kathy Gardner)
He enlisted 15 Aug. 1862 as sergeant in Co. F, 34th IA Inf.
Rgt. Widow Nancy filed for a pension for herself and five
children under 16 (NA-MSR #185-77-8).
In 1870 he was a blacksmith at Clay Tp, Sullivan Co. MO; he
later settled in Greenwood Co. KS.

Children, last five from pension application:

i.   JACOB A.[9], b. Wayne Co. IA c1859 (12 in 1870).
ii.   ANNIE J., b. Wayne Co. c1863 (7 in 1870).

iii. LUCY F., b. Wayne Co. c1865 (5 in 1870).
iv.   MARY C., b. Wayne Co. c1867 (3 in 1870).
v.   THOMAS E., b. Sullivan Co. MO c1869 (8/12 in
      1870).
vi.   (MARCELLUS) WALTER, b. Greenwood Co. KS 19 May
      1873.
vii. LYDIA M., b. Greenwood Co. 29 June 1875.
viii. EMILY E., b. Greenwood Co. 11 July 1878.
ix.   MAUD D., b. Greenwood Co. 5 Jan. 1881.
1769. x.   JAMES MILTON (called Robert in pension file),
      b. Florence CO 29 Feb. 1884.

1256. JOHN BROY[8] 1836-1920 [607 Humphrey[7] and Frances
Broy] was born in Woodford Co. IL 14 Dec. 1835, died at St.
Louis MO 4 Apr. 1920; married 29 Aug. 1855 MARY ANN TRUNNEL,
born in Brown Co. OH 26 Feb. 1839, died at St. Louis 9 June
1907, daughter of Bradford S. and Lorinda (Sargent) Trunnel
(family and Bible records from descendants Beulah Koehler and
Alpha Keller Gardiner). He is buried in the national cemetery at Jefferson Barracks.
    He served in a MO infantry regiment during the Civil War.
He was a railroad engineer.

Children:

i.   (FRANCES) LORINDA[9], b. in IA 22 Nov. 1856, d.
      St. Louis 12 Sept. 1924; m. there 24 May 1883
      JOHN DOBLER. Ch. Charles and Eva [Effie].
ii.   SARAH ELIZABETH, b. in IA 22 Mar. 1859, d. 29
      Mar. 1862, 3y 7d.
iii. NOAH, b. in IA 2 Apr. 1861, d. St. Louis 31
      May 1929; m. there 8 Jan. 1884 CLARA ---- .
      Ch. FRED[10], EDWARD, WILLIAM, NOAH, PEARL,
      THOMAS, and LORINDA.
iv.   (MARY) EMILY, b. IA 13 July 1864, d. St. Louis
      24 Jan. 1936; m. there 18 July 1882 JOHN
      PETERS. Ch. Elmer, Ruth, Ethel, Lydia,
      Emmett, Norma and Kenneth.
v.   WILLIAM THOMAS, b. MO 19 Oct. 1866, d. St.
      Louis 18 Sept. 1880.
vi.   CHARLES BROY, b. MO 16 May 1869, d. St. Louis
      8 Apr. 1920; m. there 29 Sept. 1898 ANNA
      MEEK. Ch. CHARLES[10], JOHN B. and MAY.
vii. FRANKLIN MILLARD [Frank], b. MO 2 Apr. 1871,
      d. St. Louis 22 Apr. 1929; m. MINNIE ---- .
      Ch. HARRY[10]. In 1900 Frank was at Ft. Casey
      WA, a pvt. in Co. B., 3rd Artillery Rgt.
1770. viii. JOHN COMBY, b. Jefferson City MO 10 Sept.
      1873.
ix.   AUGUSTA, b. in MO 16 May, d. 23 June, 1876.
x.   BERTHA MAY, b. St. Louis 11 May 1878, d. Oak-
      land CA in 1955; m. St. Louis 29 July 1897
      BERT COOMBS. Ch. Frank and Betty.
xi.   LYDIA ANN, b. St. Louis 28 July 1880, d. there
      7 Jan. 1959; m. there 9 July 1900 WILLIAM
      KELLER. Ch. Florence, Charles and Alpha
      Irene. Alpha, b. 11 Feb. 1911, res. Woodbury
      MN in 1987; m. Eddie J. Gardiner, b. 8 July
      1904, d. 22 Feb. 1978.

1257.   RACHEL J.[8] 1837-   [607 Humphrey[7] and Frances Broy] was born in Woodford Co. IL about 1837 (13 in 1850); married first there 7 Apr. 1853 (VRs) ANDREW M. DEWEY, born in OH, died about 1869; married second JOHN STINE, born in OH about 1815 (65 in 1880).
In 1870 she and her children were in her parents' household in Wayne Co. IA; in 1880 John and Rachel Stine, along with Albert and Jacob Dewey, lived with Humphrey at Wright Tp, Wayne Co.

Children (**Dewey**), born in IA (1870 census):

i.	SABRINA F., b. c1855 (15 in 1870).
ii.	GEORGE W., b. c1857 (13 in 1870).
iii.	JOHN V., b. c1859 (11 in 1870).
iv.	MARY A., b. c1864 (6 in 1870).
v.	ALBERT M., b. c1866 (4 in 1870).
vi.	JACOB U., b. c1869 (1 in 1870).

1258.   HUMPHREY VARNEY[8] 1839-1890 [607 Humphrey[7] and Frances Broy] was born in Woodford Co. IL 21 Nov. 1839, died at Gravette AR 24 Dec. 1890; married in Wayne Co. IA 1 Mar. 1866 (VRs) SARAH J. COOL, born in IA 7 Sept. 1848, died in OK 30 Oct. 1905 (records of descendant Larry Leighton). He was a farmer at Ottumwa IA.

Children:

	i.	ROSA F.[9], b. in IA c1868 (2 in 1870); m. ---- HARRINGTON.
	ii.	JASPER, b. in IA c1869 (7/12 in 1870).
	iii.	JOHN.
	iv.	CHARLES.
	v.	ORVILLE.
	vi.	CORA; m. ---- DEAL.
1771.	vii.	IRA, b. Ottumwa IA 27 July 1877.

1259.   FRANCES EVELYN[8] 1842-1883 [607 Humphrey[7] and Frances Broy] was born in Woodford Co. IL 17 Aug. 1842 (Bible), died at Smith Center near Athol, Smith Co. KS 10 Mar. 1883; married in Putnam Co. MO 6 Sept. 1858 WILLIAM EZRA PRINCE, born in IN 22 May 1837, died at Paris, Osborne Co. KS in Aug. 1904, son of Jacob and Sarah (Hill) Prince. He married second Rebecca Hersey (records of descendant Kathleen Gardner, including family Bible). Burials are in Myers Cemetery, Smith Co.
He served during the Civil War in Co. I, 23rd MO Inf. Rgt. He later lived at Kansas City KS.

Children (**Prince**), born in Wayne Co. IA:

i.	ROBERT WARREN, b. 20 Sept. 1860.
ii.	SARAH JANE, b. 30 Mar. 1862, d. 12 Aug. 1917; m. ---- WILLIAMS.
iii.	FRANCES EVELYN, b. Allerton 26 Aug. 1864, d. Kansas City KS 22 June 1940; m. Gaylord KS 28 Mar. 1882 DAVID WALTER TRUEBLOOD.
iv.	VIOLA TERRISSA, b. 24 Feb. 1867, d. 17 Mar. 1918; m. JOSEPH MITCHELL.

v.   ANNA SALOME, b. 4 Apr. 1869; m. 1st JUSTIN PUTNAM;
     m. 2nd JOSEPH MITCHELL.
vi. RACHEL REBECCA, b. 26 Apr. 1872, d. 19 Sept. 1901; m.
     ---- LLOYD.
vii. ALBERT WILLIAM, b. 16 Dec. 1875.

1260. DAVID^8 1830-1902 [608 <u>Jacob^7</u> and <u>Christina Peters</u>]
was born in Switzerland Co. IN 12 Apr. 1830, died at Clar-
inda, Page Co. IA 20 Apr. 1902; married at Morton, Tazewell
Co. IL 21 Jan. 1859 (VRs) MARY ELLEN MOOBERRY, born there 15
Sept. 1842, died at Colville, Stevens Co. WA 6 Apr. 1909,
daughter of Samuel and Cynthia (Flanagan) Mooberry (records
of Helen Price Joiner).   Burials are in the Clarinda (IA)
Cemetery.
     He was a carpenter. He enlisted 1 Jan. 1864 in Co. F, 23rd
IA Inf. Rgt., and was transferred to the 29th Rgt. Wounded 7
Apr. 1865 at Spanish Fort AL, he was discharged 10 Aug. that
year. He filed for an invalid pension (NA-MSR #453-141); his
widow was also pensioned.

Children:

1772. i.   ELMER ELLSWORTH^9, b. Hawleyville IA 27 Nov.
            1861.
       ii. ALVIN E., b. 11 Nov. 1863, res. Dallas, Taylor
            Co. IA in 1900; m. CELIA M$_0$FARLAND, b. in
            Oct. 1872. Ch. PERRY D.^{10} b. in Oct. 1896.
       iii. MAUDE ALICE, b. 24 Aug. 1869, d. Clarinda 6
            Apr. 1900; m. 1st JOHN MANKLE; m. 2nd VERN
            SMITH. Two Mankle daus. were in David's
            household in 1900: Winnie b. in Apr. 1890,
            Madge b. in May 1891.
       iv. VINNIE GERTRUDE, b. 23 Aug. 1875; m. MARTIN
            HOY.

1261. ANDREW J.^{8} 1832-1912 [608 <u>Jacob^7</u> and <u>Christina
Peters</u>] was born in IL 29 Nov. 1832 (23 Nov. 1834 per death
record), died at Columbus OH in July 1912; married at Peoria
IL 8 Mar. 1863 (HELEN) ANGELINE H---- , born in CT 16 Jan.
1844 (37 in 1880) (records of Helen Price Joiner).
     He was a soldier in the Civil War. He was a blacksmith at
Peoria in 1880, and was of Franklin Co. OH when he and his
brother Silas released a mortgage in Tazewell Co. 3 Sept.
1892. In 1900 he, Helen and Edwin were listed at Averyville,
Peoria.

Children, born in IL:

       i.   FREDERICK^9, b. c1864 (16 in 1880).
       ii. LAURA, b. c1866 (14 in 1880).
       iii. PERCY, b. c1876 (4 in 1880).
       iv. EDWIN H., b. in Feb. 1884.

1262. SILAS WASHINGTON^8 1833-1926 [608 <u>Jacob^7</u> and <u>Chris-
tina Peters</u>] was born at Groveland, Tazewell Co. IL 4 June
1833, died at Eureka, Woodford Co., 25 Mar. 1926 (hanged himself); married at Groveland 13 Apr. 1861 HARRIET EMELINE
NICHOLS, born at West Liberty, Champaign Co. OH 8 Apr. 1842,

died at Eureka 5 Apr. 1929, daughter of Philip and Sarah (Fitzpatrick) Nichols (records of Helen Price Joiner).
He was a farmer and stock raiser at Groveland (Atlas of Tazewell County, Ill., 1891). He was listed there in 1880, and at Eureka in 1900. His will named his wife and his living children. Burials are in Olio Cemetery, Eureka.

Children, born at Groveland:

      i.   ELIZABETH[9], b. 24 Feb. 1862, not named in her father's will.
1773. ii. FRANCIS M. [Frank], b. in Feb. 1864.
     iii. CHARLES P., b. c1866 (14 in 1880), not named in his father's will.
     iv. GEORGE WILLIAM, b. c1869 (11 in 1880), d. in 1930 (GS).
1774. v   ALBA J., b. 12 Aug. 1871.
     vi. NORA J., b. 31 Dec. 1876; m. CHARLES PARSONS.
     vii. ROBERT BEACHER, b. 21 Feb. 1880, d. Glendale CA in 1960; m. 1st Eureka 27 Dec. 1909 (VRs) VIDA BURTON, b. in 1885, d. in 1916 (GS); m. 2nd EDNA E. ---- , b. in 1894, a widow in 1960. Ch. RUSSELL EUGENE[10] b. 5 Oct. 1910.
     viii. ROY E., b. in June 1882, res. with Frank in 1900; m. in IL 15 Dec. 1909 MINNIE KIEF.
     ix. MAUDE L., b. 14 Mar. 1888; m. Eureka 27 Feb. 1908 (VRs) ALBERT H. DAVIDSON.

1263. MARTHA ELEANOR[8] 1845-1923 [609 Noah[7] and Amanda Ewing] was born in Logan Co. IL 2 Jan. 1845, died 13 May 1923 in an accidental shooting; married in Fremont Co. IA 8 Feb. 1869 SAMUEL CALDWELL ALSWORTH. born 22 Sept. 1829, died 7 June 1910 (records of Olive Leighton Johnson).

Children (**Alsworth**):

i.   ANN ELIZABETH, b. 23 Sept. 1871; m. 24 Oct. 1888 JAMES ROBERT BLACK, b. in Feb. 1867.
ii. RAYMOND L., b. 7 Dec. 1881; m. 13 May 1918 AUGUSTA V. ARMSTRONG.
iii. FRANCES ELZIRA [Fannie], b. 6 Aug. 1884; m. 24 July 1913 THOMAS G. LANG, who was b. 18 Dec. 1884.

1264. FRANCES ELIZA[8] 1847-1920 [609 Noah[7] and Amanda Ewing] was born in Logan Co. IL 14 Apr. 1847, died at Glendale CA 18 Mar. 1920; married at Wheeler's Grove IA 24 Feb. 1867 PETER GEORGE CONKLE, born 26 Dec. 1846, lived at Glendale, son of George and Beulah Ann (Vale) Conkle (records compiled by Peter Conkle, 1940).
He was a farmer and fruit grower in NE, CO and CA.

Children (**Conkle**), all but one born at Nebraska City, Otoe Co. NE:

i.   ELZA GREEN, b. 6 June 1868; m. Peru NE in Nov. 1897 MARY MATELLA [Mayne] PROUTY, b. 10 Sept. 1872.
ii. AMANDA VENETTA, b. 12 Aug. 1871; m. Peru 9 June 1899 DELOS DANIEL MILES.

iii. ORVILLE TAYLOR, b. 28 Sept. 1875; m. 19 Nov. 1902
     FLORENCE DEE GIBSON, b. E. Brownfield ME 26 Aug.
     1872.
 iv. ARTHUR EDWIN, b. 7 Apr. 1881; m. 29 Apr. 1906 EMMA
     JOSEPHINE ANDERSON, b. 9 July 1887.
  v. LAURA MAY, b. Peru NE 21 Nov. 1886, d. in CA 11 Mar.
     1961; unm.

1265. SIDNAH ROBINSON[8] 1851-1946 [609 Noah[7] and Amanda
Ewing] was born in Logan Co. IL 10 July 1851, died at Clarinda IA 5 Mar. 1946; married 23 Aug. 1876 HANNAH OLIVIA Van
METER, born at Tipton, Cedar Co. IA 29 Apr. 1860, died at
Griswold IA 21 July 1939, daughter of Cyrus William and Virginia (Bolton) VanMeter (Sidnah's letters--Cornman Papers;
records of granddaughter Olive Leighton Johnson).
He lived at Wheeler's Grove IA, in a sod-house at Hoxie KS,
at Trenton NE, Yuma CO, and Mountain Grove MO. In 1900 he
and Hannah were listed at Grove Tp, Pottawattamie Co. IA;
they later lived at Griswold, Cass Co.

Children:

1775.   i.   FLOYD BAXTER[9], b. Oakland IA 5 Dec. 1878.
       ii.   LEWIS WALTER, b. 19 Mar. 1881, d. 2 Feb. 1884.
      iii.   AMANDA ANN, b. 25 Dec. 1882, d. 20 Jan. 1883.
1776. iv.   EMMA GERTRUDE [Gertie], b. 2 Aug. 1884; m.
             JOHN JOSEPH JONES and DALTON L. NORDYKE.
1777.   v.   (CHARLES) ARTHUR, b. Hoxie KS 4 July 1888.
1778. vi.   CYRUS WILLIAM, b. Hoxie KS 16 Aug. 1890.
      vii.   LAURA BERYL, b. 22 Sept. 1901, d. Griswold 1
             Oct. 1921; unm. She was a teacher.

1266. FREDERICK[8] 1849-   [610 Samuel[7] and Sylvina Leigh-
ton] was born at Parkman ME 29 Mar. 1849, lived at Brockton
MA; married at Parkman 23 Sept. 1876 MARY ELIZABETH NUTTING,
born there 20 May 1853, not listed in 1900, daughter of Jesse
and Betsey E. (Thurston) Nutting [# 1234] (Thurston Gen.,
140; letter from Lizzie Ring Leighton--Cornman Papers; Parkman VRs). In 1880 and 1900 he was a carpenter at Brockton
MA.

Children:

   i.   JESSIE MAY[9], b. Sangerville ME 27 Oct. 1878;
        m. THOMAS H. CLARK. She and her ch. Florence
        May, b. Brockton 26 Dec. 1897, were in 1900
        living with her father.
  ii.   STANLEY EUGENE, b. Brockton 16 Dec. 1881.
 iii.   ERNEST VALENTINE, b. Brockton 14 Feb. 1885.

1267. (JOSEPH) BLASLAND[8] 1855-1934 [610 Samuel[7] and Sylvina Leighton] was born at Mount Vernon 8 July 1855, died at
Parkman ME 30 Sept. 1934, 79y 2m 22d; married at Cambridge 27
Nov. 1887 ELIZABETH EMMA GOULD [Lizzie] RING, born there 21
July 1867, lived at North Dexter ME in 1914 and at Parkman in
1934, daughter of William and Elmira Sands (Gould) Ring (town
and ME VRs; Lizzie Emma's letter--Cornman Papers). Burials
are in the Village Cemetery, Cambridge.

In 1880 J. Blasland Leighton lived with his brother Fred at Brockton MA; in 1900 he was a farmer at Parkman.

Child, born at E. Hartford CT (his marriage record):

    i.   FRANCIS JOSEPH[9], b. c1900; m. Corinna ME 24 Nov. 1920 THERESA F. KNOWLES, b. there c1904, dau. of Elbert and Florence A (Lyford) Knowles. Ch. FLORENCE E.[10] b. Parkman 26 June 1924. Theresa m. 2nd Newport ME 17 Sept. 1927 Fred Leavitt--div; m. 3rd Milo ME 14 Aug. 1942 Barton Gerrish Merrill.

1268. IRA GARDNER[8] 1857-1912 [610 Samuel[7] and Sylvina Leighton] was born at Parkman 23 Apr. 1857, died there 4 Nov. 1912; married at Dexter ME 25 Apr. 1885 ETTA ADELL ROGERS, born at St Albans ME 18 July 1860, died at Auburn ME 27 Mar. 1938, 77y 8m 9d, daughter of James and Lovina (Nutter) Rogers (Thurston Gen., 140: town and ME VRs).
In 1900 Ira lived at Dexter. He was sometimes called Gardner. Etta in 1908 was living with her son at South Portland.

Child, born at Parkman:

    i.   CHARLES GARDNER[9], b. 5 May 1886; m. So. Portland 26 Aug. 1908 ELLEN LOUISE WAGG, b. Corinna c1888, dau. of Frank and Mary (Lawless) Wagg. Ch. GARDNER BUTLER[10] b. Portland 24 Oct. 1910, res. Dexter.

1269. DANIEL E.[8] 1848-1880 [611 Hosea[7] and Mary Page] was born say 1848, died at New Sharon ME in 1880; married at Dexter ME int. 14 Mar. 1873 ELIZABETH S. [Lizzie] ROLLINS, born at Bangor ME in 1854, died at Farmington ME in 1909, daughter of Ichabod and Sarah (Watson) Rollins of Abbott ME (Rollins Family, 314; Cornman Ms).
They lived for a number of years on the Pacific coast.

Children:

1779. i.   DANIEL E.[9], b. Snohomish WA 11 Aug. 1874.
      ii.   CHARLES, b. Snohomish, d. there aged 4y.
      iii. RUTH E., b. in CA (mar. rec.), res. Farmington ME; m. there 3 June 1897 JUSTIN E. McLEARY JR., b. Strong ME, son of Justin E. and Ella E. (Conant) McLeary. Ch. Angie Ruth.
      iv.   FRANK E., b. New Sharon 9 June 1878, d. Farmington 6 Oct. 1924, 47y 3m 27d; m. there 27 Nov. 1901 MAE M. SNOW, b. Monckton NB c1879, dau. of Alfred and Jennie (White) Snow. No ch. In 1900 he was in the McLeary household.

1270. STEPHEN PHILBRICK[8] 1831-1914 [613 Nathan[7] and Abigail Carll] was born at Huron, Wayne Co. NY 19 Jan. 1837, died at Williamston, Ingham Co. MI 15 May 1914; married there 30 Dec. 1866 ROSILLA LORANGER, born at Henrietta, Jackson Co. MI 7 Mar. 1850, daughter of Nelson and Mary (Borceaux) Loranger (Cornman Ms).

Stephen was about 16 when his family settled in MI in 1854.
He enlisted 12 Aug. 1862 as sergeant in Co. H, 26th MI Inf.
Rgt., and was given a field commission as second lieutenant
in 1865. After being hospitalized by a severe food wound
received at Spotsylvania, he returned to his regiment as a
first sergeant; his unit was with Gen. Grant at Appomattox.
He was eventually a pensioner.

In 1900 he was at Williamston, where he had a large farm
(Portrait and Biographical Record of Ingham and Livingston
Counties, Mich. [1891], 631-2; A. E. Cowle, Past and Present
of Ingham County, Mich. [1905], 166).

Children, born at Williamston:

   i.   ELI A ^{9}, b. 11 Nov. 1867, d. 24 Mar. 1874.
   ii.   HIRAM, b. 18 July 1869, d. 25 Mar. 1874.
   iii. NELSON, b. 13 May 1871, d. 16 Aug. 1873.
   iv.   ROSILLA L. [Rose], b. 19 Sept. 1874; m. Will-
         iamston 21 June 1900 JAMES A. DANA. They
         lived on the family homestead.
   v.   STEPHEN P. JR., b. 11 Sept. 1880, d. 19 Apr.
         1894.
   vi.   ANNA BELLE, b. 3 Apr. 1883; m. Weston MI 4
         Dec. 1910 J. S. LECHLER. She was a teacher.
   vii. ISADORE R., b. 20 June 1886, res. Cobre NV; m.
         24 Aug. 1909 SARA AGNES McCULLOCH. Ch.
         ROBERT STEPHEN^{10} b. Wells NV 14 June 1912,
         res. Reno NV.

1271. NATHAN^8 1839-1912 [613 Nathan^7 and Abigail Carll]
was born at Huron NY 26 July 1839, died at Holland MI 20
Sept. 1914; married at Chelsea MI 2 July 1868 JULIA DANCER,
born there 25 June 1845, died at Holland 27 Nov. 1912, daughter of John and Jane (Cowell) Dancer (Cornman Ms).

In 1853 he settled at Ingham Co. MI, where he taught school
at Williamston and Wheatfield, became a merchant, and served
as town treasurer two terms.

Twice he attempted to join the Union army, but each time
was rejected for health reasons.

In 1883 he settled at Clyde Tp, Allegan Co., as a farmer,
and was listed there in 1900. He was the first Democrat to
be elected town supervisor (Portrait and Biographical Record
of Kalamazoo, Allegan and Van Buren Counties, Mich., 535, in
which he was called Stephen Leighton).

Children, born at Williamston, besides two who died in
   infancy:

   i.   ADAH JANE^9, b. 27 Apr. 1871, res. Whitehall
         MI; m. 27 Apr. 1893 DELBERT van VALKENBURG,
         b. Allegan 10 Oct. 1865, son of James C and
         Alida A. van Valkenburg. Ch. Ray b. Holland
         17 May 1898.
   ii.   NATHAN, b. 7 July 1875, d. 19 Aug. 1876.
   iii. SUSAN, b. 8 Dec. 1876; m. 26 June 1906 WESLEY
         R. HOLLEY. Ch. Marguerite b. Milbrook MI 25
         Sept. 1908, and Leighton R. b. Grand Rapids
         MI 28 Oct. 1910.

1272. NANCY FAIRCHILD[8] 1849-1886 [613 Nathan[7] and Abigail Carll] was born at Huron NY 6 Jan. 1849, died at Ipswich SD 3 Jan. 1886; married first at Williamston MI 28 Aug. 1870 SCOTT WALDO, son of Jerome and Emma Waldo; married second at Zurich, Wayne Co. NY 20 Dec. 1875 BENJAMIN FRANKLIN CARLL, born 2 Dec. 1854, son of Samuel and Jane (Drake) Carll (Cornman Ms). She had no Waldo children.

Child (**Carll**), born at Waltham MI:

i. CECILIA, b. 11 June 1877, res. Detroit; m. Pleasant Lake IN 16 May 1900 GEORGE W. CLEMENT, son of Columbus and Almira (Miller) Clement.

1273. RHODA RELIANCE[8] 1837-1905 [614 Benjamin[7] and Fannie Dennis] was born at Sodus NY 15 June 1837, died there 6 June 1905; married at Lyons NY in Dec. 1867 GILBERT SHAW, b. 27 Feb. 1834, died at Pierson MI 25 Sept. 1914 (Cornman Ms).

Children (**Shaw**), born at Sodus:

i.   ANDREW J., b. 25 Dec. 1870, d. 10 Apr. 1898.
ii. FANNIE JOSEPHINE, b. 6 Oct. 1874; m. 1 Sept. 1910 CORNELIUS J. BARTLESON, b. Holland MI 3 Apr. 1876, son of John and Minnie B. Bartleson.
iii. CHLOE BERTHEMA, b. 28 Apr. 1876; m. 2 Jan. 1894 HERMAN RHODES.
iv. ONER S., b. 25 Feb. 1882.

1274. ALDEN[8] 1834-   [615 Alvin[7] and Aurelia Alden] was born at Sodus NY 20 Jan. 1834, lived at Greenville SC in 1914; married first in Eaton Co. MI 15 Feb. 1857 (recorded as Florida A.) AMELIA F. COWAN, born in MI in 1836, died at Whitehall MI 6 July 1873, daughter of John W. and Julia (Westberg) Cowan (Cornman Ms); married second CALISTA (----) Pardy, who was born in NY in Feb. 1835.
He settled at Eaton MI, and then in 1866 moved to Whitehall. In 1880 and 1900 he and his family were listed at Montague, Muskegon Co. MI; the census showed MN as the birthplace for all his children but his first. His household included his wife Carrie and step-daughters Anna and Lucy Pardy, all born in NY.

Children:

1780. i.   CHESTER ALDEN[9], b. Eaton Rapids 23 Nov. 1857.
       ii. GEORGE EDGAR, b. Eaton Rapids in 1859, d. Ellendale ND 5 July 1885; unm.
1781. iii. ALVIN MYRON, b. 24 Apr. 1862.
1782. iv. EFFIE MAY, b. Whitehall 31 Jan. 1867; m. SAMUEL LOWERY.

1275. FRANKLIN S.[8] 1838-   [615 Alvin[7] and Aurelia Alden] was born at Sodus NY 8 Dec. 1838, lived at Hamelin MI in 1900; married there 11 Dec. 1867 R. MARIA BARR, born there 5 July 1843, daughter of David and Mary (Skinner) Barr (Cornman Ms; Portrait and Biographical Album of Barry and Eaton Counties, Mich. [Chicago, 1891], 689).

In 1880 his household at Hamelin in Eaton Co. included his mother-in-law Mary Barr, 71   Frank was a farmer and justice of the peace.

Children, born in Eaton County:

    i.   MARY B., b. 23 Aug. 1868, d. 26 Apr. 1873.
   ii. JESSE W., b. 15 Mar. 1870, d. 7 May 1873.
  iii. FANNIE A., b. 27 Aug. 1872; m. GUY E. ROGERS.

1276. SARAH^8 1841-   [615 Alvin^7 and Aurelia Alden] was born at Sodus NY 8 Dec. 1841, lived at Eaton Rapids MI; married there 31 Dec. 1862 LUCIUS A. GIDDINGS of OH, who was born 17 Aug. 1840, son of Josiah and Harriette (Allen) Giddings (Cornman Ms).

Children (**Giddings**):

    i.   LORETTA AURILLA, b. 8 Apr. 1867, d. 13 Dec. 1901; m.
        ---- TOPLIFF.
   ii. LILLIE GERTRUDE, b. 15 May 1868, d. 3 Dec. 1890;
        unm.

1277. MARY MELINDA^8 1843-1880 [615 Alvin^7 and Aurelia Alden] was born at Sodus NY 13 Apr. 1843, died at Parma MI 1 July 1880; married in Eaton Co. MI 27 Dec. 1866 GILBERT B. HOGLE, born at Ionia, Oakland Co. MI 21 Sept. 1839, died at Benton Harbor MI 22 Dec. 1918, son of William and Laura (Tyrril) Hogle (Cornman Ms; Portrait and Biographical Album of Jackson County, Mich. [Chicago, 1890], 627).
    Hogle was enrolled in Co. C, 9th MI Inf. Rgt., on 6 Sept. 1861, and discharged 5 Dec. 1862, after his knee was shattered in the battle of Murfreesboro TN 13 July 1862. He was living at Sandstone MI when he applied for a pension in 1909, aged 70 (NA-MSR 16999). He married second at Albion MI 29 Nov. 1881 Emma Jane Belcher, who died in Sept. 1918--divorced in 1886.

Children (**Hogle**):

    i.   HOMER E., b. 22 Aug. 1869, res. Pontiac MI.
   ii. ALICE G., b. 12 Aug. 1871; m. ---- MILLER.
  iii. JESSIE M., b. 9 Mar. 1873, res. Benton Harbor; m. C.
        Y. GAREY.

1278. JOHN BUZZELL^8 1826-1900 [617 Israel^7 and Mary Buzzell] was born at Barrington NH 24 Aug. 1826, died at Vineland NJ 8 Apr. 1900; married first at Pittsfield NH 29 July 1855 MERIBAH FOSS, born 6 Apr. 1828, died 25 Nov. 1861, daughter of Israel and Sarah (Babb) Foss of Strafford (Sargent, Babbs of New Eng., 112; married second 9 Apr. 1863 SARAH ELIZABETH [Lizzie] CLOUGH, born at Pittsfield NH 9 Sept. 1831, died in NJ 13 Apr. 1913, daughter of Daniel and Mehitable (Watson) Clough of Epsom (Cornman Ms; letter from Lura Mayhew, 1914-Cornman Papers; Carter, NH Ministry, 50).
    Rev. John was a Free Will Baptist clergyman who served as pastor in various churches in NH. He retired for health reasons in 1880 and moved to NJ.

Children by Meribah, born at Barrington:

i.   (EZRA) WALTER[9], b. 12 Aug. 1857, d. Meredith
        NH 2 Apr. 1882; unm.
ii.   JOHN FRANK [J. Frank], b. 22 Apr. 1857, res.
        Laconia NH; m. Bennington NJ 11 Dec. 1880
        ELLEN M. PEASE, b. Meredith 15 Dec. 1848, d.
        Laconia 11 May 1897, dau. of Moses Cheney and
        Betsey (Randlett) Pease (Hanaford, Meredith
        Annals, 384). Two ch. d. as infants in 1885
        and 1887.

Children by Lizzie:

iii.   LURA DEL, b. Barrington 29 Jan. 1865, res.
        Millville NJ; m. 15 Aug. 1891 MORTIMER MAYHEW
        of Morristown NJ, b. 1 June 1857, son of John
        L. and Catherine (Bright) Mayhew. Ch. Clar-
        issa Elizabeth b. Millville 4 Mar. 1903.
iv.   IRVING R., b. Belmont NH 9 Apr. 1868, res.
        Vineland NJ; m. 9 Apr. 1910 MARGARET JACKSON
        of Reading PA.
v.   CARL B., b. New Hampton NH 4 Oct. 1871, d.
        Philadelphia 21 Feb. 1909; m. 4 Oct. 1900
        SADIE GILLETT, dau. of Frank and Elizabeth
        (Armitage) Gillett. Ch. DOROTHY GILLETT[10] b.
        Philadelphia 2 July 1901.
vi.   LOUIS A., b. Madison NH 8 Nov. 1874, d. Vine-
        land 10 Jan. 1910.

1279. JAMES TWOMBLEY[8] 1829-1889 [617 Israel[7] and Mary Buz-
zell] was born at Barrington 22 Apr. 1829, died there 8 Dec.
1889; married there 4 July 1854 BETSEY A. BUZZELL, born there
14 May 1828, died there 1 Jan. 1897, daughter of Jonathan and
Polly (Hill) Buzzell (town VRs; Cornman Ms).

Children, born at Barrington:

i.   MARY S.[9], b. 27 Aug. 1857, d. 31 Mar. 1878;
        unm.
1783. ii.   (JAMES) HERBERT, b. 7 Sept. 1859.

1280. LORENZO DOW[8] 1815-1872 [620 Reuben[7] and Mary Ser-
geant] was born at Newbury VT 26 Mar. 1815, died there 19
Apr. 1872, 56y 23d; married there 2 Dec. 1857 SALINA R. LIND-
SEY, born at Whitefield NH 4 Jan. 1840, died at Deerfield NH
22 July 1888, daughter of Hardy and Letitia (Gerould) Lindsey. His widow married second at Deerfield 26 Nov. 1874 Martin W. Childs (Tracy, Reuben Leighton, 9; Wells, Newbury,
617; Newbury VRs).
Lorenzo was a farmer at Newbury.

Children, born at Newbury:

i.   HARRY BAILEY[9], b. 1 Oct. 1858, res. Amherst
        NH; m. ALICE J. PEARSON, b. Mt. Vernon NH
        c1873. Ch. THERESA ARLINE[10] b. Milford NH 28
        June 1896.

ii.   IDA MAY, b. 18 May 1860, d. 5 July 1912; m. 27
      Oct. 1891 CHARLES A. CHILDS, b. 25 June 1862,
      son of Martin W. and Georgia A. Childs. Ch.
      Martin L. b. Manchester NH 15 June 1897.
iii. GEORGE WATKINS, b. 7 Dec. 1861, res. Duluth
      MN. He lived at Newbury in 1900.
iv.   (CHARLES) HERBERT, b. 13 June 1863, res. Brad-
      ford VT in 1900; m. 1st Newbury 5 Jan. 1893
      EMMA L. BROWN, b. Bradford in Mar. 1870, d.
      25 Jan. 1901, dau. of William M. Brown; m.
      2nd GRACE DANFORTH, dau. of Thomas and Anna
      (Holmes) Danforth. Ch. by Emma b. 1897, 1899
      and 1901, all 3 d. unnamed; ch. CHARLES[10] by
      Grace b. 20 May 1912.
v.   WILLIAM C., b. 6 May 1865; m. 19 June 1889
      VELMA CHAMBERLAIN, dau. of Warren and Statira
      (Edwards) Chamberlain. Ch. HAROLD FRANK[10]
      b. Newbury 19 Sept. 1892, res. there with
      his uncle George in 1900.
1784. vi.   JENNIE INEZ, b. 19 Mar. 1867; m. GEORGE KING.
vii. KATIE BELLE, b. 20 Dec. 1870; m. Stoneham MA
      17 June 1891 JOHN WILSON CROWLEY of Newbury.
      Katie had been adopted by Alfred Chase of
      Stoneham.
1785. viii. JOHN WESLEY, b. 27 Jan. 1872.

1281.   ROSWELL[8] 1818-1897 [620 Reuben[7] and Mary Sergeant]
was born at Newbury VT 22 Oct. 1818, died at Groton VT 15
Mar. 1897, 78y 4m 9d; married at Newbury 25 Feb. 1848 MARY
ANN JAMES, born there 22 Feb. 1819, died there 14 Mar. 1889,
70y 11d, daughter of Jabez and Sally (Cummings) James (Tracy,
Reuben Leighton, 10; Wells, Newbury, 616; Newbury and Groton
VRs). Burials are in Oxbow Cemetery, Newbury.
     As a young man, he rafted lumber down the Connecticut
River. He was a brickmaker at Somerville MA from 1845 to
1849. On 17 Dec. 1846 he purchased a 100-acre farm at New-
bury, which was leased to John Wallace until Roswell married
and took it over.

Children, born at Newbury:

i.   HENRY EDWIN[9], b. 15 Apr. 1850, d. Groton VT 14
      May 1905; m. Newbury 25 Oct. 1887 MARY ANN
      CUNNINGHAM of Groton, dau. of John Cunning-
      ham. Ch. HARRY EDWARD[10] b. Newbury 14 Nov.
      1888, lived with his uncle Silas in 1900.
ii.   SILAS MITCHELL, b. 12 Sept. 1851, d. Newbury
      13 Apr. 1915; m. 1st there 20 June 1888 HAR-
      RIET [Hattie] BARTLETT, b. there 14 Oct.
      1859, d. there 5 June 1893, dau. of Charles
      and Sarah (Boyce) Bartlett; m. 2nd there 16
      Oct. 1895 ALICE JENNE, b. Derby VT 14 Oct.
      1862, d. Newbury 21 June 1898, dau. of Job
      and Eliza (Bailey) Jenne. No ch.
1786. iii. FRANKLIN PIERCE, b. 25 Sept. 1853.
iv.   JAMES MILO, b. 3 Oct. 1855, d. 17 Oct. 1891,
      36y 14d; unm.
1787. v.   MARY ETTA, b. 14 Feb. 1858; m. FRANK P. DOWNS.

1282. MARY ANN[8] 1820-1902 [620 Reuben[7] and Mary Sergeant]
was born at Newbury 29 Apr. 1820, died there 4 May 1902; married there 3 Mar. 1845 JOHN WALLACE 2ND, born 29 July 1821,
died at Newbury 21 Nov. 1903, son of William and Marion
(Whitelaw) Wallace (Newbury VRs; Cornman Ms).
They settled at Green Mountain IA in 1868, and at Grinnell
IA in 1874; they returned to VT in 1894.

Children (**Wallace**), born at Newbury:

i.   WILLIAM ROBERT, b. 4 Apr. 1847, d. 29 Jan. 1906.
      He res. Marshalltown IA.
ii.   ELMER E., b. 20 July 1848, res. Newport VT; m. St.
      Johnsbury VT 22 Jan. 1876 LOUISE ELLA STEBBINS, b.
      Royalton VT 17 Feb. 1855, dau. of John and Betsey
      Stebbins.
iii. ADELINE BELL, b. 3 Sept. 1850, d. Marshallton IA 16
      May 1877; m. 25 Dec. 1869 WILLIAM CRAWFORD, b. in
      Scotland, res. Nevada IA, son of James Crawford.
      He m. 2nd Cornelia Long.
iv.   FRANK, b. 30 Mar. 1853, res. Newbury; m. EMELINE
      LOUISE BERNARD of Sheridan IL, b. 17 Apr. 1856,
      dau. of George and Magdelene Bernard.
v.   KATE, b. 24 Sept. 1856, res. Grinnell IA; m. Litch-
      field NH 6 Apr. 1891 DANIEL SIMPSON BARTLETT, b.
      there 8 Nov. 1835, d. Grinnell 28 June 1912,
      son of Nathan and Fannie (Jones) Bartlett. He m.
      1st Hannah H. Ford, dau. of Ross C and Hannah[7]
      (Leighton) Ford [# 622].

1283. SUSAN[8] 1822-   [620 Reuben[7] and Mary Sergeant] was
born at Newbury VT say 1822; married there 2 July 1843 WIL-
LIAM WALLACE JR., born 27 Mar. 1819, died at Cambridge VT 19
Jan. 1894, son of William and Marion (Whitelaw) Wallace
(Cornman Ms).

Children (**Wallace**):

i.   ELLEN, b. Newbury; m. BARRON SULHAM.
ii.   GEORGIANNA; m. 1 Jan. 1868 HUGH CAMERON.
iii. KIRK, res. Newport VT; unm.
iv.   GERTRUDE; m. FRANK SAWIN.

1284. CHARLES[8] 1825-1858 [620 Reuben[7] and Mary Sergeant]
was born at Newbury VT 27 Oct. 1825, died there 29 Oct. 1858,
31y 10m 2d; married there 27 Aug. 1851 JANE B. LINDSEY, born
about 1832, died 12 Nov. 1886, 54y, daughter of Justin and
Amy (Meserve) Lindsey. Widow Jane married second Lafayette
Bass (Wells, Newbury, 620; Cornman Ms).

Children, born at Newbury:

i.   BELLE[9], b. 17 June 1853; m. Plymouth NH 15
      Sept. 1884 GEORGE WHEATLEY BOWMAN, b. West-
      ford VT 16 May 1854, son of Elliot and Har-
      riet (Wheatley) Bowman. He was a hotel
      keeper at Newport and Burlington VT, and at
      Denver CO (Hannibal P. Wheatley, Genealogy of
      the Wheatley Family [1902], 108).

    ii.   JUSTIN; mar. ---- . He was a merchant at
          Lancaster NH.
   iii. ?WILLIAM, res. Lancaster.
    iv. ?JENNIE, d. Newbury 23 Mar. 1864, 10y 5m 8d.
     v.   CHARLES D., d. Newbury 23 Jan. 1863, 6y.

1285. ANN B.[8] 1829-   [623 Jacob[7] and Salome Bowers] was
born at Newbury VT 24 Nov. 1829, died at No. Attleboro MA;
married ---- PHILLIPS (Cornman Ms).

Children (**Phillips**):

    i.   IDA; unm.
    ii. CHARLES, res. CA
   iii. FRANK, res. Charlestown MA; m. ---- . No ch.
    iv. EVA, d. No. Attleboro; m. Dr. ---- Foster. No ch.

1286. MARY ELIZABETH[8] 1835-1909 [623 Jacob[7] and Salome
Bowers] was born at Bath NH 10 Jan. 1835 (11 Jan. 1834 in
Newbury VT VRs), died at Bradford VT 17 May 1909; married at
Bradford 28 Sept. 1854 HARRY B. STEVENS, born at Newbury 22
Aug. 1818, died there 9 Oct. 1911, son of Simeon and Betsey
(Bagley) Stevens (Cornman Ms; Bradford VRs).

Children (**Stevens**), born at Bradford:

    i.   KATE, b. 3 Mar. 1856, res. St. James MN; m. EDWARD
         A GIBBS.
    ii. HARRY FREDERICK, b. 22 July 1859, d. 27 June 1900;
         m. San Francisco CA 17 Mar. 1890 CAROLINE JONES.
   iii. CARLOS WILSON, b. 24 Aug. 1867, d. Bradford 2 Mar.
         1899; m. there in 1898 FLOSSIE JENNIE DAVIS.

1287. GEORGE W.[8] 1829-1891 [625 Stephen[7] and Sarah Carbee]
was born at Newbury VT 27 May 1829, died at Acworth NH 5 Mar.
1891; married first at Newbury 27 Mar. 1853 (MARY) ADELINE
LANG, born there about 1836, died at Barnet VT 8 June 1859
(21 June, 23y 3m, Newbury VRs); married second LENORA A
[Lena] KEMP, born at Providence RI about 1844, died at
Alstead NH 2 Mar. 1899, 55y 4m 16d, daughter of Harmon and
Polly (Kenney) Kemp (town VRs; Cornman Ms).

Children by Adeline:

        i.   GEORGE[9], d. infant.
        ii. daughter, d. Barre VT 11 June 1859, 13d.

Children by Lenore, born at So. Acworth:

       iii. ARTHUR H., b. in June 1866, res. Bellows Falls
           VT in 1900; m. 28 Aug. 1895 MINNIE M. PER-
           SONS, b. Londonderry VT in Oct. 1868, dau. of
           John Persons. Ch. MILDRED EVELINE[10] b. Rock-
           ingham VT 19 Oct. 1896.
1788. iv. GERTRUDE F , b. 25 Apr. 1870; m. CHARLES L.
           BRACKETT.
        v.   CHARLES H. P., b. 3 Nov. 1873, d. So. Acworth
           6 Jan. 1876.

1288. ANDREW J.[8] 1831-1907 [625 Stephen[7] and Sarah Carbee] was born at Newbury VT 28 May 1831, died at Woodsville NH 3 Jan. 1907; married 3 Mar. 1853 HELEN M. BEDELL, born at Bath 24 Apr. 1835, died there 1 Mar. 1909, daughter of William and Orpha (Powers) Bedell (Cornman Ms; Whitcher, Haverhill, NH, 572; Hamilton Child, ed., Gazeteer of Grafton Co., N. H. [Syracuse NY, 1886], pt. 1:145, pt. 2:33; letter from Helen Taplin White--Cornman Papers).

He was a farmer. He served as state representative from Bath in 1884, and was selectman there for ten years.

Children:

1789. i.   EMMA C.[9], b. Newbury 11 May 1854; m. JOSEPH
             E. TAPLIN.
       ii.   FRANK A , b. 12 Dec. 1857, d. 18 Feb. 1891;
             unm.
       iii. FREDERICK M., b. Monroe NH 25 Apr. 1859, res.
             Bath in 1900; m. Barnet VT 13 Dec. 1888 EMMA
             F KIMBALL, b. in VT 29 Dec. 1862, dau. of
             William John and Lydia (Marshall) Kimball.
             No ch.
1790. iv.   HENRY A., b. Ryegate VT 28 May 1865.
1791. v.   BELLE C., b. Bath 17 July 1867; m. LLOYD KIM-
             BALL and GEORGE CONTY.

1289. STEPHEN L.[8] 1833-1905 [625 Stephen[6] and Sarah Carbee] was born at Newbury VT 24 Apr. 1833, died at Artesia CA 14 Sept. 1905; married first at Sunapee NH (ELLEN) JANE EASTMAN, born at Topsham VT, daughter of Isaac and Georgianna Eastman (Guy S. Rix, History and Genealogy of the Eastman Family [Concord NH, 1901], 1:131); married second 1 Oct. 1879 JULIA HILL, who was born at Walsingham, England, 27 Sept. 1848 (Cornman Ms).

He went west, and operated a mining camp in CA. In 1900 the family lived at Los Angeles.

Child by Jane, born at Bath NH:

1792. i.   LILLA LAURA[9], b. 25 Jan. 1859; m. Dr. WALTER
             LINDLEY.

Children by Julia:

1793. ii.   ALBERT L., b. Los Angeles 1 Dec. 1882.
       iii. NELLIE LURLINE, b. Pasadena CA 3 Jan. 1885.

1290. SARAH A.[8] 1835-   [625 Stephen[7] and Sarah Carbee] was born at Newbury VT 9 Sept. 1835, lived at Woodsville NH; married at Bath 25 Sept. 1856 DAVID G. FORSYTH, born at Topsham VT 25 Aug. 1831, died at Woodsville 4 Nov. 1910, son of James and Jeannette (Hastings) Forsyth (Cornman Ms).

Children (**Forsyth**), born at Bath:

i.   JOHN A., b. 10 May 1872.
ii.   MABEL L. (twin), b. 10 May 1872.

1291. LOIS CARBEE[8] 1837-   [625 Stephen[7] and Sarah Carbee] was born at Newbury VT 14 June 1837, lived at Los Angeles CA; married 25 June 1857 MICHAEL M. STEVENS, born at Lyman NH 13 July 1834, died at Los Angeles 3 Mar. 1908, son of Michael and Stella (Knapp) Stevens (Cornman Ms).

Children (**Stevens**):

i.   IDA KATE, b. Bath NH 16 Mar. 1858; m. 16 June 1856 WILLIAM NILES JR., b. Bath 30 Oct. 1861, son of William and Nancy Ann (Parker) Niles.

ii.   GEORGE MICHAEL, b. Grinnell IA 27 Aug. 1870; m. 19 Sept. 1896 ANNIE FRANCISCO, b. Joliet IL 19 Sept. 1872, dau. of Peter Yates and Sarah (Miles) Francisco. After receiving an MD from Bush Medical College, Chicago, in 1894, he practiced in IA and Los Angeles.

1292. (LYDIA) JANE[8] 1843-1877 [625 Stephen[7] and Sarah Carbee] was born at Bath NH 17 Dec. 1843, died at Hardy KS 10 Apr. 1877; married at Lisbon NH 4 July 1867 WILLIAM MORSE, born at Haverhill NH 22 Aug. 1849, died at Hastings NE 25 June 1914, son of Osgood and Fostina Morse (letter from her son Sewell--Cornman Papers).

Children (**Morse**):

i.   SEWELL L., b. Grinnell IA 14 May 1870, res. Lamar KS; m. 31 Dec. 1891 REGINA WAKEFIELD.

ii.   WILBUR, b. in 1873; m. ERNESTINE ---- .

1293. ALBERT HENRY[8] 1847-1917 [625 Stephen[7] and Sarah Carbee] was born at Bath NH 17 May 1847, died at Woodsville 14 Jan. 1917; married 5 Sept. 1872 ELLEN COOLEY LOTHER, born at Benton NH 26 Sept. 1845, daughter of Edward and Jane (Cross) Lother (Cornman Ms; Whitcher, Haverhill, NH, 572-3; Child, Gazeteer of Grafton Co., pt. 2:122).
He was a Woodsville clothing merchant, proprietor of A. H. Leighton & Co. until 1890. He built and managed the Hotel Wentworth, and was chairman of the board of health, a school board member for 17 years, and assistant postmaster.

Child, born at Woodsville (in Haverhill VRs):

i.   MARTHA LOUISE[9], b. 23 Feb. 1879; m. 18 Apr. 1900 FREDERICK LOWELL SARGENT, b. Lakeport NH 30 Nov. 1875, son of William Dyer and Hannah M. (Sanborn) Sargent. Ch. Karl Leighton b. Woodsville 24 Jan. 1901, d. 26 Jan. 1903. Fred was town and school board treasurer, and a chief clerk, Boston & Maine RR. Martha was county clerk of deeds and probate.

1294. HANNAH FRANCES[8] 1833-1865 [626 John[7] and Phoebe Buzzell] was born at Ossipee 27 Feb. 1833, died at Barrington NH 27 Oct. 1865; married in Apr. 1859 JOHN HENRY BUZZELL, born 26 Jan. 1834, son of Jonathan and Polly (Hill) Buzzell (Cornman Ms; Waterhouse Gen., 1:564).

Children (**Buzzell**), born at Barrington:

i.   EDNA, b. 30 June 1862, res. Bow Lake, Strafford; m.
      FREEMAN HANSON.
ii.   EMMA D., b. 3 Mar. 1864, res. Northwood NH; m. Laco-
      nia NH 17 May 1888 GEORGE NATHANIEL GARLAND, b.
      Strafford NH 7 Sept. 1867, son of Joseph and Olive
      Lydia (Buzzell) Garland (Garland Gen., 109).
iii. FRANK L., b. 26 Oct. 1865, res. WA in 1903. He was a
      Methodist clergyman.

1295.   LOTT BRIGHAM[8] 1826-1907 [627 Isaac[7] and Nancy Brig-
ham] was born at Hyde Park VT 9 June 1826, died at Redding CA
29 July 1907; married at Johnson VT 30 Nov. 1854 ISADORE
FISH, born there 7 May 1832, died at Webster City IA 4 Aug.
1898, daughter of Jonathan and Milly (Bean) Fish (Cornman Ms;
Biographical Record and Portrait Album of Webster and Hamilton Counties, Iowa [Chicago, 1888], 409; Hyde Park VRs).
    He was a merchant in MA before his marriage. In 1866 they
settled at Webster (near Ft. Dodge), where he bought and
enlarged a farm. He was justice of the peace and town clerk.
In 1900 he was living with Leon at Buckeye CA.

Children:

        i.   LEON[9], b. Hyde Park in Oct. 1855, res. Tur-
              lock, Shasta Co. CA; m. Shasta Co. 25 Dec.
              1887 IDA MAY CROSBY, b. Lake George NS 13
              Sept. 1863, dau. of Horton J. and Georgianna
              A (Davenport) Crosby. He was a teacher at
              Buckeye CA in 1900. Adopted ch. Mary Jean-
              ette b. Calistoga CA 24 Dec. 1891; m. 28 Nov.
              1912 Bertram A. Storer.
        ii.   ISAAC, b. Hyde Park 13 Aug. 1857, d. Templeton
              MA 8 Aug. 1859 (VRs).
1794.   iii. BRIGHAM, b. Templeton 4 Jan. 1860.
        iv.   son, b. and d. Hyde Park 20 Apr. 1863.
1795.   v.   ISAAC, b. Hyde Park 18 Aug. 1864.
        vi.   MARY BELL, b. Webster 16 May 1868, d. Otho IA
              21 Dec. 1885, 17y.
        vii. ERNEST E., b. Webster 14 Jan. 1874, d. Otho
              13 Feb. 1886.

1296.   ASA WALLACE[8] 1829-1903 [627 Isaac[7] and Nancy Brig-
ham] was born at Hyde Park 8 Dec. 1829, died at Lowell MA 11
Feb. 1903; married at Weathersfield VT 18 Feb. 1858 LORETTA
MORSE, born at Cavendish VT 6 Mar. 1832, died at Livermore IA
31 May 1890 (Cornman Ms).
    Asa was a tinsmith. In 1900 he was living alone, aged 80,
at Weathersfield.

Children:

1796.   i.   JOHN WALLACE[9], b. Weathersfield 19 Jan. 1859.
        ii.   SARAH D., b. Newbury 22 Oct. 1860, d.
              Weathersfield 3 Oct. 1864, 3y 11m 19d.
1797.   iii. ANNA M., b. Weathersfield 8 July 1867; m.
              DANIEL McCOMB.

1297. ARIEL HUNTON[8] 1834-   [627 Isaac[7] and Nancy Brigham was born at Hyde Park VT 29 Sept. 1834, lived at Willamina OR in 1900; married first at Peacham VT 17 Oct. 1858 LUCINDA W. MARSH, born at Craftsbury VT 1 Oct. 1839, died at Stow VT 2 May 1865, 25y 7m, daughter of John and Mary Marsh; married second at Barnet VT 10 Apr. 1866 LESTINA RICHARDSON, born at Barre VT 6 May 1836, died at Ft. Dodge IA 1 May 1881, daughter of Zadok and Hannah (Foster) Richardson (James Adams Vinton, Richardson Memorial [Portland ME, 1876], 845); married third 26 Apr. 1882 CAROLINE CHAPLER FISHER, born at Dover OH 19 June 1854 (Cornman Ms; VT VRs).
He was a tinsmith before the Civil War. He served three years in Co. I, 1st VT Cav. Rgt., and received a disability discharge (after accidentally shooting himself with his own pistol).
He and his family went to IA in 1866, and in 1880 he had a hardware and plumbing supply business at Ft. Dodge. In 1899 he purchased Highland Lodge at Willamina, Yamhill Co. OR, a prosperous 485-acre farm and cattle range (Portrait and Biographical Record of the Willamette Valley, Oregon [Chicago, 1903], 571).

Children by Lucinda:

    i.   DORA LIBBIE[9], b. Craftsbury VT 6 Oct. 1859; m.
             JOHN WALLACE[9] LEIGHTON [# 1796].
    ii.   GRACE, b. Hyde Park 13 Oct. 1861, d. there 7
             July 1863.

Children by Lestina, all but first born at Ft. Dodge:

    iii. CARRIE BELL, b. Elkhorn IA 9 Apr. 1868; m.
             9 July 1902 THOMAS ADAMS, b. Warwickshire,
             England, 14 Feb. 1855. Ch. Laurel Leighton
             b. Velva ND 25 June 1903.
    iv.   ELSIE, b. 10 June 1871, d. 9 Oct. 1872.
    v.   DELLA, b. 22 June 1872, d. 17 Oct. 1873.
1798. vi.   (LELAND) LEE, b. 24 Sept. 1873.
    vii. ELLA, b. 19 Aug. 1875, d. 11 Sept. 1876.
    viii. FRANK, b. 27 Oct., d. 25 Dec., 1876.
    ix.   BESSIE IRENE, b. 28 July 1880, res. ND.
             She was a teacher.

Children by Caroline, born at Ft. Dodge:

    x.   ROBERT A., b. 22 Nov. 1883.
    xi.   ELMIRA E., b. 21 Mar. 1886.
    xii. LESTER D., b. 22 July 1887.

1298. LUCIUS NOYES[8] 1836-1872 [627 Isaac[7] and Nancy Brigham] was born at Hyde Park VT 8 Apr. 1836, died at Waterbury VT 27 Nov. 1872, 37y; married at Eden VT 11 Dec. 1856 [as Margaret A.] MARY ANN HINDS, born there 25 Nov. 1839, died at Johnson VT 3 July 1876, 36y 7m 8d, daughter of Eli and Lydia (Hurd) Hinds (VT VRs; Cornman Ms; Eli's letter in 1905--Cornman Papers).
Lucius was a painter.

Children:

       i.   ELI HINDS^9, b. Wilton VT 22 June 1857, res.
             Mechanicsville NY in 1905; m. Hyde Park VT 24
             Dec. 1884 LIZZIE ANN GILLEN, dau. of Patrick
             and Margaret Gillen. Ch. IRENE MAY^{10} b.
             Mechanicsville 8 Nov. 1893.
       ii.   LESLIE H., b. Eden 26 June 1861, res. Pitts-
             burgh PA.
1799. iii. LEO L., b. Eden 20 June 1864.
       iv.   MARY F., b. Eden 23 Dec. 1865.
1800. v.   (ISAAC) EUGENE, b. Eden 4 Nov. 1867.
       vi.   MYRA, b. Eden 12 June 1870.
       vii. GUY W., b. Waterbury VT 12 Dec. 1871 (Eden
             VRs). He assumed the surname Fish after
             being given for adoption.

1299. HEALEY CADY^8 1838-1864 [627 Isaac^7 and Nancy Brig-
ham] was born at Hyde Park VT 2 Aug. 1838, died at Eden VT 15
Sept. 1864, 26y 1m 13d; married at Johnson VT 4 Mar. 1859
MARY A. SARGEANT, born there 26 June 1839, died at Boston 21
Mar. 1905, daughter of Samuel and Mary A (Lunt) Sargeant
(Edwin Everett Sargent, Sargent Record [St. Johnsbury VT,
1899], 85; town VRs; Cornman Ms).

       Children:

       i.   CORA M., b. Hyde Park 15 Dec. 1859, d. 12 Jan.
             1890; unm.
1801. ii.   HOMER V., b. Hyde Park 27 Jan. 1861.
       iii. EDNA E., b. Hyde Park 14 Jan. 1862, d. Eden
             29 Dec. 1864.
1802. iv.   HEALEY MARTIN, b. Eden 6 Aug. 1864.

1300. AURELIA^8 [Celia] 1843-   [627 Isaac^7 and Nancy
Brigham] was born at Hyde Park VT 15 June 1843, lived at Sno-
homish WA; married first at Hyde Park 25 Dec. 1862 CHARLES
CLINTON MORSE, born there 29 Oct. 1841, son of Aaron and
Pamelia T. (Niles) Morse; married second at Salem WI 25 Mar.
1869 LLOYD H. COLBY, born 29 Aug. 1846 (Cornman Ms).
    Morse was editor of the Southwestern Advocate, an official
Methodist publication. Colby was a grain dealer.

       Child (**Morse**), born at Hyde Park:

       i.   GEORGE LEIGHTON, b. 23 Apr. 1866; m. 7 May 1890 RILBY
             LEIDA RUSSELL, b. Franklin VT 20 Aug. 1869.

       Children (**Colby**), born at Prairie View MN:

       ii.   NANCY, b. 23 Mar., d. 19 Aug., 1870.
       iii. WARREN, b. 3 Aug. 1872.
       iv.   ARTHUR, b. 13 Feb. 1874.
       v.   MINNIE M., b. 7 Aug., d. 20 Sept., 1880.

1301. ELLEN ANNETTE^8 1847-   [627 Isaac^7 and Martha
Wright] was born at Hyde Park VT 4 July 1847, lived at Mor-
risville VT; married 19 Feb. 1867 EDGAR R. BENTLEY, born at
Cambridge VT 30 Aug. 1845 (Cornman Ms).

Children (**Bentley**), born at Hyde Park:

i.   LLOYD C., b. 4 Jan. 1872.
ii.   HOMER L., b. 15 Oct. 1879.

1301.   JANE SARAH[8] [Jennie] 1851-   [627 Isaac[7] and Martha Wright] was born at Hyde Park VT 26 Apr. 1851; married at Mapleton MN 11 Feb. 1879 JAMES MARVIN SPRAGUE, born in Essex Co. NY 11 Oct. 1840, son of Hiram S. and Lenora (Stanton) Sprague (Cornman Ms; Warren V. Sprague, Supplement: Sprague Families in America [1940-41], MHS, 22).

Children (**Sprague**), born at Mapleton:

i.   FLORENCE ALICE, b. 24 Apr. 1880.
ii.   MYRTLE WEALTHY, b. 18 Nov. 1881.
iii. MARY ADDIE, b. 3 Apr. 1889 (Ida Marion in Cornman Ms).

1303.   ELLEN FRANCES[8] 1836-   [631 Isaac[7] and Jemima Wood] was born at Hartford VT 9 Aug. 1836; married there 1 Jan. 1857 WILLIAM HENRY CHILD, born at Cornish NH 22 Dec. 1832, son of Stephen and Eliza (Atwood) Child (Elias Child, Genealogy of the Child-Childs-Childes Families [Utica NY, 1881], 162-3; William H. Child, History of the Town of Cornish, N. H. [The Town, 1910, reprinted in 1973], 2:163; Cornman Ms).
Willilam Child was superintendent of schools from 1886 to 1897, and author of the Cornish town history.

Children (**Child**), born at Cornish:

i.   WILLIAM PALMER, b. 15 Nov. 1857, d. Sidney, NSW, 4
      Dec. 1909; m. 1st ANNA SCOTT; m. 2nd LAURA HOWLAND.
      He emigrated to Australia.
ii.   EUGENE FRANK, b. 14 Apr. 1859, d. 19 Apr. 1860.
iii. HALLIE LILLIAN, b. 28 Dec. 1863; m. Lebanon NH 14
      Nov. 1883 REUBEN C TRUE.
iv.   EDWIN LEIGHTON, b. 15 May 1867; m. IDA L. FORD, b
      Danbury VT 16 Apr. 1867, dau. of Rev. Robert and
      Mary A. (Towle) Ford. He was superintendent of the
      Cornish Creamery Co.
v.   IDA LOUISE, b. 6 Feb. 1870, res. Worcester MA; m.
      White River Junction VT 15 June 1898 ALFRED W.
      SIBLEY.

1304.   EDWIN THOMAS[8] 1841-1880 [631 Isaac[7] and Jemima Wood] was born at Hartford VT 15 Aug. 1841, died at Malone NY 30 Aug. 1880; married there CARRIE HART, daughter of John Hart (Cornman Ms).

Children, born at Malone:

i.   ELLA LOUISE[9], b. 28 Sept. 1875, d. 21 Jan.
      1879.
ii.   RALPH WALDO, b. 8 Aug. 1877.

1305. HARRIET JOSEPHINE[8] [Hattie] 1839-1915 [633 Joseph[7] and Mary Lawrence] was born at Groton MA 5 Apr. 1839, died at Somerville MA 31 Jan. 1915; married at Chicago IL 31 Mar. 1857 AUSTIN CHANDLER DEWEY, born at Albany VT 22 July 1831, died at Chicago 12 Aug. 1891, son of Chandler and Diagratia (Buck) Dewey (Louis Marinus Dewey, Dewey Family History [Westfield, MA, 1898], 557; Cornman Ms).
In 1900 she and Ida were living at Somerville with her brother James.

Child (**Dewey**), born at Chicago:

i.   IDA MAY, b. 8 Dec. 1859; m. Indianapolis IN 28 Feb. 1878 JAMES KEARNEY GRAHAM, b. in England, son of James and Eliza (Cole) Graham.

1306. GEORGE NORTON[8] 1845-   [635 James[7] and Amanda Deland] was born at Ossipee NH in Mar. 1847; married ELLEN E. [Nellie] ---- , born at Madison NH in Jan. 1847 (Cornman Ms; Conway VRs).
George and his family were listed at Conway NH in 1880 and 1900.

Children:

i.   CHARLES S.[9], b. in July 1876.
ii.   SARAH J. [Sadie], b. Conway 26 Oct. 1878.
iii.   FRED G., b. in May 1882.
iv.   daughter, b. Conway 1 Sept. 1884.
v.   child, d. Conway 26 Oct. 1887, 1d.

1307. ELIZA C.[8] 1831-1862 [636 Isaac[7] and Maria Cate] was born probably at Barrington NH 26 Aug. 1831, died 26 May 1862; married in 1851 MOSES OTIS (Cornman Ms). In 1850 she was listed at Dover, aged 19.

Children (**Otis**):

i.   ANNIE J., res. Meredith NH; m. JOHN W. HAWKINS.
ii.   JESSIE, res. Dover.
iii.   MARIA, res. Manchester NH; m. ---- BRODY.
iv.   son.

1308. ABIGAIL[8] [Abby] 1831-   [638 David[7] and Dorcas Welch] was born at Ossipee NH about 1831 (19 in 1850); married REUBEN MAYBERRY, born at Cumberland ME 19 July 1819, son of Zephaniah and Rebecca (Read) Mayberry.
Mayberry had had four children by a first wife, and had two more by a third wife Lucinda Prescott (Gould, Mayberry Desc., 79).

Children (**Mayberry**):

i.   DAVID, d. infant.
ii.   WILLIAM ALMOND, b. 13 Mar. 1855, d. 11 Mar. 1899; m. 2 Sept. 1877 ALICE C. YOUNG of Ossipee.

1309.   JOHN B.[8] 1843-1904 [639 Remembrance[7] and Priscilla Fenderson] was born at Biddeford ME 3 Aug. 1843 (36 in 1880), died there in 1904; married first SARAH ---- , born in NH about 1845 (35 in 1880); married second at Portland ME 29 Dec. 1883 FANNIE CLARK, born in 1848, died in 1927 (GS) (town VRs; Biddeford Record Book, 2:14). Burials are in Greenwood Cemetery, Biddeford.

He was a machinist. In 1880 his father and his siblings Charles H., 44, and Mary, 45, lived at Biddeford with him.

Children by Sarah:

    i.   MABEL B.[9], b. in NH 22 Sept. 1872 (7 in 1880),
          d. Lynn MA 18 Nov. 1895, 23y 1m 26d (VRs).
    ii.   ANNIE G. [Gracie], b. at Biddeford c1874 (6 in
          1880), d. Manchester NH 6 Aug. 1888, 14y 2m
          17d.

1310.   HARRISON G.[8] 1849-   [639 Remembrance[7] and Priscilla Fenderson] was born at Biddeford 18 May 1849; married at Newport ME 1 May 1872 EMMA S. LOWE, born in Oct. 1852 (28 in 1880) (town VRs).

They lived at Saco in 1880, and at Chicago IL in 1900.

Children:

    i.   MARIAN[9], b. in ME in Mar. 1875 (7 in 1880).
    ii.   LEILA, b. in ME c1876 (4 in 1880).
    iii. ALBERT, b. in MA in Dec. 1881.

1311.   CHARLES H.[8] 1841-1914 [640 Isaac[7] and Mercy Chick] was born at Effingham NH 13 July 1841, died at Bradford MA (now part of Haverhill) 29 Oct. 1914; married 28 Mar. 1874 ORIANNA B. ATKINS, born at Corinth ME 28 Mar. 1846, daughter of Samuel S. and Mary Jane (Oakman) Atkins (MH&GR, 5[1894]: 271). He went to Haverhill MA as a young man, and served in Co. I, 44th MA Inf. Rgt., from which he was discharged 18 June 1863. He founded Leighton & Pinkham Co., a sole-leather business (Cornman Ms).

Children, born at Bradford MA:

1803.   i.   ETHEL M.[9] (Edith, 4, in 1880), b. 20 Nov.
             1875; m. JOHN W. WILLIAMS.
        ii. BESSIE E., b. 8 Feb. 1879, res. Haverhill; m.
             16 June 1909 FRED B. HEATH.

1312.   (ELIZA) JENNIE[8] 1845-   [640 Isaac[7] and Mercy Chick] was born at Effingham NH 21 Nov. 1845, lived there with her daughter in the Centerville section in 1908 (Town Register); married 24 July 1871 FRANK BAKER PINNEY, born 9 Mar. 1839, died at Epsom NH 7 Dec. 1887, son of Benjamin and Louise (Parker) Pinney (Cornman Ms).

Children (**Pinney**):

    i.   ARTHUR LEIGHTON, b. Manchester NH 7 Apr. 1873, d. 20
          May 1904; m. in June 1903 MARION M. HASKELL. She m.

2nd Charles Edward Meloon.
ii.   IOLIE MAY, b. Epsom 14 Dec. 1885; m. 16 Dec. 1908
      WESLEY MILLIKEN.

1313. ELLA MARY[8] 1856-   [640 Isaac[7] and Mercy Chick] was
born at Effingham 18 Nov. 1856, lived at Effingham Falls;
married 17 Dec. 1875 GEORGE C LEAVITT, born at Freedom NH 17
May 1854 (Freedom Town Register; Cornman Ms).
     In 1908 Leavitt was a merchant at Freedom (or Effingham
Falls); Ella's sister Sarah A. Leighton lived with them.

Children (**Leavitt**), born at Freedom:

i.   ADDIE M., b. 11 Dec. 1877, res. Effingham Falls; m.
      23 Dec. 1895 GEORGE ALDO MELOON.
ii.   ERNEST A., b. 26 Jan. 1883.
iii. ELSIE M., b. 28 Aug. 1889.
iv.   ROY T., b. 23 Jan. 1892.

1314. GEORGE H.[8] 1860-   [644 George[7] and Susan Moulton]
was born at Effingham 25 Apr. 1860; married 3 May 1880 CLARA
[Nellie] HARMON, born at Madison NH about 1863 (Cornman Ms).
     He was a carpenter, living in the Centerville section of
Effingham in 1908 with his son Bert (Town Register, 1908).

Children, born at Effingham:

i.   URBAN E.[9], b. 12 Oct. 1880; res. Haverhill NH
      in 1900 with his uncle William.
ii.   BERT R., b. 13 Aug. 1882.

1315. ALEMEDA JANE[8] 1839-   [649 Samuel Weeks[7] and Cynthia Heath] was born at Danville VT 20 Aug. 1839; married
OTIS F. HILL of Pittsfield NH (Cornman Ms).

Children (**Hill**):

i.   GEORGE W., b. Barnstead NH; m. Danbury VT 3 Nov. 1893
      JULIA E. EVANS.
ii.   HERMAN, res. Manchester NH.
iii. JOHN, res. Pittsfield NH.

1316. ELSA JANE WHITE[8] 1841-1898 [649 Samuel Weeks[7] and
Cynthia Heath] was born at Danville VT 2 Nov. 1841, died at
Woodstock VT in 1898; married JOHN DORWAY (Cornman Ms).
     Julia Cornman stated that Dorway was a "French soldier,"
and that all the children but Melvin were trapeze performers
in a circus.

Children (**Dorway**):

i.   MELVIN.
ii.   BLANCHE, res. Rumney Depot NH; m. HENRY BICKFORD.
iii. MINNIE.
iv.   HENRY.
v.   BERT T.

1317. ROSINA LANGMAID[8] [Rosa] 1849-   [650 Samuel Weeks[7] and Cynthia Heath] was born at Danville VT 18 Sept. 1849; married at Barnstead NH 13 July 1865 JOHN BIRCK (Cornman Ms).

Children (**Birck**):

i.   JOHN.
ii. GEORGE W.; m. 24 Oct. 1892 EDITH M. TWOMBLEY.

1318. ABBIE J.[8] 1852-1886 [650 Jeremiah[7] and Martha Harris] was born say 1852 at Danville VT, died at St. Johnsbury VT 26 July 1886; married there 17 Aug. 1872 (ROMANZO) EDWARD BALCH, born at Lyndon Vt 14 June 1852, son of Leonard and Betsey (Smith) Balch. He married second 10 Sept. 1887 Luella (Aldrich) Stanton--two children (Galusha B. Balch, Genealogy of the Balch Families in America [Salem MA 1897], 319; Cornman Ms). He was a machinist at Danville and St. Johnsbury.

Children (**Balch**), born at St. Johnsbury:

i.   HARRY EDWIN, b. 8 May 1873.
ii. LEONARD GEORGE, b. 6 June 1876.
iii. ?FRED, res. Craftsbury VT.
iv. ?EDWARD.

1319. BETSEY JANE[8] 1851-   [652 Daniel[7] and Theresa Poppy] was born at Danville VT 8 Nov. 1851; married 24 Dec. 1870 WINTHROP S. COLEMAN, son of Oliver W. and Mehitable Coleman (Cornman Ms).

Children (**Coleman**):

i.   CELIA MAUD, b. 22 Aug. 1871, d. in 1874.
ii. OLIVER D., b. 7 Nov. 1876, res. Dover NH.

1320. ANNA B.[8] 1869-   [653 William[7] and Lucinda Nason] was born at Haverhill NH 27 Feb. 1869, lived at Warren NH; married 27 Dec. 1884 ONSLOW D. PERRY, born 27 Dec. 1869, son of Davis Chandler and Sarah (Haines) Perry (Cornman Ms).

Children (**Perry**), born at Warren NH:

i.   EMMA I., b. 17 June 1886; m. 8 June 1908 CHARLES A.
     AVERY, b. 5 Sept. 1857, son of Aaron and Jane Avery.
ii. WINNIE M., b. 1 Feb. 1894.

1321. FREDERICK[8] 1864-   [654 Harrison[7] and Mary Gould] was born at Danville VT in June 1864 (1900 census), lived at Dover NH; married at Danville 19 Nov. 1890 SUSAN [Susie] TICE (Danville VRs).
He was listed alone at Danville in 1900.

Children, born at Danville:

i.   HARRY C.[9], b. 16 Oct., d. 8 Dec., 1892.
ii. ELNORA B., b. 6 May 1894.

1322. **WASHINGTON T.**[8] 1850-   [659 Andrew[7] and Sarah Tilton] was born at Deerfield NH 30 Oct. 1850, lived at East Northwood NH in 1900; married 22 Dec. 1884 ELMA F KILSEY, born at Nottingham 1 July 1860 (Northwood VRs; Cornman Ms).

Children, born at Northwood:

    i.   ALVIN KILSEY[9], b. 5 May 1891.
    ii.   RAND JULIAN, b. 15 July 1893.

1323. **FRANK EDMUND**[8] 1859-1894 [663 Matthew[7] and Hannah Cate] was born at Auburn NH 7 Jan. 1859, died at Chester NH 13 Sept. 1894; married at Lowell MA (VRs) 27 June 1878 JOSEPHINE E. WALTON, born at Mercer ME 29 Apr. 1861, died at Chester 5 May 1939, daughter of Andrew C. and Abbie C (Lewis) Walton. She married second Albert C. Saunders, born at Dayton OH 5 Mar. 1857, died at Chester 1 Aug. 1922, son of Albert and Orpha (Cross) Saunders--no children (data from Albert C Leighton, compiled by Josephine; John C Chase, History of Chester NH [Haverhill MA, 1926], 378; Hattie E. Heninger, Walton Family [1972], 341-2).
In 1900 widow Josephine and her daughter Alice were living at Chester with her mother Abbie Walton.

Children:

1804. i.   ARTHUR EDMUND[9], b. Lowell 15 Dec. 1878.
1805. ii.   ABBIE CLARA, b. Lowell 6 Dec. 1879; m. CHARLES
             T. WELLS.
1806. iii. ALICE BELL, b. Chester 8 Oct. 1888; m. LINDLEY
             A. ROBERTS.